World Historical Fiction

World Historical Fiction

An Annotated Guide to Novels for Adults and Young Adults

by
Lynda G. Adamson

ORYX PRESS
1999

*The rare Arabian Oryx is believed to have inspired the myth of the unicorn. This desert
antelope became virtually extinct in the early 1960s. At that time several groups of
international conservationists arranged to have 9 animals sent to the Phoenix Zoo
to be the nucleus of a captive breeding herd. Today the Oryx population
is over 1,000 and over 500 have been returned to the Middle East.*

© 1999 by The Oryx Press
4041 North Central at Indian School Road
Phoenix, Arizona 85012-3397

Published simultaneously in Canada
Printed and Bound in the United States of America

♾ The paper used in this publication meets the minimum requirements of
American National Standard for Information Science-Permanence
of Paper for Printed Library Materials, ANSI Z39.48, 1984.

Library of Congress Cataloging-in-Publication Data
Adamson, Lynda G.
    World historical fiction : an annotated guide to novels for adults
and young adults / by Lynda G. Adamson.
        p. cm.
    Includes bibliographical references and indexes.
    ISBN 1-57356-066-9 (alk. paper)
    1. Historical fiction—Bibliography. I. Title.
Z5917.H6A33 1998
[PN3377.5.H57]
016.80883'81—dc21   98-39981
                                                                 CIP

For Frank, Frank III, and Gregory

Contents

Preface

Historical fiction evokes a particular time period by focusing on a well-known person or event or on an ordinary person living in historical times. Through historical fiction, a reader can learn how people traveled, what they ate, and how they established relationships in a time other than the present. Readers often become fascinated with specific times and want to read additional titles with these settings.

The generally accepted definition of historical fiction is that it is about a time period at least 25 years before it was written. I have espoused a similar definition in other publications, but I no longer think it viable. If the setting is in a time earlier than that with which the reader is familiar, it is historical fiction. Many readers do not care that Jane Austen was writing about her times; what they want is a good story that gives them insight into the early 19th century. Therefore, in *World Historical Fiction: An Annotated Guide to Novels for Adults and Young Adults*, I have included a great many books with settings that are not present day, regardless of when they were written.

This book originally began as an update to *World Historical Fiction* by Daniel D. McGarry and Sarah Harriman White (1973). It has become more. Rather than merely add titles published after 1972, I examined over 6,000 titles listed under the subject heading "Historical Fiction" in the Library of Congress catalog. Since many books that could fit the subject of "Historical Fiction" are not marked as such in the Library of Congress catalog, I also examined the subject listings under "War stories," "Detective and mystery stories," "Romantic suspense novels," "Love stories," "Christian fiction," and, simply, "Fiction." I also examined the issues of *Library Journal, Publishers Weekly,* and *Booklist* published since 1970.

The main overlap between my list and the titles in McGarry and White are titles reprinted since 1970. However, some titles published prior to 1970 that have won awards or with which I was familiar were inexplicably excluded from McGarry and White. I have added these books to *World Historical Fiction* and retained books that have been reprinted since 1970 because they are classics, have sequels or prequels, or contain settings rarely appearing in more recent historical fiction. Additionally, McGarry and White included some books solely for an audience of young adult readers. All of the books detailed in *World Historical Fiction* are suitable for adults, but books also appropriate for young adults are labeled as such. As a final criterion for inclusion, books had to be either reviewed, or in the case of genres only recently earning the attention of reviewers (Christian fiction or romances, for example), appear with a summary of content in the publisher's catalog. *World Historical Fiction,* therefore, will help readers to choose from over 6,000 titles of historical fiction set in locales outside the United States in a variety of genres.

Organization

This advisory is organized according to areas of the world. Within each area, titles appear within relevant time periods for the area from prehistory through the recent past. Since the majority of books listed are set in Europe, I have separated books with settings in the British Isles from those with European locales.

The other chapters represent either broad areas with fewer available titles in English (e.g., Thailand, Cambodia, and Malaysia) or countries with a large collection of titles depicting that specific country (e.g., Japan). More specific geographic settings are listed in the Place and Time Index by countries or regions, then by time periods. For example, to find books set in Wales in the 14th century, the reader can turn to the Time and Place Index and choose "Wales" and the time period "1290–1491."

Novels are listed alphabetically according to the last name of the author within the appropriate setting and time period. (For novels spanning more than one of the designated time periods, I have used the setting dates of the time period in which the book begins.) Each entry includes the author, title, date of original publication (and most recently known reprint if applicable), number of pages, brief description of the content, main subjects, genre(s), if applicable, and any awards the book may have received. Annotations are descriptive rather than evaluative and include setting, character, and plot, and list relevant sequels or identify series to which books belong.

Since reprints appear erratically, librarians or patrons planning to purchase books are advised to check current citation sources for books, including those online that list and sell out-of-print titles. For almost all books that have been reprinted in large type, I have used the original date of publication and number of pages.

Young Adult Books

Books designated as "Young Adult" are, in almost all cases, books written for adults that young adults ninth grade and older might enjoy reading. I have included only a handful of books published specifically for young adults; these are excellent books giving an unusual point of view, generally set in a time period few other novels cover. Almost all of the adult books noted as appropriate for young adults come from professional educators' and reviewers' lists in *School Library Journal* and *Booklist*. Since adult mores and opinions about appropriate material for young adults vary, adults who plan to make selections for young adults from this guide and who have specific concerns about sexual content or language may wish to examine the entire novel. Similarly, other adults may discover books in the *Guide* not

designated as "young adult" that they think teenagers with whom they are acquainted will appreciate. Books designated as "young adult" in this *Guide* will be marked with a diamond (◆) symbol and listed alphabetically by author in Appendix II.

Appendixes and Indexes

Following the main section are two appendixes: a list of books that have won awards and the list of books that may be appropriate for young adults. Following these are five indexes: author, title, genre, place and time, and subject.

Genres

To say that a book of historical fiction belongs in a specific genre can be constraining and misleading. War stories can be romances, and romances can be mysteries or adventures. Therefore, a book may have more than one genre that fits its content. Genres and their general definitions for *World Historical Fiction* are

- Adventure Story—stories filled with action
- Allegory—stories that can be read on a symbolic level
- Bildungsroman (Coming-of-Age)— stories in which the protagonist matures, usually by means of some significant event
- Biographical Fiction—stories focusing on the life of a specific person in which the author creates dialogue rather than documentation
- Christian Fiction—stories without explicit sex or obscene language in which the protagonist from a Christian denomination faces challenges based on a faith in God
- Country Life—Stories taking place in rural areas somewhat removed from cities or large towns
- Domestic Fiction—stories focusing on the home life or immediate family situations of a character

- Epic Literature—stories with a protagonist who acts heroic against a nationalistic setting
- Erotic Literature—stories with graphic sexual encounters
- Family Saga—stories about several generations of a family within the same book or over a series of books
- Fantastic Literature—stories not known to be true but using characters who have become part of legend, such as King Arthur and Robin Hood
- Gothic Fiction—stories that include a dark atmosphere or eerie phenomena
- Horror—stories that are extremely terrifying or containing sensational events
- Humorous Fiction—stories that use humor as a basis for the characters to understand themselves and the world
- Jewish Fiction—stories focusing on Jews and Jewish culture
- Legal Story—stories with trials or lawyers as integral parts of the plot
- Love Story—stories depicting complex love affairs that are not necessarily patterned to have happy endings
- Medical Novel—stories in which one of the important characters is a healer or physician
- Musical Fiction—stories in which the protagonist is a musician
- Mystery (including Detective Fiction)—stories with an unknown factor that must be solved, such as a murder or a theft
- Picaresque Fiction—stories in which the episodic action moves from place to place without seeming to have a single climax
- Political Fiction—stories in which the protagonists must cope in some way with a hostile government, or in which political intrigue is an integral part of the plot
- Regency Novel—stories set during the English Regency period, 1811–1820, revolving around the activities of the titled elite and focusing on manners and social customs
- Religious Fiction—stories in which members of non-Christian religions reveal their faith
- Romance—stories in which two people fall in love but must overcome difficulties before they can be together
- Satire—stories that use humor to criticize society's mores
- Sea Story—stories focusing on adventures at sea or taking place on ships at sea
- Sports Fiction—stories with protagonists interested or involved in a specific sport
- Spy Fiction—stories in which espionage drives the plot
- Time Travel—stories in which a protagonist enters a different time period, which then becomes the main setting
- War Story—stories that take place during a time of a war when a protagonist either fights on the front or remains at home waiting for a loved one to return
- Western Fiction—Canadian and South American stories in which the action takes place in the western pioneer and frontier regions

Sample Entry

Place ———————— **Canada**

Time Period ———————— **1800–1932**

Publication
Information

Author ———————— Shields, Carol

Title ——————— 7. *The Stone Diaries*. New York: Viking, 1994. 361 pp.

Description ——————— Daisy Goodwill Flett, whose mother died during Daisy's birth
in 1905, moves from Canada to Indiana then back to Canada
with her stonecutter father and lives a fairly ordinary life against
the backdrop of 20th-century events.

Genre(s): Domestic Fiction. ———————————————— Genre(s)

Award(s): Pulitzer Prize; National Book Critics Circle
Award. ———————— Award(s)

Acknowledgments

I would like to express my appreciation to Merle Jacob at the Chicago Public Library for her advice and John Bartles in my college library for his help in gathering information. I also thank Anne Thompson and Jennifer Ashley at The Oryx Press for their ideas and suggestions. Without the patience and support of my husband, this project could have never begun, much less have come to completion.

Acknowledgements

MAIN ENTRY SECTION

Prehistory and the Ancient World

Egypt and Mesopotamia

Asch, Sholem

1. *Moses.* Trans. Maurice Samuel. New York: Putnam, 1951. 505 pp.
Moses, in the sequel to *Mary* leads the Jews from Egypt and wanders with them against a backdrop of Jewish tradition and law.
Genre(s): Jewish Fiction; Biographical Fiction.

Atherton, Gertrude Franklin Horn

2. *Dido, Queen of Hearts.* New York: Liveright and Boni, 1929. 384 pp.
Dido, queen of Carthage, loves Aeneas, but he leaves her.
Genre(s): Biographical Fiction; Fantastic Literature.

Brelich, Mario

3. *Navigator of the Flood.* Trans. John Shepley. Marlboro, VT: Marlboro, 1991. 114 pp.
Noah might have become drunk after God told him that all the world would be destroyed, because the heaviness of living with himself and a God who would do such a thing was unbearable.
Genre(s): Biographical Fiction; Religious Fiction; Allegory.

Buechner, Frederick

4. *The Son of Laughter.* San Francisco: HarperSanFranciso, 1993. 274 pp.
Jacob, son of Isaac and grandson of Abraham, buys Esau's birthright, gets Isaac's blessing, and serves as a slave in Egypt.
Genre(s): Biographical Fiction; Religious Fiction; Domestic Fiction.

Card, Orson Scott

5. *Stone Tables.* Salt Lake City, UT: Deseret, 1998. 432 pp.
After being raised as a favorite son in the Pharoah's court, Moses learns that he is an Israelite, and after his exile, he decides to become an Israelite leader.
Genre(s): Religious Fiction.

Dorr, Roberta Kells

6. *The Queen of Sheba.* San Francisco: Harper and Row, 1990. 275 pp.
Solomon has a relationship with Bilqis, the Queen of Sheba, who also displays wisdom and wealth.
Genre(s): Biographical Fiction; Religious Fiction; Christian Fiction.

Drury, Allen

◆ 7. *A God Against the Gods.* Garden City, NY: Doubleday, 1976. 310 pp.
In 14th-century BC Egypt, Nefertiti and Akhenaton rule while Akhenaton replaces the old gods.
Genre(s): Biographical Fiction; Political Fiction.

8. *Return to Thebes.* Garden City, NY: Doubleday, 1977. 272 pp.
In the sequel to *A God Against the Gods*, the old priesthood tries to regain power over Akhenaton and Nefertiti.
Genre(s): Biographical Fiction; Political Fiction.

Flaubert, Gustave

9. *Salammbo.* Trans. A.J. Krailsheimer. 1862. New York: Penguin, 1961. 319 pp.
Salammbo, daughter of Hamilcar, wants to save the *Tanite*, a veil of religious significance.

Gedge, Pauline

◆ 10. *Child of the Morning.* New York: Dial, 1977. 403 pp.
Hatshepsut, the only woman pharaoh, has to combat jealousy and intrigue to keep her position.

11. *Lady of the Reeds.* New York: Soho, 1995. 513 pp.
Thu gets her older brother to teach her to read in ancient Egypt, and when she escapes her village at 12, she meets the physician Hui who has had a dream about a blue-eyed woman and grooms her to be the pharaoh's concubine.
Genre(s): Political Fiction.

12. *The 12th Transforming.* New York: Harper and Row, 1984. 407 pp.
The Empress Tiye ensures that her son Akhenaton will ascend the throne, but his and Nefertiti's decadence incite plots to overthrow them.
Genre(s): Biographical Fiction.

Gill, Anton

13. *City of the Dead.* London: Bloomsbury, 1993. 173 pp.
The experienced scribe Huy returns to Thebes after Akhenaton's revolution where his interest in forensic work leads him to investigate the deaths of young girls in families of senior court officials.
Genre(s): Mystery.

Guild, Nicholas

14. **The Assyrian.** New York: Atheneum, 1987. 552 pp.
Tiglath Ashur, son of a king, escapes the 7th-century BC custom of castrating all but one son so that succession will be clear.
Genre(s): Adventure Story.

15. **The Blood Star.** New York: Atheneum, 1989. 664 pp.
The sequel to *The Assyrian* finds Tiglath escaping assassins and developing character through his adventures.
Genre(s): Adventure Story.

Haney, Lauren

16. **Right Hand of Amon.** New York: Avon, 1997. 300 pp.
Lieutenant Bak investigates the murder of a noble army officer in Egypt and uncovers a plot to kill the pharaoh and his son.
Genre(s): Romance.

Hardy, W. G.

17. **All the Trumpets Sounded.** New York: Coward-McCann, 1942. 501 pp.
Moses is adopted as an Egyptian prince before he becomes the Hebrew leader.
Genre(s): Biographical Fiction; Religious Fiction.

Hareven, Shulamith

◆ 18. **The Miracle Hater.** Trans. Hillel Halkin. New York: North Point, 1988. 96 pp.
Eshkar, once an enslaved Hebrew in Egypt, grows into manhood alone in the desert when he watches Moses' miracles cause pain for people he knows.
Genre(s): Religious Fiction.

Hawkes, Jacquetta

19. **King of the Two Lands: The Pharaoh Akhenaten.** New York: Random House, 1966. 288 pp.
The Pharaoh and his wife Nefertiti bring monotheism to Egypt.
Genre(s): Biographical Fiction.

Heatherley, Joyce Landorf

20. **Joseph.** Old Tappan, NJ: Revell, 1980. 319 pp.
Five women who love Joseph tell about his life and their relationships with him.
Genre(s): Biographical Fiction; Religious Fiction.

Henderson, Lois T.

21. **Hagar.** Chappaqua, NY: Christian Heral, 1978. 255 pp.
The tensions between Sarah and Hagar increase with Abraham's need to have an heir, and when Hagar departs, she takes her boy Ishmael with her.
Genre(s): Biographical Fiction; Religious Fiction.

22. **Miriam.** San Francisco: Harper and Row, 1983. 261 pp.
Miriam arranges for Moses' audience with the Pharaoh, and in a variety of ways, she becomes a source of support for Moses as he leads the Hebrews out of Egypt until she must face her punishment for pride with banishment and enduring leprosy.
Genre(s): Biographical Fiction; Religious Fiction.

◆ 23. **Ruth.** Chappaqua, NY: Christian Herald, 1981. 223 pp.
Ruth matures in her relationships with those around her as she readies herself to join her husband's family.
Genre(s): Biographical Fiction; Religious Fiction.

Hunt, Angela Elwell

◆ 24. **Brothers.** Minneapolis, MN: Bethany House, 1997. 368 pp.
When 10 Hebrew brothers arrive in Egypt, a young Canaanite girl who has found a home within the vizier's compound must look after the one brother held as a prisoner. (*Series:* Legacies of the Ancient River, 2)
Genre(s): Christian Fiction; Romance.

◆ 25. **Dreamers.** Minneapolis, MN: Bethany House, 1996. 395 pp.
Tuya, an Egyptian teenager, falls in love with the biblical Joseph. (*Series:* Legacies of the Ancient River, 1)
Genre(s): Christian Fiction.

◆ 26. **Journey.** Minneapolis, MN: Bethany House, 1997. 384 pp.
Ephraim and Manasseh, Joseph's sons, disagree about Israel's future and their love lives. (*Series:* Legacies of the Ancient River, 3)
Genre(s): Christian Fiction.

Hurston, Zora Neale

◆ 27. **Moses, Man of the Mountain.** New York: HarperCollins, 1991. 310 pp.
Moses becomes the leader of his people in order to rescue them from bondage.
Genre(s): Biographical Fiction; Religious Fiction.

Hylton, Sara

◆ 28. **The Talisman of Set.** New York: St. Martin's, 1984. 238 pp.
After returning to her grandmother's English home, Kathryn continues to dream of Egypt and believes that she is the reincarnated Princess Tuia, lover of a pharaoh.
Genre(s): Time Travel.

Jacobson, Sheldon A.

29. **Fleet Surgeon to Pharaoh.** Corvallis: Oregon State Univ, 1971. 320 pp.
The physician-priest Asa Ben Abdiel joins a Phoenician expedition from the Red Sea to Africa where he hopes to find out about advanced Egyptian techniques and to become closer to God.
Genre(s): Sea Story; Medical Novel; Adventure Story; Religious Fiction.

Jacq, Christian

◆ 30. *The Son of Light.* New York: Warner, 1997. 376 pp.

Ramses, the second son of the pharaoh Seti, competes with his brother Shaanar for succession, but when his tutor betrays him, his trusted friends help him reach his goal.

Genre(s): Biographical Fiction.

Jenks, Kathleen

31. *The River and the Stone.* New York: Dutton, 1977. 275 pp.

Moses is torn between his adopted Egyptian family and his interest in a mysterious being called El-Shaddai.

Genre(s): Biographical Fiction; Religious Fiction.

Kadare, Ismail

32. *The Pyramid.* Trans. David Bellos and Jusuf Vrioni. New York: Arcade, 1996. 161 pp.

The pharaoh Cheops says that he does not want a pyramid built for his corpse, but his priests argue that such a building occupies the people's time and is traditional.

Genre(s): Biographical Fiction.

Keller, W. Phillip

◆ 33. *Mighty Man of Valor.* Old Tappan, NJ: Revell, 1979. 124 pp.

Gideon leads 300 of his followers to victory over 139,000 Midianite soldiers by submitting to the will of God.

Genre(s): Biographical Fiction; Religious Fiction.

Lawrence, Joan

34. *The Scapegoat.* Chester Springs, PA: Dufour, 1988. 188 pp.

Moses has concerns about both his people and his God as he experiences the arrogance of his brother Aaron and the contempt of his sister Miriam.

Genre(s): Biographical Fiction; Religious Fiction.

Levin, Lee

35. *King Tut's Private Eye.* New York: St. Martin's, 1996. 232 pp.

Grand Vizier Eye, the world's first private investigator, must find the killer of Tutankhamen's father Akhenaton within a week and without using torture.

Genre(s): Mystery.

Mackey, Mary

36. *The Last Warrior Queen.* New York: Putnam, 1983. 240 pp.

The Sumerian Inanna's brother Paul kills her sister and her lover, and when she becomes queen, she leads an army against him.

Genre(s): War Story.

Mailer, Norman

37. *Ancient Evenings.* Boston: Little, Brown, 1983. 709 pp.

Menenhetet I rises from peasant stock to become a harem overlord between the reigns of Ramses II and Ramses IX of Egypt.

Mann, Thomas

38. *Joseph and his Brothers.* New York: Knopf, 1934. 428 pp.

Jacob serves Laban so that he can gain the hand of Rachel, but he must marry Leah first.

Genre(s): Religious Fiction; Biographical Fiction; Allegory.

39. *Joseph in Egypt.* New York: Knopf, 1938. 2 vols.

After an Ishmaelite merchant's caravan rescues Joseph, his adventures in Egypt include prison and rising to high political positions.

Genre(s): Biographical Fiction; Religious Fiction; Allegory.

40. *Joseph the Provider.* New York: Knopf, 1944. 608 pp.

After Joseph interprets the pharaoh's dreams, he becomes an important member of the court and gains power, in the sequel to *Joseph in Egypt.*

Genre(s): Biographical Fiction; Religious Fiction; Allegory.

41. *Young Joseph.* New York: Knopf, 1935. 273 pp.

In the sequel to *Joseph and His Brothers*, Joseph is 17 and faces the betrayal of his brothers when they sell him into slavery in Egypt.

Genre(s): Religious Fiction; Biographical Fiction; Allegory.

Ormonde, Czenzi

42. *Solomon and the Queen of Sheba.* New York: Farrar, Straus and Giroux, 1954. 251 pp.

The Queen of Sheba visits Solomon.

Genre(s): Biographical Fiction; Religious Fiction.

Patterson, Emma L.

43. *Sun Queen: A Novel About Nefertiti.* New York: McKay, 1967. 312 pp.

Nefertiti comes from the Kingdom of Mitanni as a young woman to join the Pharoah's harem and rises to rule Egypt during Akhenaton's religious reforms.

Genre(s): Biographical Fiction.

Rice, Anne

44. *The Servant of the Bones.* New York: Knopf, 1996. 387 pp.

When Azriel, a young Jewish man in Babylonia, must take the form of the god Marduk, he becomes a spirit instead, traveling through time when summoned by a master.

Genre(s): Fantastic Literature; Time Travel.

Robinson, Lynda Suzanne

◆ 45. *Eater of Souls.* New York: Walker, 1997. 229 pp.
Lord Meren, advisor to Tutankhamen, and his adopted son Kysen try to find a serial killer who slashes his victims and eats their hearts.
Genre(s): Mystery.

◆ 46. *Murder at the Feast of Rejoicing.* New York: Walker, 1996. 229 pp.
In Egypt's 18th dynasty, Lord Meren tries to solve a murder at a country house while his adopted son attempts to protect Tutankhamen.
Genre(s): Mystery.

◆ 47. *Murder at the God's Gate.* New York: Walker, 1995. 236 pp.
Lord Meren, whom some call the Falcon, and his adopted son Kysen investigate the murder of a priest in one of King Tut's temples.
Genre(s): Mystery.

◆ 48. *Murder in the Place of Anubis.* New York: Walker, 1994. 190 pp.
Tutankhamen asks loyal privy councilor Lord Meren to investigate the stabbing of a man found in the sacred area of the Theban embalmers.
Genre(s): Mystery.

Ross, Bette M

49. *Song of Deborah.* Old Tappan, NJ: Revell, 1981. 255 pp.
Deborah searches for her future with her Philistine husband, Lapidoth.
Genre(s): Biographical Fiction; Religious Fiction.

Sandmel, Samuel

50. *Alone atop the Mountain.* Garden City, NY: Doubleday, 1973. 228 pp.
Moses tries to get the children of Israel out of Egypt but faces problems such as wagons mired in the mud of the Sea of Reeds.
Genre(s): Biographical Fiction; Religious Fiction.

Silverberg, Robert

51. *Gilgamesh the King.* New York: Arbor House, 1984. 290 pp.
Gilgamesh knows that he will become king and die, but as he matures, he tries to avoid death.
Genre(s): Fantastic Literature.

Smith, Wilbur A.

◆ 52. *River God.* New York: St. Martin's, 1994. 530 pp.

In 1780 BC, Taita, a eunuch, serves a noble's daughter and observes her unhappy marriage to a pharaoh.
Genre(s): Adventure Story.

Tarr, Judith

◆ 53. *King and Goddess.* New York: Forge, 1996. 384 pp.
Hatshepsut takes Senenmut into her confidence as lover and advisor while she rules Egypt in the 14th century BC.
Genre(s): Biographical Fiction.

◆ 54. *Pillar of Fire.* New York: Tor, 1995. 448 pp.
Nofret, a Hittite slave of Akhenaten and Queen Nefertiti's third daughter, helps the unpopular Akhenaten disappear into the mountains when he cannot produce a male heir, and announces that he is dead.

Traylor, Ellen Gunderson

55. *Joseph, Dreamer of Dreams.* Eugene, OR: Harvest House, 1989. 247 pp.
Joseph hears God say that Joseph shall save his people, but difficulties make him wonder how.
Genre(s): Biographical Fiction.

56. *Moses, the Deliverer.* Eugene, OR: Harvest House, 1990. 321 pp.
After Moses fails in his life, God helps him recover and lead the Israelites out of Egypt.
Genre(s): Biographical Fiction; Religious Fiction.

Waltari, Mika

57. *The Egyptian.* Trans. Naomi Walford. New York: Putnam, 1949. 503 pp.
Sinuhe, a physician who lives with both the high-born and the lowly, travels and ends his life in exile.
Genre(s): Medical Novel.

Williams, W. Ronald

58. *Moses and the Great Cataclysm.* Toronto: Lugus, 1992. 232 pp.
Moses observes geological and meterological events when taking the Israelites out of Egypt.
Genre(s): Biographical Fiction; Religious Fiction.

Wyse, Marion

59. *The Prophet and the Prostitute.* Wheaton, IL: Tyndale House, 1979. 235 pp.
Hosea, a prophet, lives in the last years of the Northern Kingdom in ithe mid-eighth century BC and marries the prostitute Gomer.
Genre(s): Biographical Fiction; Religious Fiction.

Europe and the British Isles to 54 BC

Allan, Margaret

◆ 60. *The Mammoth Stone.* New York: New American Library, 1993. 400 pp.
A woman with one green eye and one blue eye carries a mammoth carved in stone as she guides prehistoric people from Siberia to North America.

Auel, Jean M.

61. *The Clan of the Cave Bear.* New York: Crown, 1980. 468 pp.
After a natural disaster kills Ayla's tribe, members of the Clan of the Cave Bear find her and mistrust her because her blonde hair and blue eyes are different, but she eventually helps them survive.
Genre(s): Epic Literature.

62. *The Mammoth Hunters.* New York: Crown, 1985. 645 pp.
In the sequel to *The Valley of Horses*, Ayla meets a group of people like herself and uses her talents for healing and animal training.
Genre(s): Epic Literature.

63. *The Plains of Passage.* New York: Crown, 1990. 760 pp.
The sequel to *The Mammoth Hunters* finds Ayla and Jondalar on their long journey returning to Jondalar's family.
Genre(s): Epic Literature.

64. *The Valley of Horses.* New York: Crown, 1982. 502 pp.
In the sequel to *The Clan of the Cave Bear*, Ayla spends three years of solitude in a cave, but she eventually meets Jondalar and nurses him back to health after her pet lion attacks him and kills his brother.
Genre(s): Epic Literature.

Baumann, Hans

◆ 65. *I Marched with Hannibal.* New York: Walck, 1962. 226 pp.
An orphan trying to survive becomes part of Hannibal's army and bonds with an elephant as they go through Spain and cross the Alps into Italy during the Second Punic War.
Genre(s): Adventure Story; War Story.

Berry, Francis

66. *I Tell of Greenland.* Boston: Routledge, 1977. 205 pp.
Lost manuscripts appear in the 20th century supporting Erik the Red's first settlement of Greenland, the arrival of Christianity, and the slow death of the colony at Greenland.
Genre(s): Adventure Story; Family Saga.

Blasco-Ibanez, Vicente

67. *Sonnica.* New York: Duffield, 1912. 331 pp.
Hannibal's bloody siege of Saguntum during the Punic Wars lasts for three months.
Genre(s): War Story.

Brennan, J. H.

◆ 68. *Shiva Accused: An Adventure of the Ice Age.* New York: HarperCollins, 1991. 275 pp.
After Shiva attempts to bury the old woman she found drowned by the river, the woman's tribe accuses Shiva of murder, but Shiva escapes during a mammoth stampede in the sequel to *Shiva*.
Genre(s): Religious Fiction.

◆ 69. *Shiva: An Adventure of the Ice Age.* Philadelphia: Lippincott, 1990. 184 pp.
The Ogres save Shiva, a left-handed orphan, and her tribe consider her an outcast until she finds the skull of a Sabre tiger and a circle of stones, but she has to devise a way to keep her tribe from killing the enemy Ogres.
Genre(s): Religious Fiction.

Cocquyt, Kathryn

70. *The Celtic Heart.* St. Paul, MN: Llwellyn, 1994. 600 pp.
The members of the Brigantes tribe, including the warrior Aonghus, try to defeat the Romans invading Britain.
Genre(s): Epic Literature.

Cooper, Brian

71. *Stones of Evil.* London: Macdonald and Jane's, 1974. 213 pp.
In prehistoric Britain, the standing stones represent different aspects of religious life.

Crace, Jim

72. *Gift of Stones.* New York: Scribner's, 1989. 169 pp.
Inhabitants of a Stone Age village must change their lives when they discover bronze.
Genre(s): Domestic Fiction.

Dickinson, Peter

73. *The Blue Knight.* Boston: Little, Brown, 1976. 236 pp.
The priestly caste in a bronze-age culture tries to take control of the secular government with Tron, a young believer, who is forced to serve on both councils.
Genre(s): Adventure Story.

Golding, William

74. *The Inheritors.* New York: Harcourt, 1955. 233 pp.

A happy group of mild-mannered Neanderthals cannot survive when the more technologically advanced beings, homo sapiens, arrive at their campsite.

Harrison, Harry, and Leon Stover

75. *Stonehenge.* New York: Scribner's, 1972. 254 pp.
Three hypotheses posited in this novel are that Stonehenge was built by a Bronze Age Arthur, that it is contemporary to Mycenae's Lion Gate, and that its builders were more sophisticated than the locals who lived in the area.

Herley, Richard

76. *The Flint Lord.* New York: Morrow, 1981. 214 pp.
A tribe fights its internal and external wars in 3000 BC.
Genre(s): Domestic Fiction.

Holland, Cecelia

77. *Pillar of the Sky.* New York: Knopf, 1985. 534 pp.
Moloquin's mother's brother Ladon banishes them from the village, but when the clan's storyteller adopts Moloquin, Moloquin overthrows Ladon to become the new chief.

Kurtén, Björn

78. *Dance of the Tiger.* New York: Pantheon, 1980. 255 pp.
In the Scandinavia of 35,000 years ago, Cro-Magnon men move into Neanderthal territory, and Tiger, a Cro-Magnon, becomes separated from his people.
Genre(s): Adventure Story.

◆ 79. *Singletusk.* New York: Pantheon, 1986. 195 pp.
In the sequel to *Dance of the Tiger,* Tiger's son Whitespear must search for a shaman to heal his wounded brother.

Lambert, Joan Dahr

◆ 80. *Circles of Stone.* New York: Pocket Books, 1997. 416 pp.
The Zenas, healers in a religion of goddesses, carry their beliefs to southern France over one million years ago, and continue to practice them in subsequent centuries.
Genre(s): Family Saga; Religious Fiction.

Leckie, Ross

81. *Hannibal.* Washington, DC: Regnery, 1996. 245 pp.
The intelligent and knowledgeable Hannibal shows his boldness and his determination to take Rome while loving his beautiful Spanish wife, Similce.
Genre(s): War Story; Biographical Fiction.

◆ 82. *Scipio.* Washington, DC: Regnery, 1998. 304 pp.
Publius Cornelius Scipio Africanus wins victories over Hannibal and his hordes in the sequel to *Hannibal,* but be-cause Scipio's enemy, Cato, accuses him of taking treasures and bribes in Rome, he must face trial.
Genre(s): War Story; Biographical Fiction.

Mackey, Mary

83. *The Year the Horses Came.* San Francisco: HarperSanFrancisco, 1993. 377 pp.
Marrah rescues Stavan in 4372 BC, and her culture's beliefs, including women choosing husbands based on their care of children, shocks him.
Genre(s): Fantastic Literature.

Masters, John

84. *The Rock.* New York: Putnam, 1970. 383 pp.
The generations of a family live near the Rock of Gibraltar, and interact with Phoenicians, Romans, Visigoths, and Moors.

McKee, Lynn Armistead

85. *Walks in Stardust.* New York: Berkley, 1994. 352 pp.
Members of a prehistoric society focus on survival and companionship.
Genre(s): Romance.

Rutherfurd, Edward

◆ 86. *Sarum.* New York: Crown, 1987. 897 pp.
The town of Salisbury, England, reveals five families residing in its environs who have lived there from the last Ice Age to the present.
Genre(s): Family Saga.

Sinclair, James

87. *Warrior Queen.* New York: St. Martin's, 1978. 352 pp.
Boadicea, queen of the Iceni, challenges the Romans and almost defeats them.
Genre(s): War Story.

Sutcliff, Rosemary

◆ 88. *Song for a Dark Queen.* New York: Crowell, 1979. 181 pp.
Boudicca, queen of the Iceni, tries to save Britain from the Romans around AD 60 after they rape her daughters and beat her, and she and supporters burn London before newly arrived Roman troops defeat them.
Genre(s): Biographical Fiction.

◆ 89. *Sun Horse, Moon Horse.* New York: Dutton, 1978. The British Isles pp.
Lubrin, an Iceni tribe member around 100 BC, loves to draw, and when the enemy Attributes capture his people, their leader agrees to save them if Lubrin will draw a horse on the hillside.

Tarr, Judith

◆ 90. *White Mare's Daughter.* New York: Forge, 1998. 496 pp.

In Eastern Europe, around 4500 BC, Sarama seres White Mare, the incarnation of the Horse Goddess, and when told to seek the civilization where women are rumored to be the rulers, Sarama departs willingly.
Genre(s): Fantastic Literature; War Story.

Tempest, John

◆ 91. *Vision of the Hunter.* New York: Harper and Row, 1989. 288 pp.
Finn's prehistoric tribe in Northern Europe depends on reindeer, and when the herds decrease, Finn contemplates how to domesticate the deer.

Thomas, Elizabeth Marshall

◆ 92. *The Animal Wife.* Boston: Houghton Mifflin, 1990. 289 pp.
In Siberia, 20,000 years ago, Kori captures from another tribe a woman whom he names Muskrat, and their relationship evolves as the tribe constantly searches for food.
Genre(s): Adventure Story.

◆ 93. *Reindeer Moon.* Boston: Houghton Mifflin, 1987. 338 pp.
Yanan becomes more important to her prehistoric Siberian tribe after she dies.
Genre(s): Adventure Story.

Treece, Henry

◆ 94. *The Dark Island.* New York: Random House, 1953. 312 pp.
The Romans invade Britain, and Caradoc, king of a Celtic tribe, attempts to repel them.
Genre(s): War Story.

◆ 95. *Red Queen, White Queen.* New York: Random House, 1958. 243 pp.
During the time of Nero, Queen Boadicea leads tribes from Celtic England against the Roman invaders.
Genre(s): War Story.

Waltari, Mika

96. *The Etruscan.* New York: Putnam, 1956. 381 pp.
A wealthy Etruscan who survives many adventures believes he is immortal before his death in 500 BC.
Genre(s): Adventure Story.

Weenolsen, Hebe

97. *The Forbidden Mountain.* New York: Morrow, 1983. 353 pp.
The Beaker king Sinnoch decides to rebuild Stonehenge to suit his sun-worshipping people around 2000 BC while placating the Blue Ax tribe by placing imported bluestones in a circle.
Genre(s): Religious Fiction.

Wolf, Joan

◆ 98. *Daughter of the Red Deer.* New York: Dutton, 1991. 420 pp.
The Tribe of the Horse has lost most of its women in an accident, and the men raid the Tribe of the Red Deer for 16 women, including the priestess's daughter Alin, whom they have difficulty controlling.

◆ 99. *The Horsemasters.* New York: Dutton, 1993. 401 pp.
Ronan, son of the Mistress of the Red Deer, is falsely accused and exiled, and he must form his own tribe with other misfits and teach them how to fight the men of the north who utilize the strength of horses in their fights, in the sequel to *Daughter of the Red Deer.*

◆ 100. *The Reindeer Hunters.* New York: Dutton, 1994. 368 pp.
The Kindred tribe in the sequel to *The Horsemasters,* threatened in prehistoric France with global warming, unites Nardo with Alane of the Norakomo tribe in marriage so that the two groups can together confront the Redu tribe which is trying to take their hunting grounds.

Greece

Apostolou, Anna

101. *A Murder in Macedon.* New York: St. Martin's, 1997. 256 pp.
Alexander the Great asks his Jewish friends Miriam and Simeon to investigate the murder of his father Philip, for they know many people who would have liked to see Philip dead.
Genre(s): Mystery.

102. *A Murder in Thebes.* New York: St. Martin's, 1998. 240 pp.
After the fall of Thebes in 331 BC, someone murders two of Alexander the Great's favorite officers, and he uses two Israelite friends to find the traitor.
Genre(s): Mystery; War Story.

Bova, Ben

103. *Orion and the Conqueror.* New York: Tor, 1994. 350 pp.
When Orion comes to the court of Philip II to ensure that Alexander is his successor, he comes under the control of Olympaias, Alexander's mother.
Genre(s): War Story; Time Travel.

Bradley, Marion Zimmer

◆ 104. *The Firebrand.* New York: Simon and Schuster, 1987. 608 pp.
Kassandra, the Trojan princess, can foresee the future for her family at the end of their war with the Greeks but has no power to change the outcome.
Genre(s): War Story; Fantastic Literature.

Bradshaw, Gillian

◆ 105. *Horses of Heaven.* Garden City, NY: Doubleday, 1991. 448 pp.
A powerful king and his beautiful wife have a son who must choose between them.

Brindel, June Rachuy

106. *Phaedra.* New York: St. Martin's, 1985. 227 pp.
Phaedra, hostile to the warrior culture of Theseus, represents the Earth Mother and stays at odds with Theseus.
Genre(s): Fantastic Literature.

Bryher

107. *The Coin of Carthage.* New York: Harcourt, 1963. 240 pp.
Two Greek traders adapt themselves to the fortunes of Rome and Carthage alternatively, in order to survive during the Second Punic War.
Genre(s): War Story.

108. *Gate to the Sea.* New York: Pantheon, 1958. 128 pp.
Harmonia, a priestess, has possession of the Poseidonian relics, which she tries to save from the conquering Italic tribe, the Lucanians.
Genre(s): War Story.

Caldecott, Moyra

◆ 109. *The Lily and the Bull.* New York: Hill and Wang, 1979. 177 pp.
During the reign of a queen grieving for her king, a teenaged girl and an acrobat have problems in the clash between two religious cults.
Genre(s): Religious Fiction.

Caldwell, Taylor

110. *Glory and the Lightning.* Garden City, NY: Doubleday, 1970. 468 pp.
After Aspasia of Miletus flees to Athens to start an academy for girls, she meets Pericles, and their life together begins.
Genre(s): Biographical Fiction; Love Story.

Craft, Elisabeth Roberts

111. *A Spy for Hannibal: A Novel of Carthage.* Silver Spring, MD: Bartleby, 1996. 290 pp.
Hasdrubal, a high priest in Carthage, becomes a spy for Hannibal in Rome while his brother serves in his army.
Genre(s): Spy Fiction.

Dimont, Madelon

112. *Darling Pericles.* New York: Atheneum, 1972. 217 pp.
Aspasia's father allows her to become educated, but when she realizes that the only way for a woman to succeed in Greece is to become a prostitute, she woos and wins Pericles with both her wiles and her wisdom.
Genre(s): Biographical Fiction.

Doody, Margaret Anne

◆ 113. *Aristotle, Detective.* New York: Harper and Row, 1978. 278 pp.
As a detective, Aristotle decides that someone of the non-Philemon class killed Boutades since Philemon did not kill him, and Stephanos, his helper, aids him in the solution.
Genre(s): Mystery.

Druon, Maurice

114. *Alexander the God.* New York: Scribner's, 1960. 319 pp.
Alexander wants his military victories and his abilities to make him look like a god.
Genre(s): War Story; Biographical Fiction.

Franklin, Sarah B.

115. *Daughter of Troy.* New York: Avon, 1998. 300 pp.
A young boy escapes a storm near Troy's ruins, and the older woman with whom he seeks shelter happens to be Briseis, who tells him about the political and personal wars at Troy as well as her relationship with Agamemnon and Achilles.
Genre(s): Fantastic Literature; Adventure Story; Biographical Fiction.

Freedman, Nancy

116. *Sappho: The Tenth Muse.* New York: St. Martin's, 1998. 352 pp.
The poet Sappho succumbs to her passions and falls in love with a succession of students, and when one of them rejects her, she kills herself.
Genre(s): Biographical Fiction.

Frye, Ellen

◆ 117. *The Other Sappho.* Ithaca, NY: Firebrand, 1989. 214 pp.
Lykaina, an independent Spartan woman, travels to see Sappho on the isle of Lesbos to learn about writing poetry, and there she finds a companion as well.
Genre(s): Biographical Fiction.

Gaines, Charles Kelsey

118. *By the Will of Apollo.* Nashville, TN: Vanderbilt University, 1976. 434 pp.
Cylon, a spearman, describes the rebellion in Athens, ca. 632 BC.
Genre(s): War Story; Biographical Fiction.

119. *Gorgo.* Nashville, TN: Vanderbilt University, 1976. 507 pp.
Theramenes falls in love in Athens, but he dies in battle during the Peloponnesian War in the fifth century.
Genre(s): Biographical Fiction; Romance; War Story.

Gardner, John Champlin

120. *The Wreckage of Agathon.* New York: Harper, 1970. 243 pp.

Agathon, a dissolute old Socratic teacher, discourses with his student, a practical youth.
Genre(s): Bildungsroman (Coming of Age).

Gemmell, David

121. **Dark Prince.** New York: Ballantine, 1993. 558 pp.
Parmenion, a great general under Alexander's father Philip, knows that Alexander is under the influence of the Dark God, Kadmilos.
Genre(s): Biographical Fiction; Fantastic Literature.

122. **Lion of Macedon.** New York: Ballantine, 1992. 516 pp.
An aging seeress shapes the career of Parmenion, who rises to head the Greek armies when Sparta scorns him for having a mixed ancestry.
Genre(s): Biographical Fiction; Fantastic Literature.

Gilchrist, Ellen

◆ 123. **Anabasis.** Jackson: University of Mississippi Press, 1994. 192 pp.
In 431 BC, Auria becomes the apprentice of Philokrates, a healer, and when Philokrates dies, Auria escapes into the mountains with a child and animals searching for a band of antislavery rebels.
Genre(s): Domestic Fiction; Medical Novel.

Golding, William

124. **The Double Tongue.** New York: Farrar, Straus and Giroux, 1995. 165 pp.
When Arieka flees an arranged marriage in Greek Aetolia, she shames her family and herself, but Ionides, the high priestess of the Delphic oracle offers her a position as a Pythia, or priestess of the oracle, and she performs so well that Arieka becomes First Pythia.
Genre(s): Religious Fiction.

Gordon, Caroline

125. **The Glory of Hera.** New York: Doubleday, 1972. 432 pp.
Heracles spends his life trying to escape Hera's hounding, and the story presents the gods and their attributes, which cannot be understood by mortals, along with mortals themselves.
Genre(s): Religious Fiction; Fantastic Literature.

Graves, Robert

126. **Hercules, My Shipmate.** Creative Age Press, 1945. 464 pp.
Hercules joins Jason and his Argonauts as a drunk on the ship that sails in quest of the Golden Fleece.
Genre(s): Fantastic Literature.

127. **Homer's Daughter.** New York: Doubleday, 1955. 204 pp.
Nausicaa, a Sicilian princess of the eighth century BC, remembers her life and her encounter with Odysseus, which she writes about in *The Odyssey.*
Genre(s): Fantastic Literature.

Green, Peter

128. **The Laughter of Aphrodite.** 1965. Berkeley: University of California Press, 1993. 274 pp.
The Greek poet Sappho lives and writes her poetry on the isle of Lesbos.
Genre(s): Biographical Fiction.

Green, Roger Lancelyn

129. **Mystery at Mycenae.** New York: Barnes, 1959. 137 pp.
The men of Mycenae rise together to return Helen to Greece after she runs away with Paris to Troy.
Genre(s): War Story.

Hambleton, Ronald

130. **The Love and Death of Orpheus.** Toronto: Green Bushell, 1979. 192 pp.
Orpheus, son of an emancipated woman, sails on the Argo with Jason before falling in love with Eurydice.
Genre(s): Fantastic Literature.

Holt, Tom

131. **Goatsong.** New York: St. Martin's, 1990. 256 pp.
When Eupolis of Pallene's first play fails, Eupolis joins the military, but when he returns home his comic dramas compete with those of Aristophanes.

132. **The Walled Orchard.** New York: St. Martin's, 1991. 304 pp.
In the sequel to *Goatsong*, Eupolis joins an expedition to Sicily where he escapes from a walled orchard and returns to Athens only to be accused and then acquitted on charges of treason before writing *The Demes*, a satire on the problems of Athens.
Genre(s): War Story; Legal Story.

Kazantzakis, Nikos

133. **Alexander the Great.** Trans. Theodora Vasils. Athens: Ohio University Press, 1982. 222 pp.
Young Stephen, son of a Royal Court physician, adores Alexander the Great and describes his accomplishments.
Genre(s): Biographical Fiction.

Maturin, Ann

134. **The Copper Clew.** Philadelphia: Dorrance, 1973. 118 pp.
In Crete, Theseus challenges and defeats the Minotaur using Ariadne's advice.
Genre(s): Fantastic Literature.

Mitchison, Naomi

135. **Cloud Cuckoo Land.** London: Hodder and Stoughton, 1967. 255 pp.
An inhabitant of an island almost crushed during the Peloponnesian War escapes with his family to Athens and then to Sparta, but he hates the attitudes of the Spartans and moves again.
Genre(s): War Story.

136. ***The Corn King and the Spring Queen.*** London: Jonathan Cape, 1931. 721 pp.
Scythia and Sparta battle in the third century BC, a conflict that pits barbarians against Hellenism.
Genre(s): War Story.

Molinaro, Ursule

137. ***The Autobiography of Cassandra.*** Danbury, CT: Archer Editions, 1979. 129 pp.
Cassandra is given the low status of Greek women while she simultaneously has the knowledge of the future.
Genre(s): War Story; Fantastic Literature.

138. ***The New Moon with the Old Moon in Her Arms.*** Kingston, NY: McPherson, 1993. 119 pp.
A Thargelia bride, also a female poet, decides that she will sacrifice herself in protest of the discrimination against women when she and a ritual groom are to be stoned to death as they walk through Athens.
Genre(s): Religious Fiction.

139. ***Power Dreamers.*** Kingston, NY: McPherson, 1994. 125 pp.
Jocasta admits to knowing that Oedipus is her son when she marries him.
Genre(s): Domestic Fiction.

Parotti, Phillip

◆ 140. ***Fires in the Sky.*** New York: Ticknor and Fields, 1990. 320 pp.
Dymas, at 18, lives in Troy prior to the Trojan War, where he becomes involved in Hecuba's court intrigues.
Genre(s): War Story.

◆ 141. ***The Greek Generals Talk.*** Urbana, IL: University of Illinois, 1986. 164 pp.
Twelve men who once served in the Trojan War tell their stories 50 years later about the war and about the people they knew.
Genre(s): Fantastic Literature.

Paton Walsh, Jill

142. ***Farewell, Great King.*** New York: Coward-McCann, 1972. 255 pp.
The Athenian general and statesman Themistocles writes to the Persian King Artaxerxes and tells him that he must take poison rather than betray his country.
Genre(s): War Story; Biographical Fiction.

Penfield, Wilder

143. ***The Torch.*** Boston: Little, Brown, 1960. 370 pp.
Hippocrates tries to heal Greeks during the fourth century BC.
Genre(s): Biographical Fiction; Medical Novel.

Powell, Richard

◆ 144. ***Whom the Gods Would Destroy.*** New York: Scribner's, 1970. 378 pp.

Helios, a young Trojan, narrates the story of the Trojan War and the roles played in it including Paris, Helen, Cassandra, and Achilles.
Genre(s): War Story.

Renault, Mary

◆ 145. ***The Bull from the Sea.*** New York: Pantheon, 1962. 343 pp.
Theseus, king of Athens, marries the Cretan princess Phaedra but loves the Amazon Hippolyta, in the sequel to *The King Must Die.*
Genre(s): Fantastic Literature.

◆ 146. ***Fire from Heaven.*** New York: Pantheon, 1969. 375 pp.
Aristotle influences the young Alexander, along with Alexander's friend and lover, his mother, and others before the death of his father, Philip of Macedonia.
Genre(s): War Story; Biographical Fiction.

◆ 147. ***Funeral Games.*** New York: Pantheon, 1981. 335 pp.
In the sequel to *The Persian Boy*, Alexander dies in Babylon and many claimants vie to take power.
Genre(s): Biographical Fiction.

◆ 148. ***The King Must Die.*** New York: Pantheon, 1958. 338 pp.
Theseus joins the bull-dancers in Crete and takes advantage of an earthquake to overthrow the kingdom.
Genre(s): Fantastic Literature.

◆ 149. ***The Last of the Wine.*** Pantheon, 1956. 389 pp.
Alexias, taught by Socrates, tells about his life as a wealthy Athenian.
Genre(s): War Story; Sea Story.

◆ 150. ***The Mask of Apollo.*** New York: Pantheon, 1966. 371 pp.
The antique mask of Apollo which the actor Nikeratos carries with him when he travels begins to represent his attitude as an artist.

◆ 151. ***The Persian Boy.*** New York: Pantheon, 1972. 419 pp.
In the sequel to *Fire from Heaven*, Bagoas the eunuch tells of Alexander the Great's expedition into Asia.
Genre(s): Biographical Fiction.

◆ 152. ***The Praise Singer.*** New York: Pantheon, 1978. 290 pp.
Simonides, a famous bard, praises the ancient tyrants in his memorized songs of them and of Greek history.
Genre(s): Biographical Fiction.

Rofheart, Martha

153. ***My Name Is Sappho.*** New York: Putnam, 1974. 382 pp.
Sappho has a lifelong friendship with her fellow poet Alchaeus.
Genre(s): Biographical Fiction.

Sallaska, Georgia

◆ 154. *Priam's Daughter.* New York: Doubleday, 1970. 353 pp.
Cassandra, daughter of Priam and Hecuba, endures much both during the Trojan War and afterward when Agamemnon takes her with him to Greece, because she can see into the future, but no one believes her.
Genre(s): War Story; Fantastic Literature.

Seymour, Miranda

155. *The Goddess.* New York: Coward-McCann, 1979. 365 pp.
Although Helen thinks that Menelaus might have had something to do with the death of her brothers, she decides to leave her country and marry him, but when Paris and his passion overcome her, she goes to Troy with him.
Genre(s): War Story; Fantastic Literature.

156. *Medea.* New York: St. Martin's, 1982. 247 pp.
Medea's passion and desire for power cause the tragedies of her life with Jason and the death of her two sons in ancient Greece.
Genre(s): Fantastic Literature.

Shipway, George

157. *Warrior in Bronze.* New York: Walker, 1977. 276 pp.
Around 1300 BC, Agamemnon rises to the Mycenaen throne after a series of family horrors.
Genre(s): Fantastic Literature; Political Fiction.

Somtow, S. P.

158. *The Shattered Horse.* New York: Tor, 1986. 464 pp.
After the Trojan War, Astyanax survives to avenge the losses of the Trojans and sets in motion another cycle of war as the Bronze Age evolves into the Iron Age.
Genre(s): Fantastic Literature.

Sutcliff, Rosemary

◆ 159. *The Flowers of Adonis.* New York: Coward-McCann, 1970. 383 pp.
Alcibiades makes an expedition to Sicily during the Peloponnesian War before going to Sparta and Ionia and dying in exile at Thrace.
Genre(s): Biographical Fiction.

Taleb, Mirza

160. *Hannibal, Man of Destiny.* Boston: Branden, 1974. 348 pp.

Hannibal fights for Carthage during the second Punic War from 218 to 201 BC.
Genre(s): Biographical Fiction; War Story.

Tarr, Judith

◆ 161. *Lord of the Two Lands.* New York: T. Doherty, 1993. 317 pp.
The Egyptian princess Meriamon, daughter of Pharaoh Nectanebo, reveals the destiny of Alexander the Great.
Genre(s): Biographical Fiction; Fantastic Literature.

Twose, Anna

162. *The Lion of Athens.* London: Chatto and Windus, 1976. 236 pp.
Aspasia, consort of Pericles, enjoys her conversations with Sophocles, Euripides, and Aristophanes in ancient Athens.
Genre(s): Biographical Fiction.

Vidal, Gore

163. *Creation.* New York: Random House, 1981. 510 pp.
In 445 BC, 75-year-old Cyrus Spitama of Periclean Athens dictates memoirs of his exciting experiences to his young nephew, Democritus.

Walton, Evangeline

◆ 164. *The Sword Is Forged.* New York: Timescape, 1983. 347 pp.
Theseus voyages with Hercules and abducts Antiope, Queen of the Amazons, who bears him his son Hippolytos.
Genre(s): Fantastic Literature.

Wolf, Christa

165. *Medea.* New York: Doubleday, 1998. 192 pp.
Medea, trained in the healing arts, helps citizens of Corinth, but when she speaks against injustice, they revile her.
Genre(s): Fantastic Literature; Biographical Fiction.

Wolfe, Gene

◆ 166. *Soldier of the Mist.* New York: Tor, 1986. 355 pp.
Latro, a mercenary soldier in Greece during 479 BC, loses his memory after a head injury, but from his journal, he is able to tell what happened the previous day.
Genre(s): Adventure Story.

Palestine and the Near East

Arthur, Kay

167. *Israel, My Beloved.* Eugene, OR: Harvest House, 1997. 450 pp.

Strong men and women like Sarah, gentle Enoch, and Rebecca are some of the people who help to establish the nation of Israel.
Genre(s): Religious Fiction.

Asch, Sholem

168. *The Prophet.* Trans. Arthur Saul Super. New York: Putnam, 1955. 343 pp.
In the sequel to *Moses*, the second Isaiah, in the fifth century BC, reveals life in Babylon under Cyrus the Persian as the Israelites prepare to return to their homeland.
Genre(s): Religious Fiction; War Story.

Austin, Lynn N.

169. *The Lord Is My Salvation.* Kansas City, MO: Beacon Hill, 1996. 272 pp.
King Hezekiah continues trying to reunite his people with their God while Assyrians march toward Jerusalem (*Series:* Chronicles of the King, 3)
Genre(s): Biographical Fiction; Religious Fiction.

◆ 170. *The Lord Is My Strength.* Kansas City, MO: Beacon Hill, 1995. 206 pp.
Hezekiah becomes the king of Judah. (*Series:* Chronicles of the King, 1)
Genre(s): Christian Fiction.

171. *My Father's God.* Kansas City, MO: Beacon Hill, 1997. 282 pp.
Manasseh, the young king of Judah, depends on his friend Joshua to help him, but when a fortuneteller relates to Manasseh, 12, that Joshua will cause his downfall, he believes her, and when he reaches the age of 21 he starts to purge his kingdom. (*Series:* Chronicles of the King, 4)
Genre(s): Christian Fiction; Religious Fiction; Jewish Fiction.

Brelich, Mario

172. *The Holy Embrace.* Marlboro, VT: Marlboro, 1994. 229 pp.
Abraham, stricken with a vision of holiness, tells his wife Sarah that in their old age, they must have a son whose name will be Isaac, which means laughter.
Genre(s): Biographical Fiction; Religious Fiction.

Bremkamp, Gloria Howe

173. *Merari.* San Francisco: Harper and Row, 1986. 190 pp.
The Sunammite woman, Merari, shelters the prophet Elisha after he restores her son to life and helps her family regain its lands.
Genre(s): Religious Fiction.

Cassill, R. V.

174. *After Goliath.* New York: Ticknor and Fields, 1985. 208 pp.
David rules as king of Israel, but his strong personality conflicts with others who also want control.
Genre(s): Religious Fiction.

Chamberlin, Ann

175. *Tamar.* New York: Forge, 1994. 463 pp.

Tamar, David's stepdaughter, is princess of Judah and high priestess of the goddess whom she supports, rather than of the patriarch of Judah.
Genre(s): Religious Fiction.

Chinn, Laurene

176. *The Unanointed.* New York: Crown, 1959. 351 pp.
Joab remains faithful to David as his military commander.
Genre(s): Religious Fiction.

177. *Voice of the Lord.* New York: Crown, 1961. 381 pp.
Jeremias, gentle but fearless, prophesies the destruction of Jerusalem.
Genre(s): Religious Fiction.

Coelho, Paulo

178. *The Fifth Mountain.* New York: HarperCollins, 1998. 240 pp.
Elijah prophesizes about the Israelites.
Genre(s): Religious Fiction; Biographical Fiction.

Danielson, Peter

179. *The Death of Kings.* New York: Bantam, 1994. 256 pp.
Saul is jealous of the young David and pursues him while the Philistines advance.
Genre(s): Religious Fiction.

Dial, James L.

180. *The Harlot of Jericho.* Radford, VA: Commonwealth, 1974. 177 pp.
When Joshua's men come to Jericho to spy on the locals, Rahab, the prostitute, defies the orders of the king and helps them escape.
Genre(s): Biographical Fiction; Religious Fiction.

Diamant, Anita

◆ 181. *The Red Tent.* New York: St. Martin's, 1997. 320 pp.
Dinah grows up with the strong aid of her mothers, Leah, Rachel, Zilpah, and Bilhah, in the red women's tent, but when she falls in love with a Canaanite, her brothers betray her by murdering him and others.
Genre(s): Christian Fiction; Family Saga.

Dorr, Roberta Kells

182. *Solomon's Song.* San Francisco: Harper and Row, 1989. 322 pp.
Solomon falls in love with Shulamit, the woman his father David is supposed to marry.
Genre(s): Biographical Fiction; Religious Fiction; Christian Fiction.

Fast, Howard

◆ 183. *My Glorious Brothers.* 1948. New York: Bonim, 1977. 280 pp.

Judas Maccabeus liberates the Jews from their Syrian-Greek conquerors.
Genre(s): Biographical Fiction.

Graves, Robert

184. *My Head! My Head.* New York: Haskell House, 1974. 141 pp.
Elisha meets the Shunammite woman, and in his discussions with her, finds that she is well-educated for the time in which she lives.
Genre(s): Religious Fiction.

Hamilton, Wallace

185. *David at Olivet.* New York: St. Martin's, 1979. 202 pp.
Saul and David most likely have a homosexual relationship, and their situation causes Absalom to revolt and further discord in Jonathan and David's friendship.
Genre(s): Biographical Fiction; Religious Fiction.

Hareven, Shulamith

186. *Prophet.* New York: North Point, 1990. 112 pp.
Hivai, a Gibeonite prophet, kills a slave child and leads the way for the nation of Ai to conquer the Gibeonite people, but when he leaves in disguise, he hears that the invisibile God of Moses disdains murder.
Genre(s): Religious Fiction.

Harris, Elbert L.

187. *Sojourn in Persepolis.* Chicago: Adams, 1976. 95 pp.
After the battle of Salamis, Xerxes goes to Persepolis.
Genre(s): Biographical Fiction.

Heller, Joseph

188. *God Knows.* New York: Knopf, 1984. 353 pp.
King David, on his deathbed, recalls his deeds and exploits.
Genre(s): Religious Fiction; Humorous Fiction.

Heym, Stefan

189. *The King David Report.* New York: Putnam, 1973. 254 pp.
King Solomon employs the poet-historian Ethan ben Hoshaiah to write the true story of King David.
Genre(s): Biographical Fiction; Religious Fiction.

Hutchison, Polly A.

190. *Oh, King, Live Forever.* San Diego, CA: Beta, 1977. 146 pp.
Esther risks her life but saves her people from destruction when she pleads for them to her husband, Xerxes, king of Persia.
Genre(s): Biographical Fiction; Religious Fiction.

Jacobson, Dan

191. *The Rape of Tamar.* New York: Macmillan, 1970. 224 pp.
King David's nephew Yonadab tells his version of David's story.
Genre(s): Religious Fiction.

Levine, Faye

192. *Solomon and Sheba.* New York: R. Marek, 1980. 227 pp.
The Queen of Sheba arrives in Jerusalem to test Solomon's wisdom, and their meeting reveals their radically different political and cultural views.
Genre(s): Biographical Fiction; Religious Fiction.

Lindgren, Torgny

193. *Bathsheba.* New York: Harper and Row, 1989. 249 pp.
Bathsheba, a woman of beauty, intelligence, and strength intrigues King David.
Genre(s): Biographical Fiction; Religious Fiction.

Lofts, Norah

194. *Esther.* New York: Macmillan, 1950. 163 pp.
Esther remains devoted to her Jewish people at the Persian court of Artaxerxes.
Genre(s): Religious Fiction.

Martin, Malachi

195. *King of Kings.* New York: Simon and Schuster, 1980. 480 pp.
David works to create the settlement of Zion by defeating his enemies, protecting his family, and advancing his love affairs.
Genre(s): Biographical Fiction; Religious Fiction.

Schmitt, Gladys

196. *David, the King.* New York: Dial, 1973. 631 pp.
David, a shepherd boy, comes to Saul's court to soothe him with song, and even though the jealous man drives David out, the boy eventually returns as king of Israel.
Genre(s): Biographical Fiction; Religious Fiction.

Shott, James R.

197. *Abigail.* Scottdale, PA: Herald, 1996. 144 pp.
Abigail's abusive husband Nabal dies, and she becomes one of David's wives, bearing him a son and becoming his first choice. (*Series:* People of the Promise)
Genre(s): Biographical Fiction; Religious Fiction.

198. *Bathsheba.* Scottdale, PA: Herald, 1997. 152 pp.
King David sees the unhappily married Bathsheba bathing, and after he takes her as a mistress, he sends her husband into battle and to a certain death, an event for which Bathsheba feels responsible.
Genre(s): Religious Fiction; Biographical Fiction.

◆ 199. *Othniel.* Scottdale, PA: Herald, 1994. 168 pp.

The judge Othniel succeeds Joshua, but his son Meonothai has difficulty living in peacetime after so much war. (*Series:* People of the Promise, 6)
Genre(s): Biographical Fiction; Religious Fiction; Christian Fiction.

Slaughter, Frank G.

200. *The Song of Ruth.* Garden City, NY: Doubleday, 1954. 317 pp.
Ruth, the Moabite, marries Mahlon, an Israelite, and after his death, she goes to her mother-in-law's home.
Genre(s): Jewish Fiction.

Stephens, William H.

201. *The Mantle.* Wheaton, IL: Tyndale House, 1976. 303 pp.
Elijah is a prophet of the ninth century BC during the reigns of Kings Ahab and Ahaziah.
Genre(s): Biographical Fiction; Religious Fiction.

Tarr, Herbert

202. *A Time for Loving.* New York: Random House, 1973. 189 pp.
Solomon's wisdom shines in his experiences and in the decisions he makes.
Genre(s): Religious Fiction.

Traylor, Ellen Gunderson

203. *Esther.* Eugene, OR: Harvest House, 1988. 206 pp.
When the emperor of Persia chooses Esther for his queen, she is adored for her beauty and her innocence and she saves thousands from annihilation.
Genre(s): Biographical Fiction; Religious Fiction.

204. *Jerusalem the City of God.* Eugene, OR: Harvest House, 1995. 631 pp.
The city of Jerusalem is witness to many scenes incorporated in Biblical stories including the romance between David and Bathsheba and the tale of Melchizedek.
Genre(s): Religious Fiction; Jewish Fiction; Christian Fiction.

205. *Jonah.* Wheaton, IL: Tyndale House, 1987. 257 pp.
Jonah, a prophet in the eighth century BC, tells Israel that it will expand under the leadership of Jeroboam II.
Genre(s): Biographical Fiction; Religious Fiction.

206. *Joshua, God's Warrior.* Eugene, OR: Harvest House, 1991. 279 pp.
Joshua travels throughout Palestine and battles at the walls of Jericho for his people.
Genre(s): Religious Fiction; Biographical Fiction; Allegory.

207. *Melchizedek.* Eugene, OR: Harvest House, 1997. 178 pp.
The grandson of Canaan, Melchizedek, tells stories about his times while remaining an obscure figure.
Genre(s): Biographical Fiction; Christian Fiction.

208. *Noah.* Wheaton, IL: Tyndale House, 1985. 332 pp.
As the son of Lamech and the grandson of Methuselah, Noah's birth is the first recorded after Adam's death, and he and his family are the only suvivors of the Flood.
Genre(s): Biographical Fiction; Religious Fiction.

209. *Samson.* Eugene, OR: Harvest House, 1993. 351 pp.
Although God has chosen Samson to work for him, Samson has trouble controlling his passions.
Genre(s): Biographical Fiction; Religious Fiction; Love Story.

Traylor, Ruth Gunderson

210. *Ruth.* Wheaton, IL: Tyndale House, 1986. 278 pp.
Ruth goes to live with her mother-in-law, Naomi, and learns more than she had ever anticipated.
Genre(s): Religious Fiction.

211. *Song of Abraham.* Wheaton, IL: Tyndale House, 1981. 456 pp.
Abraham has strength and will in his dealings with God and his family.
Genre(s): Religious Fiction.

Weil, Grete

212. *The Bride Price.* Boston: David R. Godine, 1991. 183 pp.
The author compares her life as first a German and then a Jew with that of David's first wife Michal, who loves him as the narrator loves Germany, but who is inexplicably scorned.
Genre(s): Biographical Fiction; Religious Fiction.

Wright, Patricia

213. *Shadow of the Rock.* Garden City, NY: Doubleday, 1979. 383 pp.
David's kinsman Joab describes their battles with Saul, their loves, and Joab's decision to murder David's treacherous son, Absalom.
Genre(s): Biographical Fiction; Religious Fiction.

Roman Empire to AD 476

Egypt

Bradshaw, Gillian

◆ 214. *The Beacon at Alexandria.* Boston: Houghton Mifflin, 1986. 376 pp.
Betrothed in the fourth century to the Roman governor she hates, Charis flees with her brother's help to Alexandria, where, disguised as a eunuch, she begins studying Hippocratic medicine.
Genre(s): Medical Novel.

Cash, Johnny

215. *Man in White.* San Francisco: Harper and Row, 1986. 226 pp.
Saul of Tarsus, a hated enemy of Jesus's followers, begins to wonder what the people are like who are willing to die for such a man.
Genre(s): Biographical Fiction; Christian Fiction.

George, Margaret

◆ 216. *The Memoirs of Cleopatra.* New York: St. Martin's, 1997. 976 pp.
When she is three, Cleopatra witnesses her mother's death, and this event stays with her throughout her life as she fights for her place in society.
Genre(s): Biographical Fiction; Family Saga.

Kingsley, Charles

217. *Hypatia.* 1853. New York: Dutton, 1968. 438 pp.
The pagans and Christians clash in Alexandria during the fifth century when Hypatia, a female mathematician, lives.
Genre(s): War Story.

Lindsay, Kathleen

218. *Enchantress of the Nile.* London: Hurst and Blackett, 1965. 184 pp.
Cleopatra survives by using her intelligence and by exploiting information she hears about those with enough power to control her.
Genre(s): Biographical Fiction.

Nelson, Ray Faraday

◆ 219. *Dogheaded Death.* Portland, OR: Strawberry Hill, 1989. 184 pp.
In Alexandria, Egypt, during the first century AD, Nero's top palace guard, Gaius Hesperian, has to investigate the murder of a shipping magnate, Odysseus, who was married to a much younger wife.
Genre(s): Mystery.

Niven, Marian

220. *The Altar and the Crown.* Sewanee, TN: University Press, 1972. 407 pp.
Lord Sesostris and Tenatos compete with Ptolemy for the crown in the first century BC, which they do not want, but they will do whatever is necessary to keep peace and security in their Greek and Egyptian world.

Rofheart, Martha

221. *The Alexandrian.* New York: Crowell, 1976. 280 pp.
Cleopatra is an expert linguist and diplomat who manipulates both Caesar and Mark Anthony, who fail when they ignore her wise advice.
Genre(s): Biographical Fiction.

Tarr, Judith

◆ 222. *Throne of Isis.* New York: Forge, 1994. 349 pp.
Cleopatra, somewhat homely, has a regality that blinds the brawny Antony and keeps him by her side.
Genre(s): Biographical Fiction.

Warner, Rex

223. *The Converts.* Boston: Little, Brown, 1967. 337 pp.
Alypius, friend of Augustine, Bishop of Hippo, describes Augustine's conversion to Christianity.
Genre(s): Biographical Fiction; Christian Fiction.

Europe and the British Isles

Bradley, Marion Zimmer

◆ 224. *The Forest House.* New York: Viking, 1994. 416 pp.
Eilan, a druid priestess, falls in love with Gaius Marcellius in Roman Britain while they both wait for a legendary king to unite the island.
Genre(s): Love Story.

◆ **225.** *Lady of Avalon.* New York: Viking, 1997. 412 pp.
Between AD 200 and 500, a priestess, a mother, and a son live through times during which Avalon is threatened, but they discover that personal sacrifice helps it survive.
Genre(s): Fantastic Literature; Family Saga.

Brand, Irene B.

226. *In This Sign Conquer.* Grand Rapids, MI: Kregel, 1996. 301 pp.
The Trento family, especially Lucius, endures many trials of faith under Roman emperors.
Genre(s): Christian Fiction.

Bryher

227. *Roman Wall.* New York: Pantheon, 1954. 219 pp.
Valerius, the officer in charge, his sister Julia, and her ward experience the fall of Orba, a Roman outpost to the barbarians from the north and east.
Genre(s): War Story.

Costain, Thomas Bertram

228. *The Darkness and the Dawn.* Garden City, NY: Doubleday, 1959. 478 pp.
Two young horse breeders live east of the Danube and serve Attila.
Genre(s): Biographical Fiction.

Crow, Donna Fletcher

229. *Glastonbury.* Wheaton, IL: Crossway, 1992. 859 pp.
Austin Ringwode, a Glastonbury monk, recalls the major periods of Christianity in England beginning with the Celts and ending with the time of Henry VIII.
Genre(s): Christian Fiction.

Davis, Lindsey

◆ **230.** *The Iron Hand of Mars.* New York: Crown, 1992. 305 pp.
Marcus Didius Falco goes to Germany in AD 71 to stop a rebel chieftain and find a missing legate.
Genre(s): Mystery.

De Carvalho, Mário

231. *A God Strolling in the Cool of the Evening.* Trans. Gregory Rabassa. Baton Rouge: Louisiana State University Press, 1997. 265 pp.
Lucius Valerius Quintius rules Tarcisis, a small Portuguese city, and faces a variety of problems, but he wants to be just and tries to make decisions based on what he believes his hero, Marcus Aurelius, would do.
Award(s): Pegasus Prize.
Genre(s): Political Fiction; Love Story.

Duggan, Alfred Leo

232. *Conscience of the King.* New York: Coward-McCann, 1951. 250 pp.

In the fifth century AD Cedric rises to power and establishes the West Saxon kingdom, but only by murdering, among others, his brothers and his wife.
Genre(s): Biographical Fiction.

Gloag, John

233. *Caesar of the Narrow Seas.* New York: St. Martin's, 1972. 235 pp.
Lucius Priscus, subordinate of Carausius, helps to establish Carausius as the emperor of Britain in the third century AD, a period in which Maximian and Diocletian also compete for power.
Genre(s): Biographical Fiction; Political Fiction.

Godwin, Parke

◆ **234.** *The Last Rainbow.* New York: Bantam, 1985. 421 pp.
In the sequel to *Beloved Exile*, Patrick goes north to preach to the Picts, and when he offends them, they break his legs and place him within a ring of stones.
Genre(s): Fantastic Literature; Christian Fiction.

Grundy, Stephan

235. *Attila's Treasure.* New York: Bantam, 1996. 512 pp.
Hagan, slayer of Sigifrith, trains as a child in the camp of Attila the Hun.
Genre(s): Fantastic Literature.

Hamilton, Joan Lesley

236. *The Lion and the Cross.* Garden City, NY: Doubleday, 1979. 372 pp.
Patrick, a young slave boy, challenges the Irish rulers and their magic before fleeing Ireland and becoming a sailor, a monk, and a lord in his native Britain before returning to tell Ireland about God.
Genre(s): Biographical Fiction.

Holland, Cecelia

◆ **237.** *The Death of Attila.* New York: Knopf, 1973. 273 pp.
Attila the Hun threatens the Romans and the Germans in the mid-fifth century AD.
Genre(s): Biographical Fiction.

Holland, Jack

238. *Druid Time.* New York: Dodd, Mead, 1986. 256 pp.
Suetonius falls in love with Nero's mother Agrippina before being named as governor to Great Britain where he has to deal with Druids and difficult weather.
Genre(s): Adventure Story.

Llywelyn, Morgan

◆ **239.** *Druids.* New York: Morrow, 1991. 456 pp.
Ainvar, a young Canute orphan, prepares for tribal rituals with Vercingetorix of the Arverni, a process that unites them in freeing Celtic Gaul from the Romans.
Genre(s): Bildungsroman (Coming of Age).

◆May be suitable for young adult readers

◆ 240. *Finn Mac Cool.* New York: Forge, 1994. 400 pp.
In the third century, Finn Mac Cool leads the first Irish army *Fianna*, after deciding to fear no one and becoming the strongest man in Ireland.
Genre(s): Biographical Fiction; Fantastic Literature.

Merezhkovsky, Dmitry

241. *The Death of the Gods.* Trans. Herbert Trench. 1901. Blauvelt, NY: Spiritual Fiction, Putnam, 1989. 463 pp.
The Emperor Julian controls the political and theological developments of the period in which Constantius and Julian rule successfully before Julian's death in an expedition against the Persians.
Genre(s): Biographical Fiction.

Paxson, Diana L.

242. *The Lord of Horses.* New York: Morrow, 1996. 373 pp.
King Gundohar of the Burgundians and his half brother, Hagano, coerce Gudrun, their sister still mourning Sigrid, to marry Attila, khan of the Western Huns, which unites the Niflungars with the Huns to avenge Sigfrid's death. (*Series:* Wodan's Children, 3)
Genre(s): Biographical Fiction; Fantastic Literature.

◆ 243. *The Shield between the Worlds.* New York: Morrow, 1994. 317 pp.
Fionn mac Cumhal falls in love with Sadh when he is 24, and his grandfather tries to thwart him through his wife, in the sequel to *Master of Earth and Water.*
Genre(s): Biographical Fiction; Fantastic Literature.

Paxson, Diana L., and Adrienne Martine-Barnes

◆ 244. *Master of Earth and Water.* New York: Morrow, 1993. 395 pp.
Two women rush Finn Mac Cumhaill (Fionn mac Cumhal) away from a jealous druid when he is born in Ireland during the third century so that he may grow up to be a poet, prophet, and warrior for his country.
Genre(s): Biographical Fiction; Fantastic Literature.

◆ 245. *Sword of Fire and Shadow.* New York: Morrow, 1995. 426 pp.
In the final work in the Fionn cycle, Fionn makes difficult third-century choices as he is sometimes cruel or foolish, but eventually goddesses take him to sleep where he can gather the strength that Ireland might need from him in the future.
Genre(s): Fantastic Literature.

Rutherfurd, Edward

◆ 246. *London.* New York: Crown, 1997. 800 pp.
London passes through 2,000 years of history in the lives of several families who become enmeshed.
Genre(s): Family Saga.

247. *Russka.* New York: Crown, 1991. 760 pp.

The lives of families inhabiting a small Ukrainian village are chronicled through the centuries from AD 180 to the Russian Revolution.
Genre(s): Family Saga.

Sutcliff, Rosemary

◆ 248. *The Eagle of the Ninth.* New York: Henry Z. Walck, 1961. 264 pp.
After Marcus is wounded, he resigns from the Roman army but stays in Britain and buys a defeated gladiator for a servant, and the man helps him search for his father.

◆ 249. *Frontier Wolf.* New York: Dutton, 1981. 196 pp.
Alexios takes charge of a Roman outpost in Britain during the fourth century and learns to work with the local leaders to obtain his goals.

◆ 250. *The Lantern Bearers.* New York: Henry Z. Walck, 1959. 248 pp.
When the Romans leave Britain in AD 410, Aquila decides to desert the army but remain in Rome since he has never lived there, but Saxons capture and enslave him.
Award(s): Carnegie Medal.
Genre(s): War Story.

◆ 251. *The Silver Branch.* New York: Henry Z. Walck, 1959. 215 pp.
Justin goes to Britain to serve in the Roman army as a surgeon, and when he discovers that the finance minister is betraying them to the local tribes, Justin asserts himself and gains self-confidence in his decisions.

Taylor, Anna

252. *The Gods Are Not Mocked.* New York: Morrow, 1969. 312 pp.
Lucius serves with Caesar in his invasion of Britain and meets Becca, a Druid priestess, who becomes his mistress.
Genre(s): Love Story; Religious Fiction.

Turton, Godfrey

253. *The Festival of Flora.* New York: Doubleday, 1972. 360 pp.
Richard Saltwick owns land dating from the third century, and when he decides to sell it to a corporation making chemicals for warfare, he travels back to the third century and falls in love with Flora, he must decide between the third century and his own time.
Genre(s): Time Travel; Love Story.

Whyte, Jack

◆ 254. *The Singing Sword.* New York: Forge, 1996. 352 pp.
As the Roman empire fails in Britain, the Camulod colony grows, its leaders have problems with the return of Claudius Seneca, and Uther Pendragon and Merlyn Britannicus are born. (*Series:* Camulod Chronicles, 2)
Genre(s): Fantastic Literature.

◆ 255. *The Skystone.* New York: Forge, 1996. 352 pp.

Caius Britannicus becomes friends with Gaius Publius Varrus, the man who saved him in Africa, and as he tries to begin a new community, Varrus, now an ironsmith, hunts for the strong iron from which his grandfather made an exquisite sword later to become Excalibur. (*Series:* Camulod Chronicles, 1)
Genre(s): Fantastic Literature.

Greece

Asch, Sholem

256. *The Apostle.* Trans. Maurice Samuel. New York: Putnam, 1943. 804 pp.
After Jesus's death in the sequel to *The Nazarene*, Paul hears the disciples' teachings, and he begins to develop Christianty throughout the Roman Empire.
Genre(s): Christian Fiction; Biographical Fiction.

Caldwell, Taylor

◆ 257. *Great Lion of God.* Garden City, NY: Doubleday, 1970. 629 pp.
Paul, first a non-believer, becomes one of Jesus's strongest advocates.
Genre(s): Biographical Fiction; Christian Fiction.

Chinn, Laurene

258. *The Soothsayer.* New York: Morrow, 1972. 240 pp.
After Paul meets the half-Jewish, half-Greek youth Timothy, the two travel throughout the Greek and Roman world in the first century AD.
Genre(s): Biographical Fiction; Christian Fiction.

Vrettos, Theodore

259. *Origen.* New Rochelle, NY: Caratzas, 1978. 299 pp.
Origen, with his ceaseless travel and his many volumes of writing, becomes the most important mystical Christian philosopher of the third century.
Genre(s): Biographical Fiction; Christian Fiction.

Palestine and the Near East

Absire, Alain

260. *Lazarus.* Trans. Barbara Bray. San Diego, CA: Harcourt, 1988. 230 pp.
Lazarus goes in search of Jesus to ask why he has suffered since his rising from the dead, but he arrives at Golgotha too late.
Genre(s): Biographical Fiction; Christian Fiction.

Asch, Sholem

261. *Mary.* Trans. Leo Steinberg. New York: Putnam, 1949. 436 pp.
In the sequel to *The Apostle*, Mary's early married years and her attempts to understand her son, Jesus, reveal a devout Jewish mother concerned about her family.
Genre(s): Biographical Fiction; Christian Fiction.

262. *The Nazarene.* Trans. Maurice Samuel. New York: Putnam, 1939. 698 pp.
Three people tell the story of Jesus and place him in the real world of Jerusalem during Roman occupation.
Genre(s): Biographical Fiction; Religious Fiction.

Ashcroft, Mary Ellen

263. *The Magdalene Gospel.* Garden City, NY: Doubleday, 1995. 129 pp.
Among the women at Jesus's tomb were Mary Magdalene, Martha, and Mary, and they tell their stories.
Genre(s): Biographical Fiction; Christian Fiction.

Bekessy, Emery

264. *Barabbas.* Trans. Richard and Clara Winston. Englewood Cliffs, NJ: Prentice Hall, 1946. 324 pp.
Barabbas contrasts to Jesus with his materialism and belief in violence as a way to defend the people against foreign rulers.
Genre(s): Religious Fiction; Allegory.

Betty, L. Stafford

265. *The Rich Man.* New York: St. Martin's, 1984. 209 pp.
Jonah ben Jonathan, a wealthy man, receives a warning from Jesus that getting to heaven and being wealthy is like a camel passing through the eye of a needle.
Genre(s): Religious Fiction.

Bouwer, Sigmund

266. *The Weeping Chamber.* Dallas, TX: Word, 1998. 350 pp.
After the wealthy Simeon of Cyrene's son dies in a fire and his daughter is lamed, he goes to Jerusalem where he witnesses Jesus performing some of his miracles.
Genre(s): Christian Fiction.

Bradshaw, Gillian

◆ 267. *Imperial Purple.* Boston: Houghton Mifflin, 1988. 324 pp.

An official forces Demetrias, a slave and silk weaver, to help in attempting to overthrow the Emperor Theodosius II in Tyre.

Brelich, Mario

268. *The Work of Betrayal.* Marlboro, VT: Marlboro, 1988. 238 pp.
Dupin, from Poe's *Murders in the Rue Morgue*, wonders about the relationship of Judas Iscariot to Jesus.
Genre(s): Biographical Fiction; Christian Fiction.

Burgess, Anthony

269. *Man of Nazareth.* New York: McGraw Hill, 1979. 357 pp.
Jesus is a man of deep compassion and many emotions as he interacts with people around him.
Genre(s): Biographical Fiction; Christian Fiction.

Caldwell, Taylor

270. *I, Judas.* New York: Atheneum, 1977. 371 pp.
Judas seems to have been betrayed himself and may have believed that the man who made Lazarus live would not die.
Genre(s): Biographical Fiction; Christian Fiction.

Callaghan, Morley

271. *A Time for Judas.* New York: St. Martin's, 1984. 247 pp.
Instead of traitor, Judas is Jesus's trusted friend in first-century Jerusalem.
Genre(s): Biographical Fiction; Christian Fiction.

Carse, James P

272. *The Gospel of the Beloved Disciple.* San Francisco: HarperSanFrancisco, 1997. 160 pp.
A Samaritan woman is Jesus' confidant throughout his ministry, and she relates his different teachings to appropriate audiences in her day, interpreting his meanings pragmatically.
Genre(s): Christian Fiction.

Chinn, Laurene

273. *Marcus.* New York: Morrow, 1965. 370 pp.
The apostle Mark becomes converted and begins his labors which earn him the position of Bishop of Alexandria.
Genre(s): Christian Fiction.

Costain, Thomas Bertram

274. *The Silver Chalice.* Garden City, NY: Doubleday, 1952. 533 pp.
Basil, an artisan who fashions the silver cup from which Jesus drinks at the last supper, moves around Antioch, Rome, and Jerusalem after the event.
Genre(s): Christian Fiction; Love Story.

Crace, Jim

275. *Quarantine.* New York: Farrar, Straus and Giroux, 1998. 256 pp.

The land of Judea during the life of Jesus has many unique inhabitants.
Genre(s): Religious Fiction; Political Fiction.

Douglas, Lloyd C.

276. *The Big Fisherman.* Boston: Houghton Mifflin, 1948. 581 pp.
In the sequel to *The Robe*, Simon Peter wanders throughout the Roman empire after the death of Jesus.
Genre(s): Christian Fiction; Biographical Fiction.

277. *The Robe.* Boston: Houghton Mifflin, 1942. 695 pp.
Marcellus, a young Roman soldier, wins the robe of Jesus Christ at dice, and it changes his life.
Genre(s): Christian Fiction.

Edwards, Gene

278. *The Triumph.* Wheaton, IL: Tyndale House, 1995. 186 pp.
The crucifixion of Jesus becomes a dramatic moment in Christian history. (*Series:* Chronicles of the Door, 4)
Genre(s): Biographical Fiction; Christian Fiction.

Elwood, Roger

279. *Darien: Guardian Angel of Jesus.* Dallas: Word, 1994. 396 pp.
Darien, Jesus' guardian angel, is with Jesus throughout his life, but he cannot foretell the future.
Genre(s): Biographical Fiction; Christian Fiction.

280. *The Road to Masada.* Chicago: Moody, 1994. 454 pp.
Pontius Pilate, his wife, and Roman legionnaries attend Jesus' crucifixion and become involved with the conquering of Masada.
Genre(s): Christian Fiction.

Feuchtwanger, Lion

281. *Josephus.* Trans. Willa and Edwin Muir. New York: Viking, 1932. 504 pp.
In AD 64, Josephus visits Rome, then goes to Jerusalem, staying until it falls in AD 70, when he returns to Rome to begin his life as a writer.
Genre(s): Biographical Fiction; War Story.

Finegan, Jack

282. *Mark of the Taw.* Richmond, VA: John Knox, 1972. 272 pp.
When Mark flees from Jerusalem with Simon Peter after Jesus's death, he writes down everything he hears about the man and his followers.
Genre(s): Biographical Fiction; Christian Fiction.

Flynn, Cleta

283. *The Parable.* Virginia Beach, VA: Donning, 1979. 157 pp.
At 13, Yeshua ben Josephus (Jesus) knows his birth circumstances and takes the vow of the Nazarite.
Genre(s): Biographical Fiction; Christian Fiction.

Fredman, John

284. **The Wolf of Masada.** New York: Morrow, 1979. 439 pp.
When Romans capture Simon ben Eleazar from the Judean hills, make him a slave, and demand that he perform to the death in an arena, he escapes through the graces of the Emperor Caligula and eventually becomes friends with Vespasian before dying at Masada.
Genre(s): War Story.

Gann, Ernest Kellogg

285. **The Antagonists.** New York: Simon and Schuster, 1970. 287 pp.
Flavius Silva, a Roman general, fights Eleazar ben Yair at Masada in AD 73.
Genre(s): War Story.

Graves, Robert

286. **King Jesus.** 1946. New York: Farrar, Straus and Giroux, 1981. 424 pp.
Jesus is the son of Mary's first husband, a son of Herod, which makes Jesus a grandson of the king and the legitimate bearer of the title "King of the Jews."
Genre(s): Biographical Fiction; Christian Fiction.

Grimes, Nikki

287. **Portrait of Mary.** New York: Harcourt, 1994. 116 pp.
Mary, unsure of how to react to all of the strange things happening to her, does not actually understand her part in history until Jesus returns to her after his death.
Genre(s): Biographical Fiction; Christian Fiction.

Gross, Joel

288. **The Lives of Rachel.** New York: New American Library, 1984. 424 pp.
In the sequel to *The Books of Rachel*, the first of the five Rachels in the Cuheno (Cohen) family refuses to betray her Maccabee husband to Antiochus.
Genre(s): Jewish Fiction; Family Saga.

Halter, Marek

◆ 289. **The Book of Abraham.** Trans. Lowell Bair. New York: Holt, Rinehart and Winston, 1986. 722 pp.
Beginning with the scribe Abraham, who flees the Roman army in AD 70, a long line of descendants continue scribal work until one, a printer, dies in the Warsaw ghetto in 1943.
Genre(s): Jewish Fiction; Family Saga.

Haugaard, Erik

◆ 290. **The Rider and His Horse.** Boston: Houghton Mifflin, 1968. 243 pp.
Rather than submit to the Romans, the Jews Eleazar ben Ya'ir and the Zealots defend Masada until death.
Genre(s): War Story.

Holmes, Marjorie

◆ 291. **The Messiah.** New York: Harper and Row, 1987. 396 pp.
Before his betrayal, Jesus preaches to those around him, including Peter and his wife and Mary and Martha.
Genre(s): Biographical Fiction; Christian Fiction.

◆ 292. **Three from Galilee.** New York: Harper and Row, 1985. 230 pp.
The sequel to *Two from Galilee* reveals Jesus in his youth as he begins to understand his role in society.
Genre(s): Christian Fiction.

293. **Two from Galilee.** Old Tappan, NJ: Revell, 1986. 223 pp.
Mary and Joseph live ordinary lives before Mary becomes the mother of Jesus.
Genre(s): Biographical Fiction; Christian Fiction.

Jacobs, Joseph

294. **Jesus as Others Saw Him.** New York: B. G. Richards, 1903. 230 pp.
A series of letters written in AD 54 describes the life of Jesus.
Genre(s): Biographical Fiction; Christian Fiction.

Johnson, Grace

295. **The Rebel.** Wheaton, IL: Tyndale House, 1996. 426 pp.
Barabbas becomes involved in the Roman intrigue and trial surrounding the Jew Jesus in Jerusalem.
Genre(s): Biographical Fiction; Christian Fiction.

Kazantzakis, Nikos

296. **The Last Temptation of Christ.** Trans. P.A. Bien. New York: Simon and Schuster, 1960. 506 pp.
Jesus lives and works in Nazareth where, as any man might, he asserts his beliefs.
Genre(s): Biographical Fiction; Christian Fiction.

Kinstler, Clysta

297. **The Moon under Her Feet.** New York: Harper and Row, 1989. 315 pp.
In a feminist view of Jesus' story, Almah Mari bears Yeshua after her union in sacred marriage at the Temple in Jerusalem, and her husband sacrifices himself for his people.
Genre(s): Biographical Fiction; Christian Fiction.

Kossoff, David

298. **The Book of Witnesses.** New York: St. Martin's, 1972. 174 pp.
A group of 40 people describe their relationships to Jesus from his youth until his death.
Genre(s): Religious Fiction.

299. **The Little Book of Sylvanus (Died 41 AD).** New York: St. Martin's, 1975. 144 pp.

Sylvanus, a skeptic and lifetime civil servant in King Herod's court, investigates the recently crucified man Jesus and the mysteries surrounding him.
Genre(s): Religious Fiction.

300. *The Voices of Masada.* New York: St. Martin's, 1973. 236 pp.
Zealots hiding on Masada decide to take their own lives under Eleazar's leadership rather than succumb to the Romans.
Genre(s): War Story.

Lagerkvist, Par

301. *Barabbas.* 1951. New York: Vintage, 1989. 144 pp.
Barabbas becomes interested in Jesus after being freed because of him, but is then imprisoned again for participation in a Christian mob.
Genre(s): Biographical Fiction; Christian Fiction.

302. *Herod and Mariamne.* New York: Knopf, 1968. 115 pp.
Even though Mariamne does not love King Herod, she pities him enough to marry him.
Genre(s): Biographical Fiction.

Landorf, Joyce

303. *I Came to Love You Late.* Grand Rapids, MI: Revell, 1980. 224 pp.
Martha tells of her relationship with Jesus.
Genre(s): Christian Fiction.

Lang, Theo

304. *The Word and the Sword.* New York: Delacorte, 1974. 509 pp.
Pontius Pilate has the difficult problem of what to do with the man Jesus, and he consults his wife, Claudia Procula, before deciding.
Genre(s): Biographical Fiction; Christian Fiction.

Leslie, Desmond

305. *The Jesus File.* London: Sidgwick and Jackson, 1975. 208 pp.
Pilate, his aide Scipio, Caiaphas, and a secret agent who infiltrates the Christians but becomes a convert send memos to each other during their involvement with the man named Jesus.
Genre(s): Biographical Fiction; Christian Fiction.

Linney, Romulus

306. *Jesus Tales.* San Francisco: North Point, 1980. 146 pp.
Jesus grows up with his parents and enjoys adventures with Peter.
Genre(s): Biographical Fiction; Christian Fiction.

Lliteras, D. S.

307. *The Thieves of Golgotha.* Charlottesville, VA: Hampton Road, 1998. 208 pp.

The three men at the crucifixion of Jesus have lives which include crime and slavery before they die on the cross.
Genre(s): Christian Fiction.

Lovelace, Merline

308. *Somewhere in Time.* New York: Silhouette, 1994. 250 pp.
On a routine Middle East mission, Captain Aurora Durant crash lands and finds herself in the middle of a Roman Army of AD 180.
Genre(s): Time Travel; Romance.

Maier, Paul L.

309. *Pontius Pilate.* Garden City, NY: Doubleday, 1968. 370 pp.
Jews, Christians, and Romans react to Pontius Pilate and his decision to put Jesus to death.
Genre(s): Biographical Fiction; Christian Fiction.

Malinski, Mieczyslaw

310. *Witnesses to Jesus.* New York: Crossroad, 1982. 307 pp.
Five people who knew Jesus—Pilate, Judas, Mary Magdalene, Annas, and Simon Peter—tell his story.
Genre(s): Biographical Fiction; Christian Fiction.

Meyer, Gabriel

311. *The Gospel of Joseph.* New York: Crossroad, 1994. 203 pp.
Joseph, husband of Mary and father of Jesus, relates in his letters that his family was prosperous and socially respectable, being descendants of King David.
Genre(s): Biographical Fiction; Religious Fiction; Christian Fiction.

Monhollon, Michael L.

312. *Divine Invasion.* Abilene, TX: Reflection, 1997. 352 pp.
During the three years before his crucifixion, Jesus becomes known in his community.
Genre(s): Christian Fiction.

Nash, N. Richard

313. *Behold the Man.* Garden City, NY: Doubleday, 1986. 376 pp.
After Romans rape her, Mary Magdalene joins the Zealots and goes to Egypt where she despairs with no recourse but prostitution, but when she returns, she meets Judas and Mary who have also had little success in their lives.
Genre(s): Biographical Fiction; Christian Fiction.

Park, Paul

314. *The Gospel of Corax.* New York: Soho, 1996. 297 pp.
A runaway Roman slave, fluent in many languages, travels with Jeshua (Jesus) to the Himalayas, where they hear

Buddhist teachings during the period before Jesus begins his preaching.
Genre(s): Biographical Fiction; Christian Fiction.

Ripley, Alexandra

315. *A Love Divine.* New York: Warner, 1997. 722 pp.
Joseph of Arimathea loves the sea and enjoys a life of adventure until his crippled daughter leads him to Jesus.
Genre(s): Christian Fiction.

Rivers, Francine

◆ 316. *A Voice in the Wind.* Wheaton, IL: Tyndale House, 1993. 514 pp.
Hadassah lives in Jerusalem while the Emperor Titus is sacking it and is transported on a slave ship. (*Series:* Mark of the Lion, 1)
Genre(s): Christian Fiction; Love Story.

Rogers, Margaret

317. *The Magdalene Woman.* New York: St. Martin's, 1980. 278 pp.
Mary's neighbor is the man Jesus who becomes impatient with his followers when they fail to understand his divine mission.
Genre(s): Biographical Fiction; Christian Fiction.

Roland, Nicholas

318. *Who Came by Night.* New York: Holt, Rinehart and Winston, 1972. 223 pp.
A Pharisee rabbi refuses to reject the laws of his religion by refuting the teachings of Jesus Christ.
Genre(s): Biographical Fiction; Christian Fiction.

Ronalds, Mary Teresa

319. *The Eyewitness: The Testimony of John.* Nashville, TN: Abingdon, 1967. 320 pp.
John, the apostle, tells of his journey with Jesus to hear John the Baptist and his prophecies about a Messiah.
Genre(s): Biographical Fiction; Christian Fiction.

Slaughter, Carolyn

320. *Magdalene.* New York: Evans, 1979. 206 pp.
Mary Magdalene leads an eventful life before she begins following Jesus.
Genre(s): Biographical Fiction; Christian Fiction.

Slaughter, Frank G.

321. *The Galileans: A Novel of Mary Magdalene.* Garden City, NY: Doubleday, 1953. 307 pp.
Mary Magdalene enjoys her dancing until Gaius Flaccus ravishes her, but she later hears about a Galilean preacher.
Genre(s): Religious Fiction; Biographical Fiction.

Smith, Herbert F.

322. *Hidden Victory.* Philadelphia: St. Joseph's University Press, 1984. 469 pp.

Jesus and his disciples, along with others they meet, live in Palestine in times of Roman domination.
Genre(s): Biographical Fiction; Christian Fiction.

Spencer, Edith T.

323. *The Other Mary.* Philadelphia: Dorrance, 1975. 409 pp.
Mary, the mother of James, goes to the cross of Jesus with the other women disciples and with Mary Magdalene to the empty tomb.
Genre(s): Biographical Fiction; Christian Fiction.

Steen, John Warren

324. *Barnabas.* Nashville, TN: Broadman, 1971. 127 pp.
Paul and Barnabus together try to tell people in Tarsus about the teachings of Jesus.
Genre(s): Biographical Fiction; Christian Fiction.

Tournier, Michel

325. *The Four Wise Men.* Garden City, NY: Doubleday, 1982. 255 pp.
Gaspar, Balthazar, and Melchior follow a comet to Bethlehem while a fourth wise man, a former salt mine prisoner, looks for a Turkish delight recipe.
Genre(s): Christian Fiction.

Traylor, Ellen Gunderson

326. *John, Son of Thunder.* Wheaton, IL: Tyndale House, 1979. 447 pp.
John the Apostle is one of Jesus' disciples, and Jesus nicknames him Boanerges, son of thunder, before he is exiled on Patmos.
Genre(s): Biographical Fiction; Christian Fiction; Adventure Story.

327. *Mark.* Wheaton, IL: Tyndale House, 1989. 304 pp.
Mark, a companion of Peter and his translator in Rome, records what he remembers about Jesus and his teaching for the Christians.
Genre(s): Biographical Fiction; Christian Fiction.

328. *Mary Magdalene.* Wheaton, IL: Tyndale House, 1985. 319 pp.
Mary Magdalene becomes a follower of Jesus after experiencing many sorrows in her life.
Genre(s): Biographical Fiction; Christian Fiction.

Wallace, Lew

329. *Ben-Hur.* 1880. New York: Buccaneer, 1985. 552 pp.
Judah Ben-Hur faces a life in the galleys after being falsely accused of trying to assassinate the governor of Jerusalem during the time of Jesus.
Genre(s): Biographical Fiction; Christian Fiction.

Walsh, John Evangelist

◆ 330. *The Man Who Buried Jesus.* New York: Collier, 1989. 152 pp.

Nicodemus, a member of the council of elders, hears that Jesus has risen from the tomb, and he visits the spot, after which he investigates the situation.
Genre(s): Biographical Fiction; Christian Fiction.

Whitten, Les

331. *The Lost Disciple.* New York: Atheneum, 1989. 445 pp.
Demas, mentioned three times in the New Testament, becomes a different man depending on the storyteller.
Genre(s): Biographical Fiction; Christian Fiction.

Wibberley, Leonard

332. *The Testament of Theophilus.* New York: Morrow, 1973. 335 pp.
Theophilus, although born a slave, becomes a wealthy Roman citizen, and Jesus tells Theophilus that when he comes before Pilate he will be his friend.
Genre(s): Christian Fiction.

Wile, Mary Lee

333. *Ancient Rage.* Burdett, NY: Larson, 1996. 144 pp.
Elizabeth is furious at her son John's death, and in later years, she wonders why Jesus did not raise him from the dead as he did Lazarus and why God informed Zechariah rather than her that her son would be a prophet.
Genre(s): Biographical Fiction; Christian Fiction.

Williman, Anne C.

334. *The Touch.* Nashville, TN: Thomas Nelson, 1985. 224 pp.
Susanna, daughter of Jairus, desires a child after her arranged marriage but also wonders about Jesus, the man who raised her from the dead when she was 12.
Genre(s): Biographical Fiction; Christian Fiction.

Wise, Robert L.

335. *The Fall of Jerusalem.* Nashville, TN: Nelson, 1994. 280 pp.
Josephus, a Pharisee, commands the Jewish forces when they revolt against Rome in AD 66. (*Series:* The People of the Covenant, 3)
Genre(s): Christian Fiction.

Zeldis, Chayym

336. *The Brothel.* New York: Putnam, 1979. 448 pp.
Mara (Mary) is the daughter of a murdered whore and sister of the local brothel's favorite attraction, but she hears God talking to her, and she loves Yosef, the Rabbi's son, whom the Romans castrate.
Genre(s): Biographical Fiction; Christian Fiction.

337. *Brothers.* New York: Random House, 1976. 497 pp.
Judas claims to have authored John's gospel and to have been the brother of Jesus.
Genre(s): Biographical Fiction; Christian Fiction.

Rome

Ball, Charles Ferguson

338. *The Life and Times of the Apostle Paul.* Wheaton, IL: Tyndale House, 1996. 200 pp.
After his conversion, Paul preaches Christianity around the Mediterranean.
Genre(s): Christian Fiction; Biographical Fiction.

Benton, Kenneth

339. *Death on the Appian Way.* London: Chatto and Windus, 1974. 223 pp.
Marcus Caelius describes the feud between Cicero and Clodia's incestuous brother Clodius in Rome.
Genre(s): Biographical Fiction.

Bulwer-Lytton, Edward

340. *The Last Days of Pompeii.* New York: Van Nostrand Reinhold, 1979. 521 pp.
Glaucus and Ione enjoy each other's company in Pompeii before Vesuvius erupts in AD 79, but Ione's jealous guardian loves her and has criminal interests.

Bunn, T. Davis

341. *To the Ends of the Earth.* Nashville: T. Nelson, 1996. 335 pp.
In AD 300, Cletus, a North African merchant, sends his son Travis to Constantinople to find new ways to earn money, and on his trip, he learns how to deal with treacherous half brothers and with being a slave for a short time.
Genre(s): Christian Fiction; Bildungsroman (Coming of Age).

Burgess, Anthony

342. *The Kingdom of the Wicked.* New York: Arbor House, 1985. 379 pp.
During the period from the founding of Christianity to the destruction of Pompeii, the Roman empire continues under the leadership of the five Julii.
Genre(s): Christian Fiction.

Burns, Ron

343. *Roman Shadows.* New York: St. Martin's, 1992. 261 pp.
In the sequel to *Roman Nights,* Cicero suggests that Gaius Livinius Severus keep an eye on the politician Gaius Scribonius Curio, and when Livinius becomes Curio's confidant, he finds himself in the midst of a murder intrigue.
Genre(s): Mystery.

Burroughs, Edgar Rice

344. *I Am a Barbarian.* Tarzana, CA: E. R. Burroughs, 1967. 287 pp.
Caligula, the Emperor of Rome, unites the Roman armies under his command and plunders Gaul in AD 40.
Genre(s): Biographical Fiction.

Caldwell, Taylor

345. *Dear and Glorious Physician.* Garden City, NY: Doubleday, 1959. 574 pp.
Luke, author of one of the gospels, was a physician who lived in Antioch, Rome, Alexandria, and Judaea.
Genre(s): Biographical Fiction; Christian Fiction.

346. *A Pillar of Iron.* Garden City, NY: Doubleday, 1965. 649 pp.
Cicero's life as a statesman takes place against a backdrop of Imperial Rome.
Genre(s): Biographical Fiction; Political Fiction.

Comfort, Alex

347. *Imperial Patient.* London: Duckworth, 1987. 206 pp.
Callimachus goes to Rome from Cos to treat Nero's wife Octavia for infertility, but he dislikes the political machinations.
Genre(s): Biographical Fiction; Medical Novel.

Coolidge, Olivia E.

348. *Caesar's Gallic War.* North Haven, CT: Shoe String, 1991. 245 pp.
Julius Caesar fights the Gallic Wars from 58 to 51 BC.
Genre(s): War Story.

Davis, Lindsey

◆ 349. *A Dying Light in Corduba.* New York: Mysterious Press, 1998. 448 pp.
Marcus Didius Falco goes to Baetica from Rome with his pregnant girlfriend to find out if an illegal oil cartel is functioning.
Genre(s): Mystery.

◆ 350. *Last Act in Palmyra.* New York: Mysterious Press, 1996. 476 pp.
Marcus Didius Falco works for Vespasian as his spy in Rome and searches for a circus musician, but when he and his girlfriend go to Syria, they are accused of murder.
Genre(s): Mystery.

◆ 351. *Poseidon's Gold.* New York: Crown, 1994. 352 pp.
Marcus Didius Falco and his girlfriend Helena Justina, daughter of a Roman senator, attempt to clear his name as a murder suspect in a death connected to his dead brother's illegal dealings.
Genre(s): Mystery.

◆ 352. *The Silver Pigs.* New York: Crown, 1989. 258 pp.

Marcus Didius Falco, detective in first-century Rome, works for the new emperor Vespasian on a trip to Britain's silver mines.
Genre(s): Mystery.

◆ 353. *Time to Depart.* New York: Mysterious Press, 1997. 631 pp.
Marcus Didius Falco joins public officer Petronius Longus to investigate the outbreak of crime in Rome after the Emperor Vespasian exiles the notorious Balbinus Pius.
Genre(s): Mystery.

◆ 354. *Venus in Copper.* New York: Crown, 1991. 277 pp.
Marcus Didius Falco investigates the intended bride of the business partner to two nouveaux riches men, but the partner is murdered, and Falco's job changes.
Genre(s): Mystery.

De Chair, Somerset Struben

355. *Friends, Romans, Concubines.* London: Constable, 1973. 274 pp.
The Empress Galla Placidia experiences rape, slavery, love, and the hatred of her daughter before Alaric's Sack of Rome AD 410.
Genre(s): Biographical Fiction.

De Hartog, Jan

◆ 356. *The Centurion.* New York: HarperCollins, 1989. 288 pp.
A retired captain, Martinus Harixma, decides to explore, and he researches in detail the life of a fourth-century Roman centurion, in the sequel to *The Commodore*.
Genre(s): Adventure Story.

Drake, David

357. *Birds of Prey.* New York: Simon and Schuster, 1984. 352 pp.
Aulus Perennius has a mission in Rome during the third century to travel to the distant future.
Genre(s): Fantastic Literature.

Duggan, Alfred Leo

358. *Children of the Wolf.* New York: Coward-McCann, 1959. 238 pp.
A spearman tells about Romulus slaying his twin brother Remus in order to found Rome and begin planning the city.
Genre(s): Fantastic Literature.

359. *Family Favourites.* 1961. New York: Pantheon, 1973. 280 pp.
Heliogabalus becomes emperor of Rome at 14 in a brief but notorious reign during the third century.
Genre(s): Biographical Fiction.

Fast, Howard

◆ 360. *Spartacus.* Armonk, NY: North Castle, 1996. 363 pp.

Spartacus leads a revolt against his Roman masters after being used for their pleasures as gladiator and slave.
Genre(s): War Story.

Feuchtwanger, Lion

361. *The Jew of Rome.* Trans. Willa and Edwin Muir. New York: Viking, 1936. 565 pp.
In the sequel to *Josephus*, the Jewish historian Josephus tries to reconcile a high position in the Roman world with being Jewish.
Genre(s): Jewish Fiction; Biographical Fiction.

362. *Josephus and the Emperor.* New York: Viking, 1942. 446 pp.
No longer a favorite of Domitian in the sequel to *The Jew of Rome*, Josephus cannot reconcile the conflicts arising from being both a Jewish teacher and a Roman soldier.
Genre(s): Jewish Fiction; Biographical Fiction.

Gaarder, Jostein

363. *That Same Flower.* New York: Farrar, Straus and Giroux, 1997. 256 pp.
After they have lived apart for several years and their son has died, Floria Aemilia, St. Augustine's ex-lover, writes a letter to him in which she argues that his God of the *Confessions* should not demand abstinence.
Genre(s): Biographical Fiction.

Gann, Ernest Kellogg

364. *The Triumph.* New York: Simon and Schuster, 1986. 382 pp.
After Masada, Flavius Silva, in the sequel to *The Antagonists*, falls in love with the emperor's married daughter Domitillia when she comes to Judea.
Genre(s): Biographical Fiction.

Ghnassia, Maurice

365. *Arena.* New York: Viking, 1969. 303 pp.
The Thracian gladiator Spartacus leads a slave revolt in 73 BC which lasts for two years.
Genre(s): Biographical Fiction; War Story.

Gillespie, Donna

366. *The Light Bearer.* New York: Berkley, 1994. 788 pp.
Auriane leads her Chattian tribe against Rome while Marcus Julianus tries to preserve justice under Nero and Domitian before the two meet after Auriane's capture.
Genre(s): Fantastic Literature; Epic Literature.

Graves, Robert

367. *Claudius, the God, and His Wife Messalina.* New York: H. Smith and R. Haas, 1935. 538 pp.
In the sequel to *I, Claudius*, Claudius describes his reign and his murder by Agrippina, mother of Nero.
Award(s): James Tate Black Award.
Genre(s): Biographical Fiction.

368. *I, Claudius.* New York: H. Smith and R. Haas, 1937. 427 pp.

The story of the Emperor Claudius, an historian, can finally be told when his famous lost autobiography is located.
Award(s): James Tate Black Award.
Genre(s): Biographical Fiction.

Groseclose, Elgin Earl

369. *Olympia.* Elgin, IL: Cook, 1980. 248 pp.
Olympia interacts with Saint John Chrysostom in 5th century Constantinople.
Genre(s): Biographical Fiction.

Haasse, Hella S.

370. *Threshold of Fire.* Trans. Anita Miller and Nini Blinstrub. Chicago, IL: Academy, 1993. 255 pp.
Hadrian, a devout Christian, wants to eradicate paganism, while Claudius Claudianus, an exiled Roman poet, writes about the ill effects of Christianity on the Roman state.
Genre(s): Political Fiction; Religious Fiction.

Hardy, W. G.

371. *The Bloodied Toga.* Toronto: Macmillan of Canada, 1979. 510 pp.
In the sequel to *The Scarlet Mantle*, Caesar and Cleopatra stay in the royal palace at Alexandria and have a son before Caesar is assassinated on the Ides of March, but at the battle of Philippi, Caesar is avenged.
Genre(s): Biographical Fiction.

372. *The City of Libertines.* New York: Appleton, 1957. 437 pp.
Caesar comes to power and glory with all of his conquests.
Genre(s): War Story.

373. *Turn Back the River.* New York: Dodd, Mead, 1938. 385 pp.
Clodia is mistress of Catiline and wife of Metellus Celer before Julius Caesar comes to power, and Cicero rails against her.
Genre(s): Biographical Fiction.

Henderson, Lois T.

◆ **374.** *Priscilla and Aquila.* San Francisco: Harper and Row, 1985. 345 pp.
After her arranged marriage to Aquila, Priscilla and he convert to Christianity and risk their lives for the apostle Paul.
Genre(s): Christian Fiction.

Hersey, John

375. *The Conspiracy.* New York: Knopf, 1972. 274 pp.
Nero's men become involved in conspiracies against Rome's intellectual leaders.
Genre(s): Political Fiction.

Jaro, Benita Kane

◆ **376.** *The Door in the Wall.* Sag Harbor, NY: Permanent Press, 1994. 323 pp.
Caelius, a Roman politician, wants power, but when he associates himself with Julius Caesar to get it, he becomes disgusted with Caesar's cruelty and personal depravities.
Genre(s): War Story.

377. *The Key.* New York: Dodd, Mead, 1988. 240 pp.
Catullus's best friend, lawyer Marcus Caelius Rufus, tells about Catullus from his birth in Verona until his refusal to relinquish Clodia who refuses to marry him.
Genre(s): Biographical Fiction.

Koestler, Arthur

378. *The Gladiators.* New York: Macmillan, 1939. 351 pp.
Spartacus leads a slave revolt in Rome during the first century BC.
Genre(s): War Story.

Lindsay, Jack

379. *Rome for Sale.* New York: Harper, 1934. 416 pp.
Catiline rebels in Rome in 60 BC because of the social and economic distress of the people in the Roman Empire.
Genre(s): Political Fiction.

Lloyd, Roger Bradshaigh

380. *Letters from the Early Church.* New York: Macmillan, 1960. 171 pp.
A series of imaginary letters describes the lives of those who worked to establish the Christian Church in Rome.
Genre(s): Christian Fiction.

Maier, Paul L.

381. *The Flames of Rome.* Garden City, NY: Doubleday, 1981. 443 pp.
During the early days of the Christian church in the reigns of Claudius and Nero, some Romans support the Christians' rights.

Massie, Allan

◆ **382.** *Caesar.* New York: Carroll and Graf, 1994. 228 pp.
The Roman general Decimus Junius Brutus, a close friend of Julius Caesar's, was also a conspirator against him on the Ides of March, and in his memoirs, he tries to justify his decision by accusing Caesar.
Genre(s): Biographical Fiction.

383. *Let the Emperor Speak.* Garden City, NY: Doubleday, 1987. 339 pp.
Augustus tries to explain and justify his actions, first to his grandsons, and then to people in general.
Genre(s): Biographical Fiction.

384. *Tiberius.* New York: Carroll and Graf, 1993. 256 pp.

Tiberius appears not as the villain of history but as a man who could not divorce his name from the horrors of his reign in Rome.
Genre(s): Biographical Fiction.

McCullough, Colleen

385. *Caesar.* New York: Morrow, 1997. 752 pp.
From 54 to 48 BC, Julius Caesar oversees the uprising of Gaul under Vercingetorix and crosses the Rubicon while facing personal trials, including the death of his daughter Julia.
Genre(s): Political Fiction; Biographical Fiction.

386. *Caesar's Women.* New York: Morrow, 1996. 696 pp.
Caesar rises to power from 68 to 58 BC by outsmarting his enemies, but each of them, once defeated, begins plans to ruin him. (*Series:* Masters of Rome, 4)
Genre(s): Love Story; Political Fiction; Biographical Fiction.

387. *The First Man in Rome.* New York: Morrow, 1990. 896 pp.
Two men, Gaius Marius and Lucius Cornelius Sulla, both want to become the First Man in Rome even with their questionable social backgrounds. (*Series:* Masters of Rome, 1)
Genre(s): Biographical Fiction; Political Fiction.

388. *Fortune's Favorites.* New York: Morrow, 1993. 878 pp.
Sulla returns from exile and becomes Rome's first dictator in two hundred years while Pompey the Great becomes a wealthy provincial, and Gaius Julius Caesar matures. (*Series:* Masters of Rome, 3)
Genre(s): Political Fiction.

389. *The Grass Crown.* New York: Morrow, 1991. 894 pp.
Lucius Cornelius Sulla gains power as Gaius Marius ages, and he must protect his position of leadership during the first century BC (*Series:* Masters of Rome, 2)
Genre(s): Political Fiction; Biographical Fiction.

Munn, H. Warner

390. *The Lost Legion.* Garden City, NY: Doubleday, 1980. 621 pp.
Commander Manlius Varro takes his 13th Legion into the Far East to find a lost Roman legion to gain the Emperor Caligula's favor.
Genre(s): War Story; Political Fiction.

Murphy, Walter F.

391. *Upon this Rock.* New York: Macmillan, 1987. 538 pp.
Quintus, a Gentile follower of Jesus, tells the story of Peter and the first century of the church.
Genre(s): Biographical Fiction; Christian Fiction.

Neilson, Winthrop, and Frances Neilson

392. *The Woman Who Loved Paul.* Garden City, NY: Doubleday, 1978. 255 pp.

Priscilla, wife of Aquila the tentmaker, helps Paul to establish Christianity in Corinth, Ephesus, and Rome.
Genre(s): Biographical Fiction; Christian Fiction.

Neville, Katherine

393. *The Magic Circle.* New York: Ballantine, 1998. 560 pp.
After Ariel Behn's cousin Sam is murdered, she becomes owner of manuscripts revealing secrets of first-century Rome and the Holy Land as well as the coming millennium.
Genre(s): Mystery.

Nield, Howard

394. *Year of the Four Caesars.* New York: St. Martin's, 1981. 287 pp.
In AD 69, four emperors, Galba, Otho, Vitellius, and Vespasian, rule during a civil war in which Veturius, a Praetorian Guard soldier, tries to gain his own power.
Genre(s): War Story.

Pater, Walter

395. *Marius the Epicurean.* New York: Dutton, 1934. 267 pp.
Marius, a Roman noble during the time of Marcus Aurelius, becomes interested in Christianity and investigates it with his friend Cornelius.
Genre(s): Religious Fiction.

Pilpel, Robert H.

396. *Between Eternities.* San Diego, CA: Harcourt, 1985. 559 pp.
Lucius Celer, a retired plebian runner and trainer, incurs the irritation of Commodus, son of Marcus Aurelius, in AD 180, when he suggests to Marcus that he choose someone else as his successor.
Genre(s): Biographical Fiction.

Rice, Anne

397. *Pandora.* New York: Knopf, 1998. 288 pp.
Pandora tells of her life as a woman of privilege in the Rome of Augustus Caesar.
Genre(s): Horror; Fantastic Literature.

Rivers, Francine

◆ 398. *As Sure as the Dawn.* Wheaton, IL: Tyndale House, 1995. 488 pp.
The German Atretes, a champion gladiator, challenges Rome after Hadassah has become a martyr. (*Series:* Mark of the Lion, 3)
Genre(s): Christian Fiction; War Story.

◆ 399. *An Echo in the Darkness.* Wheaton, IL: Tyndale House, 1994. 446 pp.
Hadassah has a difficult romance with Marcus Valerian, a Roman noble who converts to Christianity after the crucifixion of Jesus. (*Series:* Mark of the Lion, 2)
Genre(s): Christian Fiction.

Robinson, Kathleen

400. *Dominic.* New York: St. Martin's, 1991. 439 pp.
Dominic, an orphaned Christian child, is also a dwarf, and after he is sold into slavery, he is trained as an acrobat to perform with pagans.
Genre(s): Picaresque Fiction.

401. *Heaven's Only Daughter.* New York: St. Martin's, 1993. 326 pp.
The Roman emperor, Honorius, refuses to ransom his sister from the Visigoths in 410, and during the rampage of Italy, she falls in love with Atawulf, King Alaric's foster brother.
Genre(s): Romance; Love Story.

Saylor, Steven

◆ 402. *Arms of Nemesis.* New York: St. Martin's, 1992. 305 pp.
Gordianus the Finder must go south of Rome, as the Spartacus slave revolt rages, to clear two slaves accused of murdering wealthy Lucius Licinius with only three days in which to work.
Genre(s): Mystery.

◆ 403. *Catilina's Riddle.* New York: St. Martin's, 1993. 430 pp.
Gordianus the Finder has become a gentleman farmer after working for Cicero and others, but when headless bodies appear on his farm, he must reenter the world of Roman politics and intrigue.
Genre(s): Mystery.

◆ 404. *A Murder on the Appian Way.* New York: St. Martin's, 1996. 304 pp.
In 52 BC, when Clodius is murdered, his family wants Gordianus the Finder to investigate Titus Annius Milo and others, but Cicero finally helps uncover the truth.
Genre(s): Mystery.

◆ 405. *Roman Blood.* New York: St. Martin's, 1991. 357 pp.
In the first century BC, Gordianus the Finder gathers evidence for Cicero to support the defense of Sextus Roscius, a wealthy farmer accused of patricide, and what he finds reveals deeper conspiracies.
Genre(s): Mystery.

◆ 406. *The Venus Throw.* New York: St. Martin's, 1995. 308 pp.
Gordianus the Finder must try to discover the murderer of several Egyptian envoys in Rome during 56 BC.
Genre(s): Mystery.

Segal, Brenda Lesley

407. *If I Forget Thee.* New York: St. Martin's, 1983. 407 pp.
In the second century, before Bar Kokhba leads a Jewish rebellion in Rome, he looks after the young girl Jara.
Genre(s): War Story; Biographical Fiction.

Sienkiewicz, Henryk

408. *Quo Vadis.* Trans. Stanley F. Conrad. 1941. New York: Hippocrene, 1992. 493 pp.
In the time of Nero, the Roman noble Petronius retains his pagan beliefs even though they conflict with Christianity.
Genre(s): Christian Fiction.

Small, Bertrice

409. *Beloved.* New York: Ballantine, 1983. 465 pp.
A Roman centurion rapes and kills Zenobia's Alexandrian heiress mother, and as daughter of a Bedawi warrior chief, she hates the Romans, declaring that when she becomes queen of Palmyra in the third century AD, she will free her city.
Genre(s): Biographical Fiction.

Sutcliff, Rosemary

◆ 410. *The Mark of the Horse Lord.* New York: Henry Z. Walck, 1965. 276 pp.
Phaedrus wins his freedom when he kills his gladiator opponent, and when Dalraidian leaders see his resemblance to their disfigured king Midir, they recruit him to become the public Midir, so that the people will not perceive a weakened leader, and destroy the real Midir.

Vidal, Gore

411. *Julian.* New York: Modern Library, 1962. 502 pp.
Julian the Apostate, raised as a Christian, tries to restore the pagan gods when he becomes emperor in AD 361.
Genre(s): Biographical Fiction.

Waltari, Mika

412. *The Roman.* New York: Putnam, 1966. 637 pp.
Minutus comes to Rome from Antioch when 15, fights in Jerusalem and Britain with the army, and wins many honors before helping Nero persecute the Christians.
Genre(s): Adventure Story.

Ware, William

413. *Aurelian.* New York: G. Munro, 1886. 358 pp.
In the third century, Emperor Aurelian persecutes the Christians of Rome.
Genre(s): Christian Fiction.

Warner, Rex

414. *Imperial Caesar.* Boston: Little, Brown, 1960. 343 pp.
The sequel to *Young Caesar* covers Julius Caesar's last 15 years of great military conquests and his liaison with Cleopatra.
Award(s): James Tate Black Award.
Genre(s): Biographical Fiction.

415. *The Young Caesar.* Boston: Little, Brown, 1958. 353 pp.
Prior to the Ides of March in 44 BC, Caesar remembers the life he lived before leaving for Gaul.
Genre(s): Biographical Fiction.

Wilder, Thornton

416. *The Ides of March.* New York: Harper and Row, 1948. 246 pp.
Julius Caesar interacts with other Romans during the months prior to his assassination.
Genre(s): Biographical Fiction.

Williams, John Edward

417. *Augustus.* New York: Viking, 1972. 302 pp.
The Roman Emperor Augustus, great-nephew of Julius Caesar, reveals that Augustus's own opinion of himself was higher than that of those around him.
Award(s): National Book Award.
Genre(s): Biographical Fiction.

Winn, Derek

418. *I Served Caesar.* London: Stacey, 1972. 316 pp.
A trusted slave of the young Julius Caesar relates Caesar's early years and his politically motivated affairs.
Genre(s): Biographical Fiction.

Wise, Leonard

419. *Dumachas and Sheba.* Garden City, NY: Doubleday, 1976. 276 pp.
Dumachas becomes the second man to die with Jesus when the Roman Marcellus wants Dumachas's love, Sheba, and needs to get rid of him.
Genre(s): Biographical Fiction; Romance.

Wood, Barbara

420. *Soul Flame.* New York: Random House, 1987. 372 pp.
Selene, 16, daughter of a Roman slave, discovers that she has healing powers which she uses to survive, and in Rome, is accepted as the granddaughter of Cleopatra and Caesar.
Genre(s): Medical Novel; Adventure Story.

Yarbro, Chelsea Quinn

◆ 421. *Blood Games.* New York: St. Martin's, 1979. 458 pp.
In the Rome of Nero, Saint Germain Franciscus supplies the Circus Maximus with dancers and drivers before he falls in love with Olivia, whose husband Justus has had her raped by over 350 gladiators for his own enjoyment.
(Series: Saint-Germain, 3)
Genre(s): Gothic Fiction; Love Story.

Yourcenar, Marguerite

422. *Memoirs of Hadrian.* Trans. Grace Frick. 1963. New York: Modern Library, 1984. 347 pp.

In a letter to his adopted grandson (later Marcus Aurelius), Hadrian tells about his life.
Award(s): Prix Goncourt.
Genre(s): Biographical Fiction.

Europe

476-1289

Andrews, John

423. *A Viking's Daughter.* New York: Doubleday, 1989. 307 pp.
Strong-willed Gudrid, daughter of an Icelandic chieftain, travels with her father to Erik the Red's settlement in Greenland and then with her second husband to Vinland.
Genre(s): Adventure Story.

Aridjis, Homero

424. *The Lord of the Last Days.* Trans. Betty Ferber. New York: Morrow, 1995. 259 pp.
In the year 1000, Alfonso de Leon records encounters with his twin, Abd Allah of Cordoba, a Muslim who has decided to slay him in a symbolic ritual.
Genre(s): Religious Fiction.

Arnold, Michael P.

425. *Against the Fall of Night.* New York: Doubleday, 1975. 699 pp.
The Comneni family rules in Byzantium in the 11th century, and the historian of the family, Nicetas Acominatus, tells about their intelligence and caring.
Genre(s): Political Fiction.

Barroll, Clare

426. *The Iron Crown.* New York: Scribner's, 1975. 438 pp.
A young Viking who loves the princess promised to his brother leaves home for the court of Empress Zoe in Byzantium on a personal quest.
Genre(s): Adventure Story.

Bengtsson, Frans Gunnar

427. *The Long Ships.* Trans. Michael Meyer. New York: Knopf, 1954. 503 pp.
Red Orm of Danish Skania sails from 980 to 1010 and becomes, in turn, a Muslim and a Christian so that he can survive and then marry one of King Harald's daughters.
Genre(s): Sea Story; Humorous Fiction; Adventure Story.

428. *Red Orm.* New York: Knopf, 1954. 333 pp.
In the 10th century, Red Orm, a former Spanish galley slave, lives in Denmark before invading and settling in England.
Genre(s): Sea Story; Adventure Story.

Borchardt, Alice

429. *Beguiled.* New York: Dutton, 1997. 482 pp.
When Hakon attacks with his Vikings, Owen goes to Britanny for allies, and he is offered help in turn for sacrificing Elin if he will marry a nobleman's daughter.
Genre(s): War Story; Fantastic Literature.

430. *Devoted.* New York: Dutton, 1995. 467 pp.
Viking prisoner Elin warns Owen, a bishop, that Vikings will overcome him so he takes her as a wife but is eventually captured anyway.
Genre(s): Romance.

431. *The Silver Wolf.* New York: Ballantine, 1998. NA pp.
A female werewolf wanders Rome during the Dark Ages and tries to escape being burned at the stake.
Genre(s): Fantastic Literature; Horror.

Bradshaw, Gillian

◆ 432. *The Bearkeeper's Daughter.* Boston: Houghton Mifflin, 1987. 310 pp.
Theodora's illegitimate son arrives in Byzantium from Arabia, and although she fears acknowledging him, she gets him a job.
Genre(s): Biographical Fiction.

Brown, George Mackay

433. *Vinland.* London: Murray, 1992. 232 pp.
Ranald ventures to the new world which he and his compatriots call Vinland because of its grapes, but after an altercation with the Native Americans, they must sail home, and Ranald goes to the Norwegian court, returns to Orkney, and becomes a respected farmer before he fights in the Irish battle of Clontarf in 1014.
Genre(s): Sea Story; Adventure Story.

Byrne, Donn

434. *Messer Marco Polo.* New York: Century, 1921. 147 pp.
Marco Polo loves Golden Bells, the daughter of Kubla Khan, the only one whom he converts on his trip to China.
Genre(s): Biographical Fiction.

Canning, Victor

435. *Raven's Wind.* New York: Morrow, 1983. 185 pp.
After Justus falls in love with Riada, the Danes kidnap him and take him to Denmark where his adoptive father treats him kindly and teaches him shipbuilding in AD 866, but Justen longs to return to England, and when he does, he serves Alfred before Alfred becomes king.
Genre(s): War Story.

Chadwick, Elizabeth

436. *The Champion.* New York: St. Martin's, 1998. 512 pp.
Not until years after his one night with Monday in Normandy, which leaves her with a child, does Alexander de Montroi face the consequences of his actions.
Genre(s): Adventure Story; Political Fiction.

Chaikin, L. L.

437. *Behind the Veil.* Minneapolis, MN: Bethany House, 1998. 256 pp.
Lady Irene abducts Helena and presents her to Prince Kalid as a bride, but in Antioch, Helena discovers Paul's additions to the New Testament before Tancred Redwan, a Crusader, rescues her. (*Series:* Royal Pavilions, 3)
Genre(s): Christian Fiction; Romance.

438. *Golden Palaces.* Minneapolis, MN: Bethany House, 1996. 352 pp.
Helena's aunt Irene arranges a marriage for her with a Muslim prince, but a Norman warrior helps her escape. (*Series:* Royal Pavilions, 2)
Genre(s): Christian Fiction.

439. *Swords and Scimitars.* Minneapolis, MN: Bethany House, 1993. 320 pp.
Tancred Redwan rescues Helena, a Byzantine heiress, from western barbarians but finds that his courage is no match for hers. (*Series:* The Royal Pavilions, 1)
Genre(s): Christian Fiction; Romance.

Closs, Hannah Priebsch

440. *Deep Are the Valleys.* New York: Vanguard, 1960. 261 pp.
A knight seeking to avenge his friend during the Albigensian Wars thinks about joining the Cathari in the sequel to *High Are the Mountains.*
Genre(s): Western Fiction; Political Fiction; Christian Fiction.

441. *High Are the Mountains.* New York: Vanguard, 1959. 302 pp.
Catharist heretics in southern France near Toulouse form to oppose the clergy in the 12th century.
Genre(s): War Story; Political Fiction; Christian Fiction.

442. *The Silent Tarn.* New York: Vanguard, 1963. 317 pp.
The illegitimate son of the Count of Foix, Wolf, becomes involved in the politics and controversy surrounding the Albigensian heresy and the Inquisition, in the sequel to *Deep Are the Valleys.*
Genre(s): War Story; Political Fiction; Christian Fiction.

Coulter, Catherine

◆ 443. *Lord of Hawkfell Island.* New York: Jove, 1993. 400 pp.
In 900, Rorik Haraldsson moves his family and supporters to Hawkfell Island off the coast of Ireland and then kidnaps his enemy Einer's half-sister, who tries to reform him and the Viking women.
Genre(s): Romance.

444. *Lord of Raven's Peak.* New York: Jove, 1994. 304 pp.
In the sequel to *Lord of Hawkfell Island*, Merrik buys a slave in a Kiev market in AD 916 and also takes the boy's older brother, who is actually female and a gifted skald who soon finds the murderer of Merrik's brother.
Genre(s): Romance.

Crichton, Michael

445. *Eaters of the Dead.* New York: Knopf, 1976. 193 pp.
Ibn Fadlan, emissary of the caliph of Bagdad, records the habits of the Vikings in his journal, presenting a different view from that of Europeans who knew them.
Genre(s): Fantastic Literature.

Cross, Donna Woolfolk

◆ 446. *Pope Joan.* New York: Crown, 1996. 422 pp.
Berated for being intelligent and scholarly, Joan dons her dead brother's clothes, assumes a man's identity, and gains respect and authority as well as the title of pope.
Genre(s): Biographical Fiction.

Dandrea, Don

◆ 447. *Orlok.* Englewood, FL: Pineapple, 1986. 319 pp.
In 13th-century Siberia, Subotai the Bold, general to Genghis Khan, grows up an orphan before becoming a warrior for the khan.
Genre(s): Biographical Fiction; War Story.

De Haan, Tom

448. *A Mirror for Princes.* New York: Knopf, 1988. 421 pp.
As an elderly king writes his memoirs, he recollects life at court, his family, and living under his dictatorial father.
Genre(s): Political Fiction.

Delacroix, Claire

449. *The Sorceress.* New York: Harlequin, 1994. 350 pp.
Sophie and Hugues de Pontesse live normally in 13th-century France until they encounter a sorceress who reveals Sophie's magical abilities.
Genre(s): Romance; Fantastic Literature.

Dickinson, Peter

◆ 450. *The Dancing Bear.* Boston: Little, Brown, 1973. 253 pp.
In AD 558, when Huns kidnap Addie, a teenager in a wealthy Byzantine family, her servant Silvester, the household priest, and her pet dancing bear all search for her in the Hun camps.
Genre(s): War Story.

Dodson, DeAnna Julie

451. *In Honor Bound.* Wheaton, IL: Crossway, 1997. 320 pp.

Delighted that the king has said she could marry Prince Philip, Rosalynde is disappointed when Philip continues to love a dead servant girl and denies his Christianity. *Genre(s):* Christian Fiction.

Duggan, Alfred Leo

452. *The Lady for Ransom.* New York: Coward-McCann, 1953. 278 pp.
Mercenary soldiers in Byzantium serving the emperor kidnap a young woman and demand a ransom. *Genre(s):* War Story.

Eddison, Eric Rucker

453. *Styrbiorn the Strong.* New York: Boni, 1926. 284 pp.
The heir to the Swedish throne tries to claim his heritage. *Genre(s):* Fantastic Literature; Biographical Fiction.

Ennis, Michael

454. *Byzantium.* New York: Atlantic Monthly, 1989. 768 pp.
Harald Sigurdarson, a Norse prince, goes to Constantinople as a mercenary and meets Maria, the Mistress of the Robes. *Genre(s):* War Story.

Fleetwood, Frances

455. *Concordia.* New York: St. Martin's, 1973. 275 pp.
Concordia Malatesta relates the story of her parents and continues to love her father in 13th-century Italy even after he kills her mother and her brother. *Genre(s):* Biographical Fiction; Love Story.

456. *Concordia Errant.* New York: Allen, 1973. 304 pp.
The only daughter of Giovanni Malatesta and Rancesca da Rimini leaves her convent in the 13th century where she has adventures as a strolling player with a gypsy troop and as a wife and mother. *Genre(s):* Biographical Fiction; Domestic Fiction.

Fridegard, Jan

457. *Land of Wooden Gods.* Trans. Robert E. Bjork. Lincoln: University of Nebraska Press, 1989. 211 pp.
The thrall, Holme, rebels against his oppressors during the ninth century. *Genre(s):* Domestic Fiction.

458. *People of the Dawn.* Trans. Robert E. Bjork. Lincoln: University of Nebraska Press, 1990. 203 pp.
Holme, a dark-skinned smith, rescues his beautiful but weak wife from thralldom and takes her into a cave to hide while emissaries of Louis the Pious are beginning to preach for Christianity to replace pagan beliefs. *Genre(s):* Domestic Fiction.

459. *Sacrificial Smoke.* Trans. Robert E. Bjork. Lincoln: University of Nebraska Press, 1991. 190 pp.
Conflicts between the Christians and native Scandinavian paganism escalate in 9th-century Uppsala as Holme seeks to free the thralls and limit Christianity in his small Viking kingdom. *Genre(s):* Domestic Fiction.

Gardner, John Champlin

♦ 460. *Grendel.* New York: Knopf, 1971. 174 pp.
The monster Grendel expresses his isolation and loneliness in a dark and bleak northern world. *Genre(s):* Fantastic Literature.

Gellis, Roberta

461. *Fire Song.* New York: Berkley, 1984. 667 pp.
Fenice D'Aix and her husband Aubrey of Marlowe, an honorable knight, live in Gascony in the 13th century where, as previously married spouses, each harbors several secrets. *Genre(s):* Romance.

Gerson, Noel

462. *Theodora.* Englewood Cliffs, NJ: Prentice-Hall, 1969. 275 pp.
Theodora becomes the charming but politic empress to Justinian I, the Great. *Genre(s):* Biographical Fiction; Political Fiction.

Gissing, George

463. *Veranilda.* New York: Dutton, 1904. 348 pp.
Part of the scene around the Byzantine attempt to take Italy in the sixth century is the love of Veranilda. *Genre(s):* Romance; War Story.

Godwin, Parke

♦ 464. *The Tower of Beowulf.* New York: Morrow, 1995. 246 pp.
After Beowulf survives his comrades in a losing battle, he becomes obsessed with proving himself. *Genre(s):* Epic Literature.

Graves, Robert

465. *Count Belisarius.* New York: Farrar, Straus and Giroux, 1982. 564 pp.
Belisarius leads the armies of the Emperor Justinian in the 6th century. *Genre(s):* Biographical Fiction.

Griffiths, Paul

466. *Myself and Marco Polo.* New York: Random House, 1990. 274 pp.
Rustichello, the scribe to whom Marco Polo dictated his adventures, embellishes the tales when he inserts contemporary concepts into Polo's story. *Genre(s):* Biographical Fiction.

Grundy, Stephan

467. *Rhinegold.* New York: Bantam, 1994. 721 pp.

Wodan makes each of the Walsings mighty, and then one by one, he betrays all of them.
Genre(s): Fantastic Literature.

Haugaard, Erik

◆ 468. *A Slave's Tale.* Boston: Houghton Mifflin, 1965. 217 pp.

After gaining her freedom, Helga stows on a ship from Scandanavia to Frankland in 997 where she becomes interested in the new religion of priests she meets.
Genre(s): Christian Fiction.

Haughton, Rosemary

469. *Elizabeth's Greeting.* Philadelphia: Lippincott, 1968. 256 pp.

Elizabeth of Hungary becomes the wife of Ludwig, Landgraf of Thuringia in the 13th century, but by showing compassion for the poor and hungry, she attains sainthood.
Genre(s): Biographical Fiction; Christian Fiction.

Hill, Pamela

470. *The Woman in the Cloak.* New York: St. Martin's, 1988. 157 pp.

Margaret of Metola is born blind and hunchbacked to the Lord Parisio and his wife, Lady Emilia, and her embarrassed military father locks her up, attempts cures for her, and then abandons her on church steps after which she begins to help the poor and to work miracles.
Genre(s): Biographical Fiction; Love Story; Christian Fiction.

Hoban, Russell

471. *Pilgermann.* New York: Summit, 1983. 240 pp.

A German Jew, castrated for having seduced a tax collector's wife, finds himself in Antioch trying to protect the Turks from the Christians in the First Crusade.
Genre(s): War Story.

Holland, Cecelia

472. *The Firedrake.* New York: Atheneum, 1966. 243 pp.

In the 11th century, Laeghaire fights for William of Normandy's forces.

◆ 473. *The Golden Belt.* New York: Knopf, 1984. 305 pp.

When Hagen, a noble Frank, meets one of Irene's maidens, he becomes involved with the struggle over Irene, the Byzantine empress.
Genre(s): Biographical Fiction.

474. *Great Maria.* New York: Knopf, 1974. 519 pp.

Maria, daughter of an 11th-century Italian baron, marries Richard, who plans to use the marriage as a means of conquest.

◆ 475. *A Novel of the Antichrist.* New York: Atheneum, 1970. 299 pp.

The Emperor Frederick II speaks six languages, writes poetry, studies mathematics, and philosophizes in the 13th century.
Genre(s): Biographical Fiction.

◆ 476. *Two Ravens.* New York: Knopf, 1977. 199 pp.

After Bjarni sails in the 12th century to the Hebrides with his four brothers, they leave him for dead, but he eventually makes his way home to find they have already divided their deceased father's possessions among themselves.

477. *Until the Sun Falls.* New York: Atheneum, 1969. 491 pp.

In the 13th century, Psin and his son Tshant accompany Genghis Khan when the Mongols invade Europe, and when the two are not fighting the enemy, they are combatting each other.
Genre(s): War Story.

Hurley, Frank X.

478. *The Crusader.* Philadelphia: Dorrance, 1975. 102 pp.

In the 11th century, men gather to fight the infidels in the First Crusade beginning in 1069 and ending in 1099.
Genre(s): War Story.

Hutchins, Linda

479. *Mortal Love.* Garden City, NY: Doubleday, 1980. 376 pp.

Eleanor of Aquitaine muses about all of the people she knows and the way she passes her days.
Genre(s): Biographical Fiction.

Ian, V.

480. *Batu-Khan.* Westport, CT: Hyperion, 1977. 320 pp.

Batu Khan leads the Mongols in the 13th century.
Genre(s): Biographical Fiction.

Irwin, Constance H.

481. *Gudrid's Saga.* New York: St. Martin's, 1974. 287 pp.

Gudrid, Leif Eriksson's widowed sister-in-law, and her husband, Thorfinn Karlsefni, have the first child whose birth is recorded in the new world.
Genre(s): Biographical Fiction.

Jennings, Gary

482. *Raptor.* New York: Doubleday, 1992. 980 pp.

The bisexual Thorn preys on males and females while serving as a soldier, spy, and companion to Theodoric, the king of the Ostrogoths, who is taking over Europe. *Genre(s):* Adventure Story.

Johnson, Eyvind

483. *The Days of His Grace.* New York: Vanguard, 1970. 319 pp.
Johannes Lupigis, secretary to Charlemagne in the late eighth century, misses his boyhood love from Lombardy. *Genre(s):* Adventure Story.

Kaufman, Pamela

◆ 484. *Shield of Three Lions.* New York: Crown, 1983. 474 pp.
Lady Alix, in disguise, serves as a page to Richard during the Messina and Acre campaigns and must withstand his homosexual advances toward her. *Genre(s):* War Story.

Kazantzakis, Nikos

485. *God's Pauper.* Trans. P.A. Bien. Oxford: Cassirer, 1975. 390 pp.
Francis of Assisi rejects his worldly inheritance to represent God to the poor of Italy in the 13th century. *Genre(s):* Biographical Fiction; Christian Fiction.

486. *Saint Francis.* Trans. P.A. Bien. New York: Simon and Schuster, 1962. 379 pp.
Brother Leo tells about the struggles that Francis of Assisi faced in medieval Europe. *Genre(s):* Christian Fiction; Biographical Fiction.

King, Bernard

487. *Starkadder.* New York: St. Martin's, 1987. 243 pp.
Starkadder must betray three times before he is allowed to die in the Norse Dark Ages, and the gods know that when he falls, they also will die. *Genre(s):* Fantastic Literature.

Kinsale, Laura

488. *For My Lady's Heart.* New York: Berkley, 1993. 423 pp.
The wife of Ruck, an English knight, goes into a convent, and he decides to marry Princess Melanthe, the widowed head of an Italian family, but Gian, patriarch of another family, decides he wants to marry Melanthe and declares to kill anyone who challenges him. *Genre(s):* Romance.

L'Amour, Louis

489. *The Walking Drum.* New York: Bantam, 1984. 423 pp.
Mathurin Kerbouchard, captured and made a galley slave after his mother's death in 12th-century Brittany, takes control of the boat and lands in Spain. *Genre(s):* Adventure Story.

Le Porrier, Herbert

490. *The Doctor from Cordova.* Garden City, NY: Doubleday, 1979. 280 pp.
The Rabbi Moses ben Maimon, a Spanish-Jewish physician, philosopher, Talmudist, and legal codifer, lives in Moorish Cordova as a child, but when exiled from Spain, he travels through the Islamic world before settling in Cairo as court physician to Saladin. *Genre(s):* Biographical Fiction.

Lindsey, Johanna

491. *Defy Not the Heart.* New York: Avon, 1990. 411 pp.
Ranulf decides to marry Reina because he wants her fiefdom, and she agrees because she wants his protection, but she uses her wiles to ensure that he will not brutalize her. *Genre(s):* Romance.

492. *Fires of Winter.* New York: Avon, 1980. 362 pp.
A rival Viking chief in Norway abducts Brenna, King Angus's favorite daughter, and makes her a house slave for his son Garrick, but she refuses to do women's work. *Genre(s):* Romance.

493. *So Speaks the Heart.* New York: Avon, 1983. 358 pp.
Rowland de Montville, a brutish Norman, carries off Brigitte de Louroux from her Berry estate, thinking she is a servant, but after many altercations, the two fall in love in 10th-century France. *Genre(s):* Romance.

494. *Until Forever.* New York: Avon, 1995. 416 pp.
History professor Roseleen White waves an ancient sword and conjures up a Viking warrior with whom she falls in love. *Genre(s):* Romance.

Mackin, Jeanne

◆ 495. *The Queen's War.* New York: St. Martin's, 1991. 452 pp.
Eleanor of Aquitaine, wife of two kings and mother of two more, presides over a cultivated court, and with her sons, revolts against her husband, Henry II, in 1173. *Genre(s):* Biographical Fiction.

Marmontel, Jean Francois

496. *Belisarius.* 1767. New York: Garland, 1975. 240 pp.
Belisarius, a general in the Byzantine Empire, serves Justinian I in the sixth century, leading major campaigns against several enemies. *Genre(s):* Biographical Fiction.

Maturin, Charles Robert

497. *The Albigenses.* New York: Arno, 1974. 3 vols.

A civil war in Languedoc follows Montfort's crusade against the Albigenses in the 13th century.
Genre(s): Adventure Story.

Meade, Marion

498. *Stealing Heaven.* New York: Morrow, 1979. 415 pp.
Héloise and Abelard fall in love, face the wrath of Héloise's guardian, and must separate after a gang castrates Abelard.
Genre(s): Biographical Fiction; Love Story.

499. *Sybille.* New York: Morrow, 1983. 444 pp.
Sybille, a talented, aristocratic poet, suffers the losses of war in 13th-century France.
Genre(s): Domestic Fiction.

Michaels, Fern

500. *Tender Warrior.* New York: Severn House, 1997. 384 pp.
Sancho, son of King Ferdinado, receives Castile, and loyal to him is El Cid, a man who estabishes himself as a warrior but must marry the woman chosen for him for political reasons rather than the one he loves.
Genre(s): Romance; Biographical Fiction.

Michener, James A.

501. *Poland.* New York: Random House, 1983. 556 pp.
The story of the development of Poland since the 1200s is told from a small village on the Vistula River, with information on the Lubonski, Bukowski, and the Buk families.
Genre(s): Family Saga.

Mittermeyer, Helen

502. *The Veil.* New York: Warner, 1995. 287 pp.
Viking Einar Thorhallsson leaves home to find a sacred chalice which once belonged to his family and goes to Rome and Antioch on his journey.
Genre(s): Romance; Adventure Story.

Moore, George

503. *Héloise and Abelard.* London: Liveright, 1921. 2 vols.
Héloise and Abelard have a love affair that ends with her return to the convent and his to the monastery.
Genre(s): Love Story.

Morazzoni, Marta

504. *The Invention of Truth.* Trans. M. J. Fitzgerald. New York: Knopf, 1993. 112 pp.
A queen in Amiens, France, calls for people to help her create the Bayeux tapestry in the 11th century while 800 years later in 1879, the art critic John Ruskin admires the other art object of the town, the cathedral.

Munthe, Adam John

505. *A Note That Breaks the Silence.* London: Bodley Head, 1977. 240 pp.

A hunchbacked juggler remembers his master, the troubadour of Carcassonne, singing of the troubles to come when Simon de Montfort and his Crusaders invade Languedoc to fight the Cathar heresy.
Genre(s): Christian Fiction; War Story.

Newman, Sharan

◆ 506. *Death Comes as Epiphany.* New York: Tor, 1993. 320 pp.
Catherine LeVendeur, the most promising student in Héloise's convent, Paraclete, has the responsibility of discovering who has altered the text of a psalter given to the Abbot of Suger during the 12th century.
Award(s): Macavity Award.
Genre(s): Mystery.

◆ 507. *The Devil's Door.* New York: Forge, 1994. 384 pp.
In 1140, Catherine LeVendeur investigates the beating of a wealthy countess brought into the convent for help, and Catherine suspects the woman's husband, and after her investigation Catherine and her new husband Edgar attend the heresy trial for Abelarde.
Genre(s): Mystery.

◆ 508. *Strong as Death.* New York: Forge, 1996. 384 pp.
In the 12th century, as Catherine LeVendeur and her Scottish husband Edgar make a pilgrimage to Santiago de Compostela to pray for a child, a murder occurs, which they must solve.
Genre(s): Mystery.

◆ 509. *The Wandering Arm.* New York: Forge, 1995. 351 pp.
After Catherine Le Vendeur has a stillborn daughter in Paris, her father's Jewish relatives encourage her husband Edgar to come help them search for a stolen relic, the arm of Saint Aldhelm, encased in gold.
Genre(s): Mystery.

O'Faolain, Julia

510. *Women in the Wall.* New York: Viking, 1975. 326 pp.
Born in 518, Radegund is captured and forced to marry the Frankish king Clotair, but she devotes herself to others and becomes a patron saint of prisoners and captives.
Genre(s): Biographical Fiction.

Ohannenson, Joan

511. *Scarlet Music.* New York: Crossroad, 1997. 334 pp.
Hildegard of Bingen has visions, demonstrates political courage, and composes music in the 12th century.
Genre(s): Biographical Fiction; Musical Fiction; Christian Fiction.

Oldenbourg, Zoé

512. *The Cornerstone.* Trans. Edward Hyams. New York: Pantheon, 1955. 482 pp.

In the sequel to *The World Is Not Enough*, Alis and her Crusader spouse live in the splendor and squalor of 13th-century France.

513. *Destiny of Fire.* Trans. Peter Green. New York: Pantheon, 1961. 378 pp.
Pope Innocent III tries to suppress the Albigensian heresy in the 13th century by using avaricious barons to find the heretics.

514. *The Heirs of the Kingdom.* Trans. Anne Carter. New York: Pantheon, 1971. 563 pp.
A group of Arras weavers joins the First Crusade, and after three years, helps to storm Jerusalem.
Genre(s): War Story.

515. *The World Is Not Enough.* Trans. Willard R. Trask. New York: Pantheon, 1948. 509 pp.
Alis, married at 14, bears and buries children and then manages her 13th-century fief when her husband becomes a Crusader.

Paton Walsh, Jill

◆ **516. *Knowledge of Angels.*** Boston: Houghton Mifflin, 1994. 268 pp.
When a child raised by wolves without human contact is found on a Mediterranean island, the Inquisition decides that an atheist prince will be condemned if the child shows any awareness of God.
Genre(s): Christian Fiction.

Paxson, Diana L.

◆ **517. *The Dragons of the Rhine.*** New York: Morrow, 1995. 371 pp.
In the sequel to *The Wolf and the Raven*, a witch influences Sigrid to fall in love with Gudrun and betray Brunahild who has borne him a girl. (*Series:* Wodan's Children, 2)
Genre(s): Fantastic Literature; War Story.

◆ **518. *The Wolf and the Raven.*** New York: Morrow, 1993. 320 pp.
Sigfrid and Brunahild meet while the Burgunds and Huns fight their wars.
Genre(s): Fantastic Literature; War Story.

Pei, Mario

519. *Swords of Anjou.* San Diego, CA: Beta, 1977. 310 pp.
Huon and Thierry of Anjou, brother knights, find love at the court of the Saracen emir, but the plots of Roland's treacherous uncle Ganelon keep them at war in Charlemagne's time.
Genre(s): Fantastic Literature.

Phillips, Jill M.

520. *The Rain Maiden.* Secaucus, NJ: Citade, 1987. 592 pp.
Isabel of Hainault, 12th-century descendant of Charlemagne, comes to France to wed King Philippe-Auguste, a

homosexual who has stripped his mother, Adele, of her lands and titles.
Genre(s): Political Fiction.

Pouillon, Fernand

521. *The Stones of the Abbey.* San Diego, CA: Harcourt, 1970. 218 pp.
In the 12th century, a monk architect designs the Abbey of Le Thoronet in Provence and helps to build it.
Genre(s): Christian Fiction.

Powys, John Cowper

522. *Porius.* Hamilton, NY: Colgate University Press, 1994. 873 pp.
In 499 Merlin reveals his uncanny abilities.
Genre(s): Fantastic Literature.

Prescott, H. F. M.

523. *Son of Dust.* New York: Macmillan, 1956. 288 pp.
In 11th-century Normandy, Alde elopes with Fulcun after her husband dies, but her husband turns out not to be dead, and the three of them confront an awkward situation.
Genre(s): Romance.

Rhodes, Evan H.

◆ **524. *Army of Children.*** New York: Dial, 1978. 433 pp.
Roger, a Christian, and Jonathan, a Jew, go with other children in 1212 on their crusade to Jerusalem.
Genre(s): War Story.

Rivele, Stephen J.

525. *A Booke of Days.* New York: Carroll and Graf, 1997. 436 pp.
In 1096, during Pope Urban II's First Crusade, Roger L'Escrivel tries to atone for his affair by joining the hordes on their way to Jerusalem.
Genre(s): War Story.

Rotondi, Cesar J.

526. *The Garden of Persephone.* New York: St. Martin's, 1982. 336 pp.
The Englishman Julien becomes the secretary and diplomat for King Roger II of Sicily in the 12th century.
Genre(s): Political Fiction.

Sargent, Pamela

◆ **527. *Ruler of the Sky.*** New York: Crown, 1993. 703 pp.
Genghis Khan's charismatic leadership guides the warring Mongols in their conquering ways.
Genre(s): Biographical Fiction; Family Saga.

Schaefer, Frank

528. *Whose Song Is Sung.* New York: Tor, 1996. 300 pp.

◆May be suitable for young adult readers

Musculus the Dwarf tells about his adventures in life and his experiences at the court of Beowulf, a cruel place.
Genre(s): Fantastic Literature; Epic Literature.

Shwartz, Susan

529. *Cross and Crescent.* New York: St. Martin's, 1998. 382 pp.
In 1096, as pilgrims arrive in Constantinople on their way to free Jerusalem from the Muslims, Anna, daughter of Alexius, Emperor of Byzantium, schemes to take her weakening father's throne from her ineffectual brother.
Genre(s): War Story; Political Fiction.

530. *Shards of Empire.* New York: T. Doherty, 1996. 383 pp.
After Leo's uncle betrays the emperor Romanus in the battle of Manzikert, Leo tries to help him, and when Romanus dies, Leo searches for the young Jewish woman who helped them in the Byzantine Empire during the 11th century.
Genre(s): Fantastic Literature.

Silver, Warren A.

531. *The Green Rose.* New York: Dial, 1977. 305 pp.
Jewish poet and philospher Gabirol becomes an envoy to Tashfent before Tashfent burns Granada in the 11th century and only Gabirol and his love escape.
Genre(s): Biographical Fiction.

Simpson, Rosemary

532. *Seven Hills of Paradise.* New York: Doubleday, 1980. 496 pp.
During the Fourth Crusade, greed for the wealth of Constantinople overcomes the rationality of such men as Robert of Clari and Geoffrey of Villehardouin.
Genre(s): War Story.

Small, Bertrice

533. *The Love Slave.* New York: Ballantine, 1995. 451 pp.
Regan MacDuff's family sends her to a Scottish convent in the 10th century, and the abbess sells her to a slaver who in turn sells her to a Moor who asks the passion master Karim al-Malina to train her as a love slave so that she will be a proper gift for the caliph.
Genre(s): Romance; Erotic Literature.

Smiley, Jane

534. *The Greenlanders.* New York: Knopf, 1988. 558 pp.
The Norseman Erik the Red and his colonists settle Greenland in the 10th century.

Speer, Flora

535. *A Love Beyond Time.* New York: Dorchester, 1994. 448 pp.

Mike Bailey, an archaeologist, wakes up in the eighth-century France of Charlemagne with no memory of his past, meets Danise, and falls in love.
Genre(s): Romance; Time Travel.

Tarr, Judith

536. *The Eagle's Daughter.* New York: Forge, 1995. 352 pp.
To escape from a bleak future, Theophano agrees to go from Constantinople to Rome in 983 and wed Otto II, leading the way to her regency for Otto III.
Genre(s): Political Fiction.

Taylor, Georgia Elizabeth

537. *The Infidel.* New York: St. Martin's, 1979. 469 pp.
Jimena Gomez, the subservient Spanish daughter in the 11th century who obeys her father and marries his killer, El Cid, is kidnaped by one of El Cid's enemies, and in Hasan's harem she finds beauty and learning and begins to fall in love with her captor.
Genre(s): Romance.

Treece, Henry

◆ 538. *Swords from the North.* New York: Pantheon, 1967. 192 pp.
Harald serves in the Varangian Guard in 1034, and after a series of incidents, decides to return home to Norway and his betrothed.
Genre(s): Adventure Story.

◆ 539. *Westward to Vinland.* New York: S. G. Phillips, 1967. 192 pp.
Erik the Red flees Norway for Iceland in AD 960, and his son Lief the Lucky continues their exploration to America, landing on the southern coast of contemporary New England.
Genre(s): Adventure Story; Biographical Fiction.

Turtledove, Harry

540. *Thessalonica.* Riverdale, NY: Baen, 1997. 416 pp.
George, a Christian shoemaker living in Thessalonica during the 7th century AD, learns from a satyr that Avars and Slavs will soon invade in the coming days, and after they arrive, the satyrs and the centaurs help George.
Genre(s): Fantastic Literature; Christian Fiction.

Undset, Sigrid

541. *The Axe.* 1928. New York: Random House, 1994. 296 pp.
Olav and Ingunn grow up as brother and sister in Norway during the 13th century. (*Series:* The Master of Hestviken, 1)
Genre(s): Family Saga.

542. *In the Wilderness.* Trans. Arthur G. Chater. 1929. New York: Random House, 1995. 197 pp.
Olav Audunsson becomes middle aged in Norway. (*Series:* The Master of Hestviken, 3)
Genre(s): Family Saga.

543. *The Snake Pit.* 1929. New York: Random House, 1994. 223 pp.
In the 13th-century world of Norwegian paganism and emerging Christianity, Olav and Ingunn become lovers. (*Series:* The Master of Hestviken, 2)
Genre(s): Family Saga.

544. *The Son Avenger.* 1930. New York: Random House, 1995. 276 pp.
Olav Audunsson grows old in Norway. (*Series:* The Master of Hesviken, 4)
Genre(s): Family Saga.

Unsworth, Barry

545. *Pascali's Island.* New York: Norton, 1997. 192 pp.
As the Ottoman Empire decays, a Constantinople spy becomes caught in his own paranoia when spying on a village.
Genre(s): Political Fiction.

Vollmann, William T.

546. *The Ice-Shirt.* New York: Viking, 1990. 404 pp.
The Norsemen discover Vinland and try to live there, in an unusual retelling of their arrival. (*Series:* Seven Dreams, 1)
Genre(s): Family Saga.

Waddell, Helen

547. *Peter Abelard.* New York: Holt, Rinehart and Winston, 1933. 303 pp.
Peter Abelard passionately loves Héloise, but her guardian betrays them.
Genre(s): Love Story.

Williamson, Glen

548. *Repair My House.* Carol Stream, IL: Creation House, 1973. 173 pp.
Saint Francis of Assisi leaves his wealthy home and becomes a patron of the poor and ill in 12th-century Italy.
Genre(s): Biographical Fiction; Christian Fiction.

Yarbro, Chelsea Quinn

◆ 549. *Better in the Dark.* New York: Tor, 1993. 412 pp.
Count Saint-Germain is shipwrecked on the coast of northern Saxony in AD 938, and when he washes ashore and tastes Ranagonda's blood, he forms a bond with her and she nurses him back to health. (*Series:* Saint-Germain, 10)
Genre(s): Gothic Fiction.

◆ 550. *Crusader's Torch.* New York: Tor, 1988. 459 pp.
Olivia Clemens goes to Tyre where Richard the Lion-Hearted is leading the Fourth Crusade in the sequel to *A Flame in Byzantium.*
Genre(s): Gothic Fiction.

◆ 551. *A Flame in Byzantium.* New York: Tor, 1987. 470 pp.
Rome is sacked in 545, and vampire Olivia Clemens flees to Constantinople where she dislikes being curtailed by the culture's restrictions on women.
Genre(s): Gothic Fiction; Romance.

552. *Path of the Eclipse.* New York: St. Martin's, 1981. 447 pp.
Count de Saint-Germain resists Genghis Khan and his hordes in helping T'en Chih-Yu, daughter of a dead general. (*Series:* Saint-Germain, 4)
Genre(s): Gothic Fiction.

1290-1491

Aulnoy, Madame d' (Marie-Catherine)

553. *The Prince of Carency.* 1719. New York: Garland, 1973. 382 pp.
Jean de Bourbon is a 15th-century French prince.
Genre(s): Biographical Fiction.

Baumann, Hans

◆ 554. *The Barque of Brothers.* New York: Walck, 1958. 245 pp.
When Henry the Navigator begins to explore the coast of Africa, two brothers join his expedition.
Genre(s): Sea Story.

Bennetts, Pamela

555. *The Borgia Prince.* New York: St. Martin's, 1975. 254 pp.

When Bianca di Marco kills one of Cesare Borgia's captains during his capture of the castle of San Savarno, he falls in love with her.
Genre(s): Biographical Fiction.

Boccaccio, Giovanni

556. *The Elegy of Lady Fiammetta.* Trans. Mariangela Causa-Steindler and Thomas Mauch. 1345. Chicago: University of Chicago Press, 1991. 200 pp.
Lady Fiammetta suffers after her young lover rejects her in the early 14th century.
Genre(s): Romance.

Boland, Bridget

557. *Caterina.* New York: St. Martin's, 1975. 331 pp.

Caterina Sforza, mother of many and married three times, wields influence in Renaissance Italy and especially charms Machiavelli.
Genre(s): Biographical Fiction.

Bowen, Marjorie

558. *The Viper of Milan.* New York: McClure, Phillips, 1906. 362 pp.
The Count of Milan battles with the free towns of northern Italy.
Genre(s): Adventure Story; War Story.

Briggs, Jean

559. *The Flame of the Borgias.* New York: Harper and Row, 1975. 336 pp.
Pietro Bembo falls in love with Lucrezia Borgia during the Italian Renaissance.
Genre(s): Biographical Fiction.

Burman, Edward

560. *The Image of Our Lord.* New York: St. Martin's, 1991. 304 pp.
As the King of France, Philip the Fair wants the same relic belonging to the Order of the Knights of the Templar that the Catholic Church wants.
Genre(s): War Story.

Cohen, Matt

◆ 561. *The Spanish Doctor.* New York: Beaufort, 1985. 344 pp.
Avram Halavi, an illegitimate Spanish Jew, was conceived when his mother was raped during the massacre of Jews at Toledo in 1391, and after being baptized Catholic, he grows up to be a surgeon who eventually identifies with the suffering of the Jews.

Cole, Hubert

562. *Hawkwood and the Towers of Pisa.* London: Eyre Methuen, 1973. 204 pp.
Hawkwood and his White Company of mercenaries fight when he serves as Pisa's War Captain and overthrows the government while wooing Caterina in the 14th century.
Genre(s): Biographical Fiction.

Condon, Richard

563. *A Trembling upon Rome.* New York: Putnam, 1983. 398 pp.
Pope John XXIII, a pirate's son, treats his church position, with Cosimo di Medici's help, as a place from which to plunder booty in the early 15th century.
Genre(s): Biographical Fiction; Religious Fiction.

Corti, Maria

564. *Otranto.* Trans. Jessie Bright. New York: Italica, 1993. 270 pp.
In 1480, the Turks attack Otranto, and Colangelo describes how he and fellow fishermen protected their homes, while others tell of their year of occupation.
Genre(s): War Story.

Costain, Thomas Bertram

565. *The Moneyman.* Garden City, NY: Doubleday, 1947. 434 pp.
Jacques Coeur is a business tycoon during the time of Charles VII in France.
Genre(s): Biographical Fiction.

Damioli, Carol

566. *Rogue Angel.* Boston, MA: Dante University, 1994. 247 pp.
Fra Filippo Lippi, an orphan, lives in a Carmelite monastery where he discovers his ability to paint, and when he leaves, he becomes obsessed with women and drink.
Genre(s): Biographical Fiction.

Dann, Jack

◆ 567. *The Memory Cathedral.* New York: Bantam, 1995. 485 pp.
From his deathbed, da Vinci recalls his youth and the flying machine he designed, which the Medicis thought would improve their military powers.
Genre(s): Biographical Fiction; Fantastic Literature.

Davis, Genevieve

568. *A Passion in the Blood.* New York: Simon and Schuster, 1977. 360 pp.
Lucrezia Borgia is the victim of her family's political needs which keeps her from maturing into a woman with much depth of character.
Genre(s): Political Fiction.

De Treviño, Elizabeth

◆ 569. *Among the Innocent.* Garden City, NY: Doubleday, 1981. 358 pp.
Jews and Christians both face difficulties with the zeal of the inquisitors, which spreads from Spain to the New World.
Genre(s): Religious Fiction.

De Wohl, Louis

570. *Lay Siege to Heaven.* Philadelphia: Lippincott, 1961. 315 pp.
Catherine Benincasa enters a Dominican order and has a role in helping to end the civil war between the Italian city-states while persuading Pope Gregory XI to return to Rome.
Genre(s): Biographical Fiction; Christian Fiction.

Doherty, P. C.

571. *Satan's Fire.* New York: St. Martin's, 1996. 250 pp.
Sir Hugh Corbett searches for a counterfeiter distributing currency throughout the countryside and finds that the culprit is connected to the Order of Templars.
Genre(s): Mystery.

572. *The Serpent Amongst the Lilies.* New York: St. Martin's, 1990. 189 pp.

Matthew Jankyn tells of having spied on Jehanne d'Arc for his former lord, Henry Beaufort, and although he tried to find out if she were a witch or a true deliverer, he could never be certain.
Genre(s): Biographical Fiction; Adventure Story.

Doyle, Arthur Conan

573. **The White Company.** 1891. New York: Dodd, Mead, 1962. 441 pp.
The Hampshire hero wanders through France and the Pyrenees during the 14th century when the Black Prince supports Pedro the Cruel of Castile.
Genre(s): Mystery; Adventure Story.

Druon, Maurice

574. **The Iron King.** Trans. Humphrey Hare. New York: Scribner's, 1956. 269 pp.
Before he burns at the stake in 1314, Jacques de Molay curses Philip IV, the Iron King, and affects 13 generations of the House of Valois.
Genre(s): Biographical Fiction.

575. **The Lily and the Lion.** Trans. Humphrey Hare. New York: Scribner's, 1961. 313 pp.
In the sequel to *The She-Wolf of France*, Edward III marries his cousin in York on 24 January 1328, before the beginning of his rivalry with Philippe VI of Valois for the French throne and the start of the Hundred Years' War.
Genre(s): Biographical Fiction.

576. **The Poisoned Crown.** Trans. Humphrey Hare. New York: Scribner's, 1957. 224 pp.
In the sequel to *The Strangled Queen*, Louis X marries Clemence of Hungary and finds among the court intrigues a plot for his own poisoning.
Genre(s): Biographical Fiction.

577. **The Royal Succession.** Trans. Humphrey Hare. New York: Scribner's, 1957. 224 pp.
In the sequel to *The Poisoned Crown*, Louis X in 1316 incites pretenders to the crown to vie for position and to try to murder his posthumous child.
Genre(s): Biographical Fiction.

578. **The She-Wolf of France.** Trans. Humphrey Hare. New York: Scribner's, 1960. 335 pp.
In the sequel to *The Royal Succession* Isabella, sister of Charles IV of France, goes to England to marry Edward II but plots with Sir Roger Mortimer, her lover, to depose Edward.
Genre(s): Biographical Fiction.

579. **The Strangled Queen.** Trans. Humphrey Hare. New York: Scribner's, 1957. 213 pp.
In the sequel to *The Iron King*, Louis X of France wants to remarry after his wife is convicted of adultery, but the pope will not annul the first marriage of Louis.
Genre(s): Biographical Fiction.

Dunnett, Dorothy

580. **Caprice and Rondo.** New York: Knopf, 1998. 592 pp.

Nicholas Vander Poele participates in 15th-century intrigue. (*Series:* House of Niccolò, 7)
Genre(s): Adventure Story.

581. **Niccolò Rising.** London: M. Joseph, 1986. 470 pp.
As an apprentice in the 15th century, Claus begins a courier service for the Charetty company. (*Series:* House of Niccolò, 1)
Genre(s): Adventure Story.

582. **Race of Scorpions.** New York: Knopf, 1990. 534 pp.
In the sequel to *The Spring of the Ram*, Niccolò uses the force of his personality to restore his fortunes in Venice after the death of his wife and the loss of her inheritance. (*Series:* House of Niccolò, 3)
Genre(s): Adventure Story.

583. **Scales of Gold.** New York: Knopf, 1992. 519 pp.
Nicholas Vander Poele, merchant banker and adventurer, returns to Venice and finds competitors for his business, but he soon departs to search for gold in Africa. (*Series:* House of Niccolò, 4)
Genre(s): Adventure Story.

584. **The Spring of the Ram.** New York: Knopf, 1988. 469 pp.
At 19, Nicholas flees from his foe in Flanders to Florence and then to the East, using Medici funds, in the sequel to *Niccol Rising*. (*Series:* House of Niccolò, 2)
Genre(s): Adventure Story.

585. **To Lie with Lions.** New York: Knopf, 1996. 626 pp.
Beginning in 1471, Nicholas Vander Poele's enemies use both his legitimate and illegitimate sons as pawns, and Nicholas must protect himself and them. (*Series:* House of Niccolò, 6)
Genre(s): Adventure Story.

586. **The Unicorn Hunt.** New York: Knopf, 1994. 656 pp.
In the 15th century, Nicholas Vander Poele travels through Scotland, Venice, Flanders, and the Tyrol on business and family matters. (*Series:* House of Niccolò, 5)
Genre(s): Adventure Story.

Eco, Umberto

587. **The Name of the Rose.** Trans. A.W. Wheen. San Diego: Harcourt, 1983. 502 pp.
In the early 14th century, the English monk William, visiting at a Clunic abbey in Italy, solves a murder.
Genre(s): Mystery.

Eliot, George

588. **Romola.** 1863. New York: Oxford, 1994. 656 pp.
In the Florence of Lorenzo de' Medici, Romola falls in love with a handsome, seemingly intellectual young man,

but as their marriage disintegrates, Romola becomes intrigued by Savonarola and his teachings.
Genre(s): Biographical Fiction; Domestic Fiction.

Ennis, Michael

589. **Duchess of Milan.** New York: Viking, 1992. 580 pp.
Isabella of Aragon, wife of Gian Galeazzo Sforza, and her cousin Beatrice d'Este, wife of Lodovico Sforza, vie to become Duchess of Milan in the 15th century.
Genre(s): Biographical Fiction.

Eyre, Elizabeth

590. **Axe for an Abbot.** New York: St. Martin's, 1996. 339 pp.
When someone uses Sigismondo's axe to kill an important abbott, his reputation as a detective is at stake in Renaissance Italy.
Genre(s): Mystery.

◆ 591. **Dirge for a Doge.** New York: St. Martin's, 1997. 320 pp.
Sigismondo, Renaissance detective, must find out who stabbed recently married Niccolo Ermolin, a deceitful aristocrat, in his locked Venetian study.
Genre(s): Mystery.

Feyrer, Gayle

592. **The Prince of Cups.** New York: Dell, 1995. 471 pp.
In Italy during the 15th century, Mama Lucia reads the cards and tells her great-granddaughter Lucia that difficult times may be ahead, and Lucia then faces murder, betrayal, and attempted rape.
Genre(s): Romance.

Frazer, Margaret

◆ 593. **The Prioress' Tale.** New York: Berkley, 1997. 256 pp.
Sister Frevisse dislikes St. Frideswide Abbey's prioress, Alys, because she only wants to expand the abbey, and when Alys's family arrives and commits murder in the church, Sister Frevisse must expose them.
Genre(s): Mystery.

Frohlich, Newton

◆ 594. **1492.** New York: St. Martin's, 1990. 404 pp.
In the 15 years before Columbus sailed to the New World, recently converted Christians had to disguise their origins in order to survive the Inquisition and to keep their assets from Ferdinand and Isabella.
Genre(s): Biographical Fiction.

Golding, Michael

595. **Simple Prayers.** New York: Warner, 1994. 304 pp.
In the 14th century, a corpse with black welts on its body washes up on the shore of an island near Venice and forebodes doom the for people there.
Genre(s): Domestic Fiction.

Haasse, Hella S.

596. **In a Dark Wood Wandering.** Trans. Lewis C. Kaplan. Chicago: Academy, 1989. 574 pp.
Having promised his mother that he will avenge his father's murder in 1407, Charles d'Orléans is captured in battle and spends life in prison, where he writes many of his poems.
Genre(s): Biographical Fiction.

Hars Anyi, Zsolt de

597. **The Star-Gazer.** Trans. Paul Tabor. New York: Putnam, 1939. 572 pp.
Galileo follows his scientific pursuits in a world refusing to acknowledge religious doubt.
Genre(s): Biographical Fiction.

Hesse, Hermann

598. **Narcissus and Goldmund.** Trans. Ursule Molinaro. New York: Farrar, Straus and Giroux, 1968. 315 pp.
In the late Middle Ages, conflicts occur between body and intellect and between scholar and artist.
Genre(s): Picaresque Fiction.

Holland, Cecelia

◆ 599. **The Lords of Vaumartin.** Boston: Houghton Mifflin, 1982. 344 pp.
An evil uncle tricks Everard, who prefers being a scholar, into combat, but he survives battle at Crécy in 1346 and goes to Paris in disguise to follow his interests.

Hugo, Victor

600. **The Hunchback of Notre Dame.** 1930. New York: Hyperion, 1996. 583 pp.
In 1482, Quasimodo, a hunchback, mingles with the innocent Esmeralda and her antithesis, Claude Frollo.
Genre(s): Love Story.

Huntford, Roland

601. **Sea of Darkness.** New York: Scribner's, 1975. 255 pp.
In a secret journal, Columbus reveals his religious beliefs and other aspects of life in the 15th century.
Genre(s): Biographical Fiction.

Kadare, Ismail

602. **The Three-Arched Bridge.** Trans. John Hodgson. Boston: Little, Brown, 1997. 184 pp.
When engineers build a bridge in Albania, a monk records its construction and the people's belief that a body buried in it gave the bridge a soul.
Genre(s): Political Fiction.

Keneally, Thomas

◆ 603. **Blood Red, Sister Rose.** New York: Viking, 1974. 384 pp.

The voices Joan of Arc hears both torment and console her while she waits to fulfill her destiny.
Genre(s): Biographical Fiction; Christian Fiction.

Kenyon, Frank Wilson

604. *The Naked Sword.* New York: Dodd, Mead, 1968. 255 pp.
Lucrezia Borgia is the illegitmate daughter of Pope Alexander VI and has an unscrupulous brother, Cesare Borgia.
Genre(s): Biographical Fiction; Political Fiction.

La Mure, Pierre

605. *The Private Life of Mona Lisa.* Boston: Little, Brown, 1976. 406 pp.
The Mona Lisa lives in Florence and typifies the woman of her era in Renaissance Florence.
Genre(s): Biographical Fiction.

Leslie, Doris

606. *Vagabond's Way.* New York: Doubleday, 1962. 263 pp.
The gifted poet, François Villon, lives rather unconventionally in Paris while writing his poetry about the transience of life embodied in the snows of yesteryear.
Genre(s): Biographical Fiction.

Lofts, Norah

607. *Crown of Aloes.* Garden City, NY: Doubleday, 1974. 310 pp.
Isabella I helps to unite parts of Spain and make reforms in the Catholic Church with her husband Ferdinand in the late 15th century.
Genre(s): Biographical Fiction.

López-Medina, Sylvia

◆ 608. *Siguiriya.* New York: HarperCollins, 1997. 320 pp.
In 15th-century Spain, a Muslim general marries an independent Jewish woman and helps her get other Jews out of the country while their own children suffer.
Genre(s): Family Saga.

Lucie-Smith, Edward

609. *The Dark Pageant.* London: Blond and Briggs, 1977. 281 pp.
Gilles de Rais, a sadistic ghoul, commits murders in France during the reign of Charles VII.
Genre(s): Biographical Fiction; Horror.

Lytton, Edward Bulwer

610. *Rienzi, the Last of the Roman Tribunes.* Philadelphia: Lippincott, 1885. 366 pp.
Cola di Rienzo attempts to unite Italy in the 14th century.
Genre(s): Biographical Fiction.

MacAvoy, R. A.

611. *Damiano.* New York: Bantam, 1984. 243 pp.

Damiano, a 14th-century Italian wizard, must flee when a mercenary takes control of his village.
Genre(s): Fantastic Literature.

612. *Damiano's Lute.* New York: Bantam, 1984. 254 pp.
In the sequel to *Damiano*, Damiano has saved his village from a mercenary with his magic, but he wants to renounce his occult gifts as he journeys to France.
Genre(s): Fantastic Literature.

Maltz, Maxwell

613. *The Time Is Now.* New York: Simon and Schuster, 1975. 415 pp.
Gasparo Tagliacozzi, a 16th-century Italian surgeon, perfects the art of skin grafting, and a former friend, Flaminio, persecutes him in the Inquisition.
Genre(s): Biographical Fiction; Medical Novel.

Mannix, Daniel P.

614. *The Wolves of Paris.* New York: Dutton, 1978. 234 pp.
Roaming wolves enter Paris searching for food after feeding on corpses remaining from the Hundred Years' War of the 14th century.
Genre(s): War Story.

Marcantel, Pamela

◆ 615. *An Army of Angels.* New York: St. Martin's, 1997. 578 pp.
Jehanne begins hearing voices when she is 13, and these lead her to Charles VII and the rescue of France.
Genre(s): Biographical Fiction.

Martorell, Joanot, and Marti Joan de Galba

616. *Tirant lo Blanc.* Trans. David H. Rosenthal. 1984. Baltimore, MD: Johns Hopkins University Press, 1996. 642 pp.
Tirant lo Blanc, a young knight from Brittany, fights across Europe and Africa in the 15th century.
Genre(s): Adventure Story; Picaresque Fiction.

Merezhkovsky, Dmitry

617. *The Romance of Leonardo da Vinci.* Trans. Herbert Trench. New York: Putnam, 1902. 463 pp.
During the 15th century, Leonardo's artistic temperament develops in his Florentine home.
Genre(s): Biographical Fiction.

Morris, Roderick Conway

618. *Jem: Memoirs of an Ottoman Secret Agent.* New York: St. Martin's, 1989. 312 pp.
When Jem, Mehmed II's second son, attempts to seize the Turkish throne at his father's death in 1481, competing forces drive him into exile where Christian groups use him in their attempt to organize a crusade.
Genre(s): Adventure Story.

Morris, William

619. *A Dream of John Ball.* Portland, ME: Mosher, 1908. 142 pp.
Jack Ball, Jack Straw, and Wat Tyler lead in Tyler's Insurrection, the Peasant's Revolt of 1381.
Genre(s): Biographical Fiction; Political Fiction.

Mullins, Edwin B.

620. *The Master Painter.* New York: Doubleday, 1989. 373 pp.
Philip, Duke of Burgundy, hires Jan van Eyck as First Painter and asks him to depict Joan of Arc so that Philip can decide if she tells the truth.
Genre(s): Biographical Fiction.

Nye, Robert

621. *The Life and Death of My Lord, Gilles De Rais.* London: Hamish Hamilton, 1990. 322 pp.
In his youth, Gilles de Rais, is companion to Joan of Arc, and he becomes one of Europe's wealthiest men before dying at the stake in 1440 for crimes of witchcraft, sodomy, and child sexual abuse.
Genre(s): Biographical Fiction.

Park, Jacqueline

622. *The Secret Book of Grazia Dei Rossi.* New York: Simon and Schuster, 1997. 576 pp.
In the 14th century, Grazia Dei Rossi, daughter in a wealthy Jewish family, must take orders from court patrons, and she records their lives and political situations for her son in her memoirs.
Genre(s): Domestic Fiction.

Perutz, Leo

623. *Leonardo's Judas.* New York: Arcade, 1989. 154 pp.
Leonardo searches for a model who can embody the images of secrecy and treachery in Judas, and a German horsedealer who arrives in Milan qualifies as this model.
Genre(s): Biographical Fiction.

Plaidy, Jean

◆ 624. *Epitaph for Three Women.* New York: Putnam, 1983. 333 pp.
Katherine of Valois loses her husband Henry V and becomes interested in Owen Tudor, Joan of Arc struggles, and Eleanor of Gloucester is both passionate and treasonous. (*Series:* Plantagenet Saga, 12)
Genre(s): Biographical Fiction.

Reade, Charles

625. *The Cloister and the Hearth.* 1861. New York: Dutton, 1906. 703 pp.
Erasmus's father, receiving a forged letter saying that his love Margaret is dead, joins a monastery but after 20 years, he discovers that Margaret is still alive.
Genre(s): Love Story; Picaresque Fiction.

Rice, Anne

626. *The Vampire Armand.* New York: Knopf, 1998. 384 pp.
The vampire Armand travels across centuries to the Kiev Rus of his youth, to Constantinople, and to Venice on his way into 19th-century Paris and contemporary New Orleans.
Genre(s): Fantastic Literature; Adventure Story; Time Travel.

Ripley, Alexandra

627. *The Time Returns.* Garden City, NY: Doubleday, 1985. 334 pp.
In 15th-century Florence, after Ginevra's family plots to kill Lorenzo de'Medici, he finds her and nurses her to health after a rape, and she becomes his confidant but not his lover.
Genre(s): Domestic Fiction.

Schoonover, Lawrence

628. *The Burnished Blade.* New York: Macmillan, 1948. 371 pp.
Pierre enters the service of Jacques Coeur in 15th-century France and undergoes a variety of adventures before returning to France as a wealthy man.
Genre(s): Picaresque Fiction; Adventure Story.

629. *The Queen's Cross.* New York: Sloane, 1955. 377 pp.
Isabella becomes a queen who endures her king's weaknesses while she unites Aragon and Castile, rids Spain of the Moors and Jews, and sends Columbus on his journey.
Genre(s): Biographical Fiction; Romance; Political Fiction.

630. *The Spider King.* New York: Macmillan, 1954. 403 pp.
Louis XI excels in a variety of positions and brings peace to his country, in spite of his epilepsy.
Genre(s): Biographical Fiction.

Scott, Walter

631. *Quentin Durward.* 1823. New York: Oxford, 1992. 566 pp.
Young Quentin Durward belongs to the Scottish Guards, and when he saves Louis XI during a boar hunt, he wins the hand of his love, Isabelle of Croye.
Genre(s): Romance.

Seymour, Miranda

632. *Daughter of Shadows.* New York: Coward-McCann, 1977. 255 pp.
Cesare's designs on his sister Lucrezia come to fruition in Renaissance Italy.
Genre(s): Biographical Fiction.

633. *The Stones of Maggiare.* London: Hutchinson, 1975. 212 pp.

Beatrice, the consort of Lodovico Sforza il Moro, Duke of Milan, heads the Milanese court, the most splendid in Europe during the 15th century.
Genre(s): Biographical Fiction.

Shelley, Mary Wollstonecraft

634. *Valperga.* New York: Woodstock, 1995. 348 pp.
Castruccio Castracani becomes involved with the political intrigues of the Guelfs and Ghibellines in medieval Italy.
Genre(s): Adventure Story.

Shulman, Sandra

635. *The Florentine.* New York: Morrow, 1973. 314 pp.
Francesca de Narni disguises herself as a male for protection when Lorenzo de' Medici blames her family for a plot against him.
Genre(s): Domestic Fiction.

636. *Francesca: The Madonna of the Shadows.* London: New English Library, 1973. 205 pp.
While disguised as a man, Francesca de Narni has the freedom to develop her artistic talent although she is attracted to Ridolfo, in the sequel to *The Florentine.*
Genre(s): Domestic Fiction.

Sienkiewicz, Henryk

637. *The Teutonic Knights.* Trans. Alicia Tyszkiewicz. New York: Hippocrene, 1993. 786 pp.
In the 15th century, the Order of Teutonic Knights rules Prussia, but Macko of Bogdaniec and his nephew Zbyszko from the Polish-Lithuanian kingdom finally challenge the Order's supremacy.
Genre(s): Family Saga.

Szczypiorski, Andrezej

638. *A Mass for Arras.* Trans. Richard Lourie. New York: Grove, 1993. 188 pp.
Jan nearly loses his life when the people of Arras begin killing each other in 1461 because of plague and the spreading rumor that Jews caused a curse.

Twain, Mark

639. *Personal Recollections of Joan of Arc.* 1896. New York: Oxford, 1997. 461 pp.
Joan of Arc recounts her participation in the battle to regain France's independence from England.
Genre(s): Biographical Fiction; Christian Fiction.

Undset, Sigrid

640. *Kristin Lavransdatter.* New York: Knopf, 1935. 3 pp.
The compilation of three novels *Bridal Wreath*, *The Mistress of Husaby*, and *The Cross*, tells the story of Kristin, a beautiful young Norwegian in the 14th century who

marries the fickle Erland for love and suffers through the years.
Genre(s): Domestic Fiction; Love Story.

Unruh, Fritz von

641. *The Saint.* New York: Random House, 1950. 396 pp.
Catherine of Siena becomes a 14th-century mystic and attains sainthood.
Genre(s): Biographical Fiction; Christian Fiction.

Vansittart, Peter

642. *A Safe Conduct.* Chester Springs, PA: Dufour, 1995. 184 pp.
Mysterious Albrecht incites the children to burn a barn when the graf raises taxes in the German village, and when the graf offers safe conduct for negotiation to young Hans, the pipe-playing shepherd, the graf kills him immediately.
Genre(s): Political Fiction.

White, Richard

643. *Sword of the North.* Ottawa, IL: Pegma, 1983. 400 pp.
Henry Sinclair, a Scots baron and Norwegian Jarl of Orkney, tries to keep his fortune in the 14th century.
Genre(s): Biographical Fiction.

Woodhouse, Martin, and Robert Ross

644. *The Medici Emerald.* New York: Dutton, 1976. 223 pp.
Da Vinci must find the secret navigating device for which his friend was murdered and which people in both Venice and Florence want to own.
Genre(s): Biographical Fiction; Mystery.

645. *The Medici Guns.* New York: Dutton, 1975. 277 pp.
Leonardo da Vinci becomes fascinated with military engineering and helps to capture Castelmonte with his inventions in 15th-century Florence.
Genre(s): Biographical Fiction.

646. *The Medici Hawks.* New York: Dutton, 1978. 202 pp.
The Sultan Mohammad II sacks Otranto in 1480, and Leonardo must reclaim his love, Bianca, who has been sold into slavery.
Genre(s): Mystery.

◆May be suitable for young adult readers

1492-1649

Acland, Alice

647. *The Ruling Passion.* London: P. Davies, 1976. 200 pp.
Diane de Poitiers becomes the mistress of Henry IV of France in the 16th century, and Henry's wife, Catherine de' Medici, is one of the most powerful women in the country.
Genre(s): Biographical Fiction.

Alexander, Sidney

648. *The Hand of Michelangelo.* Athens: Ohio University Press, 1977. 693 pp.
In the sequel to *Michelangelo the Florentine,* Michelangelo has become a respected artist.
Genre(s): Biographical Fiction.

649. *Michelangelo: The Florentine.* Athens: Ohio University Press, 1985. 464 pp.
Michelangelo grows up in Florence during the 16th century.
Genre(s): Biographical Fiction.

650. *Nicodemus: The Roman Years of Michelangelo Buonarroti.* Athens: University of Ohio Press, 1984. 293 pp.
In the sequel to *The Hand of Michelangelo,* Michelangelo presents the last 30 years of his life, the times in which he lived, and the people he knew.
Genre(s): Biographical Fiction.

Andahazi, Federico

651. *The Anatomist.* New York: Doubleday, 1998. 256 pp.
A physician scandalizes Venetian society in the 16th century when he discovers the clitoris.
Genre(s): Medical Novel; Erotic Literature.

Anthony, Evelyn

◆ 652. *The Cardinal and the Queen.* New York: Coward-McCann, 1968. 221 pp.
Anne of Austria, married to Louis XIII, has a passionate affair with Jules Mazarin, her minister, in 17th-century Paris, after Louis' death.
Genre(s): Biographical Fiction; Political Fiction.

Aridjis, Homero

653. *1492: The Life and Times of Juan Cabezón of Castile.* Trans. Betty Ferber. New York: Summit, 1991. 263 pp.
Near the end of the 15th century, two Jewish converts to Christianity escape the Spanish Inquisition and forced exile from Spain.
Genre(s): Picaresque Fiction; Love Story.

Arnott, Peter D.

654. *Ballet of Comedians.* New York: Macmillan, 1971. 320 pp.
Molière (Jean Baptiste Poquelin) ignores his family and chooses a theatrical career, but when his acting proves to be only average, he develops his extraordinary playwriting ability.
Genre(s): Biographical Fiction.

Banti, Anna

655. *Artemisia.* Lincoln: University of Nebraska Press, 1988. 219 pp.
While desiring love from her distant father in Rome, Artemisia Gentileschi allows herself to be seduced, publically humiliated, and married to Orazio of Florence, before she begins to establish herself as a painter.
Genre(s): Biographical Fiction.

Banville, John

656. *Doctor Copernicus.* New York: Norton, 1976. 241 pp.
Copernicus, canon, doctor, and astronomer, avoided conflict with others as he steeped himself in study, but when he overturned established ideas about the universe, he exposed himself to the condemnation of his society.
Award(s): James Tate Black Award.
Genre(s): Biographical Fiction.

657. *Kepler.* Boston: David R. Godine, 1983. 192 pp.
Johannes Kepler has various problems while trying to establish some kind of order in a world of upheaval when he discovers that the planets orbit eliptically.
Genre(s): Biographical Fiction.

Bartos-Höppner, B.

◆ 658. *The Cossacks.* New York: Walck, 1963. 195 pp.
Yermak Timofeyevich serves as chieftain of the Cossacks, an outlaw band of Christians fighting to avenge Ivan IV's destruction.
Genre(s): War Story.

◆ 659. *Save the Khan.* New York: Walck, 1964. 240 pp.
When Daritai is asked to kill his ailing grandfather, Kuchum Khan, he refuses, and he withdraws to become a shepherd in the late 16th century while the Russians try to overcome the Tatars.
Genre(s): War Story.

Bataille, Christophe

660. *Hourmaster.* Trans. Richard Howard. New York: New Directions, 1998. 208 pp.
In the duchy of Montferrato in the 17th century, Gog becomes Duke Gonzaga's hourmaster with the responsibil-

ity of keeping 218 clocks working, and he marries and has a beautiful daughter who attracts the duke.
Genre(s): Adventure Story.

Beahn, John E.

◆ 661. *A Man of Good Zeal.* New York: Newman, 1958. 236 pp.
Francis de Sales struggles against Calvinism and establishes the Order of Visitation nuns in the late 16th century.
Genre(s): Biographical Fiction.

Bellonci, Maria

662. *Private Renaissance.* Trans. William Weaver. New York: Morrow, 1989. 462 pp.
Isabella d'Este, bride at the lively court of Mantua in the 16th century, manages to maintain the city's independence while those around her often shift their loyalties.
Genre(s): Biographical Fiction.

Berry, R. M.

663. *Leonardo's Horse.* Normal, IL: FC2, 1997. 317 pp.
While a contemporary academic has problems of lethargy, disappointed Leonardo da Vinci is unable to make his bronze horse for the Duke of Ludovico Sforza seem alive.
Genre(s): Adventure Story.

Braider, Donald

664. *Color from a Light Within.* New York: Putnam, 1967. 379 pp.
Greco reveals his religious faith in the images he chooses to paint during the 16th century.
Genre(s): Biographical Fiction.

665. *An Epic Joy.* New York: Putnam, 1971. 352 pp.
Peter Paul Rubens becomes the most notable Flemish artist of his time while also serving as a diplomat.
Genre(s): Biographical Fiction.

Brod, Max

666. *Redemption of Tycho Brahe.* New York: Knopf, 1928. 289 pp.
The Danish astronomer, Tycho Brahe, moves to a Bohemian castle, and has a conflict with his student, Johannes Kepler, over the heliocentric theory of the solar system.
Genre(s): Biographical Fiction.

Buchanan, Marie

667. *Morgana.* Garden City, NY: Doubleday, 1977. 287 pp.
As illegitimate daughter of James I and servant of her half-sister, Bess McLintock eventually becomes the wife of the Elector of the Rhenish Palatinate and the queen of Bohemia.
Genre(s): Biographical Fiction.

Caldwell, Taylor

668. *The Arm and the Darkness.* 1943. New York: Scribner's, 1975. 604 pp.
Cardinal Richelieu rules France while Louis XIII mans the throne.
Genre(s): Biographical Fiction.

Calitri, Charles J.

669. *The Goliath Head.* New York: Crown, 1972. 346 pp.
Michelangelo Caravaggio practices his rebellious art during the Counter Reformation in 16th-century Italy.
Genre(s): Biographical Fiction.

Cervantes Saavedra, Miguel de

670. *Don Quixote De La Mancha.* Trans. Charles Jarvis. 1605. New York: Barnes & Noble, 1995. 710 pp.
Don Quixote of 16th-century Spain decides to become a knight with a horse and squire who honors a lady, but his horse is a nag, his squire a peasant, and his lady a prostitute.
Genre(s): Picaresque Fiction.

671. *The History of That Ingenious Gentleman Don Quijote De La Mancha.* Trans. Burton Raffel. 1621. New York: Norton, 1995. 800 pp.
Don Quijote decides to become a knight, choosing Sancho Panza as his servant and Dulcinea, a local prostitute, as his lady to adore.
Genre(s): Picaresque Fiction; Romance.

Chamberlin, Ann

672. *Sofia.* New York: Forge, 1996. 368 pp.
Giorgio Veniero is 15 when he sails with 14-year-old Sofia Baffo from Venice to Corfu in 1562, but Turks capture their ship, and after they are sold into slavery, the ambitious Sofia begins her rise in the sultan's harem.
Genre(s): Adventure Story; Romance.

673. *The Sultan's Daughter.* New York: Forge, 1997. 352 pp.
Abdullah, a eunuch, tells the story of the barren Esmikhan, granddaughter of the Sultan Suleiman in the 1560s, whom Abdullah protects during the intrigue to take over the throne.
Genre(s): Domestic Fiction.

Chapman, Robin

674. *The Duchess's Diary.* Boston: Faber and Faber, 1985. 126 pp.
In 1616, Duchess Maria Isabel of Caparroso writes of her anger at Cervantes's portrayal of her in book two of *Don Quixote* by recalling the visit of Cervantes to her home in 1608.
Genre(s): Biographical Fiction.

Codrescu, Andrei

675. *The Blood Countess.* New York: Simon and Schuster, 1995. 347 pp.

When Drake returns to Hungary after 35 years, he researches the Countess Bathory, who in the 16th century drank the blood of young girls to preserve her youth.
Genre(s): Mystery.

Cohen, Jamey

676. *Dmitri.* New York: Seaview, 1980. 310 pp.
A Russian monk convinces people in 1605 that he is the Russian prince Dmitri supposedly murdered 14 years previously.
Genre(s): Biographical Fiction.

Connell, Evan S.

677. *The Alchymist's Journal.* San Francisco: North Point, 1991. 214 pp.
Seven diarists write about their relationships to alchemy and science, beginning with Paraclesus in 16th-century Switzerland.
Genre(s): Biographical Fiction.

Cowan, James

678. *A Mapmaker's Dream.* Boston, MA: Shambhala, 1996. 151 pp.
Fra Mauro, a 16th-century monk in Venice, tries to create a map of the world using stories that he hears about various places.
Genre(s): Christian Fiction.

Crawley, Aileen

679. *The Bride of Suleiman.* New York: St. Martin's, 1981. 271 pp.
The Russian girl Kharrem is enslaved and sold to a Turkish harem in the late 15th century, but her independence and refusal to act like other Muslim women make her attractive to Suleiman, heir to the throne.
Genre(s): Biographical Fiction; Romance.

680. *The Shadow of God.* New York: St. Martin's, 1983. 319 pp.
In the sequel to *The Bride of Suleiman*, former Russian slave Khurrem becomes Suleiman's favorite wife, mother of Mehmed, and his confidant on political matters, as he tries to make prudent decisions as ruler of his people.
Genre(s): Biographical Fiction; Romance.

De Treviño, Elizabeth

◆ 681. *I, Juan de Pareja.* New York: Farrar, Straus and Giroux, 1965. 192 pp.
Juan de Pareja serves as Velasquez's slave at the Spanish court of Philip IV, and he learns to paint in secret because slaves are forbidden to pursue trade.
Award(s): Newbery Medal.
Genre(s): Biographical Fiction.

Denys, Teresa

682. *The Flesh and the Devil.* New York: St. Martin's, 1981. 488 pp.
Juana de Arrelanos wants to free herself from her betrothal to a dim-witted duke in mid-17th-century Spain,

and a mercenary who both attracts and repulses her comes to the rescue.
Genre(s): Romance.

DiPerna, Paula

◆ 683. *The Discoveries of Mrs Christopher Columbus: His Wife's Version.* Sag Harbor, NY: Permanent Press, 1994. 287 pp.
Fellipa Moniz Perestrello died in 1484; however, if she had lived to travel with Columbus, her adventurous nature might have told this story of Columbus.
Genre(s): Biographical Fiction; Adventure Story; Romance.

Dumas, Alexandre

684. *Diana of Meridor, or The Lady of Monsoreau.* New York: Monro, 1880. 488 pp.
In the sequel to *Queen Margot, or Marguerite de Valois*, the French court continues to have its conflicts in the 16th century.
Genre(s): Political Fiction.

685. *The Forty-Five Guardsmen.* Boston: Houghton Mifflin, 1889. 438 pp.
The sequel to *Diana of Meridor, or The Lady of Monsoreau* continues the background and intrigue of the French court in the 16th century under Henry III's bodyguard, the Forty-Five.
Genre(s): Political Fiction.

686. *Queen Margot (Marguerite de Valois).* 1846. New York: Hyperion, 1994. 542 pp.
Marguerite de Valois marries on the day of the Saint Bartholomew's massacre in 1572, but neither her union nor her life are ever particularly happy.
Genre(s): Biographical Fiction.

687. *The Three Musketeers.* 1844. New York: Penguin, 1996. 224 pp.
D'Artagnan comes to Paris in 1625, duels with three men and becomes their best friend for many adventures.
Genre(s): Adventure Story; Picaresque Fiction.

688. *Twenty Years After.* 1845. New York: Oxford, 1993. 467 pp.
In the sequel to *The Three Musketeers*, Anne of Austria becomes regent after the death of Louis XIII, and she survives the Fronde as Charles I is executed in England.
Genre(s): Biographical Fiction.

689. *The Vicomte de Bragelonne.* 1857. New York: Oxford, 1998. 738 pp.
In the sequel to *Twenty Years After*, the lives of the four musketeers close against a backdrop of Louis XIV and his court.
Genre(s): Adventure Story.

Dunnett, Dorothy

690. *Pawn in Frankincense.* New York: Putnam, 1969. 486 pp.

Francis Crawford continues his adventures in the Middle East as he pursues a kidnapped child that is possibly his son.
Genre(s): Adventure Story.

691. *Queens' Play.* New York: Putnam, 1964. 432 pp.
In the sequel to *The Game of Kings*, Francis Crawford of Lymond, Scottish agent, protects his future monarch Mary Stuart in France during Henry II's reign.
Genre(s): Adventure Story.

692. *The Ringed Castle.* New York: Putnam, 1972. 521 pp.
In the sequel to *Pawn in Frankincense*, Francis Crawford of Scotland takes his mercenaries to Russia and becomes commander of the Tsar's armies.
Genre(s): Adventure Story.

Dussane, Beatrix

693. *An Actor Named Molière.* Trans. Lewis Galantiere. New York: Scribner's, 1937. 304 pp.
Molière rushes around writing his plays and rehearsing them with little time prior to 17th-century command performances before Louis XIV at Versailles.
Genre(s): Biographical Fiction.

Elegant, Robert S.

694. *Bianca.* North Pomfret, VT: Trafalgar Square, 1992. 348 pp.
Bianca Capello is mistress and second wife to Francesco de' Medici in Venice during the 16th century.

Eyre, Elizabeth

695. *Curtains for the Cardinal.* New York: Harcourt, 1993. 260 pp.
Sigismondo rescues a princess from her father who is trying to kill her, but a corrupt cardinal is murdered, and Sigismondo and Benno must investigate.
Genre(s): Mystery.

696. *Death of the Duchess.* New York: Harcourt, 1992. 241 pp.
Sigismondo investigates the kidnapping of a young woman from one of the noble houses of 15th-century Italy.
Genre(s): Mystery.

697. *Poison for the Prince.* New York: Harcourt, 1994. 309 pp.
When Prince Scipione seems to be weakening and sickly, Sigismondo, a courtier and private investigator, suspects poisoning.
Genre(s): Mystery.

Feather, Jane

698. *The Emerald Swan.* New York: Bantam, 1998. 448 pp.
Twenty years after the St. Bartholomew's Eve massacre, when a duchess was murdered and one of her twins disappeared, the twins' English second cousin, Gareth Har-

court, tries to marry the other twin, but she is a Catholic uninterested in the Huguenot court.
Genre(s): Political Fiction; Romance.

Flores, Angel

699. *Lope De Vega, Monster of Nature.* 1930. Port Washington, NY: Kensington, 1969. 214 pp.
Lope de Vega creates his drama and makes his time the Golden Age for Spain.
Genre(s): Biographical Fiction.

Fuentes, Carlos

700. *Terra Nostra.* Trans. Margaret Sayers Peden. New York: Farrar, Straus and Giroux, 1976. 777 pp.
Felipé, the Spanish king, administers from El Escorial as he tries to create Spain.
Genre(s): Biographical Fiction.

Gidley, Charles

◆ **701.** *Armada.* New York: Viking, 1988. 437 pp.
Tristam Pascoe, a Cornish sailor, ends up as the servant and lover of a Portugese nobleman's Irish wife, and the knowledge he gains thereby makes him a prime spy for Elizabeth I as an armada is assembled in Spain.
Genre(s): Sea Story.

Godwin, William

702. *St Leon, a Tale of the Sixteenth Century.* 1831. New York: Oxford, 1994. 478 pp.
A man becomes wealthy but discovers that he is still not happy.

Gogol, Nikolai

703. *Taras Bulba.* 1886. New York: Gilberton, 1968. 48 pp.
The Cossacks fight against the invading Poles in the 16th century.
Genre(s): War Story.

Grass, Günter

704. *The Meeting at Telgte.* Trans. Ralph Manheim. New York: Harcourt, 1981. 147 pp.
In 1649, at the end of the 30 Years' War, a group of theorists, poets, and prose writers meets to strengthen the language and literature of the German nation.

Greene, Liz

705. *The Dreamer of the Vine.* New York: Norton, 1981. 283 pp.
Nostradamus, a 16th-century prophet, physician, alchemist, and astrologer is involved in an underground pagan religion.
Genre(s): Biographical Fiction.

Gross, Joel

706. *The Books of Rachel.* New York: Seaview, 1979. 440 pp.

Jewish diamond merchants through six centuries name the first-born female in each generation Rachel.
Genre(s): Jewish Fiction; Family Saga.

Haasse, Hella S.

707. *The Scarlet City.* Chicago: Academy, 1990. 367 pp.
During the early-16th-century Italian Wars, Michelangelo, Machiavelli, and Vittoria Colonna work while Giovanni Borgia pursues adventure.
Genre(s): Adventure Story.

Hankiss, Agnes

708. *A Hungarian Romance.* Trans. Emma Roper-Evans. Columbia, LA: Readers International, 1992. 222 pp.
Susanna Forgach's marriage remains unconsummated in the early 17th century, and during her affair with Peter Bakics, Istvan Illeshazy is tried for political activities.
Genre(s): Romance; Legal Story.

Herman, George

709. *Carnival of Saints.* New York: Ballantine, 1993. 448 pp.
In 1501, Harlequin gathers a group of performers who wander throughout Italy during the time of Cesare Borgia and Pope Alexander VI, and these performers create the commedia dell'arte.
Genre(s): Political Fiction.

◆ 710. *A Comedy of Murders.* New York: Carroll and Graf, 1994. 355 pp.
Artist Leonardo da Vinci and a dwarf named Niccolo investigate homicides in the Milanese court and are subjected to threats from the pope.
Genre(s): Mystery.

◆ 711. *The Tears of the Madonna.* New York: Carroll and Graf, 1996. 288 pp.
Leonardo da Vinci and his friend, Niccolo, search for a missing necklace to use as collateral in the warring Italian city-states.
Genre(s): Mystery.

Hill, Pamela

712. *Here Lies Margot.* New York: Putnam, 1958. 254 pp.
Margaret of Burgundy becomes a major influence in keeping France from taking Belgium with her three state marriages and her regency for her nephew, Emperor Charles V.
Genre(s): Domestic Fiction; Political Fiction.

Hoeg, Peter

713. *The History of Danish Dreams.* Trans. Barbara Haveland. New York: Farrar, Straus and Giroux, 1995. 356 pp.

In four centuries, a Danish family, beginning with a 16th-century landowner who tries to stop time, into the 20th century with the birth of a golden child, questions life.

Hofmann, Gert

714. *The Parable of the Blind.* New York: Fromm International, 1986. 152 pp.
On the day depicted in Pieter Brueghel's *The Parable of the Blind*, blind beggars journey to a small village in Flanders where they pose for an artist to paint them.
Genre(s): Biographical Fiction.

Holland, Cecelia

715. *City of God.* New York: Knopf, 1979. 273 pp.
Nicholas, an aide to the Florentine ambassador, helps Pope Alexander and his son Cesare Borgia plan political intrigues.
Genre(s): Biographical Fiction.

716. *Rakóssy.* New York: Atheneum, 1967. 243 pp.
János Rakóssy tries to protect his family and other Magyars against Turkish invasions during the 16th century.
Genre(s): War Story.

◆ 717. *The Sea Beggars.* New York: Knopf, 1982. 305 pp.
After the Spanish Inquisiton results in the hanging of Jan and Hanneke van Cleef's father in Antwerp, they struggle to combat Catholic infiltration.
Genre(s): War Story.

Ingman, Heather

718. *The Dance of the Muses.* Chester Springs, PA: Dufour, 1987. 197 pp.
Ronsard, a melancholy and reflective man of the 16th century who is often ill, sees his reputation as principal poet of the French Renaissance diminish as a new generation turns to trivialization.
Genre(s): Biographical Fiction.

Irwin, Margaret

719. *The Bride.* New York: St. Martin's, 1984. 356 pp.
Visitors at the Queen of Bohemia Elizabeth's court in Holland include Prince Charles, who is about to lose his throne on his father's death, and James Graham, the Marquis of Montrose, who senses the difficulties ahead, although he is intrigued with Princess Louise, one of Elizabeth's daughters.
Genre(s): War Story.

Jacobsen, J. P.

720. *Marie Grubbe.* Trans. Hanna Astrup Larsen. 1876. New York: Twayne, 1975. 261 pp.
Marie Grubbe, a Danish woman of the 17th century, has difficulty controlling her natural instincts, and she descends in social status from that of a viceroy's consort to a ferryman's wife.
Genre(s): Domestic Fiction.

Kernan, Michael

721. *The Lost Diaries of Franz Hals*. New York: St. Martin's, 1994. 316 pp.
Franz Hals's diaries reveal him to be an opinionated man interested in the neighbors whose portraits he paints in 17th-century Haarlem.
Genre(s): Biographical Fiction.

Keyes, Frances Parkinson

722. *I, the King*. New York: McGraw Hill, 1966. 404 pp.
Philip IV, King of Spain, becomes involved with several women during his reign, including Elizabeth of France and Maria de Jésus de Agreda.
Genre(s): Biographical Fiction.

Kircher, Susanne

723. *A Roman Scandal*. New York: Mason, 1976. 306 pp.
Beatrice Cenci's father leads a despicable life, and three of his four children die because of a murder he committed in the late 16th century.
Genre(s): Biographical Fiction.

La Fayette, Madame de

724. *The Princess of Clèves*. Trans. Nancy Mitford. 1678. New York: New Directions, 1951. 210 pp.
The Princess of Clèves remains loyal to her husband although she has fallen in love with the duc de Nemours.

Lamming, R. M.

725. *The Notebook of Gismondo Cavalletti*. New York: Atheneum, 1985. 248 pp.
Gismondo Cavalletti, a member of Florence's privileged class, meets the leaders of the day including Leonardo and Michelangelo, while bearing the burden of a disfigured face.
Award(s): David Higham Prize.

Lehmann, Marcus

726. *Rabbi Joselman of Rosheim*. New York: Feldheim, 1974. 494 pp.
Joseph ben Gershon serves as a rabbi in Rosheim, Germany, in the early 16th century.
Genre(s): Biographical Fiction; Jewish Fiction.

Lennox, Judith

◆ **727. *The Italian Garden*.** New York: St. Martin's, 1993. 470 pp.
Joanna Zulian's uncle exploits her artistic ability within his own Renaissance studio, and to suvive in society, she must accept this more traditional role.

Lewis, Janet

728. *The Trial of Soren Qvist*. New York: Doubleday, 1947. 256 pp.

In Denmark, during the 17th-century reign of Christian IV, Soren Qvist faces trial.
Genre(s): Legal Story; Biographical Fiction.

729. *The Wife of Martin Guerre*. Chicago: Swallow, 1984. 110 pp.
After he marries as a child in the 1530s and has a son, Martin argues with his father, Bertrande, and leaves his wife and home, and when he apparently returns, not looking quite like himself, Bertrande accepts him, only to find that the man he thinks is his son is an impostor when Martin himself shows up.
Genre(s): Biographical Fiction.

Ludwig, Charles

730. *Queen of the Reformation*. Minneapolis, MN: Bethany House, 1986. 224 pp.
Martin Luther marries Katharina von Bora, and together they continue to denouce the heresy of the Catholic church during the Reformation.
Genre(s): Christian Fiction; Biographical Fiction.

Mallet-Joris, Françoise

731. *The Favourite*. Trans. Herma Briffault. New York: Farrar, Straus and Giroux, 1962. 282 pp.
Louise de la Fayette, maid of honor to Queen Anne, is one of Louis XIII's favorites, but their platonic relationship causes jealousy and intrigue within the court.
Genre(s): Biographical Fiction.

732. *The Witches: Three Tales of Sorcery*. New York: Farrar, Straus and Giroux, 1969. 391 pp.
Of three witches, Anne de Chantraine, Elizabeth de Ranfaing, and Jeanne Harvilliers, living in 16th- and 17th-century France, two were burned at the stake and a third had her lover burned instead.
Genre(s): Biographical Fiction.

Mann, Heinrich

733. *Henry, King of France*. Trans. Eric Sutton. 1938. Woodstock, NY: Overlook, 1985. 786 pp.
In the sequel to *Young Henry of Navarre*, Henry has just fought the battle of Arques and he continues in his pursuits until assassinated.
Genre(s): Biographical Fiction.

734. *Young Henry of Navarre*. Trans. Eric Sutton. 1937. Woodstock, NY: 1984. 585 pp.
Henry IV becomes king of France in 1589 after many intrigues at court.
Genre(s): Biographical Fiction.

Manzoni, Alessandro

735. *The Betrothed*. 1824. New York: Viking, 1984. 720 pp.
In the 1620s, Lorenzo and Lucia are betrothed, but the nobleman Don Rodrigo wants Lucia for himself.

Marlowe, Stephen

736. *The Death and Life of Miguel de Cervantes*. New York: Arcade, 1996. 495 pp.

Cervantes moves from urchin to schoolmaster and then to soldier and writer.
Genre(s): Biographical Fiction; Picaresque Fiction.

737. *The Memoirs of Christopher Columbus.*
New York: Scribner's, 1987. 569 pp.
Christopher Columbus has read all of his biographers, and he decides to tell his story as it actually happened in the 15th century.
Genre(s): Biographical Fiction.

Marshall, James Vance

738. *The Wind at Morning.* New York: Morrow, 1973. 208 pp.
Juan Vizcaya travels with Fernao de Magalhaes (Magellan), who seems driven by his dreams in the fall of 1519, and witnesses cruelties around the world.
Genre(s): Biographical Fiction.

Marston, Edward

◆ **739.** *The Laughing Hangman.* New York: St. Martin's, 1996. 248 pp.
Nicholas Bracewell must defend his drama troupe from heresy when a new playwright who tends toward Elizabethan sacrilege joins the group.
Genre(s): Mystery.

Maugham, W. Somerset

740. *Then and Now.* Garden City, NY: Doubleday, 1948. 278 pp.
In 1502, Niccolo Machiavelli, author of *The Prince*, continues his education as a political philosopher while keeping up his lechery in Florence, Italy.
Genre(s): Biographical Fiction.

Merle, Robert

741. *Vittoria.* Trans. Barbara Bray. San Diego, CA: Harcourt, 1990. 394 pp.
The beautiful Vittoria Peretti becomes frustrated in her marriage of convenience in 16th-century Italy and falls in love with Prince Orsini.
Genre(s): Domestic Fiction.

Montupet, Janine

742. *The Lacemaker.* Trans. Lowell Bair. New York: Atheneum, 1988. 448 pp.
Gilonne Perdriel, 15, owns her own lacemaking shop as the French *bourgeoisie* rises in the 17th century.
Genre(s): Domestic Fiction.

Mozeen, Thomas

743. *Young Scarron.* 1752. New York: Garland, 1974. 147 pp.
Monsieur Scarron is a French writer during the 17th century.
Genre(s): Biographical Fiction.

Murray, Linda

744. *The Dark Fire.* New York: Morrow, 1977. 418 pp.

Caravaggio becomes involved in a variety of things in his life including scandal, accusations of manslaughter, and tragedy, while completing paintings.
Genre(s): Biographical Fiction.

Naipaul, V. S.

745. *A Way in the World.* New York: Knopf, 1994. 380 pp.
Sir Walter Raleigh's search for El Dorado, Francisco de Miranda's attempt at revolution before Bolivar, and Lebrun, the Trinidadian Communist of the 1930s, are part of this story of souls who search for their roots.
Genre(s): Biographical Fiction.

Norfolk, Lawrence

746. *The Pope's Rhinoceros.* New York: Crown, 1996. 608 pp.
Hoping to win Pope Leo X's favor in the 16th century, emissaries from Portugal choose to give him a rhinoceros as an exotic gift.
Genre(s): Adventure Story; Picaresque Fiction.

O'Brien, Kate

747. *For One Sweet Grape.* New York: Penguin, 1946. 378 pp.
Ana Mendoza de la Cerda, Princess of Eboli, becomes the mistress of Philip II and of his secretary before being banished in 1579.
Genre(s): Biographical Fiction.

Orczy, Emmuska, Baroness

748. *The First Sir Percy: An Adventure of the Laughing Cavalier.* New York: Doran, 1926. 319 pp.
As Diogenes prepares to marry Gilda Eresteyn, daughter of a Dutch official, more trouble between the Dutch and the Spanish begins, and he must fight beside his friends, Pythagoras and Socrates, before taking Gilda back to England. (*Series:* Dutch War of Independence, 4)
Genre(s): Adventure Story.

749. *Flower o' the Lily.* New York: Doran, 1919. 400 pp.
The Duke of Parma sieges Cambrai in 1581 before the troops from France can rescue the people. (*Series:* Dutch War of Independence, 2)
Genre(s): Adventure Story.

750. *The Laughing Cavalier.* New York: Doran, 1914. 284 pp.
The Laughing Cavalier, made famous in Frans Hals's portrait of 1624, turns out to be the ancestor of the Scarlet Pimpernel, and he exhibits similar character traits in his own exploits. (*Series:* Dutch War of Independence, 3)
Genre(s): Adventure Story.

751. *Leatherface.* New York: Doran, 1916. 391 pp.
In the 16th century, the Prince of Orange in Flanders fights the Duke of Alva and the Spanish with secret warnings from a man known only as Leatherface because of

his mysterious mask. (*Series:* Dutch War of Independence, 1)
Genre(s): Adventure Story.

Otto, Whitney

◆ 752. *The Passion Dream Book.* New York: HarperCollins, 1997. 276 pp.
During the Renaissance, Guilietta Marcel cannot gain recognition as a female artist so she spies on Michelangelo for money, and in the early 20th century, her descendant, with her own problems of recognition, inherits one of the boxes Guilietta designed.
Genre(s): Family Saga.

Ozment, Steven

◆ 753. *The Brüghermeister's Daughter.* New York: St. Martin's, 1996. 227 pp.
Anna Büschler, a merchant's daughter, becomes a servant in a nearby castle in the 16th century, meets Erasmus, and has an affair with him.

Payne, Robert

754. *Caravaggio.* Boston: Little, Brown, 1968. 329 pp.
Caravaggio becomes famous for his juxstaposition of light and dark in his paintings during the 16th century.
Genre(s): Biographical Fiction.

Plaidy, Jean

755. *Evergreen Gallant.* New York: Putnam, 1973. 384 pp.
Henry of Navarre becomes a father at 15, and his many love affairs leave him little time to rule France.
Genre(s): Biographical Fiction; Political Fiction.

◆ 756. *The Italian Woman.* New York: Putnam, 1952. 299 pp.
When Catherine de' Medici's husband dies, she banishes his mistress and rules France through her sons, Francis and Charles. (*Series:* Medici Trilogy, 2)
Genre(s): Biographical Fiction.

◆ 757. *Light on Lucrezia.* 1958. New York: Putnam, 1976. 347 pp.
Lucrezia Borgia escapes from her family and marries happily. (*Series:* Lucrezia Borgia, 2)
Genre(s): Biographical Fiction.

◆ 758. *Madame Serpent.* 1951. New York: Berkley, 1975. 332 pp.
Catherine de' Medici, a merchant's daughter, becomes the consort of Henry II. (*Series:* Medici Trilogy, 1)
Genre(s): Biographical Fiction.

◆ 759. *Madonna of the Seven Hills.* New York: Putnam, 1974. 300 pp.
Lucrezia Borgia, although seemingly naive, becomes attracted to the lives led by her father Pope Alexander I and her brothers. (*Series:* Lucrezia Borgia, 1)
Genre(s): Biographical Fiction.

◆ 760. *Queen Jezebel.* New York: Putnam, 1976. 380 pp.

Catherine de' Medici is the widow of Henri II of France during the Religious Wars. (*Series:* Medici Trilogy, 3)
Genre(s): Biographical Fiction.

◆ 761. *The Scarlet Cloak.* London: Hale, 1969. 335 pp.
Philip II plots the overthrow of England and the re-establishment of Catholicism as the one true faith.
Genre(s): Biographical Fiction.

◆ 762. *The Spanish Bridegroom.* New York: Putnam, 1971. 301 pp.
Philip II grows up in Spain where he marries his first wife and sires Don Carlos, before he unites with Mary Tudor. (*Series:* Tudor Novels, 9)
Genre(s): Biographical Fiction.

Ponce De Leon, Napoleon Baccino

763. *Five Black Ships.* Trans. Nick Caistor. New York: Harcourt, 1994. 347 pp.
The jester with Magellan writes about their voyage to find a western passage to the Spice Islands from 1519 until 1522 when only one ship returns to Seville.
Award(s): Casa de las Americas Award.
Genre(s): Sea Story.

Posse, Abel

764. *The Dogs of Paradise.* Trans. Margaret S. Peden. New York: Atheneum, 1990. 288 pp.
After Christopher Columbus arrives in the New World in 1492, he mistreats natives as Ferdinand and Isabella have mistreated their own subjects.
Genre(s): Political Fiction.

Prokosch, Frederic

765. *A Tale for Midnight.* 1955. Westport, CT: Greenwood, 1973. 354 pp.
When Francesco Cenci is murdered, his family is tried for the crime.
Genre(s): Biographical Fiction; Legal Story.

Rojas, Carlos

766. *The Garden of Janus.* Trans. Cecelia Castro Lee. Madison, NJ: Fairleigh Dickinson, 1996. 218 pp.
Lope de Vega and Luis de Gongora wonder about the cause of the ten-year gap between the two parts of Cervantes's *Don Quixote*.
Genre(s): Biographical Fiction; Mystery.

Ross Williamson, Hugh

767. *The Florentine Woman.* New York: St. Martin's, 1973. 253 pp.
Catherine de' Medici, an important woman in France, is both an unloved wife and a bereaved widow, but she knows how to work politically for her children.
Genre(s): Biographical Fiction; Political Fiction.

768. *The Last of the Valois.* New York: St. Martin's, 1973. 246 pp.

The Massacre of Saint Bartholomew occurs most likely as a result of Catherine de' Medici's direction while her son Francis, Duke of Alencon, has disappointments including Elizabeth I's refusal to marry him in the sequel to *The Florentine Woman*.
Genre(s): Biographical Fiction.

769. *Paris Is Worth a Mass.* New York: St. Martin's, 1973. 223 pp.
In the final book of the trilogy covering the life of Catherine de' Medici, Catherine shows herself as a loving and devoted mother in contrast to Elizabeth I's demeanor as a hypocrite.
Genre(s): Biographical Fiction.

770. *The Princess a Nun.* London: Joseph, 1978. 192 pp.
Ana de Mendoza y la Cerda, Princess of Eboli, lives in Philip II's court, and when she becomes unfaithful, he banishes her.
Genre(s): Biographical Fiction.

Rothberg, Abraham

771. *The Sword of the Golem.* New York: McCall, 1971. 232 pp.
In 16th-century Prague, Rabbi Low creates Joseph Golem to combat the fanatical and brutal village priest.
Genre(s): Jewish Fiction.

Schmitt, Gladys

772. *Rembrandt.* New York: Random House, 1961. 657 pp.
Rembrandt's beginnings in Leyden lead to a life of fame and fortune in Amsterdam, until he goes bankrupt when out of favor with the populace.
Genre(s): Biographical Fiction.

Schoonover, Lawrence

773. *The Prisoner of Tordesillas.* Boston: Little, Brown, 1959. 309 pp.
Queen Juana becomes a tragic figure in the quest for power that takes place during the reigns of Ferdinand and Isabella, and then Charles V.
Genre(s): Biographical Fiction.

Scott, Chris

774. *Antichthon.* Dunvegan, Canada: Quadrant, 1982. 296 pp.
Giordano Bruno, born near Vesuvius in 1548, becomes a monk, mad philospher, poet, and guru before being burned at the stake during the Inquisition in 1600.
Genre(s): Biographical Fiction.

Seton, Anya

775. *Green Darkness.* Boston: Houghton Mifflin, 1972. 591 pp.
A 16th-century Benedictine monk Stephen Marsdon falls in love with Celia de Bohun and forsakes his vows only to be reincarnated 400 years later in a similar situation.
Genre(s): Fantastic Literature; Time Travel.

Shellabarger, Samuel

776. *Captain from Castile.* Boston: Little, Brown, 1945. 632 pp.
Pedro de Vargas helps a runaway slave exported from the New World and intrigued by the New World joins Cortés on the expedition in which Cortés destroys Montezuma's empire.

777. *The King's Cavalier.* Boston: Little, Brown, 1950. 377 pp.
Blaise, young guardsman to Francis I, remains loyal to the king, while his family joins the Bourbon conspiracy.

Shimony, Abner

◆ 778. *Tibaldo and the Hole in the Calendar.* New York: Springer-Verlag, 1997. 165 pp.
Tibaldo Bondi, a student in Bologna, faces losing his 12th birthday in 1582 when Pope Gregory XIII decides to drop 10 days from the calendar at the advice of his astronomer.
Genre(s): Adventure Story.

Smith, Haywood

779. *Shadows in Velvet.* New York: St. Martin's, 1996. 424 pp.
Anne-Marie de Bourbon-Corbay, an orphan, is ill-prepared for an arranged marriage to her cousin Phillippe during the unrest created by Anne of Austria and Cardinal Mazarin.
Genre(s): Romance.

Soister, Helena

780. *Prophecies.* New York: Bantam, 1990. 252 pp.
Two widows of English merchants see an agent on the Continent, and when Catlin answers their call, he brings with him a group of sinister, evil men.
Genre(s): Gothic Fiction; Mystery.

Stone, Irving

781. *The Agony and the Ecstasy.* Garden City, NY: Doubleday, 1961. 664 pp.
As a promising apprentice to the artist for a pope, Michaelangelo works in the 15th and early 16th centuries for the pope and others, and paints the ceiling of the Sistine Chapel.
Genre(s): Biographical Fiction.

Taylor, Georgia Elizabeth

782. *Lamia, a Witch.* New York: Dutton, 1994. 294 pp.
During the Inquisition, the Church encourages witch hunts of women trying to study science, and Marco Cellini tries to show members of his coven that science does

not require incantation, using Lamia, a wild child, as an example.

Tencin, Claudine Alexandrine Guerin de

783. *The Siege of Calais.* 1740. New York: Garland, 1974. 288 pp.
In 1558, the French at Calais under Francois de Lorraine, duke of Guise, fight against the English to reclaim their land after two hundred years of occupation.
Genre(s): War Story.

Upton, Arvin

784. *Lorenzino.* New York: Norton, 1977. 191 pp.
Lorenzo says that family pride and love of pure power led him to murder his bastard cousin Allesandro, Duke of Florence, in 1537.
Genre(s): Biographical Fiction.

Weiss, David

785. *I, Rembrandt.* New York: St. Martin's, 1979. 342 pp.
Rembrandt becomes so self-centered that only his feelings and his paintings exist, leaving little emotion remaining for his son or his mistress and certainly no sympathy for those who have lent him money.
Genre(s): Biographical Fiction.

786. *The Venetian.* New York: Morrow, 1976. 366 pp.
Titian is a self-consumed artist who makes life difficult for his family and his customers with his temperament and his delays in completing his work.
Genre(s): Biographical Fiction.

Weyman, Stanley John

787. *From the Memoirs of a Minister of France.* 1895. North Stratford, NH: Ayers, 1977. 325 pp.
Gaston de Bonne, a minster of France in Henry IV's court, recalls the dealings of the king with his wife, mistresses, and others.
Genre(s): Biographical Fiction.

Yanow, Morton Leonard

788. *The Nolan: Prisoner of the Inquisition.*
New York: Crossroad, 1998. 343 pp.
When Grand Inquistor Santa Severina orders theologian Robert Bellarmine to refute the arguments of imprisoned Giordano Bruno, Bellarmine's assistant Pietro Guidotti travels around Europe in 1597 looking for evidence against Bruno.
Genre(s): Christian Fiction; Adventure Story.

Yarbro, Chelsea Quinn

◆ **789. *Darker Jewels.*** New York: Tor, 1993. 398 pp.
During the reign of Ivan IV, Comte de Saint-Germaine goes to Russia, and Ivan forces him to marry a local girl. (*Series:* Saint-Germain, 9)
Genre(s): Gothic Fiction.

◆ **790. *The Palace.*** New York: St. Martin's, 1978. 408 pp.
Francesco Ragoczy da San Germano is a vampire whose friends include Botticelli at the time that the fanatical monk Savonarola has Florence in a turmoil. (*Series:* St. Germain, 2)
Genre(s): Gothic Fiction.

Yourcenar, Marguerite

791. *The Abyss.* Trans. Grace Frick. New York: Farrar, Straus and Giroux, 1976. 374 pp.
Zeno becomes involved with the subversive alchemists and the changes of the Renaissance in Europe during the 16th century.

Zimler, Richard

792. *The Last Kabbalist of Lisbon.* New York: Overlook, 1998. 320 pp.
In 1506 as the Inquisition rages, a young Jewish manuscript illuminator pretending to be Christian searches for the murderer of his uncle.
Genre(s): Mystery.

1650-1788

Acland, Alice

793. *The Secret Wife.* New York: St. Martin's, 1975. 203 pp.
Madame de Maintenon becomes the secret wife of Louis XIV.
Genre(s): Biographical Fiction.

Allen, Hervey

794. *Anthony Adverse.* New York: Farrar, Straus and Giroux, 1933. 1224 pp.
Anthony Adverse, an orphan, travels throughout the world as he looks for adventure.
Genre(s): Adventure Story; Epic Literature; Romance.

Andric, Ivo

795. *The Bridge on the Drina.* Trans. Lovett F. Edwards. New York: Allen and Unwin, 1959. 314 pp.
The life of a bridge near the Bosnian town of Visegrad and the events near it span three and a half centuries of Turkish rule.
Genre(s): Epic Literature.

Anthony, Evelyn

◆ **796. *Rebel Princess.*** New York: Crowell, 1953. 286 pp.

◆May be suitable for young adult readers

Catherine II of Russia, married to the mentally deficient Peter III, overthrows him to become the Empress of Russia.
Genre(s): Biographical Fiction.

◆ **797.** *Royal Intrigue.* New York: Crowell, 1954. 243 pp.
Catherine II and her son Paul oversee a court where cruelty and intrigue abound.
Genre(s): Biographical Fiction.

Auchincloss, Louis

798. *The Cat and the King.* Boston: Houghton Mifflin, 1981. 183 pp.
The duc de Saint-Simon, a somewhat catty courtier, observes King Louis XIV at the court of Versailles.
Genre(s): Biographical Fiction.

Benzoni, Juliette

799. *The Devil's Necklace.* New York: Putnam, 1980. 400 pp.
The sequel to *Lure of the Falcon* finds Gilles de Tournemine trying to conquer Juliette in 1783, having returned from America and regained the family estate in Brittany, but to raise money for such a conquest, Gilles must go to Spain.
Genre(s): Romance.

Berckman, Evelyn

800. *A Finger to Her Lips.* New York: Doubleday, 1971. 280 pp.
The Duke of Volingen-Ilm divorces Princess Sybilla-Marie and leaves her without money, but she is determined to rescue her son from him.
Genre(s): Mystery.

Blackstock, Charity

801. *The Lonely Strangers.* New York: Coward-McCann, 1972. 287 pp.
As a Stuart supporter, Coll has to leave his family after the Battle of Culloden to hide in France, and during the long exile, he becomes responsible for the young widow of a colleague.
Genre(s): War Story; Political Fiction.

Bowen, Marjorie

802. *I Will Maintain.* 1911. Pella, IA: Inheritance, 1993. 383 pp.
William III governs in his Netherlands home and marries Mary, daughter of James II.
Genre(s): Biographical Fiction.

Butler, Mildred Allen

803. *Ward of the Sun King.* New York: Funk and Wagnalls, 1970. 156 pp.
Adrienne Lavelle attends Madame de Maintenon's school at St. Cyr as one of the king's wards since she has no dowry, but when the rules suddenly change for the

worse, she decides to run away as her third cousin Pierre's male aide.
Genre(s): Biographical Fiction.

Carnegie, Sacha

804. *The Banners of Courage.* London: Davies, 1976. 158 pp.
The Polish cavalry rides into the mountains in pursuit of Catherine the Great's representative, King Poniatoyski.
Genre(s): War Story.

805. *The Banners of Power.* London: Davies, 1972. 246 pp.
Kasha Radienska, lady-in-waiting to Catherine of Russia, loves Henryk Berinski, an escapee from Siberia, and she joins him in their native Poland.
Genre(s): Biographical Fiction; Domestic Fiction.

806. *The Banners of War.* New York: Dodd, Mead, 1970. 239 pp.
Banished from St. Petersburg, Henryk Berinski reaches England but is impressed into the navy for four years before he can continue to Louix XV's France. (*Series:* Destiny of Eagles, 2)
Genre(s): Spy Fiction; Sea Story; Adventure Story.

807. *Kasia and the Empress.* New York: Dodd, Mead, 1973. 246 pp.
Catherine II is Empress of Russia.
Genre(s): Biographical Fiction.

808. *Scarlet Banners of Love.* New York: Dodd, Mead, 1968. 323 pp.
Kasia is abducted and finds herself in a sultan's harem before she can free herself and return to the man she loves in the court of Catherine the Great. (*Series:* Destiny of Eagles, 1)
Genre(s): Adventure Story.

Carr, Philippa

809. *Knave of Hearts.* New York: Putnam, 1983. 288 pp.
In the sequel to *Will You Love Me in September*, Lottie raises her children in France after her husband dies but misses her English roots during the period before the French Revolution begins. (*Series:* Daughters of England, 10)
Genre(s): Romance; Family Saga.

◆ **810.** *Will You Love Me in September.* New York: Putnam, 1981. 324 pp.
After her mother's death, in the sequel to *Song of the Siren*, Clarissa grows up with her aunt in England during the 1700s and discovers that she has a half-sister. (*Series:* Daughters of England, 8)
Genre(s): Romance.

Chandernagor, Françoise d'Aubigne

811. *The King's Way.* Trans. Barbara Bray. San Diego, CA: Harcourt, 1984. 497 pp.
After her birth in a prison, Françoise d'Aubign chooses to marry a crippled old poet when she is 16 rather than go to a convent, and through the years in her husband's sa-

lon, she becomes learned and witty, enough so that when she becomes Louis XIV's morganatic wife, she wields power over France as Madame de Maintenon.
Genre(s): Biographical Fiction.

Cooper, Dominic

812. *Men at Axlir.* New York: St. Martin's, 1980. 286 pp.
In 1740, when Sunnefa Jónsdóttir and her brother Jón are accused and tried for incest by an Icelandic court, a family feud starts which lasts for forty years.
Genre(s): Biographical Fiction.

Crnjanski, Milos

813. *Migrations.* Trans. Michael Henry Heim. New York: Harcourt, 1994. 274 pp.
In 1744, Vuk Isakovic leaves his pregnant wife and daughters to go with his brother and other Serbian mercenaries to fight in France under the cruel leadership of Austro-Hungarian officers.
Genre(s): Domestic Fiction; War Story.

Defoe, Daniel

814. *The Fortunate Mistress.* 1724. New York: AMS, 1974. 2 vols.
After her English husband leaves Lady Roxana destitute during the reign of Charles II, she makes connections on the Continent leading to marriage with a Dutch merchant.
Genre(s): Adventure Story; Picaresque Fiction.

Doherty, P. C.

815. *The Masked Man.* New York: St. Martin's, 1991. 174 pp.
Ralph Croft, a forger, questions his underground contacts in an attempt to find the identity of the Man in the Iron Mask.
Genre(s): Mystery.

Doyle, Arthur Conan

816. *The Refugees.* New York: HarperCollins, 1893. 366 pp.
After the rivalry at the French court between Madame de Maintenon and the Marquise de Montespan, the Hugenots flee to Canada.
Genre(s): Political Fiction; Christian Fiction.

Du Maurier, Daphne

817. *The Glass-Blowers.* Garden City, NY: Doubleday, 1963. 348 pp.
Madame Duval relates the story of her mother's marriage in 1747 to Robert-Mathurin Busson du Maurier who trained in the family glass business before moving to France in 1789 where he worked from the Revolution until 1802.
Genre(s): War Story.

Dukthas, Ann

◆ 818. *The Prince Lost to Time.* New York: St. Martin's, 1995. 229 pp.

Nicholas Segalla returns to France when the Dauphin, Louis Charles, 10-year-old son of Marie Antoinette is abducted.
Genre(s): Biographical Fiction; Time Travel.

Dumas, Alexandre

819. *The Black Tulip.* 1850. Cutchogue, NY: Buccaneer, 1990. 314 pp.
During the 17th century, William of Orange supports the tulip agitation against Johan de Witt and his brother in Haarlem.
Genre(s): Biographical Fiction; Love Story; Allegory.

820. *The Man in the Iron Mask.* 1850. New York: Oxford, 1991. 626 pp.
The last segment of *The Three Musketeers* involves the unsolved identity of the man in the iron mask, Raoul de Bragelonne.
Genre(s): Romance.

821. *The Memoirs of a Physician.* Boston: Little, Brown, 1893. 340 pp.
The swindler Cagliostro, count of Alessandro, relates the decline of Louis XV's power in his memoirs.
Genre(s): Political Fiction.

822. *The Queen's Necklace.* 1848. New York: Limited Editions, 1973. 300 pp.
Three members of the court of Louis XVI try to discredit Queen Marie Antoinette for adultery and theft, in the sequel to *The Memoirs of a Physician.*
Genre(s): Biographical Fiction.

Durham, Charles

823. *The Last Exile.* New York: Ballantine, 1989. 434 pp.
Gabriel Dublanche loses friends and acquaintances in France beginning in 1732, and he takes his young wife to Montreal, only to find that his new job is under Lecharbonnier, the tax collector who murdered his best friend.
Genre(s): War Story; Political Fiction.

Feather, Jane

824. *The Diamond Slipper.* New York: Bantam, 1997. 400 pp.
When Lady Cordelia Brandenburg marries by proxy, her best friend, Marie Antoinette, is pledged to the future dauphin of France, but Cordelia decides that she loves the widowed Viscount Leo Kierston, the dauphin's stand-in and father of young twin daughters.
Genre(s): Romance.

Feuchtwanger, Lion

825. *Proud Destiny.* New York: Viking, 1947. 625 pp.
Beaumarchais schemes and works for arms and support of the American armies during the American Revolution, although Benjamin Franklin never quite trusts him.
Genre(s): War Story; Biographical Fiction.

Frank, Bruno

826. *The Days of the King.* Freeport, NY: Books For Librar, 1970. 165 pp.
Frederick the Great is slovenly, shrill, and poorly spoken, but his subjects, for whom he has little love, believe that he improves their lives.
Genre(s): Biographical Fiction.

Freuchen, Peter

827. *White Man.* New York: Rinehart, 1946. 275 pp.
Peter, a Danish soldier convicted of desertion and shipped to Greenland, attempts to create a settlement near the Eskimos.

Gardner, Richard

828. *The Adventures of Don Juan.* New York: Viking, 1974. 438 pp.
As Don Juan continues to look for women in bordellos and in nunneries, he begins to realize that life is meaningless, and that no one can be perfect, even in 17th-century Spain.
Genre(s): Fantastic Literature.

Gary, Romain

829. *The Enchanters.* Trans. Helen Eustus. New York: Putnam, 1975. 320 pp.
In the 18th century, the Venetian Giuseppe Zaga serves Catherine the Great by helping her defecate properly, a process his son reports in detail.
Genre(s): Humorous Fiction.

Germany, Jo

◆ 830. *City of Golden Cages.* New York: St. Martin's, 1978. 182 pp.
A young Englishwoman arrives in Russia while the overthrow of Peter III is in progress, and she is caught up in court intrigue as she falls in love with her cousin's husband.
Genre(s): Romance.

Goldman, Lawrence

831. *The Castrato.* New York: John Day, 1973. 264 pp.
Farinelli becomes a male soprano in the 18th century after being castrated as a child and performs opera after his extraordinary debut in 1720.
Genre(s): Biographical Fiction; Musical Fiction.

Golon, Anne

832. *Angélique.* Trans. Rita Barisse. New York: Bantam, 1971. 820 pp.
Angélique lives in the court of Louis XIV where her beauty enchants many.
Genre(s): Romance; War Story.

833. *Angélique and the King.* New York: Bantam, 1971. 505 pp.

Angélique becomes a favorite of Louis XIV while attending his court.
Genre(s): Romance.

834. *Angélique in Revolt.* New York: Bantam, 1971. 470 pp.
After escaping from Morocco, Angélique returns to France and becomes the king's enemy when she sides with the Huguenots.
Genre(s): Romance.

Grafigny, Madame de

835. *Letters From a Peruvian Woman.* Trans. David Kornacker. New York: Modern Language Association, 1993. 174 pp.
After Spaniards in Peru capture an Incan princess in the 18th century, they lose her to the French during a sea battle, and in France, she learns French while protected by a nobleman whom she refuses to marry.
Genre(s): Adventure Story.

Gramont, Sanche de

836. *The Way Up.* New York: Putnam, 1972. 384 pp.
Count Gramont relates his memoirs of the 18th century and the court of Louis XV with its duels, plotting, and sexual encounters.
Genre(s): Picaresque Fiction.

Harrison, Kathryn

837. *Poison.* New York: Random House, 1995. 319 pp.
While Francisca de Luarca, daughter of a silk grower, lives in prison accused of witchcraft during the 17th-century Spanish Inquisition, she reviews her life and that of her queen, Maria Luisa, the barren wife of Carlos II, who is dying from poisoning.
Genre(s): Domestic Fiction.

Herr, Ethel

◆ 838. *The Dove and the Rose.* Minneapolis, MN: Bethany House, 1996. 334 pp.
During the reign of William of Orange, Pieter-Lucas and Aletta Engelshofen are parted when Pieter's father sends him away for not supporting the Beggars, a radical Calvinist group. (*Series:* The Seekers, 1)
Genre(s): Christian Fiction.

839. *The Maiden's Sword.* Minneapolis, MN: Bethany House, 1997. 320 pp.
When the Dutch revolt against the Spanish, Pieter-Lucas and Aletta struggle to survive. (*Series:* Seekers, 2)
Genre(s): Christian Fiction; Political Fiction; War Story.

Hersey, John

840. *Antonietta.* New York: Knopf, 1991. 304 pp.
Antonietta is a violin made by Antonio Stradivari in 1699, and its adventures include Mozart playing it and Berlioz being taught on it.
Genre(s): Musical Fiction.

Heyer, Georgette

841. *These Old Shades.* New York: Small, 1926. 362 pp.
Members of Louis XV's court become involved with one another.
Genre(s): Romance.

Hill, Pamela

842. *The Crown and the Shadow.* New York: Putnam, 1955. 314 pp.
Madame de Maintenon creates a social life at the court of Louis XIV.
Genre(s): Domestic Fiction.

843. *Tsar's Woman.* New York: St. Martin's, 1985. 207 pp.
After being chosen by one of Peter's friends, Catherine becomes Peter's bedmate, wife, and helper before his death when she becomes Catherine I.
Genre(s): Biographical Fiction.

Holt, Victoria

844. *The Queen's Confession.* Garden City, NY: Doubleday, 1968. 430 pp.
Marie Antoinette reveals feelings of being a misunderstood queen.
Genre(s): Biographical Fiction.

Hoyle, Peter

845. *The Man in the Iron Mask.* Manchester: Carcanet, 1984. 159 pp.
A man moves upstairs from the narrator, declaring that he is the unhappy twin of Louis XIV, the masked prisoner.
Genre(s): Romance.

Irwin, Margaret

846. *Royal Flush.* New York: St. Martin's, 1932. 352 pp.
Minette, the sister of Charles II and wife of Philippe d'Orléans, keeps the families of Britain and France closely united during her short marriage before her death.
Genre(s): Biographical Fiction.

Kaplick, Vaclav

847. *Witch Hammer.* Trans. John Newton. Boulder, CO: Harbinger, 1990. 416 pp.
In 1680, a woman saves a communion wafer to help the midwife's cow start giving milk, and a judge wanting to revive his career makes the women confess to witchcraft.
Genre(s): Horror.

Kurzweil, Allen

848. *A Case of Curiosities.* San Diego, CA: Harcourt, 1992. 358 pp.
In the 18th century, Claude Page, a young man, begins working for a priest by painting illicit sex scenes on watches and clocks, and as he matures, he becomes entangled with others on the fringes of society.
Genre(s): Adventure Story.

Laker, Rosalind

◆ 849. *The Golden Tulip.* New York: Doubleday, 1991. 585 pp.
Francesca Visser wants to become a master artist in 17th-century Holland, and her family helps her overcome the machinations of Ludolf van Deventer, who tries to get her father in debt so that he can marry her.
Genre(s): Romance.

850. *To Dance with Kings.* New York: Doubleday, 1988. 564 pp.
The descendants of a fan maker from a village near Versailles are hired by the courts of Louis XIV, XV, and XVI, and the family's fortunes slowly rise through the French Revolution.
Genre(s): Romance.

◆ 851. *The Venetian Mask.* Garden City, NY: Doubleday, 1993. 422 pp.
In the 18th century, three girls meet in a Venetian music conservatory for orphans, and as they mature, they marry, while remaining loyal to one another.
Genre(s): Love Story.

Law, Janice

852. *All the King's Ladies.* New York: St. Martin's, 1986. 310 pp.
Athénaïs, the Marquise of Montespan, becomes Louis XIV's official mistress for over a decade, but her influence ends with a witchcraft scandal and her husband's increasing religious beliefs.
Genre(s): Biographical Fiction.

Le Sage, Alain René

853. *The Adventures of Gil Blas of Santillane.* Trans. Tobias Smollett. 1774. New York: Routledge, 1890. 629 pp.
Gil Blas, a quiet student, becomes involved in a series of adventures that take him to all levels of society.
Genre(s): Adventure Story; Picaresque Fiction.

Lofts, Norah

854. *The Lost Queen.* Garden City, NY: Doubleday, 1969. 302 pp.
Caroline Mathilde, sister of George III, goes to Denmark to marry Christian VII, a mentally unbalanced monarch.
Genre(s): Biographical Fiction.

Mackin, Jeanne

◆ 855. *The Frenchwoman.* New York: St. Martin's, 1989. 387 pp.
As a seamstress in the court of Queen Marie Antoinette, Julienne marries a young officer who fought with Lafayette in America, and when he dies, she flees to Pennsylvania where royalists try to recreate their lives in France.
Genre(s): War Story.

◆May be suitable for young adult readers

Markish, David

856. *Jesters.* Trans. Antonina W. Bouis. New York: Holt, 1988. 246 pp.
Peter the Great trusts only three Jews, and even while confiding in these three, he treats them as jesters, or men living only at his pleasure.
Genre(s): Political Fiction.

Marshall-Andrews, Bob

857. *The Palace of Wisdom.* New York: Dutton, 1990. 336 pp.
Four people join together to stop the Inquistion from destroying the great literary works collected in Florence during the late 17th century.
Genre(s): Political Fiction.

Meynell, Esther

858. *The Little Chronicle of Magdalena Bach.* New York: F. Ungar, 1970. 245 pp.
Magdalena Bach adores her husband Johann Sebastian, and feels that their marriage is blessed with music and happiness.
Genre(s): Biographical Fiction; Domestic Fiction; Musical Fiction.

Miller, Andrew

859. *Casanova in Love.* San Diego, CA: Harcourt, 1998. 288 pp.
The Venetian lover, Casanova, falls in love.
Genre(s): Domestic Fiction.

Neider, Charles

860. *Mozart and the Archbooby.* New York: Penguin, 1991. 87 pp.
Mozart writes to his father and reveals his hatred of the Archbishop of Salzburg along with his aspirations and career goals.
Genre(s): Biographical Fiction.

Newth, Mette

◆ 861. *The Abduction.* Trans. Tina Nunnally and Steve Murray. New York: Farrar, Straus and Giroux, 1989. 248 pp.
In the 17th century, Norwegians capture Inuits, rape and kill some of them, and take others to Holland to become slaves.

O'Doherty, Brian

862. *The Strange Case of Mademoiselle P.* New York: Pantheon, 1992. 228 pp.
At the Viennese court in the 18th century, Dr. Anton Mesmer treats the blind Maria Theresa von Paradis with his new science of animal magnetism.
Genre(s): Biographical Fiction; Gothic Fiction.

Pamuk, Orhan

863. *The White Castle.* Trans. Victoria Holbrook. New York: Braziller, 1991. 161 pp.

In the 17th century, Ottoman Turks capture an Italian Christian but treat him kindly by allowing him to do research for the Pasha.

Paretti, Sandra

864. *The Drums of Winter.* Trans. Sophie Wilkins. New York: M. Evans, 1974. 441 pp.
Anna Haynow discovers in 1775 that the husband who left for America 20 years prior is not dead, but that his letters have been intercepted by her new husband.
Genre(s): War Story.

Pell, Sylvia

865. *The Shadow of the Sun.* New York: Coward-McCann, 1978. 343 pp.
Three women influence Louis XIV as his mistresses, Louise de la Valliere, Athénaïs de Montespan, and Françoise Scarron, governess to his children by Athénaïs.
Genre(s): Biographical Fiction.

Perutz, Leo

866. *The Swedish Cavalier.* Trans. John Brownjohn. New York: Arcade, 1993. 181 pp.
Christian von Tornfeld deserts from the Swedish army in the 18th century, and a thief takes his identity, makes him a slave in the bishop's lime kilns, steals gold from churches, and marries von Tornfeld's intended.
Genre(s): Gothic Fiction.

Prévost, Abbé

867. *Manon Lescaut.* Trans. Helen Waddell. 1731. New York: Dutton, 1935. 262 pp.
The Chevalier des Grieux falls in love with the harlot Manon who will not remain faithful as long as others can provide her with luxuries.
Genre(s): Love Story.

Quignard, Pascal

◆ 868. *All the World's Mornings.* Trans. James Kirkup. St. Paul, MN: Graywolf, 1993. 96 pp.
Monsieur de Sainte Columbe, a 17th-century composer, arrogantly chooses to hide his talents on his remote retreat with his turkeys and his chickens.
Genre(s): Biographical Fiction; Musical Fiction.

Rebolledo, Francisco

869. *Rasero.* Trans. Helen R. Lane. Baton Rouge: Louisiana State University Press, 1995. 552 pp.
Rasero helps Diderot edit the *Encyclopedia*, inters Voltaire's body, hears the child Mozart, and tries to save Lavoisier from Robespierre in this novel of France in the 18th century.
Award(s): Pegasus Prize.
Genre(s): Adventure Story.

Rice, Anne

870. *Cry to Heaven.* New York: Knopf, 1982. 533 pp.

Tonio Treschi, a young Venetian prince kidnapped and castrated for training as a male soprano in the 18th century, seeks revenge but falls in love with music.
Genre(s): Musical Fiction; Horror.

Riley, Judith Merkle

◆ **871.** *The Oracle Glass.* New York: Viking, 1994. 510 pp.
Genevieve Pasquia, imprisoned after her beloved father's death by relatives who think she has a fortune, becomes known as the Marquise de Morville with fortunetelling gifts desired by Louis XIV's court.
Genre(s): Romance.

Saramago, Jos

872. *Baltasar and Blimunda.* Trans. Giovanni Pontiero. San Diego, CA: Harcourt, 1987. 400 pp.
Churches and priests dominate 18th-century Portugal from the Hugh Convent in the tiny village of Mafra to the priest trying to build a flying machine.
Genre(s): Family Saga.

Schreiner, Samuel Agnew

873. *Angelica.* New York: Arbor House, 1978. 346 pp.
Angela Kauffmann flouts convention to become one of the most important painters of her age.
Genre(s): Biographical Fiction.

Sciascia, Leonardo

874. *The Council of Egypt.* Trans. Adrienne Foulke. New York: Carcanet, 1988. 212 pp.
Giuseppe Vella, an unscrupulous Palermo priest forges an ancient Arabic manuscript to justify the domination of Sicily by Naples prior to the French Revolution.
Genre(s): Biographical Fiction.

Selimovic, Mesa

875. *Death and the Dervish.* Trans. Bogdan Rakic and Stephen M. Dickey. Chicago: Northwestern University Press, 1996. 473 pp.
As dervish and spiritual leader of the Islamic contingency in Turkish-occupied Bosnia in the 18th century, Sheikh Ahmed Nuruddin avoids controversy until the arrest of his brother.
Genre(s): Religious Fiction.

Shellabarger, Samuel

876. *Lord Vanity.* Boston: Little, Brown, 1953. 467 pp.
Richard Morandi, only son of a dressmaker and an English nobleman, becomes a soldier, British spy, and gentleman.
Genre(s): Adventure Story.

Sienkiewicz, Henryk

877. *The Deluge.* Trans. Jeremiah Curtin. Boston: Little, Brown, 1891. 2 vols.

In the sequel to *With Fire and Sword*, five years after the Polish-Lithuanian knights defeat the Cossacks, Swedish troops arrive and allow Andrei Kmita to save his country.

878. *Fire in the Steppe.* Trans. W.S. Kuniczak. 1887. New York: Hippocrene, 1992. 717 pp.
In the sequel to *The Deluge*, during the Polish struggle against Cossacks, Tartars, and Turks during the 1670s Basia, a fearless heroine fights more aggressively than her indecisive husband.
Genre(s): Biographical Fiction; War Story; Adventure Story.

879. *With Fire and Sword.* Trans. W.S. Kuniczak. 1883. New York: Macmillan, 1993. 1135 pp.
Ukrainian Cossacks rebel against the Poles and eventually take the city of Zbaraz after capturing Yan Skshetuski as their prisoner.
Genre(s): War Story; Adventure Story.

Singer, Isaac Bashevis

880. *Reaches of Heaven.* New York: Farrar, Straus and Giroux, 1980. 95 pp.
Israel ben Eliezer leads Jews in 18th-century Poland.
Genre(s): Biographical Fiction.

881. *Satan in Goray.* Trans. Jacob Sloan. New York: Noonday, 1955. 239 pp.
After the Chmielnicki massacres in 17th-century Poland, Jews search for salvation and choose a false messiah.
Genre(s): Jewish Fiction.

Susac, Andrew

882. *God's Fool.* Garden City, NY: Doubleday, 1972. 146 pp.
Cagliostro, an apostolic, so disrupts the court of Marie Antoinette that someone steals her diamond necklace and accuses him of the theft, charges of which he is eventually cleared, although the Church finds him guilty of heresy.
Genre(s): Biographical Fiction.

Süskind, Patrick

883. *Perfume.* Trans. John E. Woods. New York: Knopf, 1986. 255 pp.
Jean-Baptiste Grenouille spends his life pursuing the perfect perfume and investigates all methods of making it.

Suthren, Victor

884. *Admiral of Fear.* New York: St. Martin's, 1991. 239 pp.
Edward Mainwaring, a Royal Navy officer, attacks the combined fleets of France and Spain in Toulon during 1742, in the sequel to *The Golden Galleon.*
Genre(s): Sea Story.

885. *A King's Ransom.* New York: St. Martin's, 1981. 217 pp.

Paul Gallant tries to find the valuable golden statue, intended as a gift from the king of Spain to the king of France, and the ship on which it was cargo.
Genre(s): Sea Story; War Story.

Tomizza, Fulvio

886. *Heavenly Supper.* Trans. Anne Jacobson Schutte. Chicago: University of Chicago Press, 1991. 184 pp.
The peasant Maria Janis claims that she has had nothing but communion wine and wafers to eat during the five years before her trial in the Venetian inquisition.
Award(s): Premio Strega Prize.
Genre(s): Religious Fiction; Legal Story.

Trollope, Anthony

887. *La Vendée.* 1850. New York: Penguin, 1993. 967 pp.
Insurgents from La Vendée fight successfully during their own wars before the French Revolution.
Genre(s): War Story; Romance.

Vassalli, Sebastiano

888. *The Chimera.* Trans. Patrick Creagh. New York: Scribner's, 1995. 320 pp.
In 17th-century Italy, the infant Antonia, left at a monastery gate, believes her dark skin is ugly, but a couple finally adopts her, and she, actually lovely, becomes friends with a mentally retarded boy and a shiftless man.
Award(s): Strega Prize.
Genre(s): Domestic Fiction.

Veryan, Patricia

◆ 889. *The Dedicated Villain.* New York: St. Martin's, 1989. 416 pp.
Roly searches for Bonnie Prince Charlie's treasure for himself after the Battle of Culloden in 1746 while among the Jacobites also searching for it is Fiona Bradford's father. (*Series:* Golden Chronicles, 6)
Genre(s): Romance.

Waldeck, R. G.

890. *Lustre in the Sky.* Garden City, NY: Doubleday, 1946. 434 pp.
Charles Maurice de Talleyrand-Perigord goes to Vienna during the final phase of Napoleon's era to attend the Congress of Vienna.
Genre(s): Biographical Fiction.

Weiss, David

891. *Sacred and Profane.* New York: Morrow, 1968. 639 pp.

Mozart begins his career at five and, after great fame, dies at 35, poor and sick.
Genre(s): Biographical Fiction; Musical Fiction.

Whitnell, Barbara

892. *Freedom Street.* North Pomfret, VT: Trafalgar Square, 1991. 412 pp.
Living in England during the early 18th century, Charlotte Bonnet marries a castrated silk weaver and happily creates patterns for Queen Anne until her Huguenot friend who escaped from France in childhood reappears.
Genre(s): Religious Fiction.

Wilson, Robert Anton

893. *The Earth Will Shake.* Boston: Little, Brown, 1982. 363 pp.
Sigismundo wants revenge for his priest uncle's death, and both the murderers (Sigismundo's biological father and half-brother) and 18th-century inquisitors hunt for him.
Genre(s): Bildungsroman (Coming of Age).

Wolf, Leonard

894. *The False Messiah.* Boston: Houghton Mifflin, 1982. 278 pp.
Nathan of Gaza declares that Shabbatai Zevi is the messiah of the millennium in 1666, but Mehmet, the Turkish emperor decides that he will sentence Zevi to death if he refuses to convert to Islam.

Yarbro, Chelsea Quinn

◆ 895. *A Candle for D'Artagnan.* New York: Tor, 1989. 485 pp.
In the sequel to *Crusader's Torch*, Atta Olivia Clemens arrives in France to serve Cardinal Mazarin, meets D'Artagnan, and finds a way to end her vampire existence.
Genre(s): Love Story; Gothic Fiction.

Zola, Émile

896. *The Rougon-Macquart Family.* New York: T.B. Peterson, 1871. 368 pp.
Adela de Fouqué, daughter of an insane man, marries Rougon, a stupid gardener in 1786 and bears him a son, Pierre, but after her husband dies, she has two illegitimate children. (*Series:* Rougon-Macquart Family, 1)
Genre(s): Family Saga.

1789-1859

Acland, Alice

897. *The Corsican Ladies.* London: Davies,
1974. 185 pp.
Laure, Duchesse d'Abrantes, writes her memoirs about
her affair with Balzac and about her neighbors, the turbulent Bonaparte family.
Genre(s): Biographical Fiction.

Agnon, Shmuel Yosef

898. *The Bridal Canopy.* Trans. I.M. Lask. New
York: Doubleday, 1937. 389 pp.
Reb Yudel, a Hasidic Jew, travels around Galicia to find
dowries for his three daughters while sharing stories with
his companion, the teamster Nuta.
Genre(s): Jewish Fiction; Picaresque Fiction.

Alarcon, Pedro Antonio de

899. *The Three-Cornered Hat.* Trans. Harriet de
Onis. 1874. Great Neck, NY: Barron's, 1958. 107
pp.
The miller and his wife escape the evil mayor of their
town with the help of two donkeys.
Genre(s): Humorous Fiction; Love Story.

Almqvist, C. J. L.

900. *The Queen's Diadem.* Columbia, SC: Cam-
den House, 1992. 247 pp.
Men who plot the assassination King Gustav III of Sweden at a masked ball in 1792 suffer the consequences.
Genre(s): Biographical Fiction.

Andric, Ivo

901. *Bosnian Chronicle.* New York: Knopf,
1963. 429 pp.
In the sequel to *The Bridge on the Drina*, Daville serves
in the oriental city of Travnik as Napoleon's western-ori-
ented consul.
Genre(s): Epic Literature; War Story.

Anthony, Evelyn

902. *Far Flies the Eagle.* New York: Crowell,
1955. 208 pp.
When Alexander I becomes czar of Russia, he maintains
his idealism and expresses interest in unification with
neighboring countries through the Holy Alliance.
Genre(s): Political Fiction; Biographical Fiction.

Artom, Guido

903. *Napoleon Is Dead in Russia.* Trans. Muriel
Grindrod. New York: Atheneum, 1970. 256 pp.
Claude-Francois de Malet announces on October 23,
1812, that Napolen has died in Moscow, and his conspir-
acy to overthrow Napoleon's goverment begins.
Genre(s): Biographical Fiction.

Asch, Sholem

904. *Mottke: The Thief.* Trans. Willa and Edwin
Muir. New York: Putnam, 1935. 314 pp.
Mottke, 14, has experienced everything but murder in
Warsaw's underworld during his affairs with two women.
Genre(s): Jewish Fiction; Picaresque Fiction; Love Story.

Bacchelli, Riccardo

905. *The Mill on the Po.* Trans. Frances Frenaye.
New York: Pantheon, 1950. 590 pp.
The Scacerni family, Po Valley millers, witness the
changes in Italy from the end of Napoleon's wars through
World War I and contribute to its emergence as a modern
nation.
Genre(s): Family Saga; War Story.

Balzac, Honoré de

906. *Beatrix.* Trans. Beth Archer. 1839. Englewood Cliffs, NJ: Prentice Hall, 1970. 374 pp.
A young man who loves a heartless coquette has several
women pursuing him.
Genre(s): Love Story.

907. *The Chouans.* Trans. Marion Ayton Craw-
ford.1896. New York: Penguin, 1972. 389 pp.
Royalists continue their activities after the French Revolution to retake the government.
Genre(s): War Story.

908. *Cousin Bette.* 1846. New York: Knopf,
1991. 437 pp.
Lisbeth Fischer (Cousin Bette) is jealous of the money
and beauty of her aristocratic cousin.
Genre(s): Allegory.

909. *Cousin Pons.* Trans. Herbert J. Hunt. 1847.
Baltimore, MD: Penguin, 1968. 333 pp.
Cousin Pons, an old musician, has a strong friendship
with Schmucke, another old musician, against a backdrop
of Parisian sleaze and lowlife.

910. *Eugénie Grandet.* Trans. Ellen Marriage.
1833. New York: Knopf, 1992. 237 pp.
Eugénie falls in love with her spoiled cousin whose father goes bankrupt, and after she lends him her savings,
he leaves for the West Indies.
Genre(s): Allegory.

911. *Old Goriot.* Trans. Ellen Marriage. 1935.
London: Everyman, 1991. 237 pp.
Goriot spends his money on dowries for his two ungrate-
ful daughters and then suffers humiliation at the hands of
their husbands.
Genre(s): Bildungsroman (Coming of Age).

Banis, Victor J.

912. *This Splendid Earth.* New York: St. Martin's, 1978. 439 pp.
When the vintner de Brussac family must flee after supporting the royalty during the French Revolution, its

members take cuttings from the vineyard to California and build a wine empire.

Bartos-Höppner, B.

◆ 913. *Storm over the Caucasus.* New York: Walck, 1968. 272 pp.
A shepherd boy becomes a messenger in the 19th-century conflict between the Muslims and the Russians.
Genre(s): War Story.

Blackstock, Charity

914. *A House Possessed.* Philadelphia: Lippincott, 1962. 222 pp.
On the banks of the Loch Ness, a priest attempts to exorcise the spirits of a disowned daughter and her husband who died at Waterloo.
Genre(s): Mystery; Romance.

Braider, Donald

915. *Rage in Silence.* New York: Putnam, 1969. 318 pp.
Francisco Goya becomes attached to the Duchess of Alba, and after her death, he is loyal to his mistress as well, in the 19th century.
Genre(s): Biographical Fiction.

Brandewyne, Rebecca

916. *Desire in Disguise.* 1987. New York: Severn House, 1994. 460 pp.
A male and female buccaneer meet during the French Revolution and fall in love.
Genre(s): Romance.

Brontë, Charlotte

917. *The Professor.* 1857. NewYork: Modern Library, 1997. 266 pp.
A professor, William Crimsworth, takes a position in a Brussels day school where he falls in love with a young British girl, but a jealous rival thwarts their union.
Genre(s): Love Story.

918. *Villette.* 1853. New York: Modern Library, 1997. 624 pp.
When Lucy Snowe teaches in Brussels, she falls in love with a professor.
Genre(s): Love Story.

Bryher

919. *The Colors of Vaud.* New York: Harcourt, 1969. 136 pp.
A French girl and a Swiss boy experience the liberation of the Swiss Canton of Vaud during the French Revolution.
Genre(s): War Story.

Burgess, Anthony

920. *Napoleon Symphony.* New York: Knopf, 1974. 365 pp.

Napoleon's life is divided into four parts from his forays into Italy and Egypt to his exile on the rock of St. Helena.
Genre(s): Biographical Fiction.

Burney, Fanny

921. *The Wanderer: Or, Female Difficulties.* New York: Oxford, 1991. 957 pp.
When Napoleon becomes upset with the verbosity of women in Paris during his reign, he banishes them from France.
Genre(s): War Story.

Carpentier, Alejo

922. *The Harp and the Shadow.* San Francisco: Mercury House, 1990. 159 pp.
Pope Pius IX must decide if he will proclaim that Christopher Columbus coming to the New World to convert the natives to Catholicism was the greatest event in Western history.
Genre(s): Biographical Fiction.

Carroll, Susan

923. *The Painted Veil.* New York: Fawcett, 1995. 362 pp.
A widow trying to regain custody of her daughter in London becomes involved with a man tormented by his mother's murder in the Reign of Terror and by a murderer known as The Hook.
Genre(s): Romance.

Chapman, Hester W.

924. *Fear No More.* New York: Reynal, 1968. 349 pp.
The young son of Louis XVI and Marie Antoinette leads a tragic life—kidnapping, imprisonment, and the Royalists' claim for the throne after the Revolution.
Genre(s): Biographical Fiction.

Chase-Riboud, Barbara

925. *Valide.* New York: Morrow, 1986. 429 pp.
A young girl captured by pirates in Martinque in the 1700s rises to the position of Valide for Selim III, and manages his harem of hundreds.
Genre(s): Biographical Fiction; Romance.

Chester, Deborah

926. *French Slippers.* New York: Coward-McCann, 1981. 288 pp.
Julia Swanton's father dies in a duel and, although she is left penniless in Napoleon's France, she determines to return to London and find a wealthy husband.
Genre(s): Romance.

Clavel, Bernard

927. *Lord of the River.* Trans. Elizabeth Walter. Boston: Little, Brown, 1974. 255 pp.

Christian Merlin captains horse-drawn barges on the Rhone in the 1840s until steam-powered ships replace him in his livelihood.
Genre(s): Adventure Story.

Cleeve, Brian Talbot

928. *Hester.* New York: Coward-McCann, 1980. 377 pp.
Hester marries a Royalist soldier and rides with him in the French Revolution where she barely escapes the guillotine.
Genre(s): War Story; Romance.

Coffman, Virginia

929. *The Alpine Coach.* New York: Dell, 1976. 208 pp.
After breaking her engagement, the heroine escapes from Paris to Switzerland unchaperoned.
Genre(s): Romance.

Conrad, Joseph

930. *The Rover.* Garden City, NY: Doubleday, 1923. 286 pp.
A former sea-captain, the Rover, who tried to outwit Nelson and blockade Toulon, lives on lonely Giens peninsula where an old woman and her niece brood over the revolution.

Cornwell, Bernard

931. *Sharpe's Battle.* New York: HarperCollins, 1996. 320 pp.
Richard Sharpe, in the spring of 1811 in the Peninsular War, tries to keep Napoleon from invading Portugal from his Spanish base.
Genre(s): War Story.

932. *Sharpe's Company.* New York: Viking, 1982. 280 pp.
Richard Sharpe attempts to seize the impenetrable Badajoz fortress in 1812 during the Peninsular war in the sequel to *Sharpe's Gold.*
Genre(s): War Story.

933. *Sharpe's Eagle.* New York: Viking, 1982. 270 pp.
Richard Sharpe mans the Talavera campaign in July 1809 after separation from his battalion in Portugal.
Genre(s): War Story.

934. *Sharpe's Enemy.* New York: Viking, 1984. 351 pp.
The sequel to *Sharpe's Sword* finds Richard Sharpe trying to rescue Lady Farthingale while defending Portugal at Christmas in 1812.
Genre(s): War Story.

935. *Sharpe's Gold.* New York: Viking, 1982. 250 pp.
In the sequel to *Sharpe's Eagle*, Richard Sharpe tries to destroy the Almeida in August 1810 by stealing Bonaparte's gold.
Genre(s): War Story.

936. *Sharpe's Honour.* New York: Viking, 1985. 320 pp.
In the sequel to *Sharpe's Enemy*, Richard Sharpe faces a strong adversary in Captain Leroux during the Vitoria Campaign of February 1813.
Genre(s): War Story.

937. *Sharpe's Revenge.* New York: Viking, 1989. 348 pp.
Richard Sharpe, in the sequel to *Sharpe's Rifles*, tries to clear his name after false accusations that he stole from Napoleon.
Genre(s): War Story.

938. *Sharpe's Rifles.* New York: Viking, 1988. 304 pp.
In 1809, in the sequel to *Sharpe's Seige*, Richard Sharpe has his first command when the French invade Galicia.
Genre(s): War Story.

939. *Sharpe's Siege.* New York: Viking, 1987. 319 pp.
In the sequel to *Sharpe's Regiment*, Sharpe fights French forces after attacking a coastal fort in the winter of 1814.
Genre(s): War Story.

940. *Sharpe's Sword.* New York: Viking, 1983. 319 pp.
Captain Sharpe tries to overcome the French enemy while protecting the Spanish El Mirador in the sequel to *Sharpe's Company.*
Genre(s): War Story.

941. *Sharpe's Waterloo.* New York: Viking, 1990. 378 pp.
Richard Sharpe, in the sequel to *Sharpe's Revenge*, advises the Dutch prince of Orange at Waterloo before deciding that the prince has no concept of military strategy.
Genre(s): War Story.

Costain, Thomas Bertram

942. *The Last Love.* Garden City, NY: Doubleday, 1963. 434 pp.
Lucia Elizabeth Balcombe becomes Napoleon's last love while he stays with her family waiting for his own quarters when in exile.
Genre(s): Biographical Fiction; Love Story.

Crow, Donna Fletcher

943. *Encounter the Light.* Wheaton, IL: Crossway, 1997. 240 pp.
Afer nursing soldiers in the Crimea, including Richard Greystone who has been left blinded, Jennifer Neville and Richard return to Victorian England and devote their lives to helping the poor of London.
Genre(s): War Story; Christian Fiction.

Delderfield, R. F.

944. *Fairwell the Tranquil Mind.* New York: Dutton, 1950. 319 pp.
An English smuggler takes part in the French Revolution.
Genre(s): War Story.

Der Nister

945. *The Family Mashber.* New York: Simon and Schuster, 1987. 690 pp.
Jews in 19th-century Russia carry on family and religious traditions.
Genre(s): Jewish Fiction; Domestic Fiction; Religious Fiction.

Desmond, Alice Curtis

946. *Marie Antoinette's Daughter.* New York: Dodd, Mead, 1967. 291 pp.
The daughter of Marie Antoinette and Louis XVI of France, Marie-Thérèse Angouleme, supports the Bourbon cause and becomes France's queen for 10 minutes.
Genre(s): Biographical Fiction.

Dickens, Charles

◆ **947.** *A Tale of Two Cities.* 1859. New York: Oxford, 1993. 254 pp.
Two men who look alike love Lucie Manette, and during the French Revolution one of them goes to the guillotine in place of the other for Lucie's happiness.
Genre(s): War Story.

Dinesen, Isak

948. *The Angelic Avengers.* New York: Random House, 1946. 304 pp.
In the 1840s, two beautiful girls travel to France, find an evil situation, and eventually help quell it.
Genre(s): Horror; Allegory.

949. *Ehrengard.* New York: Random House, 1963. 111 pp.
Early in the 19th century, a couple stay in seclusion to hide the woman's pregnancy caused by premarital indiscretion.

Dostoyevsky, Fyodor

950. *The House of the Dead.* Trans. Jessie Coulson. 1861. New York: Oxford, 1965. 361 pp.
The Russian government exiles a landowner to Siberia where he hears the stories of other prisoners.
Genre(s): Political Fiction.

951. *The Idiot.* Trans. Constance Garnett. 1868. New York: Oxford, 1992. 638 pp.
Prince Myshkin suffers from epilepsy but maintains a keen insight about humanity.

◆ **952.** *Netochka Nezvanova.* Trans. Ann Dunnigan. Englewood Cliffs, NJ: Prentice Hall, 1970. 201 pp.
Abandoned by her alcoholic father, Netochka Nezvanova is adopted by a prince's family, and when she moves to the home of the prince's married daughter, she learns a secret which makes her want to find stability in early 19th-century Russia.

Dumas, Alexandre

953. *Camille.* 1848. North Stratford, NH: Ayer, 1977. 64 pp.
Camille, a fashionable Paris courtesan, escapes to the country with her poor lover Armand Duval, from a Count who wants her as his mistress, but she later leaves Duval to placate his family.
Genre(s): Love Story.

954. *The Chevalier de Maison-Rouge.* Boston: Little, Brown, 1890. 369 pp.
After Marie Antoinette escapes and Louis XVI is executed, attempts to rescue her are unsuccessful, and she joins Louis XVI on the guillotine.
Genre(s): War Story; Political Fiction.

955. *The Count of Monte Cristo.* 1844. New York: Oxford, 1998. 1130 pp.
Imprisoned unjustly for supposedly having helped the exiled Napoleon, Edmond Danté escapes after 15 years, finds funds in the cavern of Monte Cristo, and punishes his enemies.
Genre(s): Adventure Story.

956. *The Countess de Charny, or The Fall of the French Monarchy.* New York: T.B. Peterson, 1853. 392 pp.
Louis XVI and Marie Antoinette flee to Varennes before Louis is captured and returned to be beheaded in the sequel to *Six Years Later, or The Taking of the Bastille.*
Genre(s): War Story; Political Fiction.

957. *Six Years Later, or The Taking of the Bastille.* Boston: Little, Brown, 1890. 290 pp.
The sequel to *The Queen's Necklace* reveals the populace of Paris overtaking the Bastille to free political prisoners.
Genre(s): Political Fiction.

Dymoke, Juliet

958. *Two Flags for France.* New York: Severn House, 1987. 304 pp.
Louis de la Rouelle first acts as guardian to Julie Varas, but when Louis becomes involved in a plot to kidnap Napoleon after his return from exile, Julie betrays him.
Genre(s): Romance.

Endore, S. Guy

959. *King of Paris.* New York: Simon and Schuster, 1956. 504 pp.
Alexandre Dumas, famous author, and his son live in 19th-century Paris.
Genre(s): Biographical Fiction.

Feather, Jane

960. *Violet.* New York: Bantam, 1995. 448 pp.
Tamsyn, the orphaned child of a Spanish robber baron and an English aristocrat, takes the leadership of her father's brigands, plunders the wealthy, and reprimands careless soldiers.
Genre(s): Romance; War Story.

Fitzgerald, Penelope

961. *The Blue Flower.* Boston: Houghton Mifflin, 1997. 227 pp.

Novalis, living in 18th-century Germany in a rambunctious family, decides to marry Sophie, a child of 12, because she seems to him like a blue flower, the one thing he wants to see in his life.
Award(s): Whitbread Book of the Year.
Genre(s): Love Story; Biographical Fiction.

Flaubert, Gustave

962. *Madame Bovary.* 1857. New York: Doubleday, 1997. 384 pp.
Emma Bovary becomes bored with her life and embarks on an affair.
Genre(s): Domestic Fiction.

Forrest, Anthony

◆ 963. *Captain Justice.* New York: Hill and Wang, 1981. 294 pp.
In 1804, Captain John Justice runs his dinghy aground near Boulogne, in an effort to thwart Napoleon, who plans to stage his invasion of England there.
Genre(s): Adventure Story; War Story.

Galdos, Benito Perez

964. *A Royalist Volunteer.* Trans. Lila Wells Guzman. Lewiston, NY: Edwin Mellen, 1993. 475 pp.
Spain tries to free itself of Napoleon's domination in the early 19th century.
Genre(s): War Story.

Garfield, Leon

965. *The Prisoners of September.* New York: Viking, 1975. 279 pp.
Richard Mortimer and Lewis Boston, Britishers bored with their lives, are in Paris when the French Revolution begins, and each decides to join opposite sides.
Genre(s): War Story.

Gellis, Roberta

966. *Fortune's Bride.* New York: Dell, 1983. 395 pp.
Captain the Honorable Robert Francis Edward Moreton marries Merry after he arrives in Spain during the Napoleonic Wars because he feels sorry for the shipwrecked and homely woman, but she waits until he falls in love with her before she tells him she is wealthy.
Genre(s): Romance.

Gielgud, Val Henry

967. *Confident Morning.* 1943. New York: White Lion, 1976. 224 pp.
Napoleon I rules France after the French Revolution.
Genre(s): Biographical Fiction.

Giono, Jean

968. *The Straw Man.* Trans. Phyllis Johnson. San Francisco: North Point, 1983. 461 pp.
Italians fight for their freedom in the Revolution of 1848.
Genre(s): War Story.

Gogol, Nikolai

969. *Dead Souls.* Trans. Ruth Hein. 1842. New York: Modern Library, 1997. 324 pp.
A Russian landowner buys the souls of dead but registered and counted peasants and raises money on the certificates.
Genre(s): Humorous Fiction; Satire.

Gorham, Charles

970. *Wine of Life: A Novel about Balzac.* New York: Dial, 1958. 598 pp.
Honoré de Balzac lives a full life as an intellectual and a novelist.
Genre(s): Biographical Fiction.

Grant, Tracy

971. *Shores of Desire.* New York: Dell, 1997. 384 pp.
Robert Lescaut falls in love with a woman whose family may have killed his wife in 1815.
Genre(s): Romance.

Gulbranssen, Trygve

972. *Beyond Sing the Woods.* New York: Putnam, 1936. 313 pp.
Dag Björndal overcomes the stigma of living in a country area of Norway and gains great power and wealth in the 19th century.

973. *The Wind from the Mountains.* New York: Putnam, 1937. 412 pp.
The sequel to *Beyond Sing the Woods* begins in 1809 when Adelaide Barr marries Young Dag and gains enough strength from his father to lead the Björndal family business.

Harrod-Eagles, Cynthia

◆ 974. *Anne.* New York: St. Martin's, 1991. 631 pp.
Count Kirov rescues Anne Peters in Paris as the Napoleonic Wars begin in 1803 and he takes her to Russia to become his family's governess. (*Series:* Kirov Saga, 1)
Genre(s): War Story; Romance; Family Saga.

◆ 975. *Fleur.* New York: St. Martin's, 1993. 406 pp.
Fleur Hamilton falls in love with Count Sergei Kirov when he rescues her from criminals in Victorian London, and when he marries someone else, Fleur stays with him and his wife as the Crimean War begins. (*Series:* Kirov Saga, 2)
Genre(s): Romance; War Story; Family Saga.

Hartling, Peter

976. *Schubert: Twelve Moments Musicaux and a Novel.* New York: Holmes and Meier, 1995. 248 pp.
Schubert's *Lieder* seem to show his emotional states at the time he composed them and indicate the various stages of his life in Vienna.
Genre(s): Biographical Fiction; Musical Fiction.

Harwood, Ronald

977. *César and Augusta.* Boston: Little, Brown, 1978. 276 pp.
Augusta Holmès desires to be a composer, and César Franck, a composer henpecked by his wife, becomes attracted to her until he completes his F Minor Piano Quintet, after which he seems to blossom into a man independent of both Augusta and his wife.
Genre(s): Biographical Fiction; Musical Fiction.

Hearne, John

978. *The Sure Salvation.* New York: St. Martin's, 1982. 224 pp.
While a slave ship is becalmed in the South Atlantic, the captain, crew, and slaves on board reveal their fears.
Genre(s): Sea Story.

Heaven, Constance

979. *The Astrov Legacy.* New York: Coward-McCann, 1973. 216 pp.
Sophie Weston comes to Russia for a visit and falls in love with the heir to the House of Astrov, Leon, but in pre-Revolutionary Russia, he is supposed to marry a wealthy woman who will fill the family coffers in the sequel to *The House of Kuragin.*
Genre(s): Romance.

◆ **980. *Castle of Doves.*** New York: Putnam, 1985. 328 pp.
Charlotte Starr, 22, goes with her cousin and his wife to Spain where her cousin's support of Don Carlos for the throne dismays her, but for diversion, she meets the Marques de Merenda, Don Lorenzo.
Genre(s): Romance.

981. *Castle of Eagles.* New York: Coward-McCann, 1974. 254 pp.
Lisa, an English orphan, comes to Vienna and thinks she may be in love with the pianist Rudi or with his uncle in the mid-19th century.
Genre(s): Romance.

982. *The House of Kuragin.* New York: Coward-McCann, 1972. 256 pp.
Rilla Weston goes to St. Petersburg to be governess for a sickly child in 1820 and she falls in love with her employer's younger brother.
Genre(s): Romance.

Hodge, Jane Aiken

◆ **983. *The Adventurers.*** Garden City, NY: Doubleday, 1965. 283 pp.
When French and Russian troops sack her home during Napoleon's retreat from Leipzig to Paris, Sonia, 17, and her young governess attach themselves to Charles, a monarchist spy, and earn a livelihood by winning at cards.
Genre(s): Romance; War Story.

◆ **984. *Escapade.*** New York: St. Martin's, 1993. 231 pp.

Charlotte Comyn, 17, leaves for London in 1811 and works in disguise for her mother's friend Beth, an actress and spy, in Palermo, Sicily.
Genre(s): Adventure Story.

◆ **985. *Greek Wedding.*** Garden City, NY, Doubleday, 1970. 303 pp.
Turks capture Phyllida Vannick, an American heiress searching for her brother in Greece during its early-19th-century war for independence, and an unwilling British yachtsman rescues her.
Genre(s): War Story; Romance.

◆ **986. *The Winding Stair.*** Garden City, NY: Doubleday, 1969. 328 pp.
When Juana Brett arrives in Portugal to care for her ailing grandmother, the grandmother wants her to spy for the English as a way of saving Portugal from Napoleon.
Genre(s): Romance.

Holland, Tom

987. *Lord of the Dead.* New York: Pocket Books, 1996. 324 pp.
Lord Byron, the English Romantic poet, tells a young woman about his life, emphasizing his meeting in Greece with an old Turk who led him into the world of vampires.
Genre(s): Horror; Biographical Fiction.

Holt, Victoria

◆ **988. *The Devil on Horseback.*** Garden City, NY: Doubleday, 1977. 358 pp.
A young British schoolmistress becomes involved with a French count and in July 1789 finds herself in the middle of the revolution.
Genre(s): War Story; Romance.

989. *The King of the Castle.* Garden City, NY: Doubleday, 1967. 310 pp.
When Dallas Lawson comes to restore the Chateau Gaillard, she meets the widower owner, who is accused of murdering his wife.
Genre(s): Romance.

Hugo, Victor

990. *Les Misérables.* 1862. New York: Random House, 1995. 106 pp.
Escaped convict Jean Valjean risks his life to take care of a motherless young girl during the first half of the 19th century.

Johnson, Susan

991. *Taboo.* New York: Bantam, 1997. 352 pp.
Russian Countess Teo Korsakova meets French General André Duras after the French Revolution and falls in love with him.
Genre(s): Romance.

Jolis, Alan

992. *Love and Terror.* New York: Atlantic Monthly, 1998. 288 pp.

When Marie Antoinette's lover Fersen hides her from revolutionary zealots, Joseph Fouch, one of Robespierre's henchmen, frantically searches for her.
Genre(s): War Story; Political Fiction.

Joyce, Brenda

993. *Splendor.* New York: St. Martin's, 1997. 486 pp.
Radical Carolyn Browne, a commoner, faces Russian Prince Sverayov's family, including his conniving wife, his daughter Katya, and his handsome brother Alexi, during the Napoleonic wars.
Genre(s): Romance.

Kalpakian, Laura

994. *Cosette.* New York: HarperCollins, 1995. 652 pp.
Cosette, from Hugo's *Les Misérables,* and Marius, editor of a progressive newspaper, endure the Revolution of 1848 and the Second Empire when Marius is in prison most of the time and Cosette sneaks his radical writings out of prison for the paper.
Genre(s): War Story.

Kay, Susan

◆ 995. *Phantom.* New York: Delacorte, 1991. 446 pp.
In 1831 Erik lives under the Paris Opera after having traveled with a circus and served as a magician in the Persian court.

Kells, Susannah

996. *The Fallen Angels.* New York: St. Martin's, 1984. 341 pp.
Lady Campion Lazender nurses her terminally ill father while her brother serves as a British diplomat in Paris, but when the French Revolution begins and meetings of a group calling itself the Fallen Ones occur at her grandfather's French chateau, she discovers that her brother is a spy.
Genre(s): Adventure Story; War Story.

Kenyon, Frank Wilson

997. *Passionate Rebel.* New York: Dodd, Mead, 1972. 255 pp.
Hector Berlioz decides to become a musician rather than a physician, but when he tries to change the Paris School with its traditions dating back to the 1780s, he has problems.
Genre(s): Musical Fiction; Biographical Fiction.

998. *Shadow of the Corsican.* London: Hutchinson, 1973. 251 pp.
Napoleon's first love is his brother Joseph's fiancée, Désirée Clary, and after she marries the Emperor's marshal Bernadotte and becomes Sweden's queen, Napoleon still remembers her.
Genre(s): Biographical Fiction.

Kertzer, David I.

999. *The Kidnapping of Edgardo Mortara.* New York: Knopf, 1997. 352 pp.
In 1858, when Catholic authorities in Bologna discover that the six-year-old Edgardo Mortara might have been baptized, he is removed from his Jewish family because Jews are not allowed to raise Christians.
Genre(s): Political Fiction.

Killens, John Oliver

1000. *Great Black Russian.* Detroit, MI: Wayne State University Press, 1989. 391 pp.
Alexander Pushkin considers himself African in his liberal stance toward the affairs of his day.
Genre(s): Biographical Fiction.

Kotlowitz, Robert

1001. *Somewhere Else.* New York: McKay, 1972. 384 pp.
Mendel, son of Moses and grandson of Eliezar, grows up in Lomza, near Warsaw, during the 19th century, and his generation finally leaves the town with him, going to London and joining the Jewish Legion.
Genre(s): Family Saga; Jewish Fiction.

Lagerlöf, Selma

1002. *Gosta Berling's Saga.* New York: American Scandanavia, 1891. 473 pp.
Gosta Berling lives in Sweden around 1820.
Genre(s): Domestic Fiction.

Laker, Rosalind

1003. *Tree of Gold.* Garden City, NY: Doubleday, 1986. 350 pp.
Although married, Gabrielle Roche, the head of a silk factory, falls in love with the head of a rival factory, Nicolas Devaux, and after many trials and years, they finally unite.
Genre(s): Romance.

Lamb, James Barrett

◆ 1004. *In Love and War.* Toronto: Macmillan of Canada, 1988. 182 pp.
De Lancey, a professional soldier, is badly hurt in the Battle of Waterloo when Napoleon's forces shell Wellington's men, and De Lancey's wife comes to be with him.
Genre(s): Biographical Fiction; War Story.

Lambdin, Dewey

◆ 1005. *HMS Cockerel.* New York: D. I. Fine, 1995. 360 pp.
Alan Lewrie, in the sequel to *The Gun Ketch,* continues his naval adventures fighting France.
Genre(s): Adventure Story; Sea Story.

Larreta, Antonio

1006. *The Last Portrait of the Duchess of Alba.* Bethesda, MD: Adler and Adler, 1988. 214 pp.

When the Duchess of Alba dies in 1802, speculation is that the cause was a fever, but the duchess may have been despondent over her fading beauty after posing for Goya in *The Naked Maja*.
Genre(s): Biographical Fiction.

Lee, Tanith

1007. *The Gods Are Thirsty.* Woodstock, NY: Overlook, 1996. 672 pp.
During the French Revolution, journalist Camille Desmoulins sparks the masses with his headlines, becoming known as author of the Revolution.
Genre(s): War Story; Biographical Fiction.

Leviant, Curt

1008. *The Man Who Thought He Was Messiah.* Philadelphia: Jewish Publications, 1990. 222 pp.
Reb Nachman believes that he could be the Messiah, but he loves a gentile girl, so he must test himself on a pilgrimage to Vienna, (where he meets Beethoven), and then to Turkey and Jerusalem.
Genre(s): Biographical Fiction; Religious Fiction.

Lofts, Norah

1009. *A Rose for Virtue.* Garden City, NY: Doubleday, 1971. 348 pp.
Hortense, stepdaughter of Napoleon I and mother of Napoleon III, tells about her unhappy marriage and the devotion between her mother Josephine and Napoleon I.
Genre(s): Biographical Fiction.

1010. *Silver Nutmeg.* Garden City, NY: Doubleday, 1947. 368 pp.
A Dutch trader thinks he is marrying a beautiful girl by proxy, but he arrives on the Dutch island to find her ravaged by disease.
Genre(s): Romance.

Logan, Mark

1011. *Brumaire.* New York: St. Martin's, 1978. 273 pp.
While Nick Minnett tries to stop the French Revolution, Napoleon begins his Egyptian campaign and overthrows the Directory.
Genre(s): War Story.

1012. *Guillotine.* New York: St. Martin's, 1976. 319 pp.
Nick Minnett, England's wealthiest banker, continues his exploits in the French Revolution, trying to contain it singlehandedly.
Genre(s): War Story.

1013. *Tricolour.* New York: St. Martin's, 1976. 316 pp.
Nick Minnett, member of one of England's wealthiest families, loves his boat, and he takes it with him to France during the French Revolution on his way to thwart the progress of the masses.
Genre(s): War Story; Adventure Story.

Lorrimer, Claire

1014. *Mavreen.* London: Arlington, 1976. 479 pp.
Mavreen has an affair with the Vicomte Gerard de Valle from 1779 to 1804 as he fights in Napoleon's army, but they cannot marry because she is illegitimate.
Genre(s): Romance.

Loy, Rosetta

1015. *The Dust Roads of Monferrato.* Trans. William Weaver. New York: Knopf, 1991. 256 pp.
During the 19th century, in Italy's Piedmont region, a peasant family encounters both natural and political disasters as its members work and fall in love.
Genre(s): Political Fiction; Romance.

Malvern, Gladys

◆ 1016. *Patriot's Daughter.* New York: Macrae Smith, 1960. Canada pp.
Anastasia, the daughter of the Marquis de Lafayette, experiences both the French Revolution and the Reign of Terror before her marriage in 1798.
Genre(s): Biographical Fiction.

Mankowitz, Wolf

1017. *A Night with Casanova.* London: Sinclair-Stevenson, 1991. 136 pp.
In 1798, Casanova's body shows signs of aging, and he has a conversation with a drinking companion who happens to be Ahasuerus, the Wandering Jew, a man who craves mortality while Casanova wants to regain his youth.
Genre(s): Adventure Story; Biographical Fiction; Humorous Fiction.

Mann, Thomas

1018. *The Beloved Returns.* Trans. H.T. Lowe-Porter. 1940. New York: Knopf, 1983. 453 pp.
Charlotte Buff Kestner returns to Weimar to see Goethe, who immortalized her as Lotte in his *Sorrows of Werther*.
Genre(s): Biographical Fiction; Love Story.

1019. *Buddenbrooks.* Trans. John E. Woods. 1964. New York: Knopf, 1993. 604 pp.
Four generations of the Buddenbrooks family begin with Johann in 1830, a prosperous Lübeck merchant.

Mantel, Hilary

1020. *A Place of Greater Safety.* New York: Atheneum, 1993. 749 pp.
Robespierre, Danton, and Desmoulins all have had difficult childhoods, but they unite during the French Revolution and make choices in the Reign of Terror that bring about their downfalls.
Genre(s): War Story.

Marlowe, Derek

1021. *A Single Summer with Lord B.* New York: Viking, 1970. 251 pp.

In the summer of 1816, Lord Byron, Percy Shelley, Mary Godwin, Claire Clairmont, and John Polidori stay at Lake Geneva.
Genre(s): Adventure Story.

Marlowe, Stephen

1022. *Colossus.* New York: Macmillan, 1972. 563 pp.
The intensity of Goya's career, his liaison with the Duchess of Alba, and his attempt to question the meaning of life after becoming deaf become apparent.
Genre(s): Biographical Fiction.

Meredith, George

1023. *Sandra Belloni.* New York: Roberts, 1864. 492 pp.
The Pole family adopts Emilia, a singer, and to help the family pay its debts, she agrees to sing in Milan.
Genre(s): Romance.

1024. *The Tragic Comedians.* 1898. New York: Arno, 1975. 157 pp.
Ferdinand Lassalle becomes Karl Marx's leading spokesperson for German socialism in the 19th century.
Genre(s): Political Fiction; Biographical Fiction.

1025. *Vittoria.* 1864. New York: Scribner's, 1911. 516 pp.
In the sequel to *Sandra Belloni*, after Emilia goes to Milan to sing, she becomes involved with the Italian resistance of the Austrian occupation, but her adopted brother appears and supports the Austrians.
Genre(s): War Story; Romance.

Michaels, Fern

1026. *Captive Secrets.* New York: Ballantine, 1991. 339 pp.
In the sequel to *Captive Splendors*, Furana van der Rhys, daughter of a pirate, decides to become a nun, but Luis Domingo arrives in Spain and changes her mind.
Genre(s): Family Saga; Romance.

Moberg, Vilhelm

1027. *The Emigrants.* Trans. Gustaf Lannestock. New York: Simon and Schuster, 1951. 366 pp.
In the summer of 1850, Karl Oskar Nilsson and his family leave Sweden for America.
Genre(s): Family Saga.

Morris, Ira J.

1028. *The Fortune Hunter.* New York: Saturday Review, 1972. 312 pp.
Needing money for his gambling debts, Count Nicholas marries a distant cousin, heiress Alexandra, but since the two prove incompatible, he goes back into the army for posting in Bucharest where he exhibits heroism and accumulates more debt.
Genre(s): Domestic Fiction.

Morrison, Peggy

1029. *The Veiled Sultan.* New York: Vanguard, 1969. 211 pp.
Aimee Dubuc de Rivery, born in Martinique, grows up in a French convent, and when she is kidnapped while returning to Martinique, she ends up with the Dey of Algiers and becomes a powerful ruler in Turkey, negotiating with the Europeans.
Genre(s): Biographical Fiction.

Neville, Katherine

1030. *The Eight.* New York: Ballantine, 1989. 546 pp.
A young novice during the French Revolution risks her life to keep a jeweled chess set that Moors gave Charlemagne, and in the 20th century, a computer expert and a chess master try to solve its mystery.
Genre(s): War Story.

Orczy, Emmuska, Baroness

1031. *Adventures of the Scarlet Pimpernel.* New York: Doubleday, 1929. 312 pp.
In the sequel to *Sir Percy Hits Back*, during the reign of terror, men help condemned Frenchmen escape, and one woman who wants the Scarlet Pimpernel to save her brother does not realize that the Pimpernel is her husband.
Genre(s): Adventure Story.

1032. *Eldorado: A Story of the Scarlet Pimpernel.* New York: Doran, 1913. 256 pp.
In the sequel to *The Triumph of the Scarlet Pimpernel*, the Scarlet Pimpernel rescues the dauphin from the temple in Eldorado and then must extricate himself from the situation.
Genre(s): Adventure Story.

1033. *The Elusive Pimpernel.* New York: Dodd, Mead, 1908. 351 pp.
Sir Percy Blakeney, an Englishman, rescues aristocrats from the guillotine during the French Revolution, in the sequel to *I Will Repay.*
Genre(s): Adventure Story.

1034. *I Will Repay.* Philadelphia: Lippincott, 1906. 207 pp.
In 1779 Juliette Marny vows to ruin Paul Droulde after he unwillingly kills her brother in a duel, and when the French Revolution begins and they fall in love, she realizes she has condemned him to death unless they escape in the sequel to *The Scarlet Pimpernel.*
Genre(s): Adventure Story.

1035. *Lord Tony's Wife.* New York: Doran, 1917. 332 pp.
The Scarlet Pimpernel continues his adventures with his group of friends in France.
Genre(s): Adventure Story.

1036. *Mam'zelle Guillotine.* New York: Hodder, 1940. 286 pp.

Sir Percy helps people escape from the guillotine in the French Revolution in the sequel to *The Way of the Scarlet Pimpernel*.
Genre(s): Adventure Story.

1037. *The Scarlet Pimpernel.* New York: Putnam, 1905. 256 pp.
Sir Percy Blakeney leads titled Englishmen in assisting the escape of emigrés threatened during the terrors of the French Revolution.
Genre(s): War Story.

1038. *Sheaf of Bluebells.* New York: Doran, 1917. 347 pp.
Madame La Marquise de Mortain and her son Laurent return to France, planning to plot against Napoleon, but de Mortain must first deal with the democratic ideals of her son by a former marriage who has been raised by an uncle.
Genre(s): Political Fiction.

1039. *Sir Percy Hits Back.* New York: Doran, 1927. 319 pp.
In the seqeul to *Eldorado*, the daughter of Robespierre's colleague Chauvelin acts foolishly and is imprisoned during the Reign of Terror, but the Pimpernel works to rescue her from death.
Genre(s): Adventure Story.

1040. *The Triumph of the Scarlet Pimpernel.* New York: Doran, 1922. 192 pp.
In the sequel to *Lord Tony's Wife*, Sir Percy Blakeney, the Scarlet Pimpernel, must avoid Robespierre as he tries to free men from the Reign of Terror after the French Revolution.
Genre(s): Adventure Story.

1041. *The Way of the Scarlet Pimpernel.* New York: Doubleday, 1929. 256 pp.
The Scarlet Pimpernel works to outwit Chabot, an unfrocked friar, so that he can rescue Louise De Croissy, her child, and her friends, and send them safely to England during the Revolution, in the sequel to *Adventures of the Scarlet Pimpernel*.
Genre(s): Adventure Story.

Pavíc, Milorad

1042. *Last Love in Constantinople.* Chester Springs, PA: Dufour, 1998. 184 pp.
The Tenecki and Opujic families become linked by fate and interact romantically at the beginning of the 19th century in Constantinople.
Genre(s): Political Fiction.

Perl, Joseph

1043. *Revealer of Secrets.* Trans. Dov Taylor. 1819. New York: HarperCollins, 1997. 480 pp.
The Haskala (Jewish Enlightenment) battles with the religious revival movement of Hasidism in early-19th-century Eastern Europe.
Genre(s): Jewish Fiction.

Perucho, Joan

1044. *Natural History.* Trans. David H. Rosenthal. New York: Knopf, 1989. 208 pp.
When a vampire creates chaos in the Spanish countryside during the 19th-century Carlist Wars, a scientist challenges him.
Genre(s): War Story.

Perutz, Leo

1045. *The Marquis of Bolibar.* Trans. John Brownjohn. Boston: Little, Brown, 1989. 192 pp.
German troops murder the leader of the Spanish guerrillas, the Marquis of Bolibar, and as they celebrate and try to seduce the colonel's mistress, they begin to wonder if the Marquis is actually dead.
Genre(s): War Story.

Petrakis, Harry Mark

1046. *The Hour of the Bell.* New York: Doubleday, 1976. 363 pp.
The Greek war of independence begins in 1821 and lasts for 10 years when Greek insurgents conquer Tripolitsa with great butchery.
Genre(s): War Story.

Petrie, Glen

1047. *The Fourth King.* New York: Atheneum, 1986. 433 pp.
Alexander Pushkin marries Natalya Goncharova, and her selfishness helps to place Pushkin's enemies in the position to cause his downfall in early-19th-century Russia.
Genre(s): Biographical Fiction.

Piercy, Marge

1048. *City of Darkness, City of Light.* New York: Fawcett, 1996. 479 pp.
Claire Lacombe, an actress, Pauline Lon, a chocolatemaker, and Manon Roland, along with three other men, have major roles in the French Revolution.
Genre(s): War Story.

Prince Michael of Greece

1049. *Sultana.* New York: Harper and Row, 1983. 448 pp.
Pirates take Aimee Dubuc de Riverie, 15, from Martinique to the sultan of Turkey's harem where she becomes Nakshidil, a favorite who has affairs with the Czar Alexander I and Napoleon.

Quigley, Aileen

1050. *Empress to the Eagle.* London: Hale, 1975. 192 pp.
Marie Louise of Austria becomes Napoleon I's wife when Josephine proves unable to have children.
Genre(s): Biographical Fiction.

Ross, Kate

1051. *The Devil in Music.* New York: Viking, 1997. 444 pp.
Julian Kestrel goes to Italy with a friend where he learns about the four-year-old unsolved murder of famed music lover Lodovico Malvezzi, and he decides to try his detecting skills in Milan.
Award(s): Agatha Award.
Genre(s): Mystery; Regency Novel.

Ryan, Patricia

1052. *Wild Wind.* New York: Topaz, 1998. 352 pp.
Alexandre de Perigeaux's former lover's husband asks him to seduce Nicolette and provide an heir, and although Alexandre knows that he should not, he still loves Nicolette.
Genre(s): Romance.

Sabatini, Rafael

1053. *Scaramouche.* Boston: Houghton Mifflin, 1949. 347 pp.
Scaramouche pushes the republican cause in the first years of the French Revolution, while pursuing law, politics, fencing, and entertainment.
Genre(s): Love Story; War Story; Adventure Story.

Saberhagen, Fred

1054. *A Sharpness on the Neck.* New York: Tor, 1996. 352 pp.
The vampire Vlad Dracula and his companion try to save the life of Phillip Radcliffe, an illegitimate son of Benjamin Franklin during the French Revolution.
Genre(s): Horror; Fantastic Literature.

Sahlberg, Gardar

1055. *Murder at the Masked Ball.* London: Macdonald and Jane's, 1974. 242 pp.
At a masked ball in the Stockholm Opera House in 1792, someone assassinates Gustaf III of Sweden.
Genre(s): Biographical Fiction; Mystery.

Sand, George

1056. *Horace.* Trans. Zack Rogow. San Francisco: Mercury, 1995. 352 pp.
A law student enjoys the opportunities that Paris offers him in love and in studies, but after finding passion and glory, he loses his honor.
Genre(s): Legal Story; Bildungsroman (Coming of Age).

1057. *Marianne.* 1876. New York: Carroll and Graf, 1987. 171 pp.
In 1825, Marianne Chevreuse reveals her independence but retains her feminine demeanor while selecting her mate.
Genre(s): Romance.

Schneider, Robert

1058. *Brother of Sleep.* Trans. Shaun Whiteside. Woodstock, NY: Overlook, 1995. 215 pp.

Johann Elias Alder, illegitimate son of a parish priest and a peasant woman in Austria during the early 19th century, becomes an extraordinary musical genius who is too shy to approach his true love and chooses death when she marries another.
Genre(s): Musical Fiction.

Selinko, Annemarie

1059. *Désirée.* New York: Morrow, 1953. 594 pp.
Eugénie Désirée Clary records two love affairs in her diary, one with Napoleon, who jilted her for Josephine, and a second with General Bernadotte, who married her.
Genre(s): Biographical Fiction.

Sherman, Delia

1060. *The Porcelain Dove.* New York: Dutton, 1993. 404 pp.
The maid of the duchesses de Malvoeux tells about the French Revolution and their part in it along with the ancient curse and magical quest in their family.
Genre(s): War Story.

Sholem Aleichem

1061. *The Adventures of Menahem-Mendl.* Trans. Tamara Kahana. 1909. New York: Putnam, 1969. 222 pp.
Menahem-Mendl corresponds with his wife about his adventures in Russian cities, but even though she pleads with him to be careful, he continues to attract disaster.
Genre(s): Humorous Fiction; Jewish Fiction; Picaresque Fiction.

Smith, Kay Nolte

◆ 1062. *A Tale of the Wind.* New York: Villard, 1991. 516 pp.
When Nandou, a talented actor and magician, falls in love with Jeanne Sorel, a ragpicker, he takes her home and educates her without revealing his love, and Jeanne falls in love with a man who deserts her before she returns to Nandou.
Genre(s): Family Saga.

Sontag, Susan

1063. *The Volcano Lover.* New York: Farrar, Straus and Giroux, 1992. 419 pp.
Sir William Hamilton lives in Naples with his wife Emma, mistress of Admiral Nelson, while serving as the British envoy to the Bourbon Ferdinand IV.
Genre(s): Biographical Fiction.

Stamford, Sarah

1064. *The Marshal's Lady.* New York: Dutton, 1981. 248 pp.
Eugénie de Coucy Oudinot endures her arranged marriage to Charles, seeing it as her duty, until she becomes a widow after 35 years.
Genre(s): Biographical Fiction.

Stendhal

1065. ***The Red and the Black***. Trans. C.K. Scott Moncrieff. 1830. New York: The Modern Library, 1995. 592 pp.
Julien Sorel engages in love affairs to advance professionally during the time of Napoleon.
Genre(s): Bildungsroman (Coming of Age).

Sue, Eugene

1066. ***The Wandering Jew***. 1846. New York: Hippocrene, 1991. 850 pp.
In 1832, Protestants and Catholics struggle for the control of a large sum of money invested for a descendant of Herodias, half-sister of Ahasuerus, the eternal wanderer.

Thompson, Morton

1067. ***The Cry and the Covenant***. Garden City, NY: Doubleday, 1949. 459 pp.
Ignac Semmelweis, a physician, tries to persuade other Hungarian doctors that childbed fever is caused by infection.
Genre(s): Biographical Fiction; Medical Novel.

Tolstoy, Leo

◆ 1068. ***War and Peace***. Trans. Ann Dunnigan. 1869. New York: New American Library, 1968. 1456 pp.
People from diverse social strata respond to Napoleon's invasion of Russia.
Genre(s): War Story.

Trollope, Anthony

1069. ***The Golden Lion of Granpere***. New York: Arno, 1981. 353 pp.
A family lives in the Vosges Mountains of France during the 19th century.
Genre(s): Domestic Fiction.

Trollope, Joanna

1070. ***Leaves for the Valley***. New York: St. Martin's, 1984. 254 pp.
In 1854, Edgar Drummond goes to the Crimea, and his two sisters, envisioning a glamorous life in Constantinople, go with him, only to find the battlefront different from their dreams.
Genre(s): War Story; Romance.

Troyat, Henri

1071. ***The Baroness***. Trans. Frances Frenaye. New York: Simon and Schuster, 1961. 284 pp.
Nikolai Ozarev, a Russian officer, and his French wife Sophie, in the sequel to *The Brotherhood of the Red Poppy*, go to live in his father's country house between 1819 and 1825.

1072. ***The Brotherhood of the Red Poppy***. Trans. Elisabeth Abbott. New York: Simon and Schuster, 1961. 281 pp.

In 1814, Nikolai Mikhailovitch Ozeroff marries a young French widow who is a member of the underground for the Republic.

Tuten, Frederic

1073. ***Tallien***. New York: Marion Boyars, 1995. 150 pp.
Jean-Lambert Tallien, involved with the revolution in France, recalls his father's union activity which detracted from the family.
Genre(s): Biographical Fiction; Domestic Fiction; War Story.

Veryan, Patricia

◆ 1074. ***Feather Castles***. New York: St. Martin's, 1982. 341 pp.
Aiding an amnesiac after the Battle of Waterloo, a young Englishwoman and her fiancé's brother bring him to England, but his arrival incites danger. (*Series:* Sanguinet Saga, 2)
Genre(s): Regency Novel; Romance.

Wassmo, Herbjorg

1075. ***Dina's Book***. Boston: Little, Brown, 1994. 455 pp.
After Dina of Reinsnes accidentally causes her mother's death during 1840 in Norway, she does as she pleases until she meets a Russian who refuses to let her control him.
Genre(s): Domestic Fiction; Gothic Fiction.

Weiss, David

1076. ***The Assassination of Mozart***. New York: Morrow, 1970. 384 pp.
In 1823, a young couple investigates Mozart's death to see if he was murdered, in the sequel to *Sacred and Profane*.
Genre(s): Biographical Fiction; Musical Fiction.

Wheatley, Dennis

1077. ***The Dark Secret of Josephine***. Geneva: Edito-Service, 1973. 438 pp.
Josephine, wife of Napoleon, has to learn the ways of Napoleon's court while raising her two children.
Genre(s): Biographical Fiction.

1078. ***Desperate Measures***. London: Hutchinson, 1974. 411 pp.
While Napoleon I spends 100 days on the island of Elba, he watches the mainland and returns to France at Cannes on March 1, 1815.
Genre(s): Biographical Fiction.

1079. ***The Rape of Venice***. Geneva: Edito-Service, 1974. 437 pp.
On May 15, 1797, Napoleon takes his troops into Venice and occupies it, deposing the last doge, Ludovico Manin.
Genre(s): War Story.

Wheeler, Thomas Gerald

1080.*A Fanfare for the Stalwart*. New York: S. G. Phillips, 1967. 191 pp.
Alain Dieudonné, 19 and a trumpeter in Napoelon's Imperial Guard in Moscow, walks back to Warsaw with two refugees after Cossacks shoot his horse in the bitter winter of 1812.
Genre(s): War Story.

White, Stewart Edward, and Harry DeVighne

1081.*Pole Star*. Garden City, NY: Doubleday, 1935. 452 pp.
Alexander Baranov heads the Russian Fur Company and trades in Alaska in the early 19th century.
Genre(s): Biographical Fiction.

Willumsen, Dorrit

1082.*Marie*. London: Bodley Head, 1986. 213 pp.
Marie Anne Grosholtz becomes adept at reproducing likenesses of guillotine victims in the French Revolution under the name Madame Tussaud, but her inexperience in life causes her to marry a fortune hunter.
Genre(s): Biographical Fiction; War Story.

Wolf, Christa

1083.*No Place on Earth*. Trans. Jan Van Heurck. New York: Farrar, Straus and Giroux, 1982. 129 pp.
Karoline von Gunderrode and Heinrich von Kleist feel a sense of alienation from the world in 1804, and they try to compensate through their writing.

Yarbro, Chelsea Quinn

◆ 1084. *Hotel Transylvania*. New York: St. Martin's, 1978. 279 pp.

In Paris in the mid-18th century, the innocent and beautiful Madelaine falls in love with the Comte de Saint Germain, a vampire, who helps her escape from a cult of devil-worshipers. (*Series:* Saint-Germain, 1)
Genre(s): Gothic Fiction.

◆ 1085. *Out of the House of Life*. New York: Tor, 1990. 480 pp.
Madelaine loves Comte de Saint-Germain, another vampire, and goes to Egypt hoping to find the House of Life where he supposedly toiled for 800 years. (*Series:* Saint-Germain, 7)
Genre(s): Gothic Fiction.

Zola, Émile

1086.*Abbé Mouret's Temptation*. New York: T.B. Peterson, 1875. 305 pp.
Serge Mouret is passionately in love with a woman even though he is clergy, and after he repents, he officiates at her funeral. (*Series:* Rougon-Macquart Family, 5)
Genre(s): Family Saga.

1087.*The Belly of Paris*. Trans. Ernest Alfred Vizetelly. 1873. Los Angeles: Sun and Moon, 1996. 397 pp.
An escaped prisoner hides in Paris and becomes involved with a group of socialists. (*Series:* Rougon-Macquart Family, 3)
Genre(s): Family Saga.

1088.*In the Whirlpool*. New York: T.B. Peterson, 1872. 298 pp.
Pierre Fouque's son Aristide change his name from Rougon to Saccard while he works in Paris during the time Haussmann is planning the great boulevards. (*Series:* Rougon-Macquart Family, 2)
Genre(s): Family Saga.

1860-1918

Adler, Elizabeth

1089.*Lonie*. New York: Villard, 1985. 400 pp.
After Lonie arrives in Paris to seek her fortune, she becomes a singer and the mistress of a wealthy man, before finally marrying an American.
Genre(s): Romance.

Agayev, M.

1090.*Novel with Cocaine*. Trans. Michael Henry Heim. New York: Dutton, 1985. 204 pp.
In Moscow from 1916 to 1919, while Vadim comes of age without noticing the Great War or the beginnings of the revolution, he uses cocaine and becomes cruel to his family.
Genre(s): War Story; Domestic Fiction; Bildungsroman (Coming of Age).

Agnon, Shmuel Yosef

◆ 1091.*A Simple Story*. New York: Schocken, 1985. 246 pp.
Hirshl Hurvitz loves the family's housemaid, but he must marry a girl from a wealthy family, and after having a mental breakdown and receiving advice from a doctor, he accepts his wife.
Genre(s): Jewish Fiction.

Aiken, Joan

◆ 1092. *The Girl from Paris*. Garden City, NY: Doubleday, 1982. 311 pp.
Ellen Paget, a member of British society, teaches in France in the mid-19th century, but a suicide draws her back to her father's home.
Genre(s): Romance.

Amstutz, Eveline

1093.*Caterina*. New York: Walker, 1970. 234 pp.

Caterina, widowed at 21, begins to run her upper-class Italian family estate for the next five generations.
Genre(s): Family Saga.

Andric, Ivo

1094. *The Woman from Sarajevo.* Trans. Joseph Hitrec. New York: Knopf, 1965. 245 pp.
In the sequel to *Bosnian Chronicle,* the early death of Miss Raika's father changes her into a miser who becomes a loan shark against a background of events leading to World War I.
Genre(s): Family Saga.

Anscombe, Roderick

1095. *The Secret Life of Laszlo, Count Dracula.* New York: Hyperion, 1994. 480 pp.
Laszlo, Count Dracula, returns to Hungary after studying in 19th-century Paris where he occasionally goes mad and murders someone.
Genre(s): Horror.

Anthony, Patricia

1096. *Flanders.* New York: Berkley, 1998. 384 pp.
Texan Travis Lee Stanhope graduates from Harvard and goes to France in 1916, where he at first enjoys killing Germans in their foxholes, but as his comrades are gassed and gutted, he begins to hallucinate.
Genre(s): War Story.

Appelfeld, Aharon

1097. *The Conversion.* Trans. Jeffrey M. Green. New York: Pantheon, 1998. 240 pp.
Austrian Karl converts to Christianity from Judaism in order to obtain his ideal government job, but his decision jeopardizes his relationship with the gentile Gloria.
Genre(s): Jewish Fiction.

Bacchelli, Riccardo

1098. *Nothing New Under the Sun.* New York: Pantheon, 1955. 600 pp.
In the sequel to *The Mill on the Po,* the descendants of the Scacerni family participate in the unification of Italy and the outbreak of World War I.
Genre(s): War Story; Family Saga.

Bajic-Poderegin, Milka

1099. *The Dawning.* Trans. Nadja Poderegin. New York: Interlink, 1995. 335 pp.
Savka, married at 15 to a man in his mid-30s, is widowed young and in turn marries off her own daughter at a young age, and neither woman has much power over the events in their lives.
Genre(s): Family Saga; War Story.

Baricco, Alessandro

1100. *Silk.* Trans. Guido Waldman. New York: Farrar, Straus and Giroux, 1997. 96 pp.

While making four journeys from France to Japan to obtain silkworms in the 1860s, Herve Joncour has an affair with a beautiful woman to whom he never speaks.
Genre(s): Love Story.

Baroja, Pio

1101. *Zalacan the Adventurer.* Fort Bragg, CA: Lost Coast, 1998. 192 pp.
During the Carlist wars beginning in 1872, the Basque orphan Zalacan becomes a hero.
Genre(s): War Story; Political Fiction.

Barraclough, June

◆ 1102. *Familiar Acts.* New York: St. Martin's, 1994. 240 pp.
Hetty Coppen, who believes that her mother prefers her younger sister, is in Italy with an aunt and cousin, where she finds that her family history is quite different from what she has previously heard.
Genre(s): Romance.

Baum, Vicki

1103. *Grand Hotel.* Garden City, NY: Doubleday, 1931. 309 pp.
Five diverse guests stay in a German hotel for two days after World War I.

Bayer, Valerie Townsend

1104. *Forbidden Objects.* New York: St. Martin's, 1995. 320 pp.
Two women in the 1930s edit the works of Emma Foster, which reveal Emma's unrequited love and unhappy subservience in the male-dominated society of the 19th century.
Genre(s): Family Saga.

Baylis, Sarah

1105. *Utrillo's Mother.* New Brunswick, NJ: Rutgers University Press, 1989. 246 pp.
Suzanne Valadon, self-taught French artist and friend of Degas and Toulouse-Lautrec, raises her son, Maurice Utrillo, to become an artist without letting him know his parentage.
Genre(s): Biographical Fiction.

Beaton, Roderick

1106. *Ariadne's Children.* New York: St. Martin's, 1996. 371 pp.
After witnessing the assassination of the Archduke and Duchess in Sarajevo, archaeologist Lionell Robertson escapes to Crete and discovers Ariadne's Summer Palace.
Genre(s): War Story.

Berger, John

1107. *G.* New York: Viking, 1972. 311 pp.
G. (standing for both Garabaldi and Don Giovanni), born in 1887 as an illegitimate child in Italy, is seduced by his

cousin twice his age when he is 15, and he travels around Europe seducing other women as World War I begins.
Award(s): Booker Prize.
Genre(s): Romance.

Bernstein, Marcelle

1108. *The Russian Bride.* New York: Simon and Schuster, 1987. 318 pp.
At the beginning of the 20th century, Salka leaves her Jewish parents in Russia during a pogrom, and marries in Vienna a philanderer whose father recognizes her business skills and includes her in the family business.
Genre(s): Domestic Fiction.

Biggins, John

1109. *The Emperor's Coloured Coat.* New York: St. Martin's, 1995. 374 pp.
Ottokar Prohaska learns to fly and crashes, serves on the Danube, becomes involved in the Serbian conspiracy beginning World War I, and ends up in China between 1913 and 1915.
Genre(s): Adventure Story; Sea Story.

1110. *A Sailor of Austria.* New York: St. Martin's, 1994. 369 pp.
As a lieutenant in the Austro-Hungarian navy during World War I, Ottokar Prohaska is assigned temporarily to the Flying Service where he must increase the squadron's miles flown and deliver love letters to a general's wife.
Genre(s): War Story; Sea Story.

1111. *The Two-Headed Eagle.* New York: St. Martin's, 1996. 367 pp.
Ottokar Prohaska tells about his adventures in the Great War as a resident of a Welsh nursing home, and he mentions his experiences in mid-1916 as a pilot bombarding a variety of targets.
Genre(s): War Story.

Bjarnhof, Karl

◆ 1112. *The Good Light.* Trans. Naomi Walford. New York: Knopf, 1960. 272 pp.
In the sequel to *The Stars Grow Pale*, the young boy living in an insitution for the blind in Copenhagen goes through adolescence with his introduction to sex and interaction with the sighted world.

◆ 1113. *The Stars Grow Pale.* Trans. Naomi Walford. New York: Knopf, 1958. 310 pp.
A young Danish boy leaves home for an institution for the blind in Copenhagen.

Blasco-Ibanez, Vicente

1114. *The Four Horsemen of the Apocalypse.* Trans. Charlotte Brewster Jo. New York: Dutton, 1918. 489 pp.
One segment of an Argentinian family settles in France and the other in Germany prior to World War I.
Genre(s): War Story.

Böll, Heinrich

1115. *Billiards at Half past Nine.* Trans. Leila Vennewitz. New York: McGraw Hill, 1962. 280 pp.
What the architect father in the Faehmel family carefully builds from 1880, his son eventually tears down as a demolition expert in World War II.
Genre(s): War Story.

Borgen, Johan

1116. *Lillelord.* Trans. Elizabeth B. Moen and Ronald E. Peterson. New York: New Directions, 1982. 320 pp.
In the year before World War I, Lillelord goes through a variety of psychological problems in Oslo.
Genre(s): Domestic Fiction.

Borovsky, Natasha

1117. *A Daughter of the Nobility.* New York: Holt, Rinehart and Winston, 1985. 500 pp.
Tatyana Silomirskaya, born in 1897, becomes friends with the children of Tsar Nicholas II, and after the revolution begins in 1917, she flees to France.
Genre(s): War Story.

Bridge, Ann

1118. *The Dark Moment.* New York: Macmillan, 1952. 337 pp.
A Turkish aristocrat, Frid, marries an aide to Mustafa Kemal and befriends a British girl who falls in love with Kemal during the formation of the modern state of Turkey.
Genre(s): Romance.

Brien, Alan

1119. *Lenin.* New York: Morrow, 1987. 735 pp.
Lenin writes his diary after his father's death in 1886 and continues recording the events of his life until a few months before his own death in 1924.
Genre(s): Biographical Fiction.

Buchan, John

1120. *Greenmantle.* London: Doran, 1915. 345 pp.
English secret service agents try to foil the German attempt to begin a holy war in the East.
Genre(s): Spy Fiction.

Bulgakov, Mikhail Afanasyevich

1121. *The White Guard.* Trans. Michael Glenny. New York: McGraw Hill, 1971. 319 pp.
A Russian family and their friends struggle in the midst of the revolution in Kiev between the White Guard and the Red Guard during 1918.
Genre(s): War Story.

Buloff, Joseph

1122. *From the Old Marketplace.* Cambridge, MA: Harvard, 1991. 335 pp.
In the first two decades of the 20th century, Vilnius, Lithuania, is the site of many disasters, including war, po-

---

groms, racism, and revolution, all of which Yosik endures.
Genre(s): War Story; Bildungsroman (Coming of Age).

Bunin, Ivan

1123. *The Life of Arseniev.* Chicago: Northwestern UP, 1994. 254 pp.
Arseniev, a young boy from a poor but aristocratic family, remembers his youth in Russia before the revolution.
Genre(s): Bildungsroman (Coming of Age).

Burgess, Anthony

1124. *The End of the World News.* New York: McGraw Hill, 1983. 388 pp.
Sigmund Freud works in Vienna while Trotsky leads his revolution in the Soviet Union in the early part of the 20th century.
Genre(s): Biographical Fiction; Satire.

Butler, David

1125. *Lusitania.* New York: Random House, 1982. 578 pp.
The German submarine U-20 torpedoes the *Lusitania,* flagship of the Cunard Line fleet, on May 7, 1915, and 1,200 people die, although the German Embassy warned of the war zone around the British Isles.
Genre(s): War Story.

Butler, Gwendoline

1126. *The Red Staircase.* New York: Coward-McCann, 1979. 431 pp.
Rose Gowrie takes a post as a companion to a 16-year-old in St. Petersburg in 1912 only to find that the family has hired her because her healing powers might help her break the hold of Rasputin on the Czar's family.
Genre(s): Romance.

Cahan, Abraham

1127. *The White Terror and the Red.* 1905. New York: Arno, 1975. 430 pp.
Plots against the life of Alexander II become anti-Jewish riots when Alexander III becomes czar.
Genre(s): War Story.

Carr, Philippa

1128. *A Time for Silence.* New York: Putnam, 1991. 349 pp.
When Lucinda Greenham and her friend go to finishing school in Europe, they must flee both personal troubles and the German invasion of Belgium. (*Series:* Daughters of England, 17)
Genre(s): Romance; War Story; Family Saga.

Carter, Angela

1129. *Nights at the Circus.* New York: Viking, 1985. 294 pp.

After the American journalist Walser interviews Fevvers, a circus flier, he becomes a clown and accompanies her to St. Petersburg.
Award(s): James Tate Black Award.

Céline, Louis-Ferdinand

1130. *Journey to the End of the Night.* Trans. Ralph Manheim. New York: New Directions, 1983. 446 pp.
Ferdinand Bardamu escapes from the front during World War I and enters a hospital for the mentally ill before he travels during the 1930s and ends up as a doctor in a dirty Paris suburb.
Genre(s): Adventure Story.

Cheuse, Alan

1131. *The Bohemians: John Reed and His Friends Who Shook the World.* Cambridge: Apple-Wood, 1982. 358 pp.
John Reed becomes involved with events in Mexico and Russia and has a relationship with Louise Bryant.
Genre(s): Biographical Fiction.

Coetzee, J. M.

1132. *The Master of Petersburg.* New York: Viking, 1994. 250 pp.
When Fyodor Dostoevsky goes to St. Petersburg to recover his deceased stepson's papers in 1869, he discovers that his stepson might have been murdered by the revolutionary People's Vengeance.
Genre(s): Mystery.

Colette

1133. *My Mother's House.* New York: Farrar, Straus and Giroux, 1953. 219 pp.
The author recalls her early years with her family, especially her mother, in Burgundy in the late 19th century.
Genre(s): Domestic Fiction; Biographical Fiction.

Collin, Richard Oliver

◆ 1134. *Contessa.* New York: St. Martin's, 1994. 392 pp.
Achille Leone expects to inherit his family's estate outside Rome, but he becomes a soldier in 1911, and his love for Rosaria, a peasant with a Marxist brother, causes problems.
Genre(s): Love Story; War Story; Political Fiction.

Conrad, Joseph

1135. *The Arrow of Gold.* Garden City, NY: Doubleday, 1919. 385 pp.
In the 1870s, an English sea captain carries Carlist munitions to the Spanish coast and falls in love with Doña Rita, the financier of the project.
Genre(s): Sea Story.

Cooperstein, Claire

◆ 1136. *Johanna: A Novel of the Van Gogh Family.* New York: Scribner's, 1995. 270 pp.

Johanna Bonger weds Theo van Gogh in 1889, but when Theo's close association with his brother Vincent drives him to death two years later, she saves Vincent's paintings.
Genre(s): Biographical Fiction.

Cosic, Dobrica

1137. *Into the Battle.* Trans. Muriel Heppell. San Diego, CA: Harcourt, 1977. 279 pp.
The people of Serbia are shocked when the Allies desert the country in World War I and they must fight alone.
Genre(s): War Story.

1138. *Reach to Eternity.* Trans. Muriel Heppell. New York: Harcourt, 1980. 410 pp.
In the sequel to *A Time of Death,* the Serbian army has just won a victory over the Austrian forces in 1914, but the Serbs must unite to overcome the unsanitary conditions and threat of epidemic caused by lack of facilities and medicine.
Genre(s): War Story.

1139. *South to Destiny.* Trans. Muriel Heppell. New York: Harcourt, 1981. 400 pp.
People of Yugoslavia, in the sequel to *Reach to Eternity,* feel that the Allies have betrayed them and that the German and Bulgarian forces cause their defeat in World War I.
Genre(s): War Story.

1140. *A Time of Death.* Trans. Muriel Heppell. New York: Harcourt, 1978. 437 pp.
Serbia fights for survival, in the sequel to *Into the Battle,* against the Austro-Hungarian empire in World War I.
Genre(s): War Story.

Cost, March

1141. *Two Guests for Swedenborg.* New York: Vanguard, 1971. 245 pp.
Before and after World War I, Olivia reads and agrees with Swedenborg's philosophy and meets someone else who feels the same.
Genre(s): Biographical Fiction; Love Story.

Crane, Teresa

1142. *Strange Are the Ways.* New York: St. Martin's, 1993. 569 pp.
In 1908, the Shalakov family moves to St. Petersburg from Moscow where Boris hopes to strengthen his reputation as a violin maker.
Genre(s): Romance; War Story; Family Saga.

Daniels, Kathleen

1143. *Minna's Story.* Santa Fe, NM: Health, 1992. 177 pp.
Minna Bernays has an affair with Sigmund Freud from 1895 to 1898 and keeps a diary about the experience.
Genre(s): Biographical Fiction.

Darrell, Elizabeth

1144. *The Gathering Wolves.* New York: Coward-McCann, 1980. 324 pp.
Paul Anderson goes to Russia to help build a railroad supply route from Moscow to Murmansk, then he must escape with White Russians as the Red Army advances during the Russian Revolution.
Genre(s): War Story.

Delbe, Anne

1145. *Camille Claudel, une Femme.* Trans. Carol Cosman. San Francisco: Mercury, 1992. 372 pp.
The family of the sculptress Camille Claudel, who was mistress and model to Auguste Rodin for many years, places her in a mental asylum for what is probably depression.
Genre(s): Biographical Fiction.

Dessi, Giuseppe

1146. *The Forests of Norbio.* Trans. Frances Frenaye. San Diego, CA: Harcourt, 1975. 306 pp.
When a peasant orphan inherits his benefactor's estate, he educates himself on forest conservation and civic responsibility.
Genre(s): Domestic Fiction.

Djilas, Milovan

1147. *Under the Colors.* Trans. Lovett F. Edwards. New York: Harcourt, 1971. 557 pp.
The Radak clan of Montenegro rebels against its Turkish overlords in the 1870s.

Doblin, Alfred

1148. *Karl and Rosa.* Trans. John E. Woods. New York: Fromm International, 1983. 547 pp.
In the sequel to *A People Betrayed,* Karl Liebknecht and Rosa Luxemburg come to their tragic end.
Genre(s): Biographical Fiction.

1149. *A People Betrayed.* New York: Fromm International, 1983. 642 pp.
Becker, a wounded officer, tells a story that includes much about Berlin and describes Karl Liebknecht and Rosa Luxemburg working through the war.
Genre(s): War Story.

Dostoyevsky, Fyodor

◆ 1150. *The Adolescent.* Trans. Andrew R. MacAndrew. New York: Doubleday, 1971. 624 pp.
A 19-year-old male has an indentity crisis in 1870s St. Petersburg.
Genre(s): Domestic Fiction; Bildungsroman (Coming of Age).

1151. *The Brothers Karamazov.* Trans. Constance Garnett. 1880. New York: Barnes and Noble, 1995. 729 pp.

Three sons of an old drunkard search for faith in God.

1152. *Crime and Punishment*. Trans. Richard Pevear and Larissa Volokhonsky. 1866. New York: Vintage, 1993. 564 pp.
Raskolnikoff murders an old moneylender and her sister, and after a lengthy investigation a saintly prostitute Sonya convinces him to confess.

1153. *Poor Folk*. Trans. Robert Dessaix. 1894. Dana Point, CA: Ardis, 1983. 143 pp.
Peasants live under difficult conditions in the rural areas of Russia in the 19th century.
Genre(s): Domestic Fiction.

1154. *The Possessed*. Trans. Andrew R. MacAndrew. 1913. New York: Macmillan, 1989. 702 pp.
Russians reveal their nihilistic approach to life in the midst of the revolution against royalty.
Genre(s): Domestic Fiction.

Douglas, Carole Nelson

◆ 1155. *Irene at Large*. New York: Tor, 1992. 381 pp.
People believe that Irene Adler and her lawyer-husband Godfrey Norton are dead, but instead they live outside Paris, and when a man from Afghanistan speaks Irene's name before falling unconscious on a Paris street, she, Holmes, and Watson must investigate.
Genre(s): Mystery.

◆ 1156. *Irene's Last Waltz*. New York: Forge, 1994. 480 pp.
Irene, her husband, and her friend Nell go to Prague to investigate the death of a bead girl from Paris's House of Worth, a few steps ahead of Sherlock Holmes, and they discover the villian and learn why the Countess of Bohemia's husband has not consumated their marriage.
Genre(s): Mystery.

Drozd, Volodymyr Hryhorovych

1157. *The Road to Mother*. Kiev: Dnipro, 1987. 299 pp.
Sophia Bohomolets, a Ukrainian intellectual, goes to a Siberian prison in 1881 for supporting the South Russian Workers Union, and has a daughter after she is incarcerated.
Genre(s): Biographical Fiction; Political Fiction.

Drucker, Peter Ferdinand

1158. *The Last of All Possible Worlds*. New York: Harper and Row, 1982. 218 pp.
Four families of bankers and diplomats tied to the Hapsburg monarchy live and work in Vienna during the first decade of the 20th century.
Genre(s): Domestic Fiction.

Ducornet, Rikki

1159. *The Stain*. New York: Grove, 1984. 191 pp.

Charlotte is born with a birthmark, which both her family and strangers treat as a demonic mark in late-19th-century France.
Genre(s): Gothic Fiction.

Duffy, Bruce

1160. *The World As I Found It*. New York: Ticknor and Fields, 1987. 546 pp.
Ludwig Wittgenstein moves through philosophical circles in upper-class Vienna and in the battlefields of World War I and World War II.
Genre(s): Biographical Fiction.

Dukthas, Ann

◆ 1161. *The Time of Murder at Mayerling*. New York: St. Martin's, 1996. 217 pp.
Nicholas Segalla returns to late-19th-century Austria and Mayerling to solve the murder-suicide of Archduke Rudolph and his pregnant mistress, Maria Vetsera.
Genre(s): Time Travel.

Dumas, Alexandre

1162. *Fernande*. Trans. A. Craig Bell. New York: St. Martin's, 1989. 144 pp.
When Fernande, a 19th-century French courtesan, discovers that her lover is married, she rejects him, but his despair leads his mother and wife to ask Fernande for help.
Genre(s): Satire.

Edelson, Marjorie

1163. *Malkeh and Her Children*. New York: Ballantine, 1992. 695 pp.
After Malkeh marries a tailor because he loves her, she founds a school for Jewish women and does other things Jewish women in pre-Revolutionary Russia had never done.
Genre(s): Domestic Fiction; Jewish Fiction.

Edgarian, Carol

◆ 1164. *Rise the Euphrates*. New York: Random House, 1994. 370 pp.
Grandmother Cassard Essayan is the only member of her family to have survived the Turkish massacre of Armenians in 1915, and her guilt causes reactions from her daughter and granddaughter.
Genre(s): Domestic Fiction.

Egan, Judith

1165. *Elena*. New Haven, CT: Ticknor and Fields, 1981. 314 pp.
At her first ball in Russia, Elena Shatagina falls in love with the grandson of serfs and marries him against her parents' wishes, but the revolution in 1917 changes everything, and Elena escapes to Constantinople.
Genre(s): Biographical Fiction; Love Story.

Ekman, Kerstin

1166. *Witches' Rings*. Chester Springs, PA: Dufour, 1997. 372 pp.

A narrator describes a poor Swedish soldier's wife, her ancestors, and the citizens of her town in the late 19th century.
Genre(s): Domestic Fiction.

Ellis, Julie

◆ 1167. *The Only Sin.* New York: Arbor House, 1986. 430 pp.
Lilli Landau is 16 in 1903 as she begins to feel the anti-Semitism in her German city of Marienbad, and to avoid an arranged marriage, she elopes, and while waiting for her philandering husband, discovers a beauty cream which she learns to market and sell.
Genre(s): Romance.

Fadeev, Aleksandr

1168. *The Nineteen.* Trans. R. D. Charques. New York: Hyperion, 1973. 293 pp.
Bolshevik soldiers conduct their own brand of warfare against Koltchak and the Japanese while living in an isolated area, family-like under their commander.
Genre(s): War Story.

Fagyas, M.

1169. *Court of Honor.* New York: Simon and Schuster, 1978. 377 pp.
Baroness Alexa von Godenhausen escapes an unhappy marriage with one of Kaiser Wilhelm II's officers by engaging in a series of liaisons prior to World War I.

1170. *Dance of the Assassins.* New York: Putnam, 1973. 383 pp.
A reluctant conspirator, Michael Vassilovich, a former lover of Queen Draga, tells about the 24 hours leading to Draga and Alexander's assassination prior to World War I.
Genre(s): War Story; Biographical Fiction.

1171. *The Devil's Lieutenant.* New York: Putnam, 1970. 384 pp.
When someone mails 10 army men cyanide capsules labeled as aphrodisiacs before World War I, one dies in agony, and when Captain Kunze investigates, he battles the self-possessed Dorfrichter.
Genre(s): Mystery; Adventure Story.

Faulks, Sebastian

1172. *Birdsong.* New York: Random House, 1996. 402 pp.
After loving and losing a French woman from Amiens, Stephen Wraysford serves in the French army during World War I.
Genre(s): Love Story; War Story.

Fedin, Konstantin

1173. *Cities and Years.* Trans. Michael Scammell. Evanston, IL: Northwestern University Press, 1993. 415 pp.

Andrei Startsov is stranded in Berlin during World War I, and when he returns to Russia in 1917, he finds himself in the midst of the revolution.
Genre(s): War Story.

Fisher, Alan

1174. *Three Passions of Countess Natalya.* New York: Macmillan, 1985. 349 pp.
Natalya, Countess Meretskova, ends her affair with a Cossack general to become a nurse during the Bolshevik Revolution but is sentenced to death for treason when she refuses complete allegiance to the new regime.
Genre(s): War Story.

Fitzgerald, Penelope

1175. *The Beginning of Spring.* New York: Henry Holt, 1989. 187 pp.
Frank Reid's wife deserts him in 1913, and he hires a peasant girl to look after his three children in Moscow.
Genre(s): Domestic Fiction.

Fleming, Thomas

1176. *Over There.* New York: HarperCollins, 1992. 608 pp.
A nurses' aide, Polly Warden, returns to England from World War I in France cynical and no longer innocent.
Genre(s): War Story.

Forster, E. M.

1177. *A Room with a View.* 1911. New York: Vintage, 1986. 364 pp.
Lucy Honeychurch falls in love while on a visit to Florence and must choose between fulfilling her social role or following her heart.
Genre(s): Love Story.

Freeman, Gillian

1178. *The Alabaster Egg.* New York: Viking, 1971. 173 pp.
Two plots present King Ludwig II of Bavaria and his homosexual lover and Hannah, a Jewish girl married to an Aryan who wants to advance his career during the Nazi period.
Genre(s): War Story; Love Story.

Freud, Esther

1179. *Summer at Gaglow.* New York: Norton, 1998. 256 pp.
The Jewish Belgard family summers at their retreat outside Berlin in 1914, but their world disintegrates as World War I progresses.
Genre(s): War Story; Domestic Fiction; Jewish Fiction.

Fritzhand, James

1180. *Four Sisters.* New York: Morrow, 1981. 519 pp.

The Petrov family of four sisters and a homosexual brother live in prerevolutionary Russia with their various husbands and lovers.
Genre(s): Family Saga.

Frondaie, Pierre

1181. *Port Arthur.* Trans. Elisabeth Abbott. Philadelphia: Lippincott, 1938. 283 pp.
Tselina, wife of a Russian count and sister to a half-Nipponese, becomes distressed when her brother wants her to help him as the head of the secret service in Korea during the Russo-Japanese war of 1904-1905.
Genre(s): War Story.

Frost, Mark

1182. *The List of 7.* New York: Morrow, 1993. 368 pp.
Sir Arthur Conan Doyle begins to work with Queen Victoria's favorite investigator, Jack Sparks, and becomes involved in seances and encounters a group called 7 that wants to reincarnate the devil, but whose leader is Sparks's brother.
Genre(s): Mystery.

Frutkin, Mark

1183. *Atmospheres Apollinaire.* Boston: David R. Godine, 1990. 193 pp.
Apollinaire lives in a time of cafés and artists where he creates his poetry and names the movements cubism and surrealism.
Genre(s): Biographical Fiction.

1184. *The Growing Dawn.* Dunvegan, Canada: Quadrant, 1983. 167 pp.
Guglielmo Marconi works to develop wireless telegraphy, and on December 12, 1901, he transmits the letter "S" from Poldhu, England, to Signal Hill, near St. John's, Newfoundland.
Genre(s): Biographical Fiction.

Furmanov, Dmitri

1185. *Chapayev.* Moscow: Progress, 1974. 318 pp.
Chapayev, peasant leader of the Red armies during the Bolshevik Revolution, follows his idealistic goals.
Genre(s): Biographical Fiction.

Gabriel, Marius

1186. *The Original Sin.* New York: Bantam, 1992. 672 pp.
Mercedes Eduard, her parents, and her daughter live between 1909 and 1973, when Mercedes is kidnapped for a 10 million dollar ransom.
Genre(s): Family Saga; War Story.

Galanaki, Rhea

1187. *The Life of Ismail Ferik Pasha.* Trans. Kay Cicellis. Chester Springs, PA: Dufour, 1996. 166 pp.
Ottoman officials kidnap Ismail Ferik Pasha, a Cretan boy, and force him to convert to Islam in the 19th century, and as an adult, he is expected to stop a revolt in Crete.
Genre(s): War Story; Political Fiction; Biographical Fiction.

Gann, Ernest Kellogg

1188. *In the Company of Eagles.* New York: Simon and Schuster, 1966. 342 pp.
A French aviator in World War I swears vengeance against an ace German flyer.
Genre(s): War Story.

Garnett, David

1189. *The Sons of the Falcon.* London: Macmillan, 1972. 288 pp.
In the 1860s, a barbaric Georgian prince living in his castle conflicts with his son who rejects blood feuds and oppression in favor of more contemporary European values.
Genre(s): Domestic Fiction.

Gaskin, Catherine

1190. *The Summer of the Spanish Woman.* Garden City, NY: Doubleday, 1977. 503 pp.
Charlotte loses her Irish estate to her secret love, goes to Spain, marries, and raises a family with her tempestuous husband.
Genre(s): Romance.

Gavin, Catherine Irvine

1191. *Give Me the Daggers.* New York: Morrow, 1972. 336 pp.
A Canadian war hero arrives in Finland during 1917 to smuggle out British soliders and when he meets a Finnish girl, he becomes involved in the Finnish struggle for freedom before Red Guards kill her.
Genre(s): War Story.

1192. *The Snow Mountain.* Pantheon, 1974. 509 pp.
Olga Nicolaievna, the oldest daughter of Nicholas II, has the wisdom to see the problems during the last years of the Romanovs as the Great War rages and she falls in love.
Genre(s): War Story; Domestic Fiction.

Gerhardie, William

1193. *Futility.* 1922. New York: New Directions, 1991. 194 pp.
The Vasilievich mother lives in Moscow with a lover while her husband lives in St. Petersburg with their daughters, and when their plans to marry others fail, they all move to Shanghai after the Revolution.
Genre(s): War Story; Domestic Fiction.

Germain, Sylvie

1194. *The Book of Nights.* Trans. Christine Donougher. Boston: D.R. Godine, 1993. 263 pp.
Victor-Flandrin Peniel has four wives, who die tragically between the end of the 19th century and World War II, as

well as 15 children, who all have their father's gold
flecked left eye.
Genre(s): War Story; Domestic Fiction.

Gibbs, Mary Ann

1195. *The Tempestuous Petticoat.* New York: Mason, 1977. 184 pp.
When Cecily Floyd travels to Venice as a lady's companion in Victorian times, she meets wealthy Charles Pitborough with whom she falls in love.
Genre(s): Romance.

Gideon, Nancy

1196. *Midnight Temptation.* New York: Pinnacle, 1994. 384 pp.
Nicole Radouix discovers her vampire heritage and rushes to Paris to forget, but she loves Marchand, and because of that, she must accept her destiny.
Genre(s): Romance; Horror.

Glassgold, Peter

1197. *The Angel Max.* San Diego, CA: Harcourt, 1998. 480 pp.
Max Kraft, born in Lithuania during 1866, dreams of coming to America where everyone speaks the same language, but after he arrives, he must send money to his siblings, who are members of anarchist groups that he hates.
Genre(s): Domestic Fiction; Political Fiction.

Goncharov, Ivan Aleksandrovich

1198. *Oblomov.* 1858. New York: Knopf, 1992. 586 pp.
Oblomov, a 19th-century Russian landowner, does nothing for himself, and eventually his indolence kills him.
Genre(s): Allegory; Humorous Fiction.

Gorham, Charles

1199. *Gold of Their Bodies.* New York: Dial, 1954. 318 pp.
Paul Gauguin breaks from traditional French painting, and when he goes to Taihiti, his style changes even more.
Genre(s): Biographical Fiction.

Gorky, Maksim

1200. *The Life of a Useless Man.* Trans. Moura Budberg. 1907. Garden City, NY: Doubleday, 1971. 240 pp.
In the Russian Revolution of 1905, Yevsey Klimkov becomes a spy for cruel masters.

Grahame, Lucia

1201. *The Painted Lady.* New York: Doubleday, 1993. 376 pp.
When Sir Anthony Camwell sees Fleur Brooks, wife of a French artist, he determines to have her, and after her husband dies, they marry; but when Anthony discovers that Fleur is being blackmailed because she posed for erotic paintings, he makes Fleur pay a price.
Genre(s): Romance.

Grayson, Richard

1202. *The Montmartre Murders.* New York: St. Martin's, 1982. 176 pp.
Surete Inspector Gautier finds a despised art dealer stabbed to death on the Boulevard de Clichy during La Belle Époque, and the subsequent investigation takes him to St. Tropez.
Genre(s): Mystery.

Green, William M.

1203. *The Romanov Connection.* New York: Beaufort, 1984. 264 pp.
Charles Aldonby, English cousin of the Romanovs, smitten in 1913 by Princess Marie on a visit, goes to rescue the Romanovs in April 1918, when the British refuse to help.
Genre(s): War Story.

Gross, Joel

1204. *Sarah.* New York: Morrow, 1987. 340 pp.
Sarah Bernhardt, daughter of a vain Jewish courtesan, struggles for love throughout her life, relishing her recognition as an actress.
Genre(s): Biographical Fiction.

Hackl, Erich

1205. *Aurora's Motive.* Trans. Edna McCown. New York: Knopf, 1989. 112 pp.
Aurora Rodrigues, a Spanish socialite pursuing her political beliefs, kills her only daughter in 1913 when the daughter is 17.
Genre(s): Domestic Fiction.

Hanlon, Emily

1206. *Petersburg.* New York: Putnam, 1988. 541 pp.
Four people become involved in a plot to overthrow the tsar in 1905.
Genre(s): War Story.

Harlowe, Justine

1207. *Memory and Desire.* New York: Warner, 1982. 423 pp.
Natasha de Vernay has had a wealthy childhood, but she and two generations of her family must flee Russia as the revolution develops and make new lives for themselves in the years preceding World War II.
Genre(s): War Story; Family Saga.

Harrod-Eagles, Cynthia

◆ 1208. *Emily.* New York: St. Martin's, 1993. 514 pp.
Emily, granddaughter of Nikolai and Anne, marries a Russian prince and faces the Bolshevik Revolution. (*Series:* Kirov Saga, 3)
Genre(s): Romance; War Story; Family Saga.

Hart-Davis, Duff

1209. *Horses of War.* New York: St. Martin's, 1992. 277 pp.

Englishman Joseph Clements, a runaway orphan with a love of horses, is eventually hired to oversee the construction of a thoroughbred farm in Russia, but when the Bolsheviks revolt, he must lead two prize stallions 600 miles to safety.
Genre(s): War Story; Adventure Story.

Hasek, Jaroslav

1210.*The Good Soldier Svejk and His Fortunes in the World War.* New York: Crowell, 1974. 752 pp.
Svejk, re-enrolled in the army at the beginning of World War I, seems an idiot, but his cheer and ability to go anywhere manage to entertain or frustrate those around him.
Genre(s): War Story; Picaresque Fiction; Humorous Fiction.

Hashian, Jack

1211.*Mamigon.* New York: Coward-McCann, 1982. 318 pp.
Magaros Mamigon experiences the slaughter in his Armenian village in 1915, and eight years later, he gets revenge against the Turk that he had once considered a friend.
Genre(s): War Story.

Haskin, Gretchen

1212.*An Imperial Affair.* New York: Dial, 1980. 312 pp.
Prince Romanovsky, offered money and a chance for revenge against the Bolsheviks, attempts to get the czar and his family out of Ekaterinburg and Russia in 1917.
Genre(s): Biographical Fiction.

Hasler, Eveline

1213.*Flying with Wings of Wax.* New York: Fromm International, 1993. 213 pp.
Emily Kempin, the first female to graduate with a law degree in Europe and the founder of New York City's first law school for women ends up in a Zurich mental institution in 1899, after not being allowed to practice law.
Genre(s): Biographical Fiction; Legal Story.

Heaven, Constance

1214.*Daughter of Marignac.* New York: Putnam, 1984. 342 pp.
Louise de Vallon's grandfather decides that she should have an arranged marriage to save the family's French estate, but Louise loves an American Civil War veteran.
Genre(s): War Story.

◆ 1215. *The Raging Fire.* New York: Putnam, 1988. 503 pp.
Galina falls in love with a non-practicing physician teaching her St. Petersburg University class in 1905, but another man who loves her makes her life miserable during the years prior to and during the Revolution.
Genre(s): Romance; War Story.

Hegi, Ursula

1216.*Stones from the River.* New York: Poseidon, 1994. 496 pp.
Trudi, a dwarf librarian, tells about the lives of people in the small German town of Burgdorf from World War I and into the 1950s.
Genre(s): War Story; Domestic Fiction.

Helprin, Mark

1217.*A Soldier of the Great War.* San Diego, CA: Harcourt, 1991. 792 pp.
An old man, Alessandro Giuliani, leaves a streetcar when a boy without a fare is denied entry and, while walking with the boy, tells him about the wealthy life he led until World War I altered it.
Genre(s): Bildungsroman (Coming of Age); War Story.

Hemingway, Ernest

◆ 1218. *A Farewell to Arms.* 1929. New York: Scribner, 1997. 297 pp.
Two people conduct a love affair while World War I rages around them.
Genre(s): War Story; Love Story.

Herbert, A. P.

1219.*The Secret Battle.* 1920. New York: Atheneum, 1981. 216 pp.
The young British soldier Harry Penrose fears warfare as he serves in the trenches of France and Turkey.
Genre(s): War Story.

Herlin, Hans

1220.*Grishin.* Garden City, NY: Doubleday, 1987. 324 pp.
In 1918, before the British know what the Soviets will do after the Russian Revolution they send one man to negotiate with the government and another to assassinate Lenin.
Genre(s): Biographical Fiction.

1221.*Siberian Transfer.* Trans. John Brownjohn. New York: St. Martin's, 1992. 280 pp.
Geologist and explorer Oliver Quinn searches for the tsar's gold, which the White Russians hid from the Bolsheviks in 1918.
Genre(s): Adventure Story.

High, Monique Raphel

1222.*The Four Winds of Heaven.* New York: Delacorte, 1980. 682 pp.
David Gunzburg, highly regarded by the tsarist regime, escapes much of the prevalent anti-Semitism until the Russian Revolution strikes down the Romanovs.
Genre(s): Jewish Fiction; Biographical Fiction.

Hill, Carol DeChelli

1223.*Henry James' Midnight Song.* New York: Poseidon, 1993. 448 pp.

Questions for Henry James to answer include who murdered women in Vienna and whether a murder took place at Sigmund Freud's house at the end of the 19th century. *Genre(s):* Mystery.

Hill, Reginald

◆ 1224. *No Man's Land.* New York: St. Martin's, 1986. 352 pp.
After the battle of the Somme in 1916, Arthur Aloysius Viney, an insane Australian army sergeant, leads a group known as Viney's Volunteers, who are armed Allied deserters.
Genre(s): War Story.

Hill, Susan

1225. *Strange Meeting.* New York: Saturday Review, 1972. 223 pp.
Two British soldiers meet during the confusion of World War I in France and form a friendship that transcends their predicament.
Genre(s): War Story.

Hoe, Susanna

1226. *God Save the Tsar.* New York: St. Martin's, 1978. 223 pp.
Tsarina Alexandra becomes frustrated with having to go to Ekaterinburg and then having to escape the Bolsheviks by going to Odessa for a ship to Constantinople.
Genre(s): Biographical Fiction.

Hoffman, Allen

1227. *Small Worlds.* New York: Abbeville, 1996. 280 pp.
In 1903, the rebbe has not left his study for five years, but on Tisha B'Av, he leads the service as if nothing has happened and reenters a life where his wife has had to fulfill his duties.
Genre(s): Domestic Fiction; Religious Fiction.

Holt, Victoria

◆ 1228. *The Demon Lover.* Garden City, NY: Doubleday, 1982. 377 pp.
Kate Collison, after taking over her father's commissions for minature paintings when his sight fails, goes to Paris and meets a baron who marries her to keep her away from his cousin.
Genre(s): Romance.

1229. *On the Night of the Seventh Moon.* Garden City, NY: Doubleday, 1972. 359 pp.
After a huntsman seduces a young English girl in Germany, they marry and become involved in various secretive events.
Genre(s): Romance.

Howells, William Dean

1230. *Indian Summer.* 1886. New York: Vintage, 1990. 278 pp.

Americans living in Florence, including a middle-aged bachelor and a 20-year-old girl, meet within the local expatriate community.

Huebsch, Edward

1231. *The Last Summer of Mata Hari.* New York: Crown, 1979. 371 pp.
The Mata Hari spends her last summer before execution as a spy and comes into contact with such people as Herman Hesse and Marcel Proust.
Genre(s): Biographical Fiction; Spy Fiction.

Hylton, Sara

◆ 1232. *The Crimson Falcon.* New York: St. Martin's, 1983. 272 pp.
At the beginning of the 20th century, a young girl stays in a dark Viennese castle while being wooed by a man with evil intentions.
Genre(s): Romance.

◆ 1233. *The Sunflower Girl.* New York: St. Martin's, 1997. 352 pp.
Marie Clair Moreau, a French girl home from her convent school for a holiday in 1894, becomes pregnant by an Englishman visiting the estate next door and has to leave school.
Genre(s): Romance.

Hyman, Tom

◆ 1234. *Seven Days to Petrograd.* New York: Viking, 1988. 412 pp.
In 1917, Lenin takes the train to Russia, funded by Germans who want the exile to lead a revolution which will remove Russia from the Great War.
Genre(s): War Story.

Ibbotson, Eva

◆ 1235. *Madensky Square.* New York: St. Martin's, 1988. 256 pp.
Susanna, a shop owner in Vienna, becomes concerned about a budding pianist and has her own illicit romance with an officer in the early 20th century.
Genre(s): Romance.

Ignatieff, Michael

◆ 1236. *Asya.* New York: Knopf, 1991. 320 pp.
Russian noble Asya Galitzine loses all during the Russian Revolution but has an affair with an officer before going to Paris to have their baby.
Genre(s): War Story.

Ilyin, Olga

1237. *The St Petersburg Affair.* New York: Holt, Rinehart and Winston, 1982. 280 pp.
During the 1860s, Kyra Beherev marries poorly and while pretending to be happy, meets a poet whose ideas about life change her perspective.
Genre(s): Romance.

Johnston, Velda

◆ 1238. *The House on the Left Bank.* New York: Dodd, Mead, 1975. 214 pp.
Living in Paris, Martha Hathaway nurses the poor, while her mother is mistress to a baron whose death preceeds her own murder.
Genre(s): Romance; War Story.

Jones, Mervyn

1239. *Joseph.* New York: Atheneum, 1970. 506 pp.
Joseph Stalin's early childhood experiences and his time in a seminary influence his decisions to purge anyone who challenges his view of life.
Genre(s): Biographical Fiction.

Jong, Erica

1240. *Inventing Memory.* New York: HarperCollins, 1997. 400 pp.
The history of four Jewish women, mothers and daughters, begins in Russia during a pogrom in the early 1900s when Sara flees but passes her heritage to her daughter Salome, her granddaughter Sally, and Sally's daughter Sara.
Genre(s): Family Saga.

Jovanovski, Meto

1241. *Cousins.* Trans. Sylvia W. Holton. San Francisco, CA: Mercury, 1987. 128 pp.
In 1917, two cousins have earned money abroad in Romania and want to return home to Bulgaria, but the war, for which they have little concern, halts them on the border.
Genre(s): War Story; Humorous Fiction.

Jünger, Ernst

1242. *A Dangerous Encounter.* Trans. Hilary Barr. Nyack, NY: Marsilio, 1993. 187 pp.
Gerhard, a diplomat, is just about to become involved with the bored wife of a naval officer, but a woman is shot outside their hotel room, causing a Paris scandal.
Genre(s): Mystery.

Jute, Andre

1243. *The Zaharoff Commission.* Melbourne, Australia: Hyland House, 1981. 248 pp.
Basil Zaharoff, a notorious arms dealer, supplies munitions to the French and British during World War I, then goes to Germany to convince them to end the war because of the threat of the Bolshevik Revolution in Russia.
Genre(s): Biographical Fiction; War Story.

Kalogridis, Jeanne

1244. *Lord of the Vampires.* New York: Delacorte, 1996. 368 pp.
Dracula wants to leave his castle, but two women plot to destroy him, his cousin Zsuzsanna, and the Countess Elizabeth Bathory, who killed virgins and drank their blood in an attempt to retain her youth.
Genre(s): Horror.

Kane, Carol J.

1245. *Blood and Sable.* New York: McGraw Hill, 1988. 472 pp.
In the Russian Revolution, Princess Anya meets Oleg Ivanov, recent landowner, who continues his depraved ways by kidnapping Anya's son.
Genre(s): War Story.

Kazan, Elia

1246. *America, America.* New York: Stein and Day, 1962. 213 pp.
At the beginning of the 20th century, Stavros Topouzoglou plans to go to Constantinople to learn about the rug business but he loses the money his family gives him, and has to earn his passage for the trip to America.
Genre(s): Family Saga.

Kazantzakis, Nikos

1247. *Freedom or Death.* New York: Simon and Schuster, 1983. 433 pp.
In 1889, people of Crete attack their Turkish oppressors.
Genre(s): War Story.

Kelly, Clint

1248. *Deliver Us From Evil.* Minneapolis, MN: Bethany House, 1998. 288 pp.
Tatul Sarafian flees the Turks in the mountains, Adrine Tevian falls in love with a man in a Turkish military camp only known as The Fox, and American Leslie Davis tries to help the Armenians although America is neutral. (*Series:* In the Shadow of the Mountain, 1)
Genre(s): War Story; Political Fiction; Christian Fiction.

Kempowski, Walter

1249. *Days of Greatness.* Trans. Leila Vennewitz. New York: Knopf, 1981. 309 pp.
The wealthy German merchants living at the end of Wilhelm's reign in pre–World War I Europe, exhibit continued devotion to their country and to their families.
Award(s): Lessing Prize.
Genre(s): Domestic Fiction.

Keyes, Frances Parkinson

1250. *Came a Cavalier.* New York: Messner, 1947. 577 pp.
An American Red Cross worker comes to France in World War I and, after marrying a French cavalry officer, stays on.

Koning, Hans

1251. *Death of a Schoolboy.* New York: Harcourt, 1974. 187 pp.
Gavrilo Princip fires the bullet that starts World War I because he hates imperial expansion, a situation which he observes when exiled from Bosnia.
Genre(s): War Story; Political Fiction.

Konwicki, Tadeusz

1252. *Bohin Manor.* Trans. Richard Lourie. New York: Farrar, Straus and Giroux, 1990. 230 pp.
In the late 19th century, Miss Helena must choose between a questionable Count and a stalwart Jew, each of whom loves her but represents a very different social choice in Lithuania.
Genre(s): Domestic Fiction.

Kotker, Norman

1253. *Herzl, the King.* New York: Scribner's, 1972. 280 pp.
In 1894 Theodor Herzl believes that a Jewish homeland in Palestine will answer the problems of Jews, and he spends his last 10 years working for that goal while sacrificing all other aspects of his life.
Genre(s): Biographical Fiction.

Kotzwinkle, William

1254. *Fata Morgana.* 1977. New York: Marlowe, 1997. 209 pp.
In 1861, Inspector Picard tries to find the truth about the conjurer Ric Lazare and his sexy wife.
Genre(s): Mystery.

Krell, David Farrell

1255. *Nietzsche.* Albany: State University of New York, 1996. 364 pp.
Friedrich Nietzsche is institutionalized in Basel in 1889, and after mentally and physically deteriorating, he dies in Weimar in 1900.
Genre(s): Biographical Fiction.

Kricorian, Nancy

◆ 1256. *Zabelle.* New York: Atlantic Monthly, 1998. 256 pp.
When grandmother Zabelle Chahasbanian dies, the family find out about her childhood when her Armenian family died in 1916, slaughtered by the Turks.
Genre(s): War Story; Political Fiction.

Kross, Jaan

1257. *The Czar's Madman.* Trans. Anselm Hollo. New York: Pantheon, 1993. 362 pp.
Timo von Bock, an Estonian baron, marries a peasant girl, frees all of the serfs on his estate, and when he criticizes the czar, he is imprisoned for nine years before being declared mad.
Genre(s): Political Fiction.

1258. *Professor Martens' Departure.* Trans. Anselm Hollo. New York: New Press, 1994. 295 pp.
Professor Martens muses on his train trip about his government service in Estonia and his years as a Russian treaty negotiator in the early 20th century.
Genre(s): Political Fiction.

Kyle, Duncan

1259. *The King's Commissar.* New York: St. Martin's, 1983. 286 pp.
A British naval officer goes with David Lloyd George to rescue the czar and his family by offering a huge sum of money to Lenin.
Genre(s): Adventure Story; War Story.

Laker, Rosalind

1260. *Banners of Silk.* Garden City, NY: Doubleday, 1981. 469 pp.
Charles Worth and Louise Vernet meet once when they are young and then again as successful couturiers in 19th-century Paris.
Genre(s): Romance.

1261. *Orchids and Diamonds.* New York: Doubleday, 1995. 293 pp.
Juliette Claudel meets Nikolai Karasvin in Paris during 1907, but after they fall in love, he must return to Russia, and she marries Marco Romanelli, moves to Venice, and faces World War I while still loving Nikolai.
Genre(s): Romance; War Story.

Lambton, Antony

1262. *Elizabeth and Alexandra.* New York: Dutton, 1986. 415 pp.
Grand Duchess Elizabeth, the sister of Alexandra, is unhappily married to Nicholas II's uncle Serge before a bomb kills him in 1905.
Genre(s): Biographical Fiction; War Story; Romance.

Land, Jane

◆ 1263. *These Tigers' Hearts.* New York: Doubleday, 1978. 178 pp.
Astra Padgett goes to Vienna from England in the 1860s to start a nursing school, but when Poland tries to free itself from Austria at the same time, Astra becomes entangled in the fray.
Genre(s): Romance.

Landey, Dora, and Elinor Klein

1264. *Triptych.* Boston: Houghton Mifflin, 1983. 544 pp.
The royal Sonya marries Count Gregory in Russia, but as a lowly woman in the revolutionary movement she has no access to information, and she flees to New York, arriving with her newly adopted child, who in turn, becomes an artist.
Genre(s): War Story.

Lawrence, Starling

1265. *Montenegro.* New York: Farrar, Straus and Giroux, 1997. 320 pp.
Auberon Harwell goes to Montenegro as the Ottoman empire falls apart to see what role Britain might play in the area, and after he begins living with Danilo Pekocevic, once a freedom fighter for the Montenegrin Serbs, he realizes that forces outside his control work in the area.
Genre(s): War Story.

Levine, Jacques

1266. *Hitler's Secret Diaries.* Pittsburgh, PA: Aiglon, 1988. 157 pp.
Hitler reveals his attitudes toward Austria and the "mongrel" races in a diary begun when he was 10 in 1899.
Genre(s): Biographical Fiction; War Story.

Lightman, Alan P.

◆ 1267. *Einstein's Dreams.* New York: Warner, 1994. 179 pp.
In 1905, Einstein publishes three important papers based on his dreams, each one with a different concept of time.
Genre(s): Biographical Fiction.

Lindgren, Torgny

1268. *The Way of the Serpent.* Trans. Tom Geddes. New York: Farrar, Straus and Giroux,1997. 104 pp.
When a Swedish peasant family at the end of the 19th century cannot pay rent, the landlord and his son possess the women, but eventually meet their due.
Genre(s): Domestic Fiction.

Lippi, Rosina

1269. *Homestead.* New York: HarperCollins, 1998. 224 pp.
Women living in Rosenau, a dairy farming community in the Austrian Alps, measure their lives by such things as receiving a postcard, secretly falling in love with an Italian deserter in the meadow, and making good quality cheese.
Genre(s): Family Saga; War Story.

Littell, Robert

1270. *The Revolutionist.* New York: Bantam, 1988. 467 pp.
Alexander Til, his stepbrother Leon, and their friend Atticus Tuohy leave New York in 1917 when Leon goes to Palestine and the other two to Russia for the revolution.
Genre(s): War Story; Political Fiction.

Lorrimer, Claire

1271. *Frost in the Sun.* New York: David and Charles, 1988. 534 pp.
Casilda Montero, eight, meets Joscelin Howard at an English convent school before World War I, and they remain friends through the next 30 years, even through the Spanish Civil War.
Genre(s): Domestic Fiction; War Story.

Lovesey, Peter

◆ 1272. *Bertie and the Crime of Passion.* New York: Mysterious Press, 1995. 244 pp.
Bertie, Prince of Wales, and Sarah Bernhardt investigate the death of his friend's daughter at the Moulin Rouge in 1891.
Genre(s): Mystery.

Lowndes, Natalya

1273. *Angel in the Sun.* London: Hodder and Stoughton, 1989. 426 pp.
Countess Natalya Igoryevna Alekseyeva escapes from her estate at the beginning of the Bolshevik Revolution disguised as a man, in the company of the dwarf, Yasha.
Genre(s): War Story.

MacBeth, George

1274. *The Lion of Pescara.* London: Cape, 1984. 256 pp.
In 1916, Gabriele D'Annunzio is temporarily blinded while writing an autobiographical prose poem in which he remembers his adventures and his affairs with Eleanor Duse and others.
Genre(s): Biographical Fiction; Erotic Literature.

Mackey, Mary

1275. *A Grand Passion.* New York: Simon and Schuster, 1986. 448 pp.
Natasha Ladanova, a leading dancer with the imperial ballet, loves a self-centered dancer who leaves Russia to join Diaghilev in Paris, and she follows him there when the revolution begins.
Genre(s): War Story.

Makine, Andrei

1276. *Dreams of My Siberian Summer.* Boston: Little, Brown, 1997. 256 pp.
Andrei spends evenings with his grandmother in the Russian village of Saranza, and she tells him of her life in Paris at the beginning of the 20th century before she came to Russia and fell in love with his grandfather who died during World War I.
Award(s): Prix Medicis for Best Foreign Fiction; Prix Goncourt.
Genre(s): Domestic Fiction; Bildungsroman (Coming of Age).

Malamud, Bernard

1277. *The Fixer.* New York: Farrar, Straus and Giroux, 1966. 335 pp.
In Kiev in 1913, Yakov, a Jewish odd-job man, is imprisoned for three years, and although he endures much inhumanity, he retains his belief in freedom.
Award(s): National Book Award; Pulitzer Prize.
Genre(s): Legal Story.

Malraux, André

1278. *The Walnut Trees of Altenburg.* Trans. A.W. Fielding. Chicago: University of Chicago Press, 1992. 224 pp.
The Germans use poison gas in an attack on the Russians guarding the eastern front in 1915, and Vincent Berger, who witnesses the horror, finds that his one desire in life is to be happy.
Genre(s): War Story.

Mann, Thomas

1279. *Death in Venice.* Trans. Stanley Appelbaum. 1965. New York: Dover, 1995. 118 pp.
Gustav von Aschenbach succumbs to his desires on a vacation trip to Venice.

Mansfield, Helene

1280. *Contessa.* Garden City, NY: Doubleday, 1982. 528 pp.
Valentina, a wealthy Russian aristocrat, has to escape Russia as the Bolshevik Revolution begins, and she, her impotent husband, and her two sons by a handsome lover travel to France.
Genre(s): Romance.

Martin du Gard, Roger

1281. *Summer 1914.* Trans. Stuart Gilbert. New York: Viking, 1941. 1008 pp.
In the sequel to *The Thibaults*, Antoine Thibault is dying from lung disease contracted in World War I at the time the Socialists' collapse.
Genre(s): Political Fiction; Family Saga.

1282. *The Thibaults.* New York: Viking, 1939. 871 pp.
The Thibaults in Paris before World War I hold onto certain aspirations, but in time the family disintegrates.
Genre(s): Domestic Fiction; Family Saga.

Matveev, Vladimir Pavlovich

1283. *The Commissar of the Gold Express.* Westport, CT: Hyperion, 1975. 212 pp.
A commissar fights in the Bolshevik Revolution.
Genre(s): War Story.

McLeave, Hugh

1284. *A Man and His Mountain.* New York: Macmillan, 1977. 324 pp.
Cézanne is boorish and pompous but also a genius and a great artist.
Genre(s): Biographical Fiction.

Mendoza, Eduardo

1285. *The Truth about the Savolta Case.* Trans. Alfred Mac Adam. New York: Pantheon, 1992. 332 pp.
The owners of a business complex in Barcelona become suspect in a murder.
Genre(s): War Story; Mystery.

Meyer, Nicholas

1286. *The Canary Trainer.* New York: Norton, 1993. 225 pp.
Sherlock Holmes goes to Paris between 1891 and 1894 under the disguise of Henrik Sigerson, a Norwegian violinist, and his playing wins him a position in the Paris Opera orchestra, but he soon must investigate the problems of a singer being trained by the Phantom living below the opera house.
Genre(s): Mystery.

Michaels, Barbara

1287. *Wings of the Falcon.* New York: Dodd, Mead, 1977. 314 pp.
In 1860, Francesca Fairbourn travels to Italy to join her deceased mother's family and finds herself in the battle for unification.
Genre(s): Romance; War Story.

Michaels, Fern

1288. *Sins of Omission.* New York: Ballantine, 1990. 497 pp.
Reuben Tarz and Daniel Bishop become friends in World War I, and after they are injured, a member of French nobility nurses them to health on her estate.
Genre(s): War Story; Romance.

Michalos, Peter

1289. *Psyche.* New York: Doubleday, 1993. 272 pp.
At thirty, Sigmund Freud begins to treat Lucy and her hysteria, and he becomes drawn into her world, seduces her, and follows her to Delphi where Sophie Schliemann is working.
Genre(s): Biographical Fiction.

Midwood, Bart

1290. *World in Pieces.* Sag Harbor, NY: Permanent Press, 1998. 224 pp.
The translator Midwood reads the papers of a deceased brother and sister and meets their family beginning with their rebellious grandmother in Vienna and ending with the son resulting from their incestuous relationship who lives on a kibbutz in Israel.
Genre(s): Domestic Fiction; Family Saga.

Morton, Frederic

1291. *The Forever Street.* Garden City, NY: Doubleday, 1984. 447 pp.
The Spiegelglass family moves from Slovakia to Vienna in the 19th century and prospers until the Nazis take over the city.
Genre(s): War Story; Jewish Fiction.

Murray, Frances

1292. *The Heroine's Sister.* New York: St. Martin's, 1975. 192 pp.
In Venice during 1868, a governess falls in love with a nobleman.
Genre(s): Romance.

Musil, Robert

1293. *The Man without Qualities.* Trans. Eithne Wilkins and Ernest Kaiser. 1953. New York: Vintage, 1996. 1774 pp.

A man living in Vienna prior to World War I reflects the decadence of the society.

Myrivilis, Stratis

1294. *Life in the Tomb.* Trans. Peter Bien. Boston, MA: University Press of New England, 1977. 325 pp.
A Greek soldier in Macedonia keeps a journal in which he describes the isolation and crudeness of a soldier's life.
Genre(s): War Story.

Napier, Priscilla Hayter

1295. *Imperial Winds.* New York: Coward-McCann, 1982. 300 pp.
Daisy Pelham flees heartbreak by going to Russia and becoming a governess for the royal family, who must, in turn, leave their home when Rasputin gains control of the court.
Genre(s): Romance.

Noga, Helen

1296. *Ayisha.* New York: McKay, 1972. 214 pp.
Hasmig, a married Armenian Christian, changes her name to Ayisha, attempting to escape persecution, and marries the Moslem Bayazid whom she has loved secretly all her life, but after the war, she is forced to leave for America with her legal husband, leaving her children as well as Bayazid.
Genre(s): War Story.

Nolan, Frederick W.

1297. *White Nights, Red Dawn.* New York: Macmillan, 1980. 451 pp.
Boris Abrikosov wants the Smirnoff family's wealth and women as classes disintegrate in Russia during 1917.
Genre(s): War Story.

Nordhoff, Charles, and James Norman Hall

1298. *Falcons of France.* Boston: Little, Brown, 1929. 332 pp.
The Lafayette flying corps aviators believe themselves worthy of their German opponents in World War I.
Genre(s): War Story.

Okudzhava, Bulat Shalvovich

1299. *The Extraordinary Adventures of Secret Agent Shipov.* London: Abelard-Schuman, 1973. 214 pp.
Shipov, a policeman, supposedly searching Tolstoy's home in secret during 1862, spends his time eating and drinking instead of working.
Genre(s): Biographical Fiction; Spy Fiction.

1300. *A Taste of Liberty.* Ann Arbor, MI: Ardis, 1986. Canada pp.
Avrosimov, an innocent bystander, relates details of the trial of the Decembrist leader, Pavel Pestel.
Genre(s): Biographical Fiction; Political Fiction; Legal Story.

Orde, Lewis

1301. *By Blood Divided.* New York: Kensington, 1991. 532 pp.
After escaping a Russian pogrom in 1903 and going to Rotterdam, a fire separates siblings Zalman and Rachel for over sixty years—Rachel lives in England and Zalman becomes successful in the United States.
Genre(s): Family Saga.

Pardo Bazan, Emilia

1302. *The House of Ulloa.* Trans. Roser Caminals-Heath. Athens: University of Georgia Press, 1992. 323 pp.
Dom Pedro, heir to the House of Ulloa, loses his fortune as class wars between peasants and aristocracy undermine the upper class in 19th-century Spain.
Genre(s): Political Fiction.

Paretti, Sandra

1303. *The Wishing Tree.* Trans. Ruth Hein. New York: St. Martin's, 1977. 338 pp.
On New Year's Eve of 1900, Camilla Hofmann learns that her family is bankrupt, but she brokers a marriage with a smart salesman who helps rebuild the family business.

Parini, Jay

1304. *The Last Station.* New York: Henry Holt, 1990. 290 pp.
During his last year, Tolstoy's battles with his wife continue as does his own dilemma over his privilege versus his professed virtues of chastity and poverty.
Genre(s): Biographical Fiction.

Pasternak, Boris

1305. *Doctor Zhivago.* New York: Pantheon, 1958. 568 pp.
Yuri Zhivago, doctor and poet, lives and loves during the first three decades of 20th-century Russia.
Genre(s): War Story.

Patrick, William

1306. *Blood Winter.* New York: Viking, 1990. 386 pp.
A researcher who has developed a crude form of penicillin during 1915 in Berlin's Institute for Infectious Diseases tries to escape from the German Intelligence so that her discovery can help humanity.
Genre(s): Medical Novel; Spy Fiction.

Pazzi, Roberto

1307. *The Princess and the Dragon.* New York: Knopf, 1990. 162 pp.
Grand Duke George, younger brother of Tsar Nicholas II, dreams of a new kingdom even though the Romanovs are weakening.
Genre(s): Biographical Fiction.

1308. *Searching for the Emperor.* Trans. M. J. Fitzgerald. New York: Knopf, 1988. 160 pp.
Nicholas and his family wait in their Siberian prison while Nicholas complains about his constraints.
Genre(s): Domestic Fiction.

Pella, Judith

1309. *The Dawning of Deliverance.* Minneapolis, MN: Bethany House, 1995. 432 pp.
Russian nurse Mariana Remizov falls in love with American war correspondent Daniel Trent while the revolution rages. (*Series:* The Russians, 5)
Genre(s): Christian Fiction; Family Saga; War Story.

1310. *Heirs of the Motherland.* Minneapolis, MN: Bethany House, 1993. 382 pp.
Mariana, raised as the daughter of peasants, is actually the daughter of a Russian princess. (*Series:* Russians, 4)
Genre(s): Christian Fiction.

1311. *White Nights, Red Morning.* Minneapolis, MN: Bethany House, 1996. 412 pp.
Yuri, eldest son of Anna Fedorcenko, wants a medical career badly enough to ignore the revolution brewing at the beginning of the 20th century, but his brother Andrei, with whom his foster sister is in love, is excited by the fray. (*Series:* The Russians, 6)
Genre(s): Christian Fiction; Family Saga.

Perez Galdos, Benito

1312. *The Golden Fountain Cafe.* Trans. Walter Rubin. Pittsburgh, PA: Latin American, 1989. 350 pp.
In the 1870s Lazaro comes to Madrid from the provinces, gets arrested, becomes the love object of a spinister, and risks losing his Clara.
Genre(s): War Story; Political Fiction.

Perutz, Leo

1313. *Little Apple.* Trans. John Brownjohn. Boston: Little, Brown, 1992. 208 pp.
As Vittorin arrives in Vienna after years in a Russian prison camp, he plans to return and take revenge on the sadistic camp commander, and when he does, he joins the Bolshevik Revolution.
Genre(s): War Story.

◆ 1314. *Master of the Day of Judgment.* Boston: Little, Brown, 1994. 160 pp.
The actor Eugene Bischoff describes an unexplained suicide during a musical evening at his Vienna home, and as a military engineer begins to contemplate the reasons for the incident Bischoff shoots himself, an act followed by others through the ensuing weeks of 1909.
Genre(s): Mystery.

Phillips, Michael R.

1315. *The Crown and the Crucible.* Minneapolis, MN: Bethany House, 1991. 410 pp.

In the 1870s, a peasant girl becomes friends with the daughter of a prince and an Imperial minister in Russia during the 1870s. (*Series:* The Russians, 1)
Genre(s): Christian Fiction.

Phillips, Michael R., and Judith Pella

1316. *A House Divided.* Minneapolis, MN: Bethany House, 1992. 350 pp.
When soldiers return to Russia, they find turmoil at home. (*Series:* The Russians, 2)
Genre(s): Christian Fiction; War Story.

1317. *Travail and Triumph.* Minneapolis, MN: Bethany House, 1992. 400 pp.
Two Russians retain their love for each other in the difficult period leading to the Bolshevik Revolution. (*Series:* The Russians, 3)
Genre(s): Christian Fiction; War Story.

Porter, David

◆ 1318. *The Vienna Passage.* Wheaton, IL: Crossway, 1995. 287 pp.
The British Toby Burgate takes a job in Vienna at the beginning of the 20th century, and there he learns to appreciate art and music and hate anti-Semitism.
Genre(s): Christian Fiction; Bildungsroman (Coming of Age).

Prevelakes, Pandeles

1319. *The Cretan.* Trans. Abbott Rick And Peter Mackridge. Minneapolis, MN:, Nostos, 1991. 480 pp.
Kostandis Markantonis, citizen, and Eleftherios Venizelos, statesman, each represent the ideal Cretan, as Crete tries to rid itself of Turkish rule in the insurrection of 1905.
Genre(s): Biographical Fiction; Epic Literature; War Story.

Proust, Marcel

1320. *Remembrance of Things Past.* Trans. C.K. Scott Moncrieff and Terence Kilmartin. 1981. New York: Random House, 1928. 3365 pp.
The three volumes containing *Swann's Way, Within a Budding Grove, The Guermantes Way, Cities of the Plain, The Captive, The Fugitive,* and *Time Regained* tell the story of Marcel and his family in a small French town from the end of the 19th century to the aftereffects of World War I.
Genre(s): Domestic Fiction.

Prus, Boleslaw

1321. *The Doll.* Trans. David Welsh. 1890. New York: Oxford, 1997. 680 pp.
Stas Wokulski, a wealthy merchant who wants to make scientific discoveries that will help mankind, sees Isabella Lecky at the theater, falls madly in love with her, and spends all his time trying to make more money to sat-

isfy her materialistic desires which mirror those of Warsaw's 1878 society.
Genre(s): Love Story; Epic Literature.

Ransmayr, Christoph

1322. *The Terrors of Ice and Darkness.* Trans. John E. Woods. New York: Grove Weidenfeld, 1991. 240 pp.
In 1872 the Austro-Hungarian polar expedition begins and lasts two years, and in 1981, an Italian dies while trying to reconstruct the expedition.
Genre(s): Adventure Story.

Remarque, Erich Maria

1323. *All Quiet on the Western Front.* Trans. A.W. Wheen. Boston: Little, Brown, 1929. 291 pp.
Five German students are drafted into World War I, but only one survives to question the value of war.
Genre(s): War Story.

Rigoni Stern, Mario

1324. *The Story of Tonle.* Trans. John Shepley. Marlboro, VT: Marlboro, 1998. 128 pp.
Tonle Bintarn works as a smuggler between Italy and Austria in the late 19th century, and he reveals his love of the area's beauty until World War I when devastation arrives in the battle of Mount Ortigara.
Genre(s): Adventure Story; War Story.

Romains, Jules

1325. *Death of a World.* Trans. Gerard Hopkins. New York: Knopf, 1938. 551 pp.
Abbé Mionnet goes on a secret mission to Rome to discover the papacy's attitude toward European foreign policy when Lenin is exiled to Krakow. (*Series:* Men of Good Will, 7)
Genre(s): War Story.

1326. *The Depths and the Heights.* Trans. Gerard Hopkins. New York: Knopf, 1937. 546 pp.
In 1912, Europe rushes toward war while the cultural and intellectual life in Paris seems oblivious to the inevitability of war. (*Series:* Men of Good Will, 6)
Genre(s): War Story.

1327. *The Earth Trembles.* Trans. Gerard Hopkins. New York: Knopf, 1936. 582 pp.
The social, political, and industrial life in France between 1910 and 1911 concerns government officials. (*Series:* Men of Good Will, 5)
Genre(s): War Story.

1328. *Men of Good Will.* Trans. Gerard Hopkins. New York: Knopf, 1933. 457 pp.
The events of a single day in Paris, October 6, 1908, precede Quinette's involvement with a murderer. (*Series:* Men of Good Will, 1)
Genre(s): War Story.

1329. *Passion's Pilgrims.* Trans. Warre B. Wells. New York: Knopf, 1934. 503 pp.
Both the true nature student life and the eroticism of Paris come to light through Quinette and others. (*Series:* Men of Good Will, 2)
Genre(s): War Story.

1330. *The Proud and the Meek.* Trans. Warre B. Wells. New York: Knopf, 1934. 569 pp.
Haverkamp makes daring real estate deals while the Bastide family loses its livelihood. (*Series:* Men of Good Will, 3)
Genre(s): War Story.

1331. *Verdun.* Trans. Gerard Hopkins. New York: Knopf, 1939. 500 pp.
During the second winter of World War I, a group of soldiers fights the battle of Verdun. (*Series:* Men of Good Will, 8)
Genre(s): War Story.

1332. *The World from Below.* Trans. Gerard Hopkins. New York: Knopf, 1935. 560 pp.
Students and intellectuals in Paris search unsuccessfully for something in which to believe. (*Series:* Men of Good Will, 4)
Genre(s): War Story.

Ross-Macdonald, Malcolm

◆ 1333. *Dancing on Snowflakes.* New York: St. Martin's, 1994. 341 pp.
When Katy O'Barry falls in love with a socially unacceptable fellow during the 1897 season, her parents send her from Dublin to Stockholm to stay with a strict aunt and uncle.
Genre(s): Love Story.

Roth, Joseph

1334. *The Radetzky March.* Trans. Joachim Neugroschel. New York: Viking, 1995. 352 pp.
Credited with saving the Hapsburg emperor's life, grandfather Trotta becomes a noble, the son a government official, and the profligate grandson, a gambler who meets a senseless death in World War I.
Genre(s): Family Saga; War Story.

Rouaud, Jean

◆ 1335. *Fields of Glory.* Trans. Ralph Manheim. Boston: Little, Brown, 1992. 152 pp.
A grandfather, grandmother, and aunt tell the grandchildren about World War I in the fields of glory at Verdun and Ypres.
Award(s): Prix Goncourt.
Genre(s): War Story.

Rubens, Bernice

1336. *Brothers.* New York: Delacorte, 1983. 468 pp.
The Bindel family faces anti-Semitism from the time of the czars in 19th-century Russia to the present, as the brothers of each generation teach the next a determination to survive.
Genre(s): Family Saga.

Saberhagen, Fred

◆ 1337. *Dancing Bears.* New York: Tor, 1996. 349 pp.
A family during the time of the Romanovs and then the Bolshevik Revolution have the ability to metamorphose into giant bears.
Genre(s): Fantastic Literature.

Sagan, Françoise

1338. *Dear Sarah Bernhardt.* New York: Seaver, 1988. 232 pp.
Bernhardt supposedly corresponds with the author, revealing her true self as daughter, workaholic, and spendthrift.
Genre(s): Biographical Fiction.

Said, Kurban

1339. *Ali and Nino.* Trans. Jenia Graman. New York: Random House, 1971. 237 pp.
In the 1910s, Ali, a Mohammedan of Baku, marries Nino, a Greek Orthodox Georgian he's loved since childhood, and they undergo the distress of the Bolshevik uprising.
Genre(s): Religious Fiction.

Salisbury, Carola

1340. *Count Vronsky's Daughter.* New York: Random House, 1981. 312 pp.
Anni, the daughter of Anna Karenina and Count Vronsky, goes to Paris at 18 to study art and falls in love with a revolutionary.
Genre(s): Romance.

Satta, Salvatore

1341. *The Day of Judgment.* Trans. Patrick Creagh. New York: Farrar, Straus and Giroux, 1987. 350 pp.
Don Sebastiano Sanna is a notary and leading citizen in Nuoro, and he raises his family there in the early 20th century.
Genre(s): Domestic Fiction.

Saunders, Diana

1342. *The Passion of Letty Fox.* New York: Donald I. Fine, 1987. 305 pp.
As the Franco-Prussian War begins, a prefect of police hires Letty to impersonate the Empress Eugénie.
Genre(s): War Story; Adventure Story.

Schnitzler, Arthur

1343. *The Road into the Open.* Trans. Roger Byers. Berkeley: University of California Press, 1992. 314 pp.
At the beginning of the 20th century in Germany, as anti-Semitism rises, Georg, a young musician and composer, attempts to adjust to new responsibilites as father of an illegitimate child.
Genre(s): Musical Fiction.

Scholefield, Alan

◆ 1344. *Fire in the Ice.* New York: St. Martin's, 1984. 281 pp.
David Kade returns to Russia in 1917, after being a refugee from its pogroms, as a millionaire on a mission for Britain, but he is captured and sent to Siberia.
Genre(s): War Story.

Scott, Joanna

1345. *Arrogance.* New York: Linden, 1991. 283 pp.
Egon Schiele is imprisoned in 1912 on charges of corrupting minors and seduction in Vienna.
Genre(s): Biographical Fiction.

Scott, Justin

1346. *A Pride of Royals.* New York: Arbor House, 1983. 503 pp.
King George of England asks an American naval officer to rescue Nicholas II from Russia before the revolution.
Genre(s): War Story.

Seltzer, Richard

1347. *The Name of Hero.* Boston: Houghton Mifflin, 1981. 290 pp.
Alexander Bulatovich fights in the Russo-Chinese War of 1900 and believes himself brave until faced with an ultimate situation.
Genre(s): Biographical Fiction; War Story.

Serge, Victor

1348. *Conquered City.* Trans. Richard Greeman. Garden City, NY: Doubleday, 1975. 194 pp.
Life in the Soviet Union during the civil war of 1917 is corrupt, and the people have unfulfilled ideals.
Genre(s): War Story.

Shapcott, Thomas W.

1349. *White Stag of Exile.* London: Lane, 1984. 171 pp.
Karoly Pulszky, an art historian, becomes so obsessed with creating the Szepmuveszeti Muzeum in Budapest during the late 19th century that he ends up purchasing obvious forgeries.
Genre(s): Biographical Fiction.

Shepard, Jim

1350. *Nosferatu.* New York: Knopf, 1998. 208 pp.
F.W. Murnau, a shy, intellectual boy, falls in love with Hans, but Hans dies in World War I, and Murnau begins making movies, including the first Dracula film, *Nosferatu.*
Genre(s): War Story; Biographical Fiction.

Sherman, Dan

1351. *The Man Who Loved Mata Hari.* New York: Donald I. Fine, 1985. 352 pp.

Nicholas Gray, an English painter living in Paris, falls in love with Mata Hari and believes that charges which lead to her execution for espionage are false.
Genre(s): Love Story; War Story; Spy Fiction; Biographical Fiction.

Sholem Aleichem

1352. *The Adventures of Mottel.* Trans. Tamara Kahana. New York: Abelard-Schuman, 1953. 342 pp.
Mottel tells of his poor family's emigration from a European village to America in the early 20th century.
Genre(s): Humorous Fiction; Jewish Fiction; Domestic Fiction; Picaresque Fiction.

◆ 1353. *The Bloody Hoax.* Trans. Aliza Shevrin. Purdue: Indiana University Press, 1992. 400 pp.
A Jew and a Gentile trade identities for one year after high school, and while the Gentile experiences the discrimination the Jew has endured the Jew enjoys life as a wealthy Russian.
Genre(s): Adventure Story.

Sholokhov, Mikhail

1354. *And Quiet Flows the Don.* 1934. New York: Carroll and Graf, 1996. 554 pp.
Gregor Melekhov, a young married Cossack, lives along the Don River where he engages in military adventures while having a torrid love affair.
Genre(s): War Story.

1355. *The Don Flows Home to the Sea.* New York: Knopf, 1941. 777 pp.
The sequel to *And Quiet Flows the Don* traces a group of Cossacks who fight in the Russian Revolution of 1917 and in the subsequent civil war in 1921.
Genre(s): War Story.

Siciliano, Sam

1356. *The Angel of the Opera.* New York: Scribner's, 1994. 274 pp.
The Paris Opera hires Sherlock Holmes to thwart the Phantom of the Opera's blackmail plan.
Genre(s): Mystery.

Silva, Daniel

1357. *The Unlikely Spy.* New York: Random House, 1997. 448 pp.
Mata Hari and one of her colleagues become the foil for catching the German forces during World War I.
Genre(s): Spy Fiction.

Singer, Isaac Bashevis

1358. *The Estate.* New York: Farrar, Straus and Giroux, 1969. 374 pp.
In the late 19th century, the Jacoby family, in the sequel to *The Manor*, escapes the ghetto for a new but somewhat unfulfilling life.
Genre(s): Jewish Fiction.

1359. *The Family Moskat.* Trans. A.H. Gross. New York: Knopf, 1950. 611 pp.
Reb Meshulam Moskat's wealthy family represents the thoughts and concerns of Jews from the end of the 19th century until the beginning of World War II.
Genre(s): Domestic Fiction; Jewish Fiction.

1360. *The Manor.* New York: Farrar, Straus and Giroux, 1967. 442 pp.
After the Polish insurrection of 1863, the government leases the estate of Count Jampolski to Calman Jacoby, a religious Jewish grain merchant.
Genre(s): Domestic Fiction.

1361. *Scum.* Trans. Rosaline Dukalsky Schwartz. New York: Farrar, Straus and Giroux, 1991. 195 pp.
Max Barabander leaves his adopted home of Argentina after his son dies and his wife has no interest in him and returns to Warsaw where he joins the criminal underground in 1906.

Singer, Israel Joshua

1362. *The Brothers Ashkenazi.* Trans. Joseph Singer. New York: Knopf, 1936. 642 pp.
Max and Jacob Ashkenazi live in Lodz, Poland, where they reflect the rise and fall of its economy.
Genre(s): Jewish Fiction.

Slavitt, David R.

1363. *The Hussar.* Baton Rouge: Louisiana State University Press, 1987. 179 pp.
An officer billeted with a mother and daughter preparing for the Seven Weeks' War finds himself involved with both of them, but when the daughter becomes pregnant, he marries her.
Genre(s): War Story.

Smith, Bert Kruger

1364. *A Teaspoon of Honey.* Nashville, TN: Aurora, 1970. 223 pp.
Herschel Malinsky is fun-loving and successful in Russia at the turn of the century until pogroms force him to leave for America where he eventually earns money in oil which he loses because of poor advice.
Genre(s): Jewish Fiction.

Smith, Helen Zenna

◆ 1365. *Not So Quiet.* New York: Feminist, 1989. 300 pp.
During World War I, loyal young Englishwomen work as volunteer ambulance drivers in France.
Genre(s): War Story.

Smith, Sarah

1366. *The Knowledge of Water.* New York: Ballantine, 1996. 469 pp.
In 1910, Perdita Halley and Alexander von Reisden enter flooded Paris where Perdita determines that she will be-

come a concert pianist even if her marriage is jeopardized, but other factors deter her success.
Genre(s): Mystery; Love Story.

Smith, Wilbur A.

1367. *The Burning Shore.* Garden City, NY: Doubleday, 1985. 420 pp.
During World War I, after Centaine's fiancé dies and her family chateau burns, she travels, with difficulty, to her fiancé's family in South Africa.
Genre(s): Family Saga.

Soliman, Patricia B.

1368. *Coco, the Novel.* New York: Putnam, 1990. 397 pp.
Coco Chanel and a variety of her friends recount her youth as a seamstress, her affairs, and her successful fashion business.
Genre(s): Biographical Fiction.

Solzhenitsyn, Aleksandr

1369. *August 1914.* Trans. Michael Glenny. New York: Farrar, Straus and Giroux, 1972. 854 pp.
General Samsonov and Colonel Vorotyntsev lead Russian soldiers into battle and subsequent defeat at the Battle of Tannenberg in 1914.
Genre(s): War Story.

1370. *Lenin in Zurich.* New York: Farrar, Straus and Giroux, 1976. 256 pp.
Lenin is nasty and obsessive in his desire to foist a revolution on the Russians.
Genre(s): Biographical Fiction.

Stancu, Zaharia

1371. *Barefoot.* Trans. Frank Kirk. New York: Twayne, 1972. 456 pp.
In the early 1900s, Darie sees the peasants rise against the local *boyar* (landowner) and realizes that the only way he can succeed will be to obtain an education, so he begins his struggle to become literate.
Genre(s): War Story; Domestic Fiction.

Stangerup, Henrik

1372. *The Road to Lagoa Santa.* New York: Scribner's, 1984. 288 pp.
P.W. Lund, natural scientist, wants to understand the plan of creation, and he enjoys friendships with other intellectuals, but at 44, he becomes depressed with the dearth of answers to his questions.
Genre(s): Biographical Fiction.

1373. *The Seducer.* Trans. Sean Martin. New York: Marion Boyars, 1990. 316 pp.
Peter Moller, in the 19th century an enemy of Kierkegaard and a critic, cavorts around the back streets

of Paris, having visions and visiting a motley group of people.

Steel, Danielle

1374. *Zoya.* New York: Delacorte, 1988. 446 pp.
Soon after visiting their distant cousin Tsar Nicholas II, Zoya and her grandmother flee Russia for Paris where Zoya loses everything in the stock market crash.
Genre(s): War Story.

Stendhal

1375. *The Charterhouse of Parma.* 1839. New York: Knopf, 1992. 521 pp.
Fabrice appears at a small Italian court and watches the development of the fascinating duchess and her jealous lover.
Genre(s): Love Story; Political Fiction.

Stevens, Robert Tyler

1376. *The Summer Day Is Done.* Garden City, NY: Doubleday, 1976. 424 pp.
John Kirby becomes an English undercover agent in Russia in 1911, and during his service, he develops a friendship with the tsar and his family.
Genre(s): War Story.

Stirling, Jessica

◆ 1377. *The Asking Price.* New York: St. Martin's, 1989. 279 pp.
Craig Nicholson takes his widowed mother and younger siblings into his tenement shared with his wife Kirsty until his mother remarries in the sequel to *The Good Provider.*
Genre(s): Romance.

◆ 1378. *The Good Provider.* New York: St. Martin's, 1988. 352 pp.
A young farm couple tries to survive in 19th-century Glasgow.
Genre(s): Romance.

◆ 1379. *The Wise Child.* New York: St. Martin's, 1989. 328 pp.
Kirsty Barnes and her common-law husband, Craig Nicholson, have domestic problems in the sequel to *The Asking Price.*
Genre(s): Romance.

Stone, Irving

◆ 1380. *Depths of Glory.* Garden City, NY: Doubleday, 1985. 653 pp.
Pissarro, leader of the French Impressionists in the later 19th century, shows his integrity and generosity.
Genre(s): Biographical Fiction.

1381. *The Greek Treasure.* Garden City, NY: Doubleday, 1975. 479 pp.
Henry Schliemann and his wife Sophia discover the city of Troy in their Turkish archaeological digs.
Genre(s): Biographical Fiction.

1382. *Lust for Life.* Garden City, NY: Doubleday, 1934. 500 pp.
Vincent van Gogh lives a tortured life of penury and neglect while painting extraordinary scenes of the life around him.
Genre(s): Biographical Fiction.

1383. *The Passions of the Mind.* Garden City, NY: Doubleday, 1971. 808 pp.
Sigmund Freud works and develops his psychoanalytic theories in Vienna.
Genre(s): Biographical Fiction.

Stryjkowsky, Julian

1384. *The Inn.* Trans. Celina Wieniewska. New York: Harcourt, 1972. 205 pp.
Cossacks invade and occupy east Galicia as World War I begins, and many Jews who suffered in the pogrom of 1905 refuse to believe it can happen again, especially old Tag, who remains in his Inn which has been a place of refuge for many.
Genre(s): War Story; Jewish Fiction.

Stubbs, Jean

◆ 1385. *Eleanora Duse.* New York: Stein And Day, 1970. 320 pp.
Eleanora Duse becomes one of the greatest tragediennes on the international stage in the 19th century.
Genre(s): Biographical Fiction.

1386. *The Painted Face.* New York: Stein and Day, 1974. 287 pp.
In 1902 an English painter goes to France to investigate the death of his sister in a railway accident in 1882.
Genre(s): Mystery.

Sulitzer, Paul-Loup

◆ 1387. *Hannah.* Trans. Christine Donougher. New York: Simon and Schuster, 1989. 416 pp.
Her *shtetl* destroyed in a pogrom, Hannah moves to Warsaw, discovers her business skills, and decides to open salons throughout the world to sell her cosmetics while all the while searching for her friend Taddeuz.
Genre(s): Biographical Fiction.

Sundman, Per Olof

◆ 1388. *The Flight of the Eagle.* Trans. Mary Sandbach. New York: Pantheon, 1970. 383 pp.
Knut Fraenkel keeps a diary of his relationship with Salomon August Andre and their attempt to reach the North Pole in 1897.
Genre(s): Biographical Fiction.

Tarchetti, I. U.

1389. *Passion.* Trans. Lawrence Venuti. San Francisco: Mercury House, 1994. 196 pp.
Fosca falls in love with a new officer in her brother's barracks, but he has another love who is more attractive.
Genre(s): Love Story.

Tennenbaum, Silvia

1390. *Yesterday's Streets.* New York: Random House, 1981. 528 pp.
The German-Jewish Wertheims prosper in the woolen business from the beginning of the 20th century until World War II causes the family to disperse.
Genre(s): War Story.

Thompson, Joan

1391. *Interesting Times.* New York: St. Martin's, 1981. 313 pp.
Two Harvard graduates decide to fight in France during World War I, and they, along with two women, become adults during the fray, but manage to save their lives and their relationships.
Genre(s): War Story; Bildungsroman (Coming of Age).

Tolstoy, Leo

1392. *The Cossacks.* 1862. New York: Viking, 1961. 279 pp.
An educated Russian gentleman falls in love with a beautiful girl.
Genre(s): War Story.

Tomisi di Lampedusa, Giuseppe

1393. *The Leopard.* Trans. Archibald Colquhoun. New York: Knopf, 1991. 300 pp.
Garibaldi's invasion of Sicily in 1860 affects an aristocratic family that once enjoyed the favor of Bourbon kings.

Trachtenberg, Inge

1394. *An Arranged Marriage.* New York: Norton, 1975. 272 pp.
After Lucy von Werner and Herrmann Rosenkrantz marry, Lucy finds that Herrmann suffers from an affliction, and they travel to Vienna, hoping that Sigmund Freud can help.
Genre(s): Love Story.

Trevanian

1395. *The Summer of Katya.* New York: Crown, 1983. 242 pp.
Twenty years after the outbreak of World War I, Dr. Jean-Marc Montjean remembers his love for Katya, a woman he met in a French Basque village.
Genre(s): Romance.

Trollope, Joanna

1396. *The Red and the White.* Trans. Anthony Hinton. New York: Crowell, 1956. 463 pp.
In the sequel to *My Father's House*, family members represent different political beliefs by either supporting the tsar or becoming avid revolutionists during the Bolshevik Revolution and World War I.
Genre(s): War Story.

Troyat, Henri

1397. *Amelie and Pierre.* Trans. Mary V. Dodge.
New York: Simon and Schuster, 1957. 338 pp.
Amelie manages the café when Pierre is drafted into the
army. (*Series:* The Seed and the Fruit, 2)

1398. *My Father's House.* Trans. David Hapgood.
New York: Duell, 1951. 692 pp.
From 1888 to the beginning of World War I, three friends
in Russia have an uneven relationship as they tear apart
and then rebuild their connections.

Tucci, Niccoló

1399. *Before My Time.* New York: Simon and
Schuster, 1962. 638 pp.
Sophie vo Randen, a wealthy Roman widow, decides that
she wants to get her daughter married to a poor Italian
doctor from the countryside.
Genre(s): Romance.

1400. *The Sun and the Moon.* New York: Knopf,
1977. 657 pp.
In the sequel to *Before my Time*, Mary and her suitor
Leonardo belong to two different classes of Italian soci-
ety.
Genre(s): Romance.

Turgenev, Ivan Sergeevich

1401. *Fathers and Children.* Trans. Constance
Garnett. New York: Heinemann, 1895. 358 pp.
Bazarov, a nihilist, advocates a materialistic view of life
and disappoints his adoring parents.
Genre(s): Domestic Fiction.

Valles, Jules

1402. *The Insurrectionist.* Trans. Sandy Petrey.
Englewood Cliffs, NJ: Prentice Hall, 1971. 288 pp.
Jacques Vingtras fights in the French streets during the
1870s, joins the Commune, and escapes to London when
faced with death.
Genre(s): War Story.

Vazov, Ivan

1403. *Under the Yoke.* Trans. Marguerite Alexieva
and Theodora Atanassova. New York: Twayne,
1971. 399 pp.
In 1876 Bulgarians begin an uprising against the Turks,
and the inhabitants of the small town of Byala Cherkva
contribute mightily to the cause.
Genre(s): War Story.

Viertel, Joseph

1404. *Life Lines.* New York: Simon and Schuster,
1982. 526 pp.
After his family has endured more than 100 years of intolerance, Yuri Karpeyko, a Minsk physician, decides to
leave the anti-Semitism of the Soviet Union and emigrate
to the United States.
Genre(s): Jewish Fiction.

Walpole, Hugh

1405. *Secret City.* New York: Doran, 1919. 386 pp.
In the sequel to *Dark Forest*, Henry Trenchard meets Se-
myonov, a Russian soldier, and in Petrograd during 1917,
they and their group become involved in the Russian
Revolution.
Genre(s): War Story.

Weiss, David

1406. *Naked Came I: A Novel of Rodin.* New
York: Morrow, 1963. 660 pp.
Auguste Rodin becomes an important French sculptor
with controversies and love affairs marking his life.
Genre(s): Biographical Fiction.

Werfel, Franz

1407. *The Forty Days of Musa Dagh.* New York:
Carroll and Graf, 1990. 824 pp.
Wealthy Armenian Gabriel Bagradian returns to Syria
from Paris in 1915 and becomes caught in the Turkish
campaign against the Armenians of Musa Dagh.
Genre(s): War Story.

1408. *The Song of Bernadette.* New York: St. Martin's, 1942. 575 pp.
While Bernadette undergoes intense questioning, she
keeps her faith in God.
Genre(s): Religious Fiction.

West, Rebecca

1409. *The Birds Fall Down.* New York: Viking,
1966. 435 pp.
After her grandfather dies from shock on a French train,
an 18-year-old girl forms an alliance with the Russian
double agent who distressed her grandfather.
Genre(s): Spy Fiction.

Wick, Ned Elvin

1410. *Seven Months of Sin.* Rapid City, SD:
Fenwynn, 1974. 204 pp.
In 1917, the Bolsheviks overcome the White Russians
and the czar.
Genre(s): War Story.

Willis, Ted

1411. *The Buckingham Palace Connection.* New
York: Avon, 1978. 288 pp.
When a governess needs to take her Romanov charges
from Ekaterinburg in 1918, a British peer helps them es-
cape on an armored railway train.
Genre(s): Adventure Story.

Wilmot, Anthony

1412. *The Last Bohemian.* London: Macdonald
and Jane's, 1975. 200 pp.
Amedeo Modigliani moves in a distinguished Parisian social circle during his brief career in the early 20th century.
Genre(s): Biographical Fiction.

Yalom, Irvin D.

1413. *When Nietzsche Wept.* New York: Basic, 1992. 306 pp.
Lou Salom asks Josef Breuer, a physician, to help her friend Nietzsche emerge from his depression, not knowing that Breuer is himself depressed.
Genre(s): Medical Novel; Biographical Fiction.

Yarbro, Chelsea Quinn

◆ 1414. *Writ in Blood.* New York: Tor, 1997. 544 pp.
Nicholas II asks Count Ragoczy Saint-Germain to visit Nicholas's uncle Edward VII in Great Britain and his cousin Kaiser Wilhelm of Germany to see if he can get them to agree to reduce arms and avoid a war. (*Series:* Saint-Germain, 12)
Genre(s): Gothic Fiction.

Yasar, Kemal

1415. *Iron Earth, Copper Sky.* Trans. Thilda Kemal. New York: Morrow, 1979. 220 pp.
Peasants of Yalak cannot pay a wealthy creditor after a meager cotton crop, and this causes a clash between the town's leader and a villager.
Genre(s): Country Life.

1416. *Memed, My Hawk.* Trans. Edward Roditi. New York: Pantheon, 1961. 371 pp.
The local agha in a Turkish village drives a young peasant into the hills where he becomes a brigand and local hero.
Genre(s): Country Life.

1417. *The Undying Grass.* Trans. Thilda Kemal. New York: Morrow, 1978. 322 pp.
In the summer, Yalak villagers leave the mountains to pick cotton on the plains while grandmother Meryemdje waits for their return, in the sequel to *Iron Earth, Copper Sky.*
Genre(s): Country Life.

York, Helen

1418. *A Venetian Charade.* New York: Doubleday, 1978. 181 pp.
When Teresa Weston arrives in 19th-century Venice to see her fiancé, she discovers that he is dead and that she may be next on the murderer's list.
Genre(s): Romance; Mystery.

Zencey, Eric

1419. *Panama.* New York: Farrar, Straus and Giroux, 1995. 375 pp.
Henry Adams visits Paris in 1892 and becomes involved in several unexpected situations but spends most of his time investigating the disappearance of an attractive woman on the beach.
Genre(s): Mystery.

Zilinsky, Ursula

1420. *The Long Afternoon.* Garden City, NY: Doubleday, 1984. 432 pp.

In Europe at the beginning of the 20th century, three boys, one German and two English, become friends and remain so during the Great War.
Genre(s): Epic Literature; Romance.

Zola, Émile

1421. *The Conquest of Plassans.* New York: T.B. Peterson, 1874. 328 pp.
Marthe Rougon marries Mouret, but the Abbé, Faujas manages to control her and commit her husband to an insane asylum before he has gone mad. (*Series:* Rougon-Macquart Family, 4)
Genre(s): Family Saga.

1422. *The Debacle.* Trans. John Hands. 1892. Chester Springs, PA: Dufour, 1970. 499 pp.
During the Franco-Prussian war, officers reveal their incompetence and cannot defeat the Prussians. (*Series:* Rougon-Macquart Family, 19)
Genre(s): Family Saga; War Story.

1423. *Doctor Pascal or Life and Heredity.* New York: Cassell, 1893. 471 pp.
Pierre Rougon's son, Pascal, researches the history of his family, and as he studies his own fatal disease, he records its progress hourly. (*Series:* Rougon-Macquart Family, 20)
Genre(s): Family Saga.

1424. *The Downfall.* Trans. Leonard W. Tancock. 1892. New York: Viking, 1973. 510 pp.
Jean Macquart, a corporal in the French forces, accidently kills Maurice Levasseur, one of his enlistments, and this catastrophe makes marrying Levasseur's sister impossible. (*Series:* Rougon-Macquart Family, 10)
Genre(s): War Story; Family Saga.

1425. *The Dream.* New York: T.B. Peterson, 1888. 310 pp.
Angélique, the illegitimate daughter of Sidonie Rougon, is adopted by a family that makes vestments for its church, and when she falls in love with a bishop's son, the father objects to her low birth. (*Series:* Rougon-Macquart Family, 16)
Genre(s): Family Saga.

1426. *Germinal.* Trans. Stanley Hochman and Eleanor Hochman. 1885. New York: New American Library, 1970. 448 pp.
Étienne Lenier works in the mines and leads an ultimately unsuccessful strike against the low wages and fines. (*Series:* Rougon-Macquart Family, 13)
Genre(s): Family Saga.

1427. *Gervaise.* New York: G.W. Carleton, 1877. 381 pp.
Gervaise, pregnant at 14 and driven from her father's home, marries a tinsmith, but they adopt a life of poverty that includes time in the local bar, which destroys the family. (*Series:* Rougon-Macquart Family, 7)
Genre(s): Family Saga.

1428. *Hélène: A Love Episode.* New York: T.B. Peterson, 1880. 334 pp.

Ursule's daughter Hélène succumbs to her love for a doctor, and while her child waits for her at an open window, it catches a fatal illness. (*Series:* Rougon-Macquart Family, 8)
Genre(s): Family Saga.

1429. *His Masterpiece.* New York: Vizetelly, 1888. 383 pp.
Claude Lanier, a painter, is the brother of Étienne and Nana, and although he is an artist with great vision, he becomes despondent and hangs himself. (*Series:* Rougon-Macquart Family, 14)
Genre(s): Family Saga.

1430. *Human Brutes.* New York: Laird and Lee, 1890. 258 pp.
Jacques Lanier, an engineer, inherits the streak of insanity that runs through his family, and he wants to murder women. (*Series:* Rougon-Macquart Family, 17)
Genre(s): Family Saga.

1431. *Joys of Life.* New York: T.B. Peterson, 1884. 424 pp.
Lisa, the market woman, has a daughter named Pauline Quenu, who sacrifices her lover to a friend and raises their child as her own. (*Series:* Rougon-Macquart Family, 12)
Genre(s): Family Saga.

1432. *The Ladies' Paradise.* New York: T.B. Peterson, 1883. 416 pp.
Octave marries the widow Hedouin, and when she dies, he becomes the owner of a large department store. (*Series:* Rougon-Macquart Family, 11)
Genre(s): Family Saga.

1433. *Lourdes.* 1894. Dover, NH: Sutton, 1993. 635 pp.
Pierre Froment, a priest in Paris goes to Lourdes to see if he can cure himself of doubts about his faith.
Genre(s): Christian Fiction.

1434. *Money.* New York: Laird and Lee, 1891. 428 pp.
Aristide Saccard loses his fortune, and he organizes a company to trade in the Orient, which attracts many investors until they are all ruined. (*Series:* Rougon-Macquart Family, 18)
Genre(s): Family Saga.

1435. *Nana.* New York: T.B. Peterson, 1880. 408 pp.
Nana, daughter of Gervaise and Coupeau, is beautiful enough to attract the attention of a theatrical producer of pornography. (*Series:* Rougon-Macquart Family, 9)
Genre(s): Family Saga.

1436. *Paris.* Trans. Ernest Alfred Vizetelly. 1900. Dover, NH: Alan Sutton, 1993. 488 pp.
In the sequel to *Rome*, when priest Pierre Froment returns to Paris after searching for his faith, he decides to leave the church and work for charity.
Genre(s): Christian Fiction.

1437. *Pot-Bouille.* New York: T.B. Peterson, 1882. 328 pp.
Octave, son of François Mouret, lives in a middle-class flat and has difficulty with his servants. (*Series:* Rougon-Macquart Family, 10)
Genre(s): Family Saga.

1438. *Rome.* London: Chatto and Windus, 1896. 587 pp.
In Rome, the priest Pierre Froment asks the pope to support a new Christian socialist order, but the pope refuses, in the sequel to *Lourdes*.
Genre(s): Christian Fiction.

1439. *The Soil.* New York: Vizetelly, 1888. 472 pp.
Peasants want land badly enough so that Jean Macquart's wife is murdered by her own sister. (*Series:* Rougon-Macquart Family, 15)
Genre(s): Family Saga.

Zweig, Arnold

1440. *The Case of Sergeant Grischa.* Trans. Eric Sutton. New York: Viking, 1927. 449 pp.
Grischa, a Russian prisoner-of-war captured by the Germans in 1917, faces the Prussian bureaucracy.
Genre(s): War Story.

1441. *Education before Verdun.* Trans. Eric Sutton. New York: Viking, 1928. 449 pp.
In the sequel to *Young Norman of 1914*, a soldier vows revenge when his younger brother is killed at Verdun in 1916.
Genre(s): War Story.

1442. *Young Woman of 1914.* New York: Viking, 1932. 346 pp.
Lenore Wahl and Werner Bertin fall in love at the beginning of World War I, unaware of the changes which the war will foist upon them.
Genre(s): War Story; Love Story.

Zweig, Stefan

1443. *Beware of Pity.* Trans. Phyllis and Trevor Blewitt. New York: Viking, 1939. 353 pp.
An Austrian army officer, a hero during World War I, becomes careless and causes tragedy.
Genre(s): War Story.

1919-1945

Aaron, David

1444. *Crossing by Night.* New York: Morrow, 1993. 396 pp.

Elizabeth Pack (code name of Cynthia) leaves America and becomes a spy who triumphs by getting the Enigma code from the Germans.
Genre(s): War Story; Spy Fiction; Romance.

◆May be suitable for young adult readers

Agnon, Shmuel Yosef

1445. *A Guest for the Night.* Trans. Misha Louvish. 1939. New York: Schocken, 1968. 485 pp.
A man returns from Palestine to Galacia after World War I and stays at the local inn where he observes the townspeople.
Genre(s): Jewish Fiction; Allegory.

Aksyonov, Vassily

1446. *Generations of Winter.* Trans. John Glad and Christopher Morris. New York: Random House, 1994. 656 pp.
Surgeon Boris Nikitovich Gradov must decide if he will compromise with revolutionary ideals while his children represent the disparate opinions of the Bolsheviks.
Genre(s): Epic Literature; Political Fiction.

Albert, Marvin H.

1447. *Operation Lila.* New York: Arbor House, 1983. 256 pp.
Jonas Ruyter, a British agent, tries to prevent the Nazis from seizing the neutral French fleet in the harbor of Toulon in 1942.
Genre(s): War Story.

Aldridge, James

1448. *One Last Glimpse.* New York: Penguin, 1978. 174 pp.
When Australian Kit Quayle comes to Paris in 1929, he has a letter of introduction to Ernest Hemingway, a man of whom he has never heard, and almost immediately, he becomes a passenger in a car traveling to Brittany with Hemingway and his friend, F. Scott Fitzgerald.
Genre(s): Biographical Fiction; Adventure Story.

Alexander, Lynne

1449. *Safe Houses.* New York: Atheneum, 1985. 261 pp.
Gerda Green, wine waitress at the Hotel Majestic in Budapest, becomes the mistress of both Raoul Wallenberg and Adolf Eichmann near the end of World War II.
Genre(s): Biographical Fiction; War Story.

Allbeury, Ted

1450. *A Time Without Shadows.* New York: Mysterious Press, 1991. 289 pp.
In 1940, British intelligence recruits Philip Maclean, an art student, to create Scorpio, a resistance network, but someone betrays him.
Genre(s): War Story; Mystery.

Anthony, Evelyn

◆ 1451. *The Poellenberg Inheritance.* New York: Coward-McCann, 1972. 249 pp.
Paula discovers that her father, a German general, is alive, and she searches for him throughout Europe while others look for a priceless painting, her inheritance.
Genre(s): Romance.

Appelfeld, Aharon

1452. *Badenheim 1939.* Trans. Dalya Bilu. Boston: D. R. Godine, 1980. 148 pp.
Jewish vacationers visit the resort town of Badenheim near Vienna in 1939 as they have for years, refusing to acknowledge Nazi presence, before they are all herded by the Nazi's into cattle cars bound for concentration camps.
Genre(s): Jewish Fiction.

◆ 1453. *For Every Sin.* Trans. Jeffrey M. Green. New York: Weidenfeld and Nicolson, 1989. 168 pp.
After Theo spends four years in death camps, he drags home to Baden-bei-Wein.
Genre(s): War Story.

1454. *Katerina.* Trans. Jeffrey M. Green. New York: Random House, 1992. 212 pp.
Katerina becomes a servant in a Jewish household in the early 20th century, and when someone kills her child by a Jewish lover, she takes revenge and is subsequently imprisoned.
Genre(s): War Story.

1455. *The Retreat.* Trans. Dalya Bilu. New York: Dutton, 1984. 164 pp.
Lotte Schloss, an aging actress, joins other Jewish men and women at the Retreat outside Vienna in 1937 where they let the founder try to purge them of their Jewishness, but they all backslide.

1456. *To the Land of the Cattails.* Trans. Jeffrey M. Green. New York: Weidenfeld and Nicolson, 1986. 127 pp.
When Toni Strauss leaves Vienna for her village on the river Prut, she takes her son, and although Rudi does not look Jewish, circumstances of their 1938 journey bring him face-to-face with his heritage.
Genre(s): Political Fiction.

1457. *Tzili, the Story of a Life.* Trans. Dalya Bilu. New York: Dutton, 1983. 185 pp.
Tzili, scapegoat of her brilliant family, is left behind when they flee, but she escapes the Holocaust because peasants think she is the local prostitute's daughter.
Genre(s): War Story.

Arnold, Elliott

1458. *A Night of Watching.* New York: Scribner's, 1967. 441 pp.
Various characters describe their situations during 1943 on Yom Kippur when the Danish Underground kept Nazis from transporting 8,000 Danish Jews to Germany.
Genre(s): War Story.

1459. *Proving Ground.* New York: Scribner's, 1973. 309 pp.
An American airplane's crew flies wounded from Yugoslavia to Italy during World War II, and when the plane is shot down, those on board worry about survival.
Genre(s): War Story.

Baddock, James

◆ 1460. *The Dutch Caper.* New York: Walker, 1990. 238 pp.
To defend against Germany's airborne radar, the British need a photograph so they sneak into a Dutch airfield and steal a German plane.
Genre(s): Mystery; Spy Fiction.

Barak, Michael

◆ 1461. *The Enigma.* New York: Morrow, 1978. 302 pp.
A baron goes to Paris to steal an encoding machine from the German High Command during World War II.
Genre(s): War Story.

Barber, Noel

1462. *A Farewell to France.* New York: Macmillan, 1983. 628 pp.
Larry Astell, an American journalist in Paris who grew up in France, tells the story of the occupation of France and the Resistance.
Genre(s): War Story; Love Story.

Barchilon, John

1463. *The Crown Prince.* New York: Norton, 1984. 435 pp.
When the pianist Paul von Wittgenstein loses his right arm in World War I, Maurice Ravel writes the Concerto for the Left Hand for him to perform in postwar Paris.
Genre(s): Biographical Fiction; War Story; Musical Fiction.

Barwick, James

1464. *The Hangman's Crusade.* New York: Coward-McCann, 1981. 345 pp.
Reinhard Heydrich, who wants to erase the Jews and others from Eastern Europe, begins his plot to succeed Hitler.
Genre(s): Biographical Fiction; War Story.

Bass, Ronald

1465. *The Emerald Illusion.* New York: Morrow, 1984. 298 pp.
A German double agent demands that an Allied officer tell about the Normandy invasion plans, but the officer tells the wrong plans.
Genre(s): War Story.

Bassani, Giorgio

◆ 1466. *The Garden of the Finzi-Continis.* Trans. Isabel Quigly. New York: Atheneum, 1965. 293 pp.
Celestino loves Micol Finzi-Contini, who ignores him, and is close friends with her brother Alberto in Ferrora, Italy, where anti-Jewish and facscist sentiment rises in the early 1930s.
Genre(s): Jewish Fiction.

Bates, H. E.

1467. *Fair Stood the Wind for France.* Boston: Little, Brown, 1944. 270 pp.
A British bombardier crashes in France, and the family in a small town nurses him while he falls in love with the household's daughter.
Genre(s): War Story; Love Story.

Beauvoir, Simone de

1468. *The Mandarins.* New York: World, 1954. 610 pp.
The Existentialists and others involved in the politics of the underground and of the liberation comingle in Paris during the 1940s.
Genre(s): War Story; Political Fiction.

Becker, Jurek

1469. *Jacob the Liar.* Trans. Leila Vennewitz. New York: Arcade, 1996. 244 pp.
Jacob Heym tells the people in the ghetto that he has heard a report that Russian troops will liberate them, and that lie leads to others which stop suicides but not the severe beatings.
Genre(s): War Story.

Begley, Louis

◆ 1470. *Wartime Lies.* New York: Knopf, 1991. 197 pp.
The Jewish narrator suffers from being in Poland when the Nazis take over.
Award(s): Ernest Hemingway Foundation Award.
Genre(s): War Story.

Benet, Juan

1471. *A Meditation.* Trans. Gregory Rabassa. 1970. New York: Persea, 1982. 372 pp.
The narrator remembers his life in a Spanish village during the civil war.
Award(s): Biblioteca Breve Prize.
Genre(s): War Story.

Bercovitch, Reuben

◆ 1472. *Hasen.* New York: Knopf, 1978. 142 pp.
Two preteen boys, Perchik and Ritter, live in a forest near a Nazi concentration camp, bribing the soldiers with trapped animals until Perchik's younger brother arrives in the camp.
Genre(s): War Story.

Bergman, Ingmar

1473. *Private Confessions.* Trans. Joan Tate. Boston: Little, Brown, 1997. 176 pp.
In 1925, Anna falls in love with her pastor husband's young friend, and she confesses to members of her family, while feeling revulsion toward her husband, concern for her children, and guilt.
Genre(s): Love Story.

Berliner, Janet, and George Guthridge

1474. ***Child of the Light.*** New York: St. Martin's, 1992. 389 pp.
German citizens watch the rise of Nazism in post-World War I Berlin.
Genre(s): Fantastic Literature; War Story.

Bernhard, Thomas

1475. ***Wittgenstein's Nephew.*** New York: Knopf, 1989. 99 pp.
Paul Wittgenstein, Ludwig's nephew, is also a philosopher, and he becomes friends with Bernhard.
Genre(s): Biographical Fiction.

Beyer, Marcel

1476. ***The Karnau Tapes.*** Trans. John Brownjohn. San Diego, CA: Harcourt, 1997. 256 pp.
Herr Karnau records the voices of everyone, including Hitler during his last days in World War II, and when asked to mind Goebbels's children for a few days, he meets Helga, the general's eight-year-old daughter.
Genre(s): War Story.

Bichelberger, Roger

1477. ***An Ordinary Exodus.*** Trans. Toby Garfitt. Colorado Springs, CO: Lion, 1991. 384 pp.
In the rural French area of Lorraine, Angela faces life raising her unborn child without her lover, killed on the front, and her relationship with her half-witted brother whom the priest has exonerated for drinking all of the eucharistic wine in the church.
Award(s): Prix Roland Dorgeles.
Genre(s): War Story.

Bienek, Horst

◆ 1478. ***Earth and Fire.*** Trans. Ralph Manheim. New York: Atheneum, 1988. 256 pp.
In the sequel to *September Light*, the inhabitants of Gleiwitz watch the Russian army approach in 1945, and some of them escape to other towns while some remain and see their homes destroyed.
Genre(s): War Story.

1479. ***The First Polka.*** Trans. Ralph R. Read. Seattle, WA: Fjord, 1984. 326 pp.
Irma marries a German soldier who has only been quartered in her Upper Silesian home for two weeks, and Poland prepares for the terror of German occupation.
Genre(s): War Story.

1480. ***September Light.*** Trans. Ralph R. Read. New York: Atheneum, 1987. 273 pp.
After Hitler attacks Poland, in the sequel to *The First Polka*, a small Polish town on the Polish-German border seems more interested in the doings of one of its main citizens, but soon the people must react to the Nazis.
Genre(s): War Story.

◆ 1481. *Time Without Bells.* New York: Atheneum, 1988. 352 pp.
In the sequel to *September Light*, the Nazis take the bells from the Gleiwitz church in Upper Silesia on Good Friday in 1943 and the people continue to feel the war's losses even more over the Easter weekend.
Genre(s): War Story.

Black, Campbell

1482. ***Death's Head.*** Philadelphia: Lippincott, 1972. 332 pp.
A Nazi death camp doctor searches for Grünwald the Jew, the only man who can identify him.
Genre(s): War Story; Mystery.

Böll, Heinrich

1483. ***Adam.*** Trans. Leila Vennewitz. New York: McGraw Hill, 1970. 136 pp.
Corporal Feinhals seems to enjoy killing, but the real criminal is the war itself.
Genre(s): War Story; Allegory.

1484. ***And Never Said a Word.*** Trans. Robert Graves. New York: Holt, Rinehart and Winston, 1954. 197 pp.
After a bomb destroyed their home in World War I, a German couple tries to survive with their three children in a tiny deteriorating room.
Genre(s): Domestic Fiction.

1485. ***The Clown.*** Trans. Leila Vennewitz. New York: McGraw Hill, 1965. 247 pp.
After a difficult performance tour, the clown Hans Schnier reconstructs his experiences as a Catholic during World War II and after it in a materialistic society.
Genre(s): Religious Fiction; War Story.

1486. *A Soldier's Legacy.* Trans. Leila Vennewitz. New York: Knopf, 1985. 144 pp.
Lieutenant Schelling fights for Germany in 1943, first at the Atlantic Wall in Normandy and then on the Russian front.
Genre(s): War Story.

1487. ***The Train.*** Trans. Leila Vennewitz. New York: McGraw Hill, 1970. 132 pp.
In 1935, a German soldier boards a train in the Ruhr on which he spends five days before arriving at the Eastern front.
Genre(s): War Story.

Bor, Josef

1488. ***The Terezn Requiem.*** Trans. Edith Pargeter. New York: Knopf, 1963. 112 pp.
A group of Jews rehearse and perform Verdi's *Requiem* in a Czechoslovakian concentration camp.
Genre(s): War Story; Jewish Fiction.

Bove, Emmanuel

1489. ***Armand.*** Trans. Janet Louth. New York: Harper, 1987. The British Isles pp.
Armand becomes the kept man of a middle-aged World War I widow, and when a crude friend from the war ap-

pears, Armand, at first, does not want to acknowledge him.
Genre(s): War Story.

1490. *The Stepson.* New York: Marlboro, 1994. 314 pp.
When Jean-Noel Oetinger becomes infatuated with his stepmother after returning from the army in 1920, he has trouble making decisions because of his marriage to a lower-class woman.

Bowering, Marilyn

1491. *Visible Worlds.* New York: HarperCollins, 1998. 288 pp.
Twin brothers, one a Nazi officer, and the other, a peacemaker, contend with family secrets.
Genre(s): War Story.

Boyne, Walter J.

◆ 1492. *Eagles at War.* New York: Crown, 1991. 392 pp.
Frank Bandfield and Hadley Roget begin the Allied aviation force during World War II to fight the German air force led by Bruno Hafner.
Genre(s): War Story; Adventure Story.

Bridge, Ann

1493. *The Tightening String.* New York: McGraw Hill, 1962. 250 pp.
A kind wife of a British diplomat in Budapest suffers the family's difficulties while trying to help others.
Genre(s): Domestic Fiction; Political Fiction.

Brinkley, William

1494. *The Ninety and Nine.* Garden City, NY: Doubleday, 1966. 393 pp.
Members of the crew of a landing ship tank move between Naples and Anzio and fall in love with members of the civilian population.
Genre(s): War Story; Love Story; Picaresque Fiction.

Briskin, Jacqueline

1495. *The Other Side of Love.* New York: Delacorte, 1991. 566 pp.
Some of the Kingsmith cousins participate and win at the 1936 Olympics in Hitler's Germany before falling in love.
Genre(s): War Story; Sports Fiction; Love Story.

Briskin, Mae

◆ 1496. *The Tree Still Stands.* New York: Norton, 1991. 256 pp.
As Ruth and her family move across Europe during World War II trying to escape the Nazis, they are helped by others with a sense of justice.
Genre(s): War Story.

Broner, Peter

1497. *Night of the Broken Glass.* Barrytown, NY: Station Hill, 1991. 316 pp.

Paul, raised as Jewish but biologically Aryan, Johann, a streetcar conductor turned rebel, and Martin, an industrialist trying to save Jews, react to the Nazis by overcoming their fears of fighting the regime.
Genre(s): War Story.

Brown, Harry

1498. *A Walk in the Sun.* New York: Knopf, 1944. 187 pp.
When the lieutenant and three sergeants die when an American platoon lands on an Italian beach, a corporal takes lead and helps the group accomplish its mission.
Genre(s): War Story.

Bruckner, Christine

1499. *Gillyflower Kid.* New York: Fromm International, 1982. 357 pp.
Maximiliane Quindt grows up as a Pomeranian heiress, marries an officer in the Third Reich, and raises her family until the Reich falls and she has to escape to survive.
Genre(s): War Story.

Buchheim, Lothar Gunther

1500. *The Boat.* Trans. Denver and Helen Lindley. New York: Knopf, 1975. 463 pp.
A German submarine patrols the Atlantic in 1941 searching for British convoys.
Genre(s): War Story; Sea Story.

Buckley, William F. Jr.

1501. *Brothers No More.* New York: Doubleday, 1995. 304 pp.
During World War II, Danny O'Hara, grandson of Franklin Delano Roosevelt, saves his Yale roommate, Henry Chafee when Henry turns coward, but in their lives after the war, the situation shifts.
Genre(s): War Story.

Bulatovic, Miodrag

1502. *The War Was Better.* New York: McGraw Hill, 1972. 424 pp.
Antonio's adventures begin in World War II in Montenegro, and he joins Peppe, Anna-Maria (a turtle), and a German in an exploration of the insanity of war.
Genre(s): War Story; Picaresque Fiction.

Burke, James Wakefield

1503. *Arli.* Ottawa, IL: Caroline House, 1978. 296 pp.
While the Russians besiege Berlin, Arliana Markgraf, committed to the Hitler youth, thinks of Hitler in sexual terms as she falls in love with Bruno Bassermann, the perfect Aryan, who becomes a killer after an extermination assignment.
Genre(s): War Story.

Bykov, Vasily

1504. *The Ordeal.* Trans. Gordon Clough. New York: Dutton, 1972. 170 pp.

Rybak and Sotnikov, Russian partisans, forage for food in the winter, and they encounter Russian defectors, of which Sotnikov kills one, and when they are captured, Rybak chooses to defect and Sotnikov, to hang.
Genre(s): War Story.

1505. *Sign of Misfortune.* Trans. Alan Myers. New York: Allerton, 1990. 296 pp.
During Stalin's collectivization and the time of World War II, a peasant couple, Petroc and Stepanida endure the cruelty of the Nazis and the police while managing to maintain their own kindness and sense of justice.
Genre(s): War Story.

Casey, Jane Barnes

1506. *I, Krupskaya: My Life with Lenin.* Boston: Houghton Mifflin, 1974. 327 pp.
Lenin's wife Krupskaya begins having affairs when her husband cuts her off from the political decisions of the revolution.
Genre(s): Biographical Fiction.

Caso, Adolph

1507. *The Straw Obelisk.* Boston: Branden, 1995. 390 pp.
When Samuele returns to his Neapolitan village after three years in World War II, he forgives his sister for her illegitimate child, takes the child, and tries to reunite with his love against a backdrop of preparations for the religious festival of the Straw Obelisk.
Genre(s): War Story.

Cela, Camilo Jose

1508. *Mazurka for Two Dead Men.* Trans. Patricia Haugaard. New York: New Directions, 1992. 312 pp.
Following the clues for solving two murders in Galicia during the Spanish Civil War is difficult.
Award(s): Spanish National Prize for Literature.
Genre(s): War Story; Mystery.

1509. *San Camilo, 1936: The Eve, Feast, and Octave of St Camillus.* Trans. J.H.R. Polt. Durham: Duke University Press, 1991. 302 pp.
A cynical student sees the sordid private and public attitudes in Madrid that allow the civil war to begin in Spain.
Genre(s): War Story.

Céline, Louis-Ferdinand

1510. *Castle to Castle.* Trans. Ralph Manheim. New York: Delacorte, 1957. 359 pp.
In the sequel to *North,* the narrator tries to protect his family during the war in Germany.
Genre(s): War Story.

1511. *Death on the Installment Plan.* Trans. Ralph Manheim. New York: Delacorte, 1968. 359 pp.
An old man relates memories of his youth, especially his time spent during World War II.
Genre(s): Biographical Fiction.

1512. *North.* Trans. Ralph Manheim. New York: Delacorte, 1972. 454 pp.
The narrator endures Germany from 1944 to 1945 as he tries desperately to get his family out of Nazi territory before the war ends.
Genre(s): Adventure Story; Biographical Fiction; Picaresque Fiction; War Story.

Chaix, Marie

1513. *The Laurels of Lake Constance.* Trans. Harry Mathews. New York: Viking, 1977. 196 pp.
A French family collaborates with the enemy, beginning in 1936, and endures increasing misfortunes during World War II.
Genre(s): War Story.

Charney, Ann

1514. *Dobryd.* Sag Harbor, NY: Permanent, 1996. 176 pp.
The narrator, who is five when Soviet soldiers liberate her, her mother, and her aunt from a barn where they have hidden for over two years outside Dobryd, Poland, helps to reclaim the city before moving to Canada to escape further Jewish persecution.
Genre(s): War Story.

Clark, Tom

1515. *The Exile of Céline.* New York: Random House, 1986. 214 pp.
Céline, French novelist, supposedly collaborated with the Nazis during World War II, but he actually had little respect for Hitler, and may have been accused unjustly.
Genre(s): Biographical Fiction; War Story.

Clarke, Caro

1516. *The Wolf Ticket.* Ithaca, NY: Firebrand, 1998. 216 pp.
Near the end of World War II, Pascale Tailland rescues a refugee who becomes her lesbian lover.
Genre(s): War Story; Romance.

Claus, Hugo

◆ 1517. *Sorrow of Belgium.* New York: Pantheon, 1990. 624 pp.
Louis's Flemish father is pleased to have Gestapo connections during World War II, and Louis's mother talks of her responsibility for German munitions, as Louis matures in the conflicting atmosphere of Flemish and French traditions.
Genre(s): Bildungsroman (Coming of Age); War Story.

Clavel, Bernard

1518. *The Spaniard.* Trans. W.G. Corp. Washington, DC: Regnery, 1971. 328 pp.
A Spanish refugee from the civil war comes to southern France, and during World War II, he attempts to reconcile the loss of his wife and home.
Award(s): Prix Goncourt.
Genre(s): War Story.

Cleary, Jon

1519. *City of Fading Light.* New York: Morrow, 1986. 351 pp.
In 1939, American actress Cathleen O'Dea arrives in Berlin to make a film for Goebbels, but she secretly searches for her Jewish mother.
Genre(s): War Story.

1520. *The Golden Sabre.* New York: Morrow, 1981. 300 pp.
In the Soviet Union, just after the Bolshevik Revolution, an American oil agent accidently kills a general who has tried to rape an English governess, and the two, with her charges, escape to southern Russia to find the children's parents.
Genre(s): Romance; Adventure Story.

Cordell, Alexander

1521. *To Slay the Dreamer.* New York: St. Martin's, 1980. 288 pp.
Richard Hanson, a specialist in assassination from the International Brigade in Madrid, is assigned to assassinate Franco in the Spanish Civil War.
Genre(s): War Story; Spy Fiction.

Crichton, Robert

1522. *The Secret of Santa Vittoria.* New York: Simon and Schuster, 1966. 447 pp.
Germans and Italians clash in the town of Santa Vittoria during World War II, but the townspeople have hidden their one million bottles of wine and refuse to reveal the location.
Genre(s): War Story.

Dagan, Avigdor

◆ 1523. *The Court Jesters.* Trans. Barbara Harshav. Philadelphia: Jewish Publications, 1989. 180 pp.
Four Jewish men, entertainers for Nazi troops as juggler, dwarf, astrologer, and hunchback, feel the guilt of survival after World War II when some of them meet in Jerusalem.
Genre(s): War Story.

Davis, J. Madison

1524. *The Murder of Frau Schutz.* New York: Walker, 1988. 259 pp.
Anthropologist Max von Prokofsk investigates the death of the wife of the Ostheim concentration camp's commandant and has to find out whether the prisoners or the commandant killed her.
Genre(s): War Story.

De Bernières, Louis

1525. *Corelli's Mandolin.* New York: Pantheon, 1994. 437 pp.
Corelli, an Italian army captain, falls in love with Pelagia Iannis on the island of Cephalonia after the Axis forces occupy the island in World War II.
Award(s): Commonwealth Writers' Prize.
Genre(s): War Story.

De Ferrari, Gabriella

1526. *A Cloud on Sand.* New York: Knopf, 1989. 323 pp.
In the 1920s, wealthy Donna Dora advertises her love affairs, but her children suffer, especially Antonia who tries to free herself from her mother's influence, until Donna Dora marries Arturo, a decision good for all.
Genre(s): War Story.

De Hartog, Jan

◆ 1527. *The Captain.* New York: Atheneum, 1966. 434 pp.
In 1942, after escaping from the Nazis, a Dutch captain takes command of a convoy ship slated for duty on the Iceland-Murmansk run.
Genre(s): War Story; Sea Story.

◆ 1528. *The Lamb's War.* New York: Atheneum, 1980. 443 pp.
In the sequel to *The Peculiar People*, when Laura Martens tries to help her Quaker father in a German concentration camp, a Nazi commandant rapes her, and the guards beat her father to death while she becomes an amnesiac for three years as the officer's concubine.
Genre(s): War Story.

◆ 1529. *Star of Peace.* New York: Harper and Row, 1984. 376 pp.
The captain on a small Dutch freighter becomes frustrated when no ports in North or South America will take the Jews on his ship who are trying to escape from the Nazis.
Genre(s): War Story; Sea Story; Christian Fiction.

De Luca, Teresa

◆ 1530. *A Distant Thunder.* New York: Morrow, 1990. 549 pp.
Dolores Carrasquez returns to her wealthy Spanish family's home, only to find that it is no longer the same, and when war breaks out, she flees the devastation in her country.
Genre(s): War Story.

Debreczeny, Paul

1531. *Temptations of the Past.* Ann Arbor, MI: Hermitage, 1982. 102 pp.
When Egor, a Soviet writer, returns to Paris in 1935, he remembers his first visit there when he was with Dunia.
Genre(s): Love Story.

Deighton, Len

1532. *Bomber.* New York: Harper and Row, 1970. 424 pp.
In June 1943, an RAF squadron, its German Luftwaffe counterparts, and the people in a small German town experience the thrust of the war.
Genre(s): War Story.

1533. *Winter: A Berlin Family.* London: Hutchinson, 1987. 536 pp.

Paul and Peter Winter, sons of a Berlin banker and his American wife, take divergent paths during World War II when one becomes a Nazi and the other an American informer.
Genre(s): War Story; Domestic Fiction.

Del Castillo, Michel

1534. *Child of Our Time.* Trans. Peter Green. New York: Knopf, 1958. 281 pp.
Tanguy, half Spanish and half French, goes into exile with his mother in France during the Spanish Civil War, and after his father betrays his mother to the police, Nazis intern Tanguy in a concentration camp.
Genre(s): War Story.

1535. *The Disinherited.* Trans. Humphrey Hare. New York: Knopf, 1960. 273 pp.
Olny lives in a squalid area of Madrid during the Spanish Civil War, and he is drawn into the Communist party because of his experiences.
Genre(s): War Story.

Delibes, Miguel

◆ 1536. *The Stuff of Heroes.* Trans. Francis M. Lopez-Morillas. New York: Pantheon, 1990. 295 pp.
A Spanish family becomes involved in the tragedy of civil war.
Genre(s): War Story.

Demetz, Hanna

◆ 1537. *The House on Prague Street.* New York: St. Martin's, 1980. 186 pp.
At the beginning of World War II, Helena, who is half Jewish, has to adjust to the loss of friends and fears for her mother while spending 12-hour days working in an armaments factory.
Genre(s): War Story; Jewish Fiction.

Denny, Robert

1538. *Aces.* New York: Donald I. Fine, 1991. 291 pp.
In World War II, pilots Mitchell M. Robinson and Lon Amundson, from a small Pennsylvania town, become part of the skies over Germany as they fly B-17s through flak and bad weather.
Genre(s): War Story.

1539. *Night Run.* New York: Donald I. Fine, 1992. 387 pp.
Mike Gavin, an American pilot, flies with the Soviet forces at night, but during a raid, he has to abandon his B-17 behind Soviet lines.
Genre(s): War Story.

Dial, Joan

◆ 1540. *Echoes of War.* New York: St. Martin's, 1984. 352 pp.
Royal Air Force pilot Tony Winfield saves Kate Kieron's life in Berlin, and after he is shot down, he finds her or-

ganization, and the two flee to England, marry, and try to overcome the forces against them.
Genre(s): War Story; Love Story.

Dijk, Lutz van

◆ 1541. *Damned Strong Love.* Trans. Elizabeth D. Crawford. New York: Holt, 1995. 138 pp.
Two males develop their relationship during World War II when Stephan K. falls in love with an Austrian-German soldier.
Genre(s): War Story.

Dis, Adriaan van

1542. *My Father's War.* Trans. Claire N. White. New York: New Press, 1996. 261 pp.
A mixed-race family goes to Holland after escaping a Japanese concentration camp in the Dutch East Indies, only to find that the Dutch do not accept them as full citizens when the war ends.
Genre(s): Domestic Fiction; War Story.

Doderer, Heimito von

1543. *The Demons.* Trans. Richard and Clara Winston. New York: Knopf, 1961. 1334 pp.
During the nine months prior to the burning of the Austrian Supreme Court Building on July 15, 1927, people from all aspects of Viennese life become affected by their situations.
Genre(s): Picaresque Fiction.

Durrell, Lawrence

1544. *Constance: Or, Solitary Practices.* New York: Viking, 1982. 393 pp.
World War II affects the English in Avignon, especially those at Constance's villa. (*Series:* Avignon Quintet, 3)
Genre(s): Love Story; War Story.

1545. *Livia: Or, Buried Alive.* New York: Viking, 1979. 265 pp.
In the period between World War I and World War II, an English colony gathers in Avignon with Livia and the British consul, who is destined to write a novel *Monsieur*. (*Series:* Avignon Quintet, 1)

1546. *Monsieur.* New York: Viking, 1975. 305 pp.
Bruce, an English doctor, goes to Avignon to be with his French wife after her brother dies under mysterious circumstances. (*Series:* Avignon Quintet, 2)
Genre(s): Family Saga.

◆ 1547. *White Eagles over Serbia.* 1957. New York: Arcade, 1995. 200 pp.
Meuthen spies in the mountains of Serbia after Tito and the Communists take rule, and he discovers a hostile band of royalists, the White Eagles, trying to overthrow the government.
Genre(s): Spy Fiction.

Elman, Richard M.

1548. *Lilo's Diary.* New York: Scribner's, 1968. 155 pp.

The sequel to *The 28th Day of Elul* allows Lilo to tell her version of being exchanged for Alex's parents' freedom in World War II.
Genre(s): War Story.

1549. *The Reckoning.* New York: Scribner's, 1969. 184 pp.
In the sequel to *Lilo's Diary*, Hungarian Newman Yagodah uses most of his energy in 1944 trying to conceal his gentile mistress from his Jewish wife while he ignores the world around him.
Genre(s): War Story.

1550. *The 28th Day of Elul.* New York: Scribner's, 1967. 279 pp.
Alex Yagodah, a refugee in Israel, receives the news that his uncle has left him money in a will dated the 28th day of Elul, 5700 (September 12, 1939) if he can profess himself to be a practicing Jew.
Genre(s): War Story.

Elon, Amos

1551. *Timetable.* Garden City, NY: Doubleday, 1980. 349 pp.
When Adolf Eichmann offers Joel Brand, a member of the Hungarian Jewish Aid and Rescue Committee, the trade of 100 Jews for each Allied truck he can find, Brand attempts to save one million lives.
Genre(s): Biographical Fiction; War Story.

Epstein, Leslie

1552. *King of the Jews.* New York: Coward-McCann, 1979. 350 pp.
Isaiah Chaim Trumpelman, leader of the Judenrat, a council selecting quotas for Nazi transport trains, may or may not have saved lives from his position.
Genre(s): War Story; Jewish Fiction.

Ettinger, Elzbieta

◆ 1553. *Kindergarten.* Boston: Houghton Mifflin, 1970. 320 pp.
A young Jewish girl tries to escape the German troops occupying Poland.
Genre(s): War Story.

Farrell, Michael J.

1554. *Papabile: The Man Who Would Be Pope.* New York: Crossroad, 1998. 191 pp.
Communist Hugh Ovath has the job of infiltrating the Roman Catholic Church after World War II, but when he becomes a priest, he rises in power and begins to resent the strangling Communist party.
Genre(s): Christian Fiction; Political Fiction.

Fast, Howard

◆ 1555. *The Bridge Builder's Story.* Armonk, NY: M. E. Sharpe, 1995. 210 pp.
Scott Waring and his wife go to Berlin for their honeymoon in 1939 and see the Gestapo in action, but when

Scott helps to liberate Buchenwald at the end of the war, he undergoes prolonged trauma.
Genre(s): Love Story; War Story.

Feinstein, Elaine

1556. *Loving Brecht.* London: Hutchinson, 1992. 187 pp.
Frieda Bloom, a 1920s Berlin cabaret singer, follows Brecht from Berlin to Moscow, New York, and London, where she becomes part of his extended family while attempting to keep him from dominating her.
Genre(s): Biographical Fiction; Love Story.

Fejes, Endré

1557. *Generation of Rust.* Trans. Sanford Greenburger. New York: McGraw Hill, 1970. 215 pp.
As they complain about their lives after World War I, the Habetlers always find the family to be a central refuge until one of them kills a man in 1962.
Genre(s): Political Fiction; Family Saga.

Ferguson, James

1558. *Out of the Whirlwind.* Providence, RI: INTI, 1982. 241 pp.
A young Resistance fighter gives a stream-of-consciousness account of Germans who retaliate by killing French citizens after a convoy raid in World War II.
Genre(s): War Story.

Fink, Ida

◆ 1559. *The Journey.* Trans. Francine Prose and Joanna Weschler. New York: Farrar, Straus and Giroux, 1992. 249 pp.
When two Jewish sisters escape the Polish ghetto in 1942 disguised as peasants, they search for jobs in dangerous Germany.
Genre(s): War Story.

Fitzgerald, F. Scott

1560. *Tender Is the Night.* New York: Scribner's, 1934. 315 pp.
Dick Diver, a young psychiatrist, marries a wealthy woman whose pursuit of glitter effectively destroys him.
Genre(s): Love Story.

Fleming, Thomas

1561. *Loyalties.* New York: HarperCollins, 1994. 574 pp.
In 1941, Ernst von Hoffman destroys an American ship by mistake but saves the skipper, while in Berlin, his wife opposes Hitler and is sent to Spain to contact and seduce the same man that her husband saved.
Genre(s): War Story; Family Saga.

Follett, Ken

1562. *Eye of the Needle.* New York: Arbor House, 1978. 313 pp.

British Intelligence must thwart Die Nadel, the only spy Hitler trusts, from reaching Hitler to tell about the 1944 invasion of France.
Award(s): Edgar Allan Poe Award.
Genre(s): War Story.

Forbes, Colin

1563. *The Heights of Zervos.* New York: Dutton, 1971. 246 pp.
When oil tank cars explode in a Bucharest rail yard, a German begins trailing the spy who executed it, planning to kill him and assume his identity.
Genre(s): War Story; Spy Fiction.

1564. *The Palermo Affair.* New York: Dutton, 1972. 255 pp.
To allow the Allies to invade Sicily, the last ferry between Sicily and Italy must be destroyed, and an American and a British officer achieve the almost impossible feat.
Genre(s): War Story.

Forester, C. S.

1565. *The Ship.* Boston: Little, Brown, 1943. 281 pp.
The British light cruiser *Artemis* is taking part in a convoy of supplies to Malta when the Italian fleet attacks.
Genre(s): War Story; Sea Story.

Forman, James D.

◆ 1566. *Ceremony of Innocence.* New York: Dutton, 1970. 208 pp.
Captured for treason by the Gestapo in 1943, Hans decides to die rather than be in debt to the guard who offers to free him.
Genre(s): War Story.

◆ 1567. *The Survivor.* New York: Farrar, Straus and Giroux, 1976. 272 pp.
Nazis catch David's family trying to escape in coffins, but David survives the concentration camps and discovers that his sister has left for Palestine.
Genre(s): War Story.

Frances, Stephen

1568. *La Guerra: A Spanish Saga.* New York: Delacorte, 1970. 640 pp.
The poor people who live in the Spanish village of Escoleras suffer the devastation of the civil war when it disrupts their lives.
Genre(s): War Story; Family Saga; Country Life.

Francis, Clare

1569. *Night Sky.* New York: Morrow, 1984. 631 pp.
After Julie Lescaux flees England for France during the war, so that her friends will not know that she is expecting a child out of wedlock, she becomes involved in evacuating Allied servicemen from occupied France.
Genre(s): War Story.

Frankau, Pamela

1570. *Over the Mountains.* New York: Random House, 1967. 340 pp.
In the sequel to *Slaves of the Lamp*, Thomas Weston, believed by his family to be dead, is captured at Dunkirk and escapes, only to be caught by the Spanish at the border.
Genre(s): War Story.

Fraser, David

1571. *Adam in the Breach.* Hampton, NH: Severn House, 1993. 352 pp.
Major Hardrow, a British officer, commands a company in the Normandy invasion of World War II, after which he goes to Madrid in with the hope of negotiating with antiwar Germans who want peace.
Genre(s): War Story.

Freeman, Gillian

1572. *The Confessions of Elisabeth von S.* New York: Dutton, 1978. 255 pp.
Elisabeth Von S. is the wife of a filmmaker in Goebbels's propaganda organization during World War II, and she keeps a diary of the mundaneness of life as well as the attitudes of those around her toward Jews and Slavs.
Genre(s): War Story.

Frizell, Bernard

1573. *The Grand Defiance.* New York: Morrow, 1972. 320 pp.
When Germans capture France's leading general and imprison him in Germany early in World War II, he decides that he must escape, and a French civilian helps him achieve his goal.
Genre(s): War Story; Adventure Story.

Fuks, Ladislav

1574. *The Cremator.* New York: Boyars, 1984. 179 pp.
Karel Kopfkringl loves his job running the Prague crematorium in 1939 because he likes to liberate the souls of the dead, and his German friend encourages his rationalization as Karel tries to free his own wife and son, who have Jewish blood, from their terrible fates.
Genre(s): War Story.

Fullerton, Alexander

1575. *A Share of Honour.* London: Pan, 1982. 282 pp.
In 1942, the submarine war in the Mediterranean causes St. Nazaire's destruction.
Genre(s): War Story; Sea Story.

Furst, Alan

1576. *Dark Star.* Boston: Houghton Mifflin, 1991. 417 pp.

The Soviet government forces a *Pravda* journalist to become an intelligence agent in the years prior to World War II.
Genre(s): Spy Fiction.

1577. *Night Soldiers.* Boston: Houghton Mifflin, 1988. 437 pp.
Khristo, a Bulgarian member of the Soviet espionage team, feels betrayed by the Spanish Civil War, and he disappears in Paris during World War II, while trying to expose the Soviets to their enemies.
Genre(s): War Story; Spy Fiction.

1578. *The Polish Officer.* New York: Random House, 1995. 384 pp.
Captain Alexander de Milja changes his disguise as he moves from country to country during World War II, spying on the Germans and working as a cartographer.
Genre(s): War Story; Spy Fiction.

1579. *The World at Night.* New York: Random House, 1996. 257 pp.
Jean Casson, a film producer working undercover for the French against the Germans in World War II Paris, finds himself functioning also for the British and the Germans, against his will.
Genre(s): Love Story; War Story.

Furst, Peter

1580. *Don Quixote in Exile.* Chicago: Northwestern UP, 1996. 260 pp.
When a sports journalist who happens to be Jewish goes to Monte Carlo to cover an automobile race in 1937, he realizes that returning to Berlin might be dangerous so he begins an odyssey to Spain, Austria, Czechoslovakia, and France.
Genre(s): War Story.

Gainham, Sarah

1581. *Night Falls on the City.* New York: Holt, Rinehart and Winston, 1967. 571 pp.
During World War II, Julia Homburg manages to hide her Jewish husband in her Vienna apartment.
Genre(s): War Story; Romance.

Garfield, Brian

◆ 1582. *The Romanov Succession.* New York: M. Evans, 1974. 413 pp.
British and American aid support a White Russian plot to assassinate Stalin in World War II.
Genre(s): War Story.

Gavin, Catherine Irvine

1583. *The House of War.* New York: Morrow, 1970. 350 pp.
When American Evelyn Barrett and her foreign correspondent husband go to Turkey in the 1920s, she meets Kemal Atatürk who wants to marry her after an affair, but she refuses.
Genre(s): Biographical Fiction; War Story.

1584. *None Dare Call It Treason.* New York: St. Martin's, 1978. 285 pp.
A small Resistance group fights the Germans when they occupy France in World War II.
Genre(s): War Story.

Gerson, Jack

1585. *Death's Head, Berlin.* New York: St. Martin's, 1989. 224 pp.
Lohmann, a policeman, investigates several deaths in Germany during 1934, and since he hates Nazis, he is especially pleased to reveal a party official's Jewish background.
Genre(s): Adventure Story; Mystery.

Giardina, Denise

1586. *Saints and Villains.* New York: Norton, 1998. 480 pp.
After studying at New York's Union Theological Seminary, Dietrich Bonhoeffer wonders if committing a crime for a greater good is ethical, and when he returns to Germany, he discovers changes under Hitler, starts speaking against the Nazis, and is imprisoned.
Genre(s): Christian Fiction; Biographical Fiction.

Gille, Elisabeth

◆ 1587. *Shadows of a Childhood.* Trans. Linda Coverdale. New York: New Press, 1998. 144 pp.
After her parents disappear to concentration camps, Lea goes to a Catholic boarding school in Bordeaux and becomes friends with saintly Benedicte, and when Benedicte's parents adopt Lea after the war ends, they send her to the Sorbonne where she confronts a Jew-killer.
Award(s): Grand Prix de Lectrices.
Genre(s): War Story.

Gilliatt, Penelope

1588. *A Woman of Singular Occupation.* New York: Scribner's, 1988. 180 pp.
A couple meet on the Orient Express going to Istanbul, fall in love, and suffer World War II intrigues.
Genre(s): War Story.

Gilman, J. D., and John Clive

◆ 1589. *KG 200.* New York: Simon and Schuster, 1977. 317 pp.
In World War II, members of the KG 200 Luftwaffe corps pretend to be Allied pilots while focusing on their primary target, Whitehall, Britain's command center.
Genre(s): War Story.

Gilroy, Frank D.

1590. *Private.* New York: Harcourt, 1970. 160 pp.
A draftee learns that the army is not democratic as World War II ends, and he returns from the European front.
Genre(s): War Story; Bildungsroman (Coming of Age).

◆May be suitable for young adult readers

Giovene, Andrea

1591. *The Book of Giuliano Sansevero.* Trans. Marguerite Waldman. Boston: Houghton Mifflin, 1970. 384 pp.
The second son in a Neapolitan family of nobility leaves home for a monastery, and after his travels, he returns to become a kind landlord of the family's estate.
Genre(s): Domestic Fiction; Bildungsroman (Coming of Age).

1592. *The Dice of War: The Book of Giuliano Sansevero.* Trans. Bernard Wall. Boston: Houghton Mifflin, 1974. 231 pp.
Giuliano Sansevero, stationed in the French Alps with the Italian army, moves from his boring garrison duty to a German concentration camp in the sequel to *The Dilemma of Love.*
Genre(s): War Story.

1593. *The Dilemma of Love: The Book of Giuliano Sansevero.* Trans. Bernard Wall. Boston: Houghton Mifflin, 1973. 253 pp.
Giuliano builds a house with the help of peasants and craftsmen in Licudi while World War II threatens in the sequel to *The Book of Giuliano Sansevero.*
Genre(s): War Story.

Gironella, Jos Mara

1594. *The Cypresses Believe in God.* Trans. Harriet de Onis. New York: Knopf, 1955. 1010 pp.
Ignacio Alvear, eldest son of a Catalonian middle-class family, reveals the people inhabiting his small town in the days prior to Spain's civil war.
Genre(s): War Story.

1595. *One Million Dead.* Trans. Joan MacLean. Garden City, NY: Doubleday, 1963. 684 pp.
In the sequel to *The Cypresses Believe in God,* the Alvear family divides in its allegiances during Spain's civil war.
Genre(s): War Story.

1596. *Peace after War.* Trans. Joan MacLean. New York: Knopf, 1969. 774 pp.
After the civil war ends in Spain, in the sequel to *One Million Dead,* the Alvear family reunites in Gerona and tries to function in the face of shortages and animosities left from the war.
Genre(s): Family Saga.

Glasco, Gordon

◆ 1597. *Slow Through Eden.* New York: Poseidon, 1992. 459 pp.
When students at Germany's Physics Institute, David (an American Jew) and Katherine (a German), fall in love and marry, they both work on the atomic bomb, and it irrevocably influences their lives together.
Genre(s): War Story; Love Story.

Glatstein, Jacob

1598. *Homeward Bound.* Trans. Abraham Goldstein. New York: Yoseloff, 1969. 142 pp.

Jews in Poland of all economic classes try to survive in the period before World War II.
Genre(s): Domestic Fiction.

Gold, Alison Leslie

1599. *The Devil's Mistress.* New York: Faber and Faber, 1997. 220 pp.
Scraps of Eva Braun's diary show a a photo clerk of 17 meeting members of the Nazi party and becoming Hitler's favorite.
Genre(s): Biographical Fiction.

Goldsmith, John

1600. *Exodus '43.* New York: Coward-McCann, 1982. 289 pp.
Rosa Abrahamsen, a wealthy Danish Jew, marries a gentile from a competing shipping family in 1939, but their family differences disappear when the Germans arrive.
Genre(s): War Story.

Goldstein, Arthur P.

1601. *The Shoes of Maidanek.* Lanham, MD: University Press of America, 1992. 62 pp.
Young Lon uses illustrations as well as words to describe his experiences in a concentration camp during World War II.
Genre(s): War Story.

Goldstein, Lisa

1602. *The Dream Years.* New York: Bantam, 1985. 181 pp.
While Robert St. Onge enjoys life in Paris on the fringes of the Surrealists during the 1920s, he becomes attracted to a woman who transports him into the 1960s.
Genre(s): Time Travel.

◆ 1603. *The Red Magician.* New York: Pocket Books, 1982. 156 pp.
A rabbi argues with a traveling magician who foretells the Holocaust of World War II and, after the war, the two resume their arguments.
Genre(s): Fantastic Literature.

Gorenshtein, Friedrich

1604. *Traveling Companions.* Trans. Bernard Meares. San Diego: Harcourt, 1991. 214 pp.
Sasha Chubinets tells about his life during the German invasion of Ukraine and his experiences in both German and Russian prison camps while Zabrodsky interjects with commentary on contemporary Ukrainian life, as they ride in a sleeping car on a Ukrainian train.
Genre(s): Political Fiction; War Story.

Grade, Chaim

1605. *The Yeshiva.* Trans. Curt Leviant. Indianapolis: Bobbs-Merrill, 1976. 304 pp.
After World War I, Tsemakh Atlas travels in Eastern European cities to enroll students in his Yeshiva during the Musar movement.
Genre(s): Jewish Fiction.

Gramont, Sanche de

1606. *Lives to Give.* New York: Putnam, 1971. 320 pp.
When four members of the Resistance go to a secret meeting, the Gestapo greets them, indicating that one of the four has betrayed the others.
Genre(s): War Story.

Granin, Daniil Aleksandrovich

1607. *The Bison.* Garden City, NY: Doubleday, 1990. 262 pp.
Timofeyev, a genetics researcher, works in Nazi Germany and Stalinist Russia where he makes discoveries about radioactivity as he strives to help victims of the Nazis and to avoid pseudoscience.
Genre(s): Biographical Fiction.

Grass, Günter

1608. *Dog Years.* Trans. Ralph Manheim. San Diego, CA: Harcourt Brace, 1965. 570 pp.
Eddi Amsel, a half-Jewish scarecrow maker, forms a friendship with Walter Matern that deteriorates as the Nazis rise in power. (*Series:* Danzig Trilogy, 3)
Genre(s): War Story.

Grekova, I.

1609. *The Ship of Widows.* Trans. Cathy Porter. Evanston, IL: Northwestern University Press, 1994. 192 pp.
Five women in a communal apartment in Moscow wait for husbands who do not return from World War II, but the birth of a son to one of the women causes them to react with unexpected happiness.
Genre(s): War Story.

Griffin, Gwyn

1610. *The Occupying Power.* New York: Putnam, 1968. 318 pp.
After Major Euan Lemonfield takes over an Italian colony on Baressa in the Mediterranean in 1940, he raises standards, but a British general's arrival in 1945 changes the situation.
Genre(s): War Story.

Griffin, W. E. B.

1611. *The Lieutenant.* New York: Berkley, 1982. 401 pp.
Lieutenant Robert Bellmon becomes a German prisoner in World War II, and a sympathetic German officer shows him photographic evidence of the Soviet massacre of Poles before helping him escape. (*Series:* Brotherhood of War, 1)
Genre(s): War Story; Adventure Story.

Guerard, Albert J.

1612. *Maquisard.* Novato, CA: Lyford, 1995. 192 pp.
The Maquisard, a group of French underground fighters, await replacements while holding back the Germans in World War II, but they fear that a new battle will undermine their success.
Genre(s): War Story.

Haas, Ben

1613. *The House of Christina.* New York: Simon and Schuster, 1977. 411 pp.
Christa Helmer tries to save the family home in Austria after her American husband is deported for knowing too much about Hitler.
Genre(s): War Story.

Habe, Hans

1614. *The Mission.* Trans. Michael Bullock. New York: Coward-McCann, 1966. 391 pp.
A Jewish physician tries to save Austrian and German Jews in 1938 at the Evian-les-Bains conference.
Genre(s): Jewish Fiction.

Hackl, Erich

◆ 1615. *Farewell Sidonia.* New York: Fromm International, 1991. 138 pp.
Abandoned by her Gypsy parents in 1933, Sidonia Aldersburg lives in Austria with foster parents who have different skin color, but the Nazis return her to her natural parents, which means that she will be sent to Auschwitz.
Genre(s): War Story.

Haddad, Carolyn

◆ 1616. *A Mother's Secret.* San Diego, CA: Harcourt, 1988. 502 pp.
Eliza Wolf, a Polish Jew, flees with her one-year-old daughter from the Nazis and leaves the child with peasants, and when she returns two years later, they have gone, and she spends the next 50 years trying to reunite with her daughter.
Genre(s): War Story; Family Saga.

Hamilton, Hugo

1617. *The Last Shot.* New York: Farrar, Straus and Giroux, 1992. 192 pp.
Near the end of World War II, Bertha Sommer rides her bicycle from Czechoslovakia to Germany with the help of a German officer whom she loves.
Genre(s): War Story; Love Story.

Hardy, Robin

1618. *The Education of Don Juan.* New York: Wyndom, 1980. 482 pp.
A Don Juan raised by lesbians fights in the Spanish Civil War and the French Resistance between his conquests.
Genre(s): Adventure Story.

Harrington, William

1619. *The English Lady.* New York: Harper and Row, 1982. 408 pp.
An Englishwoman married to her German cousin remains in Germany after the war begins and becomes a spy for

◆May be suitable for young adult readers

the British, assigned to sleep with Hitler and to try to kill him.
Genre(s): Spy Fiction; War Story.

Hart, Carolyn G.

1620. *Escape From Paris.* New York: St. Martin's, 1983. 191 pp.
Two American sisters challenge the Nazis in Paris during 1940 by helping British soldiers escape via an underground route.
Genre(s): War Story; Romance.

Haviaras, Stratis

1621. *The Heroic Age.* New York: Simon and Schuster, 1984. 272 pp.
In World War II and the subsequent civil war in Greece, five Greek children wander from one place to another trying to survive.
Genre(s): War Story.

Hayden, Torey L.

◆ 1622. *The Sunflower Forest.* New York: Putnam, 1984. 344 pp.
Although set in the 1950s, the story reveals the traumatic experiences of Lesley's mother during World War II when the Nazis took her son.
Genre(s): Bildungsroman (Coming of Age); War Story.

Hays, Tony

◆ 1623. *Murder in the Latin Quarter.* Bell Buckle, TN: Iris, 1993. 215 pp.
In 1922, Jack Barnett works as a freelance journalist in Paris, and Sylvia Beach requests his help when someone is murdered while trying to burn copies of James Joyce's newly published *Ulysses.*
Genre(s): Mystery.

Heller, Joseph

1624. *Catch-22.* New York: Simon and Schuster, 1961. 443 pp.
Captain Yossarian and other pilots on a small Mediterranean island in World War II face inconsistencies in military rules.
Genre(s): War Story; Satire; Humorous Fiction.

Hemingway, Ernest

1625. *Across the River and into the Trees.* New York: Scribner's, 1950. 308 pp.
Richard Cantwell comes to Venice on leave from the army to see his love and to visit the place where he was wounded in World War I.

◆ 1626. *For Whom the Bell Tolls.* 1940. New York: Scribner's, 1996. 495 pp.
Robert Jordan, an American fighting in Spain's civil war, blows up a bridge, but wounds his leg and is therefore unable to escape the Fascists.
Genre(s): War Story; Love Story.

◆ 1627. *The Sun Also Rises.* 1926. New York: Simon and Schuster, 1996. 251 pp.
Jake Barnes tells the story of a group of expatriates in Spain after World War I, one of whom, Brett Ashley, has an affair with a bull-fighter.
Genre(s): Adventure Story.

Hersey, John

1628. *The Wall.* New York: Knopf, 1950. 632 pp.
Jews try to survive inside the German-built wall of the Warsaw ghetto in Poland.
Genre(s): Jewish Fiction; War Story.

Higgins, Jack

1629. *Flight of Eagles.* New York: Putnam, 1998. 336 pp.
During World War II, American-born twins Max and Harry Kelso divide loyalties, one flying for the British, one for the Germans and both earning distinction.
Genre(s): War Story.

◆ 1630. *Luciano's Luck.* New York: Stein and Day, 1981. 238 pp.
Lucky Luciano, released from prison, goes into Sicily during 1943 to request help from the Sicilian Mafia for an Allied invasion.
Genre(s): Biographical Fiction; War Story.

◆ 1631. *Storm Warning.* New York: Holt, Rinehart and Winston, 1976. 311 pp.
A German sailing ship disguised as a Swedish vessel leaves Brazil late in World War II with passengers wanting to return to Germany.
Genre(s): War Story; Sea Story.

High, Monique Raphel

1632. *The Eleventh Year.* New York: Delacorte, 1982. 512 pp.
Three women in Paris during the 1920s show their disparate characters.
Genre(s): Romance.

Hill, Reginald

1633. *The Collaborators.* Woodstock, VT: Countryman, 1989. 448 pp.
The French Jew Jean-Paul joins the Resistance while a German officer, using information from Jean-Paul's wife to track him, falls in love with the wife himself.
Genre(s): War Story.

Hirsal, Josef

1634. *A Bohemian Youth.* Trans. Michael H. Heim. Chicago: Northwestern University Press, 1998. 87 pp.
After a man returns from World War I to his Bohemian village, he marries and has a son.
Genre(s): War Story; Domestic Fiction.

Hochhuth, Rolf

1635. *A German Love Story*. Trans. John Brown-john. Boston: Little, Brown, 1980. 269 pp.
Pauline's husband is fighting on the front when she meets a Polish prisoner of war, but she is so attracted to Stasiek that they flout the Nazi laws against such contact and face the consequences.
Genre(s): Love Story; War Story.

Hofmann, Gert

1636. *The Film Explainer*. Trans. Michael Hofmann. Evanston, IL: Northwestern University Press, 1996. 249 pp.
In the early 1930s, the narrator's grandfather who once explained silent films to theater audiences, fulfills his need to verbally control groups of people by joining the emergine Nazi party.
Genre(s): Biographical Fiction; Political Fiction.

1637. *Our Conquest*. Trans. Christopher Middleton. New York: Fromm International, 1985. 256 pp.
Boys wander around their German village near the end of World War II engaging in routine activities, as the Allies begin their occupation.
Genre(s): War Story.

Horton, David

◆ 1638. *A Legion of Honor*. Colorado Springs, CO: Victor, 1996. 324 pp.
Marcel Boussant joins the French Resistance after the Nazis kidnap his father, but as he smuggles Jews out of the country, he thinks the work is boring until he meets Isabelle Karmazin.
Genre(s): Christian Fiction; War Story.

Hotchner, A. E.

1639. *The Man Who Lived at the Ritz*. New York: Putnam, 1982. 360 pp.
Philip Weber, an expatriate living in Paris at the Ritz during World War II, unwillingly becomes part of German plans and a source for the Resistance.
Genre(s): War Story.

Household, Geoffrey

1640. *Rogue Justice*. Boston: Little, Brown, 1983. 192 pp.
An anonymous British man escapes from a Nazi prison and flees through Poland and Greece to Africa in the sequel to *Rogue Male*.
Genre(s): War Story; Adventure Story.

Hughes, Richard Arthur Warren

1641. *The Fox in the Attic*. New York: Harper, 1962. 352 pp.
Augustine, a young man, leaves his English village to visit German relatives just as Hitler comes to power.
Genre(s): Political Fiction.

1642. *The Wooden Shepherdess*. New York: Harper and Row, 1973. 389 pp.
In the sequel to *The Fox in the Attic*, Augustine travels through America in the Prohibition era, and through Bavaria and Morocco while Hitler plans his takeover of the German government.
Genre(s): Picaresque Fiction.

Hunter, Stephen

1643. *The Master Sniper*. New York: Dell, 1996. 402 pp.
Nazis accuse Lieutenant Colonel Repp of an assassination after he has practiced his shooting skills on death camp inmates, and Jim Leets, an American, must identify Repp's new gun.
Genre(s): Mystery.

1644. *The Spanish Gambit*. New York: Crown, 1985. 416 pp.
Two school friends become spies against each other in pre–World War II Europe.
Genre(s): War Story.

Hylton, Sara

1645. *Fragile Heritage*. New York: St. Martin's, 1990. 464 pp.
After going to Provence as a companion to Lisanne, Ellen Adair must stay there throughout the war, but on the way back to England, the ship sinks, and she, mistaken for Lisanne, is forced to marry Gervase.
Genre(s): War Story; Romance.

Ibbotson, Eva

◆ 1646. *Magic Flutes*. New York: St. Martin's, 1985. 255 pp.
Guy Farne, a self-made millionaire, falls in love with a lovely Viennese woman, buys a castle to impress her, and finds out that she is too shallow to marry.
Genre(s): Romance.

◆ 1647. *The Morning Gift*. New York: St. Martin's, 1993. 336 pp.
At the beginning of World War II, a paleontologist marries the Austrian Jew, Ruth Berger, to get her out of the country even though she is already engaged to someone else.
Genre(s): War Story; Love Story.

Iles, Greg

◆ 1648. *Black Cross*. New York: Dutton, 1995. 516 pp.
A physician from Georgia and a German Jew, in a risky maneuver, attempt to destroy a poison nerve gas laboratory in Hitler's Germany.
Genre(s): Adventure Story; War Story; Spy Fiction.

Irving, Clifford

1649. *The Angel of Zin*. New York: Stein and Day, 1984. 306 pp.

A detective of the Berlin Criminal Police comes to a Polish concentration camp to investigate the deaths of several Nazis and informers.
Genre(s): War Story.

Irving, Clive

1650. *Comrades.* New York: Random House, 1986. 563 pp.
An American photojournalist, Mary Brynes, falls in love with a Spanish anarchist during the Spanish Civil War.
Genre(s): War Story.

Jacot, Michael

1651. *The Last Butterfly.* Indianapolis: Bobbs-Merrill, 1974. 221 pp.
Antonin, a famous clown, must give a performance to capture children in an attempt by the Nazis to fool the International Red Cross at Terezin concentration camp near Prague.
Genre(s): War Story.

Janes, J. Robert

1652. *Carousel.* New York: Donald I. Fine, 1993. 288 pp.
A French inspector, paired with a Gestapo agent, must find out who left a dead girl naked with a Roman coin on her forehead in Paris during 1942.
Genre(s): Mystery; War Story.

1653. *Salamander.* New York: Soho, 1998. 322 pp.
The day before Christmas in 1942, Chief Inspector Jean-Louis St-Cyr and Inspector Hermann Kohler arrive in Lyon to investigate a movie house fire.
Genre(s): War Story; Mystery.

1654. *Sandman.* New York: Soho, 1997. 272 pp.
Frenchman Jean-Louis St.-Cyr and German Hermann Kohler investigate a serial killer in Paris during the Vichy government.
Genre(s): War Story; Mystery.

1655. *Stonekiller.* New York: Farrar, Straus and Giroux, 1997. 261 pp.
A woman who once discovered a cache of prehistoric art is murdered, but the investigators are hesitant to look too closely because Hitler and Goebbels want to use the art for propoganda and may therefore be involved.
Genre(s): Mystery; War Story.

Julitte, Pierre

1656. *Block 26: Sabotage at Buchenwald.* New York: Doubleday, 1971. 312 pp.
French prisoners at Buchenwald concentration camp work in a mysterious factory, and when they find out what they are doing, they try to sabotage the factory.
Genre(s): War Story.

Ka-Tzetnik, 135633

1657. *Star Eternal.* Trans. Nina De-Nur. New York: Arbor House, 1971. 120 pp.

The author, using his concentration camp number as his pseudonym, remembers the reduction of life to the need to find a crust of bread or a bit of soup in order to survive physically.
Genre(s): War Story.

Kadare, Ismail

1658. *The File on H.* Trans. David Bellos. Boston: Little, Brown, 1998. 192 pp.
In the 1930s, two American researchers go to Albania seeking the origin of the Homeric tradition and are confronted by a bureaucracy that accuses them of spying and a Serbian monk who refuses to credit Albania with having a heritage.
Genre(s): Adventure Story.

1659. *The General of the Dead Army.* 1963. New York: New Amsterdam, 1991. 251 pp.
An Italian general accompanies a priest on his mission to Albania to retrieve the remains of soldiers who had fallen 20 years previously in World War II.
Genre(s): War Story.

Karmel, Ilona

1660. *An Estate of Memory.* New York: Feminist, 1986. 457 pp.
Four women in a Polish Nazi work camp plot to deliver and save a baby during World War II.
Genre(s): War Story; Jewish Fiction.

Karmel-Wolfe, Henia

1661. *The Baders of Jacob Street.* Philadelphia: Lippincott, 1970. 321 pp.
Although Halina Bader's Jewish family has lived on the same Krakow street for generations, they must leave for the ghetto when Germans force them from their home.
Genre(s): War Story.

1662. *Marek and Lisa.* New York: Dodd, Mead, 1984. 249 pp.
Lisa Unger and Marek Rodwan marry during the cataclysmic events of World War II and use forged identity papers to survive until they are betrayed and separated.
Genre(s): War Story.

Kartun, Derek

1663. *The Courier.* New York: St. Martin's, 1985. 248 pp.
Bill Quinton is allowed to leave France after its fall if he takes bullion from the Bank of France in his 1937 Bentley to finance French resistance abroad.
Genre(s): War Story.

Katkov, Norman

1664. *The Judas Kiss.* New York: Dutton, 1991. 423 pp.
An Austrian baroness helps downed Allied pilots escape from Austria because her first love was an American movie producer, whom she presumes is dead, while her husband plans tortures for concentration camp inmates.
Genre(s): War Story.

Kaufelt, David A.

1665. *Silver Rose.* New York: Delacorte, 1982. 257 pp.
Rennie Jablonski goes to free her Jewish father in Berlin, but after the Gestapo kill him, she assumes a new identity and marries a Nazi.
Genre(s): War Story.

1666. *Souvenir.* New York: New American Library, 1983. 345 pp.
Floy Devon wants to return with her son to the United States, while the Nazis are trying to destroy the Resistance group headed by her aunt.
Genre(s): War Story; Political Fiction.

Kazan, Elia

1667. *Beyond the Aegean.* New York: Knopf, 1994. 449 pp.
In the sequel to *The Anatolian*, Stavros Topouzoglou returns to Greece from the United States after World War I, while Greece is trying to retake Anatolia from Turkey.
Genre(s): War Story; Political Fiction.

Keeley, Edmund

◆ 1668. *School for Pagan Lovers.* New Brunswick, NJ:, Rutgers University Press, 1993. 295 pp.
Hal Gogarty attends a German school in Greece in 1938 and falls in love with his lovely Jewish teacher.
Genre(s): War Story.

Keneally, Thomas

1669. *Gossip from the Forest.* London: Collins, 1975.
When Matthias Erzberger comes to negotiate the armistice with Marshal Foch of the Allies after World War I, he must overcome his lack of bargaining power.
Genre(s): Political Fiction.

1670. *Schindler's List.* New York: Simon and Schuster, 1982. 400 pp.
Oskar Schindler, a German, comes to Krakow, Poland, and helps the Jews working in his prison-camp complex.
Award(s): Booker Prize; *Los Angeles Times* Book Award.
Genre(s): Biographical Fiction; War Story; Jewish Fiction.

1671. *Season in Purgatory.* New York: Harcourt, 1977. 206 pp.
Pelham, an English surgeon who has parachuted into Yugoslavia on the Adriatic island of Mus, aids wounded partisans while slowly adjusting to the people around him.
Genre(s): Medical Novel.

Kennedy, Raymond A.

◆ 1672. *The Bitterest Age.* New York: Ticknor and Fields, 1994. 218 pp.
Ingebord Maas waits for her father to return from the Russian front during World War II, while bombs are reducing Potsdam to ashes.
Genre(s): War Story.

Kerr, Philip

1673. *March Violets.* New York: Viking, 1989. 245 pp.
In 1936 Berlin, Bernhard Gunther is a private investigator who solves a case of theft, murder, and corruption within the new Nazi supporting group, the March Violets.
Genre(s): Mystery.

1674. *The Pale Criminal.* New York: Viking, 1990. 272 pp.
Bernhard Gunther stops investigating homosexual blackmail in order to track a torturer-killer of teenage girls in Nazi Germany and learns about the government-sanctioned murder of Jews.
Genre(s): Mystery; War Story.

Kertesz, Imre

◆ 1675. *Fateless.* Trans. Christopher C. Wilson and Katharina M. Wilson. Chicago: Northwestern University Press, 1992. 189 pp.
A boy picked from a Budapest street goes to work in Zeitz as a laborer, but inside the camp, he has no allegiance and is free to wander as he pleases, a freedom that makes him happy.
Genre(s): War Story.

Kidel, Boris

1676. *A Flawed Escape.* New York: St. Martin's, 1975. 269 pp.
A young German Jew trying to flee the holocaust hesitates to leave his family and his unhappy love affairs.
Genre(s): War Story.

Kilian, Michael

1677. *Dance on a Sinking Ship.* New York: St. Martin's, 1988. 419 pp.
Edward, Duke of Windsor, Wallis Warfield, Duchess of Windsor, and others travel incognito on the *Wilhelmina* in 1935 on its doomed voyage.
Genre(s): Sea Story; Adventure Story.

Kingsley, Johanna

1678. *Loving Touches.* New York: Fawcett, 1995. 539 pp.
Kat DeVary, a Czech actress, delivers a daughter in a Czech prison during World War II and before she disappears, says that an American agent with whom she had a brief liaison is the father.
Genre(s): Romance; War Story; Family Saga.

Kirst, Hans Hellmut

1679. *The Affairs of the Generals.* Trans. J. Maxwell Brownjohn. New York: Coward-McCann, 1979. 253 pp.
In 1937 and 1938, Hitler and his supporters devise false stories so that they can kill off two of the German army's highest-ranking officers.
Genre(s): War Story.

1680. *Forward, Gunner Asch!* Trans. Robert Kee. Boston: Little, Brown, 1956. 368 pp.
In the sequel to *Revolt of Gunner Asch*, Gunner Asch and his companions fight on the Russian front in the late winter of 1941–42.
Genre(s): War Story.

1681. *Hero in the Tower.* New York: Coward-McCann, 1972. 348 pp.
While Captain Hein of a German anti-aircraft battery stays in a chateau south of Paris during the summer of 1940, a scholarly team comes to study the building, and Hein believes that he is the reincarnated Duke of Orléans.
Genre(s): War Story.

1682. *The Night of the Generals.* Trans. J. Maxwell Brownjohn. New York: Harper and Row, 1963. 319 pp.
Three Nazi generals become the main suspects in the murder of prostitutes in Warsaw in 1942, Paris in 1944, and Dresden in 1956.
Genre(s): Mystery.

1683. *The Officer Factory.* Trans. Robert Kee. Garden City, NY: Doubleday, 1963. 512 pp.
At a German officers' training institute in 1944, an anti-Nazi officer is murdered.
Genre(s): War Story.

1684. *The Return of Gunner Asch.* Trans. Robert Kee. Boston: Little, Brown, 1957. 310 pp.
In the sequel to *Forward, Gunner Asch!* Asch begins tracking two officers who left their men to die while pursuing black market opportunities.
Genre(s): War Story.

1685. *Revolt of Gunner Asch.* Boston: Little, Brown, 1955. 311 pp.
Gunner Asch, displeased with being bullied by his superiors, revolts against them.
Genre(s): War Story; Humorous Fiction.

1686. *Soldiers' Revolt.* Trans. J. Maxwell Brownjohn. New York: Harper and Row, 1966. 416 pp.
Some of the soldiers in the German army plot to assassinate Hitler on July 20, 1944.
Genre(s): War Story; Biographical Fiction.

1687. *The Wolves.* New York: Coward-McCann, 1968. 447 pp.
Alfons Materna cannot overtly fight the National Socialists after they kill his son so he joins the Wolves, a group trying to sabotage the Nazis.
Genre(s): War Story.

Kirstein, Lincoln

1688. *Flesh Is Heir.* New York: Brewer, Warren, 1932. 323 pp.
Roger Baum, a Jew, attends boarding school and travels in Europe to Paris and Venice during the 1920s.
Genre(s): Bildungsroman (Coming of Age).

Kis, Danilo

1689. *Hourglass.* Trans. Ralph Manheim. New York: Farrar, Straus and Giroux, 1990. 272 pp.
A Hungarian worker experiences his last few months before being sent to a Nazi concentration camp.
Genre(s): War Story.

Klein, Ed

1690. *The Parachutists.* Garden City, NY: Doubleday, 1981. 392 pp.
Israelis parachute into Hungary in 1944, not knowing exactly what their American covert officer wants them to do.
Genre(s): War Story; Spy Fiction.

Koestler, Arthur

1691. *Darkness at Noon.* Trans. Daphne Hardy. 1941. New York: Macmillan, 1987. 279 pp.
The Moscow show trials of the late 1930s lead to the arrest, imprisonment, and execution of N. S. Rubashov in the sequel to *The Gladiators*.
Genre(s): Legal Story.

Kohout, Pavel

1692. *The Widow Killer.* Trans. Neil Bermel. New York: St. Martin's, 1998. 400 pp.
Someone murders and mutilates the Baroness of Pomerania in Prague near the end of World War II, and a Czech detective joins a renegade Gestapo agent in searching for the killer.
Genre(s): War Story; Mystery; Political Fiction.

Koning, Hans

1693. *De Witt's War.* New York: Pantheon, 1983. 256 pp.
Jerome de Witt, mayor of a town near Amsterdam in 1941, tries to find out who wants to gain control of Dutch East Indies companies after two murders and 12 German executions.
Genre(s): War Story.

Konwicki, Tadeusz

1694. *Moonrise, Moonset.* New York: Farrar, Straus and Giroux, 1987. 384 pp.
The narrator presents what has happened to Poland in the 20th century up to 1981 and describes its succession of rulers.
Genre(s): Political Fiction.

Kosinski, Jerzy N.

1695. *The Painted Bird.* Boston: Houghton Mifflin, 1965. 272 pp.
Fair-haired Poles mistreat a stray dark-haired child while he is trying to find food and shelter during World War II.
Genre(s): Biographical Fiction; War Story.

Krall, Hanna

1696. *The Subtenant.* Trans. Lawrence and Joanna Stasinska Weschler. Chicago: Northwestern University Press, 1992. 150 pp.
During World War II, the narrator, as a Jewish child, hides in several Polish homes from the Nazis.
Genre(s): War Story.

1697. *To Outwit God.* Chicago: Northwestern University Press, 1992. 100 pp.
The narrator describes the uprisings by Jews during World War II in Poland.
Genre(s): War Story.

Krantz, Judith

1698. *Till We Meet Again.* New York: Crown, 1988. 735 pp.
A mother and daughter circulate in World War II Paris where they are involved in making movies and they then come to the United States.
Genre(s): Adventure Story; War Story.

Krotkov, Yuri

1699. *The Red Monarch.* New York: Norton, 1979. 253 pp.
Stalin's problems are caused mainly by his deputy Beria in 20 vignettes from his life.
Genre(s): Biographical Fiction.

Kundera, Milan

1700. *The Joke.* New York: Knopf, 1982. 267 pp.
Released from prison, where he'd been sent because of a joke he had written on a postcard to his girlfriend, Ludvik decides to seduce the wife of the man who fingered him.
Genre(s): Political Fiction.

Kuniczak, W. S.

1701. *The March.* Garden City, NY: Doubleday, 1979. 824 pp.
In the sequel to *The Thousand Hour Day*, the Polish army collapses and the Nazis and Russians begin their onslaught while several families try to survive exile to Siberia and repatriation into a new Polish army allied to the Russians.
Genre(s): War Story.

1702. *The Thousand Hour Day.* New York: Dial, 1966. 628 pp.
In the first 1,000 hours of World War II in 1939, Poland is able to repel the German attack.
Genre(s): War Story.

Kuznetsov, Anatolii A.

1703. *Babi Yar.* Trans. Jacob Guralsky. New York: Dial, 1967. 399 pp.
The author documents the German massacre from 1941 to 1943 of two million people, including 50,000 Jews, outside Kiev.
Genre(s): War Story.

Kyle, Duncan

◆ 1704. *Black Camelot.* New York: St. Martin's, 1978. 277 pp.
Near the end of World War II, the Nazis try to divide the Allies with a document called the White List.
Genre(s): War Story.

Labro, Philippe

1705. *Le Petit Garçon.* Trans. Linda Coverdale. New York: Farrar, Straus and Giroux, 1992. 257 pp.
Parents try to teach their children the importance of right and wrong and compassion for others, even as Germans occupy their small French town in World War II.
Genre(s): War Story; Bildungsroman (Coming of Age).

Lacaze, André

1706. *The Tunnel At Loibl Pass.* Trans. Barrett W. Downer. Garden City, NY: Doubleday, 1981. 624 pp.
During World War II, Paulo Chastagnier escapes the gas chamber when the Nazis use slave labor, including his, to build a tunnel in the mountains of Yugoslavia.
Genre(s): War Story.

Laker, Rosalind

◆ 1707. *The Shining Land.* New York: Doubleday, 1985. 374 pp.
Johanna Ryen meets Steffen Larsen as the Germans invade Normandy, and later when they join the resistance in Oslo, they reunite in dangerous circumstances.
Genre(s): War Story; Romance.

Lauterstein, Ingeborg

1708. *The Water Castle.* Boston: Houghton Mifflin, 1981. 408 pp.
A Viennese girl is six in the year of the Anschluss and lives through the next seven years with her liberal father and her swastika-wearing mother across the street from the Water Castle, until the Russians pillage the city.
Genre(s): War Story.

Leffland, Ella

1709. *The Knight, Death, and the Devil.* New York: Morrow, 1990. 718 pp.
Hermann Goering, a man of many contradictions, becomes head of the Luftwaffe and a staunch supporter of Hitler.
Genre(s): Biographical Fiction.

Lentin, Ronit

◆ 1710. *Night Train to Mother.* San Francisco: Cleis, 1990. 218 pp.
Ruth returns to her mother's birthplace in Romania where she discovers that she is unwelcome.
Genre(s): War Story.

◆May be suitable for young adult readers

Lenz, Siegfried

1711. *The German Lesson.* Trans. Ernst Kaiser
and Eithne Wilkins. 1972. New York: New Directions, 1986. 470 pp.
At 20, Siggi is in a home for delinquents, and must write
an essay, for which he spends months recording the story
of his father's betrayal of an artist friend during World
War II.

Levi, Primo

1712. *If Not Now, When?* New York: Summit,
1985. 349 pp.
From 1943 to 1945, a band of Jewish partisans engages
in guerilla warfare against the Germans in eastern Europe.
Genre(s): War Story; Romance.

Levin, Meyer

1713. *Eva.* New York: Simon and Schuster, 1959.
311 pp.
By assuming the identity of Katya, a Ukrainian peasant
girl, Eva Korngold escapes from Poland and takes refuge
in Austria before people realize she is Jewish.
Genre(s): War Story; Jewish Fiction.

Lewitt, Maria

1714. *Come Spring.* New York: St. Martin's, 1982.
272 pp.
Irena, a half-Jewish Polish teenager, and her mother hide
Jewish relatives on their Warsaw estate during World
War II.
Genre(s): War Story.

Linn, Merritt

1715. *A Book of Songs.* New York: St. Martin's,
1982. 309 pp.
The protagonist tells of his life in a concentration camp
and that he and others in the camp find some peace
through a child who is allowed to play the violin.
Genre(s): War Story.

Litewka, Albert

1716. *Warsaw.* New York: Sheridan Square, 1989.
499 pp.
To capture Abrahm Bankart, a Resistance leader who has
united Jews imprisoned in the Warsaw ghetto, Nazis
dress one of their own as a Jew and send him to search
for Bankart.
Genre(s): War Story.

LoCicero, Donald

1717. *The Twisted Star.* Haymarket, VA: E. M.,
1992. 299 pp.
From the 1920s, when anti-Semitism rises in Germany,
the Hartstein family cannot decide to leave, and finally
only Heinrich, the son, survives Treblinka.
Genre(s): War Story.

Loewen, Paul

1718. *Butterfly.* New York: St. Martin's, 1988. 271
pp.
A young boy of part-German and part-Japanese descent
learns that his mother is the daughter of Madame Butterfly and her American lover, Henry Pinkerton.
Genre(s): Romance.

Lord, Eda

1719. *Extenuating Circumstances.* New York:
Knopf, 1971. 176 pp.
Letty Innes-Gore wants to remain in Cannes during
World War II, and stays on a friend's estate, where she
seems untouched by events since the Germans do not
find the valuable art hidden there or find out that it is an
underground rest stop.
Genre(s): War Story.

Ludlum, Robert

◆ 1720. *The Rhinemann Exchange.* New York:
Dial, 1974. 460 pp.
The Germans and the Americans attempt the treasonous
exchange of a technological secret in World War II.
Genre(s): Spy Fiction.

1721. *The Scarlatti Inheritance.* New York:
World, 1971. 358 pp.
Heinrich Kroeger, heir to the Scarlatti fortune, works
with Germans by pretending to be a World War I hero
and backing Hitler between the wars, in expectation of
becoming a major power behind an international empire.
Genre(s): Political Fiction.

Lustig, Arnost

1722. *Darkness Casts No Shadow.* Washington,
DC: Inscape, 1977. 144 pp.
Two young people escape from a death train and hide in
the German and Czech countryside, but after the war,
they have to survive in a foreign land.
Genre(s): War Story.

1723. *Night and Hope.* Trans. George Theiner.
Washington: Inscape, 1977. 350 pp.
Children in the Terezin ghetto outside of Prague, although forcibly removed from their homes, supposedly
show the humane treatment of the Germans toward the
Jews.
Genre(s): War Story.

1724. *A Prayer for Katerina Horovitzova.* New
York: Harper and Row, 1973. 165 pp.
A Nazi commandant pretends that some of a captive
group of Jews will not be killed, but secretly, he plans to
take their fortunes before exterminating them.
Genre(s): War Story.

◆ 1725. *The Unloved.* 1985. Chicago: Northwestern
University Press, 1996. 196 pp.
To avoid being taken from the model concentration camp
at Theresienstadt, Perla, 17, learns to offer sexual favors

to the Jewish head of the central registry for deportation lists.
Award(s): National Jewish Book Award.
Genre(s): War Story.

Machlis, Joseph

1726. *The Career of Magda V.* New York: Norton, 1985. 313 pp.
Magda Volkmann becomes famous as an opera singer just as Hitler comes to power, and although apolitical, she comes in contact with Nazi leaders and finds herself making compromises for her career.
Genre(s): War Story; Musical Fiction.

MacInnes, Helen

1727. *Assignment in Brittany.* Boston: Little, Brown, 1942. 373 pp.
A British officer pretending to be French tries to find the Nazi plans for resisiting invasion off the coast of France during World War II.
Genre(s): War Story.

Mackay, John Henry

1728. *The Hustler.* Trans. Hubert Kennedy. Los Angeles: Alyson, 1985. 299 pp.
Gunther, 15, becomes a prostitute in Berlin during 1926 so that he can support himself, and when he joins with the pederast Hermann, Hermann can save neither Gunther nor himself.
Genre(s): Erotic Literature.

MacLean, Alistair

1729. *Force 10 from Navarone.* Garden City, NY: Doubleday, 1968. 274 pp.
Heroes from *The Guns of Navarone* drop into Yugoslavia to join the partisans.
Genre(s): War Story.

1730. *The Guns of Navarone.* Garden City, NY: Doubleday, 1957. 320 pp.
A British army team tries to destroy the guns on Navarone that control the approaches to the eastern Mediterranean islands.
Genre(s): War Story.

1731. *HMS Ulysses.* Garden City, NY: Doubleday, 1956. 316 pp.
The crew of the HMS *Ulysses* travels the dangerous sea route to Murmansk during World War II.
Genre(s): War Story; Sea Story.

◆ 1732. *Partisans.* Garden City, NY: Doubleday, 1983. 244 pp.
Major Peterson leads a commando force to help partisans in Yugoslavia who are trying to escape from the Nazis during World War II.
Genre(s): War Story.

1733. *South by Java Head.* Garden City, NY: Doubleday, 1958. 288 pp.

In 1942, a group of people escaping Singapore by tramp steamer sails to avoid the Japanese and the region's severe storms on their way to Australia.
Genre(s): War Story; Sea Story.

1734. *Where Eagles Dare.* Garden City, NY: Doubleday, 1967. 312 pp.
A crew tries to rescue an American general from Schloss Adler in Bavaria during the cold winter of 1943–44.
Genre(s): War Story.

MacMillan, Ian

1735. *Orbit of Darkness.* San Diego, CA: Harcourt, 1991. 288 pp.
People throughout Europe suffer Nazi atrocities during World War II, while a starving priest who refuses to die in Auschwitz becomes a symbol of hope.
Genre(s): War Story.

Magris, Claudio

1736. *Inferences from a Sabre.* New York: Braziller, 1991. 85 pp.
White Russians ally with the Germans in World War II, and when the communist Russians capture them, they commit suicide rather than surrender.
Genre(s): War Story.

Malaparte, Curzio

1737. *Kaputt.* 1941. Marlboro, VT: Marlboro, 1991. 407 pp.
On the border of Russia before World War II, the elite attitudes of Western Europeans create a seeding ground for conflict.
Genre(s): War Story.

Malraux, André

1738. *Days of Wrath.* Trans. Haakon M. Chevalier. New York: Random House, 1936. 174 pp.
An unknown comrade takes the place of his communist friend in a Nazi concentration camp.
Genre(s): War Story.

1739. *Man's Hope.* Trans. Stuart Gilbert and Alastair Macdonald. New York: Random House, 1938. 511 pp.
Malraux emphasizes the horrors of war during the first eight months of the Spanish Civil War.
Genre(s): War Story.

Mann, Thomas

1740. *Doctor Faustus.* Trans. H.T. Lowe-Porter. 1948. New York: Knopf, 1997. 510 pp.
Adrian Leverkuhn sacrifices his soul to create music in a story parallel to the fall of Germany during World War II.
Genre(s): Political Fiction; Allegory.

Manning, Olivia

1741. *Friends and Heroes.* New York: Doubleday, 1966. 336 pp.

In the sequel to *The Spoilt City*, Harriet and Guy Pringle have to flee Athens during World War II, and they eventually arrive in Egypt.
Genre(s): War Story.

1742. *The Great Fortune.* New York: Doubleday, 1961. 287 pp.
Harriet and Guy Pringle work in pre–World War II Romania where they fall in love.
Genre(s): War Story; Love Story.

1743. *The Spoilt City.* New York: Doubleday, 1962. 295 pp.
After Guy and Harriet Pringle flee Bucharest in World War II, they go to Athens, but the Nazis ruin that city as well, in the sequel to *The Great Fortune*.
Genre(s): War Story.

1744. *The Sum of Things.* New York: Atheneum, 1981. 203 pp.
Shortly after the battle of El Alamein in the Levant, Guy and Harriet Pringle endure separation during wartime, in the sequel to *The Battle Lost and Won*.
Genre(s): War Story.

Marshall, William Leonard

1745. *The Age of Death.* New York: Viking, 1970. 384 pp.
World War I horrifies George Gilfallan, but his son Anthony goes to Spain during the civil war where he is killed, and his friend, terrified at the destruction, cannot escape World War II.
Genre(s): War Story.

Martin-Gaite, Carmen

◆ 1746. *Behind the Curtains.* Trans. Frances Lpez-Morillas. New York: Columbia University Press, 1990. 288 pp.
In a small town in Franco's Spain, different people describe their response to the authoritarian pressure.
Genre(s): Domestic Fiction.

Martin, Malachi

1747. *Vatican.* New York: Harper and Row, 1986. 657 pp.
In 1945, Richard Lansing, a young Chicago priest, arrives in Rome to begin his Vatican training.
Genre(s): Religious Fiction.

Mason, Anita

1748. *Reich Angel.* New York: Farrar, Straus and Giroux, 1995. 374 pp.
Frederika Kurtz has an obsession to fly, and she eventually flies all of the Third Reich's planes, stopping at Hitler's bunker when the war ends.
Genre(s): War Story.

Maspero, François

◆ 1749. *Cat's Grin.* Trans. Nancy Amphoux. New York: Knopf, 1986. 308 pp.

Luc Ponte-Serra, 13, loses his parents to the Nazi death camps and his brother Antoine to the Resistance so he asks the Allies for rides to look for his brother.
Genre(s): War Story.

Matute, Ana Maria

1750. *Soldiers Cry by Night.* Trans. Robert Nugent and Maria de la Camara. Pittsburgh, PA: Latin American, 1995. 160 pp.
Manuel, from reformatory school in Spain, sees adults at war firsthand and thinks it uglier than his school experience.
Genre(s): War Story; Bildungsroman (Coming of Age).

Mauriac, François

1751. *Maltaverne.* Trans. Jean Stewart. New York: Farrar, Straus and Giroux, 1970. 200 pp.
In the 1920s, Alain realizes that his mother is no more than a hypocrite and religious fanatic interested in her lands and dominating others.
Genre(s): Domestic Fiction.

McCutchan, Philip

1752. *Cameron and the Kaiserhof.* New York: St. Martin's, 1984. 188 pp.
Cameron must go to neutral Spain to get control of the liner *Kaiserhof*, which the Nazis are converting into a ship to house miniature submarines, so that the British will have knowledge of the Germans' advanced submarine technology.
Genre(s): War Story; Sea Story.

McGivern, William P.

1753. *Soldiers of '44.* New York: Arbor House, 1979. 420 pp.
In 1944 Germans sever communications between an American gun section and its headquarters for 13 days.
Genre(s): War Story.

Melchior, Ib

1754. *Order of Battle.* New York: Harper, 1972. 352 pp.
At the end of World War II, Germany plans to place guerrilla forces in Bavaria while the Russians and Americans converge, but Erik Larsen and his people question the deserters and captured soldiers and follow clues to destroy the Werewolf guerillas.
Genre(s): War Story; Spy Fiction; Adventure Story.

Michaels, Anne

◆ 1755. *Fugitive Pieces.* New York: Knopf, 1997. 304 pp.
After witnessing his parents' murder and being rescued by Athos, a Greek geologist who smuggles him out of Poland, Jakob Beer looks back on his life as a fugitive.
Award(s): Orange Prize for Fiction.
Genre(s): War Story.

Michaels, Fern

1756. *Sins of the Flesh.* New York: Severn House, 1990. 434 pp.
In America and Europe, the characters from *Sins of Omission* interact during the 1940s.
Genre(s): War Story; Romance.

Milosz, Czeslaw

1757. *The Issa Valley.* New York: Farrar, Straus and Giroux, 1981. 288 pp.
A young boy grows up in Lithuania after it becomes an independent state at the end of World War I.
Genre(s): Bildungsroman (Coming of Age).

1758. *The Seizure of Power.* Trans. Celina Wieniewska. New York: Farrar, Straus and Giroux, 1982. 245 pp.
Polish citizens try to rise against the Nazis in Warsaw as the Red Army crosses the Vistula River in 1944.
Genre(s): War Story.

Minatra, MaryAnn

1759. *Before Night Falls.* Eugene, OR: Harvest House, 1996. 461 pp.
During World War II in Europe, the wealthy German, Max Farber, becomes involved with American photojournalist Emilie Morgan, but they have difficulty being honest with each other.
Genre(s): War Story; Christian Fiction.

Monsarrat, Nicholas

1760. *The Kappillan of Malta.* New York: Morrow, 1974. 503 pp.
At Malta, during the German-Italian siege from 1940 to 1942, Father Salvatore finds his years of faith and service tested.
Genre(s): War Story.

Moorhouse, Frank

1761. *Grand Days.* New York: Pantheon, 1994. 572 pp.
Edith, a young Australian, thinks that the League of Nations will help the world become peaceful, and to participate, she accepts a job in Geneva with the league Secretariat.
Genre(s): Political Fiction.

Moran, Thomas

◆ 1762. *The Man in the Box.* New York: Riverhead, 1997. 260 pp.
Dr. Robert Weiss performs an emergency appendectomy on the infant Niki while a paying guest in the Lukasser home, and when Niki is a teenager, Weiss asks the family to hide him from the Nazis in their rural Austrian mountain home.
Genre(s): Bildungsroman (Coming of Age); War Story.

Morante, Elsa

1763. *History.* Trans. William Weaver. New York: Knopf, 1977. 561 pp.
During World War II in Italy, difficult times destroy people's lives in both public and private ways.
Genre(s): War Story.

Moravia, Alberto

1764. *1934.* Trans. William Weaver. New York: Farrar, Straus and Giroux, 1983. 275 pp.
A writer (the narrator) and a young German woman represent the rise of despair and the fall of the artistic with the coming of the Nazis.
Genre(s): Mystery.

1765. *Two Women.* New York: Farrar, Straus and Giroux, 1958. 339 pp.
During World War II, an Italian woman and her 17-year-old daughter face corruption after being evacuated to the country in 1943.
Genre(s): War Story.

1766. *The Woman of Rome.* New York: Farrar, Straus and Giroux, 1949. 433 pp.
A prostitute in Fascist Italy wants a child and marriage.
Genre(s): Domestic Fiction.

Morgulas, Jerrold

1767. *Scorpion East.* New York: Seaview, 1981. 344 pp.
When the Russian general Alexander Golitsyn has to surrender to the Nazis in 1943, they send him to Berlin and prepare him to help them overthrow Stalin.
Genre(s): War Story.

1768. *The Siege.* New York: Holt, 1972. 531 pp.
In July 1936, 1800 men, women, and children barricade themselves in the Alcázar of Toledo for 10 weeks until Franco finally rescues the survivors from the Republican forces.
Genre(s): Epic Literature.

Moss, Robert

1769. *Carnival of Spies.* New York: Villard, 1987. 498 pp.
Johnny becomes a communist, having seen how poorly workers fare in the early 20th century, and goes to Moscow to be trained in ways to incite revolution.
Genre(s): Spy Fiction; Adventure Story.

Mourad, Kenize

◆ 1770. *Regards from the Dead Princess.* Trans. Sabine Destree and Anna Williams. New York: Arcade, 1989. 562 pp.
Selma, granddaughter of Murad V, last ruler of the Ottoman Empire, makes an arranged marriage to an Indian rajah and is imprisoned in his palace until she flees to Paris during the Nazi occupation.
Genre(s): Biographical Fiction; War Story.

Moyes, Patricia

1771. *Many Deadly Returns.* New York: Holt, 1970. 246 pp.
In the 1920s Henry Tibbitts attends the birthday party of a woman who mentions her premonitions, and he faces a crime which involves an unknown poison.
Genre(s): Mystery.

Mulisch, Harry

◆ 1772. *The Assault.* New York: Pantheon, 1985. 162 pp.
The Dutch Resistance assassinates the Chief Inspector of Police who is collaborating with the Nazis during World War II, and when the body is dumped in front of the Steenwijks' house, Nazis methodically destroy the family except for ten-year-old Anton.
Genre(s): War Story; Mystery.

Murphy, Walter F.

1773. *The Roman Enigma.* New York: Macmillan, 1981. 306 pp.
In Rome, the British have broken the German Enigma code during World War II, and they create Operation Bronze Goddess to fool the Nazis.
Genre(s): War Story.

Myrdal, Jan

1774. *Childhood.* Trans. Christine Swanson. Chicago: Lake View, 1991. 192 pp.
The young Jan tries to understand adults around him, especially his parents who have won Nobel Prizes but who think of him as a problem and foist him off on relatives until they emigrate from Sweden to New York.
Genre(s): Biographical Fiction.

Nabokov, Vladimir

1775. *The Gift.* Trans. Michael Scammell. New York: Vintage, 1991. 366 pp.
Fyodor, an impoverished poet and writer, lives in Berlin following World War I.

1776. *King, Queen, Knave.* New York: McGraw Hill, 1968. 272 pp.
In 1928, when Dreyer and his bored wife return from their vacation to Berlin, a country cousin arrives and changes their lives.

Nathanson, E. M.

1777. *The Dirty Dozen.* New York: Random House, 1965. 498 pp.
Captain John Reisman must train 12 American prisoners to drop behind German lines in France in preparation for D-Day in 1945.
Genre(s): War Story.

Nebenzal, Harold

1778. *Café Berlin.* Woodstock, NY: Overlook, 1992. 281 pp.
Pretending to be a Spaniard sympathetic to Hitler, Daniel Saporta, a Sephardic Jew, runs a cabaret in Berlin, and after trying to foil a German plot for a Middle East pogrom, he hides in a Berlin attic and writes his diary.
Genre(s): War Story.

Norman, Hilary

1779. *Chateau Ella.* New York: Delacorte, 1988. 565 pp.
Raised by Catholic Hungarian parents, Krisztina Florian is unaware of her Jewish heritage when she becomes enveloped in Europe's pre-World War II fever.
Genre(s): War Story.

Nyiri, Janos

◆ 1780. *Battlefields and Playgrounds.* Trans. William Brandon. New York: Farrar, Straus and Giroux, 1995. 536 pp.
Jozsef Sondor tells about his life in pre-World War II Hungary with his grandparents and during the war when he hid with his mother in Budapest to escape deportation to Auschwitz.
Genre(s): War Story; Bildungsroman (Coming of Age); Political Fiction.

Oberman, Wendy

1781. *Mothers and Other Loves.* New York: David and Charles, 1990. 306 pp.
The American Cassie Fleming goes to art school in Paris where she becomes friends with Londoners in 1938 and stays in touch with them through World War II and their adult lives.
Genre(s): War Story.

Oldenbourg, Zoé

1782. *The Awakened.* Trans. Edward Hyams. New York: Pantheon, 1957. 493 pp.
In the 1930s, a young Russian Jew falls in love with a German Jew converted to Catholicism, as the Germans begin to occupy France.
Genre(s): War Story.

Oxford, James

◆ 1783. *Night of the Falcon.* New York: St. Martin's, 1981. 206 pp.
In the last year of World War II, three men penetrate an Alpine castle held by the Nazis to find the plans for German fortifications on Italy's northern border.
Genre(s): War Story; Adventure Story.

Palmer, Bruce

1784. *They Shall Not Pass.* New York: Doubleday, 1971. 792 pp.
Carmen, fascist and communist, Pedro, Carlist, Paco, Russian-trained, Ortega, peasant priest, and Frank, American pilot who marries Carmen, participate in Spain's civil war.
Genre(s): War Story.

Paretti, Sandra

1785. *Maria Canossa.* Trans. Ruth Hein. New
York: St. Martin's, 1981. 294 pp.
When Maria arrives in Rome from Berlin in 1943, she
discovers that her brother is dead, and she has to find
work and meaning in her life during the war.
Genre(s): War Story.

Parini, Jay

1786. *Benjamin's Crossing.* New York: Henry
Holt, 1997. 305 pp.
Walter Benjamin escapes Paris before the Nazis arrive in
1940, but his philosophical concerns keep him disinter-
ested in the political implications of the war around him.
Genre(s): Biographical Fiction; War Story.

Parizeau, Alice

1787. *The Lilacs Are Blooming in Warsaw.* New
York: New American Library, 1985. 304 pp.
Raped and pregnant at 13 during World War II, Helen
witnesses Germans destroying Warsaw, Communists con-
tinuing the destruction, and finally, the success of Solidar-
ity.
Award(s): Prix European.
Genre(s): Political Fiction; War Story.

Parker, Thomas Trebitsch

1788. *Anna, Ann, Annie.* New York: Dutton,
1993. 325 pp.
A talented musician, Anna first flees Vienna for London
where she changes her name to Ann, but when she returns to Vienna, a Nazi rapes her, and she leaves for
America where someone calls her Annie.
Genre(s): Musical Fiction; War Story.

Pasinetti, P. M.

1789. *Venetian Red.* New York: Random House,
1960. 503 pp.
The ancient Venetian family of the Partibons watch their
fortunes decline as the nouveaux riches Fassolas, supporters of fascism, enjoy their rise politically and socially
from 1938 to 1941.
Genre(s): War Story.

Patterson, Harry

◆ 1790. *To Catch a King.* New York: Stein and Day,
1979. 237 pp.
Walter Schellenberg, a German officer, goes to Lisbon to
persuade the Duke and Duchess of Windsor to join the
Third Reich in 1940.
Genre(s): War Story; Biographical Fiction; Adventure
Story.

◆ 1791. *The Valhalla Exchange.* New York: Stein
and Day, 1976. 224 pp.
General Canning tells of his role in Martin Bormann's escape from Germany to South America during the last
days of World War II.
Genre(s): Adventure Story.

Pearson, Diane

1792. *Csardas.* Philadelphia: Lippincott, 1975. 576
pp.
The Ferenc family finds its fortunes and its class-con-
sciousness turned awry during the pre-World War II
years in Hungary.

Pemberton, Margaret

1793. *The Flower Garden.* New York: Watts,
1983. 442 pp.
Nancy Cameron, in the 1930s finds that she has one year
to live, so she leaves her controlling husband and father
for Madeira, where she falls in love with her father's old
enemy.

Phillips, Caryl

1794. *The Nature of Blood.* New York: Knopf,
1997. 224 pp.
One of a series of story lines is that of Eva Stern who survives the death of her family and the Holocaust, only to
be haunted by those scenes for the rest of her life.
Genre(s): War Story.

Phillips, Michael R.

1795. *The Eleventh Hour.* Wheaton, IL: Tyndale
House, 1993. 505 pp.
Just before World War II, the Prussian Baron von Dor-
mann and his daughter become uncertain of their future
in Germany. (*Series:* Secret of the Rose, 1)
Genre(s): Christian Fiction; War Story.

1796. *A Rose Remembered.* Wheaton, IL: Tyndale
House, 1994. 557 pp.
At the end of World War II Sabina von Dortmann
searches for her missing father, helps Jews in the underground, and hides from a man she almost married. (*Series:* Secret of the Rose, 2)
Genre(s): War Story; Christian Fiction.

Plain, Belva

1797. *Legacy of Silence.* New York: Delacorte,
1998. 384 pp.
Two sisters, one of them adopted, flee Berlin in 1939 after Nazis kill their parents.
Genre(s): War Story.

Platonov, Andrey

1798. *The Foundation Pit.* Trans. Mirra Ginsburg.
Evanston, IL: Northwestern University Press,
1994. 156 pp.
After the Bolshevik Revolution, while some workers create the foundation for a huge building, others go into the
surrounding area to destroy the *kulaks*, or rich peasants,
at the behest of the communists.
Genre(s): Political Fiction.

Polland, Madeleine A.

◆ 1799. *The Heart Speaks Many Ways.* New York:
Delacorte, 1982. 375 pp.

◆May be suitable for young adult readers

After Emily's Spanish boyfriend disappears in the Spanish Civil War, she returns to her upper-class Irish home but soon leaves again for the WAAF.
Genre(s): War Story.

Porter, Katherine Anne

1800. *Ship of Fools.* Boston: Little, Brown, 1962. 497 pp.
The 48 first-class passengers and the 900 Spaniards in steerage on a passenger-freighter crossing from Mexico to Germany in 1931 are traveling on a voyage of life.
Genre(s): Allegory.

Rabon, Israel

1801. *The Street.* Trans. Leonard Wolf. New York: Schocken, 1985. 184 pp.
A Jewish man wanders the streets of Poland after World War I, not knowing what to do in the hopelessness of the times.
Genre(s): Jewish Fiction.

Raddatz, Fritz J

1802. *The Survivor.* Boston: Little, Brown, 1989. 128 pp.
Bernd's father harshly disciplines him, and his stepmother belittles him during World War II in Berlin, but he stays alive after the war as a black marketeer while his father dies from tuberculosis, imprisoned in their bombed home.
Genre(s): War Story.

Ramati, Alexander

◆ 1803. *And the Violins Stopped Playing.* New York: Watts, 1986. 237 pp.
Mirga, a Gypsy survivor of the Holocaust, which took the lives of 500,000 Gypsies, recalls his culture and his people's capture and transfer to Auschwitz.
Genre(s): War Story.

Rand, Ayn

1804. *We the Living.* New York: Random House, 1959. 433 pp.
Kira Argounova is a young student with an aristocrat and a communist for lovers in Russia in 1922.
Genre(s): War Story; Love Story.

Rangel-Ribeiro, Victor

1805. *Tivolem.* Minneapolis, MN: Milkweed, 1998. 346 pp.
When Marie-Santana returns to her village of Tivolem in the Porguese colony of Goa, she meets amateur violinist Simon Fernandes.
Award(s): Milkweed Prize for Fiction.
Genre(s): Domestic Fiction.

Read, Piers Paul

1806. *The Free Frenchman.* New York: Random House, 1986. 586 pp.

After the Nazis invade, Bertrand de Roujay leaves France for London to join the Free French under De Gaulle, but his brother remains in France and collaborates with the Germans.
Genre(s): War Story; Family Saga.

1807. *Polonaise.* Philadelphia: Lippincott, 1976. 346 pp.
After the Kornowski family becomes bankrupt in Poland, Krystyna participates in events in Europe including the Spanish Civil War and World War II, while her brother seems unable to act.
Genre(s): War Story.

Reinhardt, Richard

1808. *The Ashes of Smyrna.* New York: Harper, 1971. 416 pp.
Two Turkish brothers and one's Greek wife suffer the intense hatreds between the two brothers in Constantinople and Anatolia after World War I as Kemal Atatürk rises to power.
Genre(s): Adventure Story; War Story.

Remarque, Erich Maria

1809. *The Black Obelisk.* Trans. Denver Lindley. New York: Harcourt, 1957. 434 pp.
In Germany, during the 1920s, a worker at a coffin and tombstone company endures the skyrocketing inflation and interacts with those around him.

1810. *The Night in Lisbon.* Trans. Ralph Manheim. New York: Harcourt, 1964. 244 pp.
In 1942, a German refugee offers to give another refugee his passport and passage to the United States if he will listen to the donor's story, which starts in the 1930s.
Genre(s): War Story.

1811. *The Road Back.* Trans. A.W. Wheen. Boston: Little, Brown, 1931. 343 pp.
In the sequel to *All Quiet on the Western Front,* German soldiers returned to peacetime after World War I cannot adjust to the country's riotous mood.

1812. *Three Comrades.* Trans. A.W. Wheen. Boston: Little, Brown, 1937. 479 pp.
In 1928, three German ex-soldiers fall in love with the same girl, but the one who wins her then watches her struggle with tuberculosis.
Genre(s): Love Story.

1813. *A Time to Love and a Time to Die.* Trans. Denver Lindley. New York: Harcourt, 1954. 378 pp.
Near the end of World War II, Ernst goes on furlough and marries Elisabeth, but after returning to the front, he kindly releases Russian prisoners, one of whom turns and kills him.
Genre(s): War Story; Love Story.

Rezvani

1814. *Light-Years.* Trans. A.M. Sheridan Smith. New York: Harcourt, 1971. 382 pp.

A young Russian immigrant in Paris during the 1940s is abandoned emotionally by his parents and supported by females who tend to betray each other.
Genre(s): War Story.

Rezzori, Gregor von

1815. *Oedipus at Stalingrad.* Trans. H.R. Broch de Rothermann. New York: Farrar, Straus and Giroux, 1994. 304 pp.
Baron Traugott von Jassilkowski attempts to establish himself in Berlin's high society prior to World War II by learning manners from a countess and choosing the right woman to marry.
Genre(s): Satire.

Richmond, Donald

◆ 1816. *The Dunkirk Directive.* New York: Stein and Day, 1978. 375 pp.
Twelve German soldiers disguised as British sail to England after Dunkirk to destroy the Spitfire bomber factory in Southampton.
Genre(s): War Story.

Roberts, Michelle

1817. *Daughters of the House.* New York: Morrow, 1993. 192 pp.
Cousins Therese and Leonie remember their childhood and the events in their village after World War II and discover among their secrets an unexpected relationship.
Award(s): W.H. Smith Prize.
Genre(s): War Story; Gothic Fiction.

Robinson, Derek

1818. *Piece of Cake.* New York: Knopf, 1984. 572 pp.
The RAF Hornet squadron resists innovation and has morale problems as it prepares to fight the Luftwaffe in 1939.
Genre(s): War Story.

Robles, Emmanuel

1819. *Vesuvius.* Trans. Milton Stansbury. Englewood Cliffs, NJ: Prentice Hall, 1970. 244 pp.
In 1944 when the Allies invade Naples, Silvia meets a French army officer, Serge Longereau, who is convalescing, and they fall in love, but his return to the front changes their love even though they eventually marry.
Genre(s): War Story; Love Story.

Rodman, Howard A.

1820. *Destiny Express.* New York: Atheneum, 1990. 224 pp.
More concerned about his marriage than the Nazis, Fritz Lang must revise the end of his movie which Dr. Goebbels does not like in Berlin during 1933.
Genre(s): Political Fiction.

Rodoreda, Merce

1821. *Camellia Street.* Trans. David H. Rosenthal. Saint Paul, MN: Graywolf, 1993. 186 pp.

Nuns raise Cecilia, a foundling, in Barcelona after the Civil War, but she becomes a prostitute and is always searching for her origins.
Genre(s): Domestic Fiction.

Romains, Jules

1822. *Aftermath.* Trans. Gerard Hopkins. New York: Knopf, 1946. 435 pp.
Individuals in postwar France try to make amends for or to confess their deeds. (*Series:* Men of Good Will, 9)
Genre(s): War Story.

1823. *Escape in Passion.* Trans. Gerard Hopkins. New York: Knopf, 1946. 557 pp.
In 1933, some are concerned with their love affairs while others worry about the eminent breakdown of French society as Europe succumbs to political and economic crises. (*Series:* Men of Good Will, 13)
Genre(s): War Story.

1824. *The New Day.* Trans. Gerard Hopkins. New York: Knopf, 1942. 553 pp.
In the 1920s, European social and political conditions and the recent revolution in Russia strongly influence France. (*Series:* Men of Good Will, 10)
Genre(s): War Story.

1825. *The Seventh of October.* Trans. Gerard Hopkins. New York: Knopf, 1946. 295 pp.
France faces troubles on October 7, 1933. (*Series:* Men of Good Will, 14)
Genre(s): War Story.

1826. *The Wind Is Rising.* Trans. Gerard Hopkins. New York: Knopf, 1945. 588 pp.
In 1928, Jallez and Jerphanion continue to work on an escape from decadent French society. (*Series:* Men of Good Will, 12)
Genre(s): War Story.

1827. *Work and Play.* Trans. Gerard Hopkins. New York: Knopf, 1944. 562 pp.
In the second decade of the 20th century, Jerphanion and his friends are concerned about Hitler's rise in Europe. (*Series:* Men of Good Will, 11)
Genre(s): War Story.

Romano, Elio

◆ 1828. *A Generation of Wrath.* New York: Salem, 1986. 288 pp.
The Nazis force Elio Romano to help build a concentration camp in Auschwitz in 1940, and during the next five years, he survives 11 camps before being rescued by Americans.
Genre(s): War Story; Biographical Fiction.

Ross, Frank

1829. *The Shining Day.* New York: Atheneum, 1981. 352 pp.
Wilhelm Sommer is a better historian than he is a Nazi, and his wife persuades him to impersonate an English professor from London as a spy.
Genre(s): War Story; Spy Fiction.

Ross, Maggie

1830. *Milena.* London: Harper Collins, 1983. 280 pp.

Milena Jesenka Polak became Franz Kafka's translator in 1920, and they engaged in a brief affair and intense correspondence which becomes the basis for Amy the Gentile, married to a Jew, becoming involved with a Jewish writer.
Genre(s): Biographical Fiction; Love Story.

Rosshandler, Felicia

◆ 1831. *Passing through Havana.* New York: St. Martin's, 1984. 240 pp.

The narrator pretends that she is not Jewish after she and her family flee from the Nazis to Cuba as she tries to assimilate in the unusual culture.
Genre(s): War Story.

Roth, Joseph

1832. *Right and Left.* Trans. Michael Hofmann. Woodstock, NY: Overlook, 1992. 120 pp.

Paul Bernheim, a Berlin banker, marries for money, while his brother Theodore becomes a brownshirt posing as pure Aryan in order to hide his mother's Jewish ancestors.
Genre(s): War Story.

Rouaud, Jean

1833. *Of Illustrious Men.* Boston: Little, Brown, 1994. 160 pp.

When his father dies at 40, a young boy remembers the illustriousness of his father's life first as an adult in Brittany selling crockery and as a young lonely boy who escaped a forced-labor train to join the Resistance during the war.
Genre(s): War Story.

Rudner, Lawrence

◆ 1834. *The Magic We Do Here.* Boston: Houghton Mifflin, 1988. 212 pp.

Chaim Turkow, a Polish Jew with Aryan looks, stays alive during World War II by pretending to be a mute and working as a servant to a Nazi sympathizer.
Genre(s): War Story.

Rumanes, George N.

1835. *The Man with the Black Worrybeads.* New York: Arthur Fields, 1973. 360 pp.

Petros Zervos, the underground leader assigned to sabotage German supply boats, works out an alliance with the German commandant's mistress as part of his plan.
Genre(s): War Story.

Rusch, Kris

1836. *Hitler's Angel.* New York: St. Martin's, 1998. 224 pp.

In 1972, when Annie Pohlman interviews old Fritz Stecher, he is obsessed by the death of Hitler's niece and possible lover Geli Raubal in 1931 and with the case

which ruined his career as he came closer to the truth about her murderer.
Genre(s): Mystery; Biographical Fiction.

Rybakov, Anatoli

1837. *Children of the Arbat.* Trans. Harold Shukman. Boston: Little, Brown, 1988. 685 pp.

Sasha Pankratov, a young student, is unjustly arrested, kept in prison, and exiled to Siberia while Stalin wields his power. (*Series:* Arbat Trilogy, 1)
Genre(s): Political Fiction.

1838. *Dust and Ashes.* Trans. Antonina W. Bouis. Boston: Little, Brown, 1996. 480 pp.

As the Germans attack in World War II, Sasha Pankratov finds himself living in exile far from Moscow. (*Series:* Arbat Trilogy, 3)
Genre(s): War Story; Political Fiction.

1839. *Fear.* Trans. Antonina Bouis. Boston: Little, Brown, 1992. 686 pp.

Sasha Pankrotov, a student exiled to Siberia, returns to Moscow where his mother and friends live in the Arbat section, and he attempts to understand how the country could have accepted Stalin's rule. (*Series:* Arbat Trilogy, 2)
Genre(s): Political Fiction.

1840. *Heavy Sand.* Trans. Harold Shukman. New York: Viking, 1981. 380 pp.

The Nazi invasion of the Soviet Union in World War II changes the way of life for a Russian Jewish family.
Genre(s): War Story.

Sabatier, Robert

1841. *The Safety Matches.* Trans. Patsy Southgate. New York: Dutton, 1972. 256 pp.

In the 1930s, Olivier, 10, takes refuge after the death of his widowed mother with recently married cousins in Montmartre, and his introduction to the adult world includes a motley group of misfits, but as long as he has his matches, a hedge against the dark, he feels safe.
Genre(s): Bildungsroman (Coming of Age).

1842. *Three Mint Lollipops.* Trans. Patsy Southgate and Joan Wright Smith. New York: Dutton, 1974. 284 pp.

In the sequel to *The Safety Matches*, Olivier Chateauneuf leaves Montmartre for his Uncle Henri's home where he must adjust to very conventional manners.
Genre(s): Domestic Fiction.

Sagan, Françoise

1843. *Evasion.* Trans. Elfreda Powell. Hampton, NH: Severn House, 1993. 256 pp.

Four Parisians flee to the countryside during the Nazi occupation of World War II where they belittle rural life until German bullets silence them.
Genre(s): War Story.

1844. *A Reluctant Hero.* Trans. Christine Donougher. New York: Dutton, 1987. 191 pp.

After Alice and Jerome arrive at the home of Jerome's friend Charles in 1942 and ask him to hide political refugees, Alice falls in love with Charles.
Genre(s): War Story.

Salisbury, Harrison E.

1845. *The Gates of Hell.* New York: Random House, 1975. 409 pp.
From the 1920s into the 1980s, Andropov, chief of the Soviet secret police, clashes with the writer Andrej Sokolov over human rights.

Samelson, William

1846. *One Bridge to Life.* New York: Kampmann, 1989. 466 pp.
Vilek Samelson's family disappears one by one during the Holocaust as he and his brother move through concentration camps, and he survives Buchenwald.
Genre(s): War Story.

Samuels, Gertrude

1847. *Mottele.* New York: Harper, 1976. 160 pp.
Mottele, 12, joins the Jewish partisans in the forests of Poland during World War II.
Genre(s): War Story.

Sarton, May

1848. *The Bridge of Years.* New York: Norton, 1946. 342 pp.
While the Duchesnes live in Brussels in the years between the world wars, they try to keep an orderly cadence to their lives.
Genre(s): Domestic Fiction.

Sartre, Jean-Paul

1849. *The Age of Reason.* Trans. Eric Sutton. New York: Knopf, 1947. 397 pp.
The French prepare for war in 1938 when the Germans begin their advances through Europe.
Genre(s): War Story.

1850. *The Reprieve.* 1947. New York: Knopf, 1992. 445 pp.
In the sequel to *The Age of Reason*, the French are frantic during the eight days in September 1938 before the Munich Pact and the Nazi invasion of Czechoslovakia.
Genre(s): War Story.

1851. *Troubled Sleep.* 1950. New York: Knopf, 1992. 421 pp.
In the sequel to *The Reprieve*, the French have to live with defeat and the fall of Paris in World War II.
Genre(s): War Story.

Satterthwait, Walter

1852. *Masquerade.* New York: St. Martin's, 1998. 272 pp.
When Jane Turner investigates the supposed suicide of American expatriate Richard Forsythe in 1923, she

makes similar discoveries to those of Phil, a Pinkerton investigator, who is searching along a different path.
Genre(s): Mystery.

Saxton, Judith

1853. *All My Fortunes.* New York: St. Martin's, 1988. 592 pp.
Soldiers shoot Pavel and Eva's family, and the kulaks who raise them end up in one of Stalin's labor camps, but Pavel and Eva survive.
Genre(s): War Story; Political Fiction; Family Saga.

Schaeffer, Susan Fromberg

◆ 1854. *Anya.* New York: Macmillan, 1974. 489 pp.
Before she goes to America, the Polish Jew Anya who has escaped several times during World War II, always searches for her little girl, given to Gentiles at the start of the war.
Genre(s): War Story; Jewish Fiction.

Scott, Douglas

1855. *Eagle's Blood.* New York: David and Charles, 1985. 346 pp.
The Allied forces planning to attack North Africa want to keep the Italian aircraft carrier *Aquila* in port so they must neutralize it.
Genre(s): War Story.

Sela, Owen

1856. *The Petrograd Consignment.* New York: Dial, 1979. 312 pp.
As the czar's government falls in 1919, the Germans send Russian exiles into the country, hoping to speed the collapse.
Genre(s): War Story.

Sender, Ramon José

1857. *Seven Red Sundays.* Trans. Peter Chalmers Mitchell. 1936. New York: Ivan R. Dee, 1989. 285 pp.
Labor movement activities and a national strike in Spain during 1931 lead to the 1937 civil war.
Genre(s): War Story; Political Fiction.

Shaham, Nathan

1858. *Bone to the Bone.* Trans. Dalya Bilu. New York: Grove Weidenfeld, 1993. 352 pp.
The Russian Jew Avigdor Barkov goes to Palestine in the 1920s to build communes but disagrees with the Zionists and returns to the Soviet Union where a friend's betrayal lands him in a labor camp for 25 years.
Genre(s): Political Fiction.

Shaw, Irwin

1859. *The Young Lions.* New York: Modern Library, 1958. 689 pp.
A German, a homeless Jew, and a Broadway playwright survive World War II and unite at the end of the story.
Genre(s): War Story.

Sheppard, Stephen

1860. *Monte Carlo.* New York: Summit, 1983. 287 pp.
Harry, an American writer in Monte Carlo, falls in love with a Russian singer during World War II, unaware that she is a secret agent.
Genre(s): War Story; Spy Fiction.

Sherlock, John

1861. *The Golden Mile.* New York: Viking, 1986. 496 pp.
In the last days of the Warsaw ghetto, four women make plans to take jewels of murdered Jews to Switzerland so that they can give money to Jews who survive the war.
Genre(s): War Story.

Sholokhov, Mikhail

1862. *Harvest on the Don.* Trans. H.C. Stevens. New York: Knopf, 1961. 367 pp.
In the sequel to *Seeds of Tomorrow,* Davidov, a party member sent to a small town, has difficulty with a woman he loves and with revolutionaries hiding in the area.

1863. *Seeds of Tomorrow.* Trans. Stephen Garry. New York: Knopf, 1959. 404 pp.
In 1930, in the sequel to *The Don Flows Home to the Sea,* Davidov, a government representative, has problems organizing a collective in a community of Don Cossacks.

Shreve, Anita

1864. *Resistance.* Boston: Little, Brown, 1995. 240 pp.
A Belgian farm wife cares for an American pilot downed in the area, and he begins an affair with a local woman involved in the Resistance, each thinking that any day might be their last.
Genre(s): War Story; Love Story.

Signoret, Simone

1865. *Adieu, Volodya.* Trans. Stanley Hochman. New York: Random House, 1986. 448 pp.
Between World War I and World War II in Paris, Jews come from Eastern Europe to escape persecution and, like Nicole, start their lives anew.
Genre(s): War Story.

Silone, Ignazio

1866. *Bread and Wine.* Trans. Harvey Fergusson II. New York: Harper and Row, 1937. 331 pp.
After 15 years of exile, Pietro Spina returns to Italy disguised as a monk in order to help Italian peasants fearful of the Fascist dictatorship.
Genre(s): War Story.

1867. *Fontamara.* Trans. Harvey Fergusson II. 1934. New York: Atheneum, 1960. 240 pp.
Fontamara residents anguish over their water, which has been diverted to a rich neighbor in Fascist Italy.
Genre(s): War Story.

1868. *The Fox and the Camellias.* Trans. Eric Mosbacher. New York: Harper and Row, 1961. 139 pp.
Daniele maintains a secret outpost for the Italian anti-Fascist underground, but his daughter falls in love with a handsome young Fascist.
Genre(s): War Story.

1869. *A Handful of Blackberries.* Trans. Darina Silone. New York: Harper and Row, 1953. 314 pp.
Rocco returns to the Naples region after visiting Poland and Russia, where he became disillusioned with his communist beliefs, and his local party decides to discredit him.
Genre(s): War Story.

1870. *The Seed beneath the Snow.* New York: Harper, 1942. 589 pp.
While Pietro Spina hides out at his grandmother's house during the 1930s as a socialist in Fascist Italy, he decides to turn himself in to the police in order to save his friend, in the sequel to *Bread and Wine.*
Genre(s): War Story.

Simon, Claude

1871. *The Acacia.* Trans. Richard Howard. New York: Pantheon, 1991. 252 pp.
A man searches for the grave of his father, killed in World War I, and thinks of his own participation in World War II.
Genre(s): War Story.

Simpson, Rosemary

1872. *Dreams and Shadows.* New York: St. Martin's, 1986. 466 pp.
In 1925 Abby Sullivan arrives in Paris and meets Joseph Kelemen who becomes aware of being Jewish when Hitler's power begins to increase.
Genre(s): War Story.

Sinclair, Jo

◆ 1873. *Anna Teller.* New York: Feminist, 1992. 612 pp.
Anna Teller, a fighter, survivor, and matriarch, becomes a leader for her own family and those around her during World War II and the Hungarian Revolt of 1956.
Genre(s): Family Saga; War Story.

Singer, Isaac Bashevis

◆ 1874. *The Certificate.* New York: Farrar, Straus and Giroux, 1992. 227 pp.
David Bendiger returns to Warsaw in the 1920s planning to become a writer, but the city has changed, and instead of studying as he expects, he becomes involved with three women, marrying one of them in order to obtain a certificate for emigration to Israel.

1875. *Shosha.* New York: Farrar, Straus and Giroux, 1978. 277 pp.

Aaron Greidinger, a young writer, has many affairs but chooses the love of his youth, Shosha, to marry.
Genre(s): War Story; Jewish Fiction; Love Story.

Skibell, Joseph

1876. *A Blessing on the Moon.* Chapel Hill, NC: Algonquin, 1997. 268 pp.
Although the Nazis think they have murdered Chaim Skibelski in a small Polish town's mass grave, he escapes.
Genre(s): War Story; Jewish Fiction.

Skimin, Robert, and Ferdie Pacheco

◆ 1877. *Renegade Lightning.* Novato, CA: Presidio, 1992. 272 pp.
When Franco, an Italian raised in America, shoots down Josh Rawlins's plane in World War II, Rawlins vows to get him before finding that the Sicilian Mafia also wants Franco.
Genre(s): War Story.

Skvorecky, Josef

◆ 1878. *The Cowards.* Trans. Jeanne Nemcova. New York: Grove, 1970. 418 pp.
Danny is only interested in Irena and playing jazz on his saxophone as World War II winds to a close in Czechoslovakia, but as he looks around him, he sees only people interested in allying themselves with those in power.
Genre(s): War Story.

Smith, Henry T.

◆ 1879. *The Last Campaign.* New York: Walker, 1985. 191 pp.
German soldiers at the end of World War II return to Germany, hoping to be captured by Americans rather than Russians.
Genre(s): War Story.

Solmssen, Arthur R. G.

1880. *A Princess in Berlin.* Boston: Little, Brown, 1980. 374 pp.
In inflation-ridden Berlin during the early 1920s, an American ex-soldier comes to study and stays with the family of a pilot whose life he saved in World War I.

St. Aubin de Teran, Lisa

1881. *Nocturne.* New York: St. Martin's, 1993. 208 pp.
While young, Alessandro Mezzanotte becomes mesmerized by the gypsy Valentina and travels to be with her for an hour while she performs in other cities, but after he is mutilated in World War II, she rejects him, and he remains closeted for 40 years.
Genre(s): War Story; Love Story.

Stachow, Hasso G.

◆ 1882. *If This Be Glory.* Trans. J. Maxwell Brownjohn. Garden City, NY: Doubleday, 1982. 257 pp.

A wounded German soldier ponders why his country has become involved in such despicable actions but knows that his most important goal is to survive.
Genre(s): War Story; Political Fiction.

Stahl, Norman

1883. *Towers.* New York: Donald I. Fine, 1987. 717 pp.
After Hannah is raped, she and Mark, both children of wealthy Austrian landowners, marry, although Mark is not her child's father, and their family endures the war and a series of separations before they reunite in New York.
Genre(s): Family Saga.

Stead, Christina

1884. *House of All Nations.* New York: Holt, 1972. 800 pp.
In the 1930s, the Parisian Banque Mercure thrives on money from European nobility, investment risks, and stock manipulation, but when a man finds its secret books as the European economy begins its decline in the 1930s, chaos follows.
Genre(s): Satire.

Steel, Danielle

1885. *Remembrance.* New York: Delacorte, 1981. 471 pp.
After Mussolini's soldiers kill her aristocratic parents, Serena works as a servant in her family's home before marrying her employer.
Genre(s): War Story.

1886. *The Ring.* New York: Delacorte, 1980. 338 pp.
In pre-World War II Germany, Kassandra von Gotthard's daughter Ariana has a love affair with her Nazi captor before she escapes to New York.

Stern, Daniel

1887. *Who Shall Live, Who Shall Die.* Houston, TX: Rice University Press, 1995. 303 pp.
Both soldiers and civilians face the terrors and horrors of World War II, one as assailant and the other, victim.
Genre(s): War Story.

Steward, Samuel M.

1888. *The Caravaggio Shawl.* Boston: Alyson, 1989. 209 pp.
Gertrude Stein and Alice B. Toklas discover that the new Caravaggio purchased by the Louvre is a forgery, and they try to find the thief of the original and the murderer of the museum guard.
Genre(s): Biographical Fiction; Mystery.

1889. *Murder Is Murder Is Murder.* Boston: Alyson, 1985. 189 pp.
In 1937 Gertrude Stein and Alice B. Toklas spend the summer at a chateau where their young deaf mute gar-

dener reports that his father is missing, and Alice was the last person to see the man.
Genre(s): Mystery.

Szczypiorski, Andrezej

◆ 1890. *The Beautiful Mrs Seidenman.* New York: Grove, 1990. 240 pp.
In Nazi-occupied Warsaw, Irma Seidenman poses as Aryan with her beautiful blond hair and blue eyes until an acquaintance from before the war reveals her background.
Genre(s): War Story.

◆ 1891. *The Shadow Catcher.* Trans. Bill Johnston. New York: Grove, 1997. 176 pp.
In 1939 Krzys visits the country home of his father's friend in Poland and during this time, he learns about himself and the world around him.
Genre(s): Bildungsroman (Coming of Age).

Szeman, Sherri

1892. *The Kommandant's Mistress.* New York: HarperCollins, 1993. 273 pp.
Rachel escapes death in a concentration camp by becoming the commander's mistress.
Genre(s): War Story.

Tabucchi, Antonio

1893. *Pereira Declares.* Trans. Patrick Creagh. New York: New Directions, 1995. 136 pp.
An Italian journalist hires a young man to write obituaries of famous writers who might die any day, but because the man can only write political opinions, he draws the journalist out of his apolitical stance.
Genre(s): Political Fiction.

Taktsis, Costas

1894. *The Third Wedding.* Trans. Leslie Finer. New York: Red Dust, 1971. 301 pp.
Hecuba Longos refuses to respond with silence to life around her, as Greek wives are expected to do, during the period after the Balkan wars before World War II.
Genre(s): Domestic Fiction.

Tarrant, John

◆ 1895. *The Rommel Plot.* Philadelphia: Lippincott, 1977. 250 pp.
A retired French schoolteacher plots to assassinate the German Field Marshal Rommel in World War II.
Genre(s): War Story.

Taube, Herman

1896. *Kyzyl Kishlak: Refugee Village.* Takoma Park, MD: Dryad, 1993. 324 pp.
Volodia Tarko, a Jewish medic raised in Lodz, Poland, is assigned to a small Uzbekistan village where he helps Jewish and Gentile refugees struggling against both Nazis and Soviet Communists.
Genre(s): Medical Novel; Jewish Fiction.

Taylor, Kressmann

1897. *Address Unknown.* 1938. Cincinnati, OH: Story, 1995. 64 pp.
Friends in Berlin and San Francisco correspond about the terrible things happening to Jews in Germany in 1938.
Genre(s): War Story.

Thayer, James

1898. *Five Past Midnight.* New York: Simon and Schuster, 1997. 352 pp.
In 1945, when rumors say that Hitler will try to manage the war from the Alps, Jack Cray, a special forces assassin, endures amazing hardships to find Hitler before he hides.
Genre(s): War Story; Adventure Story.

Thoene, Bodie

1899. *Danzig Passage.* Minneapolis, MN: Bethany House, 1991. 416 pp.
When Nazi hostilities come to the fore, Jewish children must be evacuated from Germany. (*Series:* Zion Covenant, 5)
Genre(s): Christian Fiction; War Story.

1900. *Munich Signature.* Minneapolis, MN: Bethany House, 1990. 396 pp.
Elisa Murphy has information that might stop Hitler's destruction in World War II. (*Series:* Zion Covenant, 3)
Genre(s): Christian Fiction; War Story.

1901. *Prague Counterpoint.* Minneapolis, MN: Bethany House, 1989. 380 pp.
As Nazi horrors sweep through Europe, Elisa Lindheim is caught in the center. (*Series:* Zion Covenant, 2)
Genre(s): Christian Fiction; War Story.

1902. *Vienna Prelude.* Minneapolis, MN: Bethany House, 1989. 410 pp.
When one woman is safely disguised from Nazis during Hilter's terror, she worries about others who are not. (*Series:* Zion Covenant, 1)
Genre(s): Christian Fiction.

1903. *Warsaw Requiem.* Minneapolis, MN: Bethany House, 1991. 512 pp.
People work to save Jewish children as murders of Jews escalate during World War II. (*Series:* Zion Covenant, 6)
Genre(s): Christian Fiction; War Story.

Thoene, Bodie, and Terri Brock

◆ 1904. *The Twilight of Courage.* Nashville, TN: Thomas Nelson, 1994. 620 pp.
Among the deeds completed during World War II from the invasion of Poland to the battle of Dunkirk is that of a German soldier who hands a Jewish baby to a female American journalist.
Genre(s): War Story; Christian Fiction.

Thomas, D. M.

1905. *The White Hotel.* New York: Penguin, 1993. 274 pp.

Anna G., Freud's patient and a musician, becomes a study for hysteria before her story ends at Babi Yar with the Nazi atrocities.
Award(s): Los Angeles Times Book Award.
Genre(s): Biographical Fiction; Fantastic Literature.

Thomson, George Malcolm

1906. *Kronstadt 21.* New York: David and Charles, 1985. 218 pp.
Mikhail Ivanovich, known as Michael Simpson, goes to Russia in 1921 to overthrow the Bolsheviks with help from a banker and a strangler.
Genre(s): Mystery.

Tielsch, Ilse

1907. *Memories with Trees.* Trans. David A. Scrase. Riverside, CA: Ariadne, 1993. 109 pp.
Anna goes to her Aunt Walburga's farm during World War II where the trees give her a feeling of safety.
Genre(s): War Story.

Tine, Robert

1908. *Black Market.* New York: St. Martin's, 1992. 339 pp.
An all African American army unit staying in Rome in 1944 after the Nazis leave obtain a piece of art from Harlem, when art-dealer Peony Seagrave hires an investigator to look into the authenticity of the 17th-century painting by Guido Reni.
Genre(s): War Story; Mystery.

Tisma, Aleksandar

1909. *Kapo.* Trans. Richard Williams. San Diego, CA: Harcourt, 1993. 304 pp.
In Auschwitz, Laiman becomes a *kapo,* a prisoner who guards other inmates in return for privileges, but he asks for sex in exchange for food, and years afterward, when he sees one of the women he abused, the horror returns.
Genre(s): War Story.

1910. *The Use of Man.* Trans. Bernard Johnson. San Diego, CA: Harcourt, 1988. 306 pp.
Four friends who have grown up together in a Yugoslavian town take separate routes when World War II starts.
Genre(s): War Story.

Tomin, Zdena

1911. *Stalin's Shoe.* New York: Dodd, Mead, 1987. 160 pp.
After emigrating to Wales, Linda Wren remembers her encounters with the Russian army in Prague during 1945 and her crush on Joseph Stalin as a child.
Genre(s): Bildungsroman (Coming of Age).

Tomkiewicz, Mina

1912. *Of Bombs and Mice.* Trans. Stefan F. Gazel. New York: Yoseloff, 1970. 336 pp.

Nata is caught in the Warsaw ghetto during World War II, and her main concern becomes protecting her young son, Bobush.
Genre(s): War Story.

Tournier, Michel

1913. *The Ogre.* Trans. Barbara Bray. New York: Doubleday, 1972. 384 pp.
Abel Tiffauges, conscripted in 1939, becomes a prisoner of war in East Prussia where he serves as a forester and then as a solicitor of boys for a Hitler youth camp.
Award(s): Prix Goncourt.
Genre(s): War Story.

Trachtenberg, Inge

1914. *So Slow the Dawning.* New York: Norton, 1973. 249 pp.
Ellen and her half-sister Renata have an excellent education and enjoy travel from Berlin in pre-Hitler days before they begin to realize that Hitler's rise has changed their lives when they leave for Holland.
Genre(s): War Story; Jewish Fiction.

Trifonov, Yuri

1915. *Disappearance.* Trans. David Lowe. Ann Arbor, MI: Ardis, 1991. 181 pp.
A Soviet boy and his family experience the Great Terror and Stalin's purge during the 1930s.
Genre(s): Political Fiction.

Trotter, William R.

1916. *Winter Fire.* New York: Dutton, 1993. 485 pp.
Erich Ziegler, a German intelligence officer in Finland during World War II, meets Jean Sibelius and finds that his eighth symphony may exist, and Ziegler, a conductor, wants to present the work to the world.
Genre(s): Biographical Fiction; Musical Fiction; War Story.

Troyat, Henri

1917. *Elizabeth.* Trans. Nicolas Monjo. New York: Simon and Schuster, 1959. 407 pp.
Elizabeth, the daughter of Amélie and Pierre, goes to live with relatives while her mother and father work. (*Series:* The Seed and the Fruit, 3)
Genre(s): Domestic Fiction.

1918. *The Encounter.* New York: Simon and Schuster, 1962. 411 pp.
During the German occupation, Elizabeth lives alone in Paris until she meets Boris. (*Series:* The Seed and the Fruit, 5)
Genre(s): War Story.

1919. *Strangers On Earth.* New York: Crowell, 1958. 328 pp.

The Danov family, exiles in Paris during the 1920s, have difficulty adjusting to their new situation.

Tuccille, Jerome

1920. *The Mission.* New York: D.I. Fine, 1991. 228 pp.
Rudolph Hess flies into Scotland in May 1941 to convince England to stop fighting in Europe so that Germany can concentrate on fighting the Russians.
Genre(s): Biographical Fiction; War Story.

Turnbull, Peter

1921. *The Claws of the Gryphon.* New York: St. Martin's, 1986. 352 pp.
When Lieutenant David Connor arrives from the United States in 1944, he becomes involved in the German operation during the Battle of the Bulge to use English-speaking troops dressed in American uniforms to disrupt the Allies.
Genre(s): War Story; Adventure Story.

Uhlman, Fred

◆ 1922. *Reunion.* New York: Farrar, Straus and Giroux, 1977. 112 pp.
Hans Schwarz, son of a Jewish doctor, has a close friend whose mother keeps a picture of Hitler on her dressing table in 1932.
Genre(s): Domestic Fiction.

Undset, Sigrid

1923. *Burning Bush.* New York: Knopf, 1932. 396 pp.
After World War I, Paul Selmer discovers religion and converts to Catholicism, but at the same time, he begins to grow disinterested in his young wife, in the sequel to *Wild Orchid.*
Genre(s): Domestic Fiction.

1924. *Wild Orchid.* New York: Knopf, 1931. 338 pp.
Paul Selmer has no spiritual background or experience in love, but he falls in love with Bjorg.
Genre(s): Domestic Fiction.

Unsworth, Barry

1925. *The Rage of the Vulture.* Boston: Houghton Mifflin, 1983. 443 pp.
Captain Robert Markham lives with his wife and son in Constantinople where he helps arrange a peacekeeping force for Turkey against Macedonia, but throughout his stay, the memory of his Armenian love killed by the Turks haunts him, and he spends much of his time trying to protect the Armenians from Turkish genocide.
Genre(s): War Story.

Uris, Leon

1926. *Mila 18.* Garden City, NY: Doubleday, 1961. 539 pp.

From their command post at Mila 18, several Warsaw Jews fight off the Germans in the ghetto with homemade weapons.
Genre(s): War Story.

Van Rjndt, Philippe

1927. *Last Message to Berlin.* New York: Putnam, 1984. 444 pp.
In 1940, the Germans try to capture the gold that the British are supposedly moving to America for safekeeping.
Genre(s): War Story.

Villars, Elizabeth

1928. *The Normandie Affair.* Garden City, NY: Doubleday, 1982. 319 pp.
In 1936, several passengers crossing the Atlantic on the *Normandie* experience major changes in their lives.
Genre(s): Sea Story.

Vittorini, Elio

1929. *Men and Not Men.* Trans. Sarah Henry. New York: Marlboro, 1985. 208 pp.
The Milan Resistance works in World War II to ambush the Germans.
Genre(s): War Story.

Voinovich, Vladimir

1930. *The Life and Extraordinary Adventures of Private Ivan Chonkin.* New York: Farrar, Straus and Giroux, 1977. 315 pp.
As World War II begins, a private in the Red Army encounters Stalin's military institutions.
Genre(s): Adventure Story.

Wall, Alan

1931. *Bless the Thief.* New York: Crown, 1998. 224 pp.
The work of Delaquay intrigues Tom Lynch, and he makes forgeries of it while simultaneously dwelling on his father's death in the Hindenburg.
Genre(s): Adventure Story.

Watkins, Paul

◆ 1932. *Night over Day over Night.* New York: Knopf, 1988. 320 pp.
In 1944, a boy, 17, joins the *Waffen SS*, goes to boot camp, and experiences the Ardennes offensive and its horrors.
Genre(s): War Story; Bildungsroman (Coming of Age).

Weil, Grete

1933. *Last Trolley from Beethovenstraat.* Trans. John Barrett. Lincoln, MA: David R. Godine, 1997. 176 pp.
While a journalist in Amsterdam during World War II, Andreas shelters Daniel, 17, before David dies at Mauthausen concentration camp.
Genre(s): War Story.

Weil, Jiri

1934. *Life with a Star.* Trans. Ruzena Kovarikova. New York: Farrar, Straus and Giroux, 1989. 208 pp.

Roubicek, a sickly bank clerk, records the strictures against Jews and watches them meekly acquiese in Warsaw, and when he begins to rebel, a Czech friend helps him hide.

Genre(s): War Story.

1935. *Mendelssohn Is on the Roof.* New York: Farrar, Straus and Giroux, 1991. 211 pp.

When a Nazi sees a statue of the Jewish composer Mendelssohn on top of a building, he demands that the statue be removed while rounding up all of the Jews in town.

Genre(s): War Story.

Weinberg, Marcel

♦ 1936. *Spots of Time.* New York: Macmillan, 1972. 240 pp.

The narrator, a war orphan at seven, survives refugee camps, disappointments, and life in an orphanage until he is 13, and makes connections with others who belie their youth with their worldly wisdom.

Genre(s): War Story.

Weiss, Ernst

1937. *The Eyewitness.* Boston: Houghton Mifflin, 1977. 206 pp.

Records from a hospital stay in 1918 when Hitler was diagnosed with psychopathic hysteria are destroyed and the doctor commits suicide in 1933.

Genre(s): Biographical Fiction.

Welt, Elly

1938. *Berlin Wild.* New York: Viking, 1986. 358 pp.

Josef Bernhardt's intelligence and wit help him survive in Berlin after 1943, but he feels guilty because those he loves perish.

Genre(s): War Story.

Werfel, Franz

1939. *Cella: Or, the Survivors.* Trans. Joachim Neuroschel. New York: Henry Holt, 1989. 244 pp.

Hans Bodenheim, a Jewish lawyer married to a Christian in a small Austrian town, slowly awakens to the horrors of Hitler.

Genre(s): War Story.

Wesley, Mary

1940. *A Sensible Life.* New York: Viking, 1990. 364 pp.

In 1926, a group of international vacationers meets at a Brittany resort and makes commitments to each other to remain friends forever.

West, Paul

1941. *The Very Rich Hours of Count von Stauffenberg.* New York: Harper and Row, 1980. 359 pp.

Claus von Stauffenberg, a calvary officer, tries to kill Hitler at least four times before planting a bomb that he is positive will kill Hitler with its blast.

Genre(s): Biographical Fiction; War Story.

Wetherell, W. D.

1942. *Chekhov's Sister.* Boston: Little, Brown, 1990. 288 pp.

Chekhov's sister Maria Pavlova tries to save her brother's villa and its valuable contents in Yalta from the predatator Nazis during World War II.

Genre(s): War Story.

Wharton, William

1943. *A Midnight Clear.* New York: Knopf, 1982. 230 pp.

A mistake sends a group of very intelligent youths to the French front in World War II where they, with Will Knott, entertain themselves by playing bridge with no cards before they die.

Genre(s): War Story.

White, Alan

1944. *The Long Drop.* New York: Harcourt, 1970. 220 pp.

A group of men volunteer for a dangerous mission in Belgium during World War II for which they must undergo rigorous training.

Genre(s): War Story; Adventure Story.

1945. *The Long Watch.* New York: Harcourt, 1971. 160 pp.

Four British commandos drop into Chartres, France, in 1943, to infiltrate a prison in order to talk to an old chemistry professor who can tell them about picrates, an alternative to nitrogen as material for fuse explosives.

Genre(s): War Story; Adventure Story.

Wiesel, Elie

1946. *The Forgotten.* New York: Summit, 1992. 304 pp.

A father, fearful of losing his memory, tells his son the stories of his father's murder in Carpathia, of his own life as a teenager in the army, and his return to a ghetto with no Jews left.

Genre(s): War Story.

1947. *The Gates of the Forest.* Trans. Frances Frenaye. New York: Holt, Rinehart and Winston, 1966. 226 pp.

Gregor, 17, survives in a cave in Hungary before finding safety, but not peace, in the United States.

Genre(s): War Story.

◆ 1948. *Night, Dawn, the Accident.* New York: Hill and Wang, 1972. 318 pp.
Three novels relate the story of a boy's experiences at Auschwitz and Buchenwald, a boy's resistance to shooting a British officer in Palestine, and an Auschwitz survivor's questioning of the meaning of life.
Genre(s): War Story.

1949. *The Testament.* Trans. Marion Wiesel. New York: Summit, 1981. 346 pp.
A son, reading his father's diary about life in Berlin, Paris, Spain, and Russia before he was executed in 1947, finds there an idealist.
Genre(s): War Story.

Wingate, John

◆ 1950. *Go Deep.* New York: St. Martin's, 1985. 190 pp.
British naval operations in Malta help to save the island during World War II.
Genre(s): War Story.

Winslow, Pauline Glen

1951. *The Windsor Plot.* New York: St. Martin's, 1985. 367 pp.
Hitler launches a complex plan to gain support of the Duke of Windsor during World War II.
Genre(s): War Story; Political Fiction.

Winward, Walter

1952. *The Midas Touch.* New York: Simon and Schuster, 1982. 288 pp.
The Allies plan to bomb ball-bearing factories in Schweinfurt, Germany, but Nazis capture the men sent to rescue the owner and his niece and learn about the plan.
Genre(s): War Story.

Wiseman, Thomas

1953. *The Day Before Sunrise.* New York: Holt, Rinehart and Winston, 1976. 347 pp.
The Germans try to get concessions and the best terms for themselves after World War II.
Genre(s): War Story; Spy Fiction.

1954. *The Time Before the War.* London: J. Cape, 1993. 219 pp.
During the Nazi occupation of Paris, Markus Rossack, an artist, watches his lover Betty and her other lover in the role of voyeur.
Genre(s): War Story; Love Story.

Wodin, Natascha

◆ 1955. *Once I Lived.* Baltimore, MD: Serpent's Tail, 1992. 210 pp.
As she looks at her stillborn child, conceived during a rape, the narrator tells about her own childhood in World War II when she and her Russian parents fled the Ukraine looking for food but instead found death and abuse.
Genre(s): War Story.

Wojdowski, Bogdan

1956. *Bread for the Departed.* Trans. Madeline G. Levine. Chicago: Northwestern University Press, 1997. 403 pp.
A young boy who lives in the Warsaw Ghetto from the ages of 10 to 12, grovels daily for bread.
Genre(s): War Story.

Wolff, Milton

1957. *Another Hill.* Chicago: University of Chicago Press, 1994. 395 pp.
Mitch Castle goes to Spain at 21 to fight in the civil war against Franco, and as people in his battalion die, he becomes commander for the bloodiest battle.
Genre(s): Biographical Fiction; War Story.

Wright, Patricia

1958. *Journey into Fire.* New York: Doubleday, 1977. 391 pp.
Unlike the rest of his family, Kolya Berdeyev escapes exile from St. Petersburg, by having helped kill the Kulaks and being married to a party worker during Stalin's regime.
Genre(s): Political Fiction.

1959. *While Paris Danced.* Garden City, NY: Doubleday, 1982. 360 pp.
After World War I, the New England Red Cross worker Eve Daunay marries a shell-shocked Frenchman and searches for her father-in-law's murderer.
Genre(s): Romance; Mystery.

Wylie, James

◆ 1960. *The Homestead Grays.* New York: Putnam, 1977. 382 pp.
A squadron of African American fighter pilots battles both the Germans and racism among the Allies in World War II.
Genre(s): War Story.

Yaffe, James

1961. *The Voyage of the Franz Joseph.* New York: Putnam, 1970. 448 pp.
In 1939 the German liner *St. Louis* sails from Hamburg with Jewish refugees from Hitler's Germany, which civilized nations refuse to accept for several months.
Genre(s): War Story.

Yarbro, Chelsea Quinn

1962. *Tempting Fate.* New York: St. Martin's, 1982. 662 pp.
Ragoczy escapes from a cell in Revolutionary Russia and heads to Bavaria with a little girl, Laisha Vlassevna, but he begins to fall in love with her, and when brownshirts batter her, he kills them. (*Series:* Saint-Germain, 5)
Genre(s): Gothic Fiction; Love Story.

Yasar, Kemal

1963. *They Burn the Thistles.* Trans. Margaret E. Platon. New York: Morrow, 1977. 412 pp.
In the sequel to *Memed, My Hawk*, Memed continues to fight for other Turkish peasants against an *agha* (feudal landlord) who wants more land.
Genre(s): Country Life.

Yoder, James D.

◆ 1964. *Black Spider over Tiegenhof.* Scottdale, PA: Herald, 1995. 232 pp.
A German girl reports a pacifist Mennonite family for hiding a Jewish doctor's 14-year-old daughter Ruth, and while Ruth nearly dies after being interned, the family's sons must go to war.
Genre(s): Christian Fiction; War Story.

Yolen, Jane

1965. *Briar Rose.* New York: Tor, 1992. 160 pp.
Beeca's grandmother tells her that she is a princess, and after her death, Becca investigates her grandmother's mementos and discovers her harrowing teenage years, including survival in a mass grave and Nazis killing her husband.
Genre(s): War Story; Jewish Fiction.

Yourcenar, Marguerite

1966. *A Coin in Nine Hands.* New York: Farrar, Straus and Giroux, 1982. 174 pp.
In 1933, a silver coin passes through the hands of nine people until it arrives in the hand of Marcella Ardeati, the estranged wife of a Facsist doctor, who plans to assassinate Mussolini.
Genre(s): Domestic Fiction; Political Fiction.

Yulsman, Jerry

1967. *The Last Liberator.* New York: Dutton, 1991. 268 pp.
Abe Cohen, pretending to be Jewish, participates in the Ploesti mission in Romania during World War II, and his captain, who is anti-Semitic, comes to admire his abilities.
Genre(s): War Story.

Zackheim, Michele

1968. *Violette's Embrace.* New York: Riverhead, 1996. 213 pp.
A biographer sifts through writer Violette LeDuc's notes to create a story of her life and of post-World War II France when LeDuc knew de Beauvoir, Sartre, Cocteau, and Genet.
Genre(s): Biographical Fiction.

Zalygin, Sergei

1969. *The Commission.* Trans. David Gordon. DeKalb: Northern Illinois University Press, 1993. 358 pp.
The people in Lebyazhka, during the period after the Bolshevik revolution in the 1920s, try to establish a commission to guard the nearby forest, but the group established decides to control a larger area.
Genre(s): Political Fiction.

Zeno

1970. *The Four Sergeants.* New York: Atheneum, 1977. 256 pp.
In the summer of 1943, four platoon sergeants, with precarious orders from their generals, parachute into Sicily to blow up a bridge.
Genre(s): War Story.

1946-1975

Abbott, Margot

◆ 1971. *The Last Innocent Hour.* New York: St. Martin's, 1991. 505 pp.
As Sally Jackson gathers information in 1946 to prosecute Nazi war criminals in Berlin, she finds a picture of her ex-husband murdering a child.
Genre(s): Love Story.

Abramov, Fyodor

1972. *Two Winters and Three Summers.* Trans. Jacqueline Edwards and Mitchell Schneider. New York: Harcourt, 1984. 382 pp.
In a northern village, a Russiant peasant family of mother and six children, waits for a new life after World War II, while the two eldest children sacrifice themselves for the rest.
Genre(s): Domestic Fiction.

Aksyonov, Vassily

1973. *The Winter's Hero.* New York: Random House, 1996. 496 pp.
Boris Nikitovich, in the sequel to *Generations of Winter*, stands up to the Stalinist government for his colleagues and reunites with his Bolshevik wife while his children and grandchildren suffer through the era.
Genre(s): Political Fiction; Family Saga.

Anthony, Evelyn

◆ 1974. *The Relic.* New York: HarperCollins, 1992. 277 pp.
When Lucy Warren's immigrant father dies, she takes his St. Valdimir's cross to the Ukrainian dissident leader, Dmitri Volkov, in Geneva.
Genre(s): Adventure Story; Political Fiction.

◆ 1975. *Stranger at the Gates.* New York: Coward-McCann, 1973. 320 pp.

The wife of a Nazi biochemist arrives at the Paris home of Comtesse Louise de Bernard and demands that she testify for her husband in the Nuremburg war crime trials. *Genre(s):* Romance.

Appelfeld, Aharon

1976. *The Iron Tracks.* New York: Pantheon, 1998. 224 pp.
Erwin Siegelbaum continues to ride European trains from place to place as he did during the Holocaust 50 years before, but since the war, he has been buying Jewish antiques from people who are unaware of their value to sell to collectors.
Genre(s): War Story.

Bassani, Giorgio

1977. *Behind the Door.* Trans. William Weaver. New York: Harcourt, 1972. 160 pp.
The narrator from *The Garden of the Finzi-Continis* changes schools, and after making a tenuous friendship with a new boy, he stands behind the door when other classmates encourage the new boy to talk against him in the 1950s.
Genre(s): Domestic Fiction.

Ben Amotz, Dahn

1978. *To Remember, To Forget.* Philadelphia: Jewish Publications, 1974. 399 pp.
When Uri Lam, a young architect, returns to Germany from Israel in 1959 to collect war reparations, he experiences fears that only a German student with common sense can help him quell.
Genre(s): Political Fiction.

Berger, Thomas

1979. *Crazy in Berlin.* New York: Delacorte, 1958. 438 pp.
Reinhart, stationed in Germany at the end of World War II, has strong feelings of guilt about Nazi treatment of the Jews, which his relationships with American Jews and others intensify.
Genre(s): War Story.

Böll, Heinrich

1980. *The Silent Angel.* New York: Picador, 1995. 192 pp.
Immediately after World War II, Hans returns to his German home in despair but discovers he is still able to love.
Genre(s): Love Story; War Story.

Boyle, Kay

1981. *Generation without Farewell.* New York: Knopf, 1960. 300 pp.
A German newspaper man falls in love with the wife of the colonel who heads the occupation unit in his town.

Brierley, David

1982. *Big Bear, Little Bear.* New York: Scribner's, 1981. 223 pp.

Just before the Berlin Airlift in 1948, someone in London reveals the identity of British agent George Orris, and Orris decides to lure the traitor to Berlin to expose him.
Genre(s): Mystery; Spy Fiction.

1983. *Shooting Star.* New York: Scribner's, 1983. 288 pp.
In a flashback, Steven Curtis, a London war photographer who changed his name from Istvan Ketesc, remembers the destruction of the 1956 Hungarian Uprising in Budapest after encountering ballet star Ilona Kisfaludy, who was 15 when they fought in the uprising together.
Genre(s): War Story.

Bruckner, Christine

1984. *Flight of Cranes.* Trans. Ruth Hein. New York: Fromm International, 1982. 372 pp.
Maximiliane Quindt, in a sequel to *Gillyflower Kid*, flees the advance of Soviet troops after being expelled from Pomerania for her wealth, and begins to accommodate anyone, Nazi or Jewish, who can help her survive.
Genre(s): War Story.

Buckley, William F. Jr.

◆ 1985. *High Jinx.* Garden City, NY: Doubleday, 1986. 261 pp.
In 1954, Blackford Oakes must avenge a disaster that led to the loss of 41 CIA agents, and he finds one of the culprits to be Beria, a sadist whose mentor is Stalin.
Genre(s): Mystery.

◆ 1986. *Stained Glass.* Garden City, NY: Doubleday, 1978. 322 pp.
Blackford Oakes works for the CIA in Germany in 1952 and collaborates with the KGB to assassinate the most prominent European anti-Communist.
Genre(s): Spy Fiction.

◆ 1987. *The Story of Henri Tod.* Garden City, NY: Doubleday, 1984. 254 pp.
Blackford Oakes, American CIA agent, goes to Berlin in 1961 where he hopes to learn what Warsaw Pact allies plan to do about the exodus of East Germans.
Genre(s): Spy Fiction.

◆ 1988. *Who's on First.* Garden City, NY: Doubleday, 1980. 275 pp.
In Hungary, Blackford Oakes, working for the CIA, tries to put the first satellite into orbit ahead of the Russians while others think he has caused the death of a Hungarian freedom fighter as the tanks roll into Budapest.
Genre(s): Spy Fiction.

Bukiet, Melvin Jules

1989. *After.* New York: St. Martin's, 1996. 384 pp.
Isaac Kaufman refuses help from organizations after World War II and decides to make money fast for a trip

to America, and he includes Fischl, a devout Jew, in his band of black market men.

Bunn, T. Davis

1990. *Berlin Encounter.* Minneapolis, MN: Bethany House, 1995. 190 pp.
During the Cold War, Jake Burnes works with NATO in Berlin and must find a way to rescue two scientists imprisoned in Stalin's Russia and bring them to the West. (*Series:* Rendezvous with Destiny, 4)
Genre(s): Spy Fiction; Christian Fiction.

1991. *Gibraltar Passage.* Minneapolis, MN: Bethany House, 1994. 191 pp.
After World War II, French captain Pierre Servais searches for his lost brother while seeking the help of the woman who once betrayed his trust. (*Series:* Rendezvous with Destiny, 2)
Genre(s): Adventure Story.

1992. *Istanbul Express.* Minneapolis, MN: Bethany House, 1995. 205 pp.
Col. Jake Burnes goes into eastern Europe during the Cold War where he confronts spies and double agents while trying to keep Stalin inside Russia. (*Series:* Rendezvous with Destiny, 5)
Genre(s): Christian Fiction.

◆ 1993. *Rhineland Inheritance.* Minneapolis, MN: Bethany House, 1993. 222 pp.
Captain Jake Burnes monitors the Nazis and their smuggling in Germany while establishing soup kitchens for the starving survivors of the war. (*Series:* Rendezvous With Destiny, 1)
Genre(s): War Story; Christian Fiction.

Céline, Louis-Ferdinand

1994. *Rigadoon.* Trans. Ralph Manheim. New York: Delacorte, 1974. 273 pp.
The narrator tries to leave Germany after World War II in the sequel to *Castle to Castle* and encounters unusual hardships and frustrations.
Genre(s): Biographical Fiction; Picaresque Fiction; Adventure Story.

Clifford, Francis

1995. *The Naked Runner.* New York: Coward-McCann, 1966. 255 pp.
When the East German police trap Sam Laker, a British businessman, on an errand for the British Secret Operations during the Cold War, he must do a despicable deed to save his son.
Genre(s): Adventure Story; Spy Fiction.

Creighton, Christopher, and Noel Hynd

1996. *The Khrushchev Objective.* Garden City, NY: Doubleday, 1987. 333 pp.
Irish radicals supposedly assassinate Lord Mountbatten in 1979, but some think that Mountbatten's role in a Khruschev summit meeting in England during 1956 is the real cause.
Genre(s): Biographical Fiction.

Davidson, Catherine Temma

1997. *The Priest Fainted.* New York: Holt, 1998. 240 pp.
The narrator visits Greece where she imagines her mother's life there thirty years prior and her grandmother as an immigrant.
Genre(s): Family Saga.

De Graaf, Anne

1998. *Bread upon the Waters.* Minneapolis, MN: Bethany House, 1995. 350 pp.
A couple fall in love in post-World War II Poland.
Genre(s): Christian Fiction; Romance; Spy Fiction.

1999. *Where the Fire Burns.* Minneapolis, MN: Bethany House, 1997. 320 pp.
Hanna and Tadeusz Piekarz have two sons in Poland during Stalin's Soviet regime, and one joins the Underground and the other follows his parents' faith. (*Series:* Hidden Harvest, 2)
Genre(s): Christian Fiction; Adventure Story.

De Hartog, Jan

◆ 2000. *The Inspector.* New York: Atheneum, 1960. 312 pp.
In 1946, a Dutch police officer helps a girl dying from tuberculosis contracted in a concentration camp get to Israel before she dies, although his aid will probably cost him his career.
Genre(s): War Story.

Demetz, Hanna

2001. *The Journey from Prague Street.* New York: St. Martin's, 1990. 152 pp.
Helene, the only member of her family to survive the Holocaust, lives in Prague, Munich, and New York after the war, where she marries, has children, and faces her husband's desertion.
Genre(s): Domestic Fiction.

Durrell, Lawrence

2002. *Quinx, or, the Ripper's Tale.* Boston: Faber and Faber, 1985. 201 pp.
Blanford, the writer, and Constance, the psychoanalyst, fall in love against a background of Gypsy camps as the search for the treasure of the Templars continues from the previous novels of the Avignon Quintet. (*Series:* Avignon Quintet, 5)
Genre(s): Love Story.

Fakinos, Aris

2003. *The Marked Men.* Trans. Jacquelin Lapidus. New York: Liveright and Boni, 1971. 272 pp.
In the Greek Civil War of 1947-1949, the partisans (the Reds) and the regular army (the Blacks) fight over the strategically located village of Doliani.
Genre(s): War Story.

◆May be suitable for young adult readers

Fallaci, Oriana

2004. *A Man.* Trans. William Weaver. New York: Simon and Schuster, 1980. 463 pp.
Alexandros Panagoules unsuccessfully tries to assassinate Greek dictator George Papadopoulis, but even when captured and tortured, he refuses to believe in dictatorship.
Genre(s): Political Fiction; Biographical Fiction.

Feibleman, Peter S.

2005. *The Columbus Tree.* New York: Atheneum, 1973. 472 pp.
A young American girl falls in love with an aging Spanish count in the 1950s.

Ferlinghetti, Lawrence

2006. *Love in the Days of Rage.* New York: Dutton, 1988. 116 pp.
While French students rage in Paris during 1968, an expatriate American woman and a French banker with sympathy for the students meet and fall in love.

Fitzgerald, Penelope

2007. *Innocence.* New York: Holt, 1987. 224 pp.
The youngest daughter in the aristocratic Florentine family of the Ridolfis marries a doctor who is trying to escape his family in the south.
Genre(s): Domestic Fiction; Political Fiction.

Fleutiaux, Pierrette

2008. *We Are Eternal.* Trans. Jeremy Leggatt. Boston: Little, Brown, 1994. 576 pp.
Estelle, the last member of the Helleur family to know the family's terrible past, calls out to a bodiless Madame to help her transform her story into opera.
Award(s): Prix Femina Award.
Genre(s): Gothic Fiction.

Forbath, Peter

2009. *Seven Seasons.* New York: Atheneum, 1971. 385 pp.
In 1968, a Czech playwright, American journalist, and a Slovak actress experience the brief democracy in Prague when Dubcek overthrows the totalitarian Novotny regime.
Genre(s): Political Fiction.

Forsyth, Frederick

2010. *The Day of the Jackal.* New York: Viking, 1971. 380 pp.
An Englishman plans to assassinate Charles de Gaulle, but police are alerted and begin to hunt him before he succeeds.
Award(s): Edgar Allan Poe Award.
Genre(s): Spy Fiction.

Francis, Clare

2011. *Wolf Winter.* New York: Morrow, 1988. 558 pp.
Ragna's husband, a Norwegian mountain climber, dies on the Russian-Finnish border, and she is drawn into the Cold War of the 1960s.

Friedman, Carl

◆ 2012. *Nightfather.* Trans. Arnold and Erica Pomerans. New York: Persea, 1994. 138 pp.
A young girl whose father survived a concentration camp during the Holocaust constantly tells her and her brothers that he has "had camp," so that they must carry the burden of his past even though they were not present.
Genre(s): War Story.

◆ 2013. *The Shovel and the Loom.* Trans. Jeannette Ringold. New York: Persea, 1996. 176 pp.
Chayah, the daughter of Holocaust survivors, lives in Antwerp during the 1970s, and searches for beliefs, but first she must experience a tragedy to understand her past.
Genre(s): Bildungsroman (Coming of Age).

Gainham, Sarah

2014. *A Place in the Country.* New York: Holt, Rinehart and Winston, 1969. 371 pp.
Robert Inglis, in the sequel to *Night Falls on the City*, serves as a young English officer in Vienna after World War II, where he meets Julia Homburg.

2015. *Private Worlds.* New York: Holt, Rinehart and Winston, 1971. 321 pp.
Julia Homburg returns to Vienna with her new husband, in the sequel to *A Place in the Country.* Sequel
Genre(s): Romance.

2016. *To the Opera Ball.* Garden City, NY: Doubleday, 1975. 424 pp.
Rolf, an Austrian soldier, offers to take a wealthy teenager to the Vienna Opera Ball as a favor to his friend, but then runs away with her.
Genre(s): Romance.

Grass, Günter

2017. *From the Diary of a Snail.* Trans. Ralph Manheim. New York: Harcourt Brace, 1973. 310 pp.
While making political speeches for a candidate, the narrator realizes that everything changes very slowly.
Genre(s): Political Fiction.

2018. *Local Anaesthetic.* Trans. Ralph Manheim. New York: Harcourt, Brace, 1970. 284 pp.
An old teacher recalls his life during the wars as he sits in the dentist's chair under local anaesthesia.

2019. *The Tin Drum.* Trans. Ralph Manheim. New York: Pantheon, 1963. 591 pp.
The dwarf Oskar Matzerath, who stopped growing physically at three but kept his mental faculties, plays a tin drum with which he stimulates his memory of the 20th century. (*Series:* Danzig Trilogy, 1)
Genre(s): Political Fiction.

Griffin, Gwyn

2020. *A Last Lamp Burning.* New York: Putnam, 1966. 512 pp.
A Neapolitan slum boy, half Italian, half Chinese, tries to survive against a backdrop of postwar aristocracy and the nouveaux riches.

Grossman, Vasily

2021. *Forever Flowing.* Trans. T.P. Whitney. New York: Harper, 1972. 224 pp.
After 30 years in prison for unspecified crimes, Ivan Grigoryevich returns to Moscow and then to the Ukraine, where his family home is no more than a few foundation stones and he laments the failure of Lenin and freedom.
Genre(s): Political Fiction.

Grynberg, Henryk

2022. *The Victory.* Trans. Richard Lourie. Evanston, IL: Northwestern University Press, 1993. 107 pp.
When a boy and his mother return to their Polish village after World War II, only two families survive, but all the houses have been taken, and they must move elsewhere.
Genre(s): Jewish Fiction.

Guareschi, Giovanni

2023. *Comrade Don Camillo.* Trans. Frances Frenaye. New York: Farrar, Straus and Giroux, 1964. 212 pp.
In the sequel to *Don Camillo Takes the Devil by the Tail*, communists traveling to Russia invite Don Camillo, and on the trip, he exasperates the communist leader Peppone when some of the group return to Catholicism.
Genre(s): Humorous Fiction.

2024. *Don Camillo and his Flock.* Trans. Frances Frenaye. London: Pellegrini and Cudahy, 1952. 250 pp.
A parish priest continues his verbal warfare with his Italian town's communist mayor in the sequel to *The Little World of Don Camillo*.
Genre(s): Humorous Fiction.

2025. *Don Camillo Meets the Flower Children.* New York: Farrar, Straus and Giroux, 1969. 256 pp.
In the sequel to *Comrade Don Camillo*, Don Camillo laments his loss of power in the parish as a result of the ecumenical movement.
Genre(s): Humorous Fiction; Christian Fiction.

2026. *Don Camillo Takes the Devil by the Tail.* Trans. Frances Frenaye. New York: Farrar, Straus and Giroux, 1957. 250 pp.
In the sequel to *Don Camillo's Dilemma*, Don Camillo defends the orthodoxy of his religion and democracy in the state in his arguments with the communist mayor, Peppone.
Genre(s): Humorous Fiction.

2027. *Don Camillo's Dilemma.* Trans. Frances Frenaye. New York: Farrar, Straus and Giroux, 1954. 255 pp.
While continuing his argument with the communist mayor, Peppone, Don Camillo continues to serve his parish and fight the Fascists in the sequel to *Don Camillo and His Flock*.
Genre(s): Humorous Fiction.

2028. *The Little World of Don Camillo.* Trans. Una Vincenzo Troubridge. London: Pellegrini and Cudahy, 1951. 238 pp.
In a small village in the Po Valley, a communist who happens to be a man of conscience and a priest who happens to be human interact.

Handke, Peter

2029. *Repetition.* New York: Farrar, Straus and Giroux, 1988. 246 pp.
Filip, 20, searches for his brother who disappeared 20 years before as a Slovenian patriot.

Harvey, John

2030. *Coup d'État.* New York: Atheneum, 1985. 480 pp.
After the Greek colonels' coup of 1967, Chryssa's husband tries to bring the junta into court, but the government sends him to prison while her sister's husband continues to support officers who ultimately become the losing faction.
Genre(s): War Story; Political Fiction.

Hegi, Ursula

2031. *Floating in My Mother's Palm.* New York: Poseidon, 1990. 158 pp.
In their small German town during the 1950s, no one mentions Hitler or the past, and Hanna's mother, an artist, feels both confined and protected in that place.
Genre(s): Domestic Fiction.

Hein, Christoph

2032. *The Tango Player.* Trans. Philip Boehm. New York: Farrar, Straus and Giroux, 1992. 220 pp.
After 21 months in prison, unjustly accused of political crimes, a professor, Hans-Peter Dallow, has difficulty readjusting to his East German society in 1968.
Genre(s): Political Fiction.

Hellenga, Robert

2033. *The Sixteen Pleasures.* New York: Soho, 1994. 327 pp.
In 1966, Margot Harrington, a book conservator, goes to Florence to help after the Arno River floods, and when she finds a rare manuscript of erotica in a convent, the

mother superior wants to sell it to raise money for their library.

Heywood, Joseph

2034. *The Domino Conspiracy*. New York: Random House, 1992. 552 pp.
In 1961, the Soviet Special Operations Group reforms because someone is trying to kill Khrushchev, while at the same time, CIA agents have found someone trying to kill recently elected President Kennedy.
Genre(s): Political Fiction; Spy Fiction.

Higgins, Jack

◆ 2035. *Confessional.* New York: Stein and Day, 1985. 278 pp.
In 1958, Soviet KGB agents train to infiltrate the Irish Republican Army in a mock Irish village built in the Ukraine.
Genre(s): Adventure Story; Spy Fiction.

◆ 2036. *Day of Judgment.* New York: Holt, Rinehart, and Winston, 1979. 263 pp.
A few days before John Kennedy, the American president, is to arrive in Berlin in 1963, East German police kidnap a Catholic priest and try to extort information from him.
Genre(s): Adventure Story.

Hlasko, Marek

2037. *The Eighth Day of the Week.* Trans. Norbert Guterman. New York: Dutton, 1958. 128 pp.
In 1956, three people wait in vain for liberation from their conquerors.

Hodge, Jane Aiken

◆ 2038. *Strangers in Company.* New York: Coward-McCann, 1973. 252 pp.
Stella Marten and her hired companion travel across Greece by bus and become participants in a plot to free political prisoners.
Genre(s): Romance.

Jackson, James O.

2039. *Dzerzhinsky Square.* New York: St. Martin's, 1986. 245 pp.
After World War II ends and Grigory Nikolayevich wants to return home from being a slave laborer for the Germans, he fears that he will be killed for collaborating with the enemy, and he decides to accept the Americans' offer to give him a new identity in exchange for espionage.
Genre(s): War Story; Political Fiction.

Jelinek, Elfriede

2040. *Wonderful, Wonderful Times.* Trans. Michael Hulse. New York: Consortium, 1990. 256 pp.
After World War II, a brother and sister, a teenage boy who has left school, and a bourgeois girl experience the chaotic freedom of life without war in Vienna.
Genre(s): Bildungsroman (Coming of Age).

Jones, James

2041. *The Merry Month of May.* New York: Delacorte, 1971. 361 pp.
Jonathan Hartley, editor of a literary magazine, documents the uprising of students and workers in France during 1968 while he watches the conflicts within an American family in Paris.
Genre(s): Political Fiction.

Kadare, Ismail

2042. *The Concert.* New York: Morrow, 1994. 443 pp.
In the early 1970s, Arian, brother of the Albanian foreign minister's wife, is in disgrace for disobeying army orders, but after the Albanians break with China, he admits to ignoring Chinese directives.
Genre(s): Political Fiction.

Katcher, Leo

2043. *Hot Pursuit.* New York: Atheneum, 1971. 224 pp.
After World War II, Robert Braden and others search for a group of communists herding Greek children into Albania.
Genre(s): War Story.

Kaye, M. M.

◆ 2044. *Death in Berlin.* New York: St. Martin's, 1983. 254 pp.
In 1953, Miranda Brane and Simon Lang search Berlin for Dutch diamonds stolen by the Nazis.
Genre(s): Mystery.

Kazantzakis, Nikos

2045. *The Fratricides.* Trans. Athena Gianakas Dallas. New York: Simon and Schuster, 1964. 254 pp.
In the 1940s, an elderly priest mediates between the Greek loyalists and the pro-communist rebels.
Genre(s): War Story.

Kirst, Hans Hellmut

2046. *Last Stop Camp 7.* New York: Coward-McCann, 1969. 319 pp.
The American commandant, Keller, and his deputy, Ted Harte, in a war criminal prison disagree on what to do with a former Nazi officer suspected of particular brutality during World War II.
Genre(s): War Story.

2047. *The Nights of the Long Knives.* Trans. J. Maxwell Brownjohn. New York: Coward-McCann, 1976. 279 pp.
After investigation, a German murdered in Lugano, Italy, turns out to be a former Nazi trained to murder on command.
Genre(s): Mystery.

2048. ***What Became of Gunner Asch.*** Trans. J. Maxwell Brownjohn. New York: Harper and Row, 1964. 275 pp.
In the sequel to *The Return of Gunner Asch*, Gunner Asch becomes a hotel owner and mayor of his German town after the war, and he must adjust to the new army and to young men acting as he once did.
Genre(s): War Story; Biographical Fiction.

Klima, Ivan

2049. ***Love and Garbage.*** Trans. Ewald Osers. New York: Knopf, 1991. 224 pp.
As a banned writer, the narrator must sweep streets in Prague with others whom the government has deemed outcast, but as he learns about their thwarted dreams, he better understands his own choices.
Genre(s): Political Fiction.

Kristeva, Julia

2050. ***The Samurai.*** New York: Columbia University Press, 1992. 341 pp.
In the late 1960s, Olga, an Eastern European student in Paris, falls in love with the leader of the leftist intelligentsia and joins the riots.
Genre(s): Political Fiction.

Kundera, Milan

2051. ***The Book of Laughter and Forgetting.*** Trans. Michael Henry Heim. New York: Knopf, 1980. 228 pp.
After a Communist party leader is hanged for treason, his face is airbrushed out of a photograph of prominent Communists.
Genre(s): Political Fiction.

2052. ***The Unbearable Lightness of Being.*** Trans. Michael Henry Heim. New York: Harper and Row, 1984. 320 pp.
After the 1968 Soviet invasion of Czechoslovakia, a married surgeon, Tomas, becomes a window washer while trying to reconcile himself to decisions that he and his wife must make about their relationship.
Award(s): Los Angeles Times Book Award.
Genre(s): War Story.

Lauterstein, Ingeborg

2053. ***Vienna Girl.*** New York: Norton, 1986. 383 pp.
Reyna in the sequel to *Water Castle*, Meinert, 15, comes out of hiding at the end of World War II, but can find little to stabilize her feelings about herself or the city.
Genre(s): War Story.

Lewis, Norman

2054. ***Within the Labyrinth.*** Boston: Atlantic Monthly, 1986. 212 pp.
When a British officer is posted in a small Italian town after World War II, he decides that he will not offer the lo-

cals bribes, but citizens in the town aggravate him in other ways and he begins to lose his idealistic perspective.
Genre(s): War Story.

Littell, Robert

2055. ***The October Circle.*** Boston: Houghton Mifflin, 1976. 193 pp.
A group of anti-communists in Sophia, Bulgaria, hope to liberate their country, but when one of them immolates himself over the death of his son, their mission becomes doomed.
Genre(s): Spy Fiction.

Lustig, Arnost

2056. ***Dita Saxova.*** Trans. Jeanne Nemcova. New York: Harper and Row, 1979. 189 pp.
Dita lives in a Prague house for Jewish girls and longs to experience the things that she has missed because of World War II.

Lvov, Arkady

2057. ***The Courtyard.*** Garden City, NY: Doubleday, 1988. 688 pp.
The 30-year residents of an Odessa apartment building experience the deprivations of life as they follow daily rituals.
Genre(s): Domestic Fiction.

Martinerie, Andrée

2058. ***A Life's Full Summer.*** New York: Harcourt, 1970. 287 pp.
Cecile watches her family and its frustrations in the 1960s while remembering her first love whom the Nazis murdered in the 1940s.
Genre(s): Domestic Fiction.

McCrum, Robert

2059. ***The Fabulous Englishman.*** Boston: Little, Brown, 1985. 274 pp.
After the Soviets kill his Czech girlfriend when they invade the country, Christopher Iles corresponds with a bookseller in Prague, and when he visits, he discovers who has been responding to his letters.
Genre(s): Political Fiction.

Meade, Glenn

◆ **2060.** ***Snow Wolf.*** New York: St. Martin's, 1996. 432 pp.
In 1953 Joseph Stalin dies mysteriously after Alex Slanski and Anna Khorev go into the country to assassinate him before he begins a rumored nuclear war.
Genre(s): Spy Fiction.

Meador, D. J.

2061. ***His Father's House.*** Gretna, LA: Pelican, 1994. 384 pp.
In 1973 Alabama law professor Robert Kirkman finds a letter written in World War I in his father's papers and

goes to East Germany to investigate, only to discover more questions than answers.
Genre(s): Political Fiction.

Mekler, Eva

2062. *Sunrise Shows Late.* Bridgehampton, NY: Bridge Work, 1997. 288 pp.
Communist Manya Gerson flees from anti-Semite Poland to a displaced-persons camp after the war, but she feels isolated because she worked in the underground rather than the camps and speaks little Yiddish, and she meets one man planning to go to Israel and another who is a scientist.
Genre(s): Jewish Fiction.

Mordden, Ethan

2063. *The Venice Adriana.* New York: St. Martin's, 1998. 304 pp.
In 1961, Mark Trigger, while living with her in Venice and writing her biography, searches for a recording of *Adriana, Lecouvreur* sung by Adriana Grafanas because he thinks that the record will provide a clue to her identity.
Genre(s): Mystery; Musical Fiction.

Neville, Jill

2064. *The Love Germ.* New York: Verso, 1998. 450 pp.
In May 1968, students involved in the Sorbonne uprisings include Polly, an Englishwoman, who falls in love with Giorgio, an Italian student and anarchist.
Genre(s): Adventure Story.

Oldenbourg, Zoé

2065. *Chains of Love.* New York: Pantheon, 1959. 495 pp.
Stephanie, a Jew converted to Catholicism, and Elie, the son of poor Russian refugees, reunite after World War II, in the sequel to *The Awakened.*
Genre(s): Romance.

Pal, Dolores

◆ 2066. *In Search of Mihailo.* New York: Harper, 1970. 192 pp.
When Carola goes to Paris in 1948, she falls in love with a Russian student priest, but he disappears, and after she moves to London, marries, and has four sons, a legacy leads her back to Paris in search of him.
Genre(s): Adventure Story.

Pearson, Diane

2067. *Voices of Summer.* New York: Crown, 1993. 272 pp.
In post-World War II, overweight Therese Aschmann wants to resume her interrupted opera career, but the small Austrian company with which she wants to start hesitates to pair her with a young, arrogant tenor.
Genre(s): Domestic Fiction; Musical Fiction.

Pekarkova, Iva

2068. *The World Is Round.* Trans. David Powelstock. New York: Farrar, Straus and Giroux, 1994. 229 pp.
Jitka leaves Czechoslovakia in the final years of Communist rule for Austria but enters an Italian refugee camp where she forms friendships with the few women there and tries to invent a story that will help her get a menial job in Vienna.
Genre(s): Political Fiction.

Petrovics-Ofner, László

◆ 2069. *Broken Places.* Boston: Little, Brown, 1990. 252 pp.
Pisti endures the Holocaust and communism in Hungary by creating images of the events in his mind, but by the time of the revolt in 1956, he has matured enough to understand the consequences.
Genre(s): War Story; Bildungsroman (Coming of Age).

Petrovska, Marija

2070. *Prague Diptych.* New York: Manyland, 1981. 144 pp.
In 1948, as a young Czech actress plans to defect to the West, she remembers the men in her life and the situation in Prague during the war, during Prague's uprising in 1945, and during the Communist coup of 1948.
Genre(s): War Story.

Peyrefitte, Roger

2071. *Knights of Malta.* New York: Phillips, 1959. 317 pp.
In the 1950s, an ambitious cardinal tries to gain control of the Order of Malta for the Vatican.
Genre(s): Political Fiction.

Phillips, Michael R.

2072. *Escape to Freedom.* Wheaton, IL: Tyndale House, 1994. 489 pp.
Sabina von Dortmann allies with American Matthew McCallum to rescue her father from East Germany as the Cold War begins. (*Series:* Secret of the Rose, 3)
Genre(s): Christian Fiction; Romance.

Plante, David

2073. *The Foreigner.* New York: Atheneum, 1984. 237 pp.
In 1959, in the sequel to *The Catholic*, a young American in Barcelona becomes involved in an unexpected world for which he is unprepared.
Genre(s): Adventure Story.

Price, Anthony

2074. *Soldier No More.* Garden City, NY: Doubleday, 1982. 240 pp.
In France during 1957, Chief David Audley of British Intelligence uses the contacts of one double agent to catch another double agent and a spy.
Genre(s): Spy Fiction.

Reeman, Douglas

2075. *White Guns.* London: Heinemann, 1989. 325 pp.
Lieutenant Vere Marriott feels that the peace of Kiel Harbour in 1945 is uneasy.
Genre(s): Sea Story.

Roshchin, Mikhail

◆ 2076. *First Love.* Trans. Antonina W. Bouis. New York: Marion Boyars, 1991. 140 pp.
When he is 16, a Russian students falls in love with his teacher, Anna Nikolayevna.
Genre(s): Love Story; Bildungsroman (Coming of Age).

Rouaud, Jean

2077. *The World More or Less.* Trans. Barbara Wright. Boston: Little, Brown, 1998. 224 pp.
In France during the mid-1960s, a fatherless boy copes with poor vision, his first love, and his lack of athletic ability in the sequel to *Of Illustrious Men.*
Genre(s): Bildungsroman (Coming of Age).

Roudybush, Alexandra

2078. *A Gastronomic Murder.* Garden City, NY: Doubleday, 1973. 185 pp.
A robbery followed by a murder in American-occupied Germany leads to the identity of the gluttonous thief at his *auberge* in Brittany.
Genre(s): Mystery.

Rye, Bjorn Robinson

2079. *The Expatriate.* Indianapolis: Bobbs-Merrill, 1975. 217 pp.
An older woman becomes the lover of a young man in 1954 and impresses him with the people she knew in Paris, including Hem and Zelda.
Genre(s): Romance.

Salerno, Jeanette

2080. *Appassionata.* New York: Dial, 1981. 416 pp.
In 1952, while Rome is recovering from the effects of World War II and Mussolini's dictatorship, Sean Royden meets Bruna and falls in love.
Genre(s): Love Story.

Schlink, Bernhard

◆ 2081. *The Reader.* Trans. Carol Brown Janeway. New York: Pantheon, 1997. 218 pp.
Not until he becomes a law student after World War II does Michael Berg realize that the woman who found him ill and nursed him through hepatitis was illiterate and possibly a Nazi war criminal.
Genre(s): Mystery.

Sennett, Richard

2082. *The Frog Who Dared to Croak.* New York: Farrar, Straus and Giroux, 1982. 150 pp.

Tibor Grau, converted to communism when he sees the homeless, finally realizes that communism is not the answer just before the Hungarian revolt in 1958.
Genre(s): Political Fiction; War Story.

Skvorecky, Josef

2083. *The Miracle Game.* Trans. Paul Wilson. New York: Norton , 1992. 436 pp.
In 1949, a statue in front of a Bohemian church moves, and possible culprits include the Communist party trying to discredit the church and the priest trying to create a miracle, but in the 20 years after, the people need miracles to cope with the deprivations in their lives.
Genre(s): Humorous Fiction; Political Fiction.

2084. *The Republic of Whores.* Trans. Paul Wilson. Hopewell, NJ: Ecco, 1994. 256 pp.
In the 1950s, Czechs serving under Stalin's regime try to sabotage military exercises, and Danny Smiricky, with a Ph.D. in philosophy, represents them all.
Genre(s): Political Fiction.

Solzhenitsyn, Aleksandr

2085. *Cancer Ward.* Trans. Nicholas Bethell and David Burg. New York: Farrar, Straus and Giroux, 1969. 560 pp.
During February and March of 1955, several men pass through the men's cancer ward in a Soviet hospital.
Genre(s): Political Fiction; Medical Novel.

2086. *The First Circle.* Trans. Thomas P. Whitney. New York: Harper and Row, 1968. 580 pp.
In a Soviet technical institute outside Moscow, favored political prisoners, including the scientists Nerzhin and Rubin, work in 1949 to create Stalin's scrambler phone.
Genre(s): Political Fiction.

2087. *One Day in the Life of Ivan Denisovich.* Trans. Ralph Parker. New York: Dutton, 1963. 160 pp.
One day in 1951, Ivan Denisovich continues the rituals he has created during eight years' imprisonment in a Stalinist labor camp in Siberia.

Spanidou, Irini

2088. *Fear.* New York: Knopf, 1998. 192 pp.
Anna's father, officer in the Greek military, does not allow her to fear snakes or the dark, but when she turns 13, she is surprised by her anxiety toward boys and her terror about the rumored serial killer in her neighborhood.
Genre(s): Political Fiction; Bildungsroman (Coming of Age).

Stead, Christina

2089. *The Little Hotel.* New York: Holt, Rinehart and Winston, 1975. 191 pp.

The inhabitants of a cheap pension-hotel in Montreux, Switzerland, discuss the problems of their late 1940s life with the hotel proprietress.

Stern, Daniel

2090. *After the War.* Houston, TX: Rice University Press, 1995. 247 pp.
Both soldiers and civilians try to readjust to life after World War II.
Genre(s): Domestic Fiction.

Taylor, Frederick

2091. *The Kinder Garden.* New York: Carroll and Graf, 1991. 460 pp.
In postwar Berlin just as the Soviet Blockade and Allied airlift begin, Boss Kind leads a band of orphans in theft and murder, which James Blessed of the Special Investigation Branch must investigate.
Genre(s): War Story.

Tertz, Abram

2092. *Goodnight!* Trans. Richard Lourie. New York: Viking, 1989. 364 pp.
The scholar Sinyavsky has as his alterego Abram Tertz, author of sensationalist fiction, while he reviews his life through six years of hard labor in the late 1960s.
Genre(s): Biographical Fiction; Legal Story.

Toíbín, Colm

2093. *The South.* New York: Viking, 1991. 240 pp.
Katherine Proctor flees Ireland for Spain, and, with a Catalan lover and another Irish painter in 1950, gives a sense of the connections between the Spanish Civil War, the Irish Civil War, and Catalonian nationalism.
Genre(s): Political Fiction.

Uris, Leon

2094. *Armageddon.* Garden City, NY: Doubleday, 1964. 632 pp.
Sean O'Sullivan, who hates Germans, falls in love with a German girl after World War II while the Russians and Americans clash over Berlin.
Genre(s): Love Story.

2095. *Topaz.* New York: McGraw Hill, 1967. 352 pp.
A Russian defector tries to get the French to believe that a Soviet espionage network called Topaz has infiltrated their government.
Genre(s): Spy Fiction.

Vaculik, Ludvik

2096. *The Axe.* New York: Harper, 1973. Canada pp.
A Prague journalist remembers his father, who had to become a political worker for the communist state, and the lovely Moravian village where they lived
Genre(s): Political Fiction.

Vassilikos, Vassilis

2097. *Z.* Trans. Marilyn Calmann. New York: Farrar, Straus and Giroux, 1985. 406 pp.
In 1963, Greek neo-fascists assassinate Z, a left-wing physician, and two men devote themselves to finding the hired killers.

Walter, Otto F.

2098. *Time of the Pheasant.* Trans. Leila Vennewitz. New York: Fromm International, 1991. 412 pp.
Thom Winter visits his aunt to ask about her diary entry indicating that his mother might have been murdered in 1961, and in his searching, he identifies his father's Nazi ties and Switzerland's probable violation of neutrality in World War II.
Genre(s): Mystery; Political Fiction.

West, Morris L.

2099. *The Lovers.* New York: Donald I. Fine, 1992. 295 pp.
Bryan Cavanaugh, former Australian navy man and lawyer, works on a wealthy man's yacht in the early 1950s, assigned to protect the man's Italian wife, a descendant of nobility, and they begin an affair, separate, and meet again 40 years later.
Genre(s): Romance.

Wiesel, Elie

2100. *The Fifth Son.* Trans. Marion Wiesel. New York: Simon and Schuster, 1985. 320 pp.
When the young Tamiroff finds out that his father tried to assassinate a German officer responsible for destroying his village but did not succeed, he decides that he will do it himself in the early 1960s.

Williams, Alan

2101. *The Beria Papers.* New York: Simon and Schuster, 1973. 319 pp.
When two Munich residents find memoirs of Lavrenti Beria, Stalin's chief of police, which detail the years 1945–1953, they uncover incriminating information about Soviet bureaucrats.
Genre(s): Biographical Fiction; Political Fiction.

1976 and After

Ehrenburg, Ilya

2102. *A Change of Season.* Trans. Manya Harari
and Humphrey Higgins. New York: Knopf, 1962.
299 pp.
Russians in a factory town experience a new phase of
their life when they are able to communicate with the
West.
Genre(s): Political Fiction.

Grass, Günter

2103. *Headbirths: Or, The Germans Are Dying
      Out.* Trans. Ralph Manheim. New York: Har-
court Brace, 1982. 136 pp.
As he observes Germans during their 1980 elections, the
narrator expounds on their doubts and the difficulties
they have making such decisions as whether they should
have a child.
Genre(s): Political Fiction.

James, Donald

2104. *The Fall of the Russian Empire.* New York:
Putnam, 1982. 336 pp.
A series of crises from crop failures to oil shortages and
unhappy workers leads to the fall of the Soviet Union,
even though loyal Russians still accept the ideals of the
Bolshevik Revolution.
Genre(s): Political Fiction.

Marks, John

2105. *The Wall.* New York: Putnam, 1998. 384 pp.
A few hours before the Berlin Wall falls in 1989, an
American spy defects to the East.
Genre(s): Spy Fiction.

Marsé, Juan

2106. *Golden Girl.* Trans. H. R. Lane. Boston: Little, Brown, 1981. 156 pp.
After Franco's death, Luys Forest tries to justify the time
he spent in the propaganda section for Franco and the
money he received, which was unearned.
Genre(s): Political Fiction.

Müller, Herta

2107. *The Land of Green Plums.* New York:
Henry Holt, 1996. 242 pp.
During Ceausescu's regime in Romania, the narrator recalls a childhood when her grandmother wandered in the
fields and her grandfather played chess, while city guards
and children ate green plums, and young men communi-
cated through coded letters.
Award(s): Kelist Prize; International IMPAC Dublin Literary Award.
Genre(s): Political Fiction.

Petrushevskaya, Ludmilla

2108. *The Time: Night.* New York: Pantheon,
1994. 155 pp.
Anna Andrianovna's son will soon be released from
prison, her promiscuous daughter lives at home with a
lover and children, and her mother needs to leave the insane asylum, all of which Anna feels responsible for.
Genre(s): Political Fiction; Domestic Fiction.

Pohl, Frederik

◆ 2109. *Chernobyl.* New York: Bantam, 1987. 355
pp.
While the Director of the Chernobyl nuclear reactor goes
duck-hunting and the assistant is visiting his mother, the
Chief Engineer runs an unauthorized experiment which
shuts off the reactor's automatic safety system on April
16, 1986.

The British Isles

476-1289

Abé, Shana

2110. *A Rose in Winter.* New York: Bantam, 1998. 400 pp.
In the 13th century, Solange's father marries her to the evil Stephen, Earl of Redmond, but after nine years, when her love, Damon Wolf, become a marquess and visits her, she convinces him that her husband is dead.
Genre(s): Romance.

Anand, Valerie

◆ 2111. *The Disputed Crown.* New York: Scribner's, 1982. 297 pp.
Resistance to William of Normandy continues for two decades after the Battle of Hastings, and Hereward of Bourne leads rebellions against William before making peace.
Genre(s): War Story; Political Fiction.

◆ 2112. *Gildenford.* New York: Scribner's, 1977. 392 pp.
Brand Woodcutter goes from the farm into battle and becomes involved with the succession of Edward the Confessor and Edward's enemy, Earl Godwin, in the 11th century.
Genre(s): Biographical Fiction.

◆ 2113. *King of the Wood.* New York: St. Martin's, 1988. 468 pp.
Several people might have been responsible for the arrow that killed William Rufus, son of William the Conqueror, in AD 1100.

◆ 2114. *The Norman Pretender.* New York: Scribner's, 1979. 410 pp.
After Harald Hardraada arrives on the eastern coast of England in 1066 to join Tostig, Harold II defeats them at Stamford Bridge and marches south where William defeats him in the Battle of Hastings.
Genre(s): Biographical Fiction.

◆ 2115. *The Proud Villeins.* New York: St. Martin's, 1992. 320 pp.
Ivon Oddeyes, grandson of Sir Ivon de Clairpont (*Series:* the Norman knight captured and made a slave in 1036), and his granddaughter Margaret carry out the family history under the rule of William the Conqueror. (*Series:* Bridges Over Time, 1)
Genre(s): Epic Literature.

Attanasio, A. A.

◆ 2116. *Kingdom of the Grail.* New York: Harper-Collins, 1992. 500 pp.

A young Jewish girl is carefully trained and sent into Wales to rule, but she must face the old Baroness's enemies while trying to retain her Jewish faith.
Genre(s): Fantastic Literature.

Balling, L. Christian

2117. *Champion.* New York: Atlantic Monthly, 1988. 309 pp.
William Marshall, Earl of Pembroke, returns from the crusades and discovers that John, brother of Richard the Lion-Hearted, has marshaled forces to besiege Lady Isabelle de Clare at Pembroke Castle.
Genre(s): Political Fiction; Love Story.

Baltuck, Naomi, and Deborah Baltuck

2118. *Keeper of the Crystal Spring.* New York: Viking, 1998. 416 pp.
When Gandulf's father destroys the home of the Saxon lord Aethelstan in southwestern England during 1067, a priest declares that Aethelstan has no heirs, but a daughter has been smuggled out of the castle, and 20 years later, she meets Gandulf.
Genre(s): War Story; Domestic Fiction; Fantastic Literature.

Barnes, Margaret Campbell

◆ 2119. *The Passionate Brood.* Philadelphia: Macrae-Smith, 1945. 308 pp.
The minstrel Blondel loyally serves Richard Plantagenet in the 12th century.
Genre(s): Biographical Fiction.

Bates, Brian

2120. *The Way of Wyrd.* San Francisco: Harper and Row, 1983. 208 pp.
Brand, a monk in AD 674, experiences pagan rites with the help of Wulf, a sorcerer.
Genre(s): Fantastic Literature.

Becnel, Roxanne

2121. *The Maiden Bride.* New York: St. Martin's, 1996. 326 pp.
In the 12th century, people outside Linnea de Valcourt's family shun her because they believe that the second-born twin is evil.
Genre(s): Romance.

2122. *Where Magic Dwells.* New York: Dell, 1994. 390 pp.
Cleve FitzWarin travels to Wales attempting to locate the natural child of his lord, conceived during Henry II's

campaign, and he becomes attracted to Gruffydd, Seeress of Radnor.
Genre(s): Romance; Fantastic Literature.

Bennetts, Pamela

2123. *The Barons of Runnymede.* New York: St. Martin's, 1974. 272 pp.
King John shows his cruelty in the years leading to the Magna Carta in 1215 to both his family and his subjects.
Genre(s): Biographical Fiction.

2124. *The de Montfort Legacy.* New York: St. Martin's, 1973. 287 pp.
Simon de Montfort defeats Henry III at the Battle of Lewes and rules in his name while keeping Henry and Edward, the heir to the throne, in captivity, but when Edward escapes, he and his forces defeat Simon at Evesham.
Genre(s): War Story.

2125. *A Dragon for Edward.* New York: St. Martin's, 1975. 237 pp.
Edward I struggles to unite Wales with the rest of his kingdom in the 13th century as he battles against Llywelyn Ap Gruffydd.
Genre(s): Biographical Fiction.

2126. *Richard and the Knights of God.* New York: St. Martin's, 1973. 253 pp.
During the Third Crusade, Simon Fitzalan looks for a relic in the Holy Land and falls in love.
Genre(s): Romance.

2127. *Stephen and the Sleeping Saints.* New York: St. Martin's, 1977. 190 pp.
When Geoffrey de Mandeville, Earl of Essex, needs money during the reign of King Stephen, he kidnaps Leceline de Waterville and demands a ransom from her betrothed, but instead, her betrothed and two friends come to rescue her.
Genre(s): Biographical Fiction.

Berger, Thomas

2128. *Arthur Rex.* New York: Delacorte, 1978. 499 pp.
King Arthur, Merlin, and the knights of the Round Table live in ancient Britain but have contemporary concerns because Guinevere and the other women act liberated.
Genre(s): Fantastic Literature; Satire.

Beverley, Jo

2129. *Lord of Midnight.* New York: New American Library, 1998. 384 pp.
Renald de Lisle fights as the king's champion, and after killing Clarence of Summerbourne, takes his lands and his daughter Claire, but not until their wedding night does Claire realize that Renald killed her father.
Genre(s): Romance.

Billington, Rachel

◆ 2130. *Theo and Matilda.* New York: HarperCollins, 1991. 346 pp.

Beginning in the eighth century, Theo and Matilda are two characters in a series of love stories that occur at different times during the history of the town of Abbeysfield.
Genre(s): Love Story.

Blish, James

2131. *Doctor Mirabilis.* New York: Dodd, Mead, 1971. 335 pp.
Roger Bacon, 13th-century philospher and scientist, shows more concern for his investigations and theories than for people.
Genre(s): Biographical Fiction.

Bonallack, Basil

2132. *The Flame in the Dark.* New York: St. Martin's, 1976. 212 pp.
Alfred of Wessex wages war against the invading Vikings and saves Britain.
Genre(s): Biographical Fiction.

Bradley, Marion Zimmer

◆ 2133. *The Mists of Avalon.* New York: Knopf, 1982. 876 pp.
When Morgan le Fay (Morgaine) has to sacrifice her virginity during fertility rites, the man who impregnates her is her younger brother Arthur, whom she turns against when she thinks he has betrayed the old religion of Avalon.
Genre(s): Fantastic Literature.

Bradshaw, Gillian

◆ 2134. *Hawk of May.* New York: Simon and Schuster, 1980. 313 pp.
Gwalchmai Mac Lot, a terrible warrior, transforms his heritage of sorcery into service to Arthur and his Christian court at Camlann.
Genre(s): Fantastic Literature.

◆ 2135. *In Winter's Shadow.* New York: Simon and Schuster, 1982. 379 pp.
In the sequel to *Kingdom of Summer*, Arthur and Gwynhwyfar have their differences because of her infidelity, but finally she joins Arthur in an attempt to oust Medraut from the usurped throne of Camlann.
Genre(s): Fantastic Literature.

◆ 2136. *Kingdom of Summer.* New York: Simon and Schuster, 1981. 283 pp.
The sequel to *Hawk of May* finds Gwalchmai in love with Elidan, daughter of Arthur's archenemy Bran, but she rejects him even though she carries his child since he has killed her brother.
Genre(s): Fantastic Literature.

Bragg, Melvyn

◆ 2137. *The Sword and the Miracle.* New York: Random House, 1997. 688 pp.
In 657, Bega, a Celtic princess, and Padric, a British prince, flee from Ireland to Britain where, although in love, they must fulfill different tasks of valor.
Genre(s): Adventure Story.

◆May be suitable for young adult readers

Brandewyne, Rebecca

2138. *Swan Road.* New York: Severn House, 1996. 369 pp.
In the ninth century, the Welsh princess Rhowenna falls in love with the conquering Viking, Wulfgar, who seduces instead of raping her.
Genre(s): Love Story; Romance.

Brouwer, Sigmund

◆ 2139. *Magnus.* Wheaton, IL: Victor, 1995. 571 pp.
Thomas, 14, lives in Magnus, a British kingdom ruled by Druids in the 13th century.
Genre(s): Fantastic Literature; Christian Fiction.

Brown, George

2140. *Beside the Ocean of Time.* New Brunswick, NJ: Transaction, 1996. 240 pp.
Thorfinn Ragnarson lives on the island of Orkney during the 20th century and dreams of such events from previous centuries as the Battle of Bannockburn and Norse men traveling to Constantinople.
Genre(s): Domestic Fiction.

Bryher

2141. *The Fourteenth of October.* New York: Pantheon, 1952. 223 pp.
The Normans invade Britain in 1066.
Genre(s): War Story.

2142. *Ruan.* New York: Pantheon, 1960. 192 pp.
Ruan prefers to be a sailor rather than keep his inherited post as a Druid priest.
Genre(s): Adventure Story; Sea Story.

2143. *This January Tale.* New York: Harcourt, 1966. 181 pp.
Eldred, a Saxon blacksmith, goes to a camp for exiles after the Norman conquests, and after his death, his widow returns to their Exeter home to find that fear and oppression remain.
Genre(s): Domestic Fiction.

Buechner, Frederick

2144. *Brendan.* New York: Atheneum, 1987. 240 pp.
Finn recounts the adventures and travels of his friend Brendan, who lived from 435 to 577, and was the Irish patron saint of sailors.
Genre(s): Biographical Fiction.

◆ 2145. *Godric.* New York: Atheneum, 1980. 178 pp.
In 12th-century England, the saintly Godric, at 100, refuses to lie about his life to a pious monk, and recalls all of the unpleasantries of his youth.
Genre(s): Biographical Fiction; Christian Fiction.

Burroughs, Edgar Rice

2146. *The Outlaw of Torn.* New York: Grosset and Dunlap, 1927. 298 pp.

A son of Henry III, kidnapped as a child, grows up to be an outlaw and an expert swordsman.
Genre(s): Adventure Story.

Butler, Margaret

2147. *The Lion of Christ.* New York: Coward-McCann, 1977. 334 pp.
In the sequel to *The Lion of Justice* and *The Lion of England*, Thomas à Becket flees to France for asylum and petitions Pope Alexander to punish Henry before Becket returns to Canterbury and is murdered.
Genre(s): Biographical Fiction; Christian Fiction.

2148. *The Lion of England.* New York: Coward-McCann, 1973. 344 pp.
Henry II takes as his mistress Hikenai, a woman with pagan beliefs, while appointing Thomas à Becket as chancellor and being married to Eleanor of Aquitaine whom he exiles.
Genre(s): Biographical Fiction.

2149. *The Lion of Justice.* New York: Coward-McCann, 1975. 280 pp.
In the sequel to *The Lion of England*, Henry II and Thomas à Becket become close friends before Thomas has to flee for his life to Flanders.
Genre(s): Biographical Fiction; Christian Fiction.

Cabell, James Branch

2150. *Domnei.* New York: R. M. McBride, 1925. 218 pp.
Melicent sells herself into slavery to help Perion, the outlaw she loves, and he fights for her release during medieval days.
Genre(s): Adventure Story.

Caldecott, Moyra

◆ 2151. *Etheldreda, Princess of East Anglianorthumbria.* London: Routledge and Kegan Paul, 1987. 215 pp.
Etheldreda, Princess of East Anglia, loves learning in the seventh century, but she must endure two political marriages before becoming the Queen of Northumbria and the abbess of Ely.
Genre(s): Biographical Fiction.

Canham, Marsha

2152. *The Last Arrow.* New York: Dell, 1997. 454 pp.
Brenna, sister of Robin Wardieu d'Ambroise, joins the mercenary Griffyn Renaud de Verdelay, to protect the legitimate heir to the throne of England.
Genre(s): Romance.

Canning, Victor

2153. *The Circle of the Gods.* London: Heinemann, 1977. 178 pp.
In the sequel to *The Crimson Chalice*, Arthur, still pagan, has a sense of what a nation might be, but he dislikes the

mundane, and to start his cavalry, he becomes a horse thief.
Genre(s): Fantastic Literature.

2154. *The Crimson Chalice.* New York: Morrow, 1976. 479 pp.
A young Roman woman becomes pregnant by her young Briton mate, and they travel west to Lundy where Merlin waits to deliver the baby Arthur.
Genre(s): Fantastic Literature.

Carr, Robyn

2155. *The Blue Falcon.* Boston: Little, Brown, 1981. 498 pp.
In the 12th century, Lady Chandra and Sir Conan de Corbney fall in love, but their parents force them to marry others, and not until Conan returns from the crusades can they be together.
Genre(s): Romance.

2156. *The Troubadour's Romance.* Boston: Little, Brown, 1985. 303 pp.
Henry II commands that Felise Scelfton marry Royce Leighton, a man accused of murdering his brother in the 12th century, but as she begins to restore his lands, she finds that he has redeeming qualities.
Genre(s): Love Story.

Chadwick, Elizabeth

2157. *The Conquest.* New York: St. Martin's, 1997. 464 pp.
In 1066, Ailith tries to kill herself after her husband and child die during the Norman invasion, but the womanizing Norman Rolf de Brize saves her and makes her a chatelaine at his English estate.
Genre(s): War Story; Romance.

2158. *The Leopard Unleashed.* New York: St. Martin's, 1993. 328 pp.
In the sequel to *The Running Vixen*, Renard, heir to the Welsh estate of Ravenstow, returns from the Crusades with his dancing girl wife, but he must combat Ranulf de Gernons, Earl of Chester, who will do anything, including kidnaping Renard's wife, to get his land.
Genre(s): Romance; War Story.

◆ 2159. *The Running Vixen.* New York: St. Martin's, 1992. 336 pp.
During the 12th century, in the sequel to *The Wild Hunt*, Heulwen and Adam de Lacey fall in love and marry in Wales while Henry I tries to have his daughter Maud recognized as his heir.
Genre(s): Romance.

◆ 2160. *The Wild Hunt.* New York: St. Martin's, 1991. 370 pp.
The heiress Judith of Ravenstow, 15, becomes wife of Guyon FitzMiles when given to him by King William Rufus, and Guyon tries to win her love and her money against the wishes of her jealous uncle.
Genre(s): Romance.

Chase, Nicholas

2161. *Locksley.* New York: St. Martin's, 1983. 279 pp.
Robin Hood returns from the Crusades, and angry that Prince John has sold the Locksley title to Fitz Stephen, he goes into the forest to form his band of men.
Genre(s): War Story; Domestic Fiction.

Christian, Catherine

2162. *The Pendragon.* New York: Knopf, 1979. 461 pp.
Verus (Bedivere) is the foster brother and one of the first Companions of Arthur, and he relates Arthur's story, including his trip with Celidon the Merlin to take part in the rites which make him Pendragon, and his love of Vivian (Ygern).
Genre(s): Fantastic Literature.

2163. *The Sword and the Flame.* London: Macmillan, 1978. 507 pp.
Arthur battles while Merlin attempts to make magic in ancient Briton.
Genre(s): Fantastic Literature.

Clark, Jean

2164. *Untie the Winds.* New York: Macmillan, 1976. 341 pp.
Saxons and Picts battle in Britain after the Romans leave.
Genre(s): War Story.

Closs, Hannah Priebsch

2165. *Tristan.* 1940. New York: Vanguard, 1968. 342 pp.
Tristan falls in love with the beautiful Iseult, pledged to marry his uncle Mark.
Genre(s): Fantastic Literature.

Collingwood, W. G.

2166. *The Likeness of King Elfwald.* 1917. Lampeter, Dyfed: Llanerc, 1990. 280 pp.
Vikings raid Northumbria and West Scotland while Elfwald tries to rule.

2167. *Thorstein of the Mere.* 1895. Lampeter, Dyfed: Llanerc, 1990. 203 pp.
The Vikings come to the Lake District of England in the 10th century.
Genre(s): Domestic Fiction.

Cornwell, Bernard

◆ 2168. *Enemy of God.* New York: St. Martin's, 1997. 416 pp.
While fighting the Saxons and trying to unite the Christians and the Druids, Arthur succeeds in gaining the throne for King Mordred and establishes the Round Table before Guinevere and Lancelot betray him. (*Series:* Warlord Chronicles, 2)
Genre(s): Biographical Fiction; Fantastic Literature.

◆ 2169. *The Winter King: A Novel of Arthur.* New York: St. Martin's, 1996. 431 pp.

Arthur keeps back the invading Saxons during the sixth century while dealing with his scheming wife, Guinevere, the manipulative Merlin, and the cowardly Lancelot. (*Series:* Warlord Chronicles, 1)
Genre(s): Fantastic Literature; Biographical Fiction.

Costain, Thomas Bertram

2170. *Below the Salt.* Garden City, NY: Doubleday, 1957. 480 pp.
A United States senator believes that he is the reincarnation of a Saxon freedman who saw King John sign the Magna Carta.
Genre(s): Love Story; Time Travel.

2171. *The Black Rose.* Garden City, NY: Doubleday, 1945. 403 pp.
A young English nobleman fights in the Mongol empire where he must choose between an Eastern girl and an English heiress.
Genre(s): War Story; Adventure Story.

Coulter, Catherine

2172. *Earth Song.* New York: New American Library, 1990. 416 pp.
In 1275, Philippa de Beauchamp discovers that she is the illegitimate daughter of Edward I after she finds that she is to marry a much older man.
Genre(s): Romance.

◆ 2173. *Lord of Falcon Ridge.* New York: Jove, 1995. 368 pp.
In the sequel to *Lord of Raven's Peak*, Rolly, the duke of Normandy, hires Cleve of Malverne to bring Chessa from Dublin to marry his son William, but when the repulsive Ragnor of York tries to kidnap her Cleve risks himself for Chessa with whom he has fallen in love.
Genre(s): Romance.

2174. *Rosehaven.* New York: Putnam, 1996. 372 pp.
In 1277, Severin returns from the Crusades to find his inheritance gone, and Edward I sends him to Oxborough Castle in East Anglia to wed Hastings, and instead of the submissive wife he wants, he finds a strong woman highly skilled in herbal healing.
Genre(s): Romance; Domestic Fiction.

Deveraux, Jude

2175. *The Conquest.* New York: Pocket Books, 1991. 320 pp.
Raised to fight like a man and dress as a boy, Zared goes with her brother to a tournament as his squire to help him win a wealthy wife.
Genre(s): Romance.

Doherty, P. C.

2176. *Angel of Death.* New York: St. Martin's, 1990. 176 pp.
Hugh Corbett must investigate the untimely death of the dean of St. Paul's Cathedral in London after Edward I

fires Berwick in anticipation of the dean's sermon against Edward's plan to tax the Church.
Genre(s): Mystery.

2177. *The Assassin in the Greenwood.* New York: St. Martin's, 1994. 217 pp.
Hugh Corbett, an agent of Edward I, goes to Nottingham to investigate the sheriff's murder, convinced that the killer is not Robin Hood.
Genre(s): Mystery.

2178. *The Crown in Darkness.* New York: St. Martin's, 1988. 187 pp.
Hugh Corbett goes to Scotland to investigate the death of Scots King Alexander III who supposedly fell from his horse down a steep hill.
Genre(s): Mystery.

◆ 2179. *Ghostly Murders.* New York: St. Martin's, 1998. 256 pp.
In his pilgrimage tale, Poor Parson relates the difficulties that two priests appointed to the village of Scawsby in Kent have when they start building a new church and find empty graves and graves of people buried alive in the adjoining cemetery.
Genre(s): Mystery.

2180. *Satan in St Mary's.* New York: St. Martin's, 1986. 186 pp.
In 1284, a group of Satan worshippers plans an attack on Edward I, and the King's clerk, Hugh Corbett, investigates a recent death that might be connected to the group.
Genre(s): Mystery.

Domning, Denise

2181. *A Love for All Seasons.* New York: Topaz, 1996. 368 pp.
In the 12th century, when Johanna of Stanrudde's evil husband takes her away from her convent hideout, she returns home to find her town suffering from famine and is there accused of adultery.
Genre(s): Romance.

Duggan, Alfred Leo

2182. *Cunning of the Dove.* New York: Pantheon, 1960. 251 pp.
The Saxon control of England, in the sequel to *The King of Athelney*, ends in 1066 with the Norman Conquest and the death of Edward the Confessor.
Genre(s): War Story.

2183. *Devil's Brood.* New York: Coward-McCann, 1957. 284 pp.
The children of Eleanor and Henry II exhibit their different and difficult personalities as they mature.
Genre(s): Domestic Fiction.

2184. *The King of Athelney.* New York: Faber and Faber, 1961. 302 pp.
Alfred the Great begins to rule the united Saxon kingdom in the sequel to *Conscience of the King,*

2185. *Knight with Armour.* New York: Coward-McCann, 1951. 306 pp.

Knights gather to fight in the crusades.
Genre(s): War Story.

2186.*Leopards and Lilies.* New York: Coward-McCann, 1954. 280 pp.
A selfish English noblewoman makes the lives of those around her miserable with her misplaced loyalties and unrestrained ambitions.
Genre(s): Domestic Fiction.

Dunnett, Dorothy

2187.*King Hereafter.* New York: Knopf, 1982. 721 pp.
Macbeth, son of Findlaech, and Thorfinn, son of Sigurd, seem to be the same person during the struggle to unify Scotland into a nation.
Genre(s): Adventure Story.

Durham, Marilyn

2188.*Flambard's Confession.* New York: Harcourt Brace, 1982. 779 pp.
Rannulf Flambard, chaplain to William II of England, confesses on his deathbed to having papers detailing the acts of greed and cruelty that he and the kings and leaders from William the Conqueror through William II have committed.
Genre(s): Biographical Fiction.

Dymoke, Juliet

2189.*Henry of the High Rock.* London: Dobson, 1971. 288 pp.
When Rufus is murdered after William the Conqueror dies, Henry wins the throne, acts contrite, and wins love as well.
Genre(s): Biographical Fiction.

2190.*The Lion's Legacy.* London: Dobson, 1974. 281 pp.
Matilda, daughter of Henry I of England and wife of the Holy Roman Emperor Henry V, expects to succeed to the throne when her father dies, but Stephen of Blois interferes.
Genre(s): Biographical Fiction.

2191.*Shadows on a Throne.* London: Wingate, 1976. 187 pp.
Macbeth rules Scotland in the 11th century and worries about others usurping his position.
Genre(s): Biographical Fiction.

Erskine, Barbara

2192.*Lady of Hay.* New York: Delacorte, 1987. 545 pp.
During the 12th century, King John has Matilda de Braose put to death, and in the 20th century, a writer has herself hypnotized so that she can relive Matilda's life.
Genre(s): Time Travel.

Farrington, Gene

2193.*The Breath of Kings.* Garden City, NY: Doubleday, 1982. 542 pp.

Ethelred the Unready surrenders to the Danish king Canute, and Canute's wife Emma gains power amid the bleakness of medieval Europe and England.
Genre(s): Biographical Fiction.

Feyrer, Gayle

2194.*The Thief's Mistress.* New York: Dell, 1996. 400 pp.
Robin Hood and Maid Marian form an alliance in 13th-century England.
Genre(s): Romance.

Follett, Ken

2195.*Pillars of the Earth.* New York: Morrow, 1989. 973 pp.
A prior, a master builder, and their community try to build a cathedral to protect themselves while Stephen and the Empress Maud fight for the crown of England.
Genre(s): Epic Literature.

Garwood, Julie

◆ 2196. *Saving Grace.* New York: Pocket Books, 1993. 372 pp.
King John decides to marry off Lady Johanna, widowed at 16, to a second abusive husband, but her foster brother finds her a husband in Scotland.
Genre(s): Romance.

◆ 2197. *The Secret.* New York: Pocket Books, 1992. 379 pp.
Judith goes to Scotland and decides to stay in a village with her new husband in 1200, but she unexpectedly asserts her rights.
Genre(s): Romance.

2198.*The Wedding.* New York: Pocket Books, 1996. 480 pp.
A Scottish maid in the 12th century falls for the leader of the clan who abducts her.
Genre(s): Romance.

Gellis, Roberta

2199.*Alinor.* Boston: Gregg, 1984. 558 pp.
Alinor, namesake and former ward of Alinor of Aquitaine in *Roselynde*, becomes a widow in the 13th century and she agrees to marry Ian de Vipont to keep her lands from King John. (*Series:* Roselynde Chronicles, 2)
Genre(s): Romance.

2200.*Gilliane.* Boston: Gregg, 1984. 494 pp.
Gilliane has to marry against her will for political reasons, but she falls in love with Lady Alinor's son Adam, her husband's enemy. (*Series:* Roselynde Chronicles, 4)
Genre(s): Romance.

2201.*Joanna.* Boston: Gregg, 1984. 560 pp.
After Joanna, Alinor's daughter, marries Geoffrey FitzWilliam, illegitimate nephew to the king, he joins the household of Lord Ian to oppose the evil doings of King John. (*Series:* Roselynde Chronicles, 3)
Genre(s): Romance.

2202. *Masques of Gold.* New York: Jove, 1988. 508 pp.
In the realm of King John in the 13th century, Lissa, an apothecary, meets Sir Justin, a merchant and leader of the London Watch, when he arrives to investigate the death of her husband of six weeks.
Genre(s): Romance; Mystery.

2203. *Roselynde.* Boston: Gregg, 1984. 495 pp.
While Alinor of Aquitaine marches on a Crusade and deals with her sons, Richard and John, her ward Alinor grows up as her confidant. (*Series:* Roselynde Chronicles, 1)
Genre(s): Romance; Biographical Fiction.

Gloag, John

2204. *Artorius Rex.* New York: St. Martin's, 1977. 197 pp.
Artorius, a sixth-century commander, spends his life trying to unite Britain and never succeeds.
Genre(s): Fantastic Literature.

Godwin, Parke

2205. *Beloved Exile.* New York: Bantam, 1984. 422 pp.
Guenevere reveals her feelings about Arthur's death at the moment when she thought peace would finally come, but instead, enemies plot to take Camelot and exile her.
Genre(s): Fantastic Literature.

2206. *Firelord.* Garden City, NY: Doubleday, 1980. 396 pp.
As the son of a tribal king, Artos creates an alliance which halts invasion during his lifetime.
Genre(s): Fantastic Literature.

◆ 2207. *Robin and the King.* New York: Morrow, 1993. 366 pp.
In the sequel to *Sherwood*, Robin Hood counters Ranulf of Bayeux, William the Conqueror's keeper of the chancery, when the keeper tries to take Sherwood Forest for the king.

◆ 2208. *Sherwood.* New York: Morrow, 1991. 526 pp.
Robin hates carrying out William I's edicts so he takes Marian, an orphan he met when returning from battle, and goes to Sherwood Forest where he collects a group of men who rob the rich to support the poor.
Genre(s): Adventure Story.

Goldman, James

2209. *Myself as Witness.* New York: Random House, 1979. 340 pp.
In 1212, the scholar-cleric Giraldus Cambrensis thinks that King John is undeservedly maligned and is actually a proponent of national unity.
Genre(s): Biographical Fiction.

Gordon, Noah

2210. *The Physician.* New York: Simon and Schuster, 1986. 604 pp.
While Rob Cole travels around the English countryside with a barber-surgeon in the 11th century, he yearns to learn the art of healing and arranges to study with Ibn Sina, a Moslem physician in Persia.
Genre(s): Medical Novel.

Greeley, Andrew M.

2211. *The Magic Cup.* New York: McGraw Hill, 1979. 246 pp.
In the sixth century, King Cormac MacDermot quests for a magic cup needed to win the princess Delvcaem.
Genre(s): Fantastic Literature.

Greenberg, Joanne

2212. *The King's Persons.* New York: Holt, 1985. 284 pp.
Brett, a Christian servant, and Abram, a Jew, live in York during the 12th century before citizens attack and massacre local Jews.
Genre(s): Jewish Fiction.

Hanchar, Peggy

2213. *The Scottish Bride.* New York: Fawcett, 1996. 352 pp.
Red Rafe kidnaps Lillias, who is nine, and forces her to marry his son, Iain, but the union angers Iain, who leaves and does not return until his father dies nine years later.
Genre(s): Romance.

Haycraft, Molly Costain

2214. *My Lord Brother the Lion Heart.* Philadelphia: Lippincott, 1968. 320 pp.
Richard's sister Joan, Queen of Sicily, discusses her brother's life as king and crusader.
Genre(s): Biographical Fiction.

Hayton, Sian

2215. *Cells of Knowledge.* New York: New Amsterdam, 1990. 206 pp.
In 10th century Britain, a monk searches for a strange woman who sought sanctuary in his monastery.
Genre(s): Christian Fiction; Mystery.

Henley, Virginia

2216. *A Year and a Day.* New York: Delacorte, 1998. 352 pp.
A young woman from Scotland meets an English baron, and they fall in love.
Genre(s): Romance.

Herbert, Kathleen

2217. *Bride of the Spear.* New York: St. Martin's, 1988. 297 pp.
In sixth-century England, after Taniu's father abandons her, her stepmother subjects her to pagan rites, and when Oswain, from a neighboring tribe, proposes marriage, she wrongly refuses.
Genre(s): War Story.

◆ 2218. *The Ghost in the Sunlight.* New York: St. Martin's, 1986. 355 pp.
Alchflaed, daughter of a seventh-century queen, gains courage from stories of her mother's exploits.
Genre(s): Domestic Fiction.

2219. *Queen of the Lightning.* New York: St. Martin's, 1984. 255 pp.
Reimmelth, queen of Cumbria, must marry for political reasons, but she refuses to relinquish her independence.
Award(s): Georgette Heyer Historical Novel Prize.
Genre(s): Domestic Fiction.

Heyer, Georgette

2220. *The Conqueror.* 1931. New York: Bantam, 1968. 405 pp.
William the Conqueror becomes the King of England after conquering Harold II.
Genre(s): War Story.

Highsmith, Domini

2221. *Keeper at the Shrine.* New York: St. Martin's, 1995. 498 pp.
In 1180, a hooded figure arrives in Beverley, England, and inside the church cures the lame priest, Simeon, and gives him a baby to raise, a situation which inflames other clergy with political aspirations.
Genre(s): Mystery.

Hill, Pamela

2222. *Marjorie of Scotland.* New York: Putnam, 1956. 284 pp.
Marjorie, daughter of Robert the Bruce, grows up in Scotland while her father fights for freedom from the British.
Genre(s): Domestic Fiction.

Hill, Sandra

2223. *The Tarnished Lady.* New York: Leisure, 1995. 300 pp.
When Lady Eadyth goes to Ravenshire Castle and asks Eirik, the lord, to marry her, her reason intrigues him.
Genre(s): Romance.

Holland, Cecelia

2224. *The Earl.* New York: Knopf, 1971. 301 pp.
In 12th-century England, the Earl of Stafford wants peace while King Stephen and Henry Plantagenet continue to fight over the crown.
Genre(s): War Story.

2225. *Hammer for Princes.* London: Hodder and Stoughton, 1972. 301 pp.
In the mid-12th century, Stephen struggles with Henry Plantagenet for the throne, while Ranulf's uncle, Thierry, remains intent on claiming the Stafford earldom.
Genre(s): Political Fiction.

2226. *The Kings in Winter.* New York: Atheneum, 1968. 208 pp.

Brian Boru, Munster king of Ireland, tries to protect his people from outside conquest.
Genre(s): War Story.

Hollick, Helen

◆ 2227. *The Kingmaking.* New York: St. Martin's, 1995. 604 pp.
Gwenhwyfar's father Cunedda declares that Arthur Pendragon is the rightful heir of Uther and suggests that Arthur serve Vortigern to gain experience before he becomes king.
Genre(s): Fantastic Literature.

◆ 2228. *Pendragon's Banner.* New York: St. Martin's, 1996. 547 pp.
In the sequel to *The Kingmaking,* Arthur and Gwenhwyfar have enemies, the strongest being Arthur's ex-wife Winifred, who wants her son Cedric to be heir, and Morgause, who wants to become queen of the realm.
Genre(s): Fantastic Literature.

Howell, Hannah

2229. *My Valiant Knight.* New York: Zebra, 1995. 320 pp.
In the 13th century, the handsome Norman Gabel de Amalville captures Ainslee MacNairn and holds her for ransom.
Genre(s): Romance.

Hunt, Angela Elwell

2230. *Afton of Margate Castle.* Wheaton, IL: Tyndale House, 1993. 490 pp.
Afton, a peasant girl, grows up in the home of an earl.
(*Series:* Theyn Chronicles, 1)
Genre(s): Christian Fiction; Romance.

◆ 2231. *Ingram of the Irish.* Wheaton, IL: Tyndale House, 1994. 480 pp.
A young knight who is unsure of his faith searches in the secular world to clarify his beliefs. (*Series:* The Theyn Chronicles, 3)
Genre(s): Christian Fiction.

◆ 2232. *The Troubadour's Quest.* Wheaton, IL: Tyndale House, 1993. 383 pp.
A musician and his young companion share their music and their faith as they travel through the countryside. (*Series:* Theyn Chronicles, 2)
Genre(s): Christian Fiction; Romance.

James, Cary

2233. *King and Raven.* New York: Tor, 1995. 384 pp.
After four of King Arthur's knights rape his sister, Micah of Greenfarm goes to France, rises to knighthood for his service, and returns to Camelot but cannot own land since he was originally from the peasant class.
Genre(s): Fantastic Literature.

James, Samantha

2234. *A Promise Given.* New York: Avon, 1998. 384 pp.
Unhappy Sabrina Kincaid meets Ian MacGregory in the Middle Ages, and he must prove himself to her before she will trust him.
Genre(s): Romance.

Johansen, Iris

2235. *Midnight Warrior.* New York: Bantam, 1994. 368 pp.
In 1066, Brynn of Falkhaar's master gives her to the Norman lord Gage Dumont to help his dying friend, and her healing abilities save Dumont and attract him.
Genre(s): Romance; Medical Novel; Fantastic Literature.

Johnson, Barbara Ferry

2236. *Tara's Song.* New York: Avon, 1978. 437 pp.
When Vikings raid the abbey where Tara is a novitiate, she is saved for Rorik the chief, who falls in love with her and marries her.
Genre(s): Romance.

Jones, Ellen

2237. *Beloved Enemy.* New York: Simon and Schuster, 1994. 570 pp.
Eleanor of Aquitaine marries Henry, duke of Normandy and later king of England, after her marriage to Louis of France fails to produce an heir, and although Henry is 11 years younger, they produce a large family, in the sequel to *The Fatal Crown.*
Genre(s): Biographical Fiction; Romance.

2238. *The Fatal Crown.* New York: Simon and Schuster, 1991. 556 pp.
Maud, the daughter of Henry I of England, falls in love with her cousin Stephen, but is married at nine to the Holy Roman Emperor, and when she returns to England as the heir, Stephen challenges and defeats her claim to the crown.
Genre(s): Biographical Fiction; Romance.

Kaufman, Pamela

2239. *Banners of Gold.* New York: Crown, 1986. 436 pp.
This sequel to *Shield of Three Lions* shows Alix as a strong woman who is taken to Germany to be a hostage until Richard the Lion-Heart is released from prison.

Kluger, Richard

2240. *The Sheriff of Nottingham.* New York: Viking, 1992. 485 pp.
The Sheriff of Nottingham, while serving a corrupt King John, tries to maintain his own integrity.
Genre(s): Adventure Story.

Knight, Bernard

◆ 2241. *Madoc, Prince of America.* New York: St. Martin's, 1977. 189 pp.
Madoc, a 12th-century Welsh prince, crosses the Atlantic Ocean and begins a settlement.
Genre(s): Biographical Fiction.

Kurland, Lynn

2242. *This Is All I Ask.* New York: Jove, 1997. 432 pp.
Knight Christopher, the Dragon of Blackmour, who is slowly losing his sight, despondently agrees to a dying friend's request that he marry the man's sister, Gillian of Warewick, an abused woman who lacks self-confidence.
Genre(s): Romance.

2243. *The Very Thought of You.* New York: Jove, 1998. 400 pp.
In Richard I's England, corporate raider Alexander Smith meets tough Lady Margaret of Falconberg and tries to convince her that he lives in a future time in a place not yet discovered.
Genre(s): Time Travel; Romance.

Lawhead, Steve

2244. *Arthur.* Wheaton, IL: Crossway, 1989. 446 pp.
Arthur begins his reign in Britian just about the time that Christianity arrives. (*Series:* Pendragon Cycle)
Genre(s): Fantastic Literature; Christian Fiction.

2245. *Byzantium.* New York: HarperPrism, 1996. 645 pp.
Irish monks of Kells prepare an illuminated manuscript to give to the Holy Roman Emperor at Byzantium and send Aidan on the trip where he has a variety of adventures.
Genre(s): Fantastic Literature; Adventure Story; Christian Fiction.

2246. *Merlin.* Grand Rapids, MI: Zondervan, 1996. 480 pp.
Merlin grows up in Britain and becomes the advisor to Arthur, who is destined to be king. (*Series:* Pendragon Cycle)
Genre(s): Fantastic Literature; Christian Fiction.

2247. *Pendragon.* New York: Morrow, 1994. 436 pp.
As Arthur becomes a Christian king in Britian, his Gwynwhyvar is faithful, and he fights major battles against the Vandals and the Irish. (*Series:* Pendragon Cycle)
Genre(s): Fantastic Literature; Christian Fiction.

◆ 2248. *Taliesin.* Wheaton, IL: Crossway, 1987. 448 pp.
A wise old druid rescues the baby Talesian and educates him while the Roman influence in Britain wanes, and when Talesian meets Charis, a bull-dancer who escaped from Atlantis after an earthquake, he fathers Merlin before the Atlanteans kill him. (*Series:* Pendragon Cycle)
Genre(s): Fantastic Literature; Christian Fiction.

Leland, Thomas

2249. *Longsword, Earl of Salisbury*. 1762. New York: Arno, 1974. 420 pp.
William Longespee, Earl of Salisbury, experiences unusual situations in the 13th century.
Genre(s): Biographical Fiction; Gothic Fiction.

Lewis, Hilda Winifred

2250. *Harold Was My King*. New York: McKay, 1970. 246 pp.
When Edward the Confessor dies, he leaves three claimants to the throne, Edgar the Atheling, Harold, Earl of Wessex, and William, Duke of Normandy, known later as William the Conqueror.
Genre(s): War Story; Political Fiction.

2251. *Wife to the Bastard*. New York: McKay, 1967. 284 pp.
Matilda, the daughter of the Duke of Flanders, marries William, Duke of Normandy, becomes queen of England when he conquers it, and raises two sons to be rulers, William Rufus of England and Robert of Normandy.
Genre(s): Domestic Fiction; Biographical Fiction.

Lide, Mary

◆ **2252. *Fortune's Knave*.** New York: St. Martin's, 1993. 269 pp.
Before becoming William the Conqueror, William of Normandy must overcome his illegitimacy and defend his birthright against other noblemen.
Genre(s): Biographical Fiction.

Lindsey, Johanna

2253. *Hearts Aflame*. New York: Pocket Books, 1987. 363 pp.
Since Viking Kristen is unable to find a suitable mate, she goes with her brother on a trading voyage, but she discovers too late that they are raiding instead, and she is pressed into the service of Royce of Wyndhurst, a man with whom she falls in love.
Genre(s): Romance.

Llywelyn, Morgan

◆ **2254. *Bard, the Odyssey of the Irish*.** Boston: Houghton Mifflin, 1984. 466 pp.
A fourth-century Celtic bard, Amergin, inspires his warrior clan to travel from the Iberian Peninsula to Ierne (present-day Ireland).
Genre(s): Fantastic Literature.

◆ **2255. *Brian Boru, Emperor of the Irish*.** New York: Tor, 1995. 157 pp.
Brian Boru rises to become the leader of the Irish after Vikings kill members of his family.
Genre(s): Biographical Fiction.

◆ **2256. *The Horse Goddess*.** Boston: Houghton Mifflin, 1982. 417 pp.

Epona, a Celt recently initiated into womanhood, leaves her tribe with a handsome Scythian to go to the Russian steppes.
Genre(s): Romance.

◆ **2257. *Lion of Ireland*.** Boston: Houghton Mifflin, 1980. 522 pp.
Brian Boru rises from a low position in his Irish tribe to become the king of a united Ireland in the 10th century.
Genre(s): Biographical Fiction.

◆ **2258. *Pride of Lions*.** New York: Forge, 1996. 351 pp.
After Brian Boru dies in 1014, his son Donough continues to fight for Ireland, even when his half-mad mother Gormlaith tries to interfere with his troubled marriage and his love for a druid.

◆ **2259. *Red Branch*.** Morrow, 1989. 558 pp.
Cuchulain, Ireland's mythical warrior, although born under mysterious circumstances, prepares to lead the country.
Genre(s): Epic Literature.

◆ **2260. *Strongbow: The Story of Richard and Aoife*.** New York: Tor, 1996. 155 pp.
Aoife (Red Eva) MacMurrough and Richard (Strongbow) de Clare, a Norman knight, fall in love and tell about their lives in the Middle Ages.
Genre(s): Love Story.

2261. *The Wind from Hastings*. Boston: Houghton Mifflin, 1978. 245 pp.
After King Harold faces defeat at the Battle of Hastings, his wife Aldith disappears.
Genre(s): War Story; Domestic Fiction.

Lofts, Norah

2262. *The Lute Player*. Garden City, NY: Doubleday, 1951. 465 pp.
Blondel de Nesle, a flute player; Eleanor of Aquitaine; and the fictional Duchess Anna tell the story of Richard the Lion-Hearted and his marriage to Berengaria.
Genre(s): Biographical Fiction.

2263. *Madselin*. Garden City, NY: Doubleday, 1983. 209 pp.
After the Norman invasion of England and the death of her husband, Madselin agrees to marry the king's armorer Rolf because her knowledge of French will be advantageous to him.
Genre(s): Romance.

2264. *Wayside Tavern*. Garden City, NY: Doubleday, 1980. 376 pp.
The Bull, an Irish tavern, survives from the end of Roman times to the present day, in the Gilderson family.

Lowell, Elizabeth

2265. *Enchanted*. New York: Avon, 1995. 400 pp.
Ariane the Betrayed fears marriage after rape and her people's betrayal, but she does not reveal her fears to Simon, her betrothed, in 11th-century England.
Genre(s): Romance.

◆May be suitable for young adult readers

Lytton, Edward Bulwer

2266. *Harold.* New York: Dutton, 1970. 456 pp.
William, Duke of Normandy, arrives on English shores
in 1066 and defeats Harold, the last of the Saxon kings.
Genre(s): Biographical Fiction.

MacCoun, Catherine

2267. *The Age of Miracles.* Boston: Little, Brown,
1989. 336 pp.
Sister Ingrid, 18, uses her powers of healing in the convent home she has always known, but when a troubadour
arrives, she breaks her vow of chastity and learns about
the world outside.
Genre(s): Medical Novel; Love Story.

Marston, Edward

◆ 2268. *The Dragons of Archenfield.* New York: St.
Martin's, 1995. 242 pp.
Ralph Delchard and Gervase Bret go into disputed terri-
tory to settle land claims, but someone has murdered
their main witness, and they must find who did it.
Genre(s): Mystery.

◆ 2269. *The Lions of the North.* New York: St. Martin's, 1996. 227 pp.
In the 11th century, Ralph Delchard and Gervase Bret go
to Yorkshire where they find a murder and a warrior who
owns lions.
Genre(s): Mystery.

◆ 2270. *The Ravens of Blackwater.* New York: St.
Martin's, 1994. 245 pp.
Ralph Delchard, a soldier, and Gervase Bret, a lawyer, investigate Norman overlords who illegally annex property
for King William, but they must also look into the secrets
at Blackwater Hall after the murder of the elder son there.
Genre(s): Mystery.

◆ 2271. *The Serpents of Harbledown.* New York: St.
Martin's, 1998. 288 pp.
After Ralph Delchard marries the lovely Saxon, Golde,
he takes her to Canterbury, where he and other members
of his retinue discover the murder of a young woman
who often visited the hospital for lepers.
Genre(s): Mystery.

◆ 2272. *The Wolves of Savernake.* New York: St.
Martin's, 1993. 242 pp.
Gervase Bret and Ralph Delchard go to the village of
Bedwyn to investigate land claims of the mill owner, but
when they arrive, he has been brutally killed, but a sec-
ond death tells them he has been murdered.
Genre(s): Mystery.

Medeiros, Teresa

◆ 2273. *Fairest of Them All.* New York: Fanfare,
1995. 371 pp.
Holly de Chaste discovers that her father has offered her
as a prize in a tournament of knights, and she disguises
her beauty until she meets a handsome Welsh knight.
Genre(s): Romance.

2274. *Touch of Enchantment.* New York: Pocket
Books, 1997. 328 pp.
Tabitha Lennox appears in the middle of a Scottish
meadow in 1254, and Sir Colin of Ravenshaw, the seventh laird of Castle Raven, thinks her appearance is
strange but does not know that a computer problem has
transported her from the 21st century.
Genre(s): Time Travel; Romance.

Meredith, Christopher

2275. *Griffri.* Chester Springs, PA: Dufour, 1991.
255 pp.
Griffri, a Welsh chief poet, tells a Cistercian monk about
his life and the complicated links between Welsh leaders
trying to retain their identity and autonomy from the English.
Genre(s): Political Fiction.

Meyer, Conrad Ferdinand

2276. *The Saint.* Providence, RI: Brown University, 1977. 129 pp.
Thomas à Becket becomes best friends with Henry II until he disagrees with him and Henry exiles him.
Genre(s): Biographical Fiction.

Monaco, Richard

2277. *The Grail War.* New York: Pocket Books,
1979. 319 pp.
While riding with Sir Gawain, Parsival enters a war be-
tween the armies of King Arthur and Clinschor, in which
Parsival's valor overcomes his foolishness.
Genre(s): Fantastic Literature.

2278. *Parsival.* New York: Macmillan, 1977. 343
pp.
While Parisival searches for the grail, his adventures in-
tersect Arthur and the evil Clinschor as well as Broaditch.
Genre(s): Fantastic Literature; Romance.

Monk, Karyn

2279. *The Witch and the Warrior.* New York: Bantam, 1998. 384 pp.
Laird Alex MacDunn saves Gwendolyn MacSween from
burning as a witch in 13th-century Scotland because he
needs her to heal his son.
Genre(s): Medical Novel; Romance.

Morson, Ian

2280. *Falconer and the Face of God.* New York:
St. Martin's, 1997. 256 pp.
William Falconer sees an actor murdered on-stage, and
later he becomes involved in a second murder in a travel-
ing troupe of jongleurs.
Genre(s): Mystery; War Story.

2281. *Falconer's Crusade.* New York: St. Martin's, 1995. 190 pp.
In 1264, Thomas Symon, a new student at Oxford, finds
the corpse of a young girl, and his instructor, Master William Falconer, institutes an investigation.
Genre(s): War Story; Mystery.

2282. *Falconer's Judgement.* New York: St. Martin's, 1996. 208 pp.
In 1264, ambitious men in England await Pope Alexander's death, but Master Regent William Falconer worries about defending a student accused of murdering the brother of Oxford's Cardinal Otho.
Genre(s): Mystery.

Muntz, Hope

2283. *The Golden Warrior.* 1949. New York: Scribner's, 1970. 400 pp.
William comes to England and wins at the Battle of Hastings.
Genre(s): Biographical Fiction.

Neale, Linda

2284. *The Briar Rose.* New York: St. Martin's, 1987. 288 pp.
Sir Hugh fitz Bohun saves Briallen from Gascon men who killed her mother, but his father causes her problems instead.
Genre(s): Adventure Story.

Newman, Sharan

◆ 2285. *The Chessboard Queen.* New York: St. Martin's, 1983. 296 pp.
In the sequel to *Guinevere*, Guinevere marries Arthur and gives her interpretation of the marriage.
Genre(s): Fantastic Literature.

◆ 2286. *Guinevere.* New York: St. Martin's, 1981. 256 pp.
Guinevere is the child of a noble family trying to hold off the Saxons, but she befriends a hostage Saxon princess.
Genre(s): Fantastic Literature; Romance.

◆ 2287. *Guinevere Evermore.* New York: St. Martin's, 1985. 277 pp.
Guinevere tells of the knights and their searches for the Holy Grail and of her marriage to Arthur after her affair with Lancelot, in the sequel to *The Chessboard Queen*.
Genre(s): Fantastic Literature.

Norman, Diana

2288. *Fitzempress' Law.* New York: St. Martin's, 1980. 248 pp.
Three motorcyclists find themselves in 12th-century England during Henry II's reign where they face consequences for their actions and attitudes.
Genre(s): Legal Story; Time Travel.

2289. *The Morning Gift.* New York: St. Martin's, 1985. 285 pp.
When Matilda de Rise marries a Saxon baron at 14, he gives her the estate of Dungesey as a gift on the day after their marriage, and when he dies, she struggles with the king to preserve the estate for her son while he serves in the French Plantagenet court.
Genre(s): Romance.

Pargeter, Edith

◆ 2290. *The Heaven Tree Trilogy.* New York: Warner, 1993. 899 pp.
The Heaven Tree, The Green Branch, and *The Scarlet Seed* tell of the 13th-century British Talvace family of stone carvers who strive to build a cathedral for their wealthy benefactor.

2291. *The Marriage of Meggotta.* New York: Viking, 1979. 283 pp.
Bethrothed eight-year-olds Richard de Clare and Meggotta de Burgh become pawns when nobles of Henry III plot for power.
Genre(s): Political Fiction.

2292. *Sunrise in the West.* London: Macmillan, 1974. 342 pp.
The man trying to liberate Wales, Llywelyn ap Gruffydd, must fight the English.
Genre(s): Biographical Fiction.

Paxson, Diana L.

2293. *The White Raven.* New York: Morrow, 1988. 411 pp.
Esseilte asks Branwen, illegitimate daughter of the Morholt and her maid and confidant, to stand in for her on her wedding night with Drustan since Esseilte is not a virgin.
Genre(s): Fantastic Literature; Romance.

Penman, Sharon Kay

◆ 2294. *Falls the Shadow.* New York: Holt, Rinehart and Winston, 1988. 580 pp.
In the sequel to *Here Be Dragons*, among the men who oppose the weak Henry III in the 13th century is Simon de Montfort, Earl of Leicester, who becomes Henry's brother-in-law in a marriage to Eleanor, Countess of Pembroke.
Genre(s): Epic Literature.

◆ 2295. *Here Be Dragons.* New York: Holt, Rinehart and Winston, 1985. 704 pp.
Members of the Plantagenet House war among themselves, with King Henry and his heir John fighting Henry's other three sons, while Llewelyn eventually unites Wales.
Genre(s): Epic Literature.

◆ 2296. *The Queen's Man.* New York: Holt, Rinehart and Winston, 1996. 291 pp.
In the 12th century, Eleanor of Aquitaine hires Justin de Quincey, bastard son of the bishop of Chester, to find the murderer of one of her goldsmiths.
Genre(s): Mystery.

◆ 2297. *The Reckoning.* New York: Holt, Rinehart and Winston, 1991. 592 pp.
The sequel to *Falls the Shadow* shows Llewelyn trying to save Wales from his brother Davydd and the English king, but Edward kills him and Davydd and makes his firstborn the Prince of Wales.
Genre(s): War Story.

◆ 2298. *When Christ and His Saints Slept.* New York: Henry Holt, 1995. 746 pp.
At the death of Henry I, his daughter, Maude, and his nephew, Stephen of Blois, fight for control of England.
Genre(s): War Story.

Peters, Ellis

◆ 2299. *Brother Cadfael's Penance.* New York: Mysterious Press, 1994. 292 pp.
Philip FitzRobert, a traitor to the Empress Maud, kidnaps 30 hostages including Brother Cadfael's son (from a chance encounter), and Brother Cadfael goes to rescue his offspring.
Genre(s): Mystery.

2300. *The Confession of Brother Haluin.* New York: Mysterious Press, 1989. 164 pp.
Brother Cadfael hears Brother Haluin's confession of a former love on the monk's deathbed, but when Haluin does not die, they visit his love's tomb and find more than they expect.
Genre(s): Mystery.

◆ 2301. *Dead Man's Ransom.* New York: Morrow, 1984. 189 pp.
While England and Wales fight a civil war, Brother Cadfael refuses to believe that a young Welshman has murdered the sheriff of Shropshire.
Genre(s): Mystery.

◆ 2302. *The Devil's Novice.* New York: Morrow, 1984. 191 pp.
After a political envoy and a novice arrive at Shrewsbury in 1140, someone murders the envoy, and Brother Cadfael must find the culprit to expiate the novice.
Genre(s): Mystery.

◆ 2303. *An Excellent Mystery.* New York: Morrow, 1985. 190 pp.
When a young postulant is missing while traveling between two nunneries during the civil wars of the 12th century, Brother Cadfael must search for her.
Genre(s): Mystery.

◆ 2304. *The Heretic's Apprentice.* New York: Mysterious Press, 1990. 186 pp.
When he is accused of murder and heresy, Elave asks Brother Cadfael to help him exonerate himself.
Genre(s): Mystery.

◆ 2305. *The Hermit of Eyton Forest.* New York: Mysterious Press, 1988. 224 pp.
The abbott refuses to let a 10-year-old boy leave school when he inherits the family land, and a hermit helps Brother Cadfael find a nobleman's subsequent murderer.
Genre(s): Mystery.

◆ 2306. *The Holy Thief.* New York: Mysterious Press, 1992. 246 pp.
The remains of Saint Winifred disappear from the abbey at Shrewsbury, and Brother Cadfael has to recover the casket with her bones and perhaps, in the process, expose his own dealings with the relic.
Genre(s): Mystery.

2307. *The Hounds of Sunset.* London: Macmillan, 1976. 339 pp.
Llywelyn ap Gruffydd's brothers betray him, and Edward I tricks him when he tries to free Wales before dying in 1282.
Genre(s): Biographical Fiction; War Story; Political Fiction.

◆ 2308. *The Leper of Saint Giles.* New York: Morrow, 1982. 223 pp.
The mysterious leper of Saint Giles helps Brother Cadfael decide whether to aid two young lovers after one of them has had a marriage arranged.
Genre(s): Mystery.

◆ 2309. *Monk's Hood.* New York: Morrow, 1981. 223 pp.
Monk's Hood kills Gervase Bonel just before he is to donate land to the monastery and before Brother Cadfael discovers unexpected power battles at the monastery.
Genre(s): Mystery.

◆ 2310. *A Morbid Taste for Bones.* New York: Morrow, 1977. 191 pp.
The prior of Shrewsbury wants the miraculous bones of Saint Winifred, and he sends Brother Cadfael to claim them.
Genre(s): Mystery.

◆ 2311. *One Corpse Too Many.* New York: Morrow, 1980. 191 pp.
When Brother Cadfael goes to Shrewsbury castle to bury those killed in the battle between Stephen and Maud, he finds an extra body and must investigate.
Genre(s): Mystery.

◆ 2312. *The Pilgrim of Hate.* New York: Morrow, 1984. 190 pp.
In 1141, pilgrims come to the Benedictine abbey in honor of St. Winifred, and when a supporter of the Empress Maud is murdered in Winchester, Brother Cadfael suspects a connection with the recently arrived pilgrims.
Genre(s): Mystery.

◆ 2313. *The Potter's Field.* New York: Mysterious Press, 1990. 230 pp.
Brother Cadfael has to discover the identity of a woman found buried in an abbey field and to identify who buried her.
Genre(s): Mystery.

◆ 2314. *The Raven in the Foregate.* New York: Morrow, 1986. 201 pp.
In 1141, on Christmas morning, Father Ailnoth's body appears in the River Severn, and Brother Cadfael must find out why.
Genre(s): Mystery.

◆ 2315. *The Rose Rent.* New York: Morrow, 1986. 190 pp.
Judith Perle, a benefactor of the abbey, disappears, and Cadfael believes that she may be connected to the murder of a young monk.
Genre(s): Mystery.

◆ 2316. *Saint Peter's Fair.* New York: Morrow, 1981. 219 pp.
After someone murders a merchant at a local fair, Brother Cadfael examines the merchant's daughter's relationships. *Genre(s):* Mystery.

◆ 2317. *The Sanctuary Sparrow.* New York: Morrow, 1983. 221 pp.
After the town goldsmith accuses Liliwin, a juggler and acrobat, of stealing, Brother Cadfael looks for the real thief. *Genre(s):* Mystery.

◆ 2318. *The Summer of the Danes.* New York: Mysterious Press, 1991. 251 pp.
While on a pilgrimage in Wales with two others, Brother Cadfael helps to discover the murderer of Bledri ap Rhys, a man who has offended everyone. *Genre(s):* Mystery.

◆ 2319. *The Virgin in the Ice.* New York: Morrow, 1983. 220 pp.
While helping a monk wounded by bandits, Brother Cadfael discovers a murder and starts to investigate. *Genre(s):* Mystery.

Plaidy, Jean

◆ 2320. *The Bastard King.* New York: Putnam, 1979. 319 pp.
William the Conqueror, son of Robert, Duke of Normandy, and his mistress Arlette, marries Matilda and invades England to become its king. (*Series:* Norman Trilogy, 1)
Genre(s): Biographical Fiction.

◆ 2321. *The Courts of Love.* New York: Putnam, 1988. 383 pp.
Eleanor of Aquitaine tells about her grandfather's Courts of Love, her own marriages, and her children. (*Series:* Queens of England, 5)
Genre(s): Biographical Fiction.

◆ 2322. *Edward Longshanks.* New York: Putnam, 1981. 318 pp.
Edward Longshanks becomes king of England in the late 13th century.
Genre(s): Biographical Fiction.

◆ 2323. *Hammer of the Scots.* New York: Putnam, 1981. 318 pp.
Edward Longshanks and his wife Eleanor of Castile return to England where he assumes the throne and raises a degenerate heir, Edward II. (*Series:* Plantagenet Saga, 7)
Genre(s): Biographical Fiction.

◆ 2324. *The Heart of the Lion.* New York: Putnam, 1980. 331 pp.
After Richard I is crowned king of England, he departs for the Third Crusade and leaves his mother to save the kingdom from his brother John. (*Series:* Plantagenet Saga, 3)
Genre(s): Biographical Fiction.

◆ 2325. *The Plantagenet Prelude.* New York: Putnam, 1976. 335 pp.

Eleanore of Aquitaine divorces her husband Louis VII to marry Henry because she knows that he will become king, but their marriage only sours after she grows fat with childbearing and learns of Henry's mistresses. (*Series:* Plantagenet Saga, 1)
Genre(s): Biographical Fiction.

◆ 2326. *The Prince of Darkness.* New York: Putnam, 1978. 317 pp.
King John reveals his inhumanity and his depravity through marriage to the 12-year-old Isabelle of Angoulme in whom he meets his sexual match. (*Series:* Plantagenet Saga, 4)
Genre(s): Biographical Fiction.

◆ 2327. *The Queen From Provence.* New York: Putnam, 1981. 286 pp.
When she is 13, Eleanor of Provence gains Henry III's attention, marries him, and begins to dominate both him and England. (*Series:* Plantagenet Saga, 6)
Genre(s): Biographical Fiction.

Pyle, Howard

2328. *Men of Iron.* 1965. New York: Harper, 1904. 327 pp.
When a young man achieves knighthood, he avenges his father who was wrongly accused of treason.
Genre(s): War Story.

Quick, Amanda

◆ 2329. *Mystique.* New York: Bantam, 1995. 368 pp.
Hugh the Relentless needs both a wife to make him look better and the green crystal stolen from Lady Alice, but Lady Alice plans only to study natural philosophy and never to marry, so the two make a bargain.
Genre(s): Romance; Mystery.

Ragosta, Millie J.

◆ 2330. *Witness to Treason.* Garden City, NY: Doubleday, 1977. 210 pp.
After someone attacks Julian de l'Hacche when she is four, Edward I gives her to Robert the Bruce for raising, and when she is betrothed to a Scottish rebel and attacked again, she remembers the circumstances of the first.

Raymo, Chet

2331. *In the Falcon's Claw.* New York: Viking, 1990. Canada pp.
Near the end of the Dark Ages, in the year 1000, Aileran, an Irish monk with a beautiful lover, records his memoirs while Gerbert, a priest who becomes Pope Sylvester II, jeopardizes Aileran's happiness.
Genre(s): Christian Fiction.

Rice, Robert

◆ 2332. *The Last Pendragon.* New York: Walker, 1991. 205 pp.
Bedwyr disobeys Arthur's request to cast Arthur's sword away, and then he leaves for Rome, but when he returns

11 years later, he helps Arthur's grandson, Irion, fight the Saxons.
Genre(s): Fantastic Literature.

Rice, Sile

2333. *The Saxon Tapestry.* New York: Arcade, 1992. 397 pp.
Saxon nobles try to keep their power while the common folk fear doom in the 11th century before William the Conqueror invades from Normandy.
Genre(s): Political Fiction.

Roberson, Jennifer

2334. *Lady of the Forest.* New York: Zebra, 1992. 593 pp.
Robert of Locksley or Robin Hood, now involved in the politics of England, meets Marian of Ravenskeep after returning from the Crusades with King Richard.
Genre(s): Romance.

Robinson, Suzanne

2335. *Lord of the Dragon.* New York: Bantam, 1995. 340 pp.
Upset that her betrothed rejected her because her legs were an unequal length, Lady Juliana Welles begins disguising herself as male and forcing all visiting knights to disrobe for her.
Genre(s): Romance; Mystery.

Rofheart, Martha

2336. *Lionheart! A Novel of Richard I, King of England.* New York: Simon and Schuster, 1981. 410 pp.
Prince Richard Plantagenet gains the loyalty of his men as he leads them into battle first against his father Henry II and then, as king, against the Moslems during the Crusades.
Genre(s): Biographical Fiction.

Rogers, Marylyle

2337. *The Eagle's Song.* New York: Pocket Books, 1992. 339 pp.
Prince Rhys ap Griffith (the Eagle) kidnaps Lady Linnet and her young brother because Linnet's father supposedly has seized his sister's dowry land, and after they reach an agreement and fall in love, Linnet's father reneges on his bargain.
Genre(s): Romance.

Schwarz-Bart, André

◆ 2338. *The Last of the Just.* Trans. Stephen Becker. New York: Atheneum, 1960. 374 pp.
The Levy family produces a just man onto whom each generation pours the griefs of the world from the pogrom in York, England, in 1185, to Auschwitz and its gas chambers in the 20th century.
Award(s): Prix Goncourt.
Genre(s): Jewish Fiction.

Scott, Walter

2339. *Ivanhoe.* 1819. New York: Bantam, 1997. 686 pp.
Although the Jewish Rebecca loves Ivanhoe, he decides to marry his father's ward Rowena, even though his father wants Rowena to marry Athelstane, who has Saxon royal blood.
Genre(s): War Story; Romance.

2340. *The Talisman.* 1825. New York: Charles Tuttle, 1991. 336 pp.
Sir Kenneth, the prince royal of Scotland, joins the crusades of Richard I in disguise.
Genre(s): Romance.

Seton, Anya

2341. *Avalon.* Boston: Houghton Mifflin, 1965. 440 pp.
In 10th-century England a wandering poetic French prince falls in love with a Cornish girl of Viking descent.
Genre(s): Love Story.

Shelby, Graham

2342. *The Devil Is Loose.* Garden City, NY: Doubleday, 1974. 261 pp.
During the 10 years of Richard I's reign, his family maneuvers for position in his realm while his brother John reveals his infantile attitudes.
Genre(s): Biographical Fiction; Political Fiction.

2343. *The Kings of Vain Intent.* New York: McKay, 1971. 320 pp.
In the sequel to *The Knights of Dark Renown*, knights, including Balian, Humphrey, Guy, and Marquis Conrad, whom Saladin captured at the Battle of the Horns of Hattin, continue their quest to reclaim Jerusalem.
Genre(s): War Story.

2344. *The Knights of Dark Renown.* New York: McKay, 1969. 283 pp.
Reynald of Châtillon causes Saladin to break his truce with the Holy Land, and Baldwin, the leper king, and his army must lead the fight of Jerusalem against the Muslims.
Genre(s): War Story.

2345. *The Wolf at the Door.* Garden City, NY: Doubleday, 1975. 240 pp.
In the sequel to *The Devil Is Loose*, King John clashes with Europe's rulers, especially Philip of France.
Genre(s): Biographical Fiction; Political Fiction.

Shipway, George

2346. *The Knight.* New York: Doubleday, 1970. 360 pp.
Days before he is to become a knight, Humphrey Visdelou must defend his family's honor, and after he aligns himself with Geoffrey de Mandeville, Earl of Essex, in the 12th century, he discovers that Geoffrey is a traitor to both Stephen and Matilda.
Genre(s): War Story.

2347. *The Paladin.* New York: Harcourt Brace, 1973. 494 pp.
During the 11th century, Walter Tirel at first serves William the Conqueror's son Rufus but then changes his allegiance to Robert.
Genre(s): Biographical Fiction.

2348. *The Wolf Time.* London: P. Davies, 1973. 282 pp.
A Norman baron joins King Rufus's service to guard him from his brother Henry's bid for the throne, and he becomes involved with Isabel of Conches and Rufus's quarrel with Archbishop Anselm before Rufus dies in New Forest.
Genre(s): Biographical Fiction.

Small, Bertrice

2349. *Hellion.* New York: Ballantine, 1996. 434 pp.
In 1100 when Hugh Fauconier receives Langston, the land of his Saxon ancestors, he must marry Isabelle (the Belle from Hell), but they fall in love and have a child before Belle must rescue Hugh from the descendants of Merlin's Vivienne in Britanny.
Genre(s): Romance.

2350. *A Moment in Time.* New York: Ballantine, 1991. 496 pp.
In 1060 Wynne finally marries Madoc of Powys, but while pregnant, she leaves to patch up a family feud and becomes enslaved.
Genre(s): Romance; Fantastic Literature.

Stewart, Mary

◆ 2351. *The Crystal Cave.* New York: Morrow, 1970. 521 pp.
Merlin spends his childhood in the court of his grandfather, the King of Wales, where he keeps secret his ability of "second sight."
Genre(s): Fantastic Literature.

◆ 2352. *The Hollow Hills.* New York: Morrow, 1973. 499 pp.
In the sequel to *The Crystal Cave*, Arthur is born and sent into hiding, and he and Merlin do not meet until he is almost a man.
Genre(s): Fantastic Literature.

◆ 2353. *The Last Enchantment.* New York: Morrow, 1979. 538 pp.
The sequel to *The Hollow Hills* shows Merlin helping Arthur, the High King, to battle the Saxons and to manage his private life.
Genre(s): Fantastic Literature.

◆ 2354. *The Prince and the Pilgrim.* New York: Morrow, 1995. 292 pp.
Alexander and Alice meet and fall in love during King Arthur's rule, while Alexander plots to avenge his father's assassination and Alice goes on pilgrimages to holy shrines with her father.
Genre(s): Romance; Fantastic Literature.

◆ 2355. *The Wicked Day.* New York: Morrow, 1983. 453 pp.

In the sequel to *The Last Enchantment*, Mordred, the son of King Arthur and his half-sister, returns to Arthur's kingdom to fulfill his destiny of murdering his father.
Genre(s): Fantastic Literature.

Sutcliff, Rosemary

◆ 2356. *Blood Feud.* New York: Dutton, 1977. 144 pp.
Thormod captures Jestyn on the British coast and enslaves him, taking him first to Scandinavia and then to Miklagard (Constantinople), on a blood feud pursuit where they join the Varangian guards and Jestyn learns about healing.
Genre(s): War Story.

◆ 2357. *Dawn Wind.* New York: Henry Z. Walck, 1962. 321 pp.
In the sixth century, Owain sells himself into thralldom with the Saxons for money to help him and his friend Regina after the Saxons overrun Great Britain.

◆ 2358. *The Shield Ring.* New York: Henry Z. Walck, 1962. 251 pp.
Bjorn, a spy, fears that if Normans ever capture him, he will reveal Saxon secrets, but since he plays the harp, he is the only one who can enter Norman camps without suspicion.
Genre(s): War Story.

◆ 2359. *Sword at Sunset.* New York: Coward-McCann, 1963. 495 pp.
After the Romans leave, Arthur strives to hold Britain together by fighting the Picts, Saxons, and other invading tribes.
Genre(s): Fantastic Literature.

Tarr, Judith

◆ 2360. *The Dagger and the Cross.* New York: Doubleday, 1991. 474 pp.
Prince Aidan receives papal dispensation to marry the Moslem Morgiana during the Crusades, but the document, when opened by his brother King Gwydion, is revealed as a forgery that claims the two are witches, and they separate to fight on different sides before reuniting and returning to Rhiyana, Wales.
Genre(s): War Story.

Taylor, Anna

◆ 2361. *Drustan the Wanderer.* New York: Saturday Review Press, 1972. 181 pp.
Tristan, a knight during the times of King Arthur, falls in love with Iseult, an unavailable woman.
Genre(s): Fantastic Literature; Romance.

Taylor, Timothy

◆ 2362. *Elaine the Fair.* Jacksonville, NC: Horseshoe, 1991. 990 pp.
Arthur, a mathematician from the country, the duke Roland, and Robin Hood fight in England during the late 12th century along with others over the beauty of Elaine of Anjou.
Genre(s): Epic Literature.

◆May be suitable for young adult readers

Todd, Catherine

2363. **Bond of Honour.** New York: St. Martin's, 1982. 223 pp.
Named heir by Edward the Confessor, William the Conqueror comes to England to fight Earl Harold Godwinsson for the throne at the Battle of Hastings.
Genre(s): War Story; Biographical Fiction.

Tolstoy, Nikolai

2364. **The Coming of the King.** New York: Bantam, 1989. 360 pp.
Merlin accompanies King Maelgun the Tall to the Battle of Dineirth before the British begin to drive out the heathen Saxons.
Genre(s): Fantastic Literature.

Tranter, Nigel G.

2365. **Columba.** London: Hodder and Stoughton, 1987. 427 pp.
Columba, an Irish prince, comes to Scotland in the 6th century after he is banished, and he converts the people to Christianity.
Genre(s): Biographical Fiction; Christian Fiction.

2366. **Macbeth the King.** London: Hodder and Stoughton, 1978. 395 pp.
Macbeth and his Queen are good monarchs and guardians of the Scots, protecting them from the Danes and the English, until they deal with Duncan.
Genre(s): Biographical Fiction.

2367. **Margaret the Queen.** London: Hodder and Stoughton, 1981. 421 pp.
Queen Margaret helps to bring the Celtic church in line with Roman Catholic ways in 11th-century Scotland, an action which leads to sainthood after her death.
Genre(s): Biographical Fiction; Christian Fiction.

2368. **Robert the Bruce: The Steps to the Empty Throne.** New York: St. Martin's, 1971. 351 pp.
Robert the Bruce begins his quest to help Scotland gain its freedom from the British.
Genre(s): Biographical Fiction.

2369. **True Thomas.** London: Hodder and Stoughton, 1981. 432 pp.
Thomas the Rhymer sings his ballads and legends of magic while the Crusades continue, and the Maid of Norway dies, ending hope for Celtic succession.
Genre(s): Biographical Fiction.

Treece, Henry

◆ 2370. **The Road to Miklagard.** New York: S. G. Phillips, 1957. 254 pp.
Harald sails to Ireland for the treasure belonging to the giant Grummoch, and after enslaving the giant in 785, Turks capture and sell Harald and his friend to a Spanish Muslim who sends them to Miklagard with his daughter.
Genre(s): Adventure Story.

◆ 2371. **Viking's Dawn.** New York: S. G. Phillips, 1956. 253 pp.
Harald sails from his Norse Viking home to Ireland and is the only one to survive a shipwreck before finding refuge on a Danish ship around AD 780.
Genre(s): Adventure Story.

Tremayne, Peter

◆ 2372. **Absolution by Murder.** New York: St. Martin's, 1996. 274 pp.
In 664, when an ecclesiastical conclave meets to settle divisions between the Roman and Celtic branches of Christianity at Whitby, Sister Fidelma investigates the murder of the Abbess of Kildare, a proponent of the Celtic way.
Genre(s): Mystery.

◆ 2373. **Shroud for the Archbishop.** New York: St. Martin's, 1995. 340 pp.
Sister Fidelma of Ireland's Celtic Church goes with Brother Eadulf of Canterbury to Rome in the seventh century for business reasons, but Wighard, scheduled to become an archbishop during their stay, is strangled in his quarters before the ceremony.
Genre(s): Mystery.

Trevaskis, Eve

2374. **The Lion of England.** London: Hale, 1975. 191 pp.
Edward I, 13th-century king of England, leads his people thoughtfully although he has little sympathy for weakness.
Genre(s): Biographical Fiction.

Twain, Mark

2375. **A Connecticut Yankee in King Arthur's Court.** 1889. New York: Oxford, 1996. 656 pp.
A Yankee of the late 19th century finds himself in King Arthur's English court and tries to show the people there how to change things.
Genre(s): Fantastic Literature; Time Travel.

Vansittart, Peter

2376. **Lancelot.** Chester Springs, PA: Dufour, 1989. 256 pp.
Lancelot, in old age, reflects on Arthur and remembers him as a tough cavalry leader with the main interests of drinking, wenching, and fighting.
Genre(s): Fantastic Literature.

Watson, William

2377. **Beltran in Exile.** London: Chatto and Windus, 1979. 286 pp.
Beltran, keeper of the treasure of the Knights of the Templars, guards it as he sails to Scotland to deliver the heart of a dead knight.
Genre(s): War Story.

Wein, Elizabeth E.

2378. *The Winter Prince.* New York: Atheneum, 1993. 202 pp.
Artos asks Medraut (Mordred), his bastard son by Morgause, to help his heir Lleu become well and prepare to be king of Camlann, but Lleu is an unpleasant child, and their first attempts are unsuccessful.
Genre(s): Fantastic Literature.

White, T. H.

2379. *The Once and Future King.* New York: Putnam, 1958. 677 pp.
Arthur becomes king of the Britons under the guidance of Merlin.
Genre(s): Fantastic Literature.

2380. *The Sword in the Stone.* New York: Putnam, 1939. 311 pp.
At a medieval manor, Kay and Wart (later King Arthur) learn the attributes necessary for becoming a successful knight.
Genre(s): Fantastic Literature.

Whyte, Jack

◆ 2381. *The Eagles' Brood.* New York: Tor, 1994. 643 pp.
Caius Merlyn Britannicus, an heir of Roman colonists, has the responsibility of protecting Camulod and spreading Roman Civilization, and at first, his cousin Uther Pendragon helps him. (*Series:* Camulod Chronicles, 3)
Genre(s): Fantastic Literature.

◆ 2382. *Saxon Shore.* New York: Tor, 1998. 496 pp.
In the sequel to *The Eagle's Brood*, Connor, the son of the High King of the Scots of Eire, rescues Authur Pendragon, adrift at sea with Merlin, and looks after him while Camulod begins to prosper.
Genre(s): Fantastic Literature.

Wingate, John

2383. *William, the Conqueror.* New York: Watts, 1983. 335 pp.
William the Conqueror seems to collect enemies, first his Norman and French ones, and then many Saxons.
Genre(s): Biographical Fiction; War Story.

Wolf, Joan

2384. *Born of the Sun.* New York: New American Library, 1989. 407 pp.
Niniane, a Celtic princess, and her people hide the Saxon prince Ceawlin when he is forced into exile, but he becomes a leader who gains enough trust to unite the Britons and Celts into one kingdom. (*Series:* Dark Age England Trilogy, 2)

2385. *The Edge of Light.* New York: New American Library, 1990. 371 pp.
King Alfred gathers an army which permanently stops the Viking invasion in 878. (*Series:* Dark Age England Trilogy, 3)
Genre(s): War Story.

2386. *The Road to Avalon.* New York: New American Library, 1988. 358 pp.
Arthur discovers that Morgan, whom he loves, is his aunt, and he must marry Gwenhyfar to keep the dynasty in tact. (*Series:* Dark Age England Trilogy, 1)
Genre(s): Fantastic Literature; Romance.

Woolley, Persia

◆ 2387. *Child of the Northern Spring.* New York: Poseidon, 1987. 428 pp.
Guinevere marries Arthur but the wars trouble her as does her first encounter with Queen Morgan.
Genre(s): Fantastic Literature.

◆ 2388. *Guinevere: The Legend in Autumn.* New York: Poseidon, 1991. 432 pp.
Guinevere recalls her trial and Arthur's battle with Mordred from inside her convent in the final days of her life, in the sequel to *Queen of the Summer Stars*.
Genre(s): Fantastic Literature.

◆ 2389. *Queen of the Summer Stars.* New York: Poseidon, 1990. 415 pp.
After Guinevere's marriage to Arthur, he continues to be preoccupied with concerns of the kingdom while Tristan and Isolde develop their relationship and Guinevere becomes aware of Lancelot, in the sequel to *Child of the Northern Spring*.
Genre(s): Fantastic Literature.

Wright, Patricia

◆ 2390. *I Am England.* New York: St. Martin's, 1987. 398 pp.
The smith Brac, the Saxon warrior Edred, the storyteller Rico, and the ironmonger Francis live near a pool on a ridge above a forest where Alfred's wars, the arrival of Vikings, and the Norman conquest as well as minor things shape their lives.
Award(s): Georgette Heyer Historical Novel Prize.
Genre(s): Family Saga.

1290-1491

Anand, Valerie

◆ 2391. *The Ruthless Yeomen.* New York: St. Martin's, 1993. 342 pp.
The sequel to *The Proud Villeins* follows several *villeins* as they try to obtain freedom through Tyler's Insurrection in 1381 and later peasant uprisings. (*Series:* Bridges Over Time, 2)
Genre(s): Domestic Fiction.

◆May be suitable for young adult readers

◆ 2392. *Women of Ashdon.* New York: St. Martin's, 1993. 373 pp.
Forced to marry Sir James Weston when she wants to marry Giles, Susannah Whitmead adjusts to her husband and his home, Ashdon, and begins to desire to keep Ashdon, a desire shared by her daughter and granddaughter. (*Series:* Bridges Over Time, 3)
Genre(s): Domestic Fiction.

Andrew, Prudence

2393. *The Constant Star.* New York: Putnam, 1946. 255 pp.
In 1381, Watt Tyler leads the peasants in revolt against poll taxes and the poor quality of life, and he confronts Richard II.
Genre(s): War Story; Political Fiction.

Barnes, Margaret Ayer

◆ 2394. *Isabel the Fair.* Philadelphia: Macrae-Smith, 1957. 349 pp.
Isabel, at 16, anticipates her role as wife and queen to Edward II of England, but his personal choices dismay her.
Genre(s): Biographical Fiction.

Barnes, Margaret Campbell

◆ 2395. *The King's Bed.* Philadelphia: Macrae-Smith, 1962. 286 pp.
Richard III's illegitimate son Dickon Broom and an innkeeper's daughter reveal Richard as kindly but gloomy before his death in battle.
Genre(s): Biographical Fiction.

◆ 2396. *The Tudor Rose.* Philadelphia: Macrae-Smith, 1953. 313 pp.
Elizabeth of York marries the Lancastrian king Henry VII, hoping to help England, and becomes the mother of Henry VIII.
Genre(s): Biographical Fiction.

◆ 2397. *Within the Hollow Crown.* Philadelphia: Macrae-Smith, 1947. 359 pp.
Richard II becomes the King of England under the regency of John of Gaunt but begins to assert leadership in 1381 during the Peasants' Revolt.
Genre(s): Biographical Fiction.

Beard, Julie

2398. *A Dance in Heather.* New York: Jove, 1996. 384 pp.
A royal decree forces Lady Tess Farnsworth to marry Richard Avery, Earl of Esterby, even though she detests him for not saving her father from burning to death as a Lollard heretic.
Genre(s): Romance.

Belle, Pamela

2399. *The Lodestar.* New York: St. Martin's, 1991. 533 pp.

Christie Heron becomes Richard, Duke of Glocester's aide, because he believes that he will rise in power with Richard when Richard becomes king.
Genre(s): Biographical Fiction; Romance.

Bennetts, Pamela

2400. *The Lords of Lancaster.* New York: St. Martin's, 1973. 269 pp.
Richard II rules England during the 14th century.
Genre(s): Biographical Fiction.

2401. *Royal Sword at Agincourt.* New York: St. Martin's, 1971. 252 pp.
Henry V inspires loyalty in English citizens of various classes and political factions from his Welsh battles to his marriage in 1420 to Catherine of France.
Genre(s): Biographical Fiction; Political Fiction.

Bowen, Marjorie

2402. *Dickon.* New York: Beagle, 1971. 255 pp.
Richard III rules after usurping power in the 15th century.
Genre(s): Biographical Fiction.

Brandewyne, Rebecca

2403. *Rose of Rapture.* New York: Warner, 1984. 435 pp.
Royal decree forces Lady Isabella Ashley, a Yorkist subject of Richard III, and Lord Warwick, Earl of Hawkhurst, supporter of Henry Tudor, to marry.
Genre(s): War Story; Romance.

Carr, Robyn

◆ 2404. *By Right of Arms.* Boston: Little, Brown, 1986. 354 pp.
In the 14th century, Edward the Black Prince sends his friend Sir Hyatt Laidley to conquer de La Noye in France, and after de La Noye dies, Hyatt claims his widow Aurelie as his own, a move she detests.
Genre(s): Romance; War Story.

◆ 2405. *The Everlasting Covenant.* Boston: Little, Brown, 1987. 393 pp.
Anne Gifford and Dylan DeFayne are in love, but their families detest each other and fight on opposite sides of the Wars of the Roses.
Genre(s): Romance.

Crow, Donna Fletcher

2406. *The Fields of Bannockburn.* Chicago: Moody, 1996. 707 pp.
In 1314, the Battle of Bannockburn helps Scotland achieve independence, and Mary, Brad, and Gareth contribute to the goal.
Genre(s): Christian Fiction; War Story.

Crowley, Duane

2407. *Riddle Me a Murder.* Manchaca, TX: Blue Boar, 1987. 231 pp.

Geoffrey Chaucer tells John of Gaunt that someone has hidden explosives in his home, possibly because the last of his series of mistresses was poisoned.
Genre(s): Mystery.

Darby, Catherine

◆ 2408. *The Love Knot.* New York: St. Martin's, 1991. 240 pp.
Philippa de Roet becomes pregnant by John of Gaunt, but he marries her to the young Geoffrey Chaucer, and Philippa complains that Chaucer spends so much time writing poetry.

Dodd, Christina

2409. *A Knight to Remember.* New York: Harper-Collins, 1996. 368 pp.
When a wounded knight and his servant come into her dispensary, Lady Edlyn is shocked to see that he is a man whom she once loved passionately.
Genre(s): Medical Novel.

Doherty, P. C.

◆ 2410. *An Ancient Evil.* New York: St. Martin's, 1995. 248 pp.
Travelers on a pilgrimage hear the story of the Strigoi who may be responsible for killing Oxford citizens, and a king and clerk must find and destroy it.
Genre(s): Mystery.

◆ 2411. *The Death of a King.* New York: St. Martin's, 1985. 176 pp.
Edward III asks Edmund Beche, a clerk, to find who murdered his father, Edward II, in 1327.
Genre(s): Mystery.

2412. *The Devil's Hunt.* New York: St. Martin's, 1998. 256 pp.
Hugh Corbett, servant to Edward I in 1303, must search in Oxford for the person who is hanging severed heads by the hair from trees, the murderer of an archivist, and someone calling himself the "Bellman" who invokes Edward's dead enemy Simon de Montfort.
Genre(s): Mystery.

2413. *Murder Wears a Cowl.* New York: St. Martin's, 1994. 249 pp.
After Edward I knights Hugh Corbett, Corbett goes to London in 1302 to identify the killer of courtesans serving the nobility.
Genre(s): Mystery.

2414. *The Prince of Darkness.* New York: St. Martin's, 1993. 247 pp.
For his boss Edward I, Hugh Corbett must find who murdered Lady Eleanor in her abbey bedchamber and tried to make the scene look like a suicide.
Genre(s): Mystery.

2415. *The Song of a Dark Angel.* New York: St. Martin's, 1995. 249 pp.
In 1302, Sir Hugh Corbett goes to Norfolk to investigate a pair of murders which eventually prove to be related to

the expedition of King John in 1216 during which a treasure was lost in the bog called The Wash.
Genre(s): Mystery.

◆ 2416. *Spy in Chancery.* New York: St. Martin's, 1988. 176 pp.
Hugh Corbett, senior clerk for Edward I, looks for a secret agent who has infiltrated the court and is passing information to Phillip IV of France.
Genre(s): Mystery.

◆ 2417. *A Tapestry of Murders.* New York: St. Martin's, 1996. 247 pp.
The Man of Law from Chaucer's *Canterbury Tales* relates the theft and murder that occurred after the death of the Dowager Queen Isabella in 1358.
Genre(s): Mystery; Legal Story.

◆ 2418. *A Tournament of Murders.* New York: St. Martin's, 1997. 256 pp.
In the 14th century, the franklin entertains his audience on a pilgrimage to Canterbury with the tale of Richard Greenele who, when he learns that he is a noble, vows to avenge the deaths of his parents.
Genre(s): Mystery.

◆ 2419. *The Whyte Harte.* New York: St. Martin's, 1988. 256 pp.
In 15th-century England, Matthew Jankyn tries to unravel the mystery of Richard II's supposed death in 1399 and later attempts to restore him to the throne.
Genre(s): Mystery.

Doyle, Arthur Conan

2420. *Sir Nigel.* New York: McClure, Phillips 1906. 368 pp.
An Englishman travels abroad in the 14th century during the time of the Black Death and the Battle of Poitiers.
Genre(s): War Story.

Du Maurier, Daphne

2421. *The House on the Strand.* Garden City, NY: Doubleday, 1969. 298 pp.
Richard Young tests a drug that takes him back 600 years, and he becomes involved in the lives of the people in a manor house.
Genre(s): Mystery; Time Travel.

Edwards, Rhoda

2422. *Fortune's Wheel.* Garden City, NY: Doubleday, 1979. 273 pp.
Richard III demonstrates his loyalty to his brother and enjoys his adventures before he realizes that Anne Neville is the woman he wants to marry.
Genre(s): Biographical Fiction.

Fairburn, Eleanor M.

2423. *The Rose at Harvest End.* New York: Reader's Digest, 1974. 216 pp.
Edward IV's bigamous marriage to Elisabeth Woodville-Grey causes problems during the Wars of the Roses.
Genre(s): Biographical Fiction.

◆May be suitable for young adult readers

2424. *Winter's Rose.* London: Hale, 1976. 190 pp.
In the 15th century, the Houses of York and Lancaster
fight for the throne of England in the Wars of the Roses.
Genre(s): War Story.

Farrington, Robert

◆ 2425. *The Killing of Richard the Third.* New
York: Scribner's, 1971. 286 pp.
In the two years leading to the 15th-century battle at Bos-
worth Field, Henry Morane becomes involved in a series
of adventures, as Richard III hovers in the background.
Genre(s): Adventure Story.

Figes, Eva

2426. *The Seven Ages.* New York: Pantheon,
1986. 186 pp.
Seven women whose lives span the period from the the
Middle Ages to the present illustrate dichotomies be-
tween males and females.
Genre(s): Family Saga.

Ford, John M.

2427. *The Dragon Waiting.* New York: Times-
cape, 1983. 365 pp.
A wizard, a woman doctor, a vampire expert, and a mer-
cenary soldier help Richard III escape to England in a
Byzantine plot.
Genre(s): Allegory.

Frazer, Margaret

◆ 2428. *The Outlaw's Tale.* New York: Jove, 1994.
217 pp.
In 1434, Sister Frevisse and Master Naylor go with Sister
Emma to her godchild's christening when Frevisse's
cousin asks for help obtaining a pardon for him and his
outlaw band.
Genre(s): Mystery.

Gellis, Roberta

2429. *The Dragon and the Rose.* Chicago: Play-
boy, 1977. 363 pp.
When Yorkist Edward IV forces Henry VI off the throne,
Henry returns briefly, but after Edward dies, his brother
Richard succeeds him while Henry VII waits in exile to
take the crown.
Genre(s): Biographical Fiction; Political Fiction.

Giardina, Denise

◆ 2430. *Good King Harry.* New York: Harper and
Row, 1984. 393 pp.
In the 15th century, Henry V (Harry) lives a full and af-
fectionate life before his untimely death at the age of 35.
Genre(s): Biographical Fiction.

Grace, C. L.

◆ 2431. *The Book of Shadows.* New York: St. Martin's, 1996. 195 pp.

Kathryn Swinbrooke, 15th-century physician, looks to
the king's court for suspects in the murder of the disgusting blackmailer Tenebrae.
Genre(s): Mystery; Medical Novel.

◆ 2432. *The Eye of God.* New York: St. Martin's,
1994. 198 pp.
Kathryn Swinbrooke and Colum Murtagh search for Edward IV's Eye of God, a royal talisman lost in battle during 1471, and they end up investigating the death of a
Lancastrian soldier who fled from the battle with the talisman.
Genre(s): Mystery; Medical Novel.

◆ 2433. *The Merchant of Death.* New York: St. Martin's, 1995. 182 pp.
When Sir Reginald Erpingham dies inside a locked tavern room in Canterbury during the 15th century, Kathryn
Swinbrooke and Colum Murtagh discover that many people had reasons to kill him.
Genre(s): Mystery; Medical Novel.

◆ 2434. *A Shrine of Murders.* New York: St. Mar-
tin's, 1993. 195 pp.
Kathryn Swinbrooke joins Colum Murtagh, who has
come to Canterbury to restore peace after the Wars of the
Roses, to investigate the poisoning of pilgrims visiting
Becket's shrine during the 15th century.
Genre(s): Mystery.

Graham, Alice Walworth

2435. *The Summer Queen.* Garden City, NY: Doubleday, 1973. 269 pp.
A lady-in-waiting of Edward IV's queen, Elizabeth, recounts Elizabeth's story as well as Edward's own rule
during the Wars of the Roses from 1459 until his death.
Genre(s): Biographical Fiction; Political Fiction.

Gregory, Susanna

2436. *A Bone of Contention.* New York: St. Martin's, 1997. 288 pp.
Matthew Bartholomew, physician, and Brother Michael
argue about medicine in 14th-century Cambridge while
they ascertain whether the recently discovered relics ex-
hibited at a new college are authentic.
Genre(s): Mystery; Medical Novel.

2437. *A Plague on Both Your Houses.* New York:
St. Martin's, 1998. 416 pp.
Physician Matthew Bartholomew must find who has mur-
dered a man and pinned him to a waterwheel while the
Black Death begins to afflict the population of his town.
Genre(s): Mystery; Medical Novel.

2438. *An Unholy Alliance.* New York: St. Martin's, 1996. 288 pp.
After the Black Death subsides, Cambridge residents face
a series of murders, and physician Matthew Bartholomew
and Brother Michael investigate.
Genre(s): Mystery.

Harding, Paul

◆ 2439. *The Nightingale Gallery.* New York: Morrow, 1991. 252 pp.
Brother Athelstan, poor friar, and the coroner Sir John Cranston ask questions about the poisoning of a wealthy merchant in 14th-century London.
Genre(s): Mystery.

◆ 2440. *Red Slayer.* New York: Morrow, 1992. 283 pp.
Brother Athelstan, curate, also serves as a clerk to Sir John Cranston, the Lord Coroner of London, and the two must solve the 14th-century murder of unlikeable Sir Ralph Whitton.
Genre(s): Mystery.

Hardwick, Mollie

2441. *I Remember Love.* New York: St. Martin's, 1983. 335 pp.
In the mid-15th century, Joscelyn Conyers and Yolande de Clifford are doomed lovers, but they are reincarnated in the 16th century and again in the 19th.
Genre(s): Time Travel; Romance.

Haycraft, Molly Costain

2442. *The King's Daughters.* Philadelphia: Lippincott, 1971. 247 pp.
Elizabeth, youngest daughter of Edward I of England, has little control over the political aspects of her life as a princess, but she retains her strong will.
Genre(s): Political Fiction; Domestic Fiction.

2443. *The Lady Royal.* Philadelphia: Lippincott, 1964. 255 pp.
Isabella, daughter of Edward III, is married to a Frenchman during the Hundred Years' War.
Genre(s): War Story.

Henley, Virginia

2444. *Desired.* New York: Dell, 1995. 400 pp.
Orphaned Lady Brianna of Bedford waits for the king to name her betrothed, and is pleased with the handsome Robert de Beauchamp until Christian Hawksblood appears and claims the Beauchamp name.
Genre(s): Romance.

Heyer, Georgette

2445. *My Lord John.* New York: Dutton, 1975. 383 pp.
John, Duke of Bedford, the son of King Henry IV enjoys the life of the Middle Ages.
Genre(s): Romance.

2446. *Simon, the Coldheart.* 1925. Garden City, NY: Doubleday, 1979. 286 pp.
At 14, Simon Malvallet rises from a page to a knight and then falls in love.
Genre(s): Adventure Story; Romance.

Hill, Pamela

2447. *My Lady Glamis.* New York: St. Martin's, 1987. 191 pp.
Jonet Douglas, Lady Glamis, belongs to a power-seeking clan, and she tries to calm those around her after marriage into the Campbell clan, but James IV, still angry at her rejection, foils her plans.
Genre(s): Romance.

Howard, Linda

2448. *Son of the Morning.* New York: Pocket Books, 1997. 372 pp.
Grace St. John, translator of ancient languages, finds a document that gives the location of the treasure that Niall of Scotland brought home as Guardian of the Treasure for the Knights Templar in the 14th century, and she is transported to his time to protect the relics, including the Holy Grail, after an evil group kills her husband and brother.
Genre(s): Romance; Mystery.

Jarman, Rosemary Hawley

2449. *The Courts of Illusion.* Boston: Little, Brown, 1983. 370 pp.
A Plantagenet loyalist, Nicholas Archer, supports Perkin Warbeck, the pretender to the throne, after the death of Richard III at Bosworth Field in 1485.
Genre(s): Biographical Fiction.

2450. *Crown in Candlelight.* Boston: Little, Brown, 1978. 477 pp.
Katherine of Valois bears children to both Owen Tudor and Henry V as a Welsh sorceress influences them all.
Genre(s): Biographical Fiction.

2451. *The King's Grey Mare.* Boston: Little, Brown, 1973. 448 pp.
During the 15th-century Wars of the Roses, Elizabeth Woodville, in the sequel to *We Speak No Treason*, becomes linked to more than one king.
Genre(s): Biographical Fiction.

2452. *We Speak No Treason.* Boston: Little, Brown, 1971. 575 pp.
An archer, a court fool, and Katherine the illegitimate daughter of Richard III, all tell tales about the King.
Genre(s): Biographical Fiction.

Johnson, Mary Ellen

2453. *The Lion and the Leopard.* New York: Crown, 1985. 320 pp.
When Maria's husband Philip leaves for a three-year journey to the Holy Land during the reign of Edward II, Maria enters a romance with Richard Plantagenet.
Genre(s): Romance.

Kalechofsky, Roberta

2454. *Bodmin, 1349.* Marblehead, MA: Micah, 1988. 438 pp.
During the Black Death years, while peasants suffer, priests extort, and Jews lend money, Will, a York peas-

ant, flees his happy marriage when he learns that his wife, Miriam, is Jewish.
Genre(s): Domestic Fiction; Jewish Fiction.

King, Susan

2455. *Lady Miracle.* New York: New American Library, 1997. 383 pp.
The licensed physician Lady Michaelmas helps the battle-wounded in Robert the Bruce's 14th-century Scotland.
Genre(s): Medical Novel; Political Fiction.

Lamb, Arnette

2456. *Chieftain.* New York: Pocket Books, 1995. 304 pp.
After her twin Clare dies, Johanna honors her promise and pretends to be Clare, taking care of her estate and her son, but after seven years, Clare's supposedly dead husband, imprisoned by Edward I, reappears, expecting his wife to honor his advances.
Genre(s): Domestic Fiction; Romance.

2457. *Maiden of Inverness.* New York: Pocket Books, 1995. 339 pp.
In 1296, Edward I forces Meridene Macgillivray, 8, to marry butcher's son Revas MacDuff, since she must crown whomever she marries as king of Scotland and Edward I thinks the Scots will accept him and refuse Revas.
Genre(s): Romance; Political Fiction.

Lane, Jane

2458. *A Summer Storm.* London: P. Davies, 1976. 183 pp.
In the 14th century, Wat Tyler leads a rebellion against Richard II in England.
Genre(s): Political Fiction.

Lang, Jennifer

2459. *The Peacock and the Pearl.* New York: St. Martin's, 1993. 438 pp.
Joanna Burgeys, daughter of a London mercer, becomes involved with both Sir Tristam and a sea captain in 14th-century London.
Genre(s): Romance.

Lewis, Hilda Winifred

2460. *Harlot Queen.* New York: D. McKay, 1970. 407 pp.
Isabella, wife of Edward II, becomes known as a harlot after her affair with her husband's enemy in the 14th century.
Genre(s): Biographical Fiction.

Lindsay, Philip

2461. *London Bridge Is Falling.* Boston: Little, Brown, 1934. 389 pp.
Jack Cade leads a major rebellion against the government of Henry VI of England in 1450 in support of small property owners whose taxes are too high.
Genre(s): War Story; Political Fiction; Biographical Fiction.

Lofts, Norah

2462. *The Homecoming.* Garden City, NY: Doubleday, 1976. 282 pp.
The sequel to *Knight's Acre* finds Sir Godfrey Tallboys returning from Spain to his wife but bringing with him a Moorish girl who saved him from slavery.
Genre(s): Family Saga; Romance.

2463. *Knight's Acre.* Garden City, NY: Doubleday, 1975. 253 pp.
Offered a large sum of money to appear in tourneys, Sir Godfrey Tallboys departs for Spain with his knights, but the Moors defeat them, and he is enslaved.
Genre(s): Family Saga; Romance.

2464. *The Lonely Furrow.* Garden City, NY: Doubleday, 1977. 308 pp.
In the sequel to *The Homecoming*, Henry Tallboys looks after his land when his wife suddenly dies, while his half-sister tries to marry him.
Genre(s): Family Saga; Romance.

2465. *The Town House.* Garden City, NY: Doubleday, 1959. 403 pp.
In the 15th century, Martin Reed, from a strong Suffolk family, rises from serfdom to become a wealthy merchant.
Genre(s): Family Saga; Romance.

Maughan, A. M.

2466. *Harry of Monmouth.* New York: Sloane, 1956. 440 pp.
Henry V, Shakespeare's Prince Hal, asserts his love for Katherine of France as he battles for his kingdom in 15th-century Britain.
Genre(s): Biographical Fiction.

McNaught, Judith

2467. *A Kingdom of Dreams.* New York: Pocket Books, 1989. 312 pp.
Royce Westmoreland, an English earl, falls in love with Jennifer Merrick, a Scottish countess, in 15th-century Scotland, and Royce's Aunt Elinor helps them overcome their disagreements.
Genre(s): Romance.

Neale, Linda

2468. *Briar Rose.* New York: St. Martin's, 1987. 287 pp.
Robert de Lacey, a Norman knight, encounters Briallen, the Briar rose, in her mother's cookshop during the 13th century and saves her from marriage to a Welsh rebel during the civil wars.
Genre(s): Domestic Fiction; War Story.

Nickell, Lesley J.

2469. *The White Queen.* New York: St. Martin's, 1978. 349 pp.
Anne Neville, wife of Richard III, is overshadowed by other contemporary figures in the public eye.
Genre(s): Biographical Fiction.

Nye, Robert

2470. *Falstaff*. Boston: Little, Brown, 1976. 450 pp.
Sir John Falstaff enjoys the women and the taverns in Elizabethan England while his stodgy son condemns him. *Genre(s):* Adventure Story.

Palmer, Marian

2471. *The White Boar*. Garden City, NY: Doubleday, 1968. 373 pp.
Richard III has loyal followers as he secures the throne of England during the Wars of the Roses. *Genre(s):* Biographical Fiction.

2472. *The Wrong Plantagenet*. New York: Doubleday, 1972. 321 pp.
Warbeck pretends to be one of Richard III's sons in an attempt to seize the throne from Henry VII while Phillip Lovell and his son Simon remain loyal to Richard III's memory and suffer for their efforts.

Penman, Sharon Kay

◆ 2473. *The Sunne in Splendour*. New York: Holt, Rinehart, and Winston, 1982. 936 pp.
Richard III serves his brother Edward IV faithfully but must claim the crown for himself after his brother's death by declaring Edward's children illegitimate. *Genre(s):* Biographical Fiction; War Story.

Peters, Ellis

2474. *The Bloody Field*. New York: Viking, 1973. 313 pp.
Henry Percy seems to do no wrong until he fails in battle on Bloody Field in opposition to Henry IV, and Hal, Prince of Wales, finds his loyalties divided between the two men. *Genre(s):* Political Fiction.

Plaidy, Jean

◆ 2475. *The Follies of the King*. New York: Putnam, 1982. 331 pp.
In the sequel to *Hammer of the Scots*, Edward II's wronged wife Isabella helps bring about her husband's death so that their son Edward III can take the throne. (*Series:* Plantagenet Saga, 8) *Genre(s):* Biographical Fiction.

◆ 2476. *The Goldsmith's Wife*. New York: Putnam, 1974. 318 pp.
Jane Shore becomes the mistress of Edward IV in 15th-century London. *Genre(s):* Love Story.

◆ 2477. *Passage to Pontefract*. New York: Putnam, 1982. 366 pp.
The rivalry between Edward the Black Prince and John of Gaunt for the throne of England continues through their sons, Richard II and Henry IV. (*Series:* Plantagenet Saga, 10) *Genre(s):* Biographical Fiction.

◆ 2478. *The Queen's Secret*. New York: Putnam, 1990. 303 pp.
Katherine of France is daughter of Charles VI and sister of Charles VII, sister to widowed Isabelle after Richard II of England dies, wife of Henry V of England, mother to Henry VI and grandmother to Henry VII, and lover and secret wife of Owen Tudor. (*Series:* Queens of England, 7) *Genre(s):* Biographical Fiction.

◆ 2479. *The Reluctant Queen*. New York: Putnam, 1991. 299 pp.
When Anne of York's father wants to use her as a bargaining chip for choosing a future king, she marries her friend Richard, King Edward IV's younger brother, never expecting him to become king. (*Series:* Queens of England, 8) *Genre(s):* Biographical Fiction.

◆ 2480. *The Star of Lancaster*. New York: Putnam, 1982. 320 pp.
Henry IV and Henry V, descendants of Edward III, become Lancastrian kings on the English throne. (*Series:* Plantagenet Saga, 11)

◆ 2481. *Uneasy Lies the Head*. New York: Putnam, 1984. 345 pp.
Henry VII puts down four revolts after he defeats Richard at Bosworth Field and keeps the throne for his son, Henry VIII. (*Series:* Plantagenet Saga, 15) *Genre(s):* Biographical Fiction.

◆ 2482. *The Vow on the Heron*. New York: Putnam, 1982. 350 pp.
In the sequel to *The Follies of the King*, Edward III, only 14, feels insecure on the throne especially with his mother's confidant Roger de Mortimer lurking, but he overcomes his fears and marries Philippa. (*Series:* Plantagenet Saga, 9) *Genre(s):* Biographical Fiction.

Potter, Jeremy

2483. *A Trail of Blood*. New York: McCall, 1971. 281 pp.
A successor to the Tudors claims that Richard III did not kill the Yorkist princes in the tower. *Genre(s):* Allegory.

Power, Jo-Ann

2484. *Nightingale's Song*. New York: Pocket Books, 1997. 290 pp.
In 1403, Henry IV's aide, the Dragon, retrieves wealthy Clare for marriage to the king's annoying nephew Geoffrey, but the Dragon falls in love with her before they get to Geoffrey's home. *Genre(s):* Romance.

Ragosta, Millie J.

2485. *Gerait's Daughter*. Garden City, NY: Doubleday, 1981. 192 pp.
Henry VII tests the loyalty of the Irish Earl of Kildare, a Yorkist in the Wars of the Roses, by declaring that Mar-

garet Fitzgerald, his daughter, must wed a hated Lancastrian.
Genre(s): War Story; Romance.

2486. *The Winter Rose.* Garden City, NY: Doubleday, 1982. 192 pp.
Anne de Syon, 18, learns that she is the illegitimate daughter of Edward IV and Eleanor Butler, but she must pretend that she is the natural daughter of Lord Howard, the man with whose family she will be living.

Riley, Judith Merkle

◆ 2487. *In Pursuit of the Green Lion.* New York: Delacorte, 1990. 440 pp.
The sequel to *A Vision of Light* finds Margaret married to Gregory and going to France to retrieve him after the Count of St. Medard captures him.
Genre(s): Romance; Picaresque Fiction.

◆ 2488. *A Vision of Light.* New York: Delacorte, 1989. 442 pp.
Margaret of Ashbury dictates her memoirs to Brother Gregory, a defrocked monk, and tells about her ability to heal, a gift that gained her accusations of witchcraft.
Genre(s): Medical Novel.

Robb, Candace M.

2489. *The Apothecary Rose.* New York: St. Martin's, 1993. 256 pp.
In the 14th century, one-eyed Owen Archer, new agent for the Lord Chancellor of England and the Archbishop of York, must investigate the deaths of two important men treated at an abbey nearby for an illness.
Genre(s): Mystery.

2490. *A Gift of Sanctuary.* New York: St. Martin's, 1998. 304 pp.
Owen Archer uses Geoffrey Chaucer to help him secretly inspect the Duke of Lancaster's Welsh fortifications, but when they arrive, they discover a stabbed dead man whose shoes are filled with sand.
Genre(s): Mystery.

◆ 2491. *The King's Bishop.* New York: St. Martin's, 1996. 372 pp.
Owen Archer, an agent for Edward III in the 14th century, tries to keep his personal feelings separate from his work for the king, especially when a friend is unjustly accused of a murder.
Genre(s): Mystery.

◆ 2492. *The Lady Chapel.* New York: St. Martin's, 1994. 287 pp.
In 1365, Owen Archer's patron makes him investigate the murder of Will Crounce, a young actor, and the murders of two others that follow.
Genre(s): Mystery.

2493. *The Nun's Tale.* New York: St. Martin's, 1995. 355 pp.
Owen Archer's boss, the Archbishop of York, asks him to investigate a nun who says that she has returned from the dead, and what he discovers are several murders.
Genre(s): Mystery.

◆ 2494. *The Riddle of St Leonard's.* New York: St. Martin's, 1997. 320 pp.
While York residents worry about plague in the 14th century, Owen Archer tries to find out why three wealthy patrons of St. Leonard's Hospital have died.
Genre(s): Mystery.

Rofheart, Martha

2495. *Fortune Made His Sword.* New York: Putnam, 1972. 445 pp.
Prince Hal, Catherine of Valois, and three other narrators tell the story of Henry IV's defeat of Richard II and the subsequent succession of his son, Henry of Monmouth.
Genre(s): Biographical Fiction.

2496. *Glendower Country.* New York: Putnam, 1973. 381 pp.
Geoffrey Chaucer, Owen Glendower's friend, Glendower himself, his wife Lady Margaret, his bard, his court physician, and his last mistress tell about Glendower and his service in the courts of Richard II and Henry IV.
Genre(s): Biographical Fiction.

Russell, Jennifer Ellen

2497. *The Threshing Floor.* Mahwah, NJ: Paulist, 1987. 352 pp.
In the 14th century, one of the Keldacross sons becomes a knight and the other, promised to the church, goes to Oxford to study, but a plague forces William to reassess his religious responsibility.
Genre(s): Christian Fiction.

Seare, Nicholas

2498. *1339 or So.* New York: Harcourt, 1975. 184 pp.
A peddlar saves a thane and his family before the end of the world arrives, but then the ending is postponed.
Genre(s): Romance; Satire.

Sedley, Kate

◆ 2499. *Death and the Chapman.* New York: St. Martin's, 1992. 190 pp.
In 1471, Roger the Chapman, 19 and recently released from a Benedictine monastery, wants to solve puzzles, an opportunity that he soon receives from a wealthy Bristol alderman when his son disappears.
Genre(s): Mystery.

◆ 2500. *The Eve of Saint Hyacinth.* New York: St. Martin's, 1996. 280 pp.
In 15th-century England, Roger the Chapman must find a killer who has become a member of the Duke of Gloucester's household.
Genre(s): Mystery.

2501. *The Holy Innocents.* New York: St. Martin's, 1995. 288 pp.
Roger the Chapman investigates the murder of two small children in Totnes during the 15th century.
Genre(s): Mystery.

◆ 2502. *The Plymouth Cloak.* New York: St. Martin's, 1993. 192 pp.
The Yorkist Duke of Gloucester hires Roger the Chapman to find who murdered the king's messenger on his way to stop another Lancastrian plot.
Genre(s): Mystery.

2503. *The Weaver's Tale.* New York: St. Martin's, 1994. 248 pp.
A widow and daughter nurse Roger the Chapman back to health after he becomes ill in Bristol in the 15th century, and he offers to find out why the widow's father, supposedly murdered, returned with amnesia and then died.
Genre(s): Mystery.

Seton, Anya

2504. *Katherine.* Boston: Houghton Mifflin, 1954. 588 pp.
John of Gaunt and Katherine Swynford, Chaucer's sister-in-law, fall in love in the 14th century.
Genre(s): Biographical Fiction; Romance.

Shelley, Mary Wollstonecraft

2505. *The Fortunes of Perkin Warbeck.* Brookfield, VT: Pickerin, 1996. 404 pp.
Perkin Warbeck claims to be the lost Duke of York with a claim to the English throne.
Genre(s): Romance.

Sisson, Rosemary Anne

2506. *The Queen and the Welshman.* London: W. H. Allen, 1979. 232 pp.
Henry V's widow Katherine secretly marries Owen Tudor, the man she loves.
Genre(s): Biographical Fiction.

Small, Bertrice

2507. *The Spitfire.* New York: Ballantine, 1990. 490 pp.
A band of the Earl of Dunmor's men stop the marriage of Arabella Grey and Sir Jasper Keane, saying that Jasper murdered the earl's intended bride, and they take Arabella for the earl, while Jasper still tries to get Arabella's lands.
Genre(s): Romance.

Smith, Haywood

2508. *Damask Rose.* New York: St. Martin's, 1998. 320 pp.
Laird Tynan MacDougald, a slave turned warrior, has the duty of executing the MacKay heir, innocent Lady Nara, to avenge a blood oath in the 15th century.
Genre(s): Romance.

Steele, Hunter

2509. *Chasing the Gilded Shadow.* New York: St. Martin's, 1986. 378 pp.
A landowner in love with James IV's 15-year-old ward Elizabeth has permission to marry her if he does not consummate the marriage until she is 16, but he becomes jealous of other suitors and takes revenge instead.

Stubbs, Jean

2510. *An Unknown Welshman.* New York: Stein and Day, 1972. 319 pp.
Henry VII works his way through the intrigues during his reign so that he can retain the throne for his son.
Genre(s): Political Fiction.

Tannahill, Reay

2511. *The World, the Flesh, and the Devil.* New York: Crown, 1987. 479 pp.
Gavin, a priest in James I's Scottish court, falls in love with Ninian, Queen Joan's attendant, but tries to deny his feelings because of his position.
Genre(s): Religious Fiction.

Thacker, Shelly

2512. *His Forbidden Touch.* New York: Avon, 1997. 384 pp.
In the 14th century, Princess Ciara's father is determined to stop bloodshed by betrothing her to the evil prince responsible, but since others plan to stop the marriage in any way possible, the king asks Royce Saint-Michel to deliver her safely in return for restoration of his stripped titles and lands.
Genre(s): Romance.

Thorne, Victoria

◆ 2513. *Longsword.* New York: St. Martin's, 1982. 252 pp.
Gervase Escot's devious uncle takes his fortune and when Gervase runs away to the castle of the woman to whom he had been engaged, he refuses to reveal his identity.
Genre(s): Romance.

Tranter, Nigel G.

2514. *Lords of Misrule.* London: Hodder and Stoughton, 1976. 414 pp.
In 14th-century Scotland, after Douglas is murdered on the field of Otterburn, the Stewarts and the Douglasses engage in tangled marriages.
Genre(s): Political Fiction; Romance.

2515. *Robert the Bruce: The Path of the Hero King.* New York: St. Martin's, 1972. 349 pp.
In the sequel to *Robert the Bruce: The Steps to the Empty Throne*, Robert the Bruce continues his quest for Scotland's freedom while loving his family.
Genre(s): Biographical Fiction.

2516. *Robert the Bruce: The Price of the King's Peace.* New York: St. Martin's, 1972. 348 pp.
In the sequel to *Robert the Bruce: The Path of the Hero King*, Robert the Bruce fights in the Battle of Bannockburn and endures the death of his daughter but realizes the joys of his grandchildren before the British recognize the Scots with the Declaration of Arbroath in 1320.
Genre(s): Biographical Fiction.

2517. *Tapestry of the Boar.* New York: Trafalgar Square, 1993. 320 pp.
A young Scot's diversity of skills and personality earn him both a bride and a knighthood.
Genre(s): Adventure Story.

2518. *Unicorn Rampant.* New York: Beaufort, 1984. 352 pp.
John Stewart becomes a hero in the eyes of his cousin King James I when he saves him from a fight with a local Scottish constabulary.

2519. *The Wallace.* London: Hodder and Stoughton, 1975. 464 pp.
Wallace, a patriot and guerilla fighter in Scotland, is betrayed, and the English execute him at Smithfield.
Genre(s): Biographical Fiction.

Tyler-Whittle, Michael Sidney

2520. *Richard III.* Philadelphia: Chilton, 1970. 275 pp.
Richard III is a strong king whose enemies malign him unfairly.
Genre(s): Biographical Fiction; Mystery; Romance.

Unsworth, Barry

2521. *Morality Play.* New York: Doubleday, 1995. 206 pp.
Nicholas Barber leaves monkhood to join a group of itinerant players and becomes caught in a 14th-century small-town murder which they try to solve.
Genre(s): Mystery.

Warner, Sylvia Townsend

2522. *The Corner That Held Them.* 1948. New York: Penguin, 1991. 367 pp.
In Norfolk, during the 14th century, plagues and disasters threaten a convent's inhabitants.
Genre(s): Domestic Fiction; Christian Fiction.

Widgery, Jeanne Anna

2523. *Trumpet at the Gates.* Garden City, NY: Doubleday, 1970. 370 pp.
Michael Frye dislikes the 14th-century feudal system, preferring the merchants and peasants to nobility, and although he fights for Richard II against Henry Bolingbroke, he has no loyalty.
Genre(s): War Story.

Wilson, Sandra

◆ 2524. *The Lady Cicely.* New York: St. Martin's, 1974. 190 pp.
Cicely watches the events of her times from her place as the daughter of a king.
Genre(s): Biographical Fiction; Love Story.

◆ 2525. *Less Fortunate than Fair.* New York: St. Martin's, 1974. 223 pp.
Cicely Plantagenet, the second daughter of Edward IV, lives during the Wars of the Roses.
Genre(s): Biographical Fiction.

◆ 2526. *The Queen's Sister.* New York: St. Martin's, 1974. 189 pp.
As the Wars of the Roses progress, Cicely Plantagenet shows herself to be pro-York and anti-Tudor.
Genre(s): Biographical Fiction.

2527. *Wife to the Kingmaker.* New York: St. Martin's, 1975. 238 pp.
Richard Neville, Earl of Warwick, struggles to overthrow Henry VI and place Edward Plantagenet on the throne.
Genre(s): Biographical Fiction.

Zelitch, Simone

2528. *The Confession of Jack Straw.* Seattle, WA: Black Heron, 1991. 263 pp.
Jack Straw confesses to his role in the English Peasant Revolt helping Wat Tyler and John Ball in the 14th century.
Award(s): University of Michigan's Hopwood Award.
Genre(s): Biographical Fiction.

1492-1649

Ainsworth, William Harrison

2529. *The Admirable Crichton.* New York: Routledge, 1839. 142 pp.
James Crichton, son of a Scottish Lord Advocate, goes to Paris for adventure in the 16th century.
Genre(s): Adventure Story.

2530. *Guy Fawkes.* New York: Dutton, 1841. 408 pp.
Guy Fawkes plans the Gunpowder Plot to free Catholics from severe laws, but it fails.
Genre(s): Political Fiction.

2531. *Windsor Castle.* New York: Dutton, 1843. 324 pp.

Anne Boleyn marries Henry VIII and manages his court.
Genre(s): Biographical Fiction.

Anand, Valerie

2532. *The Faithful Lovers.* New York: St. Martin's, 1994. 384 pp.
Parvati, an Indian renamed Penelope, becomes the wife of the bachelor Ninian Whitmead when he rescues her from shipwreck, but she is denounced as a witch during the fanatically Puritan religious fervor of the civil war.
(Series: Bridges Over Time, 4)
Genre(s): War Story; Domestic Fiction.

Anthony, Evelyn

◆ 2533. *All the Queen's Men.* New York: Crowell, 1960. 307 pp.
Elizabeth I's relationship with Robert Dudley changes from her accession to the throne in 1558 until his death in 1588.
Genre(s): Biographical Fiction.

◆ 2534. *Anne Boleyn.* New York: Crowell, 1957. 310 pp.
Henry VIII's relationship with his second wife Anne lasts from 1526 until 1536 when he has her beheaded.
Genre(s): Biographical Fiction.

◆ 2535. *Charles, the King.* Garden City, NY: Doubleday, 1961. 256 pp.
Charles I rules England before the Cromwellian factions behead him.
Genre(s): Biographical Fiction; War Story.

Arden, John

2536. *Books of Bale.* London: Methuen, 1988. 532 pp.
Bale, a White Friar in the 16th century, becomes a Protestant and the Bishop of Ossory in Ireland, and his granddaughter has Will Shakespeare as a friend.
Genre(s): Biographical Fiction; Political Fiction.

Augsburger, Myron S.

2537. *Pilgrims Aflame.* Scottsdale, PA: Herald, 1977. 288 pp.
Michael Sattler, Anabaptist, dies for his faith in 1527.
Genre(s): Biographical Fiction.

Balin, Beverly

2538. *King in Hell.* New York: Coward-McCann, 1971. 568 pp.
James Hepburn, Earl of Bothwell, marries Mary, Queen of Scots, probably out of ambition rather than love, but their love has passion since Mary was probably having an affair with him before her husband Darnley was murdered.
Genre(s): Biographical Fiction.

Barnes, Margaret Ayer

◆ 2539. *Brief Gaudy Hour: A Novel of Anne Boleyn.* Philadelphia: Macrae-Smith, 1949. 335 pp.
Although Anne Boleyn loves another, she marries Henry VIII and lives her short life in his court.
Genre(s): Biographical Fiction; Love Story.

Barnes, Margaret Campbell

◆ 2540. *King's Fool.* Philadelphia: Macrae-Smith, 1959. 286 pp.
Will Somers tells of his experiences as Henry VIII's jester and friend during Henry's long rule.
Genre(s): Biographical Fiction; Love Story.

◆ 2541. *Mary of Carisbrooke.* Philadelphia: Macrae-Smith, 1956. 318 pp.
Mary Floyd observes Charles I during the last two years of his reign after his escape to the Isle of Wight where he finds himself imprisoned.
Genre(s): Biographical Fiction; Love Story.

◆ 2542. *My Lady of Cleves.* Philadelphia: Macrae-Smith, 1946. 351 pp.
Anne of Cleves, an intelligent and warm woman, divorced from Henry VIII after six months, remains his friend and advisor.
Genre(s): Biographical Fiction.

Beahn, John E.

◆ 2543. *A Man Born Again: Saint Thomas More.* New York: Bruce, 1954. 208 pp.
The scholar Thomas More becomes a statesman in the court of Henry VIII, but Henry dislikes More's opinion about divorcing Katherine of Aragon.
Genre(s): Biographical Fiction.

Beatty, John, and Patricia Beatty

◆ 2544. *Campion Towers.* New York: Macmillan, 1965. 215 pp.
Penitence Hervey sails to England from Massachusetts to claim her inheritence and becomes involved in the intrigues of the war between Cromwell's Roundheads and the Royalists.
Genre(s): War Story.

Beck, L. Adams

2545. *Anne Boleyn.* Garden City, NY: Doubleday, 1934. 396 pp.
During her courtship with Henry VIII, Anne receives letters detailing his affection for her.
Genre(s): Biographical Fiction.

Bell, Sam Hanna

2546. *Across the Narrow Sea.* Wolfeboro, NH: Blackstaff, 1987. 299 pp.
In 1608, after the Irish lose at Kinsale, the English and Scottish settlers take Irish lands in Ulster and face the hostilities of those dispossessed.
Genre(s): Domestic Fiction; Political Fiction.

Belle, Pamela

◆ 2547. *The Chains of Fate.* New York: Berkley, 1984. 511 pp.
In the sequel to *Moon in the Water*, Thomazine Heron, heiress of Goldhayes, deserts her husband and son to reunite with her love Francis, but he thinks that she deserted him before his imprisonment and rushes into the war.
Genre(s): War Story.

◆ 2548. *The Moon in the Water.* New York: Berkley, 1984. 530 pp.
Orphan Thomazine Heron goes to live with her uncle's family, and she has to marry whomever her uncle chooses, but she falls in love with her cousin before he goes to prison as a traitor.
Genre(s): Romance.

2549. *Wintercombe*. New York: St. Martin's, 1988. 528 pp.
George St. Barbe leaves his family and his estate, Wintercombe, in the hands of his young wife, Silence, and when Royalists require quarters there, Silence becomes interested in one of the officers.
Genre(s): War Story; Romance.

Bennetts, Pamela

2550. *Envoy from Elizabeth*. New York: St. Martin's, 1973. 254 pp.
Nickolas Rokeby goes to Spain to learn the identity of an agent sent to murder Elizabeth I before the Spanish Armada.
Genre(s): Romance.

2551. *My Dear Lover England*. New York: St. Martin's, 1975. 224 pp.
England's citizens speculate over Elizabeth I's choice for a husband and whether she will wait for Dudley's wife to die before she marries him.
Genre(s): Biographical Fiction.

Bentley, Phyllis

2552. *The Power and the Glory*. New York: Macmillan, 1940. 473 pp.
A Royalist family and a Puritan family's relationships cause internal problems during the civil war.
Genre(s): War Story.

Birkhead, Margaret

2553. *Trust and Treason*. New York: St. Martin's, 1991. 384 pp.
The Woodfall family has contact with the lonely Elizabeth before she becomes queen, and the illegitimate son of the oldest Woodfall comes to London and works in the queen's secret service.
Award(s): Georgette Heyer Historical Novel Prize.
Genre(s): Political Fiction.

Blair, Anna

2554. *A Tree in the West*. London: Collins, 1976. 252 pp.
The peasant Blair family in Dundonald, Scotland, lives in poverty beginning in the 1580s with only the ritual of the Catholic Church to brighten their lives for the next hundred years.
Genre(s): Domestic Fiction; Family Saga.

Bowen, Marjorie

2555. *Double Dallilay*. London: Cassell, 1933. 383 pp.
Mary Stuart tries to keep her throne while remaining leery of Elizabeth I.
Genre(s): Biographical Fiction.

Bryher

2556. *The Player's Boy*. New York: Pantheon, 1953. 201 pp.
James Sands, an actor's apprentice, meets Francis Beaumont and witnesses Sir Walter Raleigh's scaffold death before his own violent death.

Buchan, John

2557. *Witch Wood*. Boston: Houghton Mifflin, 1927. 188 pp.
A man who opposes the hunting of witches incurs condemnation of his own.
Genre(s): Political Fiction.

Buckley, Fiona

◆ **2558. *To Shield the Queen*.** New York: Scribner's, 1997. 273 pp.
Ursula Blanchard, lady-in-waiting to Queen Elizabeth in 1560, goes to visit the wife of Sir Robert Dudley who is supposedly being poisoned so that Dudley can marry Elizabeth, but while Ursula is with her, Dudley's wife dies of a broken neck, rather than from poison.
Genre(s): Mystery.

Burgess, Anthony

2559. *A Dead Man in Deptford*. New York: Carroll and Graf, 1995. 272 pp.
Christopher Marlowe, secret agent in the Elizabethan government, infiltrates the Catholic underground although he is more interested in atheism and the new smoking tobacco.
Genre(s): Biographical Fiction; Spy Fiction.

2560. *Nothing Like the Sun*. 1964. New York: Norton, 1996. 240 pp.
Shakespeare enjoys life in London to its fullest while writing dramas for production in the Globe Theater.
Genre(s): Biographical Fiction.

Burton, Philip

2561. *You, My Brother*. New York: Random House, 1973. 561 pp.
Ned, the younger brother of William Shakespeare, follows him to London and becomes an actor before dying of the plague when still young.
Genre(s): Biographical Fiction.

Carr, Philippa

2562. *The Lion Triumphant*. New York: Putnam, 1973. 380 pp.
The sequel to *Miracle at St. Bruno's* finds Catharine betrothed to a handsome sea captain, whom she at first does not love, while tensions rise betwen England and Spain, Protestants and Catholics. (*Series: Daughters of England, 2*)
Genre(s): Romance; Family Saga.

2563. *The Miracle at St Bruno's*. New York: Putnam, 1972. 384 pp.
Damask Farland tells the story of life and its insecurities during the reigns of Henry VIII, Edward VI, Lady Jane Grey, and Mary I. (*Series: Daughters of England, 1*)
Genre(s): Romance; Gothic Fiction; Family Saga.

2564. *Saraband for Two Sisters.* New York: Putnam, 1976. 384 pp.
After *The Witch from the Sea*, twins Angelet and Bersaba become involed in the Royalist and Puritan conflicts around 1640. (*Series:* Daughters of England, 4)
Genre(s): Romance; Family Saga.

2565. *The Witch from the Sea.* New York: Putnam, 1975. 341 pp.
This sequel to *The Lion Triumphant* describes the circumstances in England, according to Linnet Pennlyon, after the destruction of the Spanish Armada. (*Series:* Daughters of England, 3)
Genre(s): Romance; Gothic Fiction; Family Saga.

Chaikin, L. L.

2566. *The Everlasting Flame.* Chicago: Moody, 1995. 244 pp.
A couple helps William Tyndale to translate the Bible in 16th-century England, then they face persecution from the church.
Genre(s): Biographical Fiction; Christian Fiction; Romance.

Chambers, Anne

2567. *The Geraldine Conspiracy.* Dublin: Marino, 1995. 448 pp.
Henry VIII tries to destroy the last scion of the Geraldine Dynasty of Ireland.
Genre(s): Political Fiction.

Chisholm, P. F.

◆ 2568. *A Famine of Horses.* New York: Walker, 1995. 270 pp.
Sir Robert Carey transfers to the Scottish border where he finds many problems during Elizabeth I's reign, including a murder, a dead horse, and an attack.
Genre(s): Mystery.

◆ 2569. *A Season of Knives.* New York: Walker, 1996. 231 pp.
After being accused of ordering the murder of an embezzler, Sir Robert Carey, cousin to Elizabeth I, must find the culprit and protect the woman he loves, who has married someone else.
Genre(s): Mystery.

2570. *A Surfeit of Guns.* New York: Walker, 1997. 233 pp.
In 1592, Sir Robert Carey discovers that guns moving between England and Scotland are being replaced with lesser-quality weapons, and his investigation takes him into the enemy court of James VI of Scotland.
Genre(s): Mystery.

Christopher, Kate

2571. *A Nest of Serpents.* London: Gollancz, 1977. 352 pp.
Frances Howard has an affair with Robert Carr, Duke of Somerset and supporter of James I, and Sir Thomas Overbury is poisoned in the Tower of London.
Genre(s): Biographical Fiction.

Clynes, Michael

2572. *A Brood of Vipers.* New York: St. Martin's, 1996. 247 pp.
Roger Shallot remembers 1523 when he and his employer went to Florence at Cardinal Wolsey's request to investigate the murder of a Florentine who had been at the court of Henry VIII.
Genre(s): Mystery.

◆ 2573. *The Grail Murders.* New York: O. Penzler, 1993. 244 pp.
Sir Roger Shallot remembers the youthful days during which he searched for the Holy Grail and Excalibur for Henry VIII while seven murders occurred around him.
Genre(s): Mystery.

◆ 2574. *The White Rose Murders.* New York: St. Martin's, 1993. 244 pp.
Sir Roger Shallot and his master Benjamin Daunbey, the nephew of Cardinal Wolsey, must solve several murders with only a poem and a white rose as the clues.
Genre(s): Mystery.

Cook, Judith

2575. *The Slicing Edge of Death.* New York: St. Martin's, 1993. 234 pp.
Within the sleazy taverns that Christopher Marlowe frequented in Elizabethan England is his murderer, but identifying the criminal is difficult because so many people had reasons for killing Marlowe.
Genre(s): Mystery.

Cowell, Stephanie

◆ 2576. *Nicholas Cooke.* New York: Norton, 1993. 448 pp.
Nicholas Cooke's temper gets him expelled from Canterbury Cathedral school, and any hope of the Church for a career vanishes, while in London he meets Kit Morley (Christopher Marlowe) who employs him as an actor until Nick is ready to leave again.
Genre(s): Mystery.

2577. *The Physician of London.* New York: Norton, 1995. 413 pp.
Nicholas from *Nicholas Cooke* has become a physician and a priest in London but is lonely until he meets Cecily and forms friendships with William Harvey and Thomas Wentworth, persons whose associations get them into trouble.
Genre(s): Medical Novel; Political Fiction.

2578. *The Players.* New York: Norton, 1997. 352 pp.
William Shakespeare, in London after an unhappy childhood and marriage, begins the life of a poor actor and playwright, counting among his friends Christopher Marlowe and Ben Jonson.
Genre(s): Biographical Fiction.

Creel, Catherine

2579. *The Reiver's Woman.* New York: Fawcett, 1997. 324 pp.

◆May be suitable for young adult readers

After Lady Analise Howard marries Scottish reiver (marsh fighter on the Scottish border) Laird Ronan against her will, she resists loving him.
Genre(s): Romance.

DeMaria, Robert

2580. *To Be a King.* Indianapolis: Bobbs-Merrill, 1976. 356 pp.
Christopher Marlowe moves from Canterbury to Cambridge and into London where he becomes part of an anti-Catholic spy network.
Genre(s): Biographical Fiction.

Dessau, Joanna

2581. *Absolute Elizabeth.* New York: St. Martin's, 1979. 192 pp.
Elizabeth I seems interested only in her dress and her appearance rather than being the queen, in the sequel to *The Red-Haired Brat.*
Genre(s): Biographical Fiction.

2582. *The Red-Haired Brat.* New York: St. Martin's, 1979. 237 pp.
Elizabeth I dwells on her life before becoming queen, during which time she sleeps nude and describes the contents of her face powder.
Genre(s): Biographical Fiction.

Deveraux, Jude

2583. *The Heiress.* New York: Pocket Books, 1995. 376 pp.
When poor Jamie Montgomery is hired to escort the extremely wealthy Axia across England, he falls in love with her cousin, not knowing that Axia has switched identities before their departure.
Genre(s): Romance.

2584. *Highland Velvet.* New York: Pocket Books, 1982. 359 pp.
In the sequel to *Velvet Promise*, Gavin Montgomery's brother Stephen becomes betrothed to the hot-tempered Scot Bronwyn MacCarran at King Henry's command.
Genre(s): Domestic Fiction; Romance.

◆ 2585. *Remembrance.* New York: Pocket Books, 1994. 410 pp.
When Hayden Lane travels back in time to Renaissance England, she meets her soul mate.
Genre(s): Romance; Time Travel.

2586. *Velvet Angel.* New York: Pocket Books, 1983. 296 pp.
In the sequel to *Velvet Song*, King Henry commands the youngest Montgomery, Miles, to marry Elizabeth Chatworth, a woman whose family the Montgomery family opposes.
Genre(s): Romance; Domestic Fiction.

2587. *Velvet Promise.* New York: Pocket Books, 1981. 376 pp.
Judith Revedounce plans to enter the convent, but when both of her brothers die early in the 16th century, she

must marry Gavin Montgomery to keep the family inheritance.
Genre(s): Romance; Domestic Fiction.

2588. *Velvet Song.* New York: Pocket Books, 1984. 217 pp.
Alyxandria Blackett loves Raine Montgomery, the leader of a band of forest outlaws during the reign of Henry VII in the early 16th century.
Genre(s): Domestic Fiction; Romance.

Dhondy, Farrukh

◆ 2589. *Black Swan.* Boston: Houghton Mifflin, 1993. 217 pp.
Rose transcribes the diaries of Elizabethan physician Simon Forman for her boss Mr. B and discovers that Christopher Marlowe, like Mr. B, lived a life of deceit with his black lover Lazarus.
Genre(s): Mystery.

Domning, Denise

2590. *Lady in Waiting.* New York: New American Library, 1998. 382 pp.
Heiress Anne Blanchemain comes to Elizabeth I's court to serve her, but she becomes her Protestant grandfather's pawn and the object of a nobleman's plot.
Genre(s): Romance; Political Fiction.

Du Maurier, Daphne

2591. *The King's General.* Garden City, NY: Doubleday, 1946. 371 pp.
During the Wars between Cromwell and Charles I, Honor Harris recalls her love for Sir Richard Grenville, the man she planned to marry until an accident crippled her a few days before their wedding.
Genre(s): Romance.

Duell, Marie

2592. *The Countess of Sedgwick.* New York: McGraw Hill, 1980. 404 pp.
The lovely countess of Sedgwick, Angharad, wants to meet John Donne before she wins her count, but she fails.
Genre(s): Romance.

Dukthas, Ann

◆ 2593. *In the Time of the Poisoned Queen.* New York: St. Martin's, 1998. 280 pp.
In 1558, Nicholas Segalla discovers a plot by the Pope to poison Queen Mary Tudor of England.
Genre(s): Mystery; Time Travel.

◆ 2594. *A Time for the Death of a King.* New York: St. Martin's, 1994. 226 pp.
Present at the death of Lord Darnley, Mary Stuart's husband, Nicholas Segalia shares what he knows about the alleged murder.
Genre(s): Mystery; Time Travel.

Dunnett, Dorothy

2595. *Checkmate.* New York: Putnam, 1975. 581 pp.
In the sequel to *The Ringed Castle*, Lymond, still wanting to find out about his birth and how to overcome his unconsummated marriage, finds that the solution involves a prophecy of the astrologer John Dee.
Genre(s): Romance.

2596. *The Disorderly Knights.* New York: Putnam, 1966. 503 pp.
In 1551, in the sequel to *Queen's Play*, a member of the Knights of Malta and his sister oppose Francis Crawford of Lymond as they travel between Malta, Tripoli, and Scotland.
Genre(s): Mystery.

2597. *The Game of Kings.* New York: Putnam, 1961. 543 pp.
In 1547, Francis Crawford of Lymond becomes involved with decisions about the departure of Mary, Queen of Scots, for France, and must prove his loyalty to Scotland.
Genre(s): Romance.

Eady, Carol Maxwell

2598. *Her Royal Destiny.* New York: Harmony, 1985. 387 pp.
Katherine Parr, last wife of Henry VIII, relates tales of her life.
Genre(s): Biographical Fiction.

Elsna, Hebe

2599. *Prelude for Two Queens.* London: Collins, 1972. 160 pp.
Mary I and Elizabeth I, daughters of Henry VIII, prepare through their childhoods, to serve their father's will.
Genre(s): Biographical Fiction.

2600. *The Queen's Ward.* New York: Beagle, 1971. 190 pp.
After Amy Robsart befriends a homeless girl, she dies, and the girl becomes Queen Elizabeth's ward.
Genre(s): Domestic Fiction.

Emerson, Kathy Lynn

◆ 2601. *Face Down in the Marrow-Bone Pie.* New York: St. Martin's, 1997. 218 pp.
Lady Susanna Appleton, an herbalist with a wide awareness of the medicinal values of plants, ignores her husband in Elizabethan England and investigates the possibility of poisoning in the murder of their manor's steward.
Genre(s): Mystery.

2602. *Face Down upon an Herbal.* New York: St. Martin's, 1998. 304 pp.
Elizabeth I asks Lady Susanna Appleton to visit Madderly Castle to help Lady Madderly finish her book on herbs, but after a series of murders, including that of Lady Madderly, Lady Susanna suspects treason.
Genre(s): Mystery.

Evans, Jean

2603. *The Phoenix Rising.* New York: St. Martin's, 1976. 205 pp.
In the months before Charles I is executed, his son Charles II remains in exile, trying to ally with the Scots for his return to England.
Genre(s): Biographical Fiction.

Fallon, Frederic

2604. *The White Queen.* Garden City, NY: Doubleday, 1972. 322 pp.
Mary, Queen of Scots, is Catholic, forthright, and passionate as she deals with the forces against her.
Genre(s): Biographical Fiction.

Feather, Jane

2605. *Hostage Bride.* New York: Bantam, 1998. 368 pp.
Rufus Decatur, supporter of Charles I, wants to win back his property, but his men mistakenly kidnap Portia Worth, niece of Rufus's staunch Roundhead enemy, in hope of ransom.
Genre(s): War Story; Romance.

Fecher, Constance

◆ 2606. *Heir to Pendarrow.* New York: Farrar, Straus and Giroux, 1969. 180 pp.
A nobleman who wants to secure his nephew's inheritance for himself arranges to have his nephew's father imprisoned.
Genre(s): Domestic Fiction.

Figes, Eva

2607. *The Tree of Knowledge.* New York: Pantheon, 1991. 154 pp.
When interviewers meet with Deborah, daughter of John Milton, in her old age, she describes bitterly her lack of education and the experiences she had just because she was a woman.
Genre(s): Domestic Fiction.

Finney, Patricia

2608. *Firedrake's Eye.* New York: St. Martin's, 1992. 263 pp.
Tom O'Bedlam, the mad son in a Catholic family, tries to stop his brother from carrying through a plot to assassinate Queen Elizabeth in 1583.
Genre(s): Political Fiction.

2609. *Unicorn's Blood.* New York: St. Martin's, 1998. 384 pp.
While Elizabeth I debates whether she should execute Mary, Queen of Scots, Mary's advisors search for a diary Elizabeth supposedly wrote as a young woman, which contains her will and names Mary as her heir.
Genre(s): Political Fiction.

Ford, Ford Madox

2610. *The Fifth Queen, the Fifth Queen Crowned, Privy Seal.* 1906. New York: Vanguard, 1963. 592 pp.
In this trilogy, Catherine Howard, Henry VIII's fifth wife, almost brings Henry back to the Catholic Church.
Genre(s): Biographical Fiction.

Fredman, John

2611. *Does the Queen Still Live?* London: Allen, 1979. 321 pp.
Francis Drake comes from a lusty, practical family which prepares him for his voyage in 1577 that lasts for three years.
Genre(s): Biographical Fiction.

Friedlander, Mark P.

2612. *The Shakespeare Transcripts.* Woodbridge, CT: Ox Bow, 1993. 275 pp.
A Renaissance scholar, jealous of his football hero student's dissertation, tries to discredit him by having him investigate Francis Bacon's allegations against Shakespeare.
Genre(s): Mystery.

Galford, Ellen

2613. *Moll Cutpurse, Her True History.* Ithaca, NY: Firebrand, 1985. 219 pp.
Mary Frith, alias Moll Cutpurse, is a criminal who wears both male and female clothing and her lover, Bridget, narrates her 17th-century story.
Genre(s): Biographical Fiction; Adventure Story.

Garrett, George P.

◆ 2614. *Death of the Fox.* San Diego, CA: Harcourt, 1971. 739 pp.
Having spent 13 years in the Tower of London, Sir Walter Raleigh, in the 24 hours before his death, recalls his Elizabethan service.
Genre(s): Biographical Fiction.

2615. *Entered From the Sun.* Garden City, NY: Doubleday, 1990. 349 pp.
Unidentified people question an actor and a soldier about who might have seen Christopher Marlowe stabbed four years prior, during an investigation to find out who killed Marlowe.
Genre(s): Biographical Fiction.

◆ 2616. *The Succession.* Garden City, NY: Doubleday, 1983. 538 pp.
As Queen Elizabeth prepares to die in 1603, she refuses to name a successor, but King James of Scotland wants the throne, and Sir Robert Cecil, Elizabeth's secretary, supports him.
Genre(s): Biographical Fiction.

George, Margaret

2617. *The Autobiography of Henry VIII: With Notes by His Fool, Will Somers.* New York: St. Martin's, 1986. 932 pp.
When Henry VIII becomes king, he is handsome and trusting, but the king's jester, Will, watches him become cruel and suspicious, as people try to control him.
Genre(s): Biographical Fiction.

2618. *Mary Queen of Scotland and the Isles.* New York: St. Martin's, 1992. 870 pp.
Mary lives in luxury as a child in France, but when she returns to Great Britain, she faces only hardship and unhappiness.
Genre(s): Biographical Fiction.

Girling, Richard

2619. *Sprigg's War.* New York: David and Charles, 1986. 263 pp.
During England's Civil War, the father of the strongly religious John Oxenham, makes advances toward John's wife while she waits for John at the family home.
Genre(s): War Story.

Gluyas, Constance

◆ 2620. *My Lord Foxe.* New York: McKay, 1976. 490 pp.
Henrietta Maria marries Charles I of England when she is only 15, and she scorns the English and remains a fervent Catholic during their marriage.
Genre(s): Biographical Fiction.

Goldstein, Lisa

◆ 2621. *Strange Devices of the Sun and Moon.* New York: St. Martin's, 1993. 384 pp.
In 1590, London fights the plague, and people plot against Elizabeth I, but widow Alice Wood, a bookseller, finds out that her missing son Arthur is the anticipated king of the fairies.
Genre(s): Fantastic Literature.

Goudge, Elizabeth

2622. *The White Witch.* New York: Coward-McCann, 1958. 439 pp.
Francis Leyland, a Royalist spy posing as a painter, becomes involved with Jenny, whose family supports the Puritans.
Genre(s): War Story.

Graham, Winston

2623. *The Grove of Eagles.* Garden City, NY: Doubleday, 1964. 498 pp.
Maugan Killigrew, the illegitimate son of a noble, serves under Sir Walter Raleigh during the Second Armada.
Genre(s): Adventure Story; Sea Story.

Gregory, Philippa

2624. *Earthly Joys.* New York: St. Martin's, 1998. 448 pp.

While Sir Robert Cecil serves James I, he relies on his gardener John Tradescant for advice.
Genre(s): War Story; Political Fiction.

◆ 2625. *The Wise Woman.* New York: Pocket Books, 1993. 438 pp.
Alys has healing skills and an understanding of the black arts, but in 16th-century England, she must go to a convent to keep from being tried as a witch.
Genre(s): Love Story; Romance.

Hamburger, Jean

2626. *The Diary of William Harvey.* New Brunswick, NJ: Rutgers University Press, 1992. 255 pp.
William Harvey, discoverer of the blood's circulation and the personal physician to Charles I, writes his memoirs after he is 70.
Genre(s): Biographical Fiction; Medical Novel.

Hannon, Edward G.

2627. *Man Alive-Man Dead.* London: Mitre, 1975. 189 pp.
In the 16th century, the Irishman, Shane O'Neill, battles the English who occupy his country.
Genre(s): Biographical Fiction.

Hardwick, Mollie

◆ 2628. *Blood Royal.* New York: St. Martin's, 1989. 320 pp.
Elizabeth Howard marries Thomas Boleyn, and their daughters, especially Anne, become inextricably involved with Henry VIII.
Genre(s): Biographical Fiction.

◆ 2629. *The Merrymaid.* New York: St. Martin's, 1984. 187 pp.
Alan and Jaquette lead a troupe of traveling players in Tudor England, where they face plague and religious upheaval.
Genre(s): Adventure Story.

Haycraft, Molly Costain

2630. *The Reluctant Queen.* Philadelphia: Lippincott, 1962. 256 pp.
The English princess Mary Tudor agrees to marry Louis XII, the king of France, and to form an alliance between the two countries if she may marry the man she loves after Louis dies.
Genre(s): Biographical Fiction.

2631. *Too Near the Throne.* Philadelphia: Lippincott, 1959. 237 pp.
Lady Arabella Stuart's claim to the throne is close to that of both Elizabeth I and James I.
Genre(s): Biographical Fiction; Political Fiction.

Hays, Tony

2632. *Murder on the Twelfth Night.* Bell Buckle, TN: Iris, 1993. 155 pp.

In 1602, William Shakespeare and Ben Jonson must find out who stabbed an apprentice actor before Puritans close the theater.
Genre(s): Mystery.

Heaven, Constance

2633. *The Queen and the Gypsy.* New York: Coward-McCann, 1977. 275 pp.
Elizabeth I and Robert Dudley have a long-time love affair while Dudley's young wife, Amy Robsart eventually commits suicide because of neglect.
Genre(s): Biographical Fiction.

Hewlett, Maurice Henry

2634. *The Forest Lovers.* 1899. New York: Macmillan, 1976. 384 pp.
Knights entertain themselves and fight for the love of women in the Middle Ages.
Genre(s): Romance.

Heyer, Georgette

2635. *Beauvallet.* New York: Dutton, 1968. 243 pp.
Sir Nicholas Beauvallet, a friend of Sir Francis Drake and a favorite of Elizabeth I, captures, on one of his trips, a Spanish girl with whom he falls in love.
Genre(s): Love Story.

Hill, Pamela

2636. *The Green Salamander.* New York: St. Martin's, 1977. 288 pp.
Margaret Douglas, mother of Mary, Queen of Scots's second husband, Lord Darnley, is a loving mother and wife who tries to safeguard her family's succession to the throne.
Genre(s): Domestic Fiction; Biographical Fiction.

2637. *A Place of Ravens.* New York: St. Martin's, 1981. 223 pp.
Clemency Holles, married to a mentally disabled epileptic, makes his home Ravensyard her passion during the time of James I and the discontent with the Royalists.
Genre(s): Romance.

Holt, Victoria

◆ 2638. *My Enemy the Queen.* Garden City, NY: Doubleday, 1978. 348 pp.
Lettice Knollys, cousin of Elizabeth I and wife of the Earl of Essex, narrates her story, revealing herself to be vain and vacuous.
Genre(s): Biographical Fiction.

Hunter, Mollie

2639. *The Spanish Letters.* New York: Funk and Wagnalls, 1967. 173 pp.
An Edinburgh guide discovers a plot for a Spanish invasion of Scotland and England in 1589.
Genre(s): War Story; Political Fiction.

Irwin, Margaret

2640. *Elizabeth and the Prince of Spain.* New York: Harcourt, Brace, 1953. 251 pp.
In the sequel to *Elizabeth, Captive Princess,* Mary Tudor marries Philip of Spain, who has a difficult relationship with Elizabeth I.
Genre(s): Biographical Fiction.

2641. *Elizabeth, Captive Princess.* New York: Harcourt, 1948. 246 pp.
Elizabeth's brother Edward dies in this sequel to *Young Bess,* and those who want the crown keep Elizabeth in captivity.
Genre(s): Biographical Fiction.

2642. *Young Bess.* New York: Harcourt, 1945. 274 pp.
Elizabeth Tudor lives from age 12 until the death of her brother Edward VI as a supposed illegitimate child without the recognition from her father, Henry VIII.
Genre(s): Political Fiction.

Johansen, Iris

2643. *The Magnificent Rogue.* New York: Bantam, 1993. 340 pp.
Scottish laird Robert MacDarren marries Kathryn Kentyre at Elizabeth I's request since Kathryn might be the illegitimate daughter of Mary, Queen of Scots, and the Earl of Shrewsbury.
Genre(s): Romance.

Johnston, Velda

◆ 2644. *I Came to the Highlands.* New York: Dodd, Mead, 1974. 242 pp.
Her father banished from the American colonies because of his outspoken support of Charles Stuart, Elizabeth Logan returns to Scotland.
Genre(s): Romance.

Joyce, Brenda

2645. *The Game.* New York: Avon, 1994. 480 pp.
Pirate Liam O'Neill captures Katherine FitzGerland while she is heading home to Ireland and tells her that her father has lost everything, but Katherine demands proof just as Elizabeth I's men grab them.
Genre(s): Romance; Sea Story.

Kay, Susan

◆ 2646. *Legacy.* New York: Crown, 1986. 648 pp.
Elizabeth rises to England's throne and must face all of its political intrigues.
Award(s): Georgette Heyer Historical Novel Prize; Betty Trask Award.
Genre(s): Biographical Fiction.

Kellerman, Faye

2647. *The Quality of Mercy.* New York: Morrow, 1989. 607 pp.

Rebecca Lopez and William Shakespeare first meet in a London graveyard, and then meet again while investigating the deaths of those they helped bury.
Genre(s): Biographical Fiction; Mystery.

Kerr, Robert

2648. *The Stuart Legacy.* New York: Stein and Day, 1973. 223 pp.
In the late 16th century, Jamie Stuart, a soldier of fortune, returns to Scotland to claim his heritage but faces forces that want him dead instead.
Genre(s): Adventure Story.

King, Susan

2649. *The Raven's Moon.* New York: Topaz, 1998. 381 pp.
In 1588, Mhairi Macrae stops Rowan Scott and intercepts an order to release her brother to the English to stand trial for treason, and he suspects her of complicity while his own reputation is at stake.
Genre(s): Political Fiction; Romance.

Kingsley, Charles

2650. *Westward Ho!* 1855. New York: Buccaneer, 1985. 588 pp.
British explorers and naval heroes make names for themselves at sea during Elizabeth I's reign.
Genre(s): Sea Story.

Kirby, Kate

2651. *Scapegoat for a Stuart.* New York: St. Martin's, 1976. 206 pp.
When Harry Weaver is suspected of being a Popish plotter during the Guy Fawkes gunpowder plot, Robert Cecil learns that Harry's wife is actually his half-sister.
Genre(s): Biographical Fiction; Mystery.

Knight, Alanna

2652. *The Black Duchess.* Garden City, NY: Doubleday, 1980. 272 pp.
Lady Sibella Stewart befriends Felipe when he escapes to the Orkney Islands after sailing on *The Black Duchess* in the Spanish Armada.
Genre(s): Sea Story; Adventure Story.

L'Amour, Louis

2653. *Fair Blows the Wind.* New York: Dutton, 1978. 282 pp.
Tatton Chantry, sole survivor of an Irish family, dreams of returning to Ireland to buy back his family's land during the time of Elizabeth I. (*Series:* The Chantrys, 5)
Genre(s): Family Saga.

Lane, Jane

2654. *Heirs of Squire Harry.* London: Davies, 1974. 201 pp.
Sir Thomas Seymour asks for the heroine to marry him, but King Henry impregnates her first.
Genre(s): Romance.

2655. *Parcel of Rogues.* New York: Rinehart, 1948. 448 pp.
Many intrigues develop among those who oppose Mary Stuart while she reigns in Scotland.
Genre(s): Political Fiction.

2656. *The Severed Crown.* New York: Simon and Schuster, 1973. 210 pp.
The final three years of the reign of Charles I show him as a king who paid for his stubborness with his life.
Genre(s): Biographical Fiction.

Lennox-Smith, Judith

2657. *Till The Day Goes Down.* New York: St. Martin's, 1992. 356 pp.
Lucas Ridley, a Borderer, becomes a spy after the beheading of Mary, Queen of Scots, and when he is caught in a raid, he must find the identity of those plotting to overthrow Elizabeth I to save his own life.
Genre(s): Political Fiction; Spy Fiction.

Leslie, Doris

2658. *Wreath for Arabella.* New York: Pocket Books, 1969. 350 pp.
Arabella, cousin of the aging Elizabeth I, serves in Elizabeth's court and becomes a political prisoner.
Genre(s): Biographical Fiction; Political Fiction.

Lewis, Hilda Winifred

2659. *I Am Mary Tudor.* New York: McKay, 1972. 422 pp.
Mary Tudor believes her father, Henry VIII, grows disintested in her as he becomes obsessed with having a male heir.

◆ 2660. *The Witch and the Priest.* New York: D. McKay, 1970. 304 pp.
Although Samuel Fleming regrets having condemned a woman to death in the 17th century for being a witch, the ghost of Joan Flower tells how she manipulated those around her to do evil.
Genre(s): Biographical Fiction.

Lide, Mary

2661. *Command of the King.* New York: St. Martin's, 1991. 288 pp.
Phillipa de Verne runs away from the man her father has chosen for her to marry and into the intrigue of shifting loyalties at the court of Henry VIII.
Genre(s): Adventure Story.

Lindsey, Johanna

2662. *A Gentle Feuding.* New York: Avon, 1984. 248 pp.
In the 16th century Scotland, crofter families, the Fergussons and the MacKinnions, have a long-standing feud until Jamie Mackinnion spots the beautiful Sheena, daughter of the rival chieftain, bathing in a pond.
Genre(s): Romance.

Llywelyn, Morgan

◆ 2663. *Grania.* New York: Crown, 1986. 437 pp.
Grace O'Malley, only child of a sea captain in the mid-1500s, becomes a pirate and the leader of Ireland's County Mayo where she begins to view Elizabeth I as her female rival.
Genre(s): Biographical Fiction; Political Fiction.

◆ 2664. *The Last Prince of Ireland.* New York: Morrow, 1992. 368 pp.
Donal Cam O'Sullivan marches 1,000 followers away from Queen Elizabeth's army in 1603 after the Battle of Kinsale ends any hope for Irish independence.
Genre(s): Biographical Fiction.

Lofts, Norah

2665. *Bless This House.* Garden City, NY: Doubleday, 1954. 349 pp.
A house built in 1577 in East Anglia comes back to the Rowhedges in 1953.
Genre(s): Romance.

2666. *The Concubine.* Garden City, NY: Doubleday, 1963. 310 pp.
In his dispatches, the Spanish Ambassador calls Anne Boleyn, second wife of Henry VIII, the concubine.

2667. *The House at Old Vine.* Garden City, NY: Doubleday, 1961. 382 pp.
In the sequel to *The Town House,* four women and two men occupy Old Vine at various times between 1496 and the latter part of the 17th century.
Genre(s): Family Saga.

2668. *The King's Pleasure.* Garden City NY: Doubleday, 1969. 372 pp.
Katharine of Aragon has to deal with Henry VIII's decision to divorce her.
Genre(s): Biographical Fiction.

◆ 2669. *The Old Priory.* Garden City, NY: Doubleday, 1982. 240 pp.
Three generations of a family inhabit a cursed priory in Suffolk to which they have strong loyalties.
Genre(s): Domestic Fiction; Romance.

◆ 2670. *Pargeters.* Garden City, NY: Doubleday, 1986. 334 pp.
To save the family home during the English Civil War, Sarah Woodley-Mercer marries a former Puritan worker when he acquires the estate, Pargeters, as a spoil of war.
Genre(s): War Story; Domestic Fiction.

2671. *Scent of Cloves.* Garden City, NY: Doubleday, 1957. 320 pp.
A nurse saves Julia from Cromwell's soldiers before she dies, and a Dutch sea captain later finds and raises her as his daughter.
Genre(s): Romance.

Luke, Mary M.

◆ 2672. *The Ivy Crown.* Garden City, NY: Doubleday, 1984. 439 pp.

Catherine Parr is stepmother to Mary Tudor, Elizabeth, and Prince Edward.
Genre(s): Biographical Fiction.

Macaulay, Rose

2673. *The Shadow Flies.* New York: Harper, 1932. 476 pp.
Before the English Civil War, Robert Herrick and his friends, including Julian Conybeare, 15-year-old daughter of an atheist doctor, interact with other poets.
Genre(s): Biographical Fiction.

2674. *They Were Defeated.* London: Oxford, 1981. 445 pp.
In the 17th century, poets and peasants cope with the escalation of the Civil War and witchhunts.
Genre(s): Biographical Fiction; War Story.

MacInnes, Colin

2675. *Three Years to Play.* New York: Farrar, Straus and Giroux, 1970. 365 pp.
In 1599, Aubrey comes to London from the country and meets Shakespeare, who uses Aubrey's story and Aubrey for his play, *As You Like It.*
Genre(s): Adventure Story.

Macleod, Alison

2676. *The Hireling.* Boston: Houghton Mifflin, 1968. 256 pp.
Tom Vaughn serves both Thomas Cromwell and Cardinal Reginald Pole as a spy who has few scruples about religion or government.
Genre(s): Political Fiction.

2677. *The Muscovite.* Boston: Houghton Mifflin, 1971. 319 pp.
English merchant Jeremy Horsey becomes the ambassador to the court of Ivan the Terrible, and after financial success during Ivan's brutal reign, he is accused of treason when he returns to England 18 years later.
Genre(s): Biographical Fiction.

Maguire, Liam

2678. *Icarus Flying.* Morden Park, England: Ormond, 1993. 354 pp.
Sir Francis Walsingham heads a Brotherhood in which Christopher Marlowe is initiated before dying in Bishopsgate as a victim of religious zealousness.
Genre(s): Biographical Fiction.

Major, Charles

2679. *When Knighthood Was in Flower.* Indianapolis: Bobbs-Merrill, 1898. 295 pp.
Mary Tudor, daughter of Henry VIII, falls in love with Charles Brandon.
Genre(s): Love Story; Biographical Fiction.

Malpass, Eric Lawson

2680. *The Cleopatra Boy.* New York: St. Martin's, 1974. 240 pp.

As Shakespeare rises to the heights of fame with the King's Men, he becomes involved in the politics of the times and shares sadness when the boy he trains to play Cleopatra dies of the plague.
Genre(s): Biographical Fiction.

2681. *Sweet Will.* New York: St. Martin's, 1974. 287 pp.
Will Shakespeare has difficulty deciding if he should remain loyal to his family and stay in Stratford or follow his desire to write and act by going to London.
Genre(s): Biographical Fiction.

Marston, Edward

2682. *The Fair Maid of Bohemia.* New York: St. Martin's, 1997. 256 pp.
Nicholas Bracewell and his troupe travel to Prague to perform for the King of Bohemia, but someone kills an actor during the first performance.
Genre(s): Mystery.

2683. *The Mad Courtesan.* New York: St. Martin's, 1992. 252 pp.
Nicholas Bracewell looks for the murderer of the gentleman-player in his company, Lord Westfield's Men.
Genre(s): Mystery.

◆ 2684. *The Merry Devils.* New York: St. Martin's, 1989. 236 pp.
Nicholas Bracewell, the bookholder for Lord Westfield's Men, must investigate the appearance of one too many devils on stage at a performance.
Genre(s): Mystery.

◆ 2685. *The Nine Giants.* New York: St. Martin's, 1991. 235 pp.
The stage manager for Lord Westfield's Men, Nicholas Bracewell, must settle differences among rival performers and stop a plot to assassinate the Lord Mayor-elect of London.
Genre(s): Mystery.

◆ 2686. *The Queen's Head.* New York: St. Martin's, 1989. 288 pp.
Nicholas Bracewell, bookholder for Lord Westfield's Men, a theater troupe, begins to search for a man with a red beard to avenge the death of an actor friend.
Genre(s): Mystery.

◆ 2687. *The Roaring Boy.* New York: St. Martin's, 1995. 260 pp.
Nicholas Bracewell has Lord Westfield's Men present a new kind of play, based on a murder, which leads to trouble for his actors unless he can solve the murder.
Genre(s): Mystery.

2688. *The Silent Woman.* New York: St. Martin's, 1994. 312 pp.
Lord Westfield's Men experience a fire on stage during a performance, and the landlord throws them out, but Nicholas Bracewell has his own problems when a young girl disguised as a boy dies on his doorstep.
Genre(s): Mystery.

◆ 2689. *The Trip to Jerusalem.* New York: St. Martin's, 1990. 223 pp.
During the Black Plague, Nicholas Bracewell and Lord Westfield's Men tour the North of England and discover that another troupe is stealing their best plays.
Genre(s): Mystery.

Mason, F. Van Wyck

2690. *Golden Admiral.* Garden City, NY: Doubleday, 1953. 340 pp.
The pinnacle of Sir Francis Drake's career is defeating the Spanish.
Genre(s): Biographical Fiction; Sea Story.

Maxwell, Robin

2691. *The Secret Diary of Anne Boleyn.* New York: Arcade, 1997. 288 pp.
Anne Boleyn keeps a secret diary that someone delivers to Elizabeth I when she ascends the throne, and Elizabeth realizes that to be successful, she must rule unconventionally.
Genre(s): Biographical Fiction.

McLeod, Alison

2692. *Prisoner of the Queen.* Boston: Houghton Mifflin, 1973. 191 pp.
The hero tries to save other Catholics by intervening for them in Protestant England during the 16th century, but he faces serious problems.
Genre(s): Romance.

Michaels, Barbara

◆ 2693. *The Dancing Floor.* New York: HarperCollins, 1997. 336 pp.
On an English vacation, Heather Tradescant finds the house, Trayton, locked, but after she learns from villagers that the Pendle Witches protected themselves with witchcraft, she finds a secret passage in the undergrowth.
Genre(s): Mystery; Time Travel.

Miles, Rosalind

◆ 2694. *I, Elizabeth.* New York: Doubleday, 1994. 595 pp.
Elizabeth writes a diary near the end of her life in which she records court intrigues and the burdens of political power.
Genre(s): Biographical Fiction.

Monsarrat, Nicholas

2695. *Running Proud.* New York: Morrow, 1979. 524 pp.
Matthew Lawe shows cowardice while serving Sir Francis Drake and therefore must wander the earth afterward meeting such people as Henry Hudson, Henry Morgan, Samuel Pepys, Captain Cook, and Lord Nelson. (*Series:* The Master Mariner, 1)
Genre(s): Sea Story; Fantastic Literature.

Morgan, Cynthia

◆ 2696. *Court of Shadows.* New York: Ballantine, 1992. 640 pp.
Justine Lisle travels Europe with consort Kat Langdon who happens to be spying on him to see if he is disloyal Elizabeth I.
Genre(s): Romance.

Morris, Gilbert

2697. *The Shield of Honor.* Wheaton, IL: Tyndale House, 1995. 394 pp.
The Wakefield and Morgan families continue their hostilities during the time of Charles I and the civil war. (*Series:* Wakefield Dynasty, 3)
Genre(s): Christian Fiction; War Story; Family Saga.

2698. *The Sword of Truth.* Wheaton, IL: Tyndale House, 1994. 409 pp.
Sir Robert Wakefield accepts Myles Morgan as his illegitimate son, disrupting his young cousin's inheritance expectations, and Myles then attempts to use Morgan's and Wakefield's involvement with William Tyndale to smuggle Bibles for the money. (*Series:* Wakefield Dynasty, 1)
Genre(s): Christian Fiction.

2699. *The Winds of God.* Wheaton, IL: Tyndale House, 1994. 380 pp.
The noble Wakefield family becomes involved more closely with the commoner Morgan family as the Spanish sail toward England with their Armada in 1588. (*Series:* Wakefield Dynasty, 2)
Genre(s): War Story; Christian Fiction; Family Saga.

Mortimer, John Clifford

2700. *Will Shakespeare.* New York: Dell, 1977. 256 pp.
Jack Rice, a member of Shakespeare's company, relates the story of the man and his plays within London society.
Genre(s): Biographical Fiction.

Motley, Annette

◆ 2701. *The Quickenberry Tree.* New York: St. Martin's, 1984. 699 pp.
Sir George Heron's family, including the courageous Lucy, survive the confusion of the English Civil War.
Genre(s): War Story.

Mullally, Margaret

2702. *A Crown in Darkness.* New York: St. Martin's, 1975. 305 pp.
When Lady Jane Grey's cousin Edward, heir to Henry VIII, dies, her father-in-law proclaims her queen on July 9, 1553, and Bloody Mary has her executed on February 12, 1554.
Genre(s): Biographical Fiction.

Nye, Robert

2703. *The Voyage of the Destiny.* New York: Putnam, 1982. 387 pp.

Sir Walter Raleigh awaits death on a false charge of treason and writes about his relationship with Elizabeth and his family's travails.
Genre(s): Biographical Fiction.

O'Brien, Judith

2704. *Once upon a Rose.* New York: Pocket Books, 1996. 338 pp.
While Deanie Bailey, a country-western singer, is filming a video in London, she goes to Hampton Court and falls into the arms of Christopher Neville four hundred years earlier.
Genre(s): Romance; Time Travel.

O'Connor, Garry

2705. *Campion's Ghost.* London: Hodder and Stoughton, 1993. 246 pp.
In 16th-century England, John Donne remembers his early life during which he was caught between the attractions of the court and the comfort of the Church.
Genre(s): Biographical Fiction.

O'Dell, Scott

◆ 2706. *The Hawk That Dare Not Hunt by Day.* Boston: Houghton Mifflin, 1975. 214 pp.
Tom Barton's cargo ship often carries contraband between London and the Continent, and he offers illegal Martin Luther manuscripts to William Tyndale.
Genre(s): Christian Fiction; Adventure Story.

Osborne, Maggie

2707. *Chase the Heart.* New York: Morrow, 1987. 324 pp.
In 1588, after Robert Dudley, Earl of Leicester dies, both Elizabeth I and Lady Nellanor Amesley want a silver casket that Dudley's widow has sold to Spanish agents.
Genre(s): Biographical Fiction; Romance.

Peters, Maureen

2708. *Henry VIII and His Six Wives.* New York: St. Martin's, 1972. 222 pp.
As Henry VIII lies on his deathbed, he recalls his six wives and their attributes and shortcomings.
Genre(s): Biographical Fiction.

Phillips, Tori

2709. *Midsummer's Night.* New York: Harlequin, 1998. 304 pp.
Widow Lady Katherine Fitzhugh wants to investigate the man Henry VIII has chosen for her to marry, and she changes identities with her shy cousin, but simultaneously, her intended has changed identities with his best friend to verify that Lady Katherine is not elderly and ugly.
Genre(s): Romance.

Plaidy, Jean

◆ 2710. *The Captive Queen of Scots.* New York: Putnam, 1970. 410 pp.

Mary, Queen of Scots, does not cope well with her confinement and the controlled movement to different castles during her last 18 years. (*Series:* Mary Queen of Scots, 2)
Genre(s): Biographical Fiction.

◆ 2711. *Daughter of Satan.* New York: Putnam, 1973. 284 pp.
Tamar, illegimate daughter of a maid and a country squire, expects to find peace in the New World but discovers that the Puritans retain their prejudices.

◆ 2712. *Gay Lord Robert.* New York: Putnam, 1971. 317 pp.
The Earl of Leicester's wife Amy is murdered, most likely to make way for him to marry Elizabeth I, but the crime creates a scandal. (*Series:* Tudor Novels, 10)
Genre(s): Biographical Fiction; War Story.

◆ 2713. *The King's Secret Matter.* 1962. New York: Putnam, 1995. 284 pp.
Catherine of Aragon refuses to divorce Henry VIII and strives to retain the succession to the throne for her daughter Mary. (*Series:* Tudor Novels, 3)
Genre(s): Biographical Fiction.

◆ 2714. *The Murder in the Tower.* New York: Putnam, 1974. 286 pp.
Frances Howard pursues Robert Carr, one of James I's favorites, but after a murder in the tower, her ambitions are stymied. (*Series:* Stuart Saga, 1)
Genre(s): Biographical Fiction; Family Saga.

◆ 2715. *Murder Most Royal.* New York: Putnam, 1972. 542 pp.
Anne Boleyn and her younger cousin Catherine Howard face similar fates in their lives at court. (*Series:* Tudor Novels, 4)
Genre(s): Biographical Fiction.

◆ 2716. *Myself My Enemy.* New York: Putnam, 1983. 382 pp.
Henriette Marie, daughter of Henry IV of France, comes to England as Charles I's bride and wants to convert everyone to Catholicism. (*Series:* Queens of England, 1)
Genre(s): Biographical Fiction.

◆ 2717. *Queen of this Realm.* New York: Putnam, 1985. 570 pp.
Elizabeth asserts that to rule wisely, she must retain the esteem of her people and subject herself to no man. (*Series:* Queens of England, 2)
Genre(s): Biographical Fiction.

◆ 2718. *The Rose without a Thorn.* New York: Putnam, 1994. 255 pp.
Catherine Howard becomes lady-in-waiting to Anne of Cleaves and enjoys being near Thomas Culpepper, but when Henry VIII decides to marry her, she has to give up her plans to marry Culpepper. (*Series:* Queens of England, 11)
Genre(s): Biographical Fiction.

◆ 2719. *Royal Road to Fotheringay.* New York: Putnam, 1968. 349 pp.

The young Mary, Queen of Scots, becomes involved in intrigue, bigotry, and violence first in France and then in Scotland. (*Series:* Mary Queen of Scots, 1)
Genre(s): Biographical Fiction.

◆ 2720. *The Sixth Wife.* New York: Putnam, 1969. 252 pp.
Catherine Parr becomes Henry VIII's sixth wife after the death of Catherine Howard. (*Series:* Tudor Novels, 6)
Genre(s): Biographical Fiction.

◆ 2721. *St Thomas's Eve.* New York: Putnam, 1970. 284 pp.
Sir Thomas More enjoys his family, his home, and his scholarship rather than the machinations of Henry VIII's court. (*Series:* Tudor Novels, 5)
Genre(s): Biographical Fiction; Christian Fiction.

2722. *The Thistle and the Rose.* New York: Putnam, 1973. 318 pp.
James IV of Scotland marries Margaret Tudor, the sister of Henry VIII, but when she discovers his infidelities, the marriage cools. (*Series:* Tudor Novels, 7)
Genre(s): Biographical Fiction.

Potter, Jeremy

2723. *Disgrace and Favour.* London: Constable, 1975. 235 pp.
Robert Carey, cousin to Queen Elizabeth, continues to curry favor from James, and then Charles, until the execution of Raleigh sends him back to the Scottish border.
Genre(s): Biographical Fiction; Political Fiction.

Prescott, H. F. M.

2724. *The Man on a Donkey.* New York: Macmillan, 1952. 631 pp.
In 1536-1537, the squire Robert Aske leads a rebellion, the Pilgrimage of Grace, against Henry VIII's suppression of the monastaries.
Genre(s): Biographical Fiction; Christian Fiction.

Riley, Judith Merkle

◆ 2725. *The Serpent Garden.* New York: Viking, 1996. 467 pp.
Susanna Dallet travels to France on assignment for the Crown as a miniature portrait painter and is accused of hiding valuable genealogical information in the 16th century.

Rose, Mark

2726. *Golding's Tale.* New York: Walker, 1972. 192 pp.
The captain who accompanied Sir Walter Raleigh on his last voyage to look for gold in Guiana, tells of the plague, mutiny, starvation, and hostile Indians, which led to Raleigh's downfall.
Genre(s): Biographical Fiction.

Ross Williamson, Hugh

2727. *The Cardinal in England.* London: Joseph, 1970. 255 pp.

Reginald Pole, Henry VIII's cousin, becomes cardinal before Henry decides to divorce his first wife.
Genre(s): Biographical Fiction.

2728. *The Cardinal in Exile.* London: Joseph, 1969. 217 pp.
Henry VIII's cousin Reginald Pole goes into exile to Rome where he almost becomes Pope before returning to England when Mary comes to the throne in the sequel to the *The Cardinal in England.*
Genre(s): Biographical Fiction; Christian Fiction.

Sabatini, Rafael

2729. *The Sea-Hawk.* Philadelphia: Lippincott, 1915. 362 pp.
Sir Oliver Tressilian, once a ship commander fighting the Spanish Armada, begins to follow Mahmud and earns the new name "Hawk of the Sea."
Genre(s): Sea Story; Adventure Story.

2730. *The Tavern Knight.* New York: Grosset and Dunlap, 1926. 219 pp.
During Cromwell's Rebellion, Roland Marleigh takes the disguise of Sir Crispin Galliard, the Tavern knight, after his wife's relatives murder her and abduct his son, with intent to avenge his fate.
Genre(s): Adventure Story; War Story.

Schoonover, Lawrence

2731. *To Love a Queen.* Boston: Little, Brown, 1973. 383 pp.
Sir Walter Raleigh, explorer, scientist, poet, and inventor, also loves Elizabeth his queen.
Genre(s): Biographical Fiction.

Scott, Walter

2732. *Kenilworth.* 1821. New York: Columbia, 1993. 541 pp.
The Earl of Leicester wants to become the king consort of Elizabeth I, and thus his wife Amy suffers his neglect, before she is murdered.
Genre(s): Romance.

Settle, Mary Lee

2733. *Prisons.* New York: Putnam, 1973. 256 pp.
In the Puritan army, Jonathan Church joins the democratic faction which opposes the conservative ways of Cromwell.
Genre(s): War Story.

Shrimsley, Bernard

2734. *Lion Rampant.* New York: Macmillan, 1984. 259 pp.
When Lady Frances Howard and her husband Robert Deveraux cannot consummate their marriage, she becomes enamoured with Henry, Prince of Wales, son of James I, so that the question of whether Henry dies of typhoid or is murdered becomes prominent.
Genre(s): Biographical Fiction; Mystery.

◆May be suitable for young adult readers

Small, Bertrice

2735. *All the Sweet Tomorrows.* New York: Ballantine, 1984. 610 pp.
In the sequel to *Skye O'Malley*, in 1569, Skye O'Malley's fourth husband, Niall Burke, is murdered, and she goes to London for Elizabeth I's promise that she will not appropriate the Burke lands since Skye has a six-week-old son, but when Skye hears that Niall is still alive, she travels to Fez to find him.
Genre(s): Romance.

2736. *Blaze Wyndham.* New York: New American Library, 1988. 327 pp.
Blaze, 15, marries the Earl of Langford, relieving her father's concerns about his eight daughters, but when the Earl dies suddenly, Henry VIII takes her as a mistress and marries her off when he meets Anne Boleyn.
Genre(s): Love Story; Romance.

2737. *Lost Love Found.* New York: Ballantine, 1989. 483 pp.
Valentina Barrows, a widow, gets lessons in love from her cousin and the young Earl of Kempe when she goes to court to wait on Queen Bess in the sequel to *This Heart of Mine.*
Genre(s): Romance.

2738. *A Love for All Time.* New York: Ballantine, 1986. 614 pp.
In the sequel to *All the Sweet Tomorrows*, Skye O'Malley's younger brother, Conn O'Malley, goes to Elizabeth I's court to learn manners, and he immediately becomes romantically involved with several different women before Elizabeth marries him off.
Genre(s): Romance.

2739. *Skye O'Malley.* New York: Ballantine, 1980. 461 pp.
Skye O'Malley, daughter of an Irish clan-leader, falls in love with Lord Niall Burke, but she must wed another and endure a number of difficulties before she can reunite with Niall.
Genre(s): Romance.

2740. *This Heart of Mine.* New York: Ballantine, 1985. 690 pp.
The man betrothed to Velvet de Marisco, daughter of Skye O'Malley, claims her, and when she refuses to marry him, he drags her to Scotland in the sequel to *A Love for All Time.*
Genre(s): Romance.

2741. *Wild Jasmine.* New York: Ballantine, 1992. 704 pp.
Skye O'Malley de Marisco comes to England after her half-brother kills her husband in India, and after wooing several men, she remarries and lives on the Irish estate King James deeds her.
Genre(s): Romance; Family Saga.

Smith, A. C. H.

2742. *Sebastian the Navigator.* London: Weidenfeld And Nicolson, 1985. 204 pp.

Sebastian Cabot reveals his tendencies of lying and cheating, but he has enough luck on his voyage to the Americas that he retains his unblemished reputation.
Genre(s): Biographical Fiction.

Smith, Haywood

2743. *Secrets in Satin.* New York: St. Martin's, 1997. 344 pp.
The Protestant Edward Garrett sees Catholic Elizabeth, Countess of Ravenwold, dance on her worthless husband's grave and is shocked when Charles I demands that Garrett marry her.
Genre(s): Romance; War Story.

Stewart, Stanley N.

2744. *The King James Version.* New York: Random House, 1977. 335 pp.
Frances Howard, 18, falls in love with the Viscount of Rochester and provokes the nullity trial in the court of James I.

Sutcliff, Rosemary

2745. *Lady in Waiting.* New York: Coward-McCann, 1957. 253 pp.
Bess Throckmorton secretly marries Sir Walter Raleigh and supports his struggles to gain favor from Elizabeth I for his travels to the New World.

◆ 2746. *Rider on a White Horse.* New York: Coward-McCann, 1959. 320 pp.
Sir Thomas Fairfax's wife and child go with him to fight against Charles and the Royalists at York and at Marston Moor.
Genre(s): War Story.

Sutherland, Elizabeth

2747. *The Seer of Kintail.* London: Constable, 1974. 223 pp.
Brahan the Seer disturbs fellow Scots by predicting the future in 17th-century Scotland.
Genre(s): Biographical Fiction.

Tey, Josephine

2748. *The Daughter of Time.* New York: Macmillan, 1952. 220 pp.
A 20th-century policeman sees a picture of Richard III and reinvestigates Richard's role in the murder of the princes in the Tower using all available information about Richard's time.

Thane, Elswyth

2749. *The Tudor Wench.* New York: Harcourt, 1932. 390 pp.
Elizabeth becomes queen of England, and her subjects celebrate at her coronation.
Genre(s): Biographical Fiction.

Thorpe, Helen

2750. *Elizabeth, Queen and Woman.* New York: Roy, 1972. 238 pp.

Elizabeth loves Robert Dudley, whom she calls Robin, but refuses to let her heart rule instead of her reason as she guides England.
Genre(s): Biographical Fiction.

Tourney, Leonard D.

2751. *Familiar Spirits.* New York: St. Martin's, 1984. 230 pp.
Matthew Stock and his wife investigate young Ursula's hanging when her ghost appears, one of the village elders dies, and the elder's widow and her sister become witch hunt suspects in Elizabethan England.
Genre(s): Mystery.

2752. *Frobisher's Savage.* New York: St. Martin's, 1994. 364 pp.
Joan and Matthew Stock investigate the murder of a wealthy farm family outside of Chelmsford, which the daughters blame on their deaf-mute brother and his friend whom Martin Frobisher brought to England.
Genre(s): Mystery.

2753. *Knaves Templar.* New York: St. Martin's, 1991. 282 pp.
Matthew Stock and his wife Joan must resolve a murder when three law students die in London's Inner Temple.
Genre(s): Mystery.

2754. *Low Treason.* New York: Dutton, 1982. 233 pp.
Matthew Stock, a village constable, discovers a jeweler's part in a plot to help the Spanish gain the British throne.
Genre(s): Mystery.

2755. *Old Saxon Blood.* New York: St. Martin's, 1988. 250 pp.
Matthew Stock and his wife investigate the death of the uncle of one of Elizabeth I's Maids of Honor at Elizabeth's request.
Genre(s): Mystery.

2756. *The Player's Boy Is Dead.* New York: Harper and Row, 1980. 192 pp.
When Shakespearean player Richard Mull, 14, is found murdered, the town constable Matthew Stock investigates and finds local villains.
Genre(s): Mystery.

Tranter, Nigel G.

2757. *James, by the Grace of God.* New York: Beaufort, 1985. 367 pp.
The sequel to *The Riven Realm* finds James V at 12, still protected by David Lindsay but a prize for nobles warring to control him and the country.
Genre(s): Biographical Fiction; Political Fiction.

2758. *The Riven Realm.* New York: Beaufort, 1985. 351 pp.
After James IV dies in battle against Henry VIII, his year-old son becomes king, and David Lindsay, the surrogate father of James, tries to protect him.
Genre(s): War Story.

2759. *The Wisest Fool.* London: Hodder and Stoughton, 1974. 463 pp.
James I becomes king of England after the death of Elizabeth I, and he makes demands which the English resent.
Genre(s): Biographical Fiction.

2760. *The Young Montrose.* London: Hodder and Stoughton, 1972. 416 pp.
James Graham, the Marquis of Montrose, becomes involved with Louise, Elizabeth of Holland's daughter, and rises to heroism during the English Civil War.
Genre(s): Biographical Fiction.

Turner, Judy

2761. *Ralegh's Fair Bess.* New York: St. Martin's, 1974. 192 pp.
Sir Walter Raleigh marries Elizabeth Throckmorton and continues his exploration and his service to Queen Elizabeth before being tried and executed for misdeeds.
Genre(s): Biographical Fiction.

Turton, Godfrey

2762. *My Lord of Canterbury.* Garden City, NY: Doubleday, 1967. 316 pp.
Thomas Cranmer, educated at Cambridge, becomes Henry VIII's trusted archbishop until Cranmer will not support Henry's divorce.
Genre(s): Biographical Fiction.

Twain, Mark

2763. *The Prince and the Pauper.* New York: Harper and Brothers, 1881. 309 pp.
Tom Canty, a poor boy, looks very much like Prince Edward, the heir to England's throne, and through a series of mishaps, the two change places.
Genre(s): Adventure Story.

Van Greenaway, Peter

2764. *The Destiny Man.* London: Gollancz, 1977. Canada pp.
A new Shakespeare play about the case of Sir Thomas Overbury appears, and Cherry and Sergeant Duff investigate a poisoning.
Genre(s): Biographical Fiction; Mystery.

Vining, Elizabeth Gray

◆ 2765. *Take Heed of Loving Me.* Philadelphia: Lippincott, 1964. 352 pp.
John Donne leads a decadent life until he begins to study theology and secretly marries Anne More.
Genre(s): Biographical Fiction.

Weenolsen, Hebe

◆ 2766. *The Trial of Jenny Sykes.* New York: St. Martin's, 1990. 320 pp.
Unless Jenny Sykes can provide a witness to prove that her child was stillborn in 17th-century England, she will be tried and hanged for murder.
Genre(s): Medical Novel.

Weiss, David

2767. *Myself, Christopher Wren.* New York: Coward-McCann, 1974. 922 pp.
Christopher Wren is an architect, astronomer, and mathematican who spends 33 years rebuilding St. Paul's after the Great Fire of London while serving five different kings.
Genre(s): Biographical Fiction.

2768. *Physician Extraordinary.* New York: Delacorte, 1975. 429 pp.
William Harvey practices medicine in the 17th century and endures chastisement and discredit for his discoveries about blood circulation.
Genre(s): Biographical Fiction; Medical Novel.

Welch, Robert

2769. *Groundwork.* Chester Springs, PA: Dufour, 1998. 202 pp.
The Condon and O'Dwyer clans live in Ireland from Elizabethan times after the defeat of Gaelic Ireland into the 1960s.
Genre(s): Family Saga.

West, Paul

2770. *Sporting with Amaryllis.* Woodstock, NY: Overlook, 1996. 160 pp.
While John Milton, 17, attends Cambridge in the early 17th century, his muse Amaryllis educates him in sex and politics in London during 1625.
Genre(s): Biographical Fiction.

Westcott, Jan Vlachos

2771. *The Tower and the Dream.* New York: Putnam, 1974. 322 pp.
Elizabeth Hardwick Talbot, Countess of Shrewsbury, renovates manor houses, including Hardwick Hall, as she marries four times, coming into the circle of Elizabeth I and Mary Stuart with the fourth marriage.
Genre(s): Romance.

Wiat, Philippa

2772. *Lion without Claws.* New York: St. Martin's, 1977. 230 pp.
Philip, the first Howard to become Earl of Arundel, marries Anne while still young, and when he gains favor with Elizabeth, he becomes a libertine, but after reviving his Catholic faith, he is imprisoned in the Tower where he dies.
Genre(s): Biographical Fiction.

Wick, Lori

2773. *The Knight and the Dove.* Eugene, OR: Harvest House, 1995. 345 pp.
Henry VIII commands Bracken to marry Megan, and although she pleases him, he cannot bring himself to tell her so until he almost loses her.
Genre(s): Christian Fiction; Romance.

Wiggs, Susan

2774. *Dancing on Air.* New York: HarperCollins, 1996. 402 pp.
Aidan O'Donoghue, an Irish chieftain, comes to bargain with Elizabeth I for his country, and while in London, he saves a woman from arrest who turns out to have every quality he always wanted.
Genre(s): Romance; Political Fiction.

2775. *Vows Made in Wine.* New York: HarperCollins, 1995. 400 pp.
Spencer Merrifield and Mistress Lark save Oliver de Lacey so that he can keep Blackrose Priory from Spencer's son, a loyal follower of Catholic Mary Queen of Scots.
Genre(s): Political Fiction; Romance.

Wilson, Derek A.

2776. *Her Majesty's Captain.* Boston: Little, Brown, 1978. 311 pp.
Elizabeth I decides to let the son of her deceased love, Sir Robert Dudley, take an expedition to find El Dorado because she needs the money and the young man loves the sea.
Genre(s): Biographical Fiction.

Wright, Patricia

◆ 2777. *That Near and Distant Place.* New York: St. Martin's, 1988. 432 pp.
In the sequel to *I Am England*, an old man narrates the events which have formed the history of Furnace Green, Sussex, beginning with Cromwell's rebellion.
Genre(s): Family Saga.

York, Robert

2778. *My Lord the Fox.* New York: Vanguard, 1986. 152 pp.
Anthony Woodcot, trusted relative of Elizabeth I, acts as a secret agent for Lord William Cecil and feeds him possibly incriminating information about Sir Robert Dudley.
Genre(s): Political Fiction.

1650-1788

Abernethy, Cecil

2779. *Mr Pepys of Seething Lane.* New York: McGraw Hill, 1957. 384 pp.
Although Pepys lives on Seething Lane in a deteriorating neighborhood he, a tailor's son, becomes Charles II's Secretary of the Affairs of the Admiralty.
Genre(s): Biographical Fiction.

Ainsworth, William Harrison

2780. **Beau Nash.** New York: Dutton, 1880. 314 pp.
Beau Nash entertains and enjoys social life in Bath during the 18th century.
Genre(s): Biographical Fiction.

2781. **Boscobel.** New York: Dutton, 1872. 311 pp.
Charles II escapes after the Battle of Worcester in the late 17th century.
Genre(s): Political Fiction.

2782. **Old St Paul's.** New York: Dutton, 1841. 173 pp.
A London grocer and his family must fight both the plague and the great fire of London.
Genre(s): Domestic Fiction.

Alexander, Bruce

2783. **Blind Justice.** New York: Putnam, 1994. 254 pp.
Sir John Fielding, creator of London's police force, has as his assistant Jeremy Proctor, and the two try to find out why Lord Richard Goodhope has commited suicide.
Genre(s): Mystery.

◆ 2784. **Murder in Grub Street.** New York: Putnam, 1995. 276 pp.
Ezekiel Crabb hires Jeremy Proctor for his bookselling shop, but before Jeremy begins, Crabb, his family, and two employees are murdered, so Jeremy and Sir John Fielding search for the villain.
Genre(s): Mystery.

2785. **Person or Persons Unknown.** New York: Putnam, 1997. 288 pp.
Sir John Fielding and Jeremy Proctor investigate several murders in Covent Garden and actually discover two murderers trying to kill prostitutes.
Genre(s): Mystery.

◆ 2786. **Watery Grave.** New York: Putnam, 1996. 265 pp.
Blind magistrate Sir John Fielding, with the help of his apprentice 14-year-old Jeremy Proctor, must solve a possible murder at sea by investigating why Captain Josiah Markham went overboard.
Genre(s): Mystery.

Anand, Valerie

2787. **The Cherished Wives.** New York: St. Martin's, 1996. 341 pp.
In 1742, Lucy-Anne marries her second cousin George, and she, her daughter, and her granddaughter must deal with ill treatment by husbands who see them as no more than property.
Genre(s): Domestic Fiction; Family Saga.

Anthony, Evelyn

2788. **Clandara.** New York: Doubleday, 1963. 303 pp.
The Stuarts try to recapture the English throne in the 18th century, causing problems for other Scottish families as well.
Genre(s): Political Fiction.

Ashfield, Helen

2789. **The Loving Highwayman.** New York: St. Martin's, 1983. 192 pp.
In the Epping Forest during the 18th century, members of the Duke of Kirdale's family's pretenses involve them in a variety of mishaps and misconceptions until spies and highwayman, both real and not, straighten the identities of all.
Genre(s): Romance.

2790. **The Michaelmas Tree.** New York: St. Martin's, 1982. 176 pp.
In 1772 Caroline and Patrick Kinnersley profess their love, but Patrick is forced to marry the woman his deceased brother has impregnated without telling Caroline why, and after Caroline endures her father's evil, governess jobs, and prison, they reunite.
Genre(s): Romance.

Auchincloss, Louis

2791. **Exit Lady Masham.** Boston: Houghton Mifflin, 1983. 169 pp.
Abigail Hill (later Lady Masham), a poor relation of the duchess of Marlborough, hears from those who want to stay at war with Louis XIV of France and from those who want peace, and as a confidant of Queen Anne, advises her of their opinions.
Genre(s): Biographical Fiction.

Bailey, H. C.

2792. **The Plot.** New York: Methuen, 1922. 250 pp.
When Titus Oates organizes the Popish Plot in 1678, Charles II finally complains when his wife is accused.
Genre(s): Adventure Story.

Balogh, Mary

2793. **Heartless.** New York: Berkley, 1995. 389 pp.
When Lucas Kendrick, Duke of Harndon, returns to England after 10 years in Paris, he meets Lady Anna Marlowe, a woman who, like he, has been psychologically wounded.
Genre(s): Romance.

2794. **Silent Memory.** New York: Berkley, 1997. 368 pp.
As a teenager, Lady Emily Marlowe falls in love with Lord Ashley Kendrick but he goes to India, marries, and becomes a widower, and when he returns, her independence and his feelings about his marriage keep them apart.
Genre(s): Romance.

Barke, James

2795. **The Well of the Silent Harp.** New York: Macmillan, 1954. 288 pp.

Robert Burns writes during the 18th century and becomes one of Scotland's most beloved poets.
Genre(s): Biographical Fiction.

Barnes, Margaret Campbell

◆ 2796. *With All My Heart.* Philadelphia: Macrae-Smith, 1951. 288 pp.
Catherine, daughter of Portugal's King John IV, becomes a political pawn when she marries Charles II of England.
Genre(s): Biographical Fiction.

Bell, Josephine

2797. *In the King's Absence.* London: Bles, 1973. 251 pp.
When Charles II is exiled abroad, a young man has a conflict between his love and his king.
Genre(s): War Story; Political Fiction.

2798. *A Question of Loyalties.* London: Bles, 1974. 245 pp.
The Duke of Marlborough and his wife, although old friends of Queen Anne, show their loyalty more to themselves and their own advancement than to her.
Genre(s): Biographical Fiction.

Belle, Pamela

2799. *A Falling Star.* New York: St. Martin's, 1990. 500 pp.
While James II is on the throne in 1685, Sir Alexander St. Barbe returns from the Continent to claim his inheritance, the Wintercombe estate, in the sequel to *Herald of Joy.*
Genre(s): Romance; War Story.

2800. *Herald of Joy.* New York: St. Martin's, 1990. 501 pp.
In the sequel to *Wintercombe*, Silence copes with her elderly husband's death while loving the Cavalier captain Nick Hellier, father of her child, Kate.
Genre(s): Romance; War Story.

2801. *Treason's Gift.* New York: St. Martin's, 1993. 546 pp.
After Alex and his wife separate in the sequel to *A Falling Star*, he goes to the Netherlands and joins the group encouraging William of Orange and Mary to return to England.
Genre(s): Epic Literature; Romance.

Beverley, Jo

2802. *Something Wicked.* New York: New American Library, 1997. 352 pp.
Lady Elfin Malloren, 25, longs for adventure and love so she disguises herself as a Frenchwoman, but as she hides from an unwanted suitor, she hears the man to whom she is attracted plot treason.
Genre(s): Romance.

2803. *Tempting Fortune.* New York: Zebra, 1994. 440 pp.

When a young redhead in Georgian England puts a gun in Lord Arcenbryght's face, his unlucky love life changes.
Genre(s): Regency Novel; Romance.

Bigsby, C. W. E.

2804. *Pearl.* London: Weidenfeld and Nicolson, 1995. 234 pp.
In 1660, Pearl, daughter of Hester in *The Scarlet Letter*, receives property from Roger Chillingworth, and she returns to England to assert her independence but meets preacher John Standish instead.
Genre(s): Bildungsroman (Coming of Age); Romance.

Black, Laura

◆ 2805. *Albany.* New York: St. Martin's, 1984. 244 pp.
When Leonara Albany learns at 17 that she is related to Bonnie Prince Charlie, she must adjust to being a member of royalty and try to retain her rightful inheritance.
Genre(s): Romance.

Blackmore, R. D.

2806. *Lorna Doone.* 1869. New York: Oxford, 1989. 560 pp.
On the north Devon coast, Lorna Doone grows up in a group of outlaws and falls in love with a man loyal to James II.
Genre(s): War Story; Romance.

Boland, Bridget

2807. *The Wild Geese.* 1938. New York: Penguin, 1991. 264 pp.
In Ireland during the 18th century, Catholics living under British rule must practice their religion secretly and have no rights to own land or enter a trade, so those who go to Europe and return as outlaws are called "wild geese."

Bosse, Malcolm J.

2808. *The Vast Memory of Love.* New York: Ticknor and Fields, 1992. 482 pp.
In 1753, entries from Henry Fielding's journal reveal the dissipated life of London noblemen and the poorer classes that they trample.
Genre(s): Mystery.

Bowen, Marjorie

2809. *Defender of the Faith.* New York: Metheun, 1911. 365 pp.
In the sequel to *I Will Maintain*, William becomes the king of England in the Glorious Revolution of 1688.
Genre(s): Biographical Fiction.

2810. *For God and the King.* 1911. Pella, IA: Inheritance, 1995. 351 pp.
After the Glorious Revolution of 1688, William and Mary rule England in the sequel to *Defender of the Faith.*
Genre(s): Biographical Fiction.

Brahms, Caryl

2811. *Enter a Dragon—Stage Centre.* London: Hodder and Stoughton, 1979. 192 pp.
Sarah Siddons, actor with David Garrick on Drury Lane in the 1780s, raises her family while running a business and working hard.
Genre(s): Biographical Fiction.

Bramble, Forbes

2812. *The Strange Case of Deacon Brodie.* New York: Coward-McCann, 1976. 313 pp.
In the 1780s, Deacon Brodie designs the gallows, and after a life as an accomplished gambler and late-night murderer, his life in Edinburgh ends on his invention.
Genre(s): Biographical Fiction.

Broster, D. K.

2813. *The Dark Mile.* New York: Coward-McCann, 1934. 362 pp.
After defeat at Culloden, the British decimate the Scottish clans while a group protects Bonnie Prince Charlie and tries to reinstate him, in the sequel to *The Gleam in the North.*
Genre(s): War Story.

2814. *The Flight of the Heron.* 1926. Geneva: Edito-Service, 1974. 313 pp.
Clans in Scotland unite behind Bonnie Prince Charlie in their clash with the British.
Genre(s): War Story.

2815. *The Gleam in the North.* New York: Coward-McCann, 1931. 349 pp.
In the sequel to *The Flight of the Heron*, Scottish clans continue to support Bonnie Prince Charlie of the Jacobite Rebellion.
Genre(s): War Story.

Brown, Mary

2816. *Playing the Jack.* New York: Simon and Schuster, 1985. 584 pp.
Sprat, an orphan, joins a band of traveling players in 18th-century England before going to work as a scrivener in London's most notorious brothel.
Genre(s): Adventure Story.

Brown, Molly

2817. *Invitation to a Funeral.* New York: Harper-Collins, 1998. 288 pp.
Aphra Behn plans a proper funeral for the murdered Matthew Cavell because of a kindness once bestowed but simultaneously becomes involved in court intrigues with Nell Gwyn and Charles II.
Genre(s): Mystery.

Buchan, John

2818. *Midwinter.* 1923. New York: Doran, 1971. 343 pp.
The Jacobites try to regain the throne of England for the deposed James II in the 17th century.
Genre(s): War Story.

Burney, Fanny

2819. *Evelina.* New York: Lowndes, 1791. 693 pp.
A woman enjoying the social life in London during the late 18th century writes to her friends about her experiences.
Genre(s): Domestic Fiction.

Burton, John

2820. *Ascanius.* 1746. New York: Garland, 1974. 64 pp.
Charles Edward, the grandson of James II of England, shows his adventuresome spirit by fighting in the 1745 Jacobite Rebellion.
Genre(s): Biographical Fiction; War Story.

Bushnell, O. A.

2821. *The Return of Lono.* Boston: Little, Brown, 1956. 290 pp.
When Lono returns, he tells of James Cook's last voyage when the Hawaiians were unhappy to see his return.
Genre(s): Biographical Fiction.

Cameron, Kenneth M.

2822. *Our Jo, or the Chronicle of a Coming Man.* New York: Macmillan, 1974. 311 pp.
Jo Hayne rises from obscurity to fame in the 17th century through his affairs and his services as spy and as an actor.
Genre(s): Picaresque Fiction.

Canham, Marsha

2823. *The Pride of Lions.* New York: Dell, 1997. 384 pp.
British aristocrat Catherine Ashbrooke marries Scottish lordling, Alexander Cameron, after her father catches them kissing, and she learns that although Alex poses as a London merchant, he is a Highlander, the legendary Camshroinaich Dubh (Dark Cameron), who has returned to fight for Bonnie Prince Charlie.
Genre(s): Romance.

Cannam, Helen

2824. *A High and Lonely Road.* New York: St. Martin's, 1990. 440 pp.
When the Quaker Hannah discovers that her intended husband plans to build a mill processing cotton picked by slaves, she marries his younger brother instead.
Genre(s): Romance.

Carr, Philippa

2825. *The Adulteress.* New York: Putnam, 1982. 334 pp.
Two men, neither her husband, liberate Zipporah's passions in 18th-century England. (*Series:* Daughters of England, 9)
Genre(s): Romance; Family Saga.

2826. *Lament for a Lost Lover.* New York: Putnam, 1977. 381 pp.
Arabella Tolworthy's family becomes exiled in France during the time of Cromwell, and in the Restoration, they return for unexpected adventures. (*Series:* Daughters of England, 5)
Genre(s): Romance; War Story.

2827. *The Song of the Siren.* New York: Putnam, 1980. 336 pp.
Jacobites kidnap Carlotta, and their leader seduces and impregnates her, but after marrying a family friend, she escapes to Paris with her lover and child. (*Series:* Daughters of England, 7)
Genre(s): Romance; Family Saga.

Carr, Robyn

2828. *The Bellerose Bargain.* Boston: Little, Brown, 1982. 324 pp.
Orphaned Alicia agrees to pose as Geoffrey Seavers's wife so that he can establish a trading fleet, but the two begin to care for each other before Alicia learns that she is not an orphan and sails to America.
Genre(s): Romance.

2829. *The Braeswood Tapestry.* Boston: Little, Brown, 1984. 297 pp.
After Charles II returns from exile for the Restoration, he finds his supporters reduced to thievery for money to support their titles.
Genre(s): Romance.

2830. *Chelynne.* Boston: Little, Brown, 1980. 402 pp.
Charles II tries to woo orphaned ward Chelynne Mondeloy, only to discover that she might be his daughter, and when Chelynne marries Chadwick Hawthorne, she does not know that he is a widower with a son on his Jamaican estate.
Genre(s): Romance.

Carroll, Susan

2831. *The Bride Finder.* New York: Ballantine, 1998. 449 pp.
A bride in Cornwall worries about her husband's mysterious meetings.
Genre(s): Romance.

Cashman, John

2832. *Kid Glove Charlie.* New York: Harper and Row, 1978. 280 pp.
Charlie Peace is an 18th-century burglar who is also a musician, craftsman, and actor, but in his last 10 years, he becomes involved with two women and kills one of their husbands.
Genre(s): Biographical Fiction.

Cates, Kimberly

2833. *Gather the Stars.* New York: Pocket Books, 1996. 308 pp.
After the Battle of Culloden, Gavin Carstares (the Glen Lyon) kidnaps Rachel de Lacey from a dance to use her

as a bargaining tool against the British to ensure safe passage of women and children from Scotland to America.
Genre(s): Romance.

Coleman, Bob

2834. *The Later Adventures of Tom Jones.* New York: Simon and Schuster, 1985. 347 pp.
In 1774, Tom Jones, a widower with three children, meets Benjamin Franklin and Samuel Johnson.
Genre(s): Domestic Fiction; Adventure Story.

Collett, Bill

2835. *The Last Mutiny.* New York: Norton, 1995. 294 pp.
Retired William Bligh meddles in the affairs of the women who live in his home in 1817 and tells about his career and how his crew mutinied after being overcome by the beauty of the Tahitian women they would have to leave.
Genre(s): Biographical Fiction; Sea Story.

Collins, Warwick

2836. *The Rationalist.* New York: Simon and Schuster, 1993. 251 pp.
The bachelor Dr. Grange carefully practices medicine in an English seaside town until a beautiful widow arrives.
Genre(s): Medical Novel.

Crow, Donna Fletcher

2837. *A Gentle Calling.* Wheaton, IL: Crossway, 1994. Canada pp.
In 1749, a British schoolteacher, searching for God's guidance, meets such people as John Wesley. (*Series:* Cambridge Chronicles, 1)
Genre(s): Christian Fiction.

2838. *Treasures of the Heart.* Wheaton, IL: Crossway, 1994. 224 pp.
Rowland Hill, an evangelical Anglican preacher, marries Mary Tudway in the 18th century. (*Series:* Cambridge Chronicles, 2)
Genre(s): Biographical Fiction; Christian Fiction.

De Hartog, Jan

◆ 2839. *The Peaceable Kingdom.* New York: Atheneum, 1972. 677 pp.
Margaret Fell marries the Quaker George Fox in 1652 and tries to achieve grace through good works.

De La Torre, Lillian

2840. *The Return of Dr Sam Johnson, Detector.* New York: International Polyglot, 1985. 191 pp.
Samuel Johnson and his biographer James Boswell become detectives solving the identity of a missing heir who mysteriously reappears and a kidnapped wench who has returned home with amnesia.
Genre(s): Mystery.

Defoe, Daniel

2841. *A Journal of the Plague Year.* 1722. New York: Oxford, 1991. 299 pp.
The bubonic plague decimates the English population during the summer and fall of 1665.

2842. *Moll Flanders.* 1722. New York: Random House, 1996. 384 pp.
Moll Flanders marries five times and plies the trades of thief and harlot before becoming penitent.
Genre(s): Picaresque Fiction.

Dickens, Charles

♦ 2843. *Barnaby Rudge.* 1841. New York: Oxford, 1987. 460 pp.
The "No Popery" or Gordon Riots of 1780 include orgies and fires and Lord George Gordon as a major figure.

2844. *Master Humphrey's Clock.* 1840. New York: American Liteary Society, 1960. 117 pp.
In the Gordon Riots of 1780, Protestants upset at Catholic desires to have rights in England cause upheaval during which they destroy more property than was destroyed in the French Revolution.
Genre(s): Political Fiction.

Dodd, Christina

2845. *A Well Favored Gentleman.* New York: Avon, 1998. 400 pp.
In the sequel to *A Well Pleasured Lady*, Alanna MacLeod, Lady of Fionnaway, struggles with Ian Fairchild over property as they fall in love.
Genre(s): Romance.

2846. *A Well Pleasured Lady.* New York: Avon, 1997. 384 pp.
Mary Rottenson poses as a housekeeper so that she will not have to see her family, but when Viscount Whitfield blackmails her into pretending that she is his intended, she must reenter society and face her family.
Genre(s): Romance.

Du Maurier, Daphne

2847. *Frenchman's Creek.* New York: Doubleday, 1942. 206 pp.
A lady of nobility during the reign of Charles II falls in love with a pirate.
Genre(s): Romance.

Edghill, Rosemary

2848. *Met by Moonlight.* New York: Pinnacle, 1998. 320 pp.
Wiccan Diana Crossways returns to 17th-century England during an All Hallow's Eve storm, and after joining a local coven, becomes intrigued with a handsome stranger.
Genre(s): Romance; Time Travel.

Feather, Jane

2849. *The Silver Rose.* New York: Bantam, 1997. 464 pp.

In 1709, Queen Anne decrees that Ariel, sister of the Earl of Ravenspeare, must wed Simon, Earl of Hawkesmoor, and end their feud but Ariel has achieved her own financial independence breeding racehorses.
Genre(s): Romance.

2850. *Vice.* New York: Bantam, 1996. 432 pp.
Tarquin, Duke of Redmayne, buys a virgin to marry his dying cousin Lucien, and Tarquin plans to marry the girl after Lucien dies, so that her child and he will inherit the estate.
Genre(s): Romance.

Fielding, Henry

2851. *Amelia.* 1751. New York: Viking, 1987. 608 pp.
Amelia, the virtuous wife of Captain William Booth, helps him cope with a variety of difficulties.
Genre(s): Humorous Fiction.

2852. *Joseph Andrews.* 1742. New York: Knopf, 1992. 437 pp.
Joseph Andrews resists the advances of his employer, Lady Booby, leaves London, and is eventually rescued from thieves by Parson Adams.
Genre(s): Humorous Fiction.

2853. *Tom Jones.* 1749. New York: Oxford, 1996. 912 pp.
In 1745, Tom Jones experiences a variety of situations resulting from his love for a young girl.
Genre(s): Humorous Fiction; Picaresque Fiction.

Fowles, John

2854. *A Maggot.* Boston : Little, Brown , 1985. 445 pp.
A lord's agent investigates the disappearance of the lord's son, who has traveled into Devon with actors pretending to be his relatives.
Genre(s): Legal Story.

Foxall, Raymond

2855. *Brandy for the Parson.* London: Hale, 1970. 224 pp.
Harry Adkins, Bow Street detective, goes to the south coast of England to investigate brandy smuggling activities through which Napoleon is gathering information.
Genre(s): Biographical Fiction; Mystery.

Froude, James Anthony

2856. *The Two Chiefs of Dunboy.* 1889. London: Chatto and Windus, 1969. 283 pp.
The Irish continue to feel frustrated with the British taking their lands.
Genre(s): Political Fiction.

Gabaldon, Diana

2857. *Dragonfly in Amber.* New York: Delacorte, 1992. 743 pp.
Dr. Claire Beauchamp Randall continues the search for her 18th-century Scot husband in the sequel to *Outlander*

and relates her involvement with Bonnie Prince Charlie and the battle at Culloden.
Genre(s): Time Travel; Romance.

2858. *Outlander.* New York: Delacorte, 1991. 627 pp.
In Scotland with her husband on a second honeymoon after World War II, Claire enters a circle of stones and is transported back to the Battle of Culloden 200 years earlier, where she must marry a Scot to save her husband.
Genre(s): Time Travel; Romance.

2859. *Voyager.* New York: Delacorte, 1994. 880 pp.
Claire Randall returns to Scotland 22 years after *Dragonfly in Amber* to meet Jamie, a survivor of Culloden, and stays with him in the mid-18th century rather than returning to the 20th.
Genre(s): Time Travel; Romance.

Galt, John

2860. *Ringan Gilhaize.* 1899. New York: AMS, 1968. 370 pp.
In 1688, the Covenanters lead an uprising at the Battle of Killiecrankie.
Genre(s): War Story.

Gartner, Chloe

2861. *The Woman from the Glen.* New York: Morrow, 1973. 317 pp.
Pollux and Jennifer MacAllan, born on the same day as Bonnie Prince Charlie, think their destinies are tied to his, and when he returns to Scotland in 1745, they loyally follow him to Culloden, and when they survive, Pollux goes to the New World while Jennifer stays.
Genre(s): War Story; Domestic Fiction.

Gluyas, Constance

2862. *Born to Be King.* Englewood Cliffs, NJ: Prentice Hall, 1974. 353 pp.
Elizabeth Drummond disguises herself as her twin brother to enter service under Bonnie Prince Charlie.
Genre(s): Biographical Fiction.

2863. *The King's Brat.* Englewood Cliffs, NJ: Prentice Hall, 1972. 363 pp.
A nobleman finds Angel Dawson in the gutter and educates her until she is presentable to the Restoration society court.
Genre(s): Adventure Story.

2864. *My Lady Benbrook.* Englewood Cliffs, NJ: Prentice Hall, 1975. 263 pp.
Angel Dawson becomes a lady in the court of Charles II and marries Benbrook, but after the fire of London and a kidnapping incident, she regains lost happiness.
Genre(s): Romance.

Goudge, Elizabeth

2865. *The Child from the Sea.* New York: Coward-McCann, 1970. 736 pp.

Lucy Walter, born in a Welsh castle, becomes the secret wife of Charles II before he comes to the throne.
Genre(s): Biographical Fiction; Romance.

Gregory, Philippa

2866. *The Favored Child.* New York: Pocket Books, 1989. 468 pp.
In the sequel to *Wideacre*, Julia Lacey revives Wideacre so well that the villagers wonder if she has magical powers as foretold by Wideacre's former mistress before her untimely death.
Genre(s): Romance; Gothic Fiction.

2867. *Wideacre.* New York: Simon and Schuster, 1987. 556 pp.
Since Beatrice loves the estate of Wideacre, she plots her father's death in hopes of tempting her weak brother Henry through incest so that she can circumvent the laws of entail.
Genre(s): Domestic Fiction; Gothic Fiction; Romance.

Hall, Robert Lee

◆ 2868. *Benjamin Franklin and a Case of Artful Murder.* New York: St. Martin's, 1994. 264 pp.
In mid-18th century London, Benjamin Franklin and his natural son Nicolas Handy look for a missing gem, but murder complicates their investigation.
Genre(s): Mystery.

◆ 2869. *Benjamin Franklin and a Case of Christmas Murder.* New York: St. Martin's, 1991. 279 pp.
In 1757 while in London, Benjamin Franklin listens to the ghost stories of Cassandra Fairbrass, which he does not believe, but when a ghost poisons Cassandra's father, he investigates.
Genre(s): Mystery.

◆ 2870. *Benjamin Franklin Takes the Case.* New York: St. Martin's, 1988. 227 pp.
Ben Franklin helps Nick Handy investigate the murder of his printing-shop employer, Ebeneezer Inch, in London during 1757.
Genre(s): Mystery.

◆ 2871. *London Blood.* New York: St. Martin's, 1997. 256 pp.
Benjamin Franklin helps London authorities look for a madman who has murdered two women, and with his illegitimate son Nicolas Handy, Franklin uncovers a secret society.
Genre(s): Mystery.

◆ 2872. *Murder at Drury Lane.* New York: St. Martin's, 1992. 279 pp.
In London's theater district, Benjamin Franklin and his illegitimate son Nick Handy try to solve a series of murders at the Drury Lane Theatre.
Genre(s): Mystery.

◆ 2873. *Murder by the Waters.* New York: St. Martin's, 1995. 261 pp.

In 1758, Benjamin Franklin travels to Bath with his natural son Nick and wonders about the highwayman who kidnaps Emma, the woman he is trying to protect as his friend in Bath has requested, and the nobleman who rapidly rescues her.
Genre(s): Mystery.

Hanchar, Peggy

2874. *Lady of the Mist.* New York: Fawcett, 1997. 289 pp.
Gillian MacGregor comes under the protection of warrior lord Thane Campbell, her clan's enemy, and becomes his mistress until she learns that he is betrothed to another.
Genre(s): Romance.

Hardwick, Mollie

◆ 2875. *Charlie Is My Darling.* New York: Coward-McCann, 1977. 317 pp.
During the Jacobite rebellion of 1745, Bonnie Prince Charlie has a love affair with the wife of a loyal follower.
Genre(s): Biographical Fiction.

Hawksley, Elizabeth

2876. *Lysander's Lady.* New York: St. Martin's, 1996. 190 pp.
Clemency Hastings inherits much money and enjoys her independence until she falls in love with Lysander, the eligible Marquess of Storrington.
Genre(s): Romance.

Haycraft, Molly Costain

2877. *Countess Carrots.* Philadelphia: Lippincott, 1973. 216 pp.
Elizabeth Percy, a teenaged widow with money, falls in love with a Swedish count, but although Charles II wants her to marry his seven-year-old illegitimate son, he agrees to choose someone more suitable for her.
Genre(s): Romance.

Heller, Keith

2878. *Man's Storm.* New York: Scribner's, 1986. 196 pp.
George Man, parish watchman, discovers the body of Joan Fletcher in a great storm during 1703, and as he follows the chief suspect, her husband, Man, discovers much about London's lowlife and Joan's low husband.
Genre(s): Mystery.

Henley, Virginia

2879. *Dream Lover.* New York: Delacorte, 1997. 352 pp.
After 10 years hard labor on a convict ship for a murder he did not commit, Sean O'Toole, the Earl of Kildare, vows to destroy his brother's murderer, Montague, and Montague's daughter, Emerald.
Genre(s): Romance.

Heyer, Georgette

2880. *The Great Roxhythe.* Boston: Small, Maynard, 1923. 418 pp.
The Marquis of Roxhythe remains loyal to Charles II throughout his reign, and his secretary supports him until he realizes the duplicity that surrounds him.
Genre(s): Love Story.

2881. *The Masqueraders.* New York: Dutton, 1967. 288 pp.
The Merriot brother and sister find themselves implicated in the Stuart rebellion and they must use the masquerade to save themselves.
Genre(s): Romance.

2882. *Royal Escape.* New York: Dutton, 1967. 429 pp.
Charles II escapes from Worcester and undergoes many adventures while his enemies pursue him to France.
Genre(s): Biographical Fiction.

Hill, Pamela

2883. *Daneclere.* New York: St. Martin's, 1978. 560 pp.
Honor Sawtrey, a farm girl, marries a wealthy landowner during Cromwell's reign and becomes the matriarch of three families through her strength and virtue.
Genre(s): War Story; Romance.

2884. *Norah.* New York: St. Martin's, 1976. 287 pp.
Norah Curle Stroyan's pride causes misery and ruin in her 18th-century Cumberland home, driving her husband from their home and her daughter into exile.
Genre(s): Romance; Gothic Fiction.

2885. *Strangers' Forest.* New York: St. Martin's, 1978. 224 pp.
In 1771, Primrose Tebb, 12, marries Andrew Farquharson because the only way he can inherit her entailed Scottish land is through marriage, and he plans to grow a forest of unique firs.
Genre(s): Romance.

2886. *Whitton's Folly.* New York: St. Martin's, 1975. 224 pp.
Edmund Whitton returns to Scotland from India in the 18th century to claim his grandfather's estate, marries his docile cousin, and forces her to watch the hanging of her half-brother whose child she bears.
Genre(s): Romance.

Hodge, Jane Aiken

◆ 2887. *Shadow of a Lady.* New York: Putnam, 1973. 317 pp.
Helen Telfair's adventures take her through a London season and an eruption of Mt. Vesuvius.
Genre(s): Romance.

Holdsworth, Jean

2888. *Candles for a Player.* London: Constable, 1980. 233 pp.

An actor who is acquainted with David Garrick and Dr. Johnson engages in a love affair.
Genre(s): Romance.

Innes, Hammond

◆ 2889. *The Last Voyage: Captain Cook's Lost Diary.* New York: Knopf, 1979. 253 pp.
Captain Cook's personal diary tells about his final voyage in the Pacific.
Genre(s): Biographical Fiction; Sea Story.

Irwin, Margaret

2890. *The Stranger Prince.* New York: St. Martin's, 1985. 556 pp.
Prince Rupert, nephew of Charles I, becomes one of the most brilliant soldiers of the English Civil War.
Genre(s): Biographical Fiction; War Story.

James, John

2891. *Seventeen of Leyden.* New York: St. Martin's, 1972. 289 pp.
Dr. Richard Wormset's code name in the Knot, the secret organization supporting James II of England, is Seventeen, and although he has retired from active service, he must go to the West Indies to free five maids taken there after Monmouth's rebellion, only to find that they have not survived.
Genre(s): Spy Fiction.

Johnson, Susan

2892. *Wicked.* New York: Bantam, 1997. 336 pp.
After her father dies, Serena Blythe, determined to study painting in Italy, saves money earned as a governess, but when the ship on which she has passage is captured, she stows away on a ship belonging to the handsome Beau St Jules, London's most famous rogue.
Genre(s): Romance; Sea Story.

Jose, Nicholas

2893. *The Rose Crossing.* Woodstock, NY: Overlook, 1996. 280 pp.
When Oliver Cromwell takes control of the government, horticulturist Edward Popple goes on a voyage as a ship's doctor to support his family, and his daughter stows away, but after a mutiny, the two end up on an island in the Indian Oean.
Genre(s): War Story.

Kells, Susannah

2894. *A Crowning Mercy.* New York: Viking, 1983. 480 pp.
During the Civil War, the Puritan Dorcas Slythe becomes involved in intrigue after her strict father's death.
Genre(s): War Story.

Kent, Alexander

◆ 2895. *Command a King's Ship.* New York: Putnam, 1974. 320 pp.

Richard Bolitho, in the sequel to *To Glory We Steer*, goes to India in 1784 where he learns that Britain hopes to strengthen an outpost in Indonesia.
Genre(s): Sea Story; War Story.

◆ 2896. *In Gallant Company.* New York: Putnam, 1977. 287 pp.
In 1777, in the sequel *Stand into Danger*, Richard Bolitho's ship is held responsibile for keeping military supplies from reaching General Washington in the American colonies.
Genre(s): Sea Story; War Story.

◆ 2897. *Sloop of War.* New York: Putnam, 1972. 319 pp.
In 1778, in the sequel to *In Gallant Company*, Richard Bolitho receives his first command at Antigua on the sloop-of-war *Sparrow* which he sails up and down the Atlantic coast for three years keeping the French away.
Genre(s): Sea Story; War Story.

◆ 2898. *Stand into Danger.* New York: Putnam, 1981. 296 pp.
Richard Bolitho, in 1774, is 18 and sailing on the frigate *Destiny* where he meets his faithful companion Stockdale as they sail to the Caribbean, in the sequel to *Midshipman Bolitho and the Avenger*.
Genre(s): Sea Story; Romance.

◆ 2899. *To Glory We Steer.* New York: Putnam, 1968. 328 pp.
In 1782, in the sequel to *Sloop of War*, Captain Richard Bolitho takes command of a frigate ordered to the Caribbean to combat French, Spanish, and American forces.
Genre(s): Sea Story; War Story.

◆ 2900. *A Tradition of Victory.* New York: Putnam, 1982. 296 pp.
In the sequel to *The Inshore Squadron*, Richard Bolitho and his crew attempt to stop the French invasion fleet.
Genre(s): War Story; Sea Story.

Kenyon, Frank Wilson

2901. *Mistress Nell.* New York: Appleton, 1961. 253 pp.
Nell Gwyn becomes the mistress of Charles II of England while pursuing her career as one of the greatest stage figures of her day.
Genre(s): Political Fiction; Domestic Fiction.

Keppel, Charlotte

◆ 2902. *The Villains.* New York: St. Martin's, 1982. 226 pp.
Two orphans, Nannette and Leonie, living with their cold-hearted aunt find that in 18th century England inquisitiveness helps them identify their enemies.
Genre(s): Romance.

Kerr, Robert

2903. *The Dark Lady.* New York: Stein and Day, 1976. 222 pp.

Jamie Stuart foils a Spanish plot to burn the British shipping vessels on the Thames.
Genre(s): Political Fiction; Adventure Story.

Koen, Karleen

2904. ***Through a Glass Darkly.*** New York: Random House, 1986. 738 pp.
When Barbara Alderley is 15, her mother barters her in marriage to a handsome older man who covets Barbara's dowry, the family seat, Bentwoodes.
Genre(s): Romance.

Ladd, Linda

2905. ***Lilacs on Lace.*** New York: Topaz, 1996. 385 pp.
By 1691, Ainsley Campbell, raised in a convent and accused as a witch due to her healing abilities, is kidnaped by an enemy clan.
Genre(s): Romance.

Laker, Rosalind

◆ 2906. ***Circle of Pearls.*** Garden City, NY: Doubleday, 1990. 519 pp.
Julia Pallister's Royalist family has political conflicts with Roundheads as well as social and religious conflicts with others.

2907. ***Gilded Splendour.*** Garden City, NY: Doubleday, 1982. 382 pp.
Thomas Chippendale designs and builds furniture, but while attracted to Isabella he marries her best friend Catherine.
Genre(s): Biographical Fiction.

◆ 2908. ***The Silver Touch.*** Garden City, NY:, Doubleday, 1987. 356 pp.
After bearing six children, Hester Bateman becomes a silversmith in 18th-century London, and establishes a reputation as an artisan.
Genre(s): Biographical Fiction.

Lamb, Arnette

2909. ***Beguiled.*** New York: Pocket Books, 1996. 303 pp.
When bodyguard Agnes MacKenzie saves Edward Napier's life by jumping in front of the arrow meant for him, he nurses her, and she falls in love.
Genre(s): Romance.

2910. ***The Betrothal.*** New York: Pocket Books, 1992. 368 pp.
Lady Marjorie Entwhistle wants only to be postmistress in 1730s Bath, but her father resorts to blackmail to get her engaged, and after escaping marriage six times, she finds herself betrothed to Lord Blake Chesterfield.
Genre(s): Romance.

Lambdin, Dewey

◆ 2911. ***The King's Coat.*** New York: Donald I. Fine, 1989. 397 pp.

In 1780, Alan Lewrie unwillingly becomes a midshipman in the British navy, but he slowly becomes a competent and proud sailor.
Genre(s): Sea Story; Adventure Story.

◆ 2912. ***The King's Commission.*** New York: Donald I. Fine, 1991. 400 pp.
In the sequel to *The French Admiral,* Alan Lewrie, still reluctant to be in the Royal Navy, becomes first officer on the brig *Shrike,* and in 1783, when the war with the colonies is almost over, he wonders if all he has learned in his new career will be useless.
Genre(s): Sea Story; War Story.

Lane, Jane

2913. ***Bridge of Sighs.*** New York: John Day, 1975. 198 pp.
Mary of Modena, the second wife of James II of England, encourages her husband to flee during the Revolution of 1688, later called the Glorious Revolution.
Genre(s): Biographical Fiction.

2914. ***The Sealed Knot.*** New York: Beagle, 1971. 304 pp.
Members of the Sealed Knot, a secret organization, work to restore the king during the time of the Protectorate.
Genre(s): Political Fiction; War Story.

2915. ***Thunder on St Paul's Day.*** New York: Newman, 1954. 256 pp.
In 1678, people believe that Jesuits are planning to assassinate King Charles II to bring the Duke of York, later James II, to the throne because he is Roman Catholic.
Genre(s): War Story.

Langenus, Ron

◆ 2916. ***Mission West.*** Trans. Niesje C. Horsman-Delmonte. Chester Springs, PA: Wolfhound, 1990. 144 pp.
Rory, 17, walks across Ireland to save a valuable parchment while Cromwell threatens the country during 1649.
Award(s): Belgian Book Prize.
Genre(s): War Story.

Laurence, Janet

2917. ***Canaletto and the Case of Westminster Bridge.*** New York: St. Martin's, 1998. 400 pp.
After Venetian artist Canaletto arrives in London, he is attacked and robbed twice, and when Fanny Rooker saves him, he helps her discover who is stalling work on the uncompleted Westminister Bridge.
Genre(s): Mystery.

Lehr, Helene

2918. ***Princess of Hanover.*** New York: St. Martin's, 1989. 302 pp.
Dorothea, daughter of William of Celle, marries her cousin George of Hanover, and since he houses his mistress down the hall from his 16-year-old bride, she begins a disastrous affair with Count Philip Konigsmark.
Genre(s): Biographical Fiction.

Leslie, Doris

2919. *The Incredible Duchess.* London: Heinemann, 1974. 277 pp.
The Duchess of Kingston, Elizabeth Chudleigh Bristol, experiences the life of the nobility.
Genre(s): Biographical Fiction.

2920. *The Sceptre and the Rose.* New York: Pocket Books, 1968. 323 pp.
Catherine of Braganza marries Charles II of England.
Genre(s): Biographical Fiction.

Lewis, Hilda Winifred

2921. *Catherine.* New York: McKay, 1966. 351 pp.
As the wife of Charles II, Catherine of Braganza must tolerate his numerous mistresses, including Nell Gwyn.
Genre(s): Domestic Fiction; Political Fiction.

Lindsey, Johanna

2922. *Silver Angel.* New York: Avon, 1989. 423 pp.
In 18th-century Turkey, Derek, an Englishman, impersonates a desert monarch with whom a young Englishwoman, sold as a concubine, falls in love.
Genre(s): Romance.

Lofts, Norah

2923. *The House at Sunset.* Garden City, NY: Doubleday, 1972. 315 pp.
In the sequel to *The House at Old Vine*, dramatic episodes occur in the lives of people who live in the house sometime between the 18th century and the present day.
Genre(s): Family Saga.

Macleod, Alison

2924. *The Changeling.* New York: St. Martin's, 1996. 336 pp.
Anne Bonny pretends to be male when she's a child and again after her marriage, while she pursues her pirating career.
Genre(s): Adventure Story.

2925. *The Portingale.* London: Hodder and Stoughton, 1976. 381 pp.
After Catherine of Braganza becomes the wife of Charles II and gives England Tangier and Bombay, she is unable to produce an heir and openly practices her Catholic religion.
Genre(s): Biographical Fiction.

Martin, Kat

2926. *Gypsy Lord.* New York: St. Martin's, 1992. 375 pp.
Catherine Barrington hears rumors that Dominic Edgemont is part gypsy, and when his relatives kidnap her, she realizes the rumors are true, but he still manages to woo and win her.
Genre(s): Romance.

2927. *Nothing but Velvet.* New York: St. Martin's, 1997. 362 pp.

When Jason Sinclair returns incognito after his brother murders their father and blames him, he stops his brother's marriage to Velvet Moran by kidnapping her, and the two soon join forces to clear Jason's name.
Genre(s): Romance.

Masefield, John

2928. *Captain Margaret.* London: G. Richards, 1909. 405 pp.
Captain Margaret unhappily transports his former love and her new husband on his ship as they set out for the New World, but the husband reveals his negative traits, and disaster prevails.
Genre(s): Romance; Sea Story.

Mason, F. Van Wyck

2929. *Manilla Galleon.* Boston: Little, Brown, 1961. 495 pp.
George Anson begins his career as father of the British Navy by leaving Britain for the Pacific where he works on containment of the Spaniards in 1740.
Genre(s): Sea Story.

Maughan, A. M.

2930. *Young Pitt.* New York: John Day, 1975. 270 pp.
William Pitt serves as the prime minister to George III of England in the late 18th century as the colonies fight for independence.
Genre(s): Biographical Fiction; Political Fiction.

McBain, Laurie

2931. *Dark Before the Rising Sun.* New York: Avon, 1982. 528 pp.
Kidnapped from her parents' home, Rhea Claire Dominick returns with the man who rescued her from slavery, a reformed pirate.
Genre(s): Romance.

McKemy, Kay

2932. *Samuel Pepys of the Navy.* New York: Warner, 1970. 242 pp.
Samuel Pepys describes his life and that of the English around him in the 17th century, especially in the court of Charles II.
Genre(s): Biographical Fiction.

Miller, Andrew

2933. *Ingenious Pain.* New York: Harcourt, 1997. 337 pp.
James Dyer cannot feel pain after his birth as the result of his mother's rape on a frozen river in 1739 so as a surgeon, he cannot understand the pain of his patients, until an Eastern European woman teaches him how to feel.
Genre(s): Medical Novel; Bildungsroman (Coming of Age).

Morris, Gilbert

2934. *The Fields of Glory.* Wheaton, IL: Tyndale House, 1995. 376 pp.
When Jenny, Evan, and Amos face a love triangle, the minister John Bunyan helps them reach their faith on a deeper level. (*Series:* Wakefield Dynasty, 4)
Genre(s): Christian Fiction; Romance; War Story; Family Saga.

2935. *The Ramparts of Heaven.* Wheaton, IL: Tyndale House, 1997. 400 pp.
Andrew Wakefield begins to work with the Methodist movement and John Wesley. (*Series:* Wakefield Dynasty, 5)
Genre(s): Christian Fiction; Family Saga.

2936. *Song of the Princes.* Wheaton, IL: Tyndale House, 1997. 386 pp.
Twins Paul and David Wakefield compete to become the master of the family home, Wakefield, and for the hand of Stella Fairfax, during the reign of George II. (*Series:* Wakefield Dynasty, 6)
Genre(s): Christian Fiction; Romance; Family Saga.

Morse, David

2937. *The Iron Bridge.* San Diego, CA: Harcourt, 1998. 448 pp.
Maggie Foster travels back to Coalbrookdale, England, in 1773, where she tries to stop the first iron bridge from being built, and in turn, the beginning of the Industrial Revolution.
Genre(s): Romance; Fantastic Literature; Time Travel.

Mullin, Arthur

2938. *Spy.* Santa Barbara, CA: Capra, 1987. 375 pp.
Although born in Massachusetts and a friend of Benjamin Franklin, Dr. Edward Bancroft has returned to England where he jumps at the opportunity to spy on the American delegation in France, and then, to doublecross the British.
Genre(s): Biographical Fiction; Spy Fiction.

Neill, Robert

◆ **2939.** *Devil's Door.* New York: Arrow, 1981. 182 pp.
During Charles II's reign, Sir Laurence Linley prepares for his daughter Mary's marriage, but things begin to go awry, and when a former Roundhead preacher starts accusing people of witchcraft, they are both tried.
Genre(s): Romance; Horror.

2940. *The Golden Days.* New York: St. Martin's, 1973. 244 pp.
England has great hostility toward James, Charles II's Catholic brother, who becomes king in 1685.
Genre(s): Political Fiction.

Noonan, Michael

2941. *The Sun Is God.* New York: Delacorte, 1973. 218 pp.

Billy Turner details the influences in his life which transfer to his paintings in Victorian England.
Genre(s): Biographical Fiction.

Norfolk, Lawrence

2942. *Lempriere's Dictionary.* New York: Harmony, 1992. 432 pp.
John Lempriere publishes a dictionary of mythology in 1788 which comes to life.
Genre(s): Adventure Story.

O'Donoghue, Maureen

2943. *Jedder's Land.* New York: Simon and Schuster, 1983. 320 pp.
Rachel Jedder, orphan, travels across England on foot during the 18th century when her grandfather leaves her his Devon farm.
Genre(s): Domestic Fiction.

Oliver, Jane

2944. *The Blue Heaven Bends over All.* New York: Putnam, 1971. 384 pp.
Sir Walter Scott exhibits his enjoyment of life with courage as well as humor in his writing of romantic novels.
Genre(s): Biographical Fiction.

2945. *Candleshine No More.* New York: Putnam, 1967. 316 pp.
Bonnie Prince Charlie attempts to recover the English throne from the Hanoverians.
Genre(s): Adventure Story; Political Fiction.

Parker, Laura

2946. *The Gamble.* New York: Zebra, 1998. 416 pp.
Highwayman Black Jack misses the necklace hiding in Sabrina Lyndsey's bodice when he robs her, but when he thinks he will use and betray her, he finds otherwise in the 1740s.
Genre(s): Romance.

Partington, Norman

2947. *Master of Bengal.* New York: St. Martin's, 1974. 303 pp.
Robert Clive rises in power in the British military and goes to India to help establish an empire.
Genre(s): Biographical Fiction.

Pears, Iain

2948. *An Instance of the Fingerpost.* New York: Putnam, 1998. 704 pp.
In the 1660s, as Charles II and the Church of England try to quell residual opposition, Robert Grove, fellow of New College, is murdered, and four different people give their versions of the incident.
Genre(s): Mystery.

Phillips, Jill M.

2949. *Walford's Oak.* Secaucus, NJ: Carol, 1990. 217 pp.

Cybele becomes a wealthy man's mistress before marrying an older widowed yeoman in the 18th century and falling in love with his son.
Genre(s): Gothic Fiction.

Plaidy, Jean

◆ 2950. *Caroline, the Queen.* New York: Putnam, 1986. 413 pp.
Queen Caroline flatters George II so that he agrees with decisions that she and Prime Minister Robert Walpole have secretly discussed, but George continues to show his disdain for the English he rules. (*Series:* Georgian Saga, 4)
Genre(s): Biographical Fiction.

◆ 2951. *A Health unto His Majesty.* New York: Putnam, 1972. 284 pp.
Charles II rejects his shy wife Catherine of Braganza for his ambitious mistress Barbara Palmer. (*Series:* Stuart Saga, 3)
Genre(s): Biographical Fiction; Family Saga.

◆ 2952. *Here Lies Our Sovereign Lord.* New York: Putnam, 1973. 317 pp.
Nell Gwyn remains an actress but becomes Charles II's well-known mistress. (*Series:* Stuart Saga, 4)
Genre(s): Biographical Fiction; Family Saga.

◆ 2953. *Perdita's Prince.* New York: Putnam, 1987. 346 pp.
While George III fights madness and the Americans, the Prince of Wales begins to fret at the puritanical court of his parents and becomes enchanted with the actress Mary Robinson in her role of Perdita in *A Winter's Tale.* (*Series:* Georgian Saga, 6)
Genre(s): Biographical Fiction.

◆ 2954. *The Pleasures of Love.* New York: Putnam, 1992. 329 pp.
Although Charles II continues to have affairs after marrying Catherine of Braganza, he loves her and refuses to divorce her merely because she is barren. (*Series:* Queens of England, 9)
Genre(s): Biographical Fiction.

◆ 2955. *The Prince and the Quakeress.* New York: Putnam, 1986. 318 pp.
As the prince of Wales, soon-to-be George III falls in love with Hannah Lightfoot, a Quaker, but his mother, Princess Augusta, will not allow the marriage. (*Series:* Georgian Saga, 3)
Genre(s): Biographical Fiction.

◆ 2956. *The Princess of Celle.* New York: Putnam, 1985. 335 pp.
Sophia Dorothea, a beautiful and innocent German, becomes the wife of George I, who divorces and exiles her. (*Series:* Georgian Saga, 1)
Genre(s): Biographical Fiction.

◆ 2957. *Queen in Waiting.* New York: Putnam, 1985. 399 pp.

Caroline, wife of George II, trains to become Queen of England under the Electress Sophia Charlotte, sister of the horrid George I. (*Series:* Georgian Saga, 2)
Genre(s): Biographical Fiction.

◆ 2958. *The Queen's Favourites.* New York: Putnam, 1966. 427 pp.
Abigail Hill challenges Sarah Jennings Churchill, duchess of Marlborough, as Queen Anne's closest confidant. (*Series:* Stuart Saga, 7)
Genre(s): Biographical Fiction; Family Saga.

◆ 2959. *The Third George.* New York: Putnam, 1987. 352 pp.
George III, married to Charlotte and father of 15 children, is a moralist who struggles with his family members, including his son's affair with Mrs. Fitzherbert, a Catholic. (*Series:* Georgian Saga, 5)
Genre(s): Biographical Fiction.

◆ 2960. *The Three Crowns.* New York: Putnam, 1965. 363 pp.
James II is the heir apparent to the three crowns of Britian, but he loses them to his daughter Mary and her husband William. (*Series:* Stuart Saga, 5)
Genre(s): Biographical Fiction; Family Saga.

◆ 2961. *The Wandering Prince.* New York: Putnam, 1971. 318 pp.
Charles II has more interest in his mistresses and in traveling to Holland and France than in ruling England. (*Series:* Stuart Saga, 2)
Genre(s): Biographical Fiction; Family Saga.

Potter, Patricia

2962. *Starcatcher.* New York: Bantam, 1997. 400 pp.
Through border raiding and kidnapping, two Scots fall in love as Charles II is restored to the throne after the grimness of Cromwell's regime.
Genre(s): Romance.

Randall, Rona

2963. *Drayton Legacy.* London: Hamilton, 1986. 341 pp.
When Joseph Drayton becomes the head of the family at his father's death, he almost destroys his sisters' happiness with bad but prudent marriages and by keeping his more talented younger brother from becoming a master potter in the 18th century.
Genre(s): Domestic Fiction; Romance.

2964. *The Potter's Niece.* London: H.Hamilton, 1987. 283 pp.
Charlotte Freeman must decide, in 18th-century England, to whom she will leave her estate, when her niece decides to become a potter in the family business and her son returns with an illegtimate child claiming rights to the home.
Genre(s): Romance.

Roberson, Jennifer

2965. *Lady of the Glen.* New York: Kensington, 1996. 420 pp.
Catriona Campbell meets Alasdair Og from the enemy MacDonald clan before William III massacres the MacDonalds in 1692 at Glencoe.
Genre(s): Romance.

Rossiter, Clare

2966. *The White Rose.* New York: St. Martin's, 1978. 190 pp.
When Bonnie Prince Charlie goes to London in 1750, he meets with Anna Stanton, a woman who became a spy for him in order to pay her brother's debts.
Genre(s): Biographical Fiction; Romance.

Sabatini, Rafael

2967. *Captain Blood.* Boston: Houghton Mifflin, 1927. 437 pp.
Peter Blood engages in many adventures, and his friend Jeremiah Pitt reports about sailing on the Spanish Main and governing Jamaica.
Genre(s): Adventure Story; Sea Story; Romance.

2968. *Captain Blood Returns.* Boston: Houghton Mifflin, 1931. 296 pp.
In the sequel to *Captain Blood*, Captain Blood continues his pirate adventures in the Caribbean and the booty he took ashore at Tortuga.
Genre(s): Adventure Story; Sea Story.

2969. *The Fortunes of Captain Blood.* Boston: Houghton Mifflin, 1936. 240 pp.
The buccaneer Captain Blood continues his adventures, and he invariably wins in the sequel to *Captain Blood Returns*.
Genre(s): Adventure Story; Sea Story.

Samson, Lisa

2970. *The Temptation of Aaron Campbell.* Eugene, OR: Harvest House, 1996. 337 pp.
Aaron Campbell makes a secret pact with his friends in the Scottish Highlands without having any idea of the real cost.
Genre(s): Christian Fiction; Adventure Story.

Scott, Amanda

2971. *The Bawdy Bride.* New York: Pinnacle, 1995. 384 pp.
Anne Davies wants to make the best of her arranged marriage to Lord Michael St. Ledgers, but sinister situations on the estate also require her efforts.
Genre(s): Romance.

Scott, Walter

2972. *The Bride of Lammermoor.* 1839. New York: Oxford, 1991. 460 pp.
During the early 18th century, the children of enemies fall in love, but find their happiness is not to be.
Genre(s): Romance.

2973. *The Heart of Midlothian.* 1813. New York: Oxford, 1983. 900 pp.
Jeannie Deans goes to London from Edinburgh to obtain a pardon for her sister who has been unjustly accused of murdering her own son.
Genre(s): Romance.

2974. *Old Mortality.* Boston: Houghton Mifflin, 1966. 392 pp.
Scots fight the Battle of Bothwell Bridge in 1679.
Genre(s): Romance; War Story.

2975. *Redgauntlet.* 1824. New York: Oxford, 1985. 560 pp.
The Young Pretender to the Scottish throne relinquishes his claim.
Genre(s): Adventure Story; Romance.

2976. *Rob Roy.* 1817. New York: Knopf, 1995. 386 pp.
After a young Englishman becomes involved in Jacobite affairs, he escapes into Scotland with Rob Roy.
Genre(s): Epic Literature.

2977. *Waverley.* 1814. New York: Oxford, 1986. 480 pp.
A multitude of events occur in Scotland during the Jacobite rebellion of 1745 at Culloden.
Genre(s): War Story; Romance.

Seton, Anya

2978. *Devil Water.* Boston: Houghton Mifflin, 1962. 526 pp.
Jenny, the daughter of Charles Radcliffe, the last Englishman beheaded for supporting the pretender James Stuart, goes to Virginia with a friend.

Sheffield, Charles

◆ 2979. *Erasmus Magister.* New York: Ace, 1982. 217 pp.
Erasmus Darwin, grandfather of Charles Darwin, uses deduction and scientific knowledge to solve supernatural problems of the 18th century.
Genre(s): Fantastic Literature; Biographical Fiction.

Shelby, Graham

2980. *The Cannaway Concern.* New York: Doubleday, 1980. 297 pp.
In the sequel to *The Cannaways*, Charlotte marries Brook Wintersill on impluse, and in 1719, she succesfully escapes from him after two attempts.
Genre(s): Family Saga.

2981. *The Cannaways.* Garden City, NY: Doubleday, 1978. 347 pp.
In 1697, Brydd Cannaway, a young wheelwright, leaves his Wilshire home for Vienna to apprentice himself to a coachmaker.
Genre(s): Family Saga.

Sherwood, Valerie

2982. *Lisbon.* New York: New American Library, 1989. 535 pp.

Around 1730, orphaned Charlotte Vayle goes to live with her uncle in England's Lake District, and after she falls in love with sailor and pirate Tom Westing, her uncle announces her marriage to a landowner, who stops her elopement with Tom and takes her to Lisbon where she must bear his brutality.
Genre(s): Romance.

2983. *Lovesong.* New York: Pocket Books, 1985. 684 pp.

Carolina Lightfoot goes from Colonial Virginia to an English boarding school where rake Lord Thomas Angevine seduces her, but while traveling home, the Spanish and then pirates capture her ship.
Genre(s): Romance.

2984. *Nightsong.* New York: Pocket Books, 1986. 490 pp.

In the sequel to *Windsong*, Carolina Lightfoot is separated from Kells when an earthquake and tidal wave destroy Port Royal, Jamaica, in 1692, and while trying to find him, she is captured and sold into slavery in the house of Don Diego Vivar.
Genre(s): Romance.

2985. *Windsong.* New York: Pocket Books, 1986. 541 pp.

In the sequel to *Lovesong*, Carolina Lightfoot and Captain Kells, buccaneer, go to England from Jamaica when they discover that an imposter using Kells's home has been attacking ships, and while clearing Kells's home, they discover that Kells's first wife is still alive.
Genre(s): Romance.

Small, Bertrice

2986. *Deceived.* New York: Kensington, 1998. 336 pp.

West Indian heiress Aurora Kimberly trades places with her sister when she is expected to marry a man she has never met, and she eventually falls in love with him.
Genre(s): Romance.

Smith, Barbara Dawson

2987. *Her Secret Affair.* New York: St. Martin's, 1998. 352 pp.

Venus Isabel Darling searches for her mother's murderer and the identity of her father while planning to publish her mother's revealing memoir, but Justin Culver, Earl of Kern, is determined to stop her.
Genre(s): Romance.

Smollett, Tobias

2988. *Roderick Random.* 1784. New York: Penguin, 1996. 476 pp.

In the 18th century, Roderick Random travels in Scotland and the West Indies with the Royal Navy and visits London.
Genre(s): Adventure Story; Picaresque Fiction.

Steen, Marguerite

2989. *The Sun Is My Undoing.* New York: Viking, 1941. 1176 pp.

When Matthew Flood discovers that his beautiful wife is an abolitionist, he leaves her and goes to Africa where he begins a life in the slave trade. (*Series:* Flood Trilogy, 1)
Genre(s): Sea Story; Picaresque Fiction; Family Saga.

Stevenson, Robert Louis

2990. *The Master of Ballantrae.* 1889. New York: Oxford, 1983. 224 pp.

Two brothers support different sides during the Stuart uprising of 1745.
Genre(s): War Story.

Stirling, Jessica

◆ 2991. *Lantern for the Dark.* New York: St. Martin's, 1992. 377 pp.

When Clare Kelso will not tell him the information he needs to defend her, Cameron Adams does not think he can save her from execution for infanticide in 18th-century Scotland.
Genre(s): Legal Story.

◆ 2992. *Shadows on the Shore.* New York: St. Martin's, 1994. 346 pp.

In the sequel to *Lantern for the Dark*, Clare Kelso Quinn is a prosperous salt dealer and a widow with a daughter when Frederick Striker reappears and tries to marry her.
Genre(s): Domestic Fiction.

Strong, Bethany

2993. *First Love.* Amherst, MA: Parable, 1976. 220 pp.

Charles II of England falls in love with Lucy Walter, a woman he cannot marry, in the 17th century.
Genre(s): Biographical Fiction; Love Story.

Stubbs, Jean

2994. *By Our Beginnings.* New York: St. Martin's, 1979. 347 pp.

In 1760, the farmer Ned Howarth defies tradition and marries beyond his social class to a woman educated in letters and social graces.
Genre(s): Domestic Fiction; Family Saga.

2995. *The Case of Kitty Ogilvie.* New York: Walker, 1971. 254 pp.

Kitty Ogilvie, from a poor manor, is charged with murder and tried in Edinburgh during the 18th century.
Genre(s): Biographical Fiction; Legal Story.

2996. *An Imperfect Joy.* New York: St. Martin's, 1981. 415 pp.

In the sequel to *By Our Beginnings*, William Howarth expands from rural blacksmith to mill owner between 1785 and 1812, while his married sister secretly supports political reform.
Genre(s): Domestic Fiction; Family Saga.

Sumner, Richard

2997. *Mistress of the Boards.* New York: Random House, 1976. 332 pp.
Nell Gwynne, mistress of Charles II, performs in London during the times of the Great Fire and the plague.
Genre(s): Biographical Fiction.

Sutcliff, Rosemary

◆ 2998. *Bonnie Dundee.* New York: Dutton, 1984. 204 pp.
In 1689, Colonel John Graham of Claverhouse supports King James instead of William of Orange, and his stable boy remembers him as a kind and helpful man.

Suthren, Victor

2999. *Royal Yankee.* New York: St. Martin's, 1987. 189 pp.
Edward Mainwaring, a Royal Navy lieutenant in 1739, begins his seafaring adventures.
Genre(s): War Story; Sea Story.

Tarkington, Booth

3000. *Monsieur Beaucaire.* Garden City, NY: Doubleday, 1900. 127 pp.
In 18th-century Bath, Louis Philippe de Valois, cousin of Louis XV but disguised as a barber, falls in love with Lady Mary who rejects him when she hears that he is a working man.
Genre(s): Adventure Story.

Thackeray, William Makepeace

3001. *The History of Henry Esmond, Esquire.* 1852. New York: Oxford, 1991. 427 pp.
Before Henry Esmond leaves for America, Henry and his friend Francis support James the Pretender.

Thomson, George Malcolm

3002. *The Ball at Glenkerran.* London: Secker and Warburg, 1982. 228 pp.
Lord Ravelston becomes a stalwart Hanoverian after once participating in the Jacobite Rebellion, but he still enjoys escaping for a night to Edinburgh, the Athens of the North.
Genre(s): Political Fiction; Domestic Fiction.

Thornton, Elizabeth

3003. *Dangerous to Love.* New York: Bantam, 1994. 448 pp.
Anti-Jacobite Julian Raynor mistakes aristocrat Serena Ward, disguised as an actress in her work for Jacobites defeated at Culloden, for a prostitute but once identified, Julian believes her father is responsible for his family's troubles.
Genre(s): Romance.

Thorpe, Adam

3004. *Ulverton.* New York: Farrar, Straus and Giroux, 1993. 390 pp.

The town of Ulverton in Wessex Downs changes through the years with public and private events such as murder, discovery, and destruction.
Genre(s): Family Saga.

Tremain, Rose

3005. *Restoration.* New York: Viking, 1990. 371 pp.
Robert Merivel must find a meaning in his life after King Charles II withdraws his patronage.

Veryan, Patricia

◆ 3006. *Ask Me No Questions.* New York: St. Martin's, 1993. 340 pp.
Ruth Allington, a penniless artist and widow, gets a job restoring a fresco in a Dover mansion in order to support her dead brother's twins, but she does not realize that the Jewelled Men killed her brother. (*Series:* Tales of the Jewelled Men, 3)
Genre(s): Romance.

◆ 3007. *Cherished Enemy.* New York: St. Martin's, 1988. 384 pp.
In the 18th century, Rosamond Albritton lost her fiancé at Culloden and hates all Jacobites, but when she is on a journey, she falls in love with Dr. Robert Victor, a man with a mysterious background. (*Series:* Golden Chronicles, 5)
Genre(s): Romance.

◆ 3008. *Had We Never Loved.* New York: St. Martin's, 1992. 310 pp.
The sequel to *Time's Fool* finds the Jewelled Men targeting the family of Lord Horatio Glendenning by calling him treasonous for his Jacobite dealings. (*Series:* Tales of the Jewelled Men, 2)
Genre(s): Romance.

◆ 3009. *Journey to Enchantment.* New York: St. Martin's, 1986. 416 pp.
The British Geoffrey Delavale, brother to Penelope Montgomery in *Practice to Deceive*, sympathizes with the Jacobites after their rebellion in 1745 when the Duke of Cumberland is merciless, so at night, he helps families escape to safety. (*Series:* Golden Chronicles, 2)
Genre(s): War Story; Romance.

◆ 3010. *Love Alters Not.* New York: St. Martin's, 1988. 448 pp.
Dimity Cranford tries to save her Jacobite friend, Lord Glendenning, and unwittingly escorts a boy to his uncle's house to unscrupulously claim the inheritance. (*Series:* Golden Chronicles, 4)
Genre(s): War Story.

◆ 3011. *Never Doubt I Love.* New York: St. Martin's, 1995. 345 pp.
Zoe Grainger's brother is the target of the Jewelled Men in the sequel to *A Shadow's Bliss*, and Zoe attempts to help him with the assistance of Lieutenant Cranford. (*Series:* Tales of the Jewelled Men, 5)
Genre(s): Romance.

3012. *Practice to Deceive.* New York: St. Martin's, 1985. 384 pp.
In 1746, after Penelope Montgomery's brother and father have died, and a greedy uncle has taken the family estate, she catches her uncle beating a Jacobite, the man she loves. (***Series:*** Golden Chronicles, 1)
Genre(s): Romance.

◆ **3013. *A Shadow's Bliss.*** New York: St. Martin's, 1994. 324 pp.
Jonathan seems foolish for not protecting himself, but when others come to his Cornwall village seeking the villanous Jewelled Men, he turns out to have been one of their victims. (***Series:*** Tales of the Jewelled Men, 4)
Genre(s): Romance.

◆ **3014. *Time's Fool.*** New York: St. Martin's, 1991. 375 pp.
Captain Gideon Rossiter returns from the Low Countries to find that his love no longer seems to care for him, but they reunite in an effort to find out who has financially ruined Gideon's father. (***Series:*** Tales of the Jewelled Men, 1)
Genre(s): Romance.

◆ **3015. *The Tyrant.*** New York: St. Martin's, 1987. 344 pp.
The defeated Jacobites in the sequel to *Journey to Enchantment* risk their lives trying to return treasures collected for Prince Charles to the rightful owners. (***Series:*** Golden Chronicles, 3)

Vivian, Daisy

3016. *Rose White, Rose Red.* New York: Walker, 1983. 203 pp.
While Blanche Montague serves as companion to her aunt, she falls in love with Gareth McQuahae, a Jacobite whose estate has been confiscated.
Genre(s): Romance.

3017. *The Wild Rose.* New York: Walker, 1986. 186 pp.
In the sequel to *Rose White, Rose Red*, Meg hides in the Countess of Ravenspur's home, and when the Countess, a Jacobite, has to flee, Meg falls in love with the son of an earl.
Genre(s): Romance.

Vrettos, Theodore

3018. *Lord Elgin's Lady.* Boston: Houghton Mifflin, 1982. 363 pp.
As Lord Elgin's face becomes disfigured from disease, he becomes more obsessed with the Parthenon antiquities that he brought from Greece to London.
Genre(s): Biographical Fiction.

Walpole, Hugh

3019. *Judith Paris.* Garden City, NY: Doubleday, 1931. 565 pp.

In the sequel to *Rogue Herries*, Judith Herries is an orphan who dedicates her life to protecting her father's descendants.
Genre(s): Domestic Fiction; Family Saga.

3020. *Rogue Herries.* Garden City, NY: Doubleday, 1930. 524 pp.
In the sequel to *Katherine Christian*, Francis (Rogue) Herries brings his family and his mistress to an old manor house in the English Lake District in the late 18th century.
Genre(s): Domestic Fiction.

Watson, Marjorie

3021. *Heir to Polventon.* New York: Saturday Review, 1974. 255 pp.
Wreckers and smugglers operate on the Cornish coast in the 18th century, and Julie Polventon comes with her husband to the area where she learns secrets about his family and hers.
Genre(s): Romance.

Williamson, Glen

3022. *Sons of Susanna.* Wheaton, IL: Tyndale House, 1991. 236 pp.
Susanna Wesley's son John begins the Methodist Movement in England, and her son Charles writes some of its most memorable hymns.
Genre(s): Biographical Fiction; Christian Fiction.

Wilson, Leslie

3023. *Malefice.* New York: Pantheon, 1992. 168 pp.
Before Alice Slade is hanged for witchcraft, she exerts a strong influence over many people in her small village.
Genre(s): War Story.

Woodiwiss, Kathleen E.

3024. *Shanna.* New York: Avon, 1977. 661 pp.
Shanna Trahern marries her choice instead of her father's, but she does not want to be his wife in reality until she falls madly in love with him after he goes to the West Indies in 1750.
Genre(s): Romance.

Wright, Patricia

3025. *The Storms of Fate.* Garden City, NY: Doubleday, 1981. 480 pp.
Arabella Sperling deserts her lover Henry Cornish when the Stuarts try him for treason, but when the monarchy is overthrown, Arabella and Henry's son Adam becomes respectable.
Genre(s): War Story.

York, Alison

3026. *The Fire and the Rope.* London: W. H. Allen, 1979. 382 pp.
Anne Bonney goes from Ireland to Charles Town with her father where she accels in self-defense and becomes a pirate.
Genre(s): Biographical Fiction.

Zochert, Donald

3027. *Murder in the Hellfire Club.* New York: Holt, 1978. 240 pp.

When Benjamin Franklin is in England in 1757, Dashwood calls upon him to investigate the murder of a member of the secret Hellfire Club.
Genre(s): Mystery.

1789-1859

Aiken, Joan

◆ 3028. *Eliza's Daughter.* New York: St. Martin's, 1994. 316 pp.
Colonel Brandon's sister's illegitimate daughter, in a sequel to *Sense and Sensibility*, discovers her background and claims her birthright.
Genre(s): Bildungsroman (Coming of Age).

◆ 3029. *Emma Watson.* New York: St. Martin's, 1996. 224 pp.
Emma and Elizabeth Watson, characters in an unfinished manuscript by Jane Austen, have talents and achievements but, as daughters of a clergyman, no money.
Genre(s): Romance.

3030. *The Five-Minute Marriage.* New York: Doubleday, 1978. 264 pp.
A music teacher with a spendthrift mother marries a noble misogynist, but their marriage of convenience turns into something more.
Genre(s): Regency Novel; Romance.

3031. *Jane Fairfax.* New York: St. Martin's, 1991. 252 pp.
A sequel to Jane Austen's *Emma* reveals Jane Fairfax's attitudes toward the village in which Emma lives.
Genre(s): Regency Novel; Romance.

3032. *Mansfield Revisited.* Garden City, NY: Doubleday, 1984. 188 pp.
Susan, sister of Fanny Price in Jane Austen's *Mansfield Park*, intrigues several young men who meet her after Fanny leaves for Antigua with her husband.
Genre(s): Romance; Regency Novel.

3033. *Midnight Is a Place.* New York: Viking, 1974. 287 pp.
Lucas Bell, 13, and Anna-Marie Murgatroyd, eight, support themselves and pay for the hospital stay of their tutor after the fire which destroyed Midnight Court in 1842 by working in a rug mill.
Genre(s): Domestic Fiction.

3034. *The Smile of the Stranger.* New York: Doubleday, 1978. 280 pp.
Juliana Paget and her father escape France in 1789 but face a variety of problems when they arrive in England.
Genre(s): Adventure Story; Mystery; Romance; Regency Novel.

◆ 3035. *The Youngest Miss Ward.* New York: St. Martin's, 1998. 320 pp.

Hattie Ward hopes to escape her contemptuous family after her mother dies, but she finds herself in competition with the condescending Lady Ursula for an attractive lord.
Genre(s): Romance.

Alcott, Louisa May

3036. *A Long Fatal Love Chase.* New York: Random House, 1995. 288 pp.
Rosamond Vivian escapes from her grandfather by running away with the adventurer Phillip Tempest, but he represents an even worse dependence, and she flees from him to a convent and then to a madhouse.
Genre(s): Romance; Adventure Story.

Anthony, Evelyn

◆ 3037. *Victoria and Albert.* New York: Cowell, 1958. 312 pp.
The autocratic and headstrong Victoria is devoted to her husband while dealing with domestic and diplomatic concerns.
Genre(s): Biographical Fiction; Love Story.

Argers, Helen

◆ 3038. *A Lady of Independence.* Garden City, NY: Doubleday, 1982. 192 pp.
Astera Claybourne refuses to marry Viscount Weston, saying that she wants a career, and in his shock, he determines that he will pursue her until he wins.
Genre(s): Regency Novel; Romance.

Arnett, Caroline

◆ 3039. *Melinda.* New York: Fawcett, 1975. 240 pp.
Melinda comes to London from America to live with her aunt after the American Revolution, and although a plan exists for her to marry the family heir, she wants to find her grandfather's jewels.
Genre(s): Romance; Gothic Fiction.

Ashfield, Helen

3040. *Beau Barron's Lady.* New York: St. Martin's, 1980. 175 pp.
In 1807 London Bess Hathaway becomes enamoured with gambler Sir Charles Beau Barron and after becoming pregnant and discarded, she marries and begins operating a chain of brothels.
Genre(s): Regency Novel; Romance.

3041. *Crystal.* New York: St. Martin's, 1987. 173 pp.
Topaz Chilcott is a young gypsy who goes to a convent before she falls in love with the most handsome man she

has ever seen, the Marquis of Rossmayne, but a series of difficulties, including scarlet fever, briefly keeps them apart.
Genre(s): Regency Novel; Romance.

3042. *Emerald.* New York: St. Martin's, 1983. 188 pp.
Emily Tregellan wants to escape the Cornwall coast, and after serving as a maid to the Feverell family and saving her money, her needlework abilities give her the chance to establish a shop in London and fall in love with the upper-class Nicholas, Viscount Asterly.
Genre(s): Regency Novel; Romance.

3043. *Garnet.* New York: St. Martin's, 1985. 190 pp.
In the early 19th century, Garnet Bradley begins working in Zachariah Speke's toy-making shop which she enjoys, but she falls in love with Roderick, a marquis's son promised to Sir Lambert's daughter Frances, which complicates her life.
Genre(s): Regency Novel; Romance.

3044. *The Marquis and Miss Jones.* New York: St. Martin's, 1982. 912 pp.
Although the hero and heroine have met, neither realizes the true identity of the other, and mistakes lead to her abduction to Paris as the French Revolution is beginning.
Genre(s): Romance.

◆ 3045. *Midsummer Morning.* New York: St. Martin's, 1984. 190 pp.
Joanna Penwarren's father, a cooper in 18th-century Cornwall, operates a smuggling ring while she hopelessly loves the marquis of Estercourt.
Genre(s): Regency Novel; Romance.

3046. *Opal.* New York: St. Martin's, 1986. 174 pp.
Opal Shannon, orphaned when parents and siblings die in a fire, supports herself in a workhouse and a scullery, but she does not forget the noble Edward, a boy whose pocket she had once picked.
Genre(s): Regency Novel; Romance.

3047. *Pearl.* New York: St. Martin's, 1985. 187 pp.
Orphan Pearl Cartwright moves in with Aunt Cissy, owner of a draper's shop in London, and becomes a London beauty who falls in love with the wrong man.
Genre(s): Regency Novel; Romance.

◆ 3048. *Regency Rogue.* New York: St. Martin's, 1982. 175 pp.
The owner of the house that both Lady Davina Temple and the earl of Dunmorrow want to buy is murdered.
Genre(s): Regency Novel; Romance.

3049. *Ruby.* New York: St. Martin's, 1984. 191 pp.
Isabella and her brother Giles find relief from their unpleasant guardian when Richard, Duke of Gloucester, takes Giles into his entourage, and Isabella marries Lord Warrick, whom the king has chosen.
Genre(s): Regency Novel; Romance.

3050. *Sapphire.* New York: St. Martin's, 1986. 173 pp.

Sapphire Grant loves Ashton, son of an earl, but class barriers keep them apart so she teaches the children of miners, and one of those she teaches discovers that he is the natural son of the Earl of Stonehurst.
Genre(s): Regency Novel; Romance.

3051. *Topaz.* New York: St. Martin's, 1987. 160 pp.
Topaz Chilcott refuses an arranged marriage, and after being cast out from her gypsy community, she meets Marquis Romayne when she tries to steal his horse in the Dartmore glens.
Genre(s): Regency Novel; Romance.

Austen, Jane

◆ 3052. *Emma.* 1815. New York: Random House, 1996. 381 pp.
Emma tries to impose her match making ideas on everyone and finds that sometimes she should desist.
Genre(s): Domestic Fiction; Love Story; Humorous Fiction.

◆ 3053. *Mansfield Park.* 1814. New York: Norton, 1997. 385 pp.
Sensible, wise, but impovershed Fanny Price goes to live with her wealthy cousins, and throughout many trials of their upper-middle-class life, she remains true to her beliefs.
Genre(s): Love Story.

◆ 3054. *Northanger Abbey.* 1818. New York: Viking, 1996. 231 pp.
As Catherine Moreland begins to mature, many of her illusions collapse under the reality of middle-class life.
Genre(s): Satire.

◆ 3055. *Persuasion.* 1818. New York: Viking, 1967. 400 pp.
Having broken her engagement with Captain Wentworth in deference to family and friends, Anne Elliott remains discontented but complaisant until Wentworth reenters her life.
Genre(s): Humorous Fiction; Love Story.

◆ 3056. *Pride and Prejudice.* 1813. New York: Viking, 1996. 400 pp.
Wealthy Mr. Darcy and spirited Elizabeth Bennett dislike each other at first sight, and each must contend with their pride and prejudices while Elizabeth's mother plots economically advantageous marriages for all her daughters.
Genre(s): Love Story.

◆ 3057. *Sense and Sensibility.* 1811. New York: Knopf, 1992. 367 pp.
Two sisters, Elinor and Marianne, fall in love, one with a man promised at a young age to another and one to a rascal.
Genre(s): Domestic Fiction.

Austen, Jane, and Another Lady

◆ 3058. *Sanditon.* Boston: Houghton Mifflin, 1975. 329 pp.

Charlotte Heywood spends time at a seaside resort where she interacts with other members of the landed gentry.

Austen-Leigh, Joan

◆ 3059. *A Visit to Highbury*. New York: St. Martin's, 1995. 182 pp.
From Highbury, Mary Goddard corresponds with her sister in London, and with characters from Jane Austen's *Emma*, they become matchmakers for two young women.
Genre(s): Regency Novel; Romance.

Bainbridge, Beryl

3060. *Watson's Apology*. New York: McGraw Hill, 1985. 222 pp.
In 1844, an English schoolmaster proposes to Irish spinster Anne Armstrong, and she mistakenly believes life with him will be more pleasant than living in a boarding house.
Genre(s): Gothic Fiction.

Baldwin, Rebecca

3061. *Dartwood's Daughters*. New York: St. Martin's, 1989. 199 pp.
When Lord Dartwood goes to Naples to excavate Roman ruins, he takes Eve, one of his twin daughters and leaves the other because of illness, and while they are away, Amy's Aunt Seale bullies her into an inappropriate engagement.
Genre(s): Regency Novel; Romance.

Balogh, Mary

3062. *Christmas Belle*. New York: New American Library, 1994. 222 pp.
Jack Frazer, visiting his grandparents' estate for Christmas confirms that his grandmother wants him married when lovely Juliana Beckworth appears, but in the company is also the lovely actress with whom he has had an unforgettable affair.
Genre(s): Regency Novel; Romance.

3063. *A Christmas Bride*. New York: Signet, 1997. 222 pp.
Attorney Edgar Downs goes to London before Christmas to find a wife with a title, and when the eligible women seem too young, an intriguing widow, Lady Helena Stapleton, beguiles him.
Genre(s): Regency Novel; Romance.

3064. *The Ideal Wife*. New York: Severn House, 1991. 224 pp.
The Earl of Severn thinks that Abigail Gardiner's need for money will help him escape a marriage planned by his mother and that he can continue his bachelor ways if married to Abigail, but she surprises him.
Genre(s): Regency Novel; Romance.

3065. *Indiscreet*. New York: Jove, 1997. 352 pp.
When Lady Catherine Winsmore refuses to marry after she is raped, she bears an illegitimate child, and when her family disowns her, she pretends to be a widow.
Genre(s): Regency Novel; Romance.

3066. *Thief of Dreams*. New York: Jove, 1998. 336 pp.
Cassandra Havelock comes of age and is released from mourning on the same day, and she plans to never marry until Nigel Wetherby appears at her birthday ball and tries to change her mind.
Genre(s): Romance.

3067. *Truly*. New York: Berkley, 1996. 352 pp.
Geraint Penderyn returns to Wales after 10 years, finds a mess on the family estate, and faces hostility, but he regains respect by masquerading as a rioter in the 1842 wars against Welsh toll roads.
Genre(s): Romance.

Banim, John

3068. *The Croppy: A Tale of 1798*. 1828. New York: D. and J. Sadlier, 1865. 435 pp.
The Irish rebel against the British in 1798, and one man becomes disturbed by the excessive violence.
Genre(s): War Story.

Banks, Lynne Reid

3069. *Dark Quartet*. New York: Delacorte, 1997. 432 pp.
The Brontës seem to live a quiet but dark life together.
Genre(s): Biographical Fiction; Domestic Fiction.

3070. *Path to the Silent Country*. New York: Delacorte, 1977. 230 pp.
In Charlotte Brontë's last years, she must cope with the death of two sisters and a brother as well as her own marriage.
Genre(s): Biographical Fiction.

Barbour, Anne

3071. *Lord Glenraven's Return*. New York: Signet, 1994. 224 pp.
Lord Glenraven disguises himself as a servant before returning to Ravencroft, his family's former estate, in order to regain it for the family, but the current owner pleasantly surprises him.
Genre(s): Regency Novel; Love Story.

3072. *A Rake's Reform*. New York: Signet, 1996. 254 pp.
The feminist Hester Blayne shelters the ward of the disapproving Earl of Bythorne against his will, but when Hester brings Chloe to London and guides her through the Season, the Earl changes his mind.
Genre(s): Regency Novel.

Barnett, Jill

3073. *Bewitching*. New York: Pocket Books, 1993. 480 pp.
A Scottish witch, Joyous Fiona MacQuarrie, makes an incorrect incantation in 1813 and ends up in Alec Castlemaine's lap, but after she invents a story about her appearance, he decides to marry her to save face.
Genre(s): Romance; Fantastic Literature.

3074. *Dreaming.* New York: Pocket Books, 1994. 325 pp.
Letty loves Richard Lennox, Earl of Downe, but he regards her as a hellion.
Genre(s): Romance.

Barrett, Julia

◆ 3075. *Presumption.* New York: M. Evans, 1993. 283 pp.
A sequel to Jane Austen's *Pride and Prejudice* centers on Georgiana Darcy and her interest in both a naval officer and an architect.
Genre(s): Domestic Fiction.

◆ 3076. *The Third Sister.* New York: Donald I. Fine, 1996. 247 pp.
When Margaret, the youngest sister in Jane Austen's *Sense and Sensibility*, is 17, she despairs of finding someone who will marry her without a dowry.
Genre(s): Domestic Fiction.

Barron, Stephanie

◆ 3077. *Jane and the Man of the Cloth.* New York: Bantam, 1997. 274 pp.
After Jane Austen's carriage is upset, she meets the secretive Mr. Sidmouth and discovers that a robber called the Reverend needs to be apprehended.
Genre(s): Mystery.

◆ 3078. *Jane and the Unpleasantness at Scargrave Manor.* New York: Bantam, 1996. 289 pp.
When Jane Austen visits her friend Isobel, Countess of Scargrave, Isobel's husband dies from poisoning, and Jane investigates the crime.
Genre(s): Mystery.

◆ 3079. *Jane and the Wandering Eye.* New York: Bantam, 1998. 272 pp.
Jane Austen helps her friend Lord Harold Trowbridge save his unjustly accused nephew from execution through her questioning of people working in the theater.
Genre(s): Mystery.

Bastable, Bernard

3080. *Dead, Mr Mozart.* New York: St. Martin's, 1995. 382 pp.
Mozart plans for the music at George IV's coronation in 1820 but becomes involved in royal scandal and murder instead.
Genre(s): Mystery.

3081. *To Die Like a Gentleman.* New York: St. Martin's, 1993. 152 pp.
Robert Barnard solves the crisis that led to the murder of the unpleasant Sir Richard Hudson.
Genre(s): Mystery.

Becnel, Roxanne

3082. *Heart of the Storm.* New York: St. Martin's, 1995. 368 pp.
Shy Eliza Thoroughgood persuades her parents to let her take her cousin Aubrey, 10, to Madeira to recover from a

riding injury in 1844, but once there, Aubrey's half-brother kidnaps both of them.
Genre(s): Romance.

Bell, Sam Hanna

3083. *A Man Flourishing.* Dover, NH: Blackstaff, 1986. 255 pp.
James Gault returns to Ireland from studying the ministry in Glasgow to join the 1798 revolution, and although he never fights, he must flee to Belfast.
Genre(s): War Story.

Bennett, Arnold

3084. *The Old Wives' Tale.* New York: Doran, 1908. 578 pp.
Residents in a village of England's midlands follow their daily rituals in the 19th century.
Genre(s): Domestic Fiction.

Beverley, Jo

◆ 3085. *The Fortune Hunter.* New York: Walker, 1991. 204 pp.
Beautiful Amy is poor and thinks that she must marry for money instead of love so that she can keep the family estate and establish dowries for her sisters.
Genre(s): Regency Novel; Romance.

3086. *The Stanforth Secrets.* New York: Walker, 1989. 252 pp.
Chloe, a Stanforth widow, awaits the arrival of the new lord so that she may leave for London, but she does not expect to fall in love with him.
Genre(s): Regency Novel; Romance.

◆ 3087. *The Stolen Bride.* New York: Walker, 1990. 193 pp.
As former governess Beth Hawley romances Sir Marius Fletcher, someone threatens to steal her former pupil, Sophie, and kill Sophie's betrothed.
Genre(s): Regency Novel; Romance; Mystery.

Black, Laura

3088. *Ravenburn.* New York: St. Martin's, 1978. 330 pp.
Katie Irvine's stepmother thinks that Kate has nervous disorders so she deprives her of society, but Katie loves the outdoors until an island's ruined castle seems threatening to her.
Genre(s): Romance.

Blackstock, Charity

3089. *The Bitter Conquest.* New York: Coward-McCann, 1968. 190 pp.
When a wife discovers that her husband is involved in criminal activities, she must decide what to do about their marriage.
Genre(s): Romance.

Blyth, Juliet

3090. *The Parfit Knight.* New York: St. Martin's, 1987. 248 pp.
After being blinded in an accident as a child, Rosalind meets the Marquis of Amberley during her London season, and after he discovers that he was indirectly involved in her mishap, he falls in love with her.
Genre(s): Regency Novel; Romance.

Bonnet, Theodore

3091. *The Mudlark.* Garden City, NY: Doubleday, 1949. 305 pp.
The mudlark, a dirty urchin from lower-class London wants to see Queen Victoria, and he succeeds.
Genre(s): Biographical Fiction.

Boucher, Rita

3092. *A Misbegotten Match.* New York: Avon, 1994. 192 pp.
When Lady Claire becomes ill, Amanda Metcalfe sends for the Lady's godson Sebastian Armitage, and although he and Amanda are attracted to one another other factors hold them apart.
Genre(s): Regency Novel; Romance.

Bowen, Marjorie

3093. *The Rake's Progress.* New York: Rider, 1912. 302 pp.
Members of fashionable society interact with an aristocratic man of dubious character.
Genre(s): Romance.

Bragg, Melvyn

3094. *The Maid of Buttermere.* New York: Putnam, 1987. 384 pp.
In the early 19th century, the scoundrel John Hatfield woos and marries Mary Robinson (Mary of Buttermere), but after his misdeeds come to light, people such as Wordsworth and Coleridge rise to her defense.
Genre(s): Biographical Fiction.

Brandewyne, Rebecca

3095. *Upon a Moon-Dark Moor.* New York: Warner, 1988. 387 pp.
Maggie Chandler's father resents her because her mother died when Maggie was born, but when her stepsister steals her fiancé, Maggie must marry her illegitimate Gypsy cousin, Draco, in the early 19th century.
Genre(s): Romance.

Brent, Madeleine

◆ 3096. *The Long Masquerade.* Garden City, NY: Doubleday, 1982. 349 pp.
When Emma Delaney believes that her unfaithful husband has been murdered in the West Indies, she goes to London, marries for convenience, and enters society, but her first husband reappears and decides to get her back.
Genre(s): Love Story; Romance.

Brindley, Louise

◆ 3097. *In the Shadow of the Brontës.* New York: St. Martin's, 1983. 272 pp.
Lizzie Godolphin, a scullery maid with her own problems, resembles Anne Brontë, and although that is her only link to the family, she also has the ability to foresee the family's future.
Genre(s): Biographical Fiction; Domestic Fiction.

Brockway, Connie

3098. *All Through the Night.* New York: Dell, 1997. 384 pp.
In 1817, a spy catches a thief, and two tormented commoners fall in love.
Genre(s): Romance.

Brodnax, Elizabeth

◆ 3099. *The Marquis of Carabas.* New York: Walker, 1991. 192 pp.
Cat Brown, daughter of a cardshark father, wants to settle in England and goes to London pretending to be the daughter of a Venetian nobleman.
Genre(s): Regency Novel; Romance.

Brontë, Charlotte

3100. *Jane Eyre.* 1847. New York: Cambridge, 1996. 528 pp.
Jane Eyre becomes a governess in Mr. Rochester's home of Thornfield and falls in love with him before she finds that he has a tragic secret.
Genre(s): Romance.

3101. *Shirley.* 1849. New York: Modern Library, 1997. 656 pp.
When Shirley Keeldar, an heiress, marries a tutor whose brother owns a mill introducing labor-saving devices, she helps the brother's campaign.
Genre(s): Domestic Fiction.

Brontë, Emily

3102. *Wuthering Heights.* 1847. New York: Modern Library, 1994. 415 pp.
When Mr. Lockwood has an encounter with the spirit of Catherine Linton at the home of the unsociable Heathcliff, he hears the story of the tempestuous love affair between Catherine and Heathcliff.
Genre(s): Love Story; Gothic Fiction.

Brontë, Anne

3103. *The Tenant of Wildfell Hall.* 1848. New York: Modern Library, 1997. 799 pp.
Gilbert Markham falls in love with a mysterious, sad woman who eventually reveals her difficult past to him.
Genre(s): Love Story.

Brown, Diana

3104. *Come Be My Love.* New York: St. Martin's, 1981. 378 pp.

◆May be suitable for young adult readers

Alexandra Cox-Neville decides to marry for love, and her education helps her escape from her father's despotism.
Genre(s): Regency Novel; Romance.

3105. *The Sandalwood Fan.* New York: St. Martin's, 1983. 272 pp.
Penelope Bramson must live under the tyranny of her deceased husband's executor, but when she decides to devote herself to painting, Lord Charles falls in love with her.
Genre(s): Regency Novel; Romance.

Brust, Steven, and Emma Bull

3106. *Freedom and Necessity.* New York: Tor, 1997. 443 pp.
In 1849, when James Cobham writes his brother to say that he cannot remember the previous two months, his brother tells him to hide because he expects foul play, and in the ensuing months he investigates his loss of memory.
Genre(s): Fantastic Literature; Mystery.

Burgess, Anthony

3107. *Abba Abba.* Boston: Little, Brown, 1977. 127 pp.
During the last months of his life in Rome, John Keats meets the Roman dialect poet Giuseppe Belli.
Genre(s): Biographical Fiction.

Burton, Hester

◆ 3108. *Riders of the Storm.* New York: Crowell, 1973. 170 pp.
In 1793, Stephen helps his friend with a school for workers' children and supports parliamentary reform, but when he is charged with sedition, he must spend his money on his defense in the sequel to *The Rebel.*

◆ 3109. *Time of Trial.* New York: Yearling, 1963. 216 pp.
In 1803, a mob burns Margaret's father's bookstore when he favors reform in London, and he goes to prison while Margaret continues to support his beliefs.
Award(s): Carnegie Medal.

Busch, Frederick

3110. *The Mutual Friend.* New York: Harper and Row, 1978. Canada pp.
Dickens, a flawed personality with greatness, has three women live with him, a prostitute as his maid, his estranged wife, and his mistress Ellen Ternan.
Genre(s): Biographical Fiction.

Byrd, Elizabeth

3111. *The Famished Land.* Philadelphia: Lippincott, 1972. 308 pp.
Irish inhabitants of Ballyfearna, especially Moira McFlaherty, 16, and her family, try to suvive the potato famine in Ireland from 1845 to 1847, but only Moira and two small brothers can live on the pond weeds.
Genre(s): Domestic Fiction.

3112. *The Long Enchantment.* London: Macmillan, 1973. 250 pp.
Linty Clarke, a jealous maid in Balmoral Castle, describes the relationship between Queen Victoria and her attendant John Brown.
Genre(s): Biographical Fiction.

Caine, Jeffrey

3113. *Heathcliff.* New York: Knopf, 1978. 245 pp.
Heathcliff, from *Wuthering Heights*, flees to London vowing revenge on both the Earnshaws and Lintons, and he spends his time becoming a master criminal.
Genre(s): Domestic Fiction.

Calvin, June

3114. *Isabella's Rake.* New York: New American Library, 1997. 220 pp.
Isabella Eardley only wants to paint, but when her first choice for a teacher declines, the teacher's student offers.
Genre(s): Regency Novel; Romance.

Cameron, Stella

3115. *Beloved.* New York: Warner, 1996. 416 pp.
Saber, Earl of Avenall, returns from India with nightmares and refuses to marry his love Ella until his problems cease.
Genre(s): Romance; Regency Novel.

3116. *Wait for Me.* New York: Warner, 1997. 432 pp.
In 1837, Gray Falconer returns to Scotland for his inheritance and his intended bride, Minerva Arbuckle, who wants to be an inventor, but someone tries to kill him.
Genre(s): Romance.

Camp, Candice

3117. *Indiscreet.* New York: Harlequin, 1997. 401 pp.
When Camilla Ferrand goes to the family estate at Chevington Park, she hires Lord Rawdon to pose as her fiancé as an appeasement to her grandfather, and since he wants to investigate rumors of a French spy in the area, he agrees.
Genre(s): Regency Novel; Romance.

Carmichael, Jeanne

3118. *Forever Yours.* New York: Fawcett, 1996. 185 pp.
Lord Blackthorn comes back into Lydia Osborne's life after five years, but she refuses to let him pretend that he has never left.
Genre(s): Regency Novel; Romance.

Carr, John Dickson

3119. *The Bride of Newgate.* New York: Harper, 1950. 308 pp.

Dick Darwent, a condemned felon, marries Lady Caroline Ross one hour before his execution, but his cousins' deaths at Waterloo grant him a last-minute clemency.

Carr, Philippa

3120. *Midsummer's Eve.* New York: Putnam, 1986. 334 pp.
Annora Cadorson wonders who jumped over a bonfire in a hooded monk's robe on the night Mother Ginny was murdered by villagers, and she does not find out until after her return from Australia. (*Series:* Daughters of England, 13)
Genre(s): Romance; Family Saga.

◆ 3121. *The Pool of St Branok.* New York: Putnam, 1987. 400 pp.
Angelet Hanson, nine, the granddaughter of Jake Cadorson from *The Return of the Gypsy*, meets Benedict Landson, and although they are mutually attracted to each other, many separations, including marriage, occur before they unite. (*Series:* Daughters of England, 14)
Genre(s): Romance; Domestic Fiction.

◆ 3122. *The Return of the Gypsy.* New York: Putnam, 1985. 352 pp.
Romany Jake, charged with killing someone planning to rape a gypsy girl, goes to the Australian penal colony for seven years while Jessica Frenshaw waits for him. (*Series:* Daughters of England, 12)
Genre(s): Romance.

3123. *Voices in a Haunted Room.* New York: Putnam, 1984. 335 pp.
In the sequel to *Knave of Hearts*, Claudine de Tournville marries one of her stepfather's twin sons although she is attracted to the other. (*Series:* Daughters of England, 11)
Genre(s): Romance; Regency Novel.

Carter, Annee

3124. *The Promise of Your Touch.* New York: Dell, 1997. 352 pp.
Healer Shivahn Armagh goes to Prevot Prison to treat a man charged with treason and scheduled for execution, but when she realizes that he is not the legendary Irish warrior, Griffin, but an Englishman who is not guilty, she, although loyal to Ireland, helps him escape.
Genre(s): Romance.

Cartland, Barbara

◆ 3125. *Love Casts out Fear.* Hampton, NH: Severn House, 1988. 192 pp.
The duke of Wellington and his men help Alecia in France.
Genre(s): Romance.

◆ 3126. *Riding to the Moon.* New York: Everest House, 1982. 158 pp.
A wager that the marquis of Ardsley will become enamoured with a nonaristocratic but well-informed Indira Rowlandson leads them to a steeplechase race.
Genre(s): Regency Novel.

Chapman, Hester W.

3127. *Lucy.* New York: Reynal, 1966. 382 pp.
When Beau Nash transforms a serving maid into a successful actress, she is unhappy with his treatment of her dog.
Genre(s): Romance.

Chase, Loretta

3128. *Isabella.* New York: Walker, 1987. 168 pp.
Isabella Latham, a spinster at 26, comes to London to chaperone her cousins for the season, but since their family fortune is in trade, she does not believe herself worthy of Edward, Earl of Hartleigh.
Genre(s): Regency Novel; Romance.

3129. *Knave's Wager.* New York: Walker, 1990. 238 pp.
A libertine loses a bet that he will be able to seduce one of the season's known prudes, because he falls in love with her.
Genre(s): Regency Novel; Romance.

3130. *The Last Hellion.* New York: Avon, 1998. 384 pp.
A crusading journalist knocks Vere Mallory, last of the Mallory Hellions, into the mud, and he decides to teach her a lesson.
Genre(s): Romance; Regency Novel.

Chernaik, Judith

3131. *Love's Children.* New York: Knopf, 1992. 229 pp.
During one year, Mary Shelley, Clare Clairmont, Harriet Westbrook, and Fanny Goodwin interact with Percy Bysshe Shelley, their husband, former husband, friend, or brother-in-law.
Genre(s): Biographical Fiction.

Chesney, Marion

◆ 3132. *The Adventuress.* New York: St. Martin's, 1987. 161 pp.
Emily Goodenough comes to the rental house at Mayfair, and the servants suspect that she and her uncle are not the gentry that they pretend to be. (*Series:* A House for the Seasons, 5)
Genre(s): Regency Novel; Romance.

◆ 3133. *Animating Maria.* New York: St. Martin's, 1990. 169 pp.
Maria has the proper manners for London society, but the Tribble sisters must reform her pushy parents before they can sponsor her. (*Series:* School for Manners, 5)
Genre(s): Regency Novel; Romance.

◆ 3134. *Back in Society.* New York: St. Martin's, 1994. 152 pp.
As Lady Jane Remney tries to commit suicide, Colonel Sandhurst tries to persuade Lady Fortesque to marry him. (*Series:* Poor Relations, 6)
Genre(s): Romance; Regency Novel.

◆ 3135. *The Banishment.* New York: St. Martin's, 1995. 151 pp.

When Sir William Beverley gambles away the huge and grand estate of Mannerling, Isabella, still unwed after a London season, must wrangle a marriage to the new owner of the family estate. (*Series:* Daughters of Mannerling)
Genre(s): Regency Novel; Romance.

◆ 3136. *Beatrice Goes to Brighton.* New York: St. Martin's, 1991. 151 pp.
Hannah Pym meets Beatrice on her way to Brighton and arranges a marriage for her. (*Series:* Travelling Matchmaker, 4)
Genre(s): Regency Novel; Romance.

◆ 3137. *Belinda Goes to Bath.* New York: St. Martin's, 1991. 155 pp.
While on a stage coach traveling to Bath, Miss Hannah Pym meets an orphaned heiress, Belinda Earle, and when they become unexpected guests at the home of a bachelor marquess, Miss Pym makes her match. (*Series:* Travelling Matchmaker, 2)
Genre(s): Regency Novel; Romance.

◆ 3138. *Colonel Sandhurst to the Rescue.* New York: St. Martin's, 1994. 152 pp.
Frederica Gray stays at a hotel to avoid marrying Lord Bewley, and Colonel Sandhurst hopes to get a ransom from him. (*Series:* Poor Relations, 5)
Genre(s): Love Story; Regency Novel.

◆ 3139. *Daphne.* New York: St. Martin's, 1984. 171 pp.
Daphne, fourth of six sisters, thinks she will marry one man until she finds another lying in the ditch her father made to trap the bishop. (*Series:* Six Sisters, 4)
Genre(s): Romance; Regency Novel.

◆ 3140. *Deborah Goes to Dover.* New York: St. Martin's, 1992. 151 pp.
On a trip to Dover, Miss Pym encounters Lady Deborah Western, disguised as a boy, on her way to a prize fight. (*Series:* Traveling Matchmaker, 5)
Genre(s): Romance; Regency Novel.

◆ 3141. *The Deception.* New York: St. Martin's, 1996. 168 pp.
The Beverley twins, Abigail and Rachel, try to win back a love and their family estate. (*Series:* Daughters of Mannerling)
Genre(s): Regency Novel; Romance.

◆ 3142. *Deirdre and Desire.* New York: St. Martin's, 1984. 206 pp.
Although Deirdre does not want to marry Lord Harry Desire, her father insists, since Lord Harry can help support his interest in hunting and hounds. (*Series:* Six Sisters, 3)
Genre(s): Regency Novel; Romance.

◆ 3143. *Diana the Huntress.* New York: St. Martin's, 1985. 192 pp.
Diana rides horses in disguise, but she falls for a cad while her intended patiently waits for her. (*Series:* Six Sisters, 5)
Genre(s): Regency Novel; Romance.

◆ 3144. *The Dreadful Debutante.* New York: Fawcett, 1995. 181 pp.
Mira, who has always tried to please her father because he wanted a son, goes to London for the season and makes a superb match.
Genre(s): Regency Novel; Romance.

◆ 3145. *Emily Goes to Exeter.* New York: St. Martin's, 1990. 151 pp.
After inheriting a large sum of money, Hannah Pym sheds her housekeeping life for one of travel, and on her first stagecoach trip, she arranges two marriages and organizes those snowed in at an inn. (*Series:* Travelling Matchmaker, 1)
Genre(s): Regency Novel; Romance.

◆ 3146. *Enlightening Delilah.* New York: St. Martin's, 1989. 165 pp.
After a neighbor breaks Delilah Wraxall's heart, she goes to London, and the Tribble sisters plan how to present her to society. (*Series:* School for Manners, 3)
Genre(s): Regency Novel; Romance.

◆ 3147. *Finessing Clarissa.* New York: St. Martin's, 1989. 168 pp.
Clarissa Vevian is especially clumsy, but in London, the Tribble sisters determine to help her. (*Series:* School for Manners, 4)
Genre(s): Regency Novel; Romance.

◆ 3148. *The Folly.* New York: St. Martin's, 1996. 165 pp.
Rachel Beverley, 19, thinks that the new owner of Mannerling is too old, but when she meets him and chastises him for neglecting his two children, she begins to change her mind. (*Series:* Daughters of Mannerling)
Genre(s): Regency Novel; Romance.

◆ 3149. *Frederica in Fashion.* New York: St. Martin's, 1985. 152 pp.
Frederica leaves her female seminary after she hears that her father plans to marry a chambermaid, deciding to become one herself in the home of the Wicked Duke of Pembury, but the duke is not as wicked as he is rumored to be. (*Series:* Six Sisters, 6)
Genre(s): Regency Novel; Romance.

◆ 3150. *Lady Fortescue Steps Out.* New York: St. Martin's, 1992. 152 pp.
Lady Fortescue, distressed at being a poor aristocrat, persuades five others in her condition to join in opening a hotel. (*Series:* Poor Relations, 1)
Genre(s): Regency Novel; Romance.

◆ 3151. *A Marriage of Inconvenience.* Hampton, NH: Severn House, 1997. 184 pp.
Isabella Chadbury must marry for convenience an older Lord Harry, but at least he is also wealthy.
Genre(s): Romance.

◆ 3152. *Marrying Harriet.* New York: St. Martin's, 1990. 167 pp.
Effa and Amy Tribble work to marry off Harriet Brown, daughter of a Methodist minister, and she wants to help

them, so she works to get them married herself. (*Series:* School for Manners, 6)
Genre(s): Regency Novel; Romance.

◆ 3153. *Minerva.* New York: St. Martin's, 1983. 192 pp.
Minerva, oldest of six sisters and two brothers, must rescue the family fortunes by going to London to find a wealthy husband. (*Series:* Six Sisters, 1)
Genre(s): Romance; Regency Novel; Domestic Fiction.

◆ 3154. *The Miser of Mayfair.* New York: St. Martin's, 1986. 167 pp.
Underpaid servants staff a rental house in Mayfair, and when the new tenant is reputed to be a miser, they expect more of the same treatment. (*Series:* A House for the Seasons, 1)
Genre(s): Regency Novel; Romance.

◆ 3155. *Miss Tonks Turns to Crime.* New York: St. Martin's, 1993. 152 pp.
When her hotel needs repair, Miss Tonks decides to steal from her wealthy sister, and she returns with what she needs plus her niece. (*Series:* Poor Relations, 2)
Genre(s): Mystery; Romance; Regency Novel.

◆ 3156. *Mrs Budley Falls from Grace.* New York: St. Martin's, 1993. 152 pp.
Mrs. Budley goes to a relative's home to secure needed objects to pawn for her hotel. (*Series:* Poor Relations, 4)
Genre(s): Regency Novel; Romance.

◆ 3157. *Penelope Goes to Portsmouth.* New York: St. Martin's, 1991. 155 pp.
On her way to Portsmouth, Miss Pym meets Miss Wilkins and Lord Augustus, and she begins her plan to get them together. (*Series:* Travelling Matchmaker, 3)
Genre(s): Regency Novel; Romance.

◆ 3158. *Perfecting Fiona.* New York: St. Martin's, 1989. 168 pp.
The Tribble sisters rescue Fiona, who seems perfect in manners and in appearance, and the Tribbles must discover her faults before getting her married off. (*Series:* The School for Manners, 2)
Genre(s): Regency Novel; Romance.

◆ 3159. *Plain Jane.* New York: St. Martin's, 1986. 171 pp.
Mrs. Hart rents a house, thought to be haunted, in Mayfair for her daughter, Euphemia, and brings her youngest daughter, considered too plain to attract admirers, but she makes the best catch and appeases the ghost. (*Series:* A House for the Seasons, 2)
Genre(s): Regency Novel; Romance.

◆ 3160. *Rainbird's Revenge.* New York: St. Martin's, 1988. 165 pp.
The servants at 67 Clarges Street in London have saved their money to buy a pub, but when they hear that the house's owner, the Duke of Pelham, is returning from Spain, they decide to stay and get revenge on his financial manager who has cheated them for years. (*Series:* A House for the Seasons, 6)
Genre(s): Regency Novel; Romance.

◆ 3161. *Rake's Progress.* New York: St. Martin's, 1987. 169 pp.
The servants at 67 Clarges Street have banded together to save money to buy a pub when Lord Guy Carlton arrives home as an invalid after the Napoleonic Wars. (*Series:* A House for the Seasons, 4)
Genre(s): Regency Novel; Romance.

◆ 3162. *Refining Felicity.* New York: St. Martin's, 1988. 167 pp.
Amy and Effie Tribble, expecting an inheritance that has not materialized, advertise to become governesses. (*Series:* The School for Manners, 1)
Genre(s): Regency Novel; Romance.

◆ 3163. *Sir Philip's Folly.* New York: St. Martin's, 1993. 148 pp.
Hotel co-owners with Sir Philip Sommerville want his annoying guest to leave while they help another guest find a husband. (*Series:* Poor Relations, 3)
Genre(s): Regency Novel; Romance.

◆ 3164. *The Taming of Annabelle.* New York: St. Martin's, 1983. 192 pp.
Annabelle falls in love with her older sister Minerva's intended, and when she realizes that Stephen loves Minerva, she settles for second best, Peter, who must use his own wiles to convince her of her luck. (*Series:* Six Sisters, 2)
Genre(s): Regency Novel; Romance.

◆ 3165. *The Wicked Godmother.* New York: St. Martin's, 1987. 166 pp.
When Harriet Metcalf goes to London to help launch two 18-year-old heiresses, a notorious rake decides to woo her. (*Series:* A House for the Seasons, 3)
Genre(s): Regency Novel; Romance.

◆ 3166. *Yvonne Goes to York.* New York: St. Martin's, 1992. 151 pp.
Hannah Pym, a matchmaker, travels in a coach accompanied by Yvonne, a French emigrant posing as an Englishman, and by an English lord with whom she falls in love. (*Series:* Travelling Matchmaker, 6)
Genre(s): Regency Novel; Romance.

Chester, Deborah

3167. *A Love So Wild.* New York: Coward-McCann, 1980. 270 pp.
The heroine grows up in Newgate Prison before falling in love.
Genre(s): Regency Novel; Romance.

Clare, Cathleen

3168. *Clarissa.* New York: Avon, 1993. 250 pp.
An eligible bachelor decides to marry Clarissa, an unattractive paid companion, and after he takes her to London, she blossoms into a lovely woman who saves her husband from Napoleon's spies.
Genre(s): Regency Novel; Romance.

Claybourne, Casey

3169. *A Ghost of a Chance.* New York: Jove, 1996. 317 pp.
Daphne's mother dies on her wedding day, and her new husband leaves without explaining, but Daphne's mother's ghost becomes involved in Daphne's life.
Genre(s): Regency Novel; Fantastic Literature; Romance.

Cleeve, Brian Talbot

3170. *Judith.* New York: Coward-McCann, 1978. 299 pp.
When Judith's wealthy relatives plan for her to marry, she escapes into a madhouse where she is tortured, and when released, she must beg in London's worst slums before reuniting with her true love, a smuggler who has become a doctor.
Genre(s): Regency Novel; Romance.

3171. *Kate.* New York: Coward-McCann, 1977. 345 pp.
Kate Harriott, orphaned during the French Revolution, escapes to her native land of Britain, but since she has an accent, a criminal blackmails her into working for him before she makes a friend who helps her when she is accused of treason.
Genre(s): Regency Novel; Romance.

3172. *Sara.* New York: Coward-McCann, 1976. 384 pp.
In the 19th century, Sara goes to England when she is eight, after her Spanish village is ransacked in the Peninsular War, grows up in an Essex village, and after her supporters die, she runs off to London.
Genre(s): Regency Novel; Romance; War Story.

Clitheroe, Susan

3173. *The Devil's Protection.* New York: St. Martin's, 1995. 224 pp.
Geneva Hartwell, 20, becomes an heiress at the death of her uncle, but she must have a guardian for six more months, and after she becomes entranced with Lord Vance, someone tells her that her stepcousin guardian, Boeman, plans to kidnap and marry her for her money.
Genre(s): Regency Novel; Romance.

Collier, G. K.

◆ 3174. *The Gamester.* New York: St. Martin's, 1994. 303 pp.
James Farendon saves Lord Justin Trevingham from death in an Italian gambling establishment, but when James later arrives in England pretending to be a count, Justin's sister suspects his guise.
Genre(s): Regency Novel; Romance.

Collins, Wilkie

3175. *The Moonstone.* 1868. New York: Knopf, 1992. 473 pp.
When the Moonstone, a huge diamond from India, disappears, Miss Verinder believes that her lover is the thief, but others are also suspected.
Genre(s): Romance; Mystery.

Comstock, Mary Chase

3176. *Fortune's Mistress.* New York: Zebra, 1996. 304 pp.
Marianne Gardiner, socially ruined because she becomes pregnant, leaves London for Cornwall to have her child and meets someone who also has a past.
Genre(s): Regency Novel; Romance.

3177. *A Midsummer's Magic.* New York: Zebra, 1994. 219 pp.
Countess of Trevalyen, Hippolyta, wants to continue her magic studies, but many things interfere before Julian St. Ives helps.
Genre(s): Regency Novel; Romance.

Condon, Richard

3178. *The Abandoned Woman.* New York: Dial, 1977. 317 pp.
During the 26 years of their marriage before she goes on trial for adultery, Princess Caroline and George IV almost never see each other, but they spend time investigating the other's actions.
Genre(s): Biographical Fiction.

Constant, Jan

3179. *The Only Hope.* New York: Ballantine, 1994. 236 pp.
Clarissa Dysart begs her aunt, previously unknown to her, to save her from a marriage, and Aunt Amy becomes Clarissa's companion contrary to the desires of Clarissa's brother.
Genre(s): Regency Novel; Romance.

Coogan, Beatrice

3180. *The Big Wind.* 1969. Boulder, CO: Roberts, 1995. 591 pp.
In Irish girl from a family of nobility falls in love with an Irish peasant during the potato famine.
Genre(s): Domestic Fiction; Love Story.

Cookson, Catherine

3181. *The Girl.* New York: Morrow, 1977. 306 pp.
After Hannah's mother takes her to Matthew's home before dying in 1850, Hannah must put up with Matthew's shrewish wife and a brutish husband before they die, which allows her to find happiness.
Genre(s): Domestic Fiction.

3182. *The Mallen Streak.* New York: Dutton, 1973. 282 pp.
Thomas Mallen loses his estate to his creditors and renews acquaintance with his illegitimate son until they cause disaster for Mallen's two wards and their governess.
Genre(s): Domestic Fiction; Family Saga.

◆ 3183. *The Maltese Angel.* New York: Simon and Schuster, 1992. 479 pp.
The woman Hayward Gibson chooses not to marry wrecks his contented life with malicious retaliation.
Genre(s): Love Story; Domestic Fiction.

◆ 3184. *Our John Willie.* Indianapolis: Bobbs-Merrill, 1974. 191 pp.
In 1852, a mine disaster orphans David Hallady and his deaf and mute younger brother John Willie, but a kindly woman helps them overcome their adversities.
Genre(s): Domestic Fiction.

◆ 3185. *The Rag Nymph.* New York: Bantam, 1991. 350 pp.
Abandoned Millie, seven, goes to live with Raggie Aggie in 1854, a rag woman who changes her way of life to protect Millie.
Genre(s): Love Story; Bildungsroman (Coming of Age); Romance.

3186. *Tilly.* New York: Morrow, 1980. 372 pp.
Tilly becomes mistress of the manor dominating Durham County, and she raises herself from the stigma of an underprivileged Victorian child.
Genre(s): Domestic Fiction.

3187. *Tilly Alone.* New York: Morrow, 1982. 265 pp.
In the sequel to *Tilly Wed*, Tilly returns to England after her husband's death with her son and her husband's half-breed daughter.
Genre(s): Domestic Fiction.

3188. *Tilly Wed.* New York: Morrow, 1981. 310 pp.
After Tilly's lover Mark dies, his son comes to settle the estate and takes Tilly back to Texas with him as his wife in the sequel to *Tilly*.
Genre(s): Domestic Fiction.

3189. *The Upstart.* New York: Simon and Schuster, 1998. 352 pp.
Although a wealthy tradesman buys a home with 34 rooms in it, neither his children nor his servants will give him the respect he thinks he deserves.
Genre(s): Domestic Fiction.

◆ 3190. *The Whip.* New York: Summit, 1983. 392 pp.
After the deaths of her parents, Emma Molinero must leave the circus life to live with her improverished grandmother, but she makes the best of her situation.
Genre(s): Domestic Fiction.

Cordell, Alexander

3191. *The Fire People.* London: Hodder and Stoughton, 1972. 381 pp.
Miners in Wales during the early 19th century debate chartism and other ills before a radical among them is hanged for participating in a riot.
Genre(s): Biographical Fiction.

3192. *Song of the Earth.* New York: Simon and Schuster, 1970. 352 pp.
In the 1850s, Welsh coal miners battle their English employers for their dignity.
Genre(s): Political Fiction.

Cornwell, Bernard

3193. *Killer's Wake.* New York: Putnam, 1989. 317 pp.
John Rosendale returns to his family home for his mother's funeral only to face false accusations of theft.
Genre(s): Sea Story; Adventure Story.

3194. *Sharpe's Regiment.* New York: Viking, 1986. 301 pp.
In the sequel to *Sharpe's Honour*, Sharpe returns to England where members of his prestigious South Essex regiment are illegally selling goods.
Genre(s): War Story.

Costain, Thomas Bertram

3195. *The Tontine.* Garden City, NY: Doubleday, 1955. 2 vols.
The stories of two English families begin during the Napoleonic Wars when they buy into an insurance lottery called the Great Waterloo Tontine.
Genre(s): Family Saga; Mystery.

Coulter, Catherine

3196. *The Heiress Bride.* New York: Putnam, 1992. 303 pp.
Sinjun (*Series:* Joan) spots Colin Kinross, Earl of Ashburnham in London in 1807, and decides to marry him and go to his castle in Scotland, where she finds hostile stepchildren and neighbors but friendly ghosts. (*Series:* Brides, 3)
Genre(s): Regency Novel; Romance.

3197. *The Hellion Bride.* New York: Jove, 1992. 378 pp.
Ryder Sherbrooke goes to Jamaica to rescue the family plantation from an islander and returns with his niece and nephew. (*Series:* Brides, 2)
Genre(s): Regency Novel; Romance.

3198. *Moonspun Magic.* 1988. Hampton, NH: Severn House, 1997. 401 pp.
In 1813, Victoria Abermarle flees from nasty Baron Damien Carstairs and goes to his loving twin.
Genre(s): Romance.

◆ 3199. *The Nightingale Legacy.* New York: Putnam, 1994. 384 pp.
After a murder in 1814, the orphan Catherine Dewent-Jones, 19, escapes from her unworthy guardian and falls in love with Lord Chilton. (*Series:* Legacy, 2)
Genre(s): Love Story; Romance; Regency Novel.

3200. *The Sherbrooke Bride.* New York: Jove, 1992. 340 pp.
When Douglas Sherbrooke, Earl of Northcliffe, goes to France on a secret mission and has to send his cousin to be his proxy in his impending marriage, his cousin falls in love with the bride and her sister becomes Sherbrooke's wife. (*Series:* Brides, 1)
Genre(s): Regency Novel; Romance.

◆ 3201. *The Valentine Legacy.* New York: Putnam, 1995. 354 pp.

When Jessie Warfield goes to England and becomes a nanny, her love comes to get her although she has previously refused to marry him. (*Series:* Legacy, 3)
Genre(s): Romance; Regency Novel; Love Story.

3202. *The Wild Baron.* New York: Jove, 1997. 384 pp.
Commoner Suzannah Hawlworth tells Rohan Carrington that she is his late brother George's widow and that people are threatening her because they believe that she has a valuable map, so Rohan marries her and discovers that her locket has both a map and a key to a magical chalice.
Genre(s): Regency Novel; Romance.

◆ 3203. *The Wyndham Legacy.* New York: Putnam, 1994. 320 pp.
Josephina Cochrain, illegitimate daughter of the Earl of Chase, becomes both legitimate and an heiress when her father dies, but she must fulfill certain requirements. (*Series:* Legacy, 1)
Genre(s): Love Story; Regency Novel; Romance.

Crace, Jim

3204. *Signals of Distress.* New York: Farrar, Straus and Giroux, 1995. 275 pp.
In 1837, Aymer Smith goes to Wherrytown, a remote coastal town in England, and says that his company will no longer need the town's kelp for its soap, but while there, he becomes attracted to two young women and emancipates an American slave from a shipwreck.
Genre(s): Sea Story.

Creasey, John

3205. *The Masters of Bow Street.* New York: Simon and Schuster, 1974. 507 pp.
One family leads the initiative for establishing the London Police Force, which later becomes Scotland Yard.

Crichton, Michael

◆ 3206. *The Great Train Robbery.* New York: Knopf, 1975. 266 pp.
In 1855, a London mobster and his gang steal 12,000 pounds of gold in transport for British troops in the Crimea.
Genre(s): Mystery.

Crow, Donna Fletcher

3207. *Where Love Begins.* Wheaton, IL: Crossway, 1995. 224 pp.
In 1824, Sir Brandley Hillard, a disabled scholar, meets Elinor Silbert in England where the evangelist Charles Simeon influences them both. (*Series:* Cambridge Chronicles, 3)
Genre(s): Christian Fiction; Love Story.

Crowley, Elaine

3208. *Kilgoran.* Garden City, NY: Doubleday, 1985. 351 pp.
After Katy, daughter of a coachman and gatekeeper at the Irish Kilgoran estate, marries, she has six children, but

her husband spends all their wages for alcohol when the potatoes fail.
Genre(s): Domestic Fiction.

Cummings, Monette

◆ 3209. *The Beauty of Her Daughter.* New York: Walker, 1985. 144 pp.
Lady Alice refuses to acknowledge her daughter Priscilla's existence for fear that her age will be emphasized and that she will lose her young suitor.
Genre(s): Regency Novel; Romance.

Darcy, Clare

◆ 3210. *Allegra.* New York: Walker, 1975. 278 pp.
After her father dies and leaves them penniless, Allegra takes her sister to Brussels and finds work before the distant cousin who inherited her father's land arrives.
Genre(s): Regency Novel; Romance.

3211. *Caroline and Julia.* New York: Walker, 1982. 185 pp.
Julia Devanter, a London actress, looks after orphan Caroline Deveraux before Caroline discovers that she may have inherited money from her late rich uncle.
Genre(s): Regency Novel; Romance.

3212. *Cressida.* New York: Walker, 1977. 217 pp.
Cressida's sweetheart becomes engaged to someone else out of spite after they fight, and then Cressida must save his new love from a rake.
Genre(s): Regency Novel; Romance.

3213. *Elyza.* New York: Walker, 1976. 240 pp.
Elyza runs away from a bad marriage, and after meeting a stranger, falls in love with him.
Genre(s): Regency Novel; Romance.

3214. *Eugenia.* New York: Walker, 1977. 219 pp.
Eugenia rescues a long-lost cousin from the Bow Street Runners, proves his legitimacy, and marries him.
Genre(s): Regency Novel; Romance.

3215. *Georgina.* New York: Walker, 1971. 274 pp.
Sent to Ireland in disgrace for refusing to marry a wealthy young man, Georgina meets Shannon, holder of the family's lands, and in her attempts to make him socially acceptable to those around them, she falls in love with him.
Genre(s): Regency Novel; Romance; Love Story.

3216. *Gwendolen.* New York: Walker, 1978. 216 pp.
When Lady Otilia Quarters's three daughters refuse their eligible suitors, she is perturbed, but their choices allow the right matches to ultimately occur.
Genre(s): Regency Novel; Romance.

◆ 3217. *Lady Pamela.* New York: Walker, 1975. 280 pp.
When a memorandum disappears from Pamela's grandfather's Foreign Office dispatch in Regency England, Pamela believes that her brother has stolen it, and she disguises herself as a lady's maid to follow him and find it.
Genre(s): Regency Novel; Romance.

◆ 3218. *Letty.* New York: Walker, 1980. 254 pp.
Lettice, a runaway, joins forces with an old baron and a gambler in Vienna to open a gaming house.
Genre(s): Regency Novel; Romance.

3219. *Lydia.* New York: Walker, 1973. 255 pp.
Lydia Leyland comes from America to London for the season and confesses to the first nobleman she meets that she hopes to marry well so that the family can recoup its fortune.
Genre(s): Regency Novel; Romance.

3220. *Regina.* New York: Walker, 1976. 217 pp.
Regina, strong and independent, becomes fretful with a cousin whom she sponsors for the season who wants to marry the wrong man.
Genre(s): Regency Novel; Romance.

3221. *Victoire.* New York: Walker, 1974. 284 pp.
Victoire, young and innocent, must participate, at her uncle's forcing, in the blackmailing of Lord Tarn, but she decides to help him in the end.
Genre(s): Regency Novel; Romance.

Davenport, Gwen

3222. *Time and Chance.* New York: Donald I. Fine, 1993. 327 pp.
A wealthy British family faces many changes when the railroad comes to their area, and Victoria ascends the throne of England.
Genre(s): Family Saga.

Delderfield, R. F.

3223. *God Is an Englishman.* New York: Simon and Schuster, 1970. 687 pp.
Adam Swann returns to England from India in 1857 and marries Henrietta Rawlinson.
Genre(s): Domestic Fiction.

Deveraux, Jude

3224. *Counterfeit Lady.* New York: Pocket Books, 1984. 375 pp.
French Revolution refugee Nicole Courtalain becomes Bianca Maleson's maid in England, and when Bianca's Virginia fiancé, Clay sends his men to kidnap her, they mistakenly take Nicole, who marries Clay.
Genre(s): Romance; Domestic Fiction; War Story.

3225. *Lost Lady.* New York: Pocket Books, 1985. 336 pp.
In London, Travis Stanford saves Regan Weston from ruffians, and when he defiles her virginity, he honorably marries her and takes her to his Virginia plantation.
Genre(s): Romance.

Devon, Marian

3226. *Deck the Halls.* New York: Ballantine, 1995. 185 pp.
Since Sir Jervis Brougham does not expect to live for another Christmas, he makes sure that his whole family comes to the estate for the holidays, and after some un-

usual pairings, he decides to live long enough to see what happens.
Genre(s): Regency Novel; Romance.

3227. *Lord Harlequin.* New York: Fawcett, 1994. 187 pp.
Falsely accused of murder, Lord Worth hides as an actor in a pantomime troupe and ends up on a country estate performing in front of his friends.
Genre(s): Regency Novel; Romance.

3228. *Miss Kendall Sets Her Cap.* New York: Fawcett Columbine, 1996. 202 pp.
Freddie Kendall, a vicar's granddaughter, decides that she wants to marry Lord Thorpe, although she does not think she has a chance until something unexpected happens in his library.
Genre(s): Regency Novel; Romance.

Diamond, Jacqueline

3229. *The Day-Dreaming Lady.* New York: Walker, 1985. 212 pp.
Sarah Rowdon imagines wonderful adventures to escape from her loneliness and her father's gambling, which undermines her attempt to attract Lord Broadmoor's interest.
Genre(s): Regency Novel; Romance; Love Story.

3230. *Lady in Disguise.* New York: Walker, 1982. 171 pp.
When a young woman meets a nobleman, they mistake identities but eventually get together.
Genre(s): Regency Novel; Romance.

3231. *Song for a Lady.* New York: Walker, 1983. 181 pp.
Deborah Martin goes to London to be with her widowed cousin, and while the cousin tries to snare another husband, Deborah auditions for a traveling opera company.
Genre(s): Regency Novel; Romance.

Dickens, Charles

3232. *Bleak House.* 1853. New York: Oxford, 1996. 976 pp.
Esther Summerson is the ward of Mr. Jarndyce whose case in Chancery Court seems to have no end.
Genre(s): Legal Story.

◆ 3233. *David Copperfield.* 1850. New York: Oxford, 1950. 878 pp.
David Copperfield, whose stepfather casts him out after the death of David's mother, lives through trials and tribulations, first at a boys' school and then as a young man in London before he goes to live with his great-aunt and eventually finds happiness.
Genre(s): Domestic Fiction.

◆ 3234. *Great Expectations.* New York: Tor, 1998. 544 pp.
Pip, a blacksmith's young nephew, falls deeply in love with the haughty and mysterious Estella, who does not re-

ciprocate his feelings, but their lives remain intertwined through the rise and fall of his fortunes.

3235. **Hard Times.** 1854. New York: Penguin, 1995. 318 pp.
Raised during the rise of industry, Louisa, whose poor choices in later life result from too practical an upbringing, cares nothing about what happens to her.
Genre(s): Domestic Fiction; Political Fiction.

3236. **Little Dorrit.** 1857. New York: Knopf, 1992. 836 pp.
Little Dorrit grows up in Marshalsea prison, where her father is confined for his debts, and she helps to feed the family with her needlework until her father receives an inheritance when she is in her teens, and more problems ensue.

3237. **Martin Chuzzlewit.** 1844. New York: Knopf, 1994. 851 pp.
Martin Chuzzlewit's wealthy grandfather forces him to emigrate to America after the selfish Martin falls in love with the wrong girl; upon his return, Martin seems to prove his worth.
Genre(s): Adventure Story.

3238. **Nicholas Nickleby.** 1839. New York: Knopf, 1993. 843 pp.
After Nicholas Nickleby's father dies bankrupt, Nicholas becomes the unhappy ward of his uncle, a moneylender, and survives many adventures before finding happiness.
Genre(s): Bildungsroman (Coming of Age).

3239. **The Old Curiosity Shop.** 1841. New York: Clarendon, 1997. 552 pp.
After Little Nell's grandfather loses his money gambling, and they roam the country as beggars, even more tragedy ensues.

◆ 3240. **Oliver Twist.** 1838. Philadelphia, PA: Courage, 1996. 478 pp.
Rogues train Oliver Twist to become a pickpocket, but he strives to escape from crime and the workhouse to which he is subject.

3241. **Our Mutual Friend.** 1859. New York: Knopf, 1994. 832 pp.
John Harmon will inherit a fortune if he marries a girl whose personality has been affected by her wealth, and friends and events conspire to prove her true worth.

Disch, Thomas M., and Charles Naylor

3242. **Neighboring Lives.** New York: Scribner's, 1981. 294 pp.
Artists and writers including Carlyle, Jewsbury, the Rosettis, Swinburne, and Meredith live in London's Chelsea section from the 1830s to the 1870s.
Genre(s): Domestic Fiction.

Drummond, June

3243. **The Bluestocking.** New York: David and Charles, 1986. 268 pp.
After her father's death, Davina Wakeford decides to sell the family heirloom, the Rigborough Missal, to pay his

debts, while Lucas returns to Rowan House next door to claim the inheritance.
Genre(s): Regency Novel; Romance.

◆ 3244. **The Impostor.** New York: St. Martin's, 1993. 237 pp.
Disguised Hector Finch must become tutor for an 11-year-old boy when he loses a bet with his brother, but he becomes involved both in a smuggling plot and with his employer's niece.
Genre(s): Regency Novel; Romance.

3245. **The Unsuitable Miss Pelham.** New York: Victor Gollancz, 1990. 272 pp.
When Lord Linslade, a very eligible bachelor, falls in love with Lucilla Pelham, he ends the family feud which began when her cousin and his sister tried to elope 15 years earlier.
Genre(s): Regency Novel; Romance.

Du Maurier, Daphne

3246. **Mary Anne.** Garden City, NY: Doubleday, 1954. 351 pp.
A young woman, Mary Anne (Thompson) Clarke, realizes that the way to succeed is to become a wealthy man's mistress.
Genre(s): Biographical Fiction; Love Story.

3247. **My Cousin Rachel.** Garden City, NY: Doubleday, 1952. 348 pp.
The charming widow of Philip's uncle comes to Cornwall from Italy, but soon Philip suspects she might have poisoned his uncle.
Genre(s): Mystery.

Dunn, Carola

◆ 3248. **Angel.** New York: Walker, 1984. 199 pp.
Lady Evangelina Brenthaven's beauty earns her the name of Angel, but her impudence makes her decide to visit her cousins in disguise as Miss Brand where she falls in love with an earl, also disguised.
Genre(s): Regency Novel; Romance.

◆ 3249. **The Black Sheep's Daughter.** New York: Walker, 1989. 210 pp.
Teresa Danville goes from Costa Rica to London, where she is more disturbed by society's ways than she was by poisonous snakes and jaguars, to look for a husband and buyers for her father's coffee.
Genre(s): Regency Novel; Romance.

3250. **The Frog Earl.** New York: Walker, 1992. 208 pp.
When his older brother dies, Simon Hurst must assume the responsibilities of the first born including going London for the season, where he falls in love with one who ignores him.
Genre(s): Regency Novel; Romance.

3251. **Lady in the Briars.** New York: Walker, 1990. 209 pp.

Rebecca Nuthall escapes her uncle for London and becomes involved with the Graylin family's intrigues after meeting Lord John Danville at their home.
Genre(s): Regency Novel; Romance.

3252. *Lord Iverbrook's Heir.* New York: Walker, 1986. 190 pp.
After Lord Hugh Iverbrook returns from Jamaica, he takes his heir, orphaned nephew Peter, five, from his brother's late wife, and the two begin a family feud.
Genre(s): Regency Novel; Romance.

◆ 3253. *Miss Hartwell's Dilemma.* New York: Walker, 1988. 224 pp.
When neither Claire nor Lizzie Sutton have attracted suitors, the older one guides the younger through her London season, and both succeed in their goals.
Genre(s): Regency Novel; Romance.

3254. *Miss Jacobson's Journey.* New York: Walker, 1992. 216 pp.
Miss Miriam Jacobson refuses to marry the Talmudic scholar chosen by a matchmaker and instead goes to Europe with her uncle, where she becomes involved in a plot to carry gold bars to Wellington's troops in Spain.
Genre(s): Romance; Adventure Story.

◆ 3255. *Two Corinthians.* New York: Walker, 1990. 217 pp.
In the sequel to *Miss Hartwell's Dilemma*, Bertram, Lord Pomeroy, and George Winterbourne fall in love with the Sutton sisters, Claire and Lizzie.
Genre(s): Regency Novel; Romance.

Dupre, Catherine

3256. *Gentleman's Child.* London: Collins, 1980. 360 pp.
While working on a farm, Miss Liddell meets a young noble who falls in love with her.
Genre(s): Romance.

Eastwood, Gail

3257. *The Captain's Dilemma.* New York: Signet, 1995. 222 pp.
Merissa Prichard decides not to marry the possessive Harlan Gatesby, and when she meets Captain Alexandre Valmont, an escaped French prisoner-of-war, she knows why.
Genre(s): Regency Novel; Romance.

3258. *The Lady From Spain.* New York: New American Library, 1997. 220 pp.
When a Spanish lady appears in a Wiltshire town asking about one of the residents, Lord Danebridge, a government official, follows her.
Genre(s): Romance; Regency Novel.

3259. *The Persistent Earl.* New York: New American Library, 1995. 220 pp.
After her husband dies in a scandalous situation, Phoebe, Lady Brodfield, stays in seclusion, but when the wounded Earl of Devenham arrives, she nurses him, and her life changes.
Genre(s): Regency Novel; Romance.

Eccles, Frank

3260. *The Mutiny Run.* New York: St. Martin's, 1994. 298 pp.
While maintaining a blockade against France, the British navy faces a mutiny at home, and Captain Brewster's HMS *Adamant* and an allied Russian ship must keep the French at bay while other ships return to England.
Genre(s): Sea Story; War Story.

Edelman, Maurice

3261. *Disraeli in Love.* New York: Stein and Day, 1972. 417 pp.
Disraeli survives debt, unhappy love affairs, anti-Semitism, and extravagance while forming his political philosophy.
Genre(s): Biographical Fiction; Political Fiction.

3262. *Disraeli Rising.* New York: Stein and Day, 1975. 348 pp.
In the sequel to *Disraeli in Love*, Disraeli advances in his political party and becomes the Chancellor of the Exchequer, against the background of Victorian England.
Genre(s): Biographical Fiction; Political Fiction.

Edgeworth, Maria

3263. *Castle Rackrent.* 1800. New York: Oxford, 1982. 200 pp.
Thady Quirk, an old Irish steward, tells about the various masters who have run Castle Rackrent during the family's declining fortunes.
Genre(s): Domestic Fiction.

3264. *Ennui.* London: J. Johnson, 1809. 400 pp.
Families become involved in the Irish Revolution of 1798 against the British.
Genre(s): War Story.

Edghill, Rosemary

◆ 3265. *The Ill-Bred Bride.* New York: St. Martin's, 1990. 288 pp.
Impoverished Lord Hanford meets middle-class Susannah, and since each needs what the other has, they marry for convenience before falling in love.
Genre(s): Regency Novel; Romance.

3266. *Turkish Delight: Or, The Earl and the Houri.* New York: St. Martin's, 1987. 263 pp.
Lady Louisa Darwen, 23, arrives in England after having lived in a Turkish harem for a few years, and she meets Gervase, Earl of Coldmeece, the conceited head of the family.
Genre(s): Regency Novel; Romance.

3267. *Two of a Kind.* New York: St. Martin's, 1970. 281 pp.
The Marquess of Barham's abominable reputation follows him to Miss Juliet Fonthill who avoids him as long as possible before falling in love.
Genre(s): Regency Novel; Romance.

Edwards, Anne

3268. *Haunted Summer.* New York: Coward-McCann, 1972. 278 pp.

Mary Shelley relates the experiences of herself, her husband, Lord Byron, his pregnant mistress Claire, and the physician Polidori during the summer of 1816.

Genre(s): Biographical Fiction.

Eliot, George

3269. *Adam Bede.* 1859. New York: Oxford, 1996. 598 pp.

Adam Bede loves Hetty, who is tried and transported for unintentionally killing her child by the local squire, and eventually, Adam finds happiness with Dinah Morris, a Methodist preacher who helps Hetty through her ordeal.

3270. *Felix Holt, the Radical.* 1866. New York: Penguin, 1995. 544 pp.

In 1832, Harold Transome arrives from the East to claim his inheritance and runs as a Radical candidate in strong contrast to Felix Holt, passionate supporter of workers and their futures.

Genre(s): Political Fiction; Love Story.

3271. *Middlemarch.* 1872. New York: Oxford, 1997. 849 pp.

Set against backdrop of small town middle-class values, idealistic, wealthy Dorothea Brooke marries badly, and an equally high-minded Dr. Lydgate embarks on an ill-considered marriage with the materialistic Rosamund Vincy.

Genre(s): Domestic Fiction; Bildungsroman (Coming of Age).

3272. *The Mill on the Floss.* 1860. New York: Oxford, 1996. 529 pp.

St. Ogg, a small town, is the main setting for the difficult relations of a brother and sister, once closely tied, and an unworthy lover.

Genre(s): Domestic Fiction.

3273. *Silas Marner.* 1861. New York: Penguin, 1996. 297 pp.

Silas Marner, unjustly accused of theft, finds redemption in the love for a foundling child.

Genre(s): Domestic Fiction.

Ellingson, Marnie

3274. *Dolly Blanchard's Fortune.* New York: Walker, 1983. 189 pp.

Dolly, an heiress, loves a poor man who believes that he loves someone else, but he eventually realizes his mistake.

Genre(s): Regency Novel; Romance.

3275. *The Wicked Marquis.* New York: Walker, 1982. 200 pp.

Esme Leonardo tries to save her handsome cousin from an arranged marriage with a young woman she does not like.

Genre(s): Regency Novel; Romance.

Elliott, Elizabeth

3276. *Scoundrel.* New York: Bantam, 1995. 352 pp.

Lady Lillian Walters, an intelligent cryptologist, becomes indispensable to the British against the French, while the Duke of Remmington protects her.

Genre(s): Regency Novel; Romance.

Enoch, Suzanne

3277. *Angel's Devil.* New York: Avon, 1995. 183 pp.

Because Simon Talbott wants to marry immediately, he decides to frighten his future in-laws by having his cousin, the Marquis of Abbonley, seem interested in Simon's own fiancée, but the plan works almost too well.

Genre(s): Regency Novel; Romance.

Epton, Nina Consuelo

3278. *The Burning Heart.* London: Macdonald and Jane's, 1974. 280 pp.

The Honorable Mrs. Jane Digby-Medjeul, a 19th-century courtesan, becomes enamored with travel, marries Bedouin Sheik Medjeul, and settles down in Damascus.

Genre(s): Biographical Fiction.

Ewing, Jean R.

3279. *Rogue's Reward.* New York: Zebra, 1995. 250 pp.

Lady Eleanor Acton tries to foil the schemes of her best friend's illegitimate stepbrother, but the stepbrother's honor makes her fall in love instead.

Genre(s): Regency Novel; Romance.

3280. *Virtue's Reward.* New York: Zebra, 1995. 250 pp.

To save Helena Trethaerin from making a terrible marriage, Captain Richard Acton marries her himself and becomes a target for murder.

Genre(s): Regency Novel; Romance.

Fairchild, Elisabeth

3281. *The Love Knot.* New York: Signet, 1995. 220 pp.

Aurora Ramsay wants a rich husband to help her save the family estate from her gambling brother, and she offers to teach an art connoisseur land management in return for assisting her in finding a suitable mate.

Genre(s): Regency Novel; Romance.

3282. *The Rakehell's Reform.* New York: Signet, 1997. 224 pp.

When Jack Ramsay loses the family fortune at cards, he crashes Selina Preston's ball merely to play the cello, and she realizes that he has worthwhile qualities.

Genre(s): Regency Novel; Musical Fiction.

Falkirk, Richard

3283. *Beau Blackstone.* New York: Stein and Day, 1974. 224 pp.

Edmund Blackstone, Bow Street Runner, helps to stop an attempt to wreck the first railroad engine to operate in England during the early 19th century.
Genre(s): Mystery.

3284. *Blackstone.* New York: Stein and Day, 1973. 239 pp.
Edmund Blackstone of the Bow Street Runners, realizes that his new assignment in the 1820s to protect Princess Alexandrina Victoria involves a number of unexpected threats.
Genre(s): Adventure Story.

3285. *Blackstone and the Scourge of Europe.* New York: Stein and Day, 1974. 192 pp.
Richard Blackstone of the Bow Street Runners becomes involved in a plot to stop Napoleon's escape from St. Helena in a primitive submarine.
Genre(s): Mystery.

Farnol, Jeffery

3286. *Heritage Perilous.* New York: McBride, 1946. 312 pp.
A soldier returns to England to claim his inherited title and its fortune.
Genre(s): Regency Novel; Romance.

3287. *The High Adventure.* Boston: Little, Brown, 1926. 376 pp.
In the southeast of England, a boxer becomes involved in a conspiracy.
Genre(s): Adventure Story; Sports Fiction.

3288. *The Ninth Earl.* London: Marston, 1950. 298 pp.
Jasper Shrig, the Bow Street Runner, tries to solve a crime.
Genre(s): Regency Novel; Romance; Mystery.

3289. *The Waif of the River.* London: Diploma, 1974. 294 pp.
In London, Jasper Shrig recruits an orphan to work for him.
Genre(s): Regency Novel; Romance; Mystery.

Feather, Jane

3290. *Virtue.* New York: Doubleday, 1993. 368 pp.
After gamester Judith Davenport becomes involved with Marcus, Lord Carrington, they marry, and he is determined that she will stop gaming and become a respectable wife.
Genre(s): Regency Novel; Romance.

Ferguson, Jo Ann

3291. *A Model Marriage.* New York: Zebra, 1998. 211 pp.
An artist wants beautiful Antonia Locke to model in the nude, but when she adamantly refuses, he plots to reach his goal by persuading her to marry him.
Genre(s): Romance; Regency Novel.

Fitzgerald, Amber

3292. *The Suspicious Heart.* Garden City, NY: Doubleday, 1981. 192 pp.
Lydia Wellington Radford decides to share her inheritance with her disinherited brother, but first she must find him and in doing so endures a series of mishaps along the way.
Genre(s): Regency Novel; Romance.

Fitzgerald, Ellen

3293. *Ardent Apparitions.* New York: Walker, 1992. 176 pp.
Arabella Arden resents having to spend time with her deceased mother's family at their Yorkshire castle until a distant cousin, Sir Francis, and the resident ghosts interest her.
Genre(s): Regency Novel; Romance.

Flanagan, Thomas

◆ 3294. *The Year of the French.* New York: Holt, Rinehart and Winston, 1979. 516 pp.
In 1798, the French arrive in Ireland ready to help overthrow the British, but Lord Cornwallis is too well organized to be defeated.
Award(s): National Book Critics Circle Award.
Genre(s): War Story.

Fleming, Georgina

3295. *The Light to My Darkness.* New York: Century, 1992. 358 pp.
Vagabonds capture Bethany Horsham and take her to their secret hideout in Dartmoor where she falls in love with one of their married members before being unjustly accused of a crime.
Genre(s): Romance.

Forester, C. S.

◆ 3296. *Beat to Quarters.* Boston: Little, Brown, 1937. 324 pp.
Hornblower, uncertain of his abilities, receives orders to go to the Pacific coast of Central America where he fights two successful battles with the same Spanish frigate. (*Series:* Hornblower, 6)
Genre(s): Sea Story; War Story.

◆ 3297. *Commodore Hornblower.* Boston: Little, Brown, 1945. 313 pp.
Horatio Hornblower reluctantly leaves his wife to go and command a squadron on the Baltic where Napoleon is lurking. (*Series:* Hornblower, 9)
Genre(s): Sea Story; War Story.

◆ 3298. *Flying Colours.* Boston: Little, Brown, 1938. 294 pp.
In the sequel to *Ship of the Line*, Captain Hornblower and some of his men escape those escorting them to Paris to be tried for piracy. (*Series:* Hornblower, 8)
Genre(s): War Story; Sea Story.

◆ 3299. *Hornblower and the Atropos.* Boston: Little, Brown, 1953. 325 pp.

Hornblower travels from Gloucester to London by canal and later engages in battles off the coast of Turkey. (*Series:* Hornblower, 5)
Genre(s): Sea Story; War Story.

◆ 3300. *Hornblower and the Hotspur.* Boston: Little, Brown, 1962. 344 pp.
The young Hornblower engages in sea battles. (*Series:* Hornblower, 3)
Genre(s): Sea Story; War Story.

◆ 3301. *Lieutenant Hornblower.* Boston: Little, Brown, 1952. 306 pp.
Before he becomes a commander, Horatio Hornblower has many adventures as a lieutenant while trying to overthrow Napoleon.
Genre(s): War Story; Sea Story.

◆ 3302. *Lord Hornblower.* Boston: Little, Brown, 1946. 322 pp.
Horatio Hornblower helps defeat Napoleon, but then Napoleon escapes from Elba, and Hornblower must wait until Waterloo to receive his honors and reunite with his wife. (*Series:* Hornblower, 10)
Genre(s): Sea Story; War Story.

◆ 3303. *Mr Midshipman Hornblower.* Boston: Little, Brown, 1950. 300 pp.
Horatio Hornblower rises to lieutenant after serving as a midshipman. (*Series:* Hornblower, 1)
Genre(s): War Story; Sea Story.

◆ 3304. *Ship of the Line.* Boston: Little, Brown, 1938. 323 pp.
In the sequel to *Beat to Quarters*, Captain Hornblower takes command of *Sutherland* and joins forces blockading the Spanish coast from Napoleon.
Genre(s): Sea Story; War Story.

Forrest, Anthony

3305. *A Balance of Dangers.* New York: Hill and Wang, 1984. 231 pp.
In 1807, John Justice sails near Denmark when that country is deciding whether to support England or Napoleon.
Genre(s): Sea Story.

3306. *The Pandora Secret.* New York: Farrar, Straus and Giroux, 1982. 285 pp.
In 1804, when Napoleon's navies threaten England, Captain John Justice, in the sequel to *Captain Justice*, goes to stand guard over Robert Fulton's work on the submarine.
Genre(s): War Story.

Forster, Margaret

◆ 3307. *Lady's Maid.* New York: Doubleday, 1991. 548 pp.
Wilson, who replaces Elizabeth Barrett's beloved maid Crow, helps Elizabeth elope with Robert Browning, but the relationship between the two women remains uneasy.
Genre(s): Biographical Fiction.

3308. *Memoirs of a Victorian Gentleman, William Makepeace Thackeray.* New York: Morrow, 1979. 391 pp.

William Makepeace Thackeray wanted no biographies, but with his letters and private papers, and his daughter's recollections, his life becomes more public.
Genre(s): Biographical Fiction.

Foxall, Raymond

3309. *The Dark Forest.* New York: St. Martin's, 1974. 251 pp.
Harry Adkins, Bow Street Runner, investigates a crime and a gang in Delamere Forest near Chester in 1807.
Genre(s): Mystery.

3310. *The Silver Goblet.* New York: St. Martin's, 1974. 191 pp.
Harry Adkins goes to Scotland to find a missing bride, using his cane instead of a gun to frighten enemies.
Genre(s): Mystery; Adventure Story.

Foxell, Nigel

3311. *Loving Emma.* Brighton, England: Harvester, 1986. 201 pp.
After joining the forces of Sir William Hamilton, Nelson meets Emma in Naples, fights battles, and cements both his naval reputation and their relationship after the Battle of the Nile in 1798.
Genre(s): Biographical Fiction; Love Story; Sea Story.

Fraser, George MacDonald

3312. *Black Ajax.* New York: Carroll and Graf, 1998. 256 pp.
Tom Molineaux, an African American boxer, comes to Regency England and challenges Tom Cribb, the English champion.
Genre(s): Sports Fiction; Biographical Fiction.

3313. *Flash for Freedom.* New York: Knopf, 1972. 287 pp.
Harry Paget Flashman, in the sequel to *Royal Flash*, has his political career aborted by Disraeli before becoming involved with the slave ship *Abe Lincoln* and with Americans connected to the slave trade.
Genre(s): Adventure Story.

3314. *Flashman.* New York: World, 1969. 256 pp.
Harry Paget Flashman, a bully from *Tom Brown's Schooldays*, tells about his commissions and his fighting in India and Afghanistan.
Genre(s): Adventure Story.

3315. *Flashman and the Angel of the Lord.* New York: Knopf, 1995. 394 pp.
In the sequel to *Flashman and the Mountain of Light*, Harry Paget Flashman goes to Harpers Ferry, West Virginia, during John Brown's raid.
Genre(s): Adventure Story.

3316. *Flashman and the Redskins.* New York: Knopf, 1982. 479 pp.
In the sequel to *Flashman's Lady*, Harry Paget Flashman uses an alias in New Orleans during 1849 to try to get back to England, although first he saves Custer's commission and survives Little Big Horn.
Genre(s): Adventure Story.

3317. *Flashman at the Charge.* New York: Knopf, 1973. 284 pp.
In 1854, Harry Paget Flashman, in the sequel to *Flash for Freedom*, leaves London for the Crimea to lead a charge of the Light Brigade before falling prisoner to the Cossacks.
Genre(s): Adventure Story.

3318. *Flashman in the Great Game.* New York: Knopf, 1975. 340 pp.
In 1857, Harry Paget Flashman, in the sequel to *Flashman at the Charge*, goes at Lord Palmerston's behest back to India as a secret agent.
Genre(s): Adventure Story.

3319. *Flashman's Lady.* New York: Knopf, 1978. 330 pp.
In the sequel to *Flashman in the Great Game*, Flashman meets an Eton-educated pirate and becomes amorous with the heathen Ranavalona, queen of Madagascar in the 1840s.
Genre(s): Adventure Story.

3320. *Royal Flash.* New York: Knopf, 1970. 256 pp.
In the sequel to *Flashman*, Harry Paget Flashman becomes embroiled in Otto von Bismarck's plan to topple Europe but finds that he is an assassin's target and flees after losing jewels to Lola Montez.
Genre(s): Adventure Story.

Freeman, Joy

3321. *The Last Frost Fair.* New York: St. Martin's, 1985. 258 pp.
Madeleine St. Cross falls in love with an army major she fears for as he fights Napoleon.
Genre(s): Regency Novel; Romance.

Fruchey, Deborah

◆ 3322. *The Unwilling Heiress.* New York: Walker, 1986. 211 pp.
Eccentric sisters rescue Lucy when she is released from her governess job and plan to send her into society and then leave her their fortune, but she is unwilling for them to offer her such luxury.
Genre(s): Romance; Regency Novel.

Fullerton, Alexander

3323. *Piper's Leave.* London: Cassell, 1974. 186 pp.
James Allan, an 18th-century piper, pursues music, women, and petty crime in the North of England.
Genre(s): Biographical Fiction; Musical Fiction.

Gaffney, Patricia

3324. *To Have and to Hold.* New York: Topaz, 1995. 378 pp.
After serving 10 years in prison for killing her husband, Rachel Wade is freed, and the magistrate, Sebastian Verlaine, intrigued by her story, hires her as a housekeeper to keep her from going to jail again for vagrancy.
Genre(s): Romance.

Garfield, Leon

3325. *The House of Cards.* New York: St. Martin's, 1985. 295 pp.
In 1847, an Englishman rescues a baby in a Polish village, and two years later he invites four people to dinner in London who have connections to the child.
Genre(s): Mystery.

Garratt, Mary A

3326. *The Asherwood Protégé.* New York: St. Martin's, 1982. 392 pp.
The duke and duchess sponsor Donna, daughter of the Asherwood vicar, during a London season, and she helps the Asherwood heir with his romance before falling in love with him herself.
Genre(s): Romance.

Garwood, Julie

3327. *The Lion's Lady.* New York: Pocket Books, 1988. 283 pp.
In 1814, Princess Christina seems an enigma to London society because its members do not know that she was raised by the Dakota Indians in Wyoming and is in England on a secret mission for her dead mother.
Genre(s): Romance.

Gibbs, Mary Ann

3328. *The Admiral's Lady.* New York: Mason, 1975. 187 pp.
Emma Hamilton becomes the mistress of Lord Nelson.
Genre(s): Romance.

3329. *The Glass Palace.* New York: Mason/Charter, 1975. 182 pp.
The Sackroyds treat their adopted daughter Tabitha like a poor relation after they spend her inheritance, but her aristocratic connection surfaces during the Crimean War.
Genre(s): Romance; War Story.

3330. *A Most Romantic City.* New York: Mason, 1976. 183 pp.
In 1794, Martha and her siblings must go to live with their grandfather, and when Martha and the grandfather clash, he makes her life miserable until a local member of the nobility rescues her.
Genre(s): Romance.

Gillespie, Jane

3331. *Aunt Celia.* New York: St. Martin's, 1991. 170 pp.
Frank Churchill, from Jane Austen's *Emma*, comes to spend the summer near his half-sister Celia and her father.
Genre(s): Regency Novel; Romance; Love Story.

◆ 3332. *Brightsea.* New York: St. Martin's, 1987. 160 pp.
Nancy Steele and her younger sister, Lucy, from Jane Austen's *Sense and Sensibility*, argue while Louise Retford quietly comes under Nancy's guardianship at the seaside one summer.
Genre(s): Romance.

◆ 3333. *Teverton Hall.* New York: St. Martin's, 1984. 224 pp.

In a sequel to *Pride and Prejudice*, Mr. Dallow has become Mr. Collin's patron, although their children are at the age to be married.

Genre(s): Regency Novel; Romance.

Girard, Paula Tanner

3334. *A Father for Christmas.* New York: Zebra, 1996. 254 pp.

The profligate Marquis of Wetherby has to take his friend's widowed sister-in-law and her son to a holiday party on the Devonshire moors and finds himself in love for the first time.

Genre(s): Regency Novel; Romance.

Glover, Judith

3335. *The Imagination of the Heart.* New York: St. Martin's, 1990. 351 pp.

Oliver van der Kleve selects Catherine for her beauty, sends her abroad to school, and regards her as a possession after marrying her but she turns to others for love and finds out about Oliver's own infidelities.

Genre(s): Domestic Fiction.

Goodman, Jo

3336. *My Steadfast Heart.* New York: Kensington, 1997. 416 pp.

Colin Thorne wins Mercedes Leyden's family estate in a boat race so she goes to an inn to murder him, but since they both have been abused and have had to live by their wits, they find mutual ground.

Genre(s): Regency Novel; Romance.

Graham, Winston

3337. *The Angry Tide.* Garden City, NY: Doubleday, 1978. 476 pp.

In the sequel to *The Four Swans*, Ross Poldark takes George Warleggan's seat in Parliament and falls in love with his wife.

Genre(s): Family Saga; Romance; Political Fiction.

3338. *The Black Moon.* London: Collins, 1973. 477 pp.

In 1794, in the sequel to *Warleggan*, Ross Poldark continues his feud with George Warleggan.

Genre(s): Family Saga; Romance.

3339. *The Four Swans.* Garden City, NY: Doubleday, 1977. 409 pp.

In the sequel to *The Black Moon*, in 1796, Ross Poldark works to quell ruthless men when Napoleon is suspected of trying to invade.

Genre(s): Family Saga; Romance.

3340. *The Loving Cup.* Garden City, NY: Doubleday, 1984. 440 pp.

In the sequel to *The Miller's Dance*, Ross Poldark and his wife care for their four children while Wellington's army triumphs against Napoleon.

Genre(s): Family Saga; Romance.

3341. *The Miller's Dance.* Garden City, NY: Doubleday, 1983. 372 pp.

Jeremy and Clowance Poldark, in the sequel to *The Stranger from the Sea*, become involved with the events of the day on the Cornish coast.

Genre(s): Family Saga; Romance.

3342. *The Stranger from the Sea.* Garden City, NY: Doubleday, 1982. 445 pp.

In the sequel to *The Angry Tide*, Jeremy Poldark becomes interested in designing a steam engine in 1810.

Genre(s): Family Saga; Romance.

3343. *The Twisted Sword.* New York: Carroll and Graf, 1991. 510 pp.

The sequel to *The Loving Cup* finds Ross Poldark and his wife in Paris on an assignment to assess the feelings of the Bourbons toward Napoleon.

Genre(s): Domestic Fiction; War Story.

Grant, Tracy

3344. *Shadows of the Heart.* New York: Dell, 1996. 373 pp.

Sophie Rutledge and Paul Lescaut become involved with each other during the last days of the French Revolution.

Genre(s): Regency Novel; Romance; War Story.

Graves, Robert

3345. *They Hanged My Saintly Billy.* Garden City, NY: Doubleday, 1957. 312 pp.

In 1856, Dr. William Palmer of Rugely is tried and accused of poisoning at least 15 people at various times throughout his life.

Genre(s): Biographical Fiction; Legal Story.

Gray, Valerie

◆ 3346. *A Spy at the Gate.* New York: St. Martin's, 1987. 297 pp.

Having loved and lost, Hester Vane becomes a writer of gothic novels in the early 19th century, but when her former love appears, wounded in the war and wearing a black mask, her adventures are no longer legal.

Genre(s): Romance.

Greene, Graham

3347. *The Man Within.* New York: Viking, 1929. 229 pp.

During the days of smuggling in Sussex, Andrews is both smuggler and informer.

Grumbach, Doris

3348. *The Ladies.* New York: Norton, 1993. 210 pp.

Lady Eleanor Butler and Sarah Ponsonby live together openly in the 18th century as the Ladies of Llangollen.

Genre(s): Biographical Fiction.

Gunn, Neil M.

3349. *Butcher's Broom.* 1934. New York: Walker, 1994. 429 pp.

Mairi, the herbalist in the rural Scottish village of Rias-gan in the early 19th century, oversees the disaster of the Highland clearances when landlords destroy communities to have more land to raise sheep.
Genre(s): Domestic Fiction.

Haines, Pamela

3350. *The Kissing Gate.* Garden City, NY: Doubleday, 1981. 638 pp.
When a servant girl saves a squire's son during the 19th century, the Rawson and the Ingham families' lives intertwine.
Genre(s): Family Saga.

Harbaugh, Karen

3351. *Cupid's Mistake.* New York: Signet, 1997. 180 pp.
Cupid tries to encourage the Marquess of Blytheland to fall in love with the innocent Cassandra Hathaway.
Genre(s): Regency Novel; Romance.

3352. *The Vampire Viscount.* New York: New American Library, 1995. 221 pp.
Nicholas St. Vire wants to regain mortal status so he contemplates marriage, and when he wins the hand of Leonore from her father in a game of cards, he realizes that he might have someone worth living for.
Genre(s): Romance; Horror; Regency Novel.

Harding, Alison

3353. *Also Georgiana.* New York: St. Martin's, 1987. 383 pp.
Georgiana Curwen, who has come of age in 1830 and learned that her grandfather had turned out her unmarried mother before Georgiana's birth, adopts her mother's independence as an artist and her concern for the poor.
Genre(s): Bildungsroman (Coming of Age).

Hardwick, Mollie

3354. *The Atkinson Heritage.* New York: Bantam, 1979. 312 pp.
In 1808, when Ephraim Atkinson marries Mary Bateman in Lancaster, England, they unite two prominent families, but their marriage is the only one that lasts.
Genre(s): Family Saga.

3355. *Beauty's Daughter.* New York: Coward-McCann, 1977. 368 pp.
Emma Hamilton's daughter must cope with her mother's beauty and renown while she matures.
Genre(s): Biographical Fiction.

◆ 3356. *Lovers Meeting.* New York: St. Martin's, 1979. 283 pp.
Four actors in a Christmas pantomime become involved in more than their performances in early 19th-century London.
Genre(s): Romance.

Hardy, Thomas

3357. *Far from the Madding Crowd.* 1874. New York: Oxford, 1993. 468 pp.
Although Gabriel Oak loves the proud Bathsheba Everdene, she willfully becomes involved with two other unsuitable men, with tragic consequences.
Genre(s): Country Life.

Harris, Marilyn

3358. *The Eden Passion.* New York: Putnam, 1979. 560 pp.
In the sequel to *The Prince of Eden*, John Eden, illegitimate son of Edward, arrives at Castle Eden to bury his father, and becomes the lover of Harriet, who happens to be his real mother.
Genre(s): Romance; Family Saga.

3359. *The Prince of Eden.* New York: Putnam, 1978. 555 pp.
In the sequel to *This Other Eden*, Edward, although illegitimate, inherits the Eden fortune while his legitimate brother James gets the title of nobility.
Genre(s): Romance; Family Saga.

3360. *This Other Eden.* New York: Putnam, 1977. 448 pp.
In the late 18th century, Lord Thomas Eden has a 16-year-old servant girl lashed for refusing his sexual advances, even as he continues to pursue her.
Genre(s): Family Saga.

Harrison, William

3361. *Burton and Speke.* New York: St. Martin's, 1982. 420 pp.
Sir Richard Burton and John Speke meet in 1854 and plan to explore the Nile, but when their divergent personalities clash, they end up bitter enemies after locating Lake Victoria.
Genre(s): Biographical Fiction.

Heath, Sandra

3362. *The Halloween Husband.* New York: New American Library, 1994. 224 pp.
When William Melcombe dies and leaves his family with no money, Lady Margaret decides to improve the situation, when, on Halloween, powers allow her to leave her portrait and try to arrange a suitable match for innocent Rowena.
Genre(s): Romance; Fantastic Literature; Regency Novel.

3363. *Halloween Magic.* New York: Signet, 1996. 224 pp.
A storm releases the beautiful Tudor Meg Ashton from her grave 200 years after her death, and she returns to Wychavon to take revenge on the descendants of those who burned her at the stake.
Genre(s): Regency Novel; Fantastic Literature; Romance.

3364. *Lucy's Christmas Angel.* New York: New American Library, 1995. 239 pp.
Emily Trevallion, 10, believes that saving her cousin Lucy from murder will let her join her parents in heaven

as a true angel, but only one person has ever seen Emily, and Lucy does not trust him.
Genre(s): Regency Novel; Romance.

Heaven, Constance

3365. *Lord of Ravensley.* New York: Coward-McCann, 1978. 373 pp.
Wealthy landowners and poor farmers conflict in the fen country during the early 19th century as the Aylshams try to keep their estate, Ravensley, functioning properly.
Genre(s): Romance.

3366. *The Ravensley Touch.* New York: Coward-McCann, 1982. 237 pp.
In the sequel to *Lord of Ravensley*, Jethro Alysham and Laurel Rutland, forbidden to marry because of family scandal, maintain an enduring love affair through a series of events, including Laurel's marriage to someone else.
Genre(s): Medical Novel; Love Story; War Story.

3367. *The Wildcliffe Bird.* New York: Coward-McCann, 1983. 248 pp.
Juliet Prior uses courage to make her way as an orphan.
Genre(s): Romance.

◆ 3368. *The Wind from the Sea.* New York: St. Martin's, 1993. 503 pp.
Isabelle de Sauvigny and her brother escape from France during the Revolution, and in England, Isabelle marries a man who spies for the British.
Genre(s): Love Story.

Hern, Candice

3369. *A Change of Heart.* New York: Signet, 1995. 223 pp.
Lady Mary Haviland, a happy spinster, agrees to help the Marquess of Pemberton find a wife but discovers that she herself is the object of his pursuit.
Genre(s): Regency Novel; Romance.

3370. *A Garden Folly.* New York: Signet, 1997. 221 pp.
To save the family, one of the Forsythe sisters must find a wealthy husband but the family has difficulty sticking to the plans when the duke they target only wants to be loved for himself.
Genre(s): Regency Novel; Romance.

Hewlett, Maurice Henry

3371. *The Fool Errant.* New York: Macmillan, 1905. 352 pp.
Francis-Anthony Strelly, an English youth in Italy, samples life in all classes as he travels and falls in love with his tutor's wife.
Genre(s): Romance.

Heyer, Georgette

3372. *April Lady.* New York: Putnam, 1957. 254 pp.

Because her mother emphasizes that she has a marriage of convenience, Lady Helen hides her affection for her husband and he for her.
Genre(s): Regency Novel; Romance.

3373. *Arabella.* New York: Putnam, 1971. 284 pp.
A country minister's daughter visits her godmother in London and decides that she will marry the most eligble but confirmed bachelor in town.
Genre(s): Regency Novel; Romance.

3374. *Bath Tangle.* New York: Putnam, 1955. 312 pp.
Serena Carlow discovers, at her father's death, that she is now ward of the marquis of Rotherham, a man she once jilted.
Genre(s): Regency Novel; Romance.

3375. *Beau Wyndham.* Garden City, NY: Doubleday, 1941. 278 pp.
Penelope Creed, teenage heiress, and Richard Wyndham flee London and unwanted marriages.
Genre(s): Regency Novel; Romance.

3376. *The Black Moth.* New York: Dutton, 1968. 326 pp.
Sir John Carstares rescues innocents after having to become a highwayman when he took on his brother's guilt at cards, while the cynical dandy, the Black Moth, adopts black and white as his only colors because of his dark hair and light skin.
Genre(s): Regency Novel; Romance.

3377. *Black Sheep.* London: Bodley Head, 1966. 255 pp.
A young aunt trying to protect her niece from a fortune hunter becomes the focus of another man who wants her money.
Genre(s): Regency Novel; Romance.

3378. *Charity Girl.* New York: Putnam, 1970. 253 pp.
Lord Desford decides to help tired Cherry Steane as she walks along the road, after serving her aunt's every whim in return for clothes and a place to live, by locating her grandfather.
Genre(s): Regency Novel; Love Story.

3379. *A Civil Contract.* New York: Putnam, 1961. 393 pp.
A Viscount who fought for Napoleon has lost his money, and he marries an heiress to replenish his title and fortune.
Genre(s): Regency Novel; Romance.

3380. *Cotillion.* New York: Putnam, 1953. 316 pp.
A young woman unexpectedly finds her love.
Genre(s): Regency Novel; Romance.

3381. *Cousin Kate.* New York: Dutton, 1968. 317 pp.
Although the Broome family has unsavory plans for poor cousin Kate, she proves the plans incapable of closure.
Genre(s): Regency Novel; Romance.

3382. *Faro's Daughter.* Garden City, NY: Doubleday, 1942. 274 pp.

Two men vie for the hand of Deb as she runs a faro table in her aunt's gaming house.
Genre(s): Regency Novel; Romance.

3383. *The Foundling.* New York: Putnam, 1948. 380 pp.
A young man brings a foundling to his fiancée for protection while they are betrothed in an arranged marriage.
Genre(s): Regency Novel; Romance.

3384. *Frederica.* New York: Dutton, 1965. 384 pp.
A wealthy bachelor falls in love with a young woman who at 24 thinks she is too old for marriage, and is therefore working to find her younger sister a suitable match.
Genre(s): Regency Novel; Romance.

3385. *Friday's Child.* New York: Putnam, 1946. 311 pp.
During social activities, a young woman and man fall in love.
Genre(s): Regency Novel; Romance.

3386. *The Grand Sophy.* New York: Putnam, 1950. 307 pp.
Sophy has learned the advantage of suprise attack from the Duke of Wellington, and she uses her knowledge to help relieve her cousins of unsuitable engagements.
Genre(s): Regency Novel; Romance.

3387. *Lady of Quality.* New York: Dutton, 1972. 254 pp.
Miss Annis Whychwood, at 29, wealthy and independent, gains a promise of reform from the man she loves after she wins a verbal contest with him.
Genre(s): Regency Novel; Romance.

3388. *The Nonesuch.* New York: Dutton, 1973. 300 pp.
A London man comes to the land he has inherited in Yorkshire and falls in love.
Genre(s): Regency Novel; Romance.

3389. *Powder and Patch.* 1923. New York: Dutton, 1968. 233 pp.
A country girl goes to London and becomes confused by all of the social whirl.
Genre(s): Regency Novel; Love Story.

3390. *The Quiet Gentleman.* New York: Putnam, 1972. 343 pp.
After the Napoleonic Wars, the seventh Earl of St. Erth returns to claim his inheritance, but he discovers enemies within his own household.
Genre(s): Regency Novel; Love Story.

3391. *Regency Buck.* 1935. New York: Dutton, 1966. 332 pp.
Orphans wishing to enjoy London society go to the home of their guardian during the Season.
Genre(s): Regency Novel; Romance.

3392. *The Reluctant Widow.* New York: Putnam, 1946. 279 pp.
Elinor Rochdale, a poor governess, applies for a post at the wrong estate, is immediately married to a dying man,

and inherits his Sussex land where subsequent murders occur.
Genre(s): Regency Novel; Romance.

3393. *Sprig Muslim.* New York: Putnam, 1956. 276 pp.
Two young people fall in love after an unusual romance in Regency England.
Genre(s): Regency Novel; Romance.

3394. *Sylvester.* New York: Putnam, 1971. 311 pp.
A pair who seem to have nothing in common fall in love after a tangled relationship.
Genre(s): Romance; Regency Novel.

3395. *The Talisman Ring.* Garden City, NY: Doubleday, 1937. 310 pp.
A young French girl and her cousins become involved in a murder involving smugglers and a lost ring.
Genre(s): Mystery; Romance.

3396. *The Toll-Gate.* New York: Putnam, 1954. 310 pp.
A Napoleonic War veteran discovers that keeping a toll-gate is one of the most exciting jobs to have.
Genre(s): Regency Novel; Romance.

3397. *The Unknown Ajax.* London: Heinemann, 1971. 314 pp.
A couple falls in love against a backdrop of the developing textile industry.
Genre(s): Regency Novel; Romance.

3398. *Venetia.* New York: HarperCollins, 1993. 384 pp.
An important relative returns to England, and Lord Damerel, noble rake, proposes to Venetia four times before she will accept.
Genre(s): Regency Novel; Romance.

Hill, Fiona

3399. *The Autumn Rose.* New York: Putnam, 1978. 255 pp.
Caroline falls in love with a blue-eyed rake in Regency England.
Genre(s): Regency Novel; Romance.

◆ 3400. *The Country Gentleman.* New York: St. Martin's, 1987. 336 pp.
Anne Guilfoyle has to leave London for Cheshire where she still retains property even though her fortune is gone, and there she meets Henry Highet, who is not what he seems.
Genre(s): Regency Novel; Romance.

◆ 3401. *The Stanbroke Girls.* New York: St. Martin's, 1981. 244 pp.
The heroine and hero care for each other from the start, and the younger sister, although seemingly romantic, shows practicality.
Genre(s): Regency Novel; Romance.

Hill, Pamela

3402. *Artemia.* New York: St. Martin's, 1990. 190 pp.

Artemia becomes a companion for Lady Feldman in the 1850s, before meeting Lady Feldman's unhappily married son and becoming his mistress.
Genre(s): Romance.

3403. ***Bride of Ae.*** New York: St. Martin's, 1983. 172 pp.
After Lord Francis Consett marries the working-class Sara Ryder and has children, he has followed the specifications to become the heir of Ae.
Genre(s): Romance.

3404. ***The Heatherton Heritage.*** New York: St. Martin's, 1974. 319 pp.
In the 19th century, William Heatherton, a famous minister, marries the innocent Marie whom he treats brutally, murders her lover whom he hides in his study, and then marries again to a woman who eventually goes mad.
Genre(s): Romance; Gothic Fiction.

Hinchman, Jane

3405. ***Rendezvous with Love.*** Garden City, NY: Doubleday, 1987. 186 pp.
Miranda Trafford travels to London, but bad weather forces her to stop at Lord Anthony Wendover's home where he awaits a bride who fails to appear.
Genre(s): Regency Novel; Romance.

Hingston, Sandy

3406. ***A Most Reckless Lady.*** New York: Dell, 1998. 384 pp.
After the friend of Lucas Strathmere, Earl of Somerleigh, makes a deathbed request, Strathmore goes to Russia to find a girl and discovers that someone is trying to kill her.
Genre(s): Romance; Regency Novel; Mystery.

Hocker, Karla

3407. ***The Incorrigible Sophia.*** New York: Walker, 1992. 216 pp.
Sophia solves the mystery of a murder related to missing military documents about British plans to foil a French invasion.
Genre(s): Regency Novel; Romance; Mystery.

Hodge, Jane Aiken

◆ 3408. ***The Lost Garden.*** New York: Coward-McCann, 1982. 319 pp.
When George III becomes mentally incapacitated, Caroline falls in love with the Duke of Cley's son before finding out that she is his half sister.
Genre(s): Romance.

◆ 3409. ***Marry in Haste.*** Garden City, NY: Doubleday, 1970. 205 pp.
Camilla Forest falls in love with her husband of convenience when she lives with him in Portugal while he tries to save the country from Napoleon's forces.
Genre(s): Romance; Regency Novel.

◆ 3410. ***Maulever Hall.*** Garden City, NY: Doubleday, 1964. 306 pp.

After a stagecoach accident, a young girl suffers amnesia and falls in love with the master of the mansion where she has found refuge.
Genre(s): Romance; Regency Novel.

◆ 3411. ***Rebel Heiress.*** New York: Coward-McCann, 1975. 256 pp.
In 1812 Henrietta Marchmont goes to London to stay with relatives and becomes involved in British politics and intrigue.
Genre(s): Romance; Regency Novel.

◆ 3412. ***Whispering.*** New York: St. Martin's, 1995. 217 pp.
A young woman travels with her father to Portugal while Wellington prepares to battle Napoleon.
Genre(s): War Story; Romance.

◆ 3413. ***Windover.*** New York: St. Martin's, 1992. 266 pp.
Kathryn, at 16, falls in love with her tutor, but her stepfather throws him over a cliff, persuading Kathryn to marry another.
Genre(s): Love Story.

Hoff, B. J.

3414. ***Song of the Silent Harp.*** Minneapolis, MN: Bethany House, 1991. 412 pp.
Nora and Daniel Kavanagh survive the Irish potato famine and join 500,000 immigrants seeking respite in America. (***Series:*** Emerald Ballad, 1)
Genre(s): Christian Fiction.

Hogg, James

3415. ***The Private Memoirs and Confessions of a Justified Sinner.*** 1824. New York: Oxford, 1969. 262 pp.
The supernatural pervades the Scottish countryside when an unbalanced human convinces others of reason.
Genre(s): Gothic Fiction.

Holt, Victoria

◆ 3416. ***Secret for a Nightingale.*** Garden City, NY: Doubleday, 1986. 371 pp.
Susanna Pleydell, a widow, begins a nursing career and goes to the Crimea where she gains admiration for the man she holds responsible for the deaths of both her husband and her child.
Genre(s): Romance; Medical Novel; War Story.

Hucker, Hazel

3417. ***Cousin Susannah.*** New York: St. Martin's, 1996. 371 pp.
After governess Susannah falls in love with James, the heir to Abbotsbridge House, and becomes pregnant, she immediately marries the social-climbing curate because she knows that James cannot marry her.
Genre(s): Romance.

Hughes, Glyn

3418. *Brontë.* New York: St. Martin's, 1996. 431 pp.
Charlotte, Emily, Anne, and Branwell Brontë face unsatisfactory lives and careers because of their isolation at Haworth.
Genre(s): Biographical Fiction; Domestic Fiction.

◆ 3419. *The Rape of the Rose.* New York: Simon and Schuster, 1993. 319 pp.
Mor Greave, a weaver and schoolmaster, flees from an attack on a mill after owners have started to use automated looms in 1812, and Mary, a prostitute, saves him.
Genre(s): Political Fiction.

3420. *Where I Used to Play on the Green.* New York: Victor Gollancz, 1983. 192 pp.
Laborers listen to William Grimshaw as the Methodist movement begins in England, and his words give them hope for their lives.
Genre(s): Christian Fiction.

Hunter, Jillian

3421. *A Deeper Magic.* New York: Pinnacle, 1994. 480 pp.
A heroine uses magic in her pursuits.
Genre(s): Romance; Fantastic Literature.

Hylton, Sara

◆ 3422. *The Whispering Glade.* New York: St. Martin's, 1985. 252 pp.
Maya Wentworth becomes governess for the Gaynor family and falls in love with the family heir, and their liaison dooms most people around them.
Genre(s): Romance; Gothic Fiction.

Inman, Robert

3423. *The Blood Endures.* New York: Simon and Schuster, 1981. 320 pp.
Tony Logan believes that his parents are a groom and a servant woman until Lord Farleigh banishes him after an affair with Farleigh's daughter, and Tony then travels to Europe and America.
Genre(s): Love Story; Adventure Story.

Iremonger, Lucille

3424. *How Do I Love Thee.* New York: Morrow, 1976. 359 pp.
Robert Browning rescues Elizabeth Barrett from her father and takes her to Italy.
Genre(s): Biographical Fiction; Love Story.

3425. *My Sister, My Love.* New York: Morrow, 1981. 312 pp.
Byron, debt-ridden and hedonistic, escapes from his creditors by fleeing to the Continent with an entourage of male and female lovers.
Genre(s): Biographical Fiction.

Jacobs, Anna

3426. *High Street.* New York: St. Martin's, 1996. 368 pp.
In the sequel to *Salem Street,* after her husband dies in 1845, Annie Gibson moves her family into their own home and establishes a stylish dress designing business, then someone tries to ruin her.
Genre(s): Domestic Fiction.

◆ 3427. *Salem Street.* New York: St. Martin's, 1995. 486 pp.
In 1820, Annie is born to millworkers on Salem Street, and as she grows up, she begins to fulfill her dream of being a dressmaker for the gentry.
Genre(s): Domestic Fiction; Romance.

Jacobs, Sherry-Anne

◆ 3428. *Persons of Rank.* New York: Century, 1994. 192 pp.
Aunt Beatrice goes to London to look for a suitor for her niece Eleanor who then falls in love with someone who's not on the social list.
Genre(s): Regency Novel; Romance.

Jagger, Brenda

3429. *Distant Choices.* New York: Morrow, 1986. 478 pp.
Separated from Evangeline Slade after the birth of their illegitimate daughter Matthew Stangway marries for wealth at his family's behest, but is finally free to marry Evangeline after his wife dies.
Genre(s): Romance; Domestic Fiction.

Jeal, Tim

3430. *Until the Colors Fade.* New York: Delacorte, 1976. 497 pp.
Citizens of a Lancashire cotton town endure affairs and the Crimean War in Victorian England.
Genre(s): Domestic Fiction.

Johansen, Iris

3431. *The Beloved Scoundrel.* New York: Bantam, 1994. 323 pp.
When Marianna Sanders, an eastern European stained-glass artisan, learns political secrets important to two warring countries, one of the leaders takes her to England and the other murders her mother and kidnaps her brother.
Genre(s): Romance.

3432. *Dark Rider.* New York: Bantam, 1995. 448 pp.
Jared Danemount, Duke of Morland, meets a bare-breasted Cassie Deville in Hawaii in the early 19th century believing that she is a Polynesian rather than the daughter of his enemy, but Cassie convinces him to take her back to England.
Genre(s): Romance.

Johnson, Alison

3433. ***The Wicked Generation.*** Chester Springs, PA: Dufour, 1992. 262 pp.
In 19th-century Scotland, Issie, a Scottish landowner's daughter, becomes enraged with her father's eviction of the peasants from their farms to a rocky island.
Genre(s): Domestic Fiction.

Johnson, Susan

3434. ***Sinful.*** New York: Doubleday, 1992. 375 pp.
Chelsea Fergusson avoids marriage to the wealthy but unpleasant Bishop Hatfield by losing her virginity to London's leading eligible bachelor, Sinjin St. John, Duke of Seth, becoming pregnant, and following Sinjin as he flees from her father.
Genre(s): Romance; Adventure Story.

Johnston, Joan

3435. ***Captive.*** New York: Dell, 1996. 416 pp.
When her father dies, Lady Charlotte Edgerton, an American, goes to England to find a husband and falls in love with her guardian.
Genre(s): Romance; Regency Novel.

Jones, Jill

3436. ***My Lady Caroline.*** New York: St. Martin's, 1996. 338 pp.
Lady Caroline's ghost appears to Alison Cunningham, a Boston heiress, and asks her to find Lord Byron's memoirs so that the world will know that he loved her.
Genre(s): Romance; Fantastic Literature.

Kane, Andrea

3437. ***The Black Diamond.*** New York: Pocket Books, 1997. 400 pp.
Slayde Huntley wants to protect his sister Aurora from the family curse by marrying her to Viscount Guillford, but she refuses to marry someone she does not love, so she chooses Lawrence Bencroft to deflower her in a tavern, then learns that he is her family's worst enemy.
Genre(s): Regency Novel; Romance; Adventure Story.

3438. ***Legacy of Diamond.*** New York: Pocket Books, 1997. 368 pp.
Slayde Huntley, Earl of Pembourne, receives notes demanding ransom for his sister, and he gives a jewel to a pirate but discovers that the woman delivered is not his sister but a lookalike, Courtney Johnston, who fears the pirate may have killed her sea captain father.
Genre(s): Regency Novel; Romance.

3439. ***Wishes in the Wind.*** New York: Pocket Books, 1996. 335 pp.
Nicole Aldridge pretends to be a man and gets a job with a horse breeder to support her father who is hiding from a criminal gang that wanted him to throw a horse race.
Genre(s): Romance; Regency Novel; Mystery.

Karr, Phyllis Ann

3440. ***Lady Susan.*** New York: Everest House, 1980. 311 pp.
Lady Susan tries to control everyone around her, especially her daughter Frederica.
Genre(s): Romance.

Kelly, Carla

3441. ***The Lady's Companion.*** New York: Signet, 1996. 223 pp.
To escape her dictatorial aunt, Susan Hampton secures a job as companion to Lady Bushnell, but when she meets the dowager's handsome bailiff, she forgets their social class differences.
Award(s): Romance Writers of America RITA Award.
Genre(s): Romance; Regency Novel.

3442. ***Mrs Drew Plays her Hand.*** New York: New American Library, 1994. 224 pp.
Rosanna Drew, the vicar's widow, moves into a dilapidated estate with her two daughters, but before winter, the estate's absentee owner, Fletcher Rand, Marquess of Winn, arrives.
Award(s): Romance Writers of America RITA Award.
Genre(s): Regency Novel; Romance.

3443. ***With this Ring.*** New York: New American Library, 1997. 240 pp.
Lydia Perkins caters to her sister's demands until she happens to visit a hospital ward filled with soldiers wounded in the Peninsular Wars, and her life changes.
Genre(s): Regency Novel; Romance.

Kelly, Rebecca

3444. ***The Wedding Chase.*** New York: Bantam, 1998. 384 pp.
Grizelda Fleetwood wants to marry someone rich, old, and flexible so that she can keep her brother out of prison and herself independent, but Wolfgang Hardwicke, Earl of Northcliffe, plots to change her mind.
Genre(s): Romance; Regency Novel.

Kent, Alexander

◆ 3445. ***Colors Aloft!*** New York: Putnam, 1986. 286 pp.
Admiral Richard Bolitho leads a new squadron of ships to the Mediterranean while his French adversary, Rear Admiral Jobert, follows.
Genre(s): Sea Story; War Story.

◆ 3446. ***Enemy in Sight!*** New York: Putnam, 1970. 350 pp.
In 1796, in the sequel to *Form Line of Battle!* Captain Richard Bolitho uses his 74-gun ship to chase the French during blockade duty off France.
Genre(s): Sea Story; War Story.

◆ 3447. ***Form Line of Battle!*** New York: Putnam, 1969. 320 pp.

In 1793, in the sequel to *Passage to Mutiny*, Captain Richard Bolitho of the Royal Navy sails from Gibraltar to fight against French forces at Toulon.
Genre(s): Sea Story; War Story.

◆ **3448. *Honor This Day.*** New York: Putnam, 1988. 287 pp.
In the sequel to *Colors Aloft*, Richard Bolitho continues his adventures in the Royal Navy.
Genre(s): Sea Story; War Story.

◆ **3449. *The Inshore Squadron.*** New York: Putnam, 1979. 256 pp.
The sequel to *Signal—Close Action* relates how, after the Battle of Copenhagen in 1801, Richard Bolitho helps recover merchantmen and keep the French out of the Baltic.
Genre(s): Sea Story.

◆ **3450. *Only Victor.*** London: Heinemann, 1990. 340 pp.
In the sequel to *With All Dispatch*, Richard Bolitho, vice-admiral, goes to the coast of South Africa to fight the Dutch and then to lead a flagship to battle near Denmark, but all he thinks about is the loss of his ship *Hyperion* and his affair with Catherine, Lady Somervell.
Genre(s): Sea Story; War Story.

◆ **3451. *Passage to Mutiny.*** New York: Putnam, 1976. 319 pp.
In the sequel to *Command a King's Ship*, Bolitho sails in the waters of New South Wales in 1789 searching for a pirate who has captured the convict ship on which Bolitho's love (the wife of an evil captain) is a passenger.
Genre(s): War Story; Sea Story.

◆ **3452. *Richard Bolitho—Midshipman.*** New York: Putnam, 1976. 158 pp.
Richard Bolitho becomes a sailor in the Royal Navy.
Genre(s): Sea Story; War Story.

◆ **3453. *Signal—Close Action.*** New York: Putnam, 1974. 320 pp.
In the sequel to *The Flag Captain*, Commodore Bolitho and his squadron of ships engage the French and Spanish while trying to keep Napoleon from stockpiling supplies for his war.
Genre(s): Sea Story; War Story.

◆ **3454. *Success to the Brave.*** New York: Putnam, 1983. 284 pp.
In 1802, a brief lull in the Napoleonic Wars allows Vice-Admiral Bolitho to take his crew to the Caribbean, aboard the *Achates*, on a mission to return the island of San Felipe to the French, in the sequel to *A Tradition of Victory*.
Genre(s): Sea Story.

◆ **3455. *With All Dispatch.*** New York: Putnam, 1989. 272 pp.
In 1792, Richard Bolitho fights a gang of smugglers known as The Brotherhood, in the sequel to *Honor This Day*.
Genre(s): Sea Story; War Story.

Kenyon, Frank Wilson

3456. *The Duke's Mistress.* New York: Dodd, Mead, 1969. 255 pp.
Mary Ann Clarke becomes the mistress of George III's playboy son, Frederick Augustus.
Genre(s): Biographical Fiction.

3457. *The Golden Years.* London: Hutchinson, 1974. 336 pp.
The poet Percy Bysshe Shelley enjoys his circle of friends and experiences in Italy.
Genre(s): Biographical Fiction.

3458. *Imperial Courtesan.* New York: Dodd, Mead, 1967. 256 pp.
The wealthy Englishwoman Harriet Howard finances Louis Napoleon's political aspirations because he makes a written promise to marry her.
Genre(s): Biographical Fiction.

Kerstan, Lynn

3459. *Francesca's Rake.* New York: Fawcett, 1997. 221 pp.
When Viscount Clayburn's father foils his son's plans and demands that he marry, Clayburn promises to do so within the year and looks for the most socially unacceptable bride he can find, but what he finds is surprising.
Genre(s): Romance; Regency Novel.

Kerstan, Lynn, and Alicia Rasley

3460. *Owen's Christmas Ghost.* New York: Zebra, 1995. 304 pp.
Valerian Caine arrives in the future of 1816 to end the family feud that he unexpectedly started a century before, hoping to remove himself from eternal boredom, but he must stop the feud before Christmas, just four weeks away.
Genre(s): Regency Novel; Romance; Time Travel.

Kidd, Elisabeth

3461. *For Love of Celia.* New York: Walker, 1988. 155 pp.
The widow Celia chaperones her orphaned sister-in-law Kitty for the season and even arranges for her engagement to an eligible young man, but Kitty plans to elope with the man to whom Celia is attracted.
Genre(s): Regency Novel; Romance.

3462. *A Hero for Antonia.* New York: Walker, 1986. 224 pp.
Years after Antonia Fairfax's London season, during which she made a fool of herself, she returns as chaperone for her niece.
Genre(s): Regency Novel; Romance.

◆ **3463. *Lady Lu.*** New York: Walker, 1989. 224 pp.
After the mourning period for her husband ends, Lady Luisa Ingram visits her sister-in-law and her neighbor, Richard Wetherell, whom Luisa once loved.
Genre(s): Romance; Regency Novel.

◆ 3464. *My Lord Guardian.* New York: Walker, 1982. 192 pp.
A young woman who becomes the ward of her dead father's handsome best friend discovers that the very qualities that make her unacceptable in society are appreciated by her guardian.
Genre(s): Regency Novel; Romance.

Kihlstrom, April

3465. *The Wicked Groom.* New York: Signet, 1996. 220 pp.
Lady Diana Westcott becomes attracted to the new stable groom only weeks before her marriage of convenience, but when she is in London, she finds out that the groom is actually her husband-to-be.
Genre(s): Regency Novel; Romance.

King, Betty

3466. *Emma Hamilton.* London: Hale, 1976. 204 pp.
The married Emma Hamilton becomes the mistress of Lord Nelson in the early 19th century.
Genre(s): Biographical Fiction.

Kingsley, Katherine

3467. *Call Down the Moon.* New York: Doubleday, 1998. 421 pp.
After Hugo Montagu returns from exile in France, he proposes to Meggie Bloom, a young woman whom he thinks is an inmate but who actually works in a mental institution, and although he knows that she has an inheritance, she does not.
Genre(s): Regency Novel; Romance.

3468. *In the Wake of the Wind.* New York: Dell, 1996. 404 pp.
Serafina Segrave accidentally meets the cynical Earl of Aubrey, the man to whom her marriage is arranged.
Genre(s): Romance; Regency Novel.

Kinsale, Laura

3469. *My Sweet Folly.* New York: Berkley, 1997. 416 pp.
Neglected wife Folie Hamilton corresponds with Robert Cambourne, a lieutenant in Calcutta, and they fall in love, and after Folie's husband and Robert's wife dies, Robert returns to England to be guardian of Folie's stepdaughter.
Genre(s): Regency Novel; Romance; Gothic Fiction.

Kirland, Martha

3470. *The Honorable Thief.* New York: Signet, 1996. 221 pp.
Honor Danforth steals from an unconscious man lying in the snow after she has lost her job as a governess, and when she is caught, her lies entangle both her and the man.
Genre(s): Regency Novel; Romance.

Kistler, Mary

◆ 3471. *The Jarrah Tree.* New York: Doubleday, 1977. 190 pp.
A governess consents to a marriage of convenience so that she can go to Australia to be near her former fiancé who is imprisoned in the penal colony.
Genre(s): Romance.

Kleypas, Lisa

3472. *Stranger in My Arms.* New York: Avon, 1998. 384 pp.
Certain that her husband has died in a shipwreck, Lara, Lady Hawksworth, is surprised when he reappears three years later, but she believe that the man is an impostor because his attention to her is so much more loving than that of her husband.
Genre(s): Romance; Regency Novel.

La Bern, Arthur J.

3473. *Hallelujah!* New York: Allen, 1973. 310 pp.
General Booth tries to help those in need in the slums of London, and when W. T. Stead abducts a young girl, Booth realizes that he cannot control everything.
Genre(s): Biographical Fiction.

LaFoy, Leslie

3474. *It Happened One Night.* New York: Bantam, 1997. 240 pp.
When CPA Alana Chapman finds herself in Ireland in 1803, she meets Kiervan des Morceaux, a privateer who thinks that marrying "up" will help him.
Genre(s): Romance; Time Travel.

Laine, Annabel

3475. *The Melancholy Virgin.* New York: St. Martin's, 1982. 220 pp.
The earl Charles Dornay's secretary Francis Mervyn is the prime suspect in a murder, but Dornay is convinced that Mervyn is innocent, while the victim's friend is sure that he is not.
Genre(s): Regency Novel; Romance.

Laker, Rosalind

3476. *The Smuggler's Bride.* New York: Doubleday, 1975. 186 pp.
When Harriette Mead leaves the country to become a London governess, she falls in love with the next-door neighbor, but when dismissed, she marries Robert on his deathbed and inherits his estate.
Genre(s): Romance.

◆ 3477. *The Sugar Pavilion.* New York: Doubleday, 1994. 370 pp.
Sophie Delcourt flees to England from France during the Revolution and takes her confectionery skills to Brighton where, as she cooks for the king, two men pursue her.
Genre(s): Romance.

Lamb, Arnette

3478. *Betrayed.* New York: Pocket Star, 1996. 198 pp.
Sarah Lachlan leaves for Edinburgh to start an orphanage, but Lady Emily Elliot is determined that one of her sons marry Sarah and her money so she sends him to Edinburgh to woo her.
Genre(s): Romance.

Lane, Allison

3479. *Lord Avery's Legacy.* New York: Signet, 1998. 224 pp.
Richard Avery, Lord Carrington, goes to Devon to save his nephew from an undesirable marriage and ends up falling in love with the girl's sister.
Genre(s): Romance; Regency Novel.

3480. *The Prodigal Daughter.* New York: Signet, 1996. 220 pp.
During the early 18th century a healer and a pompous duke are involved in a fire while Nelson fights.
Genre(s): Regency Novel; Romance.

Law, Elizabeth

3481. *The Sealed Knot.* New York: Walker, 1989. 209 pp.
The followers of the late Bonnie Prince Charlie use as their signal a sealed knot in their attempts to place the prince's grandson on the throne in 1811, and Sparrow Harvey and Simon Adair investigate the ensuing intrigues.
Genre(s): Regency Novel; Romance.

Leslie, Doris

3482. *Notorious Lady.* London: Heinemann, 1976. 275 pp.
Marguerite, Countess of Blessington, makes a living with her writing although her family and those that she meets take advantage of her kindness.
Genre(s): Biographical Fiction.

3483. *This for Caroline.* New York: Pocket Books, 1973. 291 pp.
Lord Byron's mistress is Lady Caroline Lamb.
Genre(s): Biographical Fiction.

Ley, Alice Chetwynd

3484. *Beloved Diana.* New York: Ballantine, 1977. 182 pp.
The last of the Chalfort family line's concern about inheritance leads to a murder attempt and blackmail.
Genre(s): Romance; Regency Novel.

3485. *A Fatal Assignation.* New York: St. Martin's, 1987. 221 pp.
Justin Rutherford, a scholar and sleuth, helps Bow Street Runner Joseph Watts solve the murder of Sir Aubrey Jermyn.
Genre(s): Mystery; Romance.

3486. *A Regency Scandal.* South Yarmouth, MA: J. Curley, 1978. 338 pp.
Helen Somerby expects to inherit much money, but a scandal arises.
Genre(s): Regency Novel; Romance.

3487. *A Reputation Dies.* New York: St. Martin's, 1985. 169 pp.
Justin Rutherford, his niece Anthea, and his godmother Lady Quainton offer to help the Bow Street Runners solve the murder of Yarnton, a gossip who has discussed the identity of a blackmailer.
Genre(s): Mystery; Regency Novel; Romance.

3488. *The Sentimental Spy.* New York: Ballantine, 1978. 331 pp.
Elizabeth Thorne goes to her recently inherited Sussex estate where she finds a foreign spy and a secret agent of Napoleon.
Genre(s): Romance.

Lincoln, Victoria

3489. *Charles.* Boston: Little, Brown, 1962. 438 pp.
Charles Dickens has enormous popularity with the public although his private life seems at times troubled.
Genre(s): Biographical Fiction.

Lindsey, Dawn

◆ 3490. *The Duchess of Vidal.* Garden City, NY: Doubleday, 1978. 219 pp.
As Dominique Forrester travels to her governess position, she meets the Duke of Vidal.
Genre(s): Regency Novel; Romance.

Lindsey, Johanna

3491. *Gentle Rogue.* New York: Avon, 1990. 426 pp.
James, English aristocrat and pirate, meets Georgina Anderson, only daughter in a family of sons, who is not cowed by James's bravado.
Genre(s): Romance.

3492. *Glorious Angel.* New York: Avon, 1982. 242 pp.
Jacob Maitland, devoted friend of Angela Sherrington's mother in years previous, rescues her after her father dies in a barroom, and when she moves to his home, she rekindles the flame of a childhood romance, only to be disappointed.
Genre(s): Romance.

3493. *Love Me Forever.* New York: Morrow, 1995. 338 pp.
The dictatorial father of Lady Kimberly Richards forces her into marriage, and when she meets Lachlan MacGregor, she is ill and in no mood to accept his advances.
Genre(s): Romance.

3494. *Say You Love Me.* New York: Morrow, 1996. 352 pp.
After 1811, Kelsey Langton agrees to go to a London brothel to pay her uncle's debts and earn money for her

sister's dowry, but a rogue decides he would rather pay for her to be his mistress.
Genre(s): Regency Novel; Romance.

3495. *Tender Rebel.* New York: Avon, 1988. 280 pp.
Roslynn Chadwick escapes from her cousin and goes to London to find a husband, but after the eligible Sir Anthony Malory helps her narrow her list, he decides to marry her himself.
Genre(s): Romance; Regency Novel.

3496. *When Love Awaits.* New York: Avon, 1986. 343 pp.
Lord Rolfe of Crewel decides to make a marriage of convenience with a woman he has never met and he believes is unattractive, but he discovers that he is mistaken about her appearance.
Genre(s): Romance; Regency Novel.

Lofts, Norah

3497. *The Day of the Butterfly.* Garden City, NY: Doubleday, 1980. 328 pp.
Daisy Holt becomes a dancer in a brothel, but soon her life takes on added dimensions.
Award(s): Georgette Heyer Historical Novel Prize.
Genre(s): Regency Novel; Romance.

3498. *Gad's Hall.* Garden City, NY: Doubleday, 1978. 282 pp.
The new tenants of Gad's Hall find it haunted by ghosts of its owners in the mid-19th century.
Genre(s): Romance; Family Saga.

3499. *Nethergate.* Garden City, NY: Doubleday, 1973. 256 pp.
Isabella de Savigny escapes the Reign of Terror in France and comes to Nethergate in hope of a better life.
Genre(s): Romance.

Lorraine, Marian

3500. *The Mischievous Spinster.* New York: Walker, 1983. 175 pp.
Antonia Radcliffe, beautiful and humorous, refuses to marry even though she is 29, until she finds the one love of her life.
Genre(s): Regency Novel; Romance.

Ludwig, Charles

3501. *Defender of the Faith.* Minneapolis, MN: Bethany House, 1988. 202 pp.
Queen Victoria retains her religious faith throughout her 63-year reign as England's leader.
Genre(s): Biographical Fiction; Christian Fiction.

Luke, Peter

3502. *The Other Side of the Hill.* New York: Gollancz, 1984. 250 pp.
During the early 19th century, Harry Smith serves England in Portugal and Spain where he marries a Spanish woman at the time of the Peninsular War.
Genre(s): Biographical Fiction; War Story.

Lyle, Elizabeth

3503. *Cassy.* New York: St. Martin's, 1981. 255 pp.
Left without money after her parents die in an accident, Cassy decides to become an actress, and since this occupation is unacceptable in 1813, Cassy must change her identity.
Genre(s): Regency Novel; Romance.

Lynn, Karen

◆ 3504. *Double Masquerade.* New York: Doubleday, 1981. 192 pp.
Georgie likes to masquerade as her male twin so that she can ride a horse, and when her older brother's friend arrives, she must act differently in an attempt to secure his attentions.
Genre(s): Romance.

Lyons, Genevieve

3505. *The Last Inheritance.* Garden City, NY: Doubleday, 1987. 445 pp.
To escape death during the potato famine of 1847, Michael Casey betrays his family to work as a servant for the Rennetts, and two generations after he loses the job, his great-grandson becomes master of the estate.
Genre(s): Domestic Fiction.

MacDonald, Malcolm

3506. *The Rich Are with You Always.* New York: Knopf, 1976. 483 pp.
The sequel to *The World from Rough Stones* presents the Stevensons and the Thorntons, families whose lives are opposite in almost every way.
Genre(s): Family Saga.

3507. *The Silver Highways.* New York: St. Martin's, 1987. 320 pp.
In 1789, Mary Flinders leaves County Clare for London where people are interested in either canal building or gambling.
Genre(s): Romance.

Macdonald, Shari

3508. *Forget-Me-Not.* Sisters, OR: Palisades, 1996. 274 pp.
After going to England to become an intern at a famous garden, Hayley Buckman meets the gardener who transports her into the days of *Jane Eyre* and *Northanger Abbey*.
Genre(s): Christian Fiction; Mystery.

MacInnes, Colin

3509. *Westward to Laughter.* New York: Farrar, Straus and Giroux, 1970. 237 pp.
Alexander Nairn's uncle sends him to sea, and Alexander becomes a slave, frees himself, sails to different ports, and joins pirates.
Genre(s): Picaresque Fiction.

Mack, Dorothy

3510. *The Counterfeit Widow*. New York: Signet, 1996. 221 pp.
Charity Leonard wants her sister to marry well and to escape from their abusive stepfather, so she poses as a widow and takes her sister to London for the Season.
Genre(s): Regency Novel; Romance.

Macken, Walter

3511. *The Silent People*. New York: Macmillan, 1962. 371 pp.
During the potato famine, a young man tries to survive not only the problem of hunger but also the grasping of the greedy British landlords.
Genre(s): Domestic Fiction.

MacKenna, John

3512. *Clare*. Belfast, Ireland: Blackstaff, 1993. 181 pp.
Lady Kettering, John Clare's patroness, his sister, and his wife remember him as a proud but poor poet who loved nature but dwelt too much on the nostalgic.
Genre(s): Biographical Fiction.

Marchant, Catherine

3513. *The Slow Awakening*. New York: Morrow, 1977. 281 pp.
In 1850, Kirsten becomes the maid to her son when the lady of the manor takes him to replace her own stillborn child.
Genre(s): Domestic Fiction.

Marryat, Frederick

3514. *Frank Mildmay: Or, the Naval Officer*. 1829. Ithaca, NY: McBooks, 1997. 352 pp.
Frank Mildmay serves as a British naval officer during the Napoleonic Wars.
Genre(s): Sea Story; War Story.

3515. *Mr Midshipman Easy*. 1836. New York: Penguin, 1982. 423 pp.
Frank Mildway sails with the British Navy.
Genre(s): Sea Story; War Story.

3516. *Peter Simple*. New York: Heart of Oak Sea, 1998. 467 pp.
Peter Simple is a young shipman at sea fighing for England during the Napoleonic Wars.
Genre(s): War Story; Adventure Story.

Marshall, Edison

3517. *The Infinite Woman*. New York: Farrar, Straus and Giroux, 1950. 374 pp.
Lola Montez, an Irish adventuress, tries to marry a count.
Genre(s): Biographical Fiction.

Martin, Kat

3518. *Devil's Prize*. New York: St. Martin's, 1995. 388 pp.
Damien, Earl of Falon, meets Alexa at the whist table, determined to make her suffer for refusing his brother's proposal and causing his subsequent suicide.
Genre(s): Romance.

3519. *Innocence Undone*. New York: St. Martin's, 1997. 384 pp.
Jessica Fox, daughter of a prostitute, convinces the father of Matthew Seaton, Earl of Strickland, to become her guardian, and after he has her educated and loves her like a daughter, he thinks she should marry his son.
Genre(s): Regency Novel; Romance.

Maugham, Robin

3520. *The Link: A Victorian Mystery*. New York: McGraw Hill, 1969. 202 pp.
Jamie leaves for Australia in the 1850s, having failed to overcome his homosexuality, and as he dies of alcoholism, he convinces his father's illegitimate son to return to England, impersonate Jamie and claim his inheritance.
Genre(s): Mystery.

Maxwell, Candy

3521. *You and No Other*. New York: Avon, 1996. 375 pp.
Lady Caroline Person asks the new owner of the family home to return it since he won it by gambling.
Genre(s): Romance; Regency Novel.

Mayhew, Margaret

3522. *Regency Charade*. New York: Walker, 1986. 183 pp.
After Kate Spencer's brother gambles away the family home of 500 years and then dies in a frivolous race, Kate must face the new owner of Kielder Castle.
Genre(s): Regency Novel; Romance.

Maynard, Kenneth

3523. *First Lieutenant*. New York: St. Martin's, 1985. 214 pp.
Matthew Lamb becomes the first officer on Captain Slade's ship, the *Adroit*, as it sails for the Caribbean and encounters privateers, merchant ships, and bad weather in the early 1800s.
Genre(s): Sea Story; Adventure Story.

3524. *Lamb in Command*. New York: St. Martin's, 1986. 199 pp.
Lamb, captain of the mail ship *Heron*, encounters French and Spanish privateers in the West Indies during the Napoleonic wars.
Genre(s): Sea Story; War Story.

3525. *Lieutenant Lamb*. New York: St. Martin's, 1984. 191 pp.
When Lieutenant Matthew Lamb reports to the H.M.S. *Sturdy* in 1798, he finds his captain a drunkard and the first officer fastidious as they prepare to fight French privateers.
Genre(s): War Story; Adventure Story; Sea Story.

McCutchan, Philip

♦ 3526. *Apprentice to the Sea.* New York: St. Martin's, 1995. 183 pp.
Irish Tom Chatto, 16, takes his first sea journey aboard the *Pass of Drumochter* from Liverpool to South America and experiences danger around Cape Horn when jealousies develop aboard the ship.
Genre(s): Sea Story; Adventure Story.

McDonough, James R.

3527. *The Limits of Glory.* Novato, CA: Presidio, 1991. 300 pp.
While a Scottish colonel leads his Coldstream Guards against Napoleon at Waterloo, the young wife of Wellington's chief of staff waits to hear from her husband.
Genre(s): War Story.

McGorian, Gladys

3528. *The Prince Regent's Silver Bell.* New York: Walker, 1987. 256 pp.
Katherine Martin has to become a proper lady instead of a tomboy to inherit from her uncle's will, and since she needs money to help her father, she goes to live with an unknown aunt for one year where scheming cousins await her.
Genre(s): Regency Novel; Romance.

McNaught, Judith

3529. *Until You.* New York: Pocket Books, 1994. 437 pp.
A young American woman loses her memory and an English lord rescues her because he believes she is the fiancée of the man he accidentally killed.
Genre(s): Romance; Regency Novel.

Medeiros, Teresa

3530. *Thief of Hearts.* New York: Bantam, 1995. 432 pp.
After five years in a windowless dungeon, Captain Doom stops a ship carrying the daughter of the admiral who incarcerated him, but he refuses to hurt her and reappears to become her bodyguard.
Genre(s): Romance.

Mellows, Joan

3531. *Harriet.* New York: Fawcett, 1977. 221 pp.
After deaths in her family leave her independent, Harriet enjoys herself until her brother Geoffrey causes a scandal in Rome.
Genre(s): Regency Novel; Romance.

Menen, Aubrey

3532. *Fonthill.* London: Hamilton, 1975. 188 pp.
When William Beckford loses his Jamaican plantations, he must sell his lovely home, and the man who comes to purchase it, is, like Beckford, a man interested in young boys.
Genre(s): Biographical Fiction; Humorous Fiction.

Meredith, George

3533. *Diana of the Crossways.* New York: Scribner's, 1897. 415 pp.
Diana Merion enters society in the early 19th century, marries, and fights defamation stemming from an innocent friendship.

Metzger, Barbara

3534. *Bething's Folly.* New York: Walker, 1981. 159 pp.
Although Lord Alexander Carleton wants to obey his father and marry, he thinks all women are shallow until he meets Elizabeth Bethingame, intelligent and interested only in her stable of quality race horses.
Genre(s): Regency Novel; Romance.

3535. *The Earl and the Heiress.* New York: Walker, 1982. 170 pp.
When Noelle places an ad in the paper to sell the toy Maltese dogs that her late father purchased for his now deceased wife, Justin, the Earl of Wrenthe, arrives to buy one for his Italian mistress, and although he and Noelle conflict during the transaction, later events lead to their engagement.
Genre(s): Regency Novel; Romance.

3536. *Father Christmas.* New York: Ballantine, 1995. 214 pp.
So that he will not have to worry about marriage, the Duke of Ware decides to choose one of his late cousin's twin sons as his heir, but the boy's mother has other ideas, and when she arrives to tell him, his interest changes to her.
Genre(s): Regency Novel; Romance.

3537. *Rake's Ransom.* New York: Walker, 1986. 239 pp.
Jacelyn Tremaine, 17, has a London season at her father's friend's suggestion, and she meets an impoverished earl whose uncle is a slave-trader.
Genre(s): Regency Novel; Romance.

Michaels, Barbara

3538. *Greygallows.* New York: Dodd, Mead, 1972. 279 pp.
In the early 1840s, Lucy Cartwright meets a young lawyer's assistant who comes to her aid after she is forced to marry against her will.
Genre(s): Romance; Gothic Fiction.

Michaels, Fern

3539. *Captive Embraces.* New York: Ballantine, 1979. 455 pp.
Sirena Cródez and her husband, Regan van der Rhys, become distressed by the death of her child, and after he goes to Spain, he divorces her in the sequel to *Captive Passions.*
Genre(s): Family Saga; Romance.

Michaels, Kasey

3540. *The Passion of an Angel.* New York: Pocket Books, 1995. 375 pp.
While awaiting the Battle of Waterloo, Henry MacAfee asks Banning Talbot, Marquess of Daventry, to become guardian to his little sister if MacAfee should die, and when he does, Banning finds out that she is beautiful but uncultivated.
Genre(s): Romance; Regency Novel; War Story.

Miller, Cissie

3541. *Tish.* Garden City, NY: Doubleday, 1981. 192 pp.
Tish (Lady Letitia) engages in ballooning to help support her family but refuses to let her pursuer, a handsome earl, know that she needs money.
Genre(s): Regency Novel; Romance; Love Story.

Mills, Anita

3542. *Secret Nights.* New York: New American Library, 1994. 384 pp.
Elise Rand tells barrister Patrick Hamilton that he can have her in payment for defending her father in a murder trial.
Genre(s): Regency Novel; Romance; Legal Story.

Monk, Karyn

3543. *Once a Warrior.* New York: Bantam, 1997. 370 pp.
Becuase she is female, Ariella MacKendrick cannot assume leadership of her clan, so she must find the warrior Black Wolf and make him Laird of Clan MacKendrick, but instead of bravery, what she finds is a disillusioned shell of a man.
Genre(s): Romance.

Monsarrat, Nicholas

3544. *Darken Ship.* New York: Morrow, 1981. 181 pp.
Matthew Lawe becomes captain of an illegal slave trader.
(*Series:* The Master Mariner, 2)
Genre(s): Sea Story; Fantastic Literature.

Moore, Kate

3545. *An Improper Widow.* New York: Avon, 1995. 214 pp.
His calling cards stolen and distributed throughout London in unexpected places, the Marquess of Warne begins searching for the thief and finds unexpected love.
Genre(s): Regency Novel; Romance.

3546. *A Prince Among Men.* New York: Avon, 1997. 384 pp.
Prince Alexander of Trevigna hides his identity by becoming a groom in the stables of the obstinate Lady Ophelia Brinsby, and he falls in love with her.
Genre(s): Romance; Regency Novel.

Moore, Susan

3547. *A World Too Wide.* New York: St. Martin's, 1989. 320 pp.
In the sequel to *Paths of Fortune*, Sophy and James Fraser pursue their fortunes in England while Sophy's sister Kate and her husband come to America as the Napoleonic Wars rage.
Genre(s): Adventure Story.

Nadolny, Sten

3548. *The Discovery of Slowness.* New York: Viking, 1987. 325 pp.
John Franklin has the reputation of being slow and deliberate, two traits which help him to discover the Northwest Passage in the 19th century.
Genre(s): Biographical Fiction.

Naef, Adam

3549. *The Barbury Hall Murders.* Providence, RI: Picardy, 1997. 216 pp.
Elmira Mayhew is a singer profiting from her parents' deaths, but when she visits a cousin, a murder occurs with her French accompanist the prime suspect.
Genre(s): Mystery.

Nicole, Christopher

3550. *The Sea and the Sand.* Hampton, NH: Severn House, 1988. 332 pp.
In the sequel to *Old Glory*, Toby MacGann falls in love with English Felicity Crown, 15, in the early 1800s, and before they can meet again, Barbary pirates capture the ship on which Felicity sails to Gibraltar, and Mohammed ben Idris buys her as his concubine.
Genre(s): Romance; Adventure Story; War Story; Sea Story.

Nye, Robert

3551. *The Memoirs of Lord Byron.* London: Hamish Hamilton, 1989. 224 pp.
The memoirs of Lord Byron, discovered after his death, describe his life and those around him, including his furniture, his dog, incest with his sister, and the passions of his friends.
Genre(s): Biographical Fiction.

O'Brian, Patrick

◆ 3552. *The Commodore.* New York: Norton, 1995. 281 pp.
Captain Jack Aubrey and Stephen Maturin stay in England to reconnect with their families before Aubrey leaves to stop slavers out of Africa, in the sequel to *The Wine-Dark Sea*.
Genre(s): Sea Story; War Story.

◆ 3553. *Desolation Island.* New York: Norton, 1991. 276 pp.
Captain Jack Aubrey and surgeon Stephen Maturin sail on the *Leopold* to Australia with convicts in the hold and

a beautiful female spy above, in the sequel to *The Mauritius Command*.
Genre(s): Sea Story; War Story.

◆ **3554.** *The Far Side of the World.* New York: Norton, 1992. 366 pp.
Captain Jack Aubrey and his friend, Stephen Maturin, round Cape Horn in the early 19th century during the time of Lord Nelson, to face their enemy, in the sequel to *Treason's Harbor*.
Genre(s): Sea Story; War Story.

◆ **3555.** *The Fortune of War.* New York: Norton, 1991. 329 pp.
When the War of 1812 begins, in the sequel to *Desolation Island*, Captain Jack Aubrey and Stephen Maturin rapidly sail from the Dutch East Indies to England.
Genre(s): Sea Story; War Story.

◆ **3556.** *The Golden Ocean.* New York: Norton, 1994. 285 pp.
Peter Palafox sails with the British navy in the early 19th century.
Genre(s): Sea Story.

◆ **3557.** *HMS Surprise.* New York: Norton, 1991. 318 pp.
Captain Jack Aubrey and Stephen Maturin save themselves from a local pirate in the Indian Ocean during the days of Lord Nelson, in the sequel to *Post Captain*.
Genre(s): Sea Story; War Story.

◆ **3558.** *The Ionian Mission.* New York: Norton, 1991. 367 pp.
Captain Jack Aubrey and Stephen Maturin sail to the Greek islands on a secret mission for the British navy in the sequel to *The Surgeon's Mate*.
Genre(s): Sea Story; War Story.

3559. *The Letter of Marque.* New York: Norton, 1990. 284 pp.
Jack Aubrey, dismissed unfairly from the British navy, continues his sea career as a privateer while Stephen Maturin, ship's doctor, must balance the discords in his own life while showing concern for his friend, in the sequel to *The Reverse of the Medal*.
Genre(s): Sea Story; War Story.

◆ **3560.** *Master and Commander.* New York: Norton, 1990. 412 pp.
Captain Jack Aubrey and Stephen Maturin fight in the Napoleonic Wars.
Genre(s): Sea Story; War Story.

3561. *The Mauritius Command.* New York: Stein and Day, 1978. 268 pp.
In the sequel to *HMS Surprise*, Jack Aubrey and Stephen Maturin have a charge to capture Mauritius and La Réunion, French outposts on the Indian Ocean.
Genre(s): Sea Story.

◆ **3562.** *Post Captain.* New York: Norton, 1990. 496 pp.
Captain Jack Aubrey escapes from debtors' prison in France, in the sequel to *Master and Commander*, and afterward, he and Stephen Maturin, a surgeon and a spy,

avoid a mutiny as they pursue their enemies into a French harbor.
Genre(s): Sea Story; War Story.

◆ **3563.** *The Reverse of the Medal.* New York: Norton, 1995. 287 pp.
Stephen Maturin helps Captain Jack Aubrey flee from criminals while working on a government spy project, in the sequel to *The Far Side of the World*.
Genre(s): Sea Story; War Story.

◆ **3564.** *The Surgeon's Mate.* New York: Norton, 1992. 382 pp.
In the sequel to *The Fortune of War*, two privateers chase Captain Jack Aubrey and Stephen Maturin through the fog and shallow water of the Grand Banks.
Genre(s): Sea Story; War Story.

◆ **3565.** *Thirteen Gun Salute.* New York: Norton, 1991. 320 pp.
In the sequel to *The Letter of Marque*, Jack Aubrey and Stephen Maturin sail in the Dutch East Indies during the Napoleonic Wars the on *Diane* to thwart French attacks in the area.
Genre(s): Sea Story; War Story.

◆ **3566.** *Treason's Harbour.* New York: Norton, 1992. 334 pp.
Sabotage threatens Captain Jack Aubrey and Stephen Maturin while sailing in the Red Sea in the sequel to *The Ionian Mission*.
Genre(s): Sea Story; War Story.

◆ **3567.** *The True Love.* New York: Norton, 1992. 256 pp.
Captain Jack Aubrey and Stephen Maturin sail the *Surprise* to recapture a British whaler from the French in the sequel to *The Nutmeg of Consolation*.
Genre(s): Sea Story; War Story.

◆ **3568.** *The Unknown Shore.* New York: Norton, 1995. 313 pp.
Midshipman Jack Byron and Tobias Barrow sail the *Wager*, unaware of the ship's serious problems.
Genre(s): Sea Story.

◆ **3569.** *The Wine-Dark Sea.* New York: Norton, 1993. 261 pp.
Captain Jack Aubrey and Stephen Maturin sail as privateers to the Great South Sea, in the sequel to *The True Love*, dealing with storms and icebergs, and finally arrive in Peru.
Genre(s): Sea Story; War Story.

◆ **3570.** *The Yellow Admiral.* New York: Norton, 1996. 261 pp.
In the sequel to *The Commodore*, Jack Aubrey gratefully goes back to sea to follow Napoleon after his escape from Gibraltar as an evasion from lawsuits against him for the slavers he has seized.
Genre(s): Sea Story; War Story.

O'Flaherty, Liam

3571. *Famine.* New York: Random House, 1937. 458 pp.

In the 1840s, Irish peasants must escape from the potato famine or perish.
Genre(s): Domestic Fiction.

Ogilvie, Elisabeth

◆ 3572. *Jennie About To Be.* New York: McGraw Hill, 1984. 345 pp.
Idealistic Jennie Hawthorne leaves London for Scotland but becomes outraged with her husband when he burns peasant cottages for additional land on which to raise sheep.
Genre(s): Domestic Fiction.

Overfield, Joan

3573. *Time's Tapestry.* New York: Zebra, 1996. 301 pp.
When police detective Cara Marsdale falls into Regency London dressed in her chains and green hair, she must investigate in a different environment.
Genre(s): Regency Novel; Time Travel; Mystery.

Palmer, William J.

3574. *The Highwayman and Mr. Dickens.* New York: St. Martin's, 1992. 273 pp.
Wilkie Collins, friend of Charles Dickens in the sequel to *The Detective and Mr. Dickens,* tells of his and Dickens's investigation of the murder of a society woman and her maid in London during 1852.
Genre(s): Mystery.

Parkinson, C. Northcote

3575. *Dead Reckoning.* Boston: Houghton Mifflin, 1978. 276 pp.
In the sequel to *So Near, So Far,* Richard Delancy, happily married commander of a British frigate from 1805 to 1811, serves in the East Indies where he helps capture Mauritius before becoming a knight.
Genre(s): War Story.

3576. *Devil to Pay.* Boston: Houghton Mifflin, 1973. 273 pp.
In the sequel to *The Guernsey Man,* Lt. Richard Delancey takes command of a revenue cutter and then rises to command of an English privateer during the Napoleonic Wars.
Genre(s): War Story.

◆ 3577. *The Fireship.* Boston: Houghton Mifflin, 1975. 187 pp.
Richard Delancey does not get a desired promotion in Her Majesty's Navy, but he continues his strong service in battle against the French during the 18th century, in the sequel to *Devil to Pay.*
Genre(s): War Story.

◆ 3578. *The Guernsey Man.* Boston: Houghton Mifflin, 1982. 175 pp.
Richard Delancey is purser's clerk, midshipman, and lieutenant as he is caught in the Merseyside seamen's riot.
Genre(s): War Story; Sea Story.

3579. *The Life and Times of Horatio Hornblower.* Boston: Little, Brown, 1972. 304 pp.

The fictional character Horatio Hornblower becomes the subject of this biography, which incorporates his experiences in 11 novels with factual occurences of the time.
Genre(s): War Story; Biographical Fiction.

◆ 3580. *So Near, So Far.* Boston: Houghton Mifflin, 1981. 227 pp.
In the sequel to *Touch and Go,* Richard Delancey tries to keep the French from capturing Pitt in Walmet Castle.
Genre(s): War Story.

◆ 3581. *Touch and Go.* Boston: Houghton Mifflin, 1977. 230 pp.
In the sequel to *The Fireship,* Richard Delancey commands a British sloop protecting merchant convoys on a Mediterranean trade route from Napoleon's forces.
Genre(s): War Story.

Paul, Barbara

◆ 3582. *The Frenchwoman.* New York: St. Martin's, 1978. 278 pp.
Juliette Delahousse comes to England to marry Gregory Lockington but falls in love with his brother before becoming involved in a Napoleonic plot.
Genre(s): War Story; Romance.

Pearce, Mary Emily

◆ 3583. *Apple Tree Lean Down.* New York: St. Martin's, 1976. 494 pp.
In the late 18th and early 19th century, wealthy Beth Tewkes marries a poor man, and their daughter, after moving to London, devotes herself to caring for invalid soldiers.
Genre(s): Domestic Fiction.

◆ 3584. *Polsinney Harbour.* New York: St. Martin's, 1983. 221 pp.
In the mid-19th century, Maggie Care makes a life for herself and her unborn child after her father, brother, and lover all die in an accident.
Genre(s): Domestic Fiction.

Peart, Jane

◆ 3585. *Ransomed Bride.* Grand Rapids, MI: Zondervan, 1989. 304 pp.
Lorabeth Whitaker flees England and an undesirable marriage to come to the colonies. (*Series:* Brides of Montclair, 2)
Genre(s): Christian Fiction; Romance.

3586. *Valiant Bride.* Grand Rapids, MI: Zondervan, 1989. 192 pp.
A young woman chooses duty over love. (*Series:* Brides of Montclair, 1)
Genre(s): Christian Fiction; Romance.

Perkins, Robert

3587. *Hoare and the Portsmouth Atrocity.* New York: St. Martin's, 1998. 224 pp.
On shore from sea duty in the Royal Navy, officer Bartholomew Hoare tries to stop men attacking a lady,

but the next day, he discovers that one of the attackers has been murdered.
Genre(s): Mystery; Adventure Story.

Perry, Anne

3588. *A Dangerous Mourning.* New York: Fawcett Columbine, 1991. 330 pp.
William Monk thinks that only family and servants can be suspects in the murder of aristocrat Octavia Haslett and asks his friend, nurse Hester Latterly, to help him confirm this.
Genre(s): Mystery.

◆ 3589. *The Face of a Stranger.* New York: Fawcett Columbine, 1990. 328 pp.
William Monk, a member of the London police force in 1856, develops amnesia after an accident, and, while trying to solve the murder of an aristocrat, he looks at his own character.
Genre(s): Mystery.

Pianka, Phyllis Taylor

3590. *Heather Wild.* South Yarmouth, MA: Curley, 1990. 343 pp.
Kidnapped from a London dressmaker's, Lady Elizabeth Cambridge finds herself in Devon's Heathenwood Castle because Arthur, brother of the Duke of Heathenwood, has mistaken her for her look-alike niece who is engaged to the duke but resisting marriage, a situation Arthur plans to correct.
Genre(s): Regency Novel; Romance; Love Story.

3591. *The Thackery Jewels.* New York: Harlequin, 1994. 432 pp.
When Amethyst, Emerald, and Topaz, the three Thackerys, make their debuts in London, although they are attractive and eligible, finding matches for their three different personalities is no easy task.
Genre(s): Regency Novel; Romance.

Plaidy, Jean

◆ 3592. *The Captive of Kensington Palace.* New York: Putnam, 1976. 288 pp.
The young Victoria lives in Kensington Palace. (*Series:* Queen Victoria, 1)
Genre(s): Biographical Fiction.

◆ 3593. *Indiscretions of the Queen.* New York: Putnam, 1988. 352 pp.
Caroline Brunswick and the Prince Regent George have unusual nuptials, and scandals prevail during their union. (*Series:* Georgian Saga, 8)
Genre(s): Biographical Fiction.

◆ 3594. *The Queen and Lord M.* New York: Putnam, 1977. 268 pp.
In the sequel to *The Captive of Kensington Palace*, Queen Victoria learns how to be regal. (*Series:* Queen Victoria, 2)
Genre(s): Biographical Fiction.

◆ 3595. *The Queen's Husband.* New York: Putnam, 1978. 382 pp.

The sequel to *The Queen and Lord M* introduces Albert and tells of his influence on Victoria. (*Series:* Queen Victoria, 3)
Genre(s): Biographical Fiction.

Polland, Madeleine A.

◆ 3596. *All Their Kingdoms.* New York: Delacorte, 1981. 413 pp.
In Ireland, during the 19th century, Celia Healey, escapes marriage from an old, unattractive man, but after marriage to her handsome husband of 16 years, he dies, and she and her children must combat his uncle.
Genre(s): Romance.

Pope, Dudley

3597. *Drumbeat.* Garden City, NY: Doubleday, 1968. 279 pp.
In the sequel to *Ramage*, Lieutenant Lord Nicholas and his sloop fight in the Mediterranean in 1797.
Genre(s): War Story; Sea Story.

3598. *Governor Ramage, RN 914.* New York: Simon and Schuster, 1973. 340 pp.
The sequel to *The Triton Brig* tells of the encounters experienced by Lieutenant Nicholas Ramage while he is sailing from Barbados to Jamaica.
Genre(s): Sea Story; War Story.

3599. *Ramage.* Philadelphia: Lippincott, 1965. 302 pp.
Off the coast of Italy, Lieutenant Ramage of the British Navy abandons the sinking ship he had to take command of after its senior officers died, but he faces a court-martial for his actions.
Genre(s): Sea Story; War Story.

3600. *Ramage and the Guillotine.* New York: Avon, 1975. 285 pp.
In the sequel to *Ramage's Prize*, Napoleon collects an invasion fleet at Boulogne, and Lord Ramage is smuggled ashore to quell it.
Genre(s): Sea Story; War Story.

3601. *The Ramage Touch.* New York: Walker, 1984. 226 pp.
In the sequel to *Ramage and the Rebels*, Nicholas, Lord Ramage, is ordered from the West Indies to the Mediterranean, where he is supposed to disrupt French shipping.
Genre(s): Sea Story; War Story.

3602. *Ramage's Challenge.* London: Alison, 1985. 261 pp.
In the sequel to *Ramage's Trial*, Captain Nicholas Ramage must rescue a group of English admirals, generals, and aristocrats which the French are holding as prisoners following the breakdown of the Treaty of Amiens.
Genre(s): Sea Story; War Story.

3603. *Ramage's Devil.* London: Secker and Warburg, 1982. 256 pp.
In the sequel to *Ramage and the Renegades*, Captain Ramage is forced to go into hiding while honeymooning

in Brittany when war between England and France re-starts.
Genre(s): Sea Story; War Story.

3604. *Ramage's Diamond.* New York: Avon, 1976. 307 pp.
In the sequel to *Ramage and the Guillotine*, Ramage, Post Captain, takes his crew to blockade Martinique, and his men try to persuade him to marry his love.
Genre(s): War Story; Sea Story.

3605. *Ramage's Mutiny.* London: Secker and War-burg, 1977. 232 pp.
In the sequel to *Ramage's Diamond*, Ramage becomes a pawn for his devious admiral.
Genre(s): War Story; Sea Story.

3606. *Ramage's Prize.* New York: Simon and Schuster, 1975. 344 pp.
In the sequel to *Governor Ramage, R.N. 914*, Ramage has another romantic naval adventure while battling Napo-leon.
Genre(s): Sea Story; War Story.

3607. *Ramage's Signal.* New York: Walker, 1984. 225 pp.
In the sequel to *The Ramage Touch*, Lord Nicholas Ram-age goes to the Mediterranean and finds an isolated French semaphore station from which he learns about a French merchant convoy on its way and he is prepared to capture it.
Genre(s): Sea Story; War Story.

3608. *The Triton Brig.* Garden City, NY: Dou-bleday, 1969. 378 pp.
The sequel to *Drumbeat* finds Lieutenant Lord Ramage on the *Triton* having to stop the Spithead mutiny.
Genre(s): Sea Story; War Story.

Pope, Pamela

3609. *The Rich Pass By.* North Pomfret, VT: Cen-tury, 1991. 384 pp.
In the mid-19th century, Sarah Byrne has to give her ille-gitimate daughter to the Foundling Hospital because she cannot support her, but Sarah stays nearby for the next 20 years.
Genre(s): Domestic Fiction.

Porter, Margaret Evans

3610. *Irish Autumn.* New York: Walker, 1990. 216 pp.
Garia Ivory looks after her three younger stepbrothers, abandoned by their mother after the death of her father, and when the new Lord Lindal arrives, they are attracted to one another.
Genre(s): Regency Novel; Romance.

3611. *Road to Ruin.* New York: Walker, 1990. 182 pp.
Nerissa Newby, an orphan, leaves her home village to stay with a friend, and on her journey, she meets Dominic Blythe, falsely accused of murder, who asks her to help him by pretending to be his wife.
Genre(s): Regency Novel; Romance.

◆ 3612. *Sweet Lavender.* New York: Walker, 1992. 179 pp.
Lady Beryl Rowen wants to marry below her class, a choice which her father prohibits, and Lady Beryl's sister asks for Lord Elston, a confirmed bachelor, to take her sister's mind off her loss.
Genre(s): Regency Novel; Romance.

Power, Una

3613. *The Spellbinder.* London: Century, 1993. 314 pp.
In late-18th-century Ireland, Lady Georgiana Ryden is sure that Bartley Kincaid, her despised neighbor, wants to marry her so that he can take ownership of her Castle Cloona, but when she is imprisoned for conspiracy and murder, and she escapes, he rescues her in London.
Genre(s): Romance.

Prokosch, Frederic

3614. *The Missolonghi Manuscript.* New York: Farrar, Straus and Giroux, 1984. 338 pp.
As Lord Byron dies in the Greek village of Missolonghi, he keeps notebooks in which he re-examines his past.
Genre(s): Biographical Fiction.

Pruner, Lenora

3615. *Love's Secret Storm.* Minneapolis, MN: Be-thany House, 1981. 272 pp.
After Meg marries Will, an outcast clergyman, she real-izes that she prefers her life in society to that of a rural pastor's wife.
Genre(s): Romance; Christian Fiction.

Putney, Mary Jo

3616. *One Perfect Rose.* New York: Fawcett, 1997. 421 pp.
When the doctor tells Stephen Kenyon, Duke of Ashbur-ton, that he has only a few months to live, he leaves the family estate, and when he happens to rescue a young boy, he becomes part of a travelling theater company where he meets Rosalind Jordan.
Genre(s): Romance.

3617. *River of Fire.* New York: Signet, 1996. 379 pp.
To retrieve the estate that his father has ruined, Captain Kenneth Wilding, who has returned from the Napoleonic Wars, must solve a murder in an artist's household.
Genre(s): Romance; Regency Novel; Mystery.

3618. *Shattered Rainbows.* New York: Topaz, 1996. 380 pp.
Catherine Melbourne and Lord Michael Kenyon meet in Spain in 1812 when he is wounded and she is married to another officer, but they do not acknowledge their love until she, a widow, asks for his help four years later.
Genre(s): Regency Novel; Romance; War Story.

Quick, Amanda

3619. *Dangerous.* New York: Bantam, 1993. 273 pp.

After Prudence Merryweather and Sebastian Fleetwood meet and fall in love, Prue encourages Sebastian to be benevolent rather than hostile when her aunt insults him.
Genre(s): Romance; Regency Novel.

3620.*Deception.* New York: Bantam, 1993. 342 pp.
Olympia Wingfield loves researching foreign lands, and her uncle requests that handsome aristocrat Jared Ryder deliver goods to her secured on his travels.
Genre(s): Romance.

◆ 3621. *Mischief.* New York: Bantam, 1996. 374 pp.
Imogene Waterstone asks the Earl of Colchester to help her solve murders, but both deny any love interest in the other.
Genre(s): Love Story; Regency Novel; Romance.

3622.*Mistress.* New York: Bantam, 1994. 342 pp.
Iphiginia Bright believes that the person blackmailing her aunt has killed a man, so she pretends to be the man's mistress until the man returns, not dead, and she has to explain who she is.
Genre(s): Regency Novel; Romance.

3623.*Reckless.* New York: Bantam, 1993. 400 pp.
When Lady Phoebe Layton's suitor is killed and a valuable book stolen from him, she asks another book collector to find the book and the murderer.
Genre(s): Regency Novel; Romance.

3624.*Rendezvous.* New York: Bantam, 1991. 384 pp.
Widower Harry Fleming, earl of Graystone and former spy, arranges a marriage with a reckless but loyal woman who is uninterested in marrying a scholar like Harry.
Genre(s): Regency Novel; Romance.

3625.*Surrender.* New York: Bantam, 1994. 352 pp.
Heiress Victoria Huntington has no interest in marriage, but she accepts the companionship of Lucas Colebrook and suggests a liaison.
Genre(s): Romance; Regency Novel.

3626.*With this Ring.* New York: Bantam, 1998. 368 pp.
Even though people advise her against it, a female author of gothic novels searches for a mystical set of rings.
Genre(s): Regency Novel; Romance.

Quinn, Julia

3627.*Everything and the Moon.* New York: Avon, 1997. 372 pp.
Victoria Lyndon, the vicar's daughter, falls in love with Robert Kemble, the Earl of Maccelesfield, but her father objects, and when they meet after seven years, the two have painful memories.
Genre(s): Regency Novel; Romance.

Rabe, Sheila

3628.*Bringing Out Betsy.* New York: Zebra, 1994. 251 pp.
The Duke of Littlefield placates his grandmother and ensures his inheritance by agreeing halfheartedly to sponsor

her old friend's granddaughter in London, but the naive manner of the granddaughter charms him instead.
Genre(s): Regency Novel; Romance.

Ranney, Karen

3629.*My Wicked Fantasy.* New York: Avon, 1998. 384 pp.
A carriage accident knocks Mary Kate, a young widow, unconscious, and the evil Lord of Sanderhurst rescues her.
Genre(s): Romance.

Rayner, Claire

3630.*Gower Street.* New York: Simon and Schuster, 1973. 351 pp.
Abel Lackland, a rescued slum boy, becomes a successful apothecary and surgeon. (*Series:* The Performer, 1)
Genre(s): Domestic Fiction; Medical Novel; Family Saga.

3631.*The Haymarket.* New York: Simon and Schuster, 1974. 320 pp.
In the sequel to *Gower Street,* Abel's son Jonah attends the theater, forbidden to family members, and meets Lilith Lucas who turns out to be part of his father's past. (*Series:* The Performer, 2)
Genre(s): Domestic Fiction; Medical Novel; Family Saga.

3632.*Paddington Green.* New York: Simon and Schuster, 1975. 348 pp.
The sequel to *The Haymarket* shows Abel Lackland, surgeon at St. Eleanor's in the early 19th century, and his married children as they face and overcome obstacles. (*Series:* The Performer, 3)
Genre(s): Domestic Fiction; Medical Novel; Family Saga.

3633.*Soho Square.* New York: Putnam, 1976. 311 pp.
During the 1850s, in the sequel to *Paddington Green,* the Lackland grandchild Freddie studies to be a surgeon while falling in love with his childhood friend and cousin Phoebe. (*Series:* The Performer, 4)
Genre(s): Domestic Fiction; Medical Novel; Family Saga.

Raynes, Jean

◆ 3634. *Legacy of the Wolf.* New York: Doubleday, 1977. 192 pp.
Olivia Selkirk becomes an accountant for the Countess of Dunkeigh and finds out that her Cameron blood is all that can save her.
Genre(s): Romance.

Reeman, Douglas

3635.*Badge of Glory.* New York: Morrow, 1984. 357 pp.
In 1850, Captain Philip Blackwood tries to abolish slavery in western Africa before fighting in the Crimea.
Genre(s): War Story; Sea Story.

Rees, Barbara, and Bronte, Patrick Branwell

◆ 3636. *Harriet Dark.* New York: Scribner's, 1979. 157 pp.
A gentle master brings a foundling into his household staff on a country estate.
Genre(s): Domestic Fiction.

Reeves, Barbara

3637. *The Carriage Trade.* New York: Walker, 1993. 204 pp.
Lord Maitland cannot forget the beautiful Virginia who followed her husband to the Peninsular Campaign, and afterward, when he hears that her husband is dead and she has become a caterer, he tries to restore her damaged reputation.
Genre(s): Regency Novel; Romance.

Richardson, Evelyn

3638. *My Wayward Lady.* New York: New American Library, 1997. 300 pp.
Bored in London with her sister, Lady Harriet Fareham secretly continues her work with the poor at one of the city's brothels, and the handsome Lord Adrian Chalfont becomes interested in her.
Genre(s): Romance; Regency Novel.

Roberts, Meg-Lynn

3639. *Christmas Escapade.* New York: Zebra, 1994. 317 pp.
Mary Marlowe's employer requests that she introduce his giddy daughter Belinda to society, and after the Viscount Lindford rescues them from muggers, he starts wooing Belinda, only to realize that Mary is the one he wants.
Genre(s): Regency Novel; Romance.

Ronalds, Mary Teresa

3640. *A Victorian Masque.* London: Macdonald and Jane's, 1975. 268 pp.
Arthur Sullivan breaks with William Gilbert and the D'Oly Carte opera after being deceived.
Genre(s): Biographical Fiction; Musical Fiction; Love Story.

Ross, Kate

◆ 3641. *A Broken Vessel.* New York: Viking, 1994. 289 pp.
Julian Kestrel joins with Sally, a prostitute, to find the murderer of a woman staying in a refuge for prostitutes in Regency London.
Genre(s): Mystery; Regency Novel.

◆ 3642. *Cut to the Quick.* New York: Viking, 1993. 333 pp.
In the 1820s, Mark Craddock, a former stable hand, blackmails Hugh Fontclair into affiancing Fontclair's son to Craddock's daughter, and at a party before the wedding, Julian Kestrel finds a murdered woman in his bed.
Genre(s): Mystery; Regency Novel.

◆ 3643. *Whom the Gods Love.* New York: Viking, 1995. 382 pp.
Julian Kestrel investigates the early-19th-century murder of Alexander Falkland, who was killed at a party in his own home.
Genre(s): Mystery; Regency Novel.

Ross-Macdonald, Malcolm

3644. *Tessa d'Arblay.* New York: St. Martin's, 1985. 310 pp.
Tessa d'Arblay investigates the death of her father's curate and falls in love with an artist fascinated with evil who leads her to both the killer and the methods used by a murderer of London prostitutes.
Genre(s): Mystery.

3645. *The World from Rough Stones.* New York: Knopf, 1975. 535 pp.
In 1839 John and Nora Stevenson belong to the laboring class, but they become involved with the middle-class Walter and Arabella Thornton when the railroads come to England.
Genre(s): Domestic Fiction.

Rundle, Anne

3646. *Grey Ghyll.* New York: St. Martin's, 1979. 224 pp.
Kit Talbot falls in love with a gypsy girl, and his wife hangs herself, so Kit must raise an infant daughter and a son left on his doorstep, probably his and the gypsy's, while Faro Amerwood appears, masquerading as a Frenchman.
Genre(s): Romance.

Russell, Ray

3647. *The Bishop's Daughter.* Boston: Houghton Mifflin, 1981. 311 pp.
Melissa Worthing writes her diary in 1811 and describes her relationship with Wilfrid Summerfield as well as the man she murders who raped her.
Genre(s): Romance.

Savage, Elizabeth

3648. *Willowwood.* Boston: Little, Brown, 1978. 214 pp.
Dante Gabriel Rossetti, an artist and poet, loves and marries the frail, artistic Elizabeth Siddal, while having an affair with Jane, the wife of his friend, and keeping a mistress, Fanny Cornforth.
Genre(s): Biographical Fiction; Domestic Fiction.

Savery, Jeanne

3649. *An Acceptable Arrangement.* New York: Walker, 1993. 193 pp.
Lord John and Phillida Morgan both ask their servants to look for suitable spouses for them since ambitious mothers are always trying to get them married to their children, but the servants work for Lord John and Phillida to marry each other.
Genre(s): Regency Novel; Romance.

◆May be suitable for young adult readers

3650.*A Christmas Miracle.* New York: Zebra, 1994. 320 pp.
Ernestine Matthewson goes to the Peninsula to help her sister Norry when Norry says that her husband is missing in action, and she meets an officer who entrances her.
Genre(s): Regency Novel; Romance.

3651.*A Handful of Promises.* New York: Walker, 1992. 195 pp.
Secunus Alcester returns to England after living in India for 15 years and finds that his love has waited for him.
Genre(s): Regency Novel; Romance.

3652.*The Last of the Winter Roses.* New York: Walker, 1991. 204 pp.
Lady Ardith Winter thinks that she is the ugly sister among a family of beauties, but St. John Worth convinces her otherwise.
Genre(s): Regency Novel; Romance.

Scott, Joanna

3653.*The Closest Possible Union.* New York: Ticknor and Fields, 1988. 256 pp.
A young boy traveling on his father's illegal slave ship finds out about the narrowness of life that can exist on a ship as well as in the mind.
Genre(s): Bildungsroman (Coming of Age).

Scott, Walter

3654.*The Antiquary.* New York: Columbia University Press, 1995. 541 pp.
Jonathan Oldbuck, an antiquary, lives in Scotland near the end of the 18th century.
Genre(s): Adventure Story.

3655.*The Black Dwarf.* 1816. New York: Columbia, 1993. 237 pp.
Clans along the Scottish border with England fight to protect their heritage.
Genre(s): War Story.

3656.*Saint Ronan's Well.* 1824. New York: Columbia University Press, 1995. 508 pp.
Citizens enjoy country life in Scotland during the 18th century.
Genre(s): Adventure Story.

Selwyn, Francis

3657.*Cracksman on Velvet.* New York: Stein and Day, 1974. 254 pp.
In 1857 William Verity must find an ex-army officer who plans to rob a train of its gold bullion cargo in Victorian London.
Genre(s): Mystery.

Sennett, Richard

3658.*Palais-Royal.* New York: Knopf, 1987. 320 pp.
The Courtland sons, Charles and Frederick, begin a correspondence in 1828 which extends 40 years and reveals their attitudes toward their careers—one a priest without faith and the other, an artist with aesthetic detachment.

Seymour, Arabella

3659.*A Passion in the Blood.* New York: Putnam, 1985. 375 pp.
Anna Brodie, illegitimate daughter of a landowner, raises horses, and when she unexpectedly inherits his land, she continues to breed and run racehorses in the 1830s, shocking those around her.
Genre(s): Romance.

Shannon, Dell

3660.*The Scalpel and the Sword.* New York: Morrow, 1987. 392 pp.
The Irish Con McDonough becomes a naval surgeon, and after Nelson's death, he goes with Wellington to Portugal, only to be distressed that he does not know enough to save the men.
Genre(s): War Story; Medical Novel.

Sheridan, Jane

3661.*My Lady Hoyden.* New York: St. Martin's, 1981. 319 pp.
After a slight romance with the Prince of Wales, Amanda must marry an unsuitable young noble in the late 1850s, while her sister marries the duke who loves Amanda.
Genre(s): Romance.

Sherwood, Frances

◆ 3662. *Vindication.* New York: Farrar, Straus and Giroux, 1993. 435 pp.
Mary Wollstonecraft escapes from her home into unhappy relationships until she marries William Godwin and writes *A Vindication of the Rights of Woman*, before her death at the birth of her daughter, Mary Wollstonecraft Godwin (Shelley).
Genre(s): Biographical Fiction; War Story.

Sherwood, Valerie

3663.*Rash Reckless Love.* New York: Warner, 1982. 572 pp.
Imogene's husband owns plantations in Carolina and Jamaica, which his brothers and sisters connive to inherit by trying to get rid of Imogene.
Genre(s): Romance.

3664.*This Loving Torment.* New York: Gregg, 1985. 528 pp.
Charity Woodstock sails from England to Massachusetts, and on her way, becomes the prey of a variety of men including a highwayman, burgher, trapper, planter, and a buccaneer.
Genre(s): Romance; Adventure Story.

Simonson, Sheila

3665.*The Bar Sinister.* New York: Walker, 1986. 282 pp.
After Emily loses both her husband and baby daughter, she offers to take in children to raise with her son, and

Captain Falk brings his two children before leaving to fight Napoleon.
Genre(s): Regency Novel; Romance.

3666. *A Cousinly Connexion.* New York: Walker, 1985. 195 pp.
Julian Stretton unexpectedly inherits the family wealth when both his father and older brother die within two weeks, and as he takes responsibility, he slowly comes to appreciate Jane Ash, a distant cousin by marriage.
Genre(s): Regency Novel; Romance.

3667. *Lady Elizabeth's Comet.* New York: Walker, 1985. 220 pp.
Lady Elizabeth, 28, is content with her life as an astronomer until a new earl comes to take possession of the family estate after her father dies.
Genre(s): Regency Novel; Romance.

3668. *Love and Folly.* New York: Walker, 1988. 306 pp.
While the death of George III concerns England, twin girls, a poet, and a politician become involved with politics and with each other.
Genre(s): Regency Novel; Romance.

Sinclair, Andrew

3669. *King Ludd.* New York: Four Walls Eight Windows, 1993. 352 pp.
In the 1930s, when George Gog Griffin writes his Cambridge thesis about the Luddites, he sees their movement as representative of all responses to technological advancements.
Genre(s): Political Fiction.

Skye, Christina

3670. *Come the Dawn.* New York: Dell, 1995. 402 pp.
Devlyn Carlisle, Earl of Thornewood, returns to London one year after he was reported dead at Waterloo, and although his wife is delighted, he claims amnesia.
Genre(s): Romance; Adventure Story.

3671. *Come the Night.* New York: Dell, 1994. 496 pp.
Black Lord, a highwayman, captures Silver St. Clair, but he is actually Lucien Delamere, heir to an estate, who is trying to find the men who made his life a living hell five years previously, while Silver is trying to find the recipe for perfume that died with her father.
Genre(s): Romance; Adventure Story.

Smith, Joan

3672. *Aurora.* New York: Walker, 1980. 231 pp.
Aurora falls in love with a handsome young gypsy who is probably a disguised Kenelm Derwent or his half brother.
Genre(s): Romance; Regency Novel.

3673. *Behold, A Mystery!* New York: St. Martin's, 1994. 246 pp.
Jessica Greenwood, 26, looks forward to the visit of her great-aunt Hettie's four nephews, possible suitors, for New Year's, but the morning after they arrive, Hettie is

murdered, leaving all to Jessica if she marries one of the nephews within a year, and Jessica must find the murderer.
Genre(s): Regency Novel; Romance; Mystery.

3674. *A Christmas Gambol.* New York: Fawcett Columbine, 1996. 202 pp.
In hope of furthering her career, Cicely Caldwell agrees to pretend that she has written a horrible Gothic novel but she falls in love with the novel's real author, Lord Montaigne.
Genre(s): Regency Novel; Romance.

3675. *Dame Durden's Daughter.* New York: Walker, 1978. 207 pp.
Dame Durden wants her daughter Edith to marry a man with pure Saxon blood, so when she refuses Edith's choice, the vicar's chances improve until someone discovers that the vicar is not what he seems.
Genre(s): Romance; Regency Novel.

3676. *Imprudent Lady.* New York: Walker, 1978. 236 pp.
Prudence becomes a successful novelist, and her wit attracts fellow author Lord Dammler.
Genre(s): Romance; Regency Novel.

3677. *The Kissing Bough.* New York: Fawcett Crest, 1994. 204 pp.
Nicholas Morgan's family and friends think that he will marry his old friend Jane Ramsey, but he returns from Spain with a beautiful but vulgar brewer's daughter as his fiancée.
Genre(s): Regency Novel; Romance.

3678. *Lace for Milady.* New York: Walker, 1980. 201 pp.
Priscilla finds that her neighbor, the Duke of Clavering, owns the land on which her new house stands, and after she refuses his purchase offer, she begins to hear strange noises which seem to relate to the smuggling in the area.
Genre(s): Romance; Regency Novel.

3679. *Lovers' Vows.* New York: Walker, 1981. 192 pp.
Holly McCormak, an orphan of 26, is plain but has a lovely voice, and after she takes the role of Juliet in Lord Dewar's performance, he falls in love with her.
Genre(s): Regency Novel; Romance.

3680. *Murder Will Speak.* New York: St. Martin's, 1996. 217 pp.
The Berkeley Brigade, a group of four neighbors in London, begins a search for the priceless pearl necklace stolen from one of them, and they find a body before romance begins.
Genre(s): Regency Novel; Mystery; Romance.

3681. *Talk of the Town.* New York: Walker, 1979. 201 pp.
Daphne Ingleside goes to London to stay with her notorious Aunt Effie whose numerous affairs have quieted, but Effie announces that she will write her memoirs, and all her former lovers appear, wanting to be favorably presented in print.
Genre(s): Regency Novel; Romance.

◆May be suitable for young adult readers

3682. *A Tall Dark Stranger.* New York: Fawcett, 1996. 184 pp.
The mystery surrounding a dead body and bank notes as well as a handsome stranger change Amy Talbot's quiet life.
Genre(s): Regency Novel; Mystery; Romance.

Spencer, Mary

3683. *Dark Wager.* New York: Dell, 1995. 328 pp.
Clara, eldest daughter of the Marquess of St. Genevieve, has been engaged to Lucien since her birth, but when he thinks she loves someone else, Lucien makes her marry him and take her into isolation.
Genre(s): Regency Novel; Romance.

Stevenson, Robert Louis

3684. *Weir of Hermiston.* 1896. New York: Columbia University Press, 1996. 224 pp.
During the years of 1813 and 1814, Archie Weir, banished to the remote village of Hermiston, Scotland, falls in love, but circumstances make him terminate the relationship.

Stewart, Fred Mustard

3685. *Pomp and Circumstance.* New York: Dutton, 1991. 416 pp.
Lizzie has Adam's baby in England, but situations separate them, and one ends up in Paris and the other on American Civil War battlefields.
Genre(s): Love Story.

Stewart, Mary

3686. *The Gabriel Hounds.* New York: Morrow, 1967. 320 pp.
When Cristabel Mansel goes to Damacus, she and her cousin Charles visit their aging aunt Harriet, who lives in a crumbling palace with her physician, hounds, and Arab servants.
Genre(s): Mystery.

Stickland, Caroline

3687. *An Ancient Hope.* New York: St. Martin's, 1994. 272 pp.
Charles Carnow returns to his family in Victorian England after squandering his inheritance and tries to get his father to give him him his brother's money while pursuing his brother's love, Theodosia.
Genre(s): Regency Novel; Romance.

3688. *The Darkening Leaf.* New York: St. Martin's, 1996. 286 pp.
One night in 1847, Philobeth Alleyn and her lover Frederick find a shipwreck on the Dorset coast, and the woman they find and take to Frederick's grandmother for nursing becomes Philobeth's rival.
Genre(s): Romance.

3689. *The Standing Hills.* New York: St. Martin's, 1987. 208 pp.

When Samual Delaford seduces his farm's dairy maid, the vicar takes her into his household after Delaford's sister has accepted the vicar's proposal of marriage.
Genre(s): Romance.

Stirling, Jessica

3690. *Creature Comforts.* New York: St. Martin's, 1986. 384 pp.
In the sequel to *Treasures on Earth*, Anna and Elspeth begin to adapt to married life in 1812 and to understand their husbands' choices of careers.
Genre(s): Domestic Fiction.

3691. *Hearts of Gold.* New York: St. Martin's, 1988. 480 pp.
In the sequel to *Creature Comforts*, Elspeth has left her husband, and Anna's husband has left her.
Genre(s): Domestic Fiction.

3692. *The Hiring Fair.* London: Hodder and Stoughton, 1976. 414 pp.
To earn money for their poor mining families, parents hire out their young girls to others.
Genre(s): Domestic Fiction.

3693. *The Spoiled Earth.* London: Hodder and Stoughton, 1974. 409 pp.
Villagers scarring Scotland's land in the coal mines and their families cope with tragedy and hard labor in the 19th century.
Genre(s): Domestic Fiction.

3694. *Treasures on Earth.* New York: St. Martin's, 1985. 379 pp.
Gaddy Patterson, a highlander, remains independent and a rebellious as she cares for a foundling before marrying and having a child of her own in the early 19th century.
Genre(s): Domestic Fiction.

Stirling, Jocelyn

3695. *Venture to Love.* Garden City, NY: Doubleday, 1987. 350 pp.
Argent Wood becomes part owner of a cotton mill, after being a lady's companion and a clerk, while falling in love with Rawson Carlyon, a government spy against France and Napoleon.
Genre(s): Romance.

Stone, Irving

3696. *The Origin.* Garden City, NY: Doubleday, 1980. 743 pp.
Charles Darwin travels on the H.M.S. *Beagle* and begins developing his theory on the origins of various species.
Genre(s): Biographical Fiction; Sea Story.

Stuart, Vivian

3697. *The Brave Captains.* New York: Pinnacle, 1972. 219 pp.
In the sequel to *The Valiant Sailors*, Philip Horatio Hazard demonstrates his abilities and rises to the rank of captain in the Royal Navy during the 1850s.
Genre(s): War Story.

3698.*Hazard in Circassia.* New York: Pinnacle, 1973. 206 pp.
Philip Horatio Hazard serves in the Royal navy on the Black Sea in the 1850s, in the sequel to *Victory at Sebastapol.*
Genre(s): War Story.

3699.*Hazard of Huntress.* New York: Pinnacle, 1972. 223 pp.
Philip Horatio Hazard, in the sequel to *Hazard's Command*, continues his adventures as an officer in the Royal navy.
Genre(s): War Story.

3700.*Hazard to the Rescue.* New York: Pinnacle, 1975. 206 pp.
In the sequel to *Hazard in Circassia*, Philip Horatio Hazard demonstrates his bravery at sea for the Royal navy.
Genre(s): War Story.

3701.*Hazard's Command.* New York: Pinnacle, 1972. 251 pp.
As a strong member of the Royal navy, Philip Horatio Hazard gains his on command in the sequel to *The Brave Captains.*
Genre(s): War Story.

3702.*The Valiant Sailors.* New York: Pinnacle, 1964. 272 pp.
In the 1850s, Philip Horatio Hazard joins the Royal navy as a young sailor.
Genre(s): War Story.

3703.*Victory at Sebastopol.* New York: Pinnacle, 1972. 176 pp.
Philip Horatio Hazard leads his ship in battle at Sebastapol during the 1850s in the sequel to *Hazard of Huntress*.
Genre(s): War Story.

Stubbs, Jean

3704.*The Northern Correspondent.* New York: St. Martin's, 1984. 374 pp.
The sequel to *The Vivian Inheritance* concentrates on Ambrose Longe, son of Charlotte Howarth, as he becomes the owner and editor of a newspaper in the mid-19th century.
Genre(s): Domestic Fiction; Family Saga.

3705.*The Vivian Inheritance.* New York: St. Martin's, 1982. 323 pp.
The Howarths from *An Imperfect Joy* capitalize on the changes caused by the Industrial Revolution by bringing the railroad to their valley of Wydendale.
Genre(s): Domestic Fiction; Family Saga.

Sturrock, Jeremy

3706.*Suicide Most Foul.* New York: Walker, 1981. 204 pp.
Jeremy Sturrock and his assistant Maggsy must pursue a suspicious suicide in Hanover Square before they go to Belgium in time to witness the Battle of Waterloo.
Genre(s): Mystery.

Styles, Showell

◆ 3707.*A Kiss for Captain Hardy.* Boston: Faber and Faber, 1979. 188 pp.
Lord Nelson and Emma Hamilton enjoy their relationship at the Neopolitan court while Nelson fights his sea battles and wins.
Genre(s): Biographical Fiction; Sea Story.

3708.*Mr Fitton's Commission.* London: Faber and Faber, 1977. 190 pp.
Michael Fitton, a ship's servant, is promoted to lieutenant in 1804 after his gallantry during the failed invasion of Curacao, but without patronage, he cannot succeed at sea.
Genre(s): Biographical Fiction; Sea Story.

3709.*A Sword for Mr Fitton.* London: Faber, 1975. 188 pp.
Michael Fitton sails to the Caribbean in Lord Nelson's navy.
Genre(s): Adventure Story; Sea Story.

Sutcliffe, Katherine

3710.*A Heart Possessed.* New York: Topaz, 1996. 346 pp.
After being unwillingly kept in a sanitarium for two years, Ariel Margaret Rushdon returns to her former lover's estate in 1800, pretending to be his hired model.
Genre(s): Romance; Mystery.

Tannahill, Reay

3711.*A Dark and Distant Shore.* New York: St. Martin's, 1983. 608 pp.
Vilia Cameron has an obsession with Kinveil, the family castle sold by her father to pay his debts, and when her father dies in 1811, the new owner allows her to live there with his son's family.
Genre(s): Domestic Fiction.

Tattersall, Jill

3712.*Lady Ingram's Room.* New York: Morrow, 1971. 224 pp.
Arabel Murray, young and happy, agrees to pose as the new governess at an isolated manor rather than live with a miserly uncle, and finds she is enlisted to solve the disappearance of her young charge's mother.
Genre(s): Romance; Mystery.

3713.*Lyonesse Abbey.* New York: Morrow, 1969. 248 pp.
Tessa Howard, married to Damon Tregaron to pay her father's gambling debt, goes to his Cornwall home where all is not well.
Genre(s): Romance; Gothic Fiction.

3714.*Midsummer Masque.* 1923. New York: Morrow, 1972. 253 pp.
A beautiful orphan shows up at a large house owned by a very attractive but unscrupulous man.
Genre(s): Romance; Mystery.

3715.*The Wild Hunt.* New York: Morrow, 1974. 173 pp.

In 1810 Chantal Fabian becomes the governess in a dark English house and takes a risk by remaining when strange things happen.
Genre(s): Romance; Gothic Fiction.

Tennant, Emma

◆ 3716.*Pemberley, or, Pride and Prejudice Continued.* New York: St. Martin's, 1993. 184 pp.
Uneasy Elizabeth Bennet Darcy waits for her mother, sisters, Wickham, and Lady Catherine de Bourgh to come to Pemberley for Christmas.
Genre(s): Domestic Fiction.

◆ 3717.*An Unequal Marriage, or, Pride and Prejudice Twenty Years Later.* New York: St. Martin's, 1994. 186 pp.
A second sequel to Jane Austen's *Pride and Prejudice* finds Elizabeth and Darcy with children, a lovely daughter Miranda and a problem son Edward.
Genre(s): Domestic Fiction.

Terry, Judith

3718.*Version and Diversion.* New York: Morrow, 1987. 310 pp.
Jane, a gamekeeper's daughter, becomes the maid to Julia at Mansfield Park, but when the man both Julia and her sister are trying to marry shows interest in her, she must leave for London and a possible acting career.
Genre(s): Domestic Fiction.

Thackeray, William Makepeace

3719.*The Newcomes.* 1853. New York: Tuttle, 1994. 847 pp.
Colonel Newcome's son Clive falls in love with a cousin whose brother suggests that she marry more profitably, but after bad marriages, Clive and his cousin finally unite.
Genre(s): Domestic Fiction.

3720.*Vanity Fair.* 1848. New York: Bantam, 1997. 876 pp.
Becky Sharp and her husband stand in contrast to the lives of Dobbin and Amelia in this revelation of societal classes.
Genre(s): Satire.

Thoene, Bodie, and Brock Thoene

3721.*Only the River Runs Free.* Nashville, TN: Thomas Nelson, 1997. 320 pp.
Joseph Connor comes to the small town of Ballynockanor in the 1840s, and when Kate Donovan shies away from him, embarrassed by burn scars from a fire that killed her husband, he helps her overcome her sensitivity.
Genre(s): Christian Fiction; Romance.

Thomas, Donald Serrell

3722.*Mad Hatter Summer.* New York: Viking, 1983. 310 pp.
Rev. Charles Dodgson (Lewis Carroll) likes to photograph unclothed young girls, but when he photographs Jane Ashmole, blackmail turns to murder and Inspector

Swain must discover the truth of the crimes and of the relationship between Dodgson and Ashmole.
Genre(s): Biographical Fiction; Mystery.

Thomas, Martha Lou

3723.*Waltz with a Stranger.* New York: Walker, 1986. 288 pp.
Quintilla Davenant, lame and lacking a dowry, still loves to dance, and when dancing alone in an empty library at a ball, someone begins dancing with her.
Genre(s): Regency Novel; Romance; Medical Novel.

Thompson, E. V.

3724.*Chase the Wind.* New York: Coward-McCann, 1977. 416 pp.
Josh Retallick tries to improve the dismal working conditions of Cornwall miners in the early 1800s and falls in love with Miriam Trago.
Genre(s): Romance.

Thorne, Nicola

3725.*Sisters and Lovers.* Garden City, NY: Doubleday, 1981. 589 pp.
George Vestrey takes his family to London for major events such as the Great Exhibition and the troop return from the Crimean War, and his three oldest daughters search for mates.
Genre(s): War Story; Domestic Fiction; Romance.

Thornton, Elizabeth

3726.*Dangerous to Kiss.* New York: Bantam, 1995. 384 pp.
During the murder of a boy's father, Deborah Weyman hears the man address his killer as Lord Kendall, and fearing for their lives, Deborah takes the boy into hiding.
Genre(s): Romance; Mystery.

3727.*You Only Love Twice.* New York: Bantam, 1998. 432 pp.
The amnesiac novice Sister Martha stays in a convent for three years before someone identifies her as Jessica Hayward, a suspected murderess who once loved Lucas Wilde, Lord Dundas.
Genre(s): Regency Novel; Romance.

Trevor, Meriol

3728.*The Fortunate Marriage.* New York: Dutton, 1976. Canada pp.
When nasty Caroline Dynham is murdered, her husband Rowland becomes the suspect, but when he is cleared, he pairs happily with a decent woman.
Genre(s): Regency Novel; Romance.

Trollope, Anthony

3729.*Barchester Towers.* 1881. New York: Oxford, 1989. 576 pp.
Citizens enjoy their daily lives in Barchester, an English cathedral town, during the 19th century.
Genre(s): Domestic Fiction.

3730. *Castle Richmond.* 1860. New York: Arno, 1981. 500 pp.
The Irish endure the horror of the potato famine beginning in 1845.
Genre(s): Domestic Fiction.

3731. *Doctor Thorne.* 1858. New York: Oxford, 1989. 592 pp.
Dr. Thorne treats his patients in the cathedral town of Barchester during the 19th century.
Genre(s): Domestic Fiction.

3732. *Framley Parsonage.* 1861. New York: Penguin, 1993. 544 pp.
The Vicar lives in Barchester's Framley Parsonage.
Genre(s): Domestic Fiction.

3733. *The Landleaguers.* 1883. New York: Penguin, 1994. 320 pp.
In the 19th century, the Irish unite against the British.
Genre(s): Domestic Fiction.

3734. *Last Chronicle of Barset.* 1867. New York: Knopf, 1995. 704 pp.
The people of the village of Barchester continue their daily lives.
Genre(s): Domestic Fiction.

3735. *Phineas Finn.* 1869. New York: Oxford, 1991. 323 pp.
Phineas Finn is an Irish member of Parliament.
Genre(s): Political Fiction.

3736. *Phineas Redux.* 1869. New York: Oxford, 1984. 768 pp.
Phineas Finn, a politician, works to improve the lives of his citizens.
Genre(s): Political Fiction.

3737. *Small House at Alington.* 1864. New York: Penguin, 1991. 752 pp.
A family lives in the cathedral town of Barchester during the 19th century.
Genre(s): Domestic Fiction.

3738. *The Warden.* 1885. New York: Oxford, 1989. 316 pp.
The warden interacts with citizens in the cathedral town of Barchester during the 19th century.
Genre(s): Domestic Fiction.

3739. *The Way We Live Now.* 1875. New York: Modern Library, 1984. 825 pp.
A variety of characters demonstrate the conflicts between aristocracy and tradesmen in England during the 1870s.
Genre(s): Satire.

Trollope, Joanna

3740. *Eliza Stanhope.* New York: Dutton, 1979. 223 pp.
In 1815, Eliza Stanhope meets and falls in love with Francis before he leaves to fight at Waterloo.
Genre(s): War Story; Romance.

Tyler-Whittle, Michael Sidney

3741. *The Young Victoria.* London: Heinemann, 1971. 247 pp.
As a child, Victoria establishes relationships with those around her who are preparing her for her role as queen.
Genre(s): Biographical Fiction.

Veryan, Patricia

3742. *Give All to Love.* New York: St. Martin's, 1987. 371 pp.
That his ward Josie Storm has become a lovely young woman surprises Dev, and each tries to avoid admitting love for the other. (*Series:* Sanguinet Saga, 6)
Genre(s): Regency Novel; Romance.

◆ 3743. *Lanterns.* New York: St. Martin's, 1996. 347 pp.
In 1818, Marietta Warrington must move with her newly impoverished family from London to an old Sussex estate, and there, kidnapping, treasure, romance, and other intrigues occupy her time.
Genre(s): Regency Novel; Romance.

◆ 3744. *Logic of the Heart.* New York: St. Martin's, 1990. 378 pp.
When Valentine Montclair appears, his uncle is trying to evict Priscilla's widowed mother, but he needs their help as well because someone is trying to murder him.
Genre(s): Regency Novel; Romance.

◆ 3745. *The Mandarin of Mayfair.* New York: St. Martin's, 1995. 340 pp.
The Preservers battle the League of Jewelled Men, a group trying to overthrow the monarchy, and the League tries to cause a fight between the leaders of the Preservers, August Falcon and James Morris. (*Series:* Tales of the Jewelled Men, 6)
Genre(s): Romance.

◆ 3746. *Married Past Redemption.* New York: St. Martin's, 1983. 320 pp.
Lisette Van Lindsay marries Justin Strand for convenience and then proceeds to fall in love with him. (*Series:* Sanguinet Saga, 3)
Genre(s): Regency Novel; Romance.

◆ 3747. *Nanette.* New York: Walker, 1981. 284 pp.
Nanette disguises herself as her maid and travels England to escape from her evil step-father. (*Series:* Sanguinet Saga, 1)
Genre(s): Regency Novel; Romance.

◆ 3748. *The Riddle of Alabaster Royal.* New York: St. Martin's, 1997. 256 pp.
When Jack Vespa returns to Alabaster Royal after receiving military wounds, he has difficulty finding servants because of rumors that the place is haunted, and the peace he has expected is ruined by various incidents including a woman and her grandmother hiding in his house.
Genre(s): Romance; Gothic Fiction.

3749. *The Riddle of the Lost Lover.* New York: St. Martin's, 1998. 352 pp.

After Jack Vespa returns to the family home of Alabaster Royal, he discovers that his deceased father was very different from what he had believed.
Genre(s): Regency Novel; Mystery; Romance.

3750. *Sanguinet's Crown.* New York: St. Martin's, 1985. 360 pp.
When Claude Sanguinet's henchmen try to kidnap Rachel Leith for him, they mistakenly take Charity Strand, and when her brother and her love Mitchell rescue her, they discover Sanguinet's plot to kill the Prince Regent. (*Series:* Sanguinet Saga, 2)
Genre(s): Regency Novel; Romance.

◆ 3751. *Some Brief Folly.* New York: St. Martin's, 1981. 320 pp.
Shocked at the reputation of Garret Hawkhurst, Simon Buchanan regrets that he and his sister Mia must take refuge in his home, but Mia realizes that the stories about Hawkhurst are untrue.
Genre(s): Regency Novel; Romance.

Vivian, Daisy

3752. *The Counterfeit Lady.* New York: Walker, 1987. 202 pp.
Susanna Archer's employer Lady Wycombe dies and leaves her beautiful clothes, which Susanna decides to wear at Cheyne Spa when looking for a husband.
Genre(s): Regency Novel; Romance.

3753. *Fair Game.* New York: Walker, 1986. 188 pp.
Lady Augusta Mabyn plans to regain her family's lost fortune by running a discreet gaming house in a spa.
Genre(s): Regency Novel; Romance.

3754. *The Forrester Inheritance.* New York: Walker, 1985. 209 pp.
Mariana Porter must share an inheritance with her distant cousin Brion Seymour, but before either may take a share, each must marry a relative.
Genre(s): Regency Novel; Romance.

3755. *Lady of Qualities.* New York: Walker, 1987. 210 pp.
Sabrina Fairchild lives with her sister and their aunt while her father is in the military, but when he returns, he brings home a wife with a handsome son.
Genre(s): Regency Novel; Romance.

3756. *A Marriage of Inconvenience.* New York: Walker, 1987. 216 pp.
Clarissa decides to marry Alexander in a marriage of inconvenience after the man she loves chooses someone else, but eventually, she and Alexander fall in love.
Genre(s): Regency Novel; Romance.

3757. *Return to Cheyne Spa.* New York: Walker, 1988. 231 pp.
The Duchess of Towans offers a handsome reward to Elinor Hardy, who is employed as a hostess in Lady Bassingbrook's gambing establishment, to help her arrange a match for her niece Lady Barbara.
Genre(s): Romance; Regency Novel.

Vroman, Barbara Fitz

3758. *Sons of Thunder.* Hancock, WI: Pearl-Win, 1981. 383 pp.
Siobonna Covington has no money after the death of her father, and although she has ties to the ruling British in Ireland, she begins to sympathize with the peasants who rebel against them.
Genre(s): War Story.

Walpole, Hugh

3759. *The Fortress.* Garden City, NY: Doubleday, 1932. 548 pp.
Judith Paris, in the sequel to *Judith Paris*, rules her estate at Uldale firmly until the family reunites on her 100th birthday.
Genre(s): Domestic Fiction; Family Saga.

Warady, Phylis Ann

◆ 3760. *The Earl's Comeuppance.* New York: Walker, 1992. 168 pp.
A widow travels to London with her five children for the season while trying to find a suitable husband for her oldest daughter Henrietta in the early 19th century.
Genre(s): Romance; Regency Novel.

Webb, Mary

3761. *Precious Bane.* 1924. South Bend: Notre Dame Press, 1980. 320 pp.
A family on the Welsh border with England tries to survive in the early 19th century.
Genre(s): Domestic Fiction.

West, Paul

3762. *Lord Byron's Doctor.* Garden City, NY: Doubleday, 1989. 277 pp.
John Polidori goes to the Continent with Lord Byron in 1816 as his hired companion, and in his diary, Polidori reveals himself as spoiled and jealous of Byron and his friends.
Genre(s): Biographical Fiction.

Westhaven, Margaret

3763. *The Willful Wife.* New York: Walker, 1986. 136 pp.
Cassandra, 17, must marry an older baron, and on the day of the wedding, he leaves for two years as a diplomat.
Genre(s): Regency Novel; Romance.

White, Terence De Vere

3764. *Johnnie Cross.* New York: St. Martin's, 1983. 153 pp.
After George Eliot dies, the man to whom she was married for seven months tells the story of her passion and his fear of sex.
Genre(s): Biographical Fiction; Domestic Fiction.

Williams, Jeanne

◆ 3765. *The Island Harp.* New York: St. Martin's, 1991. 338 pp.
When Mairi MacLeod's grandfather dies in 1844, she becomes head of her clan in 19th-century Scotland, but she must fight to keep their land from Scottish landlords.

Wolf, Joan

3766. *The Arrangement.* New York: Warner, 1997. 384 pp.
Although Gail Saunders, riding stable proprietress, would rather marry Raoul Melville, Earl of Saville than have an arrangement with him, she agrees until someone threatens the life of her young son.
Genre(s): Romance.

3767. *The Deception.* New York: Warner, 1996. 352 pp.
After Kate Fitzgerald's uncle tricks her into a marriage with the Earl of Greystone, they try to cope, but a murder intrudes.
Genre(s): Regency Novel; Romance.

3768. *The Gamble.* New York: Warner, 1998. 358 pp.
Georgiana Newbury becomes a blackmailer like her late father when she decides to convince the elderly Earl of Winterdale to sponsor her in society, but she discovers that a new earl holds the title, and he is young, calculating, and handsome.
Genre(s): Regency Novel; Romance.

3769. *The Guardian.* New York: Warner, 1997. 323 pp.
Stephen Grandville returns to Weston, the family estate, as guardian to Giles, his nephew, but murder attempts on Stephen's and Giles's lives delay any rekindling of the flame between Stephen and Giles's mother.
Genre(s): Regency Novel; Romance.

Wollaston, Nicholas

3770. *Thistlewood.* London: Hamish Hamilton, 1985. 149 pp.
In 1820, Arthur Thistlewood leads butchers, cobblers, and others in the Cato Street Conspiracy, a failed attempt to blow up the Tory Cabinet.
Genre(s): Political Fiction.

Woodhouse, Sarah

◆ 3771. *The Peacock's Feather.* New York: St. Martin's, 1990. 384 pp.
Jardine Savage and Alexander French try to save a coach passenger in childbirth, but she dies and leaves an infant daughter which Jardine takes to an estate he purchases without knowing anything about it.
Genre(s): Domestic Fiction.

Woodiwiss, Kathleen E.

3772. *The Flame and the Flower.* New York: Avon, 1984. 430 pp.
A Yankee rapes Heather, is forced to marry her, and brings her to America where they begin to fall in love.
Genre(s): Romance; Adventure Story.

Woodman, Richard

3773. *Arctic Treachery.* New York: Walker, 1987. 232 pp.
Nathaniel Drinkwater takes command of the captured French corvette *Melusine* and escorts the British whaling fleet to the Arctic while an enemy privateer pursues him.
Genre(s): Sea Story.

3774. *Beneath the Aurora.* London: J. Murray, 1995. 247 pp.
In the sequel to *A Flying Squadron*, Nathaniel Drinkwater takes over the Royal Navy's Secret Department, but if he must be away from his family, he prefers to be on the sea.
Genre(s): War Story; Sea Story.

3775. *The Bomb Vessel.* New York: Walker, 1986. 215 pp.
Nathaniel Drinkwater takes part in the British navy's Baltic expedition in 1801 where his leadership brings him to the attention of Lord Nelson, in the sequel to *Artic Treachery*.
Genre(s): Sea Story.

3776. *Decision at Trafalgar.* New York: Walker, 1987. 209 pp.
Nathaniel Drinkwater patrols the English Channel in 1804, and after skirmishes with the French, he participates in the Tralfalgar campaign in the sequel to *The Bomb Vessel*.
Genre(s): Sea Story; War Story.

3777. *An Eye of the Fleet.* New York: Pinnacle, 1981. 185 pp.
Nathaniel Drinkwater continues his sea adventures in the sequel to *Nathaniel Drinkwater: Midshipman*.
Genre(s): War Story; Sea Story.

3778. *In Distant Waters.* New York: St. Martin's, 1989. 246 pp.
Captain Drinkwater sails around the Horn to protect His Majesty's interests in California during 1807 when the Russians attempt to gain a foothold there in the sequel to *Baltic Mission*.
Genre(s): Sea Story; War Story.

3779. *A King's Cutter.* New York: Pinnacle, 1984. 178 pp.
In the sequel to *An Eye of the Fleet*, Nathaniel Drinkwater rejoins the navy in time to fight Napoleon and uncovers secret agent plots on the French coast before helping to win the Battle of Camperdown.
Genre(s): War Story; Sea Story.

1860-1918

Ackroyd, Peter

3780. *The Trial of Elizabeth Cree.* New York: Doubleday, 1995. 288 pp.
Lawyers for and against Elizabeth Cree, on trial for the murder of her husband in Victorian London, tell of her early life in poor surroundings and her days as a music-hall performer.
Genre(s): Legal Story.

Aiken, Joan

3781. *Castle Barebane.* New York: Viking, 1976. 312 pp.
Val Montgomery leaves New York for London to care for her niece and nephew and faces terror at the family home of Castle Barebane in Scotland.
Genre(s): Romance; Horror.

3782. *The Haunting of Lamb House.* New York: St. Martin's, 1993. 200 pp.
Toby Lamb has an experience with ghosts in the English residence of Henry James during the late 19th century.
Genre(s): Fantastic Literature.

Alexander, Kate

3783. *The House of Hope.* New York: St. Martin's, 1994. 352 pp.
Vittorio Speranza founds a London auction house in 1862 which acquires so much esteem that the family has the resources to smuggle Jews out of Germany and fight for other downtrodden groups.
Genre(s): Family Saga.

Alldritt, Keith

3784. *Elgar on the Journey to Hanley.* New York: St. Martin's, 1979. 223 pp.
Composer Edward Elgar is the obsession of Dora Penny, a vicar's daughter, although he is married to a woman who arranges for him to meet lovely women but makes certain that no relationships develop.
Genre(s): Biographical Fiction; Musical Fiction.

Amis, Kingsley

3785. *The Riverside Villas Murder.* New York: Harcourt, 1973. 224 pp.
An older woman introduces Peter Furneaux, 14, to sex while the chief constable accuses his father of a neighbor's murder.
Genre(s): Mystery; Love Story.

Argers, Helen

◆ 3786. *Noblesse Oblige.* New York: St. Martin's, 1994. 308 pp.
After meeting and romancing the Marquis of Kimston in her first London season, Caroline Richmond expects a proposal, but when it does not come, her father arranges her marriage with the Marquis's elderly father.
Genre(s): Romance.

Bainbridge, Beryl

3787. *Every Man for Himself.* New York: Carroll and Graf, 1996. 224 pp.
Morgan, a young American, tells about the situation on the *Titanic* from the time he went aboard until rescued by the *Carpathia*.

3788. *Young Adolf.* New York: Braziller, 1979. 219 pp.
During his brief visit to Liverpool when 23, Hitler lurks in the city's mazes as he mulls over his future.
Genre(s): Biographical Fiction.

Barker, Pat

3789. *The Eye in the Door.* New York: Dutton, 1994. 280 pp.
A 47,000-item list reportedly names all homosexuals in Great Britain, making them easy targets for blackmail, and the list includes war hero Billy Prior, in a sequel to *Regeneration*.
Genre(s): Biographical Fiction; War Story.

3790. *The Ghost Road.* New York: Dutton, 1996. 277 pp.
The sequel to *Regeneration* finds William Rivers, inventor of the shell shock treatment, with some of his patients and Lieutenant Billy Prior, a bisexual officer from the working class.
Award(s): Booker Prize.
Genre(s): War Story.

3791. *Regeneration.* New York: Dutton, 1992. 251 pp.
The poet Siegfried Sasson goes to a military sanitarium in 1917, supposedly suffering shell shock, but in actuality, he makes anti-war statements.
Genre(s): Biographical Fiction; War Story.

Bastable, Bernard

3792. *A Mansion and Its Murder.* New York: Carroll and Graf, 1998. 192 pp.
After Sarah Jane Fearing's uncle marries and produces a son, the uncle mysteriously dies, and she, a child in a banking family with indifferent parents, recounts the scene 50 years later.
Genre(s): Mystery.

Bayer, Valerie Townsend

3793. *City of Childhood.* New York: St. Martin's, 1992. 320 pp.

Victorian nannies raise 12 grandchildren in the garden created at their family home by a grandfather trying to escape his unhappy childhood.
Genre(s): Domestic Fiction.

3794. *The Metaphysics of Sex.* New York: St. Martin's, 1992. 384 pp.
The sequel to *City of Childhood* shows Emma Forster making the transition from a child in the garden to a young woman.
Genre(s): Domestic Fiction; Bildungsroman (Coming of Age).

Beaty, David, and Betty Beaty

3795. *Wings of the Morning.* New York: Coward-McCann, 1982. 512 pp.
In the early days of British airplanes, two lovers, separated by social class, eventually marry, and their family becomes part of aviation history.
Genre(s): Love Story.

Behan, Brian

◆ 3796. *Kathleen.* New York: St. Martin's, 1989. 304 pp.
Kathleen Coor becomes an orphan at a young age, and her struggle for independence mirrors Ireland's own struggle.
Genre(s): Domestic Fiction.

Biggle, Lloyd Jr.

3797. *The Glendower Conspiracy.* Tulsa, OK: Council Oak, 1990. 422 pp.
Sherlock Homles and his new companion, Porter Jones, travel to Wales to investigate a murder but find more problems when they arrive.
Genre(s): Mystery.

◆ 3798. *The Quallsford Inheritance.* New York: St. Martin's, 1986. 246 pp.
Edward Porter Jones, a Holmes's irregular at 16, says that Watson refused to acknowledge his closeness to Holmes, and he tells of his and Holmes's work on a triple murder.
Genre(s): Mystery.

Black, Laura

3799. *Falls of Gard.* New York: St. Martin's, 1986. 241 pp.
Bella comes from Australia to Edinburgh and unhappily tries to adjust to the stodginess of her relatives until she finally moves into an uncle's house where life is more fun, and there she meets the disagreeable Marquess of Gard.
Genre(s): Romance.

◆ 3800. *Glendraco.* New York: St. Martin's, 1977. 364 pp.
Kirstie Drummond raises questions in 19th-century Scotland about whom she will marry, her possible background of royalty, and if members of her family are insane.
Genre(s): Romance; Gothic Fiction.

Blackwell, Lawana

3801. *Jewels for a Crown.* Wheaton, IL: Tyndale House, 1996. 398 pp.
Jenny Price, a young nursing student, is asked to work with Celeste, a 12-year-old with epilepsy. (*Series:* Victorian Serenade, 3)
Genre(s): Christian Fiction; Romance; Medical Novel.

3802. *Like a River Glorious.* Wheaton, IL: Tyndale House, 1995. 333 pp.
Rachel's employers con wealthy men and steal their money, and she tries to escape from this life of deceit. (*Series:* Victorian Serenade, 1)
Genre(s): Romance; Christian Fiction.

3803. *Measures of Grace.* Wheaton, IL: Tyndale House, 1996. 368 pp.
After Corrine converts to Christianity, she tries to relinquish her life of crime, but a bitter man threatens her actions. (*Series:* Victorian Serenade, 2)
Genre(s): Christian Fiction; Romance.

3804. *Song of a Soul.* Wheaton, IL: Tyndale House, 1997. 340 pp.
After famous vocal coach Clarissa Pella agrees to train aspiring opera singer, Deborah Burke, Deborah must make a difficult decision. (*Series:* Victorian Serenade, 4)
Genre(s): Christian Fiction; Romance.

3805. *The Widow of Larkspur Inn.* Minneapolis, MN: Bethany House, 1998. 432 pp.
The widow Julia Hollis moves to her husband's only remaining property, a coaching inn in Gresham, and when the new vicar arrives from Cambridge, their children try to keep them apart. (*Series:* Gresham Chronicles, 1)
Genre(s): Christian Fiction; Romance.

Bloch, Robert

3806. *The Night of the Ripper.* Garden City, NY: Doubleday, 1984. 227 pp.
An American doctor and a policeman try to find the identity of a man who commits serial murders in the poor areas of London during the time of Jack the Ripper.
Genre(s): Mystery.

Boylan, Clare

3807. *11 Edward Street.* New York: Doubleday, 1992. 224 pp.
Daisy Devlin in the prequel to *Holy Pictures*, goes into the convent to escape working but leaves after meeting a soldier.
Genre(s): War Story; Domestic Fiction; Family Saga.

Bragg, Melvyn

3808. *The Hired Man.* New York: Knopf, 1970. 224 pp.
John Tallentire is 18, married, and a hired man in Cumberland, England, at the turn of the 20th century, and he feels caught in an endless cycle of nothing.
Genre(s): Political Fiction; Domestic Fiction.

Brent, Madeleine

3809. *The Capricorn Stone.* Garden City, NY: Doubleday, 1980. 285 pp.
The patriarch of a wealthy family in Suffolk at the beginning of the 20th century is revealed to have a career as a national jewel thief.
Genre(s): Romance.

◆ 3810. *Stranger at Wildings.* New York: Doubleday, 1976. 312 pp.
A wealthy English family at the turn of the 20th century becomes involved with a traveling circus.
Genre(s): Romance.

3811. *Tregaron's Daughter.* New York: Doubleday, 1971. 306 pp.
Caterina Tregaron, always haunted by dreams of a dark palace, sees a painting of the palace in Venice.
Genre(s): Love Story; Gothic Fiction.

Brockway, Connie

3812. *A Dangerous Man.* New York: Dell, 1996. 400 pp.
Hart Moreland, Earl of Perth, returns home to England and the betrothal party of his sister, but Mercy Coltrane appears to remind him that he once shot her during his wild life in Texas.
Genre(s): Romance.

Brown, Frances

3813. *Dancing on the Rainbow.* North Pomfret, VT: Trafalgar, 1992. 352 pp.
Mirella Granger, a tightrope walker, first tries to be a scullery maid at Windsor Castle in Victorian England, but she hates to stay in one place.
Genre(s): Romance.

Brown, Russell

3814. *Sherlock Holmes and the Mysterious Friend of Oscar Wilde.* New York: St. Martin's, 1988. 176 pp.
Oscar Wilde asks Sherlock Holmes to help one of his friends escape from a blackmailer.
Genre(s): Mystery.

Buchan, John

3815. *The Thirty-Nine Steps.* London: Doran, 1915. 145 pp.
Richard Hannay tries to foil an international conspiracy before World War I by risking capture or assassination.
Genre(s): Spy Fiction.

Buckingham, Nancy

3816. *The House Called Edenhythe.* New York: Hawthorn, 1972. 190 pp.
A young widow leaves Borneo for London to meet her in-laws, and when she arrives she meets more than she had expected.
Genre(s): Mystery.

Bugge, Carole

3817. *Star of India.* New York: St. Martin's, 1998. 208 pp.
When a priceless sapphire disappears, Sherlock Holmes recognizes the work of his enemy, Professor James Moriarty.
Genre(s): Mystery.

Burns, Patricia

3818. *Stacey's Flyer.* New York: St. Martin's, 1985. 256 pp.
After Stacey Brown returns from finishing school, she meets and marries the man hired by her father to run his coaching firm, but after they marry, they have many problems with the business and with their families.
Genre(s): Romance.

Buruma, Ian

3819. *Playing the Game.* New York: Farrar, Straus and Giroux, 1991. 234 pp.
While a student at Trinity College, Cambridge, K.S. Ranjitsinhji becomes one of the best cricket players of all time, and when he returns to India as the maharaja of Nawanagar, he is known throughout Europe.
Genre(s): Sports Fiction; Biographical Fiction.

Butler, David

3820. *Edward VII, Prince of Hearts.* London: Weidenfeld and Nicolson, 1974. 327 pp.
The Prince of Wales, to entertain himself, spends most of his time with women, before he becomes King Edward VII.
Genre(s): Biographical Fiction.

Butler, Gwendoline

3821. *Sarsen Place.* New York: Coward-McCann, 1974. 219 pp.
John Coffin must solve the murders of several women involved with Mary Lamont, governess at Sarsen Place.
Genre(s): Mystery.

Byatt, A. S.

3822. *Possession.* New York: Random House, 1990. 560 pp.
The lives of two modern scholars parallel the lives of the two Victorian poets that the scholars are researching.
Genre(s): Romance.

Cameron, Ian

◆ 3823. *The Young Eagles.* New York: St. Martin's, 1980. 249 pp.
A German and an Englishman become friends in England, even loving the same woman, but not until World War I breaks out and the German returns home do they decide that they will kill each other.
Genre(s): War Story.

Cameron, Stella

3824. *Charmed.* New York: Avon, 1995. 371 pp.

When Calum discovers that he is the rightful heir to his father's estate, having been switched at birth with another child, he determines that he will marry the impostor's intended in his attempt to recover his inheritance.
Genre(s): Romance.

3825. *Dear Stranger.* New York: Warner, 1997. 400 pp.
When handsome American Oliver Worth arrives at Blackmoor Hall to be Lily Adler's father's secretary, Lily and Oliver fall in love.
Genre(s): Romance; Mystery.

Carey, Peter

3826. *Jack Maggs.* New York: Knopf, 1998. 320 pp.
After a young thief makes friends in a wealthy London household in the mid-19th century, he meets an author interested in the criminal mind.
Award(s): Commonwealth Writers' Prize.
Genre(s): Mystery.

Carleton, William

3827. *The Tithe-Proctor.* Dublin: Duffy, 1849. 263 pp.
Irish peasants rebel when forced to pay tithes.
Genre(s): War Story.

Carr, John Dickson

3828. *The Hungry Goblin.* New York: Harper, 1972. 290 pp.
In 1869, a detective in Victorian England has an unusual and unexpected case to solve.
Genre(s): Mystery.

Carr, Philippa

◆ 3829. *The Black Swan.* New York: Putnam, 1990. 350 pp.
Lucie Lansdon's father disagrees with Prime Minister Gladstone over home rule for Ireland which leads to his assassination and Lucie's marriage to a terrorist. (*Series:* Daughters of England, 16)
Genre(s): Horror; Romance; Family Saga.

◆ 3830. *The Changeling.* New York: Putnam, 1989. 368 pp.
In the sequel to *The Pool of St. Branok*, wealthy Benedict Lansdon is a widower and absentee father campaigning for Parliament. (*Series:* Daughters of England, 15)
Genre(s): Romance; Domestic Fiction; Regency Novel.

Carroll, James

3831. *Supply of Heroes.* New York: Dutton, 1986. 403 pp.
Although Protestant Sir Hugh relinquishes his title to show his support of his Catholic tenants in Ireland, his son marries an English woman who hates Ireland, and other family members are drawn further into the mire during World War I and the Irish Rebellion.
Genre(s): War Story.

Cartland, Barbara

3832. *Love Locked In.* New York: Dutton, 1977. 159 pp.
A young woman marries the irreputable Duc de Savigne and makes him into the kind man that she knows he must be.
Genre(s): Romance.

3833. *The Peril and the Prince.* New York: Berkley, 1985. 192 pp.
Vida Anstruther crosses Europe to Russia to rescue her secret agent father and meets a Russian prince with questionable loyalties.
Genre(s): Romance.

3834. *The Wild, Unwilling Wife.* New York: Dutton, 1977. 161 pp.
A lord of the manor marries a young girl to save his family's estate.
Genre(s): Romance.

Cary, Joyce

3835. *Except the Lord.* New York: Harper, 1953. 276 pp.
In the 1870s, in the sequel to *Prisoner of Grace*, Chester Nimmo writes about his Devonshire childhood and adolescence.
Genre(s): Love Story; Political Fiction.

3836. *A Fearful Joy.* New York: Harper, 1950. 343 pp.
When Dick Bonser reveals his lack of reliability, Tabitha divorces him, but after two husbands, she wants to recapture the chemistry of their life together, so they remarry

3837. *Herself Surprised.* New York: Harper, 1948. 275 pp.
Sara Monday, an open-hearted cook, lands in jail where she examines her weaknesses.

3838. *The Horse's Mouth.* New York: Harper, 1950. 311 pp.
When an old artist attempts to retrieve nude paintings from his former model, Sara Monday, he accidently kills her, in the sequel to *To Be a Pilgrim.*

3839. *Mister Johnson.* New York: Harper, 1951. 261 pp.
Mister Johnson, an African clerk, thoughtlessly loves all things English and eventually loses his family, his job, and then his life.

3840. *Not Honour More.* New York: Harper, 1955. 309 pp.
In the sequel to *Except the Lord*, Chester Nimmo, a politician, tries to reassert himself as a labor leader during the General Strike.
Genre(s): Political Fiction; Love Story.

3841. *Prisoner of Grace.* New York: Harper, 1952. 301 pp.
Nina marries Chester Nimmo, of lower social standing, even though she loves her cousin, and even after Chester

becomes a politician, Nina leaves him periodically for Jim.
Genre(s): Political Fiction.

3842. *To Be a Pilgrim.* New York: Harper, 1949. 343 pp.
In the sequel to *Herself Suprised*, retired lawyer Tom Wilcher goes with his physician niece to his country home to await Sara Monday's release from jail.

Cashman, John

3843. *The Cook General.* New York: Harper and Row, 1974. 404 pp.
In 1879, Kate Webster, a cook-general or maidservant, kills her employer, Julia Thomas, and is subsequently executed in London.
Genre(s): Mystery.

Chatwin, Bruce

3844. *On the Black Hill.* New York: Viking, 1983. 248 pp.
Twin farmers born in 1900 live their entire lives together on the Welsh-English border.
Genre(s): Domestic Fiction.

Chernaik, Judith

3845. *The Daughter.* New York: Harper and Row, 1979. 216 pp.
Eleanor Marx gains prominence as a lecturer and a political organizer while keeping an open relationship with Edward Aveling.
Genre(s): Biographical Fiction.

Chesney, Marion

◆ 3846. *My Lords, Ladies and Marjorie.* Hampton, NH: Severn House, 1993. 224 pp.
Marjorie Montmorency-James, 18, wants to escape her sheltered life near London in the late 19th century, and she finally coerces her aunt to take her to London for the Season where she meets Lord Philip Cavendish.
Genre(s): Romance.

Clarke, Anna

3847. *The Lady in Black.* New York: McKay, 1977. 193 pp.
In 1882, George Meredith, reader for the publisher Chapman and Hall, deliberates over whether the company can publish an excellent book which is obviously the true story of a real crime.
Genre(s): Mystery.

Cloete, Stuart

3848. *The Abductors.* New York: Trident, 1966. 479 pp.
While pretending to be prudish and moral, white slave traders abduct young girls and others for their businesses.
Genre(s): Political Fiction.

Coffman, Virginia

3849. *Dark Winds.* New York: Arbor House, 1985. 300 pp.
Rachel's father almost destroys Jason's family, but because her father is dead, Jason's family decides to place its wrath on Rachel.
Genre(s): Gothic Fiction; Romance.

Colegate, Isabel

3850. *The Shooting Party.* New York: Viking, 1981. 195 pp.
During a pheasant shoot, men become competitive, and an accident occurs.

3851. *The Summer of the Royal Visit.* New York: Knopf, 1992. 256 pp.
Stephen Collinwood serves his Bath parishioners in 1876 and as all prepare for a visit from Queen Victoria, secrets begin to be revealed.
Genre(s): Domestic Fiction.

Conrad, Joseph

3852. *The Nigger of the Narcissus.* New York: Heinemann, 1897. 179 pp.
Sailors traveling from India to England try to survive a series of storms.
Genre(s): Sea Story.

Conway, Laura

3853. *The Night of the Party.* New York: McCall, 1971. 192 pp.
Juliet Alban is an orphan whose father bequeathed Privet Court, the haunted Elizabethan manor house, to a distant cousin, and she is involved in the haunting.
Genre(s): Mystery.

Cookson, Catherine

3854. *The Bannaman Legacy.* New York: Summit, 1985. 512 pp.
After the despicable squire Banneman forces Mary Ellen's love, Roddy, to leave for London, she marries and raises her family bereft of love.
Genre(s): Domestic Fiction.

◆ 3855. *The Black Candle.* New York: Summit, 1990. 488 pp.
In 1883, Joe Skinner begins managing Miss Mordaunt's candle works and marries Lily, who is carrying another man's child, but when Joe's brother kills the child's father, Joe is blamed for the murder.
Genre(s): Domestic Fiction.

3856. *The Black Velvet Gown.* New York: Summit, 1984. 345 pp.
A strange Northumberland bachelor helps the homeless and penniless widow Millican and her four children after her husband dies from cholera.
Genre(s): Domestic Fiction; Love Story.

3857. *The Cinder Path.* New York: Morrow, 1978. 244 pp.

The cinder path on which his brutal father whipped and disciplined his children and his servants haunts Charlie McFell, until his reunion with a first love after World War I helps him forget.
Genre(s): Domestic Fiction.

3858. *The Dwelling Place.* Indianapolis: Bobbs-Merrill, 1971. 313 pp.
Cissie Brodie at 15 works to keep her nine siblings together after her parents die, and when they lose their house, she moves them to a cave on the fells.
Genre(s): Domestic Fiction.

3859. *Feathers in the Fire.* Indianapolis: Bobbs-Merrill, 1972. 396 pp.
Amos McBain is born without legs, and when his father treats him like a monster, he eventually becomes one and scares people off the farm until those remaining show their understanding.
Genre(s): Domestic Fiction.

◆ 3860. *The Harrogate Secret.* New York: Summit, 1988. 352 pp.
Ten-year-old Freddy Musgrave delivers smuggled goods to the Towers mansion master and discovers a child who needs rescuing.
Genre(s): Domestic Fiction.

3861. *Love Child.* New York: Simon and Schuster, 1991. 367 pp.
Refused a divorce by his alcoholic wife, Nathaniel Martell lives openly with his mistress, and they raise six children, all of whom suffer from village gossip until an older woman advises daughter Anne about independence.
Genre(s): Romance.

3862. *The Mallen Girl.* New York: Dutton, 1973. 282 pp.
In the sequel to *The Mallen Streak*, Barbara, deaf and jealous of Sarah, throws Sarah into a pit which stores rusted machinery, causing Sarah to lose her leg.
Genre(s): Domestic Fiction.

3863. *The Mallen Lot.* New York: Dutton, 1974. 309 pp.
The sequel to *The Mallen Girl* occurs from the 1880s until World War I when Barbara Mallen Bensham destroys the lives of those around her before she commits suicide.
Genre(s): Domestic Fiction; Family Saga.

◆ 3864. *The Moth.* New York: Summit, 1986. 293 pp.
As a carpenter in his uncle's shop, Robert takes the blame for several family problems and leaves to work on a nearby estate.
Genre(s): Domestic Fiction.

3865. *The Obsession.* New York: Simon and Schuster, 1997. 320 pp.
John Falconer, a doctor, buys a practice near the estate that Beatrice Steel is trying to save after her father died penniless, and Beatrice gets Falconer to marry her (although he is in love with her sister) in order to save the house.
Genre(s): Domestic Fiction.

◆ 3866. *The Parson's Daughter.* New York: Summit, 1987. 389 pp.
Nancy Ann Howard, a parson's daughter, marries the master of the manor and changes local perceptions about crossing social classes.
Genre(s): Domestic Fiction.

3867. *The Tide of Life.* New York: Morrow, 1976. 400 pp.
After her previous employers die, Emily needs to support her ill younger sister, and she finds a position in an isolated manor home in circumstances that change her life.
Genre(s): Domestic Fiction.

◆ 3868. *The Wingless Bird.* New York: Summit, 1991. 383 pp.
Agnes, 22, is stifled by her family's unhappiness, and she marries a man above her class to escape, but other problems erupt.
Genre(s): Domestic Fiction.

Cordell, Alexander

3869. *This Sweet and Bitter Earth.* New York: St. Martin's, 1978. 447 pp.
After Toby Davies arrives in South Wales in 1900 and before the Tonypandy Riots of 1910, he falls in love with two women, one a union leader for the coal miners and the other very practical.
Genre(s): Romance.

Coughlin, Patricia

3870. *Lord Savage.* New York: Bantam, 1996. 550 pp.
Teacher Ariel Halliday has the responsibility of transforming Hawaiian-born Leon Duvanne into the aristocratic Marquis of Sage.
Genre(s): Romance.

Coulter, Catherine

◆ 3871. *Lord Harry.* New York: New American Library, 1995. 224 pp.
A young lady disguises herself as a man called Lord Harry in order to search for her brother's murderer in the 19th century.
Genre(s): Romance; Mystery.

3872. *Night Fire.* 1989. Hampton, NH: Severn House, 1995. 392 pp.
Arielle Leslie searches for love after her abusive husband dies.
Genre(s): Romance.

Crane, Teresa

3873. *Molly.* New York: Coward-McCann, 1982. 537 pp.
After British soldiers kill Molly's brother and fiancé in Ireland, she attends a London business school, securing a job as one of the first women typists and becoming owner of an employment agency before World War I.
Genre(s): War Story.

Crichton, Robert

3874. *The Camerons.* New York: Knopf, 1972. 509 pp.
Maggie Drum wants to escape from a mining town in Scotland, but her husband believes that he must remain to help others.

Darrell, Elizabeth

3875. *At the Going down of the Sun.* New York: St. Martin's, 1985. 503 pp.
Rex Sheridan enlists in World War I because of his love of flying machines, Chris enlists to escape a loveless marriage, and Roland remains home to run the family estate until their father commits suicide, leaving them in debt.
Genre(s): War Story.

Davies-Owens, Shirley

3876. *Silver Linings.* New York: St. Martin's, 1986. 292 pp.
After Emma's father dies, she and her mother fall into poverty, but her mother does not know that Emma's father abused her, and that they are better off poor.
Genre(s): Domestic Fiction.

Davis, Kathryn Lynn

◆ 3877. *All We Hold Dear.* New York: Pocket Books, 1995. 512 pp.
Eva Crawford leaves her Hebrides home, after learning that she is adopted, to go to Edinburgh to investigate her past, and she discovers her mother's journals and her 19th-century ancestors.
Genre(s): Romance.

De Rosa, Peter

3878. *Rebels: The Irish Rising of 1916.* New York: Doubleday, 1991. 535 pp.
On Easter Sunday, 1916, while expecting relief from Germans, republicans fight the British in hope of gaining control of Ireland.
Genre(s): War Story.

Delderfield, R. F.

3879. *Give Us This Day.* New York: Simon and Schuster, 1973. 767 pp.
In the sequel to *Theirs Was the Kingdom*, the lives of the third-generation offspring of Adam and Henrietta are shown during Edwardian times.
Genre(s): Domestic Fiction.

3880. *A Horseman Riding By.* New York: Simon and Schuster, 1967. 1150 pp.
When Paul Craddock returns to England from the Boer Wars, he uses his inheritance to buy a Devonshire estate that has seven tenancies.
Genre(s): Domestic Fiction.

3881. *Theirs Was the Kingdom.* New York: Simon and Schuster, 1971. 798 pp.

In the sequel to *God is an Englishman*, Adam Swann and his nine children move through Victorian England.
Genre(s): Domestic Fiction.

Denton, Kit

3882. *The Breaker.* New York: St. Martin's, 1981. 268 pp.
Harry Morant, an Australian officer fighing in the Boer Wars, faces trial for killing civilians in 1902.
Genre(s): Biographical Fiction; War Story.

Deveraux, Jude

◆ 3883. *The Duchess.* New York: Pocket Books, 1991. 316 pp.
In 1883, after an American heiress agrees to marry Harry in Scotland, she visits his home and hates its isolation, but Harry's brother Trevelyan offers adventure.
Genre(s): Romance.

3884. *Twin of Ice.* New York: Pocket Books, 1985. 309 pp.
Wealthy Kane Taggert is socially inept, but Houston Blair decides to have her twin dine with her fiancé while Houston has dinner with Kane, and both women end up with different men than they had planned.
Genre(s): Romance.

Dillon, Anna

3885. *Seasons.* New York: St. Martin's, 1989. 587 pp.
Katherine Lundy arrives in Dublin from England to work for the government agent John Lewis, sees the squalid conditions of many Dubliners, and comes in contact with reporter Dermot Corcoran before the Easter Rising in 1916.
Genre(s): War Story.

Dillon, Eilís

3886. *Across the Bitter Sea.* New York: Simon and Schuster, 1973. 571 pp.
In Ireland after the potato famine, a family deals with daily life and the political machinations of the government.
Genre(s): War Story; Political Fiction.

3887. *Blood Relations.* New York: Simon and Schuster, 1977. 479 pp.
Molly Gould, a poor Protestant, becomes involved with a wealthy Irish Catholic boy, but he dies in the Easter Rebellion of 1916, and she must find ways to adjust to her situation during the next eight years.
Genre(s): War Story.

Dodd, Christina

3888. *Move Heaven and Earth.* New York: Harper, 1995. 387 pp.
Disappointed that she has failed to save all of the soldiers for whom she has cared, Sylvan Miles begins to work with a paralyzed nobleman and falls in love with him.
Genre(s): Gothic Fiction; Romance.

Dolbier, Maurice

3889. *The Mortal Gods.* New York: Dial, 1971. 279 pp.
Robert Jovian brings a woman from the provinces to London to play Juliet to his Romeo in the late 19th century and reveals the inner workings of theater productions.
Genre(s): Romance.

Douglas, Carole Nelson

◆ 3890. *Good Morning, Irene.* New York: Tor, 1991. 374 pp.
Irene and her husband, thought to have died in the Alps, resurface in Paris with Irene's friend Nell as they try to solve the mystery of a man whose body is discovered in the Seine wearing a strange tatoo that Irene has seen previously.
Genre(s): Mystery.

◆ 3891. *Good Night, Mr Holmes.* New York: St. Martin's, 1990. 408 pp.
As the only woman that Sherlock Holmes ever admired, Irene Adler, an opera singer who earned money as a private investigator until she became famous, falls in love with the king of Bohemia before having to fool both of them.
Genre(s): Mystery.

Doyle, Arthur Conan

3892. *The Hound of the Baskervilles.* New York: McClure, Phillips, 1902. 248 pp.
When Sir Charles Baskerville is murdered, Sherlock Holmes and Dr. Watson investigate the eerie howling on the moor.
Genre(s): Mystery.

3893. *The Sign of Four.* 1890. Garden City, NY: Doubleday, 1977. 134 pp.
Mary Morstan calls Sherlock Holmes to find her vanished father.
Genre(s): Mystery.

3894. *A Study in Scarlet.* 1887. Garden City, NY: Doubleday, 1977. 145 pp.
In Utah, Mormons brutalize a girl and her lover, while in London a mysterious double murder occurs, which Sherlock Holmes must investigate.
Genre(s): Mystery.

3895. *The Valley of Fear.* 1914. Garden City, NY: Doubleday, 1977. 189 pp.
Sherlock Holmes and colleagues investigate the murder of John Douglas in Sussex while information comes to light about Douglas's past life in Pennsylvania.
Genre(s): Mystery.

Drake, Shannon

3896. *No Other Woman.* New York: Avon, 1996. 377 pp.
The head of the MacGinnis and Douglas clans, Shawna MacGinnis, mourns the death of her lover five years before, but unknown to her, he has returned from an Austra-

lian penal colony where he was mistakenly shipped and he no longer trusts anyone.
Genre(s): Romance.

Drummond, Emma

3897. *A Distant Hero.* New York: St. Martin's, 1997. 432 pp.
The Ashleigh sons from *A Question of Honour* fight in the Boer Wars while their sisters remain at home trying to maintain the family's reputation.
Genre(s): Romance.

3898. *A Question of Honour.* New York: St. Martin's, 1992. 346 pp.
When the Ashleigh family gathers in 1896 to mourn the death of the head of the family, Vorne Ashleigh, his influence continues from the grave.
Genre(s): Domestic Fiction.

3899. *That Sweet and Savage Land.* New York: St. Martin's, 1991. 285 pp.
Elizabeth Delacourte remains in England while her husband serves in India, but when John Stavenham comes home on leave, he entrances Elizabeth with himself and with his stories of India before she goes there to join her husband.
Genre(s): Adventure Story; Political Fiction.

Dwyer-Joyce, Alice

3900. *The Unwinding Corner.* New York: St. Martin's, 1983. 253 pp.
A romance erupts in the midst of the Irish Rebellion and its turmoil in the early 20th century.
Genre(s): War Story; Romance.

Eagleton, Terry

3901. *Saints and Scholars.* New York: Verso, 1987. 145 pp.
James Connolly, leader of Ireland's Easter Rising, is executed, but as the bullets fly through midair, they stop, and Wittgenstein and Connolly discuss revolution.
Genre(s): War Story; Fantastic Literature.

Eden, Dorothy

◆ 3902. *The American Heiress.* New York: Coward-McCann, 1980. 251 pp.
After surviving the *Lusitania* sinking, Hetty takes the jewels and identity of her stepsister and becomes involved with a British lord.
Genre(s): Romance.

3903. *Lady of Mallow.* New York: Coward-McCann, 1962. 256 pp.
Sarah Mildmay helps to save the inheritance of a family estate by posing as a governess in the home of the false heir.
Genre(s): Romance.

◆ 3904. *Melbury Square.* New York: Coward-McCann, 1970. 382 pp.

Against the backdrop of Victorian England, Maud Lucie grows from the pampered daughter of a pre-Raphaelite painter into an eccentric old woman.
Genre(s): Romance.

◆ 3905. *The Millionaire's Daughter.* New York: Coward-McCann, 1974. 384 pp.
At the beginning of the 20th century a father wants to overcome his own slum childhood by marrying his daughter to an earl.
Genre(s): Romance.

◆ 3906. *Ravenscroft.* New York: Coward-McCann, 1965. 253 pp.
Although a nobleman saves two orphaned sisters from procurers by marrying one, he does not get rid of the white slavers.
Genre(s): Romance.

◆ 3907. *The Salamanca Drum.* New York: Coward-McCann, 1977. 286 pp.
A mother is willing to sacrifice her entire family to military patriotic glory.
Genre(s): Romance.

◆ 3908. *Speak to Me of Love.* New York: Coward-McCann, 1972. 384 pp.
After she marries in 1881, Beatrice Bonnington continues to be strong-willed and chooses to work in her father's department store.
Genre(s): Romance.

◆ 3909. *The Storrington Papers.* New York: Coward-McCann, 1978. 253 pp.
A woman hired in contemporary times to sort the papers of the Storrington family finds herself involved in the lives of those who lived 100 years before.
Genre(s): Romance.

Edgar, Josephine

3910. *The Dark and Alien Rose.* New York: St. Martin's, 1991. 320 pp.
Rose's mother dies in Nice, and Rose, 14, goes to live with her proper British aunt where she uses her charm to diffuse comments about her dark skin and to win Tom, her cousin, before he leaves for the World War I front.
Genre(s): War Story; Romance.

3911. *Duchess.* New York: St. Martin's, 1976. 277 pp.
Viola, a charming, sophisticated shop girl in Victorian England finally rises to the station in life which she thinks she deserves.
Genre(s): Romance.

3912. *Margaret Normanby.* New York: St. Martin's, 1983. 448 pp.
Margaret Normanby works to support her family in the Victorian world of fashion where she meets a wealthy man who once pursued her mother.
Genre(s): Romance.

Estleman, Loren D.

◆ 3913. *Sherlock Holmes Versus Dracula.* New York: Doubleday, 1978. 214 pp.
Sherlock Holmes comes to England to search for Dracula.
Genre(s): Mystery.

Evans, Alan

◆ 3914. *Thunder at Dawn.* New York: Doubleday, 1979. 215 pp.
Commander Smith takes the *HMS Thunder* to the Pacific, but two German warships arrive and Smith must use the undermanned ship to overcome them and keep British supremacy in World War I.
Genre(s): War Story.

Fairbairns, Zoë

3915. *Stand We at Last.* Boston: Houghton Mifflin, 1983. 609 pp.
Five generations of women tell their stories beginning in 1855 and continuing to 1972.
Genre(s): Family Saga.

Fawcett, Quinn

◆ 3916. *Against the Brotherhood.* New York: Tor, 1997. 320 pp.
Before World War I, Mycroft Holmes, brother of Sherlock, takes the identity of a ne'er-do-well in order to infiltrate secret societies in Europe dedicated to the overthrow of European rulers.
Genre(s): Mystery.

Feuer, Lewis Samuel

3917. *The Case of the Revolutionist's Daughter.* Buffalo, NY: Prometheus, 1983. 159 pp.
Karl Marx asks Sherlock Holmes to help him find his missing daughter Tussy in 1881, but she has gone to live with the despicable Edward Aveling, and while searching for her, Marx's circle gathers for political discussions.
Genre(s): Mystery.

Fisher, Anne Kinsman

3918. *The Legend of Tommy Morris.* San Rafael, CA: Amber-Allen, 1996. 133 pp.
Tommy Morris, the only golfer ever to win the British Open four consecutive times, dies unexpectedly three months after the death of his wife in childbirth.
Genre(s): Biographical Fiction; Sports Fiction; Christian Fiction.

Fitz Gibbon, Constantine

3919. *High Heroic.* New York: Norton, 1969. 176 pp.
Michael Collins comes from West Cork to encounter and then break with Irish leader De Valera in 1921, leading to the Irish Civil War.
Genre(s): Biographical Fiction; War Story.

Fitzgerald, Nancy

◆ 3920. *Mayfair.* Garden City, NY: Doubleday, 1978. 288 pp.
The youngest two daughters of the Earl of Corrough arrive in London for the season, and when an aunt tries to pair them up with boring men, they find their own husbands.
Genre(s): Romance.

Fitzgerald, Penelope

3921. *The Gate of Angels.* New York: Doubleday, 1992. 176 pp.
In 1912 a bicycle accident introduces Fred Fairly, a physics student at St. Angelicus who is supposed to remain celibate, to Daisy Saunders, recently dismissed from her position as a nursing probationer.
Genre(s): Love Story.

Flanagan, Thomas

3922. *The End of the Hunt.* New York: Dutton, 1994. 627 pp.
Following the Easter Rebellion of 1916, in the sequel to *The Tenants of Time*, participants live through the establishment of the Irish Free State and a terrible civil war.

3923. *The Tenants of Time.* New York: Dutton, 1988. 824 pp.
In the sequel to *The Year of the French*, four men participate in the Irish Rising of 1867 and the battle of Clonbrony Wood.

Fleming, Georgina

3924. *Beyond the Shadowlands.* North Pomfret, VT: Trafalgar Square, 1993. 472 pp.
Alice Brennan escapes from the lunatic asylum in which her husband has placed her and joins a band of Gypsies who help her find her independence in Victorian England.
Genre(s): Romance.

Fleming, H. K.

3925. *The Day They Kidnapped Queen Victoria.* New York: St. Martin's, 1978. 191 pp.
While Queen Victoria travels from Balmoral after the death of Prince Albert, someone hijacks her train, and Disraeli organizes a rescue.
Genre(s): Mystery.

Follett, Ken

3926. *A Dangerous Fortune.* New York: Delacorte, 1993. 533 pp.
In 1866, after a young student drowns at Wakefield School, several boys who seem to have been involved in the incident continue their duplicity as adults.

3927. *The Man from St Petersburg.* New York: Morrow, 1982. 323 pp.
When Charlotte's real father, an anarchist-murderer, appears in London and realizes that she is related to him, he plans to use her in his attempt to kill a Russian prince.
Genre(s): War Story; Spy Fiction.

Forster, E. M.

3928. *Howards End.* 1910. New York: Knopf, 1985. 288 pp.
Howards End, an English country house, passes to the moneyed, the cultured, and then to the lower class.
Genre(s): Domestic Fiction.

3929. *Maurice.* New York: Norton, 1971. 256 pp.
While a student at Cambridge, Maurice Hall discovers that he is sexually attracted to men rather than women.
Genre(s): Domestic Fiction.

Foster, Aisling

3930. *Safe in the Kitchen.* London: Penguin, 1994. 346 pp.
Rita Fitzgerald's Dublin debut coincides with the Easter Rising in 1916, and afterward, she meets people "outside the kitchen door" by marrying a young Republican and starting to work for Ireland, eventually becoming caretaker of the Romanov jewels that De Valera smuggles into Ireland.
Genre(s): Domestic Fiction.

Fowles, John

3931. *The French Lieutenant's Woman.* Boston: Little, Brown, 1969. 467 pp.
Charles Smithson of Lyme Regis is engaged to the wealthy but shallow Ernestina while independent Sarah Woodruff, ostracized for her affair with a French sailor, fascinates him.

Fraser, George MacDonald

3932. *Mr American.* New York: Knopf, 1980. 557 pp.
Mark J. Franklin arrives in England in the early 20th century and, with unlimited wealth, acquires all of the trappings of nobility including a meeting with King Edward VII.
Genre(s): Adventure Story.

Freeborn, Richard

3933. *The Russian Crucifix.* New York: St. Martin's, 1987. 255 pp.
While Guy Seddenham's father travels to Australia trying to recoup the family fortune, Guy spends time with his younger twin sisters and aunt at Ventnor, a seaside resort where Russians come to relieve their tubercular symptoms, and while Ivan Turgenev works on a document there, Guy falls in love with two women before one is found drowned.
Genre(s): Mystery.

Freeman, Cynthia

3934. *The Days of Winter.* New York: Arbor House, 1978. 374 pp.
Of five lawyer sons in the Hack family, Rubin marries a Romanian who leaves him after he returns battered from World War I.
Genre(s): Domestic Fiction; War Story.

Frost, Mark

3935. *The Six Messiahs*. New York: Morrow, 1995. 404 pp.
Arthur Conan Doyle and Jack Sparks team together to control Sparks's brother in America.
Genre(s): Mystery.

Gaffney, Patricia

3936. *Forever and Ever*. New York: Topaz, 1996. 384 pp.
Sophie Deene inherits and runs the family copper mine in the south of England, but when Conner Pendarvis comes to town to investigate dangerous working conditions, they must adjust to each other's social status.
Genre(s): Romance.

Gardner, John E.

3937. *The Return of Moriarty*. New York: Putnam, 1974. 366 pp.
Notes from Professor James Moriarty, rival of Sherlock Holmes, reveal his criminal activities in the London area.
Genre(s): Mystery.

3938. *The Revenge of Moriarty*. New York: Putnam, 1975. 289 pp.
Moriarty, Sherlock Holmes's archenemy, returns to London with money from the United States, and he plans to annihilate Holmes, and the rest of his enemies as well.
Genre(s): Mystery.

3939. *The Secret Generations*. New York: Putnam, 1985. 383 pp.
From 1909 to 1935, almost every member of the Railton family becomes inolved in espionage and intelligence.
(*Series:* Secret Generations, 1)
Genre(s): Family Saga; Adventure Story; Spy Fiction.

Gaskin, Catherine

3940. *A Falcon for a Queen*. Garden City, NY: Doubleday, 1972. 344 pp.
After the death of her missionary father in China, Kirsty Howard returns to her ancestral Scottish home.
Genre(s): Romance.

Gilbert, Anna

3941. *A Family Likeness*. New York: St. Martin's, 1977. 223 pp.
Tessa, a gentle girl, becomes the heiress to Barmote Hall but wants to marry her former servant rather than her wealthy cousin.
Genre(s): Romance; Gothic Fiction.

◆ 3942. *Flowers for Lilian*. New York: St. Martin's, 1980. 190 pp.
In order to get everything she wants, Lilian overpowers her friend Maggie.
Genre(s): Romance.

3943. *Images of Rose*. New York: Delacorte, 1974. 275 pp.

Cousin Rose arrives after Lucy and Ellen Westerdale's mother dies in the 19th century, marries their sea captain father, and takes over after his death.
Genre(s): Romance.

◆ 3944. *The Leavetaking*. New York: St. Martin's, 1979. 192 pp.
Isobel Penrose, 16, searches for a friend and former companion in England in the late 19th century.
Genre(s): Romance; Bildungsroman (Coming of Age); Mystery.

◆ 3945. *The Long Shadow*. New York: St. Martin's, 1985. 301 pp.
Hannah admires her sister-in-law Zilla, but she discovers that a foundling has manipulated Zilla more than anyone had been aware of.
Genre(s): Romance; Gothic Fiction.

3946. *Miss Bede Is Staying*. New York: St. Martin's, 1983. 316 pp.
Newly married Florence makes friends with Miss Bede, a woman in the village, but finds eventually that Miss Bede is not what she seems.
Genre(s): Romance.

◆ 3947. *Remembering Louise*. New York: St. Martin's, 1978. 221 pp.
Hester Mallow becomes the only witness to the murder of a man looking for Hester's sister after he's been seven years absent from England.
Genre(s): Romance; Mystery.

◆ 3948. *The Treachery of Time*. New York: St. Martin's, 1996. 444 pp.
Just before World War I, an orphaned girl abandoned in a small English village becomes angry when two children show her sympathy, and she returns years later to disrupt their happiness.
Award(s): Cookson Award.
Genre(s): Romance.

Gilbert, Michael

3949. *Into Battle*. New York: Carroll and Graf, 1997. 224 pp.
Luke Pagan rushes from England to France in an attempt to fool Erick Krieger, a German spy.
Genre(s): Mystery; War Story; Spy Fiction.

◆ 3950. *Ring of Terror*. New York: Carroll and Graf, 1995. 218 pp.
Luke Pagan, 15, becomes a police detective trying to quell Russian terrorists in London while Edward VII is on the throne.
Genre(s): Mystery.

Gillespie, Jane

3951. *Ladysmead*. New York: St. Martin's, 1982. 176 pp.
In 19th-century England, Sophia, 23, has no hopes of marriage until she meets a young clergyman.
Genre(s): Romance.

Glazebrook, Philip

3952. *Byzantine Honeymoon.* New York:
Atheneum, 1979. 204 pp.
While Archie Caper honeymoons with his wife in Constantinople during 1895, a mysterious Persian persuades
him to set up a house of his own where he can enjoy all
types of pleasures.
Genre(s): Adventure Story.

3953. *Captain Vinegar's Commission.* New York:
Atheneum, 1987. 352 pp.
Tresham Pitcher goes East to seek his fortune after having to leave public school for financial reasons, and he decides to impersonate Captain Vinegar, a fictional Eastern
traveler.
Genre(s): Picaresque Fiction.

Glendinning, Victoria

3954. *Electricity.* Boston: Little, Brown, 1995. 250
pp.
Charlotte Mortimer, 19, marries the engineer Peter
Fisher, who becomes more involved with installing electricity in a nobleman's house than with her.
Genre(s): Bildungsroman (Coming of Age).

Glover, Judith

3955. *Sisters and Brothers.* New York: St. Martin's, 1984. 286 pp.
Frank and Isabelle Flynn, illegitimate children of Morgan, have passionate affairs with another brother and sister, then Isabelle goes to a brothel and the Franco-Prussian war takes the lives of those who would interfere with
their happiness.
Genre(s): Domestic Fiction; Romance.

3956. *The Stallion Man.* New York: St. Martin's,
1983. 334 pp.
Frank Morgan plots to seduce the young wife of an aged
parson, but a local farmer tries to protect the young
woman.
Genre(s): Domestic Fiction.

3957. *Tiger Lilies.* New York: St. Martin's, 1991.
320 pp.
Flora Dennison receives financial support from her father, but the daughter of her father's mistress, Roseen,
seems to have his affection, and in 1905, when the girls
are 12, they become sibling rivals.
Genre(s): Domestic Fiction.

Goddard, Robert

3958. *In Pale Battalions.* New York: Simon and
Schuster, 1988. 297 pp.
Leonora Galloway reveals her sordid past to her daughter
against a backdrop of decadent British noblitity during
World War I.
Genre(s): War Story.

3959. *Painting the Darkness.* New York: Poseidon, 1989. 446 pp.

James Davenall reappears in 1882 after an 11-year absence, calls himself Norton, and claims the family fortune
from his younger brother.

Godden, Rumer

3960. *China Court.* New York: Viking, 1961. 304
pp.
When Tracy, a young girl, returns to China Court, the
family home in England, at the death of her grandmother,
the five generations who lived in the house come alive to
her.
Genre(s): Domestic Fiction.

Gordon, Richard

3961. *Jack the Ripper.* New York: Atheneum,
1980. 278 pp.
Dr. Bertie Randolph, a respectable doctor, becomes involved in a series of murders during 1888 in London's
Whitechapel where Jack the Ripper operates.
Genre(s): Mystery.

3962. *A Question of Guilt.* New York: Atheneum,
1981. 184 pp.
When Hawley Harvey Crippen, an American doctor, is
convicted of murdering his wife in Britain in the early
20th century, another doctor who works with the needy in
London doubts that Crippen is guilty.
Genre(s): Biographical Fiction.

Goudge, Elizabeth

3963. *A City of Bells.* New York: Coward-
McCann, 1936. 380 pp.
Depressed over a wound received in the Boer Wars, Jocelyn Irwin travels to his grandfather's home and finds solace.
Genre(s): Romance.

3964. *The Dean's Watch.* New York: Coward-
McCann, 1960. 383 pp.
The dean of the cathedral and Isaac Peabody, a clockmaker, become unlikely friends in a cathedral town.
Genre(s): Religious Fiction.

3965. *The Rosemary Tree.* New York: Coward-
McCann, 1956. 381 pp.
Michael Stone, former writer and prisoner, visits a village
where he finds his former sweetheart married to someone
else.
Genre(s): Domestic Fiction.

3966. *The Scent of Water.* New York: Coward-
McCann, 1963. 348 pp.
When a woman retires to an inherited house, she finds
journals that give her insight about helping the neighbors.
Genre(s): Domestic Fiction.

Gower, Iris

◆ 3967. *Black Gold.* New York: St. Martin's, 1988.
384 pp.
In the sequel to *Fiddler's Ferry*, Welsh coal miners experience strikes, shortages, and unemployment.
Genre(s): Domestic Fiction; Romance.

◆May be suitable for young adult readers

◆ 3968. *Copper Kingdom.* New York: St. Martin's, 1983. 320 pp.
After Mali Llewelyn's mother dies, her father, a copper worker, has an affair with a streetwalker, while Mali and the copper mine's heir fall in love.
Genre(s): Domestic Fiction; Romance.

◆ 3969. *Proud Mary.* New York: St. Martin's, 1985. 372 pp.
In the sequel to *Copper Kingdom*, Mary Jenkins, Mali Richardson's laundress, rises out of difficulties in the South Wales mining town of Sweyn's Eye.
Genre(s): Domestic Fiction; Romance.

◆ 3970. *Spinners' Wharf.* New York: St. Martin's, 1985. 383 pp.
In the sequel to *Proud Mary*, Rhian Gray leaves a good job at a Yorkshire mill and returns to the mining village of Sweyn's Eye to care for an aging relative.
Genre(s): Romance; Domestic Fiction.

Gray, Alasdair

3971. *Poor Things.* New York: Harcourt, 1992. 317 pp.
Glasgow physician Archibald McCandess of Victorian Scotland describes the strange life of Bella Baxter, a woman who drowns and has the brain of her fetus transplanted into her own head when revived.
Award(s): Whitbread Award; *Guardian* Fiction Prize.
Genre(s): Horror; Medical Novel.

Greenwood, L. B.

◆ 3972. *Sherlock Holmes and the Case of the Raleigh Legacy.* New York: Atheneum, 1986. 184 pp.
Aleck Raleigh, friend of Dr. Watson, is given a letter supposedly written by Sir Walter Raleigh, and he thinks it reveals details about his family which he wants investigated.
Genre(s): Mystery.

◆ 3973. *Sherlock Homes and the Case of Sabina Hall.* New York: Morrow, 1988. 192 pp.
Holmes suggests that Dr. Watson treat an old school friend's uncle, and when the two arrive at Sabina Hall, the uncle has died, but Holmes smells poison in his medicine spoon.
Genre(s): Mystery.

Gunn, Neil M.

3974. *Blood Hunt.* New York: Walker, 1987. 250 pp.
Allan runs from the police brother of a man he has killed over a woman named Liz, while Liz finds peace with an old man in the Scottish highlands.
Genre(s): Domestic Fiction.

◆ 3975. *Morning Tide.* 1931. New York: Walker, 1993. 256 pp.
Each of three days is a milestone in Hugh's life in a small fishing village in Scotland in the early 20th century.
Genre(s): Bildungsroman (Coming of Age).

◆ 3976. *Young Art and Old Hector.* New York: Walker, 1991. 255 pp.
Old Hector helps Young Art, eight, cope with his lack of understanding as to why they cannot fish on others' lands during the 19th century in Scotland.
Genre(s): Domestic Fiction.

Gurney, Jane

3977. *The Green of the Spring.* New York: St. Martin's, 1993. 506 pp.
Upper-class Laura loves a man who marries someone else, so she marries on the rebound, while her maid Daisy has two men in love with her, but all four men are sent to France in World War I.
Genre(s): War Story.

Haines, Pamela

3978. *The Diamond Waterfall.* New York: Doubleday, 1984. 491 pp.
Lily Greenwood flees home in 1887 after falling in love with the theater, but her action begins her own downfall as well as that of two generations after her.
Genre(s): Family Saga.

3979. *The Golden Lion.* New York: Scribner's, 1986. 414 pp.
An Englishman, Eric Grainger, takes in Maria Verzotti, left an orphan with the sinking of the *Lusitania*, but after his son rapes her, she returns to Italy to have her child, one in a series of events covering five decades.
Genre(s): War Story; Family Saga.

Haire-Sargeant, Lin

◆ 3980. *H: The Story of Heathcliff's Journey Back To Wuthering Heights.* New York: Pocket Books, 1992. 280 pp.
In a letter hidden for 60 years, Heathcliff describes his experiences with Mr. Are of Thornfield as his mentor.
Genre(s): Adventure Story.

Hall, Robert Lee

◆ 3981. *Exit Sherlock Holmes.* New York: Scribner's, 1977. 224 pp.
A secret basement apartment at 221B Baker Street leads to the demise of Sherlock Holmes.
Genre(s): Mystery.

Hambly, Barbara

◆ 3982. *Those Who Hunt the Night.* New York: Ballantine, 1988. 352 pp.
People concerned about the murder of vampires in Edwardian London hire a professor to investigate.
Genre(s): Mystery; Horror.

Hamilton-Paterson, James

3983. *Gerontius.* New York: Soho, 1991. 264 pp.
Edward Elgar, dissatisfied with himself and believing his music insignificant, takes a cruise in 1923 to an Amazon port where he meets a woman from his past.
Genre(s): Biographical Fiction; Musical Fiction.

Hanna, Edward B.

◆ 3984. *The Whitechapel Horrors.* New York: Carroll and Graf, 1993. 395 pp.
As Sherlock Holmes investigates the murders of several prostitutes for Scotland Yard, he comes close to arresting Jack the Ripper and uncovering a surprisingly close connection to Buckingham Palace.
Genre(s): Mystery.

Hansen, Erik Fosnes

3985. *Psalm at Journey's End.* Trans. Joan Tate. New York: Farrar, Straus and Giroux, 1996. 371 pp.
A diverse group of people make up the *Titanic*'s orchestra on its maiden voyage in 1912.
Genre(s): Musical Fiction.

Hardwick, Michael

3986. *Prisoner of the Devil.* New York: Scribner's, 1979. 307 pp.
When the Dreyfus family and Queen Victoria ask Sherlock Holmes to reinvestigate a case, Mycroft in Whitehall threatens Holmes with time in the Tower.
Genre(s): Mystery.

◆ 3987. *Sherlock Holmes.* New York: Doubleday, 1984. 208 pp.
Sherlock Holmes recounts some of his most interesting cases, giving insights into his aide, Watson, and his nemesis, Moriarty.
Genre(s): Mystery.

Hardwick, Mollie

◆ 3988. *The Crystal Dove.* New York: St. Martin's, 1985. 224 pp.
Eleanore, 13, in trying to escape from her spinster aunts, finds a job as a magician's assistant.
Genre(s): Romance.

3989. *The Duchess of Duke Street.* New York: Holt, Rinehart and Winston, 1977. 303 pp.
In 1900, Louisa Leyton wants to be the best cook in England, which leads to her managing a hotel and catering service.

3990. *Monday's Child.* New York: St. Martin's, 1982. 286 pp.
Laura's loveliness draws wealthy suitors to her and while maintaining her naive attitude, she travels with them in Europe throughout Victorian times.
Genre(s): Romance.

3991. *Sarah's Story.* New York: Pocket Books, 1975. 189 pp.
Sarah works as a servant in a London home during the 19th century.
Genre(s): Domestic Fiction.

3992. *The Shakespeare Girl.* New York: St. Martin's, 1983. 234 pp.

Miranda Heriot enjoys Shakespeare so much that at the turn of the 20th century she runs away with a group of actors against her grandmother's wishes.

3993. *The War to End Wars.* New York: Dell, 1974. 423 pp.
Working-class and upper-class families try to cope with the changes of World War I on their lives. (*Series:* Upstairs, Downstairs)
Genre(s): War Story; Domestic Fiction.

3994. *Willowwood.* New York: St. Martin's, 1980. 316 pp.
A gardener begins to help 20-year-old Lilian de Wentworth, paralyzed since childhood, but Lilian's furious mother sends her to London to stay with an aunt, a friend of the pre-Raphaelites.

3995. *The Years of Change.* New York: Dell, 1974. 239 pp.
The aristocratic London family upstairs functions differently from the servants downstairs. (*Series:* Upstairs, Downstairs)
Genre(s): Domestic Fiction.

Hardy, Charlotte

3996. *Far From Home.* New York: St. Martin's, 1997. 432 pp.
In London, someone seduces the Irish Brid and abandons her with child, but Brid recovers to become a success on the Victorian stage.

Hardy, Thomas

3997. *Jude the Obscure.* 1895. New York: Knopf, 1992. 518 pp.
Marriage, the Church of England, and the British university system all come under criticism in a story about two cousins who love each other and want to improve their lot in life.
Genre(s): Country Life.

3998. *The Mayor of Casterbridge.* 1886. New York: Knopf, 1993. 362 pp.
After Michael Henchard becomes the mayor of Casterbridge, the wife and children he sold at a fair 18 years previously reappear.
Genre(s): Country Life.

3999. *The Return of the Native.* 1878. New York: Modern Library, 1994. 418 pp.
Clym's mother disapproves of his marriage, and when she comes to visit, Clym's wife is entertaining her lover and does not answer the door.
Genre(s): Country Life.

4000. *Tess of the d'Urbervilles.* 1891. London: Everyman's Library, 1991. 254 pp.
The son in the family for which Tess Durbeyfield works assaults her, and she has a child who dies in infancy, but her husband is unforgiving.
Genre(s): Country Life.

4001. *Under the Greenwood Tree.* 1872. New York: Oxford, 1985. 218 pp.

The people of Dorset include a carrier's family and a choir, who comment on the love affair of a young boy and girl.
Genre(s): Country Life.

Harper, Karen

4002. *The Wings of Morning.* New York: Dutton, 1993. 368 pp.
Abigail MacQueen marries her love, but he drowns, and then her son dies from St. Kilda's disease, a malady killing four of every five infants on their Outer Hebrides island, so she decides to find the cause of the disease from Queen Victoria's physician.
Genre(s): Romance; Medical Novel.

Harris, Marilyn

4003. *Eden and Honor.* Garden City, NY: Doubleday, 1989. 587 pp.
When the Eden family meets again at Eden Castle, in the sequel to *American Eden*, the proud John Murrey Eden causes hostility.
Genre(s): Romance.

4004. *Eden Rising.* New York: Putnam, 1982. 398 pp.
John Eden, in the sequel to *The Women of Eden*, has a relationship with nurse-midwife Susan Mantle.
Genre(s): Romance.

4005. *The Women of Eden.* New York: Putnam, 1980. 515 pp.
The sequel to *The Eden Passion* finds John Murrey Eden in 1870 trying to run not only the lives of his wife, sister, and mistress, but also his business.
Genre(s): Romance; Family Saga.

Harrison, Ray

4006. *Counterfeit of Murder.* New York: St. Martin's, 1987. 234 pp.
Sergeant Bragg and Constable Morton search for the leader of a counterfeiting ring which is passing thousand-pound Bank of England notes, and Morton goes underground to join the group.
Genre(s): Mystery.

4007. *Death of a Dancing Lady.* New York: Scribner's, 1986. 235 pp.
Sergeant Bragg and Constable Morton investigate a murder resulting from the destruction of a ship and an unidentified cargo of rifles at the beginning of the 20th century in London.
Genre(s): Mystery.

4008. *Death of an Honorable Member.* New York: Scribner's, 1985. 154 pp.
In the 1890s, Sergeant Bragg and Constable Morton investigate the supposedly accidental death of a member of Parliament and find a history of corrupt finances.
Genre(s): Mystery.

4009. *Deathwatch.* New York: Scribner's, 1986. 239 pp.

Sergeant Bragg and the wealthy Constable Morton must solve the murder of an undercover policeman who was investigating participants in labor union demonstrations.
Genre(s): Mystery.

4010. *Harvest of Death.* New York: St. Martin's, 1988. 288 pp.
Sergeant Bragg goes to Dorset for a vacation and to recover from a stab wound, but his enjoyment is brief when he has to investigate the murder of a local tradesman and the village midwife.
Genre(s): Mystery.

◆ 4011. *Patently Murder.* New York: St. Martin's, 1991. 255 pp.
Catherine Marsden gives money to a young London girl sitting in a doorway, and when she discovers that the girl has died, she and the police search for a murderer of child prostitutes.
Genre(s): Mystery.

◆ 4012. *Why Kill Arthur Potter?* New York: Scribner's, 1984. 155 pp.
Sergeant Joseph Bragg and Constable James Morton investigate the brutal death of Arthur Potter, a lowly shipping clerk, and end up in Monte Carlo at the gaming tables during their search for the murderer.
Genre(s): Mystery.

Harrison, Sarah

4013. *The Flowers of the Field.* New York: Putnam, 1980. 490 pp.
As an English family experiences World War I, two sisters who try to plot their lives cannot account for the subsequent frustrations.
Genre(s): Domestic Fiction; Romance; War Story.

4014. *An Imperfect Lady.* New York: Warner, 1989. 544 pp.
A Devon woman born in 1900 first marries a man of whom her mother disapproves and, at his death, develops her artistic side before marrying twice more.
Genre(s): Romance.

Harrod-Eagles, Cynthia

4015. *I, Victoria.* New York: St. Martin's, 1996. 415 pp.
Victoria writes about her family and contemporary political situations in the last year of her life.
Genre(s): Biographical Fiction.

Hastings, Michael

4016. *Tussy Is Me.* New York: Delacorte, 1971. 342 pp.
Eleanor Marx marries British scientist and writer Edward Aveling in the late 19th century, and he spends her money on his mistress while she becomes dependent on drugs.
Genre(s): Biographical Fiction.

Hattersley, Roy

4017. *The Maker's Mark.* New York: Simon and Schuster, 1991. 592 pp.
Frederick never recovers from having his first son stillborn and expects his other sons to live up to their father's fantasies, but they break from him and try to have their own lives, in the priesthood and in business.
Genre(s): Family Saga.

Hayden, Thomas

4018. *The Killing Frost.* New York: St. Martin's, 1992. 534 pp.
After years of frustration and containment, members of the Irish Republican Brotherhood decide to strike England in Dublin on Easter Sunday in 1916.
Genre(s): War Story.

Heaven, Constance

◆ 4019. *The Craven Legacy.* New York: Doubleday, 1987. 327 pp.
When Della's father is arrested for a murder he did not commit, she moves from London to Yorkshire, and while she is teaching, she uncovers the family secrets and falls in love with a married man.
Genre(s): Romance.

Hennessy, Max

4020. *The Bright Blue Sky.* New York: Atheneum, 1983. 250 pp.
Nicholas Dicken Quinney joins the Royal Air Force in World War I and rises from mechanic to navigator.
Genre(s): War Story; Adventure Story.

4021. *The Dangerous Years.* New York: Atheneum, 1979. 292 pp.
In the sequel to *The Lion at Sea*, Ginger Maguire helps refugees escape from the Bolshevik Revolution.
Genre(s): War Story; Adventure Story.

4022. *The Lion at Sea.* New York: Atheneum, 1977. 314 pp.
Kelly Maguire, a member of the Royal Navy, lives through exciting and dangerous assignments as his duties take him to many places during World War I.
Genre(s): War Story; Sea Story.

4023. *Soldier of the Queen.* New York: Atheneum, 1980. 279 pp.
Colby Goff becomes a member of the British Cavalry in time to fight in the charge of the Light Brigade in Balaklava.
Genre(s): War Story; Family Saga; Adventure Story.

Hewlett, Maurice Henry

4024. *Bendish.* New York: Scribner's, 1913. 306 pp.
Bendish, a peer married to the divorced Mrs. Lancelot, constantly deceives himself as he follows the actions of poets and kings.

Hill, Pamela

4025. *The Brocken.* New York: St. Martin's, 1991. Canada pp.
The London banking family of Crowbetter becomes involved in sex and odd connections in the 19th century.
Genre(s): Romance; Gothic Fiction.

4026. *The House of Cray.* New York: St. Martin's, 1982. 335 pp.
Isotta Bondone's father heads an international firm of art dealers whose members included Charles II and Louix XIV, but as World War I looms, problems occur.
Genre(s): Romance.

4027. *The Sutburys.* New York: St. Martin's, 1988. 208 pp.
Felix Sutbury is enemy to his half brother, and after their father's death, Guy cons Felix into making him heir, and when Felix realizes what has happened, he works to change it.
Genre(s): Romance; Gothic Fiction.

4028. *Vollands.* New York: St. Martin's, 1991. 186 pp.
The Volland family members in 19th-century England become pawns to the elder son, James, after their father's death.
Genre(s): Romance; Domestic Fiction.

Hill, Rosa

4029. *House of Green Dragons.* New York: St. Martin's, 1983. 224 pp.
Rebecca Redfearn discovers that her father is an aristocrat, and in his world, she is forced to deal with such things as her half sister's jealousy.
Genre(s): Romance.

Hodge, Jane Aiken

◆ 4030. *Red Sky at Night, Lovers' Delight?* New York: Coward-McCann, 1977. 288 pp.
When an American cousin acquires their lands in 19th-century Britain, Kate Warrender and her mother move into the local lord's household while trouble brews at his mill.
Genre(s): Romance.

Holt, Victoria

◆ 4031. *The Black Opal.* New York: Doubleday, 1993. 288 pp.
Dr. and Mrs. Marline say that they found Carmel under an azalea bush, but 10 years later, Carmel discovers that she is actually a family member.
Genre(s): Romance.

4032. *Bride of Pendorric.* Garden City, NY: Doubleday, 1963. 288 pp.

Favel Farrington fears that Roc Pendorric has married her for her money and that she will die young as other brides at Pendorric Castle have.
Genre(s): Romance.

◆ 4033. **The Captive.** Garden City, NY: Doubleday, 1989. 357 pp.
Shipwrecked off Africa with the illegimate child of a nobleman unjustly accused of murder, Rosetta Cranleigh decides to go to the man's home to identify the actual killer.
Genre(s): Romance.

4034. *Daughter of Deceit.* New York: Fawcett, 1992. 349 pp.
An ingenue ingratiates herself with a London theater family in the 19th century.
Genre(s): Romance.

4035. *The House of a Thousand Lanterns.* Garden City, NY: Doubleday, 1974. 334 pp.
After her father's death, Jane Lindsay meets her mother's employer and becomes interested in studying Chinese art, culture, and history.
Genre(s): Romance.

◆ 4036. **The Judas Kiss.** Garden City, NY: Doubleday, 1981. 400 pp.
When Pippa Ewing's older sister is murdered while lying in her husband's bed, Pippa investigates and discovers that her sister was not actually married.
Genre(s): Romance.

4037. *Kirkland Revels.* Garden City, NY: Doubleday, 1962. 312 pp.
After Catherine Rockwell's husband dies at a manor house in Yorkshire, she tries to prove that he has been murdered.
Genre(s): Romance.

◆ 4038. **The Landower Legacy.** Garden City, NY: Doubleday, 1984. 374 pp.
Between 1887 and 1897, Caroline's parents banish her to the ancestral home for having made a remark that destroyed their marriage.
Genre(s): Romance.

4039. *The Legend of the Seventh Virgin.* Garden City, NY: Doubleday, 1965. 326 pp.
A Cornish girl's ambition to become the mistress of St. Larnston Abbas, once a convent, threatens to curse her with the fate of one of the seven sinful nuns who lived there in ancient times.
Genre(s): Romance.

◆ 4040. **Lord of the Far Island.** Garden City, NY: Doubleday, 1975. 277 pp.
After the suicide of her fiancé, Ellen Kellaway visits her father's relatives on Far Island and meets her mysterious cousin.
Genre(s): Romance.

4041. *Menfreya in the Morning.* Garden City, NY: Doubleday, 1966. 256 pp.

Harriet Delvaney loves her life with husband Bevil Menfrey at their Cornish coast mansion, but finds that mysterious circumstances unsettle their idyll.
Genre(s): Romance.

4042. *Mistress of Mellyn.* Garden City, NY: Doubleday, 1960. 334 pp.
After a young governess takes charge of the motherless child of the handsome master of a Cornwall mansion, she discovers that the child's mother was murdered.
Genre(s): Romance.

◆ 4043. **The Road to Paradise Island.** Garden City, NY: Doubleday, 1985. 368 pp.
Annalice Mallory finds a diary and an old map in the newly discovered, walled-up chamber of her namesake and goes to Australia to investigate the described island.
Genre(s): Romance.

4044. *The Secret Woman.* Garden City, NY: Doubleday, 1970. 355 pp.
After Anna becomes a governess to one of the children in the Crediton shipping family, two unexplained murders occur before a trip to the South Seas.
Genre(s): Romance.

4045. *The Shivering Sands.* Garden City, NY: Doubleday, 1969. 305 pp.
When Caroline Verlaine arrives at a great estate on the Kentish coast to teach piano, she meets Napier Stacy, who has just returned after having been banished from the family.
Genre(s): Romance.u

4046. *The Silk Vendetta.* Garden City, NY: Doubleday, 1987. 425 pp.
The French and English sides of a family compete in the perfection of silk, but after the Sallongers succeed, tragedies occur.
Genre(s): Romance.

◆ 4047. **Snare of Serpents.** New York: Doubleday, 1990. 373 pp.
When Davinia's mother dies in 1899 when Davinia is 16, her father hires a new governess and then mysteriously dies, so Davinia, charged but acquitted of his murder, must leave the country.
Genre(s): Romance.

◆ 4048. **The Time of the Hunter's Moon.** Garden City, NY: Doubleday, 1983. 377 pp.
Cordelia Grant continues to ignore advances from a handsome Devon landowner while she thinks of a man met in Switzerland during a hunter's moon.
Genre(s): Romance.

Hough, Richard

4049. *Buller's Dreadnought.* New York: Morrow, 1982. 247 pp.
In the sequel to *Buller's Guns*, commander Archibald Buller serves in a variety of ways for the British Royal Navy in the early 20th century and ensures that England develops the best dreadnoughts (battleships) before the beginning of World War I.
Genre(s): Sea Story; War Story.

4050. ***Buller's Guns.*** New York: Morrow, 1981. 297 pp.
As they sail during Victoria's reign, Archy Buller, scion of a clan, becomes friends with Maclewin, a Newcastle native who joins the navy to support his widowed mother.
Genre(s): Sea Story; War Story.

4051. ***Buller's Victory.*** New York: Morrow, 1985. 215 pp.
Captain Archibald Buller, in the sequel to *Buller's Dreadnought*, reports honestly about the Dardanelles campaign of 1914 and annoys his superiors, while Richard Buller fights valiantly at sea.
Genre(s): War Story; Sea Story.

Howard, Audrey

◆ 4052. ***Ambitions.*** New York: Macmillan, 1987. 540 pp.
After Lacy Hemingway's family disowns her, she and her Irish maid create a shipping business.
Genre(s): Romance.

4053. ***Tomorrow's Memories.*** New York: Trafalgar Square, 1997. 448 pp.
Sally Grimshaw's brother inherits the family inn, and she manages it so well that local gentleman Captain Adam Cooper notices her.
Genre(s): Romance.

Howatch, Susan

4054. ***Cashelmara.*** New York: Simon and Schuster, 1974. 705 pp.
The wealthy de Salis family members move among their homes in Ireland, England, and Boston between 1859 and 1891 but always return to their Irish Cashelmara estate where the conflict between Irish tenants and British landlords festers.
Genre(s): Domestic Fiction.

4055. ***Glittering Images.*** New York: Knopf, 1987. 416 pp.
Alex Jardine, a bishop, criticizes the Archbishop of Canterbury, his superior, about the marriage of Edward VII.
(*Series:* Church of England, 1)
Genre(s): Religious Fiction.

4056. ***Penmarric.*** New York: Simon and Schuster, 1971. 735 pp.
The wealthy Mark Castallack and his children and grandchildren, Janna, Adrian, Philip, and Jan-Ives, tell about their lives in Cornwall from 1890 through World War II.
Genre(s): Domestic Fiction.

4057. ***The Shrouded Walls.*** New York: Stein and Day, 1971. 179 pp.
Axel Brandson has married an English woman in order to inherit the family fortune, and after his wife, Marianne Fleury, goes to the family home, she realizes that Axel may be a murder suspect.
Genre(s): Romance.

Howells, Harvey

4058. ***The Braw and the Bonny.*** New York: Simon and Schuster, 1971. 320 pp.
The Scots widow Anna Dougal turns her farm into a showplace with the help of a farmer from whom her late husband swindled a freehold.
Genre(s): Domestic Fiction.

Hughes, Glyn

4059. ***The Antique Collector.*** New York: Simon and Schuster, 1991. 288 pp.
Jack Shuttleworth, a transvestite, addresses his memoirs to one of the persons accused of committing unnatural acts with him and tells of the difficulty of growing up in England in the early 20th century.
Genre(s): Domestic Fiction.

Hylton, Sara

◆ 4060. ***The Chosen Ones.*** New York: St. Martin's, 1992. 323 pp.
Five roommates of varying social classes attend an exclusive English boarding school and keep in touch after leaving even though their lives have changed dramatically.
Genre(s): Romance.

4061. ***The Hills Are Eternal.*** New York: St. Martin's, 1986. 498 pp.
Tessa Chalfont's mother first elopes with a married man and then marries a cruel mill owner, but when Tessa feels overcome, she is always happy at the family estate in Yorkshire at the beginning of the 20th century.
Genre(s): Romance; Family Saga.

4062. ***Jacintha.*** New York: St. Martin's, 1982. 260 pp.
While World War I rages, Jacintha Carradia feels like an outcast at her grandmother's cliff-side home until her cousin Adrian arrives.
Genre(s): Domestic Fiction; Romance; War Story.

4063. ***Summer of the Flamingoes.*** New York: St. Martin's, 1991. 320 pp.
Lisa Ralston goes to England to live with her cousin Jessica's family after her father murders her mother in Kenya, but Jessica ruins Lisa's chances to become a concert pianist by breaking Lisa's fingers, and then Lisa marries Jessica's former fiancé.
Genre(s): Romance.

Ivory, Judith

4064. ***Sleeping Beauty.*** New York: Avon, 1998. 384 pp.
When Sir James Stoker finally convinces courtesan Coco Wild to have an affair with him, he jeopardizes his career and his future.
Genre(s): Adventure Story; Romance.

Jagger, Brenda

4065. ***The Barforth Women.*** Garden City, NY: Doubleday, 1982. 570 pp.

◆ May be suitable for young adult readers

The Barforth women of Cullingford, in the sequel to *Verity*, reveal the clash of values during Victorian times between the rising middle class of industrialists and the landed gentry.
Genre(s): Romance.

4066. *Days of Grace.* New York: Morrow, 1984. 441 pp.
At the beginning of the 20th century, Olivia Heron, who has grown up in Paris, moves her family back to England when she inherits the Herons' estate.
Genre(s): Domestic Fiction.

4067. *A Song Twice Over.* New York: Morrow, 1986. 564 pp.
In the 19th century, the Irish Cara Adeane works in a Yorkshire mill to support her mother and son, refusing to sacrifice love for wealth.
Genre(s): Domestic Fiction.

4068. *Verity.* Garden City, NY: Doubleday, 1980. 593 pp.
Although she loves someone else, Verity marries Joel Barforth in Victorian England, in order to marry well.
Genre(s): Romance.

James, Janice

◆ 4069. *A Lady of Repute.* New York: Doubleday, 1980. 256 pp.
Cecilia Ashworth, a 29-year-old unmarried head of a household with a ward, seems respectable to her friends, but she secretly writes books that others read avidly but think unsuitable for women.
Genre(s): Romance.

James, Samantha

4070. *Every Wish Fulfilled.* New York: Avon, 1997. 379 pp.
When Damien Tremayne, Earl of Deverell, searches for the murderer of his brother and father, he meets lame Heather Duval, mistress of an estate deeded by her guardian, whose natural father may have committed the murders.
Genre(s): Romance.

James, Sin

◆ 4071. *A Small Country.* Chester Springs, PA: Dufour, 1990. 192 pp.
When Tom returns from Oxford before World War I, he learns that his father has deserted the family and will have a child by a mistress, and he decides to leave school to run the family farm after his mother dies from a broken heart.
Genre(s): Domestic Fiction.

Jameson, Storm

4072. *The White Crow.* New York: Harper and Row, 1968. 313 pp.
When a Britisher takes John Antigua, illegitimate son of a Portuguese servant girl, to England, the man dies, and

John has to survive on his own, which he does by working hard and eventually opening his own restaurant.
Genre(s): Domestic Fiction; War Story.

Jeal, Tim

4073. *For God and Glory.* New York: Morrow, 1996. 343 pp.
Clara Musson, only daughter of a wealthy Victorian factory owner, marries a missionary to Africa and travels with him to help convert the natives, but he becomes obsessed about converting one of them, forcing Clara and her husband to reassess their personal lives, while the natives worry about British control.
Genre(s): Domestic Fiction.

4074. *A Marriage of Convenience.* New York: Simon and Schuster, 1979. 479 pp.
A marriage has both legal and financial implications in Victorian England.
Genre(s): Domestic Fiction.

Johnson, Grace

4075. *Tempest at Stonehaven.* Wheaton, IL: Tyndale House, 1997. 262 pp.
Davey Morrison comes to Stonehaven in the 1880s to stop a group that lures ships into wrecking on the shore near Dunnottar Castle. (*Series:* Scottish Shores, 1)
Genre(s): Christian Fiction; Romance.

Johnston, Jennifer

4076. *How Many Miles to Babylon?* Garden City, NY: Doubleday, 1974. 156 pp.
A young Irish stable boy and the son in a large country house enlist in World War I for different reasons.
Genre(s): War Story.

Johnston, Joan

4077. *The Inheritance.* New York: Dell, 1994. 416 pp.
When Texas rancher Nicholas Calloway inherits his father's vast English estate, he wants to sell it because his father disowned him, but his cousin Daisy will do anything, including marrying Nick, to keep the land in the family.
Genre(s): Romance.

Johnston, Velda

4078. *The House on Bostwick Square.* New York: Dodd, Mead, 1987. 256 pp.
After Laura Parrington's husband supposedly commits suicide, Laura takes her daughter to the family home in London on Bostwick Square and discovers that her husband was probably murdered.
Genre(s): Romance.

Jones, Elwyn

4079. *The Ripper File.* London: Barker, 1975. 204 pp.
Detectives in 1975 use modern techniques in an attempt to solve the Jack the Ripper murders of 1888 and dis-

cover that they fare no better than the original investigators.
Genre(s): Mystery.

Jones, Jonah

4080. *A Tree May Fall.* London: Bodley Head, 1980. 213 pp.
William Dobie, a Quaker, decides to join the military to save Belgium in World War I but instead finds himself trying to keep Ireland from gaining its freedom in the 1916 uprising.
Genre(s): War Story; Romance.

Joseph, Marie

◆ 4081. *Maggie Craig.* New York: St. Martin's, 1982. 268 pp.
At the turn of the 20th century, Maggie Craig lives in an industrial town and grows from a saucy young girl into a strong grandmother.
Genre(s): Romance.

Joyce, Brenda

4082. *Beyond Scandal.* New York: Avon, 1995. 432 pp.
Anne St. George's husband leaves her after their wedding and returns four years later at the death of his father, discovering that her development during these years makes him want to remain.
Genre(s): Romance; Gothic Fiction.

4083. *Finer Things.* New York: St. Martin's, 1997. 375 pp.
Violet Cooper, a hungry child, falls in love with nobleman Theodore Blake, and after she marries an elderly knight, she sees Blake again and falls even more in love.
Genre(s): Romance.

Julian, Jane

4084. *Ellen Bray.* New York: Morrow, 1986. 256 pp.
Ellen, a bal-maiden who dresses ore coming from the tin mines of Cornwall, loves both a man who is imprisoned for speaking against the mine owners and one who thinks of running for Parliament on behalf of the miners.

Kane, Andrea

4085. *The Music Box.* New York: Pocket Books, 1998. 402 pp.
Bryce Lyndley goes to the estate of his benefactor, Lady Nevon, expecting to help her sort out her finances, but she has more in mind.
Genre(s): Romance.

Kavaler, Rebecca

4086. *Doubting Castle.* New York: Schocken, 1984. 320 pp.
Ada, after being expelled from medical school without reason in the late 19th century, solves the mystery of several deaths in her father's household before being reinstated.
Genre(s): Medical Novel; Gothic Fiction; Mystery.

Keane, Molly

4087. *Good Behaviour.* New York: Knopf, 1981. 256 pp.
As Aroon St. Charles grows up in the Edwardian era, she has difficulty knowing what to take seriously and what to ignore, but her father's death changes that.
Genre(s): Domestic Fiction.

Keathing, Henry Raymond Fitzwalter

4088. *A Remarkable Case of Burglary.* New York: Doubleday, 1976. 185 pp.
Thieves carefully plan to rob a London house in 1871.
Genre(s): Mystery.

Kennedy, William P.

4089. *Rules of Encounter.* New York: St. Martin's, 1992. 357 pp.
William Day, a naval hero and a commoner, is transferred to the Irish coast when he falls in love with his aristocratic boss's daughter, and there he suspects that the Germans are receiving coded messages before the *Lusitania* is attacked.
Genre(s): War Story.

Kennett, Frances

4090. *A Woman by Design.* New York: Random House, 1988. 512 pp.
In 1885 Alice and Anne Hardy go to their Irish ancestral home after their father dies to live with a sullen grandmother, and after a bad marriage, Alice begins to design clothes and becomes a famous London couturiere named Alys.
Genre(s): Family Saga.

Kettle, Jocelyn

4091. *The Athelsons.* New York: Putnam, 1972. 320 pp.
The Athelsons have always promised their tenants that they will inherit the land, and they have protected it through careful management and marriage to wealthy people, but the last Athelson realizes that he can neither hold the estate together nor marry the cousin he loves.
Genre(s): Domestic Fiction; Romance.

Kitchen, Paddy

4092. *The Golden Veil.* London: H. Hamilton, 1981. 286 pp.
In her private life, Lizzie Siddal, Rossetti's favorite model, enjoys drawing, painting, and writing poetry.
Genre(s): Biographical Fiction.

Knight, Alanna

◆ 4093. *Castle of Foxes.* Garden City, NY: Doubleday, 1981. 279 pp.

Tanya discovers after her husband's death that she has inherited an estate in Scotland, and when she visits it, she encounters a ghost, a fox, and Queen Victoria.
Genre(s): Gothic Fiction.

◆ 4094. *Estella.* New York: St. Martin's, 1986. 237 pp.
Estella from Charles Dickens's *Great Expectations* has lived with Miss Havisham and seen her vengeance toward males before she makes her own mistakes in marriage.
Genre(s): Gothic Fiction; Romance.

Knight, Stephen

◆ 4095. *Rogano.* New York: Doubleday, 1979. 307 pp.
Brough, a retired Scotland Yard detective, helps his journalist nephew investigate the death in 1454 of Rogano, a duke, and finds that it parallels the deaths attributed a contemporary strangler in Victorian London.
Genre(s): Mystery.

Krahn, Betina

4096. *The Last Bachelor.* New York: Bantam, 1994. 528 pp.
Lady Antonia Paxton, who is widowed, knows the consequences for unmarried women in Victorian England, so she sets out to find husbands for her friends and comes into conflict with Lord Remington Carr, society's most eligible bachelor.
Genre(s): Romance.

4097. *The Mermaid.* New York: Bantam, 1997. 366 pp.
Because Celeste Ashton works with dolphins, the press begins calling her a mermaid, but when ichthyology professor Thorne arrives to observe her dolphins, he notices more than the animals.
Genre(s): Romance.

4098. *The Perfect Mistress.* Rockland, MA: Wheeler, 1995. 482 pp.
Gabrielle LeCoeur, courtesan, teams with the earl of Sandborne when he seeks information against the prime minister, but their bargain evolves into something more.
Genre(s): Romance.

Laker, Rosalind

4099. *Jewelled Path.* Garden City, NY: Doubleday, 1983. 348 pp.
Irene, daughter of a London jeweler, wants to be a jeweler herself, against her father's wishes.
Genre(s): Romance.

4100. *Warwyck's Choice.* Garden City, NY: Doubleday, 1980. 383 pp.
In the sequel to *Claudine's Daughter*, Tom, Warwyck's heir, falls in love with an enemy of the family in Sussex in 1884.
Genre(s): Domestic Fiction; Family Saga; Romance.

4101. *What the Heart Keeps.* Garden City, NY: Doubleday, 1984. 376 pp.

Subjected to rape after escaping from an orphanage, Lisa Shaw meets a young Norwegian who helps her.
Genre(s): Love Story.

Laymon, Richard

4102. *Savage.* New York: St. Martin's, 1993. 352 pp.
Brit Trevor Bentley, 15, meets Jack the Ripper in London during 1888, and the Ripper kidnaps him and brings him to America where the Ripper continues his atrocities before disappearing.
Genre(s): Mystery; Picaresque Fiction.

Lehmann, Rosamond

4103. *The Ballad and the Source.* New York: Reynal and Hitchcock, 1945. 312 pp.
Sybil Jardine, a grandmother once considered a beautiful Victorian lady, has a history that is pieced together from servants' talk and other sources by a schoolgirl named Rebecca.
Genre(s): Domestic Fiction.

Leonard, Hugh

◆ 4104. *Parnell and the Englishwoman.* New York: Atheneum, 1991. 265 pp.
In the 1880s, Charles Stewart Parnell hates the British but believes in nonviolence and unites the Irish until they find out about his affair with the married English woman Katherine O'Shea.
Genre(s): Biographical Fiction; Love Story.

Lescroart, John T.

◆ 4105. *Son of Holmes.* New York: Donald I. Fine, 1986. 195 pp.
Sherlock Holmes's illegitimate son becomes one of the most successful spies of World War I.
Genre(s): Mystery; Spy Fiction.

Lewis, Kim

4106. *Loving Becky.* New York: Dell, 1996. 375 pp.
Alex Hunter, second son of the Earl of Ruxton, must marry the daughter of a local squire when his father loses a bet.
Genre(s): Romance.

Lewis, Roy

4107. *Cock of the Walk.* Chester Springs, PA: Dufour, 1995. 154 pp.
Statesmen and clerics in Victorian London try to attain and assert their powers, actions that lead to entertaining political cartoons.
Genre(s): Political Fiction.

Lide, Mary

◆ 4108. *The Legacy of Tregaran.* New York: St. Martin's, 1991. 239 pp.
After Mr. Craddock retires to a Cornish village from his London legal practice, he finds himself supporting one of

the local families in a legal conflict, while World War I continues in the background.
Genre(s): Legal Story; War Story; Family Saga.

◆ **4109.** *The Sea Scape.* New York: St. Martin's, 1992. 204 pp.
When Julian Poleven leaves to fight in the Boer Wars, Jenny Ellis has to protect herself and her unborn child from a lecherous farmer in Cornwall.
Genre(s): Romance.

Lingard, Joan

◆ **4110.** *Greenyards.* New York: Putnam, 1981. 396 pp.
In the mid-19th century, Catrionia Ross stays in Scotland and marries rather than following her lover to Canada after the tenant farmers are forced from their lands in the Scottish Highlands.

Linscott, Gillian

◆ **4111.** *Crown Witness.* New York: St. Martin's, 1995. 218 pp.
Nell Bray defends her assistant, Simon Frater, when he is unjustly accused of the murder of a radical son of a cabinet member in George V's coronation procession.
Genre(s): Mystery.

4112. *Dance on Blood.* New York: St. Martin's, 1998. 256 pp.
After being in retirement for nine years, Nell Bray tries to keep Emmeline Pankhurst out of prison and returns to work when the British government asks her to investigate letters revealing the inner workings of secret cabinet meetings.
Genre(s): Mystery.

◆ **4113.** *Dead Man's Sweetheart.* New York: St. Martin's, 1996. 240 pp.
Nell Bray visits her family home at the beginning of the 20th century and helps defend a man accused of murdering the local mill owner.
Genre(s): Mystery.

◆ **4114.** *An Easy Day for a Lady.* New York: St. Martin's, 1995. 210 pp.
When Nell Bray leaves Britain for a vacation after woman suffrage is defeated in 1910, she becomes involved in solving the murder of a man found in the ice of the French Alps.
Genre(s): Mystery.

◆ **4115.** *Hanging on the Wire.* New York: St. Martin's, 1993. 215 pp.
Nell Bray helps her friend in a military hospital who is accused of sabotage when someone is murdered there during World War I.
Genre(s): War Story; Mystery.

◆ **4116.** *Sister Beneath the Sheet.* New York: St. Martin's, 1991. 224 pp.
Nell Bray goes to Biarritz for money left for the suffragettes, but she discovers on arrival that the donor did not commit suicide as reported, but was murdered.
Genre(s): Mystery.

◆ **4117.** *Stage Fright.* New York: St. Martin's, 1993. 188 pp.
Bernard Shaw asks Nell Bray to protect his play's leading lady from the husband she has just left, so that she will be available on opening night.
Genre(s): Mystery.

Livingston, Nancy

◆ **4118.** *The Far Side of the Hill.* New York: St. Martin's, 1988. 480 pp.
John and Davie McKie move to Darlington, open a department store, and raise their families in Victorian England as woman suffrage emerges but class distinctions remain the same.
Genre(s): Domestic Fiction.

◆ **4119.** *Never Were Such Times.* New York: St. Martin's, 1991. 464 pp.
Albert, Esther, and Chas attempt to survive the misery of back-breaking labor in 19th-century Victorian England and pass a positive legacy to their children.
Genre(s): Domestic Fiction.

Llewellyn, Richard

4120. *And I Shall Sleep Down Where the Moon Is Small.* New York: Doubleday, 1966. 423 pp.
As Huw Morgan grows old in Wales, he reflects on his life and his current situation in the sequel to *Green, Green My Valley Now*.
Genre(s): Domestic Fiction.

◆ **4121.** *Green, Green, My Valley Now.* Garden City, NY: Doubleday, 1975. 236 pp.
The sequel to *Up, into the Singing Mountain* finds Huw Morgan and his wife returning to Wales and becoming inadvertently involved with Irish revolutionaries.
Genre(s): Domestic Fiction.

◆ **4122.** *How Green Was My Valley.* 1940. New York: Macmillan, 1986. 495 pp.
Huw Morgan, the son of a miner, comes of age in South Wales and watches the land deteriorate after 1870.
Genre(s): Domestic Fiction.

4123. *None but the Lonely Heart.* New York: Macmillan, 1969. 518 pp.
Ernie Mott, having lost his job after his father's death at Verdun, becomes involved in crime.
Genre(s): War Story.

4124. *Up, into the Singing Mountain.* Garden City, NY: Doubleday, 1960. 378 pp.
In the sequel to *How Green Was My Valley*, Huw Morgan leaves his home for Patagonia, unable to share a house with his widowed sister-in-law, whom he loves but cannot marry.
Genre(s): Domestic Fiction.

Llywelyn, Morgan

4125. *1916.* New York: Tor, 1998. 384 pp.
Revolutionaries fight in the Easter Rising in an attempt to release Ireland from England's rule.
Genre(s): War Story; Political Fiction.

Lofts, Norah

4126. *The Fall of Midas.* New York: Coward-McCann, 1975. 253 pp.
In Victorian England, Edwin Orford, a merchant, and Bill Thorley, a clerk, both suffer from the restrictions of class, and eventually they both commit suicide.

4127. *Haunting of Gad's Hall.* Garden City, NY: Doubleday, 1979. 281 pp.
In the sequel to *Gad's Hall*, subsequent generations of Thorleys have problems with love and money, but eventually new tenants rid Gad's Hall of evil.
Genre(s): Family Saga; Romance.

4128. *Lovers All Untrue.* Garden City, NY: Doubleday, 1970. 252 pp.
Sick of her father's strict Victorian morals, a young woman sneaks out of her home to meet a young pharmacist.
Genre(s): Romance; Bildungsroman (Coming of Age).

4129. *Out of the Dark.* Garden City, NY: Doubleday, 1972. 343 pp.
Suspected of murdering her brother, Charlotte Cornwall runs away and changes her name.
Genre(s): Romance.

Lovesey, Peter

4130. *Abracadaver.* New York: Dodd, Mead, 1972. 220 pp.
Sergeant Cribb and Thackeray of Scotland Yard try to solve a late-19th-century murder.
Genre(s): Mystery.

◆ 4131. *Bertie and the Seven Bodies.* New York: Mysterious Press, 1990. 196 pp.
Bertie, the Prince of Wales, goes on a hunt in Buckinghamshire and brings home a murderer.
Genre(s): Mystery.

◆ 4132. *Bertie and the Tin Man.* New York: Mysterious Press, 1987. 212 pp.
Prince Albert is so surprised to hear that his friend Fred Archer, a superb jockey, has committed suicide that he begins his own investigation.
Genre(s): Mystery.

4133. *A Case of Spirits.* New York: Dodd, Mead, 1975. 160 pp.
Sergeant Cribb and Constable Thackeray investigate a murder at a seance and a burglary at the home of Dr. Probert, a man interested in the occult.
Genre(s): Mystery.

4134. *The Detective Wore Silk Drawers.* New York: Dodd, Mead, 1971. 187 pp.
Cribb and his colleagues discover a clandestine boxing center in the 1880s while investigating several headless corpses.
Genre(s): Mystery.

4135. *Invitation to a Dynamite Party.* London: Macmillan, 1974. 188 pp.

Constable Thackeray and Sergeant Collins must cope with a bomb placed by the Irish inside Scotland Yard during 1884.
Genre(s): Mystery.

4136. *Mad Hatter's Holiday.* New York: Macmillan, 1973. 192 pp.
In 1882 Sergeant Cribb and Constable Thackeray must solve a murder in the fashionable seaside resort of Brighton.
Genre(s): Mystery.

4137. *Swing, Swing Together.* New York: Dodd, Mead, 1976. 217 pp.
In 1889, when a teacher goes swimming nude in the Thames, she witnesses a crime, and the police can hardly focus on the case because of her attractiveness.
Genre(s): Mystery.

4138. *The Tick of Death.* New York: Dodd, Mead, 1974. 188 pp.
In 1884, Sergeant Cribb investigates the Clan-na-Gael, a secret society of Irish Americans working for Ireland's independence.
Genre(s): Mystery.

4139. *Wobble to Death.* New York: Dodd, Mead, 1970. 190 pp.
Sergeant Cribb investigates the death of the leading contestant in a six-day freestyle walking race (wobble) in 1879, which he must solve before the race ends.
Genre(s): Mystery.

Ludwig, Charles

4140. *Mother of an Army.* Minneapolis, MN: Bethany House, 1987. 237 pp.
Catherine Booth, wife of William Booth, helps to establish the Salvation Army and becomes recognized as one of the most accomplished preachers in London.
Genre(s): Biographical Fiction; Christian Fiction.

Lynn, Karen

◆ 4141. *The Scottish Marriage.* Garden City, NY: Doubleday, 1982. 192 pp.
While traveling to become the gentlewoman in a Scottish family, a woman ends up by circumstance in the bedchamber of Lord Maplethorpe, who declares her his wife (a legal union in Scotland) to men who burst into the room.
Genre(s): Romance.

MacDonald, George

4142. *The Fisherman's Lady.* Minneapolis, MN: Bethany House, 1993. 304 pp.
In the late 19th century, a fisherman's family goes about its daily life.
Genre(s): Christian Fiction; Domestic Fiction.

4143. *The Highlander's Last Song.* Minneapolis, MN: Bethany House, 1986. 272 pp.
The Scots reveal their deep faith in their daily lives.
Genre(s): Christian Fiction.

MacDonald, Malcolm

◆ 4144. *Abigail.* New York: Knopf, 1979. 389 pp.
Nora and John Stevenson's daughter Abigail becomes liberated, but as a woman writer in the Victorian era, she must learn to cope with obstacles.
Genre(s): Romance.

4145. *All Desires Known.* New York: St. Martin's, 1994. 346 pp.
Dr. Michael Raven and his wife Lucy leave Dublin, where they have spent too much money entertaining, and move to a clinic in the country.
Genre(s): Domestic Fiction.

4146. *The Carringtons of Helston.* New York: St. Martin's, 1998. 416 pp.
Americans who move to a Cornwall village as World War I begins conflict with a local over the farm they want to purchase.
Genre(s): Domestic Fiction; War Story.

4147. *For They Shall Inherit.* New York: St. Martin's, 1984. 591 pp.
Working-class Freddy and the aristocrat Clive fall in love with the same woman.
Genre(s): Romance.

◆ 4148. *Hell Hath No Fury.* New York: St. Martin's, 1992. 374 pp.
In 1885, Daisy O'Lindon wants to be independent from her family's genteel poverty, so she takes her first job as an artist's model.
Genre(s): Domestic Fiction.

4149. *An Innocent Woman.* New York: St. Martin's, 1991. 378 pp.
After his wife dies, Willifred Hervey moves himself and his 19-year-old daughter to Cornwall, where he reveals to her the secrets of her mother's background.
Genre(s): Domestic Fiction; Bildungsroman (Coming of Age).

4150. *Kernow and Daughter.* New York: St. Martin's, 1996. 391 pp.
Jessica Kernow decides that she will also be a businessperson in Cornwall even though her father only wants his sons in the family business at the beginning of the 20th century.
Genre(s): Domestic Fiction.

4151. *A Notorious Woman.* New York: St. Martin's, 1989. 480 pp.
After being left pregnant by a man gone to America, Johanna Rosewarne finds that she has a business sense and establishes a brewing business in Cornwall during the 19th century.
Genre(s): Family Saga.

4152. *Sons of Fortune.* New York: Knopf, 1978. 466 pp.
In the sequel to *The Rich Are with You Always*, the Stevensons gain financial security but complicate their lives.
Genre(s): Family Saga.

4153. *Tomorrow's Tide.* New York: St. Martin's, 1997. 336 pp.
While helping to run a home for convalescent soldiers, Jennifer Owens takes up acting, and looks for the parents of a foundling in World War I.
Genre(s): Domestic Fiction; Bildungsroman (Coming of Age).

◆ 4154. *The Trevarton Inheritance.* New York: St. Martin's, 1996. 395 pp.
In the 1880s, Crissy Moore, after suddenly losing her parents and grandfather, plans to keep her six siblings together, asking for help from her grandmother who had disowned her mother years before.
Genre(s): Domestic Fiction.

◆ 4155. *A Woman Alone.* New York: St. Martin's, 1991. 377 pp.
When Roseanne Kitto and Stephen Morvah, the squire's son, attend the local fair as a joke, they are surprised to find they enjoy each other's company.
Genre(s): Romance.

4156. *A Woman Possessed.* New York: St. Martin's, 1993. 375 pp.
At the beginning of the 20th century, Maurice Petifer, Laura's poor impoverished first love, returns from South Africa a millionaire and buys the property next door.
Genre(s): Romance.

◆ 4157. *A Woman Scorned.* New York: St. Martin's, 1992. 422 pp.
In 1881, four members of the Bellingham family are murdered during a birthday party, but Rick, 14, and Henrietta, 16, survive along with friend Judith Carty, who returns later to find the gunmen's identities.
Genre(s): Romance; Family Saga.

Macintyre, Lorn

4158. *The Blind Bend.* New York: St. Martin's, 1982. 272 pp.
Mary Rose, new bride of Niall, the 17th lord of Invernevis, becomes traumatized by the overgrown corner (blind bend) on the way to the mansion, in the sequel to *Cruel in the Shadow.*
Genre(s): Romance.

4159. *Cruel in the Shadow.* New York: St. Martin's, 1979. 287 pp.
In 1899, the old laird of the Macdonald family dies, and the new laird brings home an innocent bride, who people hope will put an end to the family's corruption.
Genre(s): Romance.

MacKinnon, Charles Roy

4160. *Mereford Tapestry.* New York: Delacorte, 1974. 466 pp.
Beginning in Victorian England, two families comingle for five generations until after World War II, when a marriage unites them.
Genre(s): Family Saga.

Martin, Valerie

◆ 4161. *Mary Reilly.* New York: Doubleday, 1990. 244 pp.
The servant of Dr. Jekyll, Mary Reilly, records his strange case as she sees it.
Genre(s): Horror.

Masefield, John

4162. *The Bird of Dawning.* New York: Macmillan, 1933. 310 pp.
When the second mate of a ship sinking in a race from China to England in the 1860s finds a drifting ship, he and his crew board and win the race.
Genre(s): Sea Story.

Masters, John

4163. *By the Green of the Spring.* New York: McGraw Hill, 1981. 599 pp.
The sequel to *Heart of War* chronicles both the end and the aftermath of World War I on British families.
Genre(s): War Story; Family Saga.

4164. *Heart of War.* New York: McGraw Hill, 1980. 617 pp.
The sequel to *Now, God Be Thanked* recreates the middle years of World War I and the effect of this time on the Rowlands and other families.
Genre(s): War Story; Family Saga.

4165. *Now, God Be Thanked.* New York: McGraw Hill, 1979. 589 pp.
Four families—industrialists, aristocrats, and reprobates—become mingled in the war years of England during World War I.
Genre(s): War Story; Family Saga.

Masterton, Graham

4166. *Lady of Fortune.* New York: Morrow, 1985. 554 pp.
Effie Watson wants to run Scotland's Watson's Bank in 1901, but although she eventually gains command, she cannot control her family.
Genre(s): Domestic Fiction.

Mayerson, Evelyn Wilde

4167. *Princess in Amber.* Garden City, NY: Doubleday, 1985. 298 pp.
Princess Beatrice, youngest daughter of Queen Victoria, becomes Victoria's support after the death of Albert, but Beatrice meets the Prince of Battenberg and decdies to marry.
Genre(s): Biographical Fiction.

Mayhew, Margaret

◆ 4168. *The Railway King.* New York: Doubleday, 1979. 385 pp.
A Quaker heiress refuses to marry a railroad magnate in the mid-18th century until they repair their differences.
Genre(s): Romance.

McCutchan, Philip

4169. *The Guns of Arrest.* New York: St. Martin's, 1976. 233 pp.
The sequel to *Halfhyde's Island* finds St. Vincent Halfhyde tracking Sir Russell Savory, who has fled with plans for rebuilding the British fleet and is demanding a ranson.
Genre(s): Sea Story.

4170. *Halfhyde and the Admiral.* New York: St. Martin's, 1990. 187 pp.
St. Vincent Halfhyde, in the sequel to *Halfhyde on the Amazon,* has a conflict with the admiral.
Genre(s): Sea Story.

4171. *Halfhyde and the Chain Gangs.* New York: St. Martin's, 1986. 184 pp.
Halfhyde's job to ferry treacherous convicts to South Africa near the beginning of the Boer Wars becomes complicated by a female stowaway and the discovery of gold bullion in the sequel to *The Halfhyde Line.*
Genre(s): Sea Story.

4172. *Halfhyde and the Flag Captain.* New York: St. Martin's, 1981. 183 pp.
Halfhyde sails in South American waters with a Flag Captain and an admiral who cannot agree, in the sequel to *Halfhyde Ordered South.*
Genre(s): Sea Story.

4173. *Halfhyde and the Fleet Review.* New York: St. Martin's, 1992. 216 pp.
St. Vincent Halfhyde has orders to attend the Jubilee of Victoria whose fleet review will contain several important participants, one perhaps an assassination target.
Genre(s): Sea Story.

4174. *Halfhyde Goes to War.* New York: St. Martin's, 1986. 163 pp.
In *Halfhyde and the Chain Gangs*, Halfhyde found gold bullion on his ship, and in this sequel he must take it across land, but when he returns to his ship, Boers demand that he take them back to Amsterdam.
Genre(s): Sea Story; War Story.

4175. *The Halfhyde Line.* New York: St. Martin's, 1985. 182 pp.
In the sequel to *Halfhyde Outward Bound*, St. Vincent Halfhyde buys a commercial steamship with the help of his uncle and becomes the porter of guns from Australia for Irish rebels with a crew that is loyal to another captain on board.
Genre(s): Sea Story.

4176. *Halfhyde on the Amazon.* New York: St. Martin's, 1988. 188 pp.
Halfhyde takes his ship, the *Taronga Park*, and a beautiful Australian, Victoria, with him to the Amazon to spy on a German outpost in the sequel to *Halfhyde Goes to War.*
Genre(s): Sea Story.

4177. *Halfhyde on Zanatu.* New York: St. Martin's, 1982. 165 pp.

In the sequel to *Halfhyde on the Yangtze*, St. Vincent Halfhyde faces his nemesis, Admiral Prince Gorsinski, in the Pacific while trying to save Zanatu from the Russians.
Genre(s): Sea Story.

4178. **Halfhyde Ordered South.** New York: St. Martin's, 1980. 220 pp.
St. Vincent Halfhyde fights the Germans over South American trading concerns in the sequel to *Halfhyde for the Queen*.
Genre(s): Sea Story.

4179. **Halfhyde Outward Bound.** New York: St. Martin's, 1984. 165 pp.
In the sequel to *Halfhyde on Zanatu*, St. Vincent Halfhyde escapes from his new bride by going away on a merchant vessel but then faces smugglers and murderers.
Genre(s): Sea Story.

4180. **Halfhyde to the Narrows.** New York: St. Martin's, 1977. 180 pp.
In the sequel to *The Guns of Arrest*, St. Vincent Halfhyde, recalled to active duty in the 1890s, goes to the Black Sea to retrieve a merchant ship commandeered by the Russians.
Genre(s): Sea Story.

◆ 4181. **The Last Farewell.** New York: St. Martin's, 1991. 308 pp.
Captain Pacey guides the *Laurentia* through treacherous water back to England in 1915.
Genre(s): Sea Story; War Story.

4182. **The Second Mate.** New York: St. Martin's, 1996. 186 pp.
Tom Chatto rises to officer ranks in the British Royal Navy and becomes second mate on the *Orvega* bound to Valparaiso, a voyage during which many become ill and the ship begins malfunctioning.
Genre(s): Sea Story.

McKinney, Meagan

◆ 4183. **The Ground She Walks Upon.** New York: Delacorte, 1994. 409 pp.
Flickering lights on an old Druid cross bind Nial Trevallyn and the local witch's newborn granddaughter Ravenna, and although he avoids her, circumstances often unite them.
Genre(s): Romance; Love Story.

McLeay, Alison

4184. **The Summer House.** New York: St. Martin's, 1997. 320 pp.
As World War I begins, the nouveau riche Dunstan family comes to the Lake District where Chrissie Ascham and her family live, and the industrialist Dunstan father precipitates a series of tragic events.
Genre(s): Bildungsroman (Coming of Age).

Melville, Anne

4185. **Alexa.** New York: Doubleday, 1977. 328 pp.

Margaret Lorimer decides to invest her energy in the opera career of her ward, Alexa, in the sequel to *The Lorimer Line*.
Genre(s): Domestic Fiction.

4186. **Blaize.** Garden City, NY: Doubleday, 1981. 541 pp.
The Lormier family members all seem to marry the wrong persons as they wander through the first half of the 20th century or die in war or tragic accidents, in the sequel to *Alexa*.
Genre(s): Domestic Fiction.

4187. **The Lorimer Line.** Garden City, NY: Doubleday, 1977. 360 pp.
In 1887 the Lorimer family struggles to survive after losing its money, especially Margaret, a physician who faces the prejudices against women doctors.
Genre(s): Domestic Fiction.

4188. **Lorimers in Love.** London: Heinemann, 1981. 253 pp.
The Lorimers fall in love, but their choices are not always the best.
Genre(s): Domestic Fiction; War Story.

Meyer, Nicholas

◆ 4189. **The West End Horror.** New York: Dutton, 1976. Canada pp.
Sherlock Holmes tries to find the murderer of a West End theater critic in London in 1895.
Genre(s): Mystery.

Michaels, Barbara

4190. **Black Rainbow.** New York: St. Martin's, 1982. 277 pp.
Megan O'Neill, a governess, marries the guardian of her charge, only to find that he is not what she expects.
Genre(s): Gothic Fiction.

◆ 4191. **The Wizard's Daughter.** New York: Dodd, Mead, 1980. 279 pp.
Marianne Ransom goes to London to start a singing career, a position unacceptable in English society, but a dowager believes she is the illegitimate daughter of a medium and can help her contact the other side.
Genre(s): Romance; Gothic Fiction.

Miller, Hugh

4192. **The District Nurse.** New York: St. Martin's, 1984. 318 pp.
When Megan Roberts becomes a servant, the estate owner notices her abilities and tutors her, then Megan meets Alun, falls in love, and waits for him to finish school, neither foreseeing the terrors of the Great War.
Genre(s): Domestic Fiction; Romance.

4193. **Home Ground.** New York: St. Martin's, 1991. 352 pp.
In her forties, Megan Roberts, a district nurse, hopes for a brighter future, and is surprised to have two suitors.
Genre(s): Domestic Fiction.

Minton, Mary

4194. *Yesterday's Road.* New York: David and Charles, 1987. 340 pp.

In the early 20th century, Kitty becomes a scullery maid and begins glassblowing with the help of a houseguest. *Genre(s):* Domestic Fiction.

Mitchell, James

4195. *A Woman to Be Loved.* North Pomfret, VT: Trafalagar Square, 1991. 640 pp.

After driving ambulances on the front in World War I, Jane Whitcomb suffers shellshock, but with family help, she begins to heal, and then she becomes involved in work to help the poor. (*Series:* When the Boat Comes In, 1)
Genre(s): Domestic Fiction.

Monger, Christopher

4196. *The Englishman Who Went up a Hill but Came down a Mountain.* New York: Miramax, 1995. 265 pp.

A young man goes to Wales as an assistant to measure the heights of hills, and when the supposed mountain in a small village measures as a hill, the townspeople correct the problem.
Genre(s): Humorous Fiction.

Moore, Margaret

4197. *The Dark Duke.* New York: Harlequin, 1997. 304 pp.

Adrian Fitzwalter falls in love with his stepmother's rather plain companion, and society, infuriated with his choice and her lack of beauty, rejects her.
Genre(s): Romance.

Moore, Susan

4198. *Paths of Fortune.* New York: St. Martin's, 1985. 320 pp.

After the death of their father, Kate becomes a governess and Sophy marries during the 19th century while their brother goes to London.
Genre(s): Domestic Fiction.

Murdoch, Iris

4199. *The Red and the Green.* New York: Viking, 1965. 311 pp.

During Easter week of 1916, Andrew Chase-White and a cousin whom he hopes to marry live in Ireland as an Anglo-Irish couple before the fighting between the two factions begins.
Genre(s): Domestic Fiction.

Murray, Frances

◆ 4200. *The Belchamber Scandal.* New York: St. Martin's, 1985. 224 pp.

When Amelia Belchamber's father commits suicide in financial ruin, Amelia goes to the north to become govern-

ess to an industrialist's family, and after troubles, returns to London to become housekeeper to a handsome painter.
Genre(s): Romance.

Myers, Amy

4201. *Murder Makes an Entree.* New York: St. Martin's, 1996. 275 pp.

Auguste Didier, a cooking school instructor, and Inspector Egbert Rose from Scotland Yard must discover who murdered the school's chairman right in front of Prince Albert.
Genre(s): Mystery.

Naslund, Sena Jeter

4202. *Sherlock in Love.* Boston: David R. Godine, 1993. 225 pp.

When Dr. Watson decides to write a biography of his late partner, Sherlock Holmes, an ad in the newspaper for information brings about unexpected threats, and in his investigations, Dr. Watson discovers a secret love affair.
Genre(s): Mystery; Love Story.

Newby, P. H.

4203. *Coming in with the Tide.* North Pomfret, VT: Trafalgar Square, 1991. 265 pp.

After Charles White marries Hannah Jones in the early 20th century, they are unable to bear children, but an Irish maid who works for them in Wales has James for them, a child who brings more trouble than joy.
Genre(s): Domestic Fiction; War Story.

Nicole, Christopher

4204. *The Regiment.* New York: St. Martin's, 1989. 132 pp.

Murdoch Mackinder serves in the family regiment, the Royal Western Dragoon Guards, by going to the Boer Wars, but he sympathizes with the Boers before returning to fight in the Great War.
Genre(s): War Story.

O'Brien, Judith

4205. *To Marry a British Lord.* New York: Pocket Books, 1997. 311 pp.

American Constance Lloyd moves to England after the American Civil War to work as a governess, and after becoming engaged to a duke's son, she realizes that she loves his best friend, a Welsh scientist.
Genre(s): Romance.

O'Donoghue, Maureen

4206. *Winner.* New York: Simon and Schuster, 1988. 414 pp.

Orphaned Macha Sheridan loves horses, and contrary to convention, she stays with thoroughbred horse breeding and racing at the beginning of the 20th century.
Genre(s): Adventure Story.

O'Faolain, Julia

4207. *No Country For Young Men.* New York: Carroll and Graf, 1986. 369 pp.
Sister Judith Clancy moves from a convent where she was forcibly placed, to the home of her niece and nephew at the time an American film maker records oral histories of the Irish Troubles.
Genre(s): War Story; Political Fiction.

O'Flaherty, Liam

4208. *The Informer.* New York: Knopf, 1925. 272 pp.
During 1916, after Gypo Nolan is expelled from a secret communist society, he exposes a comrade to the police and endures the consequences.
Genre(s): War Story.

O'Grady, Leslie

4209. *The Artist's Daughter.* New York: St. Martin's, 1979. 301 pp.
Nora Woburn escapes from her abusive husband and his estate, Raven's Chase, and begins working for Sir Mark Gerricle in a situation almost as bad as the one she left.
Genre(s): Romance.

4210. *Lord Raven's Widow.* New York: St. Martin's, 1983. 288 pp.
Nora Derrick joins her late husband's worst enemy in a partnership and learns to run a shipping empire in the sequel to *The Artist's Daughter.*
Genre(s): Romance.

◆ 4211. *The Second Sister.* New York: St. Martin's, 1984. 352 pp.
Cassandra Clark returns to London from Cairo when her guardians tell her that she is not an orphan and that she has a sister.
Genre(s): Romance; Mystery.

O'Neal, Katherine

4212. *Bride of Danger.* New York: Bantam, 1998. 384 pp.
Mylene, Johnny, and Daggett, three Dublin street urchins in 1870, grow up to become spies for Home Rule as they use their skills of survival.
Genre(s): Political Fiction; Romance.

Oppenheim, E. Phillips

4213. *The Great Impersonation.* Boston: Little, Brown, 1920. 322 pp.
Educated at Eton and Oxford, Baron Leopold von Ragastein decides that by impersonating one of his school friends, he can fight with the British in World War I instead of Germany.
Genre(s): War Story.

Padfield, Peter

4214. *Salt and Steel.* New York: David and Charles, 1986. 629 pp.

Henrietta Steel commits to social causes in early-20th-century England, while her brothers join the navy or study, until she falls in love with a naval career man.
Genre(s): War Story; Sea Story.

Palliser, Charles

4215. *The Quincunx.* New York: Ballantine, 1990. 788 pp.
A young boy tells about a codicil to a will which indicates that a second will may exist with the key to a vast inheritance.
Genre(s): Mystery.

Palmer, William J.

4216. *The Detective and Mr Dickens.* New York: St. Martin's, 1990. 290 pp.
Charles Dickens and Wilkie Collins help London's Inspector Field solve a brutal murder.
Genre(s): Mystery.

4217. *The Hoydens and Mr Dickens.* New York: St. Martin's, 1997. 241 pp.
Charles Dickens elicits Wilkie Collins's help in clearing his lover, actress Ellen Ternan, of murder after he takes her out of Angela Burdett-Coutts's home for women.
Genre(s): Mystery.

Parker, Robert B.

4218. *All Our Yesterdays.* New York: Delacorte, 1994. 401 pp.
During the Time of Troubles in the 1920s, Conn, an Irish Revolutionary Army captain and an American, have an affair that goes awry and Conn's son and grandson continue the legacy of IRA blackmail tactics in America.
Genre(s): Family Saga.

Pearce, Mary Emily

4219. *Cast a Long Shadow.* New York: St. Martin's, 1983. 246 pp.
Ellen Lancy's husband, a miller, throws her out one cold night, and when the blacksmith protects her, they begin a relationship which infuriates the miller.
Genre(s): Domestic Fiction.

◆ 4220. *The Old House at Railes.* New York: St. Martin's, 1994. 410 pp.
In the mid-19th century, the Tarrants in the Railes manor home lose their fortune and must sell the house to the quarryman's son Martin.
Genre(s): Country Life; Love Story.

4221. *The Two Farms.* New York: St. Martin's, 1986. 190 pp.
Jim Lundy's management of the Sutton farm in Gloucestershire during the 19th century keeps it flourishing while the Riddler's farm declines, but when Sutton's son takes Lundy's love, he goes to rebuild the Riddler property.
Genre(s): Domestic Fiction.

◆ May be suitable for young adult readers

Pearson, Diane

4222. *The Summer of the Barshinskeys.* New York: Crown, 1984. 465 pp.
In 1902, the Russian Mr. Barshinskey arrives with his family in Sophie's English village, but his ebulient behavior belies the sullenness of the other family members except for Galina, the child who is different.
Genre(s): Adventure Story; Gothic Fiction.

Pearson, John

4223. *The Bellamy Saga.* New York: Praeger, 1976. 314 pp.
The Bellamy family, from 1884 to 1929, undergoes love affairs and ups and downs in their careers as well as World War I.
Genre(s): Domestic Fiction; Family Saga.

Pearson, Michael

4224. *The Store.* New York: Simon and Schuster, 1981. 480 pp.
Thomas Kingston borrows money to open his own shop as a draper, and as his business grows, he must deal with unions, suffragists, and social change.

Peart, Jane

◆ 4225. *A Perilous Bargain.* Grand Rapids, MI: Revell, 1997. 288 pp.
An American girl becomes stranded in London, but she makes her way to Ireland and finds both a mystery and a job in a castle.
Genre(s): Mystery; Romance.

◆ 4226. *Shadow of Fear.* Grand Rapids, MI: Revell, 1996. 176 pp.
After escaping from her stepfather, Challys Winthrop works in an inn run by thieves but becomes a blackmailer's victim.
Genre(s): Romance; Christian Fiction.

4227. *Web of Deception.* Grand Rapids, MI: F. H. Revell, 1996. 204 pp.
Rachel Penniston becomes a governess who enjoys her job until her employer's sister arrives and draws her into a circle of deceit.
Genre(s): Romance; Christian Fiction.

Peck, Richard

4228. *This Family of Women.* New York: Delacorte, 1983. 393 pp.
Five women present four generations of their family as they go west, or east to London, and experience the upheavals of settlement and relationships with men.
Genre(s): Family Saga.

Perry, Anne

◆ 4229. *Ashworth Hall.* New York: Fawcett Columbine, 1997. 384 pp.

When Charlotte Pitt attends a meeting between Catholics and Protestants in Ireland, Thomas Pitt receives an assignment to guard a man who will also be attending.
Genre(s): Mystery.

◆ 4230. *Belgrave Square.* New York: Fawcett Columbine, 1992. 361 pp.
Thomas Pitt, with his wife Charlotte's help, uncovers the habits of a usurer, killed with one of his own gold coins.
Genre(s): Mystery.

4231. *Bethlehem Road.* New York: St. Martin's, 1990. 309 pp.
When three members of Parliament who voted against woman suffrage are crossing Westminster Bridge, their throats are slit, and Thomas Pitt needs Charlotte's help to solve the murder.
Genre(s): Mystery.

4232. *Bluegate Fields.* New York: St. Martin's, 1984. 308 pp.
Charlotte and Thomas Pitt reopen the murder investigation of a teenager in a bathtub when the accused man's mother urges Charlotte to show that the wrong man has been arrested.
Genre(s): Mystery.

4233. *Brunswick Gardens.* New York: Fawcett, 1998. 400 pp.
When scholar of ancient languages Unity Bellwood dies at the bottom of the stairs in her employer's home, she is three months pregnant, but when other murders follow, Thomas Pitt and his wife Charlotte investigate.
Genre(s): Mystery.

◆ 4234. *Cain his Brother.* New York: Fawcett Columbine, 1995. 390 pp.
Genevieve Stonefield fears that her missing husband has been killed by his brother Caleb and begs William Monk to investigate.
Genre(s): Mystery.

4235. *Callander Square.* New York: St. Martin's, 1980. 221 pp.
In the 1880s after two dead babies are discovered in the gardens of a square housing the wealthy, Inspector Pitt and his wife must investigate.
Genre(s): Mystery.

4236. *Cardington Crescent.* New York: St. Martin's, 1987. 314 pp.
Charlotte and Thomas Pitt discover corruption in Charlotte's sister's life when she is suspected of poisoning her womanizing husband.
Genre(s): Mystery.

4237. *Death in the Devil's Acre.* New York: St. Martin's, 1985. 248 pp.
Charlotte Pitt and her sister Emily work separately from Charlotte's husband Thomas to solve brutal murders of wealthy ladies working as prostitutes out of boredom.
Genre(s): Mystery.

◆ 4238. *Defend and Betray.* New York: Fawcett Columbine, 1992. 385 pp.

William Monk decides to help a kind upper-class woman who confesses to murdering her respected husband.
Genre(s): Mystery.

◆ 4239. *Farriers' Lane.* New York: Fawcett Columbine, 1993. 374 pp.
In 1884, a wave of anti-Semitic sentiment leads to the quick condemnation of a young Jew for killing a gentleman, but when the case is reopened five years later, the judge is murdered.
Genre(s): Mystery.

4240. *Highgate Rise.* New York: Fawcett Columbine, 1991. 330 pp.
Thomas Pitt must find an arsonist who burned the house of a physician and his wife known for helping slum tenants.
Genre(s): Mystery.

◆ 4241. *The Hyde Park Headsman.* New York: Fawcett Columbine, 1994. 392 pp.
Thomas Pitt uses Charlotte's help to work on a murder in Hyde Park that is followed by three more murders.
Genre(s): Mystery.

4242. *Paragon Walk.* New York: St. Martin's, 1981. 204 pp.
When Inspector Thomas Pitt investigates the murder of an upper-class 17-year-old girl, a crime that has terrorized the neighborhood, he finds suprising suspects.
Genre(s): Mystery.

◆ 4243. *Pentecost Alley.* New York: Fawcett Columbine, 1996. 405 pp.
Thomas Pitt is relieved when a pimp confesses to the brutal slaying of a prostitute, but after the man is executed, another murder just like the first occurs.
Genre(s): Mystery.

4244. *Resurrection Row.* New York: St. Martin's, 1981. 204 pp.
Thomas Pitt has difficulty solving the case of a murdered artist and dead bodies appear in public places until his wife Charlotte changes his perceptions of the crimes.
Genre(s): Mystery.

4245. *Rutland Place.* New York: St. Martin's, 1983. 235 pp.
When Charlotte Pitt goes to her parents' home to find a lost trinket, she unwittingly opens a difficult criminal case for herself and her husband Thomas.
Genre(s): Mystery.

4246. *Silence in Hanover Close.* New York: St. Martin's, 1988. 341 pp.
Inspector Pitt's superiors refuse to let him investigate a diplomatic murder so Charlotte's sister poses as a lady's maid in a house where she can find information for him.
Genre(s): Mystery.

4247. *The Silent Cry.* New York: Fawcett Columbine, 1997.
Gentlemen are the suspects in the rapes and beatings of women in the slums of St. Giles, but because the police

do not care, a sweatshop owner hires William Monk to investigate.
Genre(s): Mystery.

◆ 4248. *The Sins of the Wolf.* New York: Fawcett Columbine, 1994. 374 pp.
William Monk comes to Hester Latterly's aid when she is accused of killing the aging Mary Farraline with an incorrect dosage of medicine on a train to London.
Genre(s): Mystery.

◆ 4249. *A Sudden, Fearful Death.* New York: Fawcett Columbine, 1993. 383 pp.
After solving a rape case, William Monk must investigate the strangling of a nurse who served in the Crimea with Florence Nightingale.
Genre(s): Mystery.

4250. *Traitor's Gate.* New York: Fawcett Columbine, 1995. 411 pp.
When the father of Thomas Pitt's good friend is poisoned at his club, the investigation points to the Inner Circle, a group of aristocrats with a strong loyalty oath.
Genre(s): Mystery.

4251. *Weighed in the Balance.* New York: Fawcett, 1996. 355 pp.
Private investigator William Monk investigates a murder among the royals in Victorian England, and his friend, Sir Oliver, decides to represent Countess Zorah Rostova against a slander charge.
Genre(s): Mystery; Political Fiction.

Peters, Elizabeth

◆ 4252. *The Deeds of the Disturber.* New York: Atheneum, 1988. 289 pp.
Amelia Peabody refuses to believe that at the British Museum a priest has issued a curse for the desecration of an ancient mummy, but then she discovers a murderer.
Genre(s): Mystery.

Petrie, Glen

4253. *Marianne.* New York: Coward-McCann, 1977. 405 pp.
Mariamne Jenkins, daughter of an architect, falls in love with an ambitious law clerk, but she marries the wealthy man next door and is accused of murdering the clerk after he refuses to destroy her letters.
Genre(s): Biographical Fiction.

Phillips, Michael R.

4254. *Wild Grows the Heather in Devon.* Minneapolis, MN: Bethany House, 1998. 320 pp.
Amanda Rutherford becomes independent as the 20th century begins and becomes involved in woman suffrage before World War I and her cousin's claim to the family estate of Heathersleigh.
Genre(s): War Story; Christian Fiction.

Phillips, Michael R., and Judith Pella

4255. *Flight from Stonewycke.* Minneapolis, MN: Bethany House, 1985. 256 pp.

A Scots family becomes involved in an unexpected predicament. (*Series:* The Stonewycke Trilogy, 2)
Genre(s): Christian Fiction; Gothic Fiction.

4256. *The Heather Hills of Stonewycke.* Minneapolis, MN: Bethany House, 1985. 255 pp.
Inhabitants of a Scottish castle experience an unexplained situation. (*Series:* Stonewycke Trilogy, 1)
Genre(s): Christian Fiction; Gothic Fiction.

4257. *The Lady of Stonewycke.* Minneapolis, MN: Bethany House, 1986. 262 pp.
The situation in Scotland at a castle is resolved. (*Series:* Stonewycke Trilogy, 3)
Genre(s): Christian Fiction.

4258. *Robbie Taggart: Highland Sailor.* Minneapolis, MN: Bethany House, 1987. 384 pp.
Robbie Taggart goes to sea and finds adventure and romance.
Genre(s): Christian Fiction; Sea Story; Romance.

Plaidy, Jean

◆ 4259. *Lilith.* New York: Putnam, 1990. 317 pp.
Two women, Lilith Tremourney, a cottager's daughter, and Amanda Leigh, a wealthy child, become friends across class lines and continue their friendship in London as young women and mothers.
Genre(s): Domestic Fiction.

◆ 4260. *Victoria Victorious.* New York: Putnam, 1986. 569 pp.
Victoria matures from a rotund young girl to the grandmother of Europe during her 64 years. (*Series:* Queens of England, 3)
Genre(s): Biographical Fiction.

◆ 4261. *The Widow of Windsor.* New York: Putnam, 1978. 351 pp.
The sequel to *The Queen's Husband* follows Victoria's reign after the death of her husband Albert. (*Series:* Queen Victoria, 4)
Genre(s): Biographical Fiction.

Plunkett, James

4262. *Strumpet City.* New York: Delacorte, 1969. 533 pp.
Irish workers, both Catholic and Protestant, struggle during the labor movements of early 20th-century Ireland.
Genre(s): Political Fiction.

Polland, Madeleine A.

4263. *Sabrina.* New York: Delacort, 1979. 353 pp.
Although Sabrina's mother has promised her to God, Sabrina loves Gerrard, and she must make her choice as Ireland and the world enter World War I.
Genre(s): Domestic Fiction; Romance.

Potter, Patricia

4264. *The Marshall and the Heiress.* New York: Bantam, 1996. 448 pp.

Marshall Ben Masters takes the four-year-old orphan Sarah Ann to Scotland to claim her inheritance.
Genre(s): Romance.

Power, Jo-Ann

4265. *Treasures.* New York: Pocket Books, 1996. 324 pp.
Catherine Farrell's father is accused of stealing an ancient Egyptian papyrus, and three years later, her former fiancé asks her to help him find the papyrus.
Genre(s): Romance; Mystery.

Powys, John Cowper

4266. *Wolf Solent.* New York: Simon and Schuster, 1929. 966 pp.
When Wolf Solent returns to the Dorset village that once ostracized his father, he quickly takes on all of the vices and narrowmindedness of his people.
Genre(s): Epic Literature.

Prole, Lozania

◆ 4267. *The Queen's Daughters.* London: Hale, 1973. 206 pp.
Victoria's daughters—Victoria, Alice, Helena, Louise, and Beatrice—must learn to live within the spotlight of nobility during the 19th century.
Genre(s): Biographical Fiction.

Quiller-Couch, Arthur, and Daphne du Maurier

4268. *Castle Dor.* Garden City, NY: Doubleday, 1962. 274 pp.
When Amyot Trestane, a Breton sailor, jumps ship at Castle Dor and meets Linnet, who is married to an older man, their fate follows that of the legendary Tristan and Iseult.

Rae, Hugh C.

4269. *The Rookery.* New York: St. Martin's, 1975. 255 pp.
In Victorian England, Susanna Farebrother detests Edward Royde, but after her father's identical twin impersonates her father, she changes her mind about Edward.
Genre(s): Mystery.

Raison, Jennifer

4270. *Caraboo.* Brooklyn: Interlink, 1995. 220 pp.
Mary Baker, a servant girl rescued from the workhouse by the wealthy Elizabeth Worrall, convinces everyone that she is a princess from Javasu.
Genre(s): Biographical Fiction.

Randall, Rona

◆ 4271. *The Eagle at the Gate.* New York: Coward-McCann, 1978. 320 pp.
Aphra Coleman marries David Hillyard in the early 20th century, but finds that her father's secrets control her life.
Genre(s): Romance.

4272. *Ladies of Hanover Square*. New York: Coward-McCann, 1981. 364 pp.
Three women live on Hanover Square from 1901 until World War I where one is the mistress to Lord Justin Ashleigh, a man with an evil secret.
Genre(s): Romance.

4273. *The Mating Dance*. New York: Coward-McCann, 1979. 427 pp.
The actress Lucinda and her half sister, the promiscuous Clementine, live in Victorian London and display their unique personalities.
Genre(s): Romance.

◆ 4274. *Watchman's Stone*. New York: Simon and Schuster, 1975. 285 pp.
Elizabeth MacArthur marries Calum, Lord of Faillie, against the advice of those who know her, and when her father is soon killed in an accident, she realizes her own danger in the Scottish Highlands.
Genre(s): Romance; Gothic Fiction.

Rathbone, Irene

4275. *We That Were Young*. New York: Feminist, 1989. 500 pp.
Joan, Barbara, Pamela, and Betty work in France during World War I in the YMCA canteens, and at home in Britain, they spend long and arduous days in military hospitals and munitions factories.
Genre(s): War Story.

Raymond, Ernest

4276. *Gentle Greaves*. New York: Saturday Review, 1972. 534 pp.
A publisher on his deathbed at the end of World War II tells his daughter about two cousins, once childhood sweethearts, who met again during World War I and conceived a child, but could not marry because they were already married to others.
Genre(s): Love Story; War Story.

4277. *A Georgian Love Story*. New York: McCall, 1971. 294 pp.
An impoverished upper-class boy in Edwardian and Georgian London, falls in love with a shopkeeper but they must convince people of their right to be together.
Genre(s): Love Story.

Rayner, Claire

4278. *Bedford Row*. New York: Putnam, 1977. 278 pp.
In the sequel to *Soho Square*, Martha Lackland leaves her father's London clinic to help at Scutari during the Crimean War. (*Series:* The Performer, 5)
Award(s): Pulitzer Prize.
Genre(s): Domestic Fiction; Medical Novel; Love Story; Family Saga; War Story.

4279. *Charing Cross*. New York: Putnam, 1979. 306 pp.
The sequel to *Covent Garden* reveals that Sophie, Abel Lackland's grandchild, wants to become a surgeon and af-

ter many roadblocks, she succeeds. (*Series:* The Performer, 7)
Genre(s): Domestic Fiction; Medical Novel; Family Saga.

4280. *Covent Garden*. New York: Putnam, 1978. 276 pp.
In the sequel to *Bedford Row*, Amy and Fenton Lucas seek fame in London but meet the Lackland family when Amy needs brain surgery. (*Series:* The Performer, 6)
Genre(s): Domestic Fiction; Medical Novel; Family Saga.

4281. *The Enduring Years*. New York: Delacorte, 1982. 579 pp.
Hannah, young and poor, marries into an unwelcoming aristocratic family, but the inheritance she receives at her husband's early death allows her independence as a dressmaker.
Genre(s): Domestic Fiction.

4282. *London Lodgings*. New York: St. Martin's, 1995. 377 pp.
After a difficult childhood and an unpleasant arranged marriage, Tilly's lot changes with the help of the scullery maid.
Genre(s): Domestic Fiction.

4283. *The Strand*. New York: Putnam, 1981. 259 pp.
The sequel to *Charing Cross* finds a young Lackland surgeon who has returned from Australia struggling with the underside of Victorian London while becoming involved with an actress and the Lackland beauty of the 1892 season. (*Series:* The Performer, 8)
Genre(s): Domestic Fiction; Medical Novel; Family Saga.

Reed, Jeremy

4284. *Dorian*. Chester Springs, PA: Dufour, 1996. 176 pp.
Dorian Gray's portrait is slashed, and he begins to age, a process that revolts him enough to cause him to become an opium addict, voyeur, and transvestite.
Genre(s): Gothic Fiction.

Reilly, Robert

4285. *The God of Mirrors*. New York: Penguin, 1987. 403 pp.
Oscar Wilde becomes a tragic hero after London's accolades turn to damnations when he falls in love with Lord Alfred Douglas.
Genre(s): Biographical Fiction.

Rhys, Jean

4286. *Voyage in the Dark*. New York: Morrow, 1935. 266 pp.

In 1914, Anna leaves her West Indian home for England where she becomes a member of a second-rate theatrical touring company and drifts from place to place.

Richards-Akers, Nancy

4287. *Wild Irish Skies*. New York: Avon, 1997. 384 pp.
Annora Picot wants to escape marriage to one of the king's relatives because she does not love him, and she and her uncle concoct a scheme for her to be kidnapped out of Ireland.
Genre(s): Romance.

Rinehold, Connie

4288. *Forever and a Day*. New York: Dell, 1995. 352 pp.
Betina Wells, daughter of a Wyoming landowner, dies, but she then appears in England in 1878 to claim her inheritance and prevent her lover from being caught in time.
Genre(s): Time Travel; Romance.

Roberts, Ann Victoria

◆ 4289. *Louisa Elliott*. Chicago: Contemporary, 1989. 650 pp.
Louisa and Edward Elliott, both illegitimate, keep their secret, but after Louisa falls in love with an Irish military officer married to a mentally ill wife and has his children, she becomes aware of her love for Edward.
Genre(s): Love Story; Romance.

◆ 4290. *Morning's Gate*. New York: Morrow, 1992. 639 pp.
Cousins meet in New York in the 1980s and start investigating their family from *Louisa Elliott* and discover illegitimacy and incest which occurred during World War I in Australia, England, and Europe.
Genre(s): Domestic Fiction.

Roberts, Cynthia S.

◆ 4291. *The Fox-Red Hills*. New York: St. Martin's, 1993. 480 pp.
Orphans Mostyn and Carne Havard spar in the coal-mining industry, one heartless and planning to reclaim the family home through marriage and the other deciding to marry an orphan of unknown parentage.

Roberts, J. M.

4292. *Without Sanction*. Boston: Alyson, 1993. 320 pp.
Kit St. Denys loves Nick Stewart, a country doctor, but Kit's dark moods drive him away to America in the 19th century.
Genre(s): Love Story.

Roberts, Janet Louise

4293. *The Jade Vendetta*. New York: Pocket Books, 1976. 255 pp.

Cecilia Treat, a Shakespearean actress, marries the marquess Hugo Kinnaird, and finds that his temper may have killed his first wife.
Genre(s): Gothic Fiction; Romance.

Robinson, Derek

4294. *Goshawk Squadron*. New York: Viking, 1972. 246 pp.
A British pilot flies in France during 1918, and his squadron has contempt for the war and corrupt leadership.
Genre(s): War Story.

4295. *War Story*. New York: Knopf, 1988. 416 pp.
During the Great War, Oliver Paxton wins his wings, takes a plane to France, and plans to become a hero until he finally understands the futility of his desires.
Genre(s): War Story.

Robinson, Suzanne

4296. *The Rescue*. New York: Bantam, 1998. 304 pp.
Luke Hawthorne, son of a charwoman and a dockworker, steals, works for the government, and earns a knighthood before someone asks him to find an old maid lost in London who is actually neither lost nor old.
Genre(s): Romance.

Rock, Phillip

4297. *The Passing Bells*. New York: Seaview, 1978. 433 pp.
Those living around the estate of Antony Greville, Earl of Stanhope, are drawn into the changes caused by World War I as some stay at home and others fight in the trenches on the Western front.
Genre(s): War Story.

Rogow, Roberta

◆ 4298. *The Problem of the Missing Miss*. New York: St. Martin's, 1998. 259 pp.
In 1885, Arthur Conan Doyle helps Charles Dodgson search for Alicia Marbury who is abducted from the Brighton train station after the death of her maidservant.
Genre(s): Mystery.

Ross-Macdonald, Malcolm

4299. *The Dukes*. New York: Simon and Schuster, 1981. 559 pp.
Alfred Boyce is quite surprised to become the fifth Duke of St. Ormer, and he and his family must adjust to this new role as the Victorian era turns into World War I and afterward.
Genre(s): Domestic Fiction.

Routh, Jonathan

4300. *The Secret Life of Queen Victoria*. London: Sidgwick and Jackson, 1979. 110 pp.
Queen Victoria's missing diaries record her attempt to get away from her responsibilities in a two-month secret visit to Jamaica.
Genre(s): Biographical Fiction.

Rowland, Peter

◆ 4301. *The Disappearance of Edwin Drood.* New York: St. Martin's, 1992. 176 pp.
Dr. Watson and Sherlock Holmes can find no place to stay in the Cloisterham Inn on Christmas Eve because people are portraying Dickens and searching for the solution to the Edwin Drood disappearance.
Genre(s): Mystery.

Rundle, Anne

◆ 4302. *The Singing Swans.* New York: Putnam, 1975. 256 pp.
A beautiful orphan goes to Paris from the Isle of Skye where she falls in love, but the romance is initially thwarted.
Genre(s): Romance; Domestic Fiction.

Sackville-West, Vita

4303. *The Edwardians.* Garden City, NY: Doubleday, 1930. 314 pp.
The old house of Chevron, inhabited by Sebastian and his mother, a famous hostess, represents the decadent society of the days before George becomes king.

Salisbury, Carola

4304. *An Autumn in Araby.* Garden City, NY: Doubleday, 1983. 264 pp.
Suzanna Copley studies nursing with Florence Nightingale before beginning to look after a painter's son who she thinks is abused.
Genre(s): Romance.

◆ 4305. *The Shadowed Spring.* New York: Doubleday, 1980. 275 pp.
An honest teacher at a Cornwall school for young ladies in 1878 accepts a job as a governess for a lord's young daughter and ends up on a train from Paris to St. Petersburg as a special interpreter.
Genre(s): Romance.

◆ 4306. *The Winter Bride.* Garden City, NY: Doubleday, 1978. 233 pp.
When a young woman decides to become secretary to a rich poet in Cornwall, she encounters danger.
Genre(s): Romance.

Sallis, Susan

4307. *April Rising.* New York: St. Martin's, 1984. 304 pp.
April Rising of Gloucester, England, is the youngest daughter of an interesting family and she finds happiness with a Jewish tailor in the early 20th century.
Genre(s): War Story; Romance.

Satterthwait, Walter

4308. *Escapade.* New York: St. Martin's, 1995. 355 pp.
Sir Arthur Conan Doyle and Harry Houdini attend a weekend house party in Devon where they must test their abilities when someone murders the host.
Genre(s): Mystery.

Saunders, Kate

4309. *Night Shall Overtake Us.* New York: Dutton, 1994. 501 pp.
In 1907, four schoolgirls decide to remain friends forever, and during the years, many different events and incidents test their loyalty.
Genre(s): War Story; Domestic Fiction.

Savory, Teo

4310. *To a High Place.* New York: Unicorn, 1972. 96 pp.
When a young son is born into aristocracy with a deformed hand, he cannot join the military as expected, so he cultivates an interest in botany which makes him famous and which leads him on a spiritual quest to Tibet.
Genre(s): Bildungsroman (Coming of Age); Religious Fiction.

Saxe, Coral Smith

4311. *Enchantment.* New York: Love Spell, 1994. 448 pp.
Adam Hawthorne wants to prove that the Hag of Cold Springs Hollow, Bryony Talcott, is a fraud, and when he meets her, she claims to have no powers, but he falls in love with her anyway.
Genre(s): Romance.

Saxton, Judith

4312. *Harvest Moon.* New York: St. Martin's, 1996. 544 pp.
When Laurie's lazy father tries to take his trust fund, Laurie protects the manor home and goes to fight in the Spanish Civil War.
Genre(s): Domestic Fiction; War Story; Romance.

Schlee, Ann

4313. *Rhine Journey.* New York: Holt, Rinehart and Winston, 1981. 465 pp.
When Charlotte goes on a steamboat cruise with her brother 20 years after he banished her from his house for loving an unsuitable man, he suggests that she return to his home.

Schwartz, Irwin

4314. *The Piltdown Confession.* New York: St. Martin's, 1994. 210 pp.
Charles Dawson confesses on his deathbed that the Piltdown man is a hoax after evangelicals threaten Pierre Teilhard du Chardin, and Arthur Conan Doyle protects him.
Genre(s): Biographical Fiction; Mystery.

Scrimgeour, G. J.

4315. *A Woman of her Times.* New York: Putnam, 1982. 408 pp.
When Elizabeth Wingate finds out that her husband has been unfaithful, she takes her baby to London where the daughter grows up to be a beautiful actress.
Genre(s): Romance.

Seaman, Donald

4316. *Chase Royal.* New York: St. Martin's, 1982. 319 pp.
In Victorian England, members of the Irish Republican Army scheme to destroy the British.
Genre(s): War Story.

Sebald, W. G.

4317. *The Rings of Saturn.* Trans. Michael Hulse. New York: New Directions, 1998. 256 pp.
An unnamed traveler wanders across Suffolk, England, and back into time as he examines subjects such as the silk industry, the Chinese opium wars, and Joseph Conrad.
Genre(s): Adventure Story; Time Travel.

Seil, William

◆ 4318. *Sherlock Holmes and the Titanic Tragedy.* Chicago: Breese, 1996. 253 pp.
In 1912, Dr. Watson leaves retirement to help the disguised Sherlock Holmes take secret government plans about submarines to the United States, but someone steals them before boarding the *Titanic.*
Genre(s): Mystery.

Selwyn, Francis

◆ 4319. *Sergeant Verity and the Blood Royal.* New York: Stein and Day, 1979. 272 pp.
In the late 19th century, Sergeant Verity must find the location of stolen Indian treasure that has a curse attached to it.
Genre(s): Mystery.

4320. *Sergeant Verity and the Swell Mob.* New York: Stein and Day, 1981. 275 pp.
Sergeant Verity must face an unfriendly group in his criminal investigation.
Genre(s): Mystery.

4321. *Sergeant Verity Presents His Compliments.* New York: Stein and Day, 1977. 266 pp.
In Victorian England, Verity investigates a blackmailer who chooses nasty victims.
Genre(s): Mystery.

Sharp, Margery

4322. *Britannia Mews.* Boston: Little, Brown, 1946. 377 pp.
Adelaide Culver runs away from her Victorian family in 1865 and lives in Britannia Mews, an upcoming area where her father's coachman had once lived.
Genre(s): Domestic Fiction.

4323. *The Faithful Servants.* Boston: Little, Brown, 1975. 202 pp.
When the dying Jacob Arbuthnot sets up a foundation for female servants in the City of Westminster, he creates a new group of unusual women.

4324. *Rosa.* Boston: Little, Brown, 1970. 249 pp.
In the 1890s, Rosa, daughter of a Ramillies family groomsman, comes back to England and ends up marrying a noble who is trying to provide an heir to his land.
Genre(s): Domestic Fiction.

4325. *Summer Visits.* Boston: Little, Brown, 1978. 220 pp.
Cotton Hall's master, Old John Braithwaite, allows himself to be duped into believing that two children born to his mistress are his.
Genre(s): Domestic Fiction.

Shaughnessy, Alfred

4326. *Hugo.* Cinncinnati, OH: Seven Hills, 1996. 235 pp.
Hugh lives with his stepfather after his mother's death when he is eight and must adjust to his half brother as the heir of the land Hugh loves.
Genre(s): Bildungsroman (Coming of Age).

Sheppard, Stephen

4327. *The Four Hundred.* New York: Summit, 1979. 414 pp.
Four Americans plot to defraud the Bank of England, which in 1872 is the most important bank in the world, and they almost succeed until Scotland Yard intervenes.
Genre(s): Mystery.

Sheridan, Jane

4328. *Love at Sunset.* New York: St. Martin's, 1982. 288 pp.
Clarissa, daughter of Amanda in *My Lady Holden* and illegitimate daughter of the Duke of Camberly, falls in love with the duke's son, but the duke stops the marriage although not the ensuing scandal.
Genre(s): Romance.

Simone, Sonia

4329. *Stealing Midnight.* New York: HarperCollins, 1996. 256 pp.
Darius Lovejoy determines to kill the man who seduced his sister but has not planned on falling in love with the man's niece.
Genre(s): Romance.

Sinclair, Andrew

4330. *The Far Corners of the Earth.* London: Hodder and Stoughton, 1991. 216 pp.
The Sinclairs disperse from Scotland during the Highland clearances, and family members go to Peking, British Colombia, Sebastopol, and Gettysburg to reestablish their lives.
Genre(s): Domestic Fiction.

Smith, Joan

◆ 4331. *Love's Way.* New York: Walker, 1982. 192 pp.

Black Jack Gamble returns from India to protect his estate, and disdainful Chloe initially finds him disgusting. *Genre(s):* Romance; Regency Novel.

Smith, Martin Cruz

4332. *Rose.* New York: Random House, 1996. 364 pp.

In 1872, Jonathan Blair wants only to return to Africa, but his employer demands that he go to Lancashire to find out about a missing minister, which leads to information on a recent mining disaster. *Genre(s):* Love Story; Mystery.

Sole, Linda

4333. *The Last Summer of Innocence.* New York: St. Martin's, 1992. 325 pp.

When Kate is 16, her mother sends her to Cambridgeshire to live with wealthy cousins, without immediately telling her the real reason for her going. *Genre(s):* Domestic Fiction; War Story.

4334. *This Land, This Love.* New York: St. Martin's, 1998. 336 pp.

After Rebecca Cottrel returns from boarding school, her father is murdered, she marries local farmer Aden although she wanted a higher station, and then finds that aristocrat Victor Roth wanted to marry her. *Genre(s):* Romance.

Speer, Flora M.

4335. *Time and Time Again.* New York: M. Evans, 1991. 302 pp.

American Elspeth Brown comes to Tynant Manor just after learning of her English connections, and her uncle wants to make amends for the past while his friend Jordan creates new tensions. *Genre(s):* Romance.

Spellman, Cathy Cash

4336. *An Excess of Love.* New York: Delacorte, 1985. 526 pp.

Two upper-class sisters become involved in the cause of Irish independence when they fall in love with men who support it. *Genre(s):* Domestic Fiction.

Sprott, Duncan

4337. *The Rise of Mr Warde.* New York: St. Martin's, 1992. 220 pp.

Charles Warde, son of a village minister, receives a sum of money when he turns 21 and marries a village beauty, but their divorce 13 years later reveals his cruelty to his wife and children in the 19th century. *Genre(s):* Domestic Fiction.

St. James, Ian

4338. *The Killing Anniversary.* New York: Morrow, 1985. 658 pp.

A journalist, an IRA chief, an aristocrat, and a woman reveal the politics and hostilites in Ireland during the 20th century. *Genre(s):* Political Fiction; Family Saga.

St. John, Nicole

4339. *Guinevere's Gift.* New York: Random House, 1977. 245 pp.

In 1909 Lydian marries a recluse searching for the tomb of King Arthur but falls in love with his young assistant to recreate the Guinevere-King Arthur-Lancelot triangle. *Genre(s):* Romance.

Stevenson, D. E.

4340. *Celia's House.* New York: Farrar and Rinehart, 1943. 307 pp.

In 1905, Celia's heir and grandnephew begin their 40 years at Dunnian, an estate on the Scottish border. *Genre(s):* Domestic Fiction.

4341. *Listening Valley.* New York: Farrar and Rinehart, 1944. 256 pp.

In the sequel to *Celia's House,* Tony marries a wealthy man and goes to London while her sister marries and moves to India from Scotland. *Genre(s):* Domestic Fiction.

Stewart, Fred Mustard

4342. *Lady Darlington.* New York: World, 1971. 312 pp.

When Margaret Suffield agrees to nurse the difficult Lady Darlington, she does not know that Lady Darlington wants to destroy her husband. *Genre(s):* Mystery; Political Fiction.

Stirling, Jessica

4343. *Call Home the Heart.* New York: St. Martin's, 1977. 414 pp.

In the sequel to *Strathmore,* the Stalker family struggles in the mills until Mirrin begins acting and Drew earns a law scholarship. *Genre(s):* Romance.

4344. *The Dark Pasture.* New York: St. Martin's, 1978. 384 pp.

The Stalker family, in the sequel to *Call Home the Heart,* become involved with a miner's strike in 1896 and Neill Stalker, illegitimate son of a Scottish barrister, is arrested for murder. *Genre(s):* Romance.

4345. *The Island Wife.* New York: St. Martin's, 1998. 416 pp.

When a shepherd arrives on the island of Mull, off the coast of Scotland, two sisters fall in love with him, but he has secrets which disrupt their lives. *Genre(s):* Adventure Story.

◆ May be suitable for young adult readers

Stone, Lyn

4346. *The Arrangement.* New York: Harlequin, 1997. 297 pp.
Violinist Jonathan Chadwick tries to outwit gossip columnist Kathryn Wainwright by pretending to be the idiot savant, Pip.
Genre(s): Romance; Musical Fiction.

4347. *The Wilder Wedding.* New York: Harlequin, 1998. 304 pp.
After overhearing a conversation, Laura Middlebrook thinks she has only a few months to live, and she immediately proposes to handsome Sean Wilder, but after their marriage, her good health and pregnancy baffle Wilder.
Genre(s): Romance.

Stroud, John

◆ 4348. *The Waif.* London: Hodder and Stoughton, 1973. 286 pp.
A young boy in London tries to survive during the 1880s.

Stubbs, Jean

4349. *Dear Laura.* New York: Stein and Day, 1973. 287 pp.
Inspector Lintott peals away the layers hiding the real marriage of Laura and Theodore Crozier when he investigates Theodore's death in Victorian England.
Genre(s): Mystery; Gothic Fiction.

Sully, Sue

4350. *The Barleyfield.* New York: Heinemann, 1991. 352 pp.
Elizabeth Thorne hates the restrictions on women in 19th-century England, and after making love to her intended's younger brother Edward, she leaves for Australia in a loveless marriage, but Edward does not forget her.
Genre(s): Romance.

4351. *The Shingle Beach.* New York: St. Martin's, 1993. 352 pp.
Elizabeth Pengelly refuses to follow Victorian standards, but she is unhappy when her daughters do likewise, and she finally reveals to one of them that she is the daughter of her mother's lover not her mother's husband.
Genre(s): Domestic Fiction.

Summerson, Rachel

4352. *Belgrave Square.* New York: St. Martin's, 1981. 295 pp.
Sisters in a Victorian household have a variety of interests, and Flora is happy with her lot although she shocks others by reading Darwin.
Genre(s): Romance; Domestic Fiction.

Symons, Julian

4353. *The Blackheath Poisonings.* New York: Harper and Row, 1978. 302 pp.
After a doctor says gastric upset caused one death, and poison seems to have caused a second death, complications in a family's life begin to surface in Victorian Britain.
Genre(s): Mystery.

4354. *The Detling Secret.* New York: Viking, 1983. 225 pp.
Dolly Detling marries Bernard Ross against her politician father's wishes, and two deaths immediately occur.
Genre(s): Mystery.

4355. *Sweet Adelaide.* New York: Harper and Row, 1980. 284 pp.
Adelaide Blanche de la Tremille Bartlett is tried for the murder of her husband but acquitted because no one knows how she could have given him the chloroform.
Genre(s): Mystery.

Tannahill, Reay

◆ 4356. *In Still and Stormy Waters.* New York: St. Martin's, 1994. 520 pp.
Rachel Macmillan falls in love with the dark Scottish highland castle of Juran, but her step-siblings who live there hate her presence, knowing that she is the castle's legal heir.

4357. *Return of the Stranger.* New York: St. Martin's, 1996. 376 pp.
When Tassie's father dies and leaves everything to an unknown relative, Tassie and her mother must move from their home.
Genre(s): Domestic Fiction.

Tanner, Janet

◆ 4358. *The Emerald Valley.* New York: St. Martin's, 1986. 534 pp.
In the 1920s, widow Amy Roberts tries to run a British transport business, and she succeeds in both business and in marrying the richest man in town in the sequel to *Hours of Light.*
Genre(s): Family Saga.

◆ 4359. *Hours of Light.* New York: St. Martin's, 1981. 469 pp.
In 1900, Charlotte goes from Bath to Hillsbridge where she tries to earn enough money throughout World War I to keep her son Jack out of the mining pits and help him become a teacher.
Genre(s): Family Saga.

Taylor, Liza Pennywitt

4360. *The Drummer Was the First to Die.* New York: St. Martin's, 1992. 309 pp.
Men in various professions try to thwart the research of John Snow, the first epidemiologist, as he tries to find a cure for cholera.
Genre(s): Biographical Fiction; Medical Novel; Romance.

Thomas, Donald

4361. *Captain Wunder.* New York: Viking, 1981. 268 pp.

The Germans hire Richard Gaudeans (Captain Wunder) in 1907 to steal the Irish state jewels while the King visits Dublin in order to embarrass the British.
Genre(s): Political Fiction.

◆ 4362. *Jekyll, Alias Hyde.* New York: St. Martin's, 1989. 224 pp.
Albert Swain, a Scotland Yard investigator, becomes intrigued with the somewhat perverse daughter of Dr. Jekyll's attorney, and with her he looks into the mysterious case of Dr. Jekyll.
Genre(s): Mystery.

◆ 4363. *The Ripper's Apprentice.* New York: St. Martin's, 1989. 256 pp.
A criminal uses strychnine to kill prostitutes in Victorian England, and while in prison for other crimes, he plans to escape and choose new victims.
Genre(s): Mystery.

Thompson, E. V.

4364. *Ben Retallick.* New York: St. Martin's, 1981. 400 pp.
Ben Retallick and Jesse Henna fall in love in Cornwall during the 19th century and spend four years searching for each other after a landlord and his evil gamekeeper keep them separated, in the sequel to *Chase the Wind.*
Genre(s): Romance.

Treherne, John

4365. *The Walk to Acorn Bridge.* New York: Trafalgar Square, 1990. 153 pp.
J. Clack's friends accompany him as he moves from the family farm to working in a factory to life as a soldier in the early 20th century.
Genre(s): Bildungsroman (Coming of Age).

Trevelyan, Robert

4366. *Pendragon.* New York: Saturday Review, 1975. 220 pp.
Captain Pendragon's wounds received in the Crimean War do not stop his search for the murderer of a spy-catcher in London.
Genre(s): Mystery.

Trevor, Elleston

4367. *Bury Him among Kings.* New York: Doubleday, 1970. 384 pp.
Aubrey and Victor Talbot, British aristocrats, enter World War I and while realizing the horrors of war, they begin to accept each other.
Genre(s): War Story.

Trevor, William

4368. *The Silence in the Garden.* New York: Viking, 1988. 204 pp.
The Rolleston family slowly loses its Irish vitality as the elder sons refuse to marry and the daughter chooses a man too old to have children.
Genre(s): Domestic Fiction.

Trollope, Joanna

4369. *The Taverners' Place.* New York: St. Martin's, 1987. 560 pp.
From 1870 to 1939, the Taverner family gathers repeatedly at its Bath estate after each, of almost every possible, misfortune occurs to its members.
Genre(s): Domestic Fiction.

Trow, M. J.

4370. *The Supreme Adventure of Inspector Lestrade.* New York: Stein and Day, 1985. 224 pp.
In 1891, Inspector Sholto Lestrade, butt of many of Sherlock Holmes's jokes, trails a mass murderer and finally confronts him in a London circus.
Genre(s): Mystery.

Turnbull, Agnes Sligh

4371. *Whistle and I'll Come to You.* Boston: Houghton Mifflin, 1970. 256 pp.
In 1900, Robin comes to visit the wealthy Adair sisters in their village, claiming to be a distant cousin, and he falls in love with the banker's daughter before someone tries to kill the sisters.
Genre(s): Romance.

Tyler-Whittle, Michael Sidney

4372. *Albert's Victoria.* New York: St. Martin's, 1972. 263 pp.
The sequel to *The Young Victoria* presents Victoria and Albert from their wedding day until Albert's death 21 years later.
Genre(s): Biographical Fiction.

4373. *Bertie, Albert Edward, Prince of Wales.* New York: St. Martin's, 1974. 327 pp.
Albert Edward, nicknamed Bertie, is first the Prince of Wales who indulges in notorious affairs, and then becomes Edward VII after his mother, Queen Victoria, dies.
Genre(s): Biographical Fiction.

4374. *Edward.* New York: St. Martin's, 1975. 278 pp.
Edward rules for nine years with a great sense of duty, common sense, and a character that endears him to his subjects.
Genre(s): Biographical Fiction.

4375. *The Widow of Windsor.* New York: St. Martin's, 1973. 287 pp.
Victoria secludes herself after Albert's death, in the sequel to *Albert's Victoria*, but she eventually emerges and rules for the next 40 years.
Genre(s): Biographical Fiction.

Uris, Leon

4376. *Redemption.* New York: HarperCollins, 1995. 848 pp.
In the sequel to *Trinity*, Rory Larkin leaves New Zealand to fight for the British in World War I under the leader-

ship of a despicable Protestant and joins the revolutionaries in the Easter uprising of 1916.
Genre(s): Family Saga; Political Fiction.

◆ **4377.** *Trinity.* Garden City, NY: Doubleday, 1976. 751 pp.
The Larkens, the Hubbles, and the Weeds are Catholic hill-farmers, Presbyterian industralists, and British aristocracy fighting before and during the Easter Rising of Ireland in 1916.
Genre(s): War Story; Family Saga.

Van Ash, Cay

4378. *Ten Years beyond Baker Street.* New York: Harper and Row, 1984. 339 pp.
Dr. Petrie begs Sherlock Holmes to come out of retirement to help him find his flat mate, Nayland Smith, suspecting Fu Manchu of abducting him.
Genre(s): Mystery; Adventure Story.

Vaughan, Matthew

4379. *Chalky.* Boston: Little, Brown, 1975. 248 pp.
A young man in Victorian England endures jail and an orphanage before enjoying army service where he becomes a hero.
Genre(s): Romance.

Walpole, Hugh

4380. *The Dark Forest.* London: M. Secker, 1916. 316 pp.
In the sequel to *Young Enchanted*, Henry Trenchard goes to war, where he must face both the enemy and his penchant for poetry.
Genre(s): War Story; Family Saga.

4381. *Green Mirror.* New York: Doran, 1918. 473 pp.
Henry Trenchard grows up at the beginning of the 20th century and falls in love.
Genre(s): Family Saga.

4382. *Vanessa.* Garden City, NY: Doubleday, 1933. 620 pp.
In the sequel to *The Fortress*, Judith's granddaughter is loved by two men, one who wanders and another who is steady.
Genre(s): Domestic Fiction.

4383. *Young Enchanted.* New York: Doran, 1922. 427 pp.
When Henry Trenchard falls in love, he does not seem to notice that the girl does not return his affections, and he and his sister also ignore the wishes of their parents, in the sequel to *Green Mirror*.
Genre(s): Family Saga.

Walsh, Ray

4384. *The Mycroft Memoranda.* New York: St. Martin's, 1985. 186 pp.
The police ask Sherlock Holmes to help them find Jack the Ripper, who looks like Watson.
Genre(s): Mystery.

Walter, Elizabeth

4385. *A Season of Goodwill.* New York: Scribner's, 1986. 252 pp.
In an English country home at Christmas in 1907, a lovely but poor girl falls in love and has to overcome her rival.
Genre(s): Romance.

Warady, Phylis Ann

◆ **4386.** *Scandal's Daughter.* New York: Walker, 1990. 172 pp.
After Diantha marries, her husband leaves for London on business, and when she hears rumors about his behavior, she joins his brother in a wild cart race.
Genre(s): Romance.

Webster, Jan

◆ **4387.** *Muckle Annie.* New York: St. Martin's, 1986. 299 pp.
Muckle Annie is so poor in Glasgow that she takes a common-law vow with a man going to Canada, and she spends much time trying to reunite with her real love before her husband dies.
Genre(s): Romance.

4388. *Saturday City.* New York: St. Martin's, 1979. 350 pp.
Kate Kilgour's children move away from the mining pits and become involved with the political and technological discussions of the day.
Genre(s): Domestic Fiction.

West, Anthony C.

4389. *David Rees, among Others.* New York: Random House, 1970. 309 pp.
David Rees has difficulty becoming independent and confident until after World War I because of his feelings about his illegitimacy, his boarding school experiences, and his bout with tuberculosis.
Genre(s): War Story; Bildungsroman (Coming of Age).

West, Pamela Elizabeth

4390. *Yours Truly, Jack the Ripper.* New York: St. Martin's, 1987. 323 pp.
Inspector West records all of the horrible details of Jack the Ripper's murders as he searches for the Ripper in Victorian London.
Genre(s): Mystery.

West, Paul

4391. *Love's Mansion.* New York: Random House, 1992. 339 pp.
Harry and Hilly's son tries to piece together his parents' lives and the major change that World War I made in their relationship.
Genre(s): War Story; Love Story.

4392. *The Women of Whitechapel and Jack the Ripper.* New York: Random House, 1991. 420 pp.

A painter, fascinated with the dark side of Victorian life, introduces the son of Princess Alexandra to London prostitutes, and the events that follow lead to murder.
Genre(s): Mystery.

West, Rebecca

◆ 4393. *This Real Night.* New York: Viking, 1985. 267 pp.
The sequel to *The Fountain Overflows* shows Rose Aubrey and her family as they react to the horror of World War I.
Genre(s): War Story; Domestic Fiction.

Whitehouse, Arch

4394. *Hero without Honor.* New York: Doubleday, 1972. 312 pp.
Max Kenyon, an American, wins honors from the British in World War I, but he does not mind changing records if it will help him, and he does not mind ruining the career of the woman who loves and marries him.
Genre(s): War Story.

4395. *Wings for the Chariots.* New York: Doubleday, 1973. 256 pp.
Captain Clement prefers cavalry, and in World War I, he reluctantly accepts the value of a plane for attack, while Lieutenant Brower uses his skill with farm machines for driving tanks.
Genre(s): War Story.

Whitnell, Barbara

◆ 4396. *The Ring of Bells.* New York: Coward-McCann, 1982. 400 pp.
Jenny's life from her mother's death in 1887 until the day World War II begins in Britain is relatively happy against a backdrop of woman suffrage and World War I.
Genre(s): Domestic Fiction.

Wick, Lori

4397. *The Hawk and the Jewel.* Eugene, OR: Harvest House, 1993. 347 pp.
Sunny and Brandon find their relationship turning from friendship to love after their experience at Ravenscroft, a shipboard adventure, and the discovery of important documents.
Genre(s): Christian Fiction; Romance.

4398. *Who Brings Forth the Wind.* Eugene, OR: Harvest House, 1994. 396 pp.
When the volatile Tanner Richardson, Duke of Cambridge, sees his pregnant wife with another man, he makes her leave before learning the reason.
Genre(s): Christian Fiction.

Williams, Jeanne

◆ 4399. *Daughter of the Storm.* New York: St. Martin's, 1994. 311 pp.
Mairi McDonald's unborn child dies while Mairi fights for the rights of the crofters in the Hebrides, and she

adopts the orphaned Christy who always stretches to win Mairi's approval, in the sequel to *The Island Harp.*
Genre(s): Domestic Fiction.

Williams, Mary

4400. *Trenhawk.* New York: St. Martin's, 1982. 322 pp.
After Adelaide Hawksley's husband David is killed in the Crimean War, the family mansion passes to David's cousin Rupert, but when Adelaide offers to buy the estate and its mine, penniless Rupert refuses to sell, and their conflicts begin.
Genre(s): Romance.

Willis, Ted

4401. *The Green Leaves of Summer.* New York: St. Martin's, 1989. 319 pp.
In 1918, Rosie Carr learns in the sequel to *Spring at the Winged Horse* that she is a war widow, and her struggle to support her family, including her mother-in-law, begins in earnest.
Genre(s): Humorous Fiction; Family Saga.

4402. *Spring at the Winged Horse.* New York: Morrow, 1983. 286 pp.
In 1906, when she is 13, Rosie Carr's uncle makes her board and work in a local pub, but she makes friends with a variety of people, including the piano player, the jellied-eel seller, and Tommo the Toff, a handsome con-artist.
Genre(s): Humorous Fiction; Family Saga.

Willman, Marianne

4403. *The Mermaid's Song.* New York: St. Martin's, 1997. 374 pp.
In 1894, Flora O'Donnell, fearing arrest for a murder she did not commit, changes her identity and begins teaching in a girls' school, but a detective inquires about her past, and when she marries a French man for a chance to flee to Paris, she is exposed to his family's dangers as well.
Genre(s): Romance.

Wilson, T. R.

4404. *Beauty for Ashes.* New York: St. Martin's, 1992. 348 pp.
Hannah wants to marry upper-class Lawrence in 1877, but his family disagrees, so she marries a yeoman, and their two children repeat the expectations of rising from their social class.
Genre(s): Family Saga; War Story.

Wilson, Timothy

4405. *Master of Morholm.* New York: St. Martin's, 1987. 352 pp.
George Hardwick returns from London to become the Squire of Morholm and has to feed his relatives, make loans to his friends, and try to understand his relationship with his orphaned cousin.
Genre(s): Domestic Fiction.

Wood, Barbara

◆ 4406. *Domina.* Garden City, NY: Doubleday, 1983. 485 pp.
Samantha Hargrave, wanting to become a doctor, leaves Victorian London for America.
Genre(s): Medical Novel.

Woodhouse, Sarah

4407. *The Native Air.* New York: St. Martin's, 1991. 298 pp.
Dr. Alexander French returns to Norwich in the sequel to *Peacock's Feather* to consolidate his affairs before rejoining the army and returning to India, but he must first solve a kidnapping and admit that he has been in love with Ann Gerard.
Genre(s): Romance; Mystery.

Woodman, Richard

4408. *A Private Revenge.* New York: St. Martin's, 1989. 247 pp.
Nathaniel Drinkwater is convoy commander for merchantmen sailing to China, and he must cope with pirates, the French, and the Dutch before he arrives, in the sequel to *In Distant Waters.*
Genre(s): Sea Story.

Zumwalt, Eva

4409. *Love's Sweet Charity.* New York: Simon and Schuster, 1982. 192 pp.
When Lord Waverly anonymously sponsors Helena Dendridge for the London season after her father loses the family money, he falls in love with her.
Genre(s): Romance.

1919-1945

Ackroyd, Peter

4410. *English Music.* New York: Knopf, 1992. 399 pp.
Timothy Harcombe's father is a London spiritualist during the 1920s, but Timothy seems to have the greater gifts.
Genre(s): Domestic Fiction; Bildungsroman (Coming of Age).

Alexander, Kate

4411. *Fields of Battle.* New York: St. Martin's, 1981. 490 pp.
Although unsuited for each other, Rilla and Barnaby marry before the war in 1939, and while he serves in France, she becomes a nurse after the death of their infant son.
Genre(s): War Story; Spy Fiction.

Alyn, Marjory

◆ 4412. *The Sound of Anthems.* New York: St. Martin's, 1983. 209 pp.
Jennifer Marshall, 11, lives with her Catholic grandmother in Northern Ireland at the end of World War II, but she has difficulty understanding the shift of loyalties from country to religion when partisan feelings resurge.
Genre(s): War Story; Bildungsroman (Coming of Age).

Anthony, Evelyn

◆ 4413. *Exposure.* New York: HarperCollins, 1994. 256 pp.
Lord Western, Julia Hamilton's *Sunday Herald* publisher, has given her a story to investigate titled "Exposure," and her work takes her into Germany near the end of World War II.
Genre(s): War Story.

◆ 4414. *The Return.* New York: Coward-McCann, 1978. 255 pp.

Anna marries a White Russian count conspiring with others to overthrow the Soviet government by staging a kidnapping at Chartres.
Genre(s): Spy Fiction.

Bainbridge, Beryl

4415. *The Secret Glass.* New York: Braziller, 1974. 152 pp.
Nellie seems calm to outsiders, but she rules her family rigidly and even resorts to murder to keep the status quo in 1944.
Genre(s): War Story.

Barnard, Robert

◆ 4416. *The Skeleton in the Grass.* New York: Scribner's, 1988. 191 pp.
Sarah Causeley, governess to the pacificist Hallam family in Oxford, becomes involved in solving a murder in the family because of their political beliefs.
Genre(s): Political Fiction; Mystery.

Barstow, Stan

4417. *Next of Kin.* New York: Joseph, 1991. 296 pp.
As World War II ends, war widow Ella meets and rekindles her relationship with an old love, who has returned from battle and is now impotent.
Genre(s): War Story; Domestic Fiction.

Baxt, George

4418. *The Bette Davis Murder Case.* New York: St. Martin's, 1994. 200 pp.
While Bette Davis visits London, Agatha Christie helps a medium with the investigation of an anthropologists's murder.
Genre(s): Mystery.

Bell, Sam Hanna

4419. *The Hollow Ball.* Chester Springs, PA: Dufour, 1990. 248 pp.
David Minnis, 16, works in a Belfast clothing factory in the 1930s, and plays soccer to escape his life's monotony.
Genre(s): Sports Fiction.

Binchy, Maeve

4420. *Light a Penny Candle.* New York: Viking, 1983. 542 pp.
Evacuated from London during the Blitz, Elizabeth White, 10, goes to her mother's former schoolmate in Ireland, and there she begins a friendship with the daughter that helps them sustain themselves as young widows.
Genre(s): Domestic Fiction; War Story.

Blackstock, Charity

◆ 4421. *The Shirt Front.* New York: Coward-McCann, 1977. 223 pp.
Victoria Katona, 17, falls in love with a handsome journalist on the eve of World War II.
Genre(s): Mystery; Romance.

Bowling, Harry

4422. *Paragon Place.* North Pomfret, VT: Trafalgar Square, 1991. 384 pp.
During World War II, eight people with diverse interests and backgrounds live and interact in a building leased by the Catholic Church near the London docks.
Genre(s): War Story.

Boylan, Clare

4423. *Holy Pictures.* New York: Summit, 1983. 201 pp.
In the sequel to *11 Edward Street*, Daisy marries faithless Cecil Cantwell and their daughters later learn to face disappointment when Cecil's business fails after World War I.
Genre(s): Domestic Fiction.

Bragg, Melvyn

4424. *A Place in England.* New York: Knopf, 1971. 247 pp.
John Tallentire from *The Hired Man* begins to manage a pub in Cumberland, and he and his family observe the changes in the village from 1930 as they try to better themselves through education.
Genre(s): Family Saga.

Broderick, John

4425. *The Flood.* New York: Marion Boyers, 1987. 368 pp.
People in rural Ireland try to sell an Englishman land on the Shannon River, which they know will flood.
Genre(s): Domestic Fiction.

4426. *The Irish Magdalen.* New York: Marion Boyars, 1991. 269 pp.

In the 1930s, Canon Sharkey wins an illegal sweepstakes and funds a village church with it, but his housekeeper dies almost immediately, and an American arrives to extort some of the money.
Genre(s): Domestic Fiction.

Bryher

4427. *Beowulf.* New York: Pantheon, 1956. 201 pp.
The Warming Pan, a tea shop, becomes the meeting place for a variety of people who discuss their difficulties in war-time England until it is blitzed.
Genre(s): War Story.

Buchan, Elizabeth

4428. *Consider the Lily.* New York: Crown, 1993. 480 pp.
In post–World War I England, two women, one wealthy and the other vivacious, become attracted to and compete for the same man.
Genre(s): Love Story; Country Life.

Callison, Brian

4429. *A Flock of Ships.* New York: Putnam, 1970. 255 pp.
When four ships rush from England to Australia carrying cash and secrets about Pacific World War II battles, two of them are sunk, and those on board begin to suspect that one passenger must be a German spy.
Genre(s): War Story; Sea Story; Mystery.

Carey, Helen

4430. *On a Wing and a Prayer.* New York: Trafalgar Square, 1997. 407 pp.
Lady Helen de Burrel trains with the Inter-Services Research Bureau as a spy before going to France on a dangerous mission during Nazi occupation.
Genre(s): War Story; Romance.

Carr, James Lloyd

4431. *A Month in the Country.* New York: St. Martin's, 1980. 111 pp.
Tom Birkin comes to a small village after World War I to restore the local church's wall painting.

Carr, Philippa

◆ 4432. *The Gossamer Cord.* New York: Putnam, 1992. 368 pp.
In the late 1930s, the privileged twin sisters Violletta and Dorabella separate when Dorabella marries and goes to Cornwall to her husband's haunted estate. (*Series:* Daughters of England, 18)
Genre(s): Gothic Fiction; War Story.

◆ 4433. *We'll Meet Again.* New York: Putnam, 1993. 304 pp.
The Denver twins live on adjoining estates in Cornwall in World War II where one awaits her fiancé's return, and the other becomes a widow. (*Series:* Daughters of England, 19)
Genre(s): Love Story; Romance.

Cary, Joyce

4434. *Charley Is My Darling.* New York: Harper, 1960. 342 pp.
Charley regains position with the evacuees in the West Country after having his head shaved for lice.

Charteris, Hugo

4435. *The Coat.* New York: Harcourt, 1970. 224 pp.
Tim Loxley, 14, leaves England in 1941, with his philandering stepmother, wearing a coat with jewels sewn inside so that his aristocratic father may save his money if the Germans invade.
Genre(s): War Story; Adventure Story.

Chevalier, Paul

◆ 4436. *The Grudge.* New York: St. Martin's, 1981. 350 pp.
During World War II, while an escaped Luftwaffe pilot tries to hide from those who want him dead, a power feud erupts over him between Himmler and Goering.
Genre(s): War Story.

Clark, Catherine Clifton

4437. *The Saturday Treat.* New York: St. Martin's, 1993. 374 pp.
During World War II, Kate and Sally grow up, fall in love, and marry, one happy and the other not, but when Sally dies, Kate reexamines her life.
Genre(s): War Story.

Cleary, Jon

◆ 4438. *High Road to China.* New York: Morrow, 1977. 276 pp.
To save her father, Eve must arrive in China with an ancient statue, so she buys three surplus Bristol fighters to help her make the 8,000 mile trip.
Genre(s): Adventure Story; Sea Story.

Clifford, Francis

4439. *A Wild Justice.* New York: Coward-McCann, 1972. 142 pp.
When three resistance fighters take refuge in an abandoned hotel in Ireland during the rebellion, one of them is dying, and to save him, the other man sacrifices the girl to two guerilla fighters for food, and she plans revenge for her treatment.
Genre(s): War Story.

Collenette, Eric J.

4440. *Atlantic Encounter.* New York: Walker, 1987. 190 pp.
In World War II, a cruel Nazi U-boat commander, a British naval officer only interested in career advancement, and a merchant ship captain only serving the navy in wartime have a confrontation in the Atlantic.
Genre(s): War Story; Sea Story.

4441. *Ninety Feet to the Sun.* New York: Walker, 1986. 192 pp.
Germans cripple a British submarine off the coast of Norway in 1940, and Ben Grant, coxswain, must take command of the crew and make them perform their mission before returning to England.
Genre(s): War Story; Sea Story.

Collins, Larry

4442. *Fall from Grace.* New York: Simon and Schuster, 1985. 475 pp.
Catherine Pradier works with the British to cover up the Normandy invasion.
Genre(s): Spy Fiction.

Cookson, Catherine

4443. *Pure as the Lily.* Indianapolis: Bobbs-Merrill, 1973. 283 pp.
Mary Walton becomes the only source of support for her family at 16, and even though forced to marry after conceiving a child, she continues to give strength to her father, brother, and husband before and during World War II.
Genre(s): Domestic Fiction.

Cranny, Robert

4444. *On Us Thy Poor Children.* New York: Dial, 1982. 228 pp.
Jackie Guiney's lack of a future and his feelings toward his working-class family help him to realize that he cannot remain in Dublin during the 1940s.
Genre(s): Domestic Fiction.

Crosby, Caroline

◆ 4445. *The Haldanes.* New York: St. Martin's, 1993. 352 pp.
After Pauline Verity's father travels to India in the 1920s, her mother's family sends her to a Scottish boarding school where she begins investigating the disappearance of her mother's youngest child and her new stepfather.
Genre(s): Bildungsroman (Coming of Age).

Crowley, Elaine

4446. *The Ways of Women.* North Pomfret, VT: Trafalgar, 1993. 408 pp.
When Jack Harte and Barney Daly return to Ireland from World War I and reunite with their sweethearts, one of the women, Sarah, has developed ambitions that lead to their destruction.
Genre(s): Political Fiction.

Dahl, Roald

4447. *My Uncle Oswald.* New York: Knopf, 1980. 245 pp.
As a young Cambridge student, Oswald supports himself by selling aphrodisiacs and the semen from the world's greatest geniuses and surviving kings.
Genre(s): Humorous Fiction.

Daish, Elizabeth

4448. *Emma's War.* New York: David and Charles, 1990. 385 pp.
Emma begins her nurse's training in 1939, and when she moves to London during the war, she considers marrying a childhood sweetheart, but prefers romance to comfort in her life.
Genre(s): Medical Novel; Romance.

Darrell, Elizabeth

4449. *And in the Morning.* New York: St. Martin's, 1987. 608 pp.
Chris Sheridan from *At the Going Down of the Sun* works in military intelligence during World War II while his son joins the Royal Air Force and his daughter, a gifted painter, becomes an army corporal.
Genre(s): War Story; Romance.

◆ 4450. *The Flight of Flamingo.* New York: St. Martin's, 1989. 480 pp.
Three people meet in England during the 1930s and form an aviation business from which they make an important rescue in World War II.
Genre(s): War Story.

Dawson, Suleika

4451. *The Forsytes.* New York: Dell, 1996. 450 pp.
When the wife of Fleur Forsyte Mont's second cousin, Jon, dies, he becomes part of her life again.
Genre(s): Domestic Fiction; War Story.

DeCarlo, Elisa

◆ 4452. *Strong Spirits.* New York: Morrow, 1993. 160 pp.
In 1928, Aubrey Octavian Arbuthnot, penniless at his father's death, starts cavorting with his father's ghost.
Genre(s): Gothic Fiction.

Deeping, Warwick

4453. *Sorrell and Son.* New York: Knopf, 1925. 400 pp.
Stephen Sorrell has to rebuild his life after World War I and the departure of his wife so that he can give his son a gentleman's opportunites.

Deighton, Len

4454. *Goodbye, Mickey Mouse.* New York: Knopf, 1982. 337 pp.
Two American flyers stationed in England during World War II are superb aviators but have little else in common.
Genre(s): War Story; Spy Fiction.

◆ 4455. *XPD.* New York: Knopf, 1981. 339 pp.
Near the beginning of World War II, Winston Churchill proposes a deal to Hitler, which would be detrimental to Churchill's allies, but when it does not occur, some agents want the minutes of the meeting very badly.
Genre(s): War Story; Spy Fiction.

Delderfield, R. F.

4456. *The Avenue.* New York: Simon and Schuster, 1964. 1032 pp.
This double novel containing *The Dreaming Suburb* and *The Avenue Goes to War* concerns 20 people who live in a south London suburb from 1919 to 1947 and reveal Jim Carver's determination that the war had not have been in vain.
Genre(s): Domestic Fiction; War Story.

4457. *Charlie, Come Home.* New York: Simon and Schuster, 1976. 299 pp.
In a Welsh town in 1929, Charlie Pritchard rents from his employer and wife, and, while trying to avoid marriage to their dull daughter, he manages to seduce the attractive owner of the coffee shop.
Genre(s): Adventure Story; Domestic Fiction.

4458. *The Green Gauntlet.* New York: Simon and Schuster, 1968. 475 pp.
In the sequel to *A Horseman Riding By*, the Craddock family of Shallowford, Devon, survives the war years.
Genre(s): Domestic Fiction.

4459. *To Serve Them All My Days.* New York: Simon and Schuster, 1972. 638 pp.
A teacher at a public school in the West Country of England experiences both joy and tragedy.
Genre(s): Domestic Fiction.

Dickinson, Peter

4460. *The Yellow Room Conspiracy.* New York: Mysterious Press, 1994. 272 pp.
Against a backdrop of murder, Paul Ackerley and Lucy Vereker recall the incidences that brought them together through the years, including his tour of duty in World War II.
Genre(s): Mystery.

Donnelly, Frances

4461. *Shake Down the Stars.* New York: St. Martin's, 1988. 305 pp.
Three young women, all friends, find new life and independence during World War II.
Genre(s): War Story.

Dunmore, Spencer

4462. *Bomb Run.* New York: Morrow, 1971. 217 pp.
A Royal Air Force bomber crew undergoes a particularly dangerous night raid over Berlin midway through World War II.
Genre(s): War Story; Adventure Story.

4463. *The Last Hill.* New York: Morrow, 1973. 215 pp.
British defending a hill near Singapore in World War II expect reinforcements to arrive, and when told that Singapore has fallen, they refuse to surrender, and only David Cornish survives.
Genre(s): War Story.

◆ May be suitable for young adult readers

Dunn, Carola

4464. *Damsel in Distress.* New York: St. Martin's, 1997. 234 pp.
In 1923 Gloria travels with her wealthy father to England where, after she falls in love with Philip, she is kidnapped and Philip must ask his friend Daisy Dalrymple for help.
Genre(s): Mystery; Romance.

4465. *Dead in the Water.* New York: St. Martin's, 1998. 256 pp.
In 1923, Daisy Dalrymple goes to the Henley-on-Thames races with her fiancé, Alec Fletcher, but when a murder occurs on her cousin's team, she must forego her weekend of rest.
Genre(s): Mystery.

4466. *Death at Wentwater Court.* New York: St. Martin's, 1994. 216 pp.
When Daisy Dalrymple goes to Wentwater Court to write about the family at Christmas, another unwelcome guest arrives and is soon found floating under the ice on the lake's estate, but Daisy identifies ax marks on the ice and becomes invaluable in the 1922 investigation.
Genre(s): Mystery.

4467. *Murder on the Flying Scotsman.* New York: St. Martin's, 1997. 240 pp.
The Honourable Daisy Dalrymple is traveling on the Flying Scotsman in 1923 when someone murders the heir to a family fortune, and Daisy must help uncover the culprit.
Genre(s): Mystery.

4468. *Requiem for a Mezzo.* New York: St. Martin's, 1996. 212 pp.
Daisy Dalrymple sees her next-door neighbor die on stage from poisoning, and she and a partner investigate the opera star's death, in London during the 1920s.
Genre(s): Mystery.

4469. *The Winter Garden Mystery.* New York: St. Martin's, 1995. 224 pp.
In 1923, Daisy Dalrymple calls Scotland Yard after police near a British manor house arrest the innocent gardener for the murder of a pregnant maid.
Genre(s): Mystery.

Eden, Marc

4470. *The Spy.* New York: M. Evans, 1992. 192 pp.
Valerie Sinclair, chosen to become a spy because of her photographic memory, is given the mission of locating information about Germany's progress on the atomic bomb.
Genre(s): Spy Fiction; War Story.

Eden, Matthew

4471. *The Murder of Lawrence of Arabia.* New York: Crowell, 1979. 271 pp.
Lawrence of Arabia's motorcycle crashes under mysterious circumstances in 1935, and some believe that his associations with Palestinian Jews and Arabs as well as British Cabinet ministers indicate that he was murdered.
Genre(s): Biographical Fiction; Mystery.

Edwards, Anne

4472. *Wallis.* New York: Morrow, 1991. 478 pp.
Although born an American, Wallis Warfield attracts the attention of the Prince of Wales in London.
Genre(s): Adventure Story.

Elliott, Janice

4473. *Secret Places.* New York: St. Martin's, 1982. 192 pp.
Boarding-school girls center their fears of World War II on a German refugee, Laura Meister, and Patience Mackenzie tries to lessen the hostility.
Genre(s): War Story.

Everett, Peter

4474. *A Death in Ireland.* Boston: Little, Brown, 1981. 222 pp.
In 1920, Michael Collins hires an American mercenary to kill a British commander-in-chief.
Genre(s): War Story.

Facos, James

4475. *The Silver Lady.* New York: Atheneum, 1972. 365 pp.
The Eighth Air Force has its home base in England as it bombs European targets during World War II.
Genre(s): War Story.

Farrell, J. G.

4476. *Troubles.* New York: Knopf, 1971. 446 pp.
A collection of strange people remain at a dilapidated Irish seaside hotel during the Irish Rebellion (the Troubles) in 1919 before Sinn Fein members arrive.
Genre(s): Domestic Fiction; War Story.

Finlay, Lilian Roberts

4477. *Always in My Mind.* New York: St. Martin's, 1989. 352 pp.
Although Liz declares that she will love her Jewish scholar, Tadek Vashinsky, forever, Dublin society will not let a Catholic marry a Jew, and Tadek becomes trapped in Eastern Europe during World War II where he suffers before they are reunited.
Genre(s): Love Story; War Story.

Fleischer, Leonore

4478. *Shadowlands.* New York: Signet, 1993. 263 pp.
The Oxford don C. S. Lewis falls in love with American Joy Davidson and marries her, but she dies of cancer three years later.
Genre(s): Biographical Fiction; Christian Fiction; Domestic Fiction.

Follett, James

◆ 4479. *Churchill's Gold.* Boston: Houghton Mifflin, 1981. 218 pp.

When the British need reserves during World War II, they decide to move gold from South Africa, and the Germans plan to intercept the cargo.
Genre(s): War Story.

Forester, C. S.

4480. *The Last Nine Days of the Bismarck.* Boston: Little, Brown, 1959. 138 pp.
When the German battleship *Bismarck* breaks through British Naval defenses on its way to Brest, the whole British Home Fleet pursues.
Genre(s): Sea Story.

Forrester, Larry

◆ 4481. *Battle of the April Storm.* New York: John Day, 1970. Canada pp.
In 1940, the H.M.S. *Glowworm*, a destroyer, rams a German cruiser in the North Sea, which keeps the Germans from reaching England, and the German vessel commander recommends the dead British captain for the Victoria Cross.
Genre(s): War Story; Sea Story.

Frankau, Pamela

◆ 4482. *Sing for Your Supper.* New York: Random House, 1964. 311 pp.
A widow and her three children, who live in London theater society, cope with the arrival of a group of rich Americans in 1926.

◆ 4483. *Slaves of the Lamp.* New York: Random House, 1965. 405 pp.
In the sequel to *Sing for Your Supper*, Tom Weston exhibits healing powers that are, in the London theater circles of 1937, improperly appreciated.

Fraser, David

4484. *The Fortunes of War.* New York: Norton, 1985. 475 pp.
In 1937, a German and a British family become intertwined when two sons grow close at Oxford, but they face World War II with different perspectives.
Genre(s): War Story.

Gadney, Reg

4485. *Victoria.* New York: Coward-McCann, 1975. 279 pp.
On the east coast of England during World War II, Victoria Wymering becomes a widow but restarts her life and meets someone new.
Genre(s): War Story; Romance.

Gaffney, Robert

4486. *A World of Good.* New York: Dial, 1970. 352 pp.
David Keenan becomes involved in the campaigns of France during World War II, and his experiences mature his perspectives on life.
Genre(s): War Story; Bildungsroman (Coming of Age).

Gardiner, Judy

◆ 4487. *All on a Summer's Day.* New York: St. Martin's, 1992. 272 pp.
Miranda Whittaker and Natalie Ellenberg become friends in boarding school, and when an accident in which Miranda is involved kills Natalie's younger brother, Miranda's guilt forces her to go to France to search for the missing Natalie in the extermination camps.
Genre(s): War Story.

Gardner, John E.

4488. *The Secret Houses.* New York: Putnam, 1987. 399 pp.
A double agent destroys the French resistance group Tarot, and members of the Railton and Farthing families assist in the investigation. (*Series:* Secret Generations, 2)
Genre(s): Spy Fiction; Adventure Story; Family Saga.

Garfield, Brian

4489. *The Paladin.* New York: Simon and Schuster, 1979. 381 pp.
Winston Churchill hires Christopher Creighton, 16, to spy in Belgium prior to the Nazi occupation, and Creighton is so successful that he becomes a member of the Secret Service and trains for all special tasks.
Genre(s): Biographical Fiction; War Story.

Gaskin, Catherine

4490. *The Ambassador's Women.* New York: Scribner's, 1986. 537 pp.
Dena Ponrose and Ginny Glayton meet during their last month of pregnancy, bear daughters on the same day, and continue their friendship through World War II.
Genre(s): Domestic Fiction.

4491. *The Charmed Circle.* New York: Scribner's, 1989. 646 pp.
The Seymour family seems idyllic to outsiders, but its members face repeated tragedies during and after World War II.
Genre(s): War Story; Family Saga.

4492. *The Lynmara Legacy.* Garden City, NY: Doubleday, 1976. 398 pp.
After a lord spurns her as a poor Russian immigrant, Anne raises her daugther in America and later sends her back to England to claim her inheritance.
Genre(s): Romance.

4493. *Promises.* Garden City, NY: Doubleday, 1982. 471 pp.
As an abandoned child, Lily has little hope until the prosperous miller Black Jack rescues her.
Genre(s): Romance.

Gershon, Karen

◆ 4494. *The Bread of Exile.* New York: David and Charles, 1986. 184 pp.

◆ May be suitable for young adult readers

Inge Stein, 13, leaves her parents in Germany, where she was despised, to come to England, where people see her as an enemy.
Genre(s): War Story.

Gilbert, Anna

4495. *A Walk in the Wood.* New York: St. Martin's, 1989. 263 pp.
Kate Borrow replaces a male teacher called into the military in World War II and discovers that the village has secrets that she cannot unravel.
Genre(s): Romance.

◆ 4496. *The Wedding Guest.* New York: St. Martin's, 1993. 298 pp.
After the deaths of her parents, Elinor moves in with her two eccentric spinster aunts, who have been keeping family secrets.
Genre(s): Romance.

Goddard, Robert

4497. *Beyond Recall.* New York: Holt, 1998. 320 pp.
When Chris Napier returns to his Cornish town of Truro for a wedding in the 1960s, he witnesses a suicide which causes him to begin unraveling the tale of his family from before World War II.
Genre(s): Family Saga; War Story.

4498. *Closed Circle.* New York: Poseidon, 1993. 331 pp.
Two World War I veterans, Guy Horton and Max Wingate, participate in a variety of con games, and during the Depression, while courting an English heiress, they become involved in murder and discover who killed Archduke Franz Ferdinand.

4499. *A Debt of Dishonor.* New York: Simon and Schuster, 1992. 463 pp.
When architect Geoffrey Staddon reads in a 1923 London newspaper that his friend Consuela Caswell has been accused of poisoning her niece and attempting to murder her husband, he knows that he must defend her.
Genre(s): Mystery.

Golding, William

4500. *Darkness Visible.* New York: Farrar, Straus and Giroux, 1979. 265 pp.
Wartime firestorms in London mutilate a child, Matty, whose physical appearance keeps others from forming relationships with him.
Award(s): James Tate Black Award.
Genre(s): War Story.

4501. *The Pyramid.* New York: Harcourt, 1967. 183 pp.
Oliver lives in an English village from the 1920s through the late 1940s, living through many experiences as he matures.
Genre(s): Domestic Fiction.

Goodwin, Suzanne

4502. *While the Music Lasts.* New York: St. Martin's, 1993. 376 pp.
Four sisters, Julia, Vivien, Claire, and Isobelle, strictly raised in Brighton and London, survive their parents' divorce and mother's death in the 1920s, and in the 1930s, with both inheritance and financial difficulty, they gain strength in different ways.
Genre(s): Domestic Fiction.

Goudge, Elizabeth

4503. *The Bird in the Tree.* New York: Coward-McCann, 1940. 339 pp.
In 1938, on the Hampshire coast, the Eliot family lives in their 18th-century home, in which the grandmother's personality seems to have merged with the house.

Gower, Iris

◆ 4504. *Fiddler's Ferry.* New York: St. Martin's, 1988. 377 pp.
After ferryman Siona Llewelyn rescues Nerys Beynon from suicide in the sequel to *Morgan's Woman,* Nerys becomes involved with Siona and his seven sons following World War I.
Genre(s): Domestic Fiction; Romance.

◆ 4505. *Morgan's Woman.* New York: St. Martin's, 1986. 384 pp.
Catherine Preece, married to a man paralyzed during World War I, takes over the farm near Sweyn's Eye in the sequel to *Spinners' Wharf.*
Genre(s): Domestic Fiction; Romance.

Graham, James

4506. *A Game for Heroes.* New York: Doubleday, 1970. 240 pp.
When Owen Morgan returns to his German-occupied boyhood home on the Channel Islands, he leads a group of rangers in trying to destroy enemy shipping in the St. Pierre harbor.
Genre(s): War Story; Adventure Story.

Graham, Margaret

4507. *A Fragment of Time.* South Yarmouth, MA: Curley, 1992. 478 pp.
Helen, 18, defies her parents in the 1930s when she marries Heinze, an anti-Nazi photographer.
Genre(s): War Story; Romance.

Graham, Winston

4508. *The Merciless Ladies.* Garden City, NY: Doubleday, 1979. 257 pp.
In the 1920s, Paul Stafford, a promising artist, paints a portrait of Diana, and when he hangs it with portraits of courtesans, she sues him for libel.
Genre(s): Mystery.

Greeley, Andrew M.

◆ 4509. *Irish Gold.* New York: Forge, 1994. 334 pp.

Dermot Coyne goes to Dublin to investigate his parents' departure from Ireland during the Time of Troubles in 1922 and learns much about his Irish heritage from Nuala Anne McGrail.
Genre(s): Political Fiction; Romance.

Greene, Graham

4510. *The End of the Affair.* New York: Viking, 1951. 240 pp.
After a man is almost killed in a bombing raid, the married woman with whom he has been having an affair breaks away from him.
Genre(s): War Story; Religious Fiction.

4511. *The Ministry of Fear.* New York: Viking, 1943. 259 pp.
A band of fifth columnists captures a man who has killed his wife to relieve her misery.
Genre(s): War Story; Spy Fiction.

Guild, Nicholas

4512. *The Berlin Warning.* New York: Putnam, 1984. 349 pp.
British Intelligence hires David Steadman to steal and destroy an unread document from a German courier, but Steadman soon finds himself hunted by both governments.
Genre(s): War Story.

Hanley, Clifford

◆ 4513. *Another Street, Another Dance.* New York: St. Martin's, 1984. 320 pp.
Meg Macrae decides to educate herself and her children after World War I, in spite of their poverty and her alcoholic husband.
Genre(s): War Story; Domestic Fiction.

Harris, Robert

◆ 4514. *Enigma.* New York: Random House, 1995. 320 pp.
Tom, a mathematical genius who is somewhat delicate, has a mental breakdown from working at code breaking in World War II, but his supervisor lures him back to work on the Enigma code of the Germans.
Genre(s): War Story; Spy Fiction.

Harrison, Sarah

4515. *A Flower That's Free.* New York: Simon and Schuster, 1984. 766 pp.
In the sequel to *The Flowers of the Field*, Kate Kingsley, born in Paris but reared in Kenya, travels to England in 1936 to meet family members and friends, and she remains there through World War II.
Genre(s): Domestic Fiction; War Story; Romance.

Hawkes, Ellen

4516. *The Shadow of the Moth.* New York: St. Martin's, 1983. 279 pp.

Virginia Woolf investigates the apparent suicide of a Belgian woman and discovers that it is murder.
Genre(s): Mystery.

Hennessy, Max

4517. *Back to Battle.* New York: Atheneum, 1980. 297 pp.
In the sequel to *The Dangerous Years*, Ginger Maguire decides to fight in the Spanish Civil War before also participating in all of World War II's sea battles.
Genre(s): War Story; Adventure Story; Sea Story.

4518. *The Challenging Heights.* New York: Atheneum, 1983. 237 pp.
After World War I, in the sequel to *The Bright Blue Sky*, Nicholas Dicken Quinney travels around the world looking for adventure.
Genre(s): Adventure Story.

4519. *The Iron Stallions.* New York: Atheneum, 1982. 247 pp.
In the sequel to *Blunted Lance*, Joshua Goff serves in the 19th Lancers, a cavalry regiment changing its allegiance from horses to tanks while fighting in the Middle East and France during World War II.
Genre(s): War Story; Family Saga; Adventure Story.

4520. *Once More the Hawks.* New York: Atheneum, 1984. 256 pp.
Dicken Quinney, a veteran of World War I, happens to be in Berlin as Hitler invades Poland, in Paris for the French invasion, and in Africa by 1945, in the sequel to *The Challenging Heights*.
Genre(s): War Story; Adventure Story.

Hersey, John

4521. *The War Lover.* New York: Knopf, 1959. 404 pp.
Bowman, Marrow's copilot, tells the story of the last mission he and the war lover, Buzz Marrow, flew.
Genre(s): War Story.

Heyer, Georgette

4522. *Penhallow.* Garden City, NY: Doubleday, 1943. 309 pp.
In Cornwall of the 1930s, many of Adam Penhallow's relatives might have murdered him, but the question is why his second wife actually did the deed.
Genre(s): Romance.

Higgins, Jack

◆ 4523. *Cold Harbour.* New York: Simon and Schuster, 1990. 318 pp.
English intelligence officers hide a World War II operation in Cold Harbour, a small village on the English Channel, by impersonating Germans.
Genre(s): Spy Fiction; Adventure Story.

◆ 4524. *The Eagle Has Flown.* New York: Simon and Schuster, 1991. 335 pp.
In the sequel to *The Eagle Has Landed*, the Germans ask a man to parachute into England and free a prisoner while

the British thwart a plot to assassinate Hitler in fear that Himmler will take over.
Genre(s): War Story; Spy Fiction.

◆ **4525.** ***The Eagle Has Landed.*** New York: Holt, Rinehart, and Winston, 1975. 352 pp.
A small force of German paratroopers lands on the Norfolk coast during 1943 and attempts to kidnap Churchill who is visiting nearby.
Genre(s): War Story; Spy Fiction.

◆ **4526.** ***Night of the Fox.*** New York: Simon and Schuster, 1986. 316 pp.
Three impostors pose as Germans in German-occupied Jersey after a wounded American soldier, who knows about the impending Normandy invasion, washes onto shore.
Genre(s): War Story; Spy Fiction.

Hough, Richard

◆ **4527.** ***Wings Against the Sky.*** New York: Morrow, 1979. 297 pp.
During World War II, Keith Stewart, a Royal Air Force pilot, and Mike, his American friend, fly for the Allies and try to capture a traitor.
Genre(s): War Story.

Household, Geoffrey

4528. ***Rogue Male.*** Boston: Little, Brown, 1939. 191 pp.
The Rogue Male attempts to assassinate Hitler, but secret agents continue to search for him after he escapes to his home country of England.
Genre(s): Spy Fiction.

Howard, Elizabeth Jane

4529. ***Casting Off.*** London: Macmillan, 1995. 482 pp.
Between 1937 and 1947, the Cazalet cousins, brothers, and others live through World War II without servants and focus on food and clothes, or the lack thereof. (*Series:* Cazalet Chronicles, 4)
Genre(s): Domestic Fiction; War Story.

4530. ***Confusion.*** New York: Pocket Books, 1994. 341 pp.
In March 1942, the sequel to *Marking Time* finds the oldest three Cazalet cousins leaving home for marriage and jobs in London.
Genre(s): Domestic Fiction; War Story.

4531. ***The Light Years.*** New York: Pocket Books, 1990. 434 pp.
The three Cazalet brothers and their families come to Sussex for their annual holiday in 1937.
Genre(s): Family Saga.

4532. ***Marking Time.*** New York: Pocket Books, 1992. 405 pp.
In the sequel to *Light Years*, the nine middle-class Cazalet cousins go to their grandparents in Sussex when Britain enters World War II in 1939.
Genre(s): Domestic Fiction; War Story.

Hughes, Terence

◆ **4533.** ***The Day They Stole the Queen Mary.*** New York: Morrow, 1983. 348 pp.
Winston Churchill comes to meet Franklin D. Roosevelt aboard the *Queen Mary* in 1943, and with them on the ship are 1,000 Nazi prisoners-of-war.
Genre(s): War Story; Sea Story.

Huth, Angela

4534. ***Land Girls.*** New York: St. Martin's, 1996. 384 pp.
Three women become land girls (volunteer farm workers) during World War II and, even with their different backgrounds, they all find themselves attached to the farm and its inhabitants.
Genre(s): War Story; Love Story.

Hyde, Christopher

4535. ***A Gathering of Saints.*** New York: Pocket Books, 1996. 417 pp.
While Nazi planes shell London in 1940, bodies appear in the most recently bombed areas, and Scotland Yard's Detective Inspector Morris Black discovers communists and the secret Ultra in his search for a serial killer.
Genre(s): War Story; Mystery.

Hylton, Sara

4536. ***The Last Reunion.*** New York: St. Martin's, 1993. 474 pp.
In the sequel to *The Chosen Ones*, five girls who met at an English boarding school lead very different lives as adults, even though they keep in touch.

4537. ***Melissa.*** New York: St. Martin's, 1996. 304 pp.
During World War II, Alistair and Melissa are evacuated from London to a town where they become friends with Ginny, and Melissa becomes an opera star who eventually steals Alistair from Ginny.
Genre(s): War Story.

◆ **4538.** ***Reckmire Marsh.*** New York: St. Martin's, 1995. 438 pp.
Joanna Albemarle goes to Reckmire when her parents leave England, and, later, after the war begins, she sees her father for the last time, but her troubles have only begun because she makes poor decisions in her management of the manor.
Genre(s): Romance; War Story.

4539. ***Tomorrow's Rainbow.*** New York: St. Martin's, 1988. 488 pp.
Kathleen O'Donovan rises from cleaning a cotton mill to operating an antique and furniture restoration shop in Manchester between the wars.
Genre(s): Domestic Fiction.

Ibbotson, Eva

4540. ***A Song for Summer.*** New York: St. Martin's, 1998. 288 pp.

Suffragists raise Ellen, who travels to Austria to transform a boarding school and meets Marek, a school handyman and composer, but the war separates them.
Genre(s): Romance; War Story.

Irwin, Robert

4541. *Exquisite Corpse.* New York: Pantheon, 1997. 240 pp.
Caspar, member of the Serapion Brotherhood, believes passionately in the Surrealist movement in London during the 1930s.
Genre(s): Political Fiction; War Story.

Ishiguro, Kazuo

4542. *The Remains of the Day.* New York: Knopf, 1989. 245 pp.
Stevens, an elderly butler, hopes to rise to the top of his profession, and he remains stoic and unemotional at his father's death and neglects the opportunity to pursue a relationship with a former housekeeper.
Award(s): Booker Prize.
Genre(s): Love Story; Domestic Fiction.

Jagger, Brenda

4543. *A Winter's Child.* New York: Morrow, 1985. 468 pp.
In 1919, Claire Swanfield returns home from four years of combat nursing and becomes an assistant to a hotel manager instead of staying with her late husband's family.
Genre(s): Domestic Fiction.

James, Elizabeth

4544. *Life Class.* New York: St. Martin's, 1987. 368 pp.
After World War I, Sarah Morgan leaves her Welsh mining village for London and Paris where she paints and falls in love.
Genre(s): Romance.

Jenkins, Robin

4545. *The Cone-Gatherers.* Marlboro, NJ: Taplinger, 1981. 223 pp.
When the cone-gatherers come to the area where the gamekeeper John Duror works during World War II, he hates their attitudes toward him.
Genre(s): War Story.

Johnston, Jennifer

◆ 4546. *Fool's Sanctuary.* New York: Viking, 1988. 132 pp.
When Andrew returns from World War I, he meets his sister Miranda's boyfriend, an IRA member, and ideals turn into bloodshed.
Genre(s): Domestic Fiction.

Jolley, Elizabeth

4547. *My Father's Moon.* New York: Harper and Row, 1989. 171 pp.

Veronica Wright, a nurse in wartime Britain, becomes more introspective as the war progresses.
Genre(s): War Story.

Jones, Merle

4548. *Woman's Estate.* New York: St. Martin's, 1989. 528 pp.
That Diana Hartley's father is a spy leads her to leave London for the Far East with her childhood sweetheart to help him manage a rubber plantation, but when World War II begins, she returns to England.
Genre(s): War Story; Romance.

Jordan, Neil

4549. *Nightlines.* New York: Random House, 1995. 194 pp.
Donal Gore enlists in the Spanish Civil War after his father withdraws from the Irish troubles, but realizes his mistake and tries to reconcile with his father when he returns from Spain and prison.
Genre(s): Political Fiction; War Story.

Joseph, Marie

◆ 4550. *The Listening Silence.* New York: St. Martin's, 1983. 160 pp.
During World War II, Sally Barnes who is deaf, reads lips to discover the news, including the disappearance of her love David in Belgium and the death of her brother in North Africa.

Kennedy, Lena

4551. *Maggie.* New York: Paddington, 1979. 336 pp.
After being born into poverty in the East End of London, Maggie survives from the Depression through World War II.
Genre(s): War Story.

King, Laurie R.

◆ 4552. *The Beekeeper's Apprentice: Or, On the Segregation of the Queen.* New York: St. Martin's, 1994. 347 pp.
Sherlock Holmes and his young assistant, Mary Russell, solve a kidnapping after World War I, become targets for bombers.
Genre(s): Mystery.

◆ 4553. *A Letter of Mary.* New York: St. Martin's, 1997. 288 pp.
Oxford theologian Mary Russell's friend, Dorothy Ruskin, brings a letter from Palestine in 1923, which might have been written by Mary Magdalene, but when Ruskin dies soon after in a traffic accident, Russell, wife of Sherlock Holmes, thinks it is murder.
Genre(s): Mystery.

◆ 4554. *A Monstrous Regiment of Women.* New York: St. Martin's, 1995. 326 pp.

◆ May be suitable for young adult readers

In the 1920s, Sherlock Holmes aids the young Mary Russell as she investigates murders in the group gathered around the feminist preacher Margery Childe.
Genre(s): Mystery.

◆ 4555. *The Moor.* New York: St. Martin's, 1998. 304 pp.
Sherlock Holmes and his young wife, Mary Russell, go to Devonshire to investigate an ancient family curse at the request of Holmes's friend, parson, and folklorist Sabine Baring-Gould.
Genre(s): Mystery.

Kuniczak, W. S.

4556. *Valedictory.* Garden City, NY: Doubleday, 1983. 389 pp.
In the sequel to *The March*, Polish fighter-pilots reach England, from where they go on bombing mission and shoot down 1,500 German planes.
Genre(s): War Story.

Laine, Annabel

◆ 4557. *The Reluctant Heiress.* New York: Doubleday, 1978. 252 pp.
A young heiress wants to find her biological father, and an earl who likes to solve other people's problems decides to help her.
Genre(s): Romance.

Larsen, Gaylord

4558. *Dorothy and Agatha.* New York: Dutton, 1990. 230 pp.
In the 1930s Dorothy Sayers arrives home and finds a dead man whose note says that he and she were lovers, and in the ensuing investigation involving members of the Dectection Club, including Agatha Christie, Sayers is revealed as a liar.
Genre(s): Biographical Fiction.

Lawton, John

4559. *Black Out.* New York: Viking, 1995. 342 pp.
Frederick Troy identifies an arm found in London in 1944, and begins to investigate the murder.
Genre(s): Mystery.

Leavitt, David

◆ 4560. *While England Sleeps.* New York: Viking, 1993. 304 pp.
After upper-class Brian Botsford falls in love with lower-class Edward, they stay together until Edward goes to fight in the Spanish Civil War.
Genre(s): War Story; Love Story.

Lee, Maureen

4561. *Through the Storm.* North Pomfret, VT: Trafalgar Square, 1998. 330 pp.
Women who lose their husbands and face raising their families alone become attracted to American soldiers.
Genre(s): War Story; Domestic Fiction.

Lefebure, Molly

4562. *Blitz!* New York: St. Martin's, 1989. 352 pp.
Four families in the London blitz during World War II exhibit great courage.
Genre(s): War Story.

4563. *Thunder in the Sky.* New York: Victor Gollancz, 1993. 352 pp.
After the Americans arrive in East Anglia in 1942, they destroy Lorna Washborne's home to build an airfield, and Lorna begins an affair with the base commander.
Genre(s): War Story.

Leland, Mary

4564. *The Killeen.* New York: Atheneum, 1986. 136 pp.
In Ireland during the 1930s, Margaret, a servant, gives up her illegitimate child for the sake of his future while she, her employer, and her brother try to live decently with few resources.
Genre(s): Domestic Fiction.

Lide, Mary

◆ 4565. *Polmena Cove.* New York: St. Martin's, 1995. 240 pp.
Lily Polleven becomes upset when she finds a squatter on the nearby Cornwall shore, but when she hears of plans to develop the area, she supports Richard Chote until he proves a legal claim to the land.
Genre(s): Romance.

◆ 4566. *Tregaran.* New York: St. Martin's, 1989. 239 pp.
Phil, a miner, loves Joyalyn Tregaran, heiress of the Tregaran estate, but her grandmother refuses to let them marry because of Phil's family, but World War II comes to their rescue in the sequel to *The Legacy of Tregaran.*
Genre(s): Family Saga; Romance; War Story.

Livingston, Nancy

4567. *Two Sisters.* New York: St. Martin's, 1994. 585 pp.
After Gertie and Rose Bossom lose their parents, brother, and financial support in World War I, Gertie waits for a man not yet identified to rescue her and Rose earns money for typing lessons, marries, and goes to Australia.
Genre(s): Domestic Fiction.

Lovesey, Peter

4568. *The False Inspector Dew.* New York: Pantheon, 1982. 251 pp.
In the 1920s, the dentist Walter Baranov and his lover murder his wife and flee on the luxury liner *Mauretania*, but when a murder occurs on board the ship, Baranor's alias of Scotland Yard Inspector Dew makes him the logical investigator of the crime.
Genre(s): Mystery.

◆ 4569. *Waxwork.* New York: Pantheon, 1978. 239 pp.

Sergeant Cribb of Scotland Yard investigates Miriam Cromer's confession to the murder of her husband with potassium cyanide.
Genre(s): Mystery.

MacInnes, Helen

4570.*Above Suspicion.* Boston: Little, Brown, 1941. 339 pp.
In 1939, an Oxford don and his wife pretend to be vacationing in Germany when, in reality, they are looking for an anti-Nazi agent.
Genre(s): War Story; Spy Fiction.

MacLean, Alistair

◆ 4571. *San Andreas.* Garden City, NY: Doubleday, 1985. 326 pp.
When a British hospital ship *San Andreas* runs into trouble on its way from Halifax to Aberdeen, bo's'n Archie McKinnon steers the ship and tries to find out why the Germans have such interest in it.
Genre(s): War Story; Sea Story.

Magorian, Michelle

◆ 4572. *Good Night, Mr Tom.* New York: HarperCollins, 1982. 318 pp.
Willie Beech is eight when evacuated from London to a small town and the care of an older widower during World War II, and his stay with Mr. Tom frees him from the mentally unstable whims of his mother.
Award(s): Guardian Award.
Genre(s): War Story.

Malpass, Eric Lawson

4573.*The Wind Brings Up the Rain.* New York: St. Martin's, 1981. 248 pp.
During the days between the two world wars, Benbow grows up in England.
Genre(s): Bildungsroman (Coming of Age).

Manning, Olivia

4574.*The Wind Changes.* New York: Virago, 1992. 320 pp.
In 1921, the young revolutionary Sean persuades Riordan to come out of hiding and join a Catholic revolt in Dublin, which is still damaged from being burned in the Easter Week Rising of 1916.
Genre(s): Romance; Political Fiction.

Marsh, Jean

◆ 4575. *The House of Eliott.* New York: St. Martin's, 1994. 265 pp.
In the 1920s, Beatrice and Evangeline Eliott decide to open a dressmaking shop because they have too little money left from their father to survive.
Genre(s): Domestic Fiction.

Masters, John

4576.*High Command.* New York: Morrow, 1984. 403 pp.

Bill Miller rises in the British military to become a general in World War II after serving in World War I and India.
Genre(s): Epic Literature; War Story.

4577.*The Ravi Lancers.* Garden City, NY: Doubleday, 1972. 447 pp.
A regiment of Indians living in Britain fights in World War I under an English officer, Captain Warren Bateman, but his second-in-command, Lord Krishna Ram, is an Indian prince.
Genre(s): War Story.

McCarry, Charles

4578.*The Last Supper.* New York: Dutton, 1983. 389 pp.
When the Gestapo detains Hubbard Christopher's Prussian wife in 1939, he becomes a British spy in order to find her.
Genre(s): Spy Fiction.

McCarthy, Thomas

4579.*Asya and Christine.* Chester Springs, PA: Dufour, 1992. 217 pp.
Paudie Glenville, deputy in Cappoquin, County Waterford, enters a political war when the British decide to execute a local boy for killing a British soldier, and his daughter and a Jewish refugee become romantically involved with men loyal to the wrong side.
Genre(s): Political Fiction; War Story.

McCutchan, Philip

◆ 4580. *Cameron Comes Through.* New York: St. Martin's, 1986. 157 pp.
In the sequel to *Cameron, Ordinary Seaman*, Donald Cameron sails on a British destroyer in the Mediterranean where he must rescue a man who has information about the Nazi attack on Russia during World War II in 1941.
Genre(s): War Story.

◆ 4581. *Cameron in Command.* New York: St. Martin's, 1983. 163 pp.
In the sequel to *Orders for Cameron*, Donald Cameron's first command is to protect the Falklands from Japanese attack.
Genre(s): War Story.

4582.*Cameron in the Gap.* New York: St. Martin's, 1982. 155 pp.
Donald Cameron sails in rough Mediterranean seas for the Royal Navy, in the sequel to *Cameron of Castle Bay*, while German and Italian planes fly overhead.
Genre(s): War Story.

4583.*Cameron's Chase.* New York: St. Martin's, 1986. 182 pp.
Cameron commands a World War II destroyer that helps to escort supply and troop ships across the Atlantic when a new German warship, *Attila*, destroys his antenna, in the sequel to *Cameron's Raid.*
Genre(s): War Story; Sea Story.

◆ May be suitable for young adult readers

◆ **4584.** *Cameron's Commitment.* New York: St. Martin's, 1989. 190 pp.
Donald Cameron captains a light cruiser in World War II and takes it along the coast of occupied France to bomb Dieppe.
Genre(s): War Story.

4585. *Cameron's Convoy.* London: Barker, 1982. 243 pp.
Donald Cameron takes the *Castile* from Portsmouth to Northern Scotland during World War II for a refitting before going to Dieppe to rescue the British leader of a resistance group in the sequel to *Lieutenant Cameron RNVR.*
Genre(s): War Story; Sea Story.

◆ **4586.** *Cameron's Crossing.* New York: St. Martin's, 1993. 171 pp.
In the sequel to *Cameron's Commitment*, Donald Cameron takes charge in the mid-Atlantic when a storm disables the ship on which he sails and the commander proves unable to save the ship and its crew.
Genre(s): War Story; Sea Story.

◆ **4587.** *Cameron's Raid.* New York: St. Martin's, 1985. 184 pp.
Lieutenant Donald Cameron takes his old P-class boat into the Brest port after others have failed in an attempt to blow up the German U-boat pens, in the sequel to *Cameron and the Kaiserhof.*
Genre(s): War Story.

◆ **4588.** *Cameron's Troop Lift.* New York: St. Martin's, 1986. 185 pp.
In the Pacific, in the sequel to *Cameron's Chase*, Lieutenant Commander Donald Cameron rescues a Japanese captain and finds that the Japanese are transporting British prisoners-of-war to Rangoon to be Burmese slave laborers, and he must decide how to save them without risk to his own crew.
Genre(s): War Story.

◆ **4589.** *The Convoy Commodore.* New York: St. Martin's, 1987. 186 pp.
Commodore Mason Kemp has convoy duty between Scotland and Halifax during World War II, where he faces German surface ships as well as submarines.
Genre(s): War Story; Sea Story.

4590. *Convoy East.* New York: St. Martin's, 1989. 192 pp.
In the sequel to *Convoy South*, John Mason Kemp sails from Britain to Malta taking supplies to British troops during World War II and faces the German Luftwaffe and the Italian navy.
Genre(s): War Story; Sea Story.

4591. *Convoy Homeward.* New York: St. Martin's, 1992. 182 pp.
In the sequel to *Convoy of Fear*, Commodore Kemp is traveling from India to Scotland with a convoy of supply ships and warships holding German prisoners-of-war and British expatriates when he meets a Nazi surface raider.
Genre(s): Sea Story; War Story.

4592. *Convoy North.* New York: St. Martin's, 1988. 177 pp.
In 1942, in the sequel to *The Convoy Commodore*, John Mason Kemp, commander of a large troop convoy traveling from Australia to America, carries a canvas bag with top-secret intelligence.
Genre(s): Sea Story; War Story.

4593. *Convoy of Fear.* New York: St. Martin's, 1990. 190 pp.
In the sequel to *Convoy East*, Commodore Kemp crosses the Mediterranean and goes through the Suez Canal on his way to Ceylon, where he battles the Axis forces, cholera, and a typhoon.
Genre(s): War Story; Sea Story.

4594. *Convoy South.* New York: St. Martin's, 1988. 187 pp.
The sequel to *Convoy North* finds Commodore John Kemp meeting an Australian official who questions him about Japanese activity as he prepares to command a convoy of ships from Australia to the United States.
Genre(s): Sea Story; War Story.

4595. *Lieutenant Cameron RNVR.* New York: St. Martin's, 1985. 159 pp.
In the sequel to *Cameron Comes Through*, Cameron serves on a World War II cruiser, which sinks, leaving the captain disabled and Cameron in command while he faces rescue by a German transport ship.
Genre(s): War Story; Sea Story.

4596. *Orders for Cameron.* New York: St. Martin's, 1983. 154 pp.
In the sequel to *Cameron in the Gap*, Donald Cameron pilots his corvette to escort some of the British North African invasion ships, and he meets the Nazis.
Genre(s): War Story.

McGrath, Eamonn

4597. *The Clay Grew Tall.* New York: Herder and Herder, 1972. 245 pp.
John Foley grows up in Ireland during World War II, where he experiences first love, his family, and school life.
Genre(s): War Story; Bildungsroman (Coming of Age).

McGraw, Milena

4598. *After Dunkirk.* Boston: Houghton Mifflin, 1998. 480 pp.
The Germans capture and torture Flying Officer Luthie after shooting him down in the battle of Dunkirk, and when the war is over, he tries to make sense of his earlier life and his suffering during the war.
Genre(s): War Story.

Meyer, Nicholas

◆ **4599.** *The Seven-Per-Cent Solution.* New York: Dutton, 1974. 253 pp.

Dr. Watson dictates his memoirs in 1939 from a nursing home and recounts fabrications about Sherlock Holmes before Holmes was introduced to Freud.
Award(s): Dagger Award.
Genre(s): Mystery.

Miller, Hugh

4600. *Snow on the Wind.* New York: St. Martin's, 1988. 205 pp.
In the sequel to *The District Nurse*, Megan Roberts works with poor miners' families in Wales, in 1927.
Genre(s): Medical Novel; Domestic Fiction.

Mitchell, James

4601. *Leading Lady.* North Pomfret, VT: Trafalgar Square, 1994. 528 pp.
Jane Whitcomb, wealthy socialite who helps others, refuses to marry Charles, while some of their town's inhabitants go to fight in Spain. (*Series:* When the Boat Comes In, 2)
Genre(s): War Story.

Moline, Karen

4602. *Belladonna.* New York: Warner, 1998. 501 pp.
After His Lordship buys Isabella Ariel Nickerson in 1935 at a wealthy private club to satisfy his sexual appetites, she decides to extract revenge.
Genre(s): Horror; Erotic Literature.

Monsarrat, Nicholas

4603. *The Cruel Sea.* New York: Knopf, 1951. 509 pp.
Crews on the corvette *Compass Rose* and the frigate *Saltash* fight at sea during World War II.
Genre(s): War Story; Sea Story.

Moorcock, Michael

4604. *Mother London.* New York: Harmony, 1989. 496 pp.
David Mummery, Josef Kiss, and Mary Gasalee work and live in London from 1940, walking the streets and recording the sights and sounds.
Genre(s): War Story.

Moore, Brian

4605. *The Emperor of Ice-Cream.* New York: Viking, 1975. 250 pp.
Gavin Burke of Belfast fails his entrance exams to college, but after he joins the Irish Air Raid Precautions at the beginning of World War II, people perceive him differently.
Genre(s): War Story.

Mosley, Nicholas

4606. *Hopeful Monsters.* Elmwood Park, IL: Dalkey Archives, 1990. 550 pp.
Max and Eleanor meet as students at a production of *Faust* and continue to cross paths while encountering such people as Rosa Luxembourg, Albert Einstein, Adolph Hitler, and Karl Jung.
Award(s): Whitbread Book of the Year.
Genre(s): Love Story.

Mullally, Frederic

4607. *Clancy.* New York: Morrow, 1972. 443 pp.
Frank Clancy, member of a poor Irish-Catholic family in London beginning in the 1920s, becomes a socialist and fights in the Spanish Civil War until he becomes eminent and must reexamine his values.
Genre(s): Bildungsroman (Coming of Age).

Nicole, Christopher

4608. *The Last Battle.* Hampton, NH: Severn House, 1993. 352 pp.
The British Dawson family and the Japanese Hirada family, related through marriage, suffer the difficulties of war and accusations of treason.
Genre(s): War Story.

Nunez, Sigrid

4609. *The Marmoset of Bloomsbury.* New York: HarperCollins, 1998. 176 pp.
In 1934, the Rothschilds give Virginia and Leonard Woolf a sickly monkey, and Leonard carries the creature everywhere, including Germany where they encounter Jew-hating Nazis.
Genre(s): Domestic Fiction; Biographical Fiction.

O'Brien, Kate

4610. *The Last of Summer.* North Pomfret, VT: Virago, 1994. 243 pp.
Angele Maury returns to Ireland in the last summer before World War II where she must settle differences with her family and choose between the love of two men.
Genre(s): War Story.

O'Leary, Elizabeth

4611. *A House at War.* New York: St. Martin's, 1995. 247 pp.
Bea and Evie of the House of Elliot struggle to keep their design and dressmaking business and their families afloat during World War II.
Genre(s): War Story; Domestic Fiction.

Pargeter, Edith

4612. *She Goes to War.* London: Headline, 1989. 313 pp.
A young British soldier, Jim Bension, goes with the 4th Midshires to Libya to fight the Italian troops in World War II.
Genre(s): War Story.

Pearce, Mary Emily

◆ 4613. *The Land Endures.* New York: St. Martin's, 1978. 248 pp.

The sequel to *Apple Tree Lean Down* follows the Wayman family on Holland Farm in England as they recover from the mother's unexpected death after World War I.
Genre(s): Domestic Fiction.

◆ 4614. *Seedtime and Harvest.* New York: St. Martin's, 1982. 266 pp.
In the sequel to *The Land Endures*, Linn Mercybright and Charlie Truscotts have difficulties dealing with Linn's son during World War II.
Genre(s): War Story; Domestic Fiction.

Phelan, Tom

4615. *In the Season of the Daisies.* New York: Four Walls Eight Windows, 1996. 226 pp.
A young man who witnessed the murder of his brother by the IRA and lost his eye during the attack finally comes of age the night before the dedication of a new church wing financed by the people after being hounded by the local priest.
Genre(s): Domestic Fiction.

Phillips, Dee

◆ 4616. *The Coconut Kiss.* New York: Norton, 1983. 192 pp.
Flora, seven in the late 1920s, has to face children at a new school, including the older Ruby, a disturbed child.

Phillips, Michael R., and Judith Pella

4617. *Shadows over Stonewycke.* Minneapolis, MN: Bethany House, 1988. 400 pp.
Espionage and intrigue infiltrate Stonewycke before World War II. (*Series:* Stonewycke Legacy, 2)
Genre(s): Christian Fiction; War Story.

4618. *Stranger at Stonewycke.* Minneapolis, MN: Bethany House, 1987. 350 pp.
The family lives between the wars in Scotland. (*Series:* Stonewycke Legacy, 1)
Genre(s): Christian Fiction.

Pilcher, Rosamund

4619. *Coming Home.* New York: St. Martin's, 1996. 330 pp.
During World War II, some people experience friendship and romance.
Genre(s): Romance; War Story.

Pope, Dudley

4620. *Convoy.* New York: Walker, 1987. 335 pp.
Ned Yorke of the British Navy goes to the North Atlantic to investigate convoy sinkings and to discover how the German submarines penetrate without being detected.
Genre(s): War Story; Sea Story.

Porter, Margaret Evans

4621. *The Proposal.* New York: Avon, 1998. 384 pp.

Sophie Pinnock plans to redesign Lord Bevington's extensive gardens, but she finds herself involved in much more.
Genre(s): Romance.

Powell, Anthony

4622. *A Dance to the Music of Time: First Movement.* Boston: Little, Brown, 1962. 718 pp.
Three novels, *A Question of Upbringing*, *A Buyer's Market*, and *The Acceptance World*, show friends who meet at Eton in 1921, attend Oxford, and face the Depression together.

4623. *A Dance to the Music of Time: Second Movement.* Boston: Little, Brown, 1964. 712 pp.
At Lady Molly's, *Casanova's Chinese Restaurant*, and *The Kindly Ones* present friends hearing of the Spanish Civil War, the Abdication, and the intensification of hostilities leading to World War II.

4624. *A Dance to the Music of Time: Third Movement.* Boston: Little, Brown, 1971. 715 pp.
The third movement books, *The Valley of Bones*, *The Soldier's Art*, and *The Military Philosophers*, reveal individuals and their responses to World War II both in the military and at home.

Ramrus, Al, and John Shaner

◆ 4625. *The Ludendorff Pirates.* Garden City, NY: Doubleday, 1978. 233 pp.
In World War II, a German submarine (U-boat) rescues British special forces on a ship holding papers previously taken from the Germans.
Genre(s): War Story.

Reeman, Douglas

4626. *His Majesty's U-Boat.* New York: Putnam, 1973. 320 pp.
Steven Marshall gets command of a captured German submarine to carry out special missions against the enemy.
Genre(s): War Story.

4627. *HMS Saracen.* New York: Putnam, 1966. 320 pp.
In World War II, a naval officer becomes commander of the very ship on which he served in World War I.
Genre(s): Sea Story; War Story.

4628. *A Prayer for the Ship.* New York: Putnam, 1973. 254 pp.
Clive Royce, naive and new in the Royal navy, becomes proficient and proves his courage in battle and he obtains his own command in World War II.
Genre(s): War Story; Sea Story.

4629. *Rendezvous—South Atlantic.* New York: Putnam, 1972. 320 pp.
Commander Lindsay takes command of another ship after losing his previous craft in battle with a German raider in World War II.
Genre(s): War Story; Sea Story.

◆ 4630. *A Ship Must Die.* New York: Morrow, 1979. 284 pp.
As Captain Richard Blake prepares to hand over his cruiser to the Australian navy in the Indian Ocean, a German ship approaches and Blake receives alternate orders to destroy it.
Genre(s): War Story; Sea Story.

4631. *Strike from the Sea.* New York: Morrow, 1978. 255 pp.
On his way to Malaysia in 1941, Commander Robert Aislie captures a powerful French submarine and uses it to help the British in the Pacific.
Genre(s): War Story; Sea Story.

◆ 4632. *Surface with Daring.* New York: Putnam, 1977. 271 pp.
Lieutenant David Seaton navigates a midget submarine in Norway as part of the effort to overcome the Germans in World War II.
Genre(s): War Story; Sea Story.

◆ 4633. *Torpedo Run.* New York: Morrow, 1981. 290 pp.
Lieutenant Commander John Devane gains respect from his Russian allies in their first joint sea battle against the Germans when his torpedo boats defeat a German convoy in the Black Sea.
Genre(s): War Story; Sea Story.

Renault, Mary

4634. *The Charioteer.* New York: Pantheon, 1959. 347 pp.
An English homosexual is wounded at Dunkirk and receives treatment at a military hospital during World War II.
Genre(s): War Story.

Robinson, Derek

◆ 4635. *Kramer's War.* New York: Viking, 1977. 352 pp.
American pilot Earl Kramer falls into the English Channel and floats to Jersey where residents have been goading Germans to build strong battle emplacements and bunkers.
Genre(s): War Story.

Rock, Phillip

4636. *Circles of Time.* New York: Seaview, 1981. 309 pp.
In post-World War I times, the characters presented in *The Passing Bells* include Martin Rilke who is still suffering from his wife's death.
Genre(s): Family Saga.

4637. *A Future Arrived.* New York: Seaview, 1985. 228 pp.
The sequel to *Circles of Time* finds one of the Earl of Stanhope's grandsons joining the Royal Air Force, and another grandson becoming a prize-winning journalist during World War II.
Genre(s): War Story.

Roosevelt, Elliott

◆ 4638. *Murder at the Palace.* New York: St. Martin's, 1987. 232 pp.
Mrs. Roosevelt goes to Buckingham Palace during World War II and lends support to Sir Alan Burton when he is associated with an embarrassing murder.
Genre(s): Mystery.

Rosenbaum, Ray

4639. *Falcons.* Novato, CA: Lyford, 1993. 404 pp.
Ross Colyer's assignment is to lead a group of officers and enlisted men into Romania, flying at a low altitude, to destroy a refinery complex during World War II.
Genre(s): War Story.

Rossiter, John

4640. *Dark Flight.* New York: Atheneum, 1981. 224 pp.
When Laura's husband Philip crashes in France, he tries to return home, but Laura thinks he is dead and becomes attracted to another pilot who looks almost exactly like Philip.
Genre(s): War Story.

Ross-Macdonald, Malcolm

4641. *To the End of Her Days.* New York: St. Martin's, 1994. 407 pp.
In the 1920s, following the death of Jessica Lanyon's husband's, Lorna Sancreed arrives in town and changes the lives of those around her.
Genre(s): Romance.

Royce, Kenneth

◆ 4642. *Channel Assault.* New York: McGraw Hill, 1983. 252 pp.
George Fuller, a doctor, feels that he must help British enemies on Alderney to protect his mate.
Genre(s): War Story; Medical Novel.

Ryan, Mary

4643. *Glenallen.* New York: St. Martin's, 1993. 503 pp.
Peg, Cissie, and Mary become friends in a Catholic boarding school in Ireland during the 1930s, and after Peg marries Brian Fitzallen and moves to his family manor, strange things happen.
Genre(s): Romance.

Salisbury, Ray

4644. *Close the Door behind You.* New York: St. Martin's, 1983. 240 pp.
Near the end of World War II, Simon, four, must leave his grandfather to live with his parents after his father turns from a Japanese POW camp.
Genre(s): War Story.

Saunders, Jean

4645. *A Different Kind of Love.* New York: Severn House, 1998. 288 pp.

◆ May be suitable for young adult readers

When Kate Sullivan's intended groom jilts her, she goes alone on her honeymoon to escape the town gossip and meets a photographer who offers her a job modeling in London.
Genre(s): Bildungsroman (Coming of Age); Romance.

Saxton, Judith

◆ 4646. *The Blue and Distant Hills.* New York: St. Martin's, 1994. 517 pp.
When Questa returns to Wales from Italy and the war, she moves into the old family home where she meets a family from one thousand years before.
Genre(s): Bildungsroman (Coming of Age); Time Travel.

4647. *First Love, Last Love.* New York: St. Martin's, 1993. 396 pp.
Two families in a Welsh seaside resort become friends in the 1930s, and when World War II begins, their fates become interdependent.
Genre(s): War Story; Domestic Fiction.

4648. *Someone Special.* New York: St. Martin's, 1995. 536 pp.
Three women, one working-class, another upper-class, and the third, Princess Elizabeth are born on the same day in 1926, and they grow up and turn to different careers.
Genre(s): Romance.

◆ 4649. *Still Waters.* New York: St. Martin's, 1998. 512 pp.
In World War II, Tess and Mal meet at a dance, but after he returns from a harrowing experience in France, they marry, and understanding their childhood experiences in England and Australia becomes key to their survival.
Genre(s): War Story; Domestic Fiction.

4650. *This Royal Breed.* New York: St. Martin's, 1992. 443 pp.
Charles Laurient quickly leaves Paris in 1922 for his father's deathbed, and by the time he settles the estate, his lover has gone to the United States to have his child so he stays on the estate until the Nazis arrive and send him to a concentration camp.
Genre(s): War Story; Romance.

Scholefield, Alan

◆ 4651. *King of the Golden Valley.* New York: St. Martin's, 1986. 226 pp.
When Daniel Wynter receives a letter from his grandfather in 1939, written 50 years before but lost in central Asia, his grandfather promises to explain why his loss of an automobile race destroyed the family fortunes, and Wynter's search for the answer takes him to hostile Africa.
Genre(s): Adventure Story.

Shepard, Jim

◆ 4652. *Paper Doll.* New York: Knopf, 1986. 231 pp.
While waiting for their first assignment in World War II, a B-17 flight crew jokes about their situation and see themselves as the stars of wartime movies.
Genre(s): War Story.

Sherlock, John, and David Westheimer

◆ 4653. *The Amindra Gamble.* New York: Coward-McCann, 1982. 319 pp.
During World War II, the *Amindra* sails from Britain to Canada with much of the national wealth aboard, and secret agents with a German U-boat pursue it.
Genre(s): War Story; Sea Story.

Simpson, Robert

4654. *April's There.* New York: Harper, 1973. 215 pp.
During World War II, the blitz in London allows teenagers to meet black market operators and hustlers during an air raid.
Genre(s): War Story.

Sinclair, Emma

4655. *Her Father's House.* New York: St. Martin's, 1997. 448 pp.
During World War II, Jennie stays at her father's home, Trevellan, where she falls in love with the estate agent's son Mark, but her family disapproves, so she makes a life of her own as an artist until finally she and Mark can be together.
Genre(s): Family Saga; Romance.

Snow, C. P.

4656. *Conscience of the Rich.* New York: Scribner's, 1958. 342 pp.
In the late 1920s, Lewis Eliot's friend Charles March introduces him to the private world of the wealthy and influential Jewish March family in London. (*Series:* Strangers and Brothers, 7)
Genre(s): Political Fiction.

4657. *Homecoming.* New York: Scribner's, 1956. 399 pp.
After Lewis Eliot remarries, he observes the unhappy home lives of his colleagues.
Genre(s): Domestic Fiction.

4658. *The Light and the Dark.* New York: Macmillan, 1948. 302 pp.
A young Cambridge don tries to find meaning in his life through sex and alcohol, but when the war starts, he enlists and is killed in action. (*Series:* Strangers and Brothers, 2)
Genre(s): Domestic Fiction; War Story.

4659. *The Masters.* New York: Macmillan, 1951. 386 pp.
Lawyer Lewis Eliot observes the election of a new Master in one of Cambridge's colleges. (*Series:* Strangers and Brothers, 4)
Genre(s): Political Fiction.

4660. *The New Men.* New York: Scribner's, 1954. 311 pp.
A group of nuclear scientists and government officials try to save England during World War II. (*Series:* Strangers and Brothers, 5)
Genre(s): War Story.

4661. *The Sleep of Reason.* New York: Scribner's, 1968. 483 pp.
Two lesbians who are charged with torturing and killing an eight-year-old boy face their trial. (*Series:* Strangers and Brothers, 10)
Genre(s): Political Fiction; Legal Story.

4662. *Strangers and Brothers.* New York: Scribner's, 1940. 309 pp.
Lawyer George Passant helps young people begin their careers, then he is charged with fraud. (*Series:* Strangers and Brothers, 1)
Genre(s): Political Fiction.

4663. *Time of Hope.* New York: Scribner's, 1961. 408 pp.
Lewis Eliot typifies life in middle-class England during the 1930s. (*Series:* Strangers and Brothers, 3)
Genre(s): Political Fiction.

Spark, Muriel

4664. *The Girls of Slender Means.* London: Macmillan, 1963. 182 pp.
A group of young girls living in a London residence home at the end of World War II interact with a cynical young poet.
Genre(s): War Story.

4665. *The Prime of Miss Jean Brodie.* Philadelphia: Lippincott, 1962. 187 pp.
Miss Jean Brodie teaches school and influences the lives of young girls in Edinburgh during the 1930s, until one of them betrays her.

Stashower, Daniel

4666. *The Adventure of the Ectoplasmic Man.* New York: Penguin, 1986. 203 pp.
Harry Houdini wants to hire Sherlock Holmes to find out who stole royal letters and who killed the Countess Valenka.
Genre(s): Biographical Fiction; Mystery.

Steed, Neville

◆ 4667. *Black Eye.* New York: St. Martin's, 1990. 256 pp.
Johnny Black, former pilot, starts a detective agency in the English Riveria during the 1930s, and his first case is a wealthy woman who has died as Isadora Duncan did, with a scarf around her neck.
Genre(s): Mystery.

Stevenson, D. E.

4668. *Mrs Tim Carries On.* New York: Farrar and Rinehart, 1941. 307 pp.
In the sequel to *Mrs. Tim Christie*, Mrs. Tim waits in a Scottish garrison town while her husband fights in France.
Genre(s): War Story.

4669. *Mrs Tim Christie.* New York: Farrar and Rinehart, 1940. 378 pp.

Mrs. Tim is a British officer's wife in England and Scotland before World War II.
Genre(s): Domestic Fiction.

4670. *Vittoria Cottage.* New York: Holt, Rinehart and Winston, 1949. 250 pp.
Caroline Dering, the widowed mistress of Vittoria Cottage, meets a stranger on one of her walks.
Genre(s): Domestic Fiction.

Stirling, Jessica

4671. *The Blue Evening Gone.* New York: St. Martin's, 1981. 413 pp.
In the sequel to *The Drums of Time*, Holly sacrifices her family life for a liaison with an American dancer.
Genre(s): Family Saga.

◆ 4672. *The Drums of Time.* New York: St. Martin's, 1979. 528 pp.
When Holly Beckman's employer dies, he leaves her one-quarter interest in his antique business, and she leaves her family and others to build her business and make a name for herself in post-World War I London.
Genre(s): Romance.

4673. *The Gates of Midnight.* New York: St. Martin's, 1983. 302 pp.
In the sequel to *The Blue Evening Gone*, Holly Beckman is a widow who worries about her brother and her child fighting in World War II.
Genre(s): War Story; Family Saga.

◆ 4674. *The Marrying Kind.* New York: St. Martin's, 1996. 359 pp.
In the sequel to *The Penny Wedding*, while Alison attends medical school in Scotland during the 1930s, she becomes infatuated with a man not her fiancé.
Genre(s): Domestic Fiction.

4675. *The Penny Wedding.* New York: St. Martin's, 1995. 394 pp.
Maeve Burnside dies suddenly leaving husband and children, but Alison, 16, decides to continue school instead of giving up everything to look after the family.
Genre(s): Domestic Fiction.

Sully, Sue

4676. *The Dovecote.* New York: St. Martin's, 1995. 345 pp.
When Esther Norbrook decides to join an artists' colony in Dorset two years after her husband dies, she at first thrives in the artists' company, but as she becomes more intimate with the other artists, sinister forces arise.
Genre(s): War Story; Romance.

Summers, John

4677. *Dylan.* London: New English Library, 1970. 253 pp.
Dylan Thomas leaves University College, Wales, and only wants to write, but when his family nags him to work, he leaves for Canada and other sea voyages before returning to Wales.
Genre(s): Biographical Fiction.

Tanner, Janet

◆ 4678. *The Hills and the Valley.* New York: St. Martin's, 1990. 572 pp.
In the sequel to *Emerald Valley*, Barbara, in love with her adopted brother, tries to survive the war and its ills.
Genre(s): War Story; Family Saga.

Taylor, Thomas

4679. *Born of War.* New York: McGraw Hill, 1988. 450 pp.
Orde Wingate is adored and admired by many during the exploits he leads in Palestine during the 1930s until his death in Burma in 1944.
Genre(s): Biographical Fiction; War Story.

Thane, Elswyth

4680. *Homing.* New York: Duell, Sloan and Pearce, 1957. 272 pp.
The sequel to *This Was Tomorrow* finds Jeff Day working as a foreign correspondent in London at the outbreak of World War II.
Genre(s): War Story; Family Saga.

4681. *This Was Tomorrow.* New York: Duell, Sloan and Pearce, 1951. 319 pp.
Before World War II, in the sequel to *Kissing Kin*, two cousins who are dancers take their show to London where they meet two other cousins and fall in love.
Genre(s): Family Saga; War Story.

Thomas, D. M.

4682. *Eating Pavlova.* New York: Carroll and Graf, 1994. 231 pp.
When Sigmund Freud lies on his deathbed in 1939, his delusions while under the influence of morphine recall various people and sexual fantasies about his life.
Genre(s): Biographical Fiction.

Thomas, Rosie

4683. *The White Dove.* New York: Viking, 1986. 633 pp.
Amy Lowell wants to escape the conventionality of her upper-class English home and as a result, she becomes involved in Spain's civil war.
Genre(s): Love Story; War Story.

Thompson, Brian

◆ 4684. *Buddy Boy.* New York: St. Martin's, 1978. 160 pp.
In Cambridge during World War II, the military preparations for D-Day lead to an American pilot's breakdown and a British school boy's maturity.
Genre(s): War Story; Bildungsroman (Coming of Age).

Thorne, Nicola

4685. *Cashmere.* Garden City, NY: Doubleday, 1982. 384 pp.
Margaret Dunbar keeps the family's knitting mill operating after her father's death and through the Depression in Scotland until she can expand it during World War II by using imported Chinese cashmere wool.
Genre(s): War Story.

Todd, Charles

4686. *A Test of Wills.* New York: St. Martin's, 1996. 282 pp.
Inspector Ian Rutledge, still suffering from shell shock brought on by World War I, hopes to return to his success at Scotland Yard, but one of his superiors discovers his problem.
Genre(s): Mystery.

4687. *Wings of Fire.* New York: St. Martin's, 1998. 304 pp.
When Scotland Yard's Inspector Ian Rutledge goes to Cornwall to probe mysterious suicides and accidents, he not only finds family skeletons but he also has a chance to think about his participation in World War I.
Genre(s): Mystery.

Trollope, Joanna

4688. *A Spanish Lover.* New York: Random House, 1997. 334 pp.
Lizzie raises a family while her twin, Frances, starts a travel business in which she meets Luis Gomez Moreno, a married man 10 years older.
Genre(s): Family Saga.

Veryan, Patricia

◆ 4689. *Poor Splendid Wings.* Hampton, NH: Severn House, 1992. 512 pp.
Michael Owens, a British pilot, becomes torn between the love of his country and of a woman at the beginning of World War II.
Genre(s): Romance.

Wainwright, J. A.

4690. *A Deathful Ridge.* Buffalo, NY: Mosaic, 1997. 138 pp.
George Mallory, a British mountain climber, disappears in 1924 while trying to climb Mount Everest.
Genre(s): Adventure Story; Biographical Fiction.

Wakefield, Tom

◆ 4691. *War Paint.* New York: St. Martin's, 1994. 234 pp.
An English mining village experiences the arrival of a flashy school teacher, Miss Kay Roper, during 1942, who influences all.

Walter, Elizabeth

4692. *Homeward Bound.* New York: St. Martin's, 1990. 384 pp.
In 1924, a group of expatriates return to England from India on a luxury liner, each with something to hide and each with an opinion on topical issues.
Genre(s): Political Fiction.

Watkins, Paul

◆ 4693. ***The Promise of Light.*** New York: Random House, 1993. 271 pp.
In the 1920s Ben Sheridan goes to Ireland to his father's village on business, but caught in the initial IRA conflicts, he lies about his situation and becomes more mired in the fray.
Genre(s): Adventure Story.

Waugh, Evelyn

4694. ***Basil Seal Rides Again.*** Boston: Little, Brown, 1963. 49 pp.
When Basil Seal returns to London during World War II, in the sequel to *Put Out More Flags*, he helps to evacuate London children.
Genre(s): War Story.

4695. ***Brideshead Revisited.*** Boston: Little, Brown, 1945. 351 pp.
Captain Charles Ryder becomes involved with an aristocratic Roman Catholic family when he meets Sebastian Marchmain at Oxford.
Genre(s): Domestic Fiction.

4696. ***The End of the Battle.*** Boston: Little, Brown, 1979. 319 pp.
In the sequel to *Officers and Gentlemen*, Guy Crouchback goes to Yugoslavia to fight in World War II, and when he returns to England, he remarries his former wife.
Genre(s): War Story.

4697. ***Men at Arms.*** Boston: Little, Brown, 1952. 342 pp.
An English Catholic raised in Italy returns to England and attempts to join the military before World War II begins.

4698. ***Officers and Gentlemen.*** Boston: Little, Brown, 1955. 339 pp.
The sequel to *Men at Arms* finds Guy Crouchback training as a Commando in the Hebrides and then fighting in Crete.
Genre(s): War Story.

4699. ***Put Out More Flags.*** Boston: Little, Brown, 1977. 286 pp.
World War II affects the English upper-class family of Basil Seal, especially his sister, mother, and mistress, in the sequel to *Black Mischief*.
Genre(s): War Story; Satire.

4700. ***Vile Bodies.*** Boston: Little, Brown, 1930. 321 pp.
In the 1920s, young London socialites become involved in pointless parties and affairs.

Weatherby, William J.

◆ 4701. ***Chariots of Fire.*** New York: Granada, 1982. 126 pp.

Harold Abrahams, Cambridge student, and Eric Liddell, missionary, compete in the 1924 Olympics as runners for Great Britain.
Genre(s): Biographical Fiction; Sports Fiction; Christian Fiction.

Wesley, Mary

◆ 4702. ***Part of the Furniture.*** New York: Viking, 1997. 256 pp.
After her mother has left for Canada in World War II, naive Juno Marlowe goes to London with two friends, one of whom gets her pregnant, but after they leave for the front, she luckily secures work as a Land Girl.
Genre(s): War Story; Romance.

West, Anthony C.

4703. ***As Towns with Fire.*** New York: Knopf, 1970. 528 pp.
A young Irish poet finally becomes somewhat stable when serving as a pilot in World War II and going home on leave to his wife and children, but after the war, he reverts to his former behavior.
Genre(s): War Story; Bildungsroman (Coming of Age).

West, Rebecca

4704. ***Cousin Rosamund.*** New York: Viking, 1986. 294 pp.
In the sequel to *This Real Night* Rose Aubrey's mother and brother have died, and she and her sister are established concert pianists, and they are distressed because Cousin Rosamund has left England.
Genre(s): Domestic Fiction.

Whitnell, Barbara

4705. ***Charmed Circle.*** New York: St. Martin's, 1994. 352 pp.
The Rossiter family opposes Rachel Bond's marriage to their son Gavin, and he goes to Spain to fight, but when he returns, Rachel and Gavin decide to marry, again with objections, until Rachel discovers Gavin's secret.
Genre(s): War Story; Domestic Fiction.

4706. ***The View from the Summerhouse.*** New York: St. Martin's, 1995. 316 pp.
Caleb Carne, a famous radio personality during World War II, writes his biography in the 1980s, recalling his days during the terrible time prior to D-Day.
Genre(s): War Story; Adventure Story.

Wiggin, Helene

4707. ***Dancing at the Victory Café.*** New York: St. Martin's, 1996. 256 pp.
Belle Morton buys a tea restaurant in Lichfield during World War II and transforms it into a café where the soldiers and townspeople can have good food during wartime.
Genre(s): War Story.

Willis, Ted

4708. *The Bells of Autumn.* New York: St. Martin's, 1991. 319 pp.
Rosie Carr, in the sequel to *The Green Leaves of Summer*, plans to run for Parliament in 1934 and remarries before she goes to Germany to help rescue friends from the Nazis.
Genre(s): Humorous Fiction; Family Saga.

Wilson, Jonathan

4709. *The Hiding Room.* New York: Viking, 1995. 262 pp.
Daniel Weiss tries to discover the identity of his father, whom he never knew, and flasbacks to 1941 reveal his mother's experience with Nazi horrors and her love of a British army officer.
Genre(s): War Story; Love Story.

Windsor, Joyce

◆ 4710. *A Mislaid Magic.* New York: St. Martin's, 1994. 240 pp.
Amy is eight when her mother dies and her father remarries a social climber, and when her stepmother organizes an art festival on their country home grounds, Amy learns about sex and the boring conversations of some in the upper class.
Genre(s): Romance.

Winward, Walter

4711. *Hammerstrike.* New York: Simon and Schuster, 1979. 349 pp.
When the British take a German general as prisoner in World War II, the Germans do what they can to save him, including having him escape through a tunnel already dug by previous inmates of the prison in which he stays.
Genre(s): War Story.

Woodhouse, Sarah

4712. *Enchanted Ground.* New York: St. Martin's, 1993. 340 pp.
Three generations of women live at Bretton, their British country home, and Paddy tries to save the house in the 1920s by renting it to a mismatched family who discover secrets about Paddy's family.
Genre(s): Domestic Fiction; Family Saga.

Woodman, Richard

4713. *Captain of the Caryatid.* New York: Severn House, 1998. 224 pp.
In 1935, the master of a lighthouse and buoy-tender dislikes the new harbormaster, but both become involved with the Morgans, mother and daughter, and therefore, each other.
Genre(s): Sea Story.

Wyndham, Francis

4714. *The Other Garden.* New York: Moyer Bell, 1988. 106 pp.
A teenaged boy begins to pay attention to Kay, a woman in her 30s abused by her family, during World War II.
Award(s): Whitbread Award.
Genre(s): War Story.

1946-1975

Anthony, Evelyn

◆ 4715. *The Silver Falcon.* New York: Coward-McCann, 1977. 349 pp.
Isabel Schriber wants to win the Derby at Epsom Downs in honor of her deceased horse-breeder husband, but family and murder interfere.
Genre(s): Spy Fiction.

◆ 4716. *The Tamarind Seed.* New York: Coward-McCann, 1971. 246 pp.
Judith Farrow tries to recover from a love affair with a Russian Intelligence agent until they meet unexpectedly and make news in London, Moscow, and Washington.
Genre(s): Spy Fiction.

Atkinson, Kate

4717. *Behind the Scenes at the Museum.* New York: St. Martin's, 1996. 332 pp.
Ruby, born in York, England, in 1959, relates the story of her family living above shops in the 1960s and of her grandmother and mother living through the earlier wars.
Genre(s): Domestic Fiction.

Barker, Elspeth

4718. *O Caledonia.* San Diego, CA: Harcourt, 1992. 151 pp.
After World War II, Janet, one of five siblings growing up in a cold Scottish castle, remains aloof from her family.
Genre(s): Domestic Fiction; Bildungsroman (Coming of Age).

Bartlett, Neil

4719. *The House on Brooke Street.* New York: Dutton, 1997. 224 pp.
As Mr. Page deals with the death of his male lover at Christmas 1956 and reflects about events 30 years prior, he comes to the realization that he is a gay man who has lived secretly all his life.
Genre(s): Bildungsroman (Coming of Age).

Benedict, Helen

4720. *A World Like This.* New York: Dutton, 1990. 224 pp.

Brandy tries to survive inside and outside of a borstal, a type of prison for older teenagers that is run like a reform school.
Genre(s): Political Fiction.

Binchy, Maeve

◆ 4721. *Echoes.* New York: Viking, 1986. 477 pp.
A priest knows the secrets of many people in his small town but divulges none of them.
Genre(s): Romance.

4722. *Firefly Summer.* New York: Delacorte, 1988. 601 pp.
In the 1960s, Patrick O'Neill builds a hotel in his Irish ancestral home and disrupts the town's life.
Genre(s): Domestic Fiction.

◆ 4723. *The Glass Lake.* New York: Delacorte, 1995. 584 pp.
Kit McMahon's mother supposedly drowns, but she has been in London with her lover, and she makes contact with Kit when Kit is a teenager by pretending that she is Kit's mother's old friend.

Binding, Tim

4724. *A Perfect Execution.* New York: Doubleday, 1996. 295 pp.
Solomon Straw becomes the best of executioners after watching villagers slowly kill a wounded German war pilot in World War II.
Genre(s): War Story.

Buckley, William F. Jr.

◆ 4725. *Saving the Queen.* Garden City, NY: Doubleday, 1976. 248 pp.
Blackford Oakes works for the CIA in London to trace leaks of atomic secrets to the Soviet Union.
Genre(s): Spy Fiction.

Bunn, T. Davis

4726. *The Amber Room.* Minneapolis, MN: Bethany House, 1992. 334 pp.
After World War II, people search for the greatest work of art plundered during the war. (*Series:* Priceless, 2)
Genre(s): Mystery; Christian Fiction.

Butler, Gwendoline

◆ 4727. *Coffin in Fashion.* New York: St. Martin's, 1990. 176 pp.
Sergeant John Coffin begins renovations on his home and finds two buried bodies, and when other corpses turn up, they lead to Rose Hilaire, the owner of a discount clothing factory.
Genre(s): Mystery.

Byatt, A. S.

4728. *Babel Tower.* New York: Random House, 1996. 544 pp.
Frederica Potter becomes disenchanted with her marriage after attending Cambridge and leaves her country home for London where, in the turbulent 1960s, she struggles with single motherhood, politics, ideals, and changing sexual roles in a sequel to *Still Life.*.
Genre(s): War Story.

4729. *Still Life.* New York: Scribner, 1985. 384 pp.
In this sequel to *The Virgin in the Garden*, in the 1950s, Stephanie Potter, now married to a clergyman, is conflicted about her domestic life and her strivings for intellectual fulfillment; her brilliant sister Frederica eagerly embarks on her academic (and sexual) education at Cambridge University; and their troubled brother Marcus painfully tries to find friendship and love.
Genre(s): Domestic Fiction.

4730. *The Virgin in the Garden.* New York: Knopf, 1979. 428 pp.
Against the backdrop of an England preparing for the coronation of Elizabeth II in 1853, the young people in the brilliant, difficult Potter family struggle to find their way in life.
Genre(s): Domestic Fiction.

Carey, Lisa

4731. *The Mermaids Singing.* New York: Bard, 1998. 272 pp.
Clíona leaves Ireland in the 1950s for America planning to study nursing, but she becomes pregnant with Grace, who returns to Ireland as a teenager then comes back to America with her own daughter, Gráinne, before cutting her family ties.
Genre(s): Family Saga.

Conlon, Kathleen

4732. *A Forgotten Season.* New York: St. Martin's, 1981. 177 pp.
In the 1950s, Veronica, 10, gets a crush on handsome Charlie at the seashore, while her mother and Charlie have an affair.
Genre(s): Domestic Fiction.

Connaughton, Shane

4733. *The Run of the Country.* New York: St. Martin's, 1992. 224 pp.
In the political climate of partitioned Ireland, violence divides young lovers as they come of age.
Genre(s): Bildungsroman (Coming of Age); Political Fiction; Love Story.

Cookson, Catherine

4734. *The Year of the Virgins.* New York: Simon and Schuster, 1995. 272 pp.
Winifred Coulson's favorite son Donald marries Annette in 1960, against Winifred's will, but after Winifred enters a mental institution, she plots to leave and kill all of them.

Darrell, Elizabeth

4735. *We Will Remember.* New York: St. Martin's, 1996. 453 pp.

In 1946, three members of the Sheridan family, affected by the war, must close out the chapters of their lives during the war before they can properly face the future.
Genre(s): Domestic Fiction; Family Saga.

Davis-Goff, Annabel

4736. *The Dower House.* New York: St. Martin's, 1998. 304 pp.
Molly Hassard knows that her cousin Sophie will always have the privileges of class because Sophie's father is the eldest son and Molly experiences a second-class life as inhabitant of the dower house, the home adjacent to the estate, originally built for widows.
Genre(s): Bildungsroman (Coming of Age).

Deane, Seamus

◆ 4737. *Reading in the Dark.* New York: Knopf, 1997. 272 pp.
The narrator listens to the stories of his relatives and looks for clues to the family secrets that would make it vulnerable to terror during the Irish Catholic Time of Troubles in the 1950s and 1960s.
Genre(s): War Story; Political Fiction.

Doyle, Roddy

◆ 4738. *Paddy Clarke, Ha Ha Ha.* New York: Viking, 1993. 282 pp.
In the late 1960s, Paddy Clarke, 10, wants to be tough like his friends in their Dublin neighborhood.
Award(s): Booker Prize.
Genre(s): Bildungsroman (Coming of Age).

Elliott, Janice

◆ 4739. *The Kindling.* New York: Knopf, 1970. 224 pp.
In the 1950s, young inhabitants of a Northern England small town search for ways to escape their boredom.
Genre(s): Domestic Fiction.

Gardner, John E.

4740. *The Secret Families.* New York: Putnam, 1989. 415 pp.
After Sir Caspar Railton dies and is revealed to have been a British traitor for the Russians, his nephew and cousin try to restore the family's reputation. (*Series:* Secret Generations, 3)
Genre(s): Spy Fiction; Adventure Story; Family Saga.

Gibson, Elizabeth

4741. *The Water Is Wide.* Grand Rapids, MI: Zondervan, 1984. 299 pp.
In 1969, Kate Hamilton attends New University in Londonderry, and as a Protestant, she learns to trust, and even love, a Catholic.
Genre(s): Political Fiction; Christian Fiction.

Gill, B. M.

4742. *Nursery Crimes.* New York: Scribner's, 1987. 194 pp.
Zanny Moncrief seems to attract violent deaths to those around her, but no one believes that a sweet child in Wales could be associated with these deaths.
Genre(s): Mystery.

Goodwin, Suzanne

4743. *A Change of Season.* New York: St. Martin's, 1992. 576 pp.
When Lisa Whitfield and her brother Charles return to England from Burma in 1948, they inherit money from their father's estate and settle in Stratford where Lisa tries to forget her wartime love and Charles exhibits his selfishness.
Genre(s): Domestic Fiction.

Goudge, Elizabeth

4744. *The Heart of the Family.* New York: Coward-McCann, 1953. 337 pp.
An Austrian refugee meets the Eliot family, and its members help him overcome his painful memories.
Genre(s): Domestic Fiction.

4745. *Pilgrim's Inn.* New York: Coward-McCann, 1948. 300 pp.
In the sequel to *The Bird in the Tree*, grandmother Eliot helps the family recover from the war.
Genre(s): Domestic Fiction.

Haig, Kathryn

4746. *Apple Blossom Time.* New York: St. Martin's, 1998. 459 pp.
After Laura Ansty serves in Egypt during World War II, she returns to her English village to learn about her father, who died in World War I and whom no one in the family discusses.
Genre(s): War Story; Domestic Fiction.

Higgins, Jack

4747. *Memoirs of a Dance-Hall Romeo.* New York: Simon and Schuster, 1989. 186 pp.
Oliver Shaw gets out of the British army in 1949 and decides to devote himself to the pursuit of women.
Genre(s): Adventure Story.

Hogan, Desmond

4748. *Curious Street.* New York: Braziller, 1984. 194 pp.
In Belfast during 1977, Jeremy Hitchens, an Anglo-Irish soldier serving with the British forces, becomes obsessed with a 1940s novelist whom his mother had loved before the man went mad, and as he searches for the novelist, he begins to understand Irish history and his own past.
Genre(s): War Story; Bildungsroman (Coming of Age).

Howatch, Susan

4749. *Absolute Truths.* New York: Knopf, 1995. 559 pp.
In the sequel to *Mystical Paths*, the mid-1960s finds Charles Ashworth, an Anglican bishop, pitted against Neville Aysgarth, the dean of the Cathedral, because of Ays-

garth's interest in commercializing the church. (*Series:* Church of England, 6)
Genre(s): Christian Fiction.

4750. *Glamorous Powers.* New York: Knopf, 1987. 403 pp.
Jon Darrow, an Anglican priest with psychic abilities, thinks that God has instructed him to leave his religious order. (*Series:* Church of England, 2)
Genre(s): Christian Fiction.

4751. *Mystical Paths.* New York: Knopf, 1992. 433 pp.
Nicholas Darrow, 25, has great confidence in his psychic gifts until the widow of a friend asks him to investigate her husband's death on a sailboat. (*Series:* Church of England, 5)
Genre(s): Allegory; Romance; Bildungsroman (Coming of Age).

4752. *Scandalous Risks.* New York: Knopf, 1990. 385 pp.
Venetia Flaxton has an affair with the dean of Starbridge Cathedral. (*Series:* Church of England, 4)
Genre(s): Christian Fiction.

4753. *Ultimate Prizes.* New York: Knopf, 1989. 387 pp.
The Archdeacon of Starbury, Neville Aysgarth, meets a young woman who would love to be an archbishop's wife, and after Neville's own wife dies, they marry, only to find themselves without happiness after several years. (*Series:* Church of England, 3)
Genre(s): Christian Fiction.

Keady, Walter

4754. *Celibates and Other Lovers.* Denver, CO: MacMurray and Beck, 1997. 225 pp.
Phelim O'Brien is in training to become a Catholic priest in Ireland after World War II, but Catherine McGrath believes that Phelim will choose her instead of the church.
Genre(s): Domestic Fiction.

Keane, John B.

4755. *The Bodhran Makers.* New York: Four Walls Eight Windows, 1992. 256 pp.
In the 1950s, Canon Tett disapproves of the Irish celebration of Wren Day with a parade led by a person playing the Bodhran (drum) because he thinks it is anti-Catholic.
Genre(s): Musical Fiction; Domestic Fiction.

Kirk, Margaret P.

4756. *Gypsy.* New York: Atheneum, 1987. 536 pp.
Micah's father is expelled from the *kumpania* (Gypsy camp) after killing his wife, and when Micah wanders away, a couple whose children were lost during the war adopt him.
Genre(s): Family Saga.

Lovesey, Peter

4757. *The Last Detective.* Garden City, NY: Doubleday, 1991. 331 pp.

In 1964, Peter Diamond declares that England's loss of power is based on the abolition of capital punishment, but a murder without clues makes him resort to tools he scorns.
Award(s): Anthony Award.
Genre(s): Mystery.

4758. *On the Edge.* New York: Mysterious Press, 1989. 204 pp.
When Rosie and Antonia meet, they begin to talk, and eventually plan to kill Rosie's husband by pushing him under a tube train.
Genre(s): Mystery.

Mackay, Shena

4759. *The Orchard on Fire.* Wakefield, RI: Moyer Bell, 1996. 216 pp.
When rumors of a child molester filter through the town of Stonebridge in the 1950s, the parents of eight-year-old April do not suspect the valued customer in their new tearoom.
Genre(s): Domestic Fiction.

McAughtry, Sam

4760. *Touch and Go.* Belfast, Ireland: Blackstaff, 1993. 233 pp.
Protestant Hugh Reilly returns to Belfast after World War II, fights with his brother at his mother's funeral, kills a Catholic by mistake, and faces the death sentence.
Genre(s): Political Fiction; Domestic Fiction.

McCabe, Patrick

4761. *The Dead School.* New York: Doubleday, 1995. 368 pp.
Malachy Dudgeon comes to St. Anthony's school in Dublin in the 1960s where he challenges the head prefect's view of corporal punishment and school prayer.

Melville, Anne

4762. *Family Fortunes.* Garden City, NY: Doubleday, 1984. 349 pp.
In the sequel to *Blaize*, Lady Alexa Glanville and her descendants carry on the family's principles from the end of World War II and on into the 1970s in England.
Genre(s): Domestic Fiction.

4763. *The Last of the Lorimers.* London: Heinemann, 1983. 305 pp.
After World War II, Paula decides to become a journalist and do political work in Jamaica while Asha wants to remain a Headmistress.
Genre(s): Domestic Fiction.

Molina, Silvia

4764. *Gray Skies Tomorrow.* Kaneohe, HI: Plover, 1993. 107 pp.
In 1969 the narrator goes to England where she meets the Mexican poet José Carlos Becerra and has an affair against her aunt's wishes, but with the stigma of being Mexican female rather than an English one.
Award(s): Xavier Villaurrutia Prize.

◆ May be suitable for young adult readers

Genre(s): Love Story.

Mount, Ferdinand

4765. *The Clique.* London: Chatto and Windus, 1978. 230 pp.
Lil, Poppy, and Clara (the clique) live in Clara's husband's house in the 1960s, and there Goater reconnects with a former girlfriend, Margaret.
Genre(s): Domestic Fiction; Picaresque Fiction.

Norman, Philip

4766. *Everyone's Gone to the Moon.* New York: Random House, 1996. 356 pp.
During the 1960s, Louis Brennan begins working on a London Sunday magazine, covers the stories that remain historical markers of the times, and falls in love with a woman in the office who's being pursued by his former editor.
Genre(s): Love Story.

Pears, Tim

4767. *In a Land of Plenty.* New York: St. Martin's, 1998. 544 pp.
Charles and Mary Freeman live with their children in a small English town where their factory supplies jobs and their children grow up.
Genre(s): Family Saga.

Peters, Ellis

◆ 4768. *Fallen into the Pit.* New York: Mysterious Press, 1994. 324 pp.
George Felse's son Dominic, 13, finds the body of a loathsome German prisoner-of-war, but George has difficulty believing his neighbors might have committed the crime.
Genre(s): Mystery.

Phillips, Michael R., and Judith Pella

4769. *Treasure of Stonewycke.* Minneapolis, MN: Bethany House, 1988. 398 pp.
Allison and Logan Macintyre struggle with what seems like an unsolvable mystery. (*Series:* Stonewycke Legacy, 3)
Genre(s): Christian Fiction; Mystery.

Powell, Anthony

4770. *A Dance to the Music of Time: Fourth Movement.* Boston: Little, Brown, 1976. 772 pp.
The fourth movement includes the books *Books Do Furnish a Room*, *Temporary Kings*, and *Hearing Secret Harmonies*, which show the old friends from Eton as writers, politicians, and malcontents in post-World War II life.

Pym, Barbara

4771. *A Glass of Blessings.* New York: Dutton, 1980. 256 pp.

A young married woman, eager to add some interest to her life, becomes involved with Anglo-Catholic parish members in London during the 1950s.
Genre(s): Domestic Fiction.

Raphael, Frederic

4772. *After the War.* New York: Viking, 1989. 528 pp.
The Jordan family members, wanting to be British first and Jewish second, find themselves betraying and being betrayed after World War II.
Genre(s): Domestic Fiction.

Rathbone, Julian

4773. *A Spy of the Old School.* New York: Atheneum, 1983. 271 pp.
In 1948, British Intelligence believes that the man who gave code secrets to Russia in World War II died in 1944, but new security breaks indicate that they have suspected the wrong man.
Genre(s): Spy Fiction.

Roe, Jill

4774. *Angels Flying Slowly.* New York: St. Martin's, 1995. 224 pp.
Sisters have to leave their abusive mother to attend Catholic boarding school after World War II, and both become angry at her behavior.
Genre(s): Bildungsroman (Coming of Age).

Roy, Lucinda

4775. *Lady Moses.* New York: HarperCollins, 1998. 352 pp.
Jacinta, daughter of a British actress and an African writer, enjoys an idyllic London childhood in the 1950s, but after her father dies, she goes to America and then to Africa to find her heritage.
Genre(s): Domestic Fiction.

Saul, John Ralston

4776. *The Birds of Prey.* New York: McGraw Hill, 1977. 247 pp.
When Charles de Gaulle's Chief of Staff, General Ailleret, dies in a 1968 plane crash, investigations reveal that the crash may not have been an accident.
Genre(s): Biographical Fiction; Mystery.

Saunders, Jean

◆ 4777. *Journey's End.* New York: Severn House, 1996. 315 pp.
When Rose Foster goes from Wales to Los Angeles to live with her sister after World War II, she realizes that America requires her to compromise her values, and she returns to Wales, hoping to regain what she has lost.
Genre(s): Romance.

Settle, Mary Lee

4778. *Celebration.* New York: Farrar, Straus and Giroux, 1986. 355 pp.

When Teresa Cerrutti meets a geologist at the British Museum in the 1960s and falls in love with him, their circle of friends includes a motley group.

Snow, C. P.

4779. **The Affair.** New York: Scribner's, 1960. 317 pp.
In 1953, Lewis Eliot returns to Cambridge to investigate the firing of a young scientist for potentially unsubstantiated scientific fraud. (*Series:* Strangers and Brothers, 8)
Genre(s): Political Fiction.

4780. **Corridors of Power.** New York: Scribner's, 1964. 403 pp.
Roger Quaife, a member of the British government, controls the use of nuclear arms in Great Britain. (*Series:* Strangers and Brothers, 9)
Genre(s): Political Fiction.

4781. **Last Things.** New York: Scribner's, 1970. 544 pp.
Sir Lewis Eliot observes the actions in his upper-class world in the 1960s. (*Series:* Strangers and Brothers, 11)
Genre(s): Political Fiction; Domestic Fiction.

Stevenson, D. E.

4782. **Mrs Tim Flies Home.** New York: Farrar and Rinehart, 1952. 284 pp.
Mrs. Tim from *Mrs. Tim Gets a Job* leaves her husband in Kenya for the summer while she returns to England to be with their children.
Genre(s): Domestic Fiction.

4783. **Mrs Tim Gets a Job.** New York: Holt, Rinehart and Winston, 1974. 282 pp.
While Mrs. Tim (*Mrs. Tim Carries On*) waits for her husband to return from Egypt and the children attend school, she gets a job in a home which has been converted into a hotel on the Scottish border.
Genre(s): Humorous Fiction; Domestic Fiction.

4784. **Music in the Hills.** New York: Rinehart, 1950. 282 pp.
In the sequel to *Vittoria Cottage*, James Dering leaves the army for his uncle and aunt's farm, Mureth, to learn farming and to recover from his ended love affair.
Genre(s): Domestic Fiction.

4785. **Shoulder the Sky.** New York: Holt, Rinehart and Winston, 1951. 275 pp.
The sequel to *Music in the Hills* finds James bringing his wife Rhoda to his remote Scottish sheep farm from London.
Genre(s): Domestic Fiction.

Stewart, Mary

◆ 4786. **Thornyhold.** New York: Morrow, 1988. 207 pp.
In 1948 Gilly receives a legacy from a deceased cousin in Wiltshire.
Genre(s): Domestic Fiction.

Syal, Meera

4787. **Anita and Me.** New York: New Press, 1997. 336 pp.
In the 1960s, Meena Kumar is one of four nonwhite students in her school, and in the neighborhood, she listens to the Yard Ladies to perfect her local accent and finally joins Anita's gang after refusing to accept Anita's boyfriend's racist comments.
Genre(s): Bildungsroman (Coming of Age); Humorous Fiction.

Thomas, Donald Serrell

4788. **Dancing in the Dark.** New York: St. Martin's, 1994. 220 pp.
Three London underworld figures are murdered in the years after World War II, and although Scotland Yard bosses think they were "inside jobs," the investigators do not.
Genre(s): Mystery.

Thomas, Rosie

4789. **Bad Girls, Good Women.** New York: Bantam, 1989. 664 pp.
In 1955, Mattie and Julia run away to London where one tries to become an actress and the other attempts to become free from her parents.

Torrington, Jeff

4790. **Swing Hammer Swing!** San Diego, CA: Harcourt, 1994. 416 pp.
In Glasgow during 1969, Tom Clay, a slum-dwelling father-to-be and would-be novelist goes through a week of waiting.
Award(s): Whitbread Award.
Genre(s): Domestic Fiction.

Van Greenaway, Peter

4791. **Suffer! Little Children.** London: Gollancz, 1976. 222 pp.
Children of Northern Ireland grow up with a civil and religious war around them in the 20th century.
Genre(s): War Story.

Walsh, Jill Paton

4792. **Lapsing.** New York: St. Martin's, 1987. 224 pp.
Tessa, a Catholic at Oxford during the 1950s, keeps her faith during world crises and through a crush on a priest.
Genre(s): Religious Fiction.

1976 and After

Deighton, Len

4793. ***Berlin Game.*** New York: Knopf, 1984. 345 pp.
Bernard Samson must help an undercover agent escape from Berlin but fears that leaks in British intelligence will undermine the attempt.
Genre(s): Spy Fiction.

4794. ***London Match.*** New York: Knopf, 1985. 407 pp.
In the sequel to *Mexico Set*, Bernard Samson finds himself suspected as the second Soviet informer in British intelligence.
Genre(s): Spy Fiction.

◆ **4795.** ***Mexico Set.*** New York: Knopf, 1985. 373 pp.
In the sequel to the *Berlin Game*, Barnard Samson's ex-wife has defected to the Soviets and she plots against him, but he fears a second informer still lurks in London.
Genre(s): Spy Fiction.

4796. ***Spy Hook.*** New York: Knopf, 1989. 291 pp.
After his wife has defected to the Soviet secret police (KGB), Secret Service official Bernard Samson discovers that money has been stolen from the department and must find out if his wife or someone else took it.
Genre(s): Spy Fiction.

4797. ***Spy Line.*** New York: Knopf, 1989. 291 pp.
Bernard Samson must escape to Berlin after the British accuse him of spying for the Soviets in the sequel to *Spy Hook*.
Genre(s): Spy Fiction.

4798. ***Spy Sinker.*** New York: HarperCollins, 1990. 374 pp.
In the sequel to *Spy Line*, Bernard Samson is cleared of charges that he was spying for the Soviets, and he has a final encounter with Fiona, his wife.
Genre(s): Spy Fiction.

Le Carré, John

4799. ***The Spy Who Came in from the Cold.*** New York: Coward-McCann, 1964. 256 pp.
Alec Leamas wants to stop being a spy but he agrees to take a final assignment in order to prove to the enemy that their leader is a double agent.
Award(s): Edgar Allan Poe Award; Dagger Award.
Genre(s): Spy Fiction.

Miner, Valerie

4800. ***Blood Sisters.*** New York: St. Martin's, 1982. 224 pp.
In the mid-1970s Beth Flannigan, IRA supporter, and Liz Devlin, American journalist, are cousins living in London where they follow their grandmother Elizabeth O'Brien's idealism in vastly different ways.
Genre(s): Political Fiction.

Africa

Before 1900

Achebe, Chinua

◆ 4801. *Things Fall Apart.* New York: McDowell, 1959. 215 pp.
Okonkwo functions appropriately in his Ibo tribal world, but when European missionaries arrive in the late 19th century, and his favorite son converts to Christianity, he cannot cope with the change.

Al-Ghitani, Gamal

4802. *Zayni Barakat.* Trans. Farouk Abdel Wahab. New York: Penguin, 1990. 240 pp.
Zayni Barakat lusts for power in Cairo during 1516 and maintains a huge network of spies to help him control both businessmen and the masses.
Genre(s): War Story.

Badian, Seydou

4803. *Caught in the Storm.* Boulder, CO: Three Continents, 1998. 115 pp.
Kany grows up in the French Sudan, and as it becomes the Republic of Mali, she wants to marry a classmate, but her father expects her to marry a rich merchant who has two other wives.
Genre(s): Domestic Fiction.

Bishop, Michael

4804. *No Enemy But Time.* New York: Timescape, 1982. 397 pp.
Joshua Kampa has strange dreams of prehistoric Africa, which lead him into a situation in which he is the father of a child with a hominid female.
Genre(s): Time Travel.

Boyle, T. Coraghessan

4805. *Water Music.* New York: Penguin, 1983. 437 pp.
Mungo Park, an actual Scottish explorer, teams with a London miscreant to chart the course of the Niger River in West Africa where they have almost every possible mishap.
Genre(s): Biographical Fiction; Humorous Fiction.

Brink, André Philippus

4806. *Cape of Storms.* New York: Simon and Schuster, 1993. 141 pp.
The Khoikhoi chieftain T'kama marries a white woman, Khois, left behind by Vasco da Gama's crew in 1498, and when the whites return for her after she has borne an infant son, T'kama grieves.
Genre(s): Love Story.

4807. *A Chain of Voices.* New York: Morrow, 1982. 525 pp.
When Galant realizes that his master's white family will always treat him as a slave, he leads a revolt in South Africa during 1825.
Genre(s): War Story.

4808. *An Instant in the Wind.* 1976. New York: Penguin, 1985. 250 pp.
In 1749, after her husband dies, Elisabeth Maria Larsson is stranded on the Great Fish River and a runaway black slave saves her.
Genre(s): Biographical Fiction.

4809. *On the Contrary.* Boston: Little, Brown, 1994. 375 pp.
Awaiting execution in a South African prison in the 18th century, Étienne Barbier recalls his adventures in Africa's colonial society.
Genre(s): Adventure Story.

Brown, James Ambrose

4810. *The Ridge of Gold.* New York: St. Martin's, 1986. 328 pp.
Leonard Penlynne vows revenge against his former employer, Josiah Rawlingson, for the hardships he has faced in the boomtown of Johannesburg during the 1880s.

Bunn, T. Davis

4811. *Sahara Crosswind.* Minneapolis, MN: Bethany House, 1994. 186 pp.
Jake and Pierre risk their lives on the Sahara Desert to save a nation. (*Series:* Rendezvous With Destiny, 3)
Genre(s): Christian Fiction; Political Fiction.

Burke, Colin

4812. *Kimberley.* New York: Knopf, 1985. 480 pp.
In 1899, the Boers hold Kimberley in a siege for over 100 days and make Bart Bannock fear that the military will use his prize race-horses in the cavalry.
Genre(s): War Story.

Carter, Peter

◆ 4813. *The Sentinels.* New York: Oxford, 1980. 199 pp.
When John and Yoruba are shipwrecked on the African coast, they each survive by learning some of the other's language and working together.
Award(s): Guardian Award; Premio di Lettaratura d'Italie.

Cary, Joyce

4814. *The African Witch*. New York: Morrow, 1936. 416 pp.
Aladai finishes his education at Oxford in England and returns to his African tribe, aspiring to be its chief, but he finds competition.

Cavanaugh, Jack

4815. *The Pride and the Passion*. Chicago: Moody, 1996. 331 pp.
Margo de Campion, Jan van der Kemp, and Rachel van der Kemp face the problems of settling in South Africa in the 19th century. (*Series:* African Covenant, 1)
Genre(s): Christian Fiction; Romance.

Challoner, Robert

4816. *Give Fire!* New York: David and Charles, 1987. 204 pp.
Lord Charles Oakshott, in the sequel to *Run Out the Guns*, takes a sloop to Mameluke, Egypt in an attempt to stop Napoleon, and once there he witnesses the Battle of the Pyramids and the Battle of the Nile.
Genre(s): War Story; Sea Story.

Clews, Roy

4817. *The Golden City*. Leicester, England: Ulverscrof, 1983. 392 pp.
In the 19th century a mad missionary, Arab slavers, two women, and a British soldier travel together across the Sahara to Timbuktu.
Genre(s): Adventure Story.

Cloete, Stuart

4818. *The Fiercest Heart*. Boston: Houghton Mifflin, 1960. 435 pp.
Six Boer families leave their farms on the Great Trek from Cape Colony to the Transvaal in South Africa in the 1830s.

4819. *The Hill of Doves*. Boston: Houghton Mifflin, 1941. 508 pp.
Boer families live in the Transvall area of South Africa in 1880 in the sequel to *The Mask*.
Genre(s): Domestic Fiction.

4820. *The Mask*. Boston: Houghton Mifflin, 1957. 245 pp.
The Boers and the Kaffirs conflict between 1852 and 1854, in the sequel to *Watch for the Dawn*.
Genre(s): War Story.

4821. *The Turning Wheels*. Boston: Houghton Mifflin, 1937. 434 pp.
Dutch pioneers in South Africa leave the Cape Colony and head north to found the Orange Free States around 1836.

4822. *Watch for the Dawn*. Boston: Houghton Mifflin, 1939. 489 pp.

A young Boer tries to establish himself in a new life on the African veldt in the sequel to *The Turning Wheels*.
Genre(s): Domestic Fiction.

Condé, Maryse

4823. *Segu*. New York: Viking, 1987. 535 pp.
In the late 18th century, the four sons of Segu nobleman Dousika Traore separate when one is taken as a slave to Brazil, another becomes a Moslem, a third follows the tribe's pagan ways, and the last turns to life as a mercenary.
Genre(s): Family Saga; Domestic Fiction.

Crane, John Kenny

◆ 4824. *The Legacy of Ladysmith*. New York: Linden, 1986. 398 pp.
The American biographer Jason Glass retells the story of the enigmatic Scottish doctor, Robert Menzies, who saved many of his patients during the Boer Wars at his Ladysmith hospital, but Glass's research reveals that Menzies had a much darker side as well.
Genre(s): War Story.

De Klerk, Willem Abraham

4825. *The Thirstland*. London: Collins, 1977. 463 pp.
In the 1880s, Boers trek from the Transvaal through the Kalahari desert, looking for freedom, and a half-caste trader helps to set up a small but brief republic south of Angola.
Genre(s): Biographical Fiction; Adventure Story.

Dewhurst, Keith

4826. *Captain of the Sands*. New York: Viking, 1981. 391 pp.
Tom Derker sails throughout the Atlantic as he watches the captains of the sands save themselves while sacrificing their black cargos.
Genre(s): Sea Story; Adventure Story.

Drummond, Emma

4827. *A Captive Freedom*. New York: St. Martin's, 1987. 320 pp.
Leila Duncan, an actress in late 19th-century London, hides her past as a maid and trooper's wife in an affair with a cavalry officer before her husband reappears and they leave for South Africa.
Genre(s): War Story; Adventure Story.

Duggan, William

◆ 4828. *The Great Thirst*. New York: Delacorte, 1985. 328 pp.
The BaNare, living on the edge of the Kalahari Desert, are forced to live with threats of encroachment by the Zulu and the Boers.
Genre(s): Family Saga.

Forbath, Peter

4829. *The Last Hero.* New York: Warner, 1990. 729 pp.
In 1887, Henry Morton Stanley returns to Africa, planning to rescue Emin Pasha, the Egyptian forces leader left in the Sudan.
Genre(s): Biographical Fiction; Family Saga.

4830. *Lord of the Kongo.* New York: Simon and Schuster, 1996. 510 pp.
Gil Eanes, a Portuguese cabin boy, has a gift for languages which he uses when he becomes stranded in the Congo in 1482.
Genre(s): Epic Literature.

Forester, C. S.

4831. *The Sky and the Forest.* Boston: Little, Brown, 1948. 313 pp.
King of a Central African tribe, Loa conquers other villages and builds his empire until King Leopold's agents destroy him.
Genre(s): Political Fiction.

Fraser, George MacDonald

4832. *The Pyrates.* New York: Knopf, 1984. 405 pp.
Captain Ben Avery goes to Madagascar with a crown for the king, but pirates capture the crown, and he spends time trying to collect the six jewels from six Barbary Coast pirate captains.
Genre(s): Adventure Story.

Gleason, Judith

◆ **4833.** *Agotime.* New York: Grossman, 1970. 288 pp.
Agotime, a Dahomean queen, is exiled into slavery in Brazil.

Golon, Anne

4834. *Angélique in Barbary.* Trans. Monroe Stearns. New York: Bantam, 1968. 443 pp.
While Countess Angélique searches for her husband, pirates capture her twice and sell her as a slave to Moslems in North Africa.
Genre(s): Political Fiction; War Story.

Gurnah, Abdulrazak

4835. *Paradise.* New York: New Press, 1994. 256 pp.
Yusuf, 12, is sold as an indentured servant to Aziz although at first he is unaware of the transaction because Aziz treats him reasonably.
Genre(s): Bildungsroman (Coming of Age).

Hagerfors, Lennart

4836. *The Whales in Lake Tanganyika.* New York: Grove, 1989. 172 pp.
The arrogant Henry Stanley searches for Livingston in Africa with the help of Shaw, an alcoholic and a former sailor, who records the expedition in his diary.
Genre(s): Biographical Fiction; Adventure Story.

Haley, Alex

◆ **4837.** *Roots.* New York: Doubleday, 1976. 379 pp.
Captured in Africa, Kunte Kinte, a tribal prince, becomes a slave, and eventually generations of his family survive to become free again.
Genre(s): Family Saga.

Hansen, Brooks

4838. *The Chess Garden: Or the Twilight Letters of Gustav Uyterhoeven.* New York: Riverhead, 1996. 464 pp.
Dr. Uyterhoeven goes to Africa during the Boer Wars to minister to victims and sends a series of letters home to his wife in Dayton, Ohio, which the neighbors read in his chess garden.
Genre(s): War Story; Fantastic Literature.

Jackson-Opoku, Sandra

4839. *The River Where Blood Is Born.* New York: Ballantine, 1997. 416 pp.
The First Wife in Africa 300 years ago has a daughter, and her daughter has a daughter, and all of them face hardships and difficulties, including rape and slavery, in Barbados and in the United States, but they help each other through dreams and magic.
Genre(s): Family Saga.

Kaye, M. M.

4840. *Trade Wind.* New York: St. Martin's, 1981. 553 pp.
In 1859, Althena Hollis goes to Zanzibar to try to stop slave trading.
Genre(s): Adventure Story.

Kinsale, Laura

◆ **4841.** *The Dream Hunter.* New York: Berkley, 1994. 352 pp.
While Lord Winter searches for an Arabian horse in Africa, he hires a young Bedouin guide who turns out to be a British girl trying to return home from the desert.
Genre(s): Romance.

Laffeaty, Christina

◆ **4842.** *Far Forbidden Plains.* New York: St. Martin's, 1989. 512 pp.
Petronella van Zyl marries an outsider in Transvaal, South Africa, and after he is deported, her family suffers in the Boer Wars and into the period before World War I before they are reunited.
Genre(s): Romance.

Laye, Camra

4843. *The Guardian of the Word.* Trans. James Kirkup. New York: Random House, 1984. 223 pp.

◆ May be suitable for young adult readers

Mari-Diata founds the empire of Mali during the 13th century.
Genre(s): Biographical Fiction.

Lennox, Judith

4844. *The Glittering Strand.* New York: St. Martin's, 1994. 474 pp.
On her way from France to Italy to be married in the 16th century, Serafina Guardi, 10, is kidnapped and sold to a kind North African master who later sends her back to France to claim her inheritance and to rebuild the family silk trade.
Genre(s): Family Saga.

Lindsey, Johanna

4845. *Captive Bride.* Unity, ME: Five Star, 1996. 274 pp.
Philip Caxton, son of a Bedouin chief and his British wife, abducts Christina, also British, who after finally escaping from him, realizes that she loves him.
Genre(s): Romance; Adventure Story.

Maalouf, Amin

4846. *Leo Africanus.* Trans. Peter Sluglett. New York: New Amsterdam, 1992. 360 pp.
After much travel Hassan al-Wazzan becomes Leo Africanus when Pope Leo X christens him in Rome during the 16th century.
Genre(s): Biographical Fiction.

Mackin, Jeanne

4847. *Dreams of Empire.* New York: Kensington, 1996. 248 pp.
In Cairo during 1798, Napoleon refuses coffee, which happens to be spiked with glass, identical to a drink that killed a man in 3737 BC, and when the shiek's nephew drinks it and dies, the Verdiers wonder who wants to kill Napoleon.
Genre(s): Mystery; Romance.

Masefield, John

4848. *Dead Ned.* New York: Macmillan, 1938. 370 pp.
When young Ned Mansell finishes his medical training, he is accused and convicted of murdering an old friend, and after he is hanged, two of his father's friends take his body and restore him to life.
Genre(s): Adventure Story; Fantastic Literature.

4849. *Live and Kicking Ned.* New York: Macmillan, 1939. 462 pp.
In the sequel to *Dead Ned,* Ned continues to escape from those who chase him during his adventures before returning to England.
Genre(s): Adventure Story; Fantastic Literature.

Matthee, Dalene

4850. *Fiela's Child.* New York: Knopf, 1986. 320 pp.

Benjamin Fiela, a white foundling in South Africa, lives from ages 3 to 12 with a black family before a poor white couple claim him as a child who strayed from home.
Genre(s): Domestic Fiction.

McCutchan, Philip

4851. *The Red Daniel.* New York: St. Martin's, 1973. 221 pp.
In the second Boer Wars, James Ogilvie serves in South Africa as a double agent for the British government.
Genre(s): War Story.

McMenemy, Nickie

4852. *Assegai!* New York: Saturday Review, 1973. 216 pp.
In the early 19th century, Tshaka, King of the Zulus, takes as his favorite the lovely slave girl Thola in South Africa.
Genre(s): Biographical Fiction.

Michener, James A.

◆ 4853. *The Covenant.* New York: Random House, 1980. 877 pp.
The Nxumalos, the Van Doorns, and the Saltwoods interact during several hundred years of South African life.
Genre(s): Family Saga.

Mofolo, Thomas

◆ 4854. *Chaka.* Trans. F. H. Dutton. New York: Oxford, 1967. 198 pp.
Chaka unites many of the South African tribes into the nation of Zulu.
Genre(s): Biographical Fiction.

Moore, Brian

4855. *The Magician's Wife.* New York: Dutton, 1998. 240 pp.
Napoleon III asks Henri Lambert to go to Algeria and test his powers with those of an Arab holy man, and when he and his wife go, Henri wonders if they will be preventing war in the future as well as the present.

Mutswairo, Solomon M.

4856. *Mapondera, Soldier of Zimbabwe.* Ardbennie, Harare, Zimbabwe, 1983. 116 pp.
In the 19th century, the British prepare to take over Zimbabwe against the wishes of the area's natives.
Genre(s): War Story.

Out el Kouloub

4857. *Ramza.* Trans. Nayra Atiya. Syracuse, NY: Syracuse University Press, 1994. 222 pp.
In an Egyptian harem in her father's house in the late 19th century, Ramza sneaks into the library and learns to read and write, but when she proposes to marry the man of her choice, her father strongly objects.
Genre(s): Domestic Fiction.

4858. *Zanouba.* Syracuse, NY: Syracuse University Press, 1997. 224 pp.

Zanouba, 16, marries a cotton dealer, but the marriage lasts only a day, and with her dowry and virginity intact, she then marries Abdel Meguid and joins his harem, fueling the jealousy of one of his high-ranking wives.
Genre(s): Domestic Fiction; Mystery.

Palmer, Catherine

4859. *The Treasure of Timbuktu.* Wheaton, IL: Tyndale House, 1997. 271 pp.
Mungo Park aids Tillie Thornton during her escape from the Tuaregs of Timbuktu in the early 19th century. (*Series:* HeartQuest, 1)
Genre(s): Adventure Story; Christian Fiction.

Peters, Elizabeth

◆ 4860. *The Curse of the Pharaohs.* New York: Dodd, Mead, 1981. 357 pp.
Amelia Peabody and her husband dig in Egypt in the late 19th century at a pharaoh's tomb, but mysterious problems indicate that someone is trying to harm them.
Genre(s): Mystery.

◆ 4861. *The Hippopotamus Pool.* New York: Warner, 1996. 382 pp.
Amelia Peabody and her husband Emerson search for queen Tetisheri's lost tomb where they encounter villains and other related problems.
Genre(s): Mystery.

◆ 4862. *The Last Camel Died at Noon.* New York: Warner, 1991. 352 pp.
Amelia Peabody, her husband, and her son Ramses seach for an archaeologist in the Sudan who disappeared 14 years before.
Genre(s): Mystery.

◆ 4863. *Lion in the Valley.* New York: Atheneum, 1986. 291 pp.
When Amelia Peabody and her husband return to Egypt with their eight-year-old son, Ramses, a criminal kidnaps her.
Genre(s): Mystery.

◆ 4864. *The Mummy Case.* New York: St. Martin's, 1985. 313 pp.
Amelia Peabody, her husband, and son go to Egypt after a dealer in stolen antiquities is murdered.
Genre(s): Mystery.

◆ 4865. *Seeing a Large Cat.* New York: Warner, 1997. 416 pp.
Amelia Peabody Emerson investigates a grisly murder in 1903 while trying to keep both her adopted daughter and her lovesick son Ramses in tow.
Genre(s): Mystery.

◆ 4866. *The Snake, the Crocodile, and the Dog.* New York: Warner, 1992. 340 pp.
Amelia Peabody and her husband go to Egypt without their son, expecting to enjoy each other's company while excavating, but a criminal ruins their plans.
Genre(s): Mystery.

Picard, Hymen Willem Johannes

4867. *Man of Constantia.* New York: Purnell, 1973. 300 pp.
Simon van der Stel governs at the Cape of Good Hope in South Africa during the late 17th century.
Genre(s): Biographical Fiction.

Samkange, Stanlake

4868. *On Trial for My Country.* London: Heinemann, 1967. 160 pp.
Cecil Rhodes goes to Africa and conquers Lobengula, King of the Ndebele, and his people.
Genre(s): Biographical Fiction.

Scholefield, Alan

4869. *Great Elephant.* New York: Morrow, 1968. 214 pp.
A white family with one member a fugitive lives with the Zulus in South Africa during the early 19th century.
Genre(s): Adventure Story.

4870. *The Hammer of God.* New York: Morrow, 1973. 205 pp.
Theodore II, a brigand and self-acclaimed ruler of Abyssinia, demonstrates greatness in his concern for his people and his frustration with Queen Victoria's disregard, which are among the events that cause him to slowly go mad.
Genre(s): Biographical Fiction.

4871. *The Stone Flower.* New York: Morrow, 1982. 479 pp.
An illiterate Cockney and a Jewish refugee from Kiev become partners in a diamond business, but they turn against one another when their children, one part-Hottentot, fall in love.
Genre(s): War Story.

4872. *Wild Dog Running.* New York: Morrow, 1971. 245 pp.
An English family, escaping the Industrial Revolution by emigrating to South Africa, encounters troubles, on the way and after arrival, that require empathy and courage.

Schreiner, Olive

4873. *The Story of an African Farm.* 1883. New York: Penguin, 1983. 656 pp.
A woman on an African farm is an unmarried mother, isolated from society in the 19th century.
Genre(s): Domestic Fiction.

Silverberg, Robert

4874. *Lord of Darkness.* New York: Arbor House, 1983. 558 pp.
In the 16th century, Portuguese in Brazil capture Andrews Battell and take him to Africa where he suffers hardship before joining the cannibalistic Jaqqa.
Genre(s): Biographical Fiction.

Smith, Mason McCann

4875. *When the Emperor Dies.* New York: Random House, 1981. 393 pp.
When Queen Victoria fails to respond to the Ethiopian emperor Theodore's diplomatic requests, he imprisons the British consul.
Genre(s): Biographical Fiction.

Smith, Wilbur A.

4876. *The Angels Weep.* Garden City, NY: Doubleday, 1983. 468 pp.
The sequel to *Men of Men* shows the Ballantyne family in Rhodesia making their fortunes in 1895 and later as established citizens of Zimbabwe in 1977.
Genre(s): Family Saga.

4877. *Birds of Prey.* New York: St. Martin's, 1997. 554 pp.
In 1667 Hal becomes a man after the Dutch torture and kill his father while on his ship off the coast of Africa, and he carefully works his way overland to claim his father's treasure and to face the British captain who betrayed them.
Genre(s): War Story; Bildungsroman (Coming of Age); Sea Story.

4878. *Flight of the Falcon.* Garden City, NY: Doubleday, 1982. 545 pp.
In 1860, Robyn Ballantyne and her brother travel deep into Africa to find their lost missionary-explorer father.
Genre(s): Adventure Story.

4879. *The Roar of Thunder.* New York: Simon and Schuster, 1996. 564 pp.
In the sequel to *When the Lion Feeds*, Sean Courtney must fight in the Zulu War, and afterward, he decides to search for gold in the wilds of South Africa.
Genre(s): Adventure Story; Family Saga; War Story.

4880. *When the Lion Feeds.* New York: Dell, 1964. 564 pp.
Sean Courtney goes to South Africa in the late 19th century to begin farming.
Genre(s): Adventure Story; Family Saga.

1900 and After

Achebe, Chinua

◆ 4881. *Arrow of God.* New York: John Day, 1967. 287 pp.
Ezeulu, Chief Priest of Ulu in the 1920s, decides to send his son to the missionary school where his conversion causes conflict among Ezeulu, the tribe, and the school's English administrator.

◆ 4882. *A Man of the People.* New York: John Day, 1966. 150 pp.
In a newly independent Nigerian town, power corrupts leaders and hides inefficiency.
Genre(s): Political Fiction.

Amadi, Elechi

4883. *Estrangement.* Portsmouth, NH: Heinemann, 1986. 244 pp.
In 1970, at the end of the Nigerian Civil War, Alekiri has a child by the Hansa soldier who rescued her from the battle front, and then awaits the return of her husband who, through tradition, must accept her and her child.
Genre(s): War Story.

Antunes, António Lobo

4884. *Fado Alexandrino.* New York: Grove Weidenfeld, 1990. 576 pp.
Four ex-soldiers gather at dinner and recall the atrocities they committed in Angola when Portugal, between 1960 and 1974, sent a million men to protect its interests there.
Genre(s): War Story.

Attaway, Robert J.

4885. *I Think of Warri.* New York: Harper, 1974. 154 pp.
After living in the small town of Warri, Nigeria, and learning its traditions, Henry Christopher regrets having to leave as the war with Biafra escalates.
Genre(s): War Story.

Barber, Noel

4886. *Sakkara.* New York: Macmillan, 1984. 520 pp.
Mark Holt, British diplomat and lawyer, loves Serena, daughter of an adviser in the Egyptian court, but they each marry someone else and endure various trials, including World War II, before they can unite.
Genre(s): War Story; Love Story.

Bayer, William

4887. *Visions of Isabelle.* New York: Delacorte, 1976. 318 pp.
Isabelle Eberhardt wanders around African desert towns in the early 20th century, disguised as a man, writing articles about her experiences.
Genre(s): Biographical Fiction.

Behr, Mark

4888. *The Smell of Apples.* New York: St. Martin's, 1995. 200 pp.
In 1970s South Africa, Marnus Erasmus, an Afrikaner whose father is a general in the military, watches his family disintegrate under the ruthlessness of apartheid.
Genre(s): Bildungsroman (Coming of Age).

Beylen, Robert

4889. *The Way to the Sun.* Trans. Len Ortzen. Boston: Little, Brown, 1971. 255 pp.
A British army lieutenant, a married American woman, and a French former boxer flee from the Axis forces across North Africa in World War II.
Genre(s): War Story.

Borden, G. F.

4890. *Easter Day, 1941.* New York: Morrow, 1987. 256 pp.
An American veteran of the Spanish Civil War leads three British soldiers across the Libyan desert in a captured Italian tank, but going toward Tobruk they become lost.
Genre(s): War Story.

Boyd, William

4891. *An Ice-Cream War.* New York: Morrow, 1983. 408 pp.
Gabriel, a professional soldier, finds solace in a prison hospital of German East Africa while his less successful brother finds solace in an affair with Gabriel's wife until she commits suicide.
Genre(s): War Story; Satire.

Bull, Bartle

4892. *The White Rhino Hotel.* New York: Viking, 1992. 404 pp.
Kenya opens its doors to British veterans in 1919, and Anton Rider, a gypsy, becomes a central figure there, along with the dwarf Olivio Fonseca Alavedo.
Genre(s): Adventure Story.

Camus, Albert

4893. *The First Man.* New York: Knopf, 1994. 336 pp.
Jacques Cormery lives his first 14 years in French Algeria where his poverty and his status as a fatherless child make him feel like an outsider.
Genre(s): Bildungsroman (Coming of Age).

Cloete, Stuart

4894. *Rags of Glory.* Garden City, NY: Doubleday, 1963. 631 pp.
Turnbull, an English captain, Moolman, an ivory hunter, and a Dutch girl who betrays her country participate in the Boer Wars.
Genre(s): War Story.

Dangarembga, Tsisi

◆ 4895. *Nervous Conditions.* Seattle, WA: Seal, 1989. 204 pp.
Tambudzai, the eldest daughter in a poor rural Rhodesian family, goes to her uncle's home after her brother's mysterious death in the 1960s, and although she appreciates the education he offers, she has difficulty reconciling her culture with that of the West.
Genre(s): Bildungsroman (Coming of Age).

Dawkins, Louisa

4896. *Natives and Strangers.* Boston: Houghton Mifflin, 1985. 404 pp.
Marietta, born in Africa, treats her servants as friends and feels like an outsider, a condition that continues when she returns to England for her schooling.

Deighton, Len

◆ 4897. *City of Gold.* New York: HarperCollins, 1992. 375 pp.
While Bert Cutler, Glasgow police inspector, escorts Jimmy Ross to Cairo to stand trial for killing an officer, he dies, and Ross assumes his identity so that in Cairo, Ross finds himself trying to apprehend the spy helping Rommel in Africa.
Genre(s): Spy Fiction.

Dem, Tidiane

4898. *Masseni.* Trans. Frances Frenaye. Baton Rouge: Louisiana State University Press, 1982. 175 pp.
Masseni becomes the youngest wife of a chief and marries twice more after his death, before the traditional village life changes when the French leave.
Genre(s): Domestic Fiction.

Djebar, Assia

4899. *Fantasia: An Algerian Cavalcade.* Trans. Dorothy S. Blair. Portsmouth, NH: Heinemann, 1993. 227 pp.
Algerian women are freed by language, but simultaneously, language controls what they know because those who wrote the history of their country were oppressors rather than insiders.
Genre(s): Domestic Fiction.

4900. *A Sister to Scheherazade.* Trans. Dorothy S. Blair. Portsmouth, NH: Heinemann, 1993. 159 pp.
In the sequel to *Fantasia: An Algerian Cavalcade*, Isma, first wife of an Algerian male tells the story of his second wife, Hijila, to another wife.
Genre(s): Domestic Fiction.

Driscoll, Peter

4901. *Heritage.* Garden City, NY: Doubleday, 1982. 504 pp.
Robert Lombard, a military general, has friends who become enemies after World War II when they support different sides of a conflict.
Genre(s): Political Fiction.

4902. *Spearhead.* Boston: Little, Brown, 1989. 456 pp.
The People's Congress in South Africa sees a way to free one of its leaders from prison when he goes to a private clinic for cancer surgery.

Durrell, Lawrence

4903. *Balthazar.* New York: Dutton, 1958. 250 pp.

◆ May be suitable for young adult readers

In the sequel to *Justine* of The Alexandria Quartet, Balthazar, a psychiatrist, provides a different perspective of life in Alexandria.

4904. *Clea.* New York: Dutton, 1960. 287 pp.
In The Alexandria Quartet sequel to *Mountolive*, the Englishman Darley returns to Alexandria and has an affair with one of the women in his circle of friends.

4905. *Justine.* New York: Dutton, 1957. 253 pp.
In Alexandria, the first volume of The Alexandria Quartet presents Justine, her husband, a prostitute, and a poor young man whom Justine finds attractive.

4906. *Mountolive.* New York: Dutton, 1959. 318 pp.
The sequel to *Balthazar* in The Alexandria Quartet Series continues the story of expatriates and Europeans meeting and living in Alexandria.
Genre(s): Adventure Story.

4907. *Sebastian: Or Ruling Passions.* New York: Viking, 1984. 202 pp.
Sebastian becomes the lover of Constance, but he is a gnostic known as Affad who leaves her in Switzerland to continue her psychoanalytic training while he returns to Alexandria. (*Series:* Avignon Quintet, 4)
Genre(s): Family Saga.

Ebersohn, Wessel

4908. *Divide the Night.* New York: Pantheon, 1981. 224 pp.
When a psychologist in South Africa treats the killer of eight blacks, he knows that the man will strike again.

4909. *Store Up the Anger.* New York: Doubleday, 1981. 299 pp.
While Sam Bhengu waits to die in a South African police hospital cell, he remembers his youth and the riots at Sophiatown and Cato Manor.

Emecheta, Buchi

◆ **4910. *The Bride Price.*** New York: G. Braziller, 1976. 168 pp.
When Aku-nna's father dies, the tribe demands that she, her mother, and brother go to live with her uncle, a situation that conflicts with the views she holds in the 1950s.
Genre(s): Love Story.

4911. *Double Yoke.* New York: G. Braziller, 1983. 163 pp.
Nko wants to be wife, mother, and student when she marries another Nigerian undergraduate, but her mother warns her that her husband will want a wife like his own mother.

4912. *The Joys of Motherhood.* New York: G. Braziller, 1979. 224 pp.
Nnu Ego cannot adjust to life in Lagos after leaving her village, and while her children adapt to modern life, she remains isolated.
Genre(s): Domestic Fiction.

◆ **4913. *The Slave Girl.*** New York: G. Braziller, 1977. 179 pp.

Ojebeta's older brother sells her into slavery when she is eight, although the practice has supposedly been abolished in their Ibo tribe.

Faust, Irvin

4914. *Jim Dandy.* New York: Carroll and Graf, 1994. 297 pp.
Hollis Cleveland, known as Jim Dandy, dances for his father's musical review in 1915, but after college 20 years later, he runs from a Harlem numbers boss, and ends up in Ethiopia during its war with Italy.
Genre(s): War Story.

Follett, Ken

4915. *The Key to Rebecca.* New York: Morrow, 1980. 381 pp.
British Intelligence tries to stop a German spy in Cairo who transmits messages coded from a copy of Du Maurier's *Rebecca*.
Genre(s): Spy Fiction; War Story.

Forester, C. S.

4916. *The African Queen.* Boston: Little, Brown, 1935. 275 pp.
An English spinster and a Cockney with a steam launch travel down river in Africa to blow up a German ship carrying the man who killed the spinster's brother at his mission.
Genre(s): Love Story; War Story.

Freed, Lynn

4917. *The Bungalow.* New York: Poseidon, 1993. 210 pp.
In South Africa, a group of affluent Jews in 1975 treat blacks with the same disdain that anti-Semites had treated them, much to the dismay of Ruth Frank who lives in this society.
Genre(s): Domestic Fiction.

Freeman, David

4918. *One of Us.* New York: Carroll and Graf, 1997. 272 pp.
Vera Napier visits Egypt with her friend Emma just as World War II is starting, and the country's romance and passion surprise her.
Genre(s): War Story.

Fugard, Athol

4919. *Tsotsi.* New York: Random House, 1980. 167 pp.
Tsotsi adopts a name meaning "Thug" as he leads a small gang in murdering fellow countrymen in retribution for black ghetto life.
Genre(s): Political Fiction.

Fugard, Sheila

4920. *A Revolutionary Woman.* New York: Braziller, 1985. 144 pp.

When an African boy seduces a mentally disabled Boer girl in the 1920s, Christina Ransome, a disciple of Gandhi in South Africa, tries to protect the boy.
Genre(s): Domestic Fiction.

Gifford, Thomas

4921. *Praetorian.* New York: Bantam, 1993. 495 pp.
At Churchill's request, Rodger Godwin, a journalist, goes with General Max Hood, after an affair with Hood's wife, to kill Rommel in North Africa.
Genre(s): War Story; Adventure Story.

Gilman, Dorothy

◆ 4922. *Caravan.* Garden City, NY: Doubleday, 1992. 263 pp.
Caressa Horvath attempts to rob an anthropologist, but instead of prosecuting, he marries her and takes her with him to the Sahara Desert.
Genre(s): Adventure Story; Romance.

Givon, Thomas

4923. *Running Through Grass.* New York: HarperCollins, 1997. 304 pp.
In the 1960s, Robert Aron tries to take his girlfriend Marie to France from Algeria during the civil war, but one of his compatriots makes him prey.
Genre(s): Political Fiction.

Gordimer, Nadine

4924. *The Conservationist.* New York: Viking, 1975. 252 pp.
Mehring thinks that he will be able to continue his lifestyle by being kind but firm to his slaves and by avoiding the Boer neighbors in his South African home.
Award(s): Booker Prize.
Genre(s): Political Fiction.

4925. *The Lying Days.* New York: Simon and Schuster, 1953. 340 pp.
Against a backdrop of apartheid in South Africa, as Helen Shaw tries to grow up, she realizes that she has imposed her own ideals on everyone else.
Genre(s): Bildungsroman (Coming of Age).

4926. *Occasion for Loving.* New York: Viking, 1963. 308 pp.
A Jewish musicologist and his wife come to visit friends from the university in Johannesburg, and when the wife falls in love with an African artist, she commits unforgivable social taboos.
Genre(s): Political Fiction.

4927. *A Sport of Nature.* New York: Knopf, 1987. 341 pp.
Hillela Capran, a Jewish South African, becomes involved in African revolutionary causes.
Genre(s): Political Fiction.

Gordon, Shelia

4928. *Unfinished Business.* New York: Crown, 1975. 140 pp.
Paul, a successful doctor, illegally treats a black man and is sent to prison before being exiled to England.
Genre(s): Medical Novel.

Graham, Winston

4929. *Tremor.* New York: St. Martin's, 1996. 256 pp.
In 1960, Matthew Morris goes to Morocco for two weeks to recover from his unsuccessful writing career and failed marriage and while there he experiences the destructive power of an earthquake on February 29.
Genre(s): Adventure Story.

Griffin, W. E. B.

4930. *The New Breed.* New York: Putnam, 1987. 398 pp.
Colonel Sandy Felter goes to Vietnam and to the Congo and returns to tell the new president Johnson that the Congo is as volatile as Southeast Asia. (*Series:* Brotherhood of War, 7)
Genre(s): War Story; Political Fiction.

Hardy, Ronald

4931. *Rivers of Darkness.* New York: Putnam, 1979. 393 pp.
In 1973, during the final days of Portuguese colonization in Mozambique, Dr. Lynd tries to combat black flies while guerrillas threaten in the background.

Head, Bessie

4932. *A Bewitched Crossroad.* New York: Paragon House, 1986. 198 pp.
Sebina wisely attaches his clan to Khama the Great, who shows integrity and leadership and saves Botswana from gold-hungry whites swarming the land.
Genre(s): Family Saga.

Hennessy, Max

4933. *Blunted Lance.* New York: Atheneum, 1981. 298 pp.
In the sequel to *Soldier of the Queen*, Dabney Goff becomes a hero both in the Boer Wars and World War I while his father relates military history to Dabney's son back in Scotland.
Genre(s): War Story; Family Saga; Adventure Story.

Highland, Monica

4934. *110 Shanghai Road.* New York: McGraw Hill, 1986. 590 pp.
Matt, Harley, and Jordan, all raised in Shanghai during the early 20th century are part of the upheaval from 1926 to 1937, and they keep in contact through the years.
Genre(s): Adventure Story.

◆ May be suitable for young adult readers

Holt, Victoria

4935. *The Curse of the Kings.* Garden City, NY: Doubleday, 1973. 330 pp.
Although she loves Tybalt Travers and goes with him to Egypt on an archaeological expedition, Judith Osmond fears that he has married her for her money.
Genre(s): Romance.

Hulme, Kathryn

◆ 4936. *The Nun's Story.* Boston: Little, Brown, 1956. 339 pp.
Gabrielle Van der Mal enters a Belgian convent after an unhappy love affair and works in the Congo and Holland for 17 years before deciding that religious life is not for her.
Genre(s): Religious Fiction.

Huxley, Elspeth

4937. *The African Poison Murders.* New York: Harper and Row, 1940. 279 pp.
In Chania, East Africa, Policeman Vachell keeps an eye on the detested German, Karl Munson, before Munson is murdered.
Genre(s): Mystery.

Hylton, Sara

◆ 4938. *In the Shadow of the Nile.* New York: St. Martin's, 1994. 426 pp.
In the 1920s, Laura falls in love with an Egyptian prince whom her British family scorns.

Jones, J. D. F

4939. *The Buchan Papers.* New York: St. Martin's, 1997. 192 pp.
Buchan searches for gold stolen from the Boers after the end of the war in 1902.
Genre(s): Mystery; War Story.

Kayira, Legson

4940. *Jingala.* New York: Doubleday, 1969. 160 pp.
Gregory, the son of African widower Jingala, wants to become a priest at the mission school, and Jingala wants to keep him at home in the village.
Genre(s): Domestic Fiction.

Kiefer, Warren

4941. *The Lingala Code.* New York: Random House, 1972. 169 pp.
In the 1960s, during the struggle for independence in the Congo, a Texan is shot, and as the investigation opens, he seems more concerned about his money than freedom for those he exploits.
Genre(s): Mystery.

Lachmet, Djanet

◆ 4942. *Lallia.* Trans. Judith Still. New York: Harper, 1987. 150 pp.

Lallia, a young woman growing up in an Arab household, observes the political influences on her family as Algeria tries to win its independence from France.
Genre(s): War Story; Political Fiction.

Landsman, Anne

4943. *The Devil's Chimney.* New York: Farrar, Straus and Giroux, 1997. 304 pp.
In Oudtshoor, South Africa, a couple tries to raise ostriches, but the woman is a free spirit who breaks all of the local conventions while her husband disappears into the mountains.
Genre(s): Domestic Fiction.

Le Clézio, J. M. G.

◆ 4944. *Onitsha.* Trans. Alison Anderson. Lincoln: University of Nebraska Press, 1997. 192 pp.
As Fintan travels with his mother to Africa in 1948 to join his father at his trading company, he becomes aware of the Western intolerance of African people.
Genre(s): Bildungsroman (Coming of Age).

Leslie-Melville, Jock, and Betty Leslie-Melville

4945. *Bagamoyo.* New York: Morrow, 1983. 430 pp.
Richard Leigh moves to Kenya in 1898 and remains there after taking a job with the railroad and founding a farm, Bagamoyo.
Genre(s): Adventure Story.

Lobo Antunes, Antonio

4946. *South of Nowhere.* Trans. Elizabeth Lowe. New York: Random House, 1983. 160 pp.
A soldier loses faith in his company during the 15-year war in Angola preceding independence from Portugal in 1975.
Genre(s): War Story.

Mahfouz, Naguib

4947. *Autumn Quail.* Trans. Roger Allen. New York: Doubleday, 1990. 176 pp.
In Egypt, Isa, once a high official, has no place in the new government after the revolution in 1952, and he becomes an exile in his own country.
Genre(s): Political Fiction.

4948. *The Beggar.* Trans. Kristin Walker Henry. New York: Doubleday, 1990. 144 pp.
Omar, a successful Egyptian lawyer, loses all sense of value in his life after the revolution, and he neglects his business and marriage to search for meaning.
Genre(s): Political Fiction.

4949. *The Harafish.* Garden City, NY: Doubleday, 1994. 416 pp.
The passage of time in a Cairo alley is local and manifests itself in the rise and fall of the al-Nagi clan, beginning with the cart driver Ashur, as the clan wins and loses approval of the *harafish* (common people).
Genre(s): Domestic Fiction; Family Saga.

4950. *Palace of Desire.* Trans. William M. Hutchins and Olive E. Kenny. Garden City, NY: Doubleday, 1991. 422 pp.
In the sequel to *Palace Walk*, Al-Sayyid decides to end his five-year abstinence from women and liquor after the death of his son, while his adult children continue to struggle.
Genre(s): Family Saga.

4951. *Palace Walk.* Trans. William M. Hutchins and Olive E. Kenny. Garden City, NY: Doubleday, 1990. 498 pp.
At the end of World War I, al-Sayyid Ahmad explores Cairo at night while his family stays at home living according to the Qur'an.
Genre(s): Family Saga.

4952. *Respected Sir.* Trans. Rasheed El-Enany. New York: Doubleday, 1990. 208 pp.
Othman decides that he wants to be promoted through the Egyptian bureaucracy after the revolution, and this goal complicates other areas of his life.
Genre(s): Political Fiction.

4953. *Sugar Street.* Trans. William Maynard Hutchins and Angele Botros Samaan. Garden City, NY: Doubleday, 1992. 308 pp.
In 1935, Egypt chafes under British occupation, and the Ahmad family, in this sequel to *Palace of Desire*, splits between Muslim fundamentalism and Marxism.
Genre(s): Family Saga.

Manning, Olivia

4954. *The Battle Lost and Won.* New York: Atheneum, 1979. 185 pp.
In the sequel to *Danger Tree*, Simon Boulderstone leaves Cairo to fight in the desert during World War II.
Genre(s): War Story.

4955. *The Danger Tree.* New York: Atheneum, 1977. 196 pp.
Guy and Harriet Pringle flee Romania for Egypt when the Nazis invade in World War II.
Genre(s): War Story.

Masterton, Graham

4956. *Solitaire.* New York: Morrow, 1982. 567 pp.
Barney Blitz, a New York Jew, tries to find his brother and make a fortune at the Kimberly diamond mine in the late 1800s.

Mazrui, Ali Al'Amin

4957. *The Trial of Christopher Okigbo.* New York: Third, 1972. 141 pp.
A mock trial of Christopher Okigbo's decision to support Biafran separatism during the Nigerian civil war occurs after his death in 1967 and ultimately blames him for neglecting his art.
Genre(s): Biographical Fiction; Fantastic Literature.

Memmi, Albert

4958. *The Scorpion.* Trans. Eleanor Levieux. New York: Orion, 1971. 242 pp.
When Émile, a writer and teacher, disappears around 1956 as Tunis fights for freedom from France, his brother Marcel, a doctor, tries to recreate Émile's novel and uncovers the truths of his family and his Arab society.
Genre(s): War Story.

Monninger, Joseph

4959. *The Viper Tree.* New York: Simon and Schuster, 1991. 267 pp.
Frederich Loebus, a Nazi deserter, comes to a West African mission, nearly dead, and after he recovers, he disapears into the bush, to escape and to help the natives.
Genre(s): War Story.

Moore, Robin

4960. *The White Tribe.* Encampment, WY: Affiliated Writers of America, 1991. 522 pp.
In 1976 mercenaries fight in the Rhodesian army against Robert Mugabe and Joshua Nkomo of the Patriotic Front, but in reality, Mugabe and Nkomo support the Patriotic Front.
Genre(s): War Story.

Musser, Elizabeth

4961. *Two Crosses.* Wheaton, IL: Victor, 1996. 467 pp.
When Ophelie and Gabriella meet at an Algerian convent school during the French-Algerian conflict, they both wear Huguenot crosses, which establishes a bond between them.
Genre(s): Christian Fiction; War Story.

4962. *Two Testaments.* Wheaton, IL: Chariot Victor, 1997. 450 pp.
In 1962, in the sequel to *Two Crosses*, while Algeria fights for freedom from France, Anne-Marie Duchemin escapes to France, leaving her boyfriend in Algeria, but a woman she meets is in love with the very man that Anne-Marie has left behind.
Genre(s): Christian Fiction; War Story.

Olinto, Antonio

4963. *The Water House.* New York: Carroll and Graf, 1985. 410 pp.
A freed slave grandmother in Brazil takes her daughter and granddaughter to her Nigerian birthplace in the early 20th century, and the granddaughter gains wealth and political power as the nation changes.
Genre(s): Family Saga.

Ondaatje, Michael

4964. *The English Patient.* New York: Knopf, 1992. 307 pp.
In Cairo, a man meets a married woman with whom he falls in love, but the war keeps them apart and destroys

her while he, severely burned, lives to tell their story to a nurse caring for him in an abandoned Tuscan villa.
Award(s): Booker Prize.
Genre(s): War Story.

Paton, Alan

4965. *Ah, But Your Land Is Beautiful.* New York: Scribner's, 1982. 271 pp.
From 1952 to 1958, the Liberal Party of South Africa responds to the losses of Coloureds under the powerful Nationalist Party.

4966. *Cry, the Beloved Country.* New York: Scribner's, 1951. 248 pp.
A Zulu country parson arrives in Johannesburg and finds that his sister has become a prostitute and his son a murderer.

4967. *Too Late the Phalarope.* New York: Scribner's, 1953. 276 pp.
After a popular white policeman confides in a native South African girl, his family suffers humiliation.
Genre(s): Love Story.

Pearce, Michael

◆ 4968. *The Mamur Zapt and the Donkey-Vous.* New York: Mysterious Press, 1992. 272 pp.
in 1908, the Mamur Zapt, Cadwallader Owen, must find what happened to the French contractor Octave Moulin who disappeared from the terrace of Shepheard's Hotel.
Genre(s): Mystery.

◆ 4969. *The Mamur Zapt and the Girl in the Nile.* New York: Mysterious Press, 1994. 234 pp.
Captain Cadwallader Owen, head of Cairo's police, must investigate the murder of a woman whose body washed up on the banks of the Nile having fallen off a *dahabeeyah* belonging to Prince Narouz.
Genre(s): Mystery.

◆ 4970. *The Mamur Zapt and the Men Behind.* New York: Warner, 1993. 246 pp.
Cadwallader Owen, head of the British secret police in Cairo around 1908, must investigate shootings and a bombing in a student café while balancing the affections of two beautiful women.
Genre(s): Mystery.

4971. *The Mamur Zapt and the Night of the Dog.* New York: Doubleday, 1991. 184 pp.
Cadwallader Owen, as head of Cairo's British secret police around 1910, investigates the desecration of a Coptic tomb and the death of a Muslim dervish.
Genre(s): Mystery.

◆ 4972. *The Mamur Zapt and the Spoils of Egypt.* New York: Mysterious Press, 1995. 186 pp.
When Captain Cadwallader Owen, chief of the Cairo police, must keep an eye on Miss Skinner, an American, two attempts on her life force him to believe that her concerns about the dangers involved in the exporting of antiquities may be well-founded.
Genre(s): Mystery.

Rive, Richard

4973. *Emergency Continued.* New York: Consortium, 1991. 190 pp.
A half-white teacher, Andrew Dreyer, no longer demonstrates against apartheid, and his son and pupils believe that he has acquiesed to the government in 1985.
Genre(s): Political Fiction.

Ruark, Robert

4974. *Something of Value.* Garden City, NY: Doubleday, 1955. 566 pp.
A white Englishman and his Kenyan native friend fear the spread of the Mau Mau terrorist movement.
Genre(s): Political Fiction.

Scholefield, Alan

◆ 4975. *The Alpha Raid.* New York: Morrow, 1976. 197 pp.
In 1917 a German paddlewheel steamer on Lake Tanganyika stops an Allied offensive until specialists can sink the ship.
Genre(s): War Story.

4976. *The Eagles of Malice.* New York: Morrow, 1968. 281 pp.
In Africa in 1904, Andrew Black, sub-inspector of the Bechuanaland Protectorate Police, pretends to join a German baron planning to exterminate the Heroes, a tribe of cattle owners, because the Germans want the land.
Genre(s): Political Fiction.

4977. *Lion in the Evening.* New York: Morrow, 1974. 175 pp.
An American civil engineer works on a strategic railroad in British East Africa during World War I.
Genre(s): War Story.

4978. *The Young Masters.* New York: Morrow, 1972. 210 pp.
In the 1930s the orphan Paul goes to search for his aunt with Luther, a Zulu, and when his aunt sends Luther away, Paul remembers him as a kind man who had been treated unfairly because of his color.
Genre(s): Bildungsroman (Coming of Age).

Serhane, Abdelhak

4979. *Messaouda.* New York: Harper and Row, 1986. 167 pp.
While his father chases women and leaves the family to starve in the streets and his mother submits to Muslim law in her mansouria, Abdelhak matures in Morocco during the 1950s.
Genre(s): Bildungsroman (Coming of Age); Biographical Fiction.

Serote, Mongane

4980. *To Every Birth Its Blood.* St. Paul, MN: Thunder's Mouth, 1989. 368 pp.
In 1976, Africans struggle against apartheid in the Alexandra township outside Johannesburg and the journalist

Tuki and his young nephew Oupa, an activist, are involved.
Genre(s): Political Fiction.

Sher, Anthony

4981. *Middlepost.* New York: Knopf, 1989. 400 pp.
Smous, a Jewish peddler, leaves Lithuania during the pogroms and travels to South Africa where he encounters many people, none of whom speak Yiddish, while he searches for his uncle.
Genre(s): Picaresque Fiction.

Slavitt, David R.

4982. *The Killing of the King.* Garden City, NY: Doubleday, 1974. 335 pp.
In 1965, King Farouk invites Lawrence Streeter's daughter to his hotel with the intention of seducing her, and when Streeter discovers the jewelry that Farouk gives Kate, he confronts Farouk and is killed.
Genre(s): Biographical Fiction.

Slovo, Gillian

◆ 4983. *Ties of Blood.* New York: Morrow, 1990. 590 pp.
A white Jewish family from Europe and a black rural family come to Johannesburg in the early 20th century and struggle against apartheid.
Genre(s): Family Saga.

Smith, Wilbur A.

4984. *Cry Wolf.* Garden City, NY: Doubleday, 1977. 401 pp.
In 1935, two men supply Ethiopia with armed personnel carriers for its war against Mussolini's Italian troops.
Genre(s): Spy Fiction; Adventure Story.

4985. *Golden Fox.* New York: Random House, 1990. 433 pp.
A Spanish marquess working for the KGB promises to marry Isabella Courtney of South Africa after his divorce, but when their child is born, he kidnaps the baby and forces his wife to find secrets about the white South African government, in the sequel to *A Time to Die.*
Genre(s): Adventure Story; Spy Fiction.

4986. *Men of Men.* Garden City, NY: Doubleday, 1983. 518 pp.
In the sequel to *Flight of the Falcon,* the Ballantyne family becomes involved with the land schemes of Cecil Rhodes.
Genre(s): Family Saga.

4987. *Power of the Sword.* Boston: Little, Brown, 1986. 618 pp.
In the sequel to *The Burning Shore,* Centaine Courtney owns a diamond mine in South Africa while her children, half-brothers, begin to disagree with each other.
Genre(s): Family Saga.

4988. *Rage.* Boston: Little, Brown, 1987. 627 pp.

Sasha Courtney, son of Centaine in *Power of the Sword,* serves in the South African Parliament where he often opposes a Nationalist Party Afrikaner, his own brother.
Genre(s): Family Saga.

4989. *A Sparrow Falls.* Garden City, NY: Doubleday, 1978. 587 pp.
When Mark Anders returns to South Africa after World War I, in the sequel to *The Roar of Thunder,* he investigates why his grandfather has been swindled and murdered.
Genre(s): Domestic Fiction; Family Saga.

Stevenson, William

4990. *The Ghosts of Africa.* New York: Harcourt, 1980. 400 pp.
The Germans in East Africa try to keep natives from finding out about World War I, but when the British arrive, they decide to tell the Africans.
Genre(s): War Story.

Tyler, W. T.

4991. *The Consul's Wife.* New York: St. Martin's, 1998. 224 pp.
In the 1970s, Hugh Mathews is a foreign service officer posted in the Congo who becomes cynical of the bureacracy and forges an intellectual relationship with the unfulfilled wife of the embassy consul.
Genre(s): Political Fiction; Love Story.

Van der Vyver, Marita

◆ 4992. *Childish Things.* Trans. Madeleine Biljon. New York: Dutton, 1996. 256 pp.
Mart, a white girl protected from apartheid, attends a boarding school in South Africa during the 1970s.
Genre(s): Bildungsroman (Coming of Age); Biographical Fiction; Political Fiction.

Vassanji, M.G.

4993. *Book of Secrets.* New York: Picador, 1996. 337 pp.
When Pius Fernandes finds a diary written at the beginning of the 20th century by a colonial officer in British East Africa, he tries to finish it, based on the history of the period and any revisions that he uncovers.

Westlake, Donald E.

4994. *Kahawa.* New York: Viking, 1982. 280 pp.
When Lew Brady, a mercenary, goes to Uganda to help steal coffee while Idi Amin rules in the 1970s, he, his mistress, and his partner have a series of adventures.
Genre(s): Adventure Story.

Wiley, Richard

4995. *Ahmed's Revenge.* New York: Random, 1998. 352 pp.
When British expatriate and Kenyan coffee farmer Nora Grant sees her husband enter a smuggling warehouse in

the early 1970s, she is surprised and further puzzled when he dies in the hospital after a lioness attack.
Genre(s): Mystery.

Wood, Barbara

◆ 4996. *Green City in the Sun.* New York: Random House, 1988. 699 pp.
When Dr. Deborah Treverton returns to Kenya after 15 years, she learns about her family's life in Nairobi at the beginning of the 20th century.
Genre(s): Medical Novel.

Wood, Christopher

4997. *A Dove Against Death.* New York: Viking, 1983. 218 pp.

Two British soldiers escape from a German camp in the Cameroons during 1915 and use a glider to evade their pursuers.
Genre(s): War Story.

Wynd, Oswald

4998. *The Ginger Tree.* New York: Harper, 1977. 294 pp.
In 1903, a Scottish girl leaves her home to marry a British soldier in Africa.
Genre(s): Domestic Fiction.

Zwi, Rose

◆ 4999. *The Umbrella Tree.* New York: Penguin, 1991. 104 pp.
In 1976, the children of Soweto revolt against their apartheid past.
Genre(s): Political Fiction.

Australia, New Zealand, the Pacific Islands, and Antarctica

Before 1900

Aberdein, Keith

5000. *The Governor.* Wellington, New Zealand: Hamlet, 1977. 304 pp.
Sir George Grey serves as the governor of New Zealand in the 19th century.
Genre(s): Biographical Fiction.

Astley, Thea

5001. *A Kindness Cup.* New York: Penguin, 1974. 135 pp.
People of Queensland, Australia, settle the land in the 19th century.
Award(s): The Age (Australia) Book Award.
Genre(s): Domestic Fiction.

Attanasio, A. A.

◆ 5002. *Wyvern.* Boston: Houghton Mifflin, 1988. 422 pp.
Trained as a medicine man in Borneo, half-caste Jaki Gefjon joins the pirate Trevor Pym to fight the merchants ruining Asia.
Genre(s): Adventure Story.

Barnett, Jill

5003. *Imagine.* New York: Pocket Books, 1995. 392 pp.
In 1896, Margaret Huntington Smith decides to go on holiday in the South Seas, but the ship's boiler blows, and a stowaway rescues Margaret and three orphans who then try to adjust to each other on an island until a genie arrives.
Genre(s): Fantastic Literature; Romance.

Becke, Louis, and Walter Jeffery

5004. *The Mutineer.* Philadelphia: Lippincott, 1898. 298 pp.
Men serving on the *Bounty* follow Christian Fletcher's leadership in their mutiny against the captain before settling on Pitcairn Island in 1790.
Genre(s): Biographical Fiction; Sea Story.

Biddle, Cordelia Frances

5005. *Beneath the Wind.* New York: Simon and Schuster, 1993. 478 pp.
George and his wife, although unhappily married, sail for Borneo with their three children, and after they arrive, George drinks too much and fails to fulfill his father's directive.

Brent, Madeleine

◆ 5006. *Golden Urchin.* New York: Doubleday, 1987. 330 pp.
Raised by aborigines in Australia, Meg discovers out that her parents are English and that she has an inheritance, but those who want the money attempt to murder her.
Genre(s): Romance.

Butler, Richard

5007. *And Wretches Hang.* New York: St. Martin's, 1979. 225 pp.
When Matt Brady escapes from the prison colony at Macquarie Harbour, Tasmania, in 1840, his accomplices eventually die or are captured until he is taken and hanged.
Genre(s): Biographical Fiction.

Campion, Jane

5008. *The Piano.* New York: Hyperion, 1994. 213 pp.
In 19th century New Zealand, a mute woman copes with an arranged marriage.
Genre(s): Domestic Fiction.

Carey, Peter

5009. *Oscar and Lucinda.* New York: Harper and Row, 1988. 433 pp.
In the 1860s, Lucinda, an Australian heiress, and Oscar, a clergyman, set out to erect a glass church in New South Wales.
Award(s): Booker Prize; Festival Award for Literature; Miles Franklin Award.
Genre(s): Christian Fiction.

Cato, Nancy

5010. *Brown Sugar.* New York: St. Martin's, 1974. 240 pp.
In Australia, during the 19th century, two white families, one a family of missionaries devoted to helping the natives and the other, wealthy slave owners of a sugar cane plantation, interact.
Genre(s): Family Saga.

5011. *Forefathers.* New York: St. Martin's, 1982. 686 pp.

Joseph Forbes King, born in 1949, has among his forefathers natives and also settlers who've been in Australia since 1824.
Genre(s): Family Saga.

Cato, Nancy, and Vivienne Rae Ellis

5012. *Queen Trucanini.* London: Heinemann, 1976. 256 pp.
Queen Truganini reigns as queen of Tasmania in the 19th century and is the last full-blooded aborigine in the country.
Genre(s): Biographical Fiction.

Clarke, Marcus Andrew Hislop

5013. *His Natural Life.* New York: Penguin, 1970. 927 pp.
Convicts in Tasmania's penal colony are brutally treated in the 19th century.
Genre(s): Political Fiction.

5014. *Marcus Clarke.* 1885. St. Lucia, Queensland: University of Queensland, 1976. 687 pp.
A man falsely convicted of a crime ends up in Van Diemen's Land where he suffers a fate worse than death.
Genre(s): Political Fiction.

Codshalk, C. S.

5015. *Kalimantaan.* New York: Henry Holt, 1998. 480 pp.
In the 1800s, a young British subject founds his own private raj on the coast of Borneo.
Genre(s): Adventure Story.

Coleman, Clare

5016. *Daughter of the Reef.* New York: Jove, 1992. 354 pp.
Tepua, bride and daughter of an island chief, is shipwrecked in a storm after her wedding and washes ashore in Tahiti where she must use her dancing talents to be accepted by the community in which she lives.
Genre(s): Domestic Fiction.

Coleman, Terry

5017. *Southern Cross.* New York: Viking, 1979. 434 pp.
Susannah, the governor's daughter of New South Wales, embodies in her own life the struggles and experiences of the new colony settled chiefly with conficts during the early 19th century.

Conrad, Joseph

5018. *Almayer's Folly.* 1895. New York: Bantam, 1995. 468 pp.
In the sequel to *An Outcast of the Islands*, a European married to a Malayan wife lives with her on Borneo before his daughter forsakes him to marry a savage.
Genre(s): Political Fiction; Adventure Story.

5019. *An Outcast of the Islands.* New York: Appleton, 1896. 396 pp.

When Lingard hires men to work for him he makes poor choices because the men are corrupt.
Genre(s): Adventure Story.

Dark, Eleanor

5020. *Storm of Time.* New York: McGraw Hill, 1950. 590 pp.
English emigrants, convicts in the penal colony, and aborigines learn about each other in the early days of Australian settlement.
Genre(s): Domestic Fiction.

5021. *The Timeless Land.* New York: Macmillan, 1941. 447 pp.
Establishing a lawful community with a group of convicts makes early settlement in Australia especially difficult.
Genre(s): Political Fiction; Domestic Fiction.

Defoe, Daniel

◆ 5022. *Robinson Crusoe.* 1719. New York: Bantam, 1982. 288 pp.
Robinson Crusoe shipwrecks on an island in the early 18th century and carefully creates for himself a new home.
Genre(s): Adventure Story; Biographical Fiction.

Dengler, Sandy

5023. *Code of Honor.* Minneapolis, MN: Bethany House, 1988. 256 pp.
Samantha Connolly and her sisters emigrate to Queensland when they become indentured servants. (*Series:* Australian Destiny, 1)
Genre(s): Christian Fiction.

5024. *East of the Outback.* Minneapolis, MN: Bethany House, 1990. 334 pp.
A young man is forced to mature when he lives in Australia's Outback. (*Series:* Australian Destiny, 4)
Genre(s): Christian Fiction; Adventure Story.

5025. *The Power of Pinjarra.* Minneapolis, MN: Bethany House, 1989. 272 pp.
Prisoners who are transported to the penal colony at Sydney Cove must build their lives in whatever way they can. (*Series:* Australian Destiny, 2)
Genre(s): Christian Fiction.

5026. *Taste of Victory.* Minneapolis, MN: Bethany House, 1989. 272 pp.
Cole Sloan and Samantha Connolly experience problems that test their characters. (*Series:* Australian Destiny, 3)
Genre(s): Christian Fiction.

Drewe, Robert

5027. *The Drowner.* New York: St. Martin's, 1997. 336 pp.
In the 1880s, Will Dance is an engineer in Australia who irrigates the dry lands (drowners), and after he meets and falls in love with an actress, they travel to the Outback for him to work.
Genre(s): Adventure Story.

Druett, Joan

5028. *Abigail.* New York: Random House, 1988. 416 pp.
Abigail Sherman, at home on her father's whaling ship, goes to live with a Massachusetts cousin after her mother's death, and when she hears of her father's death, she rushes to marry so that she can return to New Zealand and claim his ship.
Genre(s): Sea Story.

Dutton, Geoffrey

5029. *Queen Emma of the South Seas.* New York: St. Martin's, 1977. 283 pp.
Daughter of a Samoan mother and an American father, Emma Coe Forsayth Kolbe flourishes as Queen Emma from 1850 to World War I when she creates a Pacific trading empire which gains international recognition.
Genre(s): Biographical Fiction.

Eden, Dorothy

◆ 5030. *An Important Family.* New York: Morrow, 1982. 288 pp.
To escape the tragic death of her fiancé, the Irish Kate O'Connor joins a family moving to New Zealand in 1862 only to discover the family's secrets.
Genre(s): Romance.

◆ 5031. *The Vines of Yarrabee.* New York: Coward-McCann, 1969. 381 pp.
Gilbert Massingham goes to New South Wales, establishes a vineyard, and raises a family.
Genre(s): Romance.

Eldershaw, M. Barnard

5032. *A House Is Built.* Sydney, Australia: Lloyd O'Neill, 1972. 358 pp.
When James Hyde, quartermaster, opens a store in Sydney, his family grows up in the area during the 19th century.
Genre(s): Adventure Story.

Franklin, Miles

◆ 5033. *My Brilliant Career.* 1901. New York: St. Martin's, 1981. 234 pp.
In the 1890s, Sybylla Melvyn lives in the Outback during a time of political and social unrest in Australia.
Genre(s): Domestic Fiction.

Golding, William

5034. *Close Quarters.* New York: Farrar, Straus and Giroux, 1987. 281 pp.
In the sequel to *Rites of Passage*, an old ship transporting cargo and passengers from England to Australia in the 19th century disintegrates after a sailor's error.
Genre(s): Sea Story.

5035. *Fire Down Under.* New York: Farrar, Straus and Giroux, 1989. 313 pp.

Edmund Talbot learns about survival in a terrible storm off the Cape of Good Hope, in the sequel to *Close Quarters.*
Genre(s): Sea Story.

5036. *Rites of Passage.* New York: Farrar, Straus and Giroux, 1980. 278 pp.
During the early 18th century, passengers on a ship to Australia include a parson whom the crew choses as a scapegoat.
Award(s): Booker Prize.
Genre(s): Sea Story.

Goudge, Elizabeth

5037. *Green Dolphin Street.* New York: Coward-McCann, 1944. 502 pp.
After William emigrates to New Zealand, he writes the father of the woman he loves for her hand in marriage, but he mistakenly puts her sister's name in the letter instead, and the sister comes to New Zealand.
Genre(s): Romance.

Grant, Maxwell

5038. *Inherit the Sun.* New York: Coward-McCann, 1981. 420 pp.
James Carlyon, born in 1897 in the Australian outback, becomes a businessman loyal to his country.
Genre(s): Family Saga.

Hall, Rodney

5039. *Captivity Captive.* New York: Farrar, Straus and Giroux, 1988. 214 pp.
Sixty years after three of his siblings were brutally murdered in 1898 on the Australian frontier, Patrick Murphy reflects about their deaths and the slave labor of the children on his father's farm.

5040. *The Second Bridegroom.* New York: Farrar, Straus and Giroux, 1991. 214 pp.
A young forger transported to Australia in 1838 escapes into the bush where aborigines adopt him and treat him like an icon until he allows himself to be recaptured.
Genre(s): Adventure Story.

Hanrahan, Barbara

5041. *Dove.* St Lucia: University of Queensland Press, 1983. 203 pp.
Dove and her family try to survive on Australia's frontier from the 1890s to the early years of the Depression, as land and climate control their lives.
Genre(s): Domestic Fiction.

Hickman, Patricia

◆ 5042. *Angel of the Outback.* Minneapolis, MN: Bethany House, 1995. 319 pp.
Although Rachel Langley wins her freedom, the situation in the wilds of Australia still threatens her. (*Series:* Land of the Far Horizon, 2)
Genre(s): Christian Fiction.

◆ May be suitable for young adult readers

◆ 5043. *Beyond the Wild Shores.* Minneapolis, MN: Bethany House, 1997. 320 pp.
The American Bailey Templeton opens a school in the young colony of Sydney Cove, only to meet hostility from the settlers, but she perseveres, while falling in love with a British naval officer. (*Series:* Land of the Far Horizon, 4)
Genre(s): Christian Fiction.

5044. *The Emerald Flame.* Minneapolis, MN: Bethany House, 1996. 288 pp.
Kelsey McBride, an Irish prisoner transported to Sydney Cove, searches for Jack Keegan, father of her unborn child, but after she escapes from the penal colony, she must save her child in the Battle of Castle Hill. (*Series:* Land of the Far Horizons, 3)
Genre(s): Christian Fiction; Adventure Story.

◆ 5045. *Voyage of the Exiles.* Minneapolis, MN: Bethany House, 1995. 320 pp.
The Prentice family members overcome severe obstacles as they settle in the new land of Australia. (*Series:* Land of the Far Horizon, 1)
Genre(s): Christian Fiction.

Holt, Victoria

5046. *The Mask of the Enchantress.* Garden City, NY: Doubleday, 1980. 327 pp.
Joel Mateland and his lover go to Vulvan Island in the South Pacific with their daughter Suewellyn, and his legitimate daughter shows up.
Genre(s): Romance.

5047. *The Pride of the Peacock.* Garden City, NY: Doubleday, 1976. 303 pp.
Jessica Clavering escapes her family by entering a platonic marriage with Joel, heir to an opal fortune.
Genre(s): Romance.

5048. *The Shadow of the Lynx.* Garden City, NY: Doubleday, 1971. 381 pp.
Nora Tamasin goes to Australia to live with a family friend, who was shipped there as a convict after Nora's father's death, and she marries the friend before his untimely death.
Genre(s): Romance.

Hyde, Robin

5049. *Check to Your King.* Auckland, NZ: Golden, 1975. 288 pp.
Charles Philip Hippolytus, baron of Thierry, comes to New Zealand in the 19th century as an adventurer and a pioneer.
Genre(s): Adventure Story; Biographical Fiction.

Irish, Lola

5050. *And the Wild Birds Sang.* New York: Watts, 1984. 452 pp.
In 1840s Australia, the kind aristocrat Barbara Merrill has all that Raunie Lorne, a gypsy immigrant, wants and everything that Brick O'Shea, a native Australian, hates.
Genre(s): Domestic Fiction.

Jos, F. Sionil

5051. *Dusk.* New York: Modern Library, 1998. 256 pp.
Istak, a member of the Ilokono tribe, speaks Spanish and Latin, and when his family is driven from their land, they travel across the Philippines and encounter the Spanish and the Americans who invade during the Spanish-American War.
Genre(s): War Story; Bildungsroman (Coming of Age).

Kalman, Yvonne

5052. *After the Rainbow.* New York: St. Martin's, 1990. 348 pp.
In the sequel to *Mists of Heaven*, Lisabeth and Rhys are married, and Rhys's spoiled daughter Daisy unknowingly falls in love with her half-brother Andrew before going to England to study medicine.
Genre(s): Romance; Family Saga.

5053. *Greenstone.* Garden City, NY: Doubleday, 1982. 480 pp.
Juliette Peridot discovers her entire family except her father murdered, and as she matures, she watches the Maoris revere her father, but her stepmother and husband side with the whites.
Genre(s): Domestic Fiction; Bildungsroman (Coming of Age); Family Saga.

5054. *Mists of Heaven.* New York: St. Martin's, 1988. 442 pp.
In New Zealand during the 1850s, members of the Morgan and Rennie families begin a complex relationship that includes an affair between Mary Rennie and Rhys Morgan that results in Mary's death during childbirth.
Genre(s): Romance; Family Saga.

Keneally, Thomas

5055. *Bring Larks and Heroes.* New York: Viking, 1968. 247 pp.
An intellectual British officer assigned to an Australian penal colony has diffculty with the brutality there and the choices he must make.
Award(s): Miles Franklin Award.
Genre(s): Political Fiction.

5056. *The Playmaker.* New York: Simon and Schuster, 1987. 353 pp.
In 1789, Lieutenant Ralph Clark recruits a cast of convicts in Australia to put on a play.
Genre(s): Biographical Fiction.

Kinsolving, W.

5057. *Mr Christian.* New York: Simon and Schuster, 1996. 384 pp.
Instead of perishing on Pitcairn Island with the crew of HMS *Bounty*, Fletcher Christian, leader of the 1789 mutiny, escapes in a canoe and proceeds to enjoy a series of intriguing adventures.
Genre(s): Sea Story; Adventure Story.

Krauth, Nigel

5058. *Matilda, My Darling.* New York: Watts, 1985. 222 pp.
In the 1890s, an investigator working on the disappearance of a swagman (itinerant worker) in Australia's Outback discovers social and political disagreements between landowners and shearers.
Award(s): Vogel Award.
Genre(s): Biographical Fiction; Mystery.

Long, William Stuart

5059. *The Adventurers.* New York: Dell, 1983. 447 pp.
In the sequel to *The Explorers*, members of English society go to 1815 Australia where they become emancipists, face the gold rush, and pursue Governor Macquarie's plan for agricultural development.
Genre(s): Family Saga; Adventure Story.

5060. *The Colonists.* New York: Pantheon, 1984. 404 pp.
Free landowners come to Australia, and their desires conflict with those of the original settlers already established there, in the sequel to *The Adventurers*.
Genre(s): Family Saga; Adventure Story.

5061. *The Exiles.* New York: Dell, 1979. 683 pp.
When Jennie Taggart falls in with the wrong crowd in London after arriving from the country, she is transported to Australia as a convict in 1787.
Genre(s): Family Saga; Adventure Story.

5062. *The Explorers.* New York: Dell, 1982. 510 pp.
In the sequel to *The Exiles*, Jenny Taggart becomes a skilled farmer and reunites with the father of her child and her former sweetheart in 18th-century Australia.
Genre(s): Family Saga; Adventure Story.

5063. *The Settlers.* New York: Dell, 1980. 544 pp.
In the sequel to *The Exiles*, Jenny Taggart reunites with her father and a childhood sweetheart, and as her life seems to gain stability, William Bligh arrives in New South Wales as governor in the late 18th century.
Genre(s): Family Saga; Adventure Story.

Malouf, David

5064. *The Conversations at Curlow Creek.* New York: Pantheon, 1996. 233 pp.
In Australia during 1827, Officer Michael Adair must oversee the execution of Daniel Carney, an Irishman accused of planning revolution, but as the two men talk, neither can provide the information that the other seems to want.
Genre(s): Political Fiction.

5065. *Remembering Babylon.* New York: Pantheon, 1993. 200 pp.
In the mid-19th century, a white child discovered on the Australian coast and raised by aborigines, reveals himself to locals and changes their lives.
Award(s): International IMPAC Dublin Literary Award; *Los Angeles Times* Book Award.

Matthews, Patricia

5066. *The Dreaming Tree.* New York: Harlequin, 1990. 384 pp.
In the beginning of the 19th century, exiled convict Faith Blackstock and her daughters, Hope and Charity, come to New South Wales, Australia, and Cotty Starke, a rum-runner, and John Myers, a half aborigine help them survive.
Genre(s): Domestic Fiction.

Maxwell, John

5067. *HMS Bounty.* London: Cape, 1977. 287 pp.
Christian leaves Pitcairn Island to follow Bligh and seek revenge while Bligh makes mistakes as governor of New South Wales.
Genre(s): War Story; Sea Story.

Medeiros, Teresa

◆ 5068. *Once an Angel.* New York: Bantam, 1993. 432 pp.
Urchins from boarding school throw Emily Scarborough overboard in 1865, and after she reappears naked on a North Island beach, a series of events finally unite her with her guardian, Justin Connor.
Genre(s): Romance.

Michaels, Fern

5069. *Captive Passions.* New York: Ballantine, 1977. 472 pp.
Sirena, a 17th-century Spanish noblewoman, marries the head of the East India Company in Java under false pretenses because she is actually the pirate Sea Siren.
Genre(s): Family Saga; Romance.

5070. *Captive Splendors.* New York: Ballantine, 1980. 393 pp.
Regan and Sirena van der Rhys devise an alternative plan to prevent their adopted daughter, Wren, from marrying Malcolm Weatherly, a scoundrel who only wants her money in the sequel to *Captive Embraces*.
Genre(s): Family Saga; Romance.

Mitchell, June

5071. *Amokura.* Auckland, NZ: Longman Paul, 1978. 204 pp.
Te akau Horohau, known as Meretini, marries English immigrant Thomas Uppadine Cook in 1842, and her children begin to forsake their Maori ties until her grandchildren in England know nothing of their Maori heritage, which the British regard as savage.
Genre(s): Domestic Fiction.

Noonan, Michael

5072. *Magwitch.* New York: St. Martin's, 1982. 222 pp.
Pip from Charles Dickens's *Great Expectations* traces the steps of Magwitch in Australia, the man who built his great expectations.
Genre(s): Adventure Story.

◆ May be suitable for young adult readers

Nordhoff, Charles, and James Norman Hall

5073. *Botany Bay.* Boston: Little, Brown, 1941. 374 pp.

Hugh Taliant, an American turned English highwayman, goes to Botany Bay as one of the first criminals shipped out of the country.

5074. *Men Against the Sea.* Boston, Little, Brown, 1940. 251 pp.

In the sequel to *Mutiny on the Bounty*, Captain Bligh and 18 men sail from the Friendly Islands of the South Pacific to Timor in the East Indies.
Genre(s): Sea Story; Biographical Fiction.

5075. *Mutiny on the Bounty.* Boston: Little, Brown, 1932. 396 pp.

A British crew mutinies against the cruel commander of the *Bounty* in 1787.
Genre(s): Biographical Fiction; Sea Story.

5076. *Pitcairn's Island.* Boston: Little, Brown, 1940. 333 pp.

The survivors from the *Bounty* mutiny reach Pitcairn Island and proceed to destroy each other, in the sequel to *Men Against the Sea.*
Genre(s): Sea Story.

O'Brian, Patrick

◆ 5077. *Nutmeg of Consolation.* New York: Norton, 1991. 315 pp.

Jack Aubrey captains his crew in the South China Sea where they battle a French frigate on their way to Botany Bay in New South Wales, in the sequel to *The Thirteen Gun Salute.*
Genre(s): Sea Story; War Story.

Park, Ruth

5078. *The Frost and the Fire.* Boston: Houghton Mifflin, 1958. 282 pp.

Many different types of people come to New Zealand in the 1860s to search for gold.
Genre(s): Adventure Story.

5079. *Missus.* New York: Harper and Row, 1987. 256 pp.

Hugh, an Irish immigrant to Australia, keeps delaying his marriage to Margaret (who refuses to marry anyone else) while his disabled brother manipulates everyone to his advantage during the late 19th century.
Genre(s): Domestic Fiction; Family Saga.

Pramoedya, Ananta Toer

5080. *Child of all Nations.* Trans. Max Lane. New York: Morrow, 1993. 352 pp.

The Dutch set the natives of the East Indies (Indonesia) against each other in the 1890s, in the sequel to *This Earth of Mankind.*
Genre(s): War Story.

Rogers, Jane

5081. *Promised Lands.* Boston: Faber and Faber, 1995. 376 pp.

Mariner and astronomer William Dawes sails with the first fleet of convicts to Australia in 1787.
Genre(s): Biographical Fiction.

Shadbolt, Maurice

5082. *The Lovelock Version.* New York: St. Martin's, 1981. 568 pp.

When Herman Lovelock hears the voice of an angel in New Zealand's gold fields, he takes his family to live with the Maoris as he searches for meaning in his life.
Genre(s): Family Saga; Adventure Story.

5083. *Monday's Warriors.* Lincoln, MA: David R. Godine, 1992. 304 pp.

Kimball Bent deserts from the British army in New Zealand in 1865 and persuades the Maori intent on killing the first Britisher they see to let him live so that he can marry the chief's daughter.
Genre(s): Humorous Fiction.

5084. *Season of the Jew.* New York: Norton, 1987. 384 pp.

After Lieutenant George Fairweather resigns his commission in the army, he goes to Poverty Bay, hoping to renew his relationship with a half-Maori woman, and finds himself defending the colonists.
Genre(s): War Story.

Shaw, Patricia

◆ 5085. *Cry of the Rain Bird.* New York: St. Martin's, 1995. 346 pp.

Corby Morgan takes his wife, her sister, and her father to Australia after buying a sugar plantation on which indentured South Sea islanders work, and they encounter vastly different experiences.
Genre(s): Romance.

5086. *The Feather and the Stone.* New York: St. Martin's, 1994. 312 pp.

In the 1870s, the ship on which Sibell Delahunty and her parents sail to Australia sinks, and only Sibell survives, helped by a lower-class man to reach Perth, and then with him, she travels into Aborigine territory.
Genre(s): Adventure Story.

5087. *Fires of Fortune.* New York: St. Martin's, 1996. 416 pp.

When half aborigine Ben Buckman's wealthy mother is ill, the local doctor refuses to treat her, and after Buckman goes to jail for his rebellious behavior, he vows to retaliate.
Genre(s): Adventure Story; Romance.

5088. *River of the Sun.* New York: St. Martin's, 1992. 378 pp.

In Australia during the 1860s, people from all places and all professions, including a housemaid and an Aborigine, gather to find gold.
Genre(s): Adventure Story.

5089. *Where the Willows Weep.* New York: St. Martin's, 1995. 376 pp.
In the mid-19th century, Laura Maskey and Amelia Roberts anticipate adulthood, but Laura falls in love with a married man in Queensland whose wife's death complicates their expectations.
Genre(s): Domestic Fiction.

Sweeney, Veronica Geoghegan

5090. *The Emancipist.* New York: Simon and Schuster, 1986. 1048 pp.
Aidan O'Brien is transported to Australia from Ireland for a crime he did not commit, and he fights for his rights as a prisoner and then as an emancipist (*Series:* former convict)
Genre(s): Family Saga.

Talbot, Michael

5091. *To the Ends of the Earth.* New York: Knopf, 1986. 519 pp.
Captain Arthur Philip travels to Australia in 1785 to become its first governor, and with him is Joe Cribb, a man who escaped hanging when fighting in America.
Genre(s): Sea Story.

5092. *A Wilful Woman.* New York: Knopf, 1989. 353 pp.
Commodore Arthur Phillip arrives in Botany Bay and becomes governor of a group of thieves, whores, and murderers, in the sequel to *To the Ends of the Earth.*

Toer, Pramoedya Ananta

5093. *This Earth of Mankind.* New York: Morrow, 1991. 367 pp.
Minke, a Javanese native, breaks with his family and seeks to rise in the Dutch colonial system, but his meeting with a family of mixed heritage changes his ideas.
Genre(s): Political Fiction.

Williams, Maslyn

◆ 5094. *Dubu.* New York: Morrow, 1971. 253 pp.
A career diplomat hopes to gain fame by helping to annex New Guinea to Queensland in the 19th century, but he faces the natives at their *dubu,* a sacred tribal meeting place.
Genre(s): Political Fiction; Adventure Story.

Wood, Barbara

◆ 5095. *The Dreaming.* New York: Random House, 1991. 453 pp.
Her parents dead in 1871, Joanna leaves India to seek her mother's past, and in Australia, she meets a man with whom she builds a sheep station as she looks for the family source in the dreaming (ancient time) of the aborigines.
Genre(s): Romance; Family Saga.

Woodman, Richard

5096. *The Antigone.* New York: Severn House, 1997. 220 pp.
The crew of the cargo liner *Antigone* tries to reach the Far East.
Genre(s): Sea Story.

Worboys, Anne

5097. *Aurora Rose.* New York: Dutton, 1988. 512 pp.
Nicholas le Grys and his bride Lady Cressida sail for New Zealand, neither knowing that Rose Snape, who carries Nicholas's child, is on board, but after they arrive, Lady Cressida and Rose's husband die, leaving Nicholas and Rose to colonize the country.
Genre(s): Adventure Story.

1900 and After

Anderson, Jim

◆ 5098. *Billarooby.* New York: Ticknor and Fields, 1988. 322 pp.
Linsay Armstrong, 11, becomes obsessed with a Japanese prisoner-of-war camp near his Australian home, and his concerns explode as he confronts his father about their family's past.
Genre(s): Bildungsroman (Coming of Age); War Story.

Bainbridge, Beryl

◆ 5099. *The Birthday Boys.* New York: Carroll and Graf, 1994. 189 pp.
Robert Scott narrates his second expedition to Antarctica from the time he and his men depart Cardiff in 1910 until they perish in 1912.
Genre(s): Biographical Fiction.

Barber, Noel

5100. *The Other Side of Paradise.* New York: Macmillan, 1987. 520 pp.
Kit Masters, a British physician, comes to Koraloona to practice in the 1930s, and falls in love with Gauguin's granddaughter, who owns paintings that could finance the hospital he and his employer want to build.
Genre(s): Medical Novel; War Story.

Boyd, William

5101. *The Blue Afternoon.* New York: Knopf, 1995. 367 pp.
In Manila during 1902, Dr. Salvador Carriscant has an affair with the wife of an American soldier and years later, after being unjustly accused of murder, he finds their daughter.
Genre(s): Romance; Medical Novel; War Story.

◆ May be suitable for young adult readers

Brainard, Cecilia Manguerra

◆ 5102. *When the Rainbow Goddess Wept.* New York: Dutton, 1994. 216 pp.
During the Japanese occupation of the Philippines in World War II, Yvonne, nine, flees with her upper-class family into the jungle.
Genre(s): War Story.

Bram, Christopher

5103. *Almost History.* New York: Donald I. Fine, 1992. 409 pp.
A foreign service officer in the Philippines during the Marcos regime discovers that he is homosexual, and he continues to work sensibly with this knowledge as he reveals the life in Manila during the period.
Genre(s): Political Fiction.

Brinkley, William

5104. *Don't Go near the Water.* New York: Random House, 1956. 373 pp.
Siegel, a member of the Public Relations section of the United States Navy on the island of Tulura, falls in love with the leading citizen's European-educated daughter.
Genre(s): Humorous Fiction; War Story; Love Story.

Bulosan, Carlos

5105. *The Cry and the Dedication.* Philadelphia: Temple University Press, 1995. 305 pp.
In the 1940s and 1950s, Huks travels, with great danger, to Philippine villages where he encourages the overthrow of foreign oppressors.
Genre(s): War Story; Political Fiction.

Cairney, John

5106. *Worlds Apart.* North Pomfret, VT: Trafalgar, 1992. 672 pp.
In 1900, Tina Keigh and Denis O'Neil meet and fall in love at Glasgow's docks as their families prepare to emigrate, but one family goes to America and the other to New Zealand.
Genre(s): Family Saga.

Cato, Nancy

5107. *All the Rivers Run.* New York: St. Martin's, 1978. 538 pp.
Philadelphia Gordon, an aspiring painter, must sacrifice her personal desires to her family in Australia working with river boats during the early 20th century.
Genre(s): Domestic Fiction; Romance.

◆ 5108. *The Heart of the Continent.* New York: St. Martin's, 1989. 604 pp.
Alix, mother, and Caro, daughter, work to bring medical aid to aborigines in the wilderness of Queensland, Australia during the early 20th century.
Genre(s): War Story.

Chai, Arlene J.

5109. *The Last Time I Saw Mother.* New York: Fawcett Columbine, 1996. 340 pp.
Caridad returns to Manila from Australia to care for her aging mother and learns that her aunt is actually her real mother and that the cousins with whom she grew up during World War II are her sisters.
Genre(s): Domestic Fiction.

Chalker, Jack L.

◆ 5110. *The Devil's Voyage.* New York: Doubleday, 1981. 328 pp.
The *Indianapolis* takes the bomb for Hiroshima and a crew of 1,200 men from San Francisco to a Pacific launch site, but on its return, the Japanese torpedo it.
Genre(s): Adventure Story.

Cleary, Jon

5111. *A Very Private War.* New York: Morrow, 1980. 276 pp.
Cornelius Mullane travels through the jungle on New Britain Island with a diverse group of people trying to avoid detection by Japanese patrols or scout planes.
Genre(s): War Story.

Coyle, William

5112. *Firestorm.* New York: Morrow, 1988. 384 pp.
Bernard Reardon, an Australian tailgunner, flies over Europe in World War II while his sister in Australia lives in the convent she joined as a promise to God if Bernard were saved from childhood meningitis.
Genre(s): War Story.

De Hartog, Jan

◆ 5113. *The Trail of the Serpent.* New York: Harper and Row, 1983. 214 pp.
Several people trying to escape Borneo when the Japanese invade include a Dutch religious newspaper editor, missionaries, and an atheistic ship captain.
Genre(s): Adventure Story; Christian Fiction.

Disher, Garry

5114. *The Sunken Road.* North Pomfret, VT: Trafalgar Square, 1997. 214 pp.
After World War II, stubborn Anna Tolley faces heartache and disappointment in South Australia.
Genre(s): Domestic Fiction.

Emery, John

5115. *The Sky People.* New York: Farrar, Straus and Giroux, 1988. 354 pp.
In 1937, patrol officers go into the New Guinea bush to subdue the headhunters who have murdered an Australian prospector.
Genre(s): Adventure Story.

Falconer, Delia

5116. *The Service of Clouds.* New York: Farrar, Straus and Giroux, 1998. 256 pp.
In 1907, photographer Harry Kitchings abandons pharmacist's assistant Eureka Jones to marry a widow from Sydney, and even though she becomes an object of derision, Eureka finds satisfaction in a career as a nurse's aide.
Genre(s): Domestic Fiction; War Story.

Flynn, Robert

5117. *The Sounds of Rescue, the Signs of Hope.* New York: Knopf, 1970. 288 pp.
Greg Wallace seeks refuge on an isolated Pacific island when his plane crashes in World War II, and he can barely communicate with the only other human, an aborigine.
Genre(s): War Story.

Franklin, Miles

5118. *All That Swagger.* 1936. New York: Salem, 1986. 418 pp.
In the 1830s, Danny Delacy decides to leave Ireland for Australia where despite the loss of a leg in the Outback, he continues to work on his land and becomes an example for future generations of his family.
Award(s): S.H. Prior Memorial Prize.
Genre(s): Domestic Fiction; Family Saga.

5119. *The End of My Career.* New York: St. Martin's, 1981. 234 pp.
In the sequel to *My Brilliant Career*, Sybylla Melvyn tells how she came to write her first book and describes the events that followed in her rural Australian area.
Genre(s): Biographical Fiction.

Glaskin, Gerald M.

5120. *Flight to Landfall.* New York: St. Martin's, 1980. 394 pp.
A plane carrying evacuees from Singapore to Australia crashes in the Great Sandy Desert, and Fiona and her Dutch ward help the seven survivors trek across the barren land.
Genre(s): War Story; Adventure Story.

Gould, Alan

5121. *The Man Who Stayed Below.* New York: St. Martin's, 1987. 208 pp.
In 1913, John Boult, 16, becomes an apprentice seaman on a sailing vessel commanded by an unsuitable crew as it hauls wood from Australia to England.
Genre(s): Bildungsroman (Coming of Age); Sea Story.

Graves, Ralph

5122. *Share of Honor.* New York: Holt, 1988. 454 pp.
During the Japanese occupation of the Philippines in World War II, some cope with prison and the Bataan Death March while others work as double agents.
Genre(s): War Story.

Griffin, W. E. B.

5123. *Battleground.* New York: Putnam, 1991. 414 pp.
Marines fight in Midway and then continue on to Guadalcanal while those on the edges of the battle do the planning. (*Series:* The Corps, 4)
Genre(s): War Story.

5124. *Behind the Lines.* New York: Putnam, 1995. 384 pp.
Generals in the Philippines struggle for power during World War II. (*Series:* The Corps, 8)
Genre(s): War Story.

5125. *Close Combat.* New York: Putnam, 1993. 383 pp.
Marine heroes from Guadalcanal take a war bond tour. (*Series:* The Corps, 6)
Genre(s): War Story.

5126. *Line of Fire.* New York: Putnam, 1992. 414 pp.
Marines fight on Guadalcanal in August and September of 1942 while other events occur around the globe involving people they know. (*Series:* The Corps, 5)
Genre(s): Adventure Story; War Story.

Hall, Rodney

5127. *The Grisly Wife.* New York: Farrar, Straus and Giroux, 1993. 261 pp.
After Catherine Byrne marries Muley Moloch, a prophet, she and his eight female disciples establish a mission in the Australian bush, and years later, when accused of murder, she tells their story to the police.
Award(s): Miles Franklin Award.
Genre(s): Mystery.

Heggen, Thomas

5128. *Mister Roberts.* Boston: Houghton Mifflin, 1946. 221 pp.
A man on an American naval cargo ship performs several roles for his colleagues while crossing and recrossing the Pacific during World War II.
Genre(s): War Story; Sea Story.

Herbert, Marie

5129. *Winter of the White Seal.* New York: Morrow, 1982. 275 pp.
In 1819, Jonathan Horn, aided only by a seal that has befriended him, tries to survive on an Antarctic island.

Herbert, Xavier

5130. *Poor Fellow my Country.* New York: St. Martin's, 1981. 1466 pp.
Prindy, a quarter aborigine, grows up in Australia during the 1930s and 1940s.
Award(s): Miles Franklin Award.
Genre(s): Bildungsroman (Coming of Age).

◆ May be suitable for young adult readers

Higgins, Jack

◆ 5131. *Exocet.* New York: Stein and Day, 1983.
260 pp.
Argentinian air force officials try to obtain French Exocet missles to fight the British during the Falklands war in 1982.
Genre(s): War Story.

Holt, Kare

5132. *The Race.* New York: Delacorte, 1976. 256 pp.
Amundsen and Scott become rivals because each wants to be the first man to reach the South Pole.
Genre(s): Biographical Fiction.

Homewood, Harry

5133. *Silent Sea.* New York: McGraw Hill, 1981.
368 pp.
In 1943, the *USS Eelfish* patrols the Leyte Gulf with a talented crew that sinks ships and delivers supplies.
Genre(s): War Story; Sea Story.

Johnson, Susan

5134. *A Big Life.* New York: Faber and Faber, 1993. 320 pp.
Billy's father returns from the war refusing to believe that five-year-old Billy is his son, and later, after Billy learns acrobatics, his father sells the 15-year-old for money to a variety act going to England.
Genre(s): War Story; Bildungsroman (Coming of Age).

Jones, James

5135. *The Thin Red Line.* New York: Scribner's, 1962. 495 pp.
In a companion novel to *From Here to Eternity*, Company C engages in the Guadalcanal campaign of World War II.
Genre(s): War Story.

Keith, Agnes Newton

5136. *Beloved Exiles.* Boston: Little, Brown, 1972.
326 pp.
Sara, an American, marries a British colonial official in Borneo in the mid-1930s, and refusing to follow British customs, she adopts her husband's son by his native wife.
Genre(s): War Story.

Keneally, Thomas

◆ 5137. *The Chant of Jimmie Blacksmith.* New York: Viking, 1972. 178 pp.
Jimmie Blacksmith, a half-caste aborigine who is frustrated with his dim-witted wife and who believes in tribal totems, kills European settlers in Australia during 1900.

5138. *A River Town.* New York: Doubleday, 1995.
324 pp.

In the early 20th century, Tim Shea leaves Ireland for New South Wales where he hopes to have a better life, but first he has to cope with several deaths.
Genre(s): Family Saga.

5139. *Victim of the Aurora.* New York: Harcourt, 1978. 219 pp.
In 1909 a poorly planned Antarctic expedition causes the deaths of all but one.
Genre(s): Adventure Story.

Kidman, Fiona

5140. *In the Clear Light.* New York: Norton, 1985. 208 pp.
Clara wans to break into New Zealand's middle class like her sister, but she ends up in a brothel where she meets an African American marine during World War II.
Genre(s): War Story.

Koch, Christopher J.

5141. *The Year of Living Dangerously.* New York: St. Martin's, 1979. 296 pp.
In 1965, two foreigners in Indonesia become involved in its civil war and the coup d'état.
Award(s): The Age (Australia) Book Award.
Genre(s): Adventure Story; War Story.

Lubis, Mochtar

5142. *A Road with No End.* Trans. Anthony H. Johns. Washington, DC: Regnery, 1970. 160 pp.
Isa and Hazil lead a movement of Indonesians to rid their country of Dutch rule in 1946.
Genre(s): War Story.

MacInnes, Patricia

5143. *The Last Night on Bikini.* New York: Morrow, 1995. 171 pp.
Lucky's father works on atomic and hydrogen bombs in the 1940s and 1950s and inadvertently destroys his family with his obsessions.
Genre(s): Domestic Fiction.

Mailer, Norman

5144. *The Naked and the Dead.* New York: Holt, Rinehart and Winston, 1948. 721 pp.
In World War II, an American general and a lieutenant try to lead American soldiers in a Pacific Island invasion.
Genre(s): War Story.

Malouf, David

5145. *Fly Away Peter.* New York: Random House, 1998. 144 pp.
Although Ashley Crowther and Jim Saddler grow up in different social classes, they recognize each other's talents before fighting together in World War I.
Award(s): Australian Literature Society Gold Medal.
Genre(s): War Story.

5146. *The Great World.* New York: Pantheon, 1991. 330 pp.

Two working-class Australians, Digger Keen and Vic Curran, meet in a Japanese prisoner-of-war camp and continue their relationship back in Australia after the war ends.
Award(s): Miles Franklin Award.
Genre(s): War Story.

Marahimin, Ismail

5147. *And the War Is Over.* Trans. John H. McGlynn. Baton Rouge: Louisiana State University Press, 1987. 173 pp.
After World War II ends, Japanese, Dutch, and Javanese soldiers in a Sumatran village must readjust their lives.
Award(s): Pegasus Prize.
Genre(s): War Story.

Marshall, Heather

5148. *Anneliese.* New York: David and Charles, 1989. 252 pp.
Overweight Shona Brackren tries to cope with her mother's hostility by retreating into a world where her father loves her as Anneliese, and then Shona tries to lose weight and actually become Anneliese, during World War II's rationing in New Zealand.
Genre(s): War Story.

Masters, Olga

5149. *Loving Daughters.* New York: Norton, 1993. 320 pp.
In 1919, when the Reverend Colin Edwards arrives from England, the Herbert sisters in Wyndham, Australia, are ready to fall in love, but one is serious and practical while the other is dreamy.
Genre(s): Domestic Fiction.

Matthews, Greg

5150. *The Wisdom of Stones.* New York: Harper-Collins, 1994. 467 pp.
Doug Farrands, a Northern Territory native, makes friends with Clive, who has come from England to claim his inheritance, and after Doug falls in love with and marries Clive's cousin, they both go to Japan to fight in World War II.
Genre(s): War Story; Domestic Fiction.

McCormick, John

5151. *The Right Kind of War.* Annapolis, MD: Naval Institute, 1992. 352 pp.
Marines fighting the Japanese in the Pacific during World War II also fight fear, illness, and boredom.
Genre(s): War Story.

McCullough, Colleen

5152. *An Indecent Obsession.* New York: Harper and Row, 1981. 317 pp.
As World War II ends in the Pacific, Sergeant Wilson enters a mental hospital and unbalances the tenuous calm.
Genre(s): War Story.

5153. *Ladies of Missalonghi.* New York: Harper and Row, 1987. 189 pp.
In the early 1900s after the male members of the family take the family inheritance, Missy Wright, her mother, and her aunt live in poverty until her cousin arrives from Sydney.
Genre(s): Domestic Fiction.

5154. *The Thorn Birds.* New York: Harper and Row, 1977. 533 pp.
Maggie, daughter of a Catholic father and a Protestant mother with deep secrets, harbors a love for a Catholic priest.
Genre(s): Love Story; Religious Fiction.

Mendelsohn, Jane

◆ 5155. *I Was Amelia Earhart.* New York: Knopf, 1996. 145 pp.
Amelia Earhart discusses her fate on a remote Pacific island in the log she writes after she and Fred Noonan crash in 1937.
Genre(s): Biographical Fiction.

Mercer, Charles

5156. *Pacific.* New York: Simon and Schuster, 1981. 320 pp.
In the Pacific during World War II, from just before Pearl Harbor and through the dropping of the A-bomb on Hiroshima, servicemen undergo a series of unexpected and entertaining adventures.
Genre(s): War Story; Humorous Fiction.

Mihardja, Achdiat K.

5157. *Atheis.* Trans. R. J. McGuire. Queensland, Australia: University of Queensland Press, 1972. 180 pp.
While Japan occupies Indonesia, a young man revels in the chants and prayers of his village until he goes to the city, where his rigidity eventually leads him to atheism.
Genre(s): War Story.

Montero, Gloria

5158. *The Villa Marini.* New York: Norton, 1997. 309 pp.
Marini Moran designs and builds a villa near a waterfall on her sugarcane plantation at the beginning of the 20th century, and after her husband succumbs to opium and his brother, to whom she was attracted, leaves, all she has left is the Queensland villa.
Genre(s): Domestic Fiction.

Nolledo, Wilfrido

5159. *But for the Lovers.* New York: Dutton, 1970. 194 pp.
In Manila, during the Japanese occupation in 1945, the Americans arrive, and the differences among the three cultures cause people to destroy themselves and each other.
Genre(s): War Story.

◆ May be suitable for young adult readers

Park, Ruth

5160. *The Harp in the South.* Boston: Houghton Mifflin, 1948. 271 pp.
In the sequel to *Missus*, the Darcys look at life positively in the slums of Sydney while daughter Roie turns from despair to happiness when she finds love.
Genre(s): Domestic Fiction; Family Saga.

5161. *12 1/2 Plymouth Street.* Boston: Houghton Mifflin, 1951. 312 pp.
In the sequel to *The Harp in the South*, Dolour Darcy, Roie's younger sister, tries to leave Sydney's slums.
Genre(s): Domestic Fiction; Family Saga.

Phillips, Sky

5162. *Secret Mission to Melbourne, November 1941.* Manhattan, KS: Sunflower University Press, 1992. 296 pp.
In 1941 military officers make a secret trip to Australia and the South Pacific to find potential airfields for the upcoming war.
Genre(s): War Story.

Pullen, Kathleen J.

5163. *Mary Reibey.* Sydney, Australia: Ure Smith, 1975. 248 pp.
Impoverished Mary Reibey, as a child steals to survive, but after she emigrates to Australia, she becomes a wealthy businesswoman.
Genre(s): Biographical Fiction.

Reidy, Sue

◆ 5164. *The Visitation.* New York: Scribner's, 1997. 272 pp.
Catherine and Teresa Flynn try to grow up in a repressed Irish Catholic family living in New Zealand during the 1960s, and when the Virgin Mary appears to them in the backyard, their father refuses to let them go to the Pope because he thinks the Virgin is trying to convince the Pope to approve contraception.
Genre(s): Bildungsroman (Coming of Age); Gothic Fiction.

Ruttle, Lee

◆ 5165. *The Private War of Dr Yamada.* San Francisco: San Francisco Book Co., 1978. 245 pp.
American-trained Dr. Yamada hates war and likes Americans and helps them in the Palau Islands during that island's last battle.
Genre(s): War Story; Medical Novel.

Satchell, William

5166. *The Greenstone Door.* Auckland, NZ: Golden, 1973, 1914. 400 pp.
A young man who spends his childhood and youth in a Maori village of New Zealand eventually must leave to be with his own people.
Genre(s): Bildungsroman (Coming of Age).

Scoales, William

5167. *Duckfoot.* Indianapolis: Bobbs-Merrill, 1971. 272 pp.
A bounty hunter searches the Australian outback during the Gold Rush of the late 19th century with his duckfoot (three-barreled minature shotgun) for another scalp.
Genre(s): Adventure Story.

Slater, Ian

5168. *Macarthur Must Die.* New York: Donald I. Fine, 1994. 336 pp.
After General Douglas MacArthur escapes from the Philippines and establishes his headquarters in Brisbane, Japanese Minister of War Tojo orders him murdered.
Genre(s): War Story.

Tanner, Janet

◆ 5169. *Women and War.* New York: St. Martin's, 1988. 352 pp.
During World War II in Australia, the lives of Tara Kelly and Alys Peterson change as they both vie for the same man.
Genre(s): War Story.

Tillman, Barrett

5170. *Dauntless.* New York: Bantam, 1992. 412 pp.
Representatives of different military branches prepare to fight at Guadalcanal and Midway during World War II.
Genre(s): Adventure Story; War Story.

Toer, Pramoedya Ananta

5171. *Footsteps.* Trans. Max Lane. New York: Morrow, 1994. 474 pp.
In the sequel to *Child of All Nations*, Minke travels to Betawi (Jakarta) to study medicine and realizes that he must become an activist in the Javanese struggle for freedom from Dutch rule.
Genre(s): Political Fiction.

5172. *House of Glass.* Trans. Max Lane. New York: Morrow, 1996. 352 pp.
In the sequel to *Footsteps*, Police Commissioner Pangemanann is a native employee of the Dutch government in the East Indies who wants to stop rising nationalism in his country in the early 20th century.

Ty-Casper, Linda

5173. *Awaiting Trespass.* New York: Persea, 1985. 180 pp.
When Don Severino Gil's casket is closed at his funeral in the Philippines, those attending wonder why and when they open his coffin, they discover that he had been severely beaten.
Genre(s): Political Fiction.

Uris, Leon

5174. *Battle Cry.* New York: Putnam, 1953. 505 pp.

In the Pacific islands during World War II, American Marines train and fight for their country.
Genre(s): War Story.

Wang, Wen-Hsing

5175. *Family Catastrophe.* Trans. Susan Wan Dolling. Honolulu: University of Hawaii Press, 1995. 259 pp.
When an elderly father in his pajamas and slippers disappears his adult son Fan Yeh begins to search for him in the shrines and monasteries mentioned by his father.
Genre(s): Domestic Fiction.

Wendt, Albert

5176. *The Banyan.* Garden City, NY: Doubleday, 1984. 400 pp.
Three generations of a Samoan family show the impact of other societies on the culture as the patriarch becomes affluent and the sons rebel.
Genre(s): Domestic Fiction; Family Saga.

White, Patrick

5177. *The Tree of Man.* New York: Viking, 1955. 499 pp.
The Parker family of rural Australia faces changes in their lives from the beginning of the 20th century.
Genre(s): Domestic Fiction.

Wilson, Sloan

◆ 5178. *Pacific Interlude.* New York: Arbor House, 1982. 256 pp.

Coast Guard Lieutenant Sylvester Grant assumes command of a gas tanker when he is 24 in a supporting role to MacArthur's attempt to retake the Philippines.
Genre(s): War Story; Sea Story.

Winton, Tim

5179. *Cloudstreet.* St. Paul, MN: Graywolf, 1992. 426 pp.
The lazy Pickles family owns a large house in Perth which they share with the Lamb family as their renters, and when the industrious Lambs open a grocery store on the first floor, the families become intertwined.
Award(s): Miles Franklin Award.
Genre(s): Domestic Fiction; War Story.

Wouk, Herman

5180. *The Caine Mutiny.* Garden City, NY: Doubleday, 1952. 498 pp.
During World War II, an American mine sweeper, the *Caine*, patrols in the Pacific under a tyrannical skipper, when an ensign leads a mutiny against him.
Award(s): Pulitzer Prize.
Genre(s): Sea Story; War Story.

Wynd, Oswald

5181. *The Blazing Air.* New Haven, CT: Ticknor and Fields, 1981. 311 pp.
When the Japanese army arrives in Malaya, the Gourlay family of tin-mine owners try to flee, but some of them are unsuccessful.
Genre(s): War Story.

◆ May be suitable for young adult readers

Canada

Before 1800

Boyer, Elizabeth

5182. *Marguerite de la Roque.* Novelty, OH: Veritie, 1975. 348 pp.
Marguerite de Roberval, cast ashore with her husband-to-be and servant in 1542 survives for three years although her child and the others die.
Genre(s): Adventure Story.

Brick, John

5183. *Ben Bryan, Morgan Rifleman.* New York: Duell, Sloan and Pearce, 1963. 159 pp.
Ben Bryan serves as a rifleman in the battle before Quebec falls in 1775.
Genre(s): War Story.

Cather, Willa

5184. *Shadows on the Rock.* New York: Knopf, 1931. 280 pp.
Frontenac must negotiate for his control of Quebec.
Genre(s): War Story.

Costain, Thomas Bertram

5185. *High Towers.* Garden City, NY: Doubleday, 1949. 403 pp.
Two of the 10 Le Moyne brothers, both explorers, help to establish Canada.

Elwood, Muriel

5186. *Deeper the Heritage.* New York: Scribner's, 1947. 344 pp.
The French arrive to settle in Montreal and eastern Canada during the 18th century.
Genre(s): Domestic Fiction.

Gear, Kathleen O'Neal

◆ 5187. *This Widowed Land.* New York: Tor, 1993. 384 pp.
In the early 18th century, three Jesuits sail from France to the New World to join Father Brebeuf in converting Indians, but they have difficulty adjusting to Huron ways.

Golon, Anne

5188. *The Countess Angélique.* New York: Putnam, 1968. 527 pp.
Angélique and the Count have to defend themselves from the Native Americans when they come to the New World.
Genre(s): Adventure Story.

5189. *The Temptation of Angélique.* New York: Bantam, 1971. 499 pp.
Angélique is exiled to New France, and while facing all of the problems of settlers, she meets a former lover.
Genre(s): Romance.

Houston, James

◆ 5190. *Running West.* New York: Pocket Books, 1990. 320 pp.
William, 17, wins a duel in 1714 and must leave Scotland before his enemy pursues him, and in Canada, he meets a woman from the Dene nation with whom he falls in love.
Genre(s): Love Story.

Kirby, William

5191. *The Golden Dog.* 1897. Montreal: McClelland, 1969. 321 pp.
Colonists and fur traders come to Quebec and settle in the 1740s.

Knox, Alexander

5192. *Totem Dream.* New York: Viking, 1973. 255 pp.
Terrified of Native Americans in the 18th century, Calvin is surprised when he meets two runaway girls and their white companion that they have similiar values, and he helps them continue their escape through the northern woods of Canada.
Genre(s): Adventure Story.

Maillet, Antonine

5193. *Pelagie.* Trans. Philip Stratford. Garden City, NY: Doubleday, 1982. 251 pp.
In the 18th century, Acadians begin a long journey back to their Canadian homeland after the British expel them in 1755 from Maine and Louisiana.
Award(s): Prix Goncourt.

Mason, F. Van Wyck

5194. *The Young Titan.* Garden City, NY: Doubleday, 1959. 621 pp.
Native Americans kill English settlers before capturing the French fortress of Louisburg in 1758.
Genre(s): War Story.

Moore, Brian

5195. *Black Robe.* New York: Dutton, 1985. 246 pp.
Father Laforgue journeys from Quebec to a remote village to find the Jesuits who disappeared while trying to save souls among the Native Americans in the 18th century.
Genre(s): Adventure Story.

Neilan, Sarah

◆ 5196. *Paradise.* New York: St. Martin's, 1982. 345 pp.
Patrick is considered a traitor, and Quality's family has problems in Canada during the 18th century before the two finally reunite.
Genre(s): War Story.

Niven, Frederick

5197. *The Flying Years.* Toronto: McClelland and Stewart, 1974. 253 pp.
Scots come to Canada and settle in the western area during the 18th century.
Genre(s): Western Fiction.

Riefe, Barbara

5198. *The Woman Who Fell from the Sky.* New York: Forge, 1994. 332 pp.
Margaret Addison survives a Mohawk raid in the late 17th century, and when Oneidas take her back toward Quebec, they experience other difficult situations.
Genre(s): Love Story.

Rosenstock, Janet

5199. *The Fire, the Sword, and the Devil.* Toronto: Personal Library, 1981. 381 pp.
In the period from 1520 to 1546, France faces many problems while colonizing, and Jean La Rocque de Roberval becomes the first viceroy to New France.
Genre(s): Biographical Fiction; War Story.

Silver, Alfred

5200. *Acadia.* New York: Ballantine, 1996. 410 pp.
In the Nova Scotia fur-trading colony of Acadia during the 17th century, Charles de La Tour and his bride argue with Charles and Jeanne d'Aulnay over the governorship of the colony.
Genre(s): Romance; Adventure Story.

Steffler, John

5201. *The Afterlife of George Cartwright.* New York: Henry Holt, 1993. 296 pp.
In 1770 George Cartwright begins trading with the Inuit, and while he imitates their ways to ensure his survival, he believes that European ways are best.
Genre(s): Adventure Story.

Suthren, Victor

◆ 5202. *The Black Cockade.* New York: St. Martin's, 1982. 246 pp.
Paul Gallant serves Louis XV by commanding the French fort of Louisbourg in New France, but he needs help in 1745, in the sequel to *A King's Ransom.*
Genre(s): Sea Story.

Vollmann, William T.

5203. *Fathers and Crows.* New York: Viking, 1992. 990 pp.
Jesuits come to French Canada to civilize the Indian tribes and meet the Iroquois saint Kateri Tekakwitha. (*Series:* Seven Dreams, 2)
Genre(s): Family Saga.

Wall, Robert

5204. *Blackrobe.* Toronto: Personal Library, 1981. 359 pp.
French Jesuits raise Stephen Nowell, who was carried off by Indians in 1730, and conceal his identity, but once he is an adult, he learns that he is English.
Genre(s): Adventure Story; Family Saga.

5205. *Bloodbrothers.* Toronto: Personal Library, 1981. 277 pp.
In the sequel to *Blackrobe*, during the years 1746 to 1759, Stephan Nowell has discovered his parents and had several relationships, but only the war to get the French out of Canada seems to interest him.
Genre(s): War Story; Family Saga.

1800-1932

Akenson, Donald H.

5206. *At Face Value.* Buffalo, NY: McGill-Queens, 1990. 245 pp.
Eliza McCormack, a female transvestite prostitute, becomes the Canadian Tory Member of Parliament, John White, in the late 19th century.
Genre(s): Biographical Fiction.

Atwood, Margaret Eleanor

5207. *Alias Grace.* New York: Nan A. Talese, 1996. 468 pp.
A young Canadian woman is accused of a vicious double murder in the 1840s, and a doctor questions her to ascer-

tain her guilt or innocence, but he ultimately reaches no conclusion.
Genre(s): Legal Story; Mystery.

Barclay, Byrna

5208. *Summer of the Hungry Pup.* Edmonton, Canada: NeWest, 1981. 304 pp.
Old Woman establishes a relationship with the young woman who allows her to stay on her Saskatchewan farm and tells of the Riel Rebellion which occurred during her own youth in 1885.
Genre(s): Domestic Fiction; War Story.

Blakenship, William D.

5209. *Yukon Gold.* New York: Dutton, 1977. 280 pp.

In 1898, gold diggers and Hannah Young confront Canadian Mountie Brian Bonner.
Genre(s): Adventure Story.

Block, Kevin James

5210. *Without Shedding Blood.* Winnipeg, Canada: Wildflower, 1994. 183 pp.
A Mennonite carpenter, Samuel Beamer, who is loyal to the British, struggles with his church's belief in pacifism during the War of 1812.
Genre(s): Christian Fiction; War Story.

Bowering, George

◆ 5211. *Shoot!* New York: St. Martin's, 1996. 297 pp.
In the 1870s, the McLean brothers who are *metis* (half white), become petty criminals, but do not commit murder until they can no longer stand the untrue tales about themselves.

Brand, Max

◆ 5212. *The Stingaree.* New York: Dodd, Mead, 1930. 216 pp.
Half Indian and half white, Jimmy Green is only 13 when the Stingaree arrives in his French-Canadian town searching for the murderer of his partner.
Genre(s): Western Fiction.

Craven, Margaret

5213. *I Heard the Owl Call My Name.* Garden City, NY: Doubleday, 1973. 166 pp.
A young priest goes into a remote Indian village where he is sensitive to the inevitable passing of the old life and the infiltration of the new, but the villagers eventually accept him.
Genre(s): Religious Fiction.

Davis-Gardner, Angela

5214. *Felice.* New York: Random House, 1982. 302 pp.
In the 1920s, Felice, an orphan, attends a convent school in Nova Scotia where the eccentric nuns influence her in unexpected ways.

Davis, Kathryn Lynn

◆ 5215. *Sing to Me of Dreams.* New York: Pocket Books, 1990. 549 pp.
In British Columbia in 1860, the prophetess Tanu is born to the Salish Indians who believe she is their queen until she cannot defeat the Red Sweating Sickness, and when she tries to help Jamie Ivy, she realizes that she must break with the Salish ways.
Genre(s): Romance.

De la Roche, Mazo

5216. *The Building of Jalna.* Boston: Little, Brown, 1944. 366 pp.

In 1850, Adeline and Captain Whiteoak go to an area on Lake Ontario's shores and start the town of Jalna.
Genre(s): Domestic Fiction; Family Saga.

5217. *Finch's Fortune.* Boston: Little, Brown, 1931. 443 pp.
In the sequel to *Whiteoaks of Jalna*, Renny, observing the jealousy of the others over the money Gran left Finch, tries to remain aloof.
Genre(s): Domestic Fiction; Family Saga.

5218. *Jalna.* Boston: Little, Brown, 1927. 347 pp.
The sequel to *The Whiteoak Brothers* includes representatives of each generation up to 99-year-old Gran.
Genre(s): Domestic Fiction; Family Saga.

5219. *Mary Wakefield.* Boston: Little, Brown, 1949. 337 pp.
In 1893, the heroine of the sequel to *Morning at Jalna* is Mary Wakefield, governess, who falls in love with the father of her motherless students.
Genre(s): Domestic Fiction; Family Saga.

5220. *The Master of Jalna.* Boston: Little, Brown, 1933. 379 pp.
In the sequel to *Finch's Fortune*, set after the death of Gran in 1932, Renny tries to carry on the traditions of his grandfather although there is little money remaining.
Genre(s): Domestic Fiction; Family Saga.

5221. *Morning at Jalna.* Boston: Little, Brown, 1960. 298 pp.
Following *The Building of Jalna*, Adeline has four small children and during the Civil War copes with visitors from the South who participate in an underground Confederate resistance movement.
Genre(s): Domestic Fiction; Family Saga.

5222. *The Whiteoak Brothers: Jalna—1923.* Boston: Little, Brown, 1953. 307 pp.
Adeline is 98 in the sequel to *Whiteoak Heritage*, and her grandson Renny heads the Jalna household.
Genre(s): Domestic Fiction; Family Saga.

5223. *Whiteoak Heritage.* Boston: Little, Brown, 1940. 325 pp.
The sequel to *Young Renny* finds Renny returning home from World War I to manage Jalna and raise his younger brothers while dealing with the problems of his jilted sister Meg.
Genre(s): Domestic Fiction; Family Saga.

5224. *Whiteoaks of Jalna.* Boston: Little, Brown, 1929. 423 pp.
Finch, the musical genius of the family, in the sequel to *Jalna* becomes the recipient of his grandmother's fortune.
Genre(s): Domestic Fiction; Family Saga.

5225. *Young Renny (Jalna—1906).* Boston: Little, Brown, 1935. 324 pp.
In the sequel to *Mary Wakefield* young Renny tries to make life unpleasant for a guest at Whiteoak, when his grandmother is 80.
Genre(s): Domestic Fiction; Family Saga.

Ellis, Peter Berresford

◆ 5226. *The Rising of the Moon.* New York: St. Martin's, 1987. 636 pp.
In 1866, Irish-American Fenians try to establish an Irish republic in Canada under the leadership of Gavin and John-Joe Devlin, American Civil War veterans.
Genre(s): War Story.

Findley, Timothy

◆ 5227. *The Piano Man's Daughter.* New York: Crown, 1996. 480 pp.
After Lily Kilworth dies in a 1939 asylum fire, her illegitimate son tries to piece together her life and, in so doing, creates a history of Canadian life from the 1890s to the 1930s.
Genre(s): Domestic Fiction.

Glover, Ruth

5228. *Bitter Thistle, Sweet Rose.* Kansas City, MO: Beacon Hill, 1996. 206 pp.
In Saskatchewan, a woman meets a young farmer who influences her choices in life.
Genre(s): Christian Fiction; Love Story.

5229. *Second Best Bride.* Kansas City, MO: Beacon Hill, 1997. 208 pp.
Royce Ferguson decides that lovely Marlys would make a perfect pioneer wife, but she, unlike her sister Meg, has no intention of moving to Wildrose, Prince Albert, Canada.
Genre(s): Christian Fiction; Domestic Fiction; Romance.

5230. *The Shining Light.* Kansas City, MO: Beacon Hill, 1994. 214 pp.
A family tries to establish its farm on the frontier of Saskatchewan in Wildrose.
Genre(s): Christian Fiction; Romance.

Houston, James

◆ 5231. *The White Dawn.* New York: Harcourt, 1971. 228 pp.
A young Eskimo boy tells about the rescue of three men from an American whaler in 1896, but after several months, his tribe decides to kill them because of their attempts to destroy the way of life which the boy describes in detail.
Genre(s): Family Saga.

Jennings, Maureen

5232. *Except the Dying.* New York: St. Martin's, 1997. 288 pp.
In the early 20th century, the wealthy Toronto Rhodes family comes under suspicion when the maid is discovered dead and pregnant and William Murdoch must decide who killed her and why.
Genre(s): Mystery.

5233. *Under the Dragon's Tail.* New York: St. Martin's, 1998. 256 pp.

In 1895, long after a secret birth in a village north of Victorian Toronto, a murder occurs as a result of it, and William Murdoch must investigate.
Genre(s): Mystery.

Kelton, Elmer

◆ 5234. *The Day the Cowboys Quit.* Garden City, NY: Doubleday, 1971. 227 pp.
In 1883, when Eastern bankers try to make the ranchers along the Canadian river use business methods, the cowboys strike.
Genre(s): Western Fiction.

Klein, Clayton

5235. *Challenge the Wilderness.* Fowlerville, MI: Wilderness, 1988. 425 pp.
George Ellison guides the Leonidas Hubbard Expedition searching for Lake Michikamau in Labrador, and although they spot the lake from a cliff on their first attempt, some die while trying to find the path to it.
Genre(s): Adventure Story; Biographical Fiction.

Laidlaw, Robert

5236. *The McGregors.* Toronto: Macmillan of Canada, 1979. 166 pp.
The McGregors, Highland Scots, arrive in Bruce County, Ontario, in 1853, and buy their farm in a primitive and untamed area.
Genre(s): Domestic Fiction.

Lancaster, Bruce

5237. *Bright to the Wanderer.* 1942. Rivercity, MA: Rivercity, 1983. 451 pp.
Loyalist refugees conflict over the Family Compact in 1837.
Genre(s): War Story.

Ledbetter, Susann

5238. *Deliverance Drive.* New York: Signet, 1996. 352 pp.
Jenna French's husband purchases longhorns to drive to British Columbia during the 1870s gold strike, but he dies, and Jenna has to drive them with only the help of cattleman Dan Brannum.
Genre(s): Romance; Western Fiction.

Lee, Sky

5239. *Disappearing Moon Café.* Seattle, WA: Seal, 1991. 237 pp.
A young girl tries to understand Vancouver's Chinese connections so that she can trace her family to her great-grandfather who arrived in Canada in 1892.
Genre(s): Domestic Fiction.

Lutz, Giles A.

5240. *The Magnificent Failure.* New York: Doubleday, 1967. 330 pp.

A group of settlers of French-Indian descent try to protect their homes in the Riel Rebellion from the Canadian army.
Genre(s): Western Fiction; War Story.

MacDonald, Ann-Marie

5241.*Fall on Your Knees.* New York: Simon and Schuster, 1997. 512 pp.
James Piper and his young Lebanese wife raise four daughters on Cape Breton Island in the early 1900s before they take separate paths, in which the youngest, a victim of polio, demonstrates the strongest moral character.
Award(s): Commonwealth Writers' Prize.
Genre(s): Family Saga.

MacLennan, Hugh

5242.*Two Solitudes.* New York: Duell, Sloane and Pearce, 1945. 370 pp.
Paul Tallard must make his own decisions about his French-Canadian farming community after his father has severed contact in 1917 and sent him to school in England.

MacNeil, Robert

5243.*Burden of Desire.* New York: Doubleday, 1992. 466 pp.
After a munitions ship blows up in Halifax, Nova Scotia, in 1917, three men read Julia Robertson's diary, which was lost in the wreckage, and they all fall in love with her beauty and sensuality.
Genre(s): War Story; Romance.

Maillet, Antonine

5244.*The Devil Is Loose!* Trans. Philip Stratford. New York: Walker, 1987. 310 pp.
A Canadian village along the coast stays alive during the Depression with help from bootleggers outsmarting Prohibition.
Genre(s): Domestic Fiction.

Michener, James A.

◆ 5245.*Journey.* New York: Random House, 1989. 244 pp.
In July of 1897, four British aristocrats begin traveling through Canada to the gold fields of the Klondike, a journey of 23 months.
Genre(s): Adventure Story.

Morris, Alan

5246.*Between Earth and Sky.* Minneapolis, MN: Bethany House, 1998. 320 pp.
After Reena O'Donnell's uncle telegraphs her to come to Wyoming and nurse him back to health, she, Hunter Stone, and two other Mounties travel south where they meet Sitting Bull before the Battle of Little Bighorn.
Genre(s): Christian Fiction; Western Fiction.

5247.*Bright Sword of Justice.* Minneapolis, MN: Bethany House, 1997. 320 pp.

Hunter Stone and his Mounties go to the Blackfoot village of the missionary Reena O'Donnell and find a half Blackfoot who seems to know where a violent gang has hidden, and when one of the outlaws turns out to be Reena's brother, Stone must decide what justice is. (*Series:* Guardians of the North, 3)
Genre(s): Christian Fiction; Western Fiction; Romance.

5248.*By Honor Bound.* Minneapolis, MN: Bethany House, 1996. 320 pp.
In the 1870s, Crow warriors kill Hunter Stone's wife, and, while seeking revenge, he nearly dies before Reena O'Donnell, a missionary, nurses him back to health. (*Series:* Guardians of the North, 1)
Genre(s): Christian Fiction.

5249.*Heart of Valor.* Minneapolis, MN: Bethany House, 1996. 320 pp.
Hunter Stone and his fellow Royal Canadian Mounties try to establish themselves as the law in the Northwest territories while Reena O'Donnell continues her missionary work with the Blackfoot Nation. (*Series:* Guardians of the North, 2)
Genre(s): Christian Fiction; Romance; Western Fiction.

Murphy, James F.

5250.*They Were Dreamers.* New York: Atheneum, 1983. 311 pp.
Brendan McMahon leaves Ireland in 1832 for Prince Edward Island after murdering an evil landlord, and after Brendon returns to Ireland, his children and grandchildren migrate to Boston, with his granddaughter becoming a teacher.
Genre(s): Family Saga.

5251.*They Were Dreamers.* New York: Atheneum, 1983. 352 pp.
Brendan McMahon, accused of killing his abusive landlord, flees Ireland for Canada in 1932 where he and his farm wife raise their five children in a group of immigrants.
Genre(s): Adventure Story; Romance.

Myles, Eugenie Louise

5252.*The Emperor of Peace River.* Saskatoon, SK: Western, 1978. 302 pp.
Julia and Sheridan Lawrence settle the Peace River Valley of Alberta while Julia functions as trader, school teacher, doctor, and ranch foreman.

Neilan, Sarah

5253.*An Air of Glory.* New York: Morrow, 1977. 192 pp.
As the 19th century begins, Polly and her friends travel to Nova Scotia to escape from Scotland during British and French hostilities, and they have a difficult journey.
Genre(s): Adventure Story.

Norman, Howard

5254.*The Bird Artist.* New York: Farrar, Straus and Giroux, 1994. 289 pp.

Fabian Vas decides that someone should be murdered when his mother starts an affair with the lighthouse keeper in 1911 while his father is on a hunting trip.
Genre(s): Mystery.

O'Brien, Michael D.

5255. *Strangers and Sojourners.* San Francisco: Ignatius, 1997. 571 pp.
In Canada, trying to forget her experiences as a World War I nurse, Anna Ashton marries the Irish Catholic Stephen Delaney, but he has difficulty committing to their union because of secrets and religious differences.
Genre(s): Christian Fiction.

Oke, Janette

5256. *The Calling of Emily Evans.* Minneapolis, MN: Bethany House, 1990. Canada pp.
A young woman missionary attending a Bible college takes on the task of opening a new place on her own. (*Series:* Women of the West, 1)
Genre(s): Christian Fiction; Western Fiction.

5257. *Drums of Change.* Minneapolis, MN: Bethany House, 1996. 320 pp.
During the mid-19th century, white settlers in Alberta, steal lands from Running Fawn's tribe, and she must resign herself to living on the reservation.
Genre(s): Christian Fiction.

◆ 5258. *Roses for Mama.* Minneapolis, MN: Bethany House, 1991. 224 pp.
A young girl must take over the responsibility of raising her family. (*Series:* Women of the West, 3)
Genre(s): Christian Fiction; Domestic Fiction.

5259. *When Breaks the Dawn.* Minneapolis, MN: Bethany House, 1986. 223 pp.
Elizabeth and Wynn face a disappointment from which they must draw on their strengths to recover. (*Series:* Canadian West, 3)
Genre(s): Christian Fiction; Western Fiction.

5260. *When Calls the Heart.* Minneapolis, MN: Bethany House, 1983. 221 pp.
A teacher arrives in the West and resolves never to marry a rowdy cowboy until she meets Wynn. (*Series:* Canadian West, 1)
Genre(s): Christian Fiction; Romance.

5261. *When Comes the Spring.* Minneapolis, MN: Bethany House, 1985. 255 pp.
Elizabeth and Wynn make commitments to each other and to God, which give their lives added meaning. (*Series:* Canadian West, 2)
Genre(s): Romance; Christian Fiction.

5262. *When Hope Springs New.* Minneapolis, MN: Bethany House, 1986. 222 pp.
Elizabeth, a frontier woman, thinks that she has overcome every adversity, but she finds out differently. (*Series:* Canadian West, 4)
Genre(s): Christian Fiction; Western Fiction; Adventure Story.

Ondaatje, Michael

5263. *In the Skin of a Lion.* New York: Knopf, 1987. 243 pp.
In 1923, Patrick Lewis arrives in Toronto and becomes one of the many individuals searching for Ambrose Small, a millionaire who has disappeared.

Robertson, Heather

5264. *Igor: A Novel of Intrigue.* Toronto: J. Lorimer, 1989. 250 pp.
In the sequel to *Lily: A Rhapsody in Red,* after Lily's secret marriage to Mackenzie King in the 1920s and her conversion to communism in the 1930s, she spends her life as a member of the Senate, meeting famous people including President Ronald Reagan in 1981 on his visit to Ottawa.
Genre(s): Biographical Fiction; Political Fiction.

5265. *Lily: A Rhapsody in Red.* Toronto: J. Lorimer, 1986. 327 pp.
In the sequel to *Willie, a Romance,* Lily Coolican marries Mackenzie King, and they become enmeshed in Canadian politics from 1919 to 1935.
Genre(s): Biographical Fiction; Political Fiction.

5266. *Willie, a Romance.* Toronto: J. Lorimer, 1983. 359 pp.
Lily Coolican comes to Ottawa just before World War I and attains a position in the Governor General Duke of Connaught's household as a companion and press agent where she meets William Lyon Mackenzie King.
Award(s): Books in Canada First Novel Award.
Genre(s): War Story; Political Fiction.

Ross, Dana Fuller

◆ 5267. *Yukon Justice.* New York: Bantam, 1992. 341 pp.
The Holt family journeys to the Yukon gold fields and helps to keep justice in a lawless setting. (*Series:* An American Dynasty, 7)
Genre(s): Domestic Fiction; Adventure Story; Western Fiction.

Ross-Macdonald, Malcolm

5268. *Goldeneye.* New York: Knopf, 1981. 544 pp.
In 1919, Catherine Hamilton flees Scotland and her despotic father for Canada where she works to hold her marriage and family together through World War II and the more prosperous 1950s.
Genre(s): Domestic Fiction.

Salverson, Laura Goodman

5269. *The Viking Heart.* 1923. Toronto: McClelland, 1975. 326 pp.
Immigrants from Iceland arrive in Manitoba and forge a new life for themselves.
Genre(s): Domestic Fiction.

Sarna, Lazar

5270. *The Man Who Lived near Nelligan.*
Toronto: Coach House, 1975. 167 pp.
Walter Burton lives near Emile Nelligan in the early
1900s when young Nelligan is writing his best poetry and
before Nelligan goes into a permanent depression.
Genre(s): Biographical Fiction.

Scott, Virginia G.

5271. *And from Such Men.* Philadelphia: Dorrance, 1973. 192 pp.
Charles Finney Gill becomes a poet in 19th-century Canada, describing his region of Quebec along with other poets in his group.
Genre(s): Biographical Fiction.

Shields, Carol

5272. *The Stone Diaries.* New York: Viking,
1994. 361 pp.
Daisy Goodwill Flett, whose mother died during Daisy's
birth in 1905, moves from Canada to Indiana and back to
Canada with her stonecutter father and lives a fairly ordi-
nary life against the backdrop of 20th-century events.
Award(s): Pulitzer Prize; National Book Critics Circle
Award.
Genre(s): Domestic Fiction.

Silver, Alfred

5273. *Red River Story.* New York: Ballantine,
1988. 528 pp.
The independent Kate MacPherson and other Scottish
crofters thrown off their land arrive in Canada in the
early 19th century to start new lives.
Genre(s): Domestic Fiction.

Urquhart, Jane

5274. *Away.* New York: Viking, 1994. 356 pp.
Before her family emigrates from Ireland to Canada in
the 1840s, Mary, a young girl, has contact with fairies
and a young sailor she cannot forget.
Genre(s): Domestic Fiction.

5275. *The Whirlpool.* New York: David R.
Godine, 1990. 214 pp.
Fleda prefers to live in a tent near Niagara Falls in 1889
while Patrick, a poet, plans to swim in the waters, and
both obsessions lead them into the whirlpool.
Genre(s): Adventure Story.

Vollmann, William T.

5276. *The Rifles.* New York: Viking, 1994. 411 pp.
In the 1840s, Sir John Franklin leads a disastrous expedition to the North Pole, and in the 1950s, the Canadians re-
locate Inuit families, but in the 1990s, Captain Subzero
finds their descendants sniffing gasoline. (*Series:* Seven
Dreams, 3)
Genre(s): Adventure Story.

Wheeler, Richard S.

5277. *Rendezvous.* New York: Forge, 1997. 352
pp.
Barnaby Skye, 20, deserts the Royal Navy in 1826 after
being pressed into service and goes west, wanting to get
to Harvard, but he meets Many Quill Woman on his journey, and his goals change.
Genre(s): Western Fiction.

Wiebe, Rudy Henry

5278. *The Mad Trapper.* Toronto: McClelland and
Stewart, 1980. 189 pp.
Albert Johnson, a trapper on Rat River, has adventures
with nature and with the people at Fort McPherson near
the Arctic Circle.
Genre(s): Biographical Fiction; Adventure Story.

York, Thomas

5279. *Trapper.* Garden City, NY: Doubleday,
1981. 417 pp.
Royal Canadian Mounted Police hunt Albert Johnson,
called the Mad Trapper, in Arctic Canada during the
early 1930s.
Genre(s): Biographical Fiction; Adventure Story.

1933 and After

Anderson-Dargatz, Gail

◆ 5280. *The Cure for Death by Lightning.* Boston:
Houghton Mifflin, 1996. 294 pp.
Beth Weeks, 14, escapes her abusive father during the
days of shortages in World War II by reading her
mother's scrapbook and visiting a friend on a reservation
near her farm.
Genre(s): War Story; Domestic Fiction.

Bonanno, Margaret Wander

◆ 5281. *Ember Days.* New York: HarperCollins,
1980. 424 pp.

Four generations of women in Newfoundland, from the
turn of the century through the 1970s, face the demands
of Catholic education and life.
Genre(s): Family Saga.

Choy, Wayson

5282. *The Jade Peony.* New York: St. Martin's,
1997. 238 pp.
Three young Chinese Canadian immigrants search for an
identity in Vancouver's Chinatown during the 1930s and
1940s.
Award(s): Trillum Prize.
Genre(s): Domestic Fiction.

Curtis, Wayne

5283. *One Indian Summer.* Charlotte, NC: Baker and Taylor, 1993. 197 pp.
Steven Moar decides to stay home from college in the mid-1950s to help his ailing father on the farm, but the confinement becomes difficult to tolerate.
Genre(s): Domestic Fiction; Bildungsroman (Coming of Age).

De la Roche, Mazo

5284. *Centenary at Jalna.* Boston: Little, Brown, 1958. 342 pp.
In the sequel to *Variable Winds at Jalna*, set in the mid-1950s, the Whiteoak clan celebrates the 100 years of Jalna.
Genre(s): Domestic Fiction; Family Saga.

5285. *Renny's Daughter.* Boston: Little, Brown, 1951. 376 pp.
In the sequel to *Return to Jalna*, Renny's daughter Adeline goes to Ireland and has her first unhappy romance.
Genre(s): Domestic Fiction; Family Saga.

5286. *Return to Jalna.* Boston: Little, Brown, 1946. 462 pp.
The Whiteoaks participate in World War II, in the sequel to *Wakefield's Course*, and then return to Jalna.
Genre(s): Domestic Fiction; Family Saga.

5287. *Variable Winds at Jalna.* Boston: Little, Brown, 1954. 359 pp.
Among the events of the mid-20th century, in the sequel to *Renny's Daughter*, Adeline plans a double wedding, old Nicholas dies, and television comes to town.
Genre(s): Domestic Fiction; Family Saga.

5288. *Wakefield's Course.* Boston: Little, Brown, 1941. 406 pp.
From the spring of 1939 through 1940, in *Whiteoak's Harvest*'s sequel, Renny has more money and wins the Grand National with his horse.
Genre(s): Domestic Fiction; Family Saga.

5289. *Whiteoak Harvest.* Boston: Little, Brown, 1936. 378 pp.
Renny and his wife in the sequel to *The Master of Jalna*, are living in the family home when young Wakefield returns after trying monastery life.
Genre(s): Domestic Fiction; Family Saga.

Eddenden, A. E.

5290. *A Good Year for Murder.* Chicago: Academy, 1988. 178 pp.
On Father's Day, Fort York, Ontario's official chaplain, Father Cosentino, is found strangled in his gift purple tie, and as the year progresses, other aldermen die on holidays, murders for the police and the traffic inspector to solve.
Genre(s): Mystery.

5291. *Murder at the Movies.* Chicago: Academy, 1996. 159 pp.

In 1939, Albert V. Tretheway, his sister, and his sidekick in Fort York, Canada, try to find a murderer who commits his crimes based on scenes in popular movies of the day.
Genre(s): Mystery.

5292. *Murder on the Thirteenth.* Chicago: Academy, 1992. 180 pp.
Inspector Albert Tretheway tries to follow the witchcraft signs and occult symbols that turn up in his investigation of serial murders during air-raid warnings in Fort York, Canada, in 1943.
Genre(s): Mystery.

Fry, Alan

5293. *How a People Die.* New York: Doubleday, 1970. 167 pp.
When people in a British Columbia Native American village are relocated from their ancestral home in the 1960s, new forces ruin their way of life.
Genre(s): Political Fiction.

Kavanagh, Patrick

5294. *Gaff Topsails.* New York: Viking, 1998. 448 pp.
After World War II, Michael Barron, a young mute, and his friends explore a huge iceberg while he remembers his father's stories about a beautiful woman who rides the ice.
Genre(s): Domestic Fiction.

Kinsella, W. P.

5295. *Box Socials.* New York: Ballantine, 1992. 224 pp.
While promising to discuss baseball, the narrator instead describes Alberta during the Depression and World War II, a time when box socials helped life seem more connected.
Genre(s): Domestic Fiction.

Kogawa, Joy

5296. *Itsuka.* New York: Anchor, 1994. 331 pp.
Naomi, in the sequel to *Obasan*, lives with her aunt and uncle on a farm after World War II while her brother Stephen escapes from the small town to Toronto, but when Naomi leaves the area, she becomes involved in the quest for reparations.
Genre(s): War Story.

5297. *Obasan.* Boston: David R. Godine, 1982. 250 pp.
Pearl Harbor changes life in Vancouver for Naomi Nakane when the government takes property from her relatives and interns them.
Genre(s): War Story.

Munro, Alice

5298. *Lives of Girls and Women.* New York: McGraw Hill, 1972. 250 pp.

◆ May be suitable for young adult readers

After Del Jordan goes to college in the 1940s, she matures and leaves behind her childhood in Jubilee.
Genre(s): Domestic Fiction.

Norman, Howard

5299. *The Museum Guard.* New York: Farrar, Straus, and, Giroux, 1998. 240 pp.
Orphan DeFoe Russet lives in Halifax with his uncle, an alcoholic museum guard, and after DeFoe becomes a guard in 1938, he meets Imogene Linny, a woman convinced she is a figure in the museum's painting of Jews on an Amsterdam street.
Genre(s): Domestic Fiction.

Silver, Alfred

◆ 5300. *Lord of the Plains.* New York: Ballantine, 1990. 406 pp.
In 1885, Louis Riel fights in a rebellion against the mixed breeds of the Saskatchewan under illiterate Gabriel Dumont and his strong wife.
Genre(s): War Story.

Skvorecky, Josef

5301. *The Engineer of Human Souls.* Trans. Robert Speaight. New York: Knopf, 1984. 571 pp.
A Czech writer teaching in a Toronto university corresponds with his boyhood friends and recalls the painful political experiences of his youth.
Genre(s): Political Fiction.

China

Before 1800

Altieri, Daniel, and Eleanor Cooney

5302. *The Court of the Lion.* New York: Morrow, 1989. 1120 pp.
Lady Wu plots the death of the prince, but when her son rejects the throne, she commits suicide, and her husband grieves while Lin Lin-fu, the chief minister, begins a reign of terror.
Genre(s): Epic Literature.

Baumann, Hans

◆ 5303. *Sons of the Steppe.* New York: Oxford, 1958. 237 pp.
Two grandsons of Genghis Khan have differing ideas for the direction of the country, one wanting to wage war and the other wanting to keep peace.
Genre(s): War Story.

Caldwell, Taylor

5304. *The Earth Is the Lord's.* New York: Scribner's, 1941. 570 pp.
Genghis Khan learns in early childhood how to survive and organize well enough to be chosen leader of the Mongols.
Genre(s): War Story; Biographical Fiction.

Calvino, Italo

5305. *Invisible Cities.* Trans. William Weaver. New York: Harcourt, 1974. 165 pp.
Marco Polo describes Kublai Khan's cities to him in terms of women's names to symbolize relationships between different people.
Genre(s): Biographical Fiction; Allegory.

Chun, Jinsie K. S.

5306. *I Am Heaven.* Philadelphia: Macrae-Smith, 1973. 266 pp.
Chao, a young Chinese noblewoman, rises to the position of Emperor in seventh century AD.
Genre(s): Biographical Fiction.

Cooney, Eleanor, and Daniel Altieri

5307. *Deception.* New York: HarperCollins, 1993. 640 pp.
Magistrate Dee investigates the murder of a transport minister and meets Madame Wu, the consort who wants to establish the Chou dynasty in place of the T'ang dynasty.
Genre(s): Mystery.

De Chair, Somerset Struben

5308. *The Legend of the Yellow River.* New York: St. Martin's, 1979. 186 pp.
During the Han Dynasty, Wang, a sculptor forced to become a soldier, goes to Persia twice on difficult missions at the request of the Emperor of China.
Genre(s): Picaresque Fiction.

Eaton, Evelyn Sybil Mary

5309. *Go Ask the River.* New York: Harcourt, 1969. 280 pp.
The poetess Hung Tu rises from the position of concubine in the Blue House to poet laureate of the Shu Province in the eighth century.
Genre(s): Biographical Fiction.

Elegant, Robert S.

5310. *Manchu.* New York: McGraw Hill, 1980. 560 pp.
Tatars or Manchus conquer the great Ming empire in 17th-century China, and Francis Arrowsmith, a soldier who arrived in China in 1624, describes the next 30 years.
Genre(s): War Story.

Elegant, Simon

5311. *A Floating Life.* Hopewell, NJ: Ecco, 1997. 312 pp.
For his part in a royal prince's treachery, Li Po (AD 701-762) sails to exile in the Yunan Province in 758, and tells his story to a young scholar on the boat.
Genre(s): Biographical Fiction.

Fast, Jonathan

5312. *The Jade Stalk.* New York: Dutton, 1988. 271 pp.
The empress of the T'ang Dynasty wants only the Boxer, a man with a reputation for pleasing women.
Genre(s): Erotic Literature.

Gulik, Robert Hans van

5313. *The Chinese Bell Murders.* New York: Scribner's, 1958. 262 pp.
Judge Dee Jen-Djieh solves three crimes to conclude a murder-rape case in Pooyang.
Genre(s): Mystery.

5314. *The Chinese Gold Murders.* New York: Harper and Row, 1961. 202 pp.
The magistrate of Pen-lai, Judge Dee works to solve murders in the seventh century.
Genre(s): Mystery.

5315. *The Chinese Lake Murders.* New York: Harper and Row, 1960. 255 pp.
Judge Dee, Chinese magistrate, tries to unravel puzzling murders.
Genre(s): Mystery.

5316. *The Chinese Nail Murders.* New York: Harper and Row, 1961. 224 pp.
Judge Dee tries to find a murderer who uses nails in his crimes.
Genre(s): Mystery.

5317. *The Emperor's Pearl.* Chicago: University of Chicago Press, 1994. 144 pp.
Judge Dee uses his head to find the villain in this T'ang dynasty murder.
Genre(s): Mystery; Legal Story.

5318. *The Haunted Monastery.* New York: Scribner's, 1969. 159 pp.
A broken axle strands Judge Dee Jen-Djieh and his family during a storm, but the judge solves three murders and an impersonation during the night.
Genre(s): Mystery.

5319. *The Lacquer Screen.* New York: Scribner's, 1970. 180 pp.
Judge Dee Jen-Djieh and his lieutenant circulate in the underworld before solving three crimes and an ugly secret hidden behind a lacquer screen.
Genre(s): Mystery.

5320. *The Monkey and the Tiger.* New York: Scribner's, 1966. 143 pp.
Judge Dee solves his murders by finding smugglers and robbers.
Genre(s): Mystery.

5321. *Murder in Canton.* New York: Scribner's, 1967. 207 pp.
A disabled Taoist sage helps Judge Dee to recover the Third Princess's stolen necklace.
Genre(s): Mystery.

5322. *Necklace and Calabash.* New York: Scribner's, 1971. 143 pp.
Judge Dee Jen-Djieh wants to relax for a while, but at his vacation spot, a princess requests that he find her stolen necklace.
Genre(s): Mystery.

5323. *The Phantom of the Temple.* New York: Scribner's, 1966. 203 pp.
During the T'ang Dynasty, Judge Dee Jen-Djieh investigates a murder that includes a decapitated body and a theft.
Genre(s): Mystery; Legal Story.

5324. *Poets and Murder.* New York: Scribner's, 1972. 173 pp.
Judge Dee Jen-Djieh investigates the deaths of a student studying fox magic and a dancer who had contracted rabies.
Genre(s): Mystery.

5325. *The Red Pavilion.* New York: Scribner's, 1968. 173 pp.
Judge Dee Jen-Djieh stays at the Red Pavilion on Paradise Island, but is unaware that mysterious deaths have occurred there.
Genre(s): Mystery.

5326. *The Willow Pattern.* New York: Scribner's, 1965. 183 pp.
When the court escapes the plague-ridden city, Judge Dee Jen-Djieh takes charge of affairs and must solve three murders.
Genre(s): Mystery.

Han, Suyin

5327. *The Enchantress.* New York: Bantam, 1985. 345 pp.
During the 18th century, Colin and his twin Bea travel from Switzerland to China and Thailand where they share their ability to commune with nature.

Inoue, Yasushi

5328. *Tun-huang.* Trans. Jean Oda Moy. New York: Harper and Row, 1978. 201 pp.
The Hsi-hsia, a barbarian tribe, tries to encroach on Sung-dynasty China, and Chao Hsing-te, a young scholar, hides precious sutras in the Thousand Buddha Caves, where they remain for 900 years.
Award(s): Mainchi Prize.
Genre(s): War Story.

Jennings, Gary

5329. *The Journeyer.* New York: Atheneum, 1984. 782 pp.
Marco Polo travels to the Orient after being banished from Venice at the age of 17.
Genre(s): Adventure Story.

Larsen, Jeanne

◆ **5330. *Bronze Mirror.*** New York: Henry Holt, 1991. 337 pp.
A storytelling contest between the Silkweb Empress and a courtier of the Yellow Emperor produces 12th-century Pomegranate, maid to lonely Lady Phoenix, who tells of a mother-in-law and her faithless son's court intrigues.

5331. *Manchu Palaces.* New York: Henry Holt, 1996. 342 pp.
After her mother's death, Lotus becomes the bondservant to the Empress Dowager in Beijing during the 18th century.

5332. *Silk Road.* New York: Henry Holt, 1989. 434 pp.
A young girl taken from her parents during the T'ang dynasty decides to seek revenge after being sold into slavery and trained as a concubine.

Levi, Jean

5333. *The Chinese Emperor.* Trans. Barbara Bray. New York: Harcourt, 1987. 341 pp.

In 221 BC, Ch'in Shih Huang Ti creates the central Chinese state from which he controls the land and people in his dynasty.
Genre(s): Biographical Fiction.

5334. *The Dream of Confucius.* New York: Harcourt, 1992. 294 pp.
In 209 BC, a rebellion and subsequent six-year struggle for control occur between Whet-Iron (Liu Pang) and Plume (Hsiang Yu), ending in Whet-Iron's founding of the Han dynasty, in the sequel to *The Chinese Emperor.*
Genre(s): Biographical Fiction.

Lin, Yutang

5335. *Lady Wu.* New York: Putnam, 1965. 255 pp.
Lady Wu determines that she will become empress in China during the seventh century, and she carefully plots her progress.

May, Rachel

5336. *Love in a Chinese Garden.* New York: Harlequin, 1997. 304 pp.
A young woman finds love in 9th-century China although her lover's mother is a villain.
Genre(s): Romance.

McCune, Evelyn B.

5337. *Empress.* New York: Fawcett, 1994. 487 pp.
Wu Jao is only 13 when summoned to serve as a concubine to the Emperor Taitsung, and she learns enough to win his affection and rise in power by befriending his son and heir.
Genre(s): Political Fiction.

Mei, Chin P'Ing

5338. *The Plum in the Golden Vase.* Trans. David Tod Roy. Princeton, NJ: Princeton University Press, 1993. 544 pp.
A greedy Sung dynasty merchant of the 10th century becomes involved in political and sexual adventures.
Genre(s): Family Saga.

Montalbano, William D., and Carl Hiaasen

5339. *A Death in China.* New York: Atheneum, 1984. 320 pp.

Qin Shi Huangdi standardizes the Chinese language and monetary system and begins building the Great Wall as emperor in 200 BC.
Genre(s): Biographical Fiction.

Motley, Annette

5340. *Green Dragon, White Tiger.* New York: Macmillan, 1986. 557 pp.
Empress Wu ascends in the seventh century as the only woman to rule China after a soothsayer prophesies about her as a baby.
Genre(s): Biographical Fiction.

Oxnam, Robert B.

◆ 5341. *Ming.* New York: St. Martin's, 1995. 270 pp.
Meihua, the daughter of an important patriarch in the 17th century, who has taught herself to read by listening behind screens to her brothers' tutor, falls in love with Longyan, the disgraced second son of a scholar who cannot read because of dyslexia.
Genre(s): War Story; Romance.

Shih, Nai-an

5342. *All Men Are Brothers.* Trans. Pearl Buck. New York: J. Day, 1933. 1279 pp.
Men fleeing an oppressive government, in the 12th century join others and form a robber band.
Genre(s): Adventure Story; Picaresque Fiction.

Ts'ao, Hsueh-ch'in

◆ 5343. *Dream of the Red Chamber.* New York: Pantheon, 1958. 329 pp.
The Chia family experiences a decline in fortune during the Ch'ing dynasty.
Genre(s): Biographical Fiction; Domestic Fiction.

Wu, Ch'eng-en

5344. *Monkey.* Trans. Arthur Waley. New York: Penguin, 1942. 350 pp.
Hsan-Tsang makes a pilgrimage to India in the 17th century to obtain Buddha's teachings for the Chinese.
Genre(s): Picaresque Fiction; Adventure Story; Allegory.

1800-1899

Barr, Pat

5345. *Jade.* New York: St. Martin's, 1982. 597 pp.
Captured Alice Greenwood, child of English missionaries, becomes a servant in a Chinese household, and as she begins to understand Chinese ways, she is exposed to various institutions such as concubinage and prostitution.
Genre(s): Romance.

Berry-Hart, Alice

5346. *Ching-a-ring-a-ring-ching.* London: Collins, 1977. 484 pp.
Three sisters from Victorian England travel to Shanghai, one to join her missionary husband and the others to try to find husbands.
Genre(s): Domestic Fiction.

◆ May be suitable for young adult readers

Bowering, Marilyn

5347. *To All Appearances a Lady.* New York: Viking, 1990. 336 pp.
When the spirit of his recently dead foster mother visits him, Robert Lam knows that he must investigate his past and search for the identity of his mother in Hong Kong and of his Chinese father.
Genre(s): Adventure Story.

Brent, Madeleine

5348. *Moonraker's Bride.* New York: Doubleday, 1973. 352 pp.
Jailed for stealing food for orphans in her care, Lucy meets a prisoner who marries her before his execution and wills her his fortune, but after her release the real adventure begins.
Genre(s): Love Story.

Broome, Susannah

5349. *The Pearl Pagoda.* New York: Simon and Schuster, 1980. 352 pp.
When a young woman arrives in China in the mid-19th century, the missionary she is intended to marry has died, and when she stays to help, she becomes unwillingly involved with a clipper-ship captain and the opium trade.
Genre(s): Romance; Adventure Story.

Buck, Pearl S.

5350. *Imperial Woman.* New York: John Day, 1956. 376 pp.
T'zu-hsi rules China in the Forbidden City as Western powers help to break up the Manchu Dynasty.
Genre(s): Biographical Fiction.

5351. *Peony.* New York: John Day, 1948. 312 pp.
A young Chinese girl, sold into a weathy Jewish home, becomes more than a servant but less than a daughter and falls in love with the son of the house whom she is forbidden by Chinese tradition to marry.
Genre(s): Love Story.

Carlisle, Carris

5352. *Party in Peking.* New York: St. Martin's, 1987. 192 pp.
After Dr. Lewis Sinclair, British outcast married to a Chinese woman, saves Olivia Harland and her family during the Boxer Rebellion, she sees the shallowness of the diplomats as she tries, in turn, to save Sinclair's son.
Genre(s): Romance.

Clavell, James

5353. *Tai-Pan.* New York: Atheneum, 1966. 590 pp.
In 1841, after the British have won the Opium War, Dick Struan, *tai-pan* (supreme ruler) of the Noble House, decides that England must expand power in other areas of the Far East.
Genre(s): Family Saga.

Clive, William

5354. *Dando and the Summer Palace.* New York: Putnam, 1972. 189 pp.
Dando serves the British in China during 1860 when the second opium war is raging, in a sequel to *Dando on Delhi Ridge.*
Genre(s): War Story.

Cohan, Tony

5355. *Opium.* New York: Morrow, 1984. 463 pp.
The Lin family of Hong Kong deals in opium, trading with the Ameircan Astors, Lodges, and Cabots, and delivering 10 to 20 tons into England every year throughout most of the 19th century.
Genre(s): Family Saga; Adventure Story.

Eden, Dorothy

◆ 5356. *The Time of the Dragon.* New York: Coward-McCann, 1975. 284 pp.
In 1899 a British merchant's family gets caught in the Boxer Rebellion, while their relatives in London harbor priceless Chinese art looted by an earlier generation.
Genre(s): War Story.

Elegant, Robert S.

5357. *Dynasty.* New York: McGraw Hill, 1977. 625 pp.
During the later 19th and first half of the 20th century, Sir Jonathan Sekloong, son of a Chinese Mother and a Irish father, establishes a successful business in China.
Genre(s): Family Saga.

5358. *Mandarin.* New York: Simon and Schuster, 1983. 527 pp.
Yehenala, a concubine of the Emperor Hsien Feng in 1854, becomes allies with leaders of the Taiping Tienkuo (the Kingdom of Heavenly Peace) movement to overthrow the Manchu Dynasty, before she becomes the Dowager Empress ruling during the Boxer Rebellion.
Genre(s): War Story; Family Saga.

Feng Jicai

5359. *The Three-Inch Golden Lotus.* Honolulu: University of Hawaii Press, 1994. 208 pp.
The bound feet of Fragrant Lotus, a poor girl, attract the wealthy Tong Ren-an, and he chooses her as a daughter-in-law, but after his death and the revolutionary changes in China, Fragrant Lotus's asset becomes a liability.
Genre(s): Political Fiction.

Fraser, George MacDonald

5360. *Flashman and the Dragon.* New York: Knopf, 1986. 320 pp.
In the sequel to *Flashman and the Redskins*, Harry Paget Flashman goes to China in the early 1860s, where he encounters the Taiping Rebellion.
Genre(s): Adventure Story.

Gaan, Margaret

5361. *Red Barbarian.* New York: Dodd, Mead, 1984. 448 pp.
After Charlie Tyson's father abandons him, Charlie is shipped to China as a servant, and he eventually marries the daughter of a Chinese family before the Opium War causes hostility between the British and the Chinese.
Genre(s): Family Saga.

5362. *White Poppy.* New York: Dodd, Mead, 1985. 274 pp.
In the sequel to *Red Barbarian*, Charlie Tyson's family becomes powerful enough to survive changes in the opium trade and in British-Chinese relations.
Genre(s): Family Saga.

Gordon, Deborah

5363. *Runaway Magic.* New York: Avon, 1996. 371 pp.
Susannah Stone, an American teacher in Hong Kong during 1871, casts spells and tries to recall a time-traveling friend that she plans to marry, but a British earl who removed his daughter from her school keeps haunting her.
Genre(s): Romance.

Leasor, James

5364. *Mandarin Gold.* New York: Morrow, 1974. 332 pp.
Robert Gunn, a British surgeon, goes to China in 1833, and although idealistic on arrival, he soon begins smuggling opium after a love affair ends.
Genre(s): Adventure Story.

Lee, C. Y.

5365. *China Saga.* New York: Weidenfeld and Nicolson, 1987. 534 pp.
Fong Tai marries in 1880, and nearly 100 years later, after other members of the family have lived through the Boxer Rebellion, World War II, and the Korean War, Fong's great-grandson arrives in Beijing, hoping to find his American father.
Genre(s): Family Saga.

◆ 5366. *The Second Son of Heaven.* New York: Morrow, 1990. 340 pp.
Hung Hsiu-ch'uan converts to Christianity as a young man, and his visions convince him that he is God's second son and destined to end the Manchu dynasty.
Genre(s): War Story.

Li, Leslie

5367. *Bittersweet.* Boston: Tuttle, 1992. 400 pp.
Born in peasant surroundings in the late 18th century, Li Xiumen becomes the wife of Li Tsung-jen, a political leader who soon prefers his second wife to Xiuwen.
Genre(s): Biographical Fiction; Political Fiction; Domestic Fiction.

Lin, Yutang

5368. *The Red Peony.* New York: World, 1961. 400 pp.
A young Chinese widow has several unconventional love affairs during the 19th century.
Genre(s): Love Story.

Lord, Bette

5369. *Spring Moon.* New York: Harper and Row, 1981. 464 pp.
The Mandarin Chinese family of Spring Moon, of the House of Chang, follows traditional Chinese ways from 1892 until 1927, when new ideas change their lives.

Mather, Berkely

5370. *The Midnight Gun.* New York: St. Martin's, 1984. 336 pp.
Bard Stafford returns to Hong Kong after dismissal from Cambridge and helps a gun runner smuggle guns into Tibet in the last years of the 19th century.
Genre(s): Adventure Story.

Mo, Timothy

5371. *An Insular Possession.* New York: Random House, 1987. 593 pp.
In the 19th century China and Britain fight opium wars, and two idealistic young Americans publish a newsletter against the British.
Genre(s): War Story.

Odell, Kathleen

5372. *Chinnery in China.* London: Murray, 1971. 226 pp.
In Macao during the late 19th century, George Chinnery, an English painter, is stranded in Calcutta because of debts.
Genre(s): Biographical Fiction.

O'Grady, Leslie

◆ 5373. *Lady Jade.* New York: St. Martin's, 1981. 320 pp.
During the 1890s, May Monckton returns to China after a bad marriage in England and becomes involved with an adventurer who may be involved in the illegal jade trade.
Genre(s): Romance.

Pemberton, Margaret

5374. *Moonflower Madness.* Hampton, NH: Severn House, 1993. 250 pp.
At the residence of Sir Arthur Hollis, botanist Zachary Cartwright and Lord Charles Rendlesham meet Serena Hollis and her orphaned cousin who decides to join them on their Chinese expedition to find the blue moonflower.
Genre(s): Romance.

Peters, Maureen

5375. *Night of the Willow.* New York: St. Martin's, 1982. 206 pp.

In Peking, during the Boxer Rebellion, Chang Liu sees Lucy O'Malley, 18, working as an accountant at a mill and suggests that his son Prince Chang Lee marry her, but after she does, the prince ignores her until she finds out about his dead European wife and that the Empress T'zu-hsi is testing her.
Genre(s): War Story; Political Fiction.

Reeman, Douglas

5376. *The First to Land.* New York: Morrow, 1985. 294 pp.
The nephew of Philip Blackwood in *Badge of Glory* continues the family tradition of military service by going to China to fight in the Boxer Rebellion and help the Europeans remaining in the country.
Genre(s): Sea Story; War Story.

Sledge, Linda Ching

◆ 5377. *Empire of Heaven.* New York: Bantam, 1990. 576 pp.

Since Rulan has a gift of healing, she is sent to spy in a wealthy household, but later she becomes a warrior in the Taiping Rebellion.
Genre(s): War Story.

Stewart, Fred Mustard

◆ 5378. *The Magnificent Savages.* New York: Forge, 1996. 383 pp.
After Sylvaner Savage's attempt to kill his younger half-brother Justin fails, Justin goes with Chinese pirates to Europe around 1850 during the Taiping Rebellion to learn the art of war from Giuseppe Garibaldi.
Genre(s): Adventure Story; Love Story.

Wilson, Leslie

5379. *The Mountain of Immoderate Desires.* London: Phoenix, 1995. 374 pp.
In colonial Hong Kong, at the end of the 19th century, Samuel Pink, a Colonial Service cadet, and Lily, mistress of an elderly sinologist, arrive, meet, and become lovers in a morass of deceit and betrayal.
Genre(s): Adventure Story.

1900 and After

Ballard, J. G.

◆ 5380. *Empire of the Sun.* New York: Simon and Schuster, 1984. 279 pp.
Jim, 11, becomes separated from his parents in Shanghai when the Japanese capture it on December 8, 1941, and he struggles for the next four years to stay alive.
Award(s): James Tate Black Award.
Genre(s): War Story; Bildungsroman (Coming of Age).

Barber, Noel

5381. *Tanamera.* New York: Macmillan, 1981. 637 pp.
Against their society's conventions, the British Johnnie Dexter and the Chinese Julie Soong become lovers in Singapore but face separation after the Japanese invasion.
Genre(s): War Story; Love Story.

Barnett, Raymond James

5382. *Jade and Fire.* New York: Random House, 1987. 370 pp.
In 1948 and 1949, the man who leads Taoist monks to murder their prior turns out to be the confidential aid of a powerful Communist field commander.
Genre(s): War Story.

Becker, Stephen D.

5383. *The Last Mandarin.* New York: Random House, 1979. 294 pp.
In 1949, Communists threaten Peking, and Major Jack Burnham goes to China to settle with Kanamori, a former Japanese military man responsible for atrocities during the fall of Nanking in 1937.
Genre(s): Adventure Story; Spy Fiction; Love Story.

Binstock, R. C.

5384. *Tree of Heaven.* New York: Soho, 1995. 212 pp.
In 1938, while Japanese troops rape and murder the conquered Chinese, the soldier Kuroda falls in love with Li, a Chinese woman who has Japanese blood.
Genre(s): Love Story; War Story.

Bodard, Lucien

5385. *The French Consul.* Trans. Barbara Bray. New York: Knopf, 1977. 405 pp.
In the early 20th century, the French consul Albert Bonnard lives with his wife and child in China as he dreams of bringing the railroad from Indochina to Chengtu.
Genre(s): Political Fiction.

Booth, Martin

5386. *Hiroshima Joe.* New York: Atlantic Monthly, 1986. 441 pp.
The Japanese capture Joe Sandingham in Hong Kong and imprison and torture him in World War II, and as he wonders why he bruises easily and loses his hair after the war, someone realizes that he is a victim of radiation sickness from being near Hiroshima.
Genre(s): War Story.

5387. *The Jade Pavilion.* Boston: Little, Brown, 1988. 466 pp.
In Hong Kong during 1937, Sean Mulrenan, an Anglo-Irish piano player whose mistress is Alice Soon, but finds that while the war separates them, one rises in society as the other begins to fall.
Genre(s): War Story.

Bosse, Malcolm J.

5388. *Fire in Heaven.* New York: Simon and Schuster, 1985. 654 pp.
The American Philip Embree, the czarist Vera Rogacheva, and General Tang survive China's wars during the rise of Mao and communism, in the sequel to *The Warlord*.
Genre(s): War Story; Political Fiction.

5389. *The Warlord.* New York: Simon and Schuster, 1983. 717 pp.
In 1927, a Chinese general, a White Russian sometime prostitute, a German gun seller, and an American missionary find themselves together in the disorganization of China.
Genre(s): Epic Literature.

Buck, Pearl S.

5390. *Dragon Seed.* New York: John Day, 1942. 378 pp.
When the Japanese take Nanking, Ling Tan and his family must adjust to the changes in their lives and become guerilla fighters.
Genre(s): Domestic Fiction; War Story.

5391. *The Good Earth.* New York: Crowell, 1931. 345 pp.
Wang Lung, a Chinese peasant, rises from poverty to become a rich landowner with the aid of his patient wife in the 1920s.
Award(s): Pulitzer Prize.
Genre(s): Domestic Fiction; Family Saga.

5392. *A House Divided.* 1935. Wakefield, RI: Moyer Bell, 1994. 353 pp.
After *The Good Earth* and *Sons*, Wang's grandson Yuan spends years in America as a student before he returns home to the New China and revolution.
Genre(s): Domestic Fiction; Family Saga.

5393. *Pavilion of Women.* New York: John Day, 1946. 316 pp.
Madame Wu, at 40, retires from married life, planning to find a concubine for her husband and become a chief manager of the house of Wu.
Genre(s): Domestic Fiction; Love Story.

5394. *Sons.* New York: John Day, 1932. 467 pp.
Wang Lung and O-lan's sons divide their land in the sequel to *The Good Earth*, but the youngest, Wang the Tiger, becomes a warlord.
Genre(s): Domestic Fiction; Family Saga.

Chand, Meira

5395. *A Choice of Evils.* New York: Trafalgar Square, 1996. 461 pp.
During the Japanese invasion in 1937, a Russian woman, a British journalist, and others are caught and tortured in China.
Genre(s): War Story.

Chang, Eileen

5396. *The Rice-Sprout Song.* Berkeley, CA: University of California, 1998. 182 pp.
Mao's land reforms ruin many of China's peasants.
Genre(s): War Story; Domestic Fiction.

5397. *The Rouge of the North.* Berkeley, CA: University of California, 1998. 185 pp.
A Chinese aristocratic family declines as the 20th century begins.
Genre(s): Domestic Fiction.

Chen, Yuan-tsung

5398. *The Dragon's Village.* New York: Pantheon, 1980. 285 pp.
Ling-ling, 17, joins a revolutionary theater group carrying out reforms in the Chinese countryside in 1949.

Cheng, Naishan

5399. *The Banker.* Trans. Britten Dean. San Francisco: China, 1993. 459 pp.
In 1937, the daughters of banker Zhu Jingchen believe that they are protected at the McTyeire School for Girls because Zhu Jingchen has carefully solicited foreign investors into his Cathay Republic Bank so that a Japanese invasion will harm him less.
Genre(s): War Story.

Clavell, James

5400. *Noble House.* New York: Delacorte, 1981. 1206 pp.
Ian Dunross, head of the respected China trade firm of Struan's makes an appearance during a typhoon in 1963, in the sequel to *Tai-Pan*, and various aspects of Chinese culture and business come to light.
Genre(s): Family Saga.

Clifford, Nicholas Rowland

5401. *The House of Memory.* New York: Ballantine, 1994. 343 pp.
Matthew Walker arrives in Shanghai in 1989, having promised his lover to investigate her great-uncle Simon's disappearance during the Chinese Revolution in 1927, but he discovers that Simon knew too much about the Nationalists.
Genre(s): Mystery.

Cordell, Alexander

5402. *The Dream and the Destiny.* New York: Doubleday, 1975. 368 pp.
A young medical student accompanies Mao on the Long March across northwest China in 1934.
Genre(s): War Story.

Darrell, Elizabeth

5403. *Concerto.* New York: St. Martin's, 1994. 498 pp.
To escape the war, Sarah Channing goes from England to Hong Kong to live with her father, but her desire to be-

come a concert pianist leads her to try to return to England just when the Japanese invade China during 1941.
Genre(s): War Story; Musical Fiction; Romance.

5404. *The Jade Alliance.* New York: Putnam, 1979. 630 pp.
The Brusilovs, exiled from Russia to Hong Kong in the early 1900s, establish a jade business as they become involved in the Chinese culture and gain the suspicion of the British around them.
Genre(s): War Story.

Drummond, Emma

5405. *The Bridge of a Hundred Dragons.* New York: St. Martin's, 1986. 352 pp.
In the 1920s, Alexandra Mostyn meets Major Mark Rawlings, the engineer assigned to her industrialist father to determine why a railroad bridge collapsed in Shanghai.
Genre(s): Romance; Adventure Story.

Gaan, Margaret

◆ 5406. *Little Sister.* New York: Dodd, Mead, 1983. 189 pp.
In 1925, Little Sister, six, visits her American grandfather, Chinese grandmother, cousin, and an adopted grandson who is a communist planning the May 30th demonstration in Shanghai.
Genre(s): War Story; Domestic Fiction.

Grant, Maxwell

◆ 5407. *Blood Red Rose.* New York: Macmillan, 1986. 418 pp.
After Dr. Kate Richmond, daughter of American medical missionaries in China, tries to help an elderly man, she and her friends must flee Shanghai only to find themselves in the Long March of 1936.
Genre(s): War Story; Medical Novel.

Grey, Anthony

5408. *Peking.* Boston: Little, Brown, 1988. 645 pp.
Jakob Kellner goes to China in 1931 as a missionary, but when communist soldiers capture him, he must participate in the Long March.
Genre(s): Political Fiction.

Han, Suyin

5409. *Till Morning Comes.* New York: Bantam, 1982. 512 pp.
During World War II and the subsequent civil war in China from 1945 to 1949, Stephanie Ryder, assigned to China as a magazine correspondent, falls in love with a physician who sympathizes with the communists.
Genre(s): War Story.

Hersey, John

5410. *The Call.* New York: Knopf, 1985. 704 pp.
David Tredup serves as a YMCA missionary in China where he faces ignorance, incarceration by the Japanese, and the death of his baby daughter while he is away.
Genre(s): War Story; Christian Fiction.

Houying, Dai

5411. *Stones of the Wall.* Trans. Frances Wood. New York: St. Martin's, 1986. 310 pp.
Sun Yue and He Jingfu are accused of being intellectuals during the Cultural Revolution, but they become rehabilitated rightists in order to remain in society.
Genre(s): War Story.

Jicai, Feng

◆ 5412. *Let One Hundred Flowers Bloom.* Trans. Christopher Smith. New York: Viking, 1996. 106 pp.
Hiz Hizyu, accused of political crimes in the Cultural Revolution, is sent to a provincial pottery factory to work although he is a graduate in fine arts.
Genre(s): War Story.

Jones, Margaret

5413. *The Confucius Enigma.* New York: St. Martin's, 1982. 257 pp.
In China in 1972, the high official Lin Piao disappears after planning an anti-Mao, pro-Soviet takeover, but a diplomat spots Lin Piao in a crowd and realizes that he is part of a larger political plot.
Genre(s): Biographical Fiction.

Kazantzakis, Nikos

5414. *The Rock Garden.* Trans. Kimon Friar. New York: Simon and Schuster, 1963. 251 pp.
When a white man visits Japan and China in the 1930s, he observes growing animosity among his friends in the two countries.
Genre(s): Political Fiction.

Lachs, Lorraine

5415. *Flowers for Mei-Ling.* New York: Carroll and Graf, 1997. 416 pp.
Mei-Ling Wang, a young Communist in Mao's Red Guards, witnesses the horrors and the hunger resulting from idealistic actions, and she emigrates to Canada and eventually becomes a Canadian businesswoman.
Genre(s): War Story; Political Fiction.

Lao, She

5416. *Rickshaw.* Trans. Jean M. James. Honolulu: University Press of Hawaii, 1979. 249 pp.
Hsiang Tsu comes to Peking to make a living as a rickshaw man, but circumstances and society thwart his goal.

Lee, C. Y.

◆ 5417. *Gate of Rage.* New York: Morrow, 1991. 309 pp.
China tries to attract foreign investors in the early 1980s, and the Hong family responds, only to face the horror of Tiananmen Square in 1989.
Genre(s): Political Fiction.

Li, Pi-hua

◆ 5418. *Farewell to My Concubine.* New York: Morrow, 1993. 255 pp.
Singers Duan Xialou and Cheng Dieyi, trained to become stars of the Peking Opera, develop a strained relationship because Cheng loves Duan and is jealous of his wife.
Genre(s): Love Story.

5419. *The Last Princess of Manchuria.* New York: Morrow, 1992. 240 pp.
Born in 1907, Yoshiko Kawashima is the daughter of Prince Su, and she grows up to be a spy and killer, captured after World War II for helping the Japanese against China.
Genre(s): Biographical Fiction; Spy Fiction.

Lin, Yutang

5420. *Moment in Peking.* New York: John Day, 1939. 815 pp.
A family of upper middle-class Chinese functions from the time of the Boxer Rebellion until the Japanese invasion.
Genre(s): Family Saga.

5421. *The Vermilion Gate.* New York: John Day, 1953. 438 pp.
In the 1930s, Jo-an flees from a warlord but learns that she is pregnant, a condition unacceptable to the family of the man she plans to marry.

Liu, Sola

5422. *Chaos and All That.* Trans. Richard King. Honolulu: University of Hawaii Press, 1994. 134 pp.
Huang Haha's prominent father commits suicide, as she and her friends practice their swear words so that they can join the Red Guard during China's Cultural Revolution, but as they mature, they begin to question everything.
Genre(s): War Story; Bildungsroman (Coming of Age).

Lord, Bette

◆ 5423. *The Middle Heart.* New York: Knopf, 1996. 370 pp.
After the Japanese conquer Manchuria in 1932, Steel Hope and his servant, Mountain Pine, become friends with Firecrackers and they soon discover that Firecrackers is female.
Genre(s): Romance.

Malraux, André

5424. *The Conquerors.* Trans. Stephen Becker. New York: Holt, Rinehart and Winston, 1976. 198 pp.
Garine and Borodin, professional revolutionists, spend time at the headquarters of the Kuomintang in Canton during the Bolshevik-Nationalist movement.
Genre(s): War Story.

5425. *Man's Fate.* Trans. Haakon M. Chevalier. New York: Random House, 1934. 283 pp.

Revolutionaries of different nationalities help Chinese workers during the Shanghai insurrection of 1927.
Genre(s): War Story.

Mao, Tun

5426. *Rainbow.* Trans. Madeleine Zelin. Berkeley: University of California Press, 1992. 235 pp.
Mei, a girl from Szechuan, enters the 1920s in an arranged marriage from which she escapes to teach outside Chungking before becoming an activist for government reform in Shanghai.
Genre(s): War Story; Political Fiction.

Mather, Berkely

5427. *Hour of the Dog.* New York: St. Martin's, 1982. 356 pp.
In 1941, when the Japanese invade Hong Kong, Vincent Stafford, a *taipan* (important person in the community), sneaks to Allied headquarters and returns as a scout.
Genre(s): War Story.

McKenna, Richard

5428. *The Sand Pebbles.* New York: Harper and Row, 1962. 597 pp.
Jake Holman serves on a gunboat in Chinese waters during the rebellion of the 1920s.
Genre(s): Sea Story.

McLeay, Alison

5429. *After Shanghai.* New York: St. Martin's, 1996. 418 pp.
Clio Oliver, member of a shipping family, lives in Shanghai in 1916, but after her grandfather dies in 1923, she goes to school in London, and then returns to China before the Japanese invade.
Genre(s): Family Saga.

New, Christopher

5430. *Shanghai.* New York: Knopf, 1985. 285 pp.
John Denton, an Englishman, comes to Shanghai in the early 20th century where the customs and attitudes toward other humans shock his sensibilities.
Genre(s): Adventure Story.

Peters, Natasha

5431. *The Immortals.* New York: Fawcett, 1983. 437 pp.
In post-war Shanghai, Amalie Berenger searches for her past, and when she meets her natural father, she becomes a supporter of the New China and the People's Liberation Army.
Genre(s): War Story.

Reeman, Douglas

5432. *The Pride and the Anguish.* New York: Putnam, 1969. 320 pp.
Lieutenant Ralph Trewin goes to China in 1942 with the Royal Navy to recover from his wife's death in the bomb-

◆ May be suitable for young adult readers

ing of London, but realizing that Singapore is vulnerable to attack, he pilots his gunboat nobly in the losing cause.
Genre(s): War Story; Sea Story.

Rosenbaum, Ray

5433. *Hawks.* Novato, CA: Lyford, 1994. 314 pp.
During World War II, American pilot Ross Colyer fights the Japanese from China where he battles for air control of the islands and he transports fuel and supplies into the country.
Genre(s): War Story.

Rui, Li

5434. *Silver City.* Trans. Howard Goldblatt. New York: Henry Holt, 1997. 276 pp.
After the Chinese republic is founded in 1912, Li Naijing tries to restore his family's wealth through salt mine ownership in Silver City, a small Chinese town, while a rival works against him.
Genre(s): Political Fiction; Domestic Fiction.

Steel, Danielle

5435. *Wanderlust.* New York: Delacorte, 1986. 382 pp.
Audrey Driscoll travels to Europe in the 1930s, falls in love with a travel writer, and follows him to China, where she rescues abandoned orphans.
Genre(s): Love Story.

Su Tong

5436. *Rice.* Trans. Howard Goldblatt. New York: Morrow, 1995. 288 pp.
In early-20th-century China, the decadence of the urban areas contrasts to the innocence of the rural areas when Five Dragons leaves his home which has been ruined by a flood for the city and a rice emporium.

Tanner, Janet

5437. *Oriental Hotel.* New York: St. Martin's, 1985. 448 pp.
While trying to escape Cairo at the beginning of World War II, married mother Elise Sanderson meets a Royal Air Force pilot on a secret mission with whom she falls in love as they travel back to Hong Kong.
Genre(s): War Story; Romance.

Tarrant, John

◆ 5438. *China Gold.* Lanham, MD: Scarborough, 1991. 252 pp.
The Hong Kong and Shanghai Bank plans to transfer gold to Sydney, Australia, in 1941, in case the Japanese invade, but police officers in charge of the transport decide they want the money for themselves.
Genre(s): War Story.

Taschdjian, Claire

5439. *The Peking Man Is Missing.* New York: Harper and Row, 1977. 280 pp.

Claire Taschdjian packs up the fossils of the 500,000-year-old Peking man in China during December of 1941 as the Japanese descend, but the package disappears.
Genre(s): Mystery.

Theroux, Paul

5440. *Saint Jack.* Boston: Houghton Mifflin, 1973. 247 pp.
In the 1960s, an American expatriate in Singapore decides to help American soldiers by establishing a resort for them on their vacations from Vietnam.

Tsukiyama, Gail

5441. *Night of Many Dreams.* New York: St. Martin's, 1998. 288 pp.
In 1940, as the Japanese occupy Hong Kong, Joan, 14, and Emma Lew, 9, flee to Macao, leaving their father, but after the war, they return and resume their lives.
Genre(s): War Story; Bildungsroman (Coming of Age).

◆ 5442. *Women of the Silk.* New York: St. Martin's, 1991. 278 pp.
Pei's peasant parents have her work in a silk factory to support them, and Pei finds strength from an older girl, Lin, as they begin to organize a union.

Tuten, Frederic

5443. *The Adventures of Mao on the Long March.* New York: Marion Boyars, 1997. 121 pp.
Mao takes his people on the Long March where he reveals to a select few his doubts and fears in his mammoth undertaking.
Genre(s): Biographical Fiction.

West, Paul

5444. *The Tent of Orange Mist.* New York: Scribner's, 1995. 263 pp.
Scald Ibis, 16, is raped by Japanese invaders in her city and forced to remain a prostitute in order to keep her father, a scholar, alive.
Award(s): National Book Critics Circle Award.
Genre(s): Bildungsroman (Coming of Age); War Story.

Worboys, Anne

◆ 5445. *China Silk.* New York: St. Martin's, 1992. 384 pp.
Hellen sails to Hong Kong to marry her lover against his uncle's will, and once there, she marries another, only to feel closed in again.
Genre(s): Romance.

Yan, Mo

5446. *Red Sorghum.* Trans. Howard Goldblatt. New York: Viking, 1993. 359 pp.
When the Japanese invade China in the 1930s and bring with them death, sorghum is food and part of potent wine, a metaphor of life, but as the narrator gains strength from her grandmother and lover, they cannot prevent a hybrid sorghum from coming to the village.
Genre(s): War Story; Political Fiction.

Yang, Belle

5447. *Baba: A Return to China upon My Father's Shoulders.* New York: Harcourt, 1994. 211 pp.
A child lives in Manchuria during the 1930s and early 1940s.
Genre(s): War Story; Domestic Fiction.

5448. *The Odyssey of a Manchurian.* New York: Harcourt, 1996. 305 pp.
A man struggles to survive China's civil war.
Genre(s): War Story; Domestic Fiction.

Zhang, Xianliang

5449. *Half of Man Is Woman.* New York: Norton, 1988. 253 pp.
When the poet Zhang Younglin is sentenced to a labor camp during the Cultural Revolution, he feels relief, and while there, he marries a woman he met eight years earlier.
Genre(s): War Story.

India, Tibet, Burma, Ceylon, Afghanistan, and Pakistan

Before 1900

Barrett, Maria

5450. ***Dishonored.*** New York: Warner, 1996. 407 pp.

British officer Mills retaliates for his wife's murder in an Indian uprising during 1857, and Shiva Rai hates the Mills family for their deeds, an anger that extends into the 1960s when both families meet again.
Genre(s): Domestic Fiction; Family Saga.

Barrett, William Edmund

5451. ***Lady of the Lotus.*** Garden City, NY: Doubleday, 1975. 376 pp.

Yasodhara, wife of Siddhartha, remains at home and raises their son until both are ready to join Buddha in his work.
Genre(s): Biographical Fiction; Domestic Fiction; Religious Fiction.

Bassett, Ronald

5452. ***Blood of an Englishman.*** London: Macmillan, 1975. 349 pp.

The British in India undergo the siege at Cawnpore in 1857 when the sepoys revolt.
Genre(s): War Story.

Blackburn, Julia

5453. ***The Book of Color.*** New York: Pantheon, 1995. 175 pp.

In the 1880s, a missionary arrives in the Seychelles determined to undermine the local witch doctor, and even though he marries a native woman and they have a child, the curse put upon him is transferred to his wife.
Genre(s): Domestic Fiction; Gothic Fiction.

Breem, Wallace

◆ 5454. ***The Leopard and the Cliff.*** New York: St. Martin's, 1978. 285 pp.

In 1919, as Lieutenant Colonel Sandeman tries to keep peace on the India-Afghanistan border, tribes begin to fight, and he must retreat on foot for 80 miles through guerrilla forces.
Genre(s): War Story.

Brent, Madeleine

◆ 5455. ***Stormswift.*** Garden City, NY: Doubleday, 1985. 326 pp.

Jemimah Lawley's parents die in the 1879 massacre of the British mission in Kabul, Afghanistan, and she becomes a slave for seven years until her master arranges for her escape and perilous trip back to England.
Genre(s): Romance.

Cadell, Elizabeth

5456. ***A Lion in the Way.*** New York: Morrow, 1982. 344 pp.

Annerley Brooke, 13, a British resident of Calcutta, enjoys unjudgemental friendships with Indians.
Genre(s): Romance.

Carnac, Nicholas

5457. ***Indigo.*** New York: St. Martin's, 1982. 404 pp.

Craig Lindsay goes to his uncle's indigo plantation in India in 1857, hoping to inherit it, when he finds himself in the midst of an uprising with strong feelings for both sides.
Genre(s): War Story.

Chaikin, L. L.

◆ 5458. ***Kingscote.*** Minneapolis, MN: Bethany House, 1994. 396 pp.

Coral Kendall decides to build a schoolhouse to educate the local Indians and to tell them about the Christian God, but a Hindu priest encourages the people to burn the house. (*Series:* Heart of India, 3)
Genre(s): Christian Fiction.

◆ 5459. ***Silk.*** Minneapolis, MN: Bethany House, 1993. 348 pp.

Daughter of a wealthy British family on a silk plantation in India, Coral becomes friends with an Indian who has recently converted to Christianity and who dies in childbirth, and Coral adopts the boy, only to have him kidnapped two years later. (*Series:* Heart of India, 1)
Genre(s): Christian Fiction.

5460. ***Under Eastern Stars.*** Minneapolis, MN: Bethany House, 1993. 378 pp.

A British woman reveals her courage during the occupation in India while two men fall in love with her. (*Series:* Heart of India, 2)
Genre(s): Christian Fiction; Romance.

Chase, Loretta

5461. *The Sandalwood Princess.* New York:
Walker, 1990. 224 pp.
Rani Simhi gives Amanda Cavencourt a going-away gift
of a fertility carving when Amanda leaves for England,
which Lord Headgrave, who has a grudge against Rani,
covets.
Genre(s): Romance; Regency Novel.

Clive, William

5462. *Dando on Delhi Ridge.* New York: Putnam,
1971. 254 pp.
Rifleman Dando serves in Meerut during the Mutiny of
1857 when native Indians revolt, because of a violation
of religious taboos, after a command to grease their guns
with animal fat.
Genre(s): War Story; Adventure Story.

Collis, Maurice

5463. *She Was a Queen.* 1937. New York: Criterion, 1962. 301 pp.
When a village girl becomes the Queen of Burma, she
tries to survive the continuing struggles of her people.
Genre(s): Biographical Fiction.

Courter, Gay

◆ 5464. *Flowers in the Blood.* New York: Dutton,
1989. 585 pp.
The opium trade makes Dinah Sassoon's family wealthy,
but no one can protect her from the scandal of her
mother's murder in 19th-century Calcutta.
Genre(s): Domestic Fiction.

Dalkey, Kara

5465. *Goa.* New York: Tor, 1996. 252 pp.
In late 16th-century Indian colony of Goa, the English
apothecary, Thomas Chinnery, meets an alchemist whose
vial of powder can revive the dead, and his knowledge
causes him to be questioned by the Inquisition before its
leader goes to search for more of the substance. (*Series:*
Blood of the Goddess, 1)
Genre(s): Fantastic Literature.

Drummond, Emma

5466. *Forget the Glory.* New York: St. Martin's,
1985. 341 pp.
Mary Clarke is the widow of a British trooper who
helped the fictional 43rd Light Dragoons when they left
India for the Crimean War in 1855.
Genre(s): War Story.

Farrell, J. G.

5467. *The Siege of Krishnapur.* New York: Harcourt, 1974. 344 pp.
An English civil servant in India during the Sepoy Rebellion of 1857 has to organize the defenses of Krishnapur
and take responsibility for the people with him.
Award(s): Booker Prize.
Genre(s): War Story.

Fast, Jonathan

5468. *Golden Fire.* New York: Arbor House, 1986.
418 pp.
In the sixth century, signs at Chandra's birth indicate that
he will be a great ruler, but his father sends him away so
that his brother will not kill him, and when Chandra
comes of age, he must overcome this brother, the Demon
King of Magadha.
Genre(s): Biographical Fiction.

Fitzgerald, Valerie

5469. *Zemindar.* New York: Bantam, 1982. 798 pp.
Miss Laura Hewitt, who has recently arrived in India,
falls in love with Oliver, a Zemindar feudal lord, who
tries to remain loyal to both England and the people on
his estate as the Sepoy Rebellion begins in 1857.
Award(s): Georgette Heyer Historical Novel Prize.
Genre(s): Romance.

Forster, E. M.

5470. *A Passage to India.* 1924. New York: Harcourt Brace, 1989. 320 pp.
Two women come to Chandrapore, India, and their lack
of understanding of the culture causes one of them to
make an unjust accusation.
Award(s): James Tate Black Award.
Genre(s): Political Fiction.

Fraser, George MacDonald

5471. *Flashman and the Mountain of Light.* New
York: Knopf, 1991. 365 pp.
In the sequel to *Flashman and the Dragon*, the Sikh army
in Punjab outnumbers the British forces with which
Harry Paget Flashman is involved as a spy around 1845.
Genre(s): Adventure Story.

Ghosh, Amitav

◆ 5472. *The Calcutta Chromosome.* New York:
Avon, 1997. 320 pp.
In the late 19th century, Ronald Ross lives in Calcutta
and discovers that the mosquito carries malaria; the contemporary New Yorker Murugan becomes obsessed with
this story and goes to Calcutta for more information; and
a professor in the future studies Murugan.
Genre(s): Medical Novel; Fantastic Literature.

Gibson, Tom

5473. *A Soldier of India.* New York: St. Martin's,
1982. 288 pp.
Irish soldier Martin Lalor accompanies Sir Julian
Wentworth of the East India Company on a tour of India,
and when the Sepoy Mutiny begins in 1857, he is
stranded with Wentworth's daughter and an Indian
widow.
Genre(s): War Story.

Gordon, Katharine

5474. *In the Shadow of the Peacock.* London:
Hodder and Stoughton, 1980. 396 pp.

◆ May be suitable for young adult readers

A British noble falls in love with a former temple harlot in India.
Genre(s): Romance.

Hill, Porter

5475. *The Bombay Marines.* New York: Walker, 1988. 220 pp.
Captain Adam Horne returns to Bombay after a mission in the Arabian Sea during 1761, and he is assigned to kidnap the captured French commander-in-chief General Thomas Nally in Madras and put him on a ship to England.
Genre(s): Sea Story; Adventure Story.

Holt, Victoria

◆ 5476. *The India Fan.* Garden City, NY: Doubleday, 1988. 404 pp.
Plain Drusilla goes to England, France, and India with the imprudent Lavinia who marries there the man who once wanted to marry Drusilla.
Genre(s): Romance.

5477. *The Spring of the Tiger.* Garden City, NY: Doubleday, 1979. 356 pp.
After Sarah Ashington marries, she goes with her husband to Ceylon where she experiences a series of terrifying incidents.
Genre(s): Romance.

Hoover, Thomas

5478. *The Moghul.* Garden City, NY: Doubleday, 1983. 473 pp.
Commissioned by King James I to open trade relations with India, Brian Hawksworth has a variety of experiences when he reaches this exotic land.

Jones, Alexandra

5479. *Mandalay.* New York: Villard, 1988. 486 pp.
Angela Featherstone, a British missionary trying to convert the Burmese Buddhists to Christianity, becomes involved with an American trader and the queen of Burma trying to gain control of Mandalay.
Genre(s): Family Saga.

Kaye, M. M.

5480. *The Far Pavilions.* New York: St. Martin's, 1978. 957 pp.
Between the Mutiny of 1857 and the second Afghan war, Ashton Pelham-Martyn lives in India where, while serving as a secret agent, he loves an Indian princess.
Genre(s): War Story.

5481. *Shadow of the Moon.* New York: St. Martin's, 1979. 614 pp.
Indian soldiers (Sepoys) rebel against the British in 1857, driving Winter de Ballesteros and her love, Alex, into the jungle.
Genre(s): War Story.

Lambdin, Dewey

◆ 5482. *The King's Privateer.* New York: Donald I. Fine, 1992. 360 pp.
In the sequel to *The King's Commission*, Royal Navy lieutenant Alan Lewrie checks French activities in the Far East on a ship disguised as a merchant vessel.
Genre(s): Sea Story; Adventure Story.

Leasor, James

5483. *Follow the Drum.* New York: Morrow, 1973. 368 pp.
Military mismanagement and daring exploits underlie both the British and Indian sides in the Sepoy Rebellion during 1857-1858.
Genre(s): War Story.

Malgonkar, Manohar

5484. *The Devil's Wind.* New York: Viking, 1972. 306 pp.
Nana Sahib, somewhat reluctant leader during the Indian mutiny of 1857-58 when Indian troops employed by the British rebelled, may have ordered the murder of British prisoners at Cawnpore or may have had little control of the men in his charge.
Genre(s): Biographical Fiction.

Masters, John

5485. *Coromandel.* New York: Viking, 1955. 295 pp.
Jason Savage explores India in the 1630s.
Genre(s): Adventure Story; Family Saga.

5486. *The Deceivers.* New York: Viking, 1952. 285 pp.
In the sequel to *Coromandel*, a group follows the cult of the goddess Kali.
Genre(s): Family Saga; Adventure Story.

5487. *The Lotus and the Wind.* New York: Viking, 1953. 283 pp.
In the sequel to *Nightrunners of Bengal*, a young Ghurka officer in 1881 is assigned to spy on Russians planning to invade India's northwest frontier.
Genre(s): Family Saga; Adventure Story.

5488. *Nightrunners of Bengal.* New York: Viking, 1951. 339 pp.
In the sequel to *The Deceivers*, Captain Rodney Savage succeeds in India with his society wife and money from a wealthy rani, as the Sepoy Mutiny breaks out in 1857.
Genre(s): War Story.

Mather, Berkely

5489. *The White Dacoit.* New York: Scribner's, 1974. 376 pp.
Wyndham, a British army officer in India, becomes a bandit (*dacoit*) and convict, and he marries Julia, who later dies in childbirth.
Genre(s): Adventure Story.

McCutchan, Philip

5490. *By Command of the Viceroy.* New York: St. Martin's, 1975. 224 pp.
Captain James Ogilvie and his troops have to learn why a Grand Duchess who is Queen Victoria's granddaughter is accompanying a detachment of Cossacks.
Genre(s): War Story.

5491. *Drums along the Khyber.* New York: St. Martin's, 1972. 189 pp.
James Ogilvie, assigned to his father's command of the 114th Highlanders, is stationed in India where the treatment of the natives upsets him.
Genre(s): War Story.

5492. *Lieutenant of the Line.* New York: St. Martin's, 1972. 224 pp.
As James Ogilvie prepares to celebrate his 21st birthday, he meets Mrs. Archdale, an attractive woman who becomes a widow in the ensuing onslaught from the Afghanistan frontier.
Genre(s): War Story.

5493. *Sadhu on the Mountain Peak.* New York: St. Martin's, 1973. 286 pp.
Tribesmen wait for a Muslim holy man to signal them to attack the British, and Ogilvie infiltrates the tribe to discover their plans.
Genre(s): War Story; Spy Fiction.

5494. *Subaltern's Choice.* New York: St. Martin's, 1974. 224 pp.
Captain Ogilvie of the Royal Strathspeys serves in India where a new officer arrives and excites the Afghan border.
Genre(s): Sea Story; War Story.

Modak, Manorama Ramkrishna

5495. *Single Is the Wheel.* New Delhi: Vikas, 1978. 266 pp.
Vinayak Shastri, chamberlain to the Maratha king Shrimanth, hates the British for invading India, and when Shrimanth ignores his advice, both must endure exile at Brahmavarto on the Ganges.
Genre(s): Political Fiction; War Story.

Mundy, Talbot

◆ 5496. *King of the Khyber Rifles.* West Kingston, RI: D. M. Grant, 1916. 394 pp.
Athelstan King must go into the hills to find out about a possible jihad as the Indians begin to revolt, and he unhappily accepts the woman Yasmini who knows all about the area as his partner.
Genre(s): War Story.

Myers, L. H.

5497. *The Root and the Flower.* New York: Oxford, 1985. 583 pp.
A compilation of four novels, *The Near and the Far*, *Prince Jali*, *The Pool of Vishnu*, and *The Rajah Amar*, take place in 16th century India and describe the Mogul Emperor Akbar's attempt to establish a new religion and the responses of his children and their wives to his attempts.
Genre(s): Political Fiction.

Ramaya, Shona

5498. *Flute.* New York: Viking, 1989. 265 pp.
When British brothers Dane and Julian meet in India for a vacation, one falls in love with a dancing girl while the other becomes interested in the flute-playing god, Krishna, but both mature through their experiences.
Genre(s): Bildungsroman (Coming of Age).

Rogers, Rosemary

5499. *Surrender to Love.* New York: Avon, 1982. 624 pp.
After her mother dies, Alexandra tries to find out who her true family is by traveling throughout Europe and Ceylon (Sri Lanka).
Genre(s): Romance.

Ryman, Rebecca

5500. *Olivia and Jai.* New York: St. Martin's, 1990. 644 pp.
In the 1840s, the American Olivia comes to India to live with British relatives and promptly falls in love with Jai, a half-caste with reasons to avenge those who have done him wrong.
Genre(s): Romance.

5501. *The Veil of Illusion.* New York: St. Martin's, 1995. 632 pp.
Amos and Maya Raventhorne, children of Olivia and Jai in *Olivia and Jai*, are outcasts of both the British and Indian establishments in the 19th century Maya tries to marry a British civil servant and Amos attempts to clear his father's name as a traitor during the Sepoy Rebellion of 1857.
Genre(s): Love Story; Family Saga.

Sealy, I. Allan

5502. *The Trotter-Nama.* New York: Knopf, 1988. 640 pp.
Begun in the 18th century by Justin Aloysius Trotter with profits from ice, indigo, and saltpeter, the Trotter family's history reflects that of India.
Genre(s): Family Saga.

Selwyn, Francis

5503. *Sergeant Verity and the Imperial Diamond.* New York: Stein and Day, 1976. 252 pp.
Sergeant Verity goes to Calcutta after the mutiny to supervise the transfer of a valuable jewel.
Genre(s): Mystery.

Shah, Hasan

5504. *The Dancing Girl.* 1790. New York: New Directions, 1993. 112 pp.
In the 1780s, the Indian dancer Khanum Jan falls in love with and secretly marries Hasan Shah, and while he is on

a trip with his employer, a British officer, she falls ill and dies.
Genre(s): Love Story.

Shipway, George

5505. *Free Lance.* New York: Harcourt, 1975. 286 pp.
In the early 1800s, Hugo Amaury becomes friends with Charles Marriott, and the two lead ostentatious lives in the Honorable East India Company's 7th Madras Native Cavalry.
Genre(s): Adventure Story.

5506. *Strangers in the Land.* London: Davies, 1976. 248 pp.
In 1806, a mutiny occurs at Vellore which presages the mutiny of 1857.
Genre(s): War Story; Political Fiction.

Stuart, Vivian

5507. *The Cannons of Lucknow.* New York: Pinnacle, 1974. 244 pp.
In the sequel to *Massacre at Cawnpore*, Alexander Sheridan fights at Lucknow in the autumn after the British at Kanpur surrender in 1857.
Genre(s): War Story; Adventure Story.

5508. *Escape from Hell.* New York: Pinnacle, 1976. 223 pp.
Finally in 1858, Alexander Sheridan sees victory in India for the British as he plans to return to England, in the sequel to *Guns to the Far East*.
Genre(s): War Story; Adventure Story.

5509. *Guns to the Far East.* New York: Pinnacle, 1976. 213 pp.
Philip Horatio Hazard must rush to India to help when the Sepoy mutiny, and he encounters Alexander Sheridan who has been fighting throughout 1857.
Genre(s): War Story; Adventure Story.

5510. *The Heroic Garrison.* New York: Pinnacle, 1975. 424 pp.
Alexander Sheridan helps to battle the Sepoy of India in the sequel to *The Cannons of Lucknow* as the British begin to win the war.
Genre(s): War Story; Adventure Story.

5511. *Massacre at Cawnpore.* New York: Pinnacle, 1973. 238 pp.
In the sequel to *The Sepoy Mutiny*, a massacre occurs in 1857 which Alexander Sheridan cannot halt.
Genre(s): War Story.

5512. *The Sepoy Mutiny.* New York: Pinnacle, 1973. 221 pp.

In the sequel to *Victors and Lords*, Alexander Sheridan experiences the revolt of the Indians serving in the British military.
Genre(s): War Story; Adventure Story.

5513. *Victors and Lords.* New York: Pinnacle, 1964. 251 pp.
Alexander Sheridan goes to India to serve in the British colonial forces.
Genre(s): War Story; Adventure Story.

Suthren, Victor

5514. *Captain Monsoon.* New York: St. Martin's, 1993. 224 pp.
In 1744, in the sequel to *Admiral of Fear*, Edward Mainwaring, American colonial officer in the British Royal Navy, captains a frigate in the Indian Ocean to help gain British control of India.
Genre(s): Sea Story.

Thurley, Jon

5515. *Household Gods.* New York: Morrow, 1988. 288 pp.
A barrister tries to trace his father's disappearance during the partition of India and Pakistan and discovers the political complexity of the era.
Genre(s): Political Fiction.

Trollope, Joanna

5516. *Mistaken Virtues.* New York: Dutton, 1980. 284 pp.
In Calcutta during 1776, Hickey's daughter enjoys a romance with a Britisher.
Genre(s): Romance.

Ward, Andrew

5517. *The Blood Seed.* New York: Viking, 1985. 576 pp.
Balbeer Rao, born in northern India after the Sepoy uprising in 1857, first lives with his widowed mother, but he wonders about his father's identity throughout all of his adventures.
Genre(s): Picaresque Fiction.

White, James Dilion

5518. *A Spread of Sail.* London: Hutchinson, 1975. 192 pp.
Kelso, officer with the East India Company, fights pirates to rescue treasure, and his Indian mistress sails with him.
Genre(s): Sea Story; Adventure Story.

1900 and After

Alexander, Meena

◆ 5519. *Nampally Road.* San Francisco: Mercury House, 1991. 120 pp.
When Mira Kannadical returns to Hyderabad in the 1970s after studying in England, she wants to teach at the university, but political forces control her choices.
Genre(s): Political Fiction.

Ali, Ahmed

5520. *Twilight in Delhi.* London: Oxford, 1967. 290 pp.
In the early 20th century during the last days of the Moguls, Mir Nihal, a Delhi resident, loves pigeons, and as his family continues its rhythm of life and the English tear down the city's ancient walls, the cats kill his pigeons.
Genre(s): Domestic Fiction.

Ballinger, W. A.

5521. *The Carrion Eaters.* New York: Putnam, 1971. 384 pp.
Tom Kinsman becomes the private pilot to the prince of the state of Chan in 1947 and becomes immediately involved in the turmoil of nationalism and drive for a free India.
Genre(s): Adventure Story.

Bearden, Milt

5522. *The Black Tulip.* New York: Random House, 1998. 336 pp.
When Alexander Fannin, former CIA agent, works in Afghanistan during the Soviet invasion of the 1980s, he finds himself bargaining for the exhange of a hostage and a Soviet soldier for his wife's cousin, a KGB colonel.
Genre(s): Spy Fiction; War Story.

Becker, Stephen D.

5523. *The Blue-Eyed Shan.* New York: Random House, 1982. 288 pp.
An American anthropologist returns with his wife and daughter to the Shan tribe in 1949 after leaving in 1945 and, while visiting with a Chinese general who took Peking man bones out of China, experiences the attack of a cannibalistic tribe.
Genre(s): Adventure Story.

Bhattacharya, Keron

5524. *The Pearls of Coromandel.* New York: St. Martin's, 1996. 254 pp.
John Sudgen, an Oxford graduate, goes to India in the 1920s hoping to use his intellect, but he falls in love with Kamala, a married woman rejected by her husband after a rape, and the two live together, causing John to lose his job and be tried for causing Kamala's rape.
Genre(s): Love Story; Religious Fiction; Political Fiction.

Brent, Madeleine

◆ 5525. *Merlin's Keep.* New York: Doubleday, 1978. 352 pp.
A British soldier raises Jani in a small Tibetan village before another helps her to reach England and the situation at the great house of Merlin's Keep.
Genre(s): Love Story; Mystery.

Buck, Pearl S.

5526. *Mandala.* New York: John Day, 1970. 361 pp.
Jagat, a prince in the Indian government before 1960, falls in love with an American, and the two search for their own identity in the new country.
Genre(s): Political Fiction; Romance.

Cartland, Barbara

5527. *Flowers for the God of Love.* New York: Dutton, 1979. 125 pp.
Rex Daviot wants to become governor of an Indian province, but he needs money, so when he meets Quenella who wants to escape from a royal suitor, they marry in 1900, never expecting to fall in love.
Genre(s): Romance.

Cleary, Jon

5528. *The Faraway Drums.* New York: Morrow, 1982. 288 pp.
When religious fanatics try to assassinate King George and Queen Mary on their visit to India, an intelligence officer and newspaperwoman thwart them.
Genre(s): Mystery.

Desai, Anita

◆ 5529. *Baumgartner's Bombay.* New York: Knopf, 1989. 229 pp.
Hugo Baumgartner escapes to Calcutta with his family during Hitler's rise, and although imprisoned as a hostile alien, he decides to move to Bombay after the war.
Genre(s): Jewish Fiction.

Dickinson, Peter

◆ 5530. *Tulku.* 1979. Magnolia, MA: Peter Smith, 1995. 300 pp.
When Theo escapes through Tibet with Mrs. Jones after his father, a missionary in China, sends him away because of the Boxer Rebellion, Tibetans believe that he is the reincarnated Tulku, one of their religous leaders.
Award(s): Whitbread Award; Carnegie Medal.
Genre(s): War Story; Religious Fiction.

Earl, Maureen

5531. *Boat of Stone.* Sag Harbor, NY: Permanent, 1993. 254 pp.

◆ May be suitable for young adult readers

During World War II, the British intern European Jews on the island of Mauritius, and Hanna survives with guilt.
Genre(s): War Story.

Easterman, Daniel

5532. *The Ninth Buddha.* Garden City, NY: Doubleday, 1989. 418 pp.
In 1921, a British intelligence agent's 10-year-old son is kidnapped because he is believed to be an incarnation of the Buddha, who will become the rightful ruler of Mongolia and the world.
Genre(s): Spy Fiction.

Falkirk, Richard

5533. *For Infamous Conduct.* New York: Coward-McCann, 1970. 447 pp.
Two British army officers try to follow their careers in India, one with the Gurkhas and the other with the Indian Medical Service, in the early decades of the 20th century, but neither succeeds.
Genre(s): Political Fiction.

Frutkin, Mark

5534. *Invading Tibet.* New York: Soho, 1993. 214 pp.
In 1904, when Edmund Candler, a British journalist, goes with British and Indian soldiers to discuss a trade agreement with the Dalai Lama, he falls in love with the country.
Genre(s): Adventure Story.

Ghosh, Amitav

5535. *The Circle of Reason.* New York: Viking, 1986. 423 pp.
Police suspect young master weaver Alu of being a terrorist, and they chase him from Bengal to North Africa, where he encounters a variety of people.
Genre(s): Adventure Story.

Godden, Rumer

5536. *The Dark Horse.* New York: Viking, 1982. 202 pp.
A horse imported to Calcutta for the Viceroy's Cup in the 1930s bolts for a nearby convent after its rider has abused it egregiously.
Genre(s): Sports Fiction.

Hanley, Gerald

5537. *Noble Descents.* New York: St. Martin's, 1983. 352 pp.
British and Indian residents of Induspur, in northern India, try to deal with the aftermath of independence.
Genre(s): Political Fiction.

Higgins, Jack

◆ 5538. *Year of the Tiger.* New York: Berkley, 1996. 288 pp.

In 1962, Paul Chavasse infiltrates Chinese Tibet to locate and sneak out under house arrest a mathematician who has created a new concept of space travel.
Genre(s): Spy Fiction.

Hudson, Christopher

5539. *Where the Rainbow Ends.* New York: Atheneum, 1987. 320 pp.
As World War II begins, Guy Tancred, a representative of the Dunlop Rubber enterprise, arrives in Ceylon and is surprised that the inhabitants seem uninterested in the war, although their attitude changes when the Japanese military head toward the island.
Genre(s): War Story.

Hylton, Sara

◆ 5540. *My Sister Clare.* New York: St. Martin's, 1989. 512 pp.
Eve Meredith tells of her unscrupulous sister who goes to India and charms her stepfather and distresses Eve and her mother between the wars.
Genre(s): War Story; Romance.

Kesavan, Mukul

5541. *Looking through Glass.* New York: Farrar, Straus and Giroux, 1995. 480 pp.
A photographer traveling with his grandmother's ashes falls through time and finds himself in 1942 during the Quit India movement and lives through the growing differences between Muslim and Hindu and the fight for independence in 1947.
Genre(s): Time Travel.

King, Francis Henry

5542. *Act of Darkness.* Boston: Little, Brown, 1983. 331 pp.
In the 1930s, someone murders the young son of a wealthy English family, and although the official story is that Indian servants killed him, no one believes it.
Genre(s): Mystery.

Kingsland, Rosemary

5543. *After the Ball Was Over.* New York: Viking, 1985. 140 pp.
In India in 1930, British civil servants spend three successive Sundays together.

Le Clézio, J. M. G.

5544. *The Prospector.* Trans. Carol Marks. New York: D.R. Godine, 1993. 320 pp.
After his father's death, a young man tries to restore the family's wealth by searching for buried gold in the *Corsair* wreckage off Mauritius in the early 20th century.
Genre(s): Bildungsroman (Coming of Age); War Story.

MacBeth, George

5545. *The Katana.* New York: Simon and Schuster, 1982. 239 pp.

In 1944, a British intelligence officer who is half Japanese and half Chinese attempts to assassinate Lord Mountbatten in India with the ritual sword of a samurai warrior.
Genre(s): Adventure Story; War Story.

Masters, John

5546. *Bhowani Junction.* New York: Viking, 1954. 394 pp.
In the sequel to *Far, Far the Mountain Peak*, Victoria Jones, an Anglo Indian confused by her racial identity, faces India's independence from Britain.
Genre(s): Adventure Story.

5547. *Far, Far the Mountain Peak.* New York: Viking, 1957. 471 pp.
In the sequel to *The Lotus and the Wind*, Peter Savage strives to be the best at everything, and he chooses his friends and even his wife because they will help him rise to the top in India.
Genre(s): Political Fiction.

5548. *The Himalayan Concerto.* New York: Doubleday, 1972. 293 pp.
In the sequel to *The Ravi Lancers*, Rodney Bateman begins intelligence work in India during World War I.
Genre(s): War Story.

Mehta, Gita

5549. *Raj.* New York: Simon and Schuster, 1989. 479 pp.
Princess Jaya, born during Queen Victoria's Diamond Jubilee in 1897, continues the traditions of the maharajas until she achieves independence along with her country.
Genre(s): Family Saga.

Mistry, Rohinton

5550. *A Fine Balance.* New York: Knopf, 1996. 603 pp.
In the 1970s, four people living in an apartment house in an Indian city slowly overcome their caste origins and hardships to understand each other.
Genre(s): Domestic Fiction.

5551. *Such a Long Journey.* New York: Knopf, 1991. 339 pp.
Gustad Noble and his family live in Bombay in 1971 where he works as a bank clerk and is eventually drawn into the corrupt politics of his country.
Award(s): Commonwealth Writers' Prize.
Genre(s): Political Fiction.

Murari, Timeri

◆ 5552. *Field of Honor.* New York: Simon and Schuster, 1981. 384 pp.
Nicky, the ex-prince of Tandhapur, must fight a boxing match with the son of his father's British mistress, but first must to learn how to box so that he can defend his race.

5553. *The Imperial Agent.* New York: St. Martin's, 1989. 414 pp.
Kimball O'Hara from Kipling's *Kim* has become a secret agent for the British in India at the beginning of the 20th century, but misinterpretation of his information causes a wrongful death and imprisonment, which he wants to correct.
Genre(s): Adventure Story; Spy Fiction.

Nahal, Chaman Lal

5554. *Azadi.* Boston: Houghton Mifflin, 1975. 371 pp.
A Punjabi family is uprooted during the partitioning of India after independence in 1947 into Hindu India and Muslim Pakistan.
Genre(s): Political Fiction.

Ram Rau, Santha

5555. *Remember the House.* New York: Harper and Row, 1956. 241 pp.
Western tastes lure a young wealthy Indian girl during the last year of British occupation, but she returns to her own traditions and moral values.

Robinson, Donald H.

5556. *The Raj.* Boston: Houghton Mifflin, 1971. 448 pp.
In the 1930s, Mary is a fishing fleeter, a woman who looks for a British husband in Calcutta, and when she finds one, she has to adjust to his *ganja* (bribe) taking; when he dies, she becomes determined to manage his plantation even though insurrections threaten British rule.
Genre(s): Political Fiction.

Sahgal, Nayantara

5557. *Plans for Departure.* New York: Norton, 1985. 192 pp.
As World War II begins, an Indian scientist and his secretary have gone to the hills for his research, and when members of the party disappear, Anna's sympathy with Indian independence surfaces.
Genre(s): War Story.

Scott, Paul

◆ 5558. *The Day of the Scorpion.* New York: Morrow, 1968. 483 pp.
The sequel to *The Jewel in the Crown* concerns the Laytons and others caught in the violence of India when the Congress Party calls for an insurrection.
Genre(s): War Story.

◆ 5559. *A Division of the Spoils.* New York: Morrow, 1975. 597 pp.
The sequel to *The Towers of Silence* concludes the Raj Quartet with Guy Perron, a young historian, reviewing the end of British rule in India.
Genre(s): War Story.

◆ 5560. *The Jewel in the Crown.* New York: Morrow, 1966. 480 pp.

In August of 1942, a young Englishwoman is raped in an Indian garden, and her fate and that of an elderly English schoolteacher entwine.
Genre(s): War Story; Domestic Fiction.

◆ 5561. *Staying On.* New York: Morrow, 1977. 215 pp.
Colonel Tusker Smalley, his wife Lucy and their servant remain in India at the hill station of Pankot after the Indians declare independence from Britain.

◆ 5562. *The Towers of Silence.* New York: Morrow, 1971. 392 pp.
In 1939 Barbie Batchelor goes to Pankot, India, to live with Mabel Layton, and after Mabel dies, Barbie becomes physically ill with grief, in the sequel to *The Day of the Scorpion.*
Genre(s): War Story.

Seth, Vikram

5563. *A Suitable Boy.* New York: HarperCollins, 1993. 1376 pp.
A Hindu family tries to find a suitable mate for the younger daughter, and everyone has a different person in mind.
Award(s): Commonwealth Writers' Prize.
Genre(s): Domestic Fiction; Family Saga.

Seymour, Gerald

5564. *In Honor Bound.* New York: Norton, 1984. 350 pp.
A British intelligence officer goes to Afghanistan to shoot down a sophisticated Russian helicopter and assess its capabilities.
Genre(s): Spy Fiction.

Shah, Idries

5565. *Kara Kush.* New York: Stein and Day, 1986. 575 pp.
Soviets invading Afghanistan do not bargain for the able chief, Kara Kush, who attracts Russian deserters to his caves, as well as peasants and cooks ready to destroy Soviet weaponry.
Genre(s): War Story.

Sidhwa, Bapsi

5566. *Cracking India.* Minneapolis, MN: Milkweed, 1991. 289 pp.
Lenny, the young girl of an affluent family of Lahore in 1947, becomes aware of the religious differences of people around her when her nanny is kidnapped.
Genre(s): Political Fiction.

Smith, Rita Pratt

◆ 5567. *In the Forest at Midnight.* New York: Donald I. Fine, 1989. 294 pp.
When Megan Manning leaves Madras to visit her aunt and her Indian husband, she discovers that the husband's family disapproves of her aunt as much as Megan's family has disapproved of him.
Genre(s): Domestic Fiction.

Srivanandan, A.

5568. *When Memory Dies.* Chester Springs, PA: Dufour, 1998. 414 pp.
Three generations of a family survive in colonial and post-colonial Sri Lanka.
Genre(s): Family Saga.

Weston, Christine

5569. *The Hoopoe.* New York: Harper, 1970. 525 pp.
Patrice grows up in India after World War I, under British rule and comes to Boston with her weak American husband, and when she returns to India, both she and the country have changed.
Genre(s): Domestic Fiction.

Wiggins, Marianne

◆ 5570. *John Dollar.* New York: Harper and Row, 1989. 214 pp.
After World War I, Charlotte Lewes goes Rangoon to teach children of English colonists and during a sailing trip, she is marooned on an island with eight girls and the seaman John Dollar.

Wolpert, Stanley

5571. *Nine Hours to Rama.* New York: Random House, 1962. 376 pp.
As Godse prepares to assassinate Gandhi in 1947, he reveals his involvement with a fanatical Hindu movement.
Genre(s): Political Fiction.

Wright, Daphne

5572. *The Distant Kingdom.* New York: Delacorte, 1988. 312 pp.
On a trip to India after her mother's death, Perdita Whitney meets and marries Lord Beaminster, unwittingly helping him hide a dark secret while she copes with her new life and the regiment.
Genre(s): Romance.

Zaman, Fakhar

5573. *The Prisoner.* Trans. Khalid Hasan. Chester Springs, PA: Dufour, 1996. 176 pp.
General Mohammad Zia ul-Haq overthrows the Pakistani government in 1977, and Z, a poet and revolutionary, is charged, confined to a tiny cell, and tortured for a murder he did not commit.
Genre(s): Biographical Fiction; Political Fiction.

Zameenzad, Adam

5574. *Cyrus Cyrus.* New York: Viking, 1991. 578 pp.
A man escapes from prison, leaving behind a manuscript telling of his mother's rape before his birth in the lowly Choodah caste of untouchables in India and his family's subsequent slaughter in the civil war of East Pakistan.
Genre(s): Family Saga; War Story.

Israel and Arab Countries

Before 1900

Barkhordar-Nahai, Gina

5575. *Cry of the Peacock.* New York: Crown, 1991. 352 pp.
From the 18th century in Iran, Jews face discrimination because of fear that they will contaminate the Muslims, and Peacock, 116 years old, sees it continue in the 20th century.
Genre(s): Epic Literature; Religious Fiction.

Beaufort, Simon

5576. *Murder in the Holy City.* New York: St. Martin's, 1998. 240 pp.
When Sir Geoffrey de Mappestone returns from a desert patrol near Jerusalem during the Crusades, he discovers a murdered soldier in a baker's bedchamber.
Genre(s): Mystery.

Harris, Norma

◆ 5577. *Trumpets of Silver.* New York: Dutton, 1990. 320 pp.
A family of three children flees Russia in the late 19th century; the son goes to Palestine and the daughters to New York, but all of them must decide what it means to be Jewish.
Genre(s): Jewish Fiction.

Holland, Cecelia

◆ 5578. *Jerusalem.* New York: Forge, 1996. 319 pp.
In 1187, Knights Templar, including Rannulf Fitzwilliam, fight with the leper-king Baudouin and his sister Sibylla against Saladin in Jerusalem.

Holman, Sheri

5579. *A Stolen Tongue.* New York: Atlantic Monthly, 1997. 343 pp.
Father Felix Fabri wants to visit the tomb of St. Katherine of Alexandria when he goes with German tourists to the Holy Land in the late 15th century, but on the way, he stops to see relics, and learns that someone has stolen them.
Genre(s): Mystery.

Hoyt, Edwin Palmer

◆ 5580. *The Voice of Allah.* New York: John Day, 1970. 468 pp.
Muhammad, the Arab prophet of Islam, works to make his beliefs known and understood.
Genre(s): Biographical Fiction; Religious Fiction.

Johansen, Iris

5581. *Lion's Bride.* New York: Bantam, 1996. 432 pp.
Thea of Dimas, indentured to a silkworm grower, goes to Damascus to start an embroidery shop, but when her caravan is destroyed, Lord Ware, hunted by the Knights Templar, rescues her and thwarts her long-range plans.
Genre(s): Romance.

Maalouf, Amin

5582. *The Rock of Tanios.* Trans. Dorothy S. Blair. New York: Braziller, 1994. 275 pp.
In the 1880s, Tanios experiences the rapid changes in traditional society within his Lebanese world during a period of poltical and social turmoil.
Award(s): Prix Goncourt.
Genre(s): War Story; Political Fiction.

◆ 5583. *Samarkand.* Trans. Russell Harris. New York: Interlink, 1996. 304 pp.
In the 11th century, Omar Khayyam secrets away a manuscript of his poetry, and in the early 20th century, a wealthy collector finds it and books passage on the *Titanic*.
Genre(s): Biographical Fiction.

Mujica Lainez, Manuel

5584. *The Wandering Unicorn.* Trans. Mary Fitton. New York: Taplinger, 1983. 322 pp.
A legendary French fairy Melusine, 800 years old, travels with the boy-knight Aiol to help Baldwin IV in his fight against Saladin in 12th-century Jerusalem.
Genre(s): War Story; Fantastic Literature.

Tarr, Judith

5585. *Queen of Swords.* New York: Forge, 1997. 464 pp.
Melisende, oldest daughter of Baldwin II, the king of Jerusalem, rules from 1129 to 1153, first as wife of Fulk of Anjou and then as regent to her son, with the French Lady Richild as her attendant.
Genre(s): Biographical Fiction.

Welch, Ronald

◆ 5586. *Knight Crusader.* New York: Oxford, 1979. 272 pp.
Philip D'Aubigny lives in Outremer (Jerusalem) in the 12th century and has never been to his home country of Wales, but not until he helps defeat the infidels at Acre in 1187 is he free to go to Wales to claim his inheritance.
Award(s): Carnegie Medal.

Genre(s): Adventure Story.

Yehoshua, A. B.

5587. *Mr Mani.* Trans. Hillel Halkin. New York: Doubleday, 1992. 368 pp.

Five people, a young Israeli female, a German soldier, a Jewish British soldier in Palestine, a Polish Jewish doctor, and the patriarch Avraham Mani, tell about the Jewish Mani family beginning in 1848.
Genre(s): Jewish Fiction; Satire.

1900 and After

Al-Qa'id, Yusuf

5588. *War in the Land of Egypt.* Trans. Olive and Lorne Kenney and Christopher Tingley. New York: Interlink, 1998. 192 pp.
When Anwar Sadat returns land nationalized by Nasser to a village politician, he uses his new power to get his son out of military service at the beginning of the Yom Kippur War.
Genre(s): War Story; Political Fiction.

Antonius, Soraya

5589. *The Lord.* New York: Henry Holt, 1988. 218 pp.
Miss Alice, a missionary school teacher in Jaffa during the 1930s, tries to answer questions about Palestinians who lived in the once peaceful small town during the British occupation, and about the outlawing of the *keffiya*, the black-and-white checked scarf of the peasant which became a symbol of nationalist resistance.
Genre(s): War Story.

Appelfeld, Aharon

5590. *The Age of Wonders.* New York: Godine, 1981. 270 pp.
An adult in Israel remembers the self-hatred of his Austrian father before World War II and his own difficulty in understanding it.
Genre(s): War Story; Jewish Fiction.

Baehr, Consuelo Saah

◆ 5591. *Daughters.* New York: Delacorte, 1988. 516 pp.
In the early 20th century, Miriam Mishwe marries Nadeem in a Christian village near Jerusalem and, during World War I, has an affair with a German doctor, after which she gives birth to Nadia, who in turn grows up and has a daughter.
Genre(s): Family Saga.

Barber, Rowland

5592. *The Midnighters.* New York: Crown, 1970. 304 pp.
In 1948, Martin Allen Ribakoff helps those in Israel trying to form a country after World War II to buy surplus airplanes and recruit pilots for their cause.
Genre(s): Adventure Story.

Blau, Eric

5593. *The Beggar's Cup.* New York: Knopf, 1993. 319 pp.
In doing research on Theodor Herzl for a movie, a screenwriter uncovers the seminal history of Israel.
Genre(s): Biographical Fiction; Religious Fiction.

Booth, Martin

5594. *Dreaming of Samarkand.* New York: Morrow, 1990. 308 pp.
James Elroy Flecker meets Lawrence of Arabia in Beirut in 1912, and the two become friends in the intellectually stifling environment.
Genre(s): Biographical Fiction.

Brenner, Yosef Haim

5595. *Breakdown and Bereavement.* Trans. Hillel Halkin. Ithaca, NY: Cornell University Press, 1971. 328 pp.
Hefetz and Esther live in orthodox Jerusalem as World War I begins.
Genre(s): War Story; Domestic Fiction; Religious Fiction.

Charchat, Isaac

5596. *A Constant Reminder.* New York: Shengold, 1985. 459 pp.
Benjamin Isaacson, a young Swedish Jew, stops in Germany on his way to Palestine where he becomes a Zionist agent and helps smuggle Jews into Palestine as World War II starts.
Genre(s): War Story; Jewish Fiction.

Clavell, James

5597. *Whirlwind.* New York: Morrow, 1986. 1147 pp.
In the sequel to *Noble House*, Andrew Cavallan must retrieve his pilots, their families, and the helicopters in his company from Iran when Khomeini comes to power after the revolution against the shah.
Genre(s): War Story; Adventure Story.

Dammaj, Zayd Mutee

5598. *The Hostage.* Trans. May Jayyusi and Christopher Tingley. Northampton, MA: Interlink, 1994. 168 pp.

A boy taken hostage in the 1940s to ensure his Yemeni clan's loyalty to the governor becomes a servant (*duway-dar*) and falls in love with the governor's sister.
Genre(s): Political Fiction.

Daneshvar, Simin

5599. *A Persian Requiem.* Trans. Roxanne Zand. New York: Braziller, 1992. 279 pp.
During World War II, while the British occupy Iran, Zari tries to keep values in her family while her brother-in-law is only concerned about his personal political gains, which lead to Zari's husband's death.
Genre(s): War Story.

5600. *Savushun.* Washington, DC: Mage, 1990. 432 pp.
An heroic father and his family try to survive in Shiraz during World War II while the Allies occupy the city.
Genre(s): War Story.

Dayan, Yaël

5601. *Death Had Two Sons.* New York: McGraw-Hill, 1967. 191 pp.
Although Daniel's father had turned him over to the Nazis (in place of his brother), Daniel survives and becomes an Israeli soldier before encountering his ill father.
Genre(s): Jewish Fiction.

5602. *Three Weeks in October.* New York: Delacorte, 1979. 242 pp.
The Israeli Amalia and her wounded husband Daniel relate their experiences in the Yom Kippur War of 1973.
Genre(s): War Story.

Easterman, Daniel

5603. *The Last Assassin.* Garden City, NY: Doubleday, 1985. 421 pp.
In the last days of the shah of Iran's rule during the 1970s, Islamic assassins plan to murder several world figures.
Genre(s): War Story.

Farhi, Moris

5604. *The Last of Days.* New York: Crown, 1983. 576 pp.
In the early 1970s, an Arab is determined to destroy Israel with nuclear arms.
Genre(s): Spy Fiction.

Fawal, Ibrahim

5605. *On the Hills of God.* Montgomery, AL: Black Belt, 1998. 450 pp.
Palestinian Yousif Safi, 17, plans to graduate from high school and marry his sweetheart until he has to face the internationalization of Jerusalem and the war erupting as the Zionists try to make their country out of occupied land.
Genre(s): War Story; Political Fiction; Bildungsroman (Coming of Age).

Fish, Robert L.

5606. *Pursuit.* Garden City, NY: Doubleday, 1978. 379 pp.
A Nazi surgeon transforms a vicious Nazi into a Jew who finds himself with a group of refugees escaping to Palestine.
Genre(s): War Story.

Follett, Ken

5607. *Triple.* New York: Arbor House, 1977. 379 pp.
A group of men who attended Oxford together in 1947 work to create nuclear weaons for the Israelis in order to combat the Egyptians.
Genre(s): Spy Fiction.

Frankel, Zygmunt

5608. *Short War, Short Lives.* New York: Abelard, 1971. 128 pp.
Eli, production manager in a factory, describes the defense of the factory and the response of both Israelis and Arabs during and after the Six-Day War in 1967.
Genre(s): War Story.

Freeman, Cynthia

5609. *No Time for Tears.* New York: Arbor House, 1981. 411 pp.
Her family having escaped from Russian pogroms to Palestine in 1905, Chavala Landau first helps the British in World War I and then goes to the United States to start a chain of jewelry stores to help support the state of Israel.
Genre(s): War Story; Domestic Fiction.

Grossman, David

5610. *The Book of Intimate Grammar.* Trans. Betsy Rosenberg. New York: Farrar, Straus and Giroux, 1994. 480 pp.
Gideon watches his friends Aron and Yaeli become involved in the Israeli Zionist youth movement while he remains outside it.
Genre(s): War Story; Bildungsroman (Coming of Age).

Hamizrachi, Yoram

5611. *The Golden Lion and the Sun.* Trans. Philip Simpson. New York: Dutton, 1982. 215 pp.
At the beginning of the Iranian revolution, a CIA-Israeli espionage team goes to the Iranian mountains where Kurds help them rescue spies from the Shah's reign.
Genre(s): Political Fiction; Spy Fiction.

Hellman, Aviva

◆ 5612. *To Touch a Dream.* New York: Donald I. Fine, 1989. 551 pp.
The Danzigers, in Palestine before World War I, work to build a homeland.
Genre(s): Romance; Family Saga.

Hernon, Peter

5613. ***Earthly Remains.*** Secaucus, NJ: Carol Publishing Group, 1992. 152 pp.
In the final days of the British occupation of Palestine, someone discovers ancient scrolls at Qumran Wadi, and an art collector, an archeologist, and a journalist then find a headless skeleton and a crucifixion victim nearby.
Genre(s): Adventure Story.

Hlasko, Marek

5614. ***All Backs Were Turned.*** Trans. Tomasz Mirkowicz. New York: Cane Hill, 1991. 118 pp.
Dov Ben Dov lives in Israel during the 1960s, and after killing his wife's lover, he protects Israel Berg who takes the blame for charges against Dov to keep him out of jail until Dov becomes involved with fishermen and a female German tourist.

Household, Geoffrey

5615. ***Doom's Caravan.*** Boston: Little, Brown, 1971. 241 pp.
An Englishman with the darker skin of an Arab deserts British Intelligence in World War II, but when captured in 1942, he must work as a spy against the Germans.
Genre(s): Adventure Story; Spy Fiction.

Irving, Clive

5616. ***Promise the Earth.*** New York: Harper and Row, 1982. 402 pp.
From 1916 to 1919, the British try to establish a Jewish Palestine, as well as an Arab one, by making promises to both Jews and Arabs in return for support against the Turks.

Jabbour, Hala Deeb

◆ 5617. ***A Woman of Nazareth.*** New York: Interlink, 1990. 272 pp.
Amal, a Palestinian woman born in 1943, lives in Beirut as a young girl when the mores for women are being questioned but not changed.

Jackman, Stuart Brooke

5618. ***A Game of Soldiers.*** New York: Atheneum, 1982. 303 pp.
Members of the same Royal Air Force maintenance unit isolated in the Middle East begin to resent each other more than the actual enemy.
Genre(s): War Story.

Johnson, Diane

5619. ***Persian Nights.*** New York: Knopf, 1987. 352 pp.
When Chloe Fowler's husband leaves her in Iran to return home unexpectedly, she becomes involved with his colleague while the revolutionary atmosphere intensifies.
Genre(s): War Story.

Kardos, György G.

5620. ***Avraham's Good Week.*** Trans. Ralph Manheim. New York: Doubleday, 1975. 284 pp.
Avraham Bogatir, a Jewish farmer in British-occupied Palestine, is caught in the chaos of Israeli independence.
Genre(s): Domestic Fiction.

Labaky, Mansour

◆ 5621. ***The Roads of Nowhere.*** Trans. Annelyse M. Allen. Petersham, MA: St. Bede's, 1988. 109 pp.
Naseen, a war orphan, remembers his life before the war and the destruction of his Lebanese village, but making friends with Jad, a boy whose father is still alive, helps him find hope.
Genre(s): War Story; Bildungsroman (Coming of Age); Christian Fiction.

Lasky, Jesse L. Jr., and Pat Silver

5622. ***The Offer.*** Garden City, NY: Doubleday, 1981. 624 pp.
The Hammadi-Nouari Trading Company founded under Arab and Jewish ownership in the mid-19th century, becomes a huge, international empire, but the conflicting desires of its owners threaten to destroy it as the area moves toward the founding of the state of Israel in 1948.
Genre(s): Political Fiction.

Levin, Meyer

5623. ***The Harvest.*** New York: Simon and Schuster, 1978. 670 pp.
Mati, in the sequel to *The Settlers*, goes to Chicago as a student but later returns to Palestine as a pilot and begins fighting the Arabs in 1948.
Genre(s): War Story.

5624. ***My Father's House.*** New York: Viking, 1947. 192 pp.
When David arrives in Palestine, he searches for his father, who had said to meet him there just as the Nazis were herding him into a Krakow square and away from David.
Genre(s): Jewish Fiction.

5625. ***The Settlers.*** New York: Simon and Schuster, 1972. 832 pp.
Before World War I, the Russian Chaimovitch family immigrates to Palestine, and their experiences contrast with those of Palestinians already in the area.
Genre(s): Family Saga; Jewish Fiction.

Liotta, P. H.

5626. ***Diamond's Compass.*** Chapel Hill, NC: Algonquin, 1993. 353 pp.
Dante Diamond leaves the Air Force Academy and wonders how to tell his father, who is stationed in Iran, but within three years, Dante returns to the area to face two different foes.
Genre(s): Political Fiction; War Story.

Matalon, Ronit

5627. *The One Facing Us*. Trans. Marsha Weinstein. New York: Holt, 1998. 304 pp.
Esther, 17, tells of the successes and failures of her Egyptian-Jewish family from Cairo after its members move to Israel, New York, and Africa after World War II.
Genre(s): Domestic Fiction.

Michael, Sami

5628. *Refuge*. Trans. Edward Grossman. Philadelphia: Jewish Publications, 1988. 376 pp.
In 1973 Marduch, a communist who has spent time in an Iraqi prison, fights for Israel, while someone asks his wife, an Ashkenazi Jew, to shelter an Arab.
Genre(s): War Story.

Mirza, William, and Thom Lemmons

5629. *Passport*. Wheaton, IL: Victor, 1995. 261 pp.
A Jewish family in Teheran in the last days of the shah become victims of Shiite fundamentalists, and while escaping, face terror and tragedy.
Genre(s): Adventure Story; Christian Fiction; War Story.

Munif, Abd-al-Rahman

5630. *Cities of Salt*. New York: Random House, 1988. 526 pp.
In the 1930s Americans begin oil exploration in an Arab emirate country, and the culture in an oasis community changes. (*Series:* Cities of Salt, 1)
Genre(s): Political Fiction.

5631. *The Trench*. New York: Pantheon, 1987. 554 pp.
In the Persian Gulf city of Mooran in the 1950s, the powerful few govern the country, and Dr. Subhi al-Mahmilji looks after the sultan's health and runs his business on the side. (*Series:* Cities of Salt, 3)
Genre(s): Political Fiction.

5632. *Variations on Night and Day*. Trans. Peter Theroux. New York: Pantheon, 1993. 333 pp.
A British surveyor in the 1930s becomes friends with Sultan Khureybit of Mooran because the British government believes that dealing with one leader is easier than dealing with several. (*Series:* Cities of Salt, 3)
Genre(s): Political Fiction; Epic Literature.

Oz, Amos

5633. *My Michael*. Trans. Nicolas de Lange. New York: Knopf, 1972. 287 pp.
Hannah, a married university student in Jerusalem during the 1950s, remembers Arab male playmates from her childhood and remains fascinated by their mysteriousness.

◆ 5634. *Panther in the Basement*. Trans. Nicholas de Lange. San Diego, CA: Harcourt, 1997. 160 pp.
Proffy, 12, tries to form his own underground resistance group in his family's basement as Israel prepares to fight for independence, but he becomes friends with a British police officer instead.
Genre(s): Bildungsroman (Coming of Age); War Story.

5635. *A Perfect Peace*. San Diego, CA: Harcourt, 1985. 374 pp.
Yonatan Lifshitz is disillusioned with life on a kibbutz in the mid-1960s until a stranger arrives and suggests that war is coming.
Genre(s): Domestic Fiction.

5636. *Touch the Water, Touch the Wind*. Trans. Nicholas de Lange. New York: Harcourt, 1974. 179 pp.
Pomeranz hides from the Germans in the Polish forest before reaching Israel where he astonishes kibbutz members with his mathematical genius.
Genre(s): War Story.

Pizishkzad, Iraj

5637. *My Uncle Napoleon*. Trans. Dick Davis. Washington, DC: Mage, 1996. 507 pp.
Uncle Napoleon dominates his family in Tehran during the 1940s and blames Iran's problems on the country's friendliness with foreign nations.
Genre(s): Humorous Fiction; Domestic Fiction.

Potter, Jennifer

5638. *The Long Lost Journey*. San Francisco: Mercury House, 1990. 176 pp.
In Mareb, to excavate a temple in 1910, Elinor Grace, with her companion James Fergussen, keeps a journal about her experiences before she is imprisoned and goes mad.
Genre(s): Adventure Story.

Rabinyan, Dorit

5639. *Persian Brides*. Trans. Yael Lotan. New York: Braziller, 1998. 200 pp.
At the beginning of the 20th century, pregnant Flora Ratoyan's cloth-merchant husband deserts her, and her young cousin of 11, before her own marriage, comforts Flora in the Jewish quarter of the Persian town of Omerijan.
Genre(s): Domestic Fiction.

Rosenbaum, Ray

5640. *Condors*. Novato, CA: Lyford, 1995. 340 pp.
Ross Colyer's Allied Air is hired to support Jewish immigrants in Palestine in 1946, and he is asked to spy on his employer, the Jewish Relief Foundation.
Genre(s): War Story.

Shaham, Nathan

5641. *Rosendorf Quartet*. Trans. Dalya Bilu. New York: Grove Weidenfeld, 1991. 357 pp.
Four German-Jewish refugees play in a quartet in Palestine during World War II, where they try to make music unencumbered by the outside world, but life refuses to stop intruding on their art.
Genre(s): Musical Fiction; War Story.

◆ May be suitable for young adult readers

Shahar, David

5642. *The Palace of Shattered Vessels*. Trans. Dalya Bilu. New York: Weidenfeld and Nicolson, 1988. 480 pp.
A compilation of two novels, *Summer in the Street of the Prophets* and *A Voyage to Ur of the Chaldees* reveals life in Jerusalem during the 1930s and life under the Ottomans with details from Jewish history.
Genre(s): Family Saga.

Shalev, Meir

5643. *The Blue Mountain*. Trans. Hillel Halkin. New York: HarperCollins, 1991. 384 pp.
At the beginning of the 20th century, four Russian immigrants settle in the Jezreel valley to farm and to work towards the establishment of the modern state of Israel.

5644. *Esau*. Trans. Barbara Harshav. New York: HarperCollins, 1994. 384 pp.
Abraham Levy marries Sarah at the beginning of World War I, and they and their twins, Esau and Jacob, go to Palestine where Abraham starts a bakery.
Genre(s): Jewish Fiction; Family Saga.

Thoene, Bodie

5645. *A Daughter of Zion*. Minneapolis, MN: Bethany House, 1987. 336 pp.
Rachel, a Jewish woman who returns to her home after World War II, meets disdain and feels despair. (*Series:* Zion Chronicles, 2)
Genre(s): War Story; Christian Fiction.

5646. *The Gates of Zion*. Minneapolis, MN: Bethany House, 1986. 368 pp.
A young woman searches for her identity in Israel after World War II and the Holocaust. (*Series:* Zion Chronicles, 1)
Genre(s): War Story; Christian Fiction.

5647. *Jerusalem Interlude*. Minneapolis, MN: Bethany House, 1990. 400 pp.
Shimon and Leah Feldstein take refuge in Jerusalem after World War II, but they face explosions in the city almost every day while Israel fights for independence. (*Series:* Zion Covenant, 4)
Genre(s): Christian Fiction; War Story.

5648. *The Key to Zion*. Minneapolis, MN: Bethany House, 1988. 352 pp.
When the British are in the final stages of evacuation from Palestine, two young people are involved. (*Series:* Zion Chronicles, 5)
Genre(s): War Story; Christian Fiction.

5649. *A Light in Zion*. Minneapolis, MN: Bethany House, 1988. 352 pp.
In April, 1948, as the British prepare to evacuate Palestine, Jews celebrate an important passover. (*Series:* Zion Chronicles, 4)
Genre(s): War Story; Christian Fiction.

5650. *The Return to Zion*. Minneapolis, MN: Bethany House, 1987. 352 pp.

Moshe and Rachel becomed trapped behind the walls of Jerusalem's Old City as British forces prepare to leave Palestine, and David requests arms from the Americans to use against the Arabs. (*Series:* Zion Chronicles, 3)
Genre(s): War Story; Christian Fiction.

Tsirkas, Strates

5651. *Drifting Cities*. Trans. Kay Cicellis. New York: Knopf, 1974. 710 pp.
During World War II, people linked together by politics or sex appear in Jerusalem, Cairo, and Alexandria as they endure both international and personal crises.
Genre(s): War Story; Epic Literature.

Uris, Leon

◆ 5652. *Exodus*. Garden City, NY: Doubleday, 1958. 626 pp.
People from different backgrounds come to Palestine to help create the Jewish state of Israel after World War II.
Genre(s): War Story.

5653. *Mitla Pass*. Garden City, NY: Doubleday, 1988. 435 pp.
A novelist in Israel in 1956 observes the Israeli forces in combat with Arab armies while researching a book on the country.
Genre(s): War Story.

West, Morris L.

5654. *The Tower of Babel*. New York: Morrow, 1968. 361 pp.
Several people in the Middle East, including Israelis, a Beirut banker, and a member of the Palestine Liberation Front, endure the tensions preceding the Six-Day War.
Genre(s): War Story; Spy Fiction.

Westheimer, David

5655. *Rider on the Wind*. New York: Walker, 1984. 284 pp.
Stationed in Palestine during 1942, Michael Tex Harris falls in love with the German Hannah Ruh, a member of the anti-British Palmach group, but he refuses to spend his life in Palestine, a decision that breaks up their relationship before Hannah dies in an enemy attack.
Genre(s): War Story; Love Story.

Wiesel, Elie

5656. *A Begger in Jerusalem*. New York: Random House, 1970. 224 pp.
As beggars and a journalist recall their experiences in the Israeli war of 1967 and other wars, they realize that all wars cause intangible losses.
Genre(s): War Story.

Wouk, Herman

5657. *The Glory*. Boston: Little, Brown, 1994. 685 pp.
In the sequel to *The Hope*, the Baraks, Luries, and the Pasternaks become part of the fighting in the aftermath of Israel's victory over the Arabs in 1967 including En-

tebbe, the Yom Kippur War, and bombing Iraq's nuclear reactor.
Genre(s): War Story.

5658. *The Hope.* Boston: Little, Brown, 1993. 693 pp.

Zev Barak, Don Kishote, and Nitzan, along with their families, participate in the establishment of the nation of Israel from 1948 through the Six-Day War in 1967.
Genre(s): War Story; Political Fiction.

Japan

Before 1199

Fell, Alison

5659. *The Pillow Boy of the Lady Onogoro.*
Trans. Arye Blower. New York: Harcourt Brace,
1994. 247 pp.
A poet and mistress in Kyoto during the 11th century,
Lady Onogoro hires a blind stable boy to tell her erotic
stories while she and a general make love.
Genre(s): Erotic Literature.

Guest, Lynn

5660. *The Sword of Hachiman.* New York:
McGraw Hill, 1981. 309 pp.
Yoritomo leads the Minamoto family against the Taira
family in 12th-century Japan, becomes the Shogun, and
begins the samurai-class control of Japan, which lasts
700 years.
Award(s): Georgette Heyer Historical Novel Prize.
Genre(s): Biographical Fiction; War Story; Family Saga.

Murasaki, Shikibu

5661. *The Tale of Genji.* New York: Knopf, 1992.
1184 pp.
In the Heian period, Prince Genji associates with a variety of court women.
Genre(s): Love Story.

Mydans, Shelley Smith

5662. *The Vermilion Bridge.* Garden City, NY:
Doubleday, 1980. 369 pp.
Princess Abe reigns, resigns, and reigns again as Empress
in 8th-century Japan before she dies at 52.
Genre(s): Political Fiction.

Rohlich, Thomas H., ed

5663. *A Tale of Eleventh-Century Japan:*
        Hamamatsu Chunagon Monogatari. Prince-
ton, NJ: Princeton University Press, 1983. 255 pp.
A man becomes involved with ladies in the Chinese court
of mixed Chinese and Japanese blood.
Genre(s): Domestic Fiction.

Willig, Rosette F., ed

5664. *The Changelings.* Stanford, CA: Stanford
University Press, 1983. 264 pp.
In 11th-century Japan, a brother and sister exchange roles
until they are older teenagers, causing unusual sexual situ-
ations.
Genre(s): Domestic Fiction.

1200-1599

Albery, Nobuko

5665. *The House of Kanze.* New York: Simon and
Schuster, 1985. 302 pp.
When Yoshimitsu sees Zeami, the greatest Noh theater
actor in the late 14th century, he takes him as a lover, and
as long as Yoshimitsu lives, the house of Kanze survives.
Genre(s): Biographical Fiction.

Endo, Shusaku

5666. *The Samurai.* Trans. Van C. Gessel. 1982.
New York: Norton, 1997. 272 pp.
The low-ranking samurai Hasekura goes to Mexico,
Spain, and the Vatican in search of Christian missionaries
to return with him to Japan.
Genre(s): Christian Fiction; Adventure Story.

McCullough, Helen Craig, Trans.

5667. *The Taiheiki.* 1959. San Francisco: Tuttle,
1979. 401 pp.
During the first half of the 14th century, civil war divides
Japan.
Genre(s): War Story; Political Fiction.

Tolosko, Edward

5668. *Sakuran.* New York: Farrar, Straus and Giroux, 1978. 273 pp.
Rival samurai take over Prince Jujiro Fugita's ancestral
fiefdom, and he loses everything, but he eventually returns home and avenges his loss to restore peace.
Genre(s): War Story.

Tsuji, Kunio

5669. *The Signore: Shogun of the Warring States.*
New York: Kodansha International, 1989. 197 pp.
The warlord Oda Nobunaga reunifies Japan after two cen-
turies as he battles rival chieftains and Buddhist soldier-
monks in the 16th century.
Genre(s): War Story.

Woodward, Ann

5670. *The Exile Way.* New York: Avon, 1996. 212 pp.

Lady Aoi tries to ease the suffering of the blind Japanese emperor, but during a fire, the scroll describing treatment is burned, and Lady Aoi is banished.

Genre(s): Mystery; Medical Novel.

Yoshikawa, Eiji

5671. *Taiko.* Trans. William Scott Wilson. New York: Kodansha International, 1992. 926 pp.

Toyotomi Hideyoshi wants to serve the emperor as a samurai in the 16th century, and through his perseverance and hard work he becomes the Taiko, the absolute ruler of Japan in the emperor's name.

Genre(s): Family Saga.

1600-1899

Ariyoshi, Sawako

◆ 5672. *The Doctor's Wife.* New York: Kodansha International, 1978. 174 pp.

The intense devotion of his mother, wife, and sisters allows Hanaoka Seishu, an 18th-century Japanese doctor, to have time to develop a general anaesthetic for surgical use.

Genre(s): Biographical Fiction.

5673. *Kabuki Dancer.* New York: Kodansha International, 1994. 348 pp.

Okuni, generally thought to have created Kabuk in the late 16th century, works on her craft, even though women were soon forbidden to perform.

Genre(s): Biographical Fiction.

Blaker, Richard

5674. *The Needle-Watcher.* New York: Doubleday, 1932. 494 pp.

William Adams, an English seaman, uses his knowledge of the compass as an introduction to the Japanese shogun.

Genre(s): Biographical Fiction.

Clavell, James

5675. *Gai-Jin.* New York: Delacorte, 1993. 1038 pp.

In 1862, a samurai murders a British citizen, and the following year, the British bombard Kagoshima which helps begin the Meiji Restoration.

Genre(s): Love Story; Family Saga.

5676. *Shogun.* New York: Atheneum, 1975. 802 pp.

After John Blackthorne shipwrecks in Japan, he makes himself useful to a feudal lord in a power struggle with another and becomes a samurai.

Genre(s): Family Saga.

Enchi, Fumiko

5677. *The Waiting Years.* Trans. John Bester. New York: Kodansha, 1972. 203 pp.

A woman obeys her wealthy husband's request for her to go to Tokyo and find him a mistress during the Meiji period, and his wanton infidelities destroy their marriage and the family.

Genre(s): Domestic Fiction.

Endo, Shusaku

5678. *Silence.* Trans. William Johnston. New York: Taplinger, 1979. 294 pp.

A Portugese priest arrives from Rome to rebuild the shattered Christian community in feudal Japan and to find out why another priest was tortured.

Genre(s): Christian Fiction.

Kata, Elizabeth

5679. *Kagami.* New York: Ballantine, 1992. 550 pp.

The families of the noble Okuras, the samurai Yamamotos, and the merchant Fukudas interact in the 19th century after the arrival of Commodore Perry and the subsequent Western changes that infilitrate Japan.

Genre(s): Family Saga.

Lancaster, Bruce

5680. *Venture in the East.* Boston: Little, Brown, 1951. 416 pp.

Members of the Dutch East India Company gain a trade foothold in Japan in the 17th century.

Genre(s): Political Fiction.

Matsubara, Hisako

5681. *Samurai.* Trans. Ruth Hein. New York: Times Books, 1980. 218 pp.

Tomiko, member of a samurai family, writes cheerful letters to her husband in America, refusing to inform him of her family's reversal of fortune.

McGill, Richard

5682. *Omamori.* New York: Bantam, 1987. 720 pp.

When the children of friends Douglas Napier and Fujio Hosokawa fall in love before World War II, the Japanese society forbids their union.

Genre(s): War Story.

Robson, Lucia St. Clair

5683. *The Tokaido Road.* New York: Ballantine, 1991. 576 pp.

Cat, daughter of Lord Asano, victim of a forced suicide, becomes a courtesan in Tokyo and vows to avenge her fa-

◆ May be suitable for young adult readers

ther's death with the help of his counselors and a peasant girl.
Genre(s): Adventure Story.

Rowland, Laura Joh

5684. *Bundori.* New York: Villard, 1996. 339 pp.
During the 18th century, Sano Ichiro, a samurai detective working for the Shogun of Edo in Tukugawaera Japan, tracks a serial killer.
Genre(s): Mystery.

◆ 5685. *The Concubine's Tattoo.* New York: St. Martin's, 1998. 336 pp.
During the wedding of Sano, the shogun's Most Honorable Investigator, a concubine is murdered, and Sano learns not only about the shogun's women but also about his unknown wife.
Genre(s): Mystery.

◆ 5686. *Shinju.* New York: Random House, 1994. 367 pp.

Sano Ichiro, the *yoriki,* or senior police commander, believes that an upper-class woman and a commoner were murdered rather than committed suicide as his boss wants him to believe, and Sano uncovers a plot at the shogun's level in the 17th century.
Genre(s): Mystery.

◆ 5687. *The Way of the Traitor.* New York: Villard, 1997. 320 pp.
Sano, famous Japanese detective, investigates the murder of a Dutch merchant in Edo in 1690.
Genre(s): Mystery.

Yoshikawa, Eiji

5688. *Musashi.* Trans. Charles S. Terry. New York: Harper and Row, 1981. 970 pp.
Musashi Miyamoto fights in 1600 for the losing side of the battle at Sekigahara when the Tokugawa Shogunate begins its reign.
Genre(s): Biographical Fiction; Adventure Story; War Story.

1900 and After

Albery, Nobuko

◆ 5689. *Balloon Top.* New York: Pantheon, 1978. 255 pp.
In an attempt to become independent, a young girl separates from her family in post-World War II Japan.
Genre(s): Bildungsroman (Coming of Age).

Boulle, Pierre

5690. *The Bridge over the River Kwai.* Trans. Xan Fielding. New York: Vanguard, 1954. 224 pp.
A proud British colonel in a Japanese prison camp builds a bridge with prison labor, and when commandos from his own side arrive to blow up the bridge, he warns the Japanese.
Genre(s): Satire; War Story.

Coppel, Alfred

5691. *The Burning Mountain.* San Diego, CA: Harcourt, 1983. 420 pp.
The Allies create a careful plan to invade Japan in 1945 and consider the social, aesthetic, and spiritual roots of Japanese culture in its design.
Genre(s): War Story.

Deford, Frank

◆ 5692. *Love and Infamy.* New York: Viking, 1993. 516 pp.
After growing up in Japan, Cotton Drake returns as a missionary, but his friend Kiyoshi leaves for Hawaii to spy on the American military, and when he hears about Pearl Harbor, he has to decide whether to stop his friend from warning the United States.
Genre(s): War Story.

Dickey, James

5693. *To the White Sea.* Boston: Houghton Mifflin, 1993. 275 pp.
After Air Force gunner Muldrow is shot down over Tokyo during World War II, he goes north to country resembling his Alaskan home where he survives by hunting and trapping game.
Genre(s): Adventure Story; War Story.

Endo, Shusaku

5694. *The Sea and Poison.* Trans. Michael Gallagher. New York: Taplinger, 1980. 167 pp.
During World War II, doctors and nurses must decide if they will practice human vivisection on American prisoners-of-war.
Genre(s): War Story.

Freedman, Nancy

5695. *The Seventh Stone.* New York: Dutton, 1992. 372 pp.
Nobaru and Momoko find love in their arranged marriage, but as a pregnant widow after the war, Momoko marries Nobaru's friend, while her son determines that he will defeat America in an economic war.
Genre(s): Domestic Fiction; War Story.

Golden, Arthur

5696. *Memoirs of a Geisha.* New York: Knopf, 1997. 434 pp.

Because her mother is dying and her father old, Chiyo, nine, is sold to a wealthy geisha house in Gion where she learns her trade and works it in the 1930s and 1940s.

Green, Wayne L.

◆ 5697. *Allegiance.* New York: Crown, 1983. 320 pp.
An American-educated, English-speaking Japanese doctor tries to protect an American pilot mistakenly admitted to a Japanese hospital during World War II.
Genre(s): War Story.

Hanley, Gerald

5698. *See You in Yasukuni.* New York: World, 1970. 224 pp.
Private Kyoga fights from Singapore to Burma, but he realizes that he is uninterested in crushing others so that his remains may be admired at the military shrine of Yusukuni.
Genre(s): War Story; Bildungsroman (Coming of Age).

Johnson, Katharine

5699. *Hiroshima.* Boston, MA: Branden, 1994. 205 pp.
Students in a Japanese girls' school in Hiroshima enjoy their lives before the atomic bomb is dropped on August 6, 1945.
Genre(s): War Story.

Kita, Morio

5700. *The Fall of the House of Nire.* Trans. Dennis Keene. New York: Kodansha, 1985. 245 pp.
In the sequel to *The House of Nire*, the patriarch Kiichiro dies, and his family begins to disintegrate because his adopted son is unfit, his daughter has moved to China, and his son is worried about being drafted into the army.
Genre(s): Family Saga.

5701. *Ghosts.* Trans. Dennis Keene. New York: Kodansha, 1992. 193 pp.
A young Japanese boy's mother abandons him and his sister to relatives after her husband dies in the 1930s, and he treasures anything that reminds him of family as he endures the war.
Genre(s): Bildungsroman (Coming of Age); War Story.

5702. *The House of Nire.* Trans. Dennis Keene. New York: Kodansha, 1984. 519 pp.
After World War I, Kiichiro, patriarch of his family, founds the Nire Mental Hospital.
Genre(s): Family Saga.

Libby, Lewis

5703. *The Apprentice.* St. Paul, MN: Graywolf, 1996. 248 pp.
In 1903, Setsuo, an apprentice innkeeper, witnesses several unusual events, including a murder, and his actions later gain him an unexpected reward.
Genre(s): Mystery.

Matsubara, Hisako

◆ 5704. *Cranes at Dusk.* Trans. Leila Vennewitz. New York: Dial, 1985. 255 pp.
Saya, 10, is confused by the Americans and Christianity that have come to Kyoto after the war in August, 1945, and she relies on her wise father to counsel her.
Genre(s): Domestic Fiction.

Matsumoto, Seicho

5705. *Points and Lines.* Trans. Makiko Yamamoto and Paul C. Blum. New York: Kodansha, 1970. 159 pp.
Torigai, an old detective in Hakaata, investigates the deaths of two people found on Kyushu's Kashii Beach from arsenic poison in Japan in the 1950s.
Genre(s): Mystery.

Melville, James

◆ 5706. *A Haiku for Hanae.* New York: Scribner's, 1989. 195 pp.
In 1968, Tetsuo Otani must solve the murder of a young Mormon missionary on the remote Awaji Island.
Genre(s): Mystery.

Michener, James A.

◆ 5707. *Sayonara.* New York: Random House, 1954. 243 pp.
When an American Air Corps major engaged to a general's daughter sets up house with a Japanese woman in occupied Japan, the Americans become concerned.
Genre(s): Love Story.

Mishima, Yukio

5708. *Runaway Horses.* Trans. Michael Gallagher. New York: Knopf, 1973. 421 pp.
In the 1930s, the sequel to *Spring Snow* presents a young zealot who tries to restore the emperor to power through assassination and ritual suicide.
Genre(s): Political Fiction.

5709. *Spring Snow.* Trans. Michael Gallager. New York: Knopf, 1972. 389 pp.
In Tokyo at the beginning of the 20th century, Satoko is betrothed to an imperial prince but immediately starts an affair with the son of a newly elite family.

5710. *The Temple of Dawn.* Trans. Michael Gallager. New York: Knopf, 1973. 344 pp.
In the sequel to *Runaway Horses*, Honda goes to Bangkok and India in the 1940s to better understand reincarnation.
Genre(s): Religious Fiction.

Morris, Edita

5711. *The Flowers of Hiroshima.* New York: Viking, 1959. 187 pp.
Thirteen years after Hiroshima, Sam Willoughby visits the city and sees the continuing tragedy for those who survived.
Genre(s): Love Story.

◆ May be suitable for young adult readers

5712. *Seeds of Hiroshima.* New York: Braziller, 1961. 118 pp.
After Yuka's husband Fumio dies as a result of the bombing of Hiroshima, she and Sam Willoughby become involved in a complex love affair in the sequel to *Flowers of Hiroshima.*
Genre(s): Love Story.

Murakami, Ryu

5713. *Sixty-Nine.* Trans. Ralph F. McCarthy. New York: Kodansha International, 1993. 184 pp.
For teenagers growing up in Japan in 1969, life is very similiar to that in the United States as Kensuke Yazaki, 17, plays in a rock band and becomes involved in political and parental disputes.
Genre(s): Domestic Fiction.

Nitta, Jiro

5714. *Death March on Mount Hakkoda.* Trans. James Westerhoven. Berkeley, CA: Stone Bridge, 1991. 208 pp.
A Japanese company of soldiers becomes lost in the deep snow of the northern Japanese Alps from blindly following a bad leader's poor planning.
Genre(s): War Story.

Oe, Kenzaburo

5715. *Nip the Buds, Shoot the Kids.* Trans. Paul St. John Mackintosh and Maki Sugiyama. New York: Marion Boyars, 1995. 189 pp.
Near the end of World War II, a group of Japanese reform school boys are evacuated to a remote village where the people treat them terribly until a plague breaks out.
Genre(s): Adventure Story.

5716. *The Silent Cry.* Trans. John Bester. New York: Kodansha International, 1974. 274 pp.
Two brothers, Mitsu, a scholar, and Takashi, a political activist, return to their village in the 1960s, and Taksashi protests a wealthy Korean's taking over of the the town.
Genre(s): Domestic Fiction.

Stroup, Dorothy

◆ 5717. *In the Autumn Wind.* New York: Scribner's, 1987. 448 pp.
Chiyo Hara looks after her three children while her husband is in a Siberian prisoner-of-war camp, and she then must try to keep her three children alive when Hiroshima is bombed in 1945.
Genre(s): War Story; Domestic Fiction.

Sumii, S.

5718. *The River with No Bridge.* Trans. Susan Wilkinson. Boston: Charles E. Tuttle, 1990. 359 pp.
An *eta* or *burakumin* family during the early 20th century is isolated in a small village.
Genre(s): Domestic Fiction.

Tanizaki, Jun'ichiro

5719. *The Makioka Sisters.* Trans. Edward G. Seidensticker. New York: Knopf, 1957. 530 pp.
With upper middle-class traditions and tastes, the two unmarried Makioka sisters no longer have the money to support their lifestyle in 1938.
Genre(s): Domestic Fiction.

Toland, John

5720. *Occupation.* Garden City, NY: Doubleday, 1987. 453 pp.
The Japanese Toda family and the American McGlynn family endure postwar problems in Japan from 1945 to 1950 during the trials for war crimes, in the sequel to *Gods of War.*
Genre(s): War Story; Legal Story.

Trew, Antony

◆ 5721. *Yashimoto's Last Dive.* New York: St. Martin's, 1988. 287 pp.
Togo Yashimoto orders his submarine to sink an American merchant ship, but one American survives, and when he reports that the Americans have hit the conning tower, the British return to revenge the sinking.
Genre(s): War Story.

Tsukiyama, Gail

5722. *The Samurai's Garden.* New York: St. Martin's, 1995. 211 pp.
Stephen, 17, leaves Hong Kong for Japan to recuperate from tuberculosis just as the Chinese prepare to invade, and in a small town, he develops strong relationships.
Genre(s): Love Story.

Uno, Chiyo

5723. *Confessions of Love.* Honolulu: University of Hawaii Press, 1989. 157 pp.
A Japanese man focuses completely on his new love.
Genre(s): Biographical Fiction.

5724. *The Story of a Single Woman.* Trans. Rebecca Copeland. Chester Springs, PA: Dufour, 1993. 132 pp.
Kadzue, a Japanese woman in the 1920s, decides not to marry, a radical decision in a society where men have control, although she has many lovers.
Genre(s): Domestic Fiction.

Wood, Christopher

5725. *North to Rabaul.* New York: Arbor House, 1979. 275 pp.
American Lieutenant Will Carter becomes one of MacArthur's special intelligence officers assigned to discover what the Japanese are doing on New Britain Island in April 1943.
Genre(s): Biographical Fiction; War Story.

Wynd, Oswald

5726. *The Forty Days.* New York: Harcourt, 1973. 254 pp.

The Japanese treatment of prisoners of war surfaces on the freighter *Oshima Maru* as it transports 1,200 British and American prisoners from Singapore to Japan. *Genre(s):* War Story.

Yamasaki, Toyoko

5727. *Bonchi.* Honolulu: University of Hawaii Press, 1982. 400 pp.

Kawachiya Kikuji wants to gain his independence from his family, and he divides his life between the teahouse and the businessworld in the two decades before World War II.

Korea

Before 1900

Brown, Diana

◆ 5728. *The Blue Dragon.* New York: St. Martin's, 1988. 448 pp.
Marigold comes to Korea as a missionary in the 1890s when Japan, Russia, and the United States are trying to gain inroads, and she falls in love with the country and with an American while teaching English to a court lady.
Genre(s): Christian Fiction; Romance.

Buck, Pearl S.

5729. *The Living Reed.* New York: John Day, 1963. 478 pp.
Four generations of the Kim family follow the history of Korea from 1881 and service to the Queen of Korea to the Korean War and 1952.
Genre(s): Family Saga.

Hahn Moo-Sook

5730. *Encounter.* Berkeley: University of California Press, 1992. 325 pp.
In the 1880s, fervent Catholics kill Korean non-believers, and the scholar Chong Yak-yong and his cousin Chong Ha-sang become part of the underlying philosophical conflict.
Award(s): Grand Prix of the Republic of Korea Literature Award.
Genre(s): Biographical Fiction; Christian Fiction.

Inoue, Yasushi

5731. *Wind and Waves.* Honolulu: University of Hawaii Press, 1989. 201 pp.
Kubilai, grandson of Genghis Khan, becomes Emperor of China after seizing Korea and using it as a stepping stone to invade Japan in 1274 and again in 1281.
Genre(s): War Story.

Mun-yol, Yi

5732. *The Poet.* Trans. Chong-wha Chung. New York: HarperCollins, 1996. 208 pp.
When Kim Pyong-yon's grandfather decides to support the rebels in the Korean insurrection of 1811, the family becomes known as traitors, but as Kim matures in these unpleasant circumstances, he discovers an ability to write poetry.
Genre(s): Biographical Fiction.

1900 and After

Ahn, Junghyo

5733. *Silver Stallion.* New York: Soho, 1990. 320 pp.
A pair of American soldiers rape a Korean widow who lives in a poor village while trying to support her children, and she then decides to become a prostitute in exchange for food.
Genre(s): War Story.

Barbeau, Clayton C.

5734. *The Ikon.* 1961. San Francisco, CA: Ikon, 1995. 255 pp.
An American soldier serving in the Korean war undergoes a religious conversion.
Genre(s): War Story; Christian Fiction.

Becker, Stephen D.

5735. *Dog Tags.* New York: Random House, 1973. 307 pp.
Benjamin Beer, a physician in New York City after World War II, becomes a prisoner-of-war in Korea and has his dog tags taken away, rendering him a non-person.
Genre(s): War Story; Medical Novel; Jewish Fiction.

Crawford, C. S.

5736. *The Four Deuces.* Novato, CA: Presidio, 1989. 288 pp.
A career Marine watches the men around him fight valiantly and capably in the Korean War.
Genre(s): War Story.

Griffin, W. E. B.

◆ 5737. *The Captains.* New York: Avon, 1982. 406 pp.
In the Korean War, those in the military fight for their honor and for that of their country. (*Series:* Brotherhood of War)
Genre(s): War Story.

Hickey, James

◆ 5738. *Chrysanthemum in the Snow.* New York: Crown, 1990. 335 pp.
The soldiers in a Korean War company all have their own individual problems while trying to fight together as a unit.
Genre(s): War Story.

Hinojosa, Rolando

5739. *The Useless Servants.* Houston, TX: Arte Publico, 1993. 191 pp.
In his diary of the Korean War, Rafe Buenostro records personal experiences in the Mobile Field Unit, including disorientation, horror, cold, and desolation.
Genre(s): War Story.

Holinger, William

5740. *The Fence Walker.* Albany: State University of New York Press, 1985. 290 pp.
Lieutenant Art Richardson patrols the fence dividing Korea in 1968, and his job reflects the monotonous but necessary nature of some military tasks.

Hooker, John

5741. *Standing Orders.* New York: Viking, 1987. 384 pp.
David Andersen, trained in military school to become an officer, has to prove himself in Korea but returns home to Australia because he cannot stand the killing.
Genre(s): War Story; Bildungsroman (Coming of Age).

Hooker, Richard

5742. *M.A.S.H.* New York: Morrow, 1968. 219 pp.
Doctors stationed at a hospital in wartime Korea become involved in many off-duty antics as relief from the seriousness of their work.
Genre(s): War Story; Medical Novel.

Kyong-Ni, Park

5743. *Land.* Trans. Agnita Tennant. New York: Keagan, 1996. 512 pp.
Pyongsan, an impoverished landowner, and others, finally win against the wealthy, selfish landowner Choi Chisoo in the early 20th century in situations leading to the Dong Hak rebellion.
Genre(s): Epic Literature.

Limón, Martin

5744. *Buddha's Money.* New York: Bantam, 1998. 320 pp.
American servicemen Ernie Bascom and George Sueo search for a jade head bearing a map to the lost tomb of Genghis Khan.
Genre(s): Adventure Story; Mystery.

5745. *Slicky Boys.* New York: Bantam, 1997. 384 pp.
In the mid-1970s, two American military police officers in Korea are assigned to investigate the death of a British soldier, and they suspect the slicky boys who deal in stolen military supplies.
Genre(s): Mystery.

McAleer, John J., and Billy Dickson

5746. *Unit Pride.* Garden City, NY: Doubleday, 1981. 515 pp.
Billy, 17, and his best friend Dewey face danger and horror together during the Korean War.
Genre(s): War Story.

Michener, James A.

◆ 5747. *The Bridges at Toko-Ri.* New York: Random House, 1953. 146 pp.
A naval task force tries to destroy the bridges at Toko-ri with jet bombers so that supplies will not reach communist front lines during the Korean War.
Genre(s): War Story.

Porcelli, Joe

◆ 5748. *The Photograph.* Charleston, SC: Wyrick, 1995. 346 pp.
Bok Chang Kimboy, orphaned at six in Korea, is adopted by an American officer and lives in Charleston, South Carolina, before fighting in Vietnam.
Genre(s): War Story.

Potok, Chaim

◆ 5749. *I Am the Clay.* New York: Knopf, 1992. 211 pp.
An old Korean peasant couple are fleeing from the Chinese when they find a wounded boy in the ditch, and although the man does not want the boy, the wife will not leave without him.
Genre(s): War Story.

Salter, James

5750. *The Hunters.* Washington, DC: Counterpoint, 1997. 244 pp.
In the Korean War, Captain Steve Connell is a rocket ace, but the more missions he flies, the more his courage ebbs.
Genre(s): War Story.

Slaughter, Frank G.

5751. *Sword and Scalpel.* New York: Doubleday, 1957. 272 pp.
An American army officer in Korea faces imprisonment by the Chinese and a trial for collaborating with the communists.
Genre(s): War Story.

Stout, Mira

5752. *One Thousand Chestnut Trees.* New York: Putnam, 1998. 336 pp.
When Anna finishes college, she visits her mother's relatives in Korea and learns about her mother's life during the Japanese invasion of the 1930s.
Genre(s): War Story; Domestic Fiction; Bildungsroman (Coming of Age).

Wiley, Richard

5753. *Festival for Three Thousand Maidens.* New York: Dutton, 1991. 240 pp.

In the 1960s, Bobby Comstock is a Peace Corps volunteer in Korea teaching English in a middle school, and he must adjust to the external loneliness as well as to his own personality.

Genre(s): Bildungsroman (Coming of Age).

South and Central America and the Caribbean

Before 1600

Alemán Velasco, Miguel

◆ 5754. *Copilli.* New York: Doubleday, 1984. 125 pp.
Prince Copilli, son of Axay Ácatl, is a warrior who ultimately sacrifices himself for his people.
Genre(s): Biographical Fiction.

Barreiro, Jose

5755. *The Indian Chronicles.* Houston, TX: Arte Publico, 1993. 303 pp.
Diego Colon, 12 when Christopher Columbus arrives in the West Indies, quickly masters the Spanish language and becomes Columbus's adopted son.
Genre(s): Biographical Fiction.

Bell, Clare E.

◆ 5756. *Jaguar Princess.* New York: Tor, 1993. 448 pp.
Mixcatl, a talented and literate Aztec, turns into a jaguar when necessary to retain her power.
Genre(s): Fantastic Literature.

Brandt, Jane Lewis

5757. *La Chingada.* New York: McGraw-Hill, 1979. 465 pp.
Malinche, one of the women given to Cortés, becomes his translator of language and custom and bears him a son while another man, a Spanish foot soldier, also loves her.
Genre(s): Biographical Fiction.

Clewes, Howard

5758. *I, the King.* New York: Morrow, 1979. 287 pp.
Gonzalo Pizarro, brother of the explorer Francisco, leads a revolt in Peru against Spain and is defeated at Jaquijahuana.
Genre(s): Biographical Fiction.

Forester, C. S.

5759. *To the Indies.* Boston: Little, Brown, 1940. 298 pp.
Narciso Rich joins the hidalgos, who sail in Columbus's third voyage to fight Indians in San Domingo, and is shipwrecked off the coast of Cuba before returning to the ship that transports Columbus in chains.
Genre(s): Sea Story.

Garrison, Omar V.

5760. *Balboa.* New York: Lyle Stuart, 1971. 256 pp.
Balboa explores Panama beginning in 1501 and realizes that he must have the trust of the Indians to get information he needs and to explore the area safely.
Genre(s): Adventure Story.

Gillies, John

5761. *The Martyrs of Guanabara.* Chicago: Moody, 1976. 174 pp.
Nicolas Durand de Villegaignon helps Hugenots escape from France and establish a colony on an island in Guanabara Bay, Brazil, which Portuguese troops destroy in 1560.
Genre(s): Biographical Fiction.

Highwater, Jamake

◆ 5762. *The Sun, He Dies.* Philadelphia: Lippincott, 1980. 319 pp.
From his position as chief orator for Montezuma, Nanautzin tells about the Spanish overpowering of the Aztecs.

Jennings, Gary

5763. *Aztec.* New York: Atheneum, 1980. 754 pp.
Mixtli lives on the outskirts of Tenochtitlan where he becomes an involuntary chronicler of his people's past for the invading Spaniards.
Genre(s): War Story; Epic Literature.

King, Kathleen

5764. *Cricket Sings.* Athens: Ohio University Press, 1983. 162 pp.
Cricket Sings, an old herbwoman, makes rounds in her pre-Columbian village in AD 900, using herb cures rather than relying on intervention from the gods as do the Sun Priests.
Genre(s): Domestic Fiction; Medical Novel.

Limón, Graciela

5765. *Song of the Hummingbird.* Houston, TX: Arte Publico, 1996. 217 pp.
Hummingbird, born an Aztec princess in Montezuma's court, tells about her 82 years of life, which spanned the time of the Spanish conquest of Mexico.
Genre(s): Biographical Fiction.

McGahan, Jerry

5766. *A Condor Brings the Sun.* San Francisco: Sierra Club, 1996. 266 pp.
Although living in the 20th century, Pilar represents the ancient, pre-Inca Ruma culture along with the 23 generations of Ruma women who have preceded her.
Genre(s): Domestic Fiction; Family Saga.

Michener, James A.

◆ 5767. *Caribbean.* New York: Random House, 1989. 672 pp.
From the days of the Arawak through the arrival of the Spanish marauders, the Caribbean faces those who seek its beauty and riches.
Genre(s): Epic Literature.

◆ 5768. *Mexico.* New York: Random House, 1992. 625 pp.
Norman Clay, a New York journalist born in Mexico, returns to tell the story of two rival matadors in 1961, but he also includes vast amounts of Mexican history from the past 1,500 years.
Genre(s): Epic Literature.

O'Dell, Scott

◆ 5769. *The Amethyst Ring.* Boston: Houghton Mifflin, 1983. 212 pp.
Julian Escobar, in the sequel to *The Feathered Serpent,* tries to save his city from Cortés, but he fails.
Genre(s): Adventure Story.

◆ 5770. *The Captive.* Boston: Houghton Mifflin, 1979. 210 pp.
Julian Escobar, a seminarian, leaves Seville for the New World in 1506, where after a shipwreck, he learns Mayan from a local girl.
Genre(s): Adventure Story.

◆ 5771. *The Feathered Serpent.* Boston: Houghton Mifflin, 1981. 211 pp.
In the sequel to *The Captive,* Julian Escobar begins to revive the City of the Seven Serpents as its ruler, and when he visits Moctezuma, he sees Cortés.
Genre(s): Adventure Story.

◆ 5772. *The King's Fifth.* Boston: Houghton Mifflin, 1966. 264 pp.
Esteban de Sandoval awaits his trial for hoarding the king's fifth on his 17th birthday, September 27, 1541.
Genre(s): Adventure Story.

Passuth, Laszlo

5773. *Tlaloc Weeps for Mexico.* San Francisco: Pacific, 1987. 487 pp.
Cortés, an inexperienced explorer, departs Havana in 1518 to find gold, and he achieves success through his willingness to rid the invaded land of possible enemies.
Genre(s): War Story; Biographical Fiction.

Peters, Daniel

◆ 5774. *The Incas.* New York: Random House, 1991. 1072 pp.
Micay, captured daughter of a chief, and Cusi, cast off by his father, become close as the Inca empire slowly decays in the years before Pizarro arrives in the 1500s.
Genre(s): Family Saga.

5775. *The Luck of Huemac.* New York: Random House, 1982. 657 pp.
Huemac, warrior son of a servant to an evil Aztec ruler, is shunned because the local sorcerer says that his birth occurred at an unlucky time.
Genre(s): Epic Literature.

◆ 5776. *Tikal: A Novel About the Maya.* New York: Random House, 1983. 422 pp.
Balam Xoc has visions of suffering among the Mayans of Tikal over 1,000 years ago, and this causes conflict between his family and the city's ruler.
Genre(s): Epic Literature.

Portillo, José Lopez

5777. *They Are Coming: The Conquest of Mexico.* Trans. Beatrice Berler. Denton: University of North Texas Press, 1992. 400 pp.
When Spaniards arrive in the New World, they are happy to see in Mexico a city that rivals Europe, and the Mexicans welcome them because their myths told them that white men would arrive in their country.
Genre(s): Family Saga.

Shedd, Margaret Cochran

5778. *Malinche and Cortes.* Garden City, NY: Doubleday, 1971. 308 pp.
Malinche recounts her time with Cortés as his mistress and translator in 16th-century Mexico.
Genre(s): Biographical Fiction; Love Story.

Stangerup, Henrik

5779. *Brother Jacob.* Trans. Anne Born. New York: Marion Boyars, 1993. 299 pp.
Jacobus de Dacia, son of a Danish king, goes to study in Paris and becomes a Franciscan monk, but when the Reformation outlaws his order, he flees to Mexico where he champions the Tarask Indians.
Genre(s): Biographical Fiction.

Terrazas, Filiberto

5780. *Kukulcan.* Trans. Esther Terrazas. New York: Vantage, 1974. 119 pp.
The Mayans continue their faith in Kukulcan, their blond god, as they live their lives in Central America.
Genre(s): Fantastic Literature; Religious Fiction.

Thornton, Lawrence

5781. *Tales from the Blue Archives.* New York: Doubleday, 1997. 288 pp.

Delores has had both her children and grandchildren disappear or be murdered in Argentina during the 1976 civil war while the general responsible lives happily with his own family.
Genre(s): War Story; Political Fiction.

1600-1799

Arenas, Reinaldo

5782. *The Ill-Fated Peregrinations of Fray Servando.* New York: Avon, 1987. 246. pp.
Fray Servando, a Mexican priest in the 17th century, roams Europe and the New World believing that man can fly.
Award(s): Best Foreign Language Novel in French.
Genre(s): Biographical Fiction; Picaresque Fiction.

Bell, Madison Smartt

5783. *All Souls' Rising.* New York: Pantheon, 1995. 530 pp.
In the late 1700s, the struggle for Haiti's independence causes racial animosity and bloodshed.
Award(s): National Book Critics Circle Award.
Genre(s): Epic Literature; War Story.

Bernanos, Michel

5784. *The Other Side of the Mountain.* Trans. Elaine P. Halperin. Boston: Houghton Mifflin, 1968. 107 pp.
A youth and a ship's cook are the only survivors from a French galleon under Spanish rule on its way to Peru for gold.
Genre(s): Sea Story.

Bontempelli, Bruno

5785. *The Traveler's Tree.* Trans. Linda Coverdale. New York: New Press, 1994. 250 pp.
The crew of the becalmed *Entremetteuse* attempts to land on a Caribbean island in the 18th century, but coral reefs deter them while supplies rot and sailors contract scurvy.
Genre(s): Sea Story.

Boullosa, Carmen

5786. *They're Cows, We're Pigs.* Trans. Leland H. Chambers. New York: Grove/Atlantic, 1997. 192 pp.
In 1666, Jean Smeeks, 13, sells himself as an indentured servant and goes to Tortuga where an African slave teaches him herbal medicine and a French Huguenot surgeon tells him about modern medicine, preparing him to become a surgeon for pirates.
Genre(s): Satire.

Carpentier, Alejo

5787. *The Kingdom of This World.* Trans. Harriet De Onis. 1956. New York: Farrar, Straus and Giroux, 1989. 150 pp.

After the Haitians overthrow the French during the revolution from 1791 to 1804, many become obsessed by voodoo and indulge in brutality and corruption.
Genre(s): War Story.

Fowler, Robert H.

5788. *The Spoils of Eden.* New York: Dodd, Mead, 1985. 352 pp.
Charlotte Foxley, 19, accompanies her new husband to Barbados to become mistress of his sugar plantation and faces there many cultural obstacles.

Ghose, Zulfikar

5789. *The Incredible Brazilian.* New York: Holt, Rinehart and Winston, 1972. 336 pp.
Gregorio Peixoto da Silva Xavier, son of a wealthy Brazilian landowner in the 1600s, explores the land and the people of his country in a variety of adventures, his avocation being to seduce women along the way.
Genre(s): Picaresque Fiction.

Hart, Catherine

5790. *Splendor.* New York: Avon, 1993. 394 pp.
In the Caribbean in the early 18th century, Devlin Devil Kane is magically rendered invisible by lightning, and Eden Winters must banish the spell.
Genre(s): Romance.

Heckert, Eleanor

5791. *The Golden Rock.* New York: Doubleday, 1971. 240 pp.
St. Eustatius, a small Caribbean island, serves as a supply point for blockade runners taking munitions to the rebels in the colonies.
Genre(s): War Story.

Hoover, Thomas

5792. *Caribbee.* Garden City, NY: Doubleday, 1985. 396 pp.
Hugh Winston, buccaneer, and Barbados colonist Kay Bedford are involved in the revolution against England for freedom in the West Indies during the latter half of the 17th century.
Genre(s): War Story.

Hunter, M. S.

5793. *The Buccaneer.* Los Angeles: Alyson, 1989. 319 pp.

Tommy the Cutlas, a wealthy buccaneer in the West Indies during the 17th century, records his memoirs.
Genre(s): Sea Story; Adventure Story.

Kraus, Jim, and Terri Kraus

5794.*Journey to the Crimson Sea.* Wheaton, IL: Tyndale House, 1997. 475 pp.
After reformed pirate William Hawkes settles in Bridgetown with his wife Kathryne, his friend Thomas wonders if he, vicar, would be happier married, until he falls in love with a former prostitute. (*Series:* Treasures of the Caribbean, 3)
Genre(s): Christian Fiction; Love Story.

5795.*Passages of Gold.* Wheaton, IL: Tyndale House, 1997. 510 pp.
When William and Kathryne have been married only a year, he must leave to search for Spanish pirates who have stolen a treasure of gold from them. (*Series:* Treasures of the Caribbean, 2)
Genre(s): Christian Fiction; Adventure Story.

5796.*Pirates of the Heart.* Wheaton, IL: Tyndale House, 1996. 501 pp.
The seaman and privateer William Hawkes falls in love with the daughter of the governor of Barbados in the 17th century. (*Series:* Treasures of the Caribbean, 1)
Genre(s): Christian Fiction; Sea Story; Love Story.

Lambdin, Dewey

◆ 5797. *The Gun Ketch.* New York: Donald I. Fine, 1993. 312 pp.
After marrying in England, Alan Lewrie commands the ten-gun *Alacrity* sailing to the Bahamas, and his wife's presence curbs the raucous behavior on board as the men try to protect trade and stop piracy, in the sequel to *The King's Privateer.*
Genre(s): Sea Story; Adventure Story.

Mason, F. Van Wyck

5798.*Log Cabin Noble.* New York: Doubleday, 1973. 377 pp.
William Phips becomes determined to find the treasure from a Spanish ship sunk near Cuba in the 17th century.
Genre(s): Adventure Story; Sea Story.

Miller, Linda Lael

5799.*Pirates.* New York: Pocket Books, 1995. 293 pp.
Phoebe Turlow goes to the Caribbean after her divorce, dresses up for a costume party, steps off an elevator into 1780, and meets Duncan, a pirate.
Genre(s): Time Travel.

Miranda, Ana

5800.*Bay of All Saints and Every Conceivable Sin.* Trans. Giovanni Pontiero. New York: Viking, 1992. 305 pp.
The governor searches for the murder of a Portuguese captain-general in 17th-century Brazil and among those

possibly involved are the poet Matos e Guerra, a magistrate, and a lady's maid.
Genre(s): Mystery; Political Fiction.

Nicole, Christopher

5801.*Caribee.* New York: St. Martin's, 1974. 441 pp.
Tom Warner and his son Edward, known as Caribee, arrive on St. Kitts after escaping James I where they try to settle in the early 17th century. (*Series:* Hilton Family, 1)
Genre(s): Political Fiction.

5802.*The Devil's Own.* New York: St. Martin's, 1975. 436 pp.
In the sequel to *Caribee,* Kit Hilton marries the beautiful and ambitions Meg Warner in the 18th-century West Indies where he operates a sugar mill. (*Series:* Hilton Family, 2)
Genre(s): Family Saga; Romance.

5803.*Mistress of Darkness.* New York: St. Martin's, 1976. 426 pp.
Gislane, a mustee with 1/16th African blood, is rescued from Caribbean slavery, taken to London, and sold back into slavery, but Matt Hilton leaves London to trace her to the West Indies. (*Series:* Hilton Family, 3)
Genre(s): Domestic Fiction; Family Saga; Romance.

Patterson, Orlando

5804.*Die the Long Day.* New York: Morrow, 1972. 253 pp.
When Quasheba, a slave on a Jamaican sugar plantation in the 18th century, is killed while trying to protect her daughter from a lecherous landowner, the slaves protest by defying various parts of the code by which they live.
Genre(s): Political Fiction.

Pope, Dudley

5805.*Admiral.* London: Secker and Warburg, 1983. 310 pp.
Ned Yorke, a Royalist hero, becomes a buccaneer after Roundheads take his Barbados plantation but decides to continue his work when Charles II returns in expeditions against the Spanish.
Genre(s): Sea Story.

5806.*Buccaneer.* New York: Walker, 1984. 277 pp.
Ned Yorke, who must escape his family's plantation in Barbados when Cromwellians come to arrest him, takes his love and his formerly indentured servants to sea.
Genre(s): War Story; Sea Story.

5807.*Galleon.* New York: Walker, 1987. 257 pp.
Ned Yorke decides to seize a Spanish galleon which has run aground off St. Martin, but his friend Sir Thomas Whetstone is captured and sentenced.
Genre(s): Sea Story; War Story.

Ribeiro, J. Ubaldo

5808.*An Invincible Memory.* New York: Harper and Row, 1989. 576 pp.

Characters reveal Brazil's history from the colonial period to modern times and show its variety of ethnic groups and clans.
Genre(s): Family Saga.

Schwarz-Bart, André

5809.*A Woman Named Solitude.* New York: Atheneum, 1973. 178 pp.
Solitude is born en route to Guadeloupe where her mother has been sold into slavery, but when Solitude is freed temporarily during the French Revolution, she refuses to return to slavery.

Steinbeck, John

5810.*Cup of Gold.* New York: Covici, Friede, 1936. 269 pp.
Henry Morgan, a son of the Welsh glens, sails for the Indies at 15 where he is enslaved in Barbados before becoming the lieutenant governor of Jamaica.
Genre(s): Biographical Fiction.

Suthren, Victor

◆ 5811. *The Golden Galleon.* New York: St. Martin's, 1988. 192 pp.
In the sequel to *Royal Yankee*, a young American hero wins approval for a trip to the Caribbees to capture Spanish gold in 1741.
Genre(s): Sea Story.

5812.*In Perilous Seas.* New York: St. Martin's, 1983. 208 pp.

In the sequel to *The Black Cockade*, when Canadian Paul Gallant captains a frigate for King Louis in 1747, he is responsible for leading a convoy of merchantmen from the West Indies to France while trying to evade privateers and the British navy.
Genre(s): Sea Story; War Story.

Wilder, Robert

5813.*Wind from the Carolinas.* New York: Putnam, 1964. 635 pp.
Ronald Cameron, a loyalist, moves his family to the Bahamas after the revolution and continues to support the British against the United States.
Genre(s): War Story.

Wilder, Thornton

5814.*The Bridge of San Luis Rey.* New York: Harper and Row, 1927. 148 pp.
The Franciscan Brother Juniper tries to prove that the deaths of five victims of a bridge collapse in 18th-century Peru were part of God's plan.
Award(s): Pulitzer Prize.
Genre(s): Religious Fiction.

Yarbro, Chelsea Quinn

◆ 5815. *Mansions of Darkness.* New York: Tor, 1996. 432 pp.
The vampire Count Saint-Germain goes to Cuzco, Peru, in 1640, to learn about the Inca civilization before its Spanish conquerors completely destroy it. (*Series:* Saint-Germain, 11)
Genre(s): Gothic Fiction.

1800-1899

Abrahams, Peter

5816.*The View From Coyaba.* New York: Faber and Faber, 1985. 440 pp.
Former slaves David and Sarah Brown start a church in Jamaica during the 19th century and later their grandson studies in Atlanta, runs a mission in Liberia, and becomes a Ugandan bishop.
Genre(s): Domestic Fiction.

Alcalá, Kathleen

5817.*The Flower in the Skull.* New York: Chronicle, 1998. 182 pp.
Shark Tooth becomes separated from her Opata family when Apaches and Mexican soldiers drive them from their village after the Mexican Revolution, and she escapes to Tucson.
Genre(s): War Story; Domestic Fiction.

5818.*Spirits of the Ordinary.* San Francisco: Chronicle, 1997. 245 pp.
In the 1870s, the Carabajal family debates questions imposed upon it as a result of 13 generations of Spanish Inquisition through which their Jewishness has been erased.
Genre(s): Domestic Fiction; Family Saga.

Amado, Jorge

5819.*Gabriela: Clove and Cinnamon.* Trans. James L. Taylor and William L. Grossman. New York: Knopf, 1962. 425 pp.
Gabriela, from Brazil's cacao-growing region, becomes an Arab's cook, mistress, and reluctant wife in an autocratic town with double standards.
Genre(s): Humorous Fiction; Erotic Literature; Love Story.

5820.*Show Down.* Trans. Gregory Rabassa. New York: Bantam, 1988. 422 pp.
A group of unsavory settlers in Brazil endure the frontier life of Bahia to become the proletariat.
Genre(s): Political Fiction.

Anderson, Scott

5821.*Goldwalker.* St. Peters, PA: Breake, 1989. 375 pp.
Patrick Jay O'Connell, an American expatriate, lives in wild Costa Rica where he buys gold from prospectors,

and although he always carries gold with him, no one bothers him.
Genre(s): Biographical Fiction; Adventure Story.

Barnet, Miguel

5822. *Rachel's Song.* Trans. W. Nick Hill. Willimantic, CT: Curbstone, 1991. 125 pp.
Rachel, daughter of a departed German father and a Hungarian mother, grows up in Cuba before the revolution and tells her story of becoming a renowned dancer, actress, and mistress in Havana.
Genre(s): Political Fiction; Domestic Fiction.

Berry, Jim

5823. *The Moon Stallion.* New York: Dutton, 1982. 288 pp.
Argentinian immigrant ranchers war with native tribes, including the Tehuelches under a chief Harkana, by taking their lands and food.
Genre(s): War Story.

Blake, James Carlos

5824. *The Friends of Pancho Villa.* New York: Berkley, 1996. 258 pp.
Rodolfo Fierro teams with Pancho Villa to kill as many as possible during the Mexican Revolution, a war against a dictatorship that ends up sacrificing over one-third of the population.
Genre(s): Biographical Fiction.

Bourne, Peter

5825. *Drums of Destiny.* New York: Putnam, 1947. 570 pp.
A Scottish doctor seeks refuge from the French in Haiti during the last years of the slave revolt.
Genre(s): War Story.

Brawley, Ernest

5826. *The Alamo Tree.* New York: Simon and Schuster, 1984. 432 pp.
Six generations of the O'Hare and Garrizo families become entangled during Mexico's era of political and social change.
Genre(s): Family Saga.

Bryant, Dorothy

5827. *Anita, Anita.* Berkeley, CA: Ata, 1993. 300 pp.
The Brazilian Ana (Anita) Riberio de Duarte falls in love with Giuseppe Garibaldi and joins his freedom-fighting efforts in South America and Italy while bearing him four children.
Genre(s): Love Story; Biographical Fiction.

Cartland, Barbara

5828. *Love at the Helm.* New York: Everest House, 1981. 149 pp.
In 1815, Lady Delora Horn travels with her cousin, Captain Conrad Horn, on a British naval vessel to Antigua

where her despicable brother has arranged her marriage, but before they arrive the captain falls in love with her.
Genre(s): Sea Story; Romance.

Chaikin, L. L.

5829. *Captive Heart.* Eugene, OR: Harvest House, 1998. 350 pp.
As Lady Devora Ashby sails to Jamaica to visit the governor's family, Captain Marc Dubrett, a French buccaneer, plunders her ship and holds her for ransom. (*Series:* Trade Winds, 1)
Genre(s): Romance; Christian Fiction.

5830. *Jamaican Sunset.* Chicago: Moody, 1998. 236 pp.
Pirates, a child, and stolen treasure threaten Emerald Harwick's dreams. (*Series:* Buccaneers, 3)
Genre(s): Christian Fiction; Romance; Adventure Story.

5831. *The Pirate and His Lady.* Chicago: Moody, 1997. 377 pp.
Emerald Harwick worries about the pirate war over buried treasure and her own battle to win the man she loves. (*Series:* Buccaneers, 2)
Genre(s): Christian Fiction; Romance; Adventure Story.

5832. *Port Royal.* Chicago: Moody, 1995. 409 pp.
Emerald Harwick works at a Christian school in Jamaica, and she plans to secretly marry Baret, of whom her father disapproves, but circumstances change her plans. (*Series:* Buccaneers, 1)
Genre(s): Christian Fiction; Adventure Story; Romance.

Chamoiseau, Patrick

5833. *Texaco.* Trans. Rose Myriam Réjouis and Val Vinokurov. New York: Pantheon, 1997. 401 pp.
Marie-Sophie Laborieux, daughter of a freed slave, founds a shantytown in an area formed by Texaco's presence, and her story and the story of those around her covers the period from the abolition of slavery in 1848 through de Gaulle's 1964 visit.
Award(s): Prix Goncourt.
Genre(s): Family Saga.

Cornwell, Bernard

5834. *Sharpe's Devil.* New York: HarperCollins, 1992. 280 pp.
Richard Sharpe, in the sequel to *Sharpe's Waterloo*, fights in Chile in 1821 and tries to locate the kidnapped husband of a Spanish noblewoman.
Genre(s): Adventure Story.

Coulter, Catherine

◆ 5835. *Impulse.* New York: New American Library, 1990. 390 pp.
Rafaella Holland, a Pulitzer Prize-winning journalist, decides to expose her gangster father for his immoral conduct toward her mother.
Genre(s): Love Story; Romance.

Courter, Gay

5836. *River of Dreams.* Boston: Houghton Mifflin, 1984. 555 pp.
Margaret goes with her family to Brazil after the Civil War and marries a Brazilian who makes Margaret's entry into the upper-class society easy but shocking.
Genre(s): Love Story.

Domecq, Brianda

5837. *The Astonishing Story of the Saint of Cabora.* Trans. Kay S. Garcia. Tempe, AZ: Bilingual Press, 1998. 362 pp.
Teresa Urrea becomes the unofficial saint of the Mexican Revolution in the late 1800s.
Genre(s): Biographical Fiction; War Story.

Forester, C. S.

◆ 5838. *Admiral Hornblower in the West Indies.* Boston: Little, Brown, 1958. 329 pp.
Horatio Hornblower faces a new Bonapartist uprising in the West Indies while trying to stamp out slave trade and piracy. *(Series:* Hornblower, 11)
Genre(s): Sea Story; War Story.

5839. *The Captain from Connecticut.* Boston: Little, Brown, 1941. 344 pp.
Captain Josiah Peabody takes the frigate *Delaware* to the Caribbean and breaks up a British convoy off Haiti.
Genre(s): Sea Story.

Fuentes, Carlos

5840. *The Campaign.* New York: Farrar, Straus and Giroux, 1991. 246 pp.
Baltasar Bustos, son of a wealthy Argentinian ranchowner, defies the Spanish colonial regime and falls in love with a magistrate's wife after sneaking into her house and substituting her newborn with the child of a black prostitute.
Genre(s): Political Fiction.

Garcia Marquez, Gabriel

5841. *The General in His Labyrinth.* New York: Knopf, 1990. 285 pp.
In his last days, Simon Bolívar, the Liberator of South America, is prematurely aged, but though he has announced his exile, he hopes to be restored to power.
Genre(s): Biographical Fiction.

5842. *Of Love and Other Demons.* Trans. Edith Grossman. New York: Knopf, 1995. 147 pp.
A priest hired to exorcize a young girl realizes that she is not sick but instead horrified after living with superstitous nuns in their convent during colonial times.
Genre(s): Love Story; Political Fiction.

Gaskin, Catherine

5843. *Fiona.* Garden City, NY: Doubleday, 1970. 278 pp.
Fiona, 19, goes to San Cristobal in the Caribbean as a governess in 1833, and finds herself surrounded by the unrest on the island.
Genre(s): Romance.

Gavin, Catherine Irvine

5844. *The Cactus and the Crown.* Garden City, NY: Doubleday, 1962. 472 pp.
During the time of Maximilian and Carlota, Dr. Andrew Lorimer inherits a medical practice in Mexico and his sister a sugar plantation.
Genre(s): Medical Novel.

Guerard, Albert J.

5845. *The Hotel in the Jungle.* Dallas, TX: Baskerville, 1995. 392 pp.
Persons travel to Mexico in 1870, 1922, and the present, searching for people who were at one time associated with a hotel near a Mayan ruin.
Genre(s): Adventure Story.

Henke, Shirl

5846. *Bride of Fortune.* New York: St. Martin's, 1996. 425 pp.
In the 1860s, professional soldier Nicholas Fortune changes places with his Mexican brother because he prefers an estate and a wife while his brother wants the excitement of soldiering.
Genre(s): Romance; War Story.

Henry, Will

5847. *San Juan Hill.* New York: Random House, 1962. 314 pp.
An Arizona cowboy joins Theodore Roosevelt and his Rough Riders in battle at San Juan Hill, Puerto Rico.
Genre(s): War Story; Adventure Story.

Highwater, Jamake

5848. *Journey to the Sky.* New York: T. Y. Crowell, 1978. 242 pp.
John Stephens and Frederick Catherwood travel to central America in 1839 and discover the ancient Mayan ruins in Copan, Honduras, and Palenque, Mexico.
Genre(s): Biographical Fiction.

Houston, Robert

5849. *The Nation Thief.* New York: Pantheon, 1984. 241 pp.
William Walker, a surgeon and lawyer, sails to Nicaragua in 1855, bringing with him American ways.
Genre(s): War Story.

Hughes, Richard Arthur Warren

5850. *The Innocent Voyage.* New York: Harper, 1959. 399 pp.
While children from Jamaica are sailing to England after a hurricane has partially destroyed their home, pirates mistakenly capture their vessel.
Genre(s): Sea Story.

◆ May be suitable for young adult readers

Jekel, Pamela

5851. *Sea Star.* New York: Harmony, 1983. 391 pp.
Illegitimate Anne Bonny dresses as a male during her childhood and evades marriage by becoming mistress to a pirate and then a pirate herself.
Genre(s): Adventure Story; Sea Story.

Jones, Douglas C.

◆ 5852. *Remember Santiago.* New York: Holt, Rinehart and Winston, 1988. 354 pp.
As a way of escaping problems at home, Eben Pay and his faithful Osage friend, Joe Mountain, become involved in the Spanish-American War of 1898.
Genre(s): War Story.

Juarez, Tina

5853. *Call No Man Master.* Houston, TX: Arte Publico, 1995. 395 pp.
When Carmen learns that the owner of the hidalgo on which she has grown up is her real father, she becomes converted to the revolutionaries supporting the Indians against the Spanish.
Genre(s): War Story; Domestic Fiction.

Leonard, Elmore

5854. *Cuba Libra.* New York: Delacorte, 1998. 343 pp.
Ben Tyler's old partner recruits him to sell guns to Cubans under the guise of horse trading, and when they arrive in 1898 to find the *U.S.S. Maine* wrecked in the Havana harbor, they have to revise their plans.
Genre(s): War Story; Adventure Story.

Leonard, Phyllis G.

5855. *Phantom of the Sacred Well.* New York: McKay, 1976. 273 pp.
In 1879 Joanna Masters sees a witch doctor crucify her brother in Guatemala, and she flees and tries to discover the meaning of the hieroglyphics on bone slivers in her possession.
Genre(s): Mystery; Gothic Fiction.

5856. *Prey of the Eagle.* New York: McKay, 1974. 306 pp.
In Mexico in 1881, the heroine endures a cycle of events that closely resemble those which led to the terrible fate of her 16th-century ancestress.
Genre(s): Romance.

López-Medina, Sylvia

5857. *Cantora.* Albuquerque: University of New Mexico Press, 1992. 306 pp.
During the Mexican Revolution, the narrator's great-grandmother Rosario deserts her wealthy Spanish husband for a revolutionary in Villa's army, while her daughter, granddaughter, and great-granddaughter assert independence in their own ways.
Genre(s): Domestic Fiction.

Lovell, Glenville

5858. *Fire in the Canes.* New York: Soho, 1995. 261 pp.
In 1894, Peata and her daughter Midra arrive on Barbados, and although their town initially shuns them, they become the instruments to free the people from the sugar plantation owners' control.

Lynch, Daniel

5859. *Yellow.* New York: Walker, 1992. 211 pp.
Ambrose Bierce, while lying on his deathbed in Mexico, tells the story of Frederic Remington and another journalist who went into Cuba during the Spanish-American War and liberated the "Joan of Arc" of Cuba.
Genre(s): War Story.

Machado de Assis, Joaquim Maria

5860. *Counselor Ayres' Memorial.* Los Angeles: University of California Press, 1973. 196 pp.
In the 19th century in Rio de Janeiro during its emancipation, a man of 63 narrates the story of a widow and a middle-aged politician.
Genre(s): Political Fiction; Domestic Fiction.

5861. *Dom Casmurro.* Trans. John Gledson. 1899. New York: Oxford, 1997. 230 pp.
In the 1850s, a student escapes from the seminary to marry his childhood sweetheart, but he thinks that she has betrayed him, and he becomes jealous.
Genre(s): Love Story.

5862. *Esau and Jacob.* Trans. Helen Caldwell. 1904. Los Angeles: University of California Press, 1965. 287 pp.
Twin sons of Natividade, beautiful wife of a Rio banker, become rivals in love and politics in the last days of the Brazilian empire.

5863. *Helena.* 1876. Berkeley: University of California Press, 1984. 197 pp.
In Brazil during the 19th century, a young girl suffers a marriage of convenience.
Genre(s): Domestic Fiction.

5864. *The Posthumous Memoirs of Bras Cubas.* Trans. Gregory Rabassa. 1880. New York: Oxford, 1997. 219 pp.
In his memoirs, the Brazilian Bras Cubas comments on his life as politician, writer, and celebrity.

Mason, Hilary

5865. *Morisco.* New York: Atheneum, 1979. 319 pp.
A pirate and an author fall in love.
Genre(s): Romance.

Mastretta, Angeles

◆ 5866. *Lovesick.* Trans. Margaret Sayers Peden. New York: Riverhead, 1997. 292 pp.

Emilia Sauri, born in 1893, fulfills her Aunt Milagros's prophesies by having a happy Mexican childhood and an adult life of strife while loving two men.
Genre(s): Political Fiction.

Morris, Gilbert

5867. *The Rough Rider.* Minneapolis, MN: Bethany House, 1995. 303 pp.
Aaron Winslow leaves the gold fields of the Klondike for the army and fights in the battle at San Juan Hill in 1898. (*Series:* House of Winslow, 18)
Genre(s): Christian Fiction; War Story.

Nicole, Christopher

5868. *Black Dawn.* New York: St. Martin's, 1977. 373 pp.
The Warner and Hilton families in Jamaica during the early 19th-century become part of the movement toward abolishing slavery. (*Series:* Hilton Family, 4)
Genre(s): Domestic Fiction; Family Saga; Romance.

5869. *Ratoon.* New York: St. Martin's, 1962. 246 pp.
Slaves revolt in 1823 in the East Coast Insurrection against the sugar plantation owners in British Guiana.
Genre(s): Political Fiction; War Story.

Paisley, Rebecca

5870. *Bed of Roses.* New York: Dell, 1996. 389 pp.
Suffering from amnesia, Sawyer Donovan enters Zafiro Mara Quintana's hideout in the Sierra Madre mountains where she looks after her father's aging outlaws.
Genre(s): Romance; Western Fiction.

Paredes, Americo

5871. *The Shadow.* Houston, TX: Arte Publico, 1998. 128 pp.
Antonio Cuitla leads a small village created from land taken from aristocrats, but when he becomes annoyed with people for not acknowledging his accomplishments, the people support Del Toro instead.
Genre(s): Political Fiction.

Parker, F. M.

5872. *The Far Battleground.* New York: New American Library, 1988. 224 pp.
During the Mexican War of 1846 to 1848, Lieutenant Cavillin of the Texas Rangers tries to track down United States renegades led by his friend Lieutenant Chilton who are robbing Mexican towns.
Genre(s): War Story.

5873. *The Slavers.* New York: New American Library, 1989. 256 pp.

Zaldivar, a Mexican military chieftain who enslaves white women from refugee settlements, searches for Ken Larrway, the man who killed his son in 1877.

Philip, Maxwell

5874. *Emmanuel Appadocca.* 1854. Amherst: University of Massachusetts Press, 1997. 336 pp.
A young half-white man becomes a pirate and seeks vengeance on his father for abandoning him and his mother.
Genre(s): Sea Story.

Phillips, Caryl

5875. *Cambridge.* New York: Vintage, 1993. 183 pp.
When Emily Cartwright goes to the West Indies to see the plantation that her father, an absentee landlord, owns, she experiences a series of unpleasant and unexplained situations.
Genre(s): Gothic Fiction.

Piñon, Nelida

5876. *The Republic of Dreams.* Trans. Helen Lane. New York: Knopf, 1989. 672 pp.
Madruga immigrates as a young man to Brazil from a Spanish village where he seeks his fortune and establishes his family.
Genre(s): Family Saga.

Powell, James

◆ 5877. *Apache Moon.* Garden City, NY: Doubleday, 1983. 192 pp.
In the 1880s, Luther Cordalee, an American army deserter, lives with Apaches in Mexico, when the Mexicans massacre many of them.
Genre(s): War Story.

Powell, Patricia

5878. *The Pagoda.* New York: Knopf, 1998. 256 pp.
Lowe, an immigrant of 50, runs a shop near a sugar plantation when he writes his daughter about his relationship with Sylvie and his life in Jamaica since leaving China in the 1890s.
Genre(s): Love Story; Adventure Story.

Rhys, Jean

5879. *Wide Sargasso Sea.* New York: Norton, 1966. 189 pp.
In a prequel to *Jane Eyre*, Creole heiress Antoinette Cosway lives in Dominica and Jamaica in the 1830s before she travels to England, becomes Mrs. Rochester, and goes mad.
Genre(s): Love Story.

Roa Bastos, Augusto Antonio

5880. *I, the Supreme.* New York: Vintage, 1987. 433 pp.

Jose Gaspar Rodrigues de Francia, total oligarch in Paraguay for 30 years beginning in 1814, presents politics, religion, and other subjects in a monologue.
Genre(s): Biographical Fiction.

Saunders, Raymond

5881. *Fenwick Travers and the Panama Canal.*
Novato, CA: Lyford, 1995. 318 pp.
Fenwick Travers, man of adventure, travels to the Panama Canal.
Genre(s): Adventure Story; Picaresque Fiction.

Soares, Jo

5882. *A Samba for Sherlock.* Trans. Clifford E.
Landers. New York: Pantheon, 1997. 271 pp.
Sherlock Holmes and Dr. Watson go to Brazil when Sarah Bernhardt invites them to investigate the disappearance of a Stradivarius violin that Emperor Pedro II had given to his mistress, and they also become involved in a search for the serial killer of young women.
Genre(s): Mystery.

Steen, Thorvald

5883. *Don Carlos.* Los Angeles: Sun and Moon,
1997. 160 pp.
In 1833, while Charles Darwin is in Buenos Aires aboard the *Beagle*, a day laborer from Genovese, Giovanni, happens to meet the young scientist, whom he knows only as Don Carlos.
Genre(s): Adventure Story; Biographical Fiction.

Thomson, Rupert

5884. *Air and Fire.* New York: Knopf, 1994. 309
pp.
Theo Valence takes his wife Suzanne with him from France to Mexico to erect a prefabricated iron church based on the Eiffel Tower, and Suzanne unexpectedly disrupts the town when both a Mexican army commander and an American prospector fall in love with her.
Genre(s): Romance.

Traven, B.

5885. *The Carreta.* 1931. New York: Hill &
Wang, 1970. 288 pp.
Andres drives a carreta (ox-cart) in Mexico and observes the peasants' feelings of servitude in their caste system which leads them to begin the Mexican Revolution. (*Series:* Jungle Novel, 1)
Genre(s): War Story; Political Fiction.

5886. *General from the Jungle.* New York: Hill &
Wang, 1940. 280 pp.
A young general uses his intelligence to guide a group of rebels without modern equipment in their quest for freedom to attack and burn federally protected estates after taking their valuables. (*Series:* Jungle Novel, 5)
Genre(s): War Story; Political Fiction.

5887. *Government.* 1931. New York: Hill &
Wang, 1971. 320 pp.

Don Gabriel and his friend persuade or trick Indians into working in the mahogany forests, a dangerous job during which many die, and they take the money for themselves during Porfirio Daz's dictatorship. (*Series:* Jungle Novel, 2)
Genre(s): War Story; Political Fiction.

5888. *March to the Monteria.* 1931. New York:
Hill & Wang, 1971. 256 pp.
Celso, an Indian, only wants to marry his girlfriend and raise 15 children, but to earn money, he must work on a mahogany plantation for two years, and the two years lengthens as the unscrupulous owner enslaves him in a debt system (*Series:* Jungle Novel, 3)
Genre(s): War Story; Political Fiction.

Varga Llosa, Mario

5889. *The War of the End of the World.* Trans.
Helen R. Lane. New York: Farrar, Straus and Giroux, 1984. 586 pp.
In Brazil, from 1893 to 1897, an apocalyptic movement flares in the northeastern part of the country.
Genre(s): War Story.

Vaughan, Patricia

5890. *Murmur of Rain.* New York: Pocket Books,
1996. 466 pp.
Daughter of a French father and an African mother, Lauren Dufort becomes an orphan in Haiti at 17, and Roget de Martier decides to marry her although no one understands why, because she has no money and skin too dark for social acceptance.
Genre(s): Romance.

Villatoro, Marcos McPeek

5891. *A Fire in the Earth.* Houston, TX: Arte Publico, 1996. 496 pp.
The son of Romilia Vasquez, wife of a wealthy husband who treats her like an object, goes to New York where he joins the communists and returns to El Salvador to lead a worker's revolt that fails.
Genre(s): Domestic Fiction.

Whitnell, Barbara

5892. *Cross Currents.* New York: St. Martin's,
1987. 256 pp.
Someone seduces Dorcas when she is a young girl, and although she bears a child, an older man, Zach marries her, and together they build a life on a salt-producing Caribbean island.
Genre(s): Domestic Fiction.

Wilson, Carter

5893. *A Green Tree and a Dry Tree.* New York:
Macmillan, 1972. 300 pp.
Pedro Diaz Cuscat leads the Chiapas in the War of the Castes during 1870 when they try to overcome their oppression and their poverty.
Genre(s): War Story.

Zollinger, Norman

5894. *Chapultepec.* New York: Forge, 1995. 432 pp.

While the United States fights the Civil War, France takes the opportunity to enter Mexico and create a monarchy with Maximilian and Carlota as the rulers whose government never completely defeats Benito Juarez.
Genre(s): War Story; Biographical Fiction.

1900 and After

Abella, Alex

5895. *The Great American.* New York: Simon and Schuster, 1997. 400 pp.
William Morgan, AWOL from the United States Marines, goes into Cuba where he becomes enmeshed in the plot to overthrow Batista and place Castro in charge of the government.
Genre(s): Political Fiction.

Alegría, Fernando

5896. *Allende.* Stanford, CA: Stanford University Press, 1993. 303 pp.
Salvador Allende, a physician from the middle class, tries to bring socialism to Chile, and he must fight not only his Chilean enemies but also Nixon and the United States.
Genre(s): Biographical Fiction.

5897. *The Maypole Warriors.* Trans. Carlos Lozano. Pittsburgh, PA: Latin American Literary Review Press, 1993. 192 pp.
In the 1930s, Chilean families suffer the consequences of social change when their children make foolish decisions.
Genre(s): Political Fiction.

Allende, Isabel

5898. *The House of the Spirits.* Trans. Magda Bogin. New York: Knopf, 1985. 368 pp.
The Trueba family embodies strong feelings from the beginning of the 20th century through the assassination of Allende in 1973.
Genre(s): Domestic Fiction.

Alvarez, Julia

◆ 5899. *In the Time of the Butterflies.* Chapel Hill, NC: Algonquin, 1994. 325 pp.
Dede Mirabel tells about her three sisters, Minerva, Patria, and Maria Teresa, who became martyrs during the liberation of the Dominican Republic from Trujillo in 1960.
Genre(s): Political Fiction.

Amado, Jorge

5900. *Doña Flor and Her Two Husbands.* Trans. Harriet De Onis. New York: Knopf, 1969. 553 pp.
After Dona Flor's philandering husband drops dead, she continues managing her cooking school in Bahai and entertaining a variety of suitors.
Genre(s): Humorous Fiction; Erotic Literature; Fantastic Literature.

5901. *Pen, Sword, Camisole.* Trans. Helen R. Lane. New York: D.R. Godine, 1985. 250 pp.
During World War II, a seat in the Brazilian Academy of Letters opens, and the election pits a Nazi sympathizer against a leftist candidate.
Genre(s): Political Fiction; War Story.

Angelo, Ivan

5902. *The Celebration.* Trans. Thomas Colchie. New York: Avon, 1982. 223 pp.
In 1970, police interfere with both a society party and a working-class demonstration in Brazil.
Genre(s): Political Fiction.

Arenas, Reinaldo

5903. *The Palace of the White Skunks.* New York: Viking, 1990. 356 pp.
After his mother flees Cuba and Castro, Fortunato lives with his aunts and grandparents, and to escape from the horrors of the war, he retreats into his dream world.
Genre(s): War Story; Political Fiction; Domestic Fiction.

Arguedas, Jose Maria

5904. *Yawar Fiesta.* Trans. Frances H. Barraclough. Austin: University of Texas, 1985. 224 pp.
In the 1930s, a remote community of the Peruvian Andes goes into a tumult when the national government outlaws the Yawar fiesta, the annual bloody bullfight.
Genre(s): Domestic Fiction.

Azuela, Mariano

5905. *The Trials of a Respectable Family.* Trans. Frances Kellam Hendrick. 1918. San Antonio, TX: Trinity University Press, 1963. 98 pp.
A wealthy Mexican family begins to lose its money, and some of its members ignore revolutionary changes, and the others feel responsiblity for their society's breakdown.
Genre(s): War Story.

5906. *The Underdogs.* Trans. Frederick H. Fornoff. 1915. Pittsburgh, PA: University of Pittsburgh Press, 1992. 165 pp.
Demetrio Macias becomes a federal general, and Luis Cervantes changes from an idealistic medical student to a greedy thief as the two attract a group of misfits to their army fighting in the Mexican Revolution.
Award(s): Prize in Letters from Mexican National Society for Arts and Sciences.
Genre(s): War Story.

◆ May be suitable for young adult readers

Becker, Stephen D.

5907. *A Rendezvous in Haiti.* New York: Norton, 1987. 213 pp.
Two men who were allies in World War I find themselves on different sides during an attempted revolution in Haiti when one of them captures the fiancée of the other.

Benitez, Sandra

◆ 5908. *Bitter Grounds.* New York: Hyperion, 1997. 445 pp.
Three generations of El Salvadoran women endure the political uncertainty of the years between 1933 and 1977, and experience differences in education, social class, and economic benefits.
Genre(s): Political Fiction; Family Saga.

Berman, Sabina

5909. *Bubbeh.* Pittsburgh, PA: Latin American Studies, 1998. 96 pp.
Sabita, a young Jewish girl growing up in Mexico City during the 1960s, tries to understand her relationship to her family, including her demoralized grandfather who lost everything in Poland when the family fled the Nazi invasion.
Genre(s): Domestic Fiction; Bildungsroman (Coming of Age).

Bernadro, Jose Raul

5910. *The Secret of the Bulls.* New York: Simon and Schuster, 1996. 320 pp.
In prerevolutionary Cuba, Maximiliano and Delores come to Havana with their four children after a hurricane and experience the atmosphere and attitudes of the city.

Blanco, Evangeline

5911. *Caribe.* New York: Doubleday, 1998. 320 pp.
Dr. Rafael Rodriguez hates the racial prejudice of the white Puerto Ricans, and he, a black physician, sires illegitimate children in hopes of causing a revolution against the prevailing attitudes.
Award(s): University of California at Irvine's Chicano/Latino Literary Contest.
Genre(s): Adventure Story; Medical Novel.

Bridal, Tessa

◆ 5912. *The Tree of Red Stars.* Minneapolis, MN: Milkweed, 1997. 300 pp.
In the 1970s, wealthy Magdalena Ortega Grey lives in Montevideo, Uruguay, where she becomes a university student who joins the urban-guerrilla Tupamaro movement and suffers for her choice.
Genre(s): Political Fiction; Bildungsroman (Coming of Age).

Buckley, William F. Jr.

◆ 5913. *See You Later Alligator.* Garden City, NY: Doubleday, 1985. 351 pp.
Blackford Oakes goes to Cuba during the missle crisis where he meets with Che Guevara in Havana.
Genre(s): Biographical Fiction; Spy Fiction.

Cabrera, Infante G.

5914. *Infante's Inferno.* Trans. Suzanne Jill Levine. New York: Harper and Row, 1984. 410 pp.
The narrator, unnamed, tells of his adolescent development in the seedy area of Havana during the 1940s.
Genre(s): Biographical Fiction.

5915. *Three Trapped Tigers.* Trans. Donald Gardner and Susan Jill Levine. New York: Harper, 1971. 416 pp.
The saloon society in 1950s Havana includes journalists, prostitutes, and performers.

Callado, Antönio

5916. *Don Juan's Bar.* Trans. Barbara Shelby. New York: Knopf, 1972. 288 pp.
Twelve Brazilians meet in Don Juan's Bar in Rio de Janeiro and rob banks in weak attempts to finance Che Guevara's revolution in Bolivia during the late 1960s.
Genre(s): Political Fiction.

5917. *Quarup.* Trans. Barbara Shelby. New York: Knopf, 1970. 559 pp.
The priest Father Nando works with people in various areas of Brazil during the 1950s and 1960s, and after President Goulart's government collapses, he becomes a fugitive.
Genre(s): Political Fiction.

Cantor, Jay

5918. *The Death of Che Guevara.* New York: Vintage, 1984. 577 pp.
Che Guevara, an asthmatic child, comes to a revolutionary consciousness and wants justice for Latin America.
Genre(s): Biographical Fiction; War Story.

Castellanos, Rosario

5919. *The Book of Lamentations.* Trans. Esther Allen. Nyack, NY: Marsilio, 1996. 402 pp.
In the Mexican state of Chiapas during the 1930s, an Indian uprising precipitated by greed and opression occurs.
Genre(s): Domestic Fiction; Political Fiction.

5920. *The Nine Guardians.* Trans. Irene Nicholson. Columbia, LA: Readers International, 1992. 272 pp.
A girl of seven describes those who look after her, including her landowner father, her mother, and her nanny, when the Indians rise against the wealthy for their rights.
Genre(s): War Story.

Condé, Maryse

5921. *Tree of Life.* Trans. Victoria Reiter. New York: Ballantine, 1992. 384 pp.
Albert Louis, who has left Guadeloupe and the sugar cane plantation to work on the Panama Canal, falls in

love, but after his wife dies, he wanders angrily and aimlessly.
Genre(s): Love Story.

Constant, Paule

5922. *The Governor's Daughter.* Lincoln: University of Nebraska Press, 1998. 160 pp.
In the 1920s, Chrietienne goes with her parents to French Guiana where her father suffers guilt for the deaths of his soldiers in World War I and her mother shows compassion only for the dying.
Genre(s): Domestic Fiction; Bildungsroman (Coming of Age).

Costantini, Humberto

5923. *The Long Night of Francisco Sanctis.*
Trans. Norman Thomas di Giovanni. New York: Harper, 1985. 184 pp.
In Argentina during the early 1970s, a telephone call terrifies a former student activist because dissenters have been disappearing at night.
Genre(s): Political Fiction.

Cunningham, John

5924. *The Rainbow Runner.* New York: Tor, 1992. 275 pp.
In 1913, Jacko O'Donohue, a Los Angeles detective, escorts a jeweled monstrance back to Mexico during the revolution there and experiences deceit and betrayal while trying to conclude his mission.
Genre(s): Mystery; War Story.

Day, Douglas

5925. *The Prison Notebooks of Ricardo Flores Magon.* New York: Harcourt, 1991. 270 pp.
Ricardo Flores Magon, Mexican journalist and anarchist, calls for a revolt against Mexico's dictators and spends much of his life in jail, dying in Leavenworth Penitentiary in 1922 under unexplained circumstances.
Genre(s): War Story.

De Boissire, Ralph

5926. *Crown Jewel.* New York: Schocken, 1981. 364 pp.
In Trinidad, preceding World War II, citizens such as Joe Elias, Ben le Maitre, and Andre de Coudray begin to question British imperialism and want to rule themselves.

de Queiroz, Rachel

5927. *Dora, Doralina.* New York: Avon, 1984. 228 pp.
Against the background of World War II, Dora remembers her youth as the repressed daughter of northeast Brazilian plantation owners.
Genre(s): War Story.

De Treviño, Elizabeth

5928. *The House on Bitterness Street.* New York: Doubleday, 1970. 336 pp.

Marisa becomes obsessed with the house in which her family lived before the Mexican Revolution, and even during her liasion with General Soto, she is determined to own it.
Genre(s): War Story.

Detrez, Conrad

5929. *Zone of Fire.* San Diego, CA: Harcourt, 1986. 266 pp.
A French volcanologist arrives in Managua, Nicaragua, in 1972 to study an eruption but interacts with several Sandinistans and finds that other fires burn in the country.
Genre(s): Political Fiction.

Donoso, José

5930. *Curfew.* Trans. Alfred Mac Adam. New York: Weidenfeld and Nicolson, 1988. 309 pp.
When Manungo Vera, an international popular singer, returns to Chile to attend Pablo Neruda's widow's funeral, he unwittingly becomes involved in the Pinochet regime politics.
Genre(s): Political Fiction.

Dorfman, Ariel

5931. *Hard Rain.* Columbia, LA: Readers International, 1990. 270 pp.
In the middle of the Chilean revolution in the early 1970s, writers try to record its varied aspects.
Genre(s): War Story.

Durand, Loup

5932. *Jaguar.* New York: Villard, 1991. 336 pp.
Jaguar, a Brazilian playboy, falls in love with an American, and a Russian spy uses the two when he makes Jaguar the unwitting suspect for murders committed around the world.
Genre(s): Spy Fiction; Adventure Story.

Esquivel, Laura

5933. *Like Water for Chocolate.* Trans. Carol Christensen and Thomas Christensen. Garden City, NY: Doubleday, 1992. 245 pp.
At the beginning of the 20th century, Tita, the youngest of three daughters, is expected to serve her mother for the rest of her life, but in order to show her love to Pedro, who is engaged to her sister, Tita cooks for him.
Genre(s): Love Story.

Essex, Olga Berrocal

◆ 5934. *Delia's Way.* Houston, TX: Arte Publico, 1998. 176 pp.
In Panama during the 1950s, Delia's older sister Mara Elena dominates her until Delia discovers that Maria Elena is illegimate and only her half-sister.
Genre(s): Bildungsroman (Coming of Age).

Ferré, Rosario

5935. *Eccentric Neighborhoods.* New York: Farrar, Straus and Giroux, 1998. 352 pp.

Elvira Vernet describes her mother's family of landed gentry and sugar plantation owners and her father's family of politically ambitious builders who tried to rebuild Puerto Rico when Americans gave money for housing projects.
Genre(s): Domestic Fiction; Political Fiction; Family Saga.

5936. *The House on the Lagoon.* New York: Farrar, Straus and Giroux, 1995. 320 pp.
The families of Isabel and her husband, Quintin, reveal the class and race conflicts in Puerto Rico and the changes in relationships between the country and the United States and Spain.
Award(s): National Book Critics Circle Award.
Genre(s): Domestic Fiction.

Florence, Ronald

5937. *Zeppelin.* New York: Arbor House, 1982. 379 pp.
In 1936, the German Third Reich sends the *Graf Zeppelin* to Brazil with gold to purchase planes for use in the Spanish Civil War, and with vaccination serum for needy children to be used as a propaganda ploy.
Genre(s): Political Fiction; War Story.

Foster, Cecil

◆ 5938. *No Man in the House.* New York: Ballantine, 1992. 304 pp.
Howard Prescod and his two brothers live with their grandmother on Barbados, and while their parents go to England, Howard's friends know that no man lives in the house.
Genre(s): Bildungsroman (Coming of Age).

Fraxedes, J. Joaquin

5939. *The Lonely Crossing of Juan Cabrera.* New York: St. Martin's, 1993. 176 pp.
Refugees such as Juan Cabrera, a physics and astronomy professor, try to cross the 90 miles of water from Cuba to Florida, using any means of flotation, in order to escape the government.
Genre(s): Political Fiction.

Fuentes, Carlos

5940. *The Death of Artemio Cruz.* Trans. Alfred Mac Adam. New York: Farrar, Straus and Giroux, 1964. 251 pp.
As he lies dying, the rich landowner and newspaper publisher of Mexico, Artemio Cruz, recalls his life and his participation in the Mexican Revolution.

5941. *The Old Gringo.* New York: Farrar, Straus and Giroux, 1985. 199 pp.
An old American author, perhaps Ambrose Bierce, disappears in Mexico in 1913 where he becomes a father figure to an American governess and a general in Pancho Villa's army.
Genre(s): Biographical Fiction.

Fuller, Vernella

5942. *Unlike Normal Women.* New York: Trafalgar Square, 1995. 330 pp.
In Jamaica during the early 1960s, the land-owning Clearys continue to use the country women as concubines, but women, including Aunt Vie, Azora, and Miss Dee, reject the traditional ways.
Genre(s): Domestic Fiction.

Galindo, Sergio

5943. *Otilia's Body.* Trans. Carolyn Brushwood and John Brushwood. Austin: University of Texas Press, 1994. 240 pp.
Otilia, an upper-class woman with a beautiful body and a homely face, becomes obsessed with an outlaw whom she helps recover from a gunshot wound during Mexico's revolutionary turbulence in the first half of the 20th century.
Award(s): Xavier Villaurrutia Prize.
Genre(s): War Story.

Galvao, Patricia

5944. *Industrial Park.* Trans. Elizabeth Jackson and K. David Jackson. Lincoln: University of Nebraska Press, 1993. 154 pp.
In the 1930s, three Brazilian workers, Corina (a half white), Eleonora, and Otavia, try to survive in the changing city of Sao Paulo as they live through workers' strikes and their own entanglements with men.
Genre(s): Political Fiction.

Garcia, Christina

5945. *Dreaming in Cuban.* New York: Knopf, 1992. 288 pp.
The Cuban revolution affects three generations of women in the del Pino family who retain a balance in their lives between the real and the surreal.
Genre(s): War Story; Domestic Fiction.

Garcia Marquez, Gabriel

5946. *Love in the Time of Cholera.* Trans. Edith Grossman. New York: Knopf, 1988. 348 pp.
Fermina Daza and Florentino Ariza consummate their passion at the beginning of the 20th century after having waited over 50 years.
Award(s): *Los Angeles Times* Book Award.
Genre(s): Love Story.

Garro, Elena

5947. *Recollections of Things to Come.* Trans. Ruth L. C. Simms. Austin: University of Texas Press, 1970. 289 pp.
The town of Ixtepec in southern Mexico narrates the details of the Cristero rebellion during the 1920s.
Genre(s): War Story.

Ghose, Zulfikar

5948. *A Different World.* New York: Viking, 1985. 318 pp.

In the early 20th century, Gregorio Peixoto da Silvia Xavier is caught between Brazil's military dictatorship and the guerrillas who would destroy it in the sequel to *The Beautiful Empire*.
Genre(s): War Story; Political Fiction; Love Story.

Giardinelli, Mempo

5949. *Sultry Moon.* Trans. Patricia J. Duncan. Pittsburg, PA: Latin American Studies, 1998. 128 pp.
In the late 1970s, while Argentina's military dictator rules, Ramiro Bernardez returns from Paris after eight years to much acclaim, falls in love, commits murder, and must again leave the country.
Genre(s): Love Story.

Gombrowicz, Witold

5950. *Trans-Atlantyk.* Trans. Carolyn French and Nina Karsov. New Haven, CT: Yale University Press, 1994. 122 pp.
A Polish author on a trans-Atlantic cruise finds himself in Argentina when World War II erupts.
Genre(s): Biographical Fiction; War Story.

Gonzales, Laurence

5951. *El Vago.* New York: Atheneum, 1983. 309 pp.
Agustín Mentira becomes a bandit but ends up as a revolutionary in the Mexican Revolution before he finds that his allies are no more loyal than his enemies.
Genre(s): Biographical Fiction.

Graham, James

◆ 5952. *The Wrath of God.* New York: Doubleday, 1971. 277 pp.
In the 1920s, Emmet Keogh escapes from Ireland to Mexico, meets a dishonest bartender who offers him a deal, is almost killed for protecting a young Indian girl, and when he is rescued, enjoys a series of other criminal chases.
Genre(s): Adventure Story.

Griffin, W. E. B.

5953. *Honor Bound.* New York: Putnam, 1993. 474 pp.
Marine Captain Frade, in Buenos Aires after Guadalcanal, encounters the father he never knew and a beautiful girl. (*Series:* The Corps, 7)
Genre(s): War Story.

Hennessy, Max

◆ 5954. *The Crimson Wind.* New York: Atheneum, 1985. 256 pp.
While covering the 1911 revolution in Mexico, British journalist Harley Marquis meets Villa, Zapata, and Campo and also falls in love.
Genre(s): War Story.

Higgins, Jack

5955. *The Last Place God Made.* New York: Holt, 1972. 191 pp.
In 1938, a former World War I pilot attempts to rescue nuns from native Indians in the Amazon jungle.
Genre(s): Adventure Story.

Hornman, Wim

5956. *The Stones Cry Out.* Trans. J. Maxwell Brownjohn. Philadelphia: Lippincott, 1971. 323 pp.
The Catholic Church silences the rebel Antonio Valencia (representing Camilo Torres) in an imaginary country (Colombia) during the 1960s, and he must turn to rebel leaders for support.
Genre(s): Biographical Fiction.

Ibargengoitia, Jorge

5957. *The Lightning of August.* New York: Avon, 1986. 128 pp.
In the 1920s the Mexican military establishment becomes involved in a struggle over the presidential sash.
Genre(s): Political Fiction; Satire.

Icaza, Jorge

5958. *Huasipungo.* Trans. Mervyn Savill. London: D. Dobson, 1962. 171 pp.
Andrés Chiliquinga works on the road that Alfonso Pereira builds through the Andes to attract American investors, but when the Indians revolt against their poor treatment, government soldiers murder them all.
Genre(s): Political Fiction.

Irving, Clifford

5959. *Tom Mix and Pancho Villa.* New York: St. Martin's Press, 1982. 463 pp.
Tom Mix, a movie star cowboy, supposedly spends four years riding with Pancho Villa in the Mexican Revolution and believes they are the best years of his life.
Genre(s): Biographical Fiction.

Jackson, Marian J. A.

5960. *The Sunken Treasure.* New York: Walker, 1994. 180 pp.
Abigail Danforth accompanies millionaire Malcolm Tibault and his other guests on his yacht sailing from Panama to New Orleans, and when he dies mysteriously, Abigail has problems investigating because the captain buries the body at sea.
Genre(s): Mystery.

Jose, Nicholas

5961. *The Custodians.* New York: St. Martin's, 1998. 512 pp.
In 20th-century Australia, the government places aborigines in schools away from their parents and their culture, and as Cleve grows up, he must deal with this aspect of his past.
Genre(s): Family Saga.

Kaplan, Andrew

5962. *War of the Raven*. New York: Simon and Schuster, 1990. 387 pp.
As the war escalates in Europe, some residents of Buenos Aires are neutral, but others have taken sides, and an American goes there to protect an important source of information for the Allies.
Genre(s): War Story; Political Fiction.

Kozameh, Alicia

5963. *Steps under Water*. Trans. David E. Davis. Los Angeles: University of California Press, 1996. 161 pp.
The narrator, imprisoned in the 1970s, during Argentina's dirty war, tells of the experiences of various victims.
Genre(s): War Story; Political Fiction.

Krich, John

◆ 5964. *A Totally Free Man*. New York: Simon and Schuster, 1988. 171 pp.
Fidel Castro records the story of his life story onto a tape recorder.
Genre(s): Biographical Fiction.

Lewis, Norman

◆ 5965. *Cuban Passage*. New York: Pantheon, 1982. 256 pp.
Dick Frazer has been isolated in Cuba, but as the end of Batista's regime nears, the legal system in Cuba almost leads to Frazer's death.
Genre(s): Bildungsroman (Coming of Age); Political Fiction.

Lieberman, Herbert H.

5966. *The Climate of Hell*. New York: Simon and Schuster, 1978. 383 pp.
An ex-agent for Israel searches the jungles of Paraguay for Nazis protected by a South American dictator.
Genre(s): Adventure Story.

Limón, Graciela

5967. *In Search of Bernab*. Houston, TX: Arte Publico, 1993. 161 pp.
When raped by her grandfather, Luz Delcano bears a son, Lucio, who grows up to become head of the death squads during the 1980s civil strife of El Salvador, while Luz's other illegitimate son, Bernab, becomes a priest hunted by the same death squads.
Genre(s): Adventure Story; Political Fiction.

Lord, Shirley

5968. *Golden Hill*. New York: Crown, 1982. 544 pp.
Rose Bracken, the white-skinned daughter of a native family in Trinidad, attracts the master of the wealthiest estate there and their marriage in the early 20th century creates political as well as personal intrigues.
Genre(s): Political Fiction.

Martinez, Tomas Eloy

5969. *The Peron Novel*. New York: Pantheon, 1988. 357 pp.
The regime of Juan Peron includes political intrigue and moral decay in contrast to the charisma of his wife, Evita.
Genre(s): Biographical Fiction; Political Fiction.

5970. *Santa Evita*. New York: Knopf, 1996. 352 pp.
After Evita dies and her husband has her remains preserved, those who have contact with her corpse seem to have bad luck.
Genre(s): Biographical Fiction.

Massie, Allan

5971. *The Sins of the Father*. New York: Carroll and Graf, 1992. 304 pp.
In 1964, Becky and Franz meet in Buenos Aires and marry, and afterwards, when they introduce their parents, they discover that Franz's father Rudi was a Nazi and Eli, Becky's father, survived a concentration camp and wants all Nazis obliterated.
Genre(s): Legal Story.

Mastretta, Angeles

5972. *Mexican Bolero*. Trans. Ann Wright. Englewood Cliffs, NJ: Penguin, 1989. 288 pp.
Catalina, a young farm girl, marries General Ascencio while he is increasing his power base in 1926.
Genre(s): Political Fiction.

McCarthy, Cormac

5973. *All the Pretty Horses*. New York: Knopf, 1992. 301 pp.
John Grady Cole, 16, leaves Texas for Mexico in 1950 and becomes an essential vaquero in a hacienda's program.
Award(s): National Book Critics Circle Award; National Book Award.
Genre(s): Adventure Story.

McCunn, Ruthanne Lum

5974. *Sole Survivor*. San Francisco: Design, 1985. 235 pp.
Poon Lim is the only survivor when the British ship *Benlomond* is torpedoed on November 23, 1942, off the coast of South America, and he survives for 133 days before a Brazilian fisherman rescues him.
Genre(s): Biographical Fiction; War Story; Sea Story.

Meyer, Nicholas, and Barry Jay Kaplan

5975. *Black Orchid*. New York: Dial, 1977. 310 pp.
Harry Kancaid, who goes up the Amazon in the late 1800s to break a monopoly of two families by stealing rubber seeds, has his secret discovered by his new lover.
Genre(s): Adventure Story.

Montalbón, Manuel Vázquez

5976. *Galindez*. Trans. Carol Christensen and Thomas Christensen. New York: Atheneum, 1992. 320 pp.
Jésus Galindez, a Basque nationalist, comes to the Dominican Republic after the Spanish Civil War but objects to Trujillo's rule and goes to New York where he writes hostile articles about him.
Genre(s): Political Fiction.

Montemayor, Carlos

5977. *Gambusino*. Trans. John Copeland. Chicago: Academy, 1997. 128 pp.
Alfredo Motenegro is an itinerant miner who wants to find the ultimate strike in Mexico and spends 40 years searching.
Award(s): El Nacional's 50th Anniversary Novel Contest.
Genre(s): Political Fiction.

Mueller, Marnie

5978. *Green Fires*. Willimantic, CT: Curbstone, 1994. 318 pp.
When Annie Saunders returns to Ecuador with her German husband in 1969 after having worked as a Peace Corps volunteer in the early 1960s, she tries to reconcile the difficulties of her life there with the needs of the natives.
Genre(s): Political Fiction.

Myers, Edward

5979. *The Mountain Made of Light*. New York: Penguin, 1992. 416 pp.
The anthropologist Jesse O'Keefe goes to Peru after World War I to find a village to study, and he discovers an isolated community in the Andes.
Genre(s): Adventure Story.

Naipaul, V. S.

5980. *Miguel Street*. New York: Vanguard, 1959. 171 pp.
In the 1940s, eccentrics live in the slums of Port-of-Spain.

5981. *The Mystic Masseur*. New York: Vintage, 1984. 218 pp.
In the 1940s, Ganesh Ramsumair fails at several jobs until he tries faith healing, at which he wildly succeeds.
Genre(s): Religious Fiction.

5982. *The Suffrage of Elvira*. New York: Vintage, 1985. 206 pp.
During the 1940s, Surujpat Harbans, an old, absentminded man, runs for office with the help of a strong campaign manager.
Genre(s): Political Fiction.

Noah, Robert

5983. *The Man Who Stole the Mona Lisa*. New York: St. Martin's, 1998. 256 pp.
In 1911, Marquis de Valfierno, a Buenos Aires swindler and his partner, a painter who only copies other people's work, plot to steal the *Mona Lisa* from the Louvre.
Genre(s): Mystery; Adventure Story.

Nunez, Elizabeth

5984. *Bruised Hibiscus*. New York: Amistad, 1994. 192 pp.
Rosa and Zuela, once childhood friends and both suffering from abusive husbands, meet again after a murdered white woman washes up on their shore of Trinidad.
Genre(s): Domestic Fiction.

Olsen, Austin

5985. *Corcho Bliss*. New York: Simon and Schuster, 1972. 192 pp.
Corcho Bliss, a desperado, becomes the bodyguard to a gunrunner trying to sell guns to a revolutionary general.
Genre(s): Adventure Story.

Ortiz, Adalberto

5986. *Juyungo*. Trans. Susan Hill and Jonathan Tittler. 1942. New York: Three Continents, 1983. 227 pp.
The maze of early 20th-century politics in Ecuador appears in the lives of the characters through magical realism.
Genre(s): Political Fiction.

Patten, Lewis B.

5987. *Villa's Rifles*. Garden City, NY: Doubleday, 1977. 183 pp.
Pancho Villa wants guns, and the North Americans want money.

Pausewang, Gudrun

5988. *Bolivian Wedding*. Trans. Denver Lindley. New York: Knopf, 1971. 256 pp.
On November 1, 1934, Pablo and Gorina marry in the morning and then, in the afternoon, join the annual festival to honor the dead, but a veteran outside the cemetery berates the couple since Pablo will leave to fight in the war with Paraguay in which the veteran was blinded.
Genre(s): Domestic Fiction.

Plain, Belva

◆ 5989. *Eden Burning*. New York: Delacorte, 1982. 451 pp.
The Francis family has lived on St. Felice in the Caribbean for 300 years, but they face changes related to racial problems and economic revolutions.
Genre(s): Family Saga.

Poniatowska, Elena

5990. *Dear Diego*. New York: Pantheon, 1986. 86 pp.

◆ May be suitable for young adult readers

Diego Rivera's common-law wife writes him from Paris after their son dies in infancy, and she sacrifices her career for his.
Genre(s): Biographical Fiction.

5991. *Tinisima.* New York: Farrar, Straus and Giroux, 1996. 256 pp.
When photographer and political activitst Tina Modotti's husband is assassinated in 1929, Mexican authorities arrest her and question her about his murderer.
Genre(s): Biographical Fiction; Political Fiction.

Puig, Manuel

5992. *Heartbreak Tango.* Trans. Suzanne Jill Levine. New York: Dutton, 1973. 224 pp.
Nélida Fernández, Miss Spring of 1936 in a small Argentinian town, has married into a boring life by 1947 but continues to fantasize about a dead lover.

Ramis, Magali Garcia

◆ **5993.** *Happy Days, Uncle Sergio.* Fredonia, NY: White Pine, 1995. 176 pp.
Lidia and her brother live in a household of all females in Puerto Rico during the 1950s until Uncle Sergio arrives and introduces them to the outside world.
Genre(s): Bildungsroman (Coming of Age).

Raspail, J.

◆ **5994.** *Who Will Remember the People.* Trans. Jeremy Leggatt. San Francisco: Mercury House, 1988. 213 pp.
In the early 20th century, Lafko is the remaining survivor of the Keweskar, the natives who were probably the first to cross the Bering Strait and travel south to South America and Tierra del Fuego.

Revueltas, Jose

5995. *Human Mourning.* Minneapolis: University of Minnesota Press, 1990. 208 pp.
A small group of Indian peasants flees a rising flood after the Mexican Revolution, finding shelter wherever available and discussing the conflict between the Federales and the Cristeros, church-sponsored counter-revolutionaries.
Genre(s): Political Fiction; War Story.

Reynolds, Steve, and Gene Carver

5996. *The Murder of Che Guevara.* Soddy Daisy, TN: Wild Geese, 1983. 159 pp.
In 1965, two American mercenaries trying to rescue Che Guevara see Bolivian soldiers capture and execute him.
Genre(s): Biographical Fiction.

Riesco, Laura

◆ **5997.** *Ximena at the Crossroad.* Trans. Mary G. Berg. Fredonia, NY: White Pine, 1998. 272 pp.
Young and frail but wealthy Ximena stays home and reads everything, but when Indians strike, she becomes curious and investigates their revolt.
Award(s): Best Novel of the Year in Peru.

Genre(s): Bildungsroman (Coming of Age); War Story.

Rosenblatt, Paul

5998. *The Sun in Capricorn.* Wichita, KS: Watermark, 1989. 185 pp.
In the 1970s, Jonathan, a visiting lecturer in Rio de Janeiro, becomes involved in the political problems of the city while trying to reconnect emotionally with his wife.
Genre(s): Political Fiction.

Sabato, Ernesto

5999. *The Angel of Darkness.* Trans. Andrew Hurley. New York: Ballantine, 1991. 448 pp.
In Buenos Aires during 1973, a group of German refugees, alcoholics, and Hungarian aristocrats are part of the political turmoil of the country.
Genre(s): Political Fiction.

Saint Exupéry, Antoine de

6000. *Night Flight.* Trans. Stuart Gilbert. New York: Appleton, 1932. 198 pp.
In the early days of aviation, the chief of the Buenos Aires airport makes certain that night flights of mail leave on time, even after three of his planes crash in the Andes.
Genre(s): Adventure Story.

Schoendoerffer, Pierre

6001. *Farewell to the King.* Trans. Xan Fielding. New York: Stein and Day, 1970. 256 pp.
During World War II, a British officer, Sergeant Learoyd, makes himself king of the primitive Murut tribe in Borneo, and when a young botanist spies on him for the Allies, they unite to overcome the Japanese but have serious difficulties.
Award(s): Prix Interalli.
Genre(s): War Story.

Schwarz-Bart, Simone

6002. *The Bridge of Beyond.* Trans. Barbara Bray. New York: Atheneum, 1974. 246 pp.
Telumee's grandmother raises her on a small island where the only connection to civilization is a footbridge.
Genre(s): Domestic Fiction.

Scofield, Sandra

6003. *Gringa.* Sag Harbor, NY: Permanent Press, 1989. 267 pp.
Sent to Mexico for an abortion in 1968, Abilene Painter becomes involved with radicals and revolutionaries protesting in student demonstrations.
Genre(s): Political Fiction.

Shorris, Earl

6004. *Under the Fifth Sun.* New York: Delacorte, 1980. 622 pp.
Pancho Villa, a poor farm boy and mestizo, becomes a bandit and a revolutionary leader.
Genre(s): Biographical Fiction.

Skarmeta, Antonio

6005. *Burning Patience.* Trans. Katherine Silver. New York: Pantheon, 1987. 118 pp.
A Chilean postman during Allende's administration of the early 1970s tries to woo his love with Pablo Neruda's poetry.
Genre(s): Biographical Fiction; Romance.

Taibo, Paco Ignacio II

6006. *Calling All Heroes.* Trans. John Mitchell and Ruth Mitchell de Aguilar. New York: Plover, 1990. 113 pp.
A hospitalized journalist reflects on the student protests in Mexico during 1968 and their violent conflicts with the police.
Genre(s): Political Fiction.

6007. *The Shadow of the Shadow.* New York: Viking, 1991. 233 pp.
Four friends in Mexico City during 1922 meet nightly to play dominoes, and they soon find themselves involved in a series of murders that seem to be related.
Genre(s): Mystery.

Thoby-Marcelin, Philippe, and Pierre Marcelin

6008. *All Men Are Mad.* Trans. Eva Thoby-Marcelin. New York: Farrar, Straus and Giroux, 1970. 192 pp.
Catholics and voodoo advocates clash in Haiti during 1942, and all are guilty of wrongs to humanity.
Genre(s): Religious Fiction.

Thornton, Lawrence

6009. *Imagining Argentina.* New York: Doubleday, 1987. 214 pp.
Carlos Rueda, a prominent children's playwright in Buenos Aires, Argentina, claims to have visions and joins the mothers who protest in the Plaza de Mayor after the Argentinian generals begin their reign of terror in 1976.
Award(s): Ernest Hemingway Foundation Award.
Genre(s): Political Fiction; War Story.

6010. *Naming the Spirits.* New York: Doubleday, 1995. 224 pp.
A young girl, although traumatized, survives the violence of one night during Argentina's 1976 Dirty War while 12 others, before they are killed, recall their last days and hope she will tell others about them.
Genre(s): Political Fiction; War Story.

Toíbín, Colm

6011. *The Story of the Night.* New York: Henry Holt, 1997. 312 pp.
In the early 1980s, while Argentina recovers from the Falklands War, Richard Garay, an English tutor, meets Claudio Canetto, a possible next president of the country, and forms a liaison with Canetto's son.
Genre(s): Political Fiction; Love Story.

Traven, B.

6012. *Trozas.* Trans. Hugh Young. Chicago: I. R. Dee, 1994. 265 pp.
Andres Ugaldo works under the Mexican system of peonage during the Diaz regime before it is outlawed in 1917.
Genre(s): War Story.

Unger, Douglas

◆ 6013. *El Yanqui.* New York: Harper and Row, 1986. 302 pp.
An exchange student from Long Island goes to Argentina in the late 1960s and becomes involved in its political unrest.
Genre(s): Political Fiction.

Varga Llosa, Mario

6014. *Who Killed Palominolero?* Trans. Alfred Mac Adam. New York: Farrar, Straus and Giroux, 1987. 151 pp.
In the 1950s, someone crucifies Peruvian Air Force recruit Palomino Molero, and the subsequent investigation reveals the problems in Molero's life.
Genre(s): Mystery.

Washburn, L. J.

◆ 6015. *Riders of the Monte.* Boston: Little, Brown, 1990. 174 pp.
Curtis Daniels, wanted in Texas for murder, follows Guerrero's bandits who rob and kill both the rich and the poor, but with little pleasure in killing, he leaves to avenge other deaths and rescue Angelina from Guerrero.
Genre(s): Western Fiction.

Wilder, Robert

6016. *An Affair of Honor.* New York: Putnam, 1969. 383 pp.
A black man and a white man use each other to gain power in the Bahama Islands.
Genre(s): Political Fiction.

Wilson, Carter

6017. *Treasures on Earth.* New York: Knopf, 1981. 243 pp.
Willie Hickler goes with Hiram Bingham and discovers the Inca city of Michu Picchu in 1911 while discovering things about himself as well.
Genre(s): Biographical Fiction; Adventure Story.

Winegardner, Mark

6018. *The Veracruz Blues.* New York: Viking, 1996. 251 pp.
In 1946, a Mexican businessman buys the best baseball players, regardless of race, to start teams in Mexico, but he learns that the best individual players do not always form the best teams.
Genre(s): Sports Fiction.

◆ May be suitable for young adult readers

Wright, Rosalind

6019. *Veracruz.* New York: Harper and Row, 1986. 472 pp.

In 1911 Beatrice lives with her husband Lawrence on a coffee plantation in Mexico when her sister, a woman she dislikes, arrives after Francisco Madero has been elected president.

Genre(s): War Story; Domestic Fiction.

Yamashita, Karen Tei

6020. *Brazil-Maru.* Minneapolis, MN: Coffee House, 1992. 248 pp.

Japanese immigrants go to Brazil before World War II to start farming communities, and Japanese aggression during the war creates hostile attitudes toward them.

Genre(s): War Story.

Yáñez, Agustín

6021. *The Edge of the Storm.* Trans. Ethel Brinton. Austin: University of Texas Press, 1963. 332 pp.

In the early 20th century, the parish priest and his curate transfer their own fear of death to their Mexican village parishioners and ignore the sounds of the revolution.

Genre(s): War Story.

6022. *The Lean Lands.* Trans. Ethel Brinton. Austin: University of Texas Press, 1968. 328 pp.

In the early 1920s, farmers in Jalisco, Mexico, must face the changes in the area resulting from the revolution.

Zollinger, Norman

◆ 6023. *Not of War Only.* New York: Forge, 1994. 416 pp.

Jorge Martinez fights as a young soldier in the Mexican Revolution after Corey Lane, an American lawyer, chases him across the border at the outset of the war.

Genre(s): Love Story; War Story.

Thailand, Cambodia, and Malaysia

Before 1900

Bullen, Fiona

6024.*To Catch the Sun.* New York: St. Martin's, 1990. 528 pp.
As a privileged child living in Singapore before World War II, Ursula spends the war hiding from the Japanese in a native village, but after being orphaned, she returns to England and endures the trials of unpleasant relatives and a bad marriage.
Genre(s): Epic Literature.

Conrad, Joseph

6025.*The Rescue.* New York: Doubleday, 1920. 469 pp.
Tom Lingard wants to gain wealth in Malaya by dominating the market.
Genre(s): Political Fiction; Adventure Story.

Leonowens, Anna

◆ 6026. *The Romance of the Harem.* 1872. Charlottesville: Unive, 1991. 285 pp.
Anna Leonowens relates stories of her experiences in the court of the king of Siam in the mid-19th century, and these tales become the basis for the musical *The King and I.*
Genre(s): Biographical Fiction.

Nhat Hanh, Thich

6027.*Hermitage among the Clouds.* Trans. Mobi Warren and Annabel Laity. Berkeley, CA: Parallax, 1993. 140 pp.
In the 14th century Amazing Jewel, daughter of king Tran Nhan Tong, pursues peace in Cham, south of Hue, in order to start her new country after her father defends the Viet against the Mongols.
Genre(s): Political Fiction.

1900 and After

Anderson, Jack, and Bill Pronzini

◆ 6028. *The Cambodia File.* New York: Doubleday, 1981. 431 pp.
When Pol Pot's regime, the Khmer Rouge, takes over Cambodia in 1975, Than Kim barely survives the ensuing madness.
Genre(s): War Story.

Berent, Mark

◆ 6029.*Eagle Station.* New York: Putnam, 1992. 396 pp.
Air Force pilots continue to protect Eagle Station's radar in Vietnam during 1968, in the sequel to *Phantom Leader,* while prisoners-of-war wait to hear some signal that they will be rescued.
Genre(s): War Story.

Bunch, Chris, and Allan Cole

6030.*A Reckoning for Kings.* New York: Atheneum, 1987. 384 pp.
In 1967 and 1968, military on both sides of the Vietnamese conflict struggle to kill each other as the Tet Offensive climaxes their situation.
Genre(s): War Story.

Butler, Robert Olen

◆ 6031. *On Distant Ground.* New York: Knopf, 1985. 218 pp.
After letting a Viet Cong suspect escape, a soldier faces a court-martial, but during the trial, he realizes that he may have left a child behind, and he returns to Vietnam.
Genre(s): War Story; Legal Story.

Chen-ho, Wang

6032.*Rose, Rose, I Love You.* Trans. Howard Goldblatt. New York: Columbia University, 1998. 192 pp.
Dong Siwen teaches English to a group of Taiwanese prostitutes so that they can earn American dollars from GIs on R&R from Vietnam.
Genre(s): War Story.

Cheong, Fiona

◆ 6033. *The Scent of the Gods.* New York: Norton, 1991. 224 pp.
Su Yen (Esha) is 11 and has grown up in an extended family as an orphan who is baffled by the diversity and differences among the people in her home, as Singapore becomes a nation in 1965.
Genre(s): Political Fiction; Domestic Fiction.

Clavell, James

6034. **King Rat.** Boston: Little, Brown, 1962. 363 pp.
King Rat breeds prison rats to sell for food in a Singapore prison during World War II and becomes the unofficial ruler of the camp.
Genre(s): War Story.

Cramer, Lenox

6035. **Slow Dance on the Killing Ground.** Medina, OH: Alpha, 1990. 272 pp.
During the Vietnam War, Special Forces work throughout Southeast Asia to get rid of undesirable factions of all kinds.
Genre(s): War Story; Political Fiction.

D'Alpuget, Blanche

◆ 6036. **Turtle Beach.** New York: Simon and Schuster, 1981. 286 pp.
A female Australian reporter and a Vietnamese refugee mother in Malaysia have different goals amid the cultural and ethnic strife of Malays, Chinese, Vietnamese, Indians, and Australians.
Award(s): The Age (Australia) Book Award; Festival Award for Literature.

Durand, Loup

6037. **The Angkor Massacre.** Trans. Helen R. Lane. New York: Morrow, 1983. 476 pp.
As the revolution of the Khmer begins, a group of disparate people become involved with Lara, a Frenchman whose family has been in Cambodia for eight generations.
Genre(s): Family Saga.

Farrell, J. G.

6038. **The Singapore Grip.** New York: Knopf, 1979. 431 pp.
After the Japanese arrive in Singapore during the 1930s, members of a British family realize too late that they are not invincible.
Genre(s): War Story.

Heinemann, Larry

6039. **Close Quarters.** New York: Farrar, Straus and Giroux, 1977. 335 pp.
When Philip Dosier goes to Vietnam, he has images of John Wayne's war movies in his mind, and when the Viet Cong do not wage war with the same rules, he has to develop a ruthlessness that he has never known.
Genre(s): War Story.

Keeley, Edmund

6040. **A Wilderness Called Peace.** New York: Simon and Schuster, 1985. 315 pp.
Sameth tries to survive in Cambodia in 1976 when the Vietnamese invade and occupy the country while her former lover, an American diplomat, is searching for her.
Genre(s): War Story.

Koch, Christopher J.

6041. **Highways to a War.** New York: Viking, 1995. 468 pp.
Mike Langford, a photographer, disappears in Cambodia in 1976, but he sends to a friend his diary on tape covering the years 1965 to 1975 when he worked in Indonesia.
Award(s): Miles Franklin Award.
Genre(s): War Story; Political Fiction.

Le Luu

6042. **A Time Far Past.** Trans. Ngo Vinh Hai. Amherst: University of Massachusetts Press, 1997. 280 pp.
Giang Minh Sai is married at the age of 10 in rural Vietnam during the 1960s, and he must cope with the changes in rural life as the French leave, the Vietnam War rages, and the Communists take over the government.
Genre(s): Bildungsroman (Coming of Age); War Story; Political Fiction.

Lim, Catherine

6043. **The Bondmaid.** New York: Viking, 1997. 384 pp.
The heir to the House of Wu loves Han, a woman sold to his family when she was four, but in Singapore during the 1950s, he is forced to regard her merely as a bondmaid.
Genre(s): Love Story.

Michaels, Fern

6044. **For All Their Lives.** New York: Ballantine, 1992. 503 pp.
A half-French, half-American army nurse falls in love with a wealthy idealist who volunteers to fight in Vietnam.
Genre(s): War Story; Romance.

Morris, Bill

6045. **All Souls' Day.** New York: Avon, 1997. 336 pp.
Sam Malloy runs a hotel in Bangkok during 1963 while his brother, Charlie, covers the Vietnam War in Saigon, and Charlie introduces Sam to Anne, a woman who is forced to write lies for the U.S. Information Service.
Genre(s): War Story.

Somtow, S. P.

◆ 6046. **Jasmine Nights.** New York: St. Martin's, 1995. 379 pp.
Justin, living with eccentric aunts outside Bangkok in 1963 while his parents work secretly for the U.S. government, learns about American ways from his black friend Virgil from Georgia.
Genre(s): Bildungsroman (Coming of Age); Domestic Fiction; Satire.

Vietnam

Before 1900

Bataille, Christophe

6047. *Annam.* Trans. Richard Howard. New York: New Directions, 1996. 87 pp.
During the reign of Louix XIV, French monks go as missionaries to Vietnam after a request from Canh, the 7-year-old emperor who then dies of pneumonia, and when Prince Regent Nguyen Anh regains the throne, he massacres the French group.
Award(s): Prix du Premier Roman.
Genre(s): Christian Fiction.

1900 and After

Amos, James

◆ 6048. *The Memorial: A Novel of the Vietnam War.* New York: Crown, 1989. 256 pp.
As he stands in front of the Vietnam Memorial in Washington, Jake Adams remembers friends who died or became prisoners during Operation Dewey Cameron or other battles.
Genre(s): War Story.

Anderson, Ken

6049. *Sympathy for the Devil.* Garden City, NY: Doubleday, 1987. 500 pp.
Hanson enjoys the chase and the killing in the Vietnam War, but in the end when his buddies Quinn and Silver die, he realizes that he is doomed to live.
Genre(s): War Story.

Anderson, Robert A.

6050. *Cooks and Bakers.* New York: Avon, 1982. 205 pp.
A young Marine lieutenant matures while fighting in the Vietnam War.
Genre(s): War Story.

Argo, Ronald

6051. *Year of the Monkey.* New York: Simon and Schuster, 1989. 387 pp.
Payne, serving in Vietnam as an army journalist, reports on another man's activities at the request of the CIA, but when Payne is court-martialed for that man's murder, he becomes aware of multiple layers of duplicity.
Genre(s): War Story; Spy Fiction.

Baker, Kenneth Waymon

6052. *Alone in the Valley.* Sag Harbor, NY: Permanent Press, 1992. 296 pp.
Daniel Purdue, 18, goes to Vietnam where he gains self-confidence as a leader of his platoon.
Genre(s): War Story.

Berent, Mark

◆ 6053. *Phantom Leader.* New York: Putnam, 1991. 414 pp.
In the sequel to *Steel Tiger*, Viet Cong shoot down Flak's airplane and imprison him, but with help of another pilot he escapes.
Genre(s): War Story.

◆ 6054. *Rolling Thunder.* New York: Putnam, 1989. 382 pp.
Three Air Force pilots go to Vietnam in 1965 and face the horrors of the jungle, but when they return home, they face the hostility of Americans who are against the war.
Genre(s): War Story.

◆ 6055. *Steel Tiger.* New York: Putnam, 1990. 399 pp.
The sequel to *Rolling Thunder* reveals the efforts of pilots to cut the supply line along the Ho Chi Minh Trail in 1967.
Genre(s): War Story.

6056. *Storm Flight.* New York: Putnam, 1993. 383 pp.
In 1972, American pilots, in the sequel to *Eagle Station*, search for American prisoners of war whose special skills and knowledge have made them valuable to the enemy.
Genre(s): War Story.

Boulle, Pierre

6057. *Ears of the Jungle.* Trans. Michael Dobry and Lynda Cole. New York: Vanguard, 1972. 224 pp.
Madame Ngha, head of North Vietnamese intelligence, works with primitive tribesmen and others to create countermeasures to the American electronic sensors disguised in the jungle around the Ho Chi Minh trail.
Genre(s): War Story; Fantastic Literature.

Butler, Robert Olen

6058. *Alleys of Eden.* 1982. New York: Henry Holt, 1994. 256 pp.

Cliff Butler enjoys Vietnam because he speaks the language, but after his marriage fails, he lives with a bar girl in Saigon before escaping with her in one of the last helicopters ferrying people out of the doomed city.
Genre(s): War Story.

6059. *The Deep Green Sea.* New York: St. Martin's, 1998. 240 pp.
When Benjamin Cole returns to Saigon after the Vietnam War, he meets Tien, abandoned by her mother for being of mixed race.
Genre(s): Adventure Story.

Caputo, Philip

6060. *DelCorso's Gallery.* New York: Holt, Rinehart and Winston, 1983. 352 pp.
Nick DelCorso, a Vietnam veteran, returns to see the fall of Saigon in 1975 as a photojournalist and follows it with a trip to Lebanon the next year.
Genre(s): War Story.

Carroll, Gerry

6061. *Ghostrider One.* New York: Pocket Books, 1993. 458 pp.
A Marine air-controller inside Khe Sanh and other military personnel recreate life during the Vietnam War in 1968, before the Tet Offensive.
Genre(s): War Story.

6062. *No Place to Hide.* New York: Pocket Books, 1997. 419 pp.
American pilots finish their duties as the war in Vietnam ends.
Genre(s): War Story.

6063. *North SAR.* New York: Pocket Books, 1991. 323 pp.
In June of 1972, Tim Boyle, whose best friend, Mike Santy, is an attack pilot, flies off of an aircraft carrier in the South China Sea to rescue air crews crashed in North Vietnam.
Genre(s): War Story.

Cleary, Jon

6064. *Spearfield's Daughter.* New York: Morrow, 1983. 567 pp.
In 1968, Cleo Spearfield, a correspondent in Vietnam, quits her newspaper job when the editor deletes her story, moves to England, and then to Manhattan.
Genre(s): War Story.

Coonts, Stephen

◆ 6065. *Flight of the Intruder.* Annapolis, MD: Naval Institute, 1986. 329 pp.
During the war in Vietnam, Jack Grafton loves to fly and beat the enemy with his A-6 Intruder.
Genre(s): War Story.

◆ 6066. *The Intruders.* New York: Pocket Books, 1994. 344 pp.
Jake Grafton in the sequel to *Flight of the Intruder* continues to fly A-6 Intruders with a Marine squadron in the Pa-

cific, while deciding if he should stay in the military after the senselessness of Vietnam.
Genre(s): War Story.

Cooper, Michael H.

6067. *Dues.* Willimantic, CT: Curbstone, 1994. 248 pp.
David Thorne, the smartest in his family, drops out of college in 1967 and ends up in Vietnam where he uses drugs to escape both the boredom and the terror.
Genre(s): War Story.

Currey, Richard

◆ 6068. *Fatal Light.* New York: Seymour Lawrence, 1988. 176 pp.
While serving in Vietnam, a soldier from Kentucky lovingly recalls his family and sweetheart, as he watches the senseless killing.
Genre(s): War Story.

Danziger, Jeff

◆ 6069. *Rising Like the Tucson.* New York: Doubleday, 1991. 368 pp.
Uninformed enlisted men and unqualified officers try to win in Vietnam using whatever scheme someone thinks will work.
Genre(s): War Story.

Del Vecchio, John M.

6070. *For the Sake of All Living Things.* New York: Bantam, 1990. 790 pp.
In the sequel to *The 13th Valley*, a young Cambodian peasant serves for the Khmer Rouge and rises to its leadership while his sister falls in love with an American soldier.
Genre(s): War Story.

6071. *The 13th Valley.* New York: Bantam, 1982. 606 pp.
In August, 1970, an infantry unit, with people at very different stages of their lives, engages in major combat.
Genre(s): War Story.

Deutermann, P. T.

6072. *The Edge of Honor.* New York: St. Martin's, 1994. 544 pp.
In 1969, Lt. Brian Holcomb is trying to reverse his fitness report, but while serving as the weapons officer on a ship going to the Gulf of Tonkin, he discovers that drug use is rampant.
Genre(s): War Story.

Dickason, Christie

6073. *Indochine.* New York: Villard, 1987. 581 pp.
Nina, daughter of a Vietnamese father and a French mother, survives their deaths to take over her father's opium empire during the 1950s.
Genre(s): War Story.

Dinh, Tran Van

6074. *Blue Dragon White Tiger.* Philadelphia: TriAm, 1984. 334 pp.
After a Western education, Tran Van Minh returns to Vietnam where his antipathy toward American intervention leads him to join the Viet Cong.
Genre(s): War Story.

Doolittle, Jerome

6075. *The Bombing Officer.* New York: Dutton, 1982. 236 pp.
Disturbed by his decisions about illegal bombing in Laos, Fred Upson decides to give information to a reporter and suffers unexpected consequences.
Genre(s): War Story.

Duncan, W. R.

6076. *The Queen's Messenger.* New York: Delacorte, 1982. 384 pp.
A deserter wants to have the charges for his crime dropped and he offers to identify the spy who has been revealing American raids on the North Vietnamese in advance.
Genre(s): War Story; Spy Fiction.

Duong Thu Huong

6077. *Novel Without a Name.* Trans. Phan Huy Duong and Nina McPherson. New York: Morrow, 1995. 320 pp.
Quan, a North Vietnamese soldier, is an idealist early in the war, but after 10 years of loss, he becomes hardened, until he has to help those he knew in childhood.
Genre(s): War Story.

◆ 6078. *Paradise of the Blind.* Trans. Phan Huy Duong and Nina McPherson. New York: Morrow, 1992. 256 pp.
Hang grows up in Vietnam in the shadow of the love of her mother and her aunt, and when lack of money stops her education, she becomes an export worker in the Soviet Union where she manages to retain her heritage.

Duras, Marguerite

6079. *The Lover.* Trans. Barbara Bray. New York: Pantheon, 1985. 113 pp.
A French girl lives with her family in pre–World War II Indochina where she has an affair with the son of a wealthy Chinese family, which changes her life.
Genre(s): Love Story.

Eyre, David

6080. *Float.* New York: Doubleday, 1991. 400 pp.
On a U.S. Navy gunboat in the Mekong Delta in 1966, Lieutenant Dubecheck does his best to kill the enemy, but whenever he has a chance, he relaxes and enjoys himself.
Genre(s): War Story.

Farish, Terry

◆ 6081. *Flower Shadows.* New York: Morrow, 1992. 213 pp.
Three young women serving in a Red Cross unit during the Vietnam War watch the horror of the war unfold.
Genre(s): War Story.

Ferrandino, Joseph

6082. *Firefight.* New York: Farrar, Straus and Giroux, 1987. 265 pp.
Amaro, a young soldier in Vietnam, must combat the enemy, the loss of his peers, and a superior officer.
Genre(s): War Story.

Flynn, Robert

6083. *The Last Klick.* Dallas, TX: Baskerville, 1994. 363 pp.
A college professor's daughter dies, and in an attempt to find meaning in life, he goes to Vietnam as a reporter for a conservative men's magazine, but his stories seem too intellectual, until he has a war experience that changes him.
Genre(s): War Story.

Fuller, Jack

6084. *Fragments.* New York: Morrow, 1984. 225 pp.
Morgan's friend Neumann is possibly implicated in an atrocity involving Vietnamese citizens, and when Morgan returns to the States, he tries to identify the events surrounding the situation.
Genre(s): War Story.

Glasser, Ronald J.

6085. *Another War/ Another Peace.* New York: Simon and Schuster, 1985. 247 pp.
David is sent to Vietnam as an inexperienced physician, and although at first he disdains his driver, he learns that Tom is more than a mere soldier.
Genre(s): War Story; Medical Novel.

Grey, Anthony

6086. *Saigon.* Boston: Little, Brown, 1982. 789 pp.
Joseph first visits Saigon in 1925, returns to work on a dissertation, and becomes a war correspondent there after World War II.

Griffin, W. E. B.

6087. *The Aviators.* New York: Putnam, 1988. 409 pp.
Johnny's success as a helicopter pilot in Vietnam earns him a position in developing the Army's first Air Assault Division to combat the enemy's unexpected guerrilla warfare. (*Series:* Brotherhood of War, 8)
Genre(s): War Story; Adventure Story.

Grinstead, David

6088. *Promises of Freedom.* New York: Crown, 1991. 448 pp.

Five college graduates during the Vietnam War experience both the fear of fighting and the politics over which they have no control.
Genre(s): War Story; Political Fiction.

Groom, Winston

6089. *Better Times than These.* New York: Summit, 1978. 411 pp.
In Vietnam in 1966, Bravo Company has great difficulties under an inexperienced leader.
Genre(s): War Story.

Halberstam, David

6090. *One Very Hot Day.* Boston: Houghton Mifflin, 1968. 216 pp.
A Vietnamese infantry company fulfills a mission one day under the mixed command of two Americans and a North Vietnamese soldier, who has defected.
Genre(s): War Story.

Harrison, Marshall

6091. *Cadillac Flight.* San Francisco: Presidio, 1990. 344 pp.
Captain Jim Broussard flies over Hanoi with other pilots.
Genre(s): War Story.

Heath, Layne

6092. *The Blue Deep.* New York: Morrow, 1993. 382 pp.
Marsh McCall and his men go to Vietnam to train French helicopter pilots, but Marsh suspects a black market for weapons, and he investigates before the war actually begins.
Genre(s): War Story.

6093. *CW2.* New York: Morrow, 1990. 400 pp.
Helicopter pilot Billy Roark applies for reassignment as a scout in the Vietnam War and searches the jungle for Viet Cong troops.
Genre(s): War Story.

Hillerman, Tony

6094. *Finding Moon.* New York: HarperCollins, 1995. 320 pp.
Moon Mathias, an editor of a poor quality Colorado newspaper, reluctantly goes to Vietnam to search for the child of his brother killed in Southeast Asia.
Genre(s): War Story.

Huo, T. C.

6095. *A Thousand Wings.* New York: Dutton, 1998. 240 pp.
When Fong Mun meets another immigrant from Laos in San Francisco and falls in love with him, he remembers his life during the Vietnam War when Communists took Laos.
Genre(s): War Story; Love Story.

Just, Ward S.

6096. *Stringer.* Boston: Little, Brown, 1974. 199 pp.
When Stringer, a civilian intelligence agent, is forced to destroy an enemy convoy in Southeast Asia, he suffers terrible mental anguish.
Genre(s): War Story.

Kalb, Bernard, and Marvin Kalb

6097. *The Last Ambassador.* Boston: Little, Brown, 1981. 267 pp.
Hadden Walker, Washington's last ambassador to South Vietnam, tries to save the United States' position in 1975.
Genre(s): War Story.

Karlin, Wayne

6098. *US.* New York: Henry Holt, 1993. 215 pp.
Loman, an expatriate, operates a bar and brothel in Bangkok after the Vietnam War and escorts a congressman looking for proof that men who have been reported missing-in-action are living in the Burmese jungles.
Genre(s): Political Fiction.

Lawton, David

6099. *A Lovely Country.* San Diego, CA: Harcourt, 1995. 226 pp.
Giles Trent serves as the U.S. ambassador in Vietnam during America's last years there, and he thinks that government leaders there have become amoral.
Genre(s): War Story.

Martin, Ron

6100. *To Be Free!* New York: Vanguard, 1986. 256 pp.
Ramsey plans his escape as a Marine prisoner-of-war while enduring a daily routine of work and torture.
Genre(s): War Story.

McAfee, John P

◆ 6101. *Slow Walk in a Sad Rain.* New York: Warner, 1993. 239 pp.
As the narrator watches his son play in the water, he remembers with guilt his participation in the Vietnam war and the mother and child he killed.
Genre(s): War Story.

Murphy, Yannick

6102. *The Sea of Trees.* Boston: Houghton Mifflin, 1997. 227 pp.
Tian, 12, learns to survive in Indochina during the 1940s, and her intelligence helps her family survive the war and a Japanese prison camp before making their way to France and New York.
Genre(s): War Story; Bildungsroman (Coming of Age).

Nathanson, E. M.

6103. *A Dirty Distant War.* New York: Viking, 1987. 460 pp.

When John Riesman and three suvivors from World War II in the *Dirty Dozen* go into Southeast Asia, they try to establish an intelligence network while finding that deception in the area is an art form.
Genre(s): War Story; Adventure Story.

Ninh, Bao

6104. *The Sorrow of War.* Trans. Phan Thanh Hao. New York: Pantheon, 1995. 233 pp.
Kien (Sorrowful Spirit) spends 11 years after high school recovering bodies of dead soldiers and serving in the North Vietnamese infantry.
Genre(s): War Story.

O'Brien, Tim

6105. *Going After Cacciato.* New York: Delacorte, 1978. 338 pp.
Cacciato leaves his unit in Vietnam, announcing that he is going to Paris, but the men chasing him see India and Iran as well.
Award(s): National Book Award.
Genre(s): War Story.

Peterson, Michael

6106. *A Time of War.* New York: Pocket Books, 1990. 580 pp.
President Johnson sends Bradley Marshall to Vietnam to discuss the withdrawal of troops, but he fails before the Tet Offensive occurs.
Genre(s): War Story.

Proffitt, Nicholas

6107. *The Embassy House.* New York: Bantam, 1986. 399 pp.
Captain Jack Gulliver is a ruthless killer, who must support the cover-up of an innocent man's death.
Genre(s): War Story.

6108. *Gardens of Stone.* New York: Carroll and Graf, 1983. 373 pp.
Jack Willow's idealization of war leads him to join the Army, but after completion of Officer Candidate School and a trip to Vietnam, he changes his attitude.
Genre(s): War Story.

Richards, Thomas

6109. *Zero Tolerance.* New York: Farrar, Straus and Giroux, 1997. 288 pp.
An undercover organization in the Vietnam War tries to destroy the rice fields around the Mekong Delta in an attempt to ruin the river-based culture.
Genre(s): War Story.

Schaeffer, Susan Fromberg

◆ 6110. *Buffalo Afternoon.* New York: Knopf, 1989. 535 pp.

Pete Bravado goes to Vietnam to serve in the war, where he meets Li, whose water buffalo have been shot by American soldiers.
Genre(s): War Story.

Tate, Donald

6111. *Bravo Burning.* New York: Scribner's, 1986. 216 pp.
While stationed in Vietnam during 1967, Mike Ripp learns just before a big battle occurs, that his wife has left him.
Genre(s): War Story.

Taylor, Laura

6112. *Honorbound.* New York: Watts, 1988. 367 pp.
The Viet Cong shoots down Matthew Benedict and his jet in 1967 after he has recently married Eden, and he becomes a prisoner of war for whom Eden must wait five miserable years.
Genre(s): War Story; Romance.

Taylor, Robert

6113. *The Innocent.* Santa Barbara, CA: Fithian, 1997. 256 pp.
When Captain Matthew Fairchild serves in Vietnam, he falls in love with a Vietnamese busboy who gives him an understanding of Vietnamese culture, and Fairchild discovers secret information about the massacre of citizens in a village.
Genre(s): War Story; Bildungsroman (Coming of Age).

Truscott, Lucian K.

6114. *Army Blue.* New York: Crown, 1989. 436 pp.
Lieutenant Blue IV is charged in 1969 with desertion and cowardice against the North Vietnamese, but he claims that his superiors ordered actions that would have harmed the men in his charge.
Genre(s): War Story.

Walsh, Patricia L.

6115. *Forever Sad the Hearts.* New York: Avon, 1982. 400 pp.
As a civilian nurse in Da Nang in the late 1960s, Kate Shea has trouble getting supplies, which are being stolen and black marketed, for the napalm-burned victims of the war.
Genre(s): Medical Novel; War Story.

Weber, Joe

6116. *Targets of Opportunity.* New York: Jove, 1994. 335 pp.
Austin, an American pilot, uses a North Vietnamese Mig-17 to fly into Vietnam and infiltrate the Air Force, but once there, he has a difficult additional assignment.
Genre(s): War Story.

◆ May be suitable for young adult readers

APPENDIXES

Appendix I
Book Awards

Note: Numbers refer to entry numbers.

Agatha Award
Ross, Kate, *The Devil in Music*, 1051

The Age (Australia) Book Award
Astley, Thea, *A Kindness Cup*, 5001
Koch, Christopher J., *The Year of Living Dangerously*, 5141
D'Alpuget, Blanche, *Turtle Beach*, 6036

Anthony Award
Lovesey, Peter, *The Last Detective*, 4757

Australian Literature Society Gold Medal
Malouf, David, *Fly Away Peter*, 5145

Belgian Book Prize
Langenus, Ron, *Mission West*, 2916

Best Foreign Language Novel in French
Arenas, Reinaldo, *The Ill-Fated Peregrinations of Fray Servando*, 5782

Best Novel of the Year in Peru
Riesco, Laura, *Ximena at the Crossroad*, 5997

Biblioteca Breve Prize
Benet, Juan, *A Meditation*, 1471

James Tate Black Award
Ballard, J. G., *Empire of the Sun*, 5380
Banville, John, *Doctor Copernicus*, 656
Carter, Angela, *Nights at the Circus*, 1129
Forster, E. M., *A Passage to India*, 5470
Golding, William, *Darkness Visible*, 4500
Graves, Robert, *Claudius, the God, and His Wife Messalina*, 367; *I, Claudius*, 368
Warner, Rex, *Imperial Caesar*, 414

Booker Prize
Barker, Pat, *The Ghost Road*, 3790
Berger, John, *G*, 1107
Carey, Peter, *Oscar and Lucinda*, 5009
Doyle, Roddy, *Paddy Clarke, Ha Ha Ha*, 4738
Farrell, J. G., *The Siege of Krishnapur*, 5467
Golding, William, *Rites of Passage*, 5036
Gordimer, Nadine, *The Conservationist*, 4924

Ishiguro, Kazuo, *The Remains of the Day*, 4542
Keneally, Thomas, *Schindler's List*, 1670
Ondaatje, Michael, *The English Patient*, 4964

Books in Canada First Novel Award
Robertson, Heather, *Willie, a Romance*, 5266

Carnegie Medal
Burton, Hester, *Time of Trial*, 3109
Dickinson, Peter, *Tulku*, 5530
Sutcliff, Rosemary, *The Lantern Bearers*, 250
Welch, Ronald, *Knight Crusader*, 5586

Casa de las Americas Award
Ponce De Leon, Napoleon Baccino, *Five Black Ships*, 763

Commonwealth Writers' Prize
Carey, Peter, *Jack Maggs*, 3826
De Bernières, Louis, *Corelli's Mandolin*, 1525
MacDonald, Ann-Marie, *Fall on Your Knees*, 5241
Mistry, Rohinton, *Such a Long Journey*, 5551
Seth, Vikram, *A Suitable Boy*, 5563

Cookson Award
Gilbert, Anna, *The Treachery of Time*, 3948

Dagger Award
Le Carré, John, *The Spy Who Came in from the Cold*, 4799
Meyer, Nicholas, *The Seven-Per-Cent Solution*, 4599

El Nacional's 50th Anniversary Novel Contest
Montemayor, Carlos, *Gambusino*, 5977

Festival Award for Literature
Carey, Peter, *Oscar and Lucinda*, 5009
D'Alpuget, Blanche, *Turtle Beach*, 6036

Miles Franklin Award
Carey, Peter, *Oscar and Lucinda*, 5009
Hall, Rodney, *The Grisly Wife*, 5127
Herbert, Xavier, *Poor Fellow my Country*, 5130

Keneally, Thomas, *Bring Larks and Heroes*, 5055
Koch, Christopher J., *Highways to a War*, 6041
Malouf, David, *The Great World*, 5146
Winton, Tim, *Cloudstreet*, 5179

Grand Prix de Lectrices
Gille, Elisabeth, *Shadows of a Childhood*, 1587

Grand Prix of the Republic of Korea Literature Award
Hahn Moo-Sook, *Encounter*, 5730

Guardian Award
Carter, Peter, *The Sentinels*, 4813
Magorian, Michelle, *Good Night, Mr Tom*, 4572

Guardian Fiction Prize
Gray, Alasdair, *Poor Things*, 3971

Ernest Hemingway Foundation Award
Begley, Louis, *Wartime Lies*, 1470
Thornton, Lawrence, *Imagining Argentina*, 6009

Georgette Heyer Historical Novel Prize
Birkhead, Margaret, *Trust and Treason*, 2553
Fitzgerald, Valerie, *Zemindar*, 5469
Guest, Lynn, *The Sword of Hachiman*, 5660
Herbert, Kathleen, *Queen of the Lightning*, 2219
Kay, Susan, *Legacy*, 2646
Lofts, Norah, *The Day of the Butterfly*, 3497
Wright, Patricia, *I Am England*, 2390

David Higham Prize
Lamming, R. M., *The Notebook of Gismondo Cavalletti*, 725

International IMPAC Dublin Literary Award
Malouf, David, *Remembering Babylon*, 5065
Müller, Herta, *The Land of Green Plums*, 2107

Kelist Prize
Müller, Herta*The Land of Green Plums*, 2107

Lessing Prize
Kempowski, Walter, *Days of Greatness*, 1249

Los Angeles Times **Book Award**

Garcia Marquez, Gabriel, *Love in the Time of Cholera*, 5946

Keneally, Thomas, *Schindler's List*, 1670

Kundera, Milan, *The Unbearable Lightness of Being*, 2052

Malouf, David, *Remembering Babylon*, 5065

Thomas, D. M., *The White Hotel*, 1905

Macavity Award

Newman, Sharan, *Death Comes as Epiphany*, 506

Mainchi Prize

Inoue, Yasushi, *Tun-huang*, 5328

Milkweed Prize for Fiction

Rangel-Ribeiro, Victor, *Tivolem*, 1805

National Book Award

Malamud, Bernard, *The Fixer*, 1277

McCarthy, Cormac, *All the Pretty Horses*, 5973

O'Brien, Tim, *Going After Cacciato*, 6105

Williams, John Edward, *Augustus*, 417

National Book Critics Circle Award

Bell, Madison Smartt, *All Souls' Rising*, 5783

Ferré, Rosario, *The House on the Lagoon*, 5936

Flanagan, Thomas, *The Year of the French*, 3294

McCarthy, Cormac, *All the Pretty Horses*, 5973

Shields, Carol, *The Stone Diaries*, 5272

West, Paul, *The Tent of Orange Mist*, 5444

National Jewish Book Award

Lustig, Arnost, *The Unloved*, 1725

Newbery Medal

De Treviño, Elizabeth, *I, Juan de Pareja*, 681

Orange Prize for Fiction

Michaels, Anne, *Fugitive Pieces*, 1755

Pegasus Prize

De Carvalho, Mário, *A God Strolling in the Cool of the Evening*, 231

Marahimin, Ismail, *And the War Is Over*, 5147

Rebolledo, Francisco, *Rasero*, 869

Edgar Allan Poe Award

Follett, Ken, *Eye of the Needle*, 1562

Forsyth, Frederick, *The Day of the Jackal*, 2010

Le Carré, John, *The Spy Who Came in from the Cold*, 4799

Premio di Lettaratura d'Italie

Carter, Peter, *The Sentinels*, 4813

Premio Strega Prize

Tomizza, Fulvio, *Heavenly Supper*, 886

S.H. Prior Memorial Prize

Franklin, Miles, *All That Swagger*, 5118

Prix du Premier Roman

Bataille, Christophe, *Annam*, 6047

Prix European

Parizeau, Alice, *The Lilacs Are Blooming in Warsaw*, 1787

Prix Femina Award

Fleutiaux, Pierrette, *We Are Eternal*, 2008

Prix Goncourt

Chamoiseau, Patrick, *Texaco*, 5833

Clavel, Bernard, *The Spaniard*, 1518

Maalouf, Amin, *The Rock of Tanios*, 5582

Maillet, Antonine, *Pelagie*, 5193

Makine, Andrei, *Dreams of My Siberian Summer*, 1276

Rouaud, Jean, *Fields of Glory*, 1335

Schwarz-Bart, André, *The Last of the Just*, 2338

Tournier, Michel, *The Ogre*, 1913

Yourcenar, Marguerite, *Memoirs of Hadrian*, 422

Prix Interalli

Schoendoerffer, Pierre, *Farewell to the King*, 6001

Prix Medicis for Best Foreign Fiction

Makine, Andrei, *Dreams of My Siberian Summer*, 1276

Prix Roland Dorgeles

Bichelberger, Roger, *An Ordinary Exodus*, 1477

Prize in Letters from Mexican National Society for Arts and Sciences

Azuela, Mariano, *The Underdogs*, 5906

Pulitzer Prize

Buck, Pearl S., *The Good Earth*, 5391

Malamud, Bernard, *The Fixer*, 1277

Rayner, Claire, *Bedford Row*, 4278

Shields, Carol, *The Stone Diaries*, 5272

Wilder, Thornton, *The Bridge of San Luis Rey*, 5814

Wouk, Herman, *The Caine Mutiny*, 5180

Romance Writers of America RITA Award

Kelly, Carla, *The Lady's Companion*, 3441; *Mrs Drew Plays her Hand*, 3442

W.H. Smith Prize

Roberts, Michelle, *Daughters of the House*, 1817

Spanish National Prize for Literature

Cela, Camilo Jose, *Mazurka for Two Dead Men*, 1508

Strega Prize

Vassalli, Sebastiano, *The Chimera*, 888

Betty Trask Award

Kay, Susan, *Legacy*, 2646

Trillum Prize

Choy, Wayson, *The Jade Peony*, 5282

University of California at Irvine's Chicano/Latino Literary Contest

Blanco, Evangeline, *Caribe*, 5911

University of Michigan's Hopwood Award

Zelitch, Simone, *The Confession of Jack Straw*, 2528

Xavier Villaurrutia Prize

Galindo, Sergio, *Otilia's Body*, 5943

Molina, Silvia, *Gray Skies Tomorrow*, 4764

Vogel Award

Krauth, Nigel, *Matilda, My Darling*, 5058

Whitbread Award

Dickinson, Peter, *Tulku*, 5530

Gray, Alasdair, *Poor Things*, 3971

Torrington, Jeff, *Swing Hammer Swing!* 4790

Wyndham, Francis, *The Other Garden*, 4714

Whitbread Book of the Year

Fitzgerald, Penelope, *The Blue Flower*, 961

Mosley, Nicholas, *Hopeful Monsters*, 4606

Appendix II
Books Suitable for Young Adult Readers

Note: Books in this list may be appropriate for or of interest to young adult readers (ninth grade in high school and up). The selection of most of the books noted as young adult come from lists in *School Library Journal* and *Booklist* provided by professional educators and reviewers. Numbers refer to entry numbers.

Abbott, Margot, *The Last Innocent Hour*, 1971

Achebe, Chinua, *Arrow of God*, 4881; *A Man of the People*, 4882; *Things Fall Apart*, 4801

Agnon, Shmuel Yosef, *A Simple Story*, 1091

Aiken, Joan, *Eliza's Daughter*, 3028; *Emma Watson*, 3029; *The Girl from Paris*, 1092; *The Youngest Miss Ward*, 3035

Albery, Nobuko, *Balloon Top*, 5689

Alemán Velasco, Miguel, *Copilli*, 5754

Alexander, Bruce, *Watery Grave*, 2786

Alexander, Meena, *Nampally Road*, 5519

Allan, Margaret, *The Mammoth Stone*, 60

Alvarez, Julia, *In the Time of the Butterflies*, 5899

Alyn, Marjory, *The Sound of Anthems*, 4412

Amos, James, *The Memorial: A Novel of the Vietnam War*, 6048

Anand, Valerie, *The Disputed Crown*, 2111; *King of the Wood*, 2113; *The Norman Pretender*, 2114; *The Proud Villeins*, 2115; *The Ruthless Yeomen*, 2391; *Women of Ashdon*, 2392

Anderson-Dargatz, Gail, *The Cure for Death by Lightning*, 5280

Anderson, Jack, and Bill Pronzini, *The Cambodia File*, 6028

Anderson, Jim, *Billarooby*, 5098

Anthony, Evelyn, *All the Queen's Men*, 2533; *Anne Boleyn*, 2534; *The Cardinal and the Queen*, 652; *Charles, the King*, 2535; *Exposure*, 4413; *The Poellenberg Inheritance*, 1451; *Rebel Princess*, 796; *The Relic*, 1974; *Royal Intrigue*, 797; *Victoria and Albert*, 3037

Appelfeld, Aharon, *For Every Sin*, 1453

Argers, Helen, *A Lady of Independence*, 3038; *Noblesse Oblige*, 3786

Ariyoshi, Sawako, *The Doctor's Wife*, 5672

Arnett, Caroline, *Melinda*, 3039

Ashfield, Helen, *Midsummer Morning*, 3045; *Regency Rogue*, 3048

Attanasio, A. A., *Kingdom of the Grail*, 2116; *Wyvern*, 5002

Austen, Jane, *Emma*, 3052; *Mansfield Park*, 3053; *Northanger Abbey*, 3054; *Persuasion*, 3055; *Pride and Prejudice*, 3056; *Sense and Sensibility*, 3057

Austen, Jane, and Another Lady, *Sanditon*, 3058

Austen-Leigh, Joan, *A Visit to Highbury*, 3059

Baddock, James, *The Dutch Caper*, 1460

Baehr, Consuelo Saah, *Daughters*, 5591

Bainbridge, Beryl, *The Birthday Boys*, 5099

Ballard, J. G., *Empire of the Sun*, 5380

Barak, Michael, *The Enigma*, 1461

Barnes, Margaret Ayer, *Brief Gaudy Hour: A Novel of Anne Boleyn*, 2539; *Isabel the Fair*, 2394

Barnes, Margaret Campbell, *The King's Bed*, 2395; *King's Fool*, 2540; *Mary of Carisbrooke*, 2541; *My Lady of Cleves*, 2542; *The Passionate Brood*, 2119; *The Tudor Rose*, 2396; *With All My Heart*, 2796; *Within the Hollow Crown*, 2397

Barraclough, June, *Familiar Acts*, 1102

Barrett, Julia, *Presumption*, 3075; *The Third Sister*, 3076

Barron, Stephanie, *Jane and the Unpleasantness at Scargrave Manor*, 3078; *Jane and the Wandering Eye*, 3079

Bartos-Höppner, B., *The Cossacks*, 658; *Save the Khan*, 659; *Storm over the Caucasus*, 913

Bassani, Giorgio, *The Garden of the Finzi-Continis*, 1466

Baumann, Hans, *Sons of the Steppe*, 5303

Beahn, John E., *A Man Born Again: Saint Thomas More*, 2543; *A Man of Good Zeal*, 661

Begley, Louis, *Wartime Lies*, 1470

Behan, Brian, *Kathleen*, 3796

Bell, Clare E., *Jaguar Princess*, 5756

Belle, Pamela, *The Moon in the Water*, 2548

Benitez, Sandra, *Bitter Grounds*, 5908

Berent, Mark, *Phantom Leader*, 6053; *Rolling Thunder*, 6054; *Steel Tiger*, 6055

Beverley, Jo, *The Fortune Hunter*, 3085; *The Stolen Bride*, 3087

Bienek, Horst, *Earth and Fire*, 1478

Billington, Rachel, *Theo and Matilda*, 2130

Binchy, Maeve, *Echoes*, 4721; *The Glass Lake*, 4723

Bjarnhof, Karl, *The Good Light*, 1112; *The Stars Grow Pale*, 1113

Black, Laura, *Albany*, 2805; *Glendraco*, 3800

Bonanno, Margaret Wander, *Ember Days*, 5281

Bowering, George, *Shoot!* 5211

Bradley, Marion Zimmer, *The Firebrand*, 104

Bradshaw, Gillian, *The Beacon at Alexandria*, 214

Bragg, Melvyn, *The Sword and the Miracle*, 2137

Brainard, Cecilia Manguerra, *When the Rainbow Goddess Wept*, 5102

Brand, Max, *The Stingaree*, 5212

Breem, Wallace, *The Leopard and the Cliff*, 5454

Brent, Madeleine, *Golden Urchin*, 5006; *The Long Masquerade*, 3096; *Merlin's Keep*, 5525; *Stormswift*, 5455

Bridal, Tessa, *The Tree of Red Stars*, 5912

Brindley, Louise, *In the Shadow of the Brontës*, 3097

Brodnax, Elizabeth, *The Marquis of Carabas*, 3099

Brouwer, Sigmund, *Magnus*, 2139

Brown, Diana, *The Blue Dragon*, 5728

Buckley, Fiona, *To Shield the Queen*, 2558

Buckley, William F. Jr., *See You Later Alligator*, 5913; *Stained Glass*, 1986; *The Story of Henri Tod*, 1987; *Who's on First*, 1988

Bunn, T. Davis, *Rhineland Inheritance*, 1993

Burton, Hester, *Time of Trial*, 3109

Butler, Gwendoline, *Coffin in Fashion*, 4727

Caldecott, Moyra, *The Lily and the Bull*, 109

Caldwell, Taylor, *Great Lion of God*, 257

Carr, Philippa, *The Black Swan*, 3829; *The Changeling*, 3830; *The Gossamer Cord*, 4432; *The Return of the Gypsy*, 3122

Carr, Robyn, *By Right of Arms*, 2404

Carter, Peter, *The Sentinels*, 4813

Cato, Nancy, *The Heart of the Continent*, 5108

Chadwick, Elizabeth, *The Running Vixen*, 2159; *The Wild Hunt*, 2160

Chaikin, L. L., *Kingscote*, 5458; *Silk*, 5459

Cheong, Fiona, *The Scent of the Gods*, 6033

Chesney, Marion, *The Adventuress*, 3132; *Animating Maria*, 3133; *Back in Society*, 3134; *The Banishment*, 3135; *Beatrice Goes to Brighton*, 3136; *Belinda Goes to Bath*, 3137; *Colonel Sandhurst to the Rescue*, 3138; *Daphne*, 3139; *Deborah Goes to Dover*, 3140; *The Deception*, 3141; *Deirdre and Desire*, 3142; *Diana the Huntress*, 3143; *The Dreadful Debutante*, 3144; *Emily Goes to Exeter*, 3145; *Enlightening Delilah*, 3146; *Finessing Clarissa*, 3147; *The Folly*, 3148; *Frederica in Fashion*, 3149; *Lady Fortescue Steps Out*, 3150; *A Marriage of Inconvenience*, 3151; *Marrying Harriet*, 3152; *Minerva*, 3153; *The Miser of Mayfair*, 3154; *Miss Tonks Turns to Crime*, 3155; *Mrs Budley Falls from Grace*, 3156; *My Lords, Ladies and Marjorie*, 3846; *Penelope Goes to

Portsmouth, 3157; *Perfecting Fiona*, 3158; *Plain Jane*, 3159; *Rainbird's Revenge*, 3160; *Rake's Progress*, 3161; *Refining Felicity*, 3162; *Sir Philip's Folly*, 3163; *The Taming of Annabelle*, 3164; *The Wicked Godmother*, 3165; *Yvonne Goes to York*, 3166

Chevalier, Paul, *The Grudge*, 4436

Chisholm, P. F., *A Famine of Horses*, 2568; *A Season of Knives*, 2569

Claus, Hugo, *Sorrow of Belgium*, 1517

Clynes, Michael, *The Grail Murders*, 2573; *The White Rose Murders*, 2574

Cohen, Matt, *The Spanish Doctor*, 561

Collier, G. K., *The Gamester*, 3174

Collin, Richard Oliver, *Contessa*, 1134

Cookson, Catherine, *The Black Candle*, 3855; *The Harrogate Secret*, 3860; *The Maltese Angel*, 3183; *The Moth*, 3864; *The Parson's Daughter*, 3866; *The Rag Nymph*, 3185; *The Whip*, 3190; *The Wingless Bird*, 3868

Coonts, Stephen, *Flight of the Intruder*, 6065; *The Intruders*, 6066

Coulter, Catherine, *Impulse*, 5835; *Lord Harry*, 3871; *Lord of Hawkfell Island*, 443; *The Nightingale Legacy*, 3199; *The Valentine Legacy*, 3201; *The Wyndham Legacy*, 3203

Courter, Gay, *Flowers in the Blood*, 5464

Cowell, Stephanie, *Nicholas Cooke*, 2576

Crane, John Kenny, *The Legacy of Ladysmith*, 4824

Crichton, Michael, *The Great Train Robbery*, 3206

Crosby, Caroline, *The Haldanes*, 4445

Cross, Donna Woolfolk, *Pope Joan*, 446

Cummings, Monette, *The Beauty of Her Daughter*, 3209

Currey, Richard, *Fatal Light*, 6068

D'Alpuget, Blanche, *Turtle Beach*, 6036

Dangarembga, Tsisi, *Nervous Conditions*, 4895

Dann, Jack, *The Memory Cathedral*, 567

Danziger, Jeff, *Rising Like the Tucson*, 6069

Darby, Catherine, *The Love Knot*, 2408

Darcy, Clare, *Allegra*, 3210; *Lady Pamela*, 3217; *Letty*, 3218

Davis, Kathryn Lynn, *All We Hold Dear*, 3877; *Sing to Me of Dreams*, 5215

Davis, Lindsey, *A Dying Light in Corduba*, 349; *The Iron Hand of Mars*, 230; *Poseidon's Gold*, 351;

The Silver Pigs, 352; *Time to Depart*, 353

De Hartog, Jan, *The Inspector*, 2000; *The Peaceable Kingdom*, 2839; *Star of Peace*, 1529; *The Trail of the Serpent*, 5113

De Luca, Teresa, *A Distant Thunder*, 1530

De Treviño, Elizabeth, *Among the Innocent*, 569; *I, Juan de Pareja*, 681

Deane, Seamus, *Reading in the Dark*, 4737

DeCarlo, Elisa, *Strong Spirits*, 4452

Deford, Frank, *Love and Infamy*, 5692

Deighton, Len, *City of Gold*, 4897

Delibes, Miguel, *The Stuff of Heroes*, 1536

Demetz, Hanna, *The House on Prague Street*, 1537

Desai, Anita, *Baumgartner's Bombay*, 5529

Deveraux, Jude, *The Duchess*, 3883

Dial, Joan, *Echoes of War*, 1540

Dickens, Charles, *Barnaby Rudge*, 2843; *David Copperfield*, 3233; *Great Expectations*, 3234; *Oliver Twist*, 3240; *A Tale of Two Cities*, 947

Dickinson, Peter, *Tulku*, 5530

DiPerna, Paula, *The Discoveries of Mrs Christopher Columbus: His Wife's Version*, 683

Doherty, P. C., *An Ancient Evil*, 2410; *The Death of a King*, 2411; *Spy in Chancery*, 2416; *A Tapestry of Murders*, 2417; *A Tournament of Murders*, 2418; *The Whyte Harte*, 2419

Dostoyevsky, Fyodor, *The Adolescent*, 1150; *Netochka Nezvanova*, 952

Douglas, Carole Nelson, *Irene at Large*, 1155; *Irene's Last Waltz*, 1156

Doyle, Roddy, *Paddy Clarke, Ha Ha Ha*, 4738

Drummond, June, *The Impostor*, 3244

Drury, Allen, *A God Against the Gods*, 7

Duggan, William, *The Great Thirst*, 4828

Dukthas, Ann, *In the Time of the Poisoned Queen*, 2593; *The Prince Lost to Time*, 818; *A Time for the Death of a King*, 2594; *The Time of Murder at Mayerling*, 1161

Dunn, Carola, *Angel*, 3248; *The Black Sheep's Daughter*, 3249; *Miss Hartwell's Dilemma*, 3253; *Two Corinthians*, 3255

Duong Thu Huong, *Paradise of the Blind*, 6078

Durrell, Lawrence, *White Eagles over Serbia*, 1547

Eden, Dorothy, *An Important Family*, 5030; *Melbury Square*, 3904; *The

INDEXES

Author Index

Note: Numbers refer to entry numbers. Books with more than one author will be listed under each author.

Carmichael, Jeanne, *Forever Yours*, 3118

Carnac, Nicholas, *Indigo*, 5457

Carnegie, Sacha, *The Banners of Courage*, 804; *The Banners of Power*, 805; *The Banners of War*, 806; *Kasia and the Empress*, 807; *Scarlet Banners of Love*, 808

Carpentier, Alejo, *The Harp and the Shadow*, 922; *The Kingdom of This World*, 5787

Carr, James Lloyd, *A Month in the Country*, 4431

Carr, John Dickson, *The Bride of Newgate*, 3119; *The Hungry Goblin*, 3828

Carr, Philippa, *The Adulteress*, 2825; *The Black Swan*, 3829; *The Changeling*, 3830; *The Gossamer Cord*, 4432; *Knave of Hearts*, 809; *Lament for a Lost Lover*, 2826; *The Lion Triumphant*, 2562; *Midsummer's Eve*, 3120; *The Miracle at St Bruno's*, 2563; *The Pool of St Branok*, 3121; *The Return of the Gypsy*, 3122; *Saraband for Two Sisters*, 2564; *The Song of the Siren*, 2827; *A Time for Silence*, 1128; *Voices in a Haunted Room*, 3123; *We'll Meet Again*, 4433; *Will You Love Me in September*, 810; *The Witch from the Sea*, 2565

Carr, Robyn, *The Bellerose Bargain*, 2828; *The Blue Falcon*, 2155; *The Braeswood Tapestry*, 2829; *By Right of Arms*, 2404; *Chelynne*, 2830; *The Everlasting Covenant*, 2405; *The Troubadour's Romance*, 2156

Carroll, Gerry, *Ghostrider One*, 6061; *No Place to Hide*, 6062; *North SAR*, 6063

Carroll, James, *Supply of Heroes*, 3831

Carroll, Susan, *The Bride Finder*, 2831; *The Painted Veil*, 923

Carse, James P, *The Gospel of the Beloved Disciple*, 272

Carter, Angela, *Nights at the Circus*, 1129

Carter, Annee, *The Promise of Your Touch*, 3124

Carter, Peter, *The Sentinels*, 4813

Cartland, Barbara, *Flowers for the God of Love*, 5527; *Love at the Helm*, 5828; *Love Casts out Fear*, 3125; *Love Locked In*, 3832; *The Peril and the Prince*, 3833; *Riding to the Moon*, 3126; *The Wild, Unwilling Wife*, 3834

Carver, Gene, *The Murder of Che Guevara*, 5996

Cary, Joyce, *The African Witch*, 4814; *Charley Is My Darling*, 4434; *Except the Lord*, 3835; *A Fearful Joy*, 3836; *Herself Surprised*, 3837; *The Horse's Mouth*, 3838;

Mister Johnson, 3839; *Not Honour More*, 3840; *Prisoner of Grace*, 3841; *To Be a Pilgrim*, 3842

Casey, Jane Barnes, *I, Krupskaya: My Life with Lenin*, 1506

Cash, Johnny, *Man in White*, 215

Cashman, John, *The Cook General*, 3843; *Kid Glove Charlie*, 2832

Caso, Adolph, *The Straw Obelisk*, 1507

Cassill, R. V., *After Goliath*, 174

Castellanos, Rosario, *The Book of Lamentations*, 5919; *The Nine Guardians*, 5920

Cates, Kimberly, *Gather the Stars*, 2833

Cather, Willa, *Shadows on the Rock*, 5184

Cato, Nancy, *All the Rivers Run*, 5107; *Brown Sugar*, 5010; *Forefathers*, 5011; *The Heart of the Continent*, 5108; *Queen Trucanini*, 5012

Cavanaugh, Jack, *The Pride and the Passion*, 4815

Cela, Camilo Jose, *Mazurka for Two Dead Men*, 1508; *San Camilo, 1936: The Eve, Feast, and Octave of St Camillus*, 1509

Céline, Louis-Ferdinand, *Castle to Castle*, 1510; *Death on the Installment Plan*, 1511; *Journey to the End of the Night*, 1130; *North*, 1512; *Rigadoon*, 1994

Cervantes Saavedra, Miguel de, *Don Quixote De La Mancha*, 670; *The History of That Ingenious Gentleman Don Quijote De La Mancha*, 671

Chadwick, Elizabeth, *The Champion*, 436; *The Conquest*, 2157; *The Leopard Unleashed*, 2158; *The Running Vixen*, 2159; *The Wild Hunt*, 2160

Chai, Arlene J., *The Last Time I Saw Mother*, 5109

Chaikin, L. L., *Behind the Veil*, 437; *Captive Heart*, 5829; *The Everlasting Flame*, 2566; *Golden Palaces*, 438; *Jamaican Sunset*, 5830; *Kingscote*, 5458; *The Pirate and His Lady*, 5831; *Port Royal*, 5832; *Silk*, 5459; *Swords and Scimitars*, 439; *Under Eastern Stars*, 5460

Chaix, Marie, *The Laurels of Lake Constance*, 1513

Chalker, Jack L., *The Devil's Voyage*, 5110

Challoner, Robert, *Give Fire!* 4816

Chamberlin, Ann, *Sofia*, 672; *The Sultan's Daughter*, 673; *Tamar*, 175

Chambers, Anne, *The Geraldine Conspiracy*, 2567

Chamoiseau, Patrick, *Texaco*, 5833

Chand, Meira, *A Choice of Evils*, 5395

Chandernagor, Françoise d'Aubigne, *The King's Way*, 811

Chang, Eileen, *The Rice-Sprout Song*, 5396; *The Rouge of the North*, 5397

Chapman, Hester W., *Fear No More*, 924; *Lucy*, 3127

Chapman, Robin, *The Duchess's Diary*, 674

Charchat, Isaac, *A Constant Reminder*, 5596

Charney, Ann, *Dobryd*, 1514

Charteris, Hugo, *The Coat*, 4435

Chase, Loretta, *Isabella*, 3128; *Knave's Wager*, 3129; *The Last Hellion*, 3130; *The Sandalwood Princess*, 5461

Chase, Nicholas, *Locksley*, 2161

Chase-Riboud, Barbara, *Valide*, 925

Chatwin, Bruce, *On the Black Hill*, 3844

Chen-ho, Wang, *Rose, Rose, I Love You*, 6032

Chen, Yuan-tsung, *The Dragon's Village*, 5398

Cheng, Naishan, *The Banker*, 5399

Cheong, Fiona, *The Scent of the Gods*, 6033

Chernaik, Judith, *The Daughter*, 3845; *Love's Children*, 3131

Chesney, Marion, *The Adventuress*, 3132; *Animating Maria*, 3133; *Back in Society*, 3134; *The Banishment*, 3135; *Beatrice Goes to Brighton*, 3136; *Belinda Goes to Bath*, 3137; *Colonel Sandhurst to the Rescue*, 3138; *Daphne*, 3139; *Deborah Goes to Dover*, 3140; *The Deception*, 3141; *Deirdre and Desire*, 3142; *Diana the Huntress*, 3143; *The Dreadful Debutante*, 3144; *Emily Goes to Exeter*, 3145; *Enlightening Delilah*, 3146; *Finessing Clarissa*, 3147; *The Folly*, 3148; *Frederica in Fashion*, 3149; *Lady Fortescue Steps Out*, 3150; *A Marriage of Inconvenience*, 3151; *Marrying Harriet*, 3152; *Minerva*, 3153; *The Miser of Mayfair*, 3154; *Miss Tonks Turns to Crime*, 3155; *Mrs Budley Falls from Grace*, 3156; *My Lords, Ladies and Marjorie*, 3846; *Penelope Goes to Portsmouth*, 3157; *Perfecting Fiona*, 3158; *Plain Jane*, 3159; *Rainbird's Revenge*, 3160; *Rake's Progress*, 3161; *Refining Felicity*, 3162; *Sir Philip's Folly*, 3163; *The Taming of Annabelle*, 3164; *The Wicked Godmother*, 3165; *Yvonne Goes to York*, 3166

Chester, Deborah, *French Slippers*, 926; *A Love So Wild*, 3167

Cheuse, Alan, *The Bohemians: John Reed and His Friends Who Shook the World*, 1131

Chevalier, Paul, *The Grudge*, 4436

Ekman, Kerstin, *Witches' Rings*, 1166

Eldershaw, M. Barnard, *A House Is Built*, 5032

Elegant, Robert S., *Bianca*, 694; *Dynasty*, 5357; *Manchu*, 5310; *Mandarin*, 5358

Elegant, Simon, *A Floating Life*, 5311

Eliot, George, *Adam Bede*, 3269; *Felix Holt, the Radical*, 3270; *Middlemarch*, 3271; *The Mill on the Floss*, 3272; *Romola*, 588; *Silas Marner*, 3273

Ellingson, Marnie, *Dolly Blanchard's Fortune*, 3274; *The Wicked Marquis*, 3275

Elliott, Elizabeth, *Scoundrel*, 3276

Elliott, Janice, *The Kindling*, 4739; *Secret Places*, 4473

Ellis, Julie, *The Only Sin*, 1167

Ellis, Peter Berresford, *The Rising of the Moon*, 5226

Ellis, Vivienne Rae, *Queen Trucanini*, 5012

Elman, Richard M., *Lilo's Diary*, 1548; *The Reckoning*, 1549; *The 28th Day of Elul*, 1550

Elon, Amos, *Timetable*, 1551

Elsna, Hebe, *Prelude for Two Queens*, 2599; *The Queen's Ward*, 2600

Elwood, Muriel, *Deeper the Heritage*, 5186

Elwood, Roger, *Darien: Guardian Angel of Jesus*, 279; *The Road to Masada*, 280

Emecheta, Buchi, *The Bride Price*, 4910; *Double Yoke*, 4911; *The Joys of Motherhood*, 4912; *The Slave Girl*, 4913

Emerson, Kathy Lynn, *Face Down in the Marrow-Bone Pie*, 2601; *Face Down upon an Herbal*, 2602

Emery, John, *The Sky People*, 5115

Enchi, Fumiko, *The Waiting Years*, 5677

Endo, Shusaku, *The Samurai*, 5666; *The Sea and Poison*, 5694; *Silence*, 5678

Endore, S. Guy, *King of Paris*, 959

Ennis, Michael, *Byzantium*, 454; *Duchess of Milan*, 589

Enoch, Suzanne, *Angel's Devil*, 3277

Epstein, Leslie, *King of the Jews*, 1552

Epton, Nina Consuelo, *The Burning Heart*, 3278

Erskine, Barbara, *Lady of Hay*, 2192

Esquivel, Laura, *Like Water for Chocolate*, 5933

Essex, Olga Berrocal, *Delia's Way*, 5934

Esteleman, Loren D., *Sherlock Holmes Versus Dracula*, 3913

Ettinger, Elzbieta, *Kindergarten*, 1553

Evans, Alan, *Thunder at Dawn*, 3914

Evans, Jean, *The Phoenix Rising*, 2603

Everett, Peter, *A Death in Ireland*, 4474

Ewing, Jean R., *Rogue's Reward*, 3279; *Virtue's Reward*, 3280

Eyre, David, *Float*, 6080

Eyre, Elizabeth, *Axe for an Abbot*, 590; *Curtains for the Cardinal*, 695; *Death of the Duchess*, 696; *Dirge for a Doge*, 591; *Poison for the Prince*, 697

Facos, James, *The Silver Lady*, 4475

Fadeev, Aleksandr, *The Nineteen*, 1168

Fagyas, M., *Court of Honor*, 1169; *Dance of the Assassins*, 1170; *The Devil's Lieutenant*, 1171

Fairbairns, Zoë, *Stand We at Last*, 3915

Fairburn, Eleanor M., *The Rose at Harvest End*, 2423; *Winter's Rose*, 2424

Fairchild, Elisabeth, *The Love Knot*, 3281; *The Rakehell's Reform*, 3282

Fakinos, Aris, *The Marked Men*, 2003

Falconer, Delia, *The Service of Clouds*, 5116

Falkirk, Richard, *Beau Blackstone*, 3283; *Blackstone*, 3284; *Blackstone and the Scourge of Europe*, 3285; *For Infamous Conduct*, 5533

Fallaci, Oriana, *A Man*, 2004

Fallon, Frederic, *The White Queen*, 2604

Farhi, Moris, *The Last of Days*, 5604

Farish, Terry, *Flower Shadows*, 6081

Farnol, Jeffery, *Heritage Perilous*, 3286; *The High Adventure*, 3287; *The Ninth Earl*, 3288; *The Waif of the River*, 3289

Farrell, J. G., *The Siege of Krishnapur*, 5467; *The Singapore Grip*, 6038; *Troubles*, 4476

Farrell, Michael J., *Papabile: The Man Who Would Be Pope*, 1554

Farrington, Gene, *The Breath of Kings*, 2193

Farrington, Robert, *The Killing of Richard the Third*, 2425

Fast, Howard, *The Bridge Builder's Story*, 1555; *My Glorious Brothers*, 183; *Spartacus*, 360

Fast, Jonathan, *Golden Fire*, 5468; *The Jade Stalk*, 5312

Faulks, Sebastian, *Birdsong*, 1172

Faust, Irvin, *Jim Dandy*, 4914

Fawal, Ibrahim, *On the Hills of God*, 5605

Fawcett, Quinn, *Against the Brotherhood*, 3916

Feather, Jane, *The Diamond Slipper*, 824; *The Emerald Swan*, 698; *Hostage Bride*, 2605; *The Silver Rose*, 2849; *Vice*, 2850; *Violet*, 960; *Virtue*, 3290

Fecher, Constance, *Heir to Pendarrow*, 2606

Fedin, Konstantin, *Cities and Years*, 1173

Feibleman, Peter S., *The Columbus Tree*, 2005

Feinstein, Elaine, *Loving Brecht*, 1556

Fejes, Endré, *Generation of Rust*, 1557

Fell, Alison, *The Pillow Boy of the Lady Onogoro*, 5659

Feng Jicai, *The Three-Inch Golden Lotus*, 5359

Ferguson, James, *Out of the Whirlwind*, 1558

Ferguson, Jo Ann, *A Model Marriage*, 3291

Ferlinghetti, Lawrence, *Love in the Days of Rage*, 2006

Ferré, Rosario, *Eccentric Neighborhoods*, 5935; *The House on the Lagoon*, 5936

Ferrandino, Joseph, *Firefight*, 6082

Feuchtwanger, Lion, *The Jew of Rome*, 361; *Josephus*, 281; *Josephus and the Emperor*, 362; *Proud Destiny*, 825

Feuer, Lewis Samuel, *The Case of the Revolutionist's Daughter*, 3917

Feyrer, Gayle, *The Prince of Cups*, 592; *The Thief's Mistress*, 2194

Fielding, Henry, *Amelia*, 2851; *Joseph Andrews*, 2852; *Tom Jones*, 2853

Figes, Eva, *The Seven Ages*, 2426; *The Tree of Knowledge*, 2607

Findley, Timothy, *The Piano Man's Daughter*, 5227

Finegan, Jack, *Mark of the Taw*, 282

Fink, Ida, *The Journey*, 1559

Finlay, Lilian Roberts, *Always in My Mind*, 4477

Finney, Patricia, *Firedrake's Eye*, 2608; *Unicorn's Blood*, 2609

Fish, Robert L., *Pursuit*, 5606

Fisher, Alan, *Three Passions of Countess Natalya*, 1174

Fisher, Anne Kinsman, *The Legend of Tommy Morris*, 3918

Fitz Gibbon, Constantine, *High Heroic*, 3919

Fitzgerald, Amber, *The Suspicious Heart*, 3292

Fitzgerald, Ellen, *Ardent Apparitions*, 3293

Fitzgerald, F. Scott, *Tender Is the Night*, 1560

Fitzgerald, Nancy, *Mayfair*, 3920

Fitzgerald, Penelope, *The Beginning of Spring*, 1175; *The Blue Flower*, 961; *The Gate of Angels*, 3921; *Innocence*, 2007

Fitzgerald, Valerie, *Zemindar*, 5469

Flanagan, Thomas, *The End of the Hunt*, 3922; *The Tenants of Time*,

L'Amour, Louis, *Fair Blows the Wind*, 2653; *The Walking Drum*, 489

Lancaster, Bruce, *Bright to the Wanderer*, 5237; *Venture in the East*, 5680

Land, Jane, *These Tigers' Hearts*, 1263

Landley, Dora, *Triptych*, 1264

Landorf, Joyce, *I Came to Love You Late*, 303

Landsman, Anne, *The Devil's Chimney*, 4943

Lane, Allison, *Lord Avery's Legacy*, 3479; *The Prodigal Daughter*, 3480

Lane, Jane, *Bridge of Sighs*, 2913; *Heirs of Squire Harry*, 2654; *Parcel of Rogues*, 2655; *The Sealed Knot*, 2914; *The Severed Crown*, 2656; *A Summer Storm*, 2458; *Thunder on St Paul's Day*, 2915

Lang, Jennifer, *The Peacock and the Pearl*, 2459

Lang, Theo, *The Word and the Sword*, 304

Langenus, Ron, *Mission West*, 2916

Lao, She, *Rickshaw*, 5416

Larreta, Antonio, *The Last Portrait of the Duchess of Alba*, 1006

Larsen, Gaylord, *Dorothy and Agatha*, 4558

Larsen, Jeanne, *Bronze Mirror*, 5330; *Manchu Palaces*, 5331; *Silk Road*, 5332

Lasky, Jesse L. Jr., *The Offer*, 5622

Laurence, Janet, *Canaletto and the Case of Westminster Bridge*, 2917

Lauterstein, Ingeborg, *Vienna Girl*, 2053; *The Water Castle*, 1708

Law, Elizabeth, *The Sealed Knot*, 3481

Law, Janice, *All the King's Ladies*, 852

Lawhead, Steve, *Arthur*, 2244; *Byzantium*, 2245; *Merlin*, 2246; *Pendragon*, 2247; *Taliesin*, 2248

Lawrence, Joan, *The Scapegoat*, 34

Lawrence, Starling, *Montenegro*, 1265

Lawton, David, *A Lovely Country*, 6099

Lawton, John, *Black Out*, 4559

Laye, Camra, *The Guardian of the Word*, 4843

Laymon, Richard, *Savage*, 4102

Le Carré, John, *The Spy Who Came in from the Cold*, 4799

Le Clézio, J. M. G., *Onitsha*, 4944; *The Prospector*, 5544

Le Luu, *A Time Far Past*, 6042

Le Porrier, Herbert, *The Doctor from Cordova*, 490

Le Sage, Alain René, *The Adventures of Gil Blas of Santillane*, 853

Leasor, James, *Follow the Drum*, 5483; *Mandarin Gold*, 5364

Leavitt, David, *While England Sleeps*, 4560

Leckie, Ross, *Hannibal*, 81; *Scipio*, 82

Ledbetter, Susann, *Deliverance Drive*, 5238

Lee, C. Y., *China Saga*, 5365; *Gate of Rage*, 5417; *The Second Son of Heaven*, 5366

Lee, Maureen, *Through the Storm*, 4561

Lee, Sky, *Disappearing Moon Café*, 5239

Lee, Tanith, *The Gods Are Thirsty*, 1007

Lefebure, Molly, *Blitz!* 4562; *Thunder in the Sky*, 4563

Leffland, Ella, *The Knight, Death, and the Devil*, 1709

Lehmann, Marcus, *Rabbi Joselman of Rosheim*, 726

Lehmann, Rosamond, *The Ballad and the Source*, 4103

Lehr, Helene, *Princess of Hanover*, 2918

Leland, Mary, *The Killeen*, 4564

Leland, Thomas, *Longsword, Earl of Salisbury*, 2249

Lemmons, Thom, *Passport*, 5629

Lennox, Judith, *The Glittering Strand*, 4844; *The Italian Garden*, 727

Lennox-Smith, Judith, *Till The Day Goes Down*, 2657

Lentin, Ronit, *Night Train to Mother*, 1710

Lenz, Siegfried, *The German Lesson*, 1711

Leonard, Elmore, *Cuba Libra*, 5854

Leonard, Hugh, *Parnell and the Englishwoman*, 4104

Leonard, Phyllis G., *Phantom of the Sacred Well*, 5855; *Prey of the Eagle*, 5856

Leonowens, Anna, *The Romance of the Harem*, 6026

Lescroart, John T., *Son of Holmes*, 4105

Leslie, Desmond, *The Jesus File*, 305

Leslie, Doris, *The Incredible Duchess*, 2919; *Notorious Lady*, 3482; *The Sceptre and the Rose*, 2920; *This for Caroline*, 3483; *Vagabond's Way*, 606; *Wreath for Arabella*, 2658

Leslie-Melville, Betty, *Bagamoyo*, 4945

Leslie-Melville, Jock, *Bagamoyo*, 4945

Levi, Jean, *The Chinese Emperor*, 5333; *The Dream of Confucius*, 5334

Levi, Primo, *If Not Now, When?* 1712

Leviant, Curt, *The Man Who Thought He Was Messiah*, 1008

Levin, Lee, *King Tut's Private Eye*, 35

Levin, Meyer, *Eva*, 1713; *The Harvest*, 5623; *My Father's House*, 5624; *The Settlers*, 5625

Levine, Faye, *Solomon and Sheba*, 192

Levine, Jacques, *Hitler's Secret Diaries*, 1266

Lewis, Hilda Winifred, *Catherine*, 2921; *Harlot Queen*, 2460; *Harold Was My King*, 2250; *I Am Mary Tudor*, 2659; *Wife to the Bastard*, 2251; *The Witch and the Priest*, 2660

Lewis, Janet, *The Trial of Soren Qvist*, 728; *The Wife of Martin Guerre*, 729

Lewis, Kim, *Loving Becky*, 4106

Lewis, Norman, *Cuban Passage*, 5965; *Within the Labyrinth*, 2054

Lewis, Roy, *Cock of the Walk*, 4107

Lewitt, Maria, *Come Spring*, 1714

Ley, Alice Chetwynd, *Beloved Diana*, 3484; *A Fatal Assignation*, 3485; *A Regency Scandal*, 3486; *A Reputation Dies*, 3487; *The Sentimental Spy*, 3488

Li, Leslie, *Bittersweet*, 5367

Li, Pi-hua, *Farewell to My Concubine*, 5418; *The Last Princess of Manchuria*, 5419

Libby, Lewis, *The Apprentice*, 5703

Lide, Mary, *Command of the King*, 2661; *Fortune's Knave*, 2252; *The Legacy of Tregaran*, 4108; *Polmena Cove*, 4565; *The Sea Scape*, 4109; *Tregaran*, 4566

Lieberman, Herbert H., *The Climate of Hell*, 5966

Lightman, Alan P., *Einstein's Dreams*, 1267

Lim, Catherine, *The Bondmaid*, 6043

Limón, Graciela, *In Search of Bernab*, 5967; *Song of the Hummingbird*, 5765

Limón, Martin, *Buddha's Money*, 5744; *Slicky Boys*, 5745

Lin, Yutang, *Lady Wu*, 5335; *Moment in Peking*, 5420; *The Red Peony*, 5368; *The Vermilion Gate*, 5421

Lincoln, Victoria, *Charles*, 3489

Lindgren, Torgny, *Bathsheba*, 193; *The Way of the Serpent*, 1268

Lindsay, Jack, *Rome for Sale*, 379

Lindsay, Kathleen, *Enchantress of the Nile*, 218

Lindsay, Philip, *London Bridge Is Falling*, 2461

Lindsey, Dawn, *The Duchess of Vidal*, 3490

Lindsey, Johanna, *Captive Bride*, 4845; *Defy Not the Heart*, 491; *Fires of Winter*, 492; *A Gentle Feuding*, 2662; *Gentle Rogue*, 3491; *Glorious Angel*, 3492; *Hearts Aflame*, 2253; *Love Me Forever*, 3493; *Say You Love Me*, 3494; *Silver Angel*, 2922; *So*

Title Index

Note: Numbers refer to entry numbers.

Genre Index

Note: Numbers refer to entry numbers.

Adventure Story

Aiken, Joan, *The Smile of the Stranger*, 3034

Ainsworth, William Harrison, *The Admirable Crichton*, 2529

Alcott, Louisa May, *A Long Fatal Love Chase*, 3036

Aldridge, James, *One Last Glimpse*, 1448

Allen, Hervey, *Anthony Adverse*, 794

Anderson, Scott, *Goldwalker*, 5821

Andrews, John, *A Viking's Daughter*, 423

Anthony, Evelyn, *The Relic*, 1974

Attanasio, A. A., *Wyvern*, 5002

Bailey, H. C., *The Plot*, 2792

Ballinger, W. A., *The Carrion Eaters*, 5521

Barber, Rowland, *The Midnighters*, 5592

Barroll, Clare, *The Iron Crown*, 426

Bataille, Christophe, *Hourmaster*, 660

Baumann, Hans, *I Marched with Hannibal*, 65

Becker, Stephen D., *The Blue-Eyed Shan*, 5523; *The Last Mandarin*, 5383

Bengtsson, Frans Gunnar, *The Long Ships*, 427; *Red Orm*, 428

Berry, Francis, *I Tell of Greenland*, 66

Berry, R. M., *Leonardo's Horse*, 663

Biggins, John, *The Emperor's Coloured Coat*, 1109

Blakenship, William D., *Yukon Gold*, 5209

Blanco, Evangeline, *Caribe*, 5911

Bowen, Marjorie, *The Viper of Milan*, 558

Bowering, Marilyn, *To All Appearances a Lady*, 5347

Boyer, Elizabeth, *Marguerite de la Roque*, 5182

Boyne, Walter J., *Eagles at War*, 1492

Bragg, Melvyn, *The Sword and the Miracle*, 2137

Brink, André Philippus, *On the Contrary*, 4809

Broome, Susannah, *The Pearl Pagoda*, 5349

Brown, George Mackay, *Vinland*, 433

Brown, Mary, *Playing the Jack*, 2816

Bryher, *Ruan*, 2142

Bull, Bartle, *The White Rhino Hotel*, 4892

Bunn, T. Davis, *Gibraltar Passage*, 1991

Burroughs, Edgar Rice, *The Outlaw of Torn*, 2146

Butler, Robert Olen, *The Deep Green Sea*, 6059

Cabell, James Branch, *Domnei*, 2150

Carnegie, Sacha, *The Banners of War*, 806; *Scarlet Banners of Love*, 808

Céline, Louis-Ferdinand, *Journey to the End of the Night*, 1130; *North*, 1512; *Rigadoon*, 1994

Chadwick, Elizabeth, *The Champion*, 436

Chaikin, L. L., *Jamaican Sunset*, 5830; *The Pirate and His Lady*, 5831; *Port Royal*, 5832

Chalker, Jack L., *The Devil's Voyage*, 5110

Chamberlin, Ann, *Sofia*, 672

Charteris, Hugo, *The Coat*, 4435

Clavel, Bernard, *Lord of the River*, 927

Clavell, James, *Whirlwind*, 5597

Cleary, Jon, *The Golden Sabre*, 1520; *High Road to China*, 4438

Clews, Roy, *The Golden City*, 4817

Clifford, Francis, *The Naked Runner*, 1995

Clive, William, *Dando on Delhi Ridge*, 5462

Codshalk, C. S., *Kalimantaan*, 5015

Cohan, Tony, *Opium*, 5355

Coleman, Bob, *The Later Adventures of Tom Jones*, 2834

Conrad, Joseph, *Almayer's Folly*, 5018; *An Outcast of the Islands*, 5019; *The Rescue*, 6025

Cornwell, Bernard, *Killer's Wake*, 3193; *Sharpe's Devil*, 5834

Costain, Thomas Bertram, *The Black Rose*, 2171

De Graaf, Anne, *Where the Fire Burns*, 1999

De Hartog, Jan, *The Centurion*, 356; *The Trail of the Serpent*, 5113

De Klerk, Willem Abraham, *The Thirstland*, 4825

Defoe, Daniel, *The Fortunate Mistress*, 814; *Robinson Crusoe*, 5022

Delderfield, R. F., *Charlie, Come Home*, 4457

Dengler, Sandy, *East of the Outback*, 5024

Dewhurst, Keith, *Captain of the Sands*, 4826

Dickens, Charles, *Martin Chuzzlewit*, 3237

Dickey, James, *To the White Sea*, 5693

Dickinson, Peter, *The Blue Knight*, 73

DiPerna, Paula, *The Discoveries of Mrs Christopher Columbus: His Wife's Version*, 683

Doherty, P. C., *The Serpent Amongst the Lilies*, 572

Doyle, Arthur Conan, *The White Company*, 573

Drewe, Robert, *The Drowner*, 5027

Drummond, Emma, *The Bridge of a Hundred Dragons*, 5405; *A Captive Freedom*, 4827; *That Sweet and Savage Land*, 3899

Dumas, Alexandre, *The Count of Monte Cristo*, 955; *The Three Musketeers*, 687; *The Vicomte de Bragelonne*, 689

Dunmore, Spencer, *Bomb Run*, 4462

Dunn, Carola, *Miss Jacobson's Journey*, 3254

Dunnett, Dorothy, *Caprice and Rondo*, 580; *King Hereafter*, 2187; *Niccolò Rising*, 581; *Pawn in Frankincense*, 690; *Queens' Play*, 691; *Race of Scorpions*, 582; *The Ringed Castle*, 692; *Scales of Gold*, 583; *The Spring of the Ram*, 584; *To Lie with Lions*, 585; *The Unicorn Hunt*, 586

Durand, Loup, *Jaguar*, 5932

Durrell, Lawrence, *Mountolive*, 4906

Edwards, Anne, *Wallis*, 4472

Eldershaw, M. Barnard, *A House Is Built*, 5032

Emery, John, *The Sky People*, 5115

Endo, Shusaku, *The Samurai*, 5666

Fagyas, M., *The Devil's Lieutenant*, 1171

Falkirk, Richard, *Blackstone*, 3284

Farnol, Jeffery, *The High Adventure*, 3287

Farrington, Robert, *The Killing of Richard the Third*, 2425

Forrest, Anthony, *Captain Justice*, 963

Foxall, Raymond, *The Silver Goblet*, 3310

Franklin, Sarah B., *Daughter of Troy*, 115

Fraser, George MacDonald, *Flash for Freedom*, 3313; *Flashman*, 3314; *Flashman and the Angel of the Lord*, 3315; *Flashman and the Dragon*, 5360; *Flashman and the Mountain of Light*, 5471; *Flashman and the Redskins*, 3316; *Flashman at the Charge*, 3317; *Flashman in the Great Game*, 3318; *Flashman's Lady*, 3319; *Mr*

Allegory

Christian Fiction

Country Life

Domestic Fiction

Epic Literature

Erotic Literature

Family Saga

Fantastic Literature

Gothic Fiction

Kinsale, Laura, *My Sweet Folly*, 3469
Knight, Alanna, *Castle of Foxes*, 4093; *Estella*, 4094
Leland, Thomas, *Longsword, Earl of Salisbury*, 2249
Leonard, Phyllis G., *Phantom of the Sacred Well*, 5855
Michaels, Barbara, *Black Rainbow*, 4190; *Greygallows*, 3538; *The Wizard's Daughter*, 4191
O'Doherty, Brian, *The Strange Case of Mademoiselle P*, 862
Pearson, Diane, *The Summer of the Barshinskeys*, 4222
Perutz, Leo, *The Swedish Cavalier*, 866
Phillips, Caryl, *Cambridge*, 5875
Phillips, Jill M., *Walford's Oak*, 2949
Phillips, Michael R., and Judith Pella, *Flight from Stonewycke*, 4255; *The Heather Hills of Stonewycke*, 4256
Randall, Rona, *Watchman's Stone*, 4274
Reed, Jeremy, *Dorian*, 4284
Reidy, Sue, *The Visitation*, 5164
Roberts, Janet Louise, *The Jade Vendetta*, 4293
Roberts, Michelle, *Daughters of the House*, 1817
Soister, Helena, *Prophecies*, 780
Stubbs, Jean, *Dear Laura*, 4349
Tattersall, Jill, *Lyonesse Abbey*, 3713; *The Wild Hunt*, 3715
Veryan, Patricia, *The Riddle of Alabaster Royal*, 3748
Wassmo, Herbjorg, *Dina's Book*, 1075
Yarbro, Chelsea Quinn, *Better in the Dark*, 549; *Blood Games*, 421; *A Candle for D'Artagnan*, 895; *Crusader's Torch*, 550; *Darker Jewels*, 789; *A Flame in Byzantium*, 551; *Hotel Transylvania*, 1084; *Mansions of Darkness*, 5815; *Out of the House of Life*, 1085; *The Palace*, 790; *Path of the Eclipse*, 552; *Tempting Fate*, 1962; *Writ in Blood*, 1414

Horror

Aiken, Joan, *Castle Barebane*, 3781
Anscombe, Roderick, *The Secret Life of Laszlo, Count Dracula*, 1095
Borchardt, Alice, *The Silver Wolf*, 431
Carr, Philippa, *The Black Swan*, 3829
Dinesen, Isak, *The Angelic Avengers*, 948
Gideon, Nancy, *Midnight Temptation*, 1196
Gray, Alasdair, *Poor Things*, 3971
Hambly, Barbara, *Those Who Hunt the Night*, 3982
Harbaugh, Karen, *The Vampire Viscount*, 3352
Holland, Tom, *Lord of the Dead*, 987
Kalogridis, Jeanne, *Lord of the Vampires*, 1244
Kaplick, Vaclav, *Witch Hammer*, 847
Lucie-Smith, Edward, *The Dark Pageant*, 609
Martin, Valerie, *Mary Reilly*, 4161
Moline, Karen, *Belladonna*, 4602

Neill, Robert, *Devil's Door*, 2939
Rice, Anne, *Cry to Heaven*, 870; *Pandora*, 397
Saberhagen, Fred, *A Sharpness on the Neck*, 1054

Humorous Fiction

Alarcon, Pedro Antonio de, *The Three-Cornered Hat*, 899
Amado, Jorge, *Doña Flor and Her Two Husbands*, 5900; *Gabriela: Clove and Cinnamon*, 5819
Austen, Jane, *Emma*, 3052; *Persuasion*, 3055
Bengtsson, Frans Gunnar, *The Long Ships*, 427
Boyle, T. Coraghessan, *Water Music*, 4805
Brinkley, William, *Don't Go near the Water*, 5104
Dahl, Roald, *My Uncle Oswald*, 4447
Fielding, Henry, *Amelia*, 2851; *Joseph Andrews*, 2852; *Tom Jones*, 2853
Gary, Romain, *The Enchanters*, 829
Gogol, Nikolai, *Dead Souls*, 969
Goncharov, Ivan Aleksandrovich, *Oblomov*, 1198
Guareschi, Giovanni, *Comrade Don Camillo*, 2023; *Don Camillo and his Flock*, 2024; *Don Camillo Meets the Flower Children*, 2025; *Don Camillo Takes the Devil by the Tail*, 2026; *Don Camillo's Dilemma*, 2027
Hasek, Jaroslav, *The Good Soldier Svejk and His Fortunes in the World War*, 1210
Heller, Joseph, *Catch-22*, 1624; *God Knows*, 188
Jovanovski, Meto, *Cousins*, 1241
Kirst, Hans Hellmut, *Revolt of Gunner Asch*, 1685
Mankowitz, Wolf, *A Night with Casanova*, 1017
Menen, Aubrey, *Fonthill*, 3532
Mercer, Charles, *Pacific*, 5156
Monger, Christopher, *The Englishman Who Went up a Hill but Came down a Mountain*, 4196
Pizishkzad, Iraj, *My Uncle Napoleon*, 5637
Shadbolt, Maurice, *Monday's Warriors*, 5083
Sholem Aleichem, *The Adventures of Menahem-Mendl*, 1061; *The Adventures of Mottel*, 1352
Skvorecky, Josef, *The Miracle Game*, 2083
Stevenson, D. E., *Mrs Tim Gets a Job*, 4783
Syal, Meera, *Anita and Me*, 4787
Willis, Ted, *The Bells of Autumn*, 4708; *The Green Leaves of Summer*, 4401; *Spring at the Winged Horse*, 4402

Jewish Fiction

Agnon, Shmuel Yosef, *The Bridal Canopy*, 898; *A Guest for the Night*, 1445; *A Simple Story*, 1091

Appelfeld, Aharon, *The Age of Wonders*, 5590; *Badenheim 1939*, 1452; *The Conversion*, 1097
Asch, Sholem, *Moses*, 1; *Mottke: The Thief*, 904
Austin, Lynn N., *My Father's God*, 171
Bassani, Giorgio, *The Garden of the Finzi-Continis*, 1466
Becker, Stephen D., *Dog Tags*, 5735
Bor, Josef, *The Terezn Requiem*, 1488
Charchat, Isaac, *A Constant Reminder*, 5596
Dayan, Yaël, *Death Had Two Sons*, 5601
Demetz, Hanna, *The House on Prague Street*, 1537
Der Nister, *The Family Mashber*, 945
Desai, Anita, *Baumgartner's Bombay*, 5529
Edelson, Marjorie, *Malkeh and Her Children*, 1163
Epstein, Leslie, *King of the Jews*, 1552
Feuchtwanger, Lion, *The Jew of Rome*, 361; *Josephus and the Emperor*, 362
Freud, Esther, *Summer at Gaglow*, 1179
Grade, Chaim, *The Yeshiva*, 1605
Greenberg, Joanne, *The King's Persons*, 2212
Gross, Joel, *The Books of Rachel*, 706; *The Lives of Rachel*, 288
Grynberg, Henryk, *The Victory*, 2022
Habe, Hans, *The Mission*, 1614
Halter, Marek, *The Book of Abraham*, 289
Harris, Norma, *Trumpets of Silver*, 5577
Hersey, John, *The Wall*, 1628
High, Monique Raphel, *The Four Winds of Heaven*, 1222
Kalechofsky, Roberta, *Bodmin, 1349*, 2454
Karmel, Ilona, *An Estate of Memory*, 1660
Keneally, Thomas, *Schindler's List*, 1670
Kotlowitz, Robert, *Somewhere Else*, 1001
Lehmann, Marcus, *Rabbi Joselman of Rosheim*, 726
Levin, Meyer, *Eva*, 1713; *My Father's House*, 5624; *The Settlers*, 5625
Mekler, Eva, *Sunrise Shows Late*, 2062
Morton, Frederic, *The Forever Street*, 1291
Perl, Joseph, *Revealer of Secrets*, 1043
Rabon, Israel, *The Street*, 1801
Rothberg, Abraham, *The Sword of the Golem*, 771
Schaeffer, Susan Fromberg, *Anya*, 1854
Schwarz-Bart, André, *The Last of the Just*, 2338
Shalev, Meir, *Esau*, 5644
Sholem Aleichem, *The Adventures of Menahem-Mendl*, 1061; *The Adventures of Mottel*, 1352

Legal Story

Love Story

Medical Novel

Regency Novel

Religious Fiction

Satire

Western Fiction

Place and Time Index

Note: Numbers refer to entry numbers. The action of stories may take place in several different countries or over several different continents. This index lists the setting or settings in which the predominant action occurs. For each country also check under corresponding cities (e.g., for settings in "England" see also under "London, Bath, or Yorkshire"). Also check the Subject Index for place names (e.g., "Stonehenge") and for more specific locales. Stories that involve specific settings in the United States (e.g., "Philadelphia") will be listed in the subject index.

Serote, Mongane, *To Every Birth Its Blood*, 4980
Sher, Anthony, *Middlepost*, 4981
Slovo, Gillian, *Ties of Blood*, 4983
Smith, Wilbur A., *Golden Fox*, 4985; *Power of the Sword*, 4987; *Rage*, 4988; *A Sparrow Falls*, 4989
Van der Vyver, Marita, *Childish Things*, 4992
Zwi, Rose, *The Umbrella Tree*, 4999

Africa, Sub-Saharan

Before 1900
Forbath, Peter, *The Last Hero*, 4829
Hagerfors, Lennart, *The Whales in Lake Tanganyika*, 4836

Africa, West

Before 1900
Boyle, T. Coraghessan, *Water Music*, 4805
Carter, Peter, *The Sentinels*, 4813

1900 and After
Monninger, Joseph, *The Viper Tree*, 4959

Albania

1290-1491
Kadare, Ismail, *The Three-Arched Bridge*, 602

1919-1945
Kadare, Ismail; *The File on H*, 1658; *The General of the Dead Army*, 1659

1946-1975
Kadare, Ismail; *The Concert*, 2042

Alberta

1800-1932
Myles, Eugenie Louise, *The Emperor of Peace River*, 5252
Oke, Janette, *Drums of Change*, 5257

1933 and After
Kinsella, W. P., *Box Socials*, 5295

Alexandria

Prehistory and the Ancient World
Hareven, Shulamith, *The Miracle Hater*, 18

Roman Empire to AD 476
Bradshaw, Gillian, *The Beacon at Alexandria*, 214
Kingsley, Charles, *Hypatia*, 217
Nelson, Ray Faraday, *Dogheaded Death*, 219

1900 and After
Durrell, Lawrence, *Mountolive*, 4906; *Clea*, 4904; *Justine*, 4905; *Sebastian: Or Ruling Passions*, 4907; *Balthazar*, 4903
Hylton, Sara, *In the Shadow of the Nile*, 4938

Algeria

Before 1900
Moore, Brian, *The Magician's Wife*, 4855

1900 and After
Bayer, William, *Visions of Isabelle*, 4887

Camus, Albert, *The First Man*, 4893
Djebar, Assia, *Fantasia: An Algerian Cavalcade*, 4899; *A Sister to Scheherazade*, 4900
Driscoll, Peter, *Heritage*, 4901
Givon, Thomas, *Running Through Grass*, 4923
Lachmet, Djanet, *Lallia*, 4942
Musser, Elizabeth, *Two Crosses*, 4961; *Two Testaments*, 4962

Amsterdam

1919-1945
Forman, James D., *The Survivor*, 1567
Moyes, Patricia, *Many Deadly Returns*, 1771
Weil, Grete, *Last Trolley from Beethovenstraat*, 1933

Angola

Before 1900
Silverberg, Robert, *Lord of Darkness*, 4874

1900 and After
Antunes, António Lobo, *Fado Alexandrino*, 4884
Lobo Antunes, Antonio, *South of Nowhere*, 4946

Antarctica

1900 and After
Bainbridge, Beryl, *The Birthday Boys*, 5099
Herbert, Marie, *Winter of the White Seal*, 5129
Holt, Kare, *The Race*, 5132
Keneally, Thomas, *Victim of the Aurora*, 5139

Antigua

1800-1899
Cartland, Barbara, *Love at the Helm*, 5828

Arab Emirates

1900 and After
Munif, Abd-al-Rahman, *Cities of Salt*, 5630; *The Trench*, 5631; *Variations on Night and Day*, 5632

Argentina

Before 1600
Thornton, Lawrence, *Tales from the Blue Archives*, 5781

1800-1899
Berry, Jim, *The Moon Stallion*, 5823
Fuentes, Carlos, *The Campaign*, 5840

1900 and After
Costantini, Humberto, *The Long Night of Francisco Sanctis*, 5923
Giardinelli, Mempo, *Sultry Moon*, 5949
Gombrowicz, Witold, *Trans-Atlantyk*, 5950
Griffin, W. E. B., *Honor Bound*, 5953
Higgins, Jack, *Exocet*, 5131
Kaplan, Andrew, *War of the Raven*, 5962
Kozameh, Alicia, *Steps under Water*, 5963
Martinez, Tomas Eloy, *The Peron Novel*, 5969; *Santa Evita*, 5970

Massie, Allan, *The Sins of the Father*, 5971
Puig, Manuel, *Heartbreak Tango*, 5992
Sabato, Ernesto, *The Angel of Darkness*, 5999
Saint Exupéry, Antoine de, *Night Flight*, 6000
Thornton, Lawrence, *Imagining Argentina*, 6009; *Naming the Spirits*, 6010
Toíbín, Colm, *The Story of the Night*, 6011
Unger, Douglas, *El Yanqui*, 6013

Armenia

1860-1918
Kelly, Clint, *Deliver Us From Evil*, 1248

Athens

Prehistory and the Ancient World
Caldwell, Taylor, *Glory and the Lightning*, 110
Gaines, Charles Kelsey, *By the Will of Apollo*, 118
Holt, Tom, *Goatsong*, 131; *The Walled Orchard*, 132
Molinaro, Ursule, *The New Moon with the Old Moon in Her Arms*, 138
Renault, Mary, *The Last of the Wine*, 149
Seymour, Miranda, *Medea*, 156
Twose, Anna, *The Lion of Athens*, 162

1919-1945
Manning, Olivia, *Friends and Heroes*, 1741; *The Spoilt City*, 1743

1946-1975
Vassilikos, Vassilis, Z, 2097

Australia

Before 1900
Shaw, Patricia, *Where the Willows Weep*, 5089
Astley, Thea, *A Kindness Cup*, 5001
Brent, Madeleine, *Golden Urchin*, 5006
Butler, Richard, *And Wretches Hang*, 5007
Carey, Peter, *Oscar and Lucinda*, 5009
Cato, Nancy, *Brown Sugar*, 5010; *Forefathers*, 5011
Cato, Nancy, and Vivienne Rae Ellis, *Queen Trucanini*, 5012
Clarke, Marcus Andrew Hislop, *His Natural Life*, 5013; *Marcus Clarke*, 5014
Dark, Eleanor, *Storm of Time*, 5020; *The Timeless Land*, 5021
Dengler, Sandy, *Code of Honor*, 5023; *East of the Outback*, 5024; *The Power of Pinjarra*, 5025; *Taste of Victory*, 5026
Drewe, Robert, *The Drowner*, 5027
Eldershaw, M. Barnard, *A House Is Built*, 5032
Franklin, Miles, *My Brilliant Career*, 5033

1900 and After

Arguedas, Jose Maria, *Yawar Fiesta*, 5904

Myers, Edward, *The Mountain Made of Light*, 5979

Riesco, Laura, *Ximena at the Cross-road*, 5997

Varga Llosa, Mario, *Who Killed Palominolero?* 6014

Wilson, Carter, *Treasures on Earth*, 6017

Philippines

Before 1900

Jos, F. Sionil, *Dusk*, 5051

1900 and After

Boyd, William, *The Blue Afternoon*, 5101

Brainard, Cecilia Manguerra, *When the Rainbow Goddess Wept*, 5102

Bram, Christopher, *Almost History*, 5103

Bulosan, Carlos, *The Cry and the Dedication*, 5105

Chai, Arlene J., *The Last Time I Saw Mother*, 5109

Graves, Ralph, *Share of Honor*, 5122

Nolledo, Wilfrido, *But for the Lovers*, 5159

Ty-Casper, Linda, *Awaiting Trespass*, 5173

Pisa

1290-1491

Cole, Hubert, *Hawkwood and the Towers of Pisa*, 562

Poland

476-1289

Michener, James A., *Poland*, 501

1290-1491

Sienkiewicz, Henryk, *The Teutonic Knights*, 637

1492-1649

Banville, John, *Doctor Copernicus*, 656

Gogol, Nikolai, *Taras Bulba*, 703

1650-1788

Carnegie, Sacha, *The Banners of Courage*, 804; *The Banners of Power*, 805; *Scarlet Banners of Love*, 808

Sienkiewicz, Henryk, *The Deluge*, 877; *Fire in the Steppe*, 878; *With Fire and Sword*, 879

Singer, Isaac Bashevis, *Reaches of Heaven*, 880; *Satan in Goray*, 881

1789-1859

Agnon, Shmuel Yosef, *The Bridal Canopy*, 898

Asch, Sholem, *Mottke: The Thief*, 904

Kotlowitz, Robert, *Somewhere Else*, 1001

Wheeler, Thomas Gerald, *A Fanfare for the Stalwart*, 1080

1860-1918

Hoffman, Allen, *Small Worlds*, 1227

Prus, Boleslaw, *The Doll*, 1321

Singer, Isaac Bashevis, *The Estate*, 1358; *The Family Moskat*, 1359; *The Manor*, 1360; *Scum*, 1361

Singer, Israel Joshua, *The Brothers Ashkenazi*, 1362

Sulitzer, Paul-Loup, *Hannah*, 1387

1919-1945

Agnon, Shmuel Yosef, *A Guest for the Night*, 1445

Appelfeld, Aharon, *Katerina*, 1454; *Tzili, the Story of a Life*, 1457

Begley, Louis, *Wartime Lies*, 1470

Bienek, Horst, *Earth and Fire*, 1478; *The First Polka*, 1479; *September Light*, 1480

Charney, Ann, *Dobryd*, 1514

Epstein, Leslie, *King of the Jews*, 1552

Ettinger, Elzbieta, *Kindergarten*, 1553

Fink, Ida, *The Journey*, 1559

Furst, Alan, *The Polish Officer*, 1578

Glatstein, Jacob, *Homeward Bound*, 1598

Haddad, Carolyn, *A Mother's Secret*, 1616

Hersey, John, *The Wall*, 1628

Household, Geoffrey, *Rogue Justice*, 1640

Irving, Clifford, *The Angel of Zin*, 1649

Karmel, Ilona, *An Estate of Memory*, 1660

Karmel-Wolfe, Henia, *The Baders of Jacob Street*, 1661

Keneally, Thomas, *Schindler's List*, 1670

Konwicki, Tadeusz, *Moonrise, Moon-set*, 1694

Kosinski, Jerzy N., *The Painted Bird*, 1695

Krall, Hanna, *The Subtenant*, 1696; *To Outwit God*, 1697

Kuniczak, W. S., *Valedictory*, 4556; *The March*, 1701; *The Thousand Hour Day*, 1702

Levin, Meyer, *Eva*, 1713

Lewitt, Maria, *Come Spring*, 1714

Litewka, Albert, *Warsaw*, 1716

Michaels, Anne, *Fugitive Pieces*, 1755

Milosz, Czeslaw, *The Seizure of Power*, 1758

Parizeau, Alice, *The Lilacs Are Blooming in Warsaw*, 1787

Rabon, Israel, *The Street*, 1801

Read, Piers Paul, *Polonaise*, 1807

Samelson, William, *One Bridge to Life*, 1846

Samuels, Gertrude, *Mottele*, 1847

Schaeffer, Susan Fromberg, *Anya*, 1854

Sherlock, John, *The Golden Mile*, 1861

Singer, Isaac Bashevis, *The Certificate*, 1874; *Shosha*, 1875

Skibell, Joseph, *A Blessing on the Moon*, 1876

Szczypiorski, Andrezej, *The Beautiful Mrs Seidenman*, 1890; *The Shadow Catcher*, 1891

Thoene, Bodie, and Terri Brock, *The Twilight of Courage*, 1904

Tomkiewicz, Mina, *Of Bombs and Mice*, 1912

Wojdowski, Bogdan, *Bread for the Departed*, 1956

Yolen, Jane, *Briar Rose*, 1965

1946-1975

De Graaf, Anne, *Bread upon the Waters*, 1998; *Where the Fire Burns*, 1999

Grynberg, Henryk, *The Victory*, 2022

Hlasko, Marek, *The Eighth Day of the Week*, 2037

Mekler, Eva, *Sunrise Shows Late*, 2062

Portugal

1492-1649

Gidley, Charles, *Armada*, 701

Marshall, James Vance, *The Wind at Morning*, 738

Zimler, Richard, *The Last Kabbalist of Lisbon*, 792

1650-1788

Saramago, Jos, *Baltasar and Blimunda*, 872

1789-1859

Cornwell, Bernard, *Sharpe's Battle*, 931; *Sharpe's Company*, 932; *Sharpe's Eagle*, 933; *Sharpe's Enemy*, 934; *Sharpe's Revenge*, 937; *Sharpe's Rifles*, 938

Hodge, Jane Aiken, *Whispering*, 3412; *The Winding Stair*, 986

1919-1945

Kartun, Derek, *The Courier*, 1663

Patterson, Harry, *To Catch a King*, 1790

Tabucchi, Antonio, *Pereira Declares*, 1893

Potsdam

1919-1945

Kennedy, Raymond A., *The Bitterest Age*, 1672

Prague

1492-1649

Rothberg, Abraham, *The Sword of the Golem*, 771

1919-1945

Kingsley, Johanna, *Loving Touches*, 1678

Kohout, Pavel, *The Widow Killer*, 1692

Thoene, Bodie, *Prague Counterpoint*, 1901

Tomin, Zdena, *Stalin's Shoe*, 1911

Weil, Jiri, *Life with a Star*, 1934; *Mendelssohn Is on the Roof*, 1935

1946-1975

Klima, Ivan, *Love and Garbage*, 2049

Lustig, Arnost, *Dita Saxova*, 2056

McCrum, Robert, *The Fabulous Englishman*, 2059

Skvorecky, Josef, *The Miracle Game*, 2083

Puerto Rico

1900 and After

Blanco, Evangeline, *Caribe*, 5911

Subject Index

Note: Numbers refer to entry numbers.

Hawkes, Jacquetta, *King of the Two Lands: The Pharaoh Akhenaten*, 19

Tarr, Judith, *Pillar of Fire*, 54

Alaric
Robinson, Kathleen, *Heaven's Only Daughter*, 401

Alaska
White, Stewart Edward, and Harry DeVighne, *Pole Star*, 1081

Alba, Maria del Pilar, duquesa de
Larreta, Antonio, *The Last Portrait of the Duchess of Alba*, 1006

Albigensian Wars
Closs, Hannah Priebsch, *Deep Are the Valleys*, 440; *High Are the Mountains*, 441; *The Silent Tarn*, 442
Maturin, Charles Robert, *The Albigenses*, 497
Munthe, Adam John, *A Note That Breaks the Silence*, 505

Alchemy
Connell, Evan S., *The Alchymist's Journal*, 677
Godwin, William, *St Leon, a Tale of the Sixteenth Century*, 702
Yourcenar, Marguerite, *The Abyss*, 791

Alcibiades
Sutcliff, Rosemary, *The Flowers of Adonis*, 159

Aldgyth
Llywelyn, Morgan, *The Wind from Hastings*, 2261

Aleutians
Green, Wayne L., *Allegiance*, 5697

Alexander I of Russia
Anthony, Evelyn, *Far Flies the Eagle*, 902
Harrod-Eagles, Cynthia, *Anne*, 974
Prince Michael of Greece, *Sultana*, 1049
Tolstoy, Leo, *War and Peace*, 1068

Alexander II of Russia
Cahan, Abraham, *The White Terror and the Red*, 1127
Phillips, Michael R., *The Crown and the Crucible*, 1315

Alexander III of Scotland
Tranter, Nigel G., *True Thomas*, 2369

Alexander the Great
Apostolou, Anna, *A Murder in Macedon*, 101; *A Murder in Thebes*, 102
Bova, Ben, *Orion and the Conqueror*, 103
Druon, Maurice, *Alexander the God*, 114
Gemmell, David, *Dark Prince*, 121
Kazantzakis, Nikos, *Alexander the Great*, 133
Renault, Mary, *Fire from Heaven*, 146; *Funeral Games*, 147; *The Persian Boy*, 151
Tarr, Judith, *Lord of the Two Lands*, 161

Alexander VI, Pope
Davis, Genevieve, *A Passion in the Blood*, 568

Alexandra of Russia
Lambton, Antony, *Elizabeth and Alexandra*, 1262

Alfred the Great of England
Bonallack, Basil, *The Flame in the Dark*, 2132
Canning, Victor, *Raven's Wind*, 435
Duggan, Alfred Leo, *The King of Athelney*, 2184
Wolf, Joan, *The Edge of Light*, 2385
Wright, Patricia, *I Am England*, 2390

Algerian Civil War
Driscoll, Peter, *Heritage*, 4901
Givon, Thomas, *Running Through Grass*, 4923
Lachmet, Djanet, *Lallia*, 4942
Musser, Elizabeth, *Two Crosses*, 4961; *Two Testaments*, 4962

Allan, James
Fullerton, Alexander, *Piper's Leave*, 3323

Allende, Salvador
Alegría, Fernando, *Allende*, 5896
Allende, Isabel, *The House of the Spirits*, 5898
Dorfman, Ariel, *Hard Rain*, 5931

Allies
Forbes, Colin, *The Palermo Affair*, 1564
Hill, Reginald, *No Man's Land*, 1224
Katkov, Norman, *The Judas Kiss*, 1664
Scholefield, Alan, *The Alpha Raid*, 4975
Tine, Robert, *Black Market*, 1908

Amazon
Higgins, Jack, *The Last Place God Made*, 5955

Ambulance drivers
Smith, Helen Zenna, *Not So Quiet*, 1365

American Civil War
Fraser, George MacDonald, *Flashman and the Angel of the Lord*, 3315
Stewart, Fred Mustard, *Pomp and Circumstance*, 3685

American occupation (World War II)
Bulosan, Carlos, *The Cry and the Dedication*, 5105
Michener, James A., *Sayonara*, 5707
Roudybush, Alexandra, *A Gastronomic Murder*, 2078

American Revolution
Feuchtwanger, Lion, *Proud Destiny*, 825
Heckert, Eleanor, *The Golden Rock*, 5791
Lambdin, Dewey, *The King's Commission*, 2912
Mullin, Arthur, *Spy*, 2938
Paretti, Sandra, *The Drums of Winter*, 864

Americans abroad
Abbott, Margot, *The Last Innocent Hour*, 1971
Anthony, Patricia, *Flanders*, 1096
Arnold, Elliott, *Proving Ground*, 1459
Biddle, Cordelia Frances, *Beneath the Wind*, 5005
Buck, Pearl S., *Mandala*, 5526
Bunn, T. Davis, *Rhineland Inheritance*, 1993
Clifford, Nicholas Rowland, *The House of Memory*, 5401
Crace, Jim, *Signals of Distress*, 3204
Deford, Frank, *Love and Infamy*, 5692
Deveraux, Jude, *The Duchess*, 3883; *Lost Lady*, 3225
Dunn, Carola, *Damsel in Distress*, 4464
Faust, Irvin, *Jim Dandy*, 4914
Feibleman, Peter S., *The Columbus Tree*, 2005
Fraser, George MacDonald, *Mr American*, 3932
Gordon, Deborah, *Runaway Magic*, 5363
Griffin, W. E. B., *Behind the Lines*, 5124; *The Lieutenant*, 1611
Guerard, Albert J., *The Hotel in the Jungle*, 5845
Hall, Robert Lee, *Benjamin Franklin and a Case of Artful Murder*, 2868; *Benjamin Franklin and a Case of Christmas Murder*, 2869; *Benjamin Franklin Takes the Case*, 2870; *London Blood*, 2871; *Murder at Drury Lane*, 2872; *Murder by the Waters*, 2873
Hart, Carolyn G., *Escape From Paris*, 1620
Howells, William Dean, *Indian Summer*, 1230
Keith, Agnes Newton, *Beloved Exiles*, 5136
MacDonald, Malcolm, *The Carringtons of Helston*, 4146
Minatra, MaryAnn, *Before Night Falls*, 1759
Mo, Timothy, *An Insular Possession*, 5371
Mueller, Marnie, *Green Fires*, 5978
Mullin, Arthur, *Spy*, 2938
Munif, Abd-al-Rahman, *Cities of Salt*, 5630; *The Trench*, 5631
Oberman, Wendy, *Mothers and Other Loves*, 1781
Pal, Dolores, *In Search of Mihailo*, 2066
Plante, David, *The Foreigner*, 2073
Scholefield, Alan, *Lion in the Evening*, 4977
Sheppard, Stephen, *The Four Hundred*, 4327; *Monte Carlo*, 1860
Speer, Flora M., *Time and Time Again*, 4335
Stewart, Fred Mustard, *The Magnificent Savages*, 5378
Tyler, W. T., *The Consul's Wife*, 4991
Watkins, Paul, *The Promise of Light*, 4693
Westheimer, David, *Rider on the Wind*, 5655

Bierce, Ambrose

Bigamists

Bikini Atoll

Bilhah

Black market

Blackfoot

Blackmail

Blessington, Marguerite, Countess

Bligh, William

Blindness see Disabilities (Disabled)

Blitzkrieg

Boardinghouses

Boer Wars

Freud, Sigmund

Burgess, Anthony, *The End of the World News*, 1124

Daniels, Kathleen, *Minna's Story*, 1143

Hill, Carol DeChelli, *Henry James' Midnight Song*, 1223

Meyer, Nicholas, *The Seven-Per-Cent Solution*, 4599

Michalos, Peter, *Psyche*, 1289

Stone, Irving, *The Passions of the Mind*, 1383

Thomas, D. M., *Eating Pavlova*, 4682; *The White Hotel*, 1905

Trachtenberg, Inge, *An Arranged Marriage*, 1394

Friendship

Amos, James, *The Memorial: A Novel of the Vietnam War*, 6048

Anderson, Ken, *Sympathy for the Devil*, 6049

Becker, Stephen D., *A Rendezvous in Haiti*, 5907

Binchy, Maeve, *Light a Penny Candle*, 4420

Bove, Emmanuel, *Armand*, 1489

Buckley, William F. Jr., *Brothers No More*, 1501

Cadell, Elizabeth, *A Lion in the Way*, 5456

Cameron, Ian, *The Young Eagles*, 3823

Clark, Catherine Clifton, *The Saturday Treat*, 4437

Crowley, Elaine, *The Ways of Women*, 4446

Deford, Frank, *Love and Infamy*, 5692

Donnelly, Frances, *Shake Down the Stars*, 4461

Doyle, Roddy, *Paddy Clarke, Ha Ha Ha*, 4738

Forbath, Peter, *Lord of the Kongo*, 4830

Gardiner, Judy, *All on a Summer's Day*, 4487

Gaskin, Catherine, *The Ambassador's Women*, 4490

Gilbert, Anna, *Flowers for Lilian*, 3942

Golding, William, *Darkness Visible*, 4500

Gunn, Neil M., *Young Art and Old Hector*, 3976

Hill, Susan, *Strange Meeting*, 1225

Hough, Richard, *Wings Against the Sky*, 4527

Huth, Angela, *Land Girls*, 4534

Hylton, Sara, *Melissa*, 4537

Laker, Rosalind, *The Venetian Mask*, 851

Lord, Bette, *The Middle Heart*, 5423

Masters, John, *Far, Far the Mountain Peak*, 5547

McAleer, John J., and Billy Dickson, *Unit Pride*, 5746

McGill, Richard, *Omamori*, 5682

Mount, Ferdinand, *The Clique*, 4765

Nunez, Elizabeth, *Bruised Hibiscus*, 5984

Pater, Walter, *Marius the Epicurean*, 395

Pilcher, Rosamund, *Coming Home*, 4619

Plaidy, Jean, *Lilith*, 4259

Ruark, Robert, *Something of Value*, 4974

Ryan, Mary, *Glenallen*, 4643

Saxton, Judith, *First Love, Last Love*, 4647

Settle, Mary Lee, *Celebration*, 4778

Somtow, S. P., *Jasmine Nights*, 6046

Taylor, Kressmann, *Address Unknown*, 1897

Thomas, Rosie, *Bad Girls, Good Women*, 4789

Thompson, Joan, *Interesting Times*, 1391

Troyat, Henri, *My Father's House*, 1398

Uhlman, Fred, *Reunion*, 1922

Wesley, Mary, *A Sensible Life*, 1940

Zilinsky, Ursula, *The Long Afternoon*, 1420

Frobisher, Martin, Sir

Tourney, Leonard D., *Frobisher's Savage*, 2752

Frontier and pioneer life

Amado, Jorge, *Gabriela: Clove and Cinnamon*, 5819; *Show Down*, 5820

Bowering, George, *Shoot!*, 5211

Boyer, Elizabeth, *Marguerite de la Roque*, 5182

Brand, Max, *The Stingaree*, 5212

Brown, James Ambrose, *The Ridge of Gold*, 4810

Carey, Peter, *Oscar and Lucinda*, 5009

Cloete, Stuart, *The Fiercest Heart*, 4818; *The Hill of Doves*, 4819; *The Mask*, 4820; *The Turning Wheels*, 4821; *Watch for the Dawn*, 4822

Costain, Thomas Bertram, *High Towers*, 5185

Dark, Eleanor, *Storm of Time*, 5020; *The Timeless Land*, 5021

De la Roche, Mazo, *The Building of Jalna*, 5216

Dengler, Sandy, *East of the Outback*, 5024

Eldershaw, M. Barnard, *A House Is Built*, 5032

Franklin, Miles, *All That Swagger*, 5118

Glover, Ruth, *Bitter Thistle, Sweet Rose*, 5228; *Second Best Bride*, 5229; *The Shining Light*, 5230

Hanrahan, Barbara, *Dove*, 5041

Hickman, Patricia, *Angel of the Outback*, 5042

Hyde, Robin, *Check to Your King*, 5049

Krauth, Nigel, *Matilda, My Darling*, 5058

Laidlaw, Robert, *The McGregors*, 5236

Long, William Stuart, *The Adventurers*, 5059; *The Colonists*, 5060;

The Exiles, 5061; *The Explorers*, 5062; *The Settlers*, 5063

Malouf, David, *Remembering Babylon*, 5065

Matthews, Greg, *The Wisdom of Stones*, 5150

Matthews, Patricia, *The Dreaming Tree*, 5066

Moore, Brian, *Black Robe*, 5195

Morris, Alan, *Between Earth and Sky*, 5246; *Bright Sword of Justice*, 5247; *Heart of Valor*, 5249

Murphy, James F., *They Were Dreamers*, 5251

Myles, Eugenie Louise, *The Emperor of Peace River*, 5252

Neilan, Sarah, *Paradise*, 5196

Niven, Frederick, *The Flying Years*, 5197

Oke, Janette, *Roses for Mama*, 5258; *When Breaks the Dawn*, 5259; *When Calls the Heart*, 5260; *When Comes the Spring*, 5261; *When Hope Springs New*, 5262

Pullen, Kathleen J., *Mary Reibey*, 5163

Salverson, Laura Goodman, *The Viking Heart*, 5269

Shadbolt, Maurice, *The Lovelock Version*, 5082

Shaw, Patricia, *Cry of the Rain Bird*, 5085; *The Feather and the Stone*, 5086; *River of the Sun*, 5088; *Where the Willows Weep*, 5089

Wheeler, Richard S., *Rendezvous*, 5277

Fu Manchu

Van Ash, Cay, *Ten Years beyond Baker Street*, 4378

Fur traders

Kirby, William, *The Golden Dog*, 5191

Moore, Brian, *Black Robe*, 5195

White, Stewart Edward, and Harry DeVighne, *Pole Star*, 1081

Gaius Marius

McCullough, Colleen, *The First Man in Rome*, 387; *Fortune's Favorites*, 388; *The Grass Crown*, 389

Galla Placidia

De Chair, Somerset Struben, *Friends, Romans, Concubines*, 355

Gallic Wars

Coolidge, Olivia E., *Caesar's Gallic War*, 348

Gamblers and gambling

Ashfield, Helen, *Beau Barron's Lady*, 3040

Collier, G. K., *The Gamester*, 3174

Dickens, Charles, *The Old Curiosity Shop*, 3239

Fairchild, Elisabeth, *The Rakehell's Reform*, 3282

Feather, Jane, *Virtue*, 3290

Heyer, Georgette, *Faro's Daughter*, 3382

Vivian, Daisy, *Fair Game*, 3753; *Return to Cheyne Spa*, 3757

Nelligan, Emile
Sarna, Lazar, *The Man Who Lived near Nelligan*, 5270

Nelson, Horatio, Lord
Foxell, Nigel, *Loving Emma*, 3311
Sontag, Susan, *The Volcano Lover*, 1063
Styles, Showell, *A Kiss for Captain Hardy*, 3707
Woodman, Richard, *The Bomb Vessel*, 3775

Nero, Emperor of Rome
Comfort, Alex, *Imperial Patient*, 347
Gillespie, Donna, *The Light Bearer*, 366
Hersey, John, *The Conspiracy*, 375
Maier, Paul L., *The Flames of Rome*, 381
Sienkiewicz, Henryk, *Quo Vadis*, 408
Waltari, Mika, *The Roman*, 412
Yarbro, Chelsea Quinn, *Blood Games*, 421

Neruda, Pablo
Donoso, José, *Curfew*, 5930
Skarmeta, Antonio, *Burning Patience*, 6005

New France
Cather, Willa, *Shadows on the Rock*, 5184
Costain, Thomas Bertram, *High Towers*, 5185
Durham, Charles, *The Last Exile*, 823
Elwood, Muriel, *Deeper the Heritage*, 5186
Golon, Anne, *The Countess Angélique*, 5188; *The Temptation of Angélique*, 5189
Kirby, William, *The Golden Dog*, 5191
Mason, F. Van Wyck, *The Young Titan*, 5194
Rosenstock, Janet, *The Fire, the Sword, and the Devil*, 5199
Suthren, Victor, *The Black Cockade*, 5202

New World
Brown, George Mackay, *Vinland*, 433
Cairney, John, *Worlds Apart*, 5106
Gear, Kathleen O'Neal, *This Widowed Land*, 5187
O'Dell, Scott, *The Captive*, 5770

New York City
Demetz, Hanna, *The Journey from Prague Street*, 2001
Landey, Dora, and Elinor Klein, *Triptych*, 1264

Niagara Falls
Urquhart, Jane, *The Whirlpool*, 5275

Nicaraguan Revolution
Detrez, Conrad, *Zone of Fire*, 5929

Nicholas I of Russia
Harrod-Eagles, Cynthia, *Fleur*, 975
Pazzi, Roberto, *Searching for the Emperor*, 1308

Nicholas II of Russia
Borovsky, Natasha, *A Daughter of the Nobility*, 1117

Butler, Gwendoline, *The Red Staircase*, 1126
Gavin, Catherine Irvine, *The Snow Mountain*, 1192
Haskin, Gretchen, *An Imperial Affair*, 1212
Hoe, Susanna, *God Save the Tsar*, 1226
Kross, Jaan, *Professor Martens' Departure*, 1258
Lambton, Antony, *Elizabeth and Alexandra*, 1262
Pazzi, Roberto, *The Princess and the Dragon*, 1307
Pella, Judith, *The Dawning of Deliverance*, 1309; *Heirs of the Motherland*, 1310; *White Nights, Red Morning*, 1311
Saberhagen, Fred, *Dancing Bears*, 1337
Scott, Justin, *A Pride of Royals*, 1346
Stevens, Robert Tyler, *The Summer Day Is Done*, 1376
Willis, Ted, *The Buckingham Palace Connection*, 1411
Yarbro, Chelsea Quinn, *Writ in Blood*, 1414

Nicodemus
Roland, Nicholas, *Who Came by Night*, 318
Walsh, John Evangelist, *The Man Who Buried Jesus*, 330

Nietzsche, Friedrich Wilhelm
Krell, David Farrell, *Nietzsche*, 1255
Yalom, Irvin D., *When Nietzsche Wept*, 1413

Nigerian Civil War
Amadi, Elechi, *Estrangement*, 4883

Nihilism
Dostoyevsky, Fyodor, *The Possessed*, 1154

Nineteenth dynasty
Mailer, Norman, *Ancient Evenings*, 37

Nkomo, Joshua
Moore, Robin, *The White Tribe*, 4960

Noah
Brelich, Mario, *Navigator of the Flood*, 3
Traylor, Ellen Gunderson, *Noah*, 208

Nobility
Acland, Alice, *The Corsican Ladies*, 897
Auchincloss, Louis, *Exit Lady Masham*, 2791
Bell, Josephine, *A Question of Loyalties*, 2798
Bellonci, Maria, *Private Renaissance*, 662
Bennetts, Pamela, *The Borgia Prince*, 555; *My Dear Lover England*, 2551; *Stephen and the Sleeping Saints*, 2127
Boland, Bridget, *Caterina*, 557
Briggs, Jean, *The Flame of the Borgias*, 559
Carr, Robyn, *The Braeswood Tapestry*, 2829
Chapman, Robin, *The Duchess's Diary*, 674

Chisholm, P. F., *A Season of Knives*, 2569
Christopher, Kate, *A Nest of Serpents*, 2571
Codrescu, Andrei, *The Blood Countess*, 675
Davis, Genevieve, *A Passion in the Blood*, 568
Duggan, Alfred Leo, *Leopards and Lilies*, 2186
Epton, Nina Consuelo, *The Burning Heart*, 3278
Fairburn, Eleanor M., *The Rose at Harvest End*, 2423
Goddard, Robert, *In Pale Battalions*, 3958
Haycraft, Molly Costain, *Too Near the Throne*, 2631
Heaven, Constance, *The Queen and the Gypsy*, 2633
Hill, Pamela, *The Green Salamander*, 2636
Holland, Cecelia, *City of God*, 715
Holt, Victoria, *My Enemy the Queen*, 2638
Kenyon, Frank Wilson, *The Duke's Mistress*, 3456; *The Naked Sword*, 604
Kilian, Michael, *Dance on a Sinking Ship*, 1677
Lambton, Antony, *Elizabeth and Alexandra*, 1262
Leland, Thomas, *Longsword, Earl of Salisbury*, 2249
Leslie, Doris, *The Incredible Duchess*, 2919; *Notorious Lady*, 3482; *Wreath for Arabella*, 2658
Manzoni, Alessandro, *The Betrothed*, 735
McNaught, Judith, *A Kingdom of Dreams*, 2467
Mullally, Margaret, *A Crown in Darkness*, 2702
Napier, Priscilla Hayter, *Imperial Winds*, 1295
Orczy, Emmuska, Baroness, *The Elusive Pimpernel*, 1033; *The Scarlet Pimpernel*, 1037
Pargeter, Edith, *The Marriage of Meggotta*, 2291
Peters, Ellis, *The Bloody Field*, 2474
Plaidy, Jean, *Gay Lord Robert*, 2712; *Light on Lucrezia*, 757; *Madonna of the Seven Hills*, 759
Potter, Jeremy, *Disgrace and Favour*, 2723
Prokosch, Frederic, *A Tale for Midnight*, 765
Rivele, Stephen J., *A Booke of Days*, 525
Ross-Macdonald, Malcolm, *The Dukes*, 4299
Saxton, Judith, *Harvest Moon*, 4312
Seton, Anya, *Katherine*, 2504
Seymour, Miranda, *Daughter of Shadows*, 632; *The Stones of Maggiare*, 633
Shelley, Mary Wollstonecraft, *Valperga*, 634
Stewart, Mary, *The Gabriel Hounds*, 3686

Oz, Amos, *Panther in the Basement*, 5634

Rezvani, *Light-Years*, 1814

Silone, Ignazio, *The Fox and the Camellias*, 1868

Restoration (England)

Cameron, Kenneth M., *Our Jo, or the Chronicle of a Coming Man*, 2822

Carr, Philippa, *Lament for a Lost Lover*, 2826

Carr, Robyn, *The Bellerose Bargain*, 2828; *The Braeswood Tapestry*, 2829

Gluyas, Constance, *The King's Brat*, 2863

Lofts, Norah, *Pargeters*, 2670

Potter, Patricia, *Starcatcher*, 2962

Tremain, Rose, *Restoration*, 3005

Wright, Patricia, *The Storms of Fate*, 3025

Revenge

Selimovic, Mesa, *Death and the Dervish*, 875

Revolutions and revolutionaries

Abella, Alex, *The Great American*, 5895

Alvarez, Julia, *In the Time of the Butterflies*, 5899

Blake, James Carlos, *The Friends of Pancho Villa*, 5824

Brink, André Philippus, *On the Contrary*, 4809

Burgess, Anthony, *The End of the World News*, 1124

Chen, Yuan-tsung, *The Dragon's Village*, 5398

Cheuse, Alan, *The Bohemians: John Reed and His Friends Who Shook the World*, 1131

Clavell, James, *Whirlwind*, 5597

Coetzee, J. M., *The Master of Petersburg*, 1132

Ferlinghetti, Lawrence, *Love in the Days of Rage*, 2006

Fitz Gibbon, Constantine, *High Heroic*, 3919

Furmanov, Dmitri, *Chapayev*, 1185

Gavin, Catherine Irvine, *The House of War*, 1583

Ghnassia, Maurice, *Arena*, 365

Givon, Thomas, *Running Through Grass*, 4923

Gonzales, Laurence, *El Vago*, 5951

Haugaard, Erik, *The Rider and His Horse*, 290

Hornman, Wim, *The Stones Cry Out*, 5956

Irving, Clifford, *Tom Mix and Pancho Villa*, 5959

Johnson, Diane, *Persian Nights*, 5619

Jones, Mervyn, *Joseph*, 1239

Krotkov, Yuri, *The Red Monarch*, 1699

Lubis, Mochtar, *A Road with No End*, 5142

Lytton, Edward Bulwer, *Rienzi, the Last of the Roman Tribunes*, 610

Malraux, André, *The Conquerors*, 5424; *Man's Fate*, 5425

Meredith, George, *The Tragic Comedians*, 1024

Murdoch, Iris, *The Red and the Green*, 4199

Neville, Jill, *The Love Germ*, 2064

Riesco, Laura, *Ximena at the Crossroad*, 5997

Rofheart, Martha, *Glendower Country*, 2496

Sholokhov, Mikhail, *Harvest on the Don*, 1862

Shorris, Earl, *Under the Fifth Sun*, 6004

Tranter, Nigel G., *The Wallace*, 2519

Traven, B., *The Carreta*, 5885; *General from the Jungle*, 5886; *Government*, 5887; *March to the Monteria*, 5888

Valles, Jules, *The Insurrectionist*, 1402

Werfel, Franz, *The Forty Days of Musa Dagh*, 1407

West, Rebecca, *The Birds Fall Down*, 1409

Wollaston, Nicholas, *Thistlewood*, 3770

Yáñez, Agustín, *The Edge of the Storm*, 6021; *The Lean Lands*, 6022

Revolutions and revolutionaries, women

Casey, Jane Barnes, *I, Krupskaya: My Life with Lenin*, 1506

Foster, Aisling, *Safe in the Kitchen*, 3930

Rhodes, Cecil

Samkange, Stanlake, *On Trial for My Country*, 4868

Rhodesian Civil war

Moore, Robin, *The White Tribe*, 4960

Rhone River

Clavel, Bernard, *Lord of the River*, 927

Richard I of England

Barnes, Margaret Campbell, *The Passionate Brood*, 2119

Bennetts, Pamela, *Richard and the Knights of God*, 2126

Haycraft, Molly Costain, *My Lord Brother the Lion Heart*, 2214

Kaufman, Pamela, *Banners of Gold*, 2239

Kurland, Lynn, *The Very Thought of You*, 2243

Lofts, Norah, *The Lute Player*, 2262

Penman, Sharon Kay, *The Queen's Man*, 2296

Plaidy, Jean, *The Heart of the Lion*, 2324

Rofheart, Martha, *Lionheart! A Novel of Richard I, King of England*, 2336

Scott, Walter, *Ivanhoe*, 2339; *The Talisman*, 2340

Shelby, Graham, *The Devil Is Loose*, 2342

Richard II of England

Lang, Jennifer, *The Peacock and the Pearl*, 2459

Andrew, Prudence, *The Constant Star*, 2393

Barnes, Margaret Campbell, *Within the Hollow Crown*, 2397

Bennetts, Pamela, *The Lords of Lancaster*, 2400

Doherty, P. C., *The Whyte Harte*, 2419

Lane, Jane, *A Summer Storm*, 2458

Morris, William, *A Dream of John Ball*, 619

Plaidy, Jean, *Passage to Pontefract*, 2477

Widgery, Jeanne Anna, *Trumpet at the Gates*, 2523

Zelitch, Simone, *The Confession of Jack Straw*, 2528

Richard III of England

Barnes, Margaret Campbell, *The King's Bed*, 2395

Belle, Pamela, *The Lodestar*, 2399

Bowen, Marjorie, *Dickon*, 2402

Edwards, Rhoda, *Fortune's Wheel*, 2422

Farrington, Robert, *The Killing of Richard the Third*, 2425

Jarman, Rosemary Hawley, *We Speak No Treason*, 2452

Nickell, Lesley J., *The White Queen*, 2469

Palmer, Marian, *The White Boar*, 2471; *The Wrong Plantagenet*, 2472

Penman, Sharon Kay, *The Sunne in Splendour*, 2473

Plaidy, Jean, *The Reluctant Queen*, 2479

Potter, Jeremy, *A Trail of Blood*, 2483

Tey, Josephine, *The Daughter of Time*, 2748

Tyler-Whittle, Michael Sidney, *Richard III*, 2520

Richelieu, Cardinal

Anthony, Evelyn, *The Cardinal and the Queen*, 652

Dumas, Alexandre, *The Three Musketeers*, 687

Riel Rebellion

Barclay, Byrna, *Summer of the Hungry Pup*, 5208

Lutz, Giles A., *The Magnificent Failure*, 5240

Silver, Alfred, *Lord of the Plains*, 5300

Rienzo, Cola di

Lytton, Edward Bulwer, *Rienzi, the Last of the Roman Tribunes*, 610

Rimini, Francesca da

Fleetwood, Frances, *Concordia*, 455

Riots

Cordell, Alexander, *The Fire People*, 3191

River boats

Cato, Nancy, *All the Rivers Run*, 5107

Rivera, Diego

Poniatowska, Elena, *Dear Diego*, 5990; *Tinisima*, 5991

Robert Dudley, Earl of Leicester
Anthony, Evelyn, *All the Queen's Men*, 2533

Robert I of Scotland
Hill, Pamela, *Marjorie of Scotland*, 2222
King, Susan, *Lady Miracle*, 2455
Tranter, Nigel G., *Robert the Bruce: The Path of the Hero King*, 2515; *Robert the Bruce: The Price of the King's Peace*, 2516; *Robert the Bruce: The Steps to the Empty Throne*, 2368

Roberval, Jean Francois de La Roque
Rosenstock, Janet, *The Fire, the Sword, and the Devil*, 5199

Robin Hood
Canham, Marsha, *The Last Arrow*, 2152
Chase, Nicholas, *Locksley*, 2161
Feyrer, Gayle, *The Thief's Mistress*, 2194
Godwin, Parke, *Robin and the King*, 2207; *Sherwood*, 2208
Roberson, Jennifer, *Lady of the Forest*, 2334
Taylor, Timothy, *Elaine the Fair*, 2362

Rodin, Auguste
Delbe, Anne, *Camille Claudel, une Femme*, 1145
Weiss, David, *Naked Came I: A Novel of Rodin*, 1406

Roger II, King of Sicily
Rotondi, Cesar J., *The Garden of Persephone*, 526

Roland
Pei, Mario, *Swords of Anjou*, 519

Roman Army
Lovelace, Merline, *Somewhere in Time*, 308

Roman Catholics see Catholics and the Catholic Church

Roman invasions
Treece, Henry, *The Dark Island*, 94; *Red Queen, White Queen*, 95

Roman legions
Sutcliff, Rosemary, *The Eagle of the Ninth*, 248; *The Lantern Bearers*, 250; *The Silver Branch*, 251

Roman magistrates
De Carvalho, Mário, *A God Strolling in the Cool of the Evening*, 231

Roman outposts
Sutcliff, Rosemary, *Frontier Wolf*, 249

Romanian Peasants' Uprising
Stancu, Zaharia, *Barefoot*, 1371

Romanov, House of
Green, William M., *The Romanov Connection*, 1203
Pazzi, Roberto, *Searching for the Emperor*, 1308

Romans
Crow, Donna Fletcher, *Glastonbury*, 229
Whyte, Jack, *The Singing Sword*, 254; *The Skystone*, 255

Rommel, Erwin
Borden, G. F., *Easter Day, 1941*, 4890
Tarrant, John, *The Rommel Plot*, 1895

Romulus and Remus
Duggan, Alfred Leo, *Children of the Wolf*, 358

Ronalds, Mary Frances
Ronalds, Mary Teresa, *A Victorian Masque*, 3640

Ronsard, Pierre de
Ingman, Heather, *The Dance of the Muses*, 718

Roosevelt, Eleanor
Roosevelt, Elliott, *Murder at the Palace*, 4638

Roosevelt, Franklin D.
Hughes, Terence, *The Day They Stole the Queen Mary*, 4533

Roosevelt, Theodore
Henry, Will, *San Juan Hill*, 5847

Rossetti, Dante Gabriel
Savage, Elizabeth, *Willowwood*, 3648

Roster Rising
Uris, Leon, *Redemption*, 4376

Roundheads
Barnes, Margaret Campbell, *Mary of Carisbrooke*, 2541

Royal Air Force
Darrell, Elizabeth, *And in the Morning*, 4449
Dunmore, Spencer, *Bomb Run*, 4462
Hennessy, Max, *The Bright Blue Sky*, 4020
Hough, Richard, *Wings Against the Sky*, 4527

Royal Canadian Mounted Police
Morris, Alan, *By Honor Bound*, 5248
York, Thomas, *Trapper*, 5279

Royal Marines
Keneally, Thomas, *The Playmaker*, 5056

Royal Strathspreys
McCutchan, Philip, *By Command of the Viceroy*, 5490; *Subaltern's Choice*, 5494

Royalists
Barnes, Margaret Campbell, *Mary of Carisbrooke*, 2541
Irwin, Margaret, *The Bride*, 719; *The Stranger Prince*, 2890
Laker, Rosalind, *Circle of Pearls*, 2906
Lane, Jane, *The Sealed Knot*, 2914
Pope, Dudley, *Admiral*, 5805
Sutcliff, Rosemary, *Rider on a White Horse*, 2746
Tranter, Nigel G., *The Young Montrose*, 2760

Rubber industry and trade
Hudson, Christopher, *Where the Rainbow Ends*, 5539
Meyer, Nicholas, and Barry Jay Kaplan, *Black Orchid*, 5975

Rubens, Peter Paul
Braider, Donald, *An Epic Joy*, 665

Rubenstein, Helena
Sulitzer, Paul-Loup, *Hannah*, 1387

Rudolf of Austria
Dukthas, Ann, *The Time of Murder at Mayerling*, 1161

Rum Rebellion
Hickman, Patricia, *Beyond the Wild Shores*, 5043

Ruma culture
McGahan, Jerry, *A Condor Brings the Sun*, 5766

Runners
Weatherby, William J., *Chariots of Fire*, 4701

Rupert of England
Irwin, Margaret, *The Stranger Prince*, 2890

Ruskin, John
Morazzoni, Marta, *The Invention of Truth*, 504

Russian occupation
Tomin, Zdena, *Stalin's Shoe*, 1911

Russian Revolution (1905)
Gorky, Maksim, *The Life of a Useless Man*, 1200
Hanlon, Emily, *Petersburg*, 1206

Russo-Chinese War
Seltzer, Richard, *The Name of Hero*, 1347

Ruth
Henderson, Lois T., *Ruth*, 23
Traylor, Ruth Gunderson, *Ruth*, 210

Sabutai
Dandrea, Don, *Orlok*, 447

Sahara Desert
Bunn, T. Davis, *Sahara Crosswind*, 4811

Sailors
Becke, Louis, and Walter Jeffery, *The Mutineer*, 5004
Brown, George Mackay, *Vinland*, 433
Bryher, *Ruan*, 2142
Conrad, Joseph, *The Nigger of the Narcissus*, 3852
Graham, Winston, *The Grove of Eagles*, 2623
Lambdin, Dewey, *The King's Coat*, 2911
Phillips, Michael R., and Judith Pella, *Robbie Taggart: Highland Sailor*, 4258
Sabatini, Rafael, *The Sea-Hawk*, 2729

Sainte-Colombe, sieur de
Quignard, Pascal, *All the World's Mornings*, 868

Saints
Absire, Alain, *Lazarus*, 260
Asch, Sholem, *The Apostle*, 256; *Mary*, 261

Stanley, Henry M.
Forbath, Peter, *The Last Hero*, 4829
Hagerfors, Lennart, *The Whales in Lake Tanganyika*, 4836

Statesmen
Abernethy, Cecil, *Mr Pepys of Seething Lane*, 2779
Arenas, Reinaldo, *The Ill-Fated Peregrinations of Fray Servando*, 5782
Balin, Beverly, *King in Hell*, 2538
Beahn, John E., *A Man Born Again: Saint Thomas More*, 2543
Butler, Margaret, *The Lion of Christ*, 2147; *The Lion of Justice*, 2149
Caldwell, Taylor, *Glory and the Lightning*, 110; *A Pillar of Iron*, 346
Dimont, Madelon, *Darling Pericles*, 112
Leffland, Ella, *The Knight, Death, and the Devil*, 1709
Lewis, Roy, *Cock of the Walk*, 4107
MacBeth, George, *The Lion of Pescara*, 1274
McCullough, Colleen, *The First Man in Rome*, 387; *The Grass Crown*, 389
McKemy, Kay, *Samuel Pepys of the Navy*, 2932
Meyer, Conrad Ferdinand, *The Saint*, 2276
Plaidy, Jean, *St Thomas's Eve*, 2721
Ripley, Alexandra, *The Time Returns*, 627
Shulman, Sandra, *The Florentine*, 635; *Francesca: The Madonna of the Shadows*, 636
Sutcliff, Rosemary, *The Flowers of Adonis*, 159
Turton, Godfrey, *My Lord of Canterbury*, 2762
Twose, Anna, *The Lion of Athens*, 162
Zochert, Donald, *Murder in the Hellfire Club*, 3027

Statesmen's spouses
Hardy, W. G., *Turn Back the River*, 373

Stein, Gertrude
Steward, Samuel M., *The Caravaggio Shawl*, 1888; *Murder Is Murder Is Murder*, 1889

Stephen of Blois
Bennetts, Pamela, *Stephen and the Sleeping Saints*, 2127
Follett, Ken, *Pillars of the Earth*, 2195
Holland, Cecelia, *Hammer for Princes*, 2225
Jones, Ellen, *The Fatal Crown*, 2238
Norman, Diana, *The Morning Gift*, 2289
Penman, Sharon Kay, *When Christ and His Saints Slept*, 2298
Peters, Ellis, *Brother Cadfael's Penance*, 2299; *The Confession of Brother Haluin*, 2300; *Dead Man's Ransom*, 2301; *The Devil's Novice*, 2302; *An Excellent Mystery*, 2303; *The Heretic's Apprentice*, 2304; *The Hermit of Eyton Forest*, 2305; *The Holy Thief*,

2306; *The Leper of Saint Giles*, 2308; *Monk's Hood*, 2309; *A Morbid Taste for Bones*, 2310; *One Corpse Too Many*, 2311; *The Pilgrim of Hate*, 2312; *The Potter's Field*, 2313; *The Raven in the Foregate*, 2314; *The Rose Rent*, 2315; *Saint Peter's Fair*, 2316; *The Sanctuary Sparrow*, 2317; *The Summer of the Danes*, 2318; *The Virgin in the Ice*, 2319
Shipway, George, *The Knight*, 2346

Stone Age
Crace, Jim, *Gift of Stones*, 72

Stone carvers
Pargeter, Edith, *The Heaven Tree Trilogy*, 2290

Stonehenge
Harrison, Harry, and Leon Stover, *Stonehenge*, 75
Holland, Cecelia, *Pillar of the Sky*, 77
Weenolsen, Hebe, *The Forbidden Mountain*, 97

Stradivari, Antonio
Hersey, John, *Antonietta*, 840

Straw, Jack
Zelitch, Simone, *The Confession of Jack Straw*, 2528

Strikes and lockouts
Cordell, Alexander, *Song of the Earth*, 3192
Galvao, Patricia, *Industrial Park*, 5944
Gower, Iris, *Black Gold*, 3967
Kelton, Elmer, *The Day the Cowboys Quit*, 5234
Mendoza, Eduardo, *The Truth about the Savolta Case*, 1285
Riesco, Laura, *Ximena at the Crossroad*, 5997
Zola, Émile, *Germinal*, 1426

Stuart, Arabella, Lady
Haycraft, Molly Costain, *Too Near the Throne*, 2631

Stuarts
Anthony, Evelyn, *Clandara*, 2788
Blackstock, Charity, *The Lonely Strangers*, 801
Cowell, Stephanie, *The Physician of London*, 2577
Galt, John, *Ringan Gilhaize*, 2860
Kerr, Robert, *The Dark Lady*, 2903
Macaulay, Rose, *The Shadow Flies*, 2673
Potter, Jeremy, *Disgrace and Favour*, 2723
Wright, Patricia, *The Storms of Fate*, 3025

Student protests
Scofield, Sandra, *Gringa*, 6003
Taibo, Paco Ignacio II, *Calling All Heroes*, 6006

Students
Carr, Philippa, *A Time for Silence*, 1128
Gibson, Elizabeth, *The Water Is Wide*, 4741
Heaven, Constance, *The Raging Fire*, 1215

Le Sage, Alain René, *The Adventures of Gil Blas of Santillane*, 853
Neville, Jill, *The Love Germ*, 2064
Unger, Douglas, *El Yanqui*, 6013

Styrbjorn Starki
Eddison, Eric Rucker, *Styrbiorn the Strong*, 453

Submarines
Buchheim, Lothar Gunther, *The Boat*, 1500
Collenette, Eric J., *Atlantic Encounter*, 4440; *Ninety Feet to the Sun*, 4441
Fullerton, Alexander, *A Share of Honour*, 1575
Homewood, Harry, *Silent Sea*, 5133
McCutchan, Philip, *Cameron and the Kaiserhof*, 1752
Pope, Dudley, *Convoy*, 4620
Ramrus, Al, and John Shaner, *The Ludendorff Pirates*, 4625
Reeman, Douglas, *His Majesty's U-Boat*, 4626; *Strike from the Sea*, 4631
Trew, Antony, *Yashimoto's Last Dive*, 5721

Suetonius (Giaus Suetonius Tranquillus)
Holland, Jack, *Druid Time*, 238

Suez Canal
Salisbury, Carola, *An Autumn in Araby*, 4304

Suffragists see also Woman suffrage
Linscott, Gillian, *Dead Man's Sweetheart*, 4113
Pearson, Michael, *The Store*, 4224
Whitnell, Barbara, *The Ring of Bells*, 4396

Sugar plantations
Cato, Nancy, *Brown Sugar*, 5010
Ferré, Rosario, *Eccentric Neighborhoods*, 5935
Nicole, Christopher, *Ratoon*, 5869

Sugar trade
Shaw, Patricia, *Cry of the Rain Bird*, 5085

Suleiman I, Sultan of the Ottoman Empire
Chamberlin, Ann, *The Sultan's Daughter*, 673
Crawley, Aileen, *The Bride of Suleiman*, 679; *The Shadow of God*, 680

Sulla, Lucius Cornelius
McCullough, Colleen, *The Grass Crown*, 389

Sullivan, Arthur, Sir
Ronalds, Mary Teresa, *A Victorian Masque*, 3640

Sultans
Crawley, Aileen, *The Bride of Suleiman*, 679; *The Shadow of God*, 680
Mourad, Kenize, *Regards from the Dead Princess*, 1770